OTTO EISSFELDT

THE OLD TESTAMENT
AN INTRODUCTION

OTTO EISSFELDT

THE OLD TESTAMENT

An Introduction

including the Apocrypha and Pseudepigrapha, and also the works of similar type from Qumran

THE HISTORY OF THE FORMATION OF THE OLD TESTAMENT

Translated by
PETER R. ACKROYD
*Samuel Davidson Professor of Old Testament Studies
King's College, London*

HARPER AND ROW, PUBLISHERS
NEW YORK AND EVANSTON

© in this translation 1965
BASIL BLACKWELL
OXFORD

First edition 1965
Reprinted 1966

Library of Congress Catalog Card No.: 65–15399

Translated from the 3rd German edition by permission of
J. C. B. MOHR, Tübingen (PAUL SIEBECK)

PRINTED IN GREAT BRITAIN FOR
HARPER AND ROW, PUBLISHERS, INCORPORATED

*Dedicated to the Representatives
of three generations of British
Old Testament Scholarship*

THEODORE H. ROBINSON
HAROLD H. ROWLEY
AUBREY R. JOHNSON

CONTENTS

PART ONE

THE PRE LITERARY STAGE: THE SMALLEST UNITS AND THEIR SETTING IN LIFE

II. SAYINGS

III. SONGS

PART TWO

THE LITERARY PREHISTORY OF THE BOOKS OF THE OLD TESTAMENT

PART THREE

THE ANALYSIS OF THE BOOKS OF THE OLD TESTAMENT

A. THE PENTATEUCH (הַתּוֹרָה THE LAW)

III. The Four Narrative Strands

IV. The Collections of Laws

C. THE WRITINGS

(כְּתוּבִים *HAGIOGRAPHA)*

PART FOUR

THE CANON

I. The History of the Canon

II. Apocrypha and Pseudepigrapha

(a) *Apocrypha*

(b) *Pseudepigrapha*

III. Apocryphal and Pseudepigraphical Writings
among the Qumrān Texts

PART FIVE

THE TEXT

I. The Prehistory of the Text Forms which have Survived

II. The Masoretic Text (𝕸)

III. Non-masoretic Forms of the Text

TRANSLATOR'S PREFACE

The origin of this translation is linked with the decision of Professor Otto
Eissfeldt to prepare a second edition of his *Introduction*, first published in German in 1934. This second edition appeared in 1955, but the work of translation
proceeded less rapidly than might have been hoped so that when a demand
for a third German edition led to a further revision (published in 1964), it was
clear that the translation should be collated with the most recent German text
and should appear as soon as might be after it. This has the advantage of providing the reader with an up-to-date rendering of the German text. It has also
been possible to make some substantial additions in the English translation to
the supplementary bibliographical material in § 126, covering many publications
dating into the early months of 1964. *These are included in the relevant bibliography and footnotes. Where in § 126 an addition is indicated to the body of the text
a dagger † is placed against the number on the page to which reference is made.*

The work would hardly have been possible without much kindly assistance,
most of all from Professor Eissfeldt himself, for he read a large part of the
original typescript and subsequently checked the whole of the proofs, making
many corrections and suggestions for the improvement of the text. Its English
style would have been much more deficient had it not been for the patient
reading of both typescript and proof by the translator's father, the Revd.
J. R. Ackroyd, who, having no German, was more conscious of the dangers of
'translation-ese' than was the translator himself. Accuracy has been further
ensured by the Revd. H. St. John Hart, the Revd. R. J. Coggins and Mr. M. A.
Knibb who have read the final proofs, and by others, students and colleagues,
who have read parts of the proofs and have made helpful comments.

The production of the book obviously owes much to the skill and care of
printer and publisher, and especially to Mr. H. L. Schollick of Blackwell's
who has been most patient. For typing, correspondence and other assistance it
is possible to mention among those who have contributed only Mrs. Pat
Rignold of Cambridge, and Miss Carole Chanter and Miss Ann Pinkerton of
King's College, London.

PETER R. ACKROYD

1964

INTRODUCTIONS TO THE
OLD TESTAMENT*

Eichhorn, *Einleitung ins AT* (1780/83, ⁴1823/24); E.T. *Introduction to the Study of the Old Testament* . . . A fragment translated by G. T. Gollop (1888).

Bertholdt, *Historischkritische Einleitung in sämmtliche kanonische und apokryphische Schriften des A und NT* (1812/19).

Kuenen, *Historisch-kritisch Onderzoek naar het ontstaan en de verzameling van de boeken des Ouden Verbonds* (1861/65, ²1885/93); German transl. by Weber and Müller (1886/94); E.T. of Part I §§1–29 *The Pentateuch and Book of Joshua critically examined* . . . Transl. and ed. by J. W. Colenso (1865); *An historico-critical inquiry into the origin and composition of the Hexateuch* . . . Transl. by P. H. Wicksteed (1886).

Davidson, *An Introduction to the OT* (1862/63).

Nöldeke, *Die alttestamentliche Literatur* (1868); French transl. *Histoire littéraire de l'AT* by Hartwig, Derenbourg and J. Soury (1873).

—, *Untersuchungen zur Kritik des AT* (1869).

Wellhausen, *Die Composition des Hexateuchs und der historischen Bücher des ATs* (1876/77. 1878, ³1899) (cf. below p. 166, n. 38).

—, *Prolegomena zur Geschichte Israels* (1878, ⁶1905) (cf. below p. 166, n. 39); E.T. *Prolegomena to the History of Ancient Israel* by J. S. Black and A. Menzies (1885, 1957).

Robertson Smith, *The OT in the Jewish Church* (1881, ²1892).

Reuss, *Die Geschichte der heiligen Schriften AT's* (1881, ²1890).

Cornill, *Einleitung in das AT* (1891, ⁷1913); E.T. *Introduction to the Canonical Books of the Old Testament* by G. H. Box (1907).

Driver, *Introduction to the Literature of the OT* (1891, ⁹1913 (1961)).

Wildeboer, *De letterkunde des Ouden Verbonds* (1893, ³1903); German transl. *Die Literatur des AT* by Risch (1895, ²1905).

Graf Baudissin, *Einleitung in die Bücher des AT* (1901).

Gautier, *Introduction à l'AT* (1906, ³1939).

Budde, *Geschichte der althebräischen Literatur.* (Apocrypha and Pseudepigrapha by Bertholet) (1906, ²1909).

Gunkel, 'Die israelitische Literatur' in *Kultur der Gegenwart*, ed. by Hinneberg, Part I Sect. VII (1906), pp. 51–102; (²1925), pp. 53–112.

Sellin, *Einleitung in das AT* (1910, ⁹1959 (ed. by Rost)); E.T. *Introduction to the Old Testament* by W. Montgomery (1923).

Steuernagel, *Lehrbuch der Einleitung in das AT. Mit einem Anhang über die Apokryphen und Pseudepigraphen* (1912).

---

* When reference is made to the works listed here, it is done by simply citing the author's name marked with an asterisk (*). An asterisk against a biblical reference indicates that the passage referred to contains later additions, and reference is therefore to only part of the material.

Moore, *Literature of the OT* (1913, ²1948 (rev. by Brockington)).
Gray, *A Critical Introduction to the OT* (1913 (1919)).
Meinhold, *Einführung in das AT* (1919, ³1932).
Bewer, *The Literature of the OT in its Historical Development* (1922, ³1962 (completely revised by Kraeling)).
Hempel, *Die althebräische Literatur und ihr hellenistisch-jüdisches Nachleben* (Handb. d. Literaturwiss., ed. by Walzel, 1934).
Möller, *Einleitung in das AT* (1934).
—, *Grundriss für alttestamentliche Einleitung* (1958).
Oesterley and Robinson, *Introduction to the Books of the OT* (1934, ³1958).
Weiser, *Einleitung in das AT* (1939, ⁵1963); E.T. *Introduction to the OT*, transl. by D. M. Barton (1961).
Pfeiffer, *Introduction to the OT* (1941, ²1952 (1957)).
—, *The Books of the OT* (1957).
Engnell, *Gamla Testamentet: en traditionshistorisk inledning*, I (1945).
Vriezen, *Oud-israelietische Geschriften* (1948).
—, *De Literatuur van Oud-Israël* (1961).
Bentzen, *Introduction to the OT* (1948/49, ⁵1959).
Young, *An Introduction to the OT* (1949 (1954)).
Lods, *Histoire de la littérature hébraïque et juive depuis les origines jusqu'à la ruine de l'état juif (135 après J.-C.)* (1950).
Rowley, *The Growth of the OT* (1950).
Aalders, *Oud-Testamentische Kanoniek* (1952).
Kuhl, *Die Entstehung des AT* (1953, ²1960 (ed. by Fohrer)); E.T. *The OT. Its Origins and Composition*, transl. by C. T. M. Herriott (1960).
Anderson, *A Critical Introduction to the OT* (1959).
Gottwald, *A Light to the Nations. An Introduction to the OT* (1959).
Flanders, Crapps and Anthony, *People of the Covenant: An Introduction to the OT* (1963).

Scholz, *Einleitung in die Heiligen Schriften des A und NT* (1845/48).
Kaulen, *Einleitung in die Heilige Schrift des A und NT* (1876/81; AT ⁵1911/13, rev. by Hoberg).
Cornely, *Historica et critica introductio in utriusque Testamenti libros sacros* (1885/87, ²1894/97 (1925)).
—, *Introductionis in S. Scripturae libros compendium* (1889, ¹²1940 (C. et Merk)).
Fell, *Lehrbuch der allgemeinen Einleitung in das AT* (1906).
Hudal, *Kurze Einleitung in die Heiligen Bücher des AT* (1920; ⁶1948 (rev. by Sauer)).
Höpfl, *Introductionis in sacros utriusque Testamenti libros compendium* (1921/22), I: *Introductio generalis in S. Scripturam* (⁶1958 (rec. Leloir)); II: *Introductio specialis in VT* (⁵1946 (cur. Miller et Metzinger), ⁶1963 (cur. S. Bovo)).
Nikel, *Grundriss der Einleitung in das AT* (1924).
Goettsberger, *Einleitung in das AT* (1928).
Coppens, *Introduction à l'étude historique de l'AT*, I (1938, ³1942), II (1950), III (1944, ²1950).

Robert et Tricot, *Initiation Biblique* (1939, ³1954); E.T. *Guide to the Bible: An Introduction to the Study of Holy Scripture*, transl. by Arbez and McGuire, Vol. I (1952, ²1960).

Robert et Feuillet, *Introduction à la Bible.* Tome I: *Introduction générale.* Ancien Testament by Auvray et al. (1957, ²1959).

—, *Einleitung in die Heilige Schrift.* German transl. by Faschian, I (1963).

Mariani, *Introductio in Libros Sacros Veteris Testamenti* (1958).

Bratsiotis, *Εἰσαγωγὴ εἰς τὴν Παλαιὰν Διαθήκην* (1937).

—, *'Επίτομος Εἰσαγωγὴ εἰς τὴν Παλαιὰν Διαθήκην* (1955).

Geiger, *Urschrift und Übersetzungen der Bibel* (1857, ²1928).

Fürst, *Geschichte der biblischen Literatur und des jüdisch-hellenistischen Schrifttums* (1867/70).

Cassel, *Geschichte der jüdischen Literatur* (1872/73).

Margolis, *The Hebrew Scriptures in the Making* (1922, ³1948).

Segal, מבוא המקרא (1946/50, ⁴1954/6).

Sandmel, *The Hebrew Scriptures. An Introduction to their Literature and Religious Ideas* (1963).

As it has been possible in the English translation to make some substantial additions to the supplementary bibliographical material in § 126, these are included in the relevant bibliography and footnotes. Where in § 126 an addition is indicated to the body of the text a dagger † is placed against the number on the page to which reference is made.

§ 1. THE NATURE OF THE UNDERTAKING

Literature: The opening paragraphs of the textbooks on 'Introduction' mentioned on pp. xxii–xxiv and the literature to § 2; Anderson, 'Some Aspects of the Uppsala School of OT Study' HThR 42 (1950), pp. 239–56; Baumgartner, 'At. Einleitung und Literaturgeschichte' ThR 8 (1936), pp. 179–222; Bentzen, 'Skandinavische Literatur zum AT 1939–1948' ThR 17 (1948/49), pp. 273–328; Henton Davies, 'Contemporary Religious Trends: The OT' ET 67 (1955–1956), pp. 3–7; Eissfeldt, 'The Literature of Israel: Modern Criticism' *Record and Revelation* (1938), pp. 74–109; Gordon, *New Horizons in OT Literature* (1960); Gunkel, 'Die Grundprobleme der israelitischen Literaturgeschichte' *Reden und Aufsätze* (1913), pp. 29–38; Hahn, *The OT in Modern Research* (1954, 1956); Hempel, 'The Literature of Israel: The Forms of Oral Tradition' *Record and Revelation* (1938), pp. 28–44; Jassour, '"Bibelkritik" und altjüdische Geschichtsforschung' Das Altertum 6 (1960), pp. 3–13; Jepsen, 'Wissenschaft vom AT' *Aufsätze und Vorträge zur Theol. u. Religionswiss.* 1 (1958); Kittel, 'Die Zukunft der at. Wissenschaft' ZAW 39 (1921), pp. 84–99; Lindblom, 'Einige Grundfragen der at. Wissenschaft' *Bertholet-Festschr.* (1950), pp. 325–37; Rowley, 'Trends in OT Study' OTMSt (1951), pp. XV–XXXI; Saydon, 'Palaeography of the OT and its Bearing upon Textual and Literary Criticism of the OT' Melita Theologica 3 (1950), pp. 5–22; Schrey, 'Die at. Forschung der sogenannten Uppsala-Schule' ThZ 7 (1951), pp. 321–41; Segert, 'Zur Methode der at. Literarkritik (Quellenscheidung und Überlieferungsgeschichte)' ArOr 24 (1956), pp. 610–21; van der Woude, 'Vijf jaar OuT. inleidingswetenschap' JEOL 14 (1955/6), pp. 11–26. Lit. § 126.

The term Εἰσαγωγή *Introduction* as the designation of a work devoted to furthering the understanding of the Bible was first employed, so far as we know, for the writing entitled Εἰσαγωγὴ εἰς τὰς θείας γραφάς *Introduction to the divine scriptures* by the monk Adrianus († ca. 440 A.D.), a member of the Antiochene school. Since the publication of J. D. Michaelis, *Einleitung in die göttlichen Schriften des Neuen Bundes* (1750), the normal German equivalent of the Greek term has been 'Einleitung', mediated via the latinised 'Isagoge' and the Latin 'Introductio'. English works normally use simply this Latin equivalent, i.e. 'Introduction'. The subject is, however, much older than the name. The need for notes to facilitate the understanding of a work—whether on points of grammar or of lexicography, of history or of fact, or even of an exegetical nature—exists from the moment when it is read by a generation no longer directly in touch with it. A reader who belongs to the time and place in which a writing comes into being can, normally at any rate, understand it without prefatory remarks, without 'introduction'. But one who belongs to a quite different period, or a quite different environment, cannot do so. He must first be supplied with a body of preliminary information, before he is in a position to assess a work which is otherwise, in some measure at least, foreign to him.

B

1

Thus 'introduction' has always existed to the individual books of the Bible, or to certain parts of them, and to the Bible or the Old Testament as a whole, even if at first only in the form of isolated notes. Ps. xviii has a superscription which was already present at the time of the Septuagint translators: *Of David . . . who spoke unto Yahweh the words of this song on the day when Yahweh delivered him from the hand of all his enemies and from the hand of Saul.* This is an introductory comment, regardless of whether or not it is correct. Here likewise belongs all that the Synagogue tradition relates concerning authorship, place and time of origin of the individual books and sections of books, and concerning the growth of the canon.

In the early and medieval Church,[1] the information derived from the Synagogue was handed on and amplified. The notes which were felt to be necessary for the understanding of a book were frequently provided in the form of prefaces to the individual books (Jerome). But at the same time special studies were not lacking in which notes are provided on language, geography and history, and above all on exegesis. From the early Church we may mention, in addition to Adrianus, as those responsible for handing on this kind of information, Tyconius († ca. 410), Augustine († 430), Junilius Africanus († ca. 550), Magnus Aurelius Cassiodorus († ca. 585). From the medieval period[2] we may note Isidore of Seville († ca. 636) and the Franciscan Nicholas of Lyra († ca. 1340), the latter particularly because he also made available to Christians the valuable works of the Jewish scholars Rashi († 1105)[3] and Ibn Ezra († 1167),[4] and thus kept in being a contact with the original text which was otherwise being lost.

New, or at least comparatively new, questions were raised for the understanding of the Old Testament, as for the Bible as a whole, by the relevant scientific works of Humanism and of the Reformation, and by the philosophy of the Enlightenment and of Rationalism.[5] Here, much more decisively than before, the grammatical understanding of the text was pursued, and traditions concerning authorship and date of origin of the biblical books were critically examined in the light of the actual material itself as we now have it. This led to considerable doubts concerning the traditional views and to attempts to replace them with hypotheses of greater probability. From the time of the Reformation we may mention here, in addition to Luther, primarily Carlstadt, with his work *De canonicis scripturis libellus* (1520); from the philosophy of the Enlightenment Spinoza's[6] *Tractatus theologico-politicus* (1670), and from the rationalist movement J. S. Semler's *Abhandlung von freier Untersuchung des Canon* (1771–5), and

---

[1] Diestel, *Geschichte des AT in der christlichen Kirche* (1869). Lit. § 126.

[2] Smalley, *The Study of the Bible in the Middle Ages* (²1952).

[3] Dietrich, HdO III, 1 (1953), p. 98. Lit. § 126.   [4] *Ib.*, pp. 89, 94.

[5] Kraeling, *The Old Testament since the Reformation* (1955); Kraus, *Geschichte der historisch-kritischen Erforschung des AT von der Reformation bis zur Gegenwart* (1956), and on this Baumgartner, 'Eine at. Forschungsgeschichte' ThR 25 (1959), pp. 93–110. Lit. § 126.

[6] Liebeschütz, 'Die politische Interpretation des AT bei Thomas von Aquino und Spinoza' Antike und Abendland 9 (1960), pp.39–62; Nádor, 'The method and significance of Spinoza's biblical criticism' (in Russian, with German summary) AcOr (B), V, 1–2 (1955), pp. 29–42 (44); Strauss, 'How to Study Spinoza's Theologico-Political Treatise' PAAJR 17 (1947/8), pp. 69–131; Wernham, *Benedict de Spinoza. The Political Works, the Tractatus Theologico-Politicus in part and the Tractatus Politicus in full* (1958). Lit. § 126.

Apparatus ad liberalem Veteris Testamenti interpretationem (1773). To about the same time as these works by Semler, belong Herder's *Älteste Urkunde des Menschengeschlechts* (1774–6) and *(Salomons) Lieder der Liebe* (1778). These, like the earlier work of the English scholar R. Lowth, *De sacra poesi Hebraeorum* (1753),[7] provided material complementary to the scientific critical studies of the Bible on the side of emotion and sensibility, by drawing out its aesthetic value and encouraging the appreciation of it.

All this variety of questions and suggestions was then systematically gathered into a textbook of introduction by J. G. Eichhorn. In 1780–3 he published his *Einleitung in das A.T.* in three parts. Eichhorn has been described as the founder of modern introduction to the Old Testament, and rightly so. For however greatly the answers have changed during the two centuries since the first edition of his book, the main questions which are at issue have remained the same. There are in fact three matters to which Eichhorn particularly devoted his attention—the growth of the canon, the history of the text, and the origin of the individual books—and these three fields still occupy the chief place in present-day 'Introduction'.

'Introduction' could include an unlimited range of subjects, everything indeed which is in any way necessary or desirable for the understanding of the Old Testament. But it has in course of time limited itself to areas covered by these three questions: the origin of the individual books, the growth of the canon, and the history of the text. Other matters which were formerly also discussed in introductions have become the subject of special disciplines and books —grammar, lexicography, geography, archaeology, secular history, history of religion or theology, exegesis. Of these three questions, the one which concerns the origin of the individual books takes decidedly the largest place, and the treatment of the canon and the text appear by contrast almost as an addendum. But this investigation of the origins of the individual books is in the main an analytical question, and must be so in the nature of things. Thus, 'introduction', as founded by Eichhorn, is essentially an analysis of the individual books of the Old Testament.

It is obvious that to stop at criticism and analysis in this way is unsatisfactory, and must call forth a desire for a new synthesis. This desire has found repeated expression and in recent years its most persistent advocate, building upon the work of earlier scholars, has been Hermann Gunkel*.[8] His demand is that we should have not critical, analytical introduction, but a creative, synthesising history of the literature. Gunkel has at the same time sketched an outline of what he envisages as an ideal history of Israelite literature. He begins from the consideration that in view of our total ignorance of the date of origin and the authorship of practically every part of the Old Testament, a history of Israelite literature in chronological and biographical terms is quite impossible. On the other hand, in the literature of Israel the conventional and typical are much more

---

[7] Cripps, 'Two British Interpreters of the Old Testament: Robert Lowth (1710–87) and Samuel Lee (1783–1852)', BJRL 35 (1952–3), pp. 385–404; Gregory, *R. Lowth, Lectures on the Sacred Poetry of the Hebrews, translated from the Latin* (1835).

[8] For the meaning of the asterisk after an author's name, cf. p. xxii, n.

important than the individual and personal, at any rate in the beginnings of the development. He therefore defines the task to be undertaken as the history of the literary types (*Gattungen*) which were normal in Israel, and thus points to what he conceives to be the only way in which it is possible to get from the analysis and criticism of previous introductory method to a synthetic presentation of the material.

Gunkel's demand is in large measure justified. Much that remains undiscoverable by critical analysis may be achieved by the systematic examination of the types—a comprehensive survey of the examples which are found in the Old Testament and a comparison with similar phenomena in other literatures, namely those which belong to Israel's environment. This method overcomes the hindrances which are in part due to the fortuitous limitations of the actual material handed down; it takes into account the possibility and probability of patterns which do not happen to occur in a literary form; and it attempts not merely to define the nature of the literature which has come down to us but rather to comprehend the life and thought, the story and song which underlie it. Above all, it enables us, by its assumption of an oral tradition preceding the literature, to trace the history of the forms and materials which occur in the Old Testament much further back, often beyond the boundaries of Israel, far further than the method which is associated simply with the analysis of the books. It can thus explain many peculiarities of Old Testament narratives, laws, sayings and poems which only become intelligible in the light of their prehistory.

But it is not possible to make the history of the literature into a substitute for introduction, for, as Gunkel himself admits, the history of the literature presupposes in general the solving of the problems of introduction, and thus remains dependent upon it. Gunkel's own proposed method shows that his way of examining and presenting the material in literary-historical terms can only be applied to the smallest units—the single narrative, the single legal statement, the single saying, the single poem and so on. It cannot deal with the larger units and is quite unable to deal with the books as we have them. Thus, valuable as Gunkel's scheme was for the understanding of the smallest units, it has contributed little that was original to the tracing of the composition and origin of the books, at least so far as those books and groups of books are concerned which are more than merely a loose collocation of those smallest units. This is partly due to the method itself, which is primarily at least directed towards the typical, and looks at the types, and, while not overlooking personal and individual elements, nevertheless regards them as secondary. To some extent this represents a onesidedness in the approach, understandable in view of its newness, and could presumably be corrected by a presentation of the literary history which gave due emphasis to the personal and individual elements. Even so, there remains the need not merely for the analysis itself but also for the exposition of that analysis. For while the separation of the smallest units—which is itself dependent upon analysis—may in general be carried out so easily and certainly, that we may in this restrict ourselves to the presentation of its results, the determination of the larger units, moulded as they now are into our present books, is in large measure so uncertain that an understanding of the full range

of the possibilities which exist and of the problems of every synthetic presentation which is built upon them, can only be achieved as a result of analysis itself.
In this respect therefore scientific study will never be able to dispense with
analysis, and the demand for synthesis can only be met by summing up the
more detailed analytical sections with a brief sketch of the literary history in
which the probability of its results are assessed, or by prefacing the analysis
with such a sketch (pp. 239–41, 241–8).

There is another reason why Old Testament introduction cannot be replaced
by a history of Israelite-Jewish literature in which the Old Testament is regarded
as the remnant of a much richer national literature. The material with which
research is here concerned is not simply the literature of a nation or the remains
of such a literature. The Old Testament is rather an entity which has come into
being within the development of a particular political and religious history, and
which has to be understood and evaluated as such and not simply as the remains
of a richer mass of written material. This is primarily a simple statement of fact
which corresponds to the historical reality without inviting any value-judge-
ment, and without bias as regards the conception of a canon. But in view of the
fact that this entity, which has developed historically, has survived down to the
present day as the sacred scripture not merely of Judaism but also of Christendom, the point must be made with even greater emphasis. The scientific investigation of the Old Testament must be directed towards the whole process
of its development, to every phase of that process—whether it be to those which
involve pre-literary beginnings and then artificial literary shaping, or those
where learned compiling has taken place and then deliberate ecclesiastical purposes have been at work.

The demand made by Gunkel and others for the restriction of the space which
literary analysis of the books of the O.T. has hitherto occupied in O.T. introduction, in favour of the method of investigating the history of forms and types
has been followed a few decades later by another attack, no less fierce, which
seeks to replace analysis by the traditio-historical explanation of the growth of the
O.T. books. Inspired by Nyberg (*Studien zum Hoseabuche* [1935]), Birkeland
(*Zum hebräischen Traditionswesen* [1938]), and others, Engnell, in the first part
of *Gamla Testamentet: en traditionshistorisk inledning* (1945), dealing with the
Pentateuch—so far no further part has appeared—has emphatically expressed
himself in favour of such a transformation of O.T. introduction. For this
approach the determinative assumption is that in the pre-exilic period we have
not in general to do with a written fixation of the individual cycles of saga, law
codices, collections of poems, groups of sayings and the like, but with an oral
transmission of this material in definite circles of tradition. The materials are
assumed already to have reached a fixed form in the oral stage of transmission.
The growing tendency to write them down in the exilic and post-exilic period
is then assumed to have preserved them in this form, few alterations being then
made. As a warning against a too great reliance upon the scope and reliability
of the results which may be achieved by the method of literary criticism, Engnell's insistence is justified. But his assumption that even those parts of the Old
Testament which come from the early pre-exilic period were in general written

down only in the exilic and post-exilic period can hardly be right, and it is in fact remarkable that this assumption should have been made in a period when there is unambiguous archaeological evidence to show that in Canaan, and therefore also in Israel, the use of writing is certainly several centuries older (cf. § 114, 2) than Wellhausen and others of his generation assumed. Furthermore, if the later writing down of the tradition-complexes has preserved them in the form which they had through centuries of oral transmission, essentially the same methods would need to be applied to these fixed tradition-complexes as used to be employed when the attempt was being made to analyse these sections on the assumption that they had already been fixed in writing at an earlier period. To our way of thinking, these orally transmitted complexes do not present a unified pattern any more than do those which are fixed in writing. If they are to be understood, they must be analysed in the same way as the latter, and it is therefore of no importance whether the various component parts have been fitted together in the course of oral transmission or by a literary process.

We may summarise by saying that the task of the science of Old Testament introduction is the presentation of the history of the growth of the O.T. from its first beginnings to its definitive conclusion, as earlier scholars already defined it as 'Critical History of the Old Testament' (Richard Simon † 1712),[9] or 'History of the Sacred Scriptures of the Old Testament'[10] (Eduard Reuss † 1891). Introduction thus ceases to be merely a rather fortuitous gathering together of those necessary preliminary studies for the understanding of the O.T. which have not developed into separate disciplines and books, and it now becomes plain that it was not a matter of chance that introduction should gradually have concentrated upon these three spheres: analysis of the books, growth of the canon and history of the text. These are in fact the subjects which are necessary for the understanding of the history of the growth of the O.T. It only remains to preface the analysis of the books with the treatment of the types which has already been shown to be necessary, and then to infuse the whole with a proper historical understanding.

We shall therefore deal first with the pre-literary stage, where we are concerned with the smallest units of speech and where their connection with the contemporary conditions of life is still evident. In anticipation of the literary analysis which comes after, there must then be an important preliminary examination of the literary units of medium size which underlie our books— thus, for example, the narrative strand of J or the Holiness code, the autobiographical narratives of the prophets, or the medium-sized collections which have been joined together in our book of Proverbs. Then follows the analysis of the individual books which are contained in the O.T., an analysis which, where it is possible or necessary, is concluded with a short synthetic sketch. Next comes the examination and presentation of the growth of these books into one sacred book, in its various phases, and in this section dealing with the history of the canon, we must also discuss the apocrypha and pseudepigrapha which, although from their character worthy of canonicity and related to the

[9] *Histoire Critique du Vieux Testament* (1685); cf. p. 159, n. 6.
[10] *Geschichte der Heiligen Schrift des Alten Testaments* (1881).

canonical works, and even adopted into the canon in some circles related to the main tradition, did not however find a place in the definitive Jewish canon. Here we shall include not only those which have long been known, but also those writings which have come to light since 1947 (or perhaps even since 1945)[11] in the wilderness of Judaea, especially near Qumrān, in so far as they are similar to the books normally described as apocrypha and pseudepigrapha. Finally, the text of the books which are contained in this canon must be discussed, and its history traced to the point at which it became completely fixed and the Old Testament reached its final unalterable shape.

[11] Brownlee, 'Muhammad ed-Deeb's Own Story of his Scroll Discovery' JNESt 16 (1957), pp. 236–9; Trever, 'When was Qumran Cave I discovered?' RQ 3 (1960–1), pp. 131–41. Cf. below, p. 638. Lit. § 126.

PART ONE

THE PRE-LITERARY STAGE: THE SMALLEST UNITS AND THEIR SETTING IN LIFE

§ 2. GENERAL CONSIDERATIONS

Literature: Alonso-Schökel, 'Genera litteraria' VD 38 (1960), pp. 3–15; Barr, 'Tradition and Expectation in Ancient Israel' SJTh 10 (1957), pp. 24–34; Bernhardt, *Die gattungsgeschichtliche Forschung am AT als exegetische Methode* (1959); Engnell, 'Methodological Aspects of OT Study' SVT VII (1960), pp. 13–30; Flemming, 'Das Problem von Dichtungsgattung und -art' Studium Generale 12 (1959), pp. 38–60; Gressmann, 'Die Aufgaben der at. Forschung' ZAW 42 (1924), pp. 1–33, see pp. 26–8; Herrmann, 'Die Lyrik der Naturvölker' Studium Generale 12 (1959), pp. 597–610; Jolles, *Einfache Formen, Legende, Sage, Mythe, Rätsel, Spruch, Kasus, Memorabile, Märchen, Witz* (²1956); Lods, 'Le rôle de la tradition orale dans la formation des récits de l'AT' RHR 88 (1923), pp. 51–64; Muilenburg, 'Modern Issues in Biblical Studies' ET 71 (1959/60), pp. 229–33; Nielsen, *Oral Tradition. A Modern Problem in OT Introduction* (1954); van der Ploeg, 'Le rôle de la tradition orale dans la transmission du texte de l'AT' RB 54 (1947), pp. 5–41; Rinaldi, 'Alcuni termini ebraici relativi alla letteratura' Bibl 40 (1959), pp. 267–89; Ringgren, 'Oral and Written Transmission in the OT' StTh 3 (1950–1), pp. 34–59; Stendahl, 'Implications of Form-Criticism and Tradition-Criticism for Biblical Interpretation' JBL 77 (1958), pp. 33–38; Widengren, 'Oral Tradition and Written Literature in the Light of Arabic Evidence, with special regard to Prose Narratives' AcOr[H] 23 (1959), pp. 201–62; *Literary and Psychological aspects of the Hebrew Prophets* (1948); Wright, 'Archeology and OT Studies' JBL 77 (1958), pp. 39–51.
  Cf. also Literature §§ 1, 126.

Behind all literature—and this is also true of that which is gathered in the Old Testament—there lies a pre-literary stage in which the verbal compositions stand in direct relation to life, and are themselves as it were events expressed in verbal form. The prophetic oracle stands over against the concrete situation in the history of the people; the funeral dirge is heard at the bier of this man or that woman, and so on. The term 'pre-literary' is thus used first in the chronological sense, for long before the appearance of the oldest surviving stories, laws, sayings and poems of the Old Testament, there were verbal compositions among the Hebrews. But the term is also used with reference to the sub-literary stage, to point to the fact that throughout the whole period covered by the growth of the writings gathered in the Old Testament and associated with it, that is to say from about 1200 B.C. down to the rise of Christianity, new formations again and again made their way from the substratum of popular life and cultic activity into the literary sphere and took shape in the Old Testament. What varies at different times during the period involved is only the degree and extent of this process by which sub-literary forms became literature. It was considerably more marked at the beginning of the period than in the middle, and similarly more marked then than at the end. But the process never entirely

9

came to an end, and the closing of the Old Testament was not in fact brought about by the dying out of creative literary skill but by necessities brought upon the Jews in the course of their political history.

At the pre-literary stage, writing played a small part. Among the pre-Canaanite Hebrews, one or another tribal leader may have had at hand foreigners skilled in writing, Babylonians or Egyptians, or even perhaps Canaanites, for the occasional diplomatic contact with the contemporary civilised powers. After their invasion of Canaan, where they found already in use not only the Babylonian and Egyptian, but also the Phoenician or Canaanite script (cf. § 114, 2), writing will still at first have been comparatively little practised among the people. Verbal compositions were doubtless transmitted only orally at first, and we must therefore assume for a whole range of laws, stories, sayings and poems contained in the Old Testament that before their fixation in writing there was a period, in some cases a long period, during which they were handed on orally from tribe to tribe, from place to place, and from generation to generation. But even later, when the use of writing had otherwise become quite normal in Israel, the sub-literary stratum will have employed primarily the oral method alone for the transmission of its compositions.

For this reason, and also because of their direct relationship to particular circumstances of life, these compositions are in general of small compass—a single narrative, a legal precept, a saying, a short poem. Small units suffice for the concrete situation, and such units alone can be readily appropriated by an age which, unaccustomed to the use of writing, depends upon understanding something at a single hearing. We must, of course, take into account the fact that peoples which lack writing have strongly developed powers of memory, and we must therefore not exaggerate the hypothesis that there were only small units in the pre-literary and sub-literary stages. A warning is also appropriate against the all-too-easy assumption that with the earliest compositions which we can trace in Israel we have really reached an absolute beginning. It is more probable that at the moment when we can distinguish the Israelites with their traditions and poetry a long development already lay in the past, and this is entirely the case as regards the various literary materials which they took over from other cultures, as we shall see again and again. Many of the smallest forms which are to be found in the pre-literary and sub-literary stages, and many of the larger literary patterns too, Israel did not inherit from her common Semitic place of origin, nor did she produce them herself. She acquired them from the culture compounded of elements from Babylon, Egypt, Asia Minor and Canaan, into which she entered at her invasion of Canaan. Israel probably found most of this already present at the time of the invasion; other material gradually came in from the neighbouring civilisations. Towards the end of the development, Greek influences become particularly clear, though these have found much less expression in the writings incorporated in the definitive Jewish canon than in the apocrypha and pseudepigrapha, which were excluded from this canon, but were regarded as sacred by certain Jewish groups and later by the Church (§§ 76–112). If account is not taken of the external factors which have exerted their influence on the formation of the Old Testament, its growth remains incomprehensible.

The types, which we shall have to examine further, have their own history. From the moment of their first appearance to their last, which often coincides with the end of the whole development which we have to survey, they changed and became more and more comprehensive. The sagas and legends which at first are quite sparing of names and dates are filled out with a host of such details to enhance their credibility. In the poems broad reflection often takes the place of emotion. The types, which in the earlier period were at least relatively pure, become more and more intermingled and confused. Even so, it remains true on the whole that the types are remarkably constant. Many a description of a battle in I Maccabees can hardly be distinguished from the narratives of the heroic deeds of Saul and Jonathan in I Sam. xi, xiii, xiv; and the most ancient hymns and national laments like Exod. xv, 21, Hos. vi, 1–3, xiv, 3–4 are very similar —when once the difference of compass is ignored—to corresponding passages from the latest period, like the 'Song of the Three Children in the Furnace' and the 'Prayer of Azariah' in the Additions to Daniel (§ 84). It is therefore justifiable to make a systematic survey of the types, and historical perspective need only be considered in individual cases where it is possible and necessary.

In arranging the material the obvious principle of division is between prose and poetry, a comparatively neat distinction in spite of a few borderline cases; i.e. a division between the types which are in free speech and those which are in fixed form, with the proviso that a middle position between these two groups is assigned to the sayings, which often belong in content to prose but in form to poetry. These groups are treated in the order: prose, sayings, poetry, for the further reason that this order in some measure corresponds to that which is to be observed in the sections dealing with the individual books and with the canon. The Pentateuch and the older historical books contain in the main prose narratives, though they also include sayings and particularly legal sayings. The sayings, specifically prophetic sayings, predominate in the books of the writing prophets, and the last section of the canon, the 'Writings' take their stamp from the Psalms, that is, from poems, though admittedly besides these a comparatively large place is also taken up with narratives and sayings, in this case wisdom sayings. All three groups are represented in the apocrypha and pseudepigrapha, as well as in the similar writings from Qumrān (§§ 104–12).

I. Prose Types

The range of prose forms may first be subdivided into three comprehensive groups: speeches, records, and narratives. All three of these titles are to be understood in the broadest sense, so that the term 'speeches' also covers sermons and prose prayers, and in the term 'records' many forms, such as reports and messages, are included, which are primarily employed only in personal contacts by word of mouth. Of the three groups, the speeches stand nearest to real life, and the records come next—contracts, letters and such-like forms. We begin, therefore, with the speeches, consider the records next, and the narratives last.

§ 3. SPEECHES, SERMONS, PRAYERS

Literature: Ap-Thomas, 'Some Notes on the OT Attitude to Prayer' SJTh 9 (1956), pp. 422–9; Bentzen, *Die josianische Reform* (1926), pp. 95–107; Beyer, *Spruch und Predigt bei den vorexilischen Schriftpropheten* (Diss. theol. Erlangen, 1933); Boecker, 'Anklagereden und Verteidigungsreden im AT' EvTh 20 (1960), pp. 398–412; de Boer, 'De Vorbede in het OT' OTS 3 (1943); Bratsiotis, Εἰσαγωγὴ εἰς τοὺς μονολόγους τοῦ 'Ιερεμίου (Diss. Athens 1959); 'Der Monolog im AT' ZAW 73 (1961), pp. 30–70); Breit, *Die Predigt des Deuteronomisten* (1933); Greiff, *Das Gebet im AT* (1915); Barbara Hornig, 'Das Prosagebet der nachexilischen Literatur' ThLZ 83 (1958), cols. 644–6; Huijser, 'Prediking in het OT' GThT 42 (1941), pp. 165–182, 193–208, 241–55; Johnson, *Prayer in the Apocrypha and Pseudepigrapha*, 1948; Ludwig Köhler, *Die hebräische Rechtsgemeinde* (1931), pp. 7–8 = *Der hebräische Mensch* (1953), pp. 148–52 = *Hebrew Man* (1956), pp. 154–7; Plöger, 'Reden und Gebete im deuteronomistischen und chronistischen Geschichtswerk' *Festschrift Günther Dehn* (1957), pp. 35–49; von Rad, 'Die levitische Predigt in den Büchern der Chronik' *Procksch-Festschr.*, (1934), pp. 113–24 = *Ges. Stud. z. AT* (1958), pp. 248–61; *Deuteronomium-Studien*, 1947 (²1948) = *Studies in Deuteronomy* (1953); Scharbert, 'Die Fürbitte in der Theologie des AT' ThGl 50 (1960), pp. 321–38; Wendel, *Das israelitisch-jüdische Gelübde* (1931); *Das freie Laiengebet im vorexilischen Israel* (1932).
    Cf. also Literature §§ 15, 24, 34, 46, 47, 126.

1. *Speeches.* In Israel, as elsewhere, speech played a large part as a means of influencing larger or smaller groups of people, and on occasion of persuading a single individual. Men skilled in speech were sought after and respected. Among the qualities possessed by David, which encouraged Saul to bring him into his court, there is mentioned in I Sam. xvi, 18, the fact that he was נְבוֹן דָּבָר *skilled in speech*. In Exod. iv, 10–16, Moses declines the task assigned to him by God of delivering Israel from Egypt, on the grounds that he is *not eloquent* (לֹא אִישׁ דְּבָרִים, v. 10), and, although his God does not accept this objection (vv. 11 f.),[1] after his further hesitation his brother Aaron who *can speak well* (דַּבֵּר יְדַבֵּר הוּא, v. 14) is therefore appointed for him as assistant. Great skill in speech is moreover an ability especially possessed by women—in Israel too! Joab, who wishes to influence his king, David, to pardon Absalom the crown prince, makes use for this purpose of the help of *a wise woman* (אִשָּׁה חֲכָמָה, v. 2) and is successful as a result (II Sam. xiv, 1–24). Similarly, it is *a wise woman* (אִשָּׁה חֲכָמָה, v. 16) who, according to II Sam. xx, 14–22, is deputed in the hour of extreme danger at the siege of the town of Abel-beth-Maacah, to negotiate from the town wall with Joab the commander of the besieging army. She too is successful in that she persuades Joab to be satisfied with the head of the rebel who has taken refuge in the town. It is self-evident that such men and women, specially skilled in speech, possess a technique which does not depend solely upon a particular gift, but also upon tradition and 'training'; there were in other words, certain fixed forms for speech. The two examples just cited confirm this; for the two women employ what is essentially the same device, that of first obtaining from the person addressed an admission which does not appear to be relevant to the matter in hand, and this admission then compels him to grant the request which is really involved.

[1] Speier, 'פקח Ex. iv, 11' VT 10 (1960), p. 347.

It is natural to find, in view of the development of Israel from state and people to church and cult-community and the special characteristics of the Old Testament tradition which are due to this development, that we do not hear anything like so much about political speeches in the Old Testament as we do in, for example, Greek literature. Nevertheless, political speeches must have been of great importance in Israel too, and we do in fact learn more about them than we might at first expect, though, as may also be readily appreciated, the tradition has often given them a religious colouring which they certainly did not have in ancient Israel, or at least not to such a degree and in such a manner.

A farewell speech by the political leader appears to have been a normal occurrence. This is an address which often has the character of a testament, in which the leader, facing the prospect of approaching death, or handing over his office for some other reason, says farewell to his people or to his followers. The oldest example (as it occurs in the literature) is the farewell speech of Joshua in Josh. xxiv, which belongs mainly to E; one of the latest is that of Mattathias, the Hasmonean champion of independence, in I Macc. ii, 49-68. The tone of the one is different from that of the other, in that Joshua, in more pessimistic mood, foresees the coming apostasy of his people, whereas Mattathias, filled with confidence in the final downfall of the enemy, exhorts to actions demonstrating faithful adherence to the ancestral faith. They are nevertheless similar in that they both make clear what they wish to say by means of a long historical retrospect, and both call for the preservation of the religious inheritance of the fathers. It is only that Joshua is not so certain of the outcome of this exhortation as is Mattathias. Between these two examples—again as far as literary age is concerned—are to be found a second farewell speech of Joshua in Josh. xxiii, Samuel's farewell speech in I Sam. xii, David's last words in I Kings ii, 1-9, and I Chron. xxviii, 2-10; xxix, 1-5. Joshua's speech in Josh. xxiii and Samuel's farewell speech amplify our picture of this type of address in that they further show that the one who is saying farewell testifies to his fulfilment of his duty (Josh. xxiii, 4) and exonerates himself from any responsibility (I Sam. xii, 3-5); he may also mention the tasks which he himself has not been able to carry through to completion and which he must now entrust and commend to his successor. Though all these speeches, even the oldest in Josh. xxiv, are relatively late and clearly none of them, even the latest in I Macc. ii, 49-68, reproduces word for word what was actually said, there is nevertheless no doubt that they are not to be regarded as completely divorced from reality, nor as mere literary constructions. The truth is rather that in Israel, even in the earlier periods of its existence, farewell speeches of this type were actually made.

Furthermore, in Israel, as throughout the world, speeches are a means employed for the attainment of specific purposes, both in internal and external politics. They are particularly favoured and successfully applied when it is a matter of discrediting a political opponent at home among his adherents, or of weakening an external enemy and getting the better of him by destroying confidence in his leadership. An example of the former is the address which, according to Judg. ix, 7-20, was made to the Shechemites from Gerizim by Jotham, who alone among his brothers had escaped from the assassination brought upon them by Abimelech and only made possible by the treachery of the Shechemites. It begins with a parable (vv. 8–15) which will be considered later (cf. p. 37). To this, with a change from poetry to prose, there is attached with the words *and now* (וְעַתָּה) the application in vv. 16–20, to the effect that the treachery of the Shechemites will come back upon their own heads. After this there is recounted more briefly the speech by which Gaal incites the Schechemites against Abimelech (vv. 28–9). The use of the speech as an instrument in external political conflict is to be found in the one which, according to II Kings xviii (19–25), 28–35 = Isa. xxxvi (4–10), 13–20, was delivered before the gates of Jerusalem by the envoy of the Assyrian king, in order to make the inhabitants of the city doubt the rightness of Hezekiah's policy and so to incite them to deliver the city. The Assyrian envoy's intention of working upon the mass of the inhabitants is here emphasised further by the fact that he refuses to comply with the request of the Jewish representatives that the negotiations should be conducted, not in the Jewish language, but in Aramaic, which the people could not understand, but with which the Jewish leaders were conversant. The enemy refuses with the explicit statement that his words are specifically directed to the people who will have to suffer the results of Hezekiah's policy (II Kings xviii, 26–8 = Isa. xxxvi, 11–13). It is true that this is a foreigner speaking, but there can be no doubt that the Jewish narrator has shaped this speech in the form which was normal among his own people. The content and motivation of such speeches are indicated by their aim, which is to confuse men's minds with regard to their old leader and so to win their allegiance for a new one. The policy of the old leader is depicted as rotten and hopeless, and its consequences as they will affect his followers are painted in all their perversity, while the rule of the new leader is praised as bringing nothing but good fortune and blessing. It is completely natural to find that the language is especially pictorial with a view to its effect upon the masses. Furthermore, the speech which we have just discussed is delivered at the command of another, namely the Great King himself, and is presented in the guise of a message, a form which is closely related to the speech but is also a forerunner of the 'letter form' and is therefore discussed together with the 'letter' among the 'records' (p. 19). It is proper, however, to include it at this point as a pattern of the speeches employed in Israel both in external and internal politics as a means of inciting rebellion or discontent.

We hear of various other occasions for political speeches, and may gather at least something of their contents, for example at the assembly at Shechem on the occasion of the division of the kingdom (I Kings xii, especially vv. 4, 10–11, 16), and in the measures undertaken by Nehemiah against the rich creditors (Neh. v, 7). Complete speeches, however, are not frequently given. Only in one particular case does this happen more frequently, though admittedly the literary information is in general rather late, namely in the case of the address delivered by the commander at the opening of a campaign. Its main content, varied according to the particular situation by the appropriate emphasis on one point or another, is the affirmation that the battle is for the ancestral inheritance and for Yahweh; it exhorts determination and boldness, in imitation of the soldiers' ancestors, and the choice of death rather than defeat; it expresses confidence in complete success. This sentiment is to be found already in the almost proverbial saying which in II Sam. x, 12, is uttered by Joab to his brother Abishai at the beginning of the battle on two fronts against the Ammonites and Aramaeans (cf. p. 68). Addresses of this kind directed to the army are to be found in the brief utterance of Jehoshaphat before the battle against Ammonites and Moabites (II Chron. xx, 20), and in the speeches of the Maccabees—Judas, Jonathan, and Simon—before battles against the Syrian enemy (I Macc. ix, 8, 10, 44–6; xiii, 3–6). A quite different kind of speech, also belonging before the beginning of a battle, is described in Deut. xx, 5–8,[2] namely that which is addressed to the army by the *officers* (הַשֹּׁטְרִים) commanding all those to return who have built a house but not yet dedicated it, planted a vineyard but not yet used its fruit, betrothed a wife but not yet taken her home, and even all those who are fearful and fainthearted—a style of address which makes us at least ask whether it was really derived by the Deuteronomist from real life[3] or whether it simply represents a piece of wishful thinking (cf. p. 225). On the other hand, addresses directed to the enemy before the battle, like that which Abijah, King of Judah gave on mount Zemaraim to Jeroboam and his army (II Chron. xiii, 4–12), warning the enemy to desist from a hopeless battle, were no doubt really employed, and in the words which Abner shouts in II Sam. ii, 25–6 to Joab who is pursuing him we have a much older witness to this same custom.

Monologues and dialogues also belong with speeches in the broader sense. As is true for many of the other types (§ 13), we are able to recognise these mainly because prophets and poets made use of them. As an example of the monologue, we may cite the cry of woe which is uttered by Isaiah in the awe and anxiety created by the revelation of the powerful majesty of his God (Isa. vi, 5); or the boastings, bordering on hybris, in which the Assyrian glories in his seemingly unlimited power (Isa. x, 7–11). Israel's consideration of how Yahweh is to be appeased, as it is presented in Mic. vi, 6–7, also forms a monologue. But since this is occasioned by Yahweh's reproaches which precede it in vv. 3–5 and it represents the reply to these, vv. 3–7 may also be regarded as a dialogue. The boundary between monologue and dialogue is in fact unfixed, and prayer may often be equally well regarded as monologue or as dialogue. As an entity Mic. vi, 3–7 is in any case a dialogue, and more precisely a disputation about justice or a judgement speech. We may also note the similar dialogues in the form of debate, attested particularly by Job (§ 64) and Mal. (§ 61) where the relevant literature is noted. These may sometimes become ironical or satirical in character, and are then reminiscent of the Egyptian literary disputation of the thirteenth century B.C. preserved in the Papyrus Anastasi 1.[4]

2. *Sermons.* Much more numerous than the records of political speeches with which the previous section was mainly concerned, are those of speeches of a religious kind, or sermons. These were delivered in the first place by prophets,

[2] Herrmann, 'Das Aufgebot aller Kräfte. Zur Interpretation von 1 K (Krt) II, 96–103; IV, 184–91 und Dtn xx, 5–7' ZAW 70 (1958), pp. 215–20.

[3] Cf. Köhler, *Hebrew Man* (1956), pp. 116 ff.

[4] AOT, pp. 101–5; ANET, pp. 475–9. Lit. § 126.

and in the second place by priests and by Levites, three groups which in this particular respect cannot be sharply differentiated. We can observe how in the course of their development the political speeches become longer and longer. For the sermon, however, we see that it first appeared at a relatively late date, or at least only then did it acquire real importance. A rapid survey of the Old Testament material reveals in fact that so far as the contents of the prophetic books may be dated with reasonable certainty, the older ones—Amos, Hosea, Isaiah and Micah—do not contain a single sermon, whereas the later—especially Jeremiah and Ezekiel—have a fairly large number. Such sermons are to be found in no small number in the Deuteronomic sections Deut. i–xi, xxix–xxxi, which in all probability belong to the end of the seventh century and to the sixth century (cf. pp. 173–6) and also in the more or less contemporary Deuteronomistic[5] revision of the older historical books (Josh.–Kings). So the commonly held view which treats the sermon-like passages in the books of Jeremiah and Ezekiel as not genuine cannot be maintained, or at least not with reference to all these sections. We ought rather to assume that from about the beginning of the seventh century prophets and priests began to use, in addition to the saying forms (§§ 9, 10), their normal charismatic and ecstatic forms of expression, the more rational medium of the sermon, or, if it should prove that they used such a medium at an earlier period, it was at any rate at this period that they began to use it to a much greater degree. Here we must further reckon with the possibility that there appears in this the influence of the Levites or of a particular group of Levites, who as teachers and pastors may, even before this period, have made use of the sermon for the carrying out of their responsibilities.[6]

Examples of such sermons may be found first in the passages of Jeremiah and Ezekiel already mentioned. Jer. vii, 1–viii, 3, and Ezekiel xx may be cited here, and reference made to the discussion of the point in the analysis of the books (pp. 351, 376). Further examples are the sermons to be found in the framework of Deuteronomy and scattered in the older historical books. They, like Pss. lxxviii, cv, cvi (p. 125), which are similar in content, are all characterised by the combination of historical retrospect with exhortation, in which Israel's history is described as being on the one hand an unbroken chain of divine acts of grace which bind Israel to unceasing gratitude (Deut. viii, 2–20, xi), and on the other hand a similarly continuous series of examples of disobedience and punishment as a warning (Ezek. xx). We can see here the effects of the prophetic sayings and poems themselves, which, especially in Hosea (p. 386), are often so formed that they deduce threats and warnings from history. It was indeed the prophets who first fully grasped and proclaimed the character of Yahweh as God of history.

Thus the sermon, whether belonging to prophetic circles, or those of priests and Levites, is definitely to be included as a special form of speech, which

---

[5] The term Deuteronomic is used for the compiler or compilers of Deuteronomy, and the term Deuteronomistic for the redactors who worked over or completed the other books in the spirit and style of Deuteronomy.

[6] Wright, 'The Levites in Deuteronomy' VT 4 (1954), pp. 325–30. Lit. § 126.

appears alongside the forms which are proper to prophets and priests (§ 10 and § 9, 2) and increasingly becomes interwoven with these forms. Finally, besides the prophetic and priestly sayings, the wisdom sayings (§ 11, 3) are also incorporated in the sermon which can make use of so many different kinds of material. As long as the metrical form of the wisdom saying was firmly preserved, it continued to give the effect of a wisdom poem (cf. § 16) elaborated from the wisdom saying, even when it contained a considerable amount of sermon-like material, as may be seen from the Wisdom of Solomon i, 1–v, 23. But when once this form ceased to be employed, the wisdom saying inevitably contributed its share to the all-inclusive sermon, even without this process of assimilation being hastened by the influence of the hellenistic diatribe which can clearly be discerned in IV Macc. (§ 94). The sermon-like addresses of the twelve sons of Jacob in the Testaments of the Twelve Patriarchs contain much that derives from the wisdom saying, in addition to many other elements (§ 102).

3. *Prayers*. It is proper to find a place for the prayer also among the prose forms. Although as a result of its solemn nature it is inclined to fixed metrical forms and therefore appears chiefly in poetic shape (cf. § 15), there is nevertheless a considerable place accorded to the prose prayer. It is true that most of the examples of such prayers—at any rate those of any length—belong to a later period, even to a very late date. But the beginnings of this form clearly go back to very ancient times. Here we may discuss simply the three most important types: prayers of intercession, of confession, and of thanksgiving. With all these the development may be traced quite clearly from short request-like sayings to elaborate prayers.

A quite short prayer of intercession is that of Samson in Judg. xvi, 28: *O Lord Yahweh, remember me, I pray thee, and strengthen me, I pray thee only this once, O God, that I may be avenged upon the Philistines for one of my two eyes*. The elements of this short prayer are: address, petition, affirmation of Yahweh as God, petition or wish with statement of motive. The somewhat longer prayer of Solomon in I Kings iii, 6–9 adds further the recollection of earlier demonstrations of God's grace. If we then look at the much more elaborate prayers of the later and latest periods, as they are put in the mouth of Jehoshaphat in II Chron. xx, 6–12, Judith in Judith ix, Eleazar the priest in III Macc. vi, 2–15, or as we find prayers of Mordecai and Esther in the Additions to Esther, we find in general the same motives as in the shorter petitions just mentioned—a proof of the continuity of the pattern. It is just that the whole form has become much fuller. The affirmations about God are multiplied, and among them appears more frequently now the description of him as creator of heaven and earth (III Macc. vi, 2; Judith ix, 12). Above all, as in the sermon, the largest place is given to historical retrospects. Thus III Macc. vi, 4–8 first relates occasions when God prepared a sudden end for the boastful activities of presumptuous enemies— Pharaoh and Sennacherib, and then examples of deliverance—the three companions of Daniel, Daniel himself and Jonah (cf. II Chron. xx, 7–10, Judith ix, 2–4). Solomon's prayer of dedication of the temple is a special type of prayer of intercession (I Kings viii, 23–53); it reckons up in a casuistic style all the cases of need in which Israel will cry to God for help either in the temple or facing towards the temple, and asks for God's gracious hearing in anticipation of these.

The prayer of confession is a special type of prayer of intercession in which a definite request is made, namely forgiveness of guilt and the turning away of the punishment which because of the guilt threatens the people or the individual. In Judg. x, 10, the prayer of the Israelites when hard pressed by the Ammonites is limited to a simple confession of guilt: *We have sinned against thee, because we have forsaken our God and have served the Baalim.* A second prayer belonging to the same situation (x, 15) adds to a more detailed confession of guilt a prayer for deliverance: *We have sinned; do to us whatever seems good to thee; only deliver us we pray thee to-day.* A third prayer, coming from a similar situation, is quoted by Samuel in his farewell speech (I Sam. xii, 10), and adds to confession and petition the promise of gratitude to be shown in ever more faithful honouring of Yahweh: *We have sinned, because we have forsaken Yahweh, and have served the Baalim and the Ashtaroth. But now, deliver us from the hand of our enemies, and we will serve thee.* It is a long way from these short prayers of confession to the elaborate prayers of Ezra (Ezra ix, 6–15), Daniel (Dan. ix, 4–19), the High Priest Simon (III Macc. ii, 2–19) or even to the prayer attributed in the apocryphal book of Baruch (cf. § 86) to the exiles of 597 B.C. Yet the connection with the older, shorter prayers is still clear. The motives and expressions have been retained, but here too they have become much longer and new ones have been added. Historical retrospects also take up a large place here (Ezra ix, 7; III Macc. ii, 3–8; Baruch i, 19–ii, 10), the affirmations about God are multiplied (III Macc. ii, 2–3), and so on.

Finally there is the prayer of thanksgiving. A pure example of the prose form has, only by chance, not survived, but the prayers of Jacob in Gen. xxxii, 10–13, and of David in II Sam. vii, 19–29, provide prayers of thanksgiving in the first half, although they then run on into petitions. Common to them both, apart from the address to Yahweh, there is above all the fact that those who offer them stress the sense of unworthiness which has become especially plain because of the great proofs of divine grace, felt to be entirely undeserved. They thus give indirect expression to their gratitude.

§ 4. RECORDS

Our information about ancient Israel depends substantially on literary tradition, namely the Old Testament. In this the position is different from that of the peoples in Israel's environment for which archaeological documents are available directly reflecting their character and history, whereas relatively few Israelite records of any kind have been preserved. There have survived from Israel hardly any victory or building inscriptions,[1] edicts or proclamations,[2] of

---

[1] Alt, 'Die phönikischen Inschriften von Karatepe' WdO I, 4 (1949), pp. 272–87: II, 2 (1955), pp. 172–83. Lit. § 126.

[2] Kraus, *Ein Edict des Königs Ammiṣaduqa von Babylon* (1958). Lit. § 126.

which many examples are available from Israel's neighbours. The record (סֵפֶר)
in which according to Exod. xvii, 14, Moses is said to have preserved the memory
of Israel's victory over the Amalekites, is more likely to have been a report of
the kind which will be discussed below (p. 48). But the monument (יָד)
which Saul erected to himself after his victory over the Amalekites (I Sam.
xv, 12), must more probably be thought of as provided with an inscription and
thus as a victory inscription. The relatively numerous details concerning buildings, for example those concerning Solomon's palace, temple and fortress
buildings (I Kings vi–viii; ix, 15), also belong among the reports (p. 49).
But the Siloam inscription[3] found only in 1880—admittedly it is not in the Old
Testament—is a genuine building inscription. There are a relatively large
number of royal edicts and proclamations in the later books of the Old Testament. Some of them are genuine, some not, but they almost all stem from non-
Israelite rulers, Babylonian (Dan. iii, 31–iv, 34) or Persian (Ezra i, 2–4; iv,
17–22; vii, 12–26), and thus do not really provide us with information about
Israel but about its ancient oriental environment.

(a) *Contracts*

Literature: Baltzer, *Das Bundesformular* WMANT 4 (1960); Begrich, 'Berit' ZAW 60
(1944), pp. 1–11; García de la Fuente, 'Los contratos en el AT comparados con los de
Egipto, Asiria y Babilonia', *Est Bibl* 14 (1955), pp. 223–54; Fohrer, 'Der Vertrag zwischen
König und Volk in Israel' ZAW 71 (1954), pp. 1–22; Gunneweg, 'Sinaibund und Davidsbund' VT 10 (1960), pp. 335–41; Huffmon, 'The Covenant Lawsuit in the Prophets' JBL
78 (1959), pp. 285–95; Kruse, 'Novi Foederis Hora Natalis' VD 37 (1959), pp. 257–75,
321–35; Mendenhall, *Law and Covenant in Israel and the Ancient Near East* (1955); Muilenburg, 'The Form and Structure of the Covenant Formulation' VT 9 (1959), pp. 347–65;
Noth, 'Das at. Bundschließen im Lichte eines Mari-Textes' AIPhHOS 13 ([1953], 1955),
pp. 433–44 = *Ges. Studien zum AT* (1957), pp. 142–54; Widengren, 'King and Covenant'
JSSt 2 (1957), pp. 1–32; Wolff, 'Jahwe als Bundesvermittler' VT 6 (1956), pp. 316–20. Lit.
§ 126.

For the peoples of Israel's environment—Sumerians, Babylonians, Assyrians[4] and Horites,[5] Egyptians[6] and Hittites,[7] Aramaeans[8] and Canaanites[9]—
we have the actual words of a host of contracts. But in the Old Testament,

---

[3] Cf. below, p. 52; p. 675, n. 15.

[4] AOT, pp. 431–4; ANET, pp. 217–22; Finkelstein, 'Assyrian Contracts from Sultantepe' An St 7 (1957), pp. 137–45; Kraus, 'Neue Rechtsurkunden der altbabylonischen
Zeit' WdO II, 2 (1955), pp. 120–36; Meissner, *Die Babylonisch-Assyrische Literatur*
(1928), pp. 67–76; Weidner, 'Der Staatsvertrag Aššurnirâris VI. von Assyrien mit Mati'ilu
von Bît-Agusi' AfO 8 (1932/3), pp. 17–34; Wisemann, 'The Vassal-Treaties of Esarhaddon' Iraq 20 (1958), pp. 1–90, Pls. I–XII, 1–53; 'Esarhaddon's Treaties with the
Medes' A XXIV I O K (1959), pp. 134–7. Lit. § 126.

[5] Texts: *Publications of the Baghdad School. The Joint Expedition with the Iraq Museum
at Nuzi* I–V (Chiera), (1927–34); VI (Lacheman), (1939); *Excavations at Nuzi* I (Chiera),
(1929); II (Pfeiffer), (1933); III (Meek), (1935); IV (Pfeiffer and Lacheman), (1942); V, VI,
VII (Lacheman), (1950, 1955, 1958); Pfeiffer and Speiser, *One Hundred New Selected
Nuzi Texts* (1936); ANET, pp. 219 f. Reports of Excavations: Starr, *Nuzi* I (1939); II
(1937). References to literature on Nuzi and the Old Testament in Eissfeldt, *Der Beutel der
Lebendigen* (BAL 105, 6, 1960), pp. 5–7. Lit. § 126.

[6] Erman-Ranke, *Ägypten* (1923), pp. 164–71, 640–4, *et passim*. Lit. § 126.

while we have many narratives concerning the drawing up of contracts, we have only isolated examples of the contracts themselves. As far as states and their representatives are concerned, we hear, for example, of agreements made by Abraham and Isaac with Abimelech of Gerar, at Beersheba, here understood to mean *well of the oath* or *well of the contract* (Gen. xxi, 22–32; xxvi, 26–31), by Jacob with Laban (Gen. xxxi, 44–54), by Joshua with the Gibeonites (Josh. ix, 15), by Solomon with Hiram of Tyre (I Kings v, 16–23). In most cases the chief element in these contracts is indicated, but the actual record of such a contract comes only from the Graeco-Roman period, namely the treaty of the Romans with Judas Maccabaeus, set out in I Macc. viii, 22–32.[10]

Related to the treaties concluded between tribes and peoples and their representatives, and certainly influenced by the style of these, is the agreement between God and a human community, which has, however, its own special characteristics. There were certainly prescribed for this not only specific ceremonials, but also specific forms. We get a picture of the rituals from stories like Gen. xv, 9–18; Ex. xxiv, 3–8; II Kings xxiii, 1–3. The formulae are reflected in the various bodies of law which are discussed later—the Book of the Covenant (Ex. xx, 22–xxiii, 33), the Holiness Code (Lev. xvii–xxvi), and Deuteronomy (Deut. xii–xxviii)—particularly in the lists of promises and threats which stand at the end (Lev. xxvi, Deut. xxviii; cf. Ex. xxiii, 20–33, see on this p. 214). These bodies of law as we now have them are literary products, in part very complex in composition, but it is certain that they owe their form to the actual conditions of life, in this case of cultic life, and therefore that such making of agreements with Yahweh really did take place, may even have had a fixed place in the cultus and have produced a definite formula.

[7] AOT, pp. 379 f.; ANET, pp. 199–206; Freydank, 'Eine hethitische Fassung des Vertrages zwischen dem Hethiterkönig Šuppiluliuma und Aziru von Amurru' MIOF 7 (1960), pp. 356–81; Friedrich, 'Staatsverträge des Hatti-Reiches in hethitischer Sprache' MVÄG 31, 1; 34, 1 (1926, 1930); Korošec, *Hethitische Staatsverträge* (1931); 'Staatsverträge in keilschriftlicher Überlieferung' A XXIV IOK (1959), pp. 142–4; Pirenne, 'La politique d'expansion hittite envisagée travers les traités de vassalité et de protectorat' ArOr 18 I, II (1950), pp. 373–82; Weidner, *Politische Dokumente aus Kleinasien. Die Staatsverträge in akkadischer Sprache aus dem Archiv von Boghazköi* I, II (1923). Lit. § 126.

[8] ANET, pp. 503 f.; Bauer, 'Ein aramäischer Staatsvertrag aus dem 8. Jh. vChr' AfO 8 (1932/3), pp. 1–16; Bauer und Meissner, 'Ein aramäischer Pachtvertrag aus dem 7. Jahre Darius' I' SAB (1936), pp. 414–24, 2 Pls.; Dupont-Sommer, 'Un contrat de Métayage égypto-araméen de l'an 7 de Darius I' MDS, XIV (1951), pp. 61–106; 'Les inscriptions araméennes de Sfiré' MDS XV (1960), pp. 197–351, Pls. I–XXIX; Fitzmyer, 'The Aramaic Suzerainty Treaty from Sefîrê in the Museum of Beirut' CBQ 20 (1958), pp. 444–76; Rosenthal, 'Notes on the Third Aramaic Inscription from Sefîre-Sûjîn' BASOR 158 (1960), pp. 28–31; Starcky, 'Une tablette araméenne de l'an 34 de Nabuchodonosor (AO, 21. 063)' Syria 37 (1960), pp. 99–115; Yaron, 'Aramaic Deeds of Conveyance' Bibl 41 (1960), pp. 248–74, 379–94. Lit. § 126.

[9] Korošec, 'Über die neuesten keilschriftlichen Rechtsquellen aus Alalaḫ und Ugarit' Zbornik zuanstvenik razprov 29 (1959), pp. 77–103; Nougayrol, 'Les nouvelles tablettes accadiennes de Ras-Shamra' CRAI (1953), pp. 40–51; 'Les archives internationales d'Ugarit CRAI (1954), pp. 30–41, 239–53; *Textes accadiens et hourrites des archives est, ouest et centrales* (PRU III, 1955); *Textes accadiens des Archives Sud* (PRU IV, 1956); Sidney Smith, *The Statue of Idrimi* (1949), pp. 17 f., 42–58; Wiseman, *The Alalakh Tablets* (1953), pp. 55–8; 'Abban and Alalaḫ' JCSt 2 (1958), pp. 124–9. Lit. § 126.

[10] Täubler, *Imperium Romanum* I (1913), pp. 239–54: 'Der Vertrag mit den Juden 161.' Cf. p. 639, n. 6.

Further, we often hear of agreements which are concluded at the time of the choice of a king between the chosen candidate and the body responsible for the choice. Thus we are told in II Sam. v, 3, that David made a covenant with the elders of Israel who wished to anoint him in Hebron as king over Israel, and I Kings xii and Judg. ix, 8–15 reveal to us more exactly the procedure of such negotiations and agreements. But we have no actual text of such an agreement from the earlier period, the nearest being an imitation distorted by an anti-monarchical bias in I Sam. viii, 11–17. From the later period we have the document set out by the people to honour Simon as the hereditary Priest-prince in I Macc. xiv, 27–47, which is at least related to agreements of this kind.

The position is similar with regard to agreements made between private individuals. We very often read of such agreements in the Old Testament. Abraham made one with the previous owner at the purchase of the cave of Machpelah (Gen. xxiii),[11] and the agreements made between Jeremiah and Boaz and their relatives also concerned landed property (Jer. xxxii,[12] Ruth iv, 1–12). In all three cases the negotiations are described in great detail, and in the case of Jeremiah there is specific mention of a deed of purchase in duplicate, but the wording of the document is never given; at most a few phrases are quoted (Gen. xxiii, 16 f.). The position is the same with regard to the contract of service concluded between Jacob and Laban (Gen. xxx. 28–34). In this we may observe particularly clearly the enormous difference between the Old Testament and the material excavated in Mesopotamia, Egypt, Asia Minor and Syria (Ugarit and Alalakh). There is an almost unlimited wealth of agreements of precisely this kind for these areas. The position is not at all altered by the fact that the soil of Palestine has provided two clay tablets containing contracts for the sale of land,[13] which, in spite of the fact that they are in Assyrian language, may perhaps be Israelite and not Assyrian. The position is the same in regard to domestic legal agreements, such as marriage contracts and divorce records. We have a wealth of examples from Israel's environment, but in the Old Testament there are only references to such documents, a marriage contract[14] in Tob. vii, 16, and divorce records[15] in Deut. xxiv, 1, 3; Isa. l, 1; Jer. iii, 8.

[11] Evans, ' "Coming" and "Going" at the City Gate' BASOR 150 (1958), pp. 28–33; Lehmann, 'Abraham's Purchase of Machpelah and Hittite Law' BASOR 129 (1953), pp. 15–18; Speiser, ' "Coming" and "Going" at the "City" Gate' BASOR 144 (1956), pp. 20–3. Lit. § 126.

[12] Fischer, 'Die Urkunden in Jer. xxxii, 11–14, nach den Ausgrabungen und dem Talmud' ZAW 30 (1910), pp. 136–42.

[13] They were discovered during the excavations at Gezer and belong to the years around 650 B.C. Cf. S. A. Cook, Religion of Ancient Palestine in the Light of Archaeology (1930), pp. 64–5 and Pl. XII, and also AOB, Figs. 595–6.

[14] Cf. Cowley, Ar. Pap., pp. 25–9, No. 9, pp. 44–50, No. 15; ANET, pp. 222 f.; Koschaker, 'Eheschliessung und Kauf nach alten Rechten, mit besonderer Berücksichtigung der älteren Keilschriftrechte' ArOr 18 3/4 (1950), pp. 210–96; Yaron, 'Aramaic Marriage Contracts from Elephantine' JSSt 3 (1958), pp. 1–39; 5 (1960), pp. 66–70. Cf. below, p. 639. Lit. § 126.

[15] Yaron, 'On divorce in OT times' Revue Intern. des Droits de l'Antiquité, III, 4 (1957), pp. 117–28. Cf. Lit. p. 224, n. 9; § 126.

(b) *Letters*

Literature: Beer, 'Zur israelitisch-jüdischen Briefliteratur' BWAT 13 (1913), pp. 20–41; Galling, 'Brief' BRL (1937), cols. 117–22; Habermann, 'Ancient Hebrew and Aramaic Epistles and the Word "Hela"' [Hebr., Engl. summary], Eretz Israel 4 (1956), pp. 133–37, IX; Jirku, 'Briefstil, biblischer und babylonischer' RLA II (1938), p. 68; Marty, 'Contribution à l'étude de fragments épistolaires antiques, conservés principalement dans la Bible Hébraïque. Les formules de salutation' *Mél. Syriens Dussaud* II (1939), pp. 845–855; Naveh, 'A Hebrew letter from the Seventh Century B.C.' IEJ 10 (1960), pp. 129–39, pls. 17–18; Pfeiffer, 'Assyrian Epistolary Formulae' JAOS 43 (1923), pp. 26–40; Roller, *Das Formular der Paulinischen Briefe* BWANT 58 (1933); Schroeder, 'Briefe' RLA II (1938), pp. 62–8; Vogt, 'Ostracon Hebraicum saec. 7 a. C.' Bibl 41 (1960), pp. 183 f. Lit. § 126.

We are fairly well informed by the Old Testament on the subject of the letter form, in that not only do we have mention of letters from the beginning of the monarchy to the Roman period, but fragments and complete texts are also quoted. The Hebrew term for *letter* is סֵפֶר, a term which is of course more comprehensive and includes also the contracts just discussed as well as other records which are discussed later, as well as being used primarily for (*book*) *scroll* (cf. pp. 132 f.); but it is also employed for a letter. In the post-exilic period the terms מִכְתָּב and אִגֶּרֶת also appear for *letter*. The earliest letter of which we hear in the Old Testament, is the famous (or infamous) letter sent by David concerning Uriah. In II Sam. xi, 15, its most important sentence is quoted. We find the same with regard to the letter sent by Jezebel to the elders of Jezreel (I Kings xxi, 8–10), and that of the Aramaean king to the king of Israel (II Kings v, 5–6). From the letter which, according to II Kings x, 1–3, was written by Jehu to the city elders of Samaria, there is quoted in v. 2 the main part, introduced by the word וְעַתָּה *And now!* This was preceded by the address, with the name of the recipient and the proper polite formulae, as may be seen from a comparison with letters from Israel's environment, for example the Akkadian letters from Nimrud, biblical Calah (Gen. x, 11–12),[16] Mari[17] and Alalakh,[18] the Amarna-letters,[19] the Hittite letters,[20] and the letters from Ugarit,[21] partly in

---

[16] Saggs, 'The Nimrud Letters, 1952' *Iraq* 17 (1955), pp. 21–56, 126–54, Pls. IV–IX, XXX–XXXV; 18 (1956), pp. 40–56, Pls. IX–XII; 20 (1958), pp. 182–212, Pls. XXXVII–XLI; 21 (1959), pp. 158–80, Pls. XLIII–XLIX'. Cf. Mallowan, 'The Excavations at Nimrud (Kalḫu) (1949–1958)' *Iraq* 12–21 (1950/9). Lit. § 126.

[17] *Archives Royales de Mari. Transcriptions et Traductions, publiées sous la direction de Parrot et Dossin*, I–IV, XV (1950–4); ANET, pp. 482 f.; Bottéro, 'Lettres de la Salle 110 du Palais de Mari' RA 52 (1958), pp. 163–76. Lit. § 126.

[18] Wiseman, *The Alalakh Tablets* (1953), pp. 58–62. Lit. § 126.

[19] Knudtzon, *Die El-Amarna-Tafeln*, I, II (1907–15); AOT, pp. 370–9; ANET, pp. 483–90; Campbell, 'The Amarna Letters and the Amarna Period' BA 23 (1960), pp. 2–22; van der Meer, 'The Chronological Determination of the Mesopotamian Letters in the El-Amarna Archives' JEOL 15 (1957/8), pp. 74–96. Lit. § 126.

[20] Cf. Lit. § 126.

[21] Gordon, *Ugaritic Manual* (1955), pp. 129–68, Nos. 18, 26, 32, 54, 89, 95, 101, 117, 138, etc.; *Ugaritic Literature* (1949), pp. 116–19; Nougayrol, CRAI (1952), pp. 181–91; (1953), pp. 40–51; (1954), pp. 30–41, 239–53; PRU III, IV (1955, 1956); Virolleaud, PRU II (1957). From the request sent by the Ugaritic king Niqmadu to the Hittite king Shuppiluliuma to help him against neighbouring kings who had invaded his land (CRAI (1954), p. 35, lines 7–10=PRU IV, 49, lines 11–14), it is possible to form an impression of the appeal for help which, according to II Kings xvi, 17, was made by the Judaean king

Akkadian, partly in Canaanite language, and the Aramaic letters from Egypt.[22] There cannot be the least doubt that the Israelite letter style is dependent upon that of Babylonia and Canaan; in fact, it is almost identical with that style. In this respect II Kings xix, 9–14, is also significant, where, in vv. 9–10,[23] there is mention of messengers who receive the commission: *Thus shall ye speak to Hezekiah . . .*, whereas v. 14 states that this message was contained in a letter read before Hezekiah and subsequently laid before Yahweh. This is a clear proof of the fact that the Israelite letter, like the Akkadian, developed out of the message entrusted orally to the messenger and repeated by him orally to the recipient. The narrator has clearly pictured the letter sent by a king of Assyria according to what he knew to be Israelite custom. We find this point attested also by Gen. xxxii, 5–6 and Num. xx, 14–19. A complete letter of Jeremiah's is given in Jer. xxix, 1–23, and in Jer. xxix, 24–32, there are parts of two letters, one of which was sent to Shemaiah, and the other sent by him.

From the last centuries with which we are concerned, the Neo-Babylonian, Persian and Graeco-Roman periods, there have been preserved in the Old Testament and in the books which in a broad sense belong with it, a very large number of letters. In these the letter style of the earlier period is certainly continued, but at the same time, as may be seen from a comparison with the extra-biblical letters from the Neo-Babylonian and Persian periods mainly in Aramaic[24] and from the Hellenistic period in Greek,[25] the influence of the normative diction of the period becomes noticeable, and this means, since the material is in large measure diplomatic correspondence, the style of Persian and Hellenistic administration. It is sufficient to mention here the letters to the Persian king in Ezra iv–vi and his replies; the many letters cited in the first two books of Maccabees, and finally the correspondence engaged in between Ptolemy II Philadelphus and the High Priest Eleazar in the so-called Letter of Aristeas. For our purpose it is of no importance whether these letters are genuine or not. We are here concerned only with the style, and this is at least in most cases certainly genuine and suited to the appropriate period,

Ahaz to the Assyrian king Tiglathpileser, and his consent may be thought of as similar to that which Shuppiluliuma gave to the Ugaritic king (CRAI (1954), pp. 34 f. = PRU IV, pp. 48–52). Lit. § 126.

[22] See below, n. 24.

[23] Vikentiev, 'Quelques considérations à propos des Statues de Taharqa trouvées dans les ruines du palais d'Esarhaddon' Sumer 11 (1955), pp. 111–16. Cf. below, p. 296, n. 58.

[24] Cowley, *Ar. Pap.*; AOT, pp. 450–62; ANET, pp. 491 f.; Kraeling, *Ar. Pap.*; Driver, *Ar. Doc.* (1954, ²1957); Bardtke, 'Elephantine und die jüdische Gemeinde der Perserzeit' Das Altertum 6 (1960), pp. 13–31; Edda Bresciani, 'Un papiro aramaico da El Hibbeh del Museo Archeologico di Firence' Aegyptus 39 (1959), pp. 3–8, 1 Pl.; 'Papiri aramaici egiziani di epoca persiana presso el Museo civico di Padova' RStO 35 (1960), pp. 11–24, Pls. I–V; Eilers, 'Neue aramäische Urkunden aus Ägypten' AfO 17, 2 (1956), pp. 322–35; Hammershaimb, 'Some Observations on the Aramaic Elephantine Papyri' VT 7 (1957), pp. 17–34; Kutscher, 'New Aramaic Texts' JAOS 74 (1954), pp. 233–48; Malamat, 'The New Aramaic Saqqârah Papyrus from the Time of Jeremiah' [Hebr., Engl. summary] BJPES 15 (1949/50), pp. 34–9, II–III; Milik, 'Lettre araméenne d'El Hibeh' Aegyptus 40 (1960), pp. 79–81; Segert, 'Neue aramäische Texte aus Ägypten' ArOr 24 (1956), pp. 284–91; 'Aramäische Studien, I, Die neuen Editionen von Brooklyn Papyri und Arsams Briefe in ihrer Bedeutung fur die Bibelwissenschaft' ArOr 24 (1956), pp. 383–403. Lit. p. 24, n. 27; p. 639, n. 6; § 126.

[25] Roller, pp. 34–91, *et passim.*

though this may not always be the period required by the context in which they stand.

The very large majority of the letters mentioned or preserved in the Old Testament and the related literature are letters in the true sense of the word, that is to say, writings which arise out of a quite specific occasion and are sent and received by quite specific individuals or groups. Compositions which are only loosely dressed up as letters and were from the first intended for wider publication—artificial letters or epistles—are by contrast quite rare. But this latter type is not entirely lacking. The edict which Dan. iii, 31–iv, 34 (EVV. iv, 1–37)[26] puts into the mouth of king Nebuchadrezzar is an epistle. In reality it is a narrative rich in hymnic motives, with the purpose of showing that the power of all earthly kings is ephemeral and God's rule alone abides. Thus in iv, 16, 25–30, it abandons the letter style and ends without the formula appropriate to a letter. The so-called Letter of Jeremiah is also of this type, a prophetic address of warning and exhortation which warns against addressing prayer to idols and exhorts the exclusive worship of the one God (see § 87). Similarly, the letter of Baruch to the nine and a half tribes, which stands at the end of the Syriac Apocalypse of Baruch is to be termed an epistle, although it strictly preserves the letter form both at the beginning and end (see p. 629). At the end the sender calls upon the recipients to read the letter in the assemblies, especially on fast days, and this refers to an actual custom mentioned also in the book of Baruch i, 14. It must therefore have been normal in the time of the composition of the Apocalypse, about A.D. 130, to read aloud in the synagogues on such days written missives from notable leaders of the community. The content of the letter, however, which is completely concentrated upon the period of the historical Baruch, in the time of the Exile, shows clearly that it was composed for its present context. This must have been done following the pattern of what we should call 'Lenten letters', but the letter of Baruch is not itself such a 'Lenten letter', but a purely literary composition. The same is true of the letters which, according to Esther ix, 20–32, were sent out by Mordecai and Esther calling for the celebration of the feast of Purim (§ 70) and, according to II Macc. i, 1–ii, 18, were sent out by the Palestinian Jews with regard to the feast of the dedication of the temple (§ 79). Such festal letters certainly existed, but those mentioned are invented, though clearly based on the pattern of real ones.[27]

(c) Lists

Literature: Albright, 'The List of Levitic Cities' *L. Ginzberg Jub. Vol.* (1945), pp. 49–73; Alt, 'Israels Gaue unter Salomo' BWAT 13 (1913), pp. 1–19 = *Kl. Schr.* II, pp. 76–89;

[26] Rabinowitz, 'A Legal Formula in the Susa Tablets, in an Egyptian Document of the Twelfth Dynasty, in the Aramaic Papyri, and in the Book of Daniel' Bibl 33 (1955), pp. 74–7: Dan. iv, 14, 22, 29; 'The Susa Tablets, the Bible and the Aramaic Papyri' VT 11 (1961), pp. 55–76. Lit. § 126.

[27] Cf. the 'Passover letter' of Darius II from the year 419 B.C.; Cowley, *Ar. Pap.*, pp. 60–5, No. 21; AOT, p. 453; ANET, p. 491; DOTT, pp. 258–60; Eduard Meyer, *Der Papyrusfund von Elephantine* (³1912), pp. 91–7; Kraeling, *Ar. Pap.*, pp. 92–6; Ginsberg, 'The Brooklyn Museum Aramaic Papyri' JAOS 74 (1954), pp. 153–62, esp. p. 155. Cf. also p. 23, n. 24; p. 26, n. 33; p. 553, n. 29.

'Judas Gaue unter Josia' PJB 21 (1925), pp. 100–16 = *Kl. Schr.* II, pp. 276–88; 'Eine galiläische Ortsliste in Jos xix' ZAW 45 (1927), pp. 59–81; 'Bemerkungen zu einigen judäischen Ortslisten des AT.' Beiträge zur bibl. Landes- u. Altertumskunde 68 (1951), pp. 193–210 = *Kl. Schr.* II, pp. 289–305; 'Festungen und Levitenorte im Lande Juda' *ib.*, pp. 306–31 5; Brandenstein, 'Bemerkungen zur Völkertafel der Genesis' *Festschr. Debrunner* (1954), pp. 57–83; Dhorme, 'Les peuples issus de Japhet d'après le chapitre x de la Genèse' Syria 13 (1932), pp. 28–49 = *Recueil Edouard Dhorme* (1951), pp. 167–89; Elliger, 'Die dreißig Helden Davids' PJB 31 (1935), pp. 29–75; Haran, 'The Levitical Cities: Utopia and Historical Reality' [Hebr., Engl. summary], Tarbiz 27 (1957/8), pp. 421–39, I–II; Hoftijzer, 'Enige opmerkingen rond het israëlitische 12-stammensysteem' NedThT 14 (1960), pp. 241–63; Noth, 'Das System der zwölf Stämme Israels' BWANT 52 (1930), pp. 122–32; 'Studien zu den historisch-geographischen Dokumenten des Josuabuches' ZDPV 58 (1935), pp. 185–255; 'Der Wallfahrtsweg zum Sinai' PJB 36 (1940), pp. 5–28; Schmidtke, *Die Japhetiten der biblischen Völkertafel* (1926); Simons, 'The "Table of Nations" (Gen. x): Its General Structure and Meaning' OTS 10 (1954), pp. 155–84; *The Geographical and Topographical Texts of the OT* (1959); Wiseman, 'Genesis x: Some Archaeological Considerations' Journal of the Transactions of the Victoria-Institute 87 (1955), pp. 13–25. Further literature on lists is noted in the treatment of the books which contain them, especially Josh., Chron., Ezra, Neh. Lit. § 126.

The Old Testament contains a great number of lists of all kinds: genealogical lists of individuals and of communities, lists of officials and of heroes, lists of places and boundary points, lists of sacred gifts, etc. Many of these have their counterparts in Israel's environment which are valuable for their understanding.[28] Examples of genealogical lists are the 'Table of Nations' in Gen. x,[29] the enumeration of the descendants of Nahor (Gen. xxii, 20–4), of Keturah (Gen. xxv, 1–4), of Ishmael (Gen. xxv, 12–16), of Esau or Seir or Edom (Gen. xxxvi), where in addition to the genealogical lists we have the clearly ancient and reliable lists of the *Kings who reigned in the land of Edom before any king reigned over the Israelites* (xxxvi, 31–9),[30] and the main part of I Chron. i–ix. Lists of officials and heroes are to be found in II Sam. viii, 16–18; xx, 23–6;[31] xxiii, 8–39, together with I Chron. xi, 42–7; the list of Solomon's district officers in I Kings iv, 7–19 + v, 7–8, also includes a note of their districts after the names.[32] Lists of places belonging to the individual tribes are worked

[28] A reference must suffice here to the various Canaanite lists from Ugarit, to be found among the texts in Gordon, *Ug. Manual* (1955), pp. 124–80, in transcription, and translated or at any rate described in *Ug. Lit.* (1949), pp. 107–30, as well as the lists among the texts from Alalakh (p. 22, n. 18) and Mari (p. 22, n. 17).

[29] Cavaignac, 'Alishia-Élise' JA 247 (1959), pp. 297–301: on x, 4; Maurice Dunand and Nessib Saliby, 'A la recherche de Simyra' Annales Archéologiques de Syrie 7 (1957), pp. 3–16, Pls. I–VII, 1 Map: on x, 18. Lit. § 126.

[30] Moritz, 'Edomitische Genealogien I' ZAW 44 (1926), pp. 81–93; 'Die Könige von Edom' Muséon 50 (1937), pp. 101–22; 'Ergänzungen zu meinem Aufsatz "Die Könige von Edom"' ZAW 57 (1939), pp. 148–50.

[31] Begrich, 'Sofēr und Mazkīr' ZAW 58 (1940/1), pp. 1–29; Maisler, 'The Scribe of King David and the Problem of the High Officials in the Ancient Kingdom of Israel' [Hebr., Engl. summary] BJPES 13 (1946/7), pp. 105–14, IV–V; Reventlow, 'Das Amt des Mazkir' ThZ 15 (1959), pp. 161–75; de Vaux, 'Titres et fonctionaires de David et de Salomon' RB 48 (1939), pp. 394–405; *Les Institutions de l'Ancien Testament* I (1958), pp. 195–203: 'Les grands officiers du roi'; E.T. *Ancient Israel* (1961), pp. 127–32. Lit. § 126.

[32] Adler, 'The Natural Boundaries of the Administrative Divisions of Israel under Solomon' [Hebr., Engl. summary] BIES 16 (1951/2), pp. 24–9, II; Puzo, 'La segunda prefectura salomonica' Est Bíbl 7 (1949), pp. 43–73. Lit. § 126.

together in Josh. xv–xix. A list of stages in the wanderings is found in Num. xxxiii. Lists of sacred gifts[33] and the like are found in Ex. xxxv, 21–9, Ezra ii, 68–9; and Num. xxxi, 32–40 contains a list of booty, cattle and female slaves, together with the method of division.

There can be no doubt that a large proportion of these lists is genuine and that they really belong in the context in which they now stand. This is true, for example of the list of Solomon's district officers, and also of others, not so far mentioned, like the list of those who took part in the building of the wall in Neh. iii. In regard to other lists, like those in Num. i, xxvi, xxxiii, and those utilised in Josh. xv–xix, there is equally no doubt that they are not genuine in so far as they do not by any means belong to the period to which they are now assigned.[34] The decision as to whether we are dealing with purely literary compositions prepared for their present context, or with genuine pieces of material which have simply been placed in a wrong historical context, can often not be made with certainty. The lists incorporated in Josh. xv–xix are perhaps genuine in this latter sense, and present catalogues of civil divisions and localities from about the seventh century B.C. The lists in Num. i, xxvi,[35] xxxiii, on the other hand, were in all probability, at least in the form they now have, composed for the purpose to which they are now devoted, although even here older 'genuine' details will have been utilised. But in every case, it is nevertheless true that even the completely invented lists have been composed following the pattern of real ones, and they may therefore be taken into account as witnesses to this particular form.

(d) Laws

Literature: Alt, *Die Ursprünge des israelitischen Rechts* (1934) = *Kl. Schr.* I, pp. 278–332; Brongers, *Oud-Oosters en Bijbels Recht* (1960); Daube, *Studies in Biblical Law* (1947); 'Concerning Methods of Bible-Criticism. Late Law in Early Narratives' ArOr 17, I (1949), pp. 88–99; Horst, 'Recht und Religion im Bereich des AT' EvTh 16 (1956), pp. 49–75 = *Gottes Recht. Studien zum Recht im AT* (1961), pp. 260–91; Jepsen, 'Die "Hebräer" und ihr Recht' AfO 15 (1945/51), pp. 55–68; Jirku, *Das weltliche Recht im AT* (1927); Mendenhall (§ 4a); Neufeld, 'The Prohibitions against Loans at Interest in Ancient Hebrew Laws' HUCA 26 (1955), pp. 355–412; van der Ploeg, 'Studies in Hebrew Law' CBQ 12 (1950), pp. 248–59, 416–27; 13 (1951), pp. 28–43, 164–71, 296–307; Schmökel, *Das angewandte Recht im AT* (1930); Szlechter, 'Le prêt dans l'AT et dans les Codes Mésopotamiens d'avant Hammourabi' RHPhR 35 (1955), pp. 16–25.
Cf. also Literature §§ 8, 19, 24, 30, 33–5, 126.

As everywhere else in the world, from an early period in Israel there were legal precepts serving to regulate the life of the community. Before these were incorporated in the law books which have been preserved in the Old Testament —such as the Book of the Covenant (§ 33), Deuteronomy (§ 34), The Holiness

[33] Cf. the list of temple contributions from Elephantine belonging to the year 419 B.C.; Cowley, *Ar. Pap.*, pp. 65–76, No. 22; AOT, pp. 453–4; ANET, p. 491. On Cowley, No. 81 cf. Harmatta, 'Irano-Aramaica' AcAnt [B] 7 (1959), pp. 337–409.
[34] Anderson, 'The Place of Shechem in the Bible' BA 20 (1957), pp. 10–19, assigns the list in Num. xxvi to the eleventh century B.C., and notes that Noth dates it between 1125 and 1000, whereas Albright links it with David's census in II Sam. xxiv (p. 16).
[35] Mendenhall, 'The Census Lists of Numbers i and xxvi' JBL 77 (1958), pp. 52–66.

Code (§ 35), the Priestly Code (§ 30)—or rather before they were incorporated in the smaller bodies of law (§ 19) which underlay these, they must have existed singly or combined into merely quite small groups. A considerable proportion of the relevant material is not preserved in prose, but in the form of songs or more often of sayings, and this will be discussed later (§ 8). But there is no lack of precepts which have no poetic rhythm and simply regulate the particular case in matter-of-fact terms (מִשְׁפָּט). It is these with which we are for the moment concerned, and, in so far as a division is possible at all in the Old Testament material, we treat first the regulations which govern secular law, and then those which govern the law of the cultus.

An examination of the statements which are concerned with *ius* shows that the division just mentioned between precepts which are in prose and those which have a poetic form is also justified and intelligible in that it largely coincides with the division between the regulations which appear to have been taken over by Israel from its immediate Canaanite environment and from the larger world of the ancient orient, and those which may be regarded as specifically Israelite. The regulations in prose are set out mainly in the objective conditional style, in which the main situation is introduced by כִּי *supposing that*—and the subordinate cases by אִם *if*. So we have such an example as: ²*When (supposing that) you buy a Hebrew slave, he shall serve six years, but in the seventh year he shall go out free, for nothing.* ³*If he comes in single, he shall go out single; if he comes in married, then his wife shall go out with him.* ⁴*If his master gives him a wife . . .* (Ex. xxi, 2–4). Not only in their casuistic form,[36] but also in content, such regulations closely resemble the legal precepts of other oriental peoples, Sumerians,[37] Babylonians,[38] Assyrians[39] and Hittites.[40] On the other hand the

[36] Cf. Albright, 'Contributions to Biblical Archaeology and Philology' JBL 43 (1924), pp. 363–93, esp. pp. 364 f.; 'The O.T. and the Archaeology of Palestine' OTMSt (1951), pp. 38–40. Cf. Lit. p. 28, n. 41, and § 126.

[37] AOT, pp. 410 f.; ANET, pp. 159–61; Diakonoff, 'Some Remarks on the "Reforms" of Urukagina' RA 52 (1958), pp. 1–15; Klíma, 'Zu den neuentdeckten Gesetzesfragmenten von Ur-Nammu' ArOr 21 (1953), pp. 442–7; 'Urukagina, der große Reformer in der mesopotamischen Frühgeschichte' Das Altertum 3 (1957), pp. 67–78; Kramer and Falkenstein, 'Ur-Nammu Law Code' Or 23 (1954), pp. 40–51, Pls. IV–VII; Lambert, 'Les "réformes" d'Urukagina' RA 50 (1956), pp. 169–84; 'Documents pour le § 3 des "réformes" d'Urukagina' RA 51 (1957), pp. 139–44; Lettinga, 'Het sumerische wetboek van Lipitištar, Koning van Isin' JEOL 12 (1951/2) pp. 249–63; Steele, 'The Lipit-Ishtar Law Code' AJA 51 (1947), pp. 158–64; 'An additional Fragment of the Lipit-Ishtar Code from Nippur' ArOr 18, I/II (1950), pp. 489–93; Szlechter, 'À propos du code d'Ur-Nammu' RA 47 (1953), pp. 1–10; 'Le code d'Ur-Nammu' RA 49 (1955), pp. 169–77; 'Le Code de Lipit-Ištar' RA 51 (1957), pp. 57–82, 177–96; 52 (1958), pp. 74–90. Lit. § 126.

[38] AOT, pp. 380–410; ANET, pp. 161–80; David, 'The Codex Hammurabi and its Relation to the Provisions of Laws in Exodus' OTS 7/8 (1950), pp. 149–78; Driver and Miles, *The Babylonian Laws*, I (²1957), II (1955); Goetze, *The Laws of Eshnunna* AASOR 31 (1956); on this see Loewenstamm, IEJ 7 (1957), pp. 192–8, and Noth, ZDPV 73 (1957), pp. 188 f.; Koschaker, 'Zur Interpretation des Art. 59 des Codex Bilalama' JCSt 5 (1951), pp. 104–22; Kraus, 'Ein zentrales Problem des altmesopotamischen Rechts: Was ist der Codex Ḫammu-rabi?' Genava, n.s., tome VIII (1960), pp. 283–96; Laessøe, 'On the Fragments of the Hammurabi Code' JCSt 4 (1950), pp. 173–87; de Liagre Böhl, 'Het akkadische wetboek van Bilalama, Koning van Esjnunna' JEOL 11 (1949/50), pp. 95–105; Miles and Gurney, 'The Laws of Eshnunna' ArOr 17, II (1949), pp. 174–88; Nougayrol, 'Les fragments en pierre du Code hammourabien' JA 245 (1957), pp. 339–66; 246 (1958), pp. 143–53; Pfeiffer, 'The Influence of Hammurabi's Code outside of Babylonia' A XXIV,

precepts which are in rhythmic form—whether apodictic, categorical commands and prohibitions expressed with a participle like *Whoever strikes a man so that he dies, shall be put to death* (Ex. xxi, 12), or in the form of an address, like *You shall not kill* (Ex. xx, 13)—can hardly be paralleled from Israel's environment.[41] They are to be regarded rather as corresponding particularly to Israel's way of thinking. The precepts in casuistic form are in the main concerned with the regulating of legal cases which could only have become significant for Israel after her conquest of the land, whereas by contrast the apodictic precepts are concerned mainly with the relationship of Man with God or with his fellow men and so may be considered to belong to Israel from her pre-Canaanite days.

That there is an intimate historical relationship between the legal precepts in casuistic form in the Old Testament and those similar to them in form and content in the environment of Israel is clear enough.[42] But in this matter the process must not be envisaged as if the laws known from that environment— Sumerian, Babylonian, Assyrian and Hittite—had exerted a direct influence upon Israel, if only because these laws belong to a period which lies several centuries before Israel's invasion of Canaan, in other words before her appearance on the stage of history. The fact is rather that the land of Canaan was clearly already from the beginning of the third millennium permeated by the legal attitudes of the neighbouring peoples, so that Israel, when it entered the territory of Canaan, came in contact with these, and in taking over Canaanite culture inevitably took possession of these also. It is true that up to the present no Canaanite book of law has become known to us, and in this respect even the excavations of Ras Shamra-Ugarit, so uncommonly productive in other matters, as yet remain unhelpful. But even so, the assumption that it was the Canaanites who mediated to the Israelites the legal precepts which are related to those of her neighbours, must be regarded as quite certain.

IOK (1959), pp. 148 f.; von Soden, 'Kleine Beiträge zum Verständnis der Gesetze Ḥammurabis und Bililamas' ArOr 17, II (1949), pp. 359–73; Szlechter, *Les Lois d'Ešnunna* (1945). Lit. § 126.

[39] AOT, pp. 412–22; ANET, pp. 180–8; Driver and Miles, *The Assyrian Laws* (1935).

[40] AOT, pp. 423–31; ANET, pp. 188–97; Friedrich, *Die hethitischen Gesetze. Transkription, Übersetzung, sprachliche Erläuterungen und vollständiges Wörterverzeichnis* (1959); Follet, 'Les lois Hittites' MUB 30 (1953), pp. 1–19; Haase, 'Bemerkungen zu einigen Paragraphen der hethitischen Gesetzestexte' ArOr 26 (1958), pp. 28–35; Hrozný, *Code Hittite provenant de l'Asie Mineure* (1922); Neufeld, 'Notes on Hittite Laws' ArOr 18, iv (1950), pp. 116–30; *The Hittite Laws* (1951); Souček, 'Bemerkungen zur Schlußformel der hethitischen Gesetze' ArOr 29 (1961), pp. 1–29. Lit. § 126

[41] Cf. Hammershaimb, 'On the Ethics of the OT Prophets' SVT VII (1959), pp. 75–101, esp. pp. 78–80. Cf. Lit. p. 27, n. 36, and § 126.

[42] Alt, 'Eine neue Provinz des Keilschriftrechtes' WdO I, 2 (1947), pp. 78–92 = *Kl. Schr.* III (1959), pp. 141–57; Boyer, 'La place des textes d'Ugarit dans l'histoire de l'ancien droit oriental' PRU III (1955), pp. 281–308; Goetze, 'Mesopotamian Laws and the Historian' JAOS 69 (1949), pp. 115–20; Klíma, 'Über neuere Studien auf dem Gebiete des Keilschriftrechtes' ArOr 18, I/II (1950), pp. 525–38; 18, IV (1950), pp. 351–66; 20 (1952), pp. 539–71; 21 (1953), pp. 604–40; 'New Discoveries of Legal Documents from pre-Hammurapian Times' ArOr 19 (1951), pp. 37–59; 'Einige Bemerkungen zum Sklavenrecht nach den vorhammurapischen Gesetzesfragmenten' ArOr 21 (1953), pp. 143–52; 'Die jüngste Provinz des Keilschriftrechtes' ArOr 24 (1956), pp. 123–30; Koschaker, 'Keilschriftrecht' ZDMG 89 (1935), pp. 1–39; Pirenne, 'À propos de droit commercial phénicien antique' Bull Ac Belg V, 41 (1955), pp. 586–614; Speiser, 'Early Law and Civilization' Canadian Bar Review 31 (1953), pp. 863–77. Lit. § 126.

How this mediation of legal material took place in detail remains largely obscure. In particular, it can hardly be ascertained whether the Israelites took over bodies of law already of considerable extent, or whether they merely took over single precepts which were only gradually welded together in larger complexes. Nor can it be determined whether it was from the beginning a matter of the taking over of laws fixed in writing, or simply at first of oral borrowing and transmission. Since the Sumerian, Babylonian, Assyrian and Hittite law-books, which reveal such a variety of laws of the type with which we are here concerned, similar to those of the Old Testament, were fixed in written form already centuries before Israel's entry into Canaan, and the same may be assumed for the inferred Canaanite laws, the former of the two possibilities is the more probable. This would then carry with it the implication that there were taken over primarily not individual precepts like the law of slavery[43] in Ex. xxi, 2–11, or the law in Deut. xxii, 13–21, which deals with the discovery of the facts when a married woman is accused by her husband of not having been a virgin when he married her and the determining of the punishment due to him if the accusation was false or to her if it was not, but rather series of such precepts, like the basic material of Ex. xxi, 2–xxii, 16, or Deut. xxii, 13–29.

(e) *Cultic Ordinances*

Literature: Rendtorff, *Die Gesetze in der Priesterschrift* (1954). Cf. also Literature §§ 19, 24, 30, 33–5, 126.

Much more numerous than such small groups of laws of a secular kind are those which deal with the regulation of the cult. Out of the many varieties which must have existed, there have survived primarily 'ritual lists', that is requirements for the use of the priests or of the cult-personnel in general concerning the individual types of sacrifice, concerning clean and unclean animals, concerning the recognition and treatment of leprosy in people and in objects, and many more such points. The books of Leviticus and Numbers contain a whole series of such small groups of cult-laws. They are now presented, like almost all Old Testament laws, in the guise of addresses by God to Moses on or near Sinai. But in this particular case this mode of presentation can be especially easily detected, since it is only very loosely applied to the older legal material. Thus frequently it is only necessary to remove the introductory formula: *And Yahweh called Moses and spoke to him from the tent of meeting, saying: Speak to the people of Israel and say to them . . .* (Lev. i, 1–2 *et passim*), and to remove the form of address which is probably not generally original but has been introduced with the presentation of the law as a divine address, or to alter the second person forms (cf. for example Lev. i, 2; ii, 4–15; iii, 17 *et passim*) into third person singular or plural, in order to get a corpus of law which can stand on its own. Indeed the superscriptions or colophons of these independent groups of law

---

[43] Anne E. Draffkorn, 'Ilani/Elohim' JBL 76 (1957), pp. 216–24; Mendelsohn, 'The Conditional Sale into Slavery of Free-Born Daughters in Nuzi, and the Law of Ex. xxi, 7–11' JAOS 55 (1935), pp. 190–5. Lit. § 126.

frequently still survive, as in Lev. vi, 2: *This is the law of the burnt offering,*[44] covering vi, 2–6; vi, 7: *This is the law of the cereal offering*, covering vi, 7–11, or perhaps vi, 7–16; vi, 18: *This is the law of the sin-offering*, covering vi, 18–21;[45] Num. xix, 10b covering xix, 11–13; xix, 14 aα covering xix, 14–22. The superscriptions in Lev. vii, 1, 11; xiv, 2; Num. vi, 13, and the colophons in Lev. vii, 37 (38); xi, 46–7; xii, 7; xiii, 59, xiv, 32; xiv, 54–7; xv, 32–3; Num. v, 29; vi, 21; xxx, 17, may further be compared. It is true that such superscriptions and colophons are in part late redactional additions, but this does not alter the fact that they provide us with a means of sorting out the original independent small collections when we undertake a critical examination. The colophon in Lev. xiv, 54–7, gives us information concerning the purpose for which they were employed, for here the purpose of a law concerning leprosy is stated: . . . *to show when it is unclean and when it is clean.* It is naturally only the priests who are considered as carrying out the instruction (תּוֹרָה cf. pp. 73 f.), and this natural assumption is explicitly confirmed by Deut. xxiv, 8, where it is stated: *Take heed, in an attack of leprosy,*[46] *to be very careful to do according to all that the Levitical priests shall direct you.*

Thus we may consider a very large proportion of the groups which may be separated out from the Old Testament laws as 'ritual lists', instructions for worship, or however else we may describe them, for the use of the priest. Even if in their present form they are for the most part fairly late and are likely to reflect the practice normal in the Jerusalem temple towards the end of the pre-exilic period, they, or at any rate the material on which they are based, are by no means to be regarded as purely literary constructions, but as ordinances taken from the actual practice of the cult. That is all that matters in the present context. But we can go further. Even if the surviving collections of cultic laws are fairly late, we may nevertheless assume with complete confidence that such laws existed already at an earlier period, even much earlier. For the cultic ideas and customs which are regulated in the material which survives are practically all old, and even very old, and must therefore at an earlier period already have been regulated by appropriate instructions. Thus it is certain that the examples which we have go back in content to ancient times, and in many respects also in form, and there is nothing against the assumption that they even go back into the period of oral tradition. There is only one point which must here be observed, namely that it is just in this particular sphere that Israel is dependent upon Canaanite customs and forms. We must therefore assume that side by side with original Hebrew material, a great deal was taken over by the Israelites from the Canaanite cultus only after their invasion of Canaan. This corresponds to what was said in regard to the realm of secular law, about Israel's dependence upon Canaan and upon the ancient oriental ideas and forms prevalent there. But here we are not dependent merely upon assumptions, but have analogous material from the cultic practice of Canaan, in its Phoenician/Carthaginian

---

[44] Rost, 'Erwägungen zum israelitischen Brandopfer' BZAW 77 (1958), pp. 177–83. Lit. § 126.
[45] On the regulations for the sin-offering in Lev. iv–v, cf. Elliger, 'Zur Analyse des Sündopfergesetzes' *Rudolph-Festschr.* (1961), pp. 39–50.
[46] Lit. p. 205, n. 3.

form.[47] This is to be found in the sacrificial lists from Marseilles and Carthage,[48] intended at least secondarily for the laity, but particularly in a Carthaginian ordinance for festival offerings.[49] Though these documents are also relatively late, their predecessors certainly go back to the second millennium B.C., that is to say, to the time when Israel entered into this religious atmosphere, since, among the tablets found at Ras Shamra since 1929 there are some which must be described as instructions for the priests.[50]

Thus the larger part of the cultic legal material preserved in the Old Testament represents instructions for the priests, or is at any rate dependent upon such instructions. The content of these was in part intended for oral transmission to the laity. In so far as they are not divine demands and promises directly given to the cult-personnel—as for example in the precepts concerning the duties and rights of the priests and Levites in Num. xviii—they are not generally couched in the form of addresses, but present the relevant material and particular cases in the form of reports. In addition there must have been definite ordinances for the laity. It is possible that such ordinances underlie the lists of animals which may or may not be eaten, as transmitted in Lev. xi, 1–23, 41–7, and Deut. xiv, 4–20.[51] The question must here remain open, however, whether the presentation as addresses which is now to be found in Lev. xi, 1–23, 41–7; Deut. xiv, 4–20 is original to them, or, as is more probable, they were first set out in the form of reports, and were only put into the form of addresses when they were incorporated in the narrative setting in the Pentateuch and so were put into the mouth of either Yahweh or Moses. The analogy of the sacrificial lists already mentioned from Marseilles and Carthage lends weight to the assumption that Israel also was familiar with such public pronouncements, as might indeed underlie the precepts of Lev. vii, 28–36; Deut. xviii, 1–5.

One further kind of legal precept, originally independent, may be mentioned here. It is found, in the main, in the realm of cult and ritual, but also occurs for secular legal matters. This is the practice, not unlike the Islamic *Hadith*,[52] of tracing back customs and laws to the actions of ancestors, a form which is certainly not a mere literary device, but once contributed to the regulating of practical life. The derivation of festivals and customs from precise historical

---

[47] Dussaud, *Les origines Cananéenes du sacrifice Israélite* (²1941); 'Une survivance rituelle cananéenne; L'encensoir Syrien' ArOr 17, I (1949), pp. 168–71; Février, 'Remarques sur le grand tarif de Marseille' Cahiers de Byrsa 8 (1958/9), pp. 35–43. The 'Additional Note' here (p. 43) announces an investigation of Carthaginian sacrifices, with comparison with the Hebrew cultus, to be published in the Bulletin archéologique of the Comité des Travaux historiques (1959–60). Lit. § 126.

[48] Cooke, NSI, pp. 112–24, Nos. 42–3; Lidzbarski, AST, pp. 47–52, Nos. 63, 66; AOT, pp. 448–50; ANET, pp. 502 f.

[49] Cooke, NSI, pp. 125 f., No. 44; Lidzbarski, AST, p. 52, No. 67; AOT, p. 450.

[50] Gordon, *Ug. Manual* (1955), pp. 124–67, Nos. 1–3, 5, 9, 14, 17, 19, 22, 23, 41, 44, 47, 134, etc.; *Ug. Lit.* (1949), pp. 107–15.

[51] Driver, 'Birds in the Old Testament' PEQ 87 (1955), pp. 5–20, 129–40; 'Once again: Birds in the Bible' PEQ 90 (1958), pp. 56–8.

[52] RGG² III, cols. 410–11 (Schaeder), ³III, cols. 912 f. (Schimmel); *Handwörterbuch des Islam* (1941), pp. 146–51 (Juynboll); M. M. Ali, *A Manual of Hadith* (1955), cf. Fück, BiOr 14 (1957), pp. 103 f.; Paret, 'Die Lücke in der Überlieferung über den Islam' in *Westöstliche Abhandlungen Rudolph Tschudi* (1954), pp. 147–53; Robson, 'Ibn Isḥāq's Use of the *Isnād*' BJRL 38 (1955/6), pp. 449–65. Lit. § 126.

events and their explicit founding upon these belongs here, as for example the
Passover custom in Ex. xii, 27, and the sacrifice of the first-born in Ex. xiii,
14–15. The actual legal character of what purports to be a story may be quite
clearly recognised in the detailed narratives concerning cases which supposedly
occurred in the time of Moses and in the decisions which he gave, as in those
which deal with the regulating of the celebration of the Passover by those who
are unclean or on a journey, with the stoning of one who has profaned the
sabbath, and with the confirming of the right of inheritance by the daughters of
a man[53] (cf. Num. ix, 6–13; xv, 32–6; xxvii, 1–11; xxxvi, 1–12; cf. also Num.
xxxi). Even though these *Hadiths* may in the main be late and pure literary fic-
tions, we may nevertheless assume that here as elsewhere fiction is modelled on
real life.

The treatment of these *Hadiths* leads us naturally over to the narratives
proper, and these must now be discussed.

§ 5. NARRATIVES

For the purpose of discussion it is convenient to divide narratives into two
groups: poetic narratives and historical narratives. The first group consists of
those which are shaped with an imaginative or a purposeful attitude to the world
and to life—both often go closely together; the second consists of those which
adhere in a more scientific manner to what has happened, and set out to tell how
things actually took place. It is, of course, true that we make this distinction as
we look back, whereas those who were first concerned, the story-tellers and their
audience, were by no means always clear about the difference between poetic
and historical narratives, and very often regarded a poetic narrative as historical.
Even so, the distinction is justified. For the two different attitudes to the world
are present just the same; it is only that the difference is not yet consciously
observed by those who are concerned.

(a) *Poetic Narratives*

Literature: Baumann, 'Mythos in ethnologischer Sicht' Studium Generale 12 (1959),
pp. 1–17, 583–97; Bethe, *Märchen, Sage, Mythus* (²1922); von der Leyen, *Die Welt der
Märchen* I, II (1953–4); Peuckert, *Deutsches Volkstum in Märchen und Sage, Schwank und
Rätsel* (1938).
Barr, 'The Meaning of "Mythology" in Relation to the OT' VT 9 (1959), pp. 1–10;
Baumgartner, 'Israelitisch-Griechische Sagenbeziehungen' Schweiz. Archiv f. Volkskunde 41 (1944), pp. 1–29 = *Zum AT* (1959), pp. 147–78; Childs, *Myth and Reality in the
OT* (1960); Davies, 'An Approach to the Problem of OT Mythology' PEQ 88 (1956),
pp. 83–91; Eissfeldt, 'Stammessage und Novelle in den Geschichten von Jakob und von
seinen Söhnen' FRLANT 36 (1923), I, pp. 56–77 = *Kl.Schr.* I (1962), pp. 84–104; Gerleman, 'Hebreisk Berättarstil' SvTK 25 (1949), pp. 81–90; Goitein, *The Art of Narrative in
the Bible* [Hebr.], (1956); on this cf. Patterson, JSSt 3 (1958), pp. 88–90 and Rabin, JJSt 7

[53] Valk, 'The Right of Inheritance of a Daughter and Widow in Bible and Talmud'
[Hebr.] Tarbiz 23 (1951/2), pp. 9–15.

(1956), pp. 111–12; Gordon, 'Ugarit as Link between Greek and Hebrew Literatures' RStO 29 (1954), pp. 161–9; 'Homer and Bible. The Origin and Character of East Mediterranean Literature' HUCA 26 (1955), pp. 43–108; on this cf. Lesky, Gnomon 29 (1957), pp. 321–5; 'Indo-European and Hebrew Epic' Eretz-Israel 5 (1958), pp. 10*–15*; Gray, 'Canaanite Mythology and Hebrew Tradition' Transact. Glasgow Univ. Or. Soc. 14 (1953), pp. 47–57; Gressmann, 'Sage und Geschichte in den Patriarchenerzählungen' ZAW 30 (1910), pp. 1–34; Gunkel, Schöpfung und Chaos in Urzeit und Endzeit (1895); Die Sagen der Genesis. Einleitung zum Genesis-Kommentar (³1910); Das Märchen im AT (1917); Geschichten von Elisa (1922); Hempel, 'Glaube, Mythos und Geschichte im AT' ZAW 65 (1953), pp. 109–67; Herrmann, 'Die Königsnovelle in Ägypten und in Israel. Ein Beitrag zur Gattungsgeschichte in den Geschichtsbüchern des AT' WZ Leipzig 3 (1953), pp. 51–62; Hooke (ed.), Myth and Ritual (1933); The Labyrinth. Further Studies in the Relation between Myth and Ritual in the Ancient World (1935); Myth, Ritual and Kingship (1958); James, Myth and Ritual in the Ancient Near East (1958); Keller, '"Die Gefährdung der Ahnfrau." Ein Beitrag zur gattungs- und motivgeschichtlichen Erforschung at. Erzählungen' ZAW 66 (1954), pp. 181–91; 'Über einige at. Heiligtumslegenden' ZAW 67 (1955), pp. 141–68; 68 (1956), pp. 85–97; Kuhl, Die drei Männer im Feuer (BZAW 55, 1930), pp. 65–77 et pass.; de Liagre Böhl, 'Wortspiele im Alten Testament' JPOS 6 (1926), pp. 196–212 = Op. Min (1953), pp. 11–25, 475 f.; 'Het ontstaan en de geschiedkundige waarde van Oudtestamentische verhalen' NThSt 13 (1930), pp. 45–56 = Op. Min., pp. 1–10, 475; Maag, 'Jakob-Esau-Edom' ThZ 13 (1958), pp. 418–29; McKenzie, 'Myth and the OT' CBQ 21 (1959), pp. 265–82; Palache, Het karakter van het Oud-Testamentische verhaal (Rede . . . Univ. Amsterdam 26. Jan. 1925 = 'Sinai en Paran'. Op. Min. (1959), S. 15–36; van Proosdij, 'Oudoostersche vertelkunst' Kernmomenten (1947), pp. 5–18; Hans Schmidt and Kahle, Volkserzählungen aus Palästina, I, II (FRLANT, 17, 47, 1918, 30); Shochat, 'Political Motives in the Stories of the Patriarchs' [Hebr., Engl. sum.], Tarbiz 24 (1954/5), pp. 252–67, I–II.
Cf. also Literature §§ 5 (b), 126.

1. *Introductory.* The poetic narratives with which we are concerned at the pre-literary stage, are in the main short stories simply constructed and involving normally only two to four chief characters. They are therefore all very similar to one another, but may be subdivided into several groups on the grounds of clear distinctive marks, though there are frequently cases which are borderline. These groups are myths, fairy-tales, sagas, legends, anecdotes, and tales. Now these names are themselves not without a certain ambiguity, and we must therefore first define how they are used here.

If a narrative is concerned with the world of the gods, or if gods are to a considerable extent involved in it, we may speak of a myth. Because of the eminence of its chief characters and its impressive subject-matter, there is appropriate to it a lofty and powerful style, and often elements of awe and terror. It is likely to have originated in the circles of priests and other *homines religiosi* and to have been especially cultivated at the sanctuaries where it was related to the cultus. But it then finds a response among all those who worship the gods with which it is concerned, and also extends further afield so that it may develop in such a way as to approach very nearly to the fairy-tale which is otherwise different in nature. The setting of the fairy-tale is this world, the world of humanity. Even if it also has to tell of the operation of divine beings, it is concerned always with those of lower rank, friendly to man or hostile, and not with the intervention of the chief gods. Thus the fairy-tale, unlike the myth, often has a pleasant idyllic atmosphere, and there may even be jest and humour. Its home is among men who are as yet unable to see the world except through

C

the medium of their own wishes and longings, their disinclinations and fears, or who hold firmly to such a transfiguring of the world in spite of the fact that they have a better insight into the real course of events. It is, in other words, at home among children, old and young. The fairy-tale, in spite of its belonging to this world, nevertheless roves in some measure over time and space, since it is not tied down to particular places and occasions, but is of more general human application. But the saga presupposes a sense of the unusualness and significance of single phenomena in time and space, and owes its origin to reflective and imaginative individuals in the community for which the relevant phenomenon was of importance—whether it were the person of a leader, the strange form of a mountain, an animal with some remarkable characteristic, or something else of the kind. In the community to which the leader belonged, or among those who lived in the neighbourhood of the mountain, or those who observed the remarkable animal, the saga was first told and retold, but then, like the myth, it often travelled out beyond these circles and became a migratory saga, attaching itself to new objects. If the men or places or occasions which are central to the narrative are of religious significance—priests or prophets, sanctuaries or festivals—then we call such a narrative a legend. We shall have to look for the origin of the legend, and the circle in which it first spread, among the adherents of the relevant cult, or among the disciples of the *homo religiosus* with which it is concerned.

These four types, myth, fairy-tale, saga and legend, have in common that they relate, though in very different degrees, marvellous happenings and unusual circumstances, which are strange to the events of the present and the everyday. They therefore take place largely in the past and are in some measure remote from the present. The same is not true of those narratives which we are terming anecdotes and tales. These are also poetic, not historical narratives. They are intended to give pleasure and to entertain, and not really to adhere to the recalling of what has happened, nor to instruct. They present men and events just as they are in the contemporary world. They therefore often take place in the present, or even if they have as their subject people and events of the past, they describe them in such a way as to correspond with what is normal in the present. The tale and the anecdote may, however, be distinguished in that the former is more concerned with describing the events and their effect upon men, thus presenting men as relatively passive and simply reacting to their fortunes, whereas the latter brings before us men as they intervene forcibly in the events by word and deed, mastering a situation. The anecdote has in this way something masculine about it, and is generally told by men and about men, whereas the tale is rather more feminine, and often has as its subject the eternal theme of love. The tale relates the fortunes of the individual as they are interwoven in the events of the world and the life of the community, as this happens now and will happen as long as there are men on earth, and because of this universality of application it has much in common with the fairy-tale. The anecdote on the other hand is always linked to quite definite events and in the main to quite definite individuals, and in this is close to the saga. It is less closely related to the legend because in the latter in the last resort it is not the man in question, however holy or pious he may be, who occupies the central place, but the divine power which holds sway over him. The anecdote on the other hand concentrates its whole attention upon the man who is acting decisively or who speaks with such insight and pointedness.

2. *Myths.* If we arrange the relevant Old Testament material in accordance with the scheme which has just been roughly sketched out, we find that the Israelite spirit is strongly inclined towards mythical conceptions, but was never able to bring this inclination to full expression. In this respect Israel was unlike the other peoples of the ancient Near East which produced a wealth of myths, and, as for example in the case of the Sumerians and Babylonians with the Gilgamesh Epic and the Flood Myth[1] which was linked with it, influenced with their myths the whole of the ancient orient. The numerous descriptions of the theophany, such as Exod. xix; xxxiii, 19–23; Judg. v, 4–5; I Kings xix, 9–18; Ps. xviii, 8–16, are splendidly majestic and of sublime grandeur, and they show that Israel was quite capable of producing a colourful mythology. But real myths are not to be found in the Old Testament, at least none which originated in Israel, but only some borrowed from elsewhere. This no doubt is connected with the henotheistic nature of Israel's belief in God, which recognises as the really powerful and authoritative deity only the one, Israel's tribal and national God Yahweh. A real myth presupposes at least two gods, the one contesting with the other. But Israel, or at any rate its religious leaders, from an early stage allowed only to one God, its tribal and national God Yahweh, the right and at the same time the claim to worship, and recognised beside him admittedly certain subordinate divine beings, but at any rate as far as Israel's own domain was concerned, no deity who was on an equality with him. For this reason, a real myth could not come into existence in Israel. What the Old Testament offers in the way of myths or allusions to myths has quite clearly come into Israel from outside and has been in large measure at least deprived of its really mythical character. This can be most clearly seen in the myth[2] of the conflict of

---

[1] Bauer, 'Ein viertes altbabylonisches Fragment des Gilgameš-Epos' JNESt 16 (1957), pp. 254–62; Falkenstein, 'Zur Überlieferung des Epos von Gilgameš und Huwawa' JNESt 19 (1960), pp. 165–71; Frankena, 'Het epos van de pestgod Irra' JEOL 15 (1957/8), pp. 160–76; Garelli [ed.], *Gilgameš et sa légende* (Cahiers du Groupe François Thureau-Dangin I, 1960) with full bibliography; Goetze and Levy, 'The New Megiddo Fragment of the Gilgamesh Epic from Megiddo' 'Atiqot: Journal of the Israel Department of Antiquities' 2 (1959), pp. 121–8, Pl. XVIII; Gurney, 'Two Fragments of the Epic of Gilgamesh from Sultantepe' JCSt 8 (1954), pp. 87–95; Heidel, *The Gilgamesh Epic and the OT* (²1954); de Liagre Böhl, 'Het Gilgamesj-Epos bei de oude Sumeriërs' Kernmomenten (1947), pp. 145–77; *Het Gilgamesj-Epos, Nationaal Heldendicht van Babylonië* (³1958); Matouš, 'Die Entstehung des Gilgamesch-Epos' Das Altertum 4 (1958), pp. 195–208; Otten, 'Die erste Tafel des hethitischen Gilgamesch-Epos' Istanbuler Mitt. 8 (1958), pp. 93–125, Pls. 32–3; Schott, *Das Gilgamesch-Epos. Neu übersetzt und mit Anmerkungen versehen, durchgesehen und ergänzt von von Soden* (1958); von Soden, 'Beiträge zum Verständnis des babylonischen Gilgameš-Epos' ZA 53 (1959), pp. 209–35; Stamm, 'Das Gilgamesch-Epos und seine Vorgeschichte' Asiatische Studien 6 (1952), pp. 9–29. Lit. § 126.

[2] Castellino, 'Les origines de la civilisation selon les textes bibliques et les textes cunéiformes' SVT IV (1957), pp. 116–37; Kramer, *Sumerian Mythology* (²1944); *Biblical Parallels from Sumerian Literature* (1954); 'Sumerian Literature and the Bible' Anal Bibl 12 (1959), pp. 185–204; *From the Tablets of Sumer* (1956) = *History begins at Sumer* (1958); Labat, 'Les origines et la formation de la Terre, dans le poème babylonien de la création' Anal Bibl 12 (1959), pp. 205–15; Laessøe, 'The Atraḫasīs Epic: a Babylonian History of

the creator god with the monster of chaos, which came into Canaan and Israel from Babylonia. In the creation narrative of Gen. i, 1–ii, 4a, if indeed a connection is to be assumed at all here,[3] this myth has been completely transformed in the spirit of the supernatural and monotheistic religion of Israel, though in poetic passages like Ps. civ, 6–9; Job xxxviii, 10–11, it has retained clear traces of its original nature. A similarly marked transformation has affected the Babylonian myth of the flood[4] in the Biblical flood narrative. Other myths, which apparently came into Israel from northern Syria[5] tell of the rebellion of a divine being against the supreme god and of his miserable downfall. These were not subjected to such transformation, but were left in some measure in their original form so that passages like Isa. xiv, 12–15,[6] and Ezek. xxviii, 1–19,[7] stand out exceptionally as real myths. The reason for this is clearly that in these passages the subject is the overthrow of the power which is hostile to God, and this could be regarded without any reinterpretation as the triumph of the *one* God. In this way we may also appreciate how, at the end of the Old Testament development, in apocrypha and pseudepigrapha, many of the myths which in the Old Testament were suppressed rather than communicated, were related in great detail, like the fall of the angels hinted at in Gen. vi, 1–4[8] which appears in Enoch vi–xi. It may be that there was at this time a new influx of mythological material from outside, or that the hints provided by the Old Testament were simply further elaborated. It is in any case here not a delight in myth which expresses

Mankind' Bi Or 13 (1956), pp. 90–102; Lambert, 'De quelques thèmes littéraires en sumérien et dans la Bible' RHPhR 35 (1955), pp. 4–15; 'New Light on the Babylonian Flood' JSSt 5 (1960), pp. 113–23; Maag, 'Sumerische und babylonische Mythen von der Erschaffung des Menschen' Asiat. Stud. 8 (1954), pp. 85–106; 'At. Anthropogonie in ihrem Verhältnis zur altorientalischen Mythologie' *ib.* 9 (1955), pp. 15–44; MacKenzie, ' "Before Abraham was" (The Genus litterarium of Gen. i–xi)' CBQ 15 (1953), pp. 131–40; Moran, 'A New Fragment of DIN. TIR. KI=*BÁBILU* and *ENÚMA ELIŠ* VI 61–6' Anal Bibl 12 (1959), pp. 257–65, Pl. XVIII; Mowinckel and Albright, 'The Babylonian Matter in the Predeuteronomic Primeval History (JE) in Gen i–xi' JBL 58 (1939), pp. 87–103; Rost, 'Theologische Grundgedanken der Urgeschichte' ThLZ 82 (1957), cols. 321–6; Thieme, 'Nimrod, Kusch und Babel: zum universalhistorischen Ertrag der "Biblischen Urgeschichte" ' HJ 74 (1955), pp. 1–11; Woolley, 'Stories of the Creation and the Flood' PEQ 88 (1956), pp. 14–21; Lit. p. 191, n. 8; § 126.

[3] Cf. Albright, 'Contributions to Biblical Archaeology and Philology' JBL 43 (1924), pp. 363–93, esp. 363–9; Eissfeldt, 'Phönikische und griechische Kosmogonie' in *Éléments orientaux dans la religion grecque ancienne* (Trav. du Centre d'études . . . de Strasbourg, III, 1960), pp. 1–15. Lit. § 126.

[4] Cf. p. 35, n. 2.

[5] Eissfeldt, *Baal Zaphon* (1932), pp. 18–30; 'Gott und das Meer in der Bibel' *Studia Orientalia Ioanni Pedersen* (1953), pp. 76–84; Hartmann, 'Himmel und Erde im AT' SThU 30 (1960), pp. 122–4; Gray, 'Canaanite Mythology and Hebrew Tradition' Transact. Glasgow Univ. Or. Soc. 14 (1953), pp. 47–57; Kaiser, *Die mythische Bedeutung des Meeres in Ägypten, Ugarit und Israel* (BZAW 78, ²1962); Kapelrud, *Baal in the Ras Shamra Texts* (1952); de Langhe, 'La Bible et la littérature ugaritique' Orient. et Bibl. Lovanensia I (1957), pp. 65–87; Løkkegaard, 'The House of Baal' Acta Or[H] 22 (1955), pp. 10–27; Obermann, *Ugaritic Mythology* (1948). Lit. § 126.

[6] Grelot, 'Isaïe xiv, 12–15 et son arrière-plan mythologique' RHR 149 (1956), pp. 18–48.

[7] Cf. below, p. 378, n. 31.

[8] Closen, *Die Sünde der 'Söhne Gottes' (Gen vi, 1–4)* (1937); Herrmann, 'Die Göttersöhne' ZRGG 12 (1960), pp. 242–51; Speiser, 'YDWN, Gen vi, 3' JBL 75 (1956), pp. 126–9. Lit. § 126.

itself, but the desire to present the glory and victoriousness of the one and only God as vividly as possible, and to depict emphatically the criminal sinfulness of any rebellion against him. New favour is only extended at this time to such mythical material as could achieve this double purpose.

3. *Fairy-tale, fable, tale.* The fairy-tale has left far more traces in the Old Testament. Though here too we find not the really fully developed fairy-tale narratives but only fairy-tale motifs, these show nevertheless that fairy-tales must have been much loved in Israel. We hear of magical objects like the meal jar and the oil cruse which are never exhausted (I Kings xvii, 7–16; II Kings iv, 1–7), of talking animals like Balaam's ass (Num. xxii, 22–35), of helpful creatures like the ravens of Elijah (I Kings xvii, 1–6), and of many other fairy-tale matters. Furthermore the first part of the Jonah narrative is fairy-tale in character rather than mythological, and the Tobit story clearly depends upon the very widely known fairy-tale of the grateful dead man.[9] If this already demonstrates that Israel had its share of international fairy-tale lore, the story of Solomon's judgement (I Kings iii, 16–28) makes it even clearer. For here in all probability we have a fairy-tale which is of Indian origin transferred to Solomon.[10]

Among fairy-tales in the broader sense belong also the *fables* of animals and plants, two good examples of which are to be found in the metrically constructed fable of Jotham in Judg. ix, 8–15,[11] and that of Joash in II Kings xiv, 9. The popularity of such fables is attested by the allegories[12] of Ezekiel, similarly constructed in metrical form, such as that of the eagle, the cedar and the vine in xvii, 3–10. The parable of Nathan in II Sam. xii, 1–4, and Isaiah's Song of the Vineyard in v, 1–7,[13] present comparisons in which men and animals, or men and plants appear together. In this form also, while Israel's own creative ability need not be questioned, we must reckon with the probability that there were foreign patterns and influences.[14] We certainly know Babylonian-Assyrian fables[15] which are definitely older than those of Israel, and from Egypt[16] as

---

[9] But cf. Glasson, ZAW 71 (1959), pp. 275–7.

[10] Gressmann, 'Das salomonische Urteil' Deutsche Rundschau 130 (1907), pp. 212–28; Gunkel, *Das Märchen im Alten Testament* (1917), pp. 145 f.; Kirfel, 'Indische Parallelen zum AT' Saeculum 7 (1956), pp. 369–84.

[11] Adinolfi, 'Originalità dell' apologo di Jotham (Guid. ix, 8–15)' Riv Bibl 7 (1959), pp. 322–42; Maly, 'The Jotham Fable—Anti-Monarchical?' CBQ 22 (1960), pp. 299–305.

[12] On the allegory, cf. also p. 53.

[13] Junker, 'Die literarische Art von Is v, 1–7' Anal Bibl 10 (1959), pp. 125–32 = Bibl 40 (1959), pp. 259–66.

[14] Meuli, 'Herkunft und Wesen der Fabel' Schweizerisches Archiv für Volkskunde 50 (1954), pp. 65–93, on this cf. Perry, Gnomon 29 (1957), pp. 427–31; Trencsényi-Wald-apfel, 'Eine äsopische Fabel und ihre orientalischen Parallelen' Acta Antiqua Hungar. 7 (1959), pp. 317–27; Williams, 'The Fable in the Ancient Near East' in *A Stubborn Faith … W. A. Irwin* (1956), pp. 3–26. Lit. § 126.

[15] Ebeling, *Die babylonische Fabel und ihre Bedeutung für die Literaturgeschichte* (MAOG II, 3, 1927); 'Ein neuer Beitrag zur Kenntnis der akkadischen Fabelliteratur' JCSt 4 (1950), pp. 215–22; Weidner, 'Zur Tierfabelsammlung aus Assur' AfO 16 (1952/3), p. 80. Lit. § 126.

[16] Emma Brunner-Traut, 'Der Katzenmäusekrieg im Alten und Neuen Orient' ZDMG 104 (1954), pp. 347–51; 'Ägyptische Tiermärchen' ZÄS 80 (1955), pp. 5–11, Pls. I–III; 'Altägyptische Tiergeschichte und Fabel, Gestalt und Strahlkraft' Saeculum 10 (1959), pp. 124–85, 4 Pls.; Erman-Ranke, *Ägypten* (1923), p. 429, Fig. 181, and p. 474 with Fig. 186; Reingart Würfel, 'Die ägyptische Fabel in Bildkunst und Literatur' WZ Leipzig 2 (1952/3), pp. 63–77.

from Northern Mesopotamia[17] in the second millennium B.C. we have pictorial representations of animals which presumably presuppose animal fables.

We may perhaps cite as tales—which as we have seen have much in common with the fairy-tale, though they are not without connections with the saga too—many of the narratives gathered in Gen. xxxvii,[18] xxxix–xlviii, l,[19] concerning Joseph and his brothers, particularly the one about his temptation and slandering by Potiphar's wife in chapter xxxix,[20] which like the already mentioned Tobit story is based upon a fairy-tale, the universally known story of the slanderous wife. The story of Ruth and the 'folk-tale' of Job (pp. 456–7) are tales which have reminiscences of the fairy-tale. Lastly, we must also include here the story of Susanna (§ 84) or at any rate the form which underlies its present almost legendary character—for it appears to be based upon a secular story of the saving of an innocent woman falsely accused.[21] Narratives which deal with the love relationship between men and women[22] are certainly often rather crude, but free of eroticism. Erotic features are first to be found in Esther, Judith and Tobit, in other words in books which stem from the Hellenistic period and were probably influenced by Hellenistic romances.[23]

4. *Saga.* The Old Testament is particularly rich in sagas, and this proves that Israel took particular pleasure in this type of material and cultivated it vigorously. It is thus precisely in this field that Israel made distinctive contributions. If we divide the sagas into those which are connected with localities or other natural phenomena and those which centre around a human group or a single individual—in other words into place sagas or nature sagas, and tribal or leader sagas—we may get a general picture of the wealth of the material. Both these groups have in common, among other features, the fact that they are frequently aetiological, and thus arise out of the desire to explain some striking phenomenon, or at any rate one which poses some question. That such sagas are often concerned with the explanation of a name may be readily understood from the belief in the intimate connection between object and name which is common to ancient Israel and to many ancient and primitive peoples. Thus a whole series of sagas are simply etymological sagas,[24] which means that they have

[17] Freiherr von Oppenheim, *Der Tell Halaf* (1931), pp. 159–61 and Pl. 38; *Tell Halaf III: Die Bildwerke* (1955), p. 18, Pls. 100 f.; Ungnad 'Tierkapellen', *Oppenheim-Festschrift* (1933), pp. 134–7. Lit. § 126.   [18] On Dothan cf. below, p. 586, n. 4.
[19] Janssen, 'Egyptological Remarks on the Story of Joseph in Genesis' JEOL 14 (1955/6), pp. 63–72; Kaiser, 'Stammesgeschichtliche Hintergründe der Josephsgeschichte' VT 10 (1960), pp. 1–15; Montet, *L'Égypte et la Bible* (CAB 11, 1959), pp. 15–23, *et pass.*; Vergote, *Joseph en Égypte* (1959). Lit. § 126.
[20] Cf. e.g. the Egyptian 'Tale of the Two Brothers', AOT, pp. 69–71; ANET, pp. 23–5; DOTT, pp. 168–71.
[21] Blümel, 'Drei Weihreliefs an die Nymphen' Beiträge zur Altertumswissenschaft 12/13 (1960), pp. 23–8, publishes as Fig. 1 on p. 24 a nymph relief from Mycale belonging to the third century B.C., which portrays Pan spying on two nymphs bathing. He comments: 'Here we have the famous theme of Susanna at her bath presented in ancient form.'
[22] Cf. Weisweiler, 'Die früharabische Liebesgeschichte und ihr historischer Hintergrund' Saeculum 9 (1958), pp. 162–75.
[23] Ruth Stiehl, 'Esther, Judith und Daniel' in Altheim and Stiehl, *Die Aramäische Sprache unter den Achaimeniden* Fasc. II (1960), pp. 196–213.
[24] Fichtner, 'Die etymologische Ätiologie in den Namengebungen der geschichtlichen Bücher des AT' VT 6 (1956), pp. 372–96. Lit. § 126.

arisen out of the desire to explain a name and have no aim beyond this.

The story of Sodom in Gen. xix is a place or nature saga. It is designed to explain the unfruitfulness and desolation of the area on the banks of the southern part of the Dead Sea, perhaps even to explain the very existence of this southern part. This is done by the narrative of a great city which once lay in a most fruitful area, but which was so thoroughly immoral and corrupt that divine destruction overtook both it and its environment. We cannot exclude the possibility that there may be an echo of vague recollections of settlements in that area which have perished,[25] but the story is nevertheless a saga which has many parallels in the stories to be found everywhere concerning diabolical lakes and such like. In addition to explaining the general character of the locality, this particular saga is also designed to explain two other curiosities, namely the existence of an apparently well-known pillar of salt in human shape on the south-western shore of the Dead Sea, and the existence of a city named Zoar (צֹעַר) presumably to be found on the south-eastern shore of the Dead Sea in an area otherwise quite uninhabited. The remarkable shape of the pillar of salt is explained as due to Lot's wife having turned round on the flight from Sodom, contrary to the divine prohibition, and so being turned into this pillar of salt (xix, 17–26).[26] The situation of Zoar in the middle of an uninhabited area is ascribed to Lot's having been tired on the flight and having asked that this place should be spared so that he could rest himself there (xix, 18–23). In this latter incident the name, meaning *littleness, trifle*, is also explained on the grounds that Lot justified his request by pointing out that the town was only *small* (v. 20). Another good place saga is to be found in Judg. xv, 9–19. Samson, arrested by the Judaeans under Philistine pressure, freed himself at the moment when he was about to be handed over to the Philistines at Lehi, and killed a thousand Philistines with the jaw-bone of an ass (לְחִי הַחֲמוֹר) which was lying there. He then threw away the jaw-bone and since then the place bears the name Ramath-lehi (רָמַת לֶחִי) *hill of the jaw-bone*. But the story does not end with this etymology, clearly linked to the existence of a mound shaped like a jaw-bone. Samson is now in danger of dying of thirst since there is no water in the place. In answer to his prayer, Yahweh causes water to flow out of the cavity of the tooth in the jaw-bone, and the spring which thus came into being was called *the spring of the caller* (עֵין הַקּוֹרֵא), because it arose from Samson's call in prayer (וַיִּקְרָא). Finally, we may note that a feature of an aetiological animal saga has been preserved in the curse directed to the snake after the fall (Gen. iii, 14–15).[27] It is to go upon its belly, to feed only upon dust, and always to be exposed to the feet of men. What seemed to the Israelites, by contrast with other animals, to be the dreadful way of life of snakes, and also the especial hostility of men towards them, are here explained as due to the terrible guilt brought upon herself by the tribal-mother of all snakes by the seduction of the

[25] Harland, 'Sodom and Gomorrah' BA 5 (1942), pp. 17–32; 6 (1943), pp. 41–54 = BA Reader (1961), pp. 41–75.

[26] Bauer, 'Uxor Loth repetiitne Sodomam?' VD 38 (1960), pp. 28–33.

[27] Saydon, 'Gen. iii, 15 in the Light of Recent Discussions' Melita Theologica 7 (1954), pp. 69–92.

woman, and this guilt has to be atoned by her and her descendants by their gruesome fate.

The really characteristic sagas for Israel are, however, those of the tribe and people. These rest upon the view that all human communities have an ancestor or—more rarely—an ancestress, whose life and actions are decisive for the fortunes of their descendants. These fortunes are as it were anticipated or at any rate symbolically presented. This method of presentation can only be properly understood if we also assume that these ancestors are not thought to belong merely to the past, but are also considered to be living on, in and with and beyond their descendants. Thus at the centre of the tribal and national sagas there are always individuals, and it is only thus that this type of saga becomes possible; for without this, human communities hardly lend themselves to treatment in saga, at any rate in the form in which it was produced by Israel. The degree varies to which the representation of the community as an individual[28] is carried out. Often this representation is nothing but a veil loosely thrown over the material and readily allows us to see that in reality we are dealing not with individuals but with tribes and peoples. Examples of this are the quite short saga of Keturah and her sons in Gen. xxv, 1–6[29]—very differently formed from their parallels in the Hagar stories of Gen. xvi, 4–14 and xxi, 8–21. In the Keturah narrative in v. 6, instead of the plural *concubines* which now appears, there certainly originally stood the singular *concubine* referring to Keturah. The much more detailed story of Tamar in Gen. xxxviii is similar.[30] In other examples, however, the elements which belong to tribal and national history recede so much into the background that the hearer or reader can easily completely overlook them and may often in fact believe that the story is concerned only with the fortunes of an individual person.

The first kind certainly belongs to the earlier stage, and the gradual watering down of the elements which belong to tribal and national history has taken place during the course of the development. The tendency then became stronger and stronger the further it got away from the historical circumstances and conditions which were reflected in the saga in its original form. Interest in these circumstances was lost, while interest was all the more directed towards the individual human traits in stories now firmly fixed in the popular mind, for these traits remained intelligible. It is also possible to picture this process as the transformation of the tribal and national saga conditioned by historical actuality into the supra-historical and universally applicable tale or anecdote. The secret of the lasting vitality of many Old Testament sagas is indeed to be found in the fact that they did undergo this transformation, and so are now felt to be not the reflection of Israelite fortunes in a specific period of time but as the poetic presentation of ever-recurring human fortunes and characteristics.[31] It is par-

[28] Robinson, 'The Hebrew Conception of Corporate Personality' BZAW 66 (1936), pp. 49–62.
[29] Cf. II Chr. xxi, 3, and on this Loren R. Fisher, 'An Amarna Age Prodigal' JSSt 3, (1958), pp. 113–22, esp. p. 120.
[30] Stracmans, 'Un thème égyptien dans la légende de Thamar' Atti VIII Congr. Stor. Rel. (1956), pp. 279–80 = Le Flambeau 38 (1955), pp. 415–30. Lit. § 126.
[31] von Rad, Josephsgeschichte und ältere Chokma' SVT I (1953), pp. 120–27 = *Ges.*

ticularly man in his unchanging family contacts who is brought before our eyes in unsurpassed fashion in the stories with which we are here concerned. There is the mother, who cannot bear to see the death of her child and then experiences miraculous help, in the Hagar story of Gen. xxi, 8–21. In the Joseph story it is the father who prefers his youngest or next youngest son to the others, to his deep sorrow is robbed of this son, and then at last receives him back again. Here too is the brother who, trusting in his father's favour, treats his brothers haughtily and must suffer sorely for his pride, but then experiences a miraculous rise from the depths to the greatest heights and in this position of eminence not only remains the grateful son of his father, but pardons the wrong done to him by his brothers and repays it with good. Here the people are presented in their typical family relationships, so simply and straightforwardly, and at the same time so vividly and impressively, that even children can immediately understand them, and can be led on by them to the comprehension of their own little world.[32]

Genesis is thus full of tribal and national sagas. In some the history of tribe and people is central; in others it is driven into the background by the imaginative elaboration of the individualistic features. To the first kind belong, besides those already mentioned, the blessing of Shem and Japhet and the cursing of Canaan by Noah in Gen. ix, 20–7;[33] the conception and birth of Moab[34] and Ammon in Gen. xix, 30–8; Rebekah's pregnancy and the birth of Esau and Jacob in Gen. xxv, 21–6, and the adoption of Ephraim and Manasseh by Jacob in Gen. xlviii.[35] To the second kind, however, we should reckon the stealing of the blessing of the firstborn by Jacob in Gen. xxvii, and the wooing of Rebekah in Gen. xxiv, which already represent an advanced stage in the development of saga. For here the figures of the patriarchs, at first quite independent of one another, are being put into family relationships, and are conceived of as father, son and grandson, and so forth. Hence, connecting links were needed between the stories which dealt with them.

Genesis has no sagas of heroes or leaders. The centuries with which it is concerned were obviously not suited to producing heroic characters among the Hebrews, the ancestors of later Israel. They had rather to content themselves with the role of subordinates, and to be satisfied when the Canaanite rulers of the land permitted them to pasture their flocks there. Admittedly the lack of hero sagas in Genesis can also be explained differently. The recollection of the heroes who may have existed among the Hebrews before Moses is so faint that while a few names have been preserved—Abraham, Isaac and Jacob—only very

Studien zum AT (1958), pp. 272–80; *Die Josephsgeschichte* (BSt 5, ³1959); Ward, 'The Egyptian Office of Joseph' JSSt 5 (1960), pp. 144–50. Lit. § 126.

[32] Hertzberg, 'Das Buch Genesis im Unterricht' *Festgabe Gerhard Bohne* (1960), pp. 199–208.

[33] Hoftijzer, 'Some Remarks to the Tale of Noah's Drunkenness' OTS 12 (1958), pp. 22–7; Moscati, 'Sulla storia del nome Canaan' Anal Bibl 12 (1959), pp. 266–9; Rost, 'Noah der Weinbauer. Bemerkungen zu Genesis ix, 18 ff.' *Alt-Festschrift* (1953), pp. 169–78; van Selms, 'The Canaanites in the Book of Genesis' OTS 12 (1958), pp. 182–213.

[34] Van Zyl, *The Moabites* (Pretoria Or. Ser. III, 1960).

[35] Mendelsohn, 'A Ugaritic Parallel to the Adoption of Ephraim and Manasse' IEJ 9 (1959), pp. 180–3.

little was still known of their personalities, their deeds and their fortunes. They have thus become representatives of the post-Mosaic people of Israel projected back into the pre-Mosaic age; what they do and endure—in so far as it actually reflects events and conditions of the people's history—reveals indirectly the circumstances of an Israel settled in Canaan. There is, however, no sufficient reason for casting doubt on the correctness of the picture which Genesis sketches of the period of the Patriarchs. Even so, the real hero and leader sagas of Israel begin with Moses. Their classical period is that in which Israel had to fight for Canaan, conquering and defending her gains, in other words, using here the terms which have now become the normal ones, the period of Joshua and the Judges, and also further the period of the first two kings, Saul and David. Admittedly towards the end of this period the hero saga merges more and more into the anecdote. But when in the course of the later period real heroes arise in Israel, the old poetic power always revives and clothes stories which in other respects belong more to the type of the historical narrative (p. 42) with the glamour of the ancient hero saga.

Among the wealth of stories of Moses some admittedly, like the childhood story of Ex. ii, 1–10, have a fairy-tale quality, while others, like the turning of the bitter water into sweet, the giving of the manna and the quails, and the spring which flows from the rock that has been struck in Ex. xv, 22–xvii, 7, reveal God as the real protagonist and must therefore be reckoned with the legends. But the story of the victory over the Amalekites in Ex. xvii, 8–16, and that of the smashing of the tables of the law in Ex. xxxii[36] may be counted rather among the hero sagas. For although it is clear that, especially in the first of these, God stands in the background as the real protagonist, nevertheless Moses' share in the action (and Joshua's too in the first story) looms so large that here the hero may well stand beside the deity. A superb series of hero sagas is presented in the individual stories which have been worked up into Josh. i–xi; Judg. iii, 7–xvi, 31; I Sam. xi, xiii–xiv, xvii. These concern such figures as Deborah and Barak, Gideon and Jephthah, Saul and Jonathan and David, though David's victory over Goliath in I Sam. xvii may also, and perhaps with more accuracy, be reckoned among the legends. Some of the Samson stories— for example those concerning the foxes with fire-brands on their tails which he drives into the Philistines' fields, and the carrying away of the gates of Gaza, in Judg. xv, 1–8; xvi, 1–3—should perhaps rather be reckoned as anecdotes, and the same is true of the stories concerning the deeds of David's mighty men in II Sam. xxiii, 8–23. In the later period, the note of the ancient hero-saga is heard again when a story-teller with sympathy for his hero describes the really great and kingly death of Ahab (I Kings xxii, 34–5), and another of the same stamp is able to present the heroic self-sacrifice of Eleazar Avaran (I Macc. vi, 42–7) in an appropriately exalted manner.

5. *Legends.* As with the sagas, so with the legends, a distinction may be made between those which are attached to places and those which centre upon a human personality. To the first group there naturally belong above all those

---

[36] Junker, 'Traditionsgeschichtliche Untersuchung über die Erzählung von der Anbetung des Goldenen Kalbes (Ex. xxxii)' Trierer ThZ 60 (1951), pp. 232–42.

which are connected with a holy place, especially the ἱεροὶ λόγοι which set out to explain the origin of the sacredness of the place together with the customs which are observed at it.[37] These are invariably so formed that they tell how the numen which inhabits the place revealed himself there, and by means of this revelation opened the eyes of the one who received it to recognise the holiness of the place and thus made known to him the desire of the numen to be worshipped henceforth at this spot. Now without doubt such revelations actually took place in Israel, and so it might reasonably be supposed that one or other of the relevant stories preserves the memory of the real experience. But in actual fact this cannot be said with certainty of any of them. The origins of the cult-centres are normally shrouded in the mists of antiquity. In the stories which concern us, which invariably attribute the revelation to a character belonging to Israel's past and thus ascribe to him the foundation of the cult at the place, there is the added factor that at least with many of the cult-centres we must reckon with borrowing from the Canaanites. Bethel, Gilgal, Shechem and other sanctuaries were certainly Canaanite sanctuaries before they became Israelite, and the Israelites have in many cases taken over the ἱεροὶ λόγοι belonging to them together with the places and their rituals, simply by putting their Yahweh in the place of the Canaanite numen who originally appeared in the story. In some cases this can even be demonstrated in the actual wording of the story, or may at least be seen to be probable. In the story of Jacob's dream at Bethel in Gen. xxviii, 10–22, which explains the sacredness of the spot, v. 16 (J) runs: *Surely Yahweh is in this place and I knew it not*, and v. 19 which is the immediate sequel —vv. 17–18 being an insertion from the parallel narrative (E)—continues: *And he called the name of the place Beth-El (the house of El)*. V. 19 thus clearly presupposes that the God who dwells at this place is called *El*, and v. 16 will have read originally: *El is in this place*. As it now stands, v. 16 with its name *Yahweh* prepares only imperfectly for the giving of the name in v. 19 with its use of *El*, and the explanation of this discrepancy is that the Israelites when they took over the cult-centre and its ἱερὸς λόγος naturally attributed both to their Yahweh, and so replaced *El* in v. 16 with Yahweh. This change was, moreover, relatively easy. For *El* is by no means simply the name of one particular deity, but is at the same time an appellative with the meaning *god*. It was therefore only necessary to interpret the *El* of v. 19 as an appellative, and on the other hand to understand the *Yahweh* of v. 16 in the sense of *our God*—and both of these certainly took place as can be seen elsewhere—for v. 16 to be regarded as a completely satisfactory preparation for v. 19. This cannot, however, conceal the fact that in all probability *El* originally stood in v. 16, and this means that the story was not first told with reference to Yahweh, but to the Canaanite El. A like discrepancy between *Yahweh* and *El*, which may be similarly explained, is to be found in the story of Hagar in Gen. xvi, 4–14, where at the end (v. 13) Hagar says: *And she named Yahweh, who had spoken to her: Thou art El-Ro'i.*

The legend also gives information concerning the origin and history of many

---

[37] Alt, 'Die Wallfahrt von Sichem nach Bethel' *Bulmerincq-Gedenkschrift* (1938), pp. 218–30 = *Kl. Schr.* I, pp. 79–88; Nielsen, 'The Burial of the foreign Gods' StTh 9 (1955), pp. 103–22. Lit. § 126.

details of the cultus. It tells us of the origin of the bronze snake (Num. xxi, 4–9) which was revered in the Jerusalem temple until about 700 B.C. (II Kings xviii, 4); of the various marvellous effects which were produced by the Ark of Yahweh (I Sam. iv–vi; II Sam. vi). Of particular importance, however, is the fire which burns on the altars, and which in other religions too is described as coming direct from the deity or from heaven. Thus the legend which tells of the origin of the cult at Ophrah (Judg. vi, 11–24)[38] tells how the as yet unrecognised angel of Yahweh touched with his staff the gifts which had been laid by Gideon upon a rock, and then fire sprang from the rock and consumed the gifts, a fire which —for this must be the implication of the story—has not since gone out but at the time of the narrator still burns on the rock altar at Ophrah. The same thing is told in Lev. ix, 22–4 concerning the tent of revelation, the predecessor of the Jerusalem temple. After the tent, together with its courtyard and the altar of burnt offering which stands within it, has been prepared, fire comes forth from Yahweh to the great joy of the people, and consumes the sacrifice lying upon the altar. Again the meaning is that this fire has never gone out, but has burnt on continuously, and then, after the completion of the Solomonic temple, was taken over into it (cf. I Kings viii, 4). Even when the temple was destroyed by the Babylonians, this fire was not extinguished, but—so we are told in II Macc. i, 19–36—was hidden by priests in a dry place in a cistern. Then when Nehemiah, who here takes the place of Zerubbabel and appears as the re-founder of the Jerusalem Temple-cult, wished to re-establish the sacrificial cult, he sent descendants of those priests to fetch the fire from its hiding-place. But in the place of the fire they found only thick water. So at Nehemiah's command this was poured over the altar, and behold *When this was done and some time had passed and the sun, which had been clouded over, shone out, a great fire blazed up* (v. 22).

Festivals and all kinds of cultic observances such as circumcision are also important. Their true origin is in most cases lost in the obscurity of the past, but pious legend nevertheless gives an answer to inquiries about their beginnings. Legend traces the Passover and all its individual rituals back to the protective measures undertaken by Israel at their God's command in the night before their exodus from Egypt, when all the firstborn of the Egyptians, both men and beasts, were killed (Ex. xii, 1–xiii, 16).[39] Not infrequently we have several legends concerning the same thing and they provide different information about its origin. The custom of circumcision is explained no less than three times: according to Gen. xvii it was introduced by Abraham, according to Ex. iv, 24–6[40] Moses or Moses' son was the first Israelite on whom it was practised, and according to Josh. v, 2–3, 8–9—vv. 4–7 and the words *again* and *the second time* in v. 2 are an attempt to reconcile this story with the two just mentioned—

[38] Kutsch, 'Gideons Berufung und Altarbau, Jdc. vi, 11–24' ThLZ 81 (1956), cols. 75–84.

[39] Alt, 'Zelte und Hütten' BBB 1 (1950), pp. 16–25 = *Kl. Schr.* III (1959), pp. 233–42; Rost, 'Weidewechsel und altisraelitischer Festkalender' ZDPV 66 (1943), pp. 205–16. Lit. § 126.

[40] Blau, 'The *Hatan Damim* (Ex. iv, 24–6)' [Hebr., Engl. sum.] Tarbiz 26 (1956/7), pp. 1–3, I; Ben-Shabbat, 'Notes on J. Blau's Essay "*Hatan Damim*"' (Tarbiz 26, pp. 1–3)' [Hebr., Engl. sum.] Tarbiz 26 (1956/7), pp. 213, VII; H. Kosmala, 'The "Bloody Husband"' VT 12 (1962), pp. 14–28 (with bibliography). Lit. p. 192, n. 14.

Israel first began to observe circumcision in Canaan, though admittedly immediately after they had set their feet on the land to the west of Jordan.

The Old Testament is thus extremely rich in cult-legends, and this wealth of material shows what a large part was played by cult and ritual at every period in Israel, and with what love and participation they were enjoyed among the people.[41] For even if, no doubt, no small proportion of these legends derive from propagandist interests of the personnel concerned in the cult, others reveal all the more clearly that motives of simple piety have led to their composition and narration, and that this has caused them to be accepted and loved. To the pious man, however, persons are more important than things, for these have a meaning for his own piety, and so legend embroiders especially the lives of *homines religiosi*, first and foremost the priests and prophets, but also pious laymen. The stories of Moses cannot for the most part be classified in one particular type— just as he himself is too great to be understood within one of the categories, priest, prophet or layman—and they may with almost equal validity be regarded as saga or as legend. But if we except these, the legends of prophets far out-number in Israel those which tell of priests. Furthermore the latter, in so far as they are not hostile to the priests, like the story contained within I Sam. i–iv concerning the godlessness of the sons of Eli, give the impression in general of being tendentious inventions stemming from priestly circles. This impression is gained from the narrative contained in Num. xvi, 1–xvii, 15,[42] of the rebellion of Korah and his associates against Moses and Aaron and the one which follows upon it concerning the proof of Aaron's priestly authority by the marvellous sprouting of his rod. It is gained equally from those which are directed towards defending the rights of the priesthood against the claims of the kingship, as for example in the story of Uzziah's rebellion against the high priest and his punishment with leprosy in II Chron. xxvi, 16–20.

The prophetic legends, on the other hand, appear to be compositions which have developed freely and organically, though they too are naturally enough not free of tendentiousness, in that they set out to glorify their heroes, or rather the power of God which is revealed in them, not infrequently at the expense of its opponents. It is evident that in pre-exilic Israel, so long at any rate as the seers and prophets really had a contribution to make, they were more men of the people than were the priests. After the exile it is not so much the priest who becomes the hero of religious legend as the scribe or the pious layman. A man like Jesus ben Sira who belonged to the aristocratic upper class could be en-thusiastic about the high priest Simon and composed a beautiful memorial to his piety in the poem l, 1–24, but popular legends about such figures do not seem to have been very numerous, though they were not entirely lacking. To realise this, we need only to recall the stories of the prayers of Simon the high priest and of Eleazar the priest in III Macc. ii, 1–24; vi, 1–21, or the legend, so fully in Old Testament style, of Zechariah and Elisabeth in Luke i, 5–25, 57–80,

---

[41] Soggin, 'Kultätiologische Sagen und Katechese im Hexateuch' VT 10 (1960), pp. 341–7.
[42] Greta Hort, 'The Death of Qorah' ABR 7 (1959), pp. 2–26; Liver, 'Korah, Dathan and Abiram' Scripta Hierosolymitana VIII (1961), pp. 189–217.

where the storyteller shows such undisguised sympathy for the pious priestly couple, grown old in honour (p. 106, n. 11).

The books of Samuel, Kings and Chronicles are full of prophetic legends. There are some which are linked with named prophets, such as Ahijah of Shiloh (I Kings xi, 29–39; xiv, 1–18). Others are anonymous and simply speak of a prophet, as in I Kings xiii, 1–32, in which a prophet from Judah denounces the altar at Bethel, and then, because he disobeyed the divine command and went into the house of a prophet at Bethel and took food, was torn to pieces by a lion—a story which is possibly linked with the appearance of Amos at Bethel. The classical characters of the prophetic legend are, however, Samuel, Elijah, Elisha and Isaiah, and, as time went on, the figure of Jeremiah became more and more surrounded with legends. The legends which are told about the first four of these are of the most varied character. Some present them as taking part in great political events, or even as the driving force behind these events, and so, as a result, particularly in many of the Elijah narratives, they have in them something of the exalted feeling of the hero saga: thus I Sam. xv; I Kings xviii, xxi; II Kings vi, 8–23; viii, 7–15; xviii, 17–xix, 37 (cf. Isa. xxxvi, 2–xxxvii, 38). Others reveal prophets as bringing help and performing wonders in a small circle, amid their disciples, as in I Sam. xix, 18–24; I Kings xvii, 7–xviii, 1; II Kings iv;[43] vi, 1–7; viii, 1–6; xx, 1–12 (cf. Isa. xxxviii).[44] Midway between these two groups there may be placed, for example, the story in I Sam. ix, which presents Samuel and Saul with equal affection, and shows how the kingdom is promised by Samuel to Saul while he is out searching for lost asses.[45] Jeremiah became for the subsequent period not only the prophet who mourned over the fall of Jerusalem, to whom therefore the Lamentations (§ 69) could also be ascribed, but particularly the great intercessor. This is shown by the beautiful legend in II Macc. xv, 11–16, according to which Judas, before the beginning of the battle against Nicanor, had a dream. As he was praying for the Jews with outstretched hands, there appeared to him first the former high priest Onias, and then a figure distinguished by white hair and dignity, transfigured with wonderful majesty, whom Onias presented to him as *Jeremiah, the prophet of God, who loves the brethren and prays much for the people and for the holy city.* Jeremiah then handed to Judas a golden sword, with which to defeat the enemy.

The later period, and above all the time when the Jewish religion was persecuted by Antiochus IV Epiphanes (175–163), produced a new type of legend, or at any rate elaborated it and gave it a significance it had not formerly had,[46] the martyr-legend, where the word 'martyr' is to be understood in its original sense of 'witness, confessor'. These are legends which relate how pious Jews, men and women, courageous in word and deed, have arisen to suffer and die

[43] Bieler, 'Totenerweckung durch συναναχρωσις. Ein mittelalterlicher Legendentypus und das Wunder des Elisa' ARW 32 (1935), pp. 228–45; Weinreich, 'Zum Wundertypus der συναναχρωσις' ib. pp. 246–64.

[44] Iwry, 'The Qumrân Isaiah and the End of the Dial of Ahaz' BASOR 147 (1957), pp. 27–33; Yadin, '"The Dial of Ahaz"' [Hebr., Engl. sum.] Eretz-Israel 5 (1958), pp. 91–6, Pl. X, 1–4, pp. 88*–89*.

[45] Bič, 'Saul sucht die Eselinnen' VT 7 (1957), pp. 92–7.

[46] Jepsen, *Nabi* (1934), pp. 170, 183, places the origin of the idea of the martyr in the time of Ahab, i.e. in the ninth century B.C.

for their faith. A feature which can only derive from the late period to which most of these legends belong, is that they give much space to the belief in the resurrection and the life to come which had grown up in the meantime in the Jewish religion, and which appears as the force alone making possible the bearing and overcoming of suffering and death. In Dan. i, the carrying out by Daniel and his three companions of their decision to obey the Jewish food laws even at the court of the Babylonian king and hence to refuse the food which came from the royal table, is made comparatively easy and is speedily rewarded by God. But in Dan. iii the companions of Daniel, and in Dan. vi Daniel himself, have to pay for their faithfulness to their religion and their consequent disobedience of the royal command; the three are cast into the fiery furnace, and Daniel into the lions' den. Admittedly they are very soon delivered by God's own miraculous intervention, and the danger to which their life was apparently exposed is repaid a thousand times in that the two kings here concerned, Nebuchadnezzar and Darius, granted to the three companions and to Daniel freedom to practise their religion and even confessed that their God was the only true God. In these stories individuals are threatened with death for their faith. The books of Esther and III Maccabees, the one from Susa under the Persian empire, the other from Egypt, tell of pogroms which threatened all the Jews, though these disasters too were averted by divine grace and turned to the destruction of their enemies, just as in Dan. vi, the enemies of Daniel had to suffer the punishment which they had planned for him, namely, being devoured by lions. But the aged scribe Eleazar and the mother with her seven sons, whose story is told in II Macc. vi–vii and who are then presented in IV Macc. as a shining testimony to its edifying message that pious reason is the mistress of the passions, had to pay for their faithfulness after rejecting every temptation to avoid the consequences, by going defiantly to their martyr's death—and what a martyr's death it was. A similar story is told about Isaiah in a legend contained in the late Martyrdom of Isaiah (§ 92).

(b) *Historical Narratives*

Literature: Alt, 'Die Deutung der Weltgeschichte im AT' ZThK 56 (1959), pp. 129–37; Dentan (ed.), *The Idea of History in the Ancient Near East* (1955); Hans Duhm, 'Zur Geschichte der alttestamentlichen Geschichtsschreibung' *Plüss-Festschr.* (1905), pp. 118–63; Eissfeldt, *Geschichtsschreibung im AT* (1948); Fascher, 'Antike Geschichtsschreibung als Beitrag zum Verständnis der Geschichte' ThLZ 77 (1952), cols. 641–52; Gese, 'Geschichtliches Denken im Alten Orient und im AT' ZThK 55 (1958), pp. 127–45; Hölscher, *Die Anfänge der hebräischen Geschichtsschreibung* (1942); Jacob, *La tradition historique en Israël* (1946); 'Histoire et historiens dans l'AT' RHPhR 35 (1955), pp. 26–35; 'L'AT et la vision de l'histoire' RThPh 7 (1957), pp. 254–65; Lindblom, 'Historieskrivningen i Israel och dess ställning inom forntidens hävdateckning' SvTK 31 (1955), pp. 211–27; Maisler, 'Ancient Israelite Historiography' IEJ 2 (1952), pp. 82–8; Eduard Meyer, *Die kulturelle, literarische und religiöse Entwicklung des israelitischen Volkes in der älteren Königszeit* (1930); Misch, *Geschichte der Autobiographie*, I: Das Altertum (³1950) = *A History of Autobiography in Antiquity* (1950); Mowinckel, 'Hat es ein israelitisches Nationalepos gegeben?' ZAW 53 (1935), pp. 130–52; von Rad, 'Der Anfang der Geschichtsschreibung im alten Israel' AfK 33 (1944), pp. 1–22 = *Ges. Stud. z. AT* (1958), pp. 148–88; Simpson, 'OT Historiography and Revelation' HibJ 56 (1957/8), pp. 319–32; Speiser, 'The Biblical Idea of History in its Common Near Eastern Setting', IEJ 7 (1957), pp. 201–16; Täubler,

'Die Anfänge der Geschichtsschreibung' Tyche, Historische Studien (1926), pp. 17–74, 213–23.
  Cf. also Literature §§ 5a, 18, 126.

Historical narratives may be distinguished from the poetic ones which have just been discussed in that they are not fiction as these are, but purport to adhere closely to actual events or to describe real situations. They are, however, different from the forms described earlier as records in that they do not serve an immediate practical purpose, but are directed towards a more academic interest. They belong in circles whose level of culture is such that they are capable of a 'scientific' consideration of the world and of life. Whereas poetic narratives are in general intelligible and accessible to everyone, and are therefore to be found among all classes of the people, historical narrative undoubtedly demands a certain degree of education. Man is not naturally capable of this more objective attitude towards the world and life. For this reason the production and development of historical narrative is a matter for a certain upper stratum of society.

  1. *Reports.* First among the historical narratives are the reports, that is reports which, unlike military or diplomatic messages, for which we also employ the designation 'report', are not directed to the needs of an immediate situation, but are written with the intention of preserving a memory of the event. *They are written*—for here we are from the outset concerned only with written tradition, not with oral. But we have also every reason to assume that in Israel at a very early period in political and religious centres, such as the chancelleries of the kings and probably even of their predecessors the judges, and at the larger temples, such reports were already written down. We know this from the story of Wen-Amun, which took place in about 1100 B.C. since the then king of Byblos had at his disposal reports of this kind, composed by his ancestors, and was able to examine them.[47] It can be seen also from Boghazköi, Alalakh, Ugarit and other cities of the Near East and Egypt,[48] in which excavations have revealed palace and temple archives which in many cases actually contain such reports. We have evidence moreover from a fairly early period that such reports were also to be found at the royal courts of Israel. It is probably wiser to disregard the historically doubtful note that Moses was to write a report in a book or on a sheet or a tablet to preserve the memory of the victory over the Amalekites related in Ex. xvii, 8–13. But the significant point is that this note reckons with the possibility of such reports at so early a period. But the lists of Saul's and David's courts in I Sam. xiv, 49–51; II Sam. viii, 16–18; xx, 23–6, go back at any rate ultimately to such court reports. Above all, the point becomes clear in the books of Kings from Solomon onwards, in the fact that references for further information concerning a particular king are always to books, which had

[47] AOT, pp. 71–7 (p. 73: II, 5–9); ANET, pp. 25–9 (p. 27: II, 5–9); cf. also Josephus, *Contra Apionem* I, 21, § 155: τὰς τῶν Φοινίκων ἀναγραφάς. Lit. p. 52, n. 61; § 126.
[48] Harris, 'The Archive of the Sin Temple in the Khafajah' JCSt 9 (1955), pp. 31–58; Laroche, 'La Bibliothèque de Ḫattuša' ArOr 17, I, II (1949), pp. 7–23; Otten, 'Bibliotheken im Alten Orient' Das Altertum 1 (1955), pp. 67–81; Schaeffer, PRU II–IV (1955/7) contains texts from four different archives of the royal palace of Ugarit; Weidner, 'Der Kanzler Salmanassars I' AfO 19 (1959/60), pp. 33–9; Woolley, *A Forgotten Kingdom* (1953), p. 112. Cf. also §§ 114 a, b, 126.

evidently been composed on the basis of official annals. *The book of the acts of Solomon* is the name of the book mentioned at the end of the story of Solomon's reign (I Kings xi, 41). For the Israelite and Judaean kings who succeeded him the reference is always to the *book of the acts of the days of the kings of Israel* (or *Judah*) (I Kings xiv, 19, 29 *et passim*). The mention of such a book or books containing more detailed information than those provided in our books of Kings, only makes sense if these books were generally accessible. These are not the official annals, but must be unofficial works, though elaborated on the basis of the annals. Nevertheless, they have preserved the title of the official annals, *The book of the acts of the days* which, together with the other title *The book of remembrance* (cf. on this Mal. iii, 16), is also utilised in Esth. vi, 1, for the annals kept at the Persian royal courts. This title suggests simply a chronological sequence of many individual narratives, so we are not to picture these books as continuous, and as constructed on a literary plan, but simply as quite loose sequences of the accounts which were thought to be significant and memorable. A glance at our books of Kings confirms this supposition. Here the more detailed stories which they contain, in some cases very artistically composed, such as those concerning Elijah, must derive from other sources. But as far as the many single narratives are concerned, like the notes contained in I Kings ix, 15–24[49] on Solomon's fortifications, or the information provided in xi, 7, concerning the sanctuaries which he erected on the Mount of Olives for the benefit of his foreign wives, or the report of the attack by Pharaoh Shishak on Judah which took place under Rehoboam (xiv, 25–8),[50] we must assume that they are ultimately derived from the annals. It was, therefore, appropriate to mention these annals here, while we are dealing with the smallest literary units, since they are only collections of individual reports.

The excavations at Ras Shamra have demonstrated that not only Babylonian, but also Canaanite temples were directly linked with scribal schools,[51] and represented the main centres of scribal tradition. We may also assume that this was the case with the larger Israelite sanctuaries at a relatively early date. As centres of scribal activity, it will certainly not have been the last of their concerns to write down their own affairs, in so far as these seemed particularly important, to preserve them for posterity. Now, because of the development towards the centralisation of the cult in Jerusalem which took place in the religious history of Israel and Judah, we can say very little concerning the traditions which were fostered in sanctuaries outside Jerusalem, such as Shiloh, Shechem and Bethel. The narratives which concern these sanctuaries definitely depend upon their own traditions, and it is highly probable that many laws are dependent upon the traditions fostered in these sanctuaries outside Jerusalem. We can hardly now analyse out this material exactly. On the other hand, a fair amount is preserved for us of the annals kept in the temple at Jerusalem, and we are certainly indebted to the Jerusalem tradition for by far the greater part of the Old Testament laws.

[49] Yadin, 'Solomon's City Wall and Gate at Gezer' IEJ 8 (1958), pp. 80–6.
[50] Mazar, 'The Campaign of Pharao Shishak to Palestine' SVT IV (1957), pp. 57–66.
[51] Schaeffer, Syria 12 (1931), pp. 7–8, and Pls. 11–12; *The Cuneiform Texts of Ras Shamra-Ugarit* (1939), p. 35.

The information provided by the books of Kings about the Jerusalem temple will in any case have come in the main rather from its own annals than from those which were preserved at the court, although in this matter a sharp distinction is difficult to make in view of the close interconnections of temple and palace, which were not simply a result of their standing close together. But the details in I, vi–viii, concerning the building of the temple[52] must surely derive from the temple annals, and the same is true for example of the note about the preparation of the temple treasure chest by the high priest Jehoiada in II, xii, 10–17,[53] and the report of the reform of Josiah in II, xxii–xxiii.

     2. *Popular history*. Not only did these official annals in court and temple exist from a comparatively early date, but clearly there was also in Israel from an early date what may be termed unofficial, popular historical narrative or historical writing. Here at any rate the beginnings of the type may well belong to oral tradition. Stories, for example, like that of the pursuit by Gideon of the Midianite princes Zebah and Zalmunna in Judg. viii, 4–21, or that concerning Abimelech's rise and fall in Judg. ix, and above all those which are gathered together in II Sam. i–v, concerning David's rise to power, cannot be regarded as saga, in spite of many connections with that type of material. They are rather to be seen as the beginnings of what we call historical writing, in other words as historical narrative. For they really do set out to relate what happened and how. The fact that they do this in a series of comparatively independent individual stories, simply constructed and generally having only from two to four main characters in the individual scenes and revealing also a variety of other epic features, makes it proper to connect them with the poetic narratives as Gordon has recently explicitly done in 'Homer, Caphtor and Canaan'[54] and elsewhere (p. 33), but the prevailing tone is nevertheless entirely that of history. It is not so very far from them to the magnificent literary composition of the court histories in II Sam. ix–xx and I Kings i–ii, which has very properly been termed the History of the Succession to David (pp. 137–9).

     It is very striking to observe, when the Old Testament is compared with the literature of Babylonia and Assyria, or of Egypt, or the Hittites, as well as with that of the small states in the vicinity of Israel or in South Arabia,[55] that isolated beginnings towards a writing of history of just this kind do indeed also appear there.[56] But they are in general overshadowed by the autobiographical reports

---

[52] Parrot, *Le Temple de Jérusalem* (CAB 5, 1954), pp. 7–44, E.T. (1957), pp. 15–60. Cf. below, p. 289, n. 33.
[53] Cf. Lit. p. 435, n. 2.
[54] Anadolu Arastirmalari I (1955), pp. 139–46.
[55] On the beginnings of historical writing among the Arabs, cf. Blachère, 'Regards sur la littérature narrative en arabe au 1er siècle de l'hégire' Semitica 6 (1956), pp. 75–86; Caskel, 'Die einheimischen Quellen zur Geschichte Nord-Arabiens vor dem Islam' Islamica 3 (1927), pp. 331–41; 'Aijām al-'Arab' *ib.* 3, fasc. 5 (1930), pp. 1–99; Duri, 'Al-Zuhrī: a Study on the Beginnings of History Writing in Islam' BSOASt 19 (1957), pp. 1–12; Rosenthal, 'Die arabische Autobiographie' AnOr 14 (1937), pp. 1–40.
[56] Cornelius, 'Die Annalen Ḫattušilis I' Or 28 (1959), pp. 292–6; Goetze, 'Kleinasien' *Kulturgeschichte des Alten Orients* III 1 (²1957), pp. 174 f.; Güterbock, 'Die historische Tradition und ihre literarische Gestaltung bei Babyloniern und Hethitern bis 1200' ZA 42 (1934), pp. 1–91; 44 (1938), pp. 45–145; 'The Deeds of Suppiluliuma as Told by His Son, Mursili II' JCSt 10 (1956), pp. 41–68, 75–98, 107–30; Annelies Kammenhuber, 'Die

put out by the king himself,[57] whereas this is entirely lacking in the Old Testament—and so far excavations in Palestine, which admittedly have produced very little of a literary kind, have not brought anything similar to light.[58]

It is hardly possible to decide whether this difference is to be traced to the chances of preservation, in which case no further conclusion can be drawn, or whether we may assume that we have here a point at which Israel and its kingdom differ in principle from its environment in that the king in Israel did not occupy the pre-eminent position which he had among neighbouring peoples, and hence did not possess the selfconsciousness which led to autobiographical statements in building and victory inscriptions[59] as it did among neighbouring

hethitische Geschichtsschreibung' Saeculum 9 (1958), pp. 136–55; Kramer, 'Sumerian Historiography' IEJ 3 (1953), pp. 217–32; *History begins at Sumer* (1958) = *From the Tablets of Sumer* (1956); Malamat, 'Doctrines of Causality in Hittite and Biblical Historiography' VT 5 (1955), pp. 1–12. Lit. § 126.

[57] AOT, pp. 97–100, 339–59, 440–5; ANET, pp. 260–2, 446 f., 274–300, 318 f., 320 f.; Friedrich, *Aus dem hethitischen Schrifttum* I (AO 24, 3, 1925), pp. 1–14; Gadd, 'Inscribed Barrel Cylinder of Marduk-apla-iddina II' Iraq 15 (1953), pp. 1–42, Pls. I–V; 'Inscribed Prisms of Sargon II from Nimrud' Iraq 16 (1954), pp. 173–201, Pls. XLIII–LI; 'The Harran Inscriptions of Nabonidus' AnSt 8 (1958), pp. 35–92, Pls. I–XVI; Mowinckel, 'Die vorderasiatischen Königs- und Fürsteninschriften' FRLANT 36 (1923), I, pp. 278–322; and on this Baumgartner, OLZ 27 (1924), cols. 313–17; Wiseman, 'A New Stela of Aššur-naṣir-pal II' Iraq 14 (1952), pp. 24–34, Pls. II–IX; 'An Esarhaddon Cylinder from Nimrud' Iraq 14 (1952), pp. 54–60, Pl. XIX. Lit. § 126.

[58] But cf. Sukenik, 'Note on a Fragment of an Israelite Stele found at Samaria', PEFQSt 68 (1936), p. 156, Pl. III; and on this Albright, *Recent Discoveries in Bible Lands* (1955), p. 97.

[59] Alt, 'Das Königtum in den Reichen Israel und Juda' VT 1 (1951), pp. 2–22 = *Kl. Schr.* II, pp. 116–34; Andrén, 'Kungakroningar och Kröningsmässor' SvTK 34 (1958), pp. 153–77; Beek, 'Hasidic Conceptions of Kingship in the Maccabean Period' Numen Suppl. IV (1959), pp. 349–55; Bernhardt, *Das Problem der altorientalischen Königsideologie im AT* (1957); 'Kult und König im Altertum des Vorderen Orients' Das Altertum 5 (1959), pp. 67–79; *Das Problem der altorientalischen Königsideologie im AT unter besonderer Berücksichtigung der Psalmenexegese dargestellt und kritisch gewürdigt* (SVT VIII, 1961); Brunner, 'Das Gottkönigtum der Pharaonen' Universitas 11 (1956), pp. 797–806; Buber, *Königtum Gottes* (³1956); Canney, 'Ancient Conceptions of Kingship' Or. Studies . . . C. E. Pavry (1933), pp. 63–75; Cazelles, 'Mito, rituale e regalità' Bi e Or 2 (1960), pp. 121–35; Cooke, 'The Israelite King as Son of God' ZAW 73 (1961), pp. 202–25; Engnell, *Studies in Divine Kingship in the Ancient Near East* (1943); 'Die Urmenschvorstellung und das AT' SEA 22/3 (1957/8), pp. 256–89; De Fraine, *L'aspect religieux de la royauté israélite* (1954); 'Teocrazia e monarchia in Israele' Bi e Or 1 (1959), pp. 4–11; 'Peut-on parler d'un véritable sacerdoce du roi en Israël?' BEThL XII (1959), pp. 537–47; Frankfort, *Kingship and the Gods* (²1955); Gadd, *Ideas of Divine Rule in the Ancient Near East* (1948); Hempel, 'Herrschaftsform und Ichbewußtsein' Numen Suppl. IV (1959), pp. 302–315; Johnson, *Sacral Kingship in Ancient Israel* (1955); Klausner, *The Messianic Idea in Israel.* Transl. by Stinespring (1956); Koolhaas, *Theocratie en monarchie in Israël* (Diss. Utrecht, 1957); Labat, *Le Caractère religieux de la royauté assyro-babylonienne* (1939); McKenzie, 'Royal Messianism' CBQ 19 (1957), pp. 25–52; Mayer, 'Der Erlöserkönig des AT' Münchener ThZ 3 (1952), pp. 221–43, 367–84; Mowinckel, *He that Cometh. The Messianic Hope in the OT and in the Time of Jesus.* Trans. by Anderson (1956); 'General Oriental and Specific Israelite Elements in the Israelite Conception of the Sacral Kingdom' Numen Suppl. IV (1959), pp. 283–93; Noth, 'Gott, König und Volk im AT' ZThK 47 (1950), pp. 157–91 = *Ges. Stud. z. AT* (²1960), pp. 188–229; Nougayrol, 'Une forme rare de "l'hommage au roi déifié"' An Bibl 12 (1959), pp. 276–81, Pls. XIX–XX; Rengstorf, 'Old and New Testament Traces of a Formula of the Judaean Royal Ritual' NT 5 (1962), pp. 229–44; Ringgren, *The Messiah in the OT* (1956); Rosenthal, 'Some Aspects of the Hebrew Monarchy' JJSt 9 (1958), pp. 1–18; Rost, 'Königsherrschaft Jahwes in vorköniglicher Zeit?' ThLZ 85 (1960), cols. 721–4; Schmidt, *Königtum Gottes in Ugarit und Israel*

peoples. It is, however, remarkable that whereas from Israel's environment we have a great mass of building inscriptions where the king speaks in the first person, the sole example of a sort of building inscription which Israelite Palestine affords us, the Siloam inscription[60] from about 700 B.C., does not attribute the boring of the tunnel—a considerable technical achievement for that period —to a king; indeed it does not even mention the king, but tells simply of the men who worked on the tunnel, and how they, boring from both sides, came quite near to each other, and then broke through the thin rock wall which still separated the groups of workmen, so that the water could take its course through the tunnel. We may therefore reasonably assume that in Israel royal inscriptions in the first person did not have so prominent a place as in the neighbouring lands, and hence the closely related question whether, in view of the royal inscriptions from Israel's environment, the annals kept at court must have been kept in the royal first person style, may assuredly be answered in the negative.

3. *Autobiography*. We cannot be sure at what period men who had experienced and achieved much in life began to feel the need to set out what they had done and failed to do in the form of an autobiographical report—whether it was simply as a reminder to themselves and their associates, or to justify themselves to their contemporaries and their successors, or as a sort of offering to God and at the same time as a prayer to him for reward. In Egypt, examples of such memorials by high dignitaries are to be found on tombstones as early as the first half of the third millennium.[61] To the first half of the fifteenth century B.C. belongs the autobiographical report of Idrimi, king of Alalakh at the bend of the river Orontes, modern Tell-Atchana. In this he tells how he was compelled to take to flight because of a palace revolution, how he lived in privation in exile and returned triumphantly to his throne.[62] The Hittite autobiography of Ḫattušiliš III is about two centuries younger. This not only vividly describes the external events of this king's life but also gives the reader a glimpse into his mind.[63] The first person style of the story of Ahikar, set at the court of Sennacherib and Esarhaddon,[64] is not to be explained as deriving from that of Wisdom

(BZAW 80, 1961); Segert, 'Der Messias nach neueren Auffassungen' CV 2 (1959), pp. 343–53; Widengren, *Sakrales Königtum im AT und im Judentum* (1955). Cf. Lit. p. 102, n. 1; p. 105, n. 9; p. 110, nn. 28, 29; p. 526, n. 47; § 126.

[60] Cooke, NSI, pp. 15–17; No. 2; Lidzbarski, AST, pp. 10 f., No. 3; AOT, p. 465; AOB, No. 607; ANET, p. 321; ANEP, No. 275; DOTT, pp. 209–11, Pl. 11; Cf. Lit. pp. 19, 675.

[61] AOT, pp. 80–2; ANET, pp. 230, 233f. Cf. also the autobiographical reports of Sinuhe and Wen-Amon, AOT, pp. 55–61, 71–7; ANET, pp. 18–22, 25–29; and also Clère, 'Sur un cliché des biographies de la Première Période Intermédiaire et de la XIe dynastie' *Ägyptol. Stud.*, ed. by Firchow (1955), pp. 38–43; Janssen, *De traditioneele Egyptische autobiografie vóór het Nieuwe Rijk*, I, II (1946); Otto, HdO I, 2 (1952), pp. 148–57; *Die biographischen Inschriften der ägyptischen Spätzeit* (1954); Sander-Hansen, 'Bemerkungen zu der Sinuhe-Erzählung' AcOr [H] 22, 3/4 (1957), pp. 142–9. Lit. p. 48, n. 47; p. 272, n. 17; § 126.

[62] Sidney Smith, *The Statue of Idri-mi* (1949).

[63] Goetze, *Ḫattušiliš* (MVÄG 29, 4, 1924); *Neue Bruchstücke zum grossen Text des Ḫattušiliš* (MVÄG 34, 2, 1930).

[64] AOT, pp. 454–71; ANET, pp. 427–30; DOTT, pp. 270–5; Franz Altheim and Ruth Stiehl, 'Aḥīkar und Tobit' *Die aramäische Sprache unter den Achaimeniden*, Fasc. II (1960), pp. 182–95; F. C. Conybeare, J. R. Harris and Agnes S. Lewis, *The Story of Aḥīkar* (²1913) Cowley, *Ar. Pap.*, pp. 204–48; Meissner, *Das Märchen vom weisen Achiqar* (AO 16, 2, 1917); Eduard Meyer (p. 24, n. 27), pp. 102–28; Fr. Nau, *Histoire et sagesse d'Aḥīkar*

teaching, a style which will be discussed later, but seems also to presuppose the memoir form used by higher officials. In Israel we meet with the first of such memoirs in the Persian period, namely those of Nehemiah and Ezra (pp. 543–9).

4. *Accounts of dreams and visions*. But there are two kinds of autobiographical reports which are in Israel very much older, and already played an important part at the oral stage. These are the accounts of dreams and visions, which must by their very nature be given in first person style. In the poetic narratives of the Old Testament, both early and late, dreams are discussed with extraordinary frequency.[65] The Joseph story contains several (Gen. xxxvii, 5–10; xl, xli);[66] in the Gideon narrative there is one (Judg. vii, 13–14); the story of Solomon begins with a dream (I Kings iii, 4–15), and so on. Here as elsewhere, the poetic narratives have derived their colouring from real life. Jeremiah's polemic shows us, moreover, that to many of his associates dreams were a favourite means of ascertaining the future and of prophecy (Jer. xxiii, 21–32; xxix, 8), and indeed Zechariah (i, 7–vi, 8) received information about the immediate future in eight 'Night Visions' which combine dream and interpretation. Admittedly in Zechariah it is not dreams which are discussed, but there is here used the term *see* which is the normal technical term for visions. With the narrative of the dream, there is provided its interpretation. Naturally this cannot normally be in the first person, for since in general those who relate the dreams have them interpreted by others, this will be in the form of an address, though it is possible for such an address to the narrator of the dream to be absent, and for the form to be a simple statement, as in Judg. vii, 14: *This is nothing else save the sword of Gideon the Israelite*. It is an easy and reasonable assumption that the dream and its interpretation are the source of allegory, at any rate of the involved allegory with its explanation, which in a sense simply presents an imaginary dream and its interpretation. The allegory, deriving from the prose dream-narrative, may well originally have been in prose too, but since the allegory is imaginative it soon clothed itself in the rhythmic form appropriate to poetry. In the Old Testament, it is Ezekiel who on occasion employs such complicated allegories, reminiscent of dream and dream-interpretation, e.g. ch. xvii.

The example of Zechariah's Night Visions, and the use of dreams by the prophets generally as a means of divination—a use admittedly attacked by Jeremiah—show already that dream and vision are related. But the fact that Jeremiah, who himself appeals to visions (ch. i), makes a protest, shows at the

---

l'Assyrien (1909); Smend, 'Alter und Herkunft des Achikar-Romans und sein Verhältnis zu Äsop' BZAW 13 (1908), pp. 55–125; Zeitz, 'Der Äsoproman und seine Geschichte' Aegyptus 16 (1936), pp. 225–56. Cf. p. 23, n. 24; p. 84, n. 4; § 126.

[65] Cavaletti, 'Sogno e profecia nell' AT' Riv Bibl 7 (1959), pp. 356–63; 'L'incubatione nell' AT' Riv Bibl 8 (1960), pp. 42–8; Ehrlich, *Der Traum im AT* (BZAW 73, 1953); 'Der Traum im Talmud' ZNW 47 (1956), pp. 133–45; Levitte and Casaril, 'Les rêves et leur interprétation dans les textes post-bibliques' Évidences 82 (1960), pp. 18–28; Oppenheim, *The Interpretation of Dreams in the Ancient Near East* (1956); Sauneron et al., *Les songes et leur interprétation* (Sources Orientales II, 1959); Volten, *Demotische Traumdeutung* (Analecta Aegyptiaca 3, 1942).

[66] Bérard, 'De la légende grecque à la Bible. Phaéton et les sept vaches maigres' RHR 151 (1957), pp. 221–30.

same time that there is nevertheless a substantial difference between them. This
is confirmed not only by the presence of different terminology, usually sharply
distinguished (מַרְאֶה, חָזוֹן *vision*; חֲלוֹם *dream*), but above all by the fact that
whereas the dream is an experience available to every man, the vision clearly
ranks as something reserved to the charismatics who are specially gifted for it.
Visions, with which here auditions, normally closely related, must be included,
are often described in the narratives of the Pentateuch and the historical books
which deal with the ancient period. It is true that the theophanies which led to
the foundation of the cult at individual centres, as already observed, are in some
cases described not as visions but rather as real appearances of Yahweh. So
too Moses' special position over against the prophets is determined, according
to Num. xii, in that Yahweh makes himself known to them in visions and dreams,
whereas Moses had personal contact with him and might look at his form. Saga
and legend do in fact make the claim that the men of God of the past were
granted a contact with the deity which went far beyond what is normal and
possible in the present. But visions are often described as well, the best and most
detailed examples being in the Balaam narratives of Num. xxii–xxiv. The story
here, it is true, concerns a foreign seer, not an Israelite, but the narrator certainly
imagines it according to the Israelite pattern, as indeed he names Israel's God
as the giver of the visions. xxii, 31 is itself a vision, where Yahweh opens
Balaam's eyes so that he may see standing in the road the angel of Yahweh,
invisible to ordinary human eyes—just as in II Kings vi, 17 Yahweh opens
the eyes of Elisha's servant to see a marvellous sight. For the vision means insight
into the higher reality surrounding man in the present, though normally invisible
to him, and unfolding to him the future otherwise concealed from him. But
Balaam's real visions follow only in chs. xxiii–xxiv, and here we are not just told
what visions he had, but he himself describes them in the first person, or rather,
as he describes he allows what he has just seen to appear in so vivid a manner
that he seems to be describing the act of vision itself: xxiii, 9–10, 21–24; xxiv,
5–9, 17–18. The point which concerns us here is that this is done in the first
person style. We have another such prophetic account in the first person—or
rather two such accounts—of a vision in I Kings xxii, 17–22, where Micaiah ben
Imlah imparts to king Ahab first what he has seen concerning the catastrophic
result of the battle that is pending, and then too his visionary insight into the
events which made possible the favourable pronouncement of the other prophets. We may assume with certainty that this literary type, the account in the
first person of a vision experience, the vision narrative, is very ancient in Israel
and precedes by centuries the rise of the writing prophets.

But this type is nevertheless of great importance also in the writing prophets.[67]
It may be found from Amos right down to Zechariah. Of particular importance
here is the initial vision, the call vision, which summoned the prophet into the
divine service and was therefore reckoned as being worthy of preservation
above the other visions. Thus Isaiah, Jeremiah, and Ezekiel have recorded in the

[67] Horst, 'Die Visionsschilderungen der at. Propheten' Ev Th 20 (1960), pp. 193–205;
Lindblom, 'Die Gesichte der Propheten' StTh [Riga] 1 (1935), pp. 7–28; Sister, 'Die
Typen der prophetischen Visionen in der Bibel' MGWJ 78 (1934), pp. 399–430 .Lit. § 126

first person their own call visions, and it is possible and indeed probable, that the visions which Amos relates (vii, 1–9; viii, 1–3; ix, 1–4) belong at the outset of Amos' prophetic career, and thus represent his call visions.

5. *Prophetic autobiography.* The autobiographical narratives of the prophets were not restricted to call visions or to visions in general. It is clear that from an early stage more was involved than this, although nothing is preserved to us of this kind from the period before the writing prophets, since the *words, prophecies* and *visions* etc. of earlier prophets which are mentioned in the Chronicler (I xxix, 29; II ix, 29 etc.) are hardly to be regarded as such auto-biographical material (pp. 533–5). In addition to visions, these autobiographical passages appear from an early stage to have preserved other particularly significant experiences and actions.[68] In Isaiah we are at one point given some information concerning the motive of such personal writing down, namely *that it may be for the time to come as a witness for ever* (Isa. xxx, 8). We cannot now say with certainty how large a writing is here indicated. But even if it only contained a single 'name'—רַהַב הֵם שָׁבֶת *Rahab who sits still* (xxx, 7, p. 316) —as is clearly the case with *Speed-spoil, haste-prey* in Isa. viii, 1–2, it is never-the less quite sufficient to prove that the prophets early cherished the desire to preserve for posterity as a sort of 'account rendered' at least the message which came to them at particularly significant historical moments. It was another motive which, according to Jer. xxxvi, led Jeremiah in the year 605 B.C. to dictate to his disciple Baruch the words of Yahweh which had come to him since his call in the year 627 B.C.—and this may well have included visions and other experiences. This was occasioned by the desire to summon the people once more to repentance by having it read out at the most significant historical moment. This event too shows that the prophets regarded their message as possessing a significance which outlasted the moment of its first proclamation. The detailed examination of the prophetic books brings out the fact that they are based not only on collections of words of Yahweh and of stories from the circles of disciples which relate matters concerning the prophets, but also on first person narratives from the prophets themselves.

These first person narratives from the prophets appear to have developed out of the relating of visions and always devoted much space to this. They are essentially genuine, that is, they are the relation of something actually experienced. But in course of time—without any suggestion that the later prophets, and even the latest of them, did not experience real visions—they develop into a purely literary form, and it becomes more and more the fashion to present the complete message of the prophets and even more that of the apocalyptists in this style. In this, in accordance with the nature of the material, as a kind of 'account rendered', exact notes of time and place are provided. The book of Ezekiel—we are not for the moment concerned to consider how far genuinely or not—is presented as an elaborate first person message of the prophet, in the style of a diary, in which a great variety of visions play an important part. The

[68] Fohrer, 'Die Gattung der Berichte über symbolische Handlungen der Propheten' ZAW 64 (1952), pp. 101–20; *Die symbolischen Handlungen der Propheten* (1953); van den Born, *De symbolische handelingen der Oud-Testamentische profeten* (Diss. Nijmegen, 1935).

same is true of Zech. i–viii, of Dan. vii–xii, and even more of the extra-canonical pseudepigraphic apocalypses of Enoch, Esdras and Baruch. There are two main differences between the prophetic first person narratives and those of the apocalyptists—the one series ending with Zechariah and the other beginning with Daniel. In the first place, the former always present the attitude towards events of the immediate present, with which is included the end-time believed to be imminent, whereas in the latter the warnings and promises which are equally directed to the contemporaries of the actual compiler are preceded by long historical retrospects, presented as prophecies of a visionary supposed to have been active in remote antiquity (Dan. vii–xii; Ethiop. Enoch lxxxiii–xc; xciii + xci, 12–17; Syr. Bar. liii–lxxiv and other passages). In the second place, the difference is that the prophetic books, in the depicting of what was seen in the vision, are modest and discreet, and restrict themselves simply to what appears necessary to show the aims and basis of the message which is being proclaimed; but the apocalypses, no doubt under the influence of much which has come into Judaism from outside, really delight in the elaboration of the visions, the 'translations', and heavenly journeys, and deck them out with a wealth of cosmological, astronomical and calendar material (Ethiop. Enoch xvii–xxxvi, lxxii–lxxxii, Greek Bar. etc.). It is a very long way from the short vision-narratives of Micaiah ben Imlah and Amos to these apocalyptic allegories of history, 'translations' and heavenly journeys, but at bottom the latter are not different from the former, being descriptions or narratives of visions.

II. Sayings

In content and form, the saying[1] stands midway between prose and poetry, between the story and the song. As far as content is concerned, this is true in so far as it is utilised for the expression of exalted moods and solemn feelings and is the vehicle of specially important pronouncements, although it does not reach the heights of real lyrical feeling. As far as the form is concerned, this is true because it varies between formal and freer modes of expression, sometimes having a rhythmic structure, sometimes lacking it. In any event, a considerable proportion of the forms which may be gathered under the general heading of 'sayings' possess a rhythmic structure, and the discussion of them must therefore be prefaced by a short introduction to Hebrew prosody.

[1] [Bentzen (I, pp. 167 ff.) uses the term 'sentence' instead of 'saying', but 'saying' has been employed here as being less ambiguous. Tr.]

§ 6. THE LOGICAL AND METRICAL STRUCTURE OF HEBREW POETRY

Literature: Arnold, 'The Rhythmus of the Ancient Hebrews' *OT and Semitic Studies* . . . W. R. Harper, I (1908), pp. 165–204; Begrich, 'Zur hebräischen Metrik' ThR 4 (1932), pp. 67–89; 'Der Satzstil im Fünfer' ZS 9 (1934), pp. 169–209; Bickell, *Carmina VT metrice* (1882); *Dichtungen der Hebräer zum ersten Male nach den Versmaßen des Urtextes übersetzt* (3 Parts, 1882–1883); Bruno, *Rhythmische Untersuchungen von Gen, Ex, Jos, Ri, I. II Sam, I. II Kön, Jes, Jer, Ez,* 12 *Proph, Ps, Hi, Spr, Ruth, Hhld, Pred, Klgl, Esth, Dan* (1953–1959); Budde, 'Das hebräische Klagelied' ZAW 2 (1882), pp. 1–52; with addenda in ZAW 3 (1883); 11 (1891); 12 (1892); ZDPV 6 (1883); Fohrer, 'Über den Kurzvers' ZAW 66 (1954), pp. 199–236; Freedman, 'Archaic Forms in Early Hebrew Poetry' ZAW 72 (1960), pp. 101–7; Gábor, *Der hebräische Urrhythmus* (BZAW 52, 1929); Gray, *The Forms of Hebrew Poetry* (1915); Hölscher, 'Elemente arabischer, syrischer und hebräischer Metrik' BZAW 34 (1920), pp. 93–101; Horst, 'Die Kennzeichen der hebräischen Poesie' ThR 21 (1953), pp. 97–121; Ley, *Grundzüge des Rhythmus, des Vers- und Strophenbaues in der hebräischen Poesie* (1875); *Leitfaden der Metrik der hebräischen Poesie* (1887); Lund, 'Eine metrische Form im AT' AcOr [L] 17 (1939), pp. 249–303; Maecklenburg, 'Einführung in die Probleme der hebräischen Metrik' WZKM 46 (1939), pp. 1–46; Meek, 'Hebrew Poetic Structure as a Translation Guide' JBL 59 (1940), pp. 1–9; Mowinckel, 'Zum Problem der hebräischen Metrik' *Bertholet-Festschr.* (1950), pp. 379–94; *Offersang og sang-offer* (1951), pp. 418–35; E.T. *The Psalms in Israel's Worship* (1962), II, pp. 159–75; 'Metrischer Aufbau und Textkritik an Ps. viii illustriert' *Studia Or. Ioanni Pedersen* (1953), pp. 250–62; 'Der metrische Aufbau von Jes lxii, 1–12 und die neuen sog. "Kurzverse"' ZAW 65 (1953), pp. 167–87; 'Zur hebräischen Metrik II' StTh 7 (1954), pp. 54–85, 166; 'Die Metrik bei Jesus Sirach' StTh 9 (1956), pp. 137–65; 'Marginalien zur hebräischen Metrik' ZAW 68 (1956), pp. 97–123; *Real and Apparent Tricola in Hebrew Psalm Poetry* (ANVAO, 1957, No. 2); Muilenburg, 'A Study in Hebrew Rhetoric: Repetition and Style' SVT I (1953), pp. 97–111; Ridderbos, 'Kennmerken der Hebreeuwse poëzie' GThT 55 (1955), pp. 171–83; Robinson, 'Some Principles of Hebrew Metrics' ZAW 54 (1936), pp. 28–34; 'Basic Principles of Hebrew Poetic Form' *Bertholet-Festschr.* (1950), pp. 438–50; 'Hebrew Poetic Form; The English Tradition' SVT I (1953), pp. 128–49; Segert, 'Vorarbeiten zur hebräischen Metrik' Ar Or 21 (1953), pp. 481–542; 25 (1957), pp. 190–200; 'Die Methoden der althebräischen Metrik' CV 1 (1958), pp. 233–41; 'Problems of Hebrew Prosody' SVT VII (1960), pp. 283–91; Sievers, *Metrische Studien* I (1901); II (1904–5); III (1907). Lit. § 126.

1. *Parallelismus membrorum. Short verses.* We shall see that opinions concerning the character of Hebrew prosody are still divided and there are even those who entirely deny the existence of a real metrical system in Hebrew. One clear distinguishing mark does, however, exist as between prose and poetry. It was noticed long ago, but first more closely examined by R. Lowth in his book, already noted (p. 3), *De sacra poësi Hebraeorum* (1753) and described as *parallelismus membrorum*, thereby indicating that the poetic texts consist of verses formed from two—or more rarely three—stichoi combined, in which the stichoi or members are in some way 'parallel' to one another, in that they offer variations on the same idea. This may come about by the second member repeating the content of the first in different words (synonymous parallelism), or it may be that it sets it off sharply with a contrasted thought (antithetic parallelism), or it may be that it simply takes the thought further and completes it (synthetic parallelism). An example of the first kind is in Num. xxi, 28: *For*

fire went out from Heshbon, | flame from the city of Sihon; of the second, which is
in fact very common in the Proverbs of Solomon, Prov. x, 1: *A wise son makes
his father glad, | and a foolish son—his mother's sorrow*; and of the third, Ps. ii, 6:
I have set my king | on Zion, my holy mountain. It is clear that we have here a play
of ideas which does not appear in prose texts, and that we are to regard this
placing together of two or even three stichoi, parallel to one another in the
broad sense, so as to form a larger unit, which we call the verse, as the characteristic—or one of the characteristics—of Hebrew poetry.

The recognition of this is confirmed by external evidence. Hebrew manuscripts—and so a fragmentary Psalm scroll found in Qumrān cave IV (§ 104)[2]
—often distinguish the poetical books of Psalms, Job and Proverbs, and poetic
texts which appear in a prose setting, such as the song at the overwhelming of
the Egyptians in the sea in Exod. xv, 1–18, and the Song of Moses in Deut.
xxxii, 1–43, by leaving a space between the stichoi. Furthermore, parallelism of
the members is a feature known in all near-eastern poetry, Egyptian,[3] Sumero-
Akkadian, Canaanite-Phoenician[4] and Aramaic. Here too there are various
external attestations of this division of the verses. There is, for example, a whole
series of Akkadian clay tablets in which the division of the half verses is made
clear in the script,[5] and an Aramaic tomb-inscription from Egypt, belonging to
the fifth century B.C., of which the four lines are constructed entirely on the
principle of *parallelismus membrorum,* has a clearly marked space between the
two halves of the first line.[6]

It is thus quite clear that the parallelism of the members represents a particularly important feature of Hebrew poetry. But it is nevertheless plainly not the
case that the poetry invariably displays this parallelism. It cannot be said that
we only have poetry where parallel members of a verse are present. Here and
there in the Old Testament, particularly in the prophetic books, there are to be
found not long verses with parallel members, but short verses, standing independently and consisting usually of only two or three stresses, though grouped
together into the larger unity of the strophe. A particularly lively discussion is
at the present time going on as to whether it is proper to assume the existence of
sections which contain such short verses built together into strophes and which
may be differentiated on the one side from the compositions in long verses and
on the other side from prose sections. The question was already raised at an
earlier date, for example by Gray. Recently Fohrer, following suggestions made
by Balla,[7] has pointed to analogous phenomena in Sumero-Akkadian and

---

[2] Skehan, RB 63 (1956), p. 59.
[3] Erman-Ranke, *Ägypten* (1923), pp. 468–74; Golénischeff, 'Parallélisme symétrique
en ancien égyptien', *Studies pres. to Griffith* (1932), pp. 86–96; Grapow, HdO I, 2 (1952),
pp. 21–9.
[4] Albright, 'The Old Testament and Canaanite Language and Literature' CBQ 7
(1945), pp. 1–31; *Archaeology and the Religion of Israel* (²1946), pp. 14–16; Gordon, *Ug.
Manual* (1955), pp. 108–20; de Langhe, 'La Bible et la Littérature ugaritique' Or Bibl Lov
1 (1957), pp. 65–87; Patton, *Canaanite Parallels in the Book of Psalms* (1944); Young, 'Ug.
Prosody' JNESt 9 (1950), pp. 124–33; 'The Present Status of Ugaritic Studies' JKlF 2
(1953), pp. 225–45. Cf. p. 105, n. 10. Lit. § 126.
[5] Meissner, *Babylonien und Assyrien* II (1925), p. 152; *Bab.-Ass. Lit.* (1928), pp. 25–7.
[6] Hölscher, *Syrische Verskunst* (1932), pp. 3–4.
[7] Balla, 'Ezechiel viii, 1–ix, 11; xi, 24–5' *Bultmann-Festschrift* (1949), pp. 1–11.

Egyptian literature,[8] and has expressed himself just as decisively in favour of the short verse as Mowinckel has disputed its existence. The latter either redivides into long verses the sections in which Fohrer sees short-verses, or he treats them as prose.

2. *Metrical regularity.* It is open to question whether in the grouping together of short verses or in the parallelism of the members in the long verses it is also possible to go further and to recognise metrical regularity as well. This is denied by many scholars. Others, who concede that there were in all probability definite metrical patterns, declare it to be impossible to recover these metrical patterns, because of the bad state of our texts in some places, and especially in view of the fact that the establishing of the pronunciation of Hebrew which we employ was presumably fixed at about the beginning of the Christian era, though its fixation in writing with the use of vowel signs only took place some six to seven centuries later (§ 116). Those who make these points therefore maintain that it is not proper for scholarship to attempt to go beyond the parallelism of the members, the one assured feature of Hebrew poetry, and the existence of short verses which may be assumed with a high degree of probability. In one point these scholars are certainly right. The utmost caution is necessary, especially in view of the fact that no traditions concerning Hebrew prosody have come down to us. The position here is quite different from that in regard to Greek and Roman literature. When Josephus, for example, says of the song on the overthrow of the Egyptians at the sea in Ex. xv, 1–18, that it was composed by Moses in hexameters (*Ant.* II 16, 4 § 346), and describes the Song of Moses in Deut. xxxii, 1–43 as a poem in hexameters (*Ant.* IV 8, 44 § 303), he is simply applying to Hebrew poetry the concepts of classical metre, in order to make plain to his Hellenistically educated readers a literature which otherwise would be unintelligible to them, just as Philo does in his *Vita Contemplativa* in regard to the songs of the Therapeutae.[9] These and similar judgements by Josephus and others are insufficient to prove that these poems or Hebrew poetry as such was constructed on the basis of metrical laws, and we certainly cannot gain from them anything about the real nature of such laws. We are thus limited to the analysis of Hebrew poetry itself, and must consider whether a theory can be discovered which explains the given material fully or at least sufficiently. If such a theory can be discovered, then we may be justified in going beyond the limitations which many scholars observe, and may regard the theory thus discovered as the law or one of the laws of Hebrew metre, and so read the verses in accordance with this pattern. It is worth observing in this connection that in Egyptian—and this in spite of the lack of vowel signs—and in Akkadian, the metrical laws have been established with some certainty,[10] in addition to parallelism of the members. On one of the Akkadian clay tablets already mentioned,

[8] ZAW 66 (1954), pp. 206 f.

[9] Carmignac, 'Étude sur les procédés poétiques des Hymnes' RQ 2 (1959/60), pp. 515–32.

[10] Erman-Ranke and Grapow, as well as Meissner, *op. cit.* (p. 58, n. 3; p. 58, n. 5); de Liagre Böhl, 'Bijbelse en Babylonische Dichtkunst. Een metrisch Onderzoek' JEOL 15 (1957/8), pp. 133–53; 'La métrique de l'épopée Babylonienne' Cahiers du Groupe François-Thureau-Dangin 1 (1960), pp. 145–52. Lit. § 126.

the half verses are further subdivided into two, and this is presumably to be regarded as the marking of the smallest metrical unit, the foot.

Of the various systems of Hebrew metre which have been proposed, we can mention here only the three which have found most following and which are still under discussion today:

i. The system recently reaffirmed by Segert with reference to the oldest stratum of Hebrew poetry, based on the principle of a 'metre of words', in which the basic element of continuous speech is the word in itself, regardless of the number or kind of its syllables, and regardless also of the position of its accent.

ii. The system of Bickell and Hölscher, which reckons with alternating 'trochaic' and 'iambic' two-syllable feet, a system which, with various modifications of detail, has been further developed by Mowinckel, Horst and Segert.

iii. The system of accentuation originating with Ley, Budde and Sievers, which, again with modifications, has been accepted by the majority of Old Testament scholars, including Begrich and Robinson, and which assumes as the basic unit of the Hebrew verse, four-beat measures ($\int \int \int$), or feet with a final accent made up of two unaccented and one accented syllable, i.e. 'anapaests'. The use here of terminology borrowed from classical metre in inverted commas, 'trochaic' etc., is intended to show that we are in every case dealing not with long and short beats ($- \cup$), but with accented and unaccented ($\stackrel{\prime}{-} \times$).

3. *Alternation of stressed and unstressed syllables.* Bickell set out from the recognition that the quantitative systems of classical metre, working with long and short syllables, could not be applied to Hebrew poetry, and that the discussion must begin rather from languages and literatures which stood nearer to Hebrew. Being well versed in Syriac, he attempted to arrive at the nature of Hebrew metre from Syriac. In Syriac poetry, the principle of counting syllables, or rather 'alternation of syllables', is determinative. It works entirely with two-syllable verse-feet, in which one syllable is accented and the other unaccented, in such a way that sometimes the accent falls upon the first and sometimes upon the second; in other words, 'trochaic' and 'iambic' feet are present. Bickell believed that this principle could also be found in Hebrew, and that he could establish stichoi of 6, 8, 10 and 12 syllables with trochaic stress, as well as 5 and 7 syllable stichoi with iambic stress. But he could not establish this without drastic handling of the material. To achieve verse-feet consisting regularly of trochaic or iambic two-syllables, vowels had sometimes to be suppressed, sometimes supplied. The same three-syllable word had at one point to be accented at the beginning, at another point in the middle, or at the end, and so forth. In short, the theory did not work when it was applied to the material, and clearly such an imposition of a theory on the reading was wrong. Bickell has thus found few supporters. Hölscher, however, has proposed a substantial improvement on this system. On the one hand he assumed the accentuation of the final syllable everywhere—i.e. 'iambic' feet—and on the other hand he relaxed the barren restrictions of two-syllable structure by permitting syncope, recognising the presence of one-syllable feet in which the unaccented syllable was reckoned in the cadence to be included in the preceding accented syllable. The system may

be seen in the scheme of what Hölscher regarded as the commonest grouping (= stichos) in Hebrew poetry, namely the acatalectic dimeter, the placing together of two pairs of feet, in which the second pair too is complete. The scheme appears thus: × ⌣ × ⌣ / × ⌣ × ⌣ , and Job iii, 3 would be read thus: *yōbád yŏm | 'iwwăled bŏ*. The missing unaccented syllable before *yŏm* is so to speak concealed in the preceding—*bad*, which is to be read as something like *bá-ad*.

The metrical unit next larger than the smallest metrical grouping (the stichos, or half-verse) is the period or the verse, and this is described by Hölscher as of two kinds. First there is the placing together of two of the above mentioned characteristic acatalectic dimeters. Such a pair of dimeters was to him the characteristic unit of Hebrew proverbial poetry, and corresponds—if we may here anticipate for a moment—to the verse described by Sievers as a double-triplet (3 + 3). Further, he mentions the elegiac distich which underlies the larger part of the lyrical compositions, consisting of the combining of one acatalectic dimeter with one brachy-catalectic, i.e. one in which the second foot is missing. The scheme is[11] × ⌣ × ⌣ / × ⌣ × ⌣ // × ⌣ × ⌣ / × ⌣, and the opening of Lamentations is cited as an example: *'ēkă yă|šᵉbă bādăd || hā'ĭr rabbă|tĭ 'ăm* in which the second foot *yă-* is to be completed with the unaccented syllable concealed within the preceding *-kā (ka-ā)*. This elegiac distich, conceived as the combining of one acatalectic and one brachy-catalectic dimeter corresponds—if we may again anticipate the terminology—with the elegiac verse, the five-foot line of Budde and Sievers (3 + 2). Admittedly, in order to read this last as an elegiac verse or a five-foot line, either *'ēkā* at the beginning must be left out of account as anacrusis, or *hā'ĭr* must be deleted.

4. *Anapaestic rhythm*. Ley was the originator of the theory which reckoned with an anapaestic rhythm and thus regarded the number of unaccented syllables as irregular. According to him, the character of the verses in Hebrew poetry is determined solely by the correct counting of the accented syllables or stresses, whereas the number of unaccented syllables is of no importance. Thus the smallest metrical units which can be recognised, the verse-feet, reveal in general an ascending rhythm, i.e. anapaestic; the accented syllable stands at the end: × × ⌣ . Only at the end of the verse is there often to be found an unaccented syllable left over: × ×⌣ / × . Hexameters, octameters and decameters of this type are to be found. But of particular importance for the subsequent development was the discovery of what Ley called the 'elegiac pentameter', in which the caesura stands regularly after the third stress, and which is thus constructed: × ×⌣ / × ×⌣ / × ×⌣ // × ×⌣ / × ×⌣ . This verse was most thoroughly investigated as a particular type by Budde, who did not take up any particular attitude towards metrical problems and did not really wish to decide in favour of any particular theory. Ley's discovery that there was here a quite clearly defined verse which consisted of two unequal halves, the first with three stresses and the second with two, was confirmed, and to this was added the new point that almost invariably, where a *mourning song* (קִינָה) occurs and is described explicitly as such (pp. 94–8), this verse is to be found. One verse-form had thus

---

[11] / / Marks the division of the two stichoi.

been discovered, and this was one in which Ley's theory reckoning simply with the number of accented syllables and with anapaestic rhythm seemed to fit best.

Among others who worked further on the basis of what Ley and Budde had set forth, was the Germanist Sievers. He confirmed and completed the recognition of the accentuating form of Hebrew rhythm, the coincidence of the stress in the verse with the stress in the word, that is the metrical and the grammatical accents, and the anapaestic character of the verse. But he was not satisfied with the view that the number of unaccented syllables was of no importance. He believed rather that a quite strict regularity could be discovered in this respect too. He believed that the rhythm was always based upon measures in four-time, normally feet in which were two unaccented syllables each representing a quarter beat, and one accented representing a half beat. Where, between two accented syllables, there was only one unaccented, or none at all, the missing units of the measure were contained within the preceding or following accented syllables, so that the deficiency in the four-beat measure was only apparent, and in actual fact the normal time scheme was filled out. In principle this strict theory may not be without justification, but when it is applied to the material it goes decidedly too far, and one gets the impression that there is not really any very great difference between Ley's indifference regarding the number of unaccented syllables, and Sievers' unspoken assumption that his stricter theory can only be applied with the provision of a mass of explanations of the very numerous exceptions to it. In fact, more important than Sievers' own extraordinarily penetrating system was the fact that with his extended knowledge of metre and his sensitive feeling for phonetics, he confirmed and explained the older views which have been mentioned.

It does in fact appear that the 'anapaestic' theory does more justice to the facts than the 'iambic', even though this is not so very different in the form in which it is advocated by Hölscher and his followers. Above all, the structure of the Hebrew word and sentence fit better to the 'anapaestic' rhythm than to the 'iambic', and if the former is accepted, the verses may be read more easily and naturally than when a verse structure based upon the latter is applied to them. Admittedly it must be conceded (1) that the 'anapaestic' impression which is given by the structure of Hebrew words, is linked with the secondary loss of the vocalic endings and the resultant accentuation of the last syllable, and it cannot therefore be assumed without further ado for the earlier stages of Hebrew; and (2) that in this matter much depends upon a personal sensitivity to rhythm, with the result that a certain decision is hardly possible. But in favour of the anapaestic rhythm there is nevertheless an objective argument which must not be undervalued. In a Babylonian poem on the creation which is provided with musical signs or notes, between each two stresses are to be found at least one, normally two and sometimes even three unstressed units,[12] so that here the anapaestic theory makes a rhythmical reading possible, whereas the iambic can hardly do so. For the time being at least the solution to the problem of Hebrew prosody must be sought in the direction indicated by Ley and Sievers. It is therefore appropriate to apply also the terminology proposed by Sievers for the

[12] Meissner, *Babylonien und Assyrien* II (1925), p. 153.

larger metrical units beyond the verse-feet, namely the line (= stichos), and the period (= verse), or at least to apply his sigla (2, 2 + 2, etc.). Sievers recognises lines (stichoi) of 2, 3 and 4 feet: the doublet (2), triplet (3), and quadruplet (4), and as periods (verses) he speaks of the double-doublet (2 + 2) the double-triplet (3 + 3), the double-quadruplet (4 + 4), the seven (4 + 3 or 3 + 4), the five (3 + 2 normally, or more rarely 2 + 3), and the six (2 + 2 + 2). The commonest are the double-triplet, which as we saw above (p. 61), corresponds to Hölscher's 'pair of acatalectic dimeters', and the five in the form 3 + 2, Hölscher's elegiac distich. Ps. cxiv, 3, may serve as an example of the former: *hayyăm rā'ăh wayyānôs || hayyardēn yissôb lᵉ'āḥôr*; and Amos v, 2, of the latter: *nāpᵉlăh lō' tôsîp qŭm || bᵉtûlát yiśrā'ēl*. It remains only to mention the possibility which is considered by Mowinckel and Segert that Hebrew poetry in the course of its evolution underwent changes in its metrical system. Thus Segert suggests that in the earliest period the system employed was based upon the metre of the words, with identity of metrical feet and individual words, in the latest period the system was that of alternating metre, and in between perhaps the accentuating system was employed. The development of the Hebrew language, especially in regard to its accentuation and the endings of the words, is, however, too little known for precise statements to be made.

5. *The strophe.* Finally, the question has been much discussed as to whether Hebrew poetry was familiar with a metrical unit larger than that of the verse, namely whether strophes were utilised.[13] No assured positive conclusion has yet been possible. In this matter it is important that one should first have a clear conception of what a strophe is or what definition of a strophe is intended. The strophe is a metrical unit which may be recognised where the same number and type of verses, two or more in number, are repeated two or more times in such a way that the first verse of the second and subsequent groups is metrically exactly equal to the first verse of the first group, the second verse in the one corresponds to the second verse in the others, and so on. An equal number of verses is insufficient by itself; the additional point is necessary that corresponding verses should always be similarly constructed. The existence of such strophes has not yet been certainly demonstrated. On the other hand, it is clear that Hebrew poetry reveals groupings of an equal or approximately equal number of verses in larger sections, and thus employs strophes in this broader sense. This is clear from the existence of the refrain in Pss. xlii + xliii, which form one connected poem (xlii, 6, 12; xliii, 5), in Ps. xlvi (8, 12, and certainly also to be inserted after v. 4); Ps. lxxx (4, 8, 15, 20); Ps. cvii (8, 15, 21, 31). It may be further seen from those poems constructed on an alphabetic acrostic,[14] in which each new letter introduces not, as for example in Ps. xxv, merely one

[13] Condamin, *Poèmes de la Bible. Avec une introduction sur la strophique hébraïque* (1933); Kraft, *The Strophic Structure of Hebrew Poetry as illustrated in the First Book of the Psalter* (1938); 'Some Further Observations concerning the Strophic Structure of Hebrew Poetry' *A Stubborn Faith ... W. A. Irwin* (1956), pp. 62–89; Möller, 'Der Strophenbau der Psalmen' ZAW 50 (1932), pp. 240–56; Montgomery, 'Stanza-Formation in Hebrew Poetry' JBL 64 (1945), pp. 379–84.

[14] Driver, *Semitic Writing* (²1954), pp. 206–8; Munch, 'Die alphabetische Akrostichie in der jüdischen Psalmendichtung' ZDMG 90 (1936), pp. 703–10; Piatti, 'I carmi alfabetici della Bibbia chiave della metrica ebraica?' Bibl 31 (1950), pp. 281–315, 427–58.

verse, but two, as in Pss. ix + x,[15] or three as in Lam. i, ii, iii, or even eight as in Ps. cxix,[16] in which moreover each one of these eight verses begins with the appropriate letter. But all these are primarily only stylistic sections, and not metrical structures, just as in the verse the parallelism of the members is a logical, stylistic phenomenon, and not a metrical one. As far as the verse is concerned, as we have seen, research has gone beyond the recognition of this logical, stylistic structure to insight into the metrical laws. In the larger sections, often loosely called strophes, such progress has not yet been made, and for the time being at least, therefore, though we may naturally recognise the existence of sections or divisions which extend beyond the verse, the question of the strophe as a metrical unit must be left open.

Occasionally, to heighten the effect of a saying or poem, Hebrew poetry also employs the device of vocalic or consonantal assonance,[17] as well as anadiplosis,[18] anacrusis[19] and antiphony.[20] Attention will be drawn in what follows to some examples of these (pp. 68, 83 and elsewhere).

§ 7. SAYINGS OF VARIOUS KINDS

Literature: cf. §§ 8–11, 126.

The range of the saying is as comprehensive as life itself. In the life of the individual and in that of the community, there are all manner of occasions when men's thoughts need to be set forth with greater richness of expression, or feelings may be expressed with solemnity. It may be fitting to utter a general truth or a special rule of life in the form of a proverb or aphorism. It is thus extremely difficult to know how to arrange the material in such a way as to do justice to its wealth. But four varieties of saying stand out beyond the others, as a cursory glance into the Old Testament will show: the legal saying, the cultic saying, the prophetic saying and the wisdom saying together with its forerunner the popular proverb, and they must all also have played a very large part in the actual life of Israel. These four varieties of saying must therefore each be treated separately. The sayings which do not belong in these four groups may be disposed of first, divided between the two areas of life, the life of the individual and the concerns of the community. It must of course, be recognised that the larger and smaller groups thus determined often overlap, especially

---

[15] Driver (n. 14 above), pp. 200–6; Gordis, JQR 48 (1957/8), pp. 104–22; Junker, RB 60 (1953), pp. 161–9; Komlós, JSSt 2 (1957), pp. 243–6. Lit. § 126.

[16] Deissler, *Psalm 119 (118) und seine Theologie* (1955); Holm-Nielsen, StTh 14 (1960), pp. 24–35, 50–3; Mowinckel, NTT 61 (1960), pp. 95–127, 129–59; Robert, RB 46 (1937), pp. 182–206; 48 (1939), pp. 5–20; Rongy, Rev Eccl Liège 30 (1938/9), pp. 343–58. Lit. § 126.

[17] Cf. especially Boström (Literature § 11).

[18] Mirsky, 'The Origin of *Anadiplosis* in Hebrew Literature' [Hebr., Engl. sum.] Tarbiz 28 (1958/9), pp. 171–80, IV.

[19] Robinson, 'Anacrusis in Hebrew Poetry' BZAW 66 (1936), pp. 37–40.

[20] Slotki, 'Antiphony in Ancient Hebrew Poetry' JQR 26 (1935/6), pp. 199–219.

since religion does not belong in a separate sphere but extends over all other realms of experience and intrudes into them all.

1. *Sayings from the life of the individual.* We begin with the sayings which accompany the vicissitudes of individual life, both happy and sad. The Old Testament is pervaded by joy in children. Thus Ps. cxxvii, 3—exactly in the tone of a popular proverb and no doubt making use of one: *Lo, sons are a gift from Yahweh, the fruit of the womb a reward.* With what joy a child, especially a son, was greeted by its mother, and how a man's two wives compete with one another for pre-eminence in the birth of sons, may be seen above all in the story of the birth of the sons of Jacob in Gen. xxix, 31–xxx, 24; xxxv, 16–18.[1] But these stories show, no doubt reflecting actual practice, that the birth of a son was the occasion for sayings from the mother herself, or from the father or some acquaintance. Many of these were utterances of a quite special kind which are not here our concern. But in addition there were also fixed formal sayings: *Fear not, you have a son* (Gen. xxxv, 17), or: *Fear not, you have borne a son* (I Sam. iv, 20). This was said in consolation by those who surrounded a mother who lay in severe labour or was facing death. But the mother herself rejoiced: *I have acquired a man* (Gen. iv, 1),[2] and the friends joined in such rejoicing: *A child is born to us, a son is given to us* (Isa. ix, 5). An adopted child was, however, received in the place of a son by father or mother with this formula (Ps. ii, 7): *Thou art my son, I have to-day begotten* (or *borne*) *you.* Weaning and circumcision were also occasions for solemn sayings, though we have no precise knowledge of these. We can however say something about the normal formulae used at betrothal, wedding and divorce. The joy of the bridegroom is to be heard in the words with which man greets the woman formed from his rib (Gen. ii, 23):

> *This at last is   bone of my bone   and flesh of my flesh;*
> *This shall be called woman   for she is taken from her[3] man*

The parents and brothers and sisters expressed a wish something like this to the bride as she left her parents' house (Gen. xxiv, 60):

> *Thou, our sister, become   thousands of ten thousands,*
> *And thy seed possess   the gate of those that hate him.*

To a man who has just been betrothed to a young woman, the wish is expressed: *Yahweh make your wife, who comes into your house, like Rachel and like Leah, who together built the house of Israel* (Ruth iv, 11). We can reconstruct the formula with which the young woman is handed over to her husband by her father or guardian from Tob. vii, 12, where Raguel hands over his daughter Sara to Tobias with these words: *Here, take her according to the law of Moses.* In a case of divorce, the formula appears to have been used which Hosea (ii, 4) puts into

---

[1] Dossin, 'À propos du nom des Benjaminites dans les "Archives de Mari" ' RA 52 (1958), pp. 60–2; 'Les Bédouins dans les textes de Mari' Studi Semitici 2 (1959), pp. 35–51; Kupper, *Les nomades en Mésopotamie au temps des rois de Mari* (1957), pp. 47–81. Cf. p. 258, n. 1.

[2] Borger, 'Gen. iv, 1' VT 9 (1959), pp. 85–6.

[3] אִישָׁה instead of אִישׁ *man.*

D

the mouth of God in the figurative dismissal of his wife Israel: *She is not my wife, and I am not her husband.*[4] Death, as we shall see (pp. 94–8), provides the occasion for the lament over the corpse, but also gives rise to sayings. Thus the saying of Job (i, 21), which stands out from its context in view of its use of the divine name Yahweh, not normal in the book, and which in this particular reveals its fixed form, may have been taken over from popular use; it was perhaps already used then just as we use it to-day, at the death of a child:

> *Yahweh gave and Yahweh took,   blessed be the name of Yahweh.*

As among all peoples at an early stage in their development, so too in ancient Israel the *boasting saying* and the *mocking saying* played a large role. Though these may occur in every part of life, they have their special place in times of strife and war. For it is then that a man is more than usually conscious of his own superiority and of the inferiority of his associates and opponents. An example of the boasting saying is found in the words shouted by the Philistines to Jonathan as he clambered up to them with his lad: *Come up to us, and we will tell you something!* (I Sam. xiv, 12). Another is the similar summons by Goliath to David in I Sam. xvii, 44; so too Samson's triumphal saying, involving a play upon words, upon the Philistines he had slain at Lehi with the jawbone of an ass (Judg. xv, 16) and the saying of Lamech in Gen. iv, 23–4, which in extent nearly approaches the song-form, and which has been termed the 'song of the sword' because of the incorrect assumption that it is connected with the invention of the forging of weapons mentioned in iv, 22.

The mocking saying was much more common. Its name is מָשָׁל, the same word which we shall meet again as the term for the proverb (pp. 82–7). It is easy to understand why the mocking saying should have the same name as the proverb. It is a characteristic of human nature to be more ready to mock at a fellow man than to acknowledge him, and thus *to become a proverb* (Deut. xxviii, 37; Ps. lxix, 12) normally or invariably means 'to be an object of mockery'. The mocking saying and the mocking song must have possessed a quite tremendous power in Israel, being no less feared than in ancient Arabia, where even Muhammed trembled before its might.[5] Since the mocking song will be discussed in more detail later, it will be sufficient here to mention two mocking sayings: the sentence which Hosea, no doubt like many another prophet, came to hear: *The prophet is a fool, the man of the spirit is mad* (Hos. ix, 7), and the ironical question which is so often addressed by the godless to the pious man who is in the bitterest distress: *Where is now your God?* (Ps. xlii, 4, 11).

2. *Sayings from the life of the community.* In Israel's days of prosperity, the king was the leader of the community. His weal or woe determined the weal or

---

[4] Dürr, 'Altorientalisches Recht bei den Propheten Amos und Hosea' BZ 23 (1935), pp. 150–7, see pp. 154–7; Gordon, 'Hos. ii, 4–5 in the Light of New Semitic Inscriptions' ZAW 54 (1936), pp. 277–80; Kuhl, 'Neue Dokumente zum Verständnis von Hosea ii, 4–15' ZAW 52 (1934), pp. 102–9.

[5] Brockelmann, HdO III, 2–3 (1954), pp. 254–80; Jan de Goeje, 'Die arabische Literatur' *Kultur der Gegenwart*, Part I, Section VII (1906), pp. 132–59, esp. p. 135; (²1925), pp. 142–69, esp. p. 145.

woe of the community. It follows naturally, therefore, that the fortunes of the
king were the centre of interest, and were the subject both of songs (pp. 98–9)
and also of formulae of all kinds. The saying already quoted (p. 65) was in the
context in which it appears (Isa. ix, 5), in fact pronounced at the birth of a
prince or perhaps at his accession to the throne[6] marking his adoption by
Yahweh and hence his new birth: *A child is born to us, a son is given to us.* Such
a saying would echo with especial rejoicing at the birth of a son to the king, and
above all at the birth of the crown-prince. When the time came for this one or
some other to take over the government, there resounded the shout of rejoicing
at the coronation: *N.N. has become king,* or *has ascended the throne* (II Sam. xv,
10), and he was acclaimed with the words: *Long live the king!* (I Sam. x, 24;
I Kings i, 25). In a time of dire need, when there was no other way out except
an appeal to the king, it was customary to introduce this with the words:
Help, O king! (II Sam. xiv, 4; II Kings vi, 26). Fitting to the dead king there
was, in addition to the longer funeral lament (see p. 94), the people's cry of
distress: *Ah, lord* (Jer. xxii, 18).

The normal political community in the earliest period was the tribe. Thus
just as a variety of sagas (see pp. 40–1) became associated with the tribes, so
also did a variety of sayings. It must have been a favourite device for the
individual tribes to characterise one another with short sayings, normally linked
with their names; and they may well also have described themselves in a similar
manner. A series of such sayings is to be found in the so-called Blessings of
Jacob and Moses in Gen. xlix, and Deut. xxxiii. Thus of Issachar (אִישׁ־שָׂכָר
= *man of wages, wage earner*),[7] it is said:

> *Issachar, a strong ass   crouching between the sheepfolds.*[8]
> *When he saw that rest was good   and the land was pleasant,*
> *Bowed his shoulder to carry   and became a serf.*

And of Dan (= *judge*):

> *May Dan judge his people   as one of the tribes of Israel* (Gen. xlix, 14–16).

The people of Israel was, however, most conscious of itself as a whole in war-
time, and its warfare was thus also accompanied by sayings of various kinds. A
solemn pronouncement of eternal enmity against the arch-enemy Amalek has
been preserved in Ex. xvii, 16, in a saying now attributed to Moses, and certainly
very ancient:

> *A hand upon the banner of Yah*[9]   *Yahweh has war   with Amalek for ever*
> *and ever*

---

[6] Cf. below, pp. 318–19.

[7] Alt, 'Neues über Palästina aus dem Archiv Amenophis' IV', PJB 20 (1924), pp.
22–41 = *Kl. Schr.* III (1959), pp. 158–75. On the name *Issachar* cf. Albright, 'Northwest-
Semitic Names in a List of Egyptian Slaves from the Eighteenth Century B.C.' JAOS 74
(1954), pp. 222–33, see pp. 227 f., 232 f.

[8] Eissfeldt, 'Gabelhürden im Ostjordanland' FuF 25 (1949), pp. 8–10; cf. FuF 28
(1954), pp. 54–6; 29 (1955), pp. 118 f., and below, p. 199, n. 5.

[9] Instead of כֵּס יָהּ (= כִּסֵּא־יָהּ = כִּסֵּא יָהּ ?; cf. Jer. iii, 17, where apparently the conception
of the ark as כִּסֵּא יְהוָֹה *the throne of Yahweh* is presupposed) we must read נֵס יָהּ in view of

The spirit of the ancient nomadic military piety breathes also in the sayings with which Israel on its campaigns and migrations accompanied the moments when the ark was lifted up before the beginning of the migration[10] or the battle, and subsequently was lowered again (Num. x, 35–6).

> *Up, Yahweh   and let thine enemies be scattered   and let them that hate thee flee!*[11]

and:

> *Down*[12] *Yahweh, and bless*[13]   *the ten thousand thousands of Israel!*

We find what sounds like an imitation of the formula with which the warriors encouraged one another at the beginning of the battle, when Joab before the dangerous battle on two fronts against the Aramaeans and Ammonites admonishes his brother Abishai: *Let us fight manfully for our people and for the ark*[14] *of our God, but may Yahweh do what pleases him* (II Sam. x, 12). Victory was possibly proclaimed and hailed, as we may perhaps conclude from the frequent use of the expression *Yahweh has put the enemy under our feet* (cf. I Kings v, 17; Ps. xviii, 39; cx, 1). It was perhaps proclaimed with this saying. But when the fortune of war turned against Israel, or when the army was dissatisfied with its leader and refused to follow him further, then was heard the cry of despair or rebellion: *Every man to his tent, O Israel!* i.e. 'Let every man escape who can!' or 'Desert the leader, go home!' (II Sam. xviii, 17; xix, 9; xx, 1; I Kings xii, 16).

In Israel, as everywhere else in the world, the administration of law is surrounded by all manner of solemn customs and sayings, and here we have a fair quantity of material. It is not surprising that most of it refers to murders and executions. For it is in these circumstances that the need of a solemn saying would be most strongly felt. The principle is enunciated in Gen. ix, 6, where consonantal and vocalic assonance, a much-loved device in sayings, is employed:

šōpēk dām hā'ādām	*bā'ādām dāmô yiššāpēk*
kî beṣelem 'elōhîm	*'āśāh 'et hā'ādām*
He who sheds man's blood	by man shall his blood be shed!
For in the image of God	has he made man.[15]

This is no doubt borrowed from legal usage, and we may imagine that it was spoken at the pronouncement of the death sentence or at its carrying out. The formula which had to be pronounced by the elders of the appropriate town in a case of murder by a person unknown, to which a short prayer is added, is preserved in Deut. xxi, 7–8: *Our hands have not shed this blood, and our eyes have seen nothing.* Just as verdict, execution and expiation were pronounced with a

---

the reference immediately before (v. 16) to the naming of the altar יְהֹוָה נִסִּי *Yahweh my banner.*

[10] Dus, 'Der Brauch der Ladewanderung im alten Israel' ThZ 17 (1961), pp. 1–16. Lit. p. 279, n. 41; § 126

[11] Delete מִפָּנֶיךָ *before thee.*   [12] שָׁבָה for שׁוּבָה *return.*

[13] Supplying וּבֵרַכְתָּ.   [14] אֲרוֹן for עָרֵי *cities.*

[15] Gemser, 'The Importance of the Motive Clause in Old Testament Law' SVT I (1953), pp. 50–66.

set formula, so also was the accusation, or it may have culminated in a fixed formula such as we find in I Kings xxi, 13, brought against Naboth: *He has blasphemed God and the king.* But naturally the less serious offences were also accompanied by formulae. This is true, for example, of the way in which the widow, spurned by the brother-in-law who is under an obligation to marry her, gets even with him: she pulls off his shoe, spits in his face and says: *So shall it be done to every man who will not build up his brother's house* (Deut. xxv, 9).

§ 8. LEGAL SAYINGS

Literature: Alt (§ 4d), 'Zur Talionsformel' ZAW 52 (1934), pp. 303–5 = *Kl. Schr.* I pp. 341–44; 'Das Verbot des Diebstahls im Dekalog' *Kl. Schr.* I (1953), pp. 333–40; Bernhardt, *Gott und Bild. Ein Beitrag zur Begründung und Deutung des Bilderverbotes im AT* (1956); Boecker, *Redeformen des israelitischen Rechtslebens* (Diss. theol. Bonn, 1959); Eberharter, *Der Dekalog* (1929); Gese, 'Beobachtungen zum Stil at. Rechtssätze' ThLZ 85, (1960), cols. 147–50; Gottstein, 'Du sollst nicht stehlen' ThZ 9 (1953), pp. 394–5; Herrmann, 'Das zehnte Gebot' *Sellin-Festschr.* (1927), pp. 69–82; Horst, 'Der Diebstahl im AT' *Kahle-Festschr.* (1935), pp. 19–28; 'Der Eid im AT' EvTh 17 (1957), pp. 366–84; Jenni, *Die theologische Begründung des Sabbatgebotes im AT* (1956); Jepsen, 'Du sollst nicht töten' ELKZ 13 (1959), pp. 384 f.; Kessler, 'Die literarische, historische und theologische Problematik des Dekalogs' VT 7 (1957), pp. 1–16; Ludwig Köhler, 'Der Dekalog' ThR 1 (1929), pp. 161–84; Mowinckel, *Le Décalogue* (1927); 'Zur Geschichte der Dekaloge' ZAW 55 (1937), pp. 218–35; Nowack, 'Der erste Dekalog' BZAW 33 (1918), pp. 381–97; Pedersen, *Der Eid bei den Semiten* (1914); Petuchowski, 'A Note on W. Kessler's "Problematik des Dekalogs"' VT 7 (1957), pp. 397 f.; Rabast, *Das apodiktische Recht im Deuteronomium und im Heiligkeitsgesetz* (1949); von Rad, *Deuteronomium-Studien* (²1948), pp. 17–25; E.T. *Studies in Deuteronomy* (1953), pp. 25–36; Rost, 'Die Schuld der Väter' *Festg. Rudolf Hermann* (1957), pp. 229–33; Rowley, 'Moses and the Decalogue' BJRL 34 (1951/2), pp. 81–118 = 'Moïse et le Décalogue' RHPhR 32 (1952), pp. 7–40; Hans Schmidt, 'Mose und der Dekalog' FRLANT 36 (1923), I, pp. 78–119; Schmökel, 'Biblische "Du sollst"-Gebote und ihr historischer Ort' Z Sav RG 36 (1950), pp. 365–90; Segert, 'Bis in das dritte und vierte Geschlecht—Ex xx, 5' (Czech) CV 1 (1958), pp. 37–9; Stamm, 'Sprachliche Erwägungen zum Gebot "Du sollst nicht töten"' ThZ 1 (1945), pp. 81–90; *Der Dekalog im Lichte der neueren Forschung* (1958); Stoebe, 'Das achte Gebot (Exod. xx, 16)' WuD 3 (1952), pp. 108–26; Volz, *Mose und sein Werk* (²1932); Vriezen, 'Litterairhistorische vragen aangaande de Dekaloog' NThSt 22 (1939), pp. 2–24, 34–51; Welch, *Deuteronomy. The Framework to the Code* (1932), pp. 17–48; Zimmerli 'Das zweite Gebot' *Bertholet-Festschr.* (1950), pp. 550–63.
    Cf. also Literature p. 189, n. 5; §§ 19, 24, 30, 33–5, 126.

The sayings just mentioned accompany particular legal acts as solemn words. Much more significant than these are, however, the legal sentences in apodictic style. It has already been said (pp. 27–8) in the discussion of casuistic legal regulations, that they are sharply differentiated from the latter in form and content, and are to be regarded as being of specifically Israelite origin. Originally sayings in the form of an address (*Thou shalt not commit adultery!* Ex. xx, 14), or beginning with a participle (*He who smites his father or his mother shall be put to death!* Ex. xxi, 15), or with a relative clause (*Everyone . . . who gives one of his children as a Molech-sacrifice*,[1] *shall be put to death* Lev. xx, 2), or introduced by a curse (*Cursed be he who slays his neighbour in secret!* Deut. xxvii, 24) may well have existed independently. But very soon, no doubt already at the oral stage, they were gathered into groups, especially in tens and twelves, consisting of sayings which deal with cases of a similar kind. These groups have in several cases been preserved as such in the Old Testament: e.g. the dodecalogue in Deut. xxvii, 15–26, a collection of twelve crimes deserving of curses, and the collection, known in a special sense as the Decalogue, of ten religious-cultic and social-ethical prohibitions and commands, transmitted in Ex. xx, 2–17 and Deut. v, 6–21, admittedly not in their original form, but in many ways altered and expanded. Other such dodecalogues and decalogues are also preserved in the Old Testament.[2] We cannot now determine with certainty whether and how far it is justifiable to go beyond these recognised groups and to group together individual sayings, similar in form and content, though now scattered, into tens and twelves and other groups: so for example the basic content of Ex. xxi, 12, 15–17; xxii, 18–19; xxxi, 15; Lev. xx, 2, 10–13, 15–16, 27; xxiv, 16, as a group of twelve crimes worthy of death. Nor can it be decided with any more certainty whether a ten-fold arrangement was originally intended or not in the cultic prohibitions and commands which are quoted in the section Ex. xxxiv, 12–26, which has been secondarily elaborated and hence can only be analysed with difficulty. It seems probable, however, that in this latter case we have an actual decalogue.[3]

§ 9. CULTIC SAYINGS

Literature: Begrich, 'Das priesterliche Heilsorakel' ZAW 52 (1934), pp. 81–92; 'Die priesterliche Tora' BZAW 66 (1936), pp. 63–88; Blank, 'The Curse, the Blasphemy, the Spell, and the Oath' HUCA 23, 1 (1950/1), pp. 73–95; Engnell, *Israel and the Law* ([2]1954); Grant, 'Oracle in the OT' AJSL 39 (1922–3), pp. 257–81; Hempel, 'Die israelitischen Anschauungen von Segen und Fluch im Lichte altorientalischer Parallelen' ZDMG 79 (1925), pp. 20–110 = *Apoxysmata* (BZAW 81, 1961), pp. 30–113; Humbert, 'Die Herausforderungsformel "hinnenî êlékâ" ' ZAW 51 (1933), pp. 101–8 = *Opuscules* (1958), pp. 44–59; Kaiser, 'Das Orakel als Mittel der Rechtsfindung im Alten Ägypten' ZRGG 10

[1] Berthier and Charlier, *Le Sanctuaire Punique d'El-Hofra à Constantine* (Texte 1955 Planches 1952); Cazelles, 'Molok' *Suppl Dict Bible* V (1957), cols. 1337–46; Charlier 'La nouvelle série de stèles puniques de Constantine et la question des sacrifices dits "molchomor" en relation avec l'expression "bšrm btm" ' Karthago 4 (1953), pp. 1–48; Dhorme, 'Le dieu Baal et le dieu Moloch dans la tradition Biblique' AnSt 6 (1956), pp. 57–62; Dronkert, *De Molochdienst in het OuT* (1953); *Het Mensenoffer in de oudt. wereld* (1955); Eissfeldt, *Molk als Opferbegriff im Punischen und Hebräischen und das Ende des Gottes Moloch* (1935); Février, 'Molchomor' RHR 143 (1953), pp. 8–18; Henninger, 'Menschenopfer bei den Arabern' Anthropos 53 (1958), pp. 721–805, 1 Map; Hoftijzer, 'Eine Notiz zum punischen Kinderopfer' VT 8 (1958), pp. 288–92; Kornfeld, 'Der Moloch, Eine Untersuchung zur Theorie O. Eissfeldt's' WZKM 51 (1952), pp. 287–313.
[2] Lev. xviii: see Elliger, 'Leviticus xviii' ThLZ 79 (1954), cols. 303–6; 'Das Gesetz Leviticus xviii' ZAW 67 (1955), pp. 1–25; Neh. x, 31–40, cf. p. 549; Ps. xv, 2–5, cf. p. 74. Cf. Morgenstern (§ 35).
[3] Pfeiffer, 'The Oldest Decalogue' JBL 43 (1924), pp. 294–310. Lit. § 126.

(1958), pp. 193–208; Küchler, 'Das priesterliche Orakel in Israel und Juda' BZAW 33 (1918), pp. 285–301; Lods, 'Le rôle des oracles dans la nomination des rois, des prêtres et des magistrats chez les Israélites, les Égyptiens et les Grecs' *Mél. Maspéro* 1 (1934), pp. 91– 100; Mowinckel, *Psalmenstudien* V: *Segen und Fluch in Israels Kult- und Psalmdichtung* (1924 (²1961)); *Offersang og sangoffer* (1951), pp. 297–307; E.T. *The Psalms in Israel's Worship* (1962), II, pp. 44–52; Östborn, *Tora in the OT* (1945); Press, 'Das Ordal im alten Israel' ZAW 51 (1933), pp. 121–40, 227–55; Reiser, 'Eschatologische Gottessprüche in den Elisa- Legenden' ThZ 9 (1953), pp. 321–38; Scharbert, ' "Fluchen" und "Segnen" im AT' Bibl 39 (1958), pp. 1–26; *Solidarität in Segen und Fluch im AT und in seiner Umwelt*, I (1958). Lit. § 126.

1. *Divine sayings*. Formal sayings and solemn formulae appear—as one would expect—much more frequently in the realm of cult and religion than in the sphere of law. And here we must distinguish three kinds, according to whether the speaker is God, the priest, or the worshipper. Divine sayings are particu- larly frequent, sayings, that is, in which it is felt that God is the speaker, and though in practice they are spoken by his representative, yet they are sharply differentiated from the latter's own words. The representative of God was generally the priest, who spoke in the name of his God, or, rather, through whom his God spoke in the first person. This is perfectly plain in the saying mediated through the sacred lot. It is not so clear in the case of other utterances which rank as divine sayings, by whom they are spoken and in what precise circumstances. But it appears certain that words like those which are gathered in the decalogues of Ex. xx and xxxiv, which are significantly termed *words* (דְּבָרִים), i.e. God's words (Ex. xx, 1; xxiv, 3, 4, 8; xxxiv, 28), were not merely indicated as such in the narrative, transmitted first orally and subsequently in literary form, but were also at some moment proclaimed as divine words; and the occasion for this can only be a cultic occasion. It is possible to imagine, as Mowinckel and others have done, that this happened at festivals at which the divine epiphany was experienced and the address by God was received; as the mediator of this divine voice it is more probable that we should then think rather of the cult-prophet than of the priest. For there is every reason to assume, as we shall see in the discussion of the Psalms (pp. 104, 109, 113 etc.), that in the pre-exilic cult the charismatic prophet had his place beside the official priest. We have, however, already seen in the discussion of cultic records (p. 31) that by no means all such divine addresses are to be traced back to cultic actions, but that a very substantial number of them represent originally addresses directed by the priests to the laity, i.e. Torah.

The divine word is thus primarily the oracle. The ephod, together with the Urim and Thummim, is comparatively well attested from the period of Saul and David, and was a sort of sacred lot, in which the appearance of the one 'lot' denoted 'Yes', and of the other 'No'. In the use of this, a question must always be put to the deity which demands the answer yes or no: Shall I do this? Will this happen? The answer which follows upon the appearance of the one lot or the other is an affirmative or negative linked to the wording of the question: Do this! or Do not do this! This will happen! or This will not hap- pen! Thus in I Sam. xxiii, 2, David asks Yahweh: *Shall I go and smite these Philistines?* and Yahweh's answer runs: *Go, and smite the Philistines and save*

Keilah! (cf. xxiii, 4; xxx, 8; II Sam. v, 19). David's question, expanded with a prayer formula, and Yahweh's answer to it in I Sam. xxiii, 11, refer to a future event: *Will Saul come down, as thy servant hath heard? Yahweh, God of Israel, I pray thee, tell thy servant! And Yahweh answered: He will come down.* To this there is linked immediately (xxiii, 12) another similar question and answer. Thus in this ephod oracle the fixed form of question and answer is normally determined by the technique of obtaining the oracle. But even with this oracle there were cases when God, i.e. the priest as representative of God, did not restrict himself to a mere yes or no, but of his own accord gave more precise directions. This occurs in II Sam. v, 23–4, where we are also to think of an ephod oracle, although this is not explicitly stated. Here David receives from the deity the advice not to attack the Philistines from the front but from the rear, and in addition is given an indication as to the favourable moment for the beginning of the attack. Obviously the priest, in addition to possessing the duty and the ability to handle the ephod oracle technically, possessed charismatic oracular gifts,[1] and the utterances which followed from these were naturally not bound to the ephod technique. Such oracles often have a rhythmic structure. A hint of this may already be seen in the second half of II Sam. v, 24. The rhythmic form is, however, quite clear in the saying which Rebekah receives in answer to her question to the oracle in Beerlahairoi or in Beersheba, when, during her pregnancy, she was anxious about the struggling of the children within her womb (Gen. xxv, 23):

> *Two nations are in thy womb,*
> *and two peoples shall be separated from thy bowels,*
> *and one people shall be stronger than the other,*
> *and the elder shall serve the younger.*

With regard to the remaining divine addresses, whose setting in the cult, as we have seen (p. 71), can no longer be determined with certainty, we may nevertheless assume with great probability that they—or at least the originals on which they are based—are not mere literary compositions, but really formed part of the actual cultic life. These are either pronouncements[2] by Yahweh describing his being or action in the form of first person statements; or they are demands made of the people, presented in the form of prohibition and command. Quite frequently these two forms are combined, so that the self-revelation of Yahweh as the gracious and holy one provides the grounds for the demand made of the people to fulfil the will of Yahweh in thankful obedience and to emulate his exalted pattern. But each of these also appears separately: the first, for example, in the words from the narratives concerning Yahweh's self-revelations to Moses in Ex. xxxiii, 19 and Ex. xxxiv, 6 (cf. Ps. ciii, 7–8),

---

[1] A similar situation existed at the Delphic oracle, cf. Marie Delcourt, *L'Oracle de Delphes* (1955), pp. 70–85: 'Les méthodes oraculaires'; Klaffenbach, 'Das delphische Orakel' Wissenschaftliche Annalen 3 (1954), pp. 513–26; Parke and Wormell, *The Delphic Oracle* II (1956), pp. 17–25: 'The Procedure of the Oracles'. On the Egyptian oracles, cf. Roeder *Kulte, Orakel und Naturverehrung im alten Ägypten* (1960).

[2] Elliger, 'Ich bin der Herr—euer Gott' *Karl Heim-Festschr.* (1954), pp. 9–34; Zimmerli, 'Ich bin Jahwe' *Alt-Festschr.* (1953), pp. 179–209. Lit. § 126.

which have all the appearance of being solemn cult-sayings. Ex. xxxiii, 19, runs:

I will be gracious to whom I will   and I will show mercy on whom I will.

These are personal pronouncements by God, which in many respects recall the proclamations of divine favour which conclude many of the psalms of lamentation. It seems probable that these represent or imitate the voice of God resounding in the cult; or the utterance of a charismatic who represents God (pp. 113–14, 117). The difference is only that the conclusions to the psalms are of a special kind, and have reference to the particular need presented in the relevant complaint, whereas in the other passages quite general statements are made concerning God's nature and activity. For this reason it may be assumed that these statements by God himself had their setting in particular public festivals for the whole people or the whole cult-community. Divine prohibitions and commands standing on their own are to be found frequently in the Old Testament laws, e.g.: *The firstborn of thy sons shalt thou give unto me* (Ex. xxii, 28; cf. xiii, 2; xxxiv, 19; Num. iii, 13 *et passim*).

The combination of a statement by God about himself and a demand upon men is to be found in its most pregnant form in such a phrase as the formula which appears frequently, particularly in the Holiness Code: *You are to be holy, for I am holy* (Lev. xi, 44, 45; xix, 2, *et passim*). It found its classical expression in the decalogue of Ex. xx = Deut. v, which begins thus (Ex. xx, 2–Deut. v, 6): *I am Yahweh, thy God, who brought thee out of the land of Egypt, out of the house of bondage* (cf. Ex. xxxii, 4; Hos. xiii, 4), and then links to this the powerful series of *words* beginning with: *Thou shalt not.* In the same way the divine statement of Ex. xxxiv, 6–7[3] belongs originally with the decalogue of commandments beginning at v. 14 and extending to v. 26 (p. 200), though now separated from them by vv. 8–13. We may therefore regard such combinations of divine statement with divine demand as a fixed form, and it must also have become customary at a fairly early date to join together ten propositions to form a unit (p. 70), whether the divine pronouncement is to be counted in with the rest, or whether it stands as an anacrusis, a preamble, outside the counted words. As already suggested, we may then picture these divine words as being in all probability written upon tablets and proclaimed on particular festival days by a priest as representative of God. We may perhaps follow Mowinckel and others in imagining such a cultic festival to have been actually a festival for the renewal of the covenant of Yahweh with Israel. This will then have led to the elaboration by later writers of the moment of the making of the covenant on the exalted stage of Sinai after the fashion of this festal ceremony.

2. *Priestly sayings.* Sayings which are delivered by the priest in his own name take up a large place in cultic life. These are of various kinds. In the first place, there is the 'Torah', the imparting to the laity of oral information concerning cultic and ethical matters—that is the original meaning of תּוֹרָה. Though not always rhythmic in structure, it nevertheless always follows fixed and ceremonial forms. Hag. ii, 12–14, provides an example—admittedly invented (p. 427),

---

[3] Freedman, 'God Compassionate and Gracious' Western Watch 6 (1955), pp. 6–24; Scharbert, 'Formgeschichte und Exegese von Ex xxxiv, 6 f. und seiner Parallelen' Bibl 38 (1957), pp. 130–50; Walker, 'Concerning Ex. xxxiv, 6' JBL 79 (1960), p. 277.

but correct in style—of Torah-question and Torah-answer. The question, couched in casuistic style (pp. 27–8), runs: *If someone carries holy flesh in the skirt of his garment and touches with his skirt bread . . . does it become holy?* The answer is: *No.* Then follows the further question: *If someone who is unclean by contact with a dead body touches any of these, does it become unclean?* and the answer is: *It does become unclean.* Another Torah-question which is concerned with cultic matters in the narrower sense, is described in Zech. vii, 1–3, and viii, 18–19.[4] In the fourth year of king Darius I, i.e. 518 B.C., so the statement runs, a question was brought *to the priests at the temple of Yahweh of hosts and*—this is characteristic and makes us think of an organisation such as that of cult-prophets —*to the prophets,* as to whether the fast in the fifth month should continue to be observed as before. Zechariah, commanded by Yahweh, gives the answer, indicating that not only the fast-day of the fifth month, but also those of the fourth, seventh and tenth are to cease and are to be replaced by days of rejoicing. Another form of Torah, with ethical rather than cultic questions, is attested by Pss. xv, xxiv, 3–6 and Isa. xxxiii, 14–16 (cf. also Micah vi, 6–8), which has appropriately been described as a Torah-liturgy or an 'Admission Torah'. The layman, presumably having arrived at the gate of the temple, asks the priest, though in theory in many cases directing himself to Yahweh:

Yahweh, who may sojourn in thy tent,   who may dwell on thy holy hill?

and receives from him the answer:

He who walks blamelessly, and does what is right,
*   and speaks truth from his heart . . .*

It is to be noted that in Ps. xv, from the beginning of which these words are taken, the answer comprises exactly ten qualities or modes of behaviour, which give the right of entry into the sanctuary. This indicates that in this type, as in the decalogue, the placing together of ten sections was favoured. The mention of the conditions may then be followed by a promise from the priest, which rounds off the whole. So in Ps. xv:

He who does these things   shall never be moved.

The 'liturgy' comprises three sections: the question of the layman to the priest, the priestly answer, the priestly promise.

The two examples just quoted of the priest's Torah speech are perhaps fairly late, but it may quite properly be assumed that the forms themselves are old and that they have preserved their pure form from an earlier period.

In addition to this, the cultic actions of the priest were often accompanied by various sayings and formulae. Since the action of cleansing which Isaiah experienced in his vision as performed on him by a seraph is certainly modelled upon cultic practice, we may assume that the priest at such a ceremony spoke the formula: *Since this has touched your lips your guilt is taken away, and your sin atoned* (Isa. vi, 7). The warning: *Be silent, all flesh, before Yahweh; for he has roused himself from his holy dwelling* (Zech. ii, 17; cf. Hab. ii, 20; Zeph. i, 7) was recited by the priest presumably at the moment at which Yahweh's approach

---

[4] vii, 4–viii, 17 interrupt the connection of the two sections (cf. pp. 431, 433).

was expected—at the moment of sacrifice, or at some other ceremonial which anticipates a theophany (cf. pp. 35, 73). At the end of the ceremony, the priest pronounced the saying which has retained its place to the present day in Christian worship (Num. vi, 24–6; cf. Ecclus. l, 20):

> The LORD bless thee   and keep thee
> The LORD make his face to shine   upon thee and be gracious to thee,
> The LORD lift up his countenance upon thee   and give thee peace.[5]

3. *Lay sayings.* With this priestly blessing, we may make a natural transition to the religious and cultic formulae which the layman has to use. For the blessing, beginning with בָּרוּךְ *blessed* and its opposite, the curse, beginning with אָרוּר *cursed,* are by no means reserved to the priest. They point back into the magical, dynamistic atmosphere, in which the word itself, even without the power given it by a deity, was believed to be effective, and indeed irrevocable (cf. Gen. xxvii, 37). Such words were then absorbed by religion and became the expression of a desire for a blessing attributed to a deity or, though characteristically more rarely, for a curse. Blessing and curse may be used by any man, even though naturally enough particularly great powers of blessing and cursing are attributed to the seer empowered by divine charisma (Num. xxii, 6; I Sam. ix, 13) or to the priest (Num. vi, 23–7; Deut. xxi, 5; xxvii, 14–26). Moreover, in the life of the ordinary man there are moments when blessing and curse are more powerful than at other times. This is especially true of the last hours of a man's life. A blessing spoken then by father or mother is a treasure without compare for the child, while a last curse from their mouth will bring him misfortune inescapable in its disastrousness. In Genesis blessing and curse are often applied *ex eventu,* so that the patriarch in the face of death foretells, or, really, anticipates, to his children—and that means to the people of Israel or its individual tribes—their future fortunes by means of blessing or curse (Gen. xxvii, 27–9, 39–40; xlviii, 20; xlix). This is simply a case of transference to the earliest times of what the narrator knows as contemporary custom. In every realm of life a good deed can be requited with a blessing, and an evil deed with a curse (Ruth ii, 20; Prov. xi, 26), and this practice too has been projected back into the earlier ages and even into the primeval age. Yahweh punishes the offence of the snake with a curse upon it, and similarly a fearful curse from Yahweh comes upon the fratricide Cain (Gen. iii, 14–15; iv, 11). Noah requites his three sons Canaan (p. 191), Shem and Japhet exactly according to their behaviour towards him: Canaan is cursed, Shem, or Shem's God, and Japhet, however, are blessed (Gen. ix, 25–7). Of a general religious character too are the greetings like the one especially used at harvest as greeting and reply: *Yahweh be with you! May Yahweh bless you!* (Ruth ii, 4; Ps. cxxix, 8); or the pious wish, with which priest or layman let another man go and gave him courage and hope: *Go in peace!* (Judg. xviii, 6; I Sam. i, 17; xx, 42; xxv, 35, *et passim*). A particular form of curse is the self-cursing or self-execration. This occurred in everyday life, as

---

[5] Liebreich, 'The Songs of Ascents and the Priestly Blessing' JBL 74 (1955), pp. 33–6. Ringgren, 'Den aaronitiska Välsignelsen' *Eripainos teoksesta Talenta quinque* (1953), pp. 35–45.

in the oath-formula, which clearly represents an abbreviated self-cursing: אִם *If* I do this and this (may I be accursed) = certainly I will not do this; אִם־לֹא *if* I do *not* do this and this (may I be accursed) = certainly I will do this. It also had a firm place in the cult. In I Kings viii, 31–2, it is presupposed as a ceremony which takes place in the temple, and in Ps. vii, 4–6, as also in the great oath of cleansing of Job xxxi, 5–34, 38–40a, there is preserved the formula which must then have been recited.[6] Specifically cultic formulae are those which, according to Deut. xxvi, 5–10,[7] 13–15,[8] are to be spoken by the layman as he offers the firstfruits and the tithes.

§ 10. PROPHETIC SAYINGS

Literature: Ayuso, 'Los elementos extrabíblicos de los profetas' Est Bíbl 6 (1947), pp. 347–402, 455; Bach, *Die Aufforderung zur Flucht und zum Kampf im at. Prophetenspruch* (WMANT 9, 1962); Beyer (§ 3); de Boer, 'Texte et traduction des paroles attribuées à David en 2 Samuel xxiii 1–7' SVT IV (1957), pp. 47–56; Chary, *Les Prophètes et le culte à partir de l'exil* (1955); Eissfeldt, 'The Prophetic Literature' OTMSt (1951), pp. 115–61; Gressmann, *Der Messias* (FRLANT 43, 1929), pp. 65–148: 'Prophetische Gattungen'; Häussermann, *Wortempfang und Symbol in der at. Prophetie* (BZAW 58, 1932); Haldar, *Associations of Cult Prophets among the Ancient Semites* (1945); Hallevy, 'Man of God' JNESt 17 (1958), pp. 237–44; Harms, *Die falschen Propheten* (1947); Hentschke, *Die Stellung der vorexilischen Propheten zum Kultus* (BZAW 75, 1957); on this Press, ZAW 70 (1958), pp. 181–4; Hertzberg, 'Die prophetische Kritik am Kult' ThLZ 75 (1950), cols. 219–26; Hesse, 'Wurzelt die prophetische Gerichtsrede im israelitischen Kult?' ZAW 65 (1953), pp. 45–53; Jacob, 'Le Prophétisme israélite d'après les recherches récentes' RHPhR 32 (1952), pp. 59–69; 'Quelques remarques sur les faux prophètes' ThZ 13 (1957), pp. 479–486; Kapelrud, 'Cult and Prophetic Words' StTh 4 [1950] (1951/2), pp. 5–12; 'Israels profeter og retten' SEA 18/19 (1953/4), pp. 17–31; Lindblom, *Die literarische Gattung der prophetischen Literatur* (1924); 'Zur Frage des kanaanäischen Ursprungs des altisraelitischen Prophetismus' BZAW 77 (1958), pp. 89–104; Lofthouse, ' "Thus hath Jahveh said" ' AJSL 40 (1923/4), pp. 231–51; Mowinckel, 'Die letzten Worte Davids, II Sam xxiii, 1–7' ZAW 45 (1927), pp. 30–58; ' "The Spirit" and the "Word" in the Pre-Exilic Reforming Prophets' JBL 53 (1934), pp. 199–227; 'Ecstatic Experience and Rational Elaboration in the OT Prophecy' AcOr[L] 10 (1935), pp. 264–91; 'La Connaissance de Dieu chez les prophètes de l'AT' RHPhR 22 (1942), pp. 69–105; 'Ekstatiske innslag i profetenes oplevelser' NTT 49 (1948), pp. 129–43, 193–221; Noth, *Geschichte und Gotteswort im AT* (1949) = *Ges. Stud. zum AT* (1957), pp. 230–47; Quell, *Wahre und falsche Propheten* (1952); 'Der Kultprophet' ThLZ 81 (1956), cols. 401–4; Rendtorff, 'Priesterliche Kulttheologie und prophetische Kultpolemik' ThLZ 81 (1956), cols. 339–42; Ridderbos, *Israëls Profetie en "Profetie" buiten Israël* (1955); Roubos, *Profetie en cultus in Israël* (Diss. Utrecht, 1956); Rowley, 'Ritual and the Hebrew Prophets' JSSt 1 (1956), pp. 338–60; Saydon, 'Cult and Prophecy in Israel' Melita Theologica 4 (1951), pp. 75–88; 5 (1952), pp. 7–16; Seierstad, *Die Offenbarungserlebnisse der Propheten Amos, Jesaja und Jeremia* (SNVAO 46, 2, 1946); Wolff, 'Die Begründungen der prophetischen Heils- und Unheilssprüche' ZAW 52 (1934), pp. 1–22; *Das Zitat im Prophetenspruch* (1937); Würthwein, 'Der Ursprung der prophetischen Gerichtsrede' ZThK 49 (1952), pp. 1–16; Zimmerli, *Le Prophète dans 'AT et dans l'Islam* (1945); 'Gericht und Heil im at. Prophetenwort' (*Der Anfang.*

---

[6] Cf. Driver and Miles, 'Ordeal by Oath at Nuzi' Iraq 7 (1940), pp. 132–8. Lit. § 126.

[7] Beek, 'Das Problem des aramäischen Stammvaters (Deut. xxvi, 5)' OTS 8 (1950), pp. 193–212; van der Woude, *Uittocht en Sinaï* (1961). Lit. § 126.

[8] Cazelles, 'Sur un rituel du Deutéronome: Deut. xxvi, 14' RB 55 (1948), pp. 54–71.

Zehlendorfer Vorträge, 1949), pp. 21–46; *Erkenntnis Gottes nach dem Buche Ez* (1954);
'Das Wort des göttlichen Selbsterweises (Erweiswort), eine prophetische Gattung'
Mél. Bibl. Robert (1957), pp. 154–64.
    Cf. also Literature §§ 20, 42–61, 126.

1. *Ecstatic possession as the ultimate source of the prophetic saying.* The ultimate
source of the prophetic saying is the state of ecstatic possession which enables
the prophet to see pictures which lie beyond present reality and to perceive
voices otherwise inaudible to the human ear, visions and words which reveal to
him Yahweh's nature and will. The Hebrews of the pre-Canaanite period, like
the pre-Islamic Arabs, were familiar with this phenomenon of ecstasy, and
designated as *seers* (חֹזֶה, רֹאֶה, Arabic *kahin*) men who had a particular pro-
pensity for it. In Canaan, apparently at the time in which we first learn of it,
the period of Samuel and Saul, Israel came into contact with a new ecstatic
phenomenon which was widespread in its environment;[1] the agent of this was
designated as נָבִיא translated by us with the word *prophet*, which stems from
the Greek word used in LXX for the Hebrew. The ecstasy characteristic of
this movement was clearly more intense than that of the seer and also differed
from it in that large bands were possessed by it, whereas each seer stood alone.
The two lines then merged, however, and the two names *seer* and *prophet* also
merged, with the result that the most prominent figures of the now unified
movement were described equally as *prophet* or as *seer*, whereas the ecstatics
who appeared in bands continued to make do with the name *prophet*. Both
these forms of ecstatic possession originally had their own forms of expression,
and we can no doubt get an impression of the difference by a comparison of a
seer of the old kind like Balaam (Num. xxii–xxiv) on the one hand, and of the
400 prophets who encouraged Ahab for the battle against Aram, who represent
rather the new kind (I Kings xxii, 5–12) on the other hand. But we can hardly
discover more than this. What we possess of genuine prophetic sayings, the
words of the so-called writing prophets from Amos onwards, all comes from
the time when the two kinds of ecstatic possession had long since merged, and
moreover it reveals that the form of expression which may here be observed
had already long been fixed. We have therefore in describing the prophetic
saying to limit ourselves to the material provided by the writing prophets.

    [1] Prophets in Byblos, c. 1100 B.C., cf. Wen-Amon (AOT, p. 72, ANET, p. 26b), I, x,
3–5 (38–40); c. 800 B.C. in Hamath, cf. Zakir inscription (AOT, pp. 443 f.; ANET, pp.
501 f.; DOTT, pp. 242–50; A, lines 12–17. On Egypt, cf. Erman-Ranke, *Ägypten* (1923),
pp. 325–6, and below, p. 151, n. 1; on Babylonia and Assyria, cf. AOT, pp. 281–4;
Christian, 'Sum. lú-an-ná-ba-tu = akkad. maḫḫu "Ekstatiker"' WZKM 54 (1957), pp. 9
f.; on the Hittites, cf. ANET, p. 396 a, line 17; Götze, 'Die Pestgebete des Muršiliš' Kleinas.
Forsch. 1 (1930), pp. 161–251, see pp. 162, 218–19, II, § 11, 3; on Mari, cf. Dossin, 'Une
révélation du dieu Dagan à Terqa' RA 42 (1949), pp. 125–34; Kupper, *Correspondance de
Baḫdi-Lim* (ARM VI, 1954), pp. 70 f., No. 45; Lods, 'Une tablette inédite de Mari, interés-
sante pour l'histoire ancienne du prophétisme sémitique' StOTPr (1950), pp. 103–10;
Malamat, '"Prophecy" in the Mari Documents' [Hebr., Engl. sum.] Eretz-Israel 4 (1956),
pp. 74–84, VI–VII; 'History and Prophetic Vision in a Mari Letter' [Hebr., Engl. sum.]
Eretz-Israel 5 (1958), pp. 67–73, 86*–7*; Parrot, 'Les Tablettes de Mari et l'AT' RHPhR
30 (1950), pp. 1–11; 'Mari et l'AT' RHPhR 35 (1955), pp. 117–20; Rinaldi, 'Oracoli
Amorriti' Aevum 28 (1954), pp. 1–9; von Soden, 'Verkündigung des Gotteswillens durch
prophetisches Wort in den altbabylonischen Briefen aus Mâri' WdO I (1947–52), pp.
397–403.

Even among these, who have long since outgrown the most violent ecstatic state which is to be described as possession (cf. I Sam. xix, 18–24), it is nevertheless quite clear that their sayings ultimately derive from the moments of divine possession, moments whose compulsiveness is described by Amos in the words:

> *The lion has roared   who will not fear?*
> *Yahweh² has spoken   who can but prophesy?* (iii, 8).

But we cannot get a deeper insight into such moments, nor can we trace back into them the utterances which ultimately stem from them. Just as the narratives of visions which we possess have been related and written down by the prophet after the vision, so the sayings too, which undoubtedly transmit the revelation received in the moment of ecstasy, have been shaped by the prophet after this moment. A difference does indeed exist which may be seen more clearly in some sayings than in others, in so far as the stimulus of inspiration still lasts on (Isa. viii, 11–15; xxii, 14), and also in so far as some sayings owe their existence to a definite moment of divine inspiration (Jer. xxviii, 11–12; xlii, 1–7). But others which follow along the line of instructions received earlier, were no doubt proclaimed without a new divine impetus being received by the prophet who is nevertheless aware of the will of his God (Isa. i, 2–3, 10–15). The consciousness, that he was the mediator of the divine will and that he had to deliver not his own words but the word (דָּבָר) of Yahweh, was indeed so strong in him that it persisted or at any rate could persist beyond the ecstatic moments. This becomes completely clear with Jeremiah, who also of himself passes judgement upon the situation of his people (v, 4–5) and does in fact feel himself called by God to be a tester of his people (vi, 27–30),³ and thus shows in his prophetic proclamation a certain independence. For at decisive moments he has no advice to give of himself, but has to wait for the voice of God, recognisable to him quite clearly in certain criteria (xxviii, 11–12; xlii, 1–7). It must nevertheless be true that all sayings can hardly go back to special inspiration, not even all those which are introduced with the formula: *Thus says Yahweh* (כֹּה אָמַר יְהֹוָה) or have the other formula: *utterance, whisper of Yahweh* (נְאֻם יְהֹוָה) at the end or in the middle. The form of some of the sayings presents Yahweh as the speaker and thus he speaks in the first person (Amos i, 3–ii, 16; iii, 1–2), whereas in others the prophet proclaims Yahweh's will indirectly (Amos v, 14–15). But even this hardly provides a criterion for differentiating between utterances which go back to special new moments of inspiration and those which owe their origin to the lasting prophetic consciousness of being the messenger of Yahweh and which can therefore with equal right as the others be set out as direct divine speech in the first person.

2. *Prediction and warning.* The imparting of the will of Yahweh is the essential content of the prophetic saying, and in particular of his will in regard to his shaping of the future. For the future is not a matter of blind chance, but the work of Yahweh. Thus the prophetic word is predictive, and, according to the actual content, a saying of threat or of promise. In the proclamation of the

---

² אֲדֹנָי *The Lord*, is to be omitted.
³ Soggin, 'Jeremias vi, 27–30' VT 9 (1959), pp. 95–8.

writing prophets, and also of those of their predecessors who have independent standing and do not simply merge in the mass of their contemporaries, such as Micaiah ben Imlah (I Kings xxii) and Elijah (I Kings xvii–xix, xxi; II Kings i), threat preponderates. Jeremiah even on one occasion (xxviii, 8–9) states as a criterion of the genuine prophet, that he is a prophet of woe, whereas with the prophet of weal it can only be recognised when his prophecy is fulfilled whether Yahweh really sent him or whether, without Yahweh's authority, he was producing a vision from his own mind (xxiii, 16). But the word of promise is a part of the prophetic proclamation from the very beginning, and is indeed to be found in all the writing prophets, even in Amos, for though the conclusion of the book (ix, 11–15) is not genuine (pp. 400 f.), v, 15 nevertheless proclaims the possibility that Yahweh may have pity on the remnant of Joseph.

But the will of Yahweh is not only effective for the future. It makes demands also on the present, though—as we have already suggested (p. 54)—the time scheme of present and future is quite inadequate here. The proclamation of Yahweh's future activity is at the same time an act of Yahweh's will directed towards the shaping of the present, and what he demands from the present is at the same time directed towards the shaping of the future. What he has proclaimed for the future and what he demands of the present both serve the establishing of his sovereignty. The prophetic sayings in which with threats and warnings Yahweh requires something from the present—repudiation of legal and moral abuses and obedience to his will—must therefore be placed on a level with the predictive sayings, and both types must be recognised as properly belonging to the prophets. The predictive saying—including threats and promises and the warning saying—appearing as diatribe (Isa. i, 2–3; iii, 12–15) and as exhortation (Amos v, 4–5a; Zeph. ii, 3), are the basic prophetic types to which may be traced back the very manifold variations which they have undergone. In origin they are very short, often comprising only one or two lines (Amos iv, 4; v, 3; Isa. vii, 7–9), or even only a few words (Isa. viii, 1). From a very early stage, however, a threat and a warning may be placed together, so that the latter serves as basis for the former (Amos iii, 1–2; Isa. viii, 6–8). In this way the prophets appeared in public, delivering predictions and warnings which either stood singly or were grouped together, and in very many cases the originally independent units may easily be separated out from our prophetic books, though these are in the main compiled without the sections being marked off. The formulae already quoted: *Thus saith Yahweh*, *whisper (oracle) of Yahweh*, are very useful in making possible this division of the material, provided this criterion is not employed too mechanically.

3. *Oracular poems.* But the formation of larger units—the combining of several prophecies and warnings into a 'poem'—did not begin merely at the stage when the utterances of the prophets were written down for posterity—whether by the prophets themselves or by others—in other words, when they began to be literature. This process belongs to the practical activity of the prophet, directed towards the immediate present. This may be seen quite clearly from poems like Amos i, 3–ii, 16; iv, 6–12 (incomplete at the end), Isa. ix, 7–20 + v, 25–30. For in all three cases the parts could not exist without the

whole. The enumeration of the sins and punishments for the other nations in Amos i, 3–ii, 5, forms only the preamble to the reproaches and threats hurled at Israel in ii, 6–16, and similarly, in the other two examples, the enumeration of the previous catastrophes serves only to make the terrible final disaster appear even more dreadful. The final disaster which should follow Amos iv, 12, has perhaps been omitted because it was unbearable. It is not altogether impossible that Isaiah and Amos have here worked over originally independent single sayings, but at any rate they have then made them serve a quite new purpose, namely to produce their effect through the poem as a whole, whether this was done by delivering them orally, or by circulating them in the form of a sort of broad-sheet. These two alternatives are often put forward in the discussion of prophetic sections without there being any possibility of arriving at a firm decision. The point here is simply that in the course of their preaching the prophets made use of sayings built up into larger units side by side with single sayings.

4. *Other literary types employed by the prophets.* A glance at the books of the writing prophets immediately reveals, however, that their proclamation was by no means limited to the original prophetic types, namely, in addition to the narrative of the vision previously discussed (pp. 53–5), the predictive saying and the warning, together with larger poems built up out of them or issuing from them. Rather do they make use, and indeed very full use, of every other possible type. We find indictments[4] (Isa. i, 18–20), sermons (Ezek. xx), and records (Jer. xxix, 1–23), as well as non-prophetic sayings (Zeph. i, 7), and poems of all kinds: mourning songs (Amos v, 1–2), national laments (Hos. vi, 1–3; xiv, 3–4), mocking songs (Isa. xxxvii, 22–9), drinking songs (Isa. xxii, 13), and many others. Indeed, as far as the songs are concerned, as we shall see, we do in fact only know of several of these types from their use in the prophetic books, and they would therefore be lost to us if the prophets had not made use of them on occasion to make their proclamation more vivid and so had preserved these examples for us. Examples of this kind have already been discussed more than once in connection with the types already mentioned, and in regard to the songs we shall often refer to the fact that the prophetic literature has preserved for us many non-prophetic types which would otherwise have been lost. We must here content ourselves with noting that the prophets made such borrowings of types belonging to other spheres of life from an early stage. The above examples are, in fact, taken from the earliest of the writing prophets, and undoubtedly, in this as in other ways, they simply carried on what their predecessors had done. Above all, it must always be remembered that the discovery of the types, characteristic in origin of particular areas of life, and the establishing of their pure form, represents a method of scientific research which very greatly extends our knowledge; but here as elsewhere reality goes far beyond such patterns and obscures them.

5. *Cultic and liturgical formulae.* Particular reference must here be briefly made to the question of the influence on the prophetic style of cultic and liturgical formulae. This is important in view of the liveliness with which the question

---

[4] Beek, *Het twistgesprek van de mens mit zijn God* (1946); Gemser, 'The *ríb*- or controversy pattern in Hebrew mentality' SVT III (1955), pp. 120–37, see pp. 128–33.

of the relationship of the prophets to the cult has been discussed in the last three or four decades, and in view of the results of lasting value which this discussion has produced. There are still many debatable and unsolved problems here, and no doubt always will be. Nevertheless it may be recognised as established that the relationship of the prophets to the cult was by no means so exclusively hostile as was often assumed in studies of the nineteenth century and of the first two decades of the twentieth. It is true that the pre-exilic writing prophets were frequently engaged in bitter polemic against the cult, but this does not mean that they did not also stand in a positive relationship to it and performed certain definite functions within it as well (pp. 71, 74). This is true, as we shall see, not only in the case of a prophet such as Joel, but also in the case of Jeremiah (p. 356). In these circumstances, it is to be expected that cultic and liturgical formulae have exerted an influence on prophetic diction. This is especially clear in Ezekiel, as has been shown in particular by Zimmerli in his Ezekiel commentary and in various other works on this prophet (p. 367).

§ 11. PROVERB, RIDDLE, AND WISDOM SAYING

Literature: Baumgartner, *Israelitische und altorientalische Weisheit* (1933); 'Die israel-itische Weisheitsliteratur' ThR 5 (1933), pp. 259–88; 'The Wisdom Literature' OTMSt (1951), pp. 210–37; Boström, *Paranomasi i den äldre Hebreiska Maschalliteraturen* (1928); *Proverbiastudien* (1935); Cantore, 'La sapienza biblica, ideale religioso del credente' Riv Bibl 8 (1960), pp. 1–9; Causse, 'Sagesse égyptienne et sagesse juive' RHPhR 9 (1929), pp. 149–69; Cazelles, 'Bible, Sagesse, Science' RSR 48 (1960), pp. 40–54; Davidson, 'Proverbs and Aphorisms in Hebrew Literature' PAAJR 4 (1932/33), pp. 33–42; Duesberg, *Les scribes inspirés* I (1938); II (1939); Ebeling, 'Reste akkadischer Weisheitsliteratur' MAOG 4 (1928/29), pp. 21–9; Eissfeldt, *Der Maschal im AT* (BZAW 24, 1913); Fichtner, *Die altorientalische Weisheit in ihrer israelitisch-jüdischen Ausprägung* (BZAW 62, 1933); Finkel, 'A Mathematical Conundrum in the Ugaritic Keret Poem' HUCA 26 (1955), pp. 109–49; Gandz, 'The Origin of the Gnomon or The Gnomon in Hebrew Literature' PAAJR 2 (1930/1), pp. 23–38; Godbey, 'The Hebrew *mašal*' AJSL 39 (1922/3), pp. 89–108; Gressmann, *Israels Spruchweisheit im Zusammenhang der Weltliteratur* (1925); Hempel, 'Pathos und Humor in der israelitischen Erziehung' BZAW 77 (1958), pp. 63–81; Herbert, 'The "Parable" (*māšāl*) in the OT' SJTh 7 (1954), pp. 180–96; Humbert, *Recherches sur les sources égyptiennes de la littérature sapientale d'Israël* (1929); Johnson, 'מָשָׁל' SVT III (1955), pp. 162–9; Lindblom, 'Wisdom in the OT Prophets' SVT III (1955), pp. 192–204; Meinhold, *Die Weisheit Israels* (1908); Paterson, *The Book that is Alive: Studies on the OT Life and Thought as set forth by the Hebrew Sages* (1954); *The Wisdom of Israel* (1960); Pfeiffer, 'Edomitic Wisdom' ZAW 44 (1926), pp. 13–25; 'Wisdom and Vision in the OT' ZAW 52 (1934), pp. 93–101; Pirot, 'Le "Māšāl" dans l'AT' RSR 37 (1950), pp. 565–80; von Rad, 'Die ältere Weisheit Israels' Kerygma und Dogma 2 (1956), pp. 54–72; Rankin, *Israel's Wisdom Literature* (²1954); J. Schmidt, *Studien zur Stilistik der at. Spruchliteratur* (1936); Torczyner, 'The Riddle in the Bible' HUCA 1 (1924), pp. 125–49; Yeivin, 'Social, religious and cultural Trends in Jerusalem under the Davidic dynasty' VT 3 (1953), pp. 149–66; Zimmerli, 'Zur Struktur der at. Weisheit' ZAW 51 (1933), pp. 177–204.
     Cf. also Literature §§ 16, 64, 65, 68, 88, 89, 126.

The Wisdom Literature takes up a fairly large part of the Old Testament. Proverbs, Job, Ecclesiastes and Ecclesiasticus belong entirely to this type, and many sections from other books must also be reckoned to it, e.g. the warnings in Tob. iv. These books belong as they stand to the post-exilic period. They show therefore how much the artistic wisdom saying was loved at that time in Judaism.

1. *The popular proverb*. Ancient Israel too already had a partiality for such material. Even though the artistic saying, metrically constructed, known to us from the books just mentioned, did not at first perhaps play any great part, yet the less strictly formal popular proverb enjoyed very great popularity. This bears the same name as the later artistic saying—מָשָׁל—a name which perhaps originally meant *magical saying*, and which is used for many different kinds of sayings and poems, as for example the *mocking song* (pp. 66, 92). But it belongs primarily to the popular proverb and the artistic saying. This common name for the popular proverb and the artistic wisdom saying itself shows that they belong together. The proverb actually performed the same service in the earlier period which later was taken over by the artistic saying, without the proverb being, however, completely replaced. Indeed, the relationship is even closer. For among the later artistic sayings there is undoubtedly concealed a wealth of older proverbial material.

Among older proverbs, explicitly denoted as *mašal*, we find: *Is Saul also among the prophets?* (I Sam. x, 12; xix, 24). This plainly has the same sense as the one quoted by Jeremiah (xxiii, 28), though it is not explicitly called a *mašal*, but can immediately be recognised as one by its sound: *What has straw in common with wheat?*, and also as *Out of the wicked comes forth wickedness* (I Sam. xxiv, 14). Another is denoted as a proverb by the introductory formula: *Therefore it is said* (I Sam. xix, 24; II Sam. v, 8;[1] cf. I Sam. x, 12), which is often used to link proverbs to particular historical situations. This is the saying: *Like Nimrod a mighty hunter before the Lord* (Gen. x, 9). Others still stand out from their context without being precisely indicated, by their sound as fixed sayings. Thus we find: *Let not him that girds on his armour boast himself as he that puts it off* (I Kings xx, 11). A great wealth of ancient popular proverbs is further to be found in the wisdom books (Prov., Ecclus. etc.). Thus phrases which occur several times, but in different combinations, may certainly be assumed to be popular proverbs, as, for example: *The mouth of the wicked conceals violence*, which is to be found in Prov. x, 6 and x, 11, in the former having the parallel stichos: *Blessings are on the head of the righteous*, in the latter: *A fountain of life is the mouth of the righteous* (cf. x, 15 and xviii, 11; xi, 13 and xx, 19). It may be seen that these examples are in prose, or else represent short lines which cannot always be marked off with certainty from prose. Thus the metrical form which properly belongs to the later artistic saying—normally, as we have seen (p. 61), a double triplet—was not an absolute essential of the ancient proverb, though this does not of course exclude the possibility that the popular proverb also made use at an early date of that *parallelismus membrorum* which existed early in Israel as in Israel's environment, and of the rhythmic structure which no doubt always existed with it. The change over from the popular proverb to the artistic saying is thus fluid in this respect too. A saying current among the

[1] Stoebe, 'Die Einnahme Jerusalems und des Ṣinnôr' ZDPV 73 (1957), pp. 73–99.

people, which is quoted by Jeremiah (xxxi, 29) and by Ezekiel (xviii, 2) as a *mašal*, is thus in the form of a double triplet:

> *The fathers have eaten sour grapes*
> *and the children's teeth are set on edge.*

As in other kinds of saying, the popular proverb also favours consonantal and vocalic assonance. This may be seen in the first stichoi of Prov. xiii, 3 (cf. xxi, 33) and xi, 2 (cf. xiii, 10), which certainly represent older proverbs:

nōṣēr pîw	*šōmēr napšô*	He who guards his mouth keeps his life
bā' zādôn	*wayyābō' qālon*	When pride comes then comes disgrace.

The style is terse and vivid. A general truth, which is what we are concerned with, is normally made clear with pictures or examples, as may be readily seen in the words quoted concerning Saul and Nimrod, and concerning straw and wheat. It is not really necessary to look for a special setting in life for the popular proverb, since we must recognise that the whole of life is shot through with such sayings. But we must ask how far the proverbial material found in Israel was of Israelite origin and how far it came from elsewhere. Though this cannot normally be decided in any particular case, we may nevertheless venture to say that just as it is quite clear in the case of the artistic saying that Israel borrowed enormously from its environment (cf. pp. 474–5), so too at this earlier stage much will have come into Israel from outside, mainly no doubt mediated by the Canaanites.[2] By its very nature the proverb is often concerned with matters and characteristics which are of general human interest, and is therefore specially suitable for being taken over from one people to another.[3] Admittedly it is not

---

[2] Albright, 'Some Canaanite-Phoenician Sources of Hebrew Wisdom' SVT III (1955), pp. 1–15; 'The Role of the Canaanites in the History of Civilization' *Essays W. F. Albright* (1961), pp. 328–62, see p. 451.

[3] Sumerian and Accadian wisdom: AOT, pp. 284–95; ANET, pp. 402–52; DOTT, pp. 97–110; Van Dijk, *La Sagesse Suméro-Accadienne* (1953); 'Note sur la sagesse suméro-accadienne' Sumer 10 (1954), pp. 139–42; Gadd, 'Fragments of Assyrian Scholastic Literature' BSOASt 20 (1957), pp. 255–65; Gordon, 'Sumerian Proverbs: "Collection Four"' JAOS 77 (1957), pp. 67–79 (p. 67, n. 1 makes reference to "Coll. One, Two, and Three"); 'Sumerian Proverbs and Fables' ("Coll. Five") JCSt 12 (1958), pp. 1–21, 43–75, Pls. I–IV; *Sumerian Proverbs. Glimpses of Everyday Life in Ancient Mesopotamia* (Monographs of the Univ. Mus., Philadelphia, 1960); 'A New Look at the Wisdom of Sumer and Akkad' BiOr 17 (1960), pp. 122–52, Pl. II; Jestin, 'Le poème d'En-me-er-kar' RHR 151 (1957), pp. 145–220; Kramer, 'Sumerian Wisdom Literature' BASOR 122 (1951), pp. 28–31; 'Forty-eight Proverbs and their Translation' *Troisième Rencontre Assyriologique* (1954), pp. 75–84; 'Die sumerische Schule' WZ Halle 5 (1955/6), pp. 695–704; 'Sumerische Ethik und Weisheitssprüche' Wiss. Annalen 5 (1956), pp. 767–74; Lambert, 'Morals in Ancient Mesopotamia' JEOL 15 (1957/8), pp. 184–96; *Babylonian Wisdom Literature* (1960); Meissner, 'Sprichwörter bei Asarhaddon' AfO 10 (1935/6), pp. 361 f.; Nougayrol, 'Tablette bilingue accado hourrite' PRU III (1955), pp. 309–24. Egyptian wisdom: AOT, pp. 33–46; ANET, pp. 412–24; DOTT, pp. 155–61, 172–86; Anthes, 'The Legal Aspect of the Instruction of Amenemhet' JNESt 16 (1957), pp. 176–91; von Bissing, *Altägyptische Lebensweisheit* (1955); Brunner, 'Die Weisheitsliteratur' HdO I, 2 (1952), pp. 90–110; 'Eine neue Entlehnung aus der Lehre des Djedefhor' *Kees-Festschr.* (MDAI 14, 1956), pp. 17–19; *Altägyptische Erziehung* (1957); Faulkner, 'Ptaḥḥotpe and the Disputants' *Ägyptol. Stud.*, ed. by Firchow (1955), pp. 81–4; Fecht, *Der Habgierige und die Maat in der Lehre des Ptaḥḥotep* (ADAI, Abt. Kairo I, 1959); Gemser, 'The Instructions of 'Oncheshonqy and Biblical Wisdom Literature' SVT VII (1960), pp. 102–28; Glanville,

necessary always to think of mutual influence where within and outside Israel the same or similar modes of speech are to be found, for the same pictures and expressions may have come into being quite independently one of the other. Thus the Isaiah saying, which is designed to make plain most drastically the folly of Assyria's presumption (x, 15):

> *Shall the axe vaunt itself over him who hews with it,*
>   *or the saw magnify itself against him who wields it*

sounds very much like one of the Sayings of Ahikar (VII, 104):[4]

> *Why should wood strive with the fire*
>   *meat with the knife,*
>   *a man with the king?*

But here we need hardly think of the dependence of one of the sayings upon the other. Nevertheless the fact of external influence upon the formation of Israelite proverbs is well established. Nowhere else does the Old Testament itself speak so often of external influence and pattern as in this field, and this too in the earlier period: I Kings v, 10–14; x, 1–10 + 13,[5] Jer. xlix, 7; Prov. xxx, 1; xxxi, 1, though admittedly the reference is not in every case to wisdom as applied to human life, but at times, as clearly in I Kings v, 12–13, it is to wisdom as applied to nature, i.e. to the beginnings of natural science.[6]

    2. *The riddle.* Before the development of the popular proverb into the artistic saying can be discussed, a little must be said about one particular kind of popular saying which has much in common with the popular proverb, and, like the latter, was also taken up by the Wisdom literature, naturally enough without entirely disappearing as a popular type. This is the riddle, the Hebrew word for which is known to us: חִידָה. In Judg. xiv, 12–18, we have an excellent example which vividly reveals ancient Israel's partiality for riddles. In the same passage we learn on what occasions men took pleasure in setting and solving riddles, namely at marriage festivals, and we also learn that prizes could be won or lost

Catalogue of Demotic Papyri in the British Museum, Vol. II: 'The Instructions of 'Oncheshonqy' Part I (1955); Herrmann, *Untersuchungen zur Überlieferungsgestalt mittelägyptischer Literaturwerke* (1957); Lanczkowski, 'Reden und Schweigen im ägyptischen Verständnis, vornehmlich des Mittleren Reiches' *Ägyptol. Stud.,* ed. by Firchow (1955), pp. 186–96; Otto, 'Bildung und Ausbildung im alten Ägypten' ZÄS 81 (1956), pp. 41–8; Scharff, 'Voraussetzung und Gegenstand altägyptischer Wissenschaft' AMz, Jahrbuch (1951), pp. 277–95; Schott and Grapow, 'Wissenschaftliche Literatur' HdO I, 2 (1952), pp. 170–93; Stricker, 'De Wijsheid van Anchsjesjonq' JEOL 15 (1957/8), pp. 11–33; Suys, *La Sagesse d'Ani* (Anal. Or. 11, 1935); Volten, *Zwei altägyptische politische Schriften* (*Pap. Carlsberg VI und die Lehre des Königs Amenemhet*) (1945); Würthwein, *Die ägyptische Weisheit und das AT* (1959); Žába, *Les maximes de Ptaḥḥotep. Texte, Traduction et Commentaire* (1956).
    Cf. also Lit. p. 52, n. 64 (Ahikar), p. 474, n. 10 (Amenemope); §§ 65, 126.
    [4] Cowley, *Ar. Pap.,* pp. 216, 223; AOT, p. 459; ANET, p. 429a. Lit. § 126.
    [5] Albright, 'Zur Chronologie des vorislamischen Arabien' BZAW 77 (1958), pp. 1–8.
    [6] Alt, 'Syrien und Palästina im Onomastikon des Amenope' SThU 20 (1950), pp. 58–71 = *Kl. Schr.* I (1953), pp. 231–45; 'Die Weisheit Salomos' ThLZ 76 (1951), cols. 139–144 = *Kl. Schr.* II (1953), pp. 90–9; Noth, 'Die Bewährung von Salomos "Göttlicher Weisheit"' SVT III (1955), pp. 225–37; Richter, 'Die Naturweisheit des AT im Buche Hiob' ZAW 70 (1958), pp. 1–20; Scott, 'Solomon and the Beginnings of Wisdom in Israel' SVT III (1955), pp. 262–79.

in the process. The riddle, in its form here not a question but a statement or narration, is a double triplet, whose two stichoi have each two words beginning with *m*:

Mēhā'ōkēl yāṣā' ma'ªkāl   *umē'aẓ yāṣā mātôq*
From the eater came food   *and from the strong came sweetness.*

The answer, in form a question, is a double line consisting of two double units, and has altogether five words beginning with *m*:

mah-mātôq middªbaš   *ûmeh 'aẓ mē'ªrî*
What is sweeter than honey and what is stronger than a lion?

It has been doubted, and quite properly so, whether the interpretation of the riddle which is demanded by the context, and the interpretation of the question as its solution, are original. The context makes the riddle refer to the lion torn in two by Samson and then used by wild bees for the storing of their honey. But it may well be that the question itself is really a riddle, and the answer which might be suggested—'Love'—would then be extremely suitable for a wedding. It is difficult, however, to be certain about this.[7] According to I Kings x, 1, the queen of Sheba came to Solomon in order to test him with riddles (cf. I Kings x, 23–4). Even if the narrative is fiction, we are nevertheless justified in thinking that such a contest with riddles as is here described did in fact have its place at court, and even at Solomon's court. Josephus, *Ant.* VIII 5, 3 §§ 146–9, derives from older sources a story concerning a riddle contest between Solomon and an envoy from king Hiram of Tyre, and we hear of similar events from a much later period at the courts of Darius I (I Esd. iii–iv) and of Ptolemy II Philadelphos (Letter of Aristeas §§ 187–300). In the latter example, in the place of the more naïve riddle questions, problems of statecraft and of dealing with men are set out by the ruler. The story of the queen of Sheba's visit itself shows that the cultivation of wisdom and play with riddles belong together, for it is Solomon's wisdom which this story sets out to emphasise; and this is confirmed by Prov. i, 6, where חִידָה *riddle* is used as a sort of synonym for מָשָׁל *wisdom saying.* So we may assume that a type which is a favourite in the later wisdom literature, namely the numerical saying[8]—like the one which begins: *Three things are never satisfied: four never say 'Enough'* (Prov. xxx, 15), and then enumerates the three or four things or persons (Ecclus. xxv, 1–2, Prov. vi, 16–19; xxx, 15–31,[9]

---

[7] Eissfeldt, 'Die Rätsel in Jdc xiv' ZAW 30 (1910), pp. 132–5; Hans Schmidt, 'Zu Jdc xiv' ZAW 39 (1921), p. 316. Lit. § 126.

[8] Albright, 'The Role' *Essays Albright* (1961), pp. 328–62, see p. 357; Hans Bauer, 'Zu ZAW 1936, 56' ZAW 54 (1937), p. 152; Bea, 'Der Zahlenspruch im Hebräischen und Ugaritischen' Bibl 21 (1940), pp. 196–8; Buzy, 'Les machals numériques de la sangsue et de l'almah' RB 42, 1933, pp. 5–13; Ginsberg, 'Zu ZAW 1936, 152' ZAW 55 (1937), pp. 308 f.; Stevenson, 'A Mnemonic Use of Numbers in Proverbs and Ben Sira' Transact. Glasgow Univ. Or. Soc. 9 (1938/9), pp. 26–38; Stummer, *Der kritische Wert der altaramäischen Ahikartexte aus Elephantine* (1914), pp. 58 f., 85 f. Cf. the anonymous numerical sayings in the Mishna tractate Pirqê Abôth 5, 1–15. Lit. § 126.

[9] Grintz, 'The Proverbs of *'Aluqa'* [Hebr., Engl. sum.] Tarbiz 28 (1958/9), pp. 135–7, I; Schneider, 'Die "Töchter" des Blutegels in Spr xxx, 15' *Junker-Festschr.* (1961), pp. 257–64.

and also presumably xxx, 11–14) developed out of a riddle which asked: 'Which are the three which are never satisfied?' etc.

3. *The wisdom saying as an artistic form.* The popular type of the riddle, and above all of the much more important popular proverb, were developed later, though certainly already in the pre-exilic period, into the artistic wisdom saying. The development consists partly in the fact that, as we have seen already, the proverbs are now produced entirely in metrical form. But new material was also composed, and, here is the most significant point, the contact with the wisdom literature of the outside world which had already existed earlier became even closer, with the result that much new material flowed into Judaism from Egypt, from Babylonia-Persia, from Edom, and later from Hellenistic sources. The incorporation of this material borrowed from abroad was no doubt due largely to foreigners who as diplomatic or commercial representatives, as scribes (סֹפֵר) lived in Israel, as also to Israelites who had been active in such capacities in other lands and then brought their lives to a close in their homeland. Thus an Israelite who had returned home from Egypt after such activity may be regarded as responsible for the compilation of the collection Prov. xxii, 17–xxiv, 22, which, as we shall have occasion to see more closely, is so largely dependent upon an Egyptian wisdom book, that of Amenemope (pp. 474–5). I Kings v, 9–14 testifies that wisdom poetry was already deliberately cultivated by Solomon and his contemporaries, and we have already noted (pp. 84–5) that the contents of at least some of the 3,000 *mašals* there mentioned were not statements of practical wisdom and exhortations to follow them, but compilations of an encyclopaedic kind concerning phenomena and processes of the natural order, particularly from the realm of animals and plants, just as the numerical sayings and riddles mentioned on pp. 85–6 take up a sort of middle position between sayings of practical wisdom and scientific observations. The class, or better, the profession—for that is what it really was—to which the forming of such sayings belonged was that of the *wise* (חֲכָמִים). We hear of them often already in the pre-exilic period (Isa. v, 21; Jer. ix, 22; xviii, 18). Their professional ideals are later best revealed by Ecclus. xxxviii, 24–xxxix, 11. The collections which underlie our book of Proverbs and other wisdom books, and the books themselves, derive from such people, as the title in two cases (Prov. xxii, 17–xxiv, 22; xxiv, 23–34) specifically states. The compilers of the didactic psalms (i, xxxvii, xlix, lxxiii, lxxviii, xci, cxxviii, cxxxiii, cxxxix) are also to be sought in the circles of these wise men (pp. 125–7).

But this activity of the wise is by no means to be regarded as being a purely literary and learned one, abstracted from real life. On the contrary, the wise are fully involved in life. When in the wisdom books we find the picture of teacher and pupils used so often, and Dame Wisdom is depicted as the mistress of a house (Prov. ix) into which she invites men, we may infer that the wise did in fact impart instruction as in a school, and that the substance of their instruction was the rich treasury of wisdom sayings which they preserved and to which they added.[10] We may further imagine that the many small groups of wisdom

[10] Dürr, *Das Erziehungswesen im Alten Testament und im Antiken Orient* (1932), pp. 106–14; Smend, *Die Weisheit des Jesus Sirach erklärt* (1906), pp. xxxv–xxxvi.

sayings which we meet in Proverbs and Ecclesiasticus—the placing together of four single sayings which begin with *b* in Prov. xi, 9–12; the grouping of two each of whose first words are לֵב *heart* and טוֹב *good* in xv, 13–14, 16–17; the numerical sayings already mentioned (pp. 85–6), and small poems like that on the risks of lending (vi, 1–5), on the dangers of laziness (vi, 6–11),[11] on the destructiveness of falsehood (vi, 12–15), on the rewards of wisdom (Ecclus. iv, 11–19)—were designed to serve pedagogic ends. They had to be learned by heart by the pupils, and thus became a treasured possession for life. In short, even in this later period, when according to Eccles. xii, 12, there was no end to the writing of books, and we are thus in a period of purely literary activity, it is nevertheless still true that practical life produces new forms, which only subsequently become 'literature'.[12]

III. Songs

Literature: Causse, 'Les Origines de la Poésie hébraïque' RHPhR 4 (1924), pp. 393–419; 5 (1925), pp. 1–28; *Les plus vieux chants de la Bible* (1926); Mary E. Chase, *Life and Language in the OT* (1956); Oesterley, *Ancient Hebrew Poems* (1938); Robinson, *The Poetry of the OT* (1947); G. A. Smith, *The Early Poetry of Israel in its Physical and Social Origins* (⁴1913 (1927)).

The most common Hebrew term for *song* is שִׁיר or שִׁירָה. Admittedly, this term, like other Hebrew terms for literary types, does not have only one meaning.[1] Thus in Judg. v, 12, when Deborah is invoked: *Up! Up! Deborah, Up! Up! speak a* שִׁיר, it is clearly used in the sense of *saying*, or more precisely *recruiting saying*, or even *exorcism formula*, and very nearly *magical saying*, as indeed here the verb *to speak* (דִּבֶּר) is used with it. But this is an exception. Elsewhere, we are told concerning the שִׁיר that it is accompanied by instrumental music (Gen. xxxi, 27; Amos vi, 5; Isa. xxiii, 16; xxx, 29), and the verb *to sing* which corresponds to the noun is mentioned in association with dancing (I Sam. xviii, 6; Ps. lxxxvii, 7). שִׁיר is thus in fact generally identical in meaning with our word *song*.

Like other ancient peoples, Israel was one that loved singing, and its whole life was shot through with songs and singing. Naturally enough, a collection of writings such as is presented by the Old Testament, regarded by Judaism as religiously valuable, has preserved for us more religious or cultic than secular songs. But we can nevertheless get a picture of Israel's richness in secular songs, not least thanks to the fact already mentioned several times (p. 80) that

[11] Albright, 'An Archaic Hebrew Proverb in an Amarna Letter from Central Palestine' BASOR 89 (1944), pp. 29–32: on vi, 6; xxx, 25.

[12] Davidson, *Thesaurus of Proverbs and Parables from Mediaeval Jewish Literature* [Hebr.] (1958); Frankenberg, 'Die Schrift des Menander (Land anecd. syr. I, pp. 64 ff.), ein Produkt der jüdischen Spruchweisheit' ZAW 15 (1895), pp. 226–77; Widengren, 'Quelques rapports entre Juifs et Iraniens à l'époque des Parthes' SVT IV (1957), pp. 197–241; *Iranisch–semitische Kulturbegegnung in parthischer Zeit* (AFLNW 70, 1960), pp. 36–9. Lit. § 126.

[1] Albright (1945) (p. 58, n. 4), p. 20; Enciso, 'Mizmor, shir y máskil' Est Bíbl 12 (1953), pp. 185–94.

the prophets in making their proclamation vivid made use of all manner of types which were not specifically prophetic, among these some that were secular. We may look first at some examples of songs which refer to the life of the individual; then at those which are concerned with the king and the community —clan, tribe or people; and finally we may discuss the religious, cultic songs and the wisdom songs. It is, of course, perfectly clear that the distinction between secular and cultic is extremely fluid, since the whole of Israel's life was impregnated with religion, but this does not make the distinguishing of the two impossible.

§ 12. SONGS OF WORK AND HARVEST, DRINKING SONGS, SONGS OF MARRIAGE AND LOVE, WATCHMAN'S SONGS

Literature: Bücher, *Arbeit und Rhythmus* ([6]1924); Budde, 'Das Volkslied Israels im Munde der Propheten' PJ 73 (1893), pp. 460–83; 'Noch etwas vom Volksliede des alten Israel' PJ 82 (1895), pp. 491–500; Lohmann, 'Das Wächterlied Jes. xxi, 11, 12' ZAW 33 (1913), pp. 20–9. Cf. also Literature on the Song of Songs, § 67, and § 126.

1. *Work songs.* Songs were to be heard when men were at work, and with these the workers enlivened and encouraged themselves and their animals (Ecclus. xxxviii, 25). But in the earlier period, when word and song were thought of as endued with magical power and so as effective in themselves, such songs were intended to assist the work directly and to bring about its success. This is likely to be the meaning of the ancient Song of the Well in Num. xxi, 17–18, a song sung during the digging of wells. Admittedly in its present context it is associated with a particular well, or rather, with a town in Trans-Jordan which has the name בְּאֵר *well,* and the song is supposed to have been sung by Israel after her arrival at this town. But in reality this is a song sung generally at the digging of wells, or at any rate it is modelled on such a song:[2]

> *Spring up, O well!   sing to it!*
> *O well which princes dug   which nobles delved,*
> *With the sceptre,   with their staves!*

If the work itself is thus accompanied by a song, we may naturally imagine that songs and singing were heard most when it was a case of rejoicing in the success of the labour. It is Israel as an agricultural people which we can discern in this material. Thus it is no matter for surprise that harvest and vintage, threshing and treading out the grapes are the most prominent occasions for this rejoicing at the successful results of men's labour and are more particularly accompanied by joyous song. *As men rejoice at the harvest* (Isa. ix, 2) has in fact become a proverbial phrase, and there are many references to rejoicing and singing during the harvesting and treading of the grapes (Judg. ix, 27; xxi, 21; Isa. xvi, 10). The song finds its natural and proper setting in company, when wine is being

---

[2] Montgomery, *Arabia and the Bible* (1934), p. 8.

drunk.[3] We often hear of songs for drinking and banquets, not least among the prophets who often uttered the strongest attack against conviviality carried on at the expense of the poor and leading to a self-confident lack of faith (Amos vi, 4–6; Isa. v, 11–13). A few songs of this kind have also survived, based on the theme, ancient and yet always new:

> 'Gather ye rosebuds while ye may,
>   Old Time is still a-flying:
> And this same flower that smiles to-day,
>   To-morrow will be dying.'[4]

Isaiah quotes such a brief song, which the people of Jerusalem sing in their dissolute carousing and tippling, failing in their foolish blindness to see the imminent catastrophe, or refusing to see it (xxii, 13): *Let us eat and drink, for tomorrow we die.* The song which is put into the mouth of godless Jewish free-thinkers in Wisd. ii, 1–20 is clearly dependent in vv. 6–9 upon a drinking song with similar sentiments, or perhaps even actually quotes from it (cf. p. 495).

2. *Wedding songs.* But the time in men's lives when they are more than norm-ally jubilant, and the singing of their hearts flows out as a song on their lips, has always been the time of betrothal and marriage. And so it will always be, as long as men have hearts that beat. This was equally true of Israel. *The voice of the bridegroom and the voice of the bride* is an expression used by Jeremiah side by side with the more general expression *voice of mirth and voice of gladness,* when he is proclaiming the deepest distress and greatest joy. The deepest dis-tress is when the voice of the bridegroom and the voice of the bride, the voice of mirth and the voice of gladness, are silent, and greatest joy is when both may again be heard in a land which has up till then been desolate (Jer. xvi, 9; xxv, 10, for the one, vii, 3; xxxiii, 11, for the other). How great the joy was during the seven days of the marriage celebration (Gen. xxix, 27–8) we may learn from the story already mentioned (pp. 84–5) of Samson's marriage (Judg. xiv, 10–18), even though by chance nothing is said here about songs. But as far as love songs and marriage songs[5] are concerned, we are in the especially fortunate position of possessing in the Song of Songs a whole collection (pp. 486–8). In part, as will be more precisely demonstrated when we discuss this little book, they are frankly naturalistic love songs, witnessing to a strong erotic sense, natural and pure (i, 7–8; i, 9–17; ii, 8–14). In part, they are songs composed for the marriage festival and recited then (iii, 6–11; vii, 1–6). It is true that as we now have them they are relatively late, and belong perhaps to the third century B.C. But they were preceded by other older models, even very ancient ones in which ancient

[3] On wine songs and drinking songs among the ancient Arabs, cf. Brockelmann, HdO III, 2–3 (1954), pp. 263–79; Wiet, 'La vie de plaisir à la Mecque et à Médine au premier siècle de l'Islam' CRAI (1959), pp. 417–25.

[4] Herrick, *Hesperides*: 'To Virgins, to Make Much of Time.' Cf. Martin Ulsteri's 'Freut euch des Lebens' (1793): 'Freut euch des Lebens, weil noch das Lämpchen glüht, pflücket die Rose, eh sie verblüht.'

[5] Horst, 'Die Formen des althebräischen Liebesliedes' *Littmann-Festschrift* (1935), pp. 43–54 = *Gottes Recht* (1961), pp. 176–87. For the Arabs, cf. Brockelmann, HdO III, 2–3 (1954), pp. 256–79; Gabrieli, 'La letteratura beduina preislamica' Studi Semitici 2 (1959), pp. 95–114. Cf. below, p. 488, nn. 12–20.

Israel rejoiced, and which will not have looked very different. The frank love songs of this book would not be unsuitable for Samson's adventures in love, and we may also picture his wedding as being the occasion for marriage songs like those which it contains.[6]

3. *The watchman's song.* There are many indications to show that during the period of Israelite history about which the Old Testament gives information, the office of watchman was an important one. The palace and the temple equally with the camp and the town wall have a watchman at their disposal, who watches all the time what happens in and around them, and immediately gives warning if danger threatens. In the story of Gideon's attack on the Midianite camp *watchmen* are mentioned (שֹׁמְרִים Judg. vii, 19) who had been set up by the Midianites, and according to I Sam. xiv, 16, the surprise attack of Saul on the Philistines was preceded by a warning by Saul's *look-outs* (צֹפִים). II Sam. xviii, 24–7, describes very vividly how, from the battlements of the gate tower of Mahanaim, which is for the time being serving as David's residence, a *look-out* (צֹפֶה) observes the approach of the two messengers sent by Joab with a report on the outcome of the battle against Absalom, and announces to David what is happening. This description is excelled in vividness by the one in II Kings ix, 17–20, telling how the *look-out* (צֹפֶה) standing on the tower of either the wall or the palace of Jezreel informs his king Joram of the furious driving of Jehu racing up in his war-chariot. It is thus natural enough that in Israel as in other peoples and cultures the profession of watchman, clothed as it is in a certain romanticism, has produced particular songs. Unfortunately the Old Testament does not preserve such watchman's songs themselves, but we do find, in the books of the prophets and in the Psalms, various allusions to them. Thus the opening of the mocking song preserved in II Kings xix, 21–8 = Isa. xxxvii, 22–9,[7] on the ignominious departure of Sennacherib from Jerusalem (p. 94) is certainly an imitation of songs in which the watchmen were accustomed to proclaim triumphantly the failure of the enemy who has attacked their city or fortress. The conclusion of Ps. cxxx, which calls on Israel to wait for Yahweh *more than watchmen for the morning, watchmen for the morning,* not only allows us to sense something of the longing with which the watchman in the depths of the night wishes for the morning to come, but also justifies us in assuming that there were songs which gave moving expression to this longing. The same may be seen from Isa. xxi, 1–10, 11–12; Hab. ii, 1–3, where prophets are presented as watchmen,[8] and the ardent longing for a message from God which is ascribed to them vividly reflects the mood of real watchmen. This is even more clear in Isa. xxi, 11–12, where the question directed to the prophet:

[6] Cf. Mörike, 'Nimmersatte Liebe' (1828):
> So ist die Lieb', und war auch so,
> Wie lang es Liebe gibt, und anders war Herr Salomo,
> Der Weise, nicht verliebt.

(Such is love! And so it has been so long as love has existed. And even Solomon the wise did not love otherwise.)

[7] Budde, 'The Poem in 2 Kings xix, 21–8 (Isaiah xxxvii, 22–9)' JThSt 35 (1934), pp. 307–13.

[8] Cf. also the description of Ezekiel as *look-out* (עֹפֶה) in Ezek. iii, 17, etc.

Watchman, what of the night,   watchman, what of the night?

and the answer which is given:

Morning comes   and also the night
If you will inquire, inquire   come back again

clearly correspond to what actually happened in the course of the watchman's
duties. We may also sense something of the passionate longing for the morning
which must often have filled the hearts of the watchmen in Isa. lxii, 6–7, where
the poet-prophet declares:

Upon your walls, O Jerusalem   I set watchmen;
neither day nor night   shall they ever be silent;
You who put Yahweh in remembrance   no rest for you,
And give him no rest   until he establishes Jerusalem,
Until he makes it   a praise in the earth

A glad message by the watchman, namely the proclaiming of the entry of the
king returning to his residence after victorious battle is to be found in Isa. lii,
8–9:

Hark, your look-outs lift up their voice   together they sing for joy;
For eye to eye they see   the return of Yahweh to Zion.
Rejoice, sing together   you waste places of Jerusalem
For the Lord has comforted his people,   he has redeemed Jerusalem.

§ 13. MOCKING SONGS AND FUNERAL DIRGES

Literature: Maria Cramer, *Die Totenklage bei den Kopten. Mit Hinweisen auf die Toten-
klage im Orient überhaupt* (1941); Eissfeldt (§ 11), (1913); Hedwig Jahnow, *Das hebräische
Leichenlied im Rahmen der Völkerdichtung* (BZAW 36, 1923); Lohmann, *Die anonymen
Prophetien gegen Babel aus der Zeit des Exils* (Diss. phil. Rostock, 1910).

1. *General considerations.* We are very well informed concerning the types of
the mocking song and the funeral dirge, and they also provide a suitable link
to those songs whose central interest is not the individual but the community.
For it is evident that the subject of mockery and of the mocking song may
equally well be an individual or a city, a tribe or a people. Indeed, in the Old
Testament, which is in the first place concerned in maintaining the memory of
events which were and are significant for the whole people, and only in the
second place gives information about the individual, there are far more mocking
songs directed against corporate entities than there are composed against individuals. As far as the funeral dirge is concerned, the position is quite clear that
at an early date it was already applied in a transferred sense to collective entities,
to the downfall of the tribe, the city, or the people. This can be quite seriously
meant, so that, as is proper for the funeral dirge, the 'death' of the collective
entity is genuinely bewailed. Or it may be said in a mocking tone, as when the

catastrophe produces in the composer of the song not sympathy, but scorn and malicious joy, and the funeral dirge is used then only as a form, the content being mockery and scorn. So we get a mocking funeral dirge. Mocking song and funeral dirge are thus in this respect closely related, or rather have come together in the course of the development. We must again be grateful to the prophets that we have relatively so many examples of these two types, for the prophets were especially inclined to make use of them. In the process, both of them often acquire a particular stamp, corresponding to the prophetic proclamation which is directed towards the future. The prophets thus not infrequently represent the catastrophe which they threaten as if it had already occurred, and looking back upon what they represent as being already in the past, strike up a mocking song or a funeral dirge, whether the latter is intended seriously or reveals a mocking undertone. We may name such poems, in reality composed with reference to an event which lies in the future, 'prophetic' mocking songs and funeral dirges, to be set alongside other songs which are in this sense prophetic songs, as we shall see (p. 318), e.g. the 'prophetic' song of thanksgiving.

2. *Mocking songs.* The mocking song bears the name *mašal* like the mocking saying, and we have already seen (p. 66) how it is to be explained that proverb and mocking saying bear the same name: 'to become a proverb', i.e. 'to become a by-word' means the same as to become the object of men's mockery. We have also noted already what enormous power a mocking word must have represented in Israel as elsewhere in the ancient world. Such mocking speech on the subject of one's fellow men is expressed more naturally, in so far as a fixed form of speech is employed at all, in the form of a saying rather than of a song, and we have already noted a series of mocking sayings. But the song form may also be utilised, and on one occasion a mocking poem directed to an individual, namely to a harlot, is actually termed a *song* (שִׁירָה, Isa. xxiii, 15–16):

> *Take a harp   go about the city   forgotten harlot,*
> *Play well   sing loudly   that you may be remembered!*

Where mockery is expressed at the individual person, the saying form predominated, and that of the song was the exception; but we must assume that with mockery at other tribes, cities or peoples, where the saying is also to be found, the form of the song was preferred, at any rate when the event which called forth the mockery was one of some moment: the significance of the content demanded then a more significant form. It is certain that the mocking song was employed fairly frequently in ancient Israel. The tremendous events of the conquest and then of the defence of Canaan would not have been possible at all had there not been passionate enthusiasm for their own ways and an equally profound mocking and despising of their enemies, and both were expressed in songs—recruiting and victory songs on the one hand, mocking songs on the other. Both belong together, as Goethe once put it well: '. . . panegyric poetry is just as basic as satirical, to which it only forms the obverse'.[1] Indeed, the one frequently merges into the other, and the victory song in particular frequently

---

[1] Goedeke's edition, vol. 14 (1867), p. 187.

contains echoes of the motives of the mocking song. Just as in the life of the individual, the mocking saying represented a weapon of great power, so the mocking song was a terrible political weapon, which provided protection and security for one's own people, but consigned the enemy to contempt and destruction. The mocking song was for the foreign policy of ancient Israel what today is represented by newspaper propaganda which, when it becomes really intense, goes back in words and pictures to the crudities of the ancient method. As far as Israel is concerned, the ancient mocking poetry appears to have been forced more and more into the background with the rise of prophecy, and to have been replaced by the prophetic threats against foreign nations. Such threats are to be found—as is well known and will subsequently be demonstrated in detail—in considerable quantity in the books of Isaiah, Jeremiah, Ezekiel and Zechariah, and other books such as Obadiah, Nahum and Habakkuk are entirely made up of them. This shows, quite independently of the question as to how far these passages actually derive from the prophets to whom they are now attributed, that in the Assyrian and Babylonian period, and in the Persian and Greek period, this form must have had great importance. This is confirmed by the polemic of some of the writing prophets against their associates who were proclaiming blessing alone for Israel. For the prophecies of the latter may certainly be pictured in the style of these utterances, and indeed a considerable proportion of them no doubt derives from the circles of these 'prophets of weal'. Just like the mocking songs at an earlier stage, so now these prophetic threats against foreign nations were an instrument of foreign policy, and when we consider that in both cases the word itself is thought to have dwelling within it a power which shapes reality, the difference between the two is, at least in this respect, not very great, quite apart from the fact that these threats against foreign nations very frequently contain motives from the mocking song (Isa. xxxvii, 22–29; xlvii).[2]

The song cited in Num. xxi, 27–30, is an ancient mocking song, applied in its present context—whether rightly or not makes no difference—to the victory before Israelite times of the Amorite king Sihon over a Moabite king. It is introduced by the phrase: *Therefore say the* מֹשְׁלִים, and in these *composers of the mašal* we may most probably understand actual composers of mocking songs. The poem itself is thus at least indirectly described as *mašal*—mocking song; the fact that from its contents it may also be understood as a victory song does not contradict this. For the victory song, which will be examined further (pp. 99–101), is not infrequently elaborated with motives from the mocking song. We need only to recall the passages of the Song of Deborah in which the poet pours out his scorn on Reuben and Gad which remained far from the battle (Judg. v, 15–17), and the conclusion in which the contrast between the excited anticipations of the mother of Sisera and her court ladies on the one hand, and the real situation, the death of Sisera, on the other hand, is described exactly in the style of the mocking song (v, 28–30). For the mocking song delights in the vivid effect which may be produced by contrasting former glory with present dishonour, pride before downfall and pitiful disaster (pp. 96–8).

[2] Blau, '*Hōḇᵉrē šāmājim* (Jes. xlvii, 13) = Himmelsanbeter' VT 7 (1957), pp. 183 f.

The prophets also employ the mocking song like the mocking saying in the older manner, so as to make men or occurrences of their own time laughable. Thus Deutero-Isaiah pours out his sarcastic mockery of the idols with their makers and worshippers (xliv, 12–20). But the characteristic development which the mocking song undergoes in the prophets is, as we have seen, that it is composed with reference to an event which still lies in the future, and which is represented as if it had already occurred. Here we have the appearance of the 'prophetic' mocking song. An example of this is the mocking song of Yahweh on Sennacherib's departure from Jerusalem. This is ascribed to Isaiah, and in spite of various doubts as to its genuineness, it may nevertheless be attributable to him at least in its original form (II Kings xix, 21–8 = Isa. xxxvii, 22–9). It opens in the style of a mocking watchman's song (p. 90):

> *She despises you, she scorns you the virgin daughter of Zion,*
> *She wags her head behind you the daughter of Jerusalem:*
> *Whom have you mocked and reviled and against whom have you raised your*
> *voice*
> *And haughtily lifted your eyes? against the Holy One of Israel!*

It then quotes the boasting of the Assyrian king and Yahweh's reply that the king has not in fact acted by his own power but as the tool of Yahweh. The poem closes with this threat:

> *Because you have raged against me and your arrogance has come to my ears,*
> *I will put my ring in your nose and my bit in your mouth,*
> *And I will turn you back on the way by which you came.*

The conclusion makes it clear that the king's ignominious withdrawal still lies in the future, but at the beginning the king is nevertheless already depicted as engaged in retreat, and the daughter of Jerusalem shouts after him in scorn and triumph. The contrast between then and now is particularly well brought out: then like a god he was reaching up to the loftiest heights, now he is trailed along the road like a mere animal.

3. *Funeral dirges.* We have two examples of the elegy for the dead, the *qinah* (קִינָה) sung by professional mourning women (Jer ix, 16) or by relatives or friends (II Sam. i, 17; iii, 33–4), normally at the bier of the dead person. These are the two ascribed to David; in all probability they actually derive from him, but are in any case quite clearly from his time: the elegy over Saul and Jonathan (II Sam. i, 19–27)[3] and that over Abner (II Sam. iii, 33–4). The first of these is explicitly indicated as a *qinah*, and has the characteristic expression *Ah, how!* (אֵיךְ), which normally stands at the beginning, towards the end in v. 25, and right at the end in v. 27. It is possible that the expression *Ah, how are the heroes fallen* which appears there twice like a refrain originally appeared also at the beginning. The poem, which according to the note which precedes it (II Sam. i, 18) was extracted from the *Book of the Upright* (סֵפֶר הַיָּשָׁר, cf. on this, pp. 132–3), is of the highest poetic quality, clear and transparent in its structure,

---

[3] Gordon (§ 5a) (1954), p. 154.

with nobility of language and with a genuineness of emotion which is deeply moving. The fact that almost at the beginning of the history of Israel's song and story—in so far as we can trace it—such an artistic product is to be found, or indeed two such if we reckon with it the Song of Deborah (discussed a little later, pp. 100 f.) which is a century and a half older, reveals what a high level had already been attained at that time by Israel's poetry. Indeed, since David's Qinah and the Song of Deborah must presuppose a lengthy pre-history of their types—for the development cannot begin with such finished products—we must assume that this was true of an even earlier period, and that presumably means even in the Israel of pre-Canaanite days. Nothing forbids such an assumption. For, certain as it is that Israel learnt from the Canaanites, and through Canaanite mediation from the Egyptians and Babylonians in types which we either have already examined or will be examining subsequently, so too in the song-types here, in the funeral dirge and the victory song, we are dealing with forms which are not tied to any element which can only have been taken over in the settled land—like those of court ceremonial and many of the cultic ordinances—but have as their subject-matter situations which the pre-Canaanite Hebrews also knew, which are indeed common to men and peoples of all periods: death and victory.[4]

The funeral dirge, which belongs originally at the bier of the individual, has then been applied to the 'death' of communities—tribes and cities and peoples, in that their downfall is thought of as death. We may assume that this application, and so the existence of the 'political' dirge, is very ancient. We may for the moment leave on one side the *qinah* in Ezek. xix, 1–14, where there is disagreement as to how far it envisages past events and how far future, how far it is meant earnestly or as mockery, and how far the *mother* (vv. 1, 10) refers to the queen-mother and how far to the people. We may also leave on one side Ezek. xxvi, 17; xxvii, 32, and the 'prophetic' dirge. Our earliest extended example is then to be seen in Lamentations, of which the first, second and fourth (chs. i, ii, iv) are actually funeral dirges, as their characteristic opening אֵיכָה *Ah, how!* reveals, and they are in fact funeral dirges given political application. The lament is called forth over the downfall, or death, of Jerusalem pictured as a woman, and exactly in the style of the real funeral dirge there is a description of the former beauty of the living person and of the present mean appearance of the dead, though naturally enough the actual subject—the city formerly so happy, and so richly populated, but now carrying on a pitiable existence almost depopulated—again and again appears through the picture. But the type of the political dirge must be older than these examples which are the oldest we possess. For the 'prophetic' political dirge is older, a lament, that is to say, over something still in the future, but represented as the downfall, already in the past, of the people or of some other community. This can only be understood as the taking over of an already existing 'non-prophetic' political dirge into prophetic use. We find it first in Amos in the well-known words which he made to resound to the terror of the crowd gathered for the joyful autumnal festival at Bethel—

[4] For the Arabs, cf. Brockelmann, HdO III, 2–3 (1954), pp. 253–82; Gabrieli (p. 89, n. 4), pp. 95–114.

the situation has been thus envisaged and probably rightly so—speaking in the
hollow rhythm of the genuine funeral dirge, and possibly also with a simple
musical accompaniment:

> *Fallen, no more to rise   is the virgin Israel,*
> *prostrate on her land   with none to raise her up* (Amos v, 2).

This proclamation of the catastrophe about to break upon the people—for
the prophetic dirge is in fact just such a proclamation of something future—must
have had a terrifying effect upon the crowd, and this was its intention. The
prophet deliberately brings before the people with the utmost impressiveness
the alarming nearness and the terrible gravity of the judgement. He himself is
also profoundly shattered by its terror, in spite of seeing in it the victory of
Israel's God triumphing in her downfall. It is thus his own mood which he
expresses in the *qinah*. In this respect it is a genuine dirge. But in the prophets
there is to be found another type of usage of this prophetic *qinah*, and this is by
far the more common, namely where it is used in a mocking sense. It is noteworthy that this mocking dirge is almost invariably directed against an external,
non-Israelite entity—a people, a city or a king. What the prophet feels at their
downfall is not sympathy and distress, but the opposite, the bitterest scorn and
the most joyful satisfaction. Here we have the examples already mentioned,
where the mocking song and the funeral dirge overlap, and this may also be seen
expressed in the fact that both names are used for this mocking prophetic
funeral dirge—*mašal* (Isa. xiv, 4)[5] and *qinah* (Ezek. xxvii, 2; xxviii, 12; xxxii,
2, 16).[6] Such a poem is in fact both, and may equally well be termed one or
the other.

The book of Ezekiel is very rich in prophetic mocking dirges, and if we
ignore the already mentioned *qinah* in xix, 1–14 (p. 95), it is foreign kingdoms
or their rulers—Tyre and Egypt—against which he hurls these compositions,
sustained equally by their exalted poetic rhythm and by passionate anger. This
is intelligible enough. For these are the very powers which again and again
encouraged Judah in its disastrous anti-Babylonian policy, so sharply com-
bated by Ezekiel. In xxvii, 2–10, 25b–36,[7] Tyre is represented as a magnificently
equipped merchant ship, caught on the high seas by the east wind and shattered.
In xxviii, 12–19, the subject is the king of Tyre, who is thought of as a divine
being dwelling on the mountain of the gods—clearly in dependence upon a myth
similar to that which is utilised in Isa. xiv (pp. 97–8)—and he is cast down
to the earth by the High God because of his pride. Isa. xxxii, 2–16 is directed
against Egypt or rather against its Pharaoh: Egypt or Pharaoh, formerly a
crocodile, arrogantly thrashing about in the water, has now been thrown up on
to the dry land, and delivered to the birds of the air as food. In each case we
may see the enormous contrast between former glory and present darkness,
between former power and present insignificance, and to heighten the effect of

---

[5] Orlinsky, '*Madhebah* in Isaiah xiv, 4' VT 7 (1957), pp. 202 f.

[6] In Micah ii, 4 *mašal* and נְהִי, the synonym of *qinah*, stand side by side.

[7] The intermediate verses (9b) 11–25a are perhaps a later insertion. But cf. Dussaud,
'Les Phéniciens au Négeb et en Arabie' RHR 108 (1933), pp. 5–49, see pp. 44–9; Sidney
Smith, '"The Ship Tyre"' PEQ 85 (1953), pp. 97–110. Cf. below, p. 378.

the contrast, there are borrowings from myth with its vividly glaring colours; for even the picture of the crocodile apparently has indications of a mythological basis.

The most powerful prophetic dirge which we possess in the Old Testament, however, and indeed one of the most precious of all Old Testament poems, is the one which is to be found in Isa. xiv, 4–21,[8] described there, as we have seen, as a *mašal*, but beginning with אֵיךְ *Ah, how!*, the characteristic opening of the dirge. In this poem the prophetic device of picturing a future event as one that has already taken place, is particularly clearly exemplified. For it is introduced thus: *When Yahweh has given you rest from your pain and turmoil and the hard service with which you were enslaved, you will take up this taunt against the king of Babylon and say.* But whether this introduction is correct in representing a Babylonian king as the object of this mocking song, has been doubted,[9] and with good reason, since in the poem itself no allusion of this kind can be found. Thus it could equally well apply to an Assyrian king, and the poem would then derive not from the Babylonian period, before the fall of Babylon in 538 B.C., but from the Assyrian period, before the fall of Nineveh in 612 B.C. However that may be, it is clear that it is directed at one of these two world powers, represented by the person of their king, under which Israel had so terribly suffered, and it is from this that we may explain the magnificent pathos of passionate and triumphant satisfaction with which the fall of the king, presented as if it has already taken place, is derisively lamented. There is affirmed first the feeling of happiness and relief felt by the whole world, oppressed until now, at the fall of the hated tyrant (vv. 4–8), and then follows a description (vv. 9–20a) of how the princes who already dwell in the underworld hasten to meet him, now also become a shade, and greet him with a mocking *qinah* (note v. 12 אֵיךְ). Almost at once the poet himself takes the place of these princes, and whereas in v. 10 they speak or sing in the first person plural, now they are mentioned in the third person. The poem concludes with a threat directed at the successors of the tyrant (vv. 20b–21). The middle section, however, the *qinah* as it were within the *qinah* (vv. 10b–20a), in order to bring out really forcibly the contrast between the former state of glory and the present gloom, makes use of a myth similar to that in Ezek. xxviii, 12–19,[10] comparing the tyrant with 'Lucifer, son of the dawn'[11] fallen from heaven (v. 12). We must also draw attention to the fact that in this poem (vv. 8–11, 18–20) there is a very detailed account of the underworld and the grave. This is clearly a heritage from the real funeral dirge, which in deep sorrow speaks of the underworld as the future abode of the beloved dead. This motif has been retained in this mocking dirge, but plunged into a different mood, that of bitter irony. This ironical use of a motif of mourning produces a tremendous heightening of the bitterness of the poem's mockery,

[8] Quell, 'Jesaja xiv, 1–23' *Baumgärtel-Festschr.* (1959), pp. 131–57.

[9] P. Rost, MAOG 4 (1928/9), pp. 175–9, suggests that the poem looks back upon the death of the last king of Assyria, Assuruballit II, who fell in battle far from his homeland after the fall of Nineveh. Cf. below, pp. 319–20.

[10] Dus, 'Melek Ṣōr-Melqart?' Ar Or 26 (1958), pp. 179–85; McKenzie, 'Mythological Allusions in Ezek. xxviii, 12–18' JBL 75 (1956), pp. 322–7.

[11] K. L. Schmidt, 'Lucifer als gefallene Engelmacht' ThZ 7 (1951), pp. 161–79.

E

just as simply the use of the *qinah* line, taken from the real *qinah* and familiar to everyone in its intensely sorrowful tone, also brings with it a heightening of the effect.

§ 14. ROYAL SONGS AND VICTORY SONGS

Literature: Bentzen, 'King Ideology—"Urmensch"—"Troonsbestijgingsfeest"' StTh 3 (1951), pp. 143–57; Dürr, *Ursprung und Ausbau der israelitisch-jüdischen Heilandserwartung* (1925), pp. 74–124; Gressmann, *Der Messias* (FRLANT 43, 1929), pp. 7–59; Gunkel, *Einleitung in die Psalmen,* completed by Begrich (1933), pp. 140–71; Mowinckel, 'Urmensch und "Königsideologie"' StTh 2 (1949/50), pp. 71–89; *Offersang og sangoffer* (1951), pp. 51–117. E.T. *The Psalms in Israel's Worship* (1962), I, pp. 42–80.
    Cf. also Literature p. 51, n. 59; p. 102, n. 1; § 126.

1. *Royal songs.* With the mocking song and the funeral dirge we have already passed well beyond the types which are concerned with the affairs of the individual's life into those which are directed towards public concerns. If we were considering Israel's neighbours, we should have first, in surveying these, to look at the songs which celebrate the king; for there they play an important role, particularly in Egypt. But if for the moment we leave on one side the more cultic songs which are discussed later, the situation in Israel is different in this respect, just as we saw it to be in the royal reports in the first person already discussed (pp. 50 f.). We have in fact very few such songs. That there were such is quite clear. In II Sam. xix, 36, we have the evidence of the aged Gileadite Barzillai who has looked after David during his stay east of Jordan occasioned by his flight from Absalom. When David wishes to express his gratitude by taking him to Jerusalem to the court, he answers by saying that he is too old now to have any appreciation for the delights offered at the royal table or for the songs of the male and female singers evidently maintained at the court. Here we have evidence of male and female singers at the court of David, just as we know of them from Egypt and Babylonia, and from a later period this is also attested by the inscription of Sennacherib on the so-called Taylor Cylinder. Here in col. III, lines 38–9, we are informed that the Judaean king Hezekiah, hard pressed by Sennacherib in 701, sent, together with other enormous tribute, *male and female singers* to Nineveh.[1]
    Such a royal choir as we may assume to have existed also at the Israelite court would have the duty of increasing by their songs the pleasure of the king's mealtimes and banquets. But no doubt this choir was also employed at festivals of other kinds, such as the accession to the throne, marriage, the birth of the crown prince, the reception of the king returning victorious from war, and so on. On all these occasions the praise of the king must certainly have been sounded, that of the reigning monarch above all, but also that of his illustrious ancestors. In the introduction to the so-called 'Last Words of David' in II Sam. xxiii, 1–7, David is described as the *favourite of the songs of Israel*[2]—at

[1] AOT, p. 354; ANET, p. 288a; DOTT, p. 67.
[2] Cazelles, 'La titulature du roi David' *Mél. Bibl. Robert* (1957), pp. 131–6.

any rate that is the most probable meaning of the expression. Similarly in the actual text of Ps. xxii, 4, Yahweh is described as *enthroned on the praises of Israel.* There must have been songs which praised David, and we could hardly expect it to be otherwise when we consider the great affection which this king enjoyed. But not a single one of these has survived, and of other profane royal songs we possess only very few. I Macc. xiv, 6–15, preserves a poem on the victorious reign of Simon the Maccabee, and Ps. xlv[3] provides a song on the marriage of a king, in itself secular, but re-interpreted with reference to the relationship of Yahweh to his people and so preserved in the Psalter. Some scholars have considered that it refers to a foreign ruler and belongs only to the Maccabean period, but it is undoubtedly much older than this, and may be assigned with some certainty to the marriage of Ahab with the Tyrian princess Jezebel (I Kings xvi, 31). As with the royal reports in the first person (pp. 50 f.), we may ask whether the lack of such royal songs is due to the chance nature of the material which has been handed down, or whether in Israel, with its demo-cratic, or better its theocratic, character, such poems were unknown or at any rate played no great part. Such a quantity of court poetry as was possessed by the neighbouring lands is certainly not likely to have existed in Israel, but it was definitely not entirely lacking. The royal song must have entered Israel together with the remainder of the court ceremonial from the nearer environment of Canaan and from the more distant Egypt, Babylonia and Asia Minor. This is clear from the passages already cited which mention male and female singers at the court. It may also be seen in the fact that when the king is mentioned in the Old Testament, use is made of a whole series of descriptive phrases which presumably go back to the royal songs (Ps. xviii, 35; I Sam. xxix, 9; II Sam. xiv, 17, 20; Lam. iv, 20). Lastly and most important, this is seen in the Messianic prophecies. For when, as for example in Isa. ix, 3–6; xi, 1–9; Micah v, 3; Jer. xxiii, 5–6, they glorify the virtues of the Messiah and the times of happiness and peace which he is to bring about, this must certainly also be understood as an echo of the songs which glorify the reigning monarch. This point may be made without in any way detracting from the mythological character of many of the ideas and formulae.

2. *Victory songs.* Although very little has been preserved for us of the royal songs, we nevertheless possess relatively many songs which glorify all Israel or sections of it. Naturally enough these nearly all come from times of warfare and celebrate Israel's victories. We hear frequently of the reciting of such songs of victory, this being primarily an affair of the women and taking place immedi-ately on the return of the victorious army or at specially arranged festivals of victory. Exod. xv, 20 relates that after the overthrow of the Egyptians in the sea, Miriam and *all the women after her* went out and took up the song in xv, 21, which is later to be discussed with the Hymns (p. 106). Similarly Judg. xi, 34, tells how Jephthah's daughter *went out* to meet her father with drums and dan-cing as he returned home victorious. I Sam. xviii, 6–7, says that *the women came*

---

[3] Gaster, JBL 74 (1955), pp. 239–51; King, *A Study of Psalm xlv (xliv)* (Pontif. Univ. Lateranensis Diss., 1959); Morgenstern, HUCA 28 (1957), pp. 33–46: Porter, JThSt 12 (1961), pp. 51–3; Schildenberger, BZ 3 (1959), pp. 31–43.

out of all the cities of Israel with song and dance and instruments of music to meet the troops under Saul and David or under David alone, as they returned from battle against the Philistines. We also hear of a specially organised victory festival in Judg. xvi, 23–5. This is a festival of the Philistines triumphing over the capture of Samson, but the Israelite narrator no doubt pictures this according to the pattern of celebrations known to him from among his own people, while at the same time faithfully preserving the local colour of Gaza in his mention of the god Dagon and in the description of his temple.

A good impression of the nature of the songs sung at the victorious return of the troops or at special victory festivals is given us by the one which is sung to the honour of David in I Sam. xviii, 7:

> *Saul has slain his thousands   but David his ten thousands.*

It is a single verse, a double-triplet, which we must imagine as repeated incessantly by the women as they dance and touch their instruments, and for that purpose it is long enough. Somewhat longer is the Philistine triumph song, though this too is repeated (Judg. xvi, 23–4). Here we may note the fivefold repetition of *-ēnû* like a rhyme:

> *nātan 'elōhēnû beyādēnû 'ēt šimšôn 'ôyebēnû*
> *we'ēt maḥarîb 'arṣēnû wa'ašer hirbāh 'et-ḥalālēnû*
>
> *Our god has given into our hand   Samson our enemy*
> *the ravager of our country   who multiplied our slain.*

The most impressive monument of ancient Israelite war and victory poetry, and indeed one of the most valuable pieces of Israelite poetry at all, is the Song of Deborah in Judg. v.[4] It may find a place here among the victory songs, although following the pattern of the Hymn it opens with a summons to praise Yahweh (vv. 2–3), and then too, likewise in the hymn style, it describes the appearance of Yahweh (vv. 4–5), and above all finally regards Yahweh as the giver of success. But even so it is in fact the tremendous event itself and men's share in it which stand in the foreground. After the introduction which contains the summons to praise Yahweh and to listen (vv. 2–3), there follows in vv. 4–5 the description of the appearance of Yahweh who hastens from Sinai to the aid of his people. Vv. 6–8 pause for a moment to indicate the distressing conditions of need and despondency which have endured for many years. Vv. 9–15a[5] leap forward again to the present from a past which has now been successfully overcome, and describe the mobilisation of the tribes hastening to the battle. Admittedly not all were there. Reuben, Gilead, Asher and Dan had no share in

[4] Ackroyd, 'The Composition of the Song of Deborah' VT 2 (1952), pp. 160–2; Albright, 'The Song of Deborah in the Light of Archaeology' BASOR 62 (1936), pp. 26–31; Engberg and Albright, 'Historical Analysis of Archaeological Evidence: Megiddo and the Song of Deborah' BASOR 78 (1940), pp. 4–9; Gerleman, 'The Song of Deborah in the Light of Stylistics' VT 1 (1951), pp. 168–80; Goddard, 'The Critic and Deborah's Song' Westminster ThJ 3 (1941), pp. 93–112; Grether, *Das Deboralied* (1941); Rabin, 'Judges v, 2 and the "Ideology" of Deborah's War' JJSt 6 (1955), pp, 125–34; Sellin, 'Das Deboralied' *Procksch-Festschr.* (1934), pp. 149–66; Slotki, 'The Song of Deborah' JThSt 33 (1932), pp. 341–54; Weiser, 'Das Deboralied' ZAW 71 (1959), pp. 67–97. Lit. § 126.
[5] Goodwin, 'The Meaning of Judges v, 8b–13' JBL 63 (1944), pp. 257–62.

it and are mocked because of this inactivity in vv. 15b–17, whereas Zebulun and Naphtali, which make up the heart of the rising, are mentioned in v. 18 in terms of especial praise. Vv. 19–22 then describe most vividly the course of the battle, or rather the decisive moment of the destruction of the enemies. Against the background of a terrible curse (v. 22) against the town of Meroz[6] which although in a position to do so and indeed under an obligation, had contributed nothing to the exploitation of the victory, Jael is then blessed and a description is given of how she murdered Sisera, the leader of the enemies (vv. 24–7). This very vivid description ends with the words: *There he lay dead,* and immediately afterwards, with the most striking contrast, vv. 28–30 relate the high hopes with which Sisera's mother watches out with her companions for the return of her victorious son laden with booty, and so, with a link back to the description of Sisera's murder, but again in startling contrast with the verses immediately preceding it, to the expression of the wish with which the song ends (v. 31):

> *So shall perish all thine enemies, Yahweh*
>   *but thy friends be like the going up of the sun in its splendour!*

A mere indication of the contents of the song cannot give any conception of its dramatic vividness. It does not simply describe the events in an orderly chronological sequence, but repeatedly changes the point of view and of time, at one moment seeing the mountains of Edom shaking at the marching up of Yahweh, at another transporting us to the residence of Sisera.[7] At one moment it lingers on the bygone days of disgrace, at the next shows us the hosts hastening to the battle, and then plunges direct into the tumult of battle. It does not report objectively about events and people, but addresses itself to them directly, summoning them and questioning them, pouring out upon them curse or blessing. The song itself must be read, or better still, be heard. Its poet is unknown to us, and will remain unknown, for its present introduction: *Then sang Deborah and Barak ben Abinoam on that day,* which presumably is intended to designate Deborah and Barak not only as the singers but also as the composers of the song, cannot claim to be authentic, if only because in the song itself (v. 12) Deborah and Barak are themselves addressed. The statement could more easily be right in suggesting that the poem was a song recited immediately after the victory, perhaps at a festival to be pictured on the analogy of Judg. xvi, 23–5. But that too is no more than a suggestion. The one certain point is that we must relate the origin of the song very closely with the events themselves. For the sense of participation in the events is so genuine and so intense that we can hardly imagine that a later author could so well project himself into the mood which stirred men's spirits at that time.

---

[6] Alt, 'Meros' ZAW 58 (1940/1), pp. 244–7 = *Kl. Schr.* I (1953), pp. 274–7.
[7] Maisler, 'Beth She'arim, Gaba, and Harosheth of the Peoples' HUCA 24 (1952/3), pp. 75–84.

§ 15. CULTIC SONGS

Literature: Balla, *Das Ich der Psalmen* (1912); Baumgartner, *Die Klagegedichte des Jeremia* (BZAW 32, 1917); Begrich, 'Die Vertrauensäußerungen im israelitischen Klageliede des Einzelnen und in seinem babylonischen Gegenstück' ZAW 46 (1928), pp. 221–60; Blackman, 'The Psalms in the Light of Egyptian Research' in Simpson, *The Psalmists* (1926), pp. 177–97; Calès, 'Les psaumes du règne de Jahvé' RSR 25 (1935), pp. 462–89, 583–92; Causse, 'L'ancienne poésie cultuelle d'Israël et les origines du Psautier' RHPhR 6 (1926), pp. 1–37; Driver, 'The Psalms in the Light of Babylonian Research' in Simpson, *The Psalmists* (1926), pp. 109–75; Feuillet, 'Les psaumes eschatologiques du règne de Yahweh' NRTh 73 (1951), pp. 244–60, 352–63; Frost, 'Asseveration by Thanksgiving' VT 8 (1958), pp. 380–90; Gressmann, 'The Development of Hebrew Psalmody' in Simpson, *The Psalmists* (1926), pp. 1–21; Gunkel–Begrich (§14) (1933); Haller, 'Ein Jahrzehnt Psalmforschung' ThR 1 (1929), pp. 377–402; Johnson, 'The Psalms' OTMSt (1951), pp. 162–209; Kraus, *Die Königsherrschaft Gottes im AT. Untersuchungen zu den Liedern von Jahwes Thronbesteigung* (1951); McCullough, 'The "Enthronement of Yahweh" Psalms' in *A Stubborn Faith . . . Irwin* (1956), pp. 53–61; Mowinckel, *Psalmenstudien* I–VI (1921–24 (1961)); *Offersang og sangoffer* (1951); E.T. *The Psalms in Israel's Worship* (1962); *Zum israelitischen Neujahr und zur Deutung der Thronbesteigungspsalmen* (1952); 'Psalm Criticism between 1900 and 1935' VT 5 (1955), pp. 13–33; 'Notes on the Psalms' StTh 13 (1959), pp. 134–65; Paterson, 'The Psalms and the Cult' Transact. Glasgow Univ. Or. Soc. 14 (1953), pp. 42–7; Robert, 'L'exégèse des Psaumes selon les méthodes de la "Formgeschichte"' *Miscell. Bibl. Ubach* (1954), pp. 211–25; Quell, *Das kultische Problem der Psalmen* (BWAT 36, 1926); Hans Schmidt, *Die Thronfahrt Jahves* (1927); *Das Gebet der Angeklagten im AT* (BZAW 49, 1928); Stamm, 'Ein Vierteljahrhundert Psalmenforschung' ThR 23 (1955), pp. 1–68; Stummer, *Sumerisch-akkadische Parallelen zum Aufbau at. Psalmen* (1922); Volz, *Das Neujahrsfest Jahwes (Laubhüttenfest)* (1912).

Cf. also Literature §§ 63, 67, 69, 92, 108, 126, and in Kraus, BK XV (1960).

1. *Royal cult songs.* The royal cult songs[1] may conveniently mark the transition from the more secular songs to the more cultic—for a really clear division cannot here be made any more than it can between the various types of psalms and songs akin to the psalms. In these songs the subject-matter is again in fact events of a secular and political character, but seen in the light of the cult. Whereas, as we have seen, hardly anything is preserved in the Old Testament of the royal songs which are to be reckoned as secular poetry, the Psalter preserves a whole series of these royal cult songs. It is obvious why the former have to all intents and purposes been lost, whereas a fairly substantial proportion of the latter has survived; in the latter God and not man stands in the forefront. The subject-matter is what the king asks from his God, or what he thanks him for, or what he has vowed to him, or what he has received from him as a promise, and not what he himself has done by his own might. The songs thus do not conflict with the Jewish religious outlook which to an even greater degree than was the case already in ancient Israel and than was original to Israel's religion, sees all human achievements and greatness as overshadowed by the sovereignty of God, and is in particular concerned to make most emphatically clear the

[1] Johnson, 'The Rôle of the King in the Jerusalem Cultus' in *The Labyrinth*, ed. Hooke (1935), pp. 71–111; von Rad, 'Erwägungen zu den Königspsalmen' ZAW 58 (1940/1), pp. 216–22; 'Das judäische Königsritual' ThLZ 72 (1947), cols. 211–16 = *Ges. Stud. z. AT* (1958), pp. 105–213. Lit. p. 51, n. 59; p. 110, nn. 28, 29; § 126.

superiority of the heavenly king over every earthly monarch. In these songs the human pales by contrast with the divine, as in them there is drawn not the picture of one particular king, but something like the king as such, the typical king. And this fact made it possible that in post-exilic Judaism they did not have to be understood with reference to the ruling king, or rather, since Judaism had no monarchy, with reference to the kings of the past, but could easily be transferred to the king of the future, the one who should be well-pleasing to God, the Messiah. We saw with reference to the secular royal songs, that they could be so to speak rescued by Messianic prophecy and could continue to exist in it. So here too—in Ps. xlv (cf. p. 99) in the case of a secular royal song—the Messianic interpretation preserved from oblivion songs which can hardly have originated except in the period of the kings of Israel or Judah and at that time referred to the ruling monarchs.

If we leave aside less important and disputed examples, we are here concerned with the following psalms: ii, xviii, xx, xxi,[2] lxxii, ci, cx, cxxxii,[3] cxliv, 1–11. Their interpretation, it is true, is uncertain in many details, largely as a result of what is in some cases very marked textual corruption, and this is unfortunately particularly true in the case of the two very significant psalms ii,[4] and cx.[5] But even so we may affirm the following points with reasonable certainty. Psalms ii, xxi, lxxii,[6] cx, belong to the king's accession, itself a cultic celebration and indeed one which was primarily celebrated cultically, or to the festival celebrated annually as a memorial to his accession to the throne. Ps. ci also fits well in the setting of the accession festival; it presents an oath spoken by the king on this significant day. In a rather broader sense, Ps. cxxxii may also be reckoned with this group of songs, since here the foundation of the Davidic dynasty is the central point beside the foundation of the Jerusalem sanctuary, and we may believe that the Judaean kings, who, with the exception of Athaliah (II Kings xi), were all Davidites down to the fall of the southern kingdom, looked back at their accession in gratitude and pride over the long line of their

[2] Driver, AfO 18, 1 (1957), p. 129.

[3] Asensio, Gregorianum 38 (1957), pp. 310–16; Eissfeldt, WdO II 5/6 (1959), pp. 480–3; Porter, JThSt 5 (1954), pp. 161–73.

[4] Closen, Bibl 21 (1940), pp. 288–309; de Fraine, Bijdragen 16 (1955), pp. 349–56; Hesse, Luther-Jahrbuch 25 (1958), pp. 23–41; Köbert, Bibl 21 (1940), pp. 426–8; Press, ThZ 13 (1957), pp. 321–34; Robert RSR 39 (1951), pp. 88–98; Rowley, JThSt 42 (1941), pp. 143–54; Schulz, ThGl 23 (1931), pp. 87–97; Sonne, HUCA 19 (1945/6), pp. 43–55. Lit. § 126.

[5] Baneth, MGWJ 69 (1925), pp. 230–3; Caquot, Semitica 6 (1956), pp. 33–52; Coppens, (ALBO, Ser. III, 1, 1955); Suppl. to Numen IV (1958), pp. 333–48; Dürr, *Psalm 110 im Lichte der neueren altorientalischen Forschung* (Verz. d. Vorl. Akad. Braunsberg W.-S. 1929–30); Edelkoort, Vox Theol. 15 (1944), pp. 86–90; Gaster, Journal Manchester Eg. Or. Soc. 21 (1937), pp. 37–44; Hardy, JBL 64 (1945), pp. 385–90; Jefferson, JBL 73 (1954), pp. 152–6; Kissane, Irish ThQ 21 (1954), pp. 103–14; Kroeze, *Genesis Veertien* (1937), pp. 206–21; del Medico, ZAW 69 (1957), pp. 160–70; Morgenstern, JQR 32 (1941/2), pp. 371–85; HUCA 27 (1956), pp. 138–43; Rowley, *Bertholet-Festschr.* (1950), pp. 461–72; de Savignac, OTS 9 (1951), pp. 107–35; VT 7 (1957), pp. 82–90; Stoebe, *Baumgärtel-Festschr.* (1959), pp. 175–91; Tournay, RB 52 (1945), pp. 220–37; Vriezen, Vox Theol. 15 (1944), pp. 81–5; Widengren, *Psalm 110 och det sakrale kungadömet i Israel* (1941). Lit. § 126.

[6] Grelot, VT 7 (1957), pp. 319–21; van Leeuwen, NedThT 12 (1957), pp. 16–31; Murphy, *A Study of Psalm lxxii (lxxi)*, 1948; Skehan, Bibl 40 (1959), pp. 302–8. Lit. § 126.

ancestors and particularly to the first of the line, David. For he had founded sanctuary and dynasty simultaneously, or at any rate vowed to his God the founding of the former, and received the assurance of the latter as a promise from Yahweh. Ps. xx is a prayer sung by the people or more probably by a choir on behalf of the king as he goes out to the battlefield, and Ps. cxliv, 1–11, is a prayer recited by the king himself on such an occasion, in the style of the individual lament, which will be discussed later. Ps. xviii,[7] finally, presents a song of thanksgiving in the form of two parallel movements (vv. 2–31 and 32–51) which the king recites when he returns victorious from the battlefield. Thus with these royal songs the actual setting in life may be recognised with reasonable clarity.

Special attention must be drawn to one particular feature which may be observed in several of these songs and which can only be understood from cultic practice. In Ps. ii, 7–9; xx, 7; xxi, 5; cx, 1–4; cxxxii, 11–12, divine oracles are imparted to the king, or are presupposed, assuring him of divine pleasure and support. The consideration of these passages itself demands that if they are to be understood we must assume that in the Israelite cultus charismatics, i.e. cult prophets, had their place, and that they assured the king at his accession of his adoption by God (Ps. ii, 7), or promised God's help to the king as he went out to the battlefield in response to the prayer of people or choir (xx, 7), and so on. This assumption may be clearly confirmed by a consideration of the literature of Babylonia and Assyria, and in particular of a prayer addressed to the god Nabu by king Ashurbanipal.[8] For this text is basically a dialogue between the king and the god. The king presents his prayer in several stages, and in each case the god answers him and promises to hear him. This reply is in one case introduced by the words *Thus said Nabu*, and in another case by: *There answered a breath from Nabu, his lord.* The assumption can hardly be avoided that these divine answers came through the mediation of charismatics who were able to detect and to interpret the *breath of Nabu*; and this is confirmed by the fact that in another example the divine promise is made *through the mouth*, i.e., the mouth of prophets or prophetesses. This is a very good example of the common features which link together the cultic poetry of Israel and Babylonia. For as we have already repeatedly indicated and must again even more especially in the consideration of the cultic poetry (p. 113), in this matter Israel was markedly dependent upon its environment. Moreover, we shall meet again with the divine oracle clearly mediated by the cult prophet in the individual (pp. 117–18) and also in the collective lament (p. 114), and we may ask whether this may be explained as having been at first a royal privilege, later becoming a more general possession, so that it may now be heard in answer to the prayer of the ordinary pious man.

2. '*Spiritual songs.*' We thus observe that with regard to the royal cult songs, they have their primary reference to quite definite situations in the life of the king and illumine these situations in a cultic and religious manner. Subsequently

---

[7] Asensio, *Gregorianum* 33 (1952), pp. 219–60, 566–611; Cross Jr. and Freedman, JBL 72 (1953), pp. 15–34; Melamed, *Sepher Dinaburg* [Hebr.] (1949), pp. 19–30.

[8] AOT, pp. 266–7; Falkenstein and von Soden, *Sumerische und akkadische Hymnen und Gebete* (1953), pp. 292 f., 393 f., cf. AOT, pp. 281–3, ANET, pp. 449 f. Similarly in Egyptian, cf. Erman-Ranke, *Ägypten* (1923), pp. 467–8. Lit. § 126.

they lose their link with these concrete situations, and indeed their link with the king altogether, and so are understood of the Messiah[9] and hence re-interpreted in various ways with reference to religious needs. This is similarly true of other cultic songs. Originally associated with definite cultic actions, they have become detached from these and have become 'spiritual songs', and in this process such cultic matters as sacrifice and ritual dance, which are mentioned and which originally referred to actual practice, are now spiritually interpreted and have become metaphors. Exilic and post-exilic Judaism interpreted and utilised a whole series of ancient cultic songs in this way as spiritual songs, and this explains how they came to be taken up into the Psalter which is thus not merely the hymn-book (p. 448) of the post-exilic Temple—and perhaps not even primarily that—but is also that of the post-exilic synagogues. Other psalms were never actually cultic songs, but are spiritual songs in origin, though for our discussion of them it does not matter and in many cases cannot be decided whether in fact they came into existence as private outpourings of a devout spirit or whether their authors did from the first have in mind this wider use. They are definitely not cultic songs in the sense that they were to be sung in association with particular cultic actions, but the situation is that the worship of the synagogue, for which they were either primarily intended or which was at least part of the intention, was no longer a cultus of the older kind, but simply an edifying occasion held in common. Thus these songs, even in their use in public worship, still really remain spiritual songs, for this worship is itself spiritual. But even the songs which came into being without any contact with the cultus, reveal in form and content many similarities to the old genuine cult songs, and thus also themselves provide valuable clues to the nature of the older songs. So we have genuine ancient cult songs which had their setting at quite precise points in the cult, and later spiritual songs which came into being in dependence upon these. Both are to be found within the Psalter and also outside it, and they enable us to form a vivid picture of the variety of the older cult poetry of Israel and even of its most ancient forms.

3. *Hymns.* A very common form of song is the Hymn, and this form may be traced from Israel's beginnings right through to the Christian era and remained in the process essentially constant. In this too Israel's dependence upon her environment becomes especially clear.[10] The Hymn is the song which extols

[9] Bentzen, 'Kan ordet "Messiansk" anvendes om Salmernes Kongeforestillinger?' SEA 12 (1947), pp. 36–50; *Messias-Moses redivivus-Menschensohn* (1948), E.T. *King and Messiah* (1955); Colunga, 'El mesianismo en los salmos regios' Stud. Anselm. 27/8 (1951), pp. 208–30; 'Jerusalén, la ciudad del Gran Rey. Exposición mesiánica de algunos Salmos' Est Bíbl 14 (1955), pp. 255–79; Coppens, *De messiaanse verwachting in het Psalmboek* (Med. Vlaamse Ac. 17 (1955, No. 5), 1955); Miller, 'Gibt es direkt messianische Psalmen?' *Miscell. Bibl. Ubach* (1954), pp. 201–9; Šegula, 'Messias Rex in Psalmis' VD 32 (1954), pp. 21–33, 77–83, 142–54. Cf. also literature for § 14 and on p. 51, n. 59; p. 110, n. 28; p. 526, n. 47; § 126.

[10] AOT, pp. 12–18, 241–56; ANET, pp. 365–92; DOTT, pp. 142–50; Albright, 'The Egyptian Correspondence of Abimilki, Prince of Tyre' JEA 23 (1937), pp. 190–203; Böhl, 'Hymnisches und Rhythmisches in den Amarne-Briefen aus Kanaan' ThLBl 35 (1914), cols. 337–40 = *Op. Min.* (1953), pp. 375–9, 516–17; van Dijk, *Sumerische Götterlieder* II (AAH, 1960, I, 1960); Falkenstein, 'Sumerische religiöse Texte' ZA 52 (1957), pp. 58–75, 2 Pls.; *Sumerische Götterlieder* I (AAH 1959, 1, 1959); Falkenstein and von

the glory and the greatness of Yahweh as it is revealed in nature and history, and particularly in Israel's history. Its Hebrew name is תְּהִלָּה. Though at a later date this word was understood in a more general sense, and so—in the plural—was used as the title of the Psalter, yet its original reference was only to hymns or hymn-like songs, for it means *praise, song of praise.* The hymn ascribed to Miriam in Exod. xv, 21, which is certainly very old, refers to the basic saving act of Yahweh, the destruction of the Egyptians in the sea and the deliverance of Israel:

> *Sing to Yahweh! for he has exalted himself greatly   horse and chariot he has thrown into the sea.*

The advent of the Christian salvation is accompanied by hymns, in style just like those of the Old Testament, namely the Magnificat of Mary (Luke i, 46–7, 49–55) and the Benedictus of Zechariah (Luke i, 68–79).[11] Between these stands, for example, the song of the Seraphim, evidently modelled on the hymn which resounded in the earthly sanctuary of Yahweh, as heard by Isaiah in his call-vision (Isa. vi, 3):

> *Holy, holy, holy is the lord of hosts   all the earth is full of his glory.*[12]

From the Psalter, we may mention Pss. xcviii, c, cl as hymns, which, although at any rate in part coming from a later period, and even of very late date, nevertheless clearly allow the direct connection with the cult to be recognised, and were no doubt originally composed for use in the cult. In xcviii and cl all manner of musical instruments are mentioned, with which Yahweh is to be extolled, and this may certainly be understood to mean that these instruments accompanied or interwove the singing of the hymn. Ps. c mentions the doors and courts of the Temple. On the other hand, with Ps. ciii[13] and Ps. civ,[14] we are likely to be dealing with compositions which in the first place at least are to be understood as outpourings of pious spirits, and only in the second place to have found application in worship. This may perhaps be seen in their length which contrasts so greatly with those just mentioned, and furthermore in the

Soden (p. 104, n. 8); Grzegorzewski, *Elemente vorderorientalischen Hofstils auf kanaanäischem Boden* (Diss. theol. Königsberg, 1937); Jirku, 'Kana'anäische Psalmenfragmente in der vorisraelitischen Zeit Palästinas und Syriens' JBL 52 (1933), pp. 108–20; Laessøe, 'A Prayer to Ea, Shamash, and Marduk, from Hama' Iraq 18 (1956), pp. 60–7, Pl. XIV; Mowinckel, *Offersang og sangoffer* (1951), pp. 436–53, E.T. *The Psalms in Israel's Worship* (1962), II, pp. 176–92; O'Callaghan, 'Echoes of Canaanite Literature in the Psalms' VT 4 (1954), pp. 164–76. Lit. p. 58, n. 3; § 126.

[11] Gunkel, 'Die Lieder in der Kindheitsgeschichte Jesu bei Lukas' *Harnack-Festgabe* (1921), pp. 43–60; Lambertz, 'Sprachliches aus Septuaginta und NT' WZ Leipzig 2 (1952/3), pp. 79–87; Vielhauer, 'Das Benedictus des Zacharias' ZThK 49 (1952), pp. 255–72; Winter, 'Magnificat and Benedictus—Maccabaean Psalms?' BJRL 37 (1954/5), pp. 328–47. Lit. § 126.

[12] Leiser, 'The Trisagion of Isaiah's Vision' NTS 6 (1959/60), pp. 261–3; Walker, 'The Origin of the "Thrice Holy" Apc iv, 8' NTS 5 (1958/9), pp. 132 f. Lit. § 126.

[13] Parker, Canadian JTh 1 (1955), pp. 191–6; Jepsen, KuD 7 (1961), pp. 261–71.

[14] AOT, pp. 15–18; ANET, pp. 369–71; DOTT, pp. 142–50; Dell'Oca, Rev Bíbl 22 (1960), pp. 89–92; Eissfeldt, FuF 33 (1959), pp. 113–17; Grill, BZ 3 (1959), p. 102; Humbert, RHPhR 15 (1935), pp. 1–27 = *Opuscules* (1958), pp. 66–82; Nagel, *Bertholet-Festschr.* (1950), pp. 395–403; van der Voort, RB 58 (1951), pp. 321–47. Lit. § 126.

substitution of the singular imperative or cohortative form for the plural summons: *Sing, rejoice* used in Pss. xcviii, c, cl as well as in Exod. xv, 21, or for the reflexive summons *Let us sing.* This latter feature appears also in hymnic cult songs and here may perhaps be understood as spoken by a song leader or as having a collective reference; it is thus admittedly not a sure criterion. It is really the inwardness and warmth of feeling which is present in a particularly high degree in both these psalms which seems to designate them as expressions of private piety, and thus as spiritual songs: *Praise the Lord, O my soul.*

Just as here pious spirits have utilised for the expression of their personal piety the style of the hymn which primarily belongs in the cultus, so we may find in many places in the Old Testament such a literary use of the hymn style. Among the prophets it is Deutero-Isaiah who is most fond of using this style, in his desire to present before the eyes of the despondent people, as powerfully and impressively as possible, the unique greatness and glory of his God. He includes whole hymns like xlii, 10–12;[15] xliv, 23; lii, 9–10, and uses various motifs from them. In doing so he makes Yahweh pronounce with reference to himself descriptions of the greatness and glory which the hymn ascribed to Yahweh, as for example, in xliv, 24–8:

> *I am Yahweh   who creates all things*
> *who stretches out the heavens alone   who spreads out the earth—who should*
> *help me?*
> *who frustrates the omens of liars   and makes diviners fools . . .*

We noted such descriptions of Yahweh by himself already in the word of Yahweh spoken at the epiphany (cf. p. 73), but in Deutero-Isaiah, who apparently lived in the Babylonian exile, it is reasonable to ask whether he may not have been influenced also by the Babylonian hymn style, with the result that he takes from the Babylonian gods the descriptions of themselves which their own people attributed to them, and claims them for his own God, beside whom there is none other. Among the other books which belong either to the Old Testament or to its appendix, it is particularly Job (pp. 464 f.) and Jesus ben Sira who have a predilection for using the hymnic style. Ecclus. xxxix, 14b–35; xlii, 15–xliii, 33, are complete hymns of large compass, whereas xlv, 26a; l, 22, also complete hymns, do not exceed Exod. xv, 21 in length. Hymn motifs are often incorporated in his language, e.g. x, 14–17; xviii, 1–7.

The structure of the hymn is very simple. The introduction, already mentioned, may be imperative (Pss. xcviii, 1; c, 1; cl, 1–5) or jussive (Ps. cxlviii, 13), or cohortative (Ps. xcv, 1–2),[16] and contains a summons to begin the extolling of Yahweh. There follows the main section or corpus which enumerates the characteristics or acts of Yahweh as worthy of praise, and is very frequently linked to the introduction by the use of the word כִּי *for* to indicate the basis of the praise (Exod. xv, 21; Ps. xcviii, 1, 9). This enumeration, which may utilise participles (Ps. ciii, 3–6), relative clauses (Ps. viii, 2b)[17] or even main clauses

[15] Morgenstern, 'Isaiah xlii, 10–13' *Pyatt Memorial Vol.* (1953), pp. 27–38.
[16] Schilling, Bibel und Leben 2 (1961), pp. 105–20. Lit. § 126.
[17] Altheim, *Zarathustra und Alexander* (1960), pp. 20 f., points out that the use of

(Exod. xv, 21; Ps. civ, 5–6) may be interrupted by a repetition of the summons to praise Yahweh, either once (Ps. xcviii, 4–8) or several times (Ps. cxlvii, 1, 7, 12). This divides the song into two or more parallel movements and it is particularly effective when the summons appears once more at the end, rounding off the whole poem (Pss. ciii, 22; civ, 35). The introduction may, however, run over into the whole song, and so itself become a hymn. In Ps. cxlviii, which consists of 14 verses, only 3 or 4 verses at most (5b–6, 13b–14) form the main body of the hymn, all the rest is simply introduction, and Ps. cl is nothing but introduction. Yet both are complete hymns. In them the description of Yahweh appears indirectly. The number and significance of the beings summoned to extol Yahweh in Ps. cxlviii and the variety of the instruments called upon to accompany the praise in Ps. cl, reveal clearly enough how majestic is the God to whom the hymn is to refer.

We have already seen that the hymn is in origin a cultic song, but we can no longer ascertain its exact place in the cultus, probably simply because it does not belong in just one place alone, but may be sung on various occasions. In Amos v, 23, song and the playing of the harp are mentioned immediately after the sacrifices, and this shows that the sacrifice was accompanied by songs, and certainly these would include hymns (cf. II Chron. xxiii, 18; xxix, 27), as we might naturally assume even without this piece of evidence. But there were also other occasions suitable for hymns, and these are explicitly mentioned. II Sam. vi, 5, relates—according to the text as it must certainly be corrected following I Chron. xiii, 8—that at the bringing up of the Ark *David and all the house of Israel* danced before the Ark *with all their might and with songs and lyres and harps.* . . . Among the songs sung on the occasion, hymns will certainly have been included, and even though none of these has been preserved, Ps. xxiv appears to contain as its last section (vv. 7–10)[18] the song which, when the Ark was brought into Jerusalem, was struck up just at the moment when the Ark, carried in before the procession, reached the gate of the city of David. (The psalm as a whole is a comparatively late composition, with a hymnic introduction (vv. 1–2) and a Torah-liturgy (p. 74) as its central part (vv. 3–6)). Other cultic occasions on which hymns may also have been sung are mentioned in Exod. xxxii, 18; Isa. xxx, 29. The same is true of Neh. xii, 27–43, if we may mention a late passage after these others which refer to the earlier period. In this passage we are told of the festival of the dedication of the walls, celebrated with songs[19] and instrumental music. Here too are mentioned choirs of singers as the performers of the song, just as we are fairly well informed about the significance and functions of the temple singers for the post-exilic period from the Chronicler and the Psalms. Unfortunately our sources are silent in this matter too for the earlier period, and we have therefore to limit ourselves here to the assumption, based upon general considerations and upon

relative clauses and participles is characteristic of the forms of religious speech, and may be found in many contexts including the Gathas of Zoroaster.

[18] Eissfeldt, WdO II (1954–9), pp. 480–3; Podechard, *Mémorial Lagrange* (1940), pp. 143–6; Rolf Rendtorff, *Festschr. Heinrich Rendtorff* (1958), pp. 121–9; Slotki, JBL 51 (1932), pp. 214–26; Smart, JBL 52 (1933), pp. 175–80; Treves, VT 10 (1960), pp. 428–34.
[19] Lohmann (cf. p. 323, n. 76), p. 40.

the analogy, for example, of male and female singers in the royal palace (cf. p. 98), that at that time too cultic singing was undertaken by choirs of singers.[20] But perhaps we can say something more than this. For in I Chron. xxv, 1–3, which deals with the appointing by David of Temple singers who are described as descendants of Asaph, Heman and Jeduthun, the activity of these singers is designated as נָבָא—in other words, the term is used which elsewhere describes *prophetic utterance* or more generally prophetic proclamation.[21] This makes very probable the assumption which suggests itself also on other grounds, that the post-exilic singers—for it is in the main their affairs which are reflected in the measures described in I Chron. xxv as undertaken by David (pp. 538–40)—inherited the position of the earlier cult prophets whose existence and importance has already been indicated by more than one consideration (p. 104). This indicates that cultic singing was in the earlier period the responsibility of these cult prophets. Among the songs which they were required to render the hymns will in the nature of things have occupied a primary place, and there are not lacking indications which show that the hymns or at any rate many of them, were rendered antiphonally, no doubt by several choirs (Pss. lxviii, 27;[22] cxxxv, 19–20).[23]

4. *Accession songs.* Special mention should be made of the group of hymns which are termed accession songs. They do in fact deserve this name in so far as they extol the beginning of the royal rule of Yahweh or at any rate the fact of

[20] Cf. Albright, *Archaeology and the Religion of Israel* (²1946, ³1953), pp. 126–8, 210.

[21] Johnson, *The Cultic Prophet in Ancient Israel* (1944), pp. 59 f.; (²1962), pp. 69–72.

[22] Aistleitner, BZ 19 (1931), pp. 29–41; Albright, HUCA 23 1 (1951), pp. 1–39; Níl·l· 56 (1955), pp. 1–12; Eerdmans, ET 46 (1934/5), pp. 169–72; Enciso, Est Bíbl 11 (1952), pp. 127–55; Fensham, JNESt 19 (1960), pp. 292–3; Haupt, AJSL 23 (1906/7), pp. 220–40; Iwry, JBL 71 (1952), pp. 161–5; Kaminka, REJ 55 (1908), pp. 146–8; Mowinckel, *Der achtundsechzigste Psalm* (1953); Podechard, RB 54 (1947), pp. 502–20; Tournay, RB 51 (1942), pp. 227–45; Weil, RES (1935) I, pp. III–XVI; RHR, 117 (1938), pp. 75–89. Lit. § 126.

[23] In addition to the psalms which have already been mentioned and those which are next discussed—the accession songs—the following are also to be reckoned among the hymns: viii (de Boer, OTS 2 (1943), pp. 171–93; Kruse, JSSt 5 (1960), pp. 343–7; Louis, *The Theology of Psalm viii* (1946); Morgenstern, HUCA 19 (1945/6), pp. 491–523; Mowinckel, *Studia Or. Ioanni Pedersen* (1953), pp. 250–62; Stamm, ThZ 13 (1957), pp. 470–8). xix (Dürr, *Sellin-Festschr.* (1927), pp. 37–48; Morgenstern, HUCA 19 (1945/6), pp. 491–523; Tournay, *Nötscher-Festschr.* (1950), pp. 271–4; Tur-Sinai, Ar Or 17, II (1949), pp. 419–33; Weippert, ZAW 73 (1961), pp. 97–9). xxix (Caquot, Syria 33 (1956), pp. 36–41; Cross, BASOR 117 (1950), pp. 19–21; Fullerton, JBL 48 (1929), pp. 274–90; Gaster, JQR 37 (1946/7), pp. 55–65; Ginsberg, *Atti del XIX Congr. Or.* (1938), pp. 472–6; Gualandi, Bibl 39 (1958), pp. 478–85; Vogt, Bibl 41 (1960), pp. 17–24). xxxiii (Deissler, *Mél. Bibl. Robert* (1957), pp. 225–33). xxxvi (Le Mat, *Textual Criticism and Exegesis of Psalm xxxvi* (1957)). xlvi (Eissfeldt, ThBl 1 (1922), cols. 54–9; Gaster, ET 71 (1959/60) p. 287; Hans Schmidt, *Luther-Jahrbuch* (1926), pp. 98–119). xlviii (Dahood, CBQ 16 (1954), pp. 15–19; Deissler, BEThL XII (1959), pp. 495–503; Krinetzki, BZ 4 (1960), pp. 70–97; Morgenstern, HUCA 16 (1941), pp. 1–95). lxv, lxvii, lxxvi (Eissfeldt, ThLZ 82 (1957), cols. 801–8; Kroeze, *Genesis Veertien* (1937), pp. 203–5; Talmon, IEJ 10 (1960), pp. 174–80). lxxxiv (Grollenberg, VT 9 (1959), pp. 311 f.; Tournay, RB 54 (1947), pp. 521–33). lxxxvii (Kaminka, REJ 55 (1908), pp. 146–8). cv (Brinktrine, ZAW 64 (1952), pp. 251–8). cxi (Holm-Nielsen, StTh 14 (1960), pp. 35–7). cxiii, cxiv, cxvii, cxxxvi, cxlv (Holm-Nielsen, StTh 14 (1960), pp. 35–7; Liebreich, HUCA 27 (1956), pp. 181–92). cxlvi, cxlvii, cxlix (Gunkel, *Orient. Stud. Paul Haupt* (1926), pp. 47–57). Lit. § 126.

his kingship:[24] Pss. xlvii,[25] xciii,[26] xcvi,[27] xcvii, xcviii, xcix and others. During the last fifty years these songs have frequently been connected with a cultic celebration, though admittedly opinions differ as to the more exact designation of it. Volz, Mowinckel, Hans Schmidt and many others, while differing very much among themselves, think of the accession festival of Yahweh, coinciding with the autumnal and New Year festival. They assume that this festival was celebrated annually in the Jerusalem Temple at any rate by the later period of the monarchy, if not already earlier. Weiser's view also approximates to this conception, but he prefers to consider that the content of the festival was in particular the renewal of the covenant once made by Yahweh with his people, and therefore calls it a covenant-renewal festival. The assigning of the accession songs to the pre-exilic period is probable or at least possible if such a definition is given of the festival which is to be regarded as their setting, but they may also, according to Kraus, have originated only in the post-exilic period. For the celebration to which he assigns them, which he also calls the accession festival of Yahweh, arose in his view first in the post-exilic period, when, under the influence of the message of Deutero-Isaiah, and in particular of his cry of joy addressed to Zion in lii, 7–10, *Your God has become king*, the ancient festival of Zion whose content was the choice of Zion and of David, was replaced by a festival which celebrated the accession not of an earthly king, but of a heavenly king, Yahweh.

If the assigning of the psalms we are here considering to a particular annual festival, however it may exactly be conceived, were correct, then the relationship of a definite series of psalms to a particular cultic occasion would be firmly established. But for the understanding of these songs there is no necessity to assign them to a celebration which in any case is not actually attested but only surmised. The particularly emphatic singling out of the thought of Yahweh's kingly rule, which distinguishes these psalms (xlvii, 3, 7–9; xciii, 1–2; xcvi, 10; xcvii, 1; xcviii, 6; xcix, 1), is to be understood rather as vivid metaphorical actualisation of the conception of Yahweh as king which is also attested elsewhere at an early date,[28] though certainly in this the celebration of the accession of the earthly king has served as a pattern.[29] It is worthy of note that these songs frequently display an eschatological outlook (xcvi, 13; xcviii, 9); the kingly rule of Yahweh of which in the present only tokens are to be seen,

[24] Ludwig Koehler, '*Jahwäh mālāk*' VT 3 (1953), pp. 188 f.; Ridderbos, 'Jahwäh Malak' VT 4 (1954), pp. 87–9. Lit. § 126.
[25] Beaucamp, Bibl 38 (1957), pp. 457–60; Burrows, ZAW 55 (1937), p. 176; Caquot, RHR 39 (1959), pp. 311–37; Muilenburg, JBL 63 (1944), pp. 235–56; Ratschow, ZAW 53 (1935), pp. 171–80.
[26] Jefferson, JBL 71 (1952), pp. 155–60.
[27] Tournay, RB 54 (1947), pp. 533–42; Caquot, Syria 33 (1956), pp. 36–41.
[28] Alt, 'Gedanken über das Königtum Jahwes' *Kl. Schr.* I (1953), pp. 345–57.
[29] Bohl, *Nieuwjaarsfeest en Koningsdag in Babylon en in Israël* (1927) = *Op. Min.* (1953), pp. 263–81, 502–4; Bright, *The Kingdom of God* (1953 [1956]); Eissfeldt, 'Jahwe als König' ZAW 46 (1928), pp. 81–105 = *Kl. Schr.* I (1962), pp. 172–93; Gross, 'Lässt sich in den Psalmen ein "Thronbesteigungsfest Gottes" nachweisen'? Trierer ThZ 65 (1956), pp. 24–40; Michel, 'Studien zu den sogenannten Thronbesteigungspsalmen' VT 6 (1956), pp. 40–68; Pap, *Das israelitische Neujahrsfest* (Diss. Theol. Utrecht, 1933); Snaith, *The Jewish New Year Festival* (1947); Widengren (p. 51, n. 59). Lit. p. 51, n. 59; p. 102, n. 1; § 126.

will then reveal itself in glory visibly to the whole world; of this the worshipping community is quite persuaded.

5. *The 'Sentence of Judgement'*. We must mention here another kind of song which, although it does not belong with the hymn in form but appears in the guise of a 'Sentence of judgement' (p. 76), nevertheless corresponds in content with the hymns in so far as it too extols the power and glory of Yahweh. This is done—and here lies the special characteristic of this type—by presenting a conflict between Yahweh and the other gods and revealing Yahweh as gaining supremacy. There were clearly many such songs, and so it comes about that many traces of them are preserved in the Old Testament. Isa. xli, 21–8[30] belongs among them, an ironic summons by Yahweh to the other gods to produce predictions made by them of events which have actually taken place, so that these may be compared with Cyrus' victorious progress predicted by Yahweh himself. So also does the opening of Ps. lviii,[31] in which the gods—in v. 2 we must certainly read אֵלִים *gods* instead of אֵלֶם *dumbness*—are reproached because instead of being concerned with the upholding of justice, they favour rather injustice and violence. Ps. lxxxii,[32] however, is a complete composition which presents Yahweh in the assembly of the supreme god El making accusation against the other gods that they neglect justice, and declaring that they are not gods at all but are to die like men. It closes with the affirmation that Yahweh is lord over all nations. This psalm, with its recognition of El as the supreme deity—though admittedly quite clearly this is to be understood more as a poetic and mythological statement than as one representing a practical cultic attitude—gives the impression of great antiquity. It may perhaps even be ascribed to David or at any rate to his milieu, and in it may be seen an aspect of the spiritual conflict which was carried on side by side with the military struggle, by which the endeavour was being made to give an ideological justification of the incorporation of Israel's neighbours into the Israelite empire, which must signify at the same time Yahweh's victory over their gods. From this, new light is shed on the one hand upon the accession songs discussed in section 4 (pp. 109–111) and on the other hand upon Pss. xci and cxxi (p. 126) which are perhaps to be understood as 'psalms of conversion'. To the victory of Yahweh over the other gods in the heavenly sphere there corresponds on earth the acceptance by men of the cult of Yahweh.

6. *National laments*. Among the cultic songs which are preserved in the Old Testament, a large place is occupied both within the Psalter and outside it, by the songs of lamentation and of intercession. These include some which are concerned with general needs, in which the whole community, be it city or people, join, though, as for example with Ps. lxxvii,[33] the division between the

---

[30] McEleney, 'The Translation of Isaias xli, 27' CBQ 19 (1957), pp. 441–3; Whitley, 'A Note on Isa. xli, 27' JSSt 2 (1957), pp. 327 f.

[31] Dahood, CBQ 17 (1955), pp. 300–3; Grill, ThPQ 107 (1959), pp. 133–4.

[32] Eissfeldt, JSSt 1 (1956), pp. 29 f.; Gordon, JBL 54 (1935), pp. 139–54; Ludwig Koehler, Kirchenbote Schaffhausen (March 1954), p. 2; Morgenstern, HUCA 14 (1939), pp. 29–126; O'Callaghan, CBQ 15 (1953), pp. 311–14; Podechard, *Mémorial Chaine* (1950), pp. 291–6; Schmidt, BZAW 80 (1961), pp. 32–4; Wright, *The OT against its Environment* (1950), pp. 30–41. Lit. § 126.

[33] Dell'Oca, Rev Bibl 22 (1960), pp. 89–92; Goy, *Hommage à W. Vischer* (1960),

two groups cannot always be sharply made. Others, much more numerous, are concerned with the needs of the individual. We shall discuss first the former group, the collective or national songs of lamentation. Here it is quite clear to what situation they originally belong, and it is also true of them—in this unlike the individual songs of lamentation—that they hardly appear to have lost their connection with the concrete cultic situation. In the historical and prophetic books we often hear of days of fasting and repentance which are evidently specially ordained on each occasion because of some particular distress. The prayer in I Kings viii, 23–53, spoken by Solomon at the dedication of the temple, mentions this cultic custom in vv. 33–40, and enumerates a series of occasions on which such days of repentance and intercession would be held. In I Kings xxi, 9–12, in the narrative of Naboth's vineyard, this custom is presupposed, and Jer. xxxvi, 1–10, the introduction to the narrative concerning the fate of the original scroll of Jeremiah, shows that it would be possible, as Jeremiah here does, to reckon with certainty on the holding in the near future of a fast-day in politically decisive days, when great changes were taking place in the balance of power, changes which must also influence the fate of Judah. The book of Joel gives us a very vivid picture of how such a fast-day was conducted in detail, and shows that prayer and song occupied a considerable place in it. The first two chapters refer to the disaster of a plague of locusts; in i, 13–14, the priests are called upon to lament and to spend the whole night clothed in mourning garments so that they may then call together all the inhabitants of the land to a service of mourning in the temple, and in ii, 12–17, this summons for the holding of a fast-day is emphatically repeated, and in v. 17 a prayer is quoted which is to be recited by the priests, and the exact point at which the recitation is to take place is even indicated: *between the porch and the altar* (cf. also Jdth. iv, 9–15). It is on such occasions that the national lament has its place, and in actual fact the songs which are to be assigned to this type agree with what is quoted in Joel ii, 17 as the prayer of the priests. From the Psalter the following psalms are some of those which belong here: Pss. xliv, lx, lxxiv,[34] lxxix,[35] lxxx,[36] lxxxiii, lxxxix.[37] Central to these songs is always the passionate complaint at the shameful wrong brought upon Israel by the enemies (xliv, 10–17, 20, 26), accompanied by an equally passionate plea for help (xliv, 24–5, 27). To this are added the recollection of Yahweh's favour formerly shown to the people (xliv, 2–4), the expression of trust maintained even now in Yahweh's will and power to bring help in spite of the heavy burden of present trial (xliv, 5–9), the protestation of innocence (xliv, 18–19, 21–2),

pp. 56–62; Grill, BZ 3 (1959), p. 102; Weiser, ThLZ 72 (1947), cols. 133–40 = *Ausg. Schr.* (1961), pp. 280–90. Lit. § 126.
[34] Eliash, JPOS 5 (1925), pp. 55–7; Gaster, ET 68 (1956/7), p. 382; Liebschütz, AJSL 40 (1923/4), pp. 284–7; 41 (1924/5), p. 279; Willesen, VT 2 (1952), pp. 289–306. Lit. § 126.
[35] Glombitza, NThT 14 (1960), pp. 329–49. Lit. § 126.
[36] Eissfeldt, *Alt-Festschr.* (1953), pp. 65–78 (cf. below, p. 284, n. 13); Heinemann, JQR 40 (1949/50), pp. 297–302; Roifer, Tarbiz 29 (1959/60), pp. 113–24, I–II. Lit. § 126.
[37] Ahlström, *Psalm 89. Eine Liturgie aus dem Ritual des leidenden Königs* (Diss. theol. Uppsala, 1959); Baumstark, Or Chr 31 (1934), pp. 1–12; Eissfeldt, *Muilenburg-Festschr.* (1962), pp. 196–207; Hofbauer, BEThL, XII (1959), pp. 504–10; Johnson, *Sacral Kingship* (1955), pp. 22–7, 97–104. Lit. § 126.

and the assurance that the disaster has come upon the offerers of the prayer because of their faithful adherence to Yahweh (xliv, 23). In Ps. lxxix, 13 there is added to these statements which appear fairly generally, the vow of thanksgiving for the naturally anticipated hearing of the prayer, and the complaint of lx, 3–7 is answered in vv. 8–10 by a divine oracle, explicitly introduced as such, to the effect that Yahweh, and so too Israel, is lord of Canaan and the neighbouring lands, and that he will take into possession this territory of his rule. This promise reminds us very strongly of the divine sayings which appear in many of the royal songs (p. 104), and no doubt goes back like the latter to oracles mediated by cult-prophets, though we must certainly reckon with the possibility that we have here an imitation of the ancient custom which has now become simply a matter of form, and that the practice itself did not any longer exist at the date of the song.

As far as the collective songs of lamentation to be found in the Psalter—or at least some part of them—are concerned, there is indeed much which suggests origin in the late post-exilic period. Though certainty is not here attainable, one or two at least seem likely to come from so late a date as the Maccabaean period.[38] But even if this were correct, we may nevertheless prove here as in other cases that the type itself is older, indeed much older, and it may be traced back far into the pre-exilic period—quite apart from the fact that it appears that one of these psalms, Ps. lxxx, may be assigned with some certainty to the second half of the eighth century B.C. (p. 112, n. 36). In the first place, the Babylonians also had such songs of lamentation,[39] and we may assume that these exerted an influence on Israel through the mediacy of the Canaanites, and that in this respect as in others the influence is likely to have begun soon after Israel's occupation of the land. In the second place, there also appear relatively frequently in the writings of the prophets, already even in Hosea, passages which show strong reminiscences of the national songs of lamentation both in form and content, and these must be understood as imitations of the already existing type by the prophets. Among these may be mentioned Hos. vi, 1–6;[40] xiv, 3–9; Jer. iii, 22b–iv, 2; xiv, 7–10; xiv, 19–xv, 4; Isa. lxiii, 7–lxiv, 11, and to these we may also add, because it is also relatively old, ch. v of Lamentations which belongs to this type and certainly came into being shortly after the catastrophe of 587 B.C. In the examples from Hosea and Jeremiah, unlike those in the Psalter, there is expressed a contrite sense of sin and sincere repentance rather than the protestation of innocence which is in the Psalms either explicitly uttered or at least may be read between the lines. But this fact does not prevent our assigning these passages to the type of the national songs of lamentation. For in the light of Israelite beliefs concerning the interrelationship of distress and sin, we may assume *a priori* that the catastrophe which has fallen upon the community will evoke in it varying emotions, depending

[38] Cf. Ackroyd, *The Problem of Maccabaean Psalms* (Thesis Cambridge 1945); cf. VT 3 (1953), pp. 113–32.
[39] KB VI, 2 (1915), pp. 66–71, 82–91; Falkenstein and von Soden (p. 104, n. 8), pp. 183–213, 263–73.
[40] Alt, 'Hosea v, 8–vi, 6' NKZ 30 (1919), pp. 537–68 = *Kl. Schr.* II (1953), pp. 163–87; H. Schmidt, 'Hosea vi, 1–6' *Sellin-Festschr.* (1927), pp. 111–26.

upon whether it feels itself guilty or not, whether it regards the distress as deserved or as undeserved and so as completely inexplicable. If the latter is true, then at the fast which is instigated by the occurrence of the distress, expression will be given to the protestation of innocence alongside complaint and petition. If the former, the community humbly acknowledges the distress as a deserved punishment and prays both for forgiveness of sins and for the removal of the distress. For among the national songs of lamentation to be found in the Psalter we also have some in which there is not lacking the acknowledgement of guilt, at least of the guilt of the people's forefathers, and a plea for forgiveness of sins (lxxiv, 8–9). Furthermore, we shall see, as we might indeed expect, that the individual song of lamentation also has this double attitude towards distress: its recognition as a deserved punishment and the question 'Why?' which arises out of a feeling of innocence (p. 117).

The passages cited from Hosea and Jeremiah as imitations of the national songs of lamentation present, after the people's complaint and petition, a divine utterance which either promises unconditional forgiveness and help (Hos. xiv, 5–9), or else proclaims that it will be forthcoming if there is genuine and lasting conversion (Jer. iv, 1–2 and also Hos. vi, 5–6), or alternatively offers a sharp denial of any mercy (Jer. xiv, 10; xv, 1–4). We may hardly doubt that this divine utterance corresponds to the oracle attested also by Ps. lx, 8–10, by which God, through the mediation of the cult-prophet, reveals his attitude to the people's complaint. We thus have in these prophetic passages very ancient evidence not only for the national song of lamentation itself but also for the divine oracle which follows upon it. From this a new light is shed upon a series of passages from the historical books which mention fasts, questions addressed to Yahweh and his answers, just as at the same time the latter in their turn make completely clear the cultic character of the national song of lamentation together with its accompanying divine utterance. These are such passages as Josh. vii, 6–15; Judg. xx, 26–8; II Kings xix, 14–34; II Chron. xx, 3–17. This last is particularly important. Here, after the quotation of the prayer couched entirely in the style of the national song of lamentation and offered by king Jehoshaphat in his anxiety at the threatened onslaught by great hostile forces, we read: *And Jahaziel . . . the Levite from among the sons of Asaph, upon him came the spirit of Yahweh in the midst of the assembly, and he said: Hearken, all Judah and inhabitants of Jerusalem and king Jehoshaphat! Thus says Yahweh to you: Do not fear, and do not be dismayed at this great multitude; for the battle is not your affair, but God's* (vv. 14–15). Thus it is here directly stated that the divine answer to the complaint offered by the people or by the king speaking on behalf of the people, is given by means of a charismatic. In this instance, it is a Levite who does this, and this confirms the suggestion put forward in another connection that the Levites in many respects entered into the heritage of the pre-exilic cult-prophets and took over their functions (p. 109).

7. *Collective songs of trust.* The expression of confidence (cf. p. 112) which forms one motif of the national song of lamentation, may also become independent and appear as a special song, a collective song of trust. An example of this is Ps. cxxv, which admittedly incorporates a petition in its expression of con-

fidence (v. 4), but may as a whole be understood as a collective song of trust. Much more common, as we shall see (p. 120), is the individual song of trust.

8. *The 'I' of the psalms.* Before we turn to the individual songs of lamentation, we must say a little concerning a question which was for a long time much discussed, as to whether the 'I' of the psalms, and particularly of the songs of lamentation, is to be understood individually or collectively, i.e. whether it is to be regarded as referring to the individual or to the people or community.[41] At an earlier period, the collective interpretation enjoyed great popularity, but for the last fifty years, in particular as a result of the work of Gunkel, Balla and Begrich, there has been a swing of the pendulum and many scholars have wished to see in the 'I' exclusively the individual. Even if they did not entirely deny the possibility that it could sometimes also denote the people or the community, they limited it too narrowly. Recently Mowinckel, in reaction against the exaggeration of this interpretation of the 'I' of the psalms as an individual, which is very largely correct, has rightly pointed out,[42] that there is a kernel of truth in Smend's collective 'I' in the royal psalms and in the national psalms of lamentation. Indeed this is quite clear for example in the song of thankgsiving Ps. cxxix, *They have often oppressed me from my youth up let Israel now say,* for here in the 'I' the people is to be understood. We must therefore reckon with the possibility that some few of the psalms here described as individual, and particularly the songs of lamentation, are to be interpreted collectively. But in the overwhelming majority of the psalms, both within the Psalter and outside it, the 'I' certainly indicates the pious individual.

9. *Individual laments.* What the national song of lamentation means for the community, the individual song of lamentation[43] means for the individual Israelite. It is very well represented in the Psalter: some forty psalms are to be reckoned to this type.[44] But such songs also appear not infrequently outside

[41] Smend, 'Über das Ich der Psalmen' ZAW 8 (1888), pp. 49–147.

[42] *Offersang og sangoffer* (1951), pp. 50–91, 227–48; E.T. *The Psalms in Israel's Worship* (1962), I, pp. 42–80, 225–46.

[43] Wevers, 'A Study in the Form Criticism of Individual Complaint Psalms' VT 6 (1956), pp. 80–96.

[44] Ps. iii (Tournay, RB 52 (1945), pp. 214–16). v, vi, vii (Leveen, JRAS (1946), pp. 81–3). xii (Wernberg-Møller, ZAW 69 (1957), pp. 69–71). xiii, xvii (Gualandi, Bibl 37 (1956), pp. 199–208; Leveen, VT 11 (1961), pp. 48–54; Pautrel, RSR 46 (1958), pp. 78–84). xxii (Asensio, Gregorianum 33 (1952), pp. 219–260, 566–611; Beer, BZAW 41 (1925), pp. 12–20; Courte, *Le psaume vingt-deuxième* (1932); Feuillet, NRTh 70 (1948), pp. 137–49; Westermann, BSt 8 (1955)). xxv (Holm-Nielsen, StTh 14 (1960), pp. 45–8). xxvi, xxvii, 7–14 (Birkeland, ZAW 51 (1933), pp. 216–21). xxviii, xxxi, xxxv (Driver, ThZ 9 (1953), pp. 468 f.; Magne, RB 54 (1947), pp. 42–53). xxxviii, xxxix, xlii+xliii (Kruse, JSSt 5 (1960), pp. 333–43; Lákatos, RBiLit 14 (1952), pp. 105–11; Rowley, Bibl 21 (1940), pp. 45–50). li (Press, ThZ 11 (1955), pp. 241–9; Steuernagel, *Sellin-Festschr.* (1927), pp. 151–6; Stoebe (BSt 20, 1958)). liv, lv, lvii (Pautrel, RSR 44 (1956), pp. 566–72; Slotki, Journal Manchester Eg. Or. Soc. 18 (1933), pp. 61–5). lix, lxi, lxiii, lxiv (Dell'Oca, Rev Bibl 22 (1960), pp. 89–92; Strobel, RB 57 (1950), pp. 161–73). lxix, lxx, lxxi (Tournay, *Nötscher-Festschr.* (1950), pp. 274–80). lxxvii (Lit. p. 111, n. 33). lxxxv (Dahood, Bibl 37 (1956), pp. 338–40; Nober, VD 38 (1960), pp. 34–5). lxxxvi, lxxxviii (Hofbauer, BEThL XII (1959), pp. 504–10; Joüon, RSR 27 (1937), pp. 440–56). cii, 1–12, 24–9, cix (Creager, JNESt 6 (1947), pp. 121–3). cxx, cxxvi (Morgenstern, *Homenaje a Millás-Vallicrosa* II (1956), pp. 109–117; Strugnell, JThSt 7 (1956), pp. 239–43). cxxx (Cornill, BZAW 34 (1920), pp. 38–42; Porúbčan, VT 9 (1959), pp. 322–3; Volz, BZAW 41 (1925), pp. 287–96). cxl, cxli (Pautrel, RSR 44 (1956), pp. 219–28; Tournay, VT 9 (1959), pp. 58–64).

the Psalter. Jeremiah and the compiler of the book of Job were particularly fond of making use of this form. It is also represented in the last stages of Old Testament literature; thus the Prayer of Manasseh is, as far as style is concerned, a pure example of the individual psalm of lamentation. The distresses which lead to the offering of the individual lament are above all illness and the insults and mockery of enemies. These two types of distress may indeed belong together in that the sickness which has come upon the one who offers the prayer, and which according to Old Testament conceptions is regarded as divine punishment, quite naturally had as its consequence mockery and evil intrigues. However, in general at least, we seem here to be dealing with real illness, even if its severity is sometimes exaggerated, and even if the statement that the worshipper is already plunged into the underworld, stands at the point of death and the like,[45] is likely to be rather an expression directed to the evoking of divine sympathy than an exact description of reality.[46] Similarly the enemies, concerning whose dangerous attitude the worshipper complains passionately, are really his personal opponents. It is true that Gunkel and Mowinckel were right in rejecting the view formerly much favoured—set forth for example by Smend— that the 'workers of inquity' (פֹּעֲלֵי אָוֶן) often mentioned in these psalms as the opponents of the pious are to be associated with the party of the godless who stand over against the party of the pious, and so that these psalms derive from the party divisions, assumed rather than precisely demonstrated, of post-exilic Judaism. Instead they see in this the simple presence together and opposition to one another of pious and impious men, such as existed in ancient Israel, as indeed everywhere else. But it can hardly be right to interpret the evil-doers as magicians, exorcists and witches who have brought about the illness of the worshipper by their devices, as has been suggested by Mowinckel and elaborated by others, e.g. by Nicolsky.[47] It is more likely that these evil-doers are none other than the impious, who not only trouble the pious by actual hostile behaviour but cause them anxiety by reason of what the latter regard as their entirely undeserved good fortune. This also makes it clear that the view of Birkeland[48] can hardly be regarded as correct, namely that, in association with his conception of the individual songs of lamentation as entirely or largely originating in reference to the king and subsequently given a 'democratising'

cxlii, cxliii. Cf. the 'Babylonian-Assyrian songs of lamentation' AOT, pp. 257–63; ANET, pp. 383–5, 391 f.; DOTT, pp. 111–17; Falkenstein and von Soden (p. 104, n. 8), pp. 183–213, 263–73; Castellino, *Le lamentazioni individuali e gli inni in Babilonia e in Israele* (1939); Widengren, *The Accadian and Hebrew Psalms of Lamentation as Religious Documents* (1936). Lit. § 126.

[45] Barth, *Die Errettung vom Tode in den individuellen Klage- und Dankliedern des Alten Testaments* (1947); Bentzen, 'Der Tod des Beters in den Psalmen' *Eissfeldt-Festschrift* (1947), pp. 57–60.

[46] Cf. A. R. Johnson, *The Vitality of the Individual in the thought of Ancient Israel* (1949), esp. pp. 88 ff.

[47] Nicolsky, *Spuren magischer Formeln in den Psalmen* (BZAW 46, 1927).

[48] Birkeland, *Die Feinde des Individuums in der israelitischen Psalmenliteratur* (1933); *The Evildoers in the Book of Psalms* (ANVAO, 1955, No. 2, 1955); *Myt och historia i Psaltaren* (1955); Puukko, 'Der Feind in den alttestamentlichen Psalmen' OTS 8 (1950), pp. 47–65; Ridderbos, *De 'werkers der ongerechtigheid' in de individueele Psalmen* (1939). Lit. p. 448, n. 8.

interpretation with reference to the Israelites or specifically to the pious, the evil-doers mentioned in the psalms are to be understood as foreign enemies. We may say this in spite of the fact that Mowinckel has shown an inclination to agree at least in some measure with this view.

Thus central to the individual songs of lamentation is complaint of bodily suffering and assaults by enemies. So the invocation of Yahweh which stands at the beginning is followed by the complaint at this double distress (Pss. iii, 2–3; xiii, 2–3) and then further by a prayer for deliverance (Pss. iii, 8; xiii, 4–5), by expressions of trust (Pss. iii, 4–7; xiii, 6a), protestations of innocence and cursing of the enemies (Ps. xvii, 3–5, 13–14) or perhaps by a confession of guilt and a prayer for forgiveness (Pss. xxxviii, 5, 19; cxxx, 3–4, 7), and by a varied series of observations, for example on the brevity of human life (Ps. xxxix, 5–6) or on the fact that Yahweh cannot have any advantage in the death of his saints, since he would thereby merely lose one of his worshippers (Ps. vi, 6). At the end, there is normally an expression of certainty that the prayer will be heard (Ps. xxviii, 6–7; Man. 14), a promise of thanksgiving is stated (Pss. xiii, 6b; xxvi, 12; Man. 15), and this song of thanksgiving may itself in fact be spoken in anticipation (Ps. xxii, 23–5). In Ps. lv, there stands at the end a saying addressed to the worshipper assuring him of help from his God (v. 23). Among the passages from the book of Jeremiah which belong here (xi, 18–23; xii, 1–3, 5–6; xv, 10–11, 15–21; xx, 7–13), the last mentioned closes, like most of the psalms which come under consideration here, with an expression of certainty of being heard (vv. 12–13), whereas in the other three Jeremiah's complaint is followed by Yahweh's answer (xi, 21–3; xii, 5–6; xv, 19–21), and in xi, 21 and xv, 19, this answer is explicitly introduced as such. Thus we have here a situation exactly like that in the collective songs of lamentation. The prophets, in their imitations of these two types, have adhered more closely to the form of the divine utterance answering the complaint than have the two relevant groups of psalms. For it is extremely probable that in the individual songs of lamentation too the expression of certainty of being heard which forms their conclusion, ultimately derives from the adaptation of the cultic divine utterance which provides a reply to the complaint. Even if we have no other explicit evidence for this, the narrative of Hezekiah's illness (Isa. xxxviii) nevertheless points in this direction. When Hezekiah is made aware of his approaching death (v. 1) he prays to Yahweh exactly in the style of the individual songs of lamentation (vv. 2–3), and there then follows the divine answer to him mediated by Isaiah to the effect that Yahweh has heard his prayer (vv. 4–6). Later we shall see (pp. 122 f.) that there then follows the song of thanks uttered by Hezekiah after his recovery, and that this too exactly corresponds to cultic practice. The fact that the form of the divine utterance is preserved in Jeremiah, but not in general in the relevant psalms and in other passages of the Old Testament which belong in this connection, may well be explained from the fact that Jeremiah, in spite of his protests against the cultus or against the wrongly evaluated cultus (vii, 1–15), stands in fact very close to it, closer evidently than the authors of the psalms in question. We need not therefore feel any surprise if it was cult-prophets— and thus actually associates of Jeremiah—who mediated such divine utterances, quite apart from the possibility, which must seriously be considered in view of a section like xiv, 1–xv, 4, that Jeremiah too occasionally functioned as such (p. 356).

If we are right in deriving the expression of certainty which stands at the end of the majority of the individual songs of lamentation from the divine utterance which answers the complaint, then this clearly implies that the individual song of lamentation, exactly like the collective one, originally belongs in the cultus and was there pronounced by the individual sufferers themselves or by cultic officials acting as their representatives. But at the same time it is also clear that the individual songs of lamentation which are preserved in the Psalter and elsewhere in the Old Testament have become more detached from the cultus than the imitations of this type which are to be found in Jeremiah, where the divine utterance is itself clearly indicated. They have thus become 'spiritual songs' or are at any rate on the way to becoming such. This means that we may take up a position in regard to the question, often discussed recently, as to whether the individual songs of lamentation in the Psalter are cultic songs, which were recited at ceremonies such as those of protestation of innocence, purification, atonement, and the like; or whether they are the private outpourings of pious individuals. Mowinckel has opted decisively for the first alternative, and has thus made such an impact upon psalm study that many scholars relate nearly all the psalms, and especially the individual songs of lamentation, to particular cultic actions. Gunkel, on the other hand, who did in fact first point out the historical connections of the individual psalms of lamentation with the cultus, has not concealed his doubts about the assumption that the individual songs of lamentation which are preserved in the Psalter are all or mainly actual cultic songs, nor his preference for the view that they are rather to be regarded as 'spiritual songs'. It is extremely difficult to arrive at a firm decision in this matter. It depends in the main on the decision as to whether the expressions which refer to cultic matters are to be regarded as statements of fact or as metaphors, an alternative which often faces the student of Old Testament poetry in other problems too. Whereas earlier there was a tendency to treat all such material more as metaphorical statement, the tendency prevails today to find realities everywhere and so to refer the relevant expressions in the psalms to cultic practices. This has come about because, thanks to the rich results of excavations in and especially around Palestine and also to the study of comparative religion and culture which is particularly concerned with its 'primitive' elements, we may picture the cultic life of ancient Israel much more vividly and clearly than earlier generations could do.

Statements such as that the worshipper enters the house of Yahweh and may worship before his holy temple (Ps. v, 8), make it quite clear that the temple plays a part in his piety, but it by no means follows that the song in which such expressions appear must be one which belongs in the cultus, any more than, on the other hand, the prophetic threats against the temple (Micah iii, 12; Jer. vii, 14–15) are of cultic type. Each of them merely gives us some information concerning the general nature of piety in those times, but nothing concerning the exact character of the particular passages. Nor does the expres-

sion used in Pss. xxxviii, 7; xlii, 10, that the worshipper enters in mourning—
and no doubt this means clothed in mourning garments—tell us anything about
the cultic character of these two psalms or of their forerunners. Here we simply
learn something about a mourning custom then general, quite apart from the
question as to whether the expressions are really to be understood literally, or
only as a metaphor for an inner mood. More important statements, as for
example that the worshipper implores Yahweh in the morning (Pss. v, 4;
lxxxviii, 14),[49] do not in themselves mean anything precise; for outside the
psalms too, where cultic ideas do not come in question (Isa. xvii, 14; Ps. xlvi, 6),
the morning appears as the time of divine help, whereas evening and night are
times of distress (Isa. xvii, 14); and this is psychologically intelligible. More
significant is a prayer like that of Ps. li, 9: *Purge me with hyssop, that I may be
clean.* For though here too we are certainly dealing with a metaphorical expression, it is nevertheless probable that this picture goes back to a ceremony of
purification which was formerly actually carried out, and it may readily be
assumed that the prayer uttered in this psalm was originally spoken to make
effective that ceremony of purification. This is all the more clear since in Isa. vi,
6–7, we have explicit attestation of a similar ceremony of purification, which is
preceded not admittedly by the prayer that it should be undertaken but by the
expression of the need for purification (vi, 5). These considerations are all the
more impressive when we look at Babylonian individual prayers of lamentation,
which are not only very similar to those in the Old Testament, but also clearly
reveal connections with ceremonies of purification.[50]

Hans Schmidt has put forward the view, with reference to some of the individual songs of lamentation, that they belong to a procedure of legal examination, with a view to obtaining divine judgement, which took place with the
accused at a holy place, and that they were here recited by the accused or on his
behalf during the proceedings, partly—namely the complaint and prayer—
before the divine judgement decision, and in part—namely the thanksgiving
which frequently stands at the end—after the pronouncement of the oracle in
favour of the accused. He therefore calls these psalms 'prayers of the accused'.
In fact, in Pss. vii, xxxv, lvii, and lxix some part of the material can be understood as pointing to the setting of a cultic legal procedure.[51] The assumption
therefore that some of the individual songs of lamentation which are preserved
in the Psalter are prayers of the accused or—for this possibility too must also
be considered here as elsewhere—are imitations of this type which have become
'spiritual songs', deserves a certain attention even though no really convincing
proof can be given for this.

It thus appears probable that the individual song of lamentation which is so
well represented in the Old Testament, was originally a cultic song, and was
associated with quite specific cultic actions. But it is certain on the other hand

[49] Hempel, 'Die Lichtsymbolik im AT' StG 13 (1960), pp. 351–68, pp. 358–66: 'Der
rettende Morgen'; Ziegler, 'Die Hilfe Gottes "am Morgen"' *Nötscher-Festschr.* (1950),
pp. 281–8.
[50] AOT, pp. 257–81; ANET, pp. 383–5; Meissner, *Bab. und Ass.* II (1925), pp. 96–7,
238–41; *Bab.-Ass. Lit.* (1928), p. 66.
[51] Cf. I Kings viii, 31 f. (I am indebted to Ackroyd for this reference).

that a large proportion of the individual songs of lamentation which have come down to us were composed without reference to the cultus, and represent private utterances of pious individuals. Songs such as Pss. xxxix, li and cxxx are couched in such personal terms and have such a deeply religious content that the assumption that they were composed as texts to accompany cultic actions is very artificial, and alphabetic songs like Ps. xxv also do not suit the cultus very well. Here, as with other types, we must rather assume that the cultic song led to the development of a private poetry not tied to the cult. This may have begun already fairly early, and this is indeed likely even at the time when the cultic song of lamentation itself had not yet ceased to exist. We have seen (pp. 116 f.) that Jeremiah has a tendency to use this form for the expression of his inner tensions. It was thus at that time already possible to utilise it for the expression of quite personal feelings. It is then easy to understand how Jewish piety very readily made use of this form, a form particularly appropriate for the expression of distress. Post-exilic Judaism, both as a community and as far as its individual members were concerned, was burdened with much external distress and even more inner distress, and was thus glad to be able to pour out this distress before its God in song and prayer, and so to find itself filled by him with new power and new confidence.

10. *Individual songs of trust.* We have seen that in the individual songs of lamentation, as in the collective ones, there is frequent expression of trust in Yahweh, scattered among the complaints and prayers. This motif of the individual psalm of lamentation sometimes became independent, and thus was developed into complete, though normally brief, songs of trust. To such belong Pss. iv;[52] xi;[53] xxiii;[54] xxvii, 1–6;[55] lxii;[56] xci;[57] cxxi[58] and cxxxi, though, as will be shown on p. 126, this is only partly true of Ps. xci and Ps. cxxi. In these it is quite clear that we are dealing with 'spiritual songs' and this fact gives added weight to the reasonable assumption that at least quite a number of the individual songs of lamentation are also to be so understood.

11. *Collective songs of thanksgiving.* We have repeatedly noted at the end of the songs of lamentation, both collective and individual, not only the expression of certainty of being heard, but also already the thanksgiving itself for the help and deliverance awaited with such certainty, or, in the 'prayers of the accused', perhaps already experienced. It is quite natural that this thanksgiving itself has

[52] Dürr, Bibl 16 (1935), pp. 330–8; Tournay, RB 52 (1945), pp. 216–19.

[53] Morgenstern, JBL 69 (1950), pp. 221–31; Sonne, JBL 68 (1949), pp. 241–5.

[54] Asensio, Bibl 40 (1959), pp. 237–47; Dürr, Heil. Land 79 (1935), pp. 57–65; Haupt, AJSL 21 (1905/6), pp. 133–52; Ludwig Köhler, ZAW 68 (1957), pp. 227–34; Morgenstern, JBL 65 (1946), pp. 13–24; Pfeiffer, VT 8 (1958), pp. 219–20; Schildenberger, Bibel und Kirche 15 (1960), pp. 49–51; Vogt, Bibl 34 (1953), pp. 195–211. Lit. § 126.

[55] Birkeland, ZAW 51 (1933), pp. 216–21; cf. above, p. 115, n. 44.

[56] Honeyman, VT 11 (1961), pp. 348–50. Lit. § 126.

[57] Caquot, Semitica 8 (1958), pp. 21–37; Eissfeldt, WdO II, 4 (1957), pp. 343–8; de Fraine, Bibl 40 (1959), pp. 372–83; Löw, *Goldziher Mem. Vol.* I (1948), p. 328; Wensinck, *Sem. Stud. uit de Nalatenschap* (1941), pp. 14–22. On Ps. xci cf. also p. 126.

[58] Eissfeldt, *Lilje-Festschr.* (1959), pp. 9–14; Morgenstern, JBL 58 (1939), pp. 311–23; Pollock, JBL 59 (1940), pp. 411 f. On Ps. cxxi, cf. also p. 126.

soon created forms of its own, and the expectation that we should find such songs of thanksgiving[59] preserved in the Psalter too and generally in the Old Testament is not disappointed. The position is, however, that collective songs of thanksgiving corresponding to the collective songs of lamentation are far fewer in number than the individual songs of thanksgiving. This may clearly be explained by the fact that the community could express its thanksgiving, and doubtless did so, in another form, namely the hymn. For the hymn presents the exaltation of Yahweh because of his deeds in Israel's history too. Thus if the people, or at any rate a large part of it, had cause to give thanks for a deliverance which it had experienced as a unit, the hymn naturally presented itself as the medium of such thanksgiving. Nevertheless we have a group of psalms which give more particular expression to the thanksgiving for help which has been experienced by Israel as a whole, and these are to be described as collective songs of thanksgiving. Ps. cxxxvi is an example. This begins in vv. 1–3 and closes in v. 26 with a summons to give thanks. In vv. 4–25 the deeds of Yahweh, and especially his deeds of kindness to Israel, are praised in hymnlike fashion. The psalm is so constructed that the first half of each verse contains the summons to give thanks (vv. 1–3, 26) and the enumeration of the deeds of Yahweh (vv. 4–25) whereas the second half is identical throughout: *For his kindness endures for ever*. The psalm is thus clearly intended for recital by leaders and choir or by two choirs, and is thus indicated as a cultic song. In II Chron. vii, 3, 6, we do in fact hear of cultic occasions on which were recited such songs of thanksgiving, containing this refrain: *For his kindness endures for ever* (cf. Jer. xxxiii, 11; Ps. cxviii, 1–4;[60] Ecclus. li (1)–(16)). Even if Ps. cxxxvi derives from a fairly late post-exilic period, it nevertheless certainly had older forerunners. The same is true of Ps. lxvii, a national song of thanksgiving which clearly, according to v. 7, was sung at the harvest festival, and this too is to be thought of as recited antiphonally. In contrast to Pss. lxvii and cxxxvi, the short psalms cxxiv and cxxix, rich in content and inner feeling, are 'spiritual songs' of thanksgiving.

12. *Individual songs of thanksgiving*. Much more numerous than the collective songs of thanksgiving are the individual ones, and with these again the position is that although they may no longer themselves be all actually cultic, yet their connection with cultic song is completely clear. They have the same name as the *thank-offering* תּוֹדָה (Jonah ii, 10; Pss. l, 14, 23; cvii, 22), in itself a clear proof of the fact that they originally belong with the thank-offering;[61] and this conclusion is fully confirmed by the many expressions which clearly refer to the sacrifice. Ps. lxvi contains in its first part (vv. 2–12) motifs from the hymn and the collective song of lamentation, but its second part (vv. 13–20) is an individual song of thanksgiving. This second part begins:

[59] Mand, 'Die Eigenständigkeit der Danklieder des Psalters als Bekenntnislieder' ZAW 70 (1958), pp. 185–99.

[60] Becker, ZAW 70 (1958), p. 174; Meysing, VT 10 (1960), pp. 130–37; Hans Schmidt, ZAW 40 (1923), pp. 1–14.

[61] Cf. Ps. c, 1, מִזְמוֹר לְתוֹדָה (I am indebted to Ackroyd for this reference).

I come into thy house with burnt offerings,
  I pay to thee my vows,
for which my lips opened,
  and which my mouth spoke in my distress

and then, after further words concerning the offerings, it continues:

Come, hear, that I may relate   all ye who fear Yahweh
  what he has done for me.

Ps. cxvi[62] speaks similarly of the thank-offerings and vows which the worshipper presents before all the people in the courts of the temple of Yahweh (vv. 17–19), and in v. 13 the worshipper promises:

The cup of salvation I will raise   and call on the name of Yahweh.

That we are here dealing with an actual cultic action, or at least with a metaphorical expression which is based upon it, can in this case be proved. A fifth-century B.C. votive stele of Yeḥawmilk, king of Byblos, of which the text refers to a favour shown to him by his goddess Baʿalat of Byblos, has a picture on the space provided above the text, and this portrays the king standing before the goddess who sits upon her throne; he holds in his hand a libation cup, and offers it to her,[63] and the text contains the following words[64] in lines 7–8: *Yehawmilk, king of Byblos, to my lady, Baʿalat of Byblos. For when I cried to my lady, Baʿalat of Byblos, then she heard me and showed me favour.* Thus the Phoenician cultus too was familiar with the gesture of thanksgiving which the psalm passage attests, and the words quoted from the inscription lead to the surmise that there existed there too songs of thanksgiving similar to those of the Old Testament, as we have similar ones in Egypt in fair numbers and in fact from a very early date.[65] The two psalms, lxvi and cxvi, especially if they are taken together with parallels from elsewhere, give us a very clear picture of the cultic situation of the song of the thank-offering. It was recited in the presence of the people, that is we may suppose at any rate primarily the friends of the worshipper, on the occasion of sacrifices and other thanksgiving rituals. This is confirmed not only by similar passages such as Ps. cxviii, 19–21; Jonah ii, 10, but also by Ps. xl, 2–12, which presents the worshipper in vv. 7–9[66] as saying that he well knows God's disinclination for sacrifices and therefore wishes to bring to him as thanksgiving that in which he really takes pleasure, namely obedience. Such songs of thanksgiving were uttered after the averting of distress, in particular after recovery from an illness. This may be seen from Isa. xxxviii, 9, where it is stated

[62] Daiches, *Gaster Anniversary Vol.* (1936), pp. 64–7; Ina Lohr, *Pro regno, pro sanctuario*, Festschr. van der Leeuw (1950), pp. 317–21.
[63] AOB, fig. 516; cf. also Gressmann, 'Der Festbecher' *Sellin-Festschr.* (1927), pp. 55–62, and Ginsberg, 'Psalms and Inscriptions of Petition and Acknowledgment' *L. Ginzberg Jub. Vol.* I (1945), pp. 159–71.
[64] Cooke, NSI, pp. 18–26, No. 3; Lidzbarski, AST, pp. 12–15, No. 5; AOT, p. 446; ANET, p. 502.
[65] AOT, p. 32; ANET, pp. 380 f.
[66] Sofia Cavaletti, RStO 32 (1957), pp. 293–9.

concerning the song of thanksgiving which is put into the mouth of Hezekiah in xxxviii, 10–20,[67] that he prayed it after recovery from his illness.

The structure of the songs of thanksgiving is more or less constant, whether they are genuine cultic songs or 'spiritual songs' which have developed from them, the latter hardly to be differentiated from the former. In the introduction, normally short and sometimes omitted altogether, the worshipper announces his intention of giving thanks to God (Ps. xxx, 2). This is followed by the main section in which there is a narration of the worshipper's experience, the terrible distress in which he found himself (Jonah ii, 4–7a),[68] the prayer which he then directed to Yahweh (Jonah ii, 3, 8), and the deliverance which he experienced (Jonah ii, 7b). The song closes with the declaration that the worshipper now intends to return thanks (Jonah ii, 10), or with the confession that Yahweh is gracious, which summarises the worshipper's experience (Pss. xxxiv, 23; cxxxviii, 8a), or with a prayer for further help (Pss. xl, 12; cxxxviii, 8b), or even with some other formula (Pss. xxxii, 11; lxvi, 20). We may recognise how firmly fixed the form of the song of thanksgiving was by a further fact. Approximately thirty-five 'Songs of thanksgiving' came to light near Qumrān in 1947, belonging to the sectarian community which was settled in and around Qumrān and originated in about 100 B.C.[69] In spite of all the peculiarities which belong to the particular nature and fortunes of that sectarian community, these are nevertheless in all essentials constructed exactly like the songs of the Psalter which belong to this group.

One of the songs of thanksgiving in the Psalter, Ps. cvii, deserves further special mention. Here the individual worshippers appear in groups, and it is in this way at one and the same time an individual and a collective song of thanksgiving. The psalm, or more precisely its main part vv. 1–32, begins with a general summons to give thanks utilising the phrase already noted: *Give thanks to the Lord, for he is gracious and his kindness endures for ever.* It is then divided into four sections in which four groups of people are called upon to thank God for the deliverance which they have experienced in their own particular distress, viz. (1) those who had gone astray in the wilderness (vv. 4–9), (2) those who lay in prison (vv. 10–16), (3) those who had suffered from the most severe sickness (vv. 17–22), and (4) those who had experienced terrible distress at sea (vv. 23–32). In similar terms, and with a refrain, it is said by these four groups that they cried to Yahweh in their distress and that they were delivered by him (vv. 6, 13, 19, 28), and similarly all four are summoned with the same words, also in refrain form, to thank God (vv. 8, 15, 21, 31). The psalm concludes with a hymn—regarded by many, as for example by Gunkel, as a secondary addition

[67] Begrich, *Der Psalm des Hiskia* (FRLANT 42, 1926); de Boer, 'Notes on the Text and Meaning of Isaiah xxxviii, 9–20' OTS 9 (1951), pp. 170–86.

[68] On Jonah ii, 3–10, cf. A. R. Johnson, StOTPr (1950), pp. 82–102.

[69] Sukenik, אוצר המגילות הגנוזות, 1954 = *The Dead Sea Scrolls of the Hebrew University* (1955), Pls. 35–58; J. Licht, מגילת ההודיות ממגילות מדבר יהודה (1957); Translations: Bardtke, *Die Handschriftenfunde am Toten Meer* (²1953), pp. 150–66; Millar Burrows, *The Dead Sea Scrolls* (1956), pp. 400–15; Dupont-Sommer, *Les écrits esséniens découverts près de la Mer Morte* (1959), pp. 213–66; E.T. *The Essene Writings from Qumran* (1961), pp. 202–54; T. H. Gaster, *The Scriptures of the Dead Sea Sect* (1957), pp. 131–217. Cf. below, § 108. Lit. § 126.

—which extols Yahweh as the real 'worker of wonders who can both exalt and abase'[70] (vv. 33–43). It may be assumed that we have here a song which was sung at a great festival of thanksgiving, more probably on behalf of the multitude of those who have been saved than actually by them. At any rate the fact that the individual groups are summoned to give thanks and do not actually pronounce this in the first person form, suggests that it might reasonably be assumed that various choirs direct the summons to the individual groups, and that these either in silence or with the Amen expressed their agreement and then finally the whole assembly sang the hymn together.

§ 16. WISDOM POEMS

Literature: Gunkel and Begrich (§ 14), pp. 381–97; Mowinckel, *Offersang og sangoffer* (1951), pp. 368–82, E.T. *The Psalms in Israel's Worship* (1962), II, pp. 104–25; 'Psalms and Wisdom' SVT III (1955), pp. 205–24; Munch, 'Die jüdischen "Weisheitspsalmen" und ihr Platz im Leben' Ac Or [L] 15 (1936), pp. 112–40.
Cf. also Literature §§ 11, 64, 65, 88, 126.

While the main body of the psalms gathered in the Psalter is made up of cultic and spiritual songs, there are nevertheless in addition some which are of an instructional nature. Some of these, in the style of the hymn, extol the high value of wisdom, others, like the wisdom sayings, contain admonitions to goodness and warnings against evil, while others raise a problem, more precisely the vexatious problem as to why so often things go well for the godless but badly for the pious. Such wisdom poems of larger or smaller compass also appear outside the Psalter, especially frequently in Prov., Job and Ecclus., as for example Prov. viii, 1–36[1]—Wisdom recommends herself as teacher; ix, 1–18 —Dame Wisdom and Dame Folly invite men to a feast; Job xxviii—The Unattainableness of Wisdom; Ecclus. i, 1–20—The Origin of Wisdom; Job xviii, 5–21; xx, 5–29; xxvii, 11–23—The terrible end of the godless; Ecclus. xiv, 20-xv, 10—The Blessing of Wisdom; Prov. xxxi, 10–31—'The Praise of the virtuous housewife'.[2] These wisdom poems derive from the circles of the wise (p. 86), who here go beyond the form of the wisdom saying which is really their original province and make use of the song form for the expression of their feelings, reflections, admonitions and warnings. These wisdom poems reveal a whole wealth of indications to show that their compilers are very familiar with the wisdom saying. Sometimes, as in Ps. xlix, 5, such a song is in fact called a *wisdom saying* (מָשָׁל). Several of them begin with the expression *Happy is he* or *Blessed is he* (אַשְׁרֵי),[3] which belongs in the circle of the wisdom

---

[70] '. . . der rechte Wundermann, der bald erhöhen, bald stürzen kann.'
[1] Cazelles, 'L'enfantement de la Sagesse en Prov. viii' BEThL XII (1959), pp. 511–15; Scott, 'Wisdom in Creation: the *'āmôn* of Proverbs viii, 30' VT 10 (1960), pp. 213–23.
[2] Margaret B. Crook, 'The Marriageable Maiden of Proverbs xxxi, 10–31' Theology Digest 5 (1957), p. 72. Lit. § 126.
[3] Dodd, 'The Beatitudes' *Mél. Bibl. Robert* (1957), pp. 404–10; George, 'La "forme" des Béatitudes jusqu'à Jésus' *Mél. Bibl. Robert* (1957), pp. 398–403. Lit. p. 126, n. 14; § 126.

teachers—so Ps. i. Their derivation from men, or perhaps also women, who normally employ the wisdom saying, is betrayed in many of the wisdom songs by the further fact that they contain lines, which, as in Ps. xxxvii, 16, have the appearance of being independent sayings, or by the fact that they are loose collections of individual sayings rather than a connected composition with an unbroken sequence of thought. It is not surprising that the wisdom poems, as for example Pss. xxxvii, cxii; Prov. xxxi, 10–31, particularly favour the use of the alphabetic acrostic form, which does in fact make the linking together of unconnected individual sayings easy and is able to distract our attention from the lack of unified composition.

The boundaries between the types to which the songs belong within the Psalter and outside it, are everywhere fluid, so there is only a limited validity in the separating out of the wisdom songs from among them. Yet in the Psalter Pss. i,[4] xxxvii,[5] xlix,[6] lxxiii,[7] lxxviii,[8] xci,[9] cxii,[10] cxxviii and cxxxiii,[11] belong here at any rate. The same is true of Psalms cv and cvi which provide a retrospect of Israel's history (p. 16) and in this are similar to Ps. lxxviii. It is, however, to be noted that Ps. cv also has hymnic features and has for this reason been reckoned among the hymns (p. 109, n. 23). Two further psalms may also be reckoned to this group. The first is Ps. xc[12] the main section of which, vv. 1–12, presents an impressive reflection on the brevity of human life, while its conclusion, vv. 13–17, perhaps added later, implores the mercy of Yahweh in the style of the national lament. The other is Ps. cxxxix[13] which also has in other respects a largely hymnic character, but may on the whole be regarded as a devotional reflection on God's omniscience and omnipresence—perhaps occasioned by the suspicion raised against the worshipper that he has associated with the impious. Psalms xxxvii, xlix and lxxiii, with all their individual differences, have in common that they inquire concerning the reason for the good fortune of the godless and the misfortune of the pious. They answer this urgent question either with a reference to the catastrophe which will eventually fall

---

[4] Auvray, RB 53 (1946), pp. 365–71; Botterweck, ThQ 138 (1958), pp. 129–51; Engnell *Studia Or. Ioanni Pedersen* (1953), pp. 85–96; Haupt, AJSL 19 (1903/4), pp. 129–42; Joüon, RSR 27 (1937), pp. 440–56. Lit. § 126.

[5] Allegro, PEQ 86 (1954), pp. 69–75, Pl. XVIII; Holm-Nielsen, StTh 14 (1960), pp. 37–9; Munch, ZAW 55 (1937), pp. 36–46.

[6] Lindblom, *Mélanges d'histoire des religions . . . J. Pedersen* (Horae Soederblomianae I, 1944), pp. 21–7; Munch, ZAW 55 (1937), pp. 36–46; Stenzel, ThZ 10 (1954), pp. 152–4; Volz, ZAW 55 (1937), pp. 235–64. Lit. § 126.

[7] Birkeland, ZAW 67 (1955), pp. 99–103; Blank, *Pyatt Mem. Vol.* (1953), pp. 1–13; Castellino, *Stud. Or. Levi della Vida*, I (1956), pp. 141–50; Hansen, DTT 13 (1950), pp. 77–87; Jellicoe, ET 67 (1955/6), pp. 209–10; Kuhn, ZAW 55 (1937), pp. 307 f.; Munch, ZAW 55 (1937), pp. 36–46; Ringgren, VT 3 (1953), pp. 265–72; Würthwein, *Bertholet-Festschr.* (1950), pp. 532–49. Lit. § 126.

[8] Eissfeldt (BAL 104, 5, 1958); Jirku, *Die älteste Geschichte Israels im Rahmen lehrhafter Darstellungen* (1917), pp. 24, 155; Junker, Bibl 34 (1953), pp. 487–500; Kroeze, *Genesis Veertien* (1937), pp. 205–6. Lit. § 126.

[9] Lit. p. 120, n. 57.

[10] Holm-Nielsen, StTh 14 (1960), pp. 37–9.

[11] Gunkel, BZAW 34 (1920), pp. 69–74. Lit. § 126.

[12] Herrmann, *Festschr. für Otto Schmitz* (1953), pp. 57–70. Lit. § 126.

[13] Baumann, EvTh 11 (1951/2), pp. 187–90; Danell, *Psalm cxxxix* (1951); Würthwein, ThLZ 81 (1956), cols. 341 f.; VT 7 (1957), pp. 165–82. Lit. § 126.

upon the godless—what one might term a negative answer—or with the stubborn 'Nevertheless' of faith, with an exposition of the preciousness of fellowship with God which brings blessing to the pious and which exceeds all possessions and is imperishable—thus positively. With these may be compared Ps. xci, which was reckoned above (p. 120) with the psalms of trust, and in addition the section in a speech by Eliphaz which appears to be an independent poem, Job v, 17–26, in that both these compositions attempt to alleviate though not to solve the problem with a recollection of the ever-renewed experience that God does in the end remember his pious ones; he delivers them from distress and brings the godless to disaster. At the same time, Ps. xci may perhaps be described as a 'psalm of conversion' which attests how a pious man who was formerly devoted to 'Elyon-Shaddai has now turned to Yahweh and is confirmed by a priest of Yahweh in the certainty that he is indeed under the latter's protection. The same may be true of Ps. cxxi, likewise included among the songs of trust on p. 120, for here there speaks one who after a vain search in other cults has now found full satisfaction with Yahweh, and receives a friendly welcome from the priest of Yahweh to whom he has declared his allegiance. If this is correct, then it becomes especially clear with these two psalms how uncertain is their allocation to particular 'types' and how indistinct is the borderline between 'cultic' and 'spiritual' songs. For if Ps. xci and Ps. cxxi are really psalms of conversion, then they obviously belong in the temple since it is here that a transfer of allegiance to Yahweh was effected. But what we have here is the experience of individuals which is used to give a consolatory warning to others. By contrast with this the poet in Ps. lxxviii, who denotes his production in v. 2 as a *wisdom saying* (מָשָׁל), evaluates what his hearers and readers can and should learn for the conduct of their own life from the history of Israel. This history testifies to the continuous ingratitude and unfaithfulness of the people in regard to its God, so gracious and merciful, and so warns against such an attitude by this example, and admonishes to trust in God and obedience to his commandments.

Pss. i and cxxviii are introduced by the expression *Blessed is he* or *Happy is he*[14] which belongs in the circle of the wisdom teachers; Ps. cxxxiii is introduced by *See how beautiful and pleasant!* which also belongs there; and these three psalms depict in glowing colours the good fortune of those who allow the law of Yahweh to be determinative for everything in their life and action—so Ps. i, or as in Ps. cxxviii, fear Yahweh and walk in his ways, or, as in Ps. cxxxiii, praise the harmonious common life, crowned by Yahweh's blessing, of brothers in the family unit of the community. Thus here it is a religious and ethical attitude which is praised, not the ideal for life of the wise, and this might suggest that the inclusion of these psalms in the group of wisdom poems is not justified. They are in fact not real wisdom poems, but they belong with this group in so far as they reveal its special characteristics, though they have replaced the wisdom which is normally glorified in the poems of the group by faithfulness to the law and the fear of God, and they thus reflect the development which wisdom litera-

---

[14] Hans Schmidt, 'Grüsse und Glückwünsche im Psalter' ThStKr 103 (1931), pp. 141–50. Cf. p. 124, n. 3; Lit. § 126.

ture in general went through in Israel. For here, as may be seen from a rapid comparison of the book of Proverbs, and in particular of the older collections which it incorporates (pp. 472–6) with Ecclesiasticus, faithfulness to the law and fear of God have everywhere increasingly replaced the ideal of wisdom. With this fact in mind, it is possible also to treat psalms like xix, 8–15 (p. 446) and cxix, which have a hymnic character and so may be reckoned to the hymn type, as wisdom poems; and to set them beside songs which have the praise of wisdom as their content, such as Ecclus. xiv, 20–xv, 10, and Prov. viii, except that in them wisdom is replaced by the piety of the law or the fear of Yahweh. That process, characteristic of the history of Israelite-Jewish spiritual and religious development, by which wisdom dissolves into piety, also brought with it the consequence that even psalms such as xxxvii, xlix and lxxiii, which as reflections on a particular problem are genuine wisdom poems, were used in the cultus, if not of the temple at least of the synagogue, and as such were taken up in the Psalter which is a collection of such songs. But it nevertheless remains true that the real home of this type of poetry is not the cultus, but the realm of the wise.

PART TWO

THE LITERARY PREHISTORY OF THE BOOKS OF THE OLD TESTAMENT

§ 17. GENERAL CONSIDERATIONS

Literature: Saydon, 'Literary Criticism of the O.T. Old Problems and New Ways of Solution' BEThL XII (1959), pp. 316–24.

THE recognition of the nature of the smallest units which we have discussed in the previous sections, is of the greatest importance. In the first place it makes possible an assured demarcation of the individual narratives, sayings, songs and the like, and thus achieves the first prerequisites for their proper understanding. The tradition[1] which we possess for such demarcation, i.e. the traditional division of the text into larger sections, is in fact by no means everywhere satisfactory and correct, whether we follow the Jewish division into *parashoth* (see p. 692), already to be found in the Qumrān scrolls, or the division into chapters, which appeared in the Vulgate in about A.D. 1200, and from the fourteenth century onwards was gradually adopted in Hebrew manuscripts and printed editions—a division which does in fact agree in large measure with the other system. In the little book of Lamentations, where it is immediately clear that there are five independent songs, namely four alphabetic and one which is influenced by the alphabetic form in that its 22 lines correspond to the number of the letters of the alphabet, the division into *parashoth* and chapters is correct. The end, however, of the paradise and fall stories (Gen. iii, 24) is separated from the beginning of the Cain narrative (iv, 1) only by a 'closed' *parasha* (ס) whereas the conclusion of the first section, namely the expulsion from paradise in iii, 22–4, is separated from the preceding section by an 'open' *parasha* (פ); this has the effect of closely linking material which does not really belong together, and of separating material which really forms one continuous whole. Here the chapter division is better. By contrast, the division into *parashoth* is to be followed and not the chapter division in, for example, the last of the '*Ebed-Yahweh* songs, Isa. lii, 13–liii, 12, and in the section Isa. lxiii, 7–lxiv, 11, which we have already noted as a unit, namely a national song of lamentation (p. 113). But there are also cases where both divisions are misleading, and we must make a division according to our own judgement (Jer. vii, 1–viii, 3; xiv, 19–xv, 4, see pp. 351 f., 113). It is here that the recognition of the types may render excellent service, quite apart from the other cases where it prevents false divisions— as for example the separation of the song of thanksgiving which stands at the end of many of the individual songs of lamentation, showing that it belongs to

---

[1] Bardtke, 'Die Parascheneinteilung der Jesajarolle I von Qumrān' *Dornseiff-Festschrift* (1953), pp. 33–75; Ginsburg, *Introduction* (p. 678), pp. 9–108; Noth (p. 669), pp. 242 f.

the nature of the songs of lamentation to anticipate the thanks which are to be expressed in the given case (see p. 117). The recognition of the forms of speech does more than this, however. It rescues the individual passage from its isolated position, makes possible the examination together of all the examples which belong to one particular form, and so enables us to understand the type and hence to appreciate properly the structure and content of each individual example.

But this recognition of the smallest units does not end the matter. The books of the Old Testament are not to be treated as if they were merely collections of such small units. Nor are we to think that their compilers had in front of them a whole host of these smallest units, and then, entirely at their own choice, welded them together for the first time into a new larger literary unity. It is more likely that all the books presuppose the existence already of literary compilations and arrangements of the smallest units. The structure of our books, their 'composition', is quite unintelligible unless we can succeed at least in some measure in throwing light on the extent and nature, the date, place and purpose of the books or booklets utilised by them as sources. From the recognition of the nature of the individual forms, it is possible properly to understand individual sections of the books, as for example the national song of lamentation in Isa. lxiii, 7–lxiv, 11, at any rate in their typical characteristics. But the appeal to the examination of the types is not sufficient for the understanding of the book in question as a whole, nor for the understanding of the historical situation of its individual parts. Here literary criticism must be used to arrive at the sources which underlie the book in question. This method of research is not to the same extent necessary or important with all the books of the Old Testament. In the case of books which consist entirely or mainly in the placing together of the smallest units—such as Lamentations, the Psalter and to a large extent the Proverbs of Solomon, which only contain larger literary units to a very limited degree—the crucial point for understanding them naturally rests in the individual song or saying. The fact that these books too did in fact in their turn make use of earlier books, is certainly a point which is worth illuminating more precisely, but for the understanding of the really important point, namely of the individual song or saying, it does not amount to much. Nevertheless here too we must explain such points as the double occurrence of many psalms and sayings, and this is only possible with the recognition that these books too have a literary prehistory.

The illumination of the literary prehistory is however much more important in the prophetic, legal and historical books. The fact that our prophetic books do not reveal any logically consistent chronological arrangement or order of contents, is obvious, but it is equally clear that nevertheless certain principles of arrangement underlie them, or perhaps originally underlay them. Where it appears that there was clearly at an earlier stage a reasonable arrangement in the books or in parts of them, but that this order is now disturbed, the present order must be explained. This explanation, in so far as it is possible, not infrequently has important consequences for the understanding of the individual sections. It may not contribute much to our understanding of the actual material of the call vision of Isaiah (Isa. vi) to recognise that it originally stood at the beginning of the book, and then to explain how it came into its present position. But the recognition that the five visions of Amos (vii, 1–9; viii, 1–3; ix, 1–4), now divided into three sections, perhaps once formed the beginning of an autobiographical account, and certainly originally stood together, carries with it a real insight into the meaning of the deliberately climactic arrangement (see pp. 397–8). The book of Jeremiah as a whole, and also many of its individual narratives and sayings, can only be fully understood if it is recognised that it represents the placing together of a third person narrative by Baruch, a first person narrative by Jeremiah, and of other 'sources'. Disorder, and at the same time indications of an intelligible order which was once present, are furthermore not infrequently to be seen in the law books. Thus the section containing cultic regulations, Deut. xvi, 21–xvii, 7, divides the sections xvi, 18–20 and xvii, 8–13, which are concerned with the regulation of the judicial system, and seems originally to have belonged after xii, 31. The recognition of this fact not only enables us to make a more intelligible arrangement of the section in question, but also contributes to the understanding of what is the chief point of xvii, 2–7, i.e. not, as now appears, the statement concerning the necessity of producing two witnesses, but the rooting out of the idolaters. In the narrative books large sections such as II Sam. xiii–xx reveal a clear structure which is in general free of disarrangement and unevenness, repetitions and contradictions. On the other hand there are sections, for example the Flood narrative in Gen. vi–ix, or the narratives of the crossing of the Jordan and the conquest of Jericho in Josh. iii–vi, which are full of unevennesses of all kinds, and are quite unintelligible in their present form. They can only be made intelligible on the assumption that here several narratives have been combined, and by the separation and rearrangement of the various parts. In short, we must not only have in mind the preliterary and subliterary prehistory of the books of the Old Testament, but also their literary prehistory.

Now we have already indicated in the introductory remarks concerning the nature of our undertaking (§ 1), that the more detailed insight into the composition of the books and so into their literary prehistory can only be achieved by the analysis of the books as they are now. But we may nevertheless here set out some general observations, anticipating some of the precise results of the analysis. A detailed examination of the characteristics of the individual books is here neither necessary nor possible. We must be content with stating what is relevant to the four main groups of the Old Testament books, historical, legal, prophetic and poetic, including in this last the wisdom literature. Or alternatively we may pick out for the group in question one particularly characteristic example.

§ 18. THE HISTORICAL BOOKS

Literature: Auerbach, *Wüste und gelobtes Land,* I (1932), pp. 22–33; Eising, *Form-geschichtliche Untersuchung zur Jakobserzählung der Genesis* (1940); Eissfeldt, 'Die kleinste literarische Einheit in den Erzählungsbüchern des AT' ThBl 6 (1927), cols. 333–7 = 'The Smallest Literary Unit in the narrative books of the Old Testament' in *Old Testament Essays* ed. D. C. Simpson (1927), pp. 85–93 = *Kl. Schr.* I (1962), pp. 143–9; Gressmann, 'Ursprung und Entwicklung der Joseph-Sage' FRLANT 36 (1923), I, pp. 1–55; Guidi, 'L'historiographie chez les Sémites' RB 3 (1906), pp. 509–19; Gunkel, 'Jakob' PJ 176 (1919), pp. 339–62; 'Die Komposition der Joseph-Geschichten' ZDMG 76 (1922), pp. 55–71; Pfeiffer and Pollard, *The Hebrew Iliad* (1957); Rost, *Die Überlieferung von der Thronnachfolge Davids* (BWANT 42, 1926); Seeligmann, 'Phasen uit de geschiedenis van het Joodsch historische bewustzijn' Kernmomenten (1947), pp. 49–73.
Cf. also Literature §§ 5, 22–30, 37–41, 70–3, 126.

1. *Indications of sources.* So far as the historical books are concerned, we are in the fortunate position with regard to the latest of them—or at any rate the latest among the canonical books—the book of Chronicles, which originally included Ezra and Nehemiah, that we can at least with certainty recognise and describe more precisely some of the sources used. The book of Chronicles mentions together with other books the *Book of the Kings of Judah and Israel* (II Chron. xxv, 26 etc.) as the place where more may be found concerning the king in question, and thus at least indirectly as the source utilised by the Chronicler. Whether this book is intended to mean our book of Kings, or another work itself representing a revision of our book of Kings, is here of no consequence. The original here mentioned is certainly connected with our book of Kings, in fact large sections of the books of Chronicles agree with our books of Samuel and Kings. Thus in this case we have the source mentioned and utilised by the Chronicler itself actually preserved. Of the remainder of the sources utilised in Chronicles-Ezra-Nehemiah, the autobiography of Nehemiah which is made use of from Neh. i, 1, onwards, is indicated by the title which still remains at Neh. i, 1, *The words of Nehemiah ben Hacaliah,* and though the same is not true of the autobiography of Ezra, we can nevertheless separate it from Ezra-Nehemiah with some certainty. If we now work back from the Chronicler, we may note that our book of Kings also names several of its sources, namely *the book of the acts of Solomon* (I Kings xi, 41), *the book of the acts of the kings of Israel* and that of *the kings of Judah* (I Kings xiv, 19, 29). But we no longer actually possess these, and we can only form a very incomplete picture of them. If we go even further back to the books from Genesis to Samuel or Kings, we find here that two or three 'books' are mentioned as sources for certain passages, all apparently in poetic form. First, in Num. xxi, 14b–15, there is a series of geographical names, apparently rhythmically grouped, such as might be suitable in a victory song or a mocking song, introduced in v. 14a by: *Therefore so it is said in the book of the wars of Yahweh* (סֵפֶר מִלְחֲמֹת יְהוָה).[1] Then, *The Book of the Upright* (סֵפֶר הַיָּשָׁר)[2] is twice men-

---

[1] Caspari, 'Was stand im Buche der Kriege Jahwes?' ZWTh 54 (1912), pp. 110–58; Gispen, 'Het boek van de oorlogen van Jahwe' GThT 59 (1959), pp. 129–37; Tur-Sinai,

tioned as a source, namely in Josh. x, 13a, for Joshua's prayer to the sun in
Gibeon and to the moon in the valley of Aijalon to stay their course (x, 12–13),
and in II Sam. i, 18b, for David's lament over the death of Saul and Jonathan
(i, 19–27). Lastly, though this is not in the Hebrew text, in I Kings viii, 53a,
in connection with Solomon's utterance at the dedication of the Temple, the
Greek translation of the LXX includes the note that it was written *in the Book
of the Song* (I Kings viii, 12–13; LXX = viii, 53a, ἐν βιβλίῳ τῆς ᾠδῆς).
Since the Hebrew original of the Greek ᾠδή can only be שִׁיר, and the three
consonants of this Hebrew word are the same as those of the Hebrew יָשָׁר—
upright, it has been surmised that the word שִׁיר underlying ᾠδή may be
explained as having arisen from a miswriting of יָשָׁר, namely by the reversal of
the first two consonants, י and שׁ, and that thus originally here too the *Book of
the Upright* was mentioned as the source. Much as this suggestion deserves
consideration, however, it may nevertheless be proper to leave the matter as
it stands, with the text transmitted as ᾠδή = שִׁיר, and so to reckon with the
possibility that in addition to the *Book of the Wars of Yahweh* and the *Book of
the Upright* there was a third ancient collection, namely the *Book of the Song,*
or, since *Song* here is to be understood as a collective term, the *Book of the
Songs.* Solomon's utterance at the dedication of the Temple, with its cultic
religious content, is of a quite different kind from the passages which are
ascribed to the *Book of the Upright,* which are both concerned with warlike
events.

We may thus think that the *Book of the Songs* mentioned as the source of
Solomon's utterance at the dedication of the Temple, was a collection of compositions concerned with cultus and religion, whereas the *Book of the Wars of
Yahweh* and the *Book of the Upright* evidently contained songs which celebrated
on the one hand victories and heroic deeds and on the other hand the tragic
greatness of fallen warriors. That in these too there was mention of Yahweh is
of course entirely natural, in view of the close connections between religious
and national feeling which were characteristic of ancient Israel. Indeed the first
of the three collections is called the *Book of the Wars of Yahweh.* But this fact
does not exclude the possibility that in ancient Israel, alongside collections of
compositions of nationalistic religious content, there may have been others
containing specifically cultic songs, and that the book named as the source of
Solomon's utterance at the dedication of the Temple was of this kind. A pointer
to a more precise indication of the content and purpose of the *Book of the
Upright*—and this may then indirectly apply to the *Book of the Wars of Yahweh*
—is perhaps given by the words which precede the mention of the source of
David's lament over the death of Saul and Jonathan: *to teach the Judaeans the
bow.* For these words, to which objection has often wrongly been made, can
hardly have any other meaning than that the lament has power to arouse courage
and boldness in the young men, and that this power residing in it is to be made

'Was there an Ancient "Book of the Wars of the Lord"?' [Hebr., Engl. sum.] BIES 24
(1959/60), pp. 146–8, III–IV.
   [2] Mercati, 'Una congettura sopra il libro del Giusto' in *Note di Letteratura Biblica e
Cristiana Antica* (Studi e Testi 5, 1901), pp. 1–7; Thackeray, 'New Light on the Book of
Jashar' JThSt 11 (1910), pp. 518–32.

effective for the instructing and emboldening of the young manhood—for *bow* here refers to warlike fitness in general.[3] The name of the collection of song, the *Book of the Upright*, also points in the same direction.

Opinions differ with regard to Joshua's summons to the sun and moon to stand still, as to how far here the quotation from the *Book of the Upright* extends.[4] It is certain that the words:

> *Sun in Gibeon stand still   and moon in the valley of Aijalon,*
> *Then the sun stood still   and the moon stayed,*
> *Until the people took vengeance on their enemies*

belong to the quotation. But since the immediate context of these lines can also be read metrically, the suggestion made by some that the quotation should be somewhat further extended, may be regarded as justifiable. It is another question whether the complex so denoted is to be taken as a part of a larger epic whole. Here and elsewhere it has been suggested that the narratives which we possess were in general preceded by epics, and that these, quite apart from some few isolated quotations taken from them, may have influenced the narratives deeply in so far as the latter by their style and range of motifs may reveal themselves as the heirs of the older epics.[5] This question will have to be examined more thoroughly later.

We are thus given some information concerning ancient collections of songs which were utilised as sources in the compilation of the narrative to be found in the books from Genesis to Kings. But we learn nothing concerning the originals for the narrative—for the moment leaving the laws on one side. Yet it is quite certain that here too literary sources were being worked over, and that the material did not merely exist in the form of detached single reports and narratives, as a shapeless mass, to be first formed into a literary whole by the compiler or compilers of the older—i.e. pre-deuteronomic—historical work which extends from Genesis into the books of Kings. For this we are dependent simply upon analysis, and here it is inevitable that completely certain results can only be reached rarely and with difficulty, and that the majority of the insights must retain a hypothetical character. It is nevertheless permissible to assume some certainty for the main outlines.

2. *The compass of the older historical work.* Our first task, however, is to indicate rather more precisely the extent of the older historical work. This has so far been described only rather roughly as extending from the beginning of Genesis to the end of the books of Samuel or into the books of Kings. From this great complex of material, we must first remove the whole of the Priestly Code together with the Law of Holiness, i.e. in addition to substantial parts of Gen. i–Exod. xxiv, Num. x–xxxvi and Deut. xxxiv–Josh. xxiv, the large complexes

---

[3] Eissfeldt, 'Zwei verkannte militärtechnische Termini im Alten Testament' VT 5 (1955), pp. 232–8.

[4] Alfrink, 'Het "stil staan" van zon en maan in Jos x, 12–15' StC 24 (1949), pp. 238–69; van den Bussche, 'Het zogenaamd zonnewonder in Jos x, 12–15' Collationes Gandavenses II, 1 (1951), pp. 48–53; de Fraine, 'De miraculo solari Josue (Jos x, 12–15)' VD 28 (1950), pp. 227–36.

[5] Gordon (§ 5a) (1954), pp. 163–6; *New Horizons in OT Literature* (1960), pp. 23–4.

Exod. xxv–xxx and Exod. xxxv–Num. ix. It is also necessary to take out Deuteronomy and the Deuteronomic sections of the remaining books, i.e. the whole of Deut. i–xxx, substantial parts of Josh., smaller parts of Judg. and Sam., and large sections again of the books of Kings. There thus remains only the older part of Gen. i to Exod. xxiv, xxxi–xxxiv; Num. x–xxxvi; Deut. xxxi– II Kings, leaving for a moment undetermined as to where precisely in the books of Kings the end is to be placed. With the removal of the whole of the book of Leviticus, the divisions between the books of Exodus and Leviticus, Leviticus and Numbers are automatically removed. Since hardly anything remains of the book of Deuteronomy, it is impossible here again to mark off a separate book. But we must go further, and also regard the divisions between Deut. xxxiv and Josh., between Josh. and Judg., Judg. and Sam., and Sam. and Kings as no longer determinative. In the first case, the abolishing of the boundary follows closely upon the disappearance of Deuteronomy itself. Between Josh. and Judg. there is also no real division, since the beginning of Judg. (i, 1–ii, 9)[6] runs largely parallel to the content of the book of Joshua and does not, like the remainder of the book of Judges, deal with the defence of the land, but with its conquest. Furthermore, Sam. shows various connecting links with Judges. On the one hand the so-called appendices to the book of Judges (chs. xvii–xxi) with their repeated mention of the disasters of the period without a king (xvii, 6; xviii, 1; xix, 1; xxi, 25) appear to pave the way for the emergence of the monarchy. On the other hand, Samuel appears, at any rate in a number of narratives, as the last of the judges (I Sam. vii, viii, xii). Finally, it is generally recognised that I Kings i–ii form the direct sequel to II Sam. xiii–xx, and so the division between II Sam. and I Kings makes a break between material which belongs together. As far as the Pentateuch is concerned, it is in any case clear that its division into five books took place only when the whole of the material now united within it had already been incorporated, and that this division was aimed at producing sections of approximately equal length, corresponding to the normal length of the scrolls of the time.[7] But in the other cases too we must rid ourselves of the idea that the present beginnings of the books are ancient and original and that they enable us to give definitive information concerning the literary prehistory of the older historical work. On the contrary, the position is rather that the divisions which are actually present, and from which it is not so easy to get away, make the recognition of this prehistory more difficult.

Instead of these divisions, we must at any rate for the older content of Gen. to Josh., and probably also for that from Judg. to Sam. and into Kings, think in terms of strata. Only then can we get a picture of the literary sources which

---

[6] On i, 22–6 (Bethel), Albright, 'The First Month of Excavation at Bethel' BASOR 53 (1934), pp. 23–5; 'The Kyle Memorial Excavation at Bethel' BASOR 56 (1934), pp. 2–15; Kelso, 'The Second Campaign at Bethel' BASOR 137 (1955), pp. 5–10; 'Excavations at Bethel' BA 19 (1956), pp. 36–43; 'The Third Campaign at Bethel' BASOR 151 (1958), pp. 3–8. Lit. § 126.

[7] Blau, *Studien zum althebräischen Buchwesen* I (1902), pp. 48–9; Driver, *Semitic Writing* (²1954), pp. 81–4. Cf. also the description by Trever of the complete scroll of Isaiah— 7.35 m. long, and 30 cm. high—from Qumrān, in Burrows, *The Dead Sea Scrolls of St. Mark's Monastery*, I (1950), pp. XIII–XVIII, and cf. below, §§ 104, 114, 115.

were used in their task by the compilers or more properly redactors of the older basic material from Gen. to Josh.—i.e. of the Hexateuch—or of Gen. to Sam. together with a sequel which extends into Kings—i.e. of the Octateuch or Enneateuch.[8] It will appear in fact from the analysis that, ignoring amplifications due to the insertion of separate disconnected sections, the older material from Gen. to Josh. represents the combination of two or more probably three, parallel narrative strands, which all extend from the creation of the first man, or at any rate from Abraham, at least as far as the conquest of Canaan. The analysis will show further that the same features which led to the assumption of several parallel strands of narrative forming the basis of the Hexateuch—i.e. the presence of complete parallel narratives appearing more than once (Gen. xii, 10–20; xx,[9] xxvi, 1–11) on the one hand, and of narratives compiled from parts of several parallel narratives (Gen. vi–ix, Josh. iii–vi) on the other hand—also meet the observer in just the same way in the following books, right into the book of Kings. Here too it appears that the hypothesis applied in the Hexateuch for the elucidation of the present condition of the material is the most illuminating, i.e. the assumption of the combining of various parallel narrative strands. The question then forces itself upon us as to whether the parallel strands which are to be assumed for Judg. to Sam. or Kings may not be continuations of those observed in the Hexateuch. This possibility appears all the more probable in view of the fact that, as we shall see, even the oldest strand of narrative in the Hexateuch cannot have been compiled before the time of David. If that is the case, it appears almost impossible to avoid the assumption that the compiler would not have been content with finishing his presentation at some point in more ancient history, but would have brought it down to his own time.

3. *Literary sources.* We have thus illuminated the literary prehistory of the older Hexateuch or Octateuch in so far as we have indicated as its component parts two or three continuous parallel strands, i.e. books, concerning Israel's history and prehistory, beginning more or less with the creation and continuing down to the time of David and Solomon or even further. The question is whether we can go even further back and show that the compilers of these strands of narrative contained in the Hexateuch and Octateuch—particularly the earliest of them—already had literary sources in front of them. The question may on general grounds be answered in the affirmative. Even if we place the narrative strands of the Hexateuch and Octateuch very far back, and suggest that the earliest of them came into being by about 950 B.C., we must nevertheless reckon on written originals for various sections of these narrative strands. The compiler of the oldest strand, as well as the compiler or compilers of the later, will certainly have derived much from oral tradition, and have given it its first literary form. But with the narratives which approximate very closely to historical writing, as with those of Gideon and Abimelech in Judg. vi–ix, we may more readily think of literary originals. Narratives of this kind can hardly have been handed on orally. On different grounds we must assume for the beginning

[8] On the name Hexateuch, etc., see p. 156.
[9] Rabinowitz, 'The "Great Sin" in Ancient Egyptian Marriage Contracts' JNESt 18 (1959), p. 73, on xx, 9. Lit. § 126.

of the historical work, the prehistory in Gen. i, 1–xi, 9, that literary sketches, foreign in this case, served as patterns. The Babylonians know of a line of kings before the Flood and after the Flood,[10] and it can hardly be doubted that the Biblical sequence—antediluvian patriarchs, Flood, postdiluvian patriarchs —is dependent upon the Babylonian scheme, which, like other such material, is likely to have been transmitted via the Canaanites. Furthermore, the narratives which are gathered around Abraham and Lot, Jacob and Esau, Jacob and Laban, Joseph and his brothers, Israel's sojourn in Egypt, Sinai, Balaam and Joshua, as well as many other groups of narratives, may have been before the compiler of the earliest or second earliest narrative strand already in the form of literary units, 'cycles of sagas' as they have been termed. It is also possible to indicate, at any rate tentatively, the extent of the material which belongs to the literary units of medium size which are perhaps so to be assumed, but their exact wording certainly cannot be determined. Even if such cycles lay before the compilers of the two oldest narrative strands, they merely made use of these, at any rate primarily, as sources for their material, while substantially transforming their wording and fitting them into the main lines of their own presentation. This may be seen quite simply in the fact that all the cycles which may be assumed for the book of Genesis—the Abraham–Lot cycle, the Jacob–Esau cycle etc.— overlap, in that the hero of each appears as father of the hero who stands central to the next cycle, or as son of the one dealt with in the preceding cycle. Thus all these cycles presuppose the genealogical sequence of Abraham–Isaac– Jacob–the twelve sons of Jacob, whereas it is a recognised result of research that the genealogical linkage of the patriarchs is relatively late and is dependent upon the idea of Israel as a larger entity, an idea which first came into being when Israel was in Canaan. The separate cycles, in so far as they existed, must be pictured without these links binding them together, and this means that we can only reconstruct the extent of their contents, but not their literary form.

4. *The history of the succession to David.* The position is similar in regard to the complexes of narratives which are presupposed by many scholars for the books which follow, as for example by Noth, as will subsequently be demonstrated more precisely (cf. pp. 243 f.). This may be shown from an example which has often been discussed and which is in fact very significant, namely the section so rightly described as the History of the Succession to David, II Sam. xiii– xx + I Kings i–ii.[11] It is clear, and also almost generally recognised, that here we have a literary work which is all of one piece, if we ignore some small amplifications or perhaps short insertions from a parallel source. But the exact points at which it begins and ends remain very uncertain, as may immediately be seen by a review of the recent attempts at determining where it begins. Rost is firmly of the opinion that this narrative is a history of the succession to David and that it is directed to the answering of the question which stands central especially to I Kings i (vv. 5, 13, 20, 24, 27, 30, 35, 43, 46, 48), as to who is to ascend the throne in David's place. In his view, therefore, I Sam. iv–vi; II Sam.

[10] AOT, pp. 147–50; ANET, pp. 265 f.
[11] Sutcliffe, 'Simultaneity in Hebrew: a Note on I Kings i, 41' JSSt 3 (1958), pp. 80–1.

vi, vii, ix–xii also belong to it. But he maintains that the compiler already had I Sam. iv–vi; II Sam. vi; vii; x, 6b–xi, 1; xii, 26–31, and made it suitable for his purpose by small additions. Thus to the Ark-narrative of I Sam. iv–vi, II Sam. vi he added the Michal episode of II Sam. vi, 16, 20b–23 in order to explain why the successor could not be a child of Michal, and to this negative feature he then set as a contrast the positive statement of II Sam. vii. For this purpose he made use of an old narrative concerning a promise of Yahweh, given to David by the prophet Nathan, concerning the duration of his dynasty. Furthermore, he completed the narrative of the Ammonite war in II Sam. x, 6b–xi, 1; xii, 26–31 [12] by the addition of the Bathsheba narrative x, 1–6a; xi, 2–xii, 25, and developed it into a presentation of the beginnings of Solomon [13] the successor, for Bathsheba was Solomon's mother. Lastly, Rost attributes II Sam. ix to the compiler of the history of the succession, because much in II Sam. xiii–xx + I Kings i–ii would have been unintelligible (Meribbaal, Ziba) if ch. ix had not preceded. In this analysis of the section (I Sam. iv) II Sam. ix–xx + I Kings i–ii, Rost has been followed by many others; it has thus been adopted, though with certain modifications, by von Rad (Lit. p. 47) and Noth (see pp. 243–4). But in spite of its detailed examination of stylistic criteria, this defining of the limits of an apparently fixed and complete historical work rests ultimately not upon literary criteria but upon considerations of content, as to whether the narratives reveal relationships to the theme of the succession to David or not; and the conclusions are anything but certain. Alongside II Sam. ix, I Sam. i–iii or its basic material may—indeed must—equally justifiably be reckoned to the succession history, since chs. i–iii demand a continuation such as chs. iv–vi on the one hand, and on the other hand, the mention of Eli and his sons in ch. iv presupposes their mention and more detailed treatment in chs. i–iii.

Others define quite differently the exact extent of the work, of which in any case II Sam. ix (or x or xiii)–xx + I Kings i–ii is to be regarded as the core. Thus Budde [14] is inclined to accept the view first put forward by Duhm, that Abiathar, the priest of David who was exiled to Anathoth by Solomon, compiled II Sam. x–xx + I Kings i–ii, or—as Duhm himself expressed it—that this work was produced from the personal traditions of the family of Abiathar. [15] He considers that Abiathar's work also began with I Sam. iv, and thus agrees in that with Rost. But he assigns the whole of the older content from I Sam. iv to I Kings ii to this work, whereas Rost sharply differentiates the succession history—not in his view derived from Abiathar—from a second narrative, likewise independent and complete, namely the history of David's flight from Saul and his rise to power, which according to him comprises I Sam. xxiii, 1–13; xxvii, 1–xxviii, 2; xxix, 1–xxx, 26; II Sam. i, 1; ii, 4a; iii, 20–30, 31–7; iv, 1a, 5–12; [16] v, 3, 17–25 (viii ?) and which he ascribes to Abiathar. Auerbach, on

[12] Goslinga, 'Spreekt 2 Sam xii, 31 inderdaad van wrede terechtstelling der Ammonieten?' GThT 59 (1959), pp. 138–48. Lit. § 126.

[13] Stamm, 'Der Name des Königs Salomo' ThZ 16 (1960), pp. 285–97.

[14] *Die Bücher Samuel* (KHC, 1902), p. XVII.

[15] *Das Buch Jeremia* (KHC, 1901), p. 3. Klostermann, *Die Bücher Samuelis und der Könige* (1887), p. XXXII, holds, on the other hand, that Ahimaaz the son of Zadok the priest was the compiler of II Sam. x–xx + I Kings i–ii.

the other hand, who like Rost is guided in the main by historical considerations and not by the criteria of literary analysis, and who, like Duhm and Budde, regards Abiathar as the compiler of II Sam. xiii–xx + I Kings i–ii, feels his way from this firm point further and further backwards, eventually arriving at the result that the whole body of reliable ancient narratives which precede II Sam. xiii, in other words the basic material from Gen. i to II Sam. xii, comes from the compiler of the concluding composition, from Abiathar, who is identified with the Yahwist (J), who in his turn also found some part of the material already in writing. This example demonstrates that it is clearly impossible to determine exactly the beginning of the work which is in general, with a fair degree of unanimity, regarded as II Sam. ix (or x or xiii)–xx + I Kings i–ii. One of the reasons for this uncertainty is the fact that even an author of the rank of the one to whom we owe this central section must stand upon the shoulders of the narrators of those individual narratives, complete in themselves, with which we were concerned in the first part of this book (p. 50) and he pays tribute to their skill. Even II Sam. xiii–xx + I Kings i–ii falls into a series of small narratives. These stand with a fair degree of independence alongside one another and can be largely understood by themselves, so that it has been possible (see p. 270) for this section to be denied the character of a connected and complete larger composition altogether and for it to be regarded as a quite loose series of completely unconnected separate narratives. The relative independence of the separate narratives may be everywhere noted. This may be seen for example in the story of how David, when he had fled to Mahanaim, was provisioned by friends from the east of Jordan (II Sam. xvii, 27–9).[17] This makes it in any case often extremely difficult to decide whether two narratives which now succeed one another were really originally written down as belonging together, and thus form a larger unit, or whether they stand together quite by chance or merely because the chronological sequence of the events described necessarily involved their being placed together. The decision is made all the more difficult because it cannot always be decided with certainty whether the links which now exist are really original or only secondary, as for example in the anticipation in Gen. xv, 13–16,[18] of the Israelite journey to Egypt and return from thence. Nor, if they are original, can we be sure whether they must be explained as indications of the literary connections of the narratives in question or merely as references to the same subject, which may come from different hands, as for example in the case of the references in Josh. vi, 26, and I Kings xvi, 34, to the refortification of Jericho which could only be undertaken with terrible sacrifices.

5. *The oldest narrative strand.* It is therefore better to be content with more modest results. We may recognise that the compiler of the oldest strand of narrative extending from Gen. to Kings or—if the strand does not extend

---

[16] On Beeroth in iv, 2–12, cf. Elliger, 'Noch einmal Beeroth' in *Mél. Bibl. Robert* (1957), pp. 82–94, with 2 plates.

[17] Fish, *A Copy of the Umma Tablet BM 106055 and Copies of Other Tablets relating to its Subject-Matter* (Manchester Cuneiform Studies 8, 1959), pp. 83–98.

[18] Tur-Sinai, 'Auf wieviel Jahre berechnet die Bibel den Aufenthalt der Kinder Israel n Ägypten?' BiOr 18 (1961), pp. 16 f.

beyond Joshua—the compiler of this strand and the compiler or compilers of the basic strand which must be assumed for Judg.–Kings, had before them not only a wealth of oral tradition and individual sections fixed in writing but also literary compositions of larger size. But it is not at all possible for us to identify these with even a modicum of certainty, or to define more nearly their place, date and purpose. Against this, the narrative strands which run right through the Octateuch, or at least the Hexateuch, may in general be recognised and characterised with great certainty. While other points must be left to the analysis which follows later, we may here say a little simply about the oldest of these strands. This already was written from the standpoint of 'all Israel', and presupposes the united kingdom, or, if it was first compiled after the division of the kingdom, the continuing idea of this united kingdom. It thus cannot in any case have been written before David. A consideration of a general nature corroborates this conclusion. The creation of a large and powerful united Israelite empire as it was achieved by David, must have produced an atmosphere of national exaltation, which was very congenial to the composition of historical works. For it is the experience of events which deeply affect the life of a people which brings into being a lively desire for their immortalising and at the same time for a definitive account of what preceded them. Such experience also releases the power for the task. This is particularly clear in Israel. An experience like the rise to power under David happened to Israel again only in the victorious rebellion of the Maccabees, and at that time too there immediately arose a great writing of history appropriate to the greatness of the subject. Thus it is a natural assumption, and one that has often been made, that it was David's deeds or the recollection of them which first led a particular individual to set out a presentation of Israel's history linking it with the history of humanity. The result of the analysis, as we shall see, appears to point to the same conclusion. For down to the reign of David three strands of narrative may be clearly traced, but from then on only two with any certainty. This may be interpreted as indicating that the oldest strand ended at David because it was then compiled, whereas the later strand or strands carries the presentation even further.

But we may not regard this dating of the oldest strand—in the time of David or Solomon or not too much later—as being quite certain, not even if II Sam. xiii–xx + I Kings i–ii is to be assigned to the compiler of this, the oldest, or the next oldest strand. The argument which is repeatedly brought forward is that that section, because of the liveliness and realism of its presentation, must definitely be ascribed to a contemporary of the events. But this argument must be limited to the point that an eye-witness account underlies it. The possibility that a gifted writer, let us say in the ninth century B.C., compiled his great narrative on the basis of reliable information concerning the events, is by no means excluded. If about 950 B.C. or a little later—for no one places the narrative earlier—a narrator of equal rank with that of II Sam. xiii–xx + I Kings i–ii could write down, on the basis of older information, the story of Gideon and Abimelech—or more exactly the oldest of the presentations now combined in Judg. vi–ix—events which took place about 200 years before the narrator's own time, we must allow the possibility of something similar being undertaken with reference to the time of David by an author who lived in the ninth century. We certainly have not a simple eye-witness account in II Sam. xiii–xx + I Kings i–ii, but a composition presented and embellished with great narrative skill, a composition which has in it something of a *good* historical novel. The section contains much which can hardly be regarded as deriving from the compiler's personal observation, nor from the report of some other eye-witness. There is embellishment arising out of poetic fantasy, though admittedly a fantasy which is marked by good knowledge of the historical reality and a sober sense of what is possible. To this belongs, for example, the conversation between Amnon and Tamar in the bedchamber (xiii, 11–16), and the equally private conversation between Joab and the messenger, who announces that Absalom has been caught in a tree (xviii, 10–14). In the conversation too between David and the woman of Tekoa (xiv, 4–20) and in Absalom's conferring with Ahitophel and Hushai (xvii, 1–14), it is also clear that the account is not a mere verbatim report but an artistic narrative which makes use of the poet's licence. We thus encounter here a further feature which this section has in common with the poetic narratives (see p. 139).

A quite concrete point has been invoked for a later dating of the section. It is possible that the fact that in II Sam. xx, 14, the north-Israelite Abel is described as Abel of Beth-maacah = 'Abel which belongs to the (Aramaean) Beth-maacah',[19] is to be explained on the grounds that the occupation of this area by the Aramaeans, related in I Kings xv, 20, and taking place in about 900 B.C., is already presupposed. This situation would also suit the proverb quoted a few verses later (vv. 18–19): *Let them but ask in Abel and in Dan whether what the faithful of Israel have ordained has come into disuse.*[20] This was even then regarded as being very ancient (cf. v. 18), and certainly can be understood in such a way that it presupposes the Aramaean occupation of the district and so implies: in spite of occupation by an alien power, these two cities remained true to Israelite custom.[21] This possibility must certainly be seriously considered, but we cannot really be sure since the name of the city and the proverb may also be explained differently.

We should be in a better position if we could trace the narrative strands of the Octateuch with some certainty beyond I Kings ii, since the final point of their presentation would provide us with a firm *terminus ante quem non*. But unfortunately this cannot be done. The 'compiler' of the books of Kings made use of a different procedure, transforming his originals more radically than had been done by the compilers or redactors of the preceding books. In addition the material which may have been drawn from continuations of the strands of the Octateuch is largely concealed by information taken from other sources. So the sorting out of those continuations is from the start a rather profitless endeavour, at least in that it is quite impossible to recover one or more continuous

---

[19] Mazar, 'Geshur and Ma'cah' [Hebr., Engl. sum.] Zion 23/4 (1958/9), pp. 115–23, I; 'Geshur and Maacah' JBL 80 (1961), pp. 16–28.

[20] Instead of the obviously corrupt 𝔐, which must be translated: *and so they settled a matter. I, the most peaceful ones (of the faithful of Israel)*, the text must be read, following 𝔊: וּבְדָן הֵתַמּוּ אֲשֶׁר שָׂמוּ.

[21] Smend, ZAW 39 (1921), p. 204.

strands. The book of Kings does reveal signs of a mingling of sources, and this indeed just in those sections which do not appear to be taken from the 'annals' or to be the work of the compiler himself, but which have much in common with the narrative style of the preceding books. A combining of two narratives may, for example, be found in I Kings xi, 14–25, and in II Kings xi.[22] Parts also of the stories of Elijah (I Kings xvii, 1–xix, 18; xxi) and of Elisha (I Kings xix, 19–21; II Kings viii, 7–15; ix–x) stand out rather like two parallel attempts, on quite a large scale, at associating with the great figures of Elijah or Elisha the events which so deeply influenced and convulsed Israel (and Judah?) in the middle of the ninth century B.C., namely the Aramaean wars on the one hand and the religious revolutionary movement which led to Jehu's accession on the other. These might well be assigned to two of the strands of the Octateuch. If we add to this the fact that side by side with the Elijah narratives with their burning hatred against Ahab are to be found the Ahab stories of I Kings xx and xxii which show considerable sympathy for the king and do full justice to his magnanimity and valour, we might see in these the continuation of a third strand, which would certainly be the oldest. But with similar justification it would be possible also to allocate the two parallel narratives contained in II Kings xviii, 17–xix, 37,[23] concerning Isaiah's and Hezekiah's attitude in the year 701 B.C. to two strands of the Octateuch, and even assume a derivation from the third and again the oldest strand for the quite divergent note in xviii, 14–16 (see pp. 296, 328 f.). But with such surmises we do not get any further, since the condition of the book of Kings does not in any single case permit the restoration of a strand which could be the continuation of one of the strands found in the Octateuch. We must therefore simply be content with the possibility that the strands, at any rate the latest or two latest, did continue beyond Solomon, and regard this as probable for the latest or two latest, since there is much to be said for the assumption that the strands which came into being at a later date, in the ninth or the eighth century, are likely to have continued the narrative down to their own time. But precise results cannot be here achieved.

6. *The later strands*. There are thus several presentations of the story from the beginning of mankind down to Solomon or even further, which precede the predeuteronomic historical work which is preserved in Gen. to Kings and which have been incorporated into it. We have attempted to arrive at some clarity concerning the date and purpose of composition of the oldest strand. It only remains briefly to make clear also the origin of the later strands. Here again we may think of the relationship of the book of Chronicles to the complex Gen. to Kings which we have before us. Chronicles became necessary when this older complex no longer sufficed because it no longer corresponded to the alteration which had taken place meantime in religious and ethical ideas and cultic practices. The position was similar with the oldest narrative strand of the Hexateuch or Octateuch. Some time after its composition, the need for a new

---

[22] Differently Rudolph, see p. 295, n. 56.

[23] On Esarhaddon in xix, 37, cf. Parrot and Nougayrol, 'Asarhaddon et Naqi'a sur un bronze du Louvre' Syria 33 (1956), pp. 147–60, Pl. VI; Hildegard Lewy, 'Nitokris-Naqî'a' JNESt 11 (1952), pp. 264–86.

presentation came to be felt, and this in its turn was later no longer sufficient, but had to give place to a third. It is possible that instead of the chronological sequence which has just been suggested we should think of a co-existence of the strands—assuming that the second and third presentations came into existence roughly at the same time as the first, or that the third was roughly contemporary with the second, but in another locality and in another stratum of society. The second of these hypotheses is possible but not very probable. But so far as our present clarification of the position is concerned, this difference does not greatly matter. What we can define with some certainty as stages in the literary pre-history of the older history work contained in Gen. to Kings are nevertheless continuous parallel strands, which—and this is true above all of the oldest—also in their turn here and there had before them literary creations of moderate size. But this does not permit us to sort out with certainty the literary form of these originals.

7. *Various elements within the different strands.* But if it is certain that the compilers of our narrative strands in the Hexateuch or the Octateuch did not merely make use of oral tradition but also had before them and worked over material already shaped as literature, including compositions of moderate size, then the possibility must *prima facie* be reckoned with that these strands are not themselves all of one piece, but are likely occasionally to reveal different sections, which may not even fit well together. This again must not be allowed to obscure the fact that we have here historical works which are artistically constructed according to a deliberate plan, and not something like merely chance series, loosely constructed of various elements, in which only the principle of chronological sequence was operative. We shall see further that the strands all clearly reveal the marked characteristics of their compilers and of their period.

§ 19. THE COLLECTIONS (CORPORA) OF LAW

Literature: Colella, 'La legge mosaica e le legislazioni dell' Antico Oriente' in Rinaldi, *Secoli sul Mondo* (²1957), pp. 143–54, 578–9; Jepsen, *Untersuchungen zum Bundesbuch* (BWANT 41, 1927); Leovy and Taylor, 'Law and Social Development in Israel' AThR 39 (1957), pp. 9–24; Morgenstern, 'The Book of the Covenant' HUCA 5 (1928), pp. 1–151; 7 (1930), pp. 19–258; 8/9 (1931–2), pp. 1–150, 741–6; Napier, 'Community under Law' Interpretation 7 (1953), pp. 404–17; Noth, *Die Gesetze im Pentateuch. Ihre Voraussetzungen und ihr Sinn* (1940) = *Ges. Stud. zum AT* (1957), pp. 9–141; J. M. P. Smith, *The Origin and History of Hebrew Law* (1931); Waterman, 'Pre-Israelite Laws in the Book of the Covenant' AJSL 38 (1921–22), pp. 36–54; Würthwein, 'Der Sinn des Gesetzes im AT' ZThK 55 (1958), pp. 255–70; Zimmerli, 'Das Gesetz im AT' ThLZ 85 (1960), cols. 481–98; Zingg, 'Das Schuld- und Vollstreckungsrecht (Obligationen- und Exekutionsrecht)' Judaica 16 (1960), pp. 156–71.
Cf. also Literature §§ 4d, 8, 24, 30, 33–5, 126.

We have already seen (pp. 26–9, 69 f.) that the Book of the Covenant (Exod. xx, 22–xxiii, 33), the Deuteronomic Code (Deut. xii–xxvi), the Holiness Code (Lev. xvii–xxvi), and the Priestly Code, in so far as it is purely a legal corpus (i.e.

above all Lev. i–xvi) have as their basis as their smallest units, for the most part, individual laws and judicial utterances which were at first directed to the immediate practical necessities of life. We must now ask ourselves whether here too, just as in the case of the narrative books, we must assume the existence of smaller collections, literary intermediate stages between these laws and judicial utterances or groups of utterances on the one hand and our collections on the other hand; or whether we are to picture the compilers or redactors of our collections as having before them simply the individual laws and groups of judicial utterances, which they have then put together as seemed appropriate to them.

It must first be noted that not one of the collections of law reveals a clear structure, entirely free of repetitions and contradictions, or a completely intelligible and planned order. On the contrary, as we go through them, we meet with unevennesses of the most varied kind. It is clear that some of these arise from the fact that our texts have been secondarily corrected. Such corrections are intelligible enough. The desire was to fit the older precepts to newer ones which had now at a particular time become valid. There is a clear example of this in Lev. xxiii. The basic material of the festival laws set out here comes from the Holiness Code, but this basic material, to be defined roughly as xxiii, 9–12, 15–18aα, 19b, 20, 39, 40–3, has later been worked over and amplified from the point of view of the Priestly Code. For vv. 18aβb, 19a we can even point to the passage from which the amplification has been taken, viz. Num. xxviii, 27–30. There are many such cases. But in addition, there are other unevennesses where the present state of the text clearly cannot be adequately explained as due to corrections and amplifications which have dislocated a legal text originally complete and unified. Here the hypothesis suggests itself that the compiler or redactor of the collection in question did not have a free hand in the choice and arrangement of his material because it already lay before him in the form of smaller collections. Thus in the Holiness Code two series of laws concerning marriage and sexual relationships which almost exactly correspond, stand next to one another—Lev. xviii, 6–30, and xx, 10–26. This fact can surely only be explained on the assumption that here two smaller collections have been united, of which the one contained xviii, 6–30, and the other xx, 10–26. The redactors of the legal collections thus showed just the same respect for the literary material which lay before them as did the redactors of the narrative strands of the Hexateuch or Octateuch, and as did also, at least to a certain degree, the redactors of the Psalter and the book of Proverbs (see pp. 152 f.). From the literary and aesthetic point of view, this attitude of respect is a disadvantage, for it prevented the redactors from constructing out of the material before them a new and larger literary unity. But from the point of view of literary history, it is very fortunate, for it is thus still possible for us to recognise the literary stages which preceded the books which have come down to us.

There can be no doubt that the single laws do not directly underlie our collections, or at least that this does not occur everywhere but only relatively rarely. But the separating out of the smaller collections which are to be assumed as originals is extremely difficult, at least in those places where they do not just stand untouched side by side, but have been worked together. In the historical books, too, the disentangling of narratives which have been combined with one another is often very difficult, and there are cases where we have to be content with recognising a combining of sources without undertaking their analysis. But the analysis is much more difficult with the laws. With the narratives, a study of a particular example will reveal whether the analysis is correct. If it proves possible to separate out two or more narratives, fragmentary certainly but even so intelligible without difficulty, and with gaps which may be filled fairly readily, then the analysis is clearly right. But the laws do not contain a narrative development which can be checked by the chronological sequence, and in the establishing of a logical arrangement according to subject-matter such as one might expect, subjective judgement plays a much greater part than it does in the demonstration of the interconnections of a narrative. In narratives which lack unity it is possible with some certainty to distinguish between isolated glosses and secondary additions of all kinds on the one hand and insertions from a parallel narrative on the other. But it is much more difficult in the case of laws which have obviously been amplified, to say whether we have a case of expansion by the use of isolated pieces of material not belonging to a continuous source or whether we have part of a parallel law.

In this preliminary survey of the matter, therefore, it will be appropriate to mention only such small collections underlying our legal corpora as clearly stand out as such by their isolated position. Thus, in the very disparate corpus of the Book of the Covenant in Exod. xx, 22–xxiii, 33, the section xxi, 1–xxii, 16, immediately stands out as a separate unit, and is indeed so indicated by the title מִשְׁפָּטִים judgements. In Deuteronomy, in contrast to the preceding chapters which contain in the main cultic ordinances, the main part of chs. xxi–xxv contains precepts in casuistic form (p. 224) concerned with the regulating of normal civil law. So we may have the possibility in mind that these chapters already stood together, even before they were taken up in Deuteronomy. We have already seen that various small collections appear to underlie the Holiness Code, as for example xx–xxi, a collection of requirements for priests and sacrifices. Finally, as we shall see later in more detail (pp. 204 f.), the Priestly Code has not only been amplified in the course of time by a whole series of individual laws, but has also had inserted into it whole collections of moderate size. The colophon in Lev. vii, 37 f., which draws together as a unit the sacrificial laws set out in Lev. i–vii,[1] may be secondary, but it is nevertheless probable that these regulations originally formed a small independent collection. The same is certainly true of the laws of purification brought together in Lev. xi–xv. We can therefore be in no doubt that smaller collections of laws on related subjects preceded our collections of laws, and we may therefore reckon with this possibility in the analysis of these collections, even in cases where it is no longer possible to carry out a clear separation of the originals.

---

[1] Elliger, 'Zur Analyse des Sündopfergesetzes' in *Rudolph-Festschrift* (1961), pp. 39–50; on Lev. iv, 1–v, 13; Moraldi, 'Espiazione sacrificale e riti espiatori nell' ambiente biblico e nell' AT' An Bibl 5 (1956), pp. 109–32. Lit. § 126.

§ 20. THE PROPHETIC AND APOCALYPTIC BOOKS

Literature: Buber, *Sehertum, Anfang und Ausgang* (1955); Budde, 'Eine folgenschwere Redaktion des Zwölfprophetenbuchs' ZAW 39 (1921), pp. 218–29; Dürr (§ 14), pp. 1–15; Gressmann, *Der Messias* (FRLANT 43, 1929), pp. 417–45; Hölscher, 'Problèmes de la littérature apocalyptique juive' RHPhR 9 (1929), pp. 101–14; Ladd, 'Why not Prophetic Apocalyptic?' JBL 76 (1957), pp. 192–200; McCown, 'Hebrew and Egyptian Apocalyptic Literature' HThR 18 (1925), pp. 357–411; Mowinckel, *Prophecy and Tradition: The Prophetic Books in the Light of the Study of the Growth and History of the Tradition* (1946); Plöger, *Theokratie und Eschatologie* (WMANT 2, 1960); Robinson, 'Baruch's Roll' ZAW 42 (1924), pp. 209–21; 'Die prophetischen Bücher im Lichte neuer Entdeckungen' ZAW 45 (1927), pp. 3–9; Rössler, *Gesetz und Geschichte in der spätjüdischen Apokalyptik* (WMANT 4, 1960).

Cf. also Literature §§ 10, 42–61, 71, 76, 92, 95–101, 110, 126.

1. *Smaller collections.* The prophetic books also presuppose the prior existence of smaller collections of sayings which derive from the prophets in question or which are attributed to them, and of narratives which refer to them. Just as the Book of the Twelve, reckoned in the Jewish canon as one book, comprises the small books of the twelve prophets, so also the larger books of Isaiah and Jeremiah—leaving that of Ezekiel on one side for the moment (cf. pp. 380–1)—clearly represent compositions based on smaller collections. This is true not only of these latter, but also of much smaller books such as those of Amos and Hosea. Naturally enough, the separation of the original sources is here not so simple as in the Book of the Twelve, where, with the sole exception of Zech. ix–xiv, the books of the individual prophets may be recognised simply by their titles. But the search for these earlier collections is all the more important, for without knowledge of them the structure of our prophetic books is quite incomprehensible.

The books of Isaiah and Jeremiah also reveal a whole series of smaller collections provided with special titles and therefore recognisable as formerly independent. Jer. xxiii, 9, contains the title לַנְּבִאִים *Concerning the prophets*; this refers to xxiii, 9–32 or xxiii, 9–40, and marks off the section as a special collection of words against the prophets. In Jer. xxx, 1–3, we are told that Jeremiah received the command from Yahweh to write certain promises of Yahweh in a *book* (סֵפֶר), and in verse 4 there follows as the title of this book: *These are the words . . .* Introduction and title clearly apply to chs. xxx–xxxi, and show that these chapters, or at least their basic material, the 'Ephraimite booklet of salvation' as it has appropriately been called, once existed independently. Another formerly independent section begins at Jer. xlvi, 1 (cf. xxv, 13b), as is shown by the title: *That which went forth as word of Yahweh to Jeremiah the prophet concerning the nations.* This is a collection of threats against foreign nations. It comprises chs. xlvi–li, or perhaps rather only chs. xlvi–xlix. For chs. l–li have in l, 1 their own title which appears to be comparable with xlvi, 1, and this again reveals itself as a separate booklet, namely a collection of threats against Babylon. Finally, we may note that the scroll which, according to ch. xxxvi, Jeremiah dictated to Baruch, certainly cannot correspond to the whole of our book of Jeremiah, since the indications there given only fit certain parts of it. On the other hand it is probable that this scroll has been incorporated in our book of Jeremiah. This collection must subsequently be more exactly described both as regards its nature and content (pp. 350–4).

In the book of Isaiah too, the external evidence of the titles gives us some assistance in our search for the earlier collections. There is the title which, in slightly varying form, stands twice, in i, 1 and ii, 1, mentioning only words concerning *Judah and Jerusalem* and not words concerning foreign nations. This can now apply at most to chs. i–xii, whatever its original function may have been (pp. 307, 310), since from ch. xiii onwards there follow threats against foreign nations. On the other hand, the section chs. xiii–xxiii—to which the short passage xxx, 6–7 belongs although it is now separated from it—has the peculiarity that the individual sections have the title מַשָּׂא: *Oracle*. This can surely only be explained on the assumption that chs. xiii–xxiii or their basic מַשָּׂא material (p. 307) once stood independently, thus forming a collection of threats against foreign nations similar to Jer. xlvi–xlix or xlvi–li. It is well known that other sections of the book of Isaiah—xxiv–xxvii, xxxiv–xxxv, xl–lv, lvi–lxvi—stand out as literary units of particular kinds on the basis of their content, and this point must also be examined more closely at the appropriate moment.

2. *The three different kinds of prophetic writing.* The understanding of the literary prehistory of our prophetic books is thus aided to a considerable degree by the fact that the collections of moderate size which are incorporated in them are in part at least still recognisable with substantial certainty by outward indications or criteria of content or historical reference. In this respect we are in a better position than with the historical books and the law collections, where almost everything remains hypothetical since outward indications, such as titles, are only rarely available, and arguments from content or historical background do not lead to completely unambiguous results. But in our uncovering of the prehistory of the prophetic books we may go yet a step further, and establish precise results in matters in which the arguments so far put forward are of no assistance. A comparison of the prophetic books does in fact show that many of them—the majority if we consider only the larger ones—reveal elements of three different kinds. These are (1) collections of sayings which the prophet proclaimed, whether as the mouthpiece of Yahweh in the form of first person utterances of Yahweh, or as utterances of his own referring to Yahweh in the third person; (2) autobiographical accounts by the prophet himself concerning his activity or at least concerning important sections of it, and in particular concerning his call; (3) series of narratives concerning the prophet, which have been put together by others, no doubt his disciples. The extent to which these three kinds of prophetic writing appear in our books varies. But in general all three are represented, and the prehistory of our books and thus their actual structure becomes much clearer if we first get a clear picture of the nature and significance of these varied products of prophetic literary activity. We must first, however, give examples of these three kinds of prophetic writing.

Concerning the predecessors of the writing prophets—Samuel, Nathan,

Ahijah of Shiloh, Elijah, Micaiah ben Imlah, Elisha and the rest—we have only third person narratives of the saga and legend type. Scattered within these is to be found a whole range of sayings, some in prose, some in poetic form, and these sayings are often quite lengthy. Thus the narrative of Saul's rejection by Yahweh and by Samuel culminates in the saying of I Sam. xv, 22–3. Here Yahweh is referred to in the third person. But the story of David's reproof by Nathan (II Sam. xii) not only puts in the latter's mouth the well-known parable of the poor man's ewe lamb, but adds to it an utterance of Yahweh in vv. 7–10 (12) provided with the introductory formula normal to the writing pro- phets: *Thus says Yahweh, the God of Israel.* Similarly, the threat which Ahijah of Shiloh speaks to the wife of Jeroboam (I Kings xiv, 7–11) is an address by Yahweh, and the same is true of Elijah's diatribe and threat to Ahab (I Kings xxi, 19), and of the words with which Elisha's disciple accompanies the anointing of Jehu (II Kings ix, 6–9). But we are hardly justified in assuming that collec- tions of sayings existed for these prophets too, and that these were used by the compilers of the third person narratives. Or, if such collections of sayings really did exist—which in itself is quite possible—it is not thereby established that the words put into the mouths of these prophets by the narrator actually derived from such collections. For the words are entirely such as could equally well have been invented by the compilers of these biographical narratives, familiar on the one hand with the attitude of the prophet in question and on the other hand with the speech-forms of the prophets of their own time. They are likely to have been invented just like the speeches of the other persons who appear. Thus we can say nothing certain concerning collections of prophetic sayings older than those which underlie the books of the writing prophets. The matter is similar with the prophetic autobiographical narratives. The narratives, also legendary, concerning the older seers and prophets, contain autobiographical accounts of visionary experiences. Balaam describes in the first person what he has seen (Num. xxiii, 7–10, 18–24; xxiv, 3–9, 15–19), and so does Micaiah ben Imlah (I Kings xxii, 17, 19). But certain though it is that the predecessors of the writing prophets also had such experiences and described them in the first person, it nevertheless remains uncertain whether they compiled literary accounts in the first person concerning their activity. For the vision accounts of Balaam and Micaiah ben Imlah are likely also to have been imitations by the narrators from what they could observe in the prophets of their own time. Thus we cannot go further than saying that we have only biographical narratives, some of them of a legendary character, concerning the predecessors of the writing prophets, and must leave it undecided as to whether there were also in existence collections of sayings and autobiographical narratives stemming from them.

But if we look now at the books of the two earliest of the writing prophets, Amos and Hosea, the biographical narratives take a very minor place. By far the largest part of their books is occupied by their words, evidently taken from collections of sayings, and in addition there are also parts of an autobiographical narrative in each case. In Amos the section vii, 10–17, doubtless fragmentary and extracted from a larger context, is biographical, and in the book of Hosea the beginning (ch. i) contains a narrative concerning the prophet in the third person. In Amos, however, the visions are related in the form of an autobio-graphical account (vii, 1–9; viii, 1–3; ix, 1–4), and in Hosea so is the marriage story of ch. iii which presumably provides a parallel to the biographical narra-tive of ch. i (pp. 387–90). It is also true of Isaiah i–xxxix that by far the larger part of the content consists of sayings and addresses, which, as may here be more precisely recognised (pp. 306–7), come from several collections of such material. But side by side with these, there are also biographical narratives con-cerning the prophet, and personal narratives in autobiographical style. Thus, for example, we have on the one hand, ch. vii which should not, as often happens, be changed to a first person narrative to fit in with ch. vi and ch. viii, but should rather be regarded as a parallel to ch. viii, and also ch. xx and chs. xxxvi–xxxix. On the other hand we have ch. vi and ch. viii and also xiv, 28–32, if with Bewer (p. 313) we should read וָאֶחֱזֶה *then I saw*, instead of אָחָז הָיָה *Ahaz was* in v. 28. It may be recognised with certainty (pp. 399, 391, 308), in spite of the fact that the biographical and autobiographical material which has been preserved is only rather scanty in Amos, Hosea and Isaiah, that both types must have been taken from originally independent smaller books. This, as the analysis will show (cf. § 46), becomes completely clear in the book of Jeremiah, in which the three types of prophetic writing—collections of sayings, biography and autobiography—are more or less in equal proportions, and in which more particularly quite precise observations can be made concerning the nature and origin of the biographical and autobiographical material. At the same time, it becomes quite clear that without the knowledge of these three types of pro-phetic writing the structure of the present book remains unintelligible.

Among the remaining prophets, Joel, Obadiah, Nahum, Zephaniah, Zechariah ix–xiv and Malachi contain nothing but sayings. The book of Jonah, however, is a biographical account, admittedly of legendary character, and so of a quite different kind from the biographical narratives just mentioned. In Micah and Habakkuk, which also contain only sayings, we may perhaps detect traces of autobiography. In general the possibility must be borne in mind that our prophetic books may originally have contained, in addition to sayings presenting the direct word of God, more narratives concerning the prophet in the form of biography and autobiography than is now the case, but that these narratives were suppressed by a redaction which was only concerned with the word of God, or that they have at any rate been reduced to a minimum. In Micah iii, 1, for example, there is a phrase *And I said* which now stands completely isolated, and could be the remains of a piece of autobiography, and Hab. i, 2–ii, 4, is in form autobiographical and may with more justice be placed alongside those so far mentioned in that here too we are dealing with a visionary experience such as is not often the main content of an autobiographical account. The Book of Ezekiel is, in its present form, a single large autobiographical narrative, whose separate parts appear to be quite precisely dated. Zech. i–viii is also practically entirely made up of autobiography, though there are also a number of sayings included, particularly in chs. vii–viii. The little book of Zechariah's contempor-ary, Haggai, which in other respects most closely resembles the books of Ezekiel and Zech. i–viii by the dating of the individual sections, is in form a biographical account by Haggai himself, and we may perhaps assume that this prophet thought that by not using the first person style, but by giving his own account of himself in the third person, he would be underlining even more firmly the precision and objectivity which is already stressed by the dating.

3. *Apocalyptic*. If we turn from the prophetic literature to its successor, apocalyptic, it is immediately noticeable that in the apocalypses the saying, the genre which takes up the bulk of the space in the prophetic books, is entirely or almost entirely lacking. The apocalyptists thus do not set forth divine utterances ultimately received in a state of ecstatic possession, and are no longer speakers, but simply authors. It follows that no sayings of theirs could be collected. The other two types of material, biography—here entirely of a legendary character—and autobiography, do remain, but in such a way that the latter takes up more and more space, and everything, even the dullest pieces of erudition, is brought into this form (see pp. 528 f.), as had indeed already happened with Ezekiel in chs. xl–xlviii. In the book of Daniel, the first half (i–vi) is in form biographical, whereas the second half (vii–xii) is autobiographical, even though the introductions to ch. vii (vv. 1–2aα) and to chs. x–xii (x, 1) refer to Daniel in the third person. Apocalypses such as IV Ezra and Enoch are, however, compiled entirely in autobiographical form. As in the case of the prophetic books, so too with Daniel the separation of biographical and autobiographical material provides a means of recognising the prehistory of the book. For the possibility must be entertained that the collection of Daniel legends in chs. i–vi originally had an independent existence. With the other apocalypses, where this criterion is lacking, we have at least to some extent other indications which assist in illuminating their often very complicated prehistory. Thus in the book of Enoch, which is really a complex of many books, the originally independent books or booklets still bear titles, and this, together with other features, makes it possible to recognise them as separate units. The details of this will be discussed when we come to the analysis of the books.

4. *Foreign influences*. At this point, when we are simply setting out the principles which are everywhere valid for the literary prehistory of our prophetic and apocalyptic books, there is one other question which requires an answer because of its general significance. This is the question whether, in the formation of the complexes of moderate size which precede our books, some external influences may also have been determinative. We have already indicated (see p. 77) that the existence of seers and *nabis* is not a specifically Israelite phenomenon, and that, if for the moment we disregard the religious and ethical content which in Israel is so clearly of a quite special kind, the visions and sayings of the seers and prophets in Israel's environment look exactly like those in Israel itself. But the question is whether parallels may be found in Israel's environment to the literary products of this ecstatic movement, parallels which could perhaps have served as patterns. It has been thought that such parallels can be demonstrated in Egyptian literature. For here, already by about 2000 B.C., prophetic texts appear—the prophecies of Nefer-rohu (Neferti), the exhortations

of Ipu-wer and others[1]—which proclaim concerning the future first all manner of disasters and then good fortune, and in this reveal a certain similarity to many of the smaller collections of sayings which underlie our prophetic books. For these too appear to be arranged according to the pattern, first disaster and then good fortune. It is possible that there is Egyptian influence at work here, not indeed upon the proclamation of the prophets themselves, but upon the collections of their sayings which came into being largely in the circles of their disciples. But this is by no means certain, for the arrangement simply corresponds to a general human attitude. After looking forward to a hard future, there is also felt a need to be consoled and encouraged by a prospect of the good fortune which is hoped for in the period after the disaster. It is particularly intelligible in Judaism that the prophetic threats should be concluded with words of salvation, whether genuine or not. For the threats had been fulfilled, and men felt themselves heavily burdened with the hard fate which lay now upon Israel. Certainly the fate was deserved; the guilt of the fathers was great enough. But the more post-exilic Judaism expressed this mood of penitence, the more it lived in the certain hope that distress would soon, indeed very soon, come to an end, and that the salvation of the last times would break in. At that time, men could therefore hardly help thinking that the prophets, both with and after their threatening of catastrophe, had also set forth the proclamation of salvation. So, in good faith, the collections of prophetic words were arranged and elaborated accordingly.

But in one point we may with certainty recognise external influence on Israel. Those Egyptian prophecies are, at any rate in part *vaticinia ex eventu*. This is particularly true of the so-called 'demotic Chronicle'[2] which dates probably from the middle of the third century B.C. It purports to have been compiled under king Tachos (360-359 B.C.) and to proclaim in advance the events down to the beginning of the Greek period, though in reality those events already lie in the past. To this there is then added the real prophecy, the proclamation of the overthrow of foreign rule and the re-establishment of the native kingdom. This structure reveals, as we may see, great similarity to Dan. vii–xii, and to many sections from the pseudepigraphic apocalypses (cf. § 76), as well as to the Habakkuk 'Commentary' from Qumrān[3] (cf. § 109). It is thus very reasonable to assume here the dependence of Judaism on its environment, the more so since the apocalypses are influenced in their content too by their environment (see p. 620). Whether in this we should think solely of Egypt is

[1] AOT, pp. 46–55; ANET, pp. 441–9; Albright, *Recent Discoveries in Bible Lands* (1955), p. 13; Lanczkowski 'Ägyptischer Prophetismus im Lichte des alttestamentlichen' ZAW 70 (1958), pp. 31–8; Morenz, HdO, I, 2 (1952), p. 199; Otto, HdO, I, 2 (1952), pp. 112–17 *et passim*; Posener, *Littérature et politique dans l'Égypte de la XIIᵉ Dynastie* (1956). Cf. also Lit. n. 2; §§ 10, 126.

[2] Kienitz, *Die politische Geschichte Ägyptens vom 7. bis zum 4. Jahrhundert vor der Zeitwende* (1953), pp. 136–9; Eduard Meyer, *Die Israeliten und ihre Nachbarstämme* (1906), pp. 451–5; 'Eine eschatologische Prophetie über die Geschichte Ägyptens in persischer und griechischer Zeit' SAB (1915), pp. 287–311 = *Kl. Schr.* II (1924), pp. 67–91; Morenz, HdO I, 2 (1952), p. 201; Otto, HdO I, 2 (1952), pp. 118 f.; Spiegelberg, *Die sogenannte demotische Chronik* (1914). Lit. n. 1; § 126.

[3] Rabin, 'Notes on the Habakkuk Scroll and the Zadokite Documents' VT 5 (1955), pp. 148–62, esp. 148–52.

admittedly not so certain. For the writings of the Sibyllines, which will be discussed later (§ 95), and the 'Oracles of Hystaspes'[4] which are similar and reveal Iranian elements, show that at the time there was also to be found in other parts of the world this type of *vaticinia ex eventu* designed to give credibility to the genuine prophecy which it preceded and into which it led. At all events we do not seem here to be dealing with a specifically Jewish phenomenon.

§ 21. THE POETIC AND DIDACTIC BOOKS

Cf. *Literature:* §§ 11–16, 63–5, 67, 69, 88, 89, 93, 108, 112, 126.

In the poetic and didactic books of the Old Testament, to which we must now turn, it is quite clear, as with the others, that they presuppose a literary prehistory, and here the earlier stages may be particularly clearly and easily recognised. A general outline of this may be conveniently given here for the Psalter and book of Proverbs though reference must be made to the analysis of these books for the details.

1. *Collections of songs contained in the Psalter.* The division of the Psalter into five books deliberately follows the pattern of the Pentateuch or at any rate was subsequently understood as an imitation of this (Pss. i–xli, xlii–lxxii, lxxiii–lxxxix, xc–cvi, cvii–cl). The division is linked in part to older independent collections, in that it utilises their concluding doxologies (Pss. xli, 14; lxxii, 18–20 etc.) to mark the divisions, and it thus to this extent preserves a recollection of the literary prehistory of the Psalter. But other observations are more valuable. Thus a first glance reveals that groups of psalms such as cxx–cxxxiv which all have the title, only used here שִׁיר הַמַּעֲלוֹת (Ps. cxxi לַמַּעֲלוֹת) —*pilgrim songs*—originally formed an independent collection. Likewise it is almost certain that the Korah psalms (xlii, xliv–xlix, lxxxiv–lxxxv, lxxxvii–lxxxviii) and Asaph psalms (l,[1] lxxiii–lxxxiii), which still largely stand together, represent special, originally independent collections. Furthermore, the colophon to Ps. lxxii: *The prayers of David, the son of Jesse, are ended,* clearly presupposes a separate collection of Davidic psalms, which probably earlier comprised only li–lxxi (lxxii) rather than iii–xli + li–lxxi (lxxii). The Psalter is not the result of a placing together of individual psalms, available to the redactor still quite detached, but an adding together of several collections, which to some extent contained the same songs. This is quite unmistakably demonstrated by the fact that certain psalms appear twice: xiv = liii;[2] xl, 14–18 = lxx; lvii, 8–12 + lx,

---

[4] Altheim, *Weltgeschichte Asiens im griechischen Zeitalter* I (1947), p. 105; II (1948), pp. 174–84; *Alexander und Asien* (1953), pp. 284 f.; Cumont, 'La fin du monde selon les mages occidentaux' RHR 103 (1931), pp. 29–96; Cumont and Bidez, *Les mages hellénisés* (1938), I, pp. 217–22; II, pp. 361–76; Czeglédy, 'Bahrām Čōbīn and the Persian Apocalyptic Literature' AcOr[B] VIII, 1 (1958), pp. 21–43; Windisch, *Die Orakel des Hystaspes* (VAA, NR XXVIII, 3, 1929). Lit. § 126.

[1] Beaucamp, NRTh 91 (1959), pp. 897–915; Pautrel, *Mél. Bibl. Robert* (1957), pp. 234–240.

[2] Budde, 'Psalm xiv und liii' JBL 47 (1928), pp. 160–83.

7–14 = cviii. We have here exactly the same phenomenon as in the historical (pp. 134–6) and legal (pp. 143–5) books, and though this has not yet been discussed, the same feature is also to be found in the prophetic books (e.g. Amos viii, 4–14 = individual sayings in chs. iv–v, see p. 400; Jer. x, 12–16 = li, 15–19, see p. 362).

2. *Collections of sayings incorporated in the book of Proverbs.* In the book of Proverbs, we may separate out even more easily the originally independent smaller collections of sayings and poems which the redactor had in front of him. For these collections are not interwoven and hence their original form has not been destroyed—this is in part true also of those in the Psalter. They have been arranged here one after the other quite untouched, and each collection still has its special title: i–ix; x, 1–xxii, 16; xxii, 17[3]–xxiv, 22; xxiv, 23–34; xxv–xxix; xxx, 1–33; xxxi, 1–31. Furthermore, these medium-sized or small collections in their turn are in part made up from even smaller collections[4] as will be shown in the analysis. This fact which can so clearly be recognised in the Psalter and in Proverbs, must also apply to other books of the same kind.

Thus, at any rate for the majority of the books of the Old Testament, canonical or extra-canonical, we must reckon with the fact that they presuppose books of smaller compass, and it is now the task of the analysis to demonstrate this in detail.

---

[3] On xxii, 17, see pp. 86, 471.
[4] The position is similar in regard to collections of proverbs in Israel's environment, as for example the Sumerian and Arabian proverbs, cf. Blachère, 'Contribution à l'étude de la littérature proverbiale des Arabes à l'époque archaïque' Arabica 1 (1955), pp. 53–83; Bloch,' Zur altarabischen Spruchdichtung' in *Westöstliche Abhandlungen Rudolf Tschudi* (1954), pp. 181–224; Gordon, 'The Sumerian Proverb Collections' JAOS 74 (1954), pp. 82–5; *Sumerian Proverbs: Glimpses of Everyday Life in Ancient Mesopotamia* (1960); Henning, 'Eine arabische Version mittelpersischer Weisheitsschriften' ZDMG 106 (1956), pp. 73–7; Sellheim, *Die klassisch-arabischen Sprichwörtersammlungen, insbesondere die des Abū 'Ubaid* (1954). Cf. lit. p. 83, n. 3; p. 87, n. 12; § 126. Cf. also Theognis (below p. 495, n. 19).

PART THREE

THE ANALYSIS OF THE BOOKS OF THE OLD TESTAMENT

A. THE PENTATEUCH (הַתּוֹרָה THE LAW)

§ 22. NAME AND CONTENTS

Literature: Commentaries (a) Series: ATD: von Rad, *Gen* ([5]1958) E.T. (1961); Noth: *Ex* ([2]1959), E.T. (1962); COuT: Gispen, *Lev* (1950), *Num* i, 1–xx, 13 (1959); Echter-B.: Junker, *Gen, Deut* ([2]1955); Schneider, *Ex, Lev, Num* (1952); HAT: Beer and Galling, *Ex* (1939); HK: Gunkel, *Gen* ([6]1963); Baentsch, *Ex–Num* (1903); Steuernagel, *Deut* ([2]1923); HS: Heinisch, *Gen* (1930), *Ex* (1934), *Lev* (1935), *Num* (1936); Junker, *Deut* (1933); HSAT: Holzinger, *Gen–Num* (1922); Marti, *Deut* (1922); IB: Simpson, Bowie, *Gen* (1952); Rylaarsdam, Park, *Ex* (1952); Micklem, *Lev* (1953); Marsh, Butzer, *Num* (1953); Wright, Shires, Parker, *Deut* (1953); ICC: Skinner, *Gen* ([2]1930 (1951)); Gray, *Num* (1903 (1955)); Driver, *Deut* ([3]1902 (1952)); Jerusalem-B.: de Vaux, *Gen* ([2]1958); Couroyer, *Ex* ([2]1958); Cazelles, *Lev* ([2]1958), *Num* ([2]1958), *Deut* ([2]1958); KAT: Procksch, *Gen* ([2,3]1924); König, *Deut* (1917). KeH: Dillmann, *Gen* ([6]1892), *Num* ([2]1886), *Deut* ([2]1886); Dillmann-Ryssel, *Ex–Lev* ([3]1897); KHC: Holzinger, *Gen* (1898), *Ex* (1900), *Num* (1903); Bertholet, *Lev* (1901), *Deut* (1899); KV: Noordtzij, *Lev* (1940), *Num* ([2]1957); LD: Chaine, *Gen* (1948); SAT: Gunkel, *Gen* ([2]1921); Gressmann, *Ex–Deut* ([2]1922); Soncino-B.: Freedman, *Gen* ([2]1950); Rabbinowitz, *Ex* ([2]1950); Lehrman, *Lev* ([2]1950); Fisch, *Num* ([2]1950), *Deut* ([2]1950); SZ: Strack, *Gen* ([2]1905), *Ex–Num* (1894); Öttli, *Deut* (1893); Torch-B.: Richardson, *Gen* i–xi ([3]1959); Cunliffe-Jones, *Deut* ([2]1956); TU: Böhl, *Gen* I ([2]1930), II (1925), *Ex* (1928); de Wilde, *Lev* (1937); Edelkoort, *Num* (1930); WC: Driver, *Gen* ([12]1926 (1954)); McNeile, *Ex* (1908 (1931)); Elliott-Binns, *Num* (1927).

(b) Single Commentaries: Delitzsch, *Gen* (1887); König, *Gen* ([2, 3]1925); Bamberger, *Raschi's Pentateuch-Kommentar vollständig ins Deutsche übertragen* ([3]1935).

Cf. Literature § 126.

1. *Name*. The name most commonly used among the Jews for the five books of Moses is הַתּוֹרָה *The Law*, or תּוֹרַת מֹשֶׁה *The Law of Moses*, or סֵפֶר הַתּוֹרָה *The Book of the Law*, or סֵפֶר תּוֹרַת מֹשֶׁה *The Book of the Law of Moses*, or some similar phrase, a name which in the first place indicates only its legal sections, and in particular Deuteronomy, but is then also applied to the whole range of the five books. We cannot say for certain whether this more comprehensive application of the word already appears in the Old Testament, since the passages which here come in question may all be so interpreted as to indicate only the legal sections (Ezra x, 3; II Chron. xxx, 16; Neh. viii, 3; II Kings xiv, 6). The New Testament, however, clearly presupposes this wider use when it employs for the whole Old Testament the term: ὁ νόμος καὶ οἱ προφῆται *The Law and the Prophets* (Matt. v, 17). Side by side with the name *The Law* is to be found also the other name *The Book of Moses*, and here again the relevant Old Testament passages (Ezra vi, 18; Neh. xiii, 1; II Chron. xxv, 4;

xxxv, 12) possibly indicate by it only the law in the narrower sense, whereas in the New Testament, namely in Mark xii, 26, where the passage Exod. iii, 2–6 is quoted as standing *in the Book of Moses*, the whole range of the five books is clearly meant. The singular term *The Law*, *The Book*, does not, however, mean that the five-fold division of the larger whole so denoted did not exist. This division is in fact older than the Septuagint which clearly had the division before it already. Admittedly the description corresponding to this five-fold division חֲמִשָּׁה חוּמְשֵׁי הַתּוֹרָה *The five fifths of the Law*, is first to be found in Talmudic times. But it is clearly older. For the term ἡ πεντάτευχος (βίβλος) *The (book) consisting of five books*, which is probably to be understood as a translation of the Hebrew name, already appears in the second century A.D., and its Latin form *pentateuchus* (*liber*) soon after. Our entitling of the five books of Moses as the Pentateuch corresponds to the Latin name. (*Pentateuchus*, like the German *Der Pentateuch*, is a masculine form.) On the analogy of this word, and of the description Octateuch used in the early church for the eight books Gen.–Judg. + Ruth, the term Hexateuch has come to be used in recent times for the books from Gen. to Josh., which, as we shall see (p. 250) form a unit; and similarly the term Octateuch (Enneateuch) for the complex Gen. to Sam. (Kings) without Ruth, which also probably originally belonged more closely together. These terms will also occasionally be used here in the discussion which follows; they have already been used earlier (p. 136).

2. *Contents.* The dividing lines between the individual books of the Pentateuch are in general meaningful. At the end of Gen. (ch. l) there comes to an end the story which tells of the Patriarchs, i.e. the forefathers of the people, and with Exod. i there begins the history of the people itself (i, 7). The division between Exod. and Lev. is also justified in so far as the tent of meeting is completed with Exod. xl (v. 33), and from Lev. i onwards there are set out the regulations which apply to the cultus to be celebrated there—though admittedly together with other regulations. But this division does at the same time break the connection between material which belongs together. For Lev. viii, in which is related the carrying out of the directions given in Exod. xxviii–xxix,[1] namely the dedication to the priesthood of Aaron and his sons,[2] belongs as closely with Exod. xxv–xxxi as do Exod. xxxv–xl, which also give an account of the carrying out of the directions set out in Exod. xxv–xxxi. The fact too that the setting for the action of Lev. and of Exod. xix–xl is the same, namely Sinai, also binds these two together.

There is something new with the beginning of Num. For the reviewing and arrangements for marching and service related in i–iv may be considered as preparation for the departure from Sinai, and should indeed be so regarded. Admittedly in the directions given in v, 1–x, 10, there is to be found a great deal which has nothing to do with this departure, and which can hardly be related

---

[1] Elliger, 'Ephod und Choschen. Ein Beitrag zur Entwicklungsgeschichte des hohepriesterlichen Ornats' VT 8 (1958), pp. 19–35 = *Baumgärtel-Festschrift* (1959), pp. 9–23; Haran, 'The Ephod According to Biblical Sources' [Hebr., Engl. sum.] Tarbiz 24 (1954/5), pp. 380–91, II–III.

[2] Grintz, 'Aspects of the History of the High Priesthood' [Hebr., Engl. sum.] Zion 23/4 (1958/9), pp. 124–40, I–II.

to it. But the period of time between i, 1 and x, 11, is only twenty days (from 1:II:2 to 20:II:2), whereas Israel's sojourn at Sinai lasted more than three quarters of a year (Exod. xix, 1–?:III:1; Num. i, 1–1:II:2), so that the twenty days of Num. i, 1–x, 10, may simply be regarded as leading up to the departure. Although there is no change of place, Deuteronomy stands out sharply from the end of Num. in that Deut. i, 1, begins the great speech of Moses which covers chs. i–xxx. On the other hand, Deut. xxxi–xxxiv are clearly the direct continuation of Num. xxvii (xxxvi), in that here the appointment of Joshua as Moses' successor, begun in Num. xxvii, is brought to a conclusion, and besides, these chapters are concerned with the last words and death of Moses. Thus it may be seen that the division is meaningful, but at the same time it clearly appears that it has been made secondarily, and derives from the desire to divide into five approximately equal parts a complex which was felt to be too large (see p. 135).

For our understanding of the Pentateuch, this five-fold division must not in any case be determinative, and a division undertaken with reference to the contents themselves would appear differently, roughly thus: Gen. i–xi prehistory;[3] xii–l, the Patriarchs (Abraham, Isaac, Jacob and his sons); Exod. i–xviii the oppression of the Israelites in Egypt, their flight from Egypt and journey to Sinai; Exod. xix, 1, to Num. x, 10, Israel's sojourn at Sinai;[4] Num. x, 11–xxxvi + Deut. i–xxxiv, Israel's journey from Sinai into the plains of Moab opposite Jericho and Moses' death on mount Nebo. In Exod. xix, 1 to Num. x, 10, and in Num. x, 11 to Deut. xxxiv there is little action related, in contrast to Gen. i to Exod. xviii. Here a very large part is taken up with the legal material: Exod. xx, 1–17, the ethical decalogue; xx, 22–xxiii, 19 (33), the Book of the Covenant; Exod. xxv–xxxi + xxxv–xl + Lev. viii–ix, directions concerning the tent of meeting together with the cultic apparatus belonging to it, and the carrying out of these directions; Exod. xxxiv* the cultic decalogue; Lev. i–vii sacrificial laws; xi–xv purification laws; xvi[5] the great Day of Atonement; xvii–xxvi the Holiness Code; xxvii directions concerning vows, the first-born, the ban (חֵרֶם)[6] and tithes; a series of smaller groups of laws in Num. including in xviii the duties and privileges of the priests and Levites, and in xxviii–xxix the sacrificial calendar;[7] Deut. i–xxx the Deuteronomic law. It is one of the tasks of Pentateuchal criticism to explain how this interruption of the narrative by large blocks of law took place; it appears inept from a literary and aesthetic point of view, and even the young Goethe took exception to it.[8] It is to this task that we must now turn.

[3] Cramer, *Genesis i–xi: Urgeschichte?* (SGV 224/5, 1959).

[4] Jülicher, *Die Quellen von Ex i–vii*, 7 (Diss. phil. Halle, 1880); 'Die Quellen von Ex vii, 8 bis xxiv, 11' JpTh 8 (1882), pp. 79–127, 272–315.

[5] Löhr, *Das Ritual von Lev xvi* (SKG II, 1 1925).

[6] Brekelmans, *De ḥerem in het OuT* (1959).

[7] Rost, 'Zu den Festopfervorschriften von Numeri xxviii und xxix' ThLZ 83 (1958), cols. 329–34.

[8] 'Israel in der Wüste' Goethe, *West-Östlicher Diwan*, ed. by Ernst Beutler (1943), pp. 242–62, esp. p. 240. Cf. Budde, 'Goethe zu Mose's Tod' ZAW 50 (1932), pp. 300–3.

I. The History of Pentateuchal Criticism

§ 23. THE PENTATEUCH AS A WHOLE, WITH PARTICULAR REFERENCE TO THE NARRATIVE

Literature: Bea, 'Der heutige Stand der Pentateuchfrage' Bibl 16 (1935), pp. 175–200; Bentzen, 'Bemerkungen über neuere Entwicklungen in der Pentateuchfrage' ArOr 19 (1951), pp. 226–32; Carpenter and Harford, *The Composition of the Hexateuch* (1902); Cazelles, 'À propos du Pentateuque' Bibl 35 (1954), pp. 279–98; 'Les localisations de l'Exode et la critique littéraire' RB 62 (1955), pp. 321–64; 'Ras Schamra und der Pentateuch' ThQ 138 (1958), pp. 26–39; Coppens, 'Chronique de l'Ancien Testament: Le problème de l'Hexateuque' EThL 29 (1953), pp. 58–76; 'Moïse et les Origines du Pentateuque selon M. Cazelles' EThL 32 (1956), pp. 275–81 = ALBO II, 50 (1956); Daube, 'Rechtsgedanken in den Erzählungen des Pentateuchs' BZAW 77 (1958), pp. 32–41; Eissfeldt, 'Die neueste Phase in der Entwicklung der Pentateuchkritik' ThR 18 (1950), pp. 91–112, 179–215, 267–87; Galbiati, *La Struttura letteraria dell' Esodo: contributo allo studio dei criteri stilistici dell' A.T. e della composizione del Pentateuco* (1956); Holzinger, *Einleitung in den Hexateuch* (1893); Jacob, *Der Pentateuch* (1905); Kapelrud, 'Pentateuch-problemer' NTT 56 (1955), pp. 185–201; Kaufmann, *The Religion of Israel.* Translated and abridged by Moshe Greenberg (1961), pp. 153–211: 'The Sources'; König, *Ist die moderne Pentateuchkritik auf Tatsachen begründet?* (1933); I. Lewy, *The Growth of the Pentateuch.* Intr. by R. H. Pfeiffer (1955); McKenzie, *The Two-Edged Sword* (1956), pp. 72–131; Möhlenbrink, 'Josua im Pentateuch' ZAW 59 (1943), pp. 14–58; Moore, 'Tatian's Diatessaron and the Analysis of the Pentateuch' JBL 9 (1890), pp. 201–15; North, 'Pentateuchal Criticism' OTMSt (1951), pp. 48–83; Prado, 'Ultimos esbozos católicos sobre el Pentateuco' Sefarad 15 (1955), pp. 410–53; Rost, 'Die Gottesverehrung der Patriarchen im Licht der Pentateuchquellen' SVT VII (1960), pp. 346–59; Sant, 'The Pentateuch and Catholic Criticism (The Catholic Critical School 1897–1906)' Melita Theologica 10 (1951), pp. 16–21; Simpson, *Pentateuchal Criticism* (²1924); Steinmann, *Les plus anciennes Traditions du Pentateuque* (1954); Wright, 'Recent European Study of the Pentateuch' JBR 18 (1950), pp. 216–25.

Cf. also Literature §§ 5a, b, 18, 19, 22, 24–35, 126.

1. *The traditional view and early doubts expressed as to its correctness.* As the names mentioned in § 22, 1, already reveal—and as it is furthermore explicitly attested by introductory and concluding formulae which stand with the individual laws (cf. e.g. Deut. i, 1; iv, 44–5; xxxi, 24; xxxii, 45 etc.)—Moses was from an early date regarded as the compiler, or more correctly as the mediator, of the laws of the Pentateuch which issued from God himself. The name used in the New Testament clearly with reference to the whole Pentateuch—*the Book of Moses*—is certainly to be understood as meaning that Moses was the compiler of the Pentateuch. Explicit references to this conception may be found in Philo (*De vita Mosis* I § 4; IV § 291), in Josephus (*Ant. Prooem.* 4 §§ 18–26 and IV 8, 48 § 326), and in the Talmud (bab. Baba Batra 14b), where it is said that Moses wrote the five books named after him. Philo and Josephus explicitly attribute to Moses also the conclusion which relates his death (Deut. xxxiv, 5–12), whereas the Talmud regards this as having been written by Joshua. The Jewish tradition concerning the compilation of the Pentateuch by Moses was taken over by the Christian church.

Nevertheless, already at an early date, doubts were voiced both by Christians and by Jews concerning the absolute reliability of this tradition, even if at first it was only a matter of isolated and unsystematic individual points of doubt. There was to be a long wait, more than a millennium, before a positive theory concerning the composition and origin of the Pentateuch arose to replace the tradition. The doubts are in part to be explained as arising from dogmatic and ethical objections to many statements of the Pentateuch which could therefore hardly be attributed to Moses. Thus the Clementine Homilies[1] feel it to be objectionable that often there are attributed to God such strongly anthropomorphic actions as swearing, and limitations of various kinds are expressed concerning him; that there is a narrative concerning Noah's drunkenness, and that Abraham appears as the husband of three women; and the authors would like to deny these pieces of material to Moses. Other objections arise from observations of historical criticism, or from the criticism of style and literary form. It was recognised that the text itself occasionally demands a date of composition different from that of the tradition. It was noted that in the books which follow on the Pentateuch, the supposed work of Moses, the style was substantially the same as before and that no such clear difference of style was observable as one might have expected with a change of compiler. A whole series of repetitions and contradictions was discovered which could only with difficulty be understood if the Pentateuch was compiled by one author.

Thus Ibn Ezra († 1167) hints with regard to Gen. xii, 6, that the addition *The Canaanites were then in the land* to the sentence *And Abram journeyed through the land as far as the place at Shechem*,[2] *as far as the terebinth of the soothsayer*, must come from a period when the Canaanites were no longer in the land, in other words a period which lay a considerable time after Moses. Carlstadt (cf. p. 2) notes in his work *De canonicis scripturis* which appeared in 1520, that Moses could not have compiled the five books named after him, since it is nonsensical to ascribe to him the account of his own death which appears in Deut. xxxiv, 5–12, and that this account in fact reveals the same style as the preceding narrative.[3] Attention was drawn to the various repetitions and contradictions and other literary defects of all kinds, particularly by Andreas Masius (1574)[4] Isaac de la Peyrère (1655),[5] and Richard Simon,[6] and they drew from this the conclusion that the Pentateuch as we now have it could not have come from Moses, but was the work of a later author, who certainly made use of notes by

[1] III, 55–7; II, 52 (Rehm (1953), pp. 76–7, 55–6).
[2] Harrelson, Anderson, Wright, 'Shechem "Navel of the Land"' BA 20 (1957), pp. 1–32; Kee and Toombs, 'The Second Season of Excavation at Biblical Shechem' BA 20 (1957), pp. 82–105; Nielsen, *Shechem. A Traditio-Historical Investigation* (1945); Yadin, 'A Note on Dating the Shechem Temple' BASOR 150 (1958), p. 34; Wright, 'Comment on Yadin's Dating of the Shechem Temple' BASOR 150 (1958), pp. 34 f. Lit. p. 201, n. 13; § 126.
[3] § 85 (Credner (1847), pp. 368 f.)
[4] *Josuae imperatoris historia illustrata atque explicata.*
[5] *Systema theologicum ex praeadamitarum hypothesi,* pars prima.
[6] Deville, 'Richard Simon, critique catholique du Pentateuque' NRTh 73 (1951), pp. 723–39; Steinmann, *Richard Simon et les origines de l'exégèse biblique* (1960); Stummer, *Die Bedeutung Richard Simons für die Pentateuchkritik* (1912). Cf. above p. 6.

Moses, but added to them a great deal from other sources as well as material of his own.

The seventeenth century above all, into which we have already come with the mention of Peyrère, made notable contributions to Pentateuchal criticism, and the two philosophers Thomas Hobbes and Spinoza deserve to be mentioned here more than others, because they, admittedly beginning from the work of their predecessors, nevertheless recognised and stated more clearly than these had done what was the real point at issue, and in which direction the solution of the problem was to be sought. Hobbes, in his *Leviathan* of 1651 formulated the task of Pentateuchal criticism thus: 'The light that must guide us in this question, must be that which is held out to us from the Bookes themselves; And this light, though it shew us not the writer of every book, yet it is not unusefull to give us knowledge of the time, wherein they were written.'[7] The Pentateuch as a whole is accordingly post-Mosaic, but the sections which are explicitly ascribed to Moses (Exod. xxiv, 4; xxxiv, 28; xvii, 14 etc.) do come from him. As far as Spinoza is concerned, chapters 7 and 8 of his *Tractatus theologico-politicus* from the year 1670 are here relevant, and there he sets forth the following: The Pentateuch, together with the books that follow, including the books of Kings, is one large connected historical work, of which Ezra is the compiler; and by him too the various parts were named according to their content as 'Books of Moses', the 'Book of Joshua' etc. Ezra made use of sources for his work, including notes by Moses. He did not leave the sources unaltered, but fitted them to his own time. Ezra was not able to put the finishing touches to his work and this is the reason for the many literary imperfections which may be observed in the Pentateuch—lack of order and connection, repetitions, contradictions and the like.

2. *The older documentary hypothesis.* Though significant results had already been achieved by the work of those mentioned and of others, yet there was lacking up to this point any attempt to differentiate clearly between the individual component parts of which the Pentateuch is made up, or to describe them more exactly according to their period and bias. The pastor of Hildesheim, H. B. Witter, began to attempt this with his book, which appeared in 1711: *Jura Israelitarum in Palaestinam,* a commentary on the Pentateuch which remained unfinished—reaching only Gen. xvii, 27—in which he showed that in Gen. i–ii, 4, a divine name was used other than that in ii, 5–iii, 24,[8] and that ii, 5–iii, 24, was in content parallel to i, 1–ii, 4.[9] Admittedly this first attempt by a German scholar was soon completely forgotten and only brought to light again four decades ago by the French Old Testament scholar Lods.[10] The

---

[7] Part III, Ch. 33.

[8] Speiser, 'The Rivers of Paradise' *Joh. Friedrich-Festschr.* (1959), pp. 473–85; Tur-Sinai, 'Jhwh Elohim in der Paradies-Erzählung Genesis ii, 4b–iii, 24' VT 11 (1961), pp. 94–9.

[9] Campegius Vitringa had already pointed to the parallelism of i, 1–ii, 4 and ii 5–iii, 24 in his *Observationes sacrae* I of 1683 (ed. 1723, pp. 42 f.) but admittedly without making use of the difference of the divine names as an argument for this.

[10] *Jean Astruc et la critique biblique au XVIIIᵉ siècle* (1924); cf. also ZAW 43 (1925), pp. 134–5; Bardtke, 'Henning Bernhard Witter' ZAW 66 (1954), pp. 153–81; 'Henning Bernhard Witter, Pfarrer zu Hildesheim' Alt-Hildesheim, Heft 26 (Nov. 1955), pp. 1–10.

second endeavour, apparently quite independent of this, did not at first meet with a much better fate. This was the hypothesis put forward by Jean Astruc (born in 1684 at Sauve (Tarn) as the son of a protestant pastor who in 1685 became a catholic; after studying medicine at Montpellier, Astruc was from 1730 onwards private physician to Louis XV and professor of medicine in Paris),[11] in his *Conjectures sur les mémoires dont il paroit que Moyse s'est servi, pour composer le livre de la Genèse* (1753). He was inspired by the completely conservative desire to make intelligible what he regarded as a firmly established fact, namely, that Moses had compiled Genesis of which the action took place long before his own time. He had himself made afresh the observation that different names for God were used and drew from this the conclusion that there were different sources present. This he elaborated into the theory that Moses had two main sources in front of him, of which the one (A) used the divine name Elohim and the other (B) the name Jehovah. Since Astruc could not manage to assign the whole of the material of Genesis to these two sources, he assumed that there were a further ten, admittedly fragmentary sources. He pictured the process of composition of Genesis in this way: Moses set these sources (2 + 10) in four columns alongside one another, but these four columns were at a later stage combined and the present form of the book of Genesis came into being. Astruc thus follows the tradition completely in regard to his dating of Genesis and simply attempts to make this intelligible by means of an exact analysis of the book. In actual fact the analysis itself on the one hand and the assigning to a date on the other—whether of Genesis or of the Pentateuch, or of the sources discovered by the analysis—are two quite different matters, and it is as well to keep separate these two tasks of Pentateuchal criticism even in a survey of its history.

Another remark is also in place here. The dissection of the Pentateuch into parallel strands—for that is what Astruc's main sources are—took its beginning from the examination of the book of Genesis which is purely a narrative book, and this solution of the problem of the Pentateuch, reckoning with two or three (see p. 162) parallel strands which has appropriately been termed the 'older documentary hypothesis', remained dominant as long as the discussion was substantially limited to Genesis. When the other books, containing to a large extent legal material, were also brought into the investigation, there began to be confusion in the documentary hypothesis, because no parallel strands could be seen in the laws and so the solution was now sought in the 'fragment hypothesis' which we shall subsequently examine. It is clear that the composition of the legal parts of the Pentateuch is different from that of its narrative parts, and it is extremely important to keep this difference in mind and to beware of the temptation to treat everything alike.

Astruc's thesis did not fall into oblivion like that of his predecessor, and Old Testament scholarship owes this to the fact that Eichhorn in his *Introduction to*

---

[11] *Dict. de biographie française* III (1939), p. 1391; O'Doherty, 'The "Conjectures" of Jean Astruc, 1753' CBQ 15 (1953), pp. 300–4; de Savignac, 'L'œuvre et la personnalité de Jean Astruc' NC 5 (1953), pp. 138–47; de Vaux, 'À propos du second centenaire d'Astruc. Réflexions sur l'état actuel de la critique du Pentateuque' SVT I (1953), pp. 182–98.

the Old Testament[12] characterised more precisely according to style and content the two main sources proposed by Astruc, and thus for the first time proved that they existed. In this he at first assumed like Astruc that Moses had put together these two main sources and the subsidiary sources—Eichhorn assumed three or five fragmentary sources. Later he abandoned this view and ascribed the combining of the sources to a redactor otherwise unknown to us. Eichhorn pictured the redactor's method as being that he took material first from one source and then from the other, according to which offered the more complete account.

In 1798 Ilgen took a notable step forwards in his book *The documents of the Jerusalem Temple archives in their original form as a contribution to the correction of the history of religion and politics*, part I: *The Documents of the first book of Moses.*[13] Here he assigned the 17 individual documents assumed for Genesis to three authors, of whom two use the name Elohim and one uses Jehovah, but at the same time hinted that perhaps two Jehovistic authors should be reckoned with. Ilgen's recognition of these points first had its effects 50 to 100 years later, both in his apportioning of the Elohim material of Genesis to two authors and in the possibility, only hinted at, that the Jehovistic sections were also not unified but must be assigned to two parallel strands.

3. *The 'fragment' hypothesis.* For the time being, however, this attempt at solving the problem of Genesis or of the Pentateuch by assuming the presence of several parallel strands was put into the background by the so-called 'fragment hypothesis' which was originated by the English scholar Alexander Geddes and adopted by J. S. Vater in Germany. The works of these two authors which here come under review are those of Geddes from the years 1792[14] and 1800;[15] and Vater's *Commentary on the Pentateuch.*[16] These all present an examination of the whole Pentateuch and apply to the solution of the problem primarily the observations which may be made on the laws. These lead in fact to the assumption of several larger and smaller sections (fragments), independent of one another and without any continuity, but simply placed together by the hand of a redactor. Thus Geddes pictured the Pentateuch as such a collection of fragments. He did assume, making use of Astruc's recognition of the difference in the two divine names and the difference of two sources indicated by this, that the fragments belonged to two different circles, of which the one was accustomed to use Elohim and the other Jehovah; but this must not obscure the fact that the older documentary hypothesis as such is here abandoned. With Vater, the special consideration of the laws reveals itself in the fact that he regards the nucleus of the Pentateuch as a law book, namely Deuteronomy, traced back to the time of David and Solomon, to which historical and legal sections were gradually added. Only in the latest period before the exile did this process come to an end. W. M. L. de Wette too, whose significant work on

---

[12] *Einleitung in das Alte Testament* (First ed. 1780–3).
[13] *Die Urkunden des Jerusalemischen Tempelarchivs in ihrer Urgestalt als Beytrag zur Berichtigung der Geschichte der Religion und Politik*, part I. *Die Urkunden des ersten Buches von Mose*. No further volumes appeared.
[14] *The Holy Bible*, vol. I (1792).
[15] *Critical Remarks on the Hebrew*, vol. I (1800).
[16] *Commentar über den Pentateuch*, I, II (1802), III (1805).

Deuteronomy must be discussed in more detail later (p. 171), adopted the fragment hypothesis for the rest.[17]

4. *The supplementary hypothesis.* This theory was then replaced by the 'supplementary hypothesis', whose origin is to be seen in Ewald's review[18] of J. J. Stähelin's *Critical investigations of Genesis*.[19] Ewald here put forward the following points as his view: The basis of the Pentateuch—or more accurately the Hexateuch since Ewald reckons with a narrative running through to the conquest of Canaan and thus including the book of Joshua—is an Elohistic work whose compiler took up in his presentation older sections such as the decalogue and the Book of the Covenant. Later a parallel document using the divine name Jehovah came into being, and a third hand inserted sections of this Jehovistic work, together with other material, into the Elohistic work, but in such a way that the Elohistic basic document was always given preference. Since Ewald was of the opinion that the Jehovistic sections inserted in the Elohistic work were taken from a connected narrative strand, his position is basically that of the older documentary hypothesis. But it nevertheless gave the impetus to the development of the purely supplementary hypothesis, in that Ewald's successors assumed only one connected strand, the basic document itself, but denied that the Jehovistic sections were originally connected. They affirmed rather that these were from the start intended to supplement the Elohistic strand. Among others, we may mention as representatives of this supplementary hypothesis Bleek,[20] Tuch,[21] and Franz Delitzsch in his first period, represented by his commentary on Genesis of 1852.

Just as Ewald provided the impetus for the development of the supplementary hypothesis, so too he led to its shattering. For in his *History of Israel*,[22] he declared that it was necessary to assume the existence of at least two continuous Elohistic narrative strands, and he also reckoned with one Jehovist who had put together and amplified the older strands. A similar position was held by Knobel (commentaries on Exod. and Lev. (1857) and on Num.–Josh. (1861)), and Schrader (in his preparing of the 8th edition of de Wette's *Introduction* (1869)). The picture presented by Schrader is as follows: Two main strands are to be noted in the Pentateuch, that of the annalistic Elohistic narrator, which originated in the early period of David's reign, and the work, compiled soon after the division of the kingdom, of the theocratic narrator, also Elohistic. These two strands were then worked into a unity and at the same time supplemented about the middle of the eighth century by the prophetic Jehovist. We thus have a kind of combination of the older documentary hypothesis and the supplementary hypothesis presented as a solution of the Pentateuchal problem by Ewald, Knobel, Schrader and others.

[17] For a more detailed account cf. Smend, *W. M. L. de Wettes Arbeit am A und NT* (1958), pp. 112–16; cf. also Handschin, *W. M. L. de Wette als Prediger und Schriftsteller* (1958); Puknat, 'De Wette in New England' Proc. Am. Philos. Soc. 102 (1958), pp. 376–95; Staehelin, *Dewettiana* (1956); 'Kleine Dewettiana' ThZ 13 (1957), pp. 33–41.
[18] ThStKr 4 (1831), pp. 595–606. Lit. § 126.
[19] *Kritische Untersuchungen über die Genesis* (1830).
[20] *De libri Geneseos origine* (1836).
[21] *Kommentar über die Genesis* (1838).
[22] *Geschichte Israels* (first ed. 1843–55).

5. *The new documentary hypothesis.* Hupfeld[23] then went back, however, to the purely documentary hypothesis with his book *The sources of Genesis and the nature of their combination*,[24] and since his work met with much approval and deeply influenced the period that followed, it is justifiable to begin with him a new phase in the history of Pentateuchal criticism, that of the 'new documentary hypothesis'. It is here worth noting, in view of what has already been said (p. 161) that this theory came into existence with reference to Genesis, and with a neglect of the remaining books of the Pentateuch. According to Hupfeld, three narrative strands, each a complete and organic whole, underlie Genesis: the Elohistic original, a later Elohistic work, and the work which uses the divine name יהוה, the latest of the three. A fourth hand, to be distinguished from the authors of these three strands, in other words a redactor, combined these three into a single unit. From the large number of those who have adhered substantially to the new documentary hypothesis inaugurated by Hupfeld, we need mention here only two: Dillmann in his weighty commentaries on the Hexateuch (1875 ff.), and Franz Delitzsch in his *Studies in Pentateuchal Criticism*[25] and in his *Original Mosaic material in the Pentateuch*.[26] If we employ the sigla generally used today, the new documentary hypothesis—now including Deuteronomy—may be set out in the following chronological order of composition: P (= Priestly Code), E (= Elohist), J (= Jahwist, Yahwist) and D (= Deuteronomy). In so far as the solution of the Pentateuchal problem by means of a theory of sources has been adhered to at all in the subsequent period, the analysis undertaken by the new documentary hypothesis—apart from some modifications which are yet to be mentioned (pp. 169–70)—with its assigning of the Pentateuch to the four sources P, E, J and D, has retained its validity. This is even true for Mowinckel in *The Two Sources of the Predeuteronomic Primeval History (JE) in Gen. i–xi* (1937) and for Hölscher, *The beginnings of Hebrew historical writing*[27] and *Historical writing in Israel*.[28] The only point of difference is that these two to some extent go their own ways, in that in Gen. i–xi, where the duplications and unevennesses which are generally recognised in the older material (what is left after the removal of the P-material) are usually described as secondary expansions of the J narrative or similarly (pp. 169, 191–2), they assign these extra passages to E. Thus for E too they assume a 'prehistory', whereas the majority of scholars believe that its first indications are to be found in Gen. xv.[29]

6. *The dating of the sources.* With regard to the dating of these sources and their chronological order there was a marked change in the middle of the sixties of the nineteenth century. For the source P, up till then regarded as the oldest document and therefore called the basic document, was recognised to be actually

---

[23] Riehm, *Hermann Hupfeld, Lebens- und Charakterbild eines deutschen Professors* (1867), pp. 123–7. Lit. § 126.   [24] *Die Quellen der Genesis und die Art ihrer Zusammensetzung* (1853).
[25] 'Pentateuchkritische Studien I–XII' ZKWL 1 (1880), pp. 1–10, 57–66, 113–21, 173–83, 223–34, 279–89, 337–47, 393–9, 445–9, 503–9, 559–67, 617–26.
[26] 'Urmosaisches im Pentateuch I–III' ZKWL 3 (1882) pp. 113–36, 225–35, 281–99.
[27] *Die Anfänge der hebräischen Geschichtsschreibung* (1942).
[28] *Geschichtsschreibung in Israel* (1952).
[29] Kaiser, 'Traditionsgeschichtliche Untersuchung von Genesis xv' ZAW 70 (1958), pp. 107–26; Snijders, 'Genesis xv' OTS 12 (1958), pp. 261–79. Lit. p. 191, n. 9; § 126.

the latest or at any rate the next to latest, so that now JEDP or JEPD became the representation in sigla corresponding to the newer understanding—neglecting as we may for the moment the uncertainty as to whether E is earlier or later than J. The attributing to the post-exilic period, or at any rate to the latest part of the pre-exilic period, of the source which up till then had been regarded as the earliest, assigned roughly to the period of David, had as its consequence a marked transformation of the picture of the course of Israelite history. For now the information offered by P could no longer be used for the reconstruction of the earlier or even the earliest period, but had to be regarded as a deposit of the later, or latest, period. So this phase of Pentateuchal criticism, which as we shall see in a moment is to be named after Reuss, Graf, Kuenen and Wellhausen, drew the attention of very wide circles, and it must plainly be designated as epoch making. But we must not in this connection forget that the new element is concerned exclusively or at least primarily with the historical placing of the individual strands, and not with the separation of the strands themselves. So far as analysis is concerned, if we ignore some significant individual improvements, the theory of Reuss, Graf, Kuenen and Wellhausen agrees with the new documentary hypothesis which it found already to hand.

The recognition that the complexities of cultic and priestly regulations, presupposed by the stratum of the Pentateuch now called P, must lie not at the beginning but at the end of the development, had already been repeatedly stated in the first half of the nineteenth century. We must mention here, particularly because of its influence on Wellhausen, Vatke's book *The Religion of the Old Testament*,[30] strongly influenced by the Hegelian philosophy of history.[31] But here the discussion was based on intuitive insights, conditioned by historical and philosophical postulates, rather than on proofs based upon literary criticism. It was this basis in literary criticism which was provided above all by Reuss, Graf, Kuenen and Wellhausen among others, and it is just for this reason that this new phase in the history of Pentateuchal criticism is usually named after them. Reuss had already in 1833 expressed in a lecture the idea that the so-called basic document, i.e., P, was in reality the latest source.[32] But this thesis first really became known through the book by his pupil Graf entitled *The Historical books of the Old Testament*.[33] Here and in an article in a periodical[34] amplifying the book, he showed that Deuteronomy and the older historical books, i.e. Judges to Kings, did not presuppose the laws and narratives of P,[35] and the latter must therefore be later than those books. With reference to the narratives, Kosters[36] confirmed and elaborated Graf's conclusions. After

[30] *Die Religion des Alten Testaments* I (1835).
[31] Smend, 'De Wette und das Verhältnis zwischen historischer Bibelkritik und philosophischem System im 19. Jahrhundert' ThZ 14 (1958), pp. 107–19. Lit. § 126.
[32] Causse, 'La Bible de Reuss, etc.' RHPhR 9 (1929), pp. 1–31, cf. esp. p. 17, n. 44.
[33] *Die geschichtlichen Bücher des Alten Testaments* (1866).
[34] 'Die s.g. Grundschrift des Pentateuchs' AWAT 1 (1869), pp. 466–77.
[35] De Wette had already in 1806 declared that no traces of the 'Mosaic' law could be found in Josh.–II Kings xxi: cf. Smend, *Das Mosebild von Heinrich Ewald bis Martin Noth* (1959), p. 4.
[36] *De historie-beschouwing van den Deuteronomist met de berichten in Genesis-Numeri ver eleken* (1868).

Kuenen in his *The Religion of Israel*[37] had raised his powerful voice in favour of the late dating of P, it gained general recognition with Wellhausen's essays on the composition of the Hexateuch[38] and even more with his *History of Israel*[39] though we must recognise that some scholars, such as Dillmann, and at least at first Kittel[40] and Baudissin* maintained the priority of P over D, and that others, while admitting the late origin of P, pointed very firmly to the great age of much of the material contained in it (so Kittel later). Unanimity could not be achieved in the absolute dating of the individual strands, particularly J and E. Some thought that J and E had come into existence in the ninth and eighth centuries, or in the eighth and seventh, whereas others placed them one or two centuries further back. But in regard to the chronological order of the individual sources, the conception which was expressed in sigla form as JEDP gradually prevailed, although there have never been lacking those who declared E to be older than J (e.g. Baudissin*, König).

7. *Reaction against the new documentary hypothesis.* Although by and large the new documentary hypothesis expressed in sigla form as JEDP has prevailed more and more since the seventies of the last century, there has been no lack of serious objection to it nor of attempts to replace it by another theory. Many of these attempts, as for example those of Möller,[41] B. Jacob,[42] Cassuto,[43] Aalders[44] and Young*, with all their differences in detail, declare so unreservedly not only in favour of the literary unity of the Pentateuch, but also for its derivation from Moses, that although they contain in detail useful and correct observations, they hardly come into consideration as serious contributions to the solution of the Pentateuchal problem. Among other works, we may mention three here because they represent types of approach, namely that of A. Klostermann,[45] that of Eerdmans,[46] that of Volz and Rudolph,[47] and that of Robertson.[48] Klostermann's and

[37] *De Godsdienst van Israël* (1869–70), E.T. *The Religion of Israel* (3 vols.) by A. Heath (1874–5).

[38] 'Die Composition des Hexateuchs' *Jahrbücher für deutsche Theologie* 21 (1876), pp. 392–450, 531–602; 22 (1877), pp. 407–79, which appeared as a book in 1885. The 2nd (1889) and 3rd (1899) editions have the title *Die Composition des Hexateuchs und der historischen Bücher des AT*, because they also contain Wellhausen's analysis of the books from Judges to Kings which had first been published in Bleek's *Einleitung in das AT* ([4]1878).

[39] *Geschichte Israels* I (1878), published from the 2nd edition (1883) onwards under the title *Prolegomena zur Geschichte Israels* (E.T. *Prolegomena to the History of Ancient Israel* (1885), reprinted 1957).

[40] *Geschichte der Hebräer* I (1888), pp. 87–120, E.T. *A History of the Hebrews* I by J. Taylor (1895), pp. 96–132.

[41] *Die Einheit und Echtheit der fünf Bücher Mosis* (1931).

[42] *Das erste Buch der Tora. Genesis übersetzt und erklärt* (1934).

[43] 'La Questione della Genesi' (1934), and, in Hebrew, Commentaries on Gen. and Ex. (1944–51) and *The Documentary Hypothesis and the Composition of the Pentateuch* ([3]1959, Engl. ed. 1961). Cf. Artom, 'Umberto Cassuto' RStO 28 (1953), pp. 225–9; Milka Cassuto Salzmann, 'Bibliographia scelta delle pubblicazioni scientifiche di Umberto Cassuto' *ib.* pp. 229–38, p. 230 f.: 'Pentateuco'. Lit. § 126.

[44] *A Short Introduction to the Pentateuch* (1949).

[45] *Der Pentateuch* (1893); second series of studies publ. in 1907.

[46] *Alttestamentliche Studien* I–IV (1908–12); 'The Composition of Numbers' OTS 6 (1949), pp. 101–216.

[47] Volz and Rudolph, *Der Elohist als Erzähler. Ein Irrweg der Pentateuchkritik? An der*

Robertson's solution may be described as a kind of 'crystallisation hypothesis'. Around the nucleus of the basic Mosaic law, the remainder of the Pentateuch had gradually been deposited. Eerdmans' position, however, can hardly be described with a catchword. Although all his works are united in their firm and complete rejection of the new documentary hypothesis, the arguments which he brings forward against it are of a very varied kind, and his own conception of the formation of the Pentateuch involves a wealth of possibilities. In particular, he declares that the starting-point of modern Pentateuchal research—the separation of strands according to the divine names Yahweh and Elohim—is impossible, and he denies altogether the existence of continuous strands. What may actually be observed, particularly in Genesis, is that the material belongs to four different stages of religio-historical development, of which the earliest is quite poly-theistic, whereas the latest is purely monotheistic. Thus the arguments which are here brought against the new documentary hypothesis are mainly derived from a study of the material and content. Volz and Rudolph, lastly, are agreed in their denial of the existence of an independent source E, but apart from this they differ substantially from one another in their judgement of the composition of Genesis and of the Pentateuch as a whole. Volz also denies the existence of a narrative P strand, and considers P, like E, simply as an elaborator of J. He is then concerned to limit the part played by these two as much as possible, and so all the more to emphasise the artistic structure and religious value of J, the only narrative strand which he recognises. Rudolph, however, unreservedly recognises the existence of the source P, and also concedes that in the Pentateuch there is a series of E sections which appear in opposition to the narrative of J or disturb it in some other way, though they are not to be regarded as elements in a continuous E narrative, but simply as the products of various interpolators, who wished to improve or enlarge the scope of the J narrative.

8. *Modifications of the new documentary hypothesis.* In these studies there has been a radical repudiation of the new documentary hypothesis. But it has also, roughly since the turn of the century, undergone modifications from another direction, or more precisely from two other directions. In the first place, as a result of the impact of archaeological discoveries made in Palestine and the neighbouring lands, there has come to be a greater interest in the matters men-tioned in the Old Testament than in its formation. The question of the age and formation of the individual books or parts of books has often appeared rela-tively unimportant for the understanding of the contents, the more so since the study of the life of the people in the contemporary world in Palestine and the Near East, going hand in hand with archaeological research, made it clear that in many respects no real difference exists between the centuries and millennia, and that customs and outlooks in many ways remain the same, as do economic conditions. But when the previous answers to the questions concerning the origin of the Pentateuch were found to be unnecessary for the satisfying of his-torical interest, it seemed no longer necessary to spend much time on them.

Genesis erläutert (BZAW 63, 1933); Rudolph, *Der 'Elohist' von Exodus bis Josua* (BZAW 68, 1938).
   [48] *The OT Problem. A Re-Investigation* (1950).

Admittedly in earlier generations it had been in the main just this historical interest which had evoked the various theories concerning the formation of the Pentateuch, so that Pentateuchal criticism and introduction to the Old Testament in general represented an auxiliary discipline to historical research, what is normally called 'source criticism'. But now historical research no longer seemed to need this indirect route, and it was either abandoned or at any rate not followed through any further.

The tendency which became increasingly strong at the turn of the century to subordinate the personal element to the subject-matter, and so to pay attention above all to what was the common element to those times, itself forced work on the Pentateuch even further in the direction already taken. It revealed the narrative strands, understood so far as being the works of individual authors, to be nothing more than collections of popular material. So attention was directed to the separate parts of these collections—the single narrative, or saying, or song, etc.—and these were subjected to a closer examination, either exclusively or primarily, while the collections which had come into being more or less by chance were regarded as relatively unimportant. The smallest literary units, so closely linked with particular circumstances in the life of community or individual, were examined with great care, and the attempt was made to understand them from every point of view in form and content. We have already shown (pp. 129 f.) that in this many insights were achieved which are of lasting value. To this we must add that the work, directed primarily to the smallest units, has also brought a better understanding of the larger units, the strands or sources, in that it revealed the possibility, not previously sufficiently seriously considered, that the individual narratives and the other smallest units were likely to have preserved, even when they were incorporated in the context of the 'source', many peculiarities from their 'pre-source' stage of existence, peculiarities which did not therefore really fit the general outlook of the source and yet could not on that ground be regarded as not belonging to the source. But with all this it is nevertheless true that, looked at as a whole, the method of research just described, as it was expressed for example in the first volume[49] of the Göttingen series *Schriften des AT* (SAT) brought with it a modification of the new documentary hypothesis.

The other impulse to the modification of this hypothesis came from the ranks of its most ardent supporters, in that they attempted to press the literary critical examination even further. Taking up again various earlier observations, they recognised or believed they could recognise, that each of the four sources J, E, D, P presented in itself a complex picture, elaborated by many additions coming from the 'school' of the original author, and that these were not unified and complete books, constructed as it were on a deliberate plan by one author. For P, Wellhausen himself had pointed to the successive formation of large bodies of law. Kuenen (in the 2nd ed. of his introduction, 1885–93) and Procksch[50] endeavoured to trace expansions of E, and for the corresponding

---

[49] I, 1: *Die Urgeschichte und die Patriarchen* by Gunkel (1911, ²1921); I, 2: *Die Anfänge Israels* (from Exodus to Judges and Ruth) by Gressmann (1914, ²1922).
[50] *Das nordhebräische Sagenbuch. Die Elohimquelle* (1906).

examinations of the content of J we may mention Schrader[51] and Budde[52] among others. This relaxing of the new documentary hypothesis is expressed in the sigla used: P or Pg (g = ground-work, basic material), P[1], P[2], P[3] etc., E, E[1], E[2], E[3] etc., J, J[1], J[2], J[3] etc.

9. *The most recent form of the documentary hypothesis.* Deliberately repudiating such modifications of the new documentary hypothesis, Smend returned to a strict documentary hypothesis in his book *The narrative of the Hexateuch, examined with reference to its sources.*[53] Admittedly, as will be shown in more detail in a moment, this was not the new documentary hypothesis, but an elaboration of it, which may be indicated with the name 'newest documentary hypothesis'. Following the precedent set by Charles Bruston[54] and taking account also of the works by Schrader and Budde just mentioned, he attempted to show that the section of the Hexateuch narrative which uses the divine name Yahweh, i.e. the Yahwistic material, may be best understood as the combining of two continuous strands. He denoted these as J[1] and J[2], but did not by this intend to indicate supplements to the basic material of J, but two authors of parallel narrative strands extending right through the Hexateuch. At the same time as he divided the Yahwistic material strictly into two 'documents', he also denied that the E complex was to be understood as a basic document (E) expanded by additions (E[1], E[2], E[3] etc.), and here too carried through a purely documentary hypothesis in that he preferred to assign to his J[1] and J[2] large sections of material which had been characterised as E[1], E[2] etc. and thus left a unified E material. On the other hand, Smend also assumed later secondary additions to P, more even than his predecessors had done, and the position is similar for D. But here it is at least mainly a matter of legal material. The narrative of the Hexateuch he divided almost entirely between the four 'documents' J[1], J[2], E and P. Smend's views have been accepted, in some cases with not insignificant modifications of his analysis, by the following among others: Eichrodt,[55] Holzinger,[56] Meinhold[57] and Eissfeldt.[58] Eissfeldt, to obviate the confusion which can so easily arise from the use of the sigla J[1] and J[2], which suggest that it is a matter of elaborations of a basic J material, and at the same time to bring out the point that the units so denoted by Smend actually have equal standing with the sources E, D and P denoted by simple capital letters, introduced the siglum L (= lay source) for Smend's J[1], and replaced his J[2] with a simple J. The siglum L was also chosen because the strand denoted by it, in contrast to P, the Priestly Code, is least dominated by clerical and cultic tendencies.

Although they were not actually stimulated by Smend, but worked on

[51] *Studien zur Kritik und Erklärung der biblischen Urgeschichte* (1883).
[52] *Urgeschichte* (1883).
[53] *Die Erzählung des Hexateuch auf ihre Quellen untersucht* (1912).
[54] 'Les quatre sources des lois de l'Exode' RThPh 16 (1883), pp. 329–69; 'Les deux Jéhovistes' *ib.* 18 (1885), pp. 5–34, 429–528, 602–37; cf. Budde, ZAW 34 (1914), p. 253, n. 1.
[55] *Die Quellen der Genesis von neuem untersucht* (BZAW 31, 1916).
[56] *Genesis, Exodus, Leviticus, Numeri und Josua* (HSAT, 1922).
[57] 'Die jahwistischen Berichte in Gen. xii–l' ZAW 39 (1921), pp. 42–57.
[58] *Hexateuch-Synopse* (1922, 1962).

their own account, Morgenstern[59] and Pfeiffer[60] **also belong** to the adherents of the newest documentary hypothesis, in that they assume the existence of a fourth narrative strand alongside J, E and P—the former for Exodus and the latter for Genesis—and regard this strand as the oldest. Pfeiffer considers that it originated in the tenth century B.C. in Seir or in the south of Palestine, and therefore denotes it as S, whereas Morgenstern derives what he regards as the oldest Exodus narrative, dated in 899 B.C., from the Kenites and hence gives it the siglum K. On the other hand, Simpson[61] who reckons with three sources for the predeuteronomic narrative of the whole Pentateuch—J^1, J^2, E—was directly influenced by Smend. But he differs from him in that he does not treat J^2 as a parallel strand to J^1, but as an elaboration and transformation of J^1.

Whereas Smend and his followers explained the generally acknowledged disunity of P by the assumption that the basic P material had undergone various elaborations and amplifications, von Rad[62] has divided the narrative material which remains after the removal of secondary additions (which he does not entirely deny), into two parallel strands extending right through the Hexateuch, and for these he suggests the sigla P^A and P^B.

10. *Form-critical assessment of the Pentateuch.* An attempt at deepening the understanding of the documentary hypothesis, not admittedly in its latest form which is rejected tacitly rather than explicitly, but in the previous form, which is at any rate in essentials (JEDP) regarded as valid, has been made by the form-critical estimation of the Pentateuch as it is represented by von Rad[63] and by Noth.[64] This method of approach is not primarily concerned with the examination of the prehistory of the various individual pieces of material united in the Pentateuch, as has been undertaken already by Gunkel, Gressmann and others (p. 168), but is concerned with the tracing back of the original form of the Pentateuch as a whole into its beginnings which are looked for far beyond the sources, even the earliest J. These beginnings are regarded as being traditions belonging to particular festivals and shaped in confessional form, echoing on the one hand the Sinai tradition and on the other hand the conquest tradition, as they are echoed in Ps. l, lxxxi, and Deut. xxvi, 5b–9. These testimonies to the faith provided the framework for very varied traditions which were gradually incorporated in them, and so, long before the compilation of the earliest Pentateuch source, the original form of the Pentateuch actually came into being, and this, in accordance with its undeniable beginnings, is not really a historical work but rather a statement of faith, and must be so appreciated.

[59] 'The Oldest Document of the Hexateuch' HUCA 4 (1927), pp. 1–138.
[60] 'A Non-Israelite Source of the Book of Genesis' ZAW 48 (1930), pp. 66–73.
[61] *The Early Traditions of Israel. A Critical Analysis of the Pre-deuteronomic Narrative of the Hexateuch* (1948); Eissfeldt, *Die Ältesten Traditionen Israels. Ein kritischer Bericht über C. A. Simpson's The Early Traditions of Israel* (1950); Simpson, *Composition of the Book of Judges* (1957), pp. 149–96: Appendix: The Literary Structure of the J Document in the Hexateuch.
[62] *Die Priesterschrift im Hexateuch literarisch untersucht und theologisch gewertet* (BWANT 65, 1934).
[63] *Das formgeschichtliche Problem des Hexateuch* (BWANT 78, 1938) = *Ges. Stud. zum AT* (1958), pp. 9–86.
[64] *Überlieferungsgeschichte des Pentateuch* (1948, ²1960).

§ 24. THE PROBLEM OF DEUTERONOMY

Literature: In addition to that mentioned within this paragraph, and in §§ 19, 22, 23, 34, 41, cf. Erichsen, 'Eine neue demotische Erzählung' AAMz (1956), pp. 49–81, Pls. I–III, see pp. 50–2; Karl, 'The Discovery of the Torah in the Days of Josiah' (Hebr.) Tarbiz 22 (1950/1), pp. 129–35; Maag, 'Erwägungen zur deuteronomischen Kultzentralisation' VT 6 (1956), pp. 10–18; Segal, 'The Book of Deuteronomy' JQR 48 (1957/8), pp. 315–51. Lit. § 126.

Since Deuteronomy by its rather special character may easily be divided off from the remainder of the Pentateuch, it is proper to present separately the history of its critical treatment. It is also as well to treat separately in the first place the two admittedly interconnected questions which nevertheless in many respects are independent of one another, namely those of date and analysis.

1. *The chronological placing of D.* So far as the chronological placing of Deuteronomy is concerned, a fact that has been of far-reaching importance is that it was recognised as having a connection with the law book referred to in the account of Josiah's reform in II Kings xxii–xxiii. The recognition of this is ancient. That the law-book found by Josiah was Deuteronomy, compiled by Moses, was suggested already by some of the Church Fathers[1] and later for example by Hobbes (p. 160) and by Lessing.[2] But it first acquired greater significance for the understanding of Deuteronomy itself and for the study of the Pentateuch as a whole, through the work of de Wette, who in his *Dissertatio critica*[3] of 1805 maintained the thesis that 'Deuteronomy is a work which differs from the earlier books of the Pentateuch, and stems from a later author', thus regarding Deuteronomy as having originated not long before the time of its discovery, namely 621 B.C. By this suggestion the precise time of origin of Deuteronomy was established, and a fixed point was discovered by which the age of the other component parts of the Pentateuch could also be determined. De Wette's thesis thus provided Pentateuchal criticism with a 'point of Archimedes' to which it could attach itself in order to deliver it from the bonds of church and synagogue tradition, and put in its place an alternative dating of the Pentateuch and its parts. It is true that the necessary conclusions from de Wette's judgement were only gradually drawn. He himself in fact held to the view that the source we call P was older than D—hence his description in his *Dissertatio* of Deuteronomy as 'stemming from a later author'. That P rather presupposed D, and was thus later than D, was first established later, as we have seen (pp. 165 f.), by Reuss, Graf, Kuenen and Wellhausen.

De Wette's thesis came to be almost universally accepted, especially after it had been given new support by Riehm in his book *Moses' giving of the law in the land of Moab*,[4] for it may be regarded as relatively unimportant whether the book is regarded as having been compiled only in the time of Josiah, shortly

[1] Nestle, 'Das Deuteronomium und II Könige xxii' ZAW 22 (1902), pp. 170–1, 312–13.
[2] Hempel, ZAW 51 (1933), p. 299, n. 1.
[3] *Dissertatio critico-exegetica, qua Deuteronomium a prioribus Pentateuchi libris diversum, alius cuiusdam recentioris auctoris opus esse monstratur.*
[4] *Die Gesetzgebung Mosis im Lande Moab* (1854).

before its discovery, or half a century or a century earlier in the time of Manasseh or Hezekiah. Nor does it greatly matter whether it is regarded as an entirely Judaean product, or is assumed to derive from the northern kingdom (Welch, see below) or from the area of the Assyrian province of Samaria which had replaced that kingdom after its collapse, and to have been brought to Jerusalem in circumstances unknown to us and so have been discovered there in connection with Josiah's reform.[5] Even if it is dated earlier and regarded as deriving from the north, it is still only thought to have become effective after its discovery in Jerusalem in 621 B.C. But there have never been lacking those who have rejected de Wette's view of Deuteronomy, among whom some, partly with a denial of the justification for extracting the book from the Pentateuch as a separate unit, have claimed for it a much greater age, while others have firmly assigned it to the post-exilic period. Thus Oestreicher[6] sought to weaken the argument put forward as decisive by de Wette and his successors for the identifying of Deuteronomy with the law mentioned in II Kings xxii–xxiii, namely that cult centralisation was demanded by Deuteronomy and carried through according to II Kings. This he did by denying both to the narrative and to Deuteronomy the idea of a centralisation of the cultus at Jerusalem, and by regarding the law book found after or during Josiah's reform—but not before it—as a very ancient book, going back before Deuteronomy and also containing, for example, regulations found in the Holiness Code (Lev. xvii–xxvi). Loehr[7] similarly denied that Josiah's reform was occasioned by the lawbook, which he regarded as having been found only later, and regarded this book as one which went back to Moses or at any rate to the Mosaic period. The arguments which he adduced are in the main based on a critical study of the contents. In Deuteronomy, ancient legal precepts were preserved, indeed some very ancient ones, a point which is not denied by even the most determined upholder of de Wette's thesis, but which provides no justification for the conclusions drawn from it by Loehr. For Welch[8] likewise, it is mainly considerations of content which lead him to the dating of Deuteronomy, with its later additions removed, in the early period of the monarchy or even in the period of the Judges, and also to the assumption that it is to be regarded as derived from the northern kingdom. Brinker[9] regards Deuteronomy as having been compiled by Samuel for the sanctuary at Shechem, whereas D. W. B. Robinson[10] ascribes it to Moses and assumes that, having been deposited in the Temple at Jerusalem at the time of the latter's erection, it was at first read every seven years to the king, but gradually fell into oblivion and was only found again under Josiah.

Hölscher[11] in particular has argued for the origin of Deuteronomy in the exilic or post-exilic periods, though others too have held this view. Two

---

[5] Alt, 'Die Heimat des Deuteronomiums' *Kl. Schr.* II (1953), pp. 250–75; Bright, *A History of Israel* (1959), pp. 299 f.; Galling, 'Das Königsgesetz im Deuteronomium' ThLZ 76 (1951), cols. 133–8.

[6] *Das Deuteronomische Grundgesetz* (BFChTh 27, 4, 1923).

[7] *Untersuchungen zum Hexateuchproblem* II: *Das Deuteronomium* (SGK I, 6, 1925).

[8] *The Code of Deuteronomy* (1924); *Deuteronomy, the Framework to the Code* (1932).

[9] *The Influence of Sanctuaries in Early Israel* (1946).

[10] *Josiah's Reform and the Book of the Law* (1951).

[11] 'Komposition und Ursprung des Deuteronomiums' ZAW 40 (1923), pp. 161–255.

arguments in particular are put forward by him for this dating. First, it seems to him unthinkable that the regulations of Deuteronomy, in part strongly utopian, should have come into being at a time when the Judaean kingdom still existed, and when the Judaeans were familiar with the conditions of actual political and legal life. Such unworldly speculations must rather be ascribed to a later period when the Jews no longer had a state and were no longer an independent people. His second argument arises from the observation that many passages in the books of Jeremiah and Ezekiel, which doubtless originated only in the period after Josiah's reform, presuppose the evils which are forbidden by Deuteronomy, and which ought in Hölscher's view to have been removed once and for all if it really was Deuteronomy which gave the impetus to Josiah's reform and provided its standard of judgement.

Thus discussion of the correctness of de Wette's thesis, and so of one of the foundations of Pentateuchal criticism has not come to an end, and it has often appeared as if the thesis could not maintain itself against the renewed attacks brought against it from various sides. Yet it has resisted them, and today, in spite of continued attacks, appears more strongly established than ever as may be seen in the substantially similar remarks on the subject by Gressmann,[12] Budde,[13] Hans Schmidt,[14] Bewer, Dahl and Paton,[15] Baumgartner,[16] König,[17] Causse[18] and Irwin,[19] and in the relevant sections of the more recent introductions to the Old Testament.

2. *The analysis of D.* At the present time there is thus a large measure of agreement that the law book which underlay Josiah's reform, or which at any rate was utilised in it, is preserved in our Deuteronomy. But there are wide differences of opinion as to precisely how we should separate out the original Deuteronomy—that law book itself—from our book of Deuteronomy, and also in the analysis of Deuteronomy itself. It is indeed generally agreed that the law of Josiah and our Deuteronomy are not identical. On the one hand there is the impression given by the account in II Kings xxii–xxiii, according to which (xxii, 8, 10) the law was on the same day first read by the *scribe* Shaphan and then read by him to the king. This suggests that we are dealing with a relatively small corpus of laws, considerably smaller than the content of Deut. i–xxxiv. On the other hand, its designation as סֵפֶר הַתּוֹרָה *book of the law* (II Kings xxii, 8[20]) makes it seem virtually impossible that it could have contained as much narrative material as does our book of Deuteronomy at the beginning (i–xi) and at the end (xxvii–xxxiv). Although these arguments are not quite decisive, they are nevertheless worth noting, the more so since even a cursory reading of our Deuteronomy shows that there are many duplications and repetitions even in the historical section, i.e. at the beginning and the end. This point will later be discussed in detail (pp. 225–6). There is thus a fairly general inclination to

[12] ZAW 42 (1924), pp. 313–37.
[13] ZAW 44 (1926), pp. 177–224.
[14] ThBl 6 (1927), cols. 40–8.
[15] JBL 47 (1928), pp. 305–79.
[16] ThR 1 (1929), pp. 7–25.
[17] ZAW 48 (1930), pp. 43–66.
[18] RHPhR 13 (1933), pp. 1–29, 289–323.
[19] AJSL 56 (1939), pp. 337–49.
[20] S. Granild, 'Nogle forudsaetninger for Lovbogen i 2 Kong. xxii, 8' DTT 19 (1956), pp. 199–210.

deny to the original Deuteronomy substantial parts or even the whole of the beginning and end of the present book.

Duplications and unevennesses of various kinds are, however, to be found not only in the narrative sections at the beginning and end (i–xi, xxvii–xxxiv), but are also often noticeable in the central section (xii–xxvi) which contains the actual laws. Thus it is clear that there is overloading at the beginning in xii, where not only is the demand that sacrifices of all kinds are to be brought to one place only, chosen by Yahweh, expressed at least twice (xii, 5–7 and xii, 11–12), but the concession permitting profane slaughter in the individual localities is also given twice (xii, 15–17 and xii, 20–5). It is further obvious that the section containing cultic regulations in xvi, 21–xvii, 7, is out of place in a context which is concerned with legal matters and interrupts the connection between xvi, 20 and xvii, 8 (p. 131). It is difficult to believe that such unevennesses can belong to a programmatic scheme of laws of the kind which we must believe the original Deuteronomy to have been, even if we take into account the fact that we ought not to attribute to an ancient scheme of laws the same kind of order and logical arrangement which we should now expect. We must therefore assume that the original Deuteronomy has not come down to us in its original form but modified. This is indeed the opinion of the majority of scholars. But opinions differ on the questions as to what the original Deuteronomy may have looked like, and how the present form of the book has come about.

The various attempts at a solution which have been offered may be divided into two main groups, even though the boundaries between them are fluid and at the same time there are again many differences within each group. One group assumes that our Deuteronomy is a book which came into being by successive amplifications of the Josianic law-book or perhaps of its earlier forerunner. This, if we may here use the terminology already employed for the Pentateuch narrative, is a kind of supplementary hypothesis. The other group, however, describe the book which we now have as the result of the combining of two or more editions of the original Deuteronomy, and thus support a kind of documentary hypothesis. Hempel[21] may be reckoned as belonging to the first group. He regarded Josiah's law-book as the ancient Jerusalem Temple rule, elaborated in the time of Hezekiah or Manasseh in the interests of cultic centralisation, filled out with social regulations and provided with a historical introduction. He admittedly assumed at the same time that those who elaborated and added to it later included also a תּוֹעֵבָה (abomination)-source which had been compiled as a protest against the abominations practised and favoured by Manasseh. In this respect he was at the same time applying a kind of documentary hypothesis to the analysis of Josiah's book. He applied this method completely to the analysis of the book of Deuteronomy as we have it, for he explained it, just as do the representatives of the second group to be mentioned in a moment, as the combining of various editions of Josiah's book. Horst has endeavoured to prove the existence of an older, pre-deuteronomic basis for a part of Deuteronomy, namely the judicial sections contained in xii–xviii. This basic material he considered to be a decalogue containing a 'law of Yahweh's privileges', and

[21] *Die Schichten des Deuteronomiums* (1914).

he endeavoured to show that it had undergone a threefold elaboration and supplementation,[22] in which the last stage brought in the idea of centralisation. Hölscher,[23] however, with a study of the whole of Deuteronomy, has with very great acumen affirmed that only the supplementary hypothesis is justified, and by removing the remaining sections as supplements of various kinds assigns the following passages to the original Deuteronomy: the nucleus with singular forms of vi–xi, together with xii, 13–31; xiii, 2–18; xiv, 22–9; xv, 1–23; xvi, 1–15; xvii, 2–20;[24] xviii, 1–8,[25] xix, 1–20;[26] xx, 1–20; xxi, 1–23; xxii, 1–8, 13–29; xxiii, 10–26; xxiv, 1–22; xxv, 1–12;[27] xxvi, 1–18; xxviii. In most cases only parts of the passages listed belong to the original Deuteronomy, and the degree of certainty with which the individual sections are regarded as original is not everywhere the same. But the criteria for sorting out the basic material are purely literary: 'On the negative side the lack of inner contradictions, and on the positive side linguistic usage and style.'[28]

The representatives of the second group all agree in seeking the solution of the problem in the assumption that our Deuteronomy is the result of the combining of two or more editions of the original Deuteronomy, though their conceptions in some respects diverge very widely in detail. Thus it is disputed as to whether the original Deuteronomy is to be regarded as containing a historical introduction and a conclusion which includes the proclamation of reward and punishment, and, if so, which sections of the admittedly overloaded chapters (i–xi and xxvii–xxxiv) would come here into question; or whether the original Deuteronomy is to be regarded as a simple corpus of laws and so is to be sought only within xii–xxvi. An enumeration of the many shades of opinion would only confuse the issue, and so we must content ourselves here with the mention of a small selection of those who might be included as endeavouring to explain the composition of Deuteronomy by means of some kind of documentary hypothesis.

Steuernagel[29] has several times written on the Deuteronomic question, and although his various works relevant to this matter vary among themselves in detail, they nevertheless all endeavour to explain the present form of Deuteronomy by the assumption that it represents the combining of several editions of the original work, as this original itself is in its turn to be understood as a combination of various elements (laws directed towards centralisation, sayings

[22] *Das Privilegrecht Jahwes. Rechtsgeschichtliche Untersuchungen zum Deuteronomium* (FRLANT 45, 1930) = *Gottes Recht* (1961), pp. 17–154.

[23] ZAW 40 (1923), pp. 161–255 (Cf. above p. 172, n. 11).

[24] Caquot, 'Remarques sur la "loi royale" du Deutéronome (xvii, 14–20)' Semitica 9 (1959), pp. 21–33.

[25] Driver, 'Two Problems in the OT. Examined in the Light of Assyriology' Syria 33 (1956), pp. 70–8, pp. 77 f.: Deuteronomy xviii, 8.

[26] van Vliet, *No Single Testimony. A Study on the Adoption of the Law Deut. xix, 15 par. into the NT* (1958).

[27] Gordon, 'A New Akkadian Parallel to Deuteronomy xxv, 11–12' JPOS 15 (1935), pp. 29–34; Roth, 'Does the Thorah punish Impudence? Notes to Deuteronomy xxv, 11–12.' *Études Or. Hirschler* (1950), pp. 116–21.

[28] ZAW 40 (1923), p. 191.

[29] In addition to HK (1899, ²1923) and *Einleitung in das AT* (1912), cf. *Der Rahmen des Deuteronomiums* (1894), and *Die Entstehung des deuteronomischen Gesetzes* (1895, ²1901).

concerning abominations (תּוֹעֵבָה), laws of judges, laws of elders). In order to separate the individual editions, Steuernagel, like Staerk,[30] used, at any rate for a time, the criterion of singular or plural address to Israel, and on this basis denoted the editions as singular or plural. In a different and simpler way, Wellhausen had applied the documentary hypothesis to Deuteronomy, in that he defined it as the combining of two editions of the original Deuteronomy which are to be found within xii–xxvi, allocating i–iv, xii–xxvi*, xxvii to the one, and v–xi, xii–xxvi*, xxviii–xxx to the other—thus denying the introduction and conclusion to the original form of Deuteronomy, and dividing them between the two editions. At a later date, Smend accepted this view, with modifications of individual points, and for the introduction and conclusion, carried through the division of the material to the two editions in detail, whereas this division is only outlined for the legal corpus. In contrast to the optimism of earlier generations in regard to the possibility of a clear literary analysis of Deuteronomy, there has come into recent studies a certain reserve. Scholars content themselves with observing, as Noth does,[31] that the original Deuteronomy gradually grew into its present form, and abandon the attempt at making more precise statements concerning the exact nature of this development, its stages and the motives which led to it.

3. *Stalemate and advance in the study of D.* Von Rad has set himself to break away from this position of stalemate in the study of Deuteronomy by undertaking, as has happened for the Pentateuch as a whole (p. 170), to fill out the literary analysis by form critical assessment for Deuteronomy too. In his *Deuteronomium-Studien,* which appeared first in 1947,[32] he adheres to the connection of Deuteronomy with the period of Josiah as an assured result of research, and regards the particular character of Deuteronomy as consisting in the fact that it gives a homiletical interpretation of older cult-legal material and presents it parenetically. The remarkable sequence of parenesis, law, covenant obligation and curse, which is presented in Deuteronomy, is explained as the outcome of an ancient cultic procedure, namely the covenant renewal festival at Shechem which von Rad assumes. With this the possibility is opened up by means of a synthetic approach, of making intelligible some at least of the peculiarities of Deuteronomy, for which earlier attempts at explanation were made solely by critical analysis of the sections in question. An attempt at interpreting Deuteronomy along this line, though admittedly with a complete ignoring of all historical and critical matters, is presented in Kline's essay 'Dynastic Covenant'.[33] Here he declares that the book in the form in which we now have it represents a classic example of the suzerainty treaties known to us from documents from Syria and Anatolia of the fourteenth and thirteenth centuries B.C., and he ascribes it to Moses.

[30] *Das Deuteronomium. Sein Inhalt und seine literarische Form* (1894).
[31] *Überlieferungsgeschichtliche Studien* I (1943, ²1957), p. 16.
[32] (²1948). E.T. *Studies in Deuteronomy* (1953).
[33] WThJ 23 (1960), pp. 1–15.

§ 25. ASSESSMENT OF THE DEVELOPMENT OF PENTATEUCHAL CRITICISM

Literature: cf. §§ 18, 19, 22–4, 26–35, 126.

1. *Two preliminary points.* After this survey of the history of Pentateuchal criticism, which in large measure runs parallel to the development not only of the criticism of the Gospels[1] but also to that of Homer,[2] we may now consider what attitude should be adopted towards the various attempts at a solution which have appeared during its course. Two preliminary remarks must, however, be made. In the first place, it is important to be aware of the limits of what may be achieved by literary criticism of the Pentateuch. The lack of unanimity which prevails in this sphere may be very largely explained by the fact that these limits are not always recognised, and that, instead, claims are made for literary criticism which are in fact only appropriate to a consideration of the actual content. Thus it is clear—in the previous discussion this has been stressed plainly enough—that older materials, some very ancient indeed, lie behind our Pentateuch and the individual larger complexes which may be separated out from it; and this is true both of the narrative and of the legal material. The allocation of the materials of the Pentateuch to very varied periods and the assumption too of very great age for many of these, are made necessary by considerations from the point of view of the history of religion, and of cultural and intellectual development, with occasionally, though rarely, reference also to political history. In other cases, a foreign work may be recognised as the original of an Israelite narrative or legal precept, and it may then be shown that the material is perhaps much older than the literary form in which we now have it. But when we have recognised this, we have not arrived at the literary form which the material had at that clearly demonstrable earlier stage. Such an approach, coming as it were from outside the actual text, can generally arrive only at the content but not at its form, for which various possibilities must remain open. The essential points with regard to this have already been made earlier (pp. 3–7).

Pentateuchal criticism has thus a literary task to perform, namely to establish by a thorough investigation of the Pentateuch in the form in which it now lies before us, how this form actually came into being. That we are not here concerned with a unified book, compiled according to a deliberate plan by one single author, Moses for example, is in general agreed. The question is simply how this lack of uniformity is to be explained. Apart from the evaluation of the

---

[1] Loisy, *Les Évangiles Synoptiques*, I (1907), pp. 59–83; Smend, *Wilhelm Martin Lebrecht de Wettes Arbeit am A und NT* (1958), pp. 149–56; Wellhausen, *Einleitung in die drei ersten Evangelien* (1911), pp. 32–8; Wernle, *Die synoptische Frage* (1899). Lit. § 126.

[2] Lesky, 'Homer' Anzeiger für die Altertumswissenschaft 4 (1951), cols. 65–80, 195–212; 5 (1952), cols. 1–24; 6 (1953), cols. 129–50; 8 (1955), cols. 129–56; 12 (1959), cols. 129–146; 13 (1960), cols. 1–22. Schadewaldt, *Von Homers Welt und Werk* (³1959), pp. 9–202; *Neue Kriterien zur Odyssee-Analyse* (SAH 1959, 2. Abh. 1959); Verdenius, 'L'association des idées comme principe de composition dans Homère, Hésiode, Théognis' REG 73 (1960), pp. 345–61. Lit. § 126.

Pentateuch from the point of view of traditio-history and form-criticism which may here be left on one side because it is directed to other ends (pp. 168, 170), three types of hypothesis have been put forward, as we have seen (§ 23): the 'fragment', the supplementary, and the documentary. These names, which have now come to be generally used, may be retained here, but—and this is our second preliminary observation—everything depends upon our being quite clear about the methods thus designated and their difference. This has not always been observed, and yet they can in fact only be successfully applied if their special features are sharply set out. Above all it appears that in fact no one hypothesis has ever been applied quite alone in the course of Pentateuchal criticism; it is rather that the one or the other has been in the foreground, depending upon which parts of the Pentateuch—narratives or laws—have provided the starting-point and the main lines of the investigation in question, while at the same time other hypotheses too have been brought in to assist in the explanation. This recognition should temper the vehemence with which at times the struggle has been maintained for the sole validity of this or that hypothesis, and enables the investigator to consider the matter with reflection and moderation. It makes it clear that the dispute about method may to a very large extent be explained quite simply on the basis of our inability to hold in view equally and simultaneously all parts of the Pentateuch and so to set out a solution which fits them all at the same time.

2. *The hypotheses—'fragment', documentary, and supplementary.* If the 'fragment' hypothesis is really carried through to its most extreme position, it would mean that we should think of the Pentateuch as a unity first put together by an author—whether it be Moses or Ezra—from a large number of individual sections—narratives, laws, sayings, songs—which up till then had never been combined at all. In this form, however, the hypothesis has never been seriously put forward. Nor can it be maintained. It is quite clear that built-up complexes of medium size underlie our Pentateuch, exactly as is the case with the prophetic books, the psalms and the proverbs (pp. 152-3). But if these units of medium size were to be designated as 'fragments'—this has been done (pp. 162-3)— and it were to be assumed that not having been combined before they were first put together by the hand which actually shaped our Pentateuch, even this view would be untenable. A closer examination immediately reveals that these complexes are in many ways interwoven, and thus clearly did not lie before the final compiler entirely unrelated to one another. Thus the application of the pure 'fragment' hypothesis to the Pentateuch is actually impossible, and we may assert that this theory really only represents a reaction against the exaggerated application of the other hypotheses, and only finds a response when there has come a certain weariness of applying other, more positive theories, and interest in the Pentateuch is directed to questions other than the specifically literary critical ones. The inclination—though it is one which has admittedly not been clearly and explicitly expressed—to accept a kind of fragmentary hypothesis (pp. 168-9), which, as we have seen, has become stronger and stronger in the last half century, is certainly to be explained from the fact that the attention of scholars has been increasingly taken up with questions of content, form-

criticism, and traditio-history, rather than from any wish to replace the other theories by a new one, or by the renewal of an older view. Thus von Rad and Noth, as we have seen (p. 170), recognise explicitly the validity of the newer documentary hypothesis, and only wish to extend the application of the form historical approach, which had so far been applied more to the smallest literary units—the individual narrative, or the single legal saying etc.—so as to apply it to the Pentateuch as a whole, and so trace its prehistory much further back than is possible by literary analysis.

Thus, if the fragment hypothesis logically applied is not acceptable for the answering of the question of Pentateuchal criticism, there remain only the other two, the documentary and the supplementary. Here too it is important first to be quite clear about the nature of the methods thus designated. The name of the first—the documentary hypothesis—is in itself open to misunderstanding, and in any case does not clearly express what is now normally understood by it. We are not here dealing with 'documents' of the kind which have been discussed in Part I (pp. 19–32), but with literary works of considerable compass, whether they are of narrative or legal kind, or even a mixture of both. At first, as with Astruc (p. 161) and Ilgen (p. 162), these were thought of as works of a more or less official character, and they were for this reason designated as 'documents', and this description has survived in the name of the hypothesis although it has long since ceased to be justified. It is characteristic of this hypothesis that it reckons with two or more 'documents' parallel to one another, and assumes with reference to these that they have been combined in the Pentateuch as we have it and thus formed our Pentateuch. It would therefore also be possible to designate the hypothesis as an 'addition hypothesis' or 'compilation hypothesis', and this name would clearly bring out the point which differentiates it from the other, supplementary hypothesis. The documentary hypothesis came into being with reference to Genesis[3]—we may again think of Astruc and Ilgen (pp. 161–2)—and this is no accident. For it is indeed primarily the narrative part of the Pentateuch which most readily demands such an explanation of the form in which it lies before us, and of all the books of the Pentateuch it is the book of Genesis which is practically all narrative and not law.

In the strict sense, we can only speak of the adding together of parallel works in the case of compositions of a narrative kind. For here the continuity and the progress of the narrative provides a standard which is at least in some measure reliable, by which it may be determined whether the parallel strands

---

[3] Bacon, *The Genesis of Genesis* (1892); Chaine, *Le Livre de la Genèse* (1948); Eissfeldt, *Die Genesis der Genesis* ([2]1961), cf. *Interpreter's Dictionary of the Bible* II (1962), pp. 266–80; Glueck, *Rivers in the Desert: A History of the Negeb* (1959); 'The Negev' BA 22 (1959), pp. 82–97 = BA Reader (1961), pp. 1–11; Hoftijzer, *Die Verheissungen an die drei Erzväter* (1956); Humbert, 'Die neuere Genesis-Forschung' ThR 6 (1934), pp. 147–60, 207–28; Keller, 'Grundsätzliches zur Auslegung der Abraham-Überlieferung in der Genesis' ThZ 12 (1956), pp. 425–45; Mowinckel, ' "Rachelstämme" und "Leastämme" ' BZAW 77 (1958), pp. 129–50; Seale, 'The Glosses in the Book of Genesis and the JE Theory' ET 67 (1956/7), pp. 333–5; Vawter, *A Path through Genesis* (1957, 1964); Wiseman, *New Discoveries in Babylonia about Genesis* (1936); Wright, 'The Achievement of Nelson Glueck' BA 22 (1957), pp. 98–100; 'Is Glueck's Aim to Prove that the Bible is True?' *ib.* pp. 101–108 = BA Reader (1961), pp. 11–21. Lit. in Eissfeldt, *Die Genesis der Genesis* ([2]1961), pp. 73–94. Lit. § 126.

assumed really do each represent a narrative work. If the individual parts reveal continuity and progress, they thereby reveal themselves to be parts of narrative works. Where that is not the case, we cannot speak in terms of the adding together of parallel strands. In the legal corpora this standard of judgement is absent (pp. 144–5). Thus it is proper, at any rate at first, to examine the application of the documentary hypothesis only in those sections where we are concerned with the analysis of larger complexes of narrative, and only to apply it with reserve to the legal corpora. The separation of Deuteronomy, which is generally recognised as a unit of a special kind, may not be regarded as a point in favour of the documentary hypothesis. For Deuteronomy stands out sharply from its context, but is not really parallel with it, or only to a limited extent, and is even less interlocked with it. We are really applying a kind of supplementary hypothesis if we recognise Deuteronomy as a unit added to an older body of material, and hence separate it off. The documentary hypothesis in the strict sense of the term is thus only applicable where we are concerned with the analysis of the Pentateuchal narrative.

The situation is different with the supplementary hypothesis. It is true that this too originated in reference to narratives: the materials now designated J were thus supposed to be characterised as supplements to the basic work (= our P or more properly P + E) (p. 163). But it is equally applicable to the legal corpora. It assumes that underlying our Pentateuch or at any rate definite parts of it, there is a work, completely or relatively unified, and that this basic work was secondarily supplemented, by one or several hands. It is nevertheless always a matter of the addition of small, isolated pieces at a time, which have no connection with one another, and had no such connection even before their incorporation in the main body of the material. For this is the point which really distinguishes this theory from the documentary hypothesis. The latter assumes that the sections which disturb a narrative and which must be removed in order to recover its proper form, themselves belong together in a continuous whole, or did at one time form such a whole. The former regards the sections which are to be denied to the main narrative strand or to each individual main narrative as mere expansions of the basic material, like growths on the main stem. We have seen (p. 163) that those who have used the name 'supplementary hypothesis' have not always been completely clear about its real nature, but have also applied it to a method which in reality is to be regarded as a documentary hypothesis. This fact does not make it superfluous to differentiate clearly between the two theories. It only reveals the more clearly how necessary this is. For without such a clear conception of the nature of the methods applicable to Pentateuchal criticism it is impossible to employ them, and a delimitation of the various hypotheses the one from the other is completely impossible without such clarity of conception.

3. *The narrative sections.* If we now ask which of the two hypotheses we have just described more clearly may most readily explain the form of the Pentateuch as we now have it, we must observe that for the narrative sections, i.e. substantially Gen. i to Exod. xxxiv, Num. x–xxxvi, Deut. xxxi–xxxiv, we cannot get any satisfactory result from the purely supplementary hypothesis. For the

larger and smaller sections which are, with a considerable measure of agreement, separated out as interruptions of a narrative strand or of a single narrative, reveal themselves in most cases—indeed in the vast majority of cases—as elements in a continuous whole; and, although they may now often appear to supplement the main narrative, they cannot have come into being merely as expansions of the basic material, but must originally have formed a unity, in other words a narrative parallel to the main narrative. This may be made quite clear, for example, in two ways in the flood narrative. On the one hand, the two halves, now assigned to J and P into which Gen. vi, 5–ix, 19, must of necessity be divided, with relative ease, are clearly two independent narratives which admittedly have not survived intact but may be very readily reconstructed in their entirety. On the other hand, the P section of Gen. vi, 5–ix, 19—if we may now restrict ourselves to this—reveals itself quite clearly as the continuation of the first creation narrative Gen. i, 1–ii, 4a, as may be seen by the reference back (vii, 11; ix, 1–7) both to the driving back of the primeval waters there described (i, 6–10) and also to the food commands there set forth (i, 29–30). The Pentateuch narrative is thus, at all events in large sections, the result of a combination of parallel strands, though for the moment we may leave open the question as to how many such parallel strands are to be assumed (see § 27). On the other hand, however, it is certain that the Pentateuchal narrative has also been amplified with unconnected individual passages of larger and smaller compass, and this may already have taken place while the parallel strands were still independent, or only at the time of their combination or after (§ 32). The supplementary hypothesis is thus a more satisfactory basis for the explanation of a number of unevennesses in the Pentateuchal narrative than the other hypothesis, but the main part of the material may be most naturally disentangled and rearranged by the application of the documentary hypothesis, and it is no accident that Pentateuchal criticism, with all its vicissitudes, has over and over again given preference to the documentary hypothesis.

4. *The legal corpora.* So far as the legal corpora are concerned, matters are much less simple than in the narrative, as we have already seen (pp. 144–5, 180). In the largest of these, namely Deuteronomy, there is much that leads to the assumption that its present form is to be understood as the result of the combination of two law books. This is indicated particularly by the double introduction (i, 1–iv, 40; iv, 44–xi, 32). But in the corpus of law itself (xii–xxvi), it is hardly possible to bring forward arguments to demonstrate that the disagreements which repeatedly strike us are better to be explained on the assumption that here two bodies of law have been combined than on the alternative assumption that a basic corpus of law has been amplified secondarily by the addition of individual supplements of larger and smaller compass. The inclination to apply the documentary hypothesis to the corpus of law is doubtless encouraged and indeed justified on the grounds that the presence of a double introduction appears to favour this hypothesis. But against this we may be led by the character of the corpus of law itself, which defies any neat division into two basic corpora, and suggests rather amplifications of one basic corpus, to trace back to amplifications the overloading which may be observed in the introduction. The position

in the Holiness Code (Lev. xvii–xxvi) is similar to that in Deuteronomy. Here many of the duplications may be most easily explained on the assumption that two corpora of law have been combined, whereas others make it more likely that we should think rather of the presence of secondary amplifications of the basic material. It thus lies in the nature of the case that there should have been in the history of Pentateuchal criticism no real progress beyond a fluctuation between varying views in the analysis of Deuteronomy and of the legal codes as a whole, and we miss the clear line which, in spite of all the vicissitudes in the analysis of the narrative, may nevertheless there be observed. In this, the matter will no doubt have to remain as yet at a judgement of *non liquet*.

II. Analysis of the Pentateuch Narrative

§ 26. THE ARGUMENTS FOR ANALYSIS

Literature: Kräutlein, *Die sprachlichen Verschiedenheiten in den Hexateuchquellen* (Diss. phil. Rostock, 1907); Martin, *Stylistic Criteria and the Analysis of the Pentateuch* (1955). Cf. also Literature §§ 5, 18, 19, 22–25, 27–32.

1. *The changes in the divine names.* Pentateuchal criticism as we now have it began, as we have seen, when it was observed that in Genesis God is sometimes called *Yahweh* and sometimes *Elohim*, and so from this change of name two 'documents' were at first distinguished from one another. This argument, in spite of repeatedly renewed opposition,[1] still retains its great significance. It is true that the *Yahweh* and *Elohim* strata have not been preserved exactly with their original differentiation of the use of the divine name, and that sometimes an *Elohim* has crept secondarily into the *Yahweh* stratum, and a *Yahweh* into the *Elohim* stratum. Furthermore, the transmission of the divine names is not everywhere quite certain, since there are occasional differences between 𝔐 and 𝔊 (ὁ θεός, i.e. אֱלֹהִים in 𝔊 instead of יְהֹוָה in 𝔐, e.g. Gen. iv, 1, 4, 16; xii, 17). But in spite of this, the difference of usage of the divine names has on the whole been preserved amazingly well in the various strata, as may be seen by a glance at, for example, the two flood narratives (J and P) or the Hagar stories in Gen. xvi, 4–14 (J) and xxi, 8–21[2] (E). What is remarkable is not that the two strata which have now been interwoven should occasionally have exerted a mutual influence upon one another in respect of the divine names which they employ, but the fact that in spite of the combination this peculiarity should have been preserved so clearly. Admittedly the difference of divine

[1] Lacocque, 'Les noms divins et la théorie des sources dans l'AT' Veritatem in caritate 3–4 (1957/8), pp. 69–84; Segal, 'El, Elohim and Yahweh in the Bible' JQR 46 (1955/6), pp. 89–115; 'The Unitary Character of the Pentateuch' [Hebr., Engl. sum.] Tarbiz 25 (1955/6), pp. 1–10, I–III; 'The Composition of the Pentateuch: A Fresh Examination' SHier 8 (1961), pp. 68–114, esp. pp. 72–86.

[2] Haag, 'Erwägungen über Beer-Šeba' BEThL XII (1959), pp. 335–45; Yeivin, 'Beersheba, City of the Patriarchs' [Hebr., Engl. sum.] Zion 30 (1955), pp. 117–27, I–II; Zimmerli, *Geschichte und Tradition von Beerseba im AT* (1932). Lit. § 126.

names may only be used in the analysis of Genesis and the beginning of Exodus. For the two sources which we now call E and P avoid the name Yahweh at first and only use it from the moment when God makes this known as his name to Moses—E from Exod. iii, 15[3] and P from Exod. vi, 6 on. Furthermore, the application of this argument permits a division of the material into only two halves, one with *Yahweh* and one with *Elohim,* and thus makes possible, as the development of criticism has shown, only a provisional and insufficient analysis. But in spite of all this, the changes of divine name remain still a fundamental of Pentateuchal criticism.

2. *Linguistic usage.* A second factor which facilitates the separation of the sources is the further difference of linguistic usage. A whole series of places, persons and objects are differently designated, and closer examination readily reveals that the change in these designations is not accidental or arbitrary, but coincides with other peculiarities and may thus be understood as a characteristic mark of the different strata. Thus when the *Yahweh* stratum uses a comprehensive name for the earlier inhabitants of Canaan, it consistently calls them *Canaanites* (כְּנַעֲנִי Gen. xii, 6; 1, 11), whereas E uses *Amorites* (אֱמֹרִי Gen. xv, 16; xlviii, 22). The *Yahweh* stratum uses the name *Sinai* (סִינַי Exod. xix, 11, 18) for the mountain of God, E uses *Horeb* (חֹרֵב Exod. iii, 1; xvii, 6). For *female slave* the *Yahweh* stratum uses the word שִׁפְחָה (Gen. xvi, 5 of Hagar, xxxii, 23 of Zilpah and Bilhah), while E uses אָמָה (Gen. xxi, 12 of Hagar, xxx, 3 of Bilhah). The female slave who acts as a subordinate wife[4] to the husband is thus called שִׁפְחָה in the *Yahweh* stratum and אָמָה in E.[5] But it is to be noted that another designation for the subordinate wife is also to be found in the *Yahweh* stratum, namely *concubine* (פִּילֶגֶשׁ), as in Gen. xxv, 6 for Keturah who corresponds to Hagar in Gen. xvi and xxi, and in xxxv, 22 for Bilhah—a clear pointer to the lack of unity in the *Yahweh* stratum (p. 186). Apart from D, whose special diction must later be discussed (p. 220), the source P may most readily be recognised by its linguistic usage. רְכוּשׁ *goods,* אֲחֻזָּה *landed property,* הֵקִים בְּרִית *to make a covenant* and many other words, expressions and stylistic peculiarities are characteristic of P.

3. *Diversity of ideas.* A third means of recognising the individual strata and sources is the difference in level of their religious and moral ideas, their legal and political outlook, and also the difference in the contemporary conditions and events which they presuppose. So far as this last point is concerned, statements like *The Canaanites were then in the land* (Gen. xii, 6) indicate clearly that the narrators knew that the situation with which they were here concerned lay in

---

[3] Allard, 'Note sur la formule "Ehyeh Aser Ehyeh"' RSR 45 (1957), pp. 79–86; Bourke, 'Yahweh, the Divine Name' The Bridge III (1958), pp. 271–87; Freedman, 'The Name of the God of Moses' JBL 79 (1960), pp. 151–6; Irwin, 'Exodus iii, 14' AJSL 56 (1939), pp. 297–8; Pákozdy, 'אהיה אשר אהיה' Judaica 11 (1955), pp. 193–208; Reisel, *Observations on* אהיה אשר אהיה Ex. iii, 14' (Diss. Amsterdam, 1957); Schild, 'On Exodus iii, 14' VT 4 (1954), pp. 296–302; Schulze, ' "Ehejeh ascher ehejeh"' Judaica 11 (1955), pp. 209–216; Vischer, 'Eher Jahwo als Jahwe' ThZ 16 (1960), pp. 259–67; Vriezen, ' '*Ehje* ᵃ*šer 'ehje' Bertholet-Festschrift* (1950), pp. 498–512. Lit. § 126.

[4] Kardimon, 'Adoption as a Remedy for Infertility in the Period of the Patriarchs' JSSt 3 (1958), pp. 123–6.

[5] Jepsen, '*Amaʰ* und *Schiphchaʰ*' VT 8 (1958), pp. 293–7, 425.

the distant past (p. 159), and the narratives of Abraham, Hagar and Lot, the histories of Jacob, Esau and Laban, and others, clearly reflect in their present form the period in which Israel was firmly established in Canaan with Edom (Esau) as southern neighbour, the Aramaeans (Laban) on the north-east, Moab and Ammon (Lot) on the east, while the sons of Hagar, the Ishmaelites, lived still farther out to the south and east, and aspired to break from there into the cultivated land, even into Israelite territory. But this and other features are characteristics which belong to the whole Pentateuch, and in particular to Genesis, and not especially to one or other of the strata. We can scarcely find any allusions to definite political conditions or precise events belonging particularly to the individual sources and thus delimiting them the one from the other; and where such allusions are found they are not always unambiguous. Nevertheless the geographical and political horizon of the table of nations of P in Gen. x is clearly broader than that of J in the same passage, and this in its turn is broader than that of Gen. ix, 21–7⁶ (L) where the perspective is limited to Palestine-Syria and does not, like the others, embrace the whole Mediterranean area. But such differences may only be observed at isolated points, and do not characterise the sources in question as a whole. They are thus hardly sufficient to enable us to differentiate between the sources.

In regard to the total religious outlook, however, there is in fact a series of characteristics belonging to the individual sources as a whole and differentiating them from one another, and these are useful for the analysis. Thus E emphasises the remoteness of God from the world and from man more strongly than does the *Yahweh* stratum. Whereas in J's Hagar story (Gen. xvi, 4–14) the angel of Yahweh sojourns on earth and addresses Hagar there (v. 7), in the corresponding E narrative (Gen. xxi, 8–21) the angel of God speaks his words to Hagar from heaven (v. 17). Similarly in J's Bethel narrative (Gen. xxviii, 13–16, 19) Yahweh stands upon the earth before Jacob (v. 13), whereas according to E (vv. 10–12, 17–18, 20–2) a ladder bearing the angels of God represents the bond between the earth and heaven and God (v. 12). To this difference between J and E corresponds the fact that E represents men as fearful when they are honoured with a theophany, whereas J pictures them rather as attracted by it. In the narrative of the burning bush (Exod. iii), Moses appears in E as fearful (v. 6), but in J as too bold, so that he has to be warned by Yahweh (v. 5). The same is true of the attitude of the people at Yahweh's appearance at Sinai: in J the injunction not to come near the mountain has to be repeatedly brought home to them (Exod. xix, 12–13, 21–4), whereas in E the people are fearful and only reluctantly follow Moses to the foot of the mountain (xix, 17; xx, 18–21). E is also in ethical matters more sensitive than J. Whereas J simply sets down the false statement by Abraham that Sarah is his sister (Gen. xii, 10–xiii, 1), E attempts to weaken this by making Sarah into a half-sister of Abraham (Gen. xx, 12). There is a similar difference between the J and E narratives as to how Jacob acquired his wealth. In the *Yahweh* stratum (Gen. xxx, 29–43), Jacob manages to increase his cattle by all manner of artificial means such as would be

⁶ Hoftijzer, 'Some Remarks to the Tale of Noah's Drunkenness' OTS 12 (1958), pp. 22–7, Cf. p. 41, n. 33.

known to a shepherd, whereas E appears to have related (cf. Gen. xxxi, 4–16) that Jacob's herds increased by the direct intervention of God without Jacob playing any part, and that the property which came to Jacob was basically only the inheritance of his two wives which had been withheld from them by their father Laban. J is thus in ethical matters clearly more crude than E, but it appears as if even in the *Yahweh* stratum there may be detected further differences of level. A feature of the narrative like the statement that Yahweh gives the Israelites the direct command to rob the Egyptians (Exod. iii, 21–2), goes far beyond the features of J so far mentioned, and we have here to recognise a piece of the older strand of the *Yahweh* stratum, i.e. of L (pp. 192–3).

Just as P has a characteristic linguistic usage, so too it has its own quite easily recognisable religious and cultic attitude. Whereas according to the narratives of the J stratum and of E, men bring sacrifices to God from the beginning of the world, sacrifice for P begins only after the revealing of the law at Sinai (Lev. ix). The reason for this is obvious. There can be only one legitimate sacrificial and cultic law. This Israel first learnt at Sinai. If sacrifices were offered before this by the patriarchs, it could only have happened in a manner contrary to the law of Sinai. So P denies the practice of sacrifice entirely to the period before Moses. This attitude has the result also that for example in P's flood narrative, only one pair each of all beasts is to be taken into the ark, whereas J here makes a distinction between clean animals—i.e. those suitable for food and sacrifice—and unclean, and has seven pairs each of the former but only one pair each of the latter taken into the ark. For P, which allows to mankind before the flood only vegetable food (Gen. i, 29) and only permits the eating of flesh after the flood (ix, 2–3), unlike J, does not need to reckon with the fact that during and immediately after the flood a number of the clean beasts will be used for sacrifice and food. However, P does not picture mankind in the pre-Mosaic period as being entirely without definite religious observances, for three religious duties are in fact laid down earlier in it—or, with reference to the last of the duties to be mentioned, in a particular section of it. These are the observance of the sabbath (Gen. i, 1–ii, 4a), the avoidance of eating the blood and the respecting of human life (Gen. ix, 1–7), and the practice of circumcision (Gen. xvii). By letting these ordinances become known at particular periods in the pre-Mosaic history of mankind, P accords to them a validity which goes beyond Israel, the sole recipient of the Sinai revelation, and at the same time gives them a position of particular honour and significance. In this series of stages of revelation there is thus expressed also a definite total view which is characteristic only of P.

These examples are sufficient to show that the individual strata of the Pentateuchal narrative reveal their own particular religious level and are to a certain degree recognisable by this. But this can only be determined to a certain degree. There may often be very divergent opinions as to whether a particular conception does or does not accord with the whole outlook of a stratum as it may be established in other respects, and so as to whether it is to be recognised as belonging to it or is to be denied to it. The spiritual make-up of each individual is a *complexio oppositorum*, and so too a narrative work will reveal many points of tension. This is all the more likely to be the case if its compiler uses older materials, already to a large extent shaped, and so is trying to work as carefully as possible with them. This is clearly in large measure the case with the authors of our Pentateuchal narrative strands. They are authors, not collectors, but yet they are authors who shape or re-shape materials which are centuries old and have already gone through many generations orally and in written form. As they work, they leave in them much in thought and conception which hardly fits their own contemporary situation. But even if we were compelled to picture these authors differently, the accumulated momentum of the materials themselves would have resisted their complete assimilation to the time of the authors (p. 143). Under these conditions, it is naturally difficult to draw conclusions of literary lack of unity from the presence of elements belonging to different spiritual levels. Hence the argument based upon the sameness of spiritual level in the individual sources must be used with caution.

4. *Literary phenomena.* A fourth criterion, finally, of which the analysis of the Pentateuchal narrative makes use, is the observation of formal literary phenomena such as the double or more frequent occurrences of narratives, parts of narratives and references,[7] the interruption of a narrative by an element which clearly does not belong to it, and the later resumption of the thread which has been broken off, and many other similar points. So far as the double and more frequent occurrence of narratives and references is concerned, even a superficial reading shows that, for example, the imperilling of the ancestress of Israel and thus of Israel's whole future—for the ancestress is to become the mother of the one who bears Israel's future—occurs three times, twice for Sarah (Gen. xii, 10–xiii, 1; xx, 1–18) and once with Rebekah (Gen. xxvi, 6–11).[8] In addition to other laws, two different decalogues are traced to Sinai-Horeb (Exod. xx, 1–17 and xxxiv, 10–28). There is mention of the gifts of manna and quails, and of the miracle of the spring both before the revelation at Sinai and after (Exod. xvi, xvii, 1–7[9] for the one, Num. xi, 4–35; xx, 1–13 for the other), and so forth. These are complete narratives, which, though separated from one another by intervals, may nevertheless be set side by side and may be readily recognised as parallels. A closer examination, however, reveals that in other cases the parallels do not stand side by side but have been interwoven. In many cases, it cannot be doubted that we have here the combining of two or more parallel narratives, and not the expansion of a basic narrative by various disconnected individual supplements.

The flood narrative, which represents the combining of J and P, has already been mentioned as a classic example of this. Another equally telling example is the Joseph narrative, i.e. Gen. xxxvii, xxxix–l, which, with the removal of the P elements and other parts which are to be assigned to L (p. 192), clearly reveals itself as the combination of two narratives which run exactly parallel to one another, namely J and E. A third example is the Balaam narrative of Num.

[7] Jirku, 'Doppelte Überlieferungen im Mythus und im Epos von Ugarit?' ZDMG 110 (1960), pp. 20–5.
[8] Maly, 'Genesis xii, 10–20; xx, 1–18; xxvi, 7–11, and the Pentateuchal Question' CBQ 18 (1956), pp. 255–62.
[9] Lehming, 'Massa und Meriba' ZAW 73 (1961), pp. 71–7.

xxii–xxiv, which also represents an interweaving of two parallel narratives which may be readily disentangled and which also belong to J and E (p. 189, n. 6). Elsewhere, such an allocation of the material to two narrative strands cannot be made, but it is necessary to assume three or four, as in the whole complex Gen. xxxvii–l already indicated, and similarly in the primeval history in Gen. i–xi, and in the narratives of Israel's exodus from Egypt and the events which precede it in Exod. i–xv. The existence side by side in this way of separate and completely preserved parallel narratives on the one hand, and of combinations of two or more parallel narratives mutilated in the process of combination on the other hand, is what gives our Pentateuch its peculiar stamp, and this phenomenon may most readily be explained on the assumption that parallel strands have been combined and not simply parallel narratives which existed as individual pieces of material, since there are clearly connections between the parallel narratives which stand alone and those which we have only as parts of compilations, and the individual members naturally link themselves together into two or more chains of narrative. Thus, for example, the P section of the flood narrative now combined with J, clearly appears as the continuation of the P creation narrative which stands alone (p. 185). The same is true of the relationship between the unified story of the hidden cup in Gen. xliv which belongs entirely to J and xxxvii which, ignoring the P introduction, is certainly combined from J and E, and the similarly constructed xlii–xliii. In xxxvii, as in xlii–xliii,[10] one of the two parallel narratives (J) presents Judah (xxxvii, 26; xliii, 3, 8) as the chief and spokesman of the brothers, while the other (E) has Reuben (xlii, 37). Since in xliv Judah appears as spokesman, this chapter is to be regarded as the continuation of the J part of xxxvii, xlii–xliii, which reveals the same peculiarity, and this conclusion is confirmed by other indications such as linguistic usage.

An example in which one thread is allowed to drop, to be taken up only after being interrupted by a section which clearly does not fit with it, is provided in Gen. xii, 6–8; xiii, 2, 5, 7–18 (with the exception of xiii, 6, 11b, 12abα, which belong to P and do not concern us here) on the one hand, and xii, 10–xiii, 1, on the other. According to xii, 6–8; xiii, 2, 5, 7–18, Abraham and Lot belong together, and there is here no mention of Sarah; but xii, 10–xiii, 1, are concerned with Abraham and Sarah and hence know nothing of Lot; for the phrase *and Lot with him* in xiii, 1, is clearly a secondary addition, designed to link the two sections together. There is no lack of other such linkages, and this one is at the same time an illuminating example of the way in which the attempt has been made to fuse together sections which were originally quite unconnected. xii, 6–8; xiii, 2, 5, 7–18, take place in Bethel, whereas xii, 10–xiii, 1, are set in Egypt. The bridge between the two scenes of action is brought about by the insertion after xii, 8, of the words *And Abraham journeyed ever further into the Negeb* (v. 9), and by another insertion placed after xiii, 2 (vv. 3–4), which brings Abraham back to the scene of xii, 6–8; xiii, 7–18. That these are quite mechanical additions may be seen not only by the awkward nature of xiii, 3–4,

[10] Danek, 'Nicht Quellen, sondern Syntax' Judaica 3 (1947), pp. 199–209; Baumgartner, ' "Nicht Quellen, sondern Syntax" ' ThZ 3 (1947), pp. 473–4.

but also by the fact that these verses in their turn interrupt material which belongs together, for the information of v. 5 that Lot too had great possessions quite clearly represents the immediate continuation of the note in v. 2 that Abraham was very rich. Thus two completely distinct sections have been woven together, in a quite mechanical manner, though this by no means excludes the possibility that the redactor had his own reasons for undertaking the uniting of the material in the precise way in which it has been done. For he clearly saw in the bestowing of gifts on Abraham by the Pharaoh, related in xii, 16,[11] the reason for the wealth of Abraham which is mentioned in xiii, 2, i.e., in the other narrative, and for this reason placed xiii, 2, 5, 7–18 after xii, 10–xiii, 1. But the narrative xii, 6–8; xiii, 2, 5, 7–18, itself depicted Abraham as being rich from the outset, just as in the same way it produces no basis for Lot's opulence. Thus we have here a mechanical uniting of two sections which originally had nothing to do with each other, but belong to different strands of narrative. For xii, 6–8; xiii, 2, 5, 7–18 (L) clearly finds its continuation in xviii–xix (L), whereas xii, 10–xiii, 1 (J) is continued in the J strand of xv–xvi.

§ 27. ANALYSIS OF THE PENTATEUCH NARRATIVE: THE RESULTS

Literature: cf. §§ 22–6, 28–32.

It is these four criteria, just illustrated with a few examples, which have above all been employed by criticism in the analysis of the Pentateuchal narrative. The result which follows is that the material divides itself into four narrative strands. Admittedly the degree of certainty with which these strands may be separated out is not everywhere equal, and in certain cases we may ask whether the sections, recognised clearly as of the same kind and separated out as such, really form parts of a continuous whole or are only atomistic expansions, from one hand or from one 'school', of the material as it already existed. But on a closer investigation, the balance here too inclines to the documentary hypothesis and not to the supplementary hypothesis.

1. *The P-section.* As already noted several times, P may be most easily recognised as an independent entity, and hence the critics are fairly well agreed in the separation out of P. The following is P's share of the Pentateuch: Gen. i, 1–ii, 4a; v*; vi, 5–ix, 19*,[1] 28–9; x*; xi, 10–26, 27, 31–2; xii, 4b–5; xiii, 6, 11b–12abα;

---

[11] On the subject of the camels mentioned here, cf. Brentjes, 'Das Kamel im Alten Orient' Klio 38 (1960), pp. 23–52; Dostal, 'The Evolution of Bedouin Life' Studi Semitici 2 (1959), pp. 11–34; Free, 'Abraham's Camels' JNESt 3 (1944), pp. 187–93; Lambert, 'The Domesticated Camel in the Second Millennium. Evidence from Alalakh and Ugarit' BASOR 160 (1960), pp. 42–3; Walz, 'Neue Untersuchungen zum Domestikationsproblem der altweltlichen Cameliden' ZDMG 104 (1954), pp. 45–87. Lit. § 126.

[1] Lambert, 'Il n'y aura plus jamais de déluge (Genèse ix, 11)' NRTh 77 (1955), pp. 581–601, 693–724; Parrot, *Déluge et Arche de Noé* (1952), E.T. *The Flood and Noah's Ark* (1955).

xvi, 1a, 3, 15–16; xvii; xix, 29; xxi, 2b–5; xxiii; xxv, 7–10, 12–17, 19–20, 26b; xxvi, 34–5; xxvii, 46; xxviii, 1–9; xxix, 24, 28b–29; xxx, 4a, 9b; xxxi, 18aβb; xxxiii, 18aβ; xxxv, 6a, 9–13, 15, 22bβ–9; xxxvi, 1, 2a, 6–8, 40–3; xxxvii, 1–2; xli, 46a; xlvi, 6–27; xlvii, 5–11*, 27*, 28; xlviii, 3–7; xlix, 1*, 28–33*; l, 12–13; Exod. i, 1–5, 7*, 13, 14*; ii, 23aβb–25; vi, 2–30; vii, 1–13, 19–20aa, 21bβ–22; viii, 1–3, 11b–15;[2] ix, 8–12; xi, 9–xii, 20, 28; xii, 40–xiii, 2; xvi, 1*, 2–3, 6–13a, 14*; xix, 1; xxiv, 15b–18a; xxv, 1–xxxi, 17, 18a; xxxiv, 29–35;[3] xxxv–xl; Lev. i–xvi; xxvii; Num. i, 1–x, 28; xiii–xiv*; xv; xvi*;[4] xvii–xix; xx, 1–13*, 22–9; xxii, 1; xxv, 6–xxxi, 54; xxxii*; xxxiii–xxxvi; Deut. xxxii, 48–52; xxxiv, 1*, 7–9.

2. *J and E.* After the removal of the P material and of the D material which is in this context left on one side (p. 180), the remainder of Gen. i–l, Exod. i–xxiv, xxxii–xxxiv, Num. x–xxxvi, Deut. xxxi–xxxiv reveals at various points two series of parallel narratives. In Gen. xii, 10–xiii, 1; xv–xvi; xx–xxiv (Abraham, Sarah, God's covenant with Abraham, Hagar and Ishmael, Isaac, Rebekah); Gen. xxv, 27–28+xxvii; xxviii, 10–22; xxxii–xxxiii (Jacob's deception of Esau, his flight from Esau, his experience at Bethel, and, passing over here the narrative in xxix–xxxi concerning Jacob and Laban which is not easy to disentangle, his meeting with Esau on his return from Aram); Gen. xxxvii+xxxix–l (Joseph and his brothers); Exod. xix–xx; xxiv, 12–18; xxxi, 18; xxxiv (theophany at Sinai, Moses' ascent into the mountain to receive the tables of stone, or for the actual writing of them, the decalogue),[5] and Num. xxii–xxiv (the Balaam narrative),[6] the parallel narratives which may be everywhere observed group themselves naturally into two series, as shown overleaf.

These four parallel series reveal the characteristic feature (p. 186) of the existence side by side of complete parallels (e.g. Gen. xii, 10–xiii, 1//xx, 1–18) and of the interweaving of compiled parallels, which are therefore incomplete (xxvii*//xxvii*). They are furthermore to some extent to be rearranged because

---

[2] Couroyer, 'Le doigt de Dieu (Exode, viii, 15)' RB 63 (1956), pp. 481–95.

[3] de Fraine, 'Moses' "cornuta facies" (Ex xxxiv, 29–35)' Bijdragen 20 (1959), pp. 28–38; Schulz, 'Die Decke des Moses' ZNW 49 (1958), pp. 1–31. Lit. § 126.

[4] Greta Hort, 'The Death of Qorah' ABR 7 (1959), pp. 2–26; Nyberg, 'Ḳoraḥ's uppror (Num. xvi f.). Ett bidrag till frågan om traditionshistorisk metod' SEA 12 (1947), pp. 230–52.

[5] Beyerlin, *Herkunft und Geschichte der ältesten Sinaitraditionen* (1961); Eissfeldt, 'Lade und Gesetzestafeln' ThZ 16 (1960), pp. 281–4; 'Die älteste Erzählung vom Sinaibund' ZAW 73 (1961), pp. 137–46; Haelvoet, 'La Théophanie du Sinaï. Analyse littéraire des récits d'Ex. xix–xxiv' EThL 29 (1953), pp. 374–97 = ALBO, II, 39 (1953); Rudolph, 'Der Aufbau von Ex xix–xxxiv' BZAW 66 (1936), pp. 41–8. Lit. § 8.

[6] Albright, 'The Oracles of Balaam' JBL 63 (1944), pp. 207–33; Allegro, 'The Meaning of the Phrase šetūm hāʿayin in Num xxiv, 3, 15' VT 3 (1953), pp. 78 f.; Burrows, *The Oracles of Jacob and Balaam* (1938); Eissfeldt, 'Die Komposition der Bileam-Erzählung' ZAW 57 (1939), pp. 212–41; 'Sinai-Erzählung und Bileamsprüche' HUCA 32 (1961), pp. 179–90; Liver, 'The Figure of Balaam in Biblical Tradition' [Hebr., Engl. sum.] Eretz-Israel 3 (1954), pp. 97–100, IV; Löhr, 'Num xxii, 2–xxiv, 25' AfO 4 (1927), pp. 85–9; Mackensen, 'The Present Literary Form of the Balaam Story' *Macdonald Presentation Vol.* (1933), pp. 275–92; Mauchline, 'The Balaam–Balak Songs and Saga' Stud. Sem. et Orient. 2 (1945), pp. 73–94; Mowinckel, 'Der Ursprung der Bilʿām-Sage' ZAW 48 (1930), pp. 233–71; Pákozdy, 'Theologische Redaktionsarbeit in der Bileam-Perikope' BZAW 77 (1958), pp. 161–76; Sutcliffe, 'A Note on Numbers xxii' Bibl 18 (1937), pp. 439–42; Vermès, 'Deux traditions sur Balaam. Nombres xxii, 2–21 et ses interprétations midrashiques' Cahiers Sioniens 9 (1955), pp. 289–302; Yaure, 'Elymas–Nehelamite–Pethor' JBL 79 (1960), pp. 297–314, cf. pp. 310–314: 'Balaam of "Pethor"'. Lit. § 126.

	a		b
(1) Gen.		(1) Gen.	
xii, 10–xiii, 1	Endangering of Sarah		xx, 1–18
xxi, 22–34*	Abraham's treaty with Abimelech		xxi, 22–34*
xv*	God's covenant with Abraham		xv*
xvi, 4–14	Hagar and Ishmael		xxi, 8–21
xxi, 1–7*	Birth of Isaac		xxi, 1–7*
xxiv*	Wooing of Rebekah		xxiv*
(2) Gen.		(2) Gen.	
xxv, 27–8*; xxvii*	Jacob's deception of Esau and flight from him		xxv, 27–8*; xxvii*
xxviii, 13–16, 19	Theophany in Bethel		xxviii, 10–12, 17–18, 20–2
xxxii–xxxiii*	Jacob's meeting with Esau		xxxii–xxxiii*
xxxvii*, xxxix–l*	Joseph and his brothers		xxxvii*, xxxix–l*
(3) Exod.		(3) Exod.	
xix*; xx, 18–21*	Theophany at Sinai		xix*; xx, 18–21*
xxxiv, 1–4	Moses' ascent into the mountain		xxiv, 12–18*
xxxiv, 5–26*	Decalogue		xx, 1–17
xxxiv, 27–8	Decalogue tablets		xxxi, 18*
(4) Num.		(4) Num.	
xxii, 2–19*	Balak's embassy to Balaam		xxii, 2–19*
xxii, 22–35	Balaam sets out on the road		xxii, 20–1
xxii, 36–40*	Meeting of Balaam and Balak		xxii, 36–40*
xxiii, 28–xxiv, 9	Balaam blesses Israel		xxii, 41–xxiii, 10
xxiv, 10–19	Balaam's second blessing		xxiii, 11–24

as a result of the combining of the material, the original order has been disturbed here and there (e.g. the endangering of Sarah, which now in 1b comes after the making of the covenant, probably stood as in 1a before it, and the narrative of Abraham's treaty with Abimelech in xxi, 22–34*, presumably in both 1a and 1b, had its place between the 'endangering of Sarah' and 'God's covenant with Abraham'). Now these do not comprise isolated groups, for a closer examination reveals immediately that the two series are closely connected with group 1 in each case linked to groups 2, 3 and 4. Thus two large series appear: 1a, 2a, 3a, 4a and 1b, 2b, 3b, 4b. This fact itself makes it probable that we have here two continuous strands, and this becomes a certainty when we notice that in between these four groups there may be observed again and again the existence side by side or interwoven of two quite similarly constructed narratives (e.g. in Exod. 1–xv,[7] and particularly in iii–v). As far as Genesis is

[7] Eissfeldt, 'Die Komposition von Ex i–xii' ThBl 18 (1939), cols. 224–33; Mowinckel, 'Die vermeintliche "Passahlegende" Ex i–xv in bezug auf die Frage: Literarkritik und Traditionskritik' StTh 5 (1952), pp. 66–88; Pedersen, 'Passahfest und Passahlegende' ZAW 52 (1934), pp. 161–75; *Israel* III–IV (1940), pp. 726–37 and (Additions 1959), pp. 794–5. Cf. Lit. above, p. 44, n. 39; § 126.

concerned, the two strands may also be differentiated by the divine names, since a uses *Yahweh*, whereas b uses *Elohim*. a is thus J and b is E. Outside Genesis, this mark of recognition soon comes to an end, as we have seen (pp. 182–3), but a series of other indications (e.g. the replacement of the prevailing nationalistic and religious feeling of 4a by a more spiritual ethos in 4b, cf. p. 201) make it clear that the narratives indicated under 3a and 4a belong together with those of 1a and 2a, and those of 3b and 4b with those of 1b and 2b—and thus belong to J and E respectively.

3. *L*. If the material which belongs to J and E (pp. 199–204) is separated out of that part of the Pentateuch which remains after the removal of P (and D), it appears that the material is by no means all used up. There remains to be more closely defined a whole series of narratives and complexes of narratives. This is true in the first place of Gen. i–xi, the primeval history[8] E does not yet appear here, but only begins at xv[9] with the narrative of God's covenant with Abraham, and appears to have had no primeval history at all; for the efforts of Mowinckel and Hölscher to demonstrate an E share in Gen. i–xi (p. 164) may be regarded as without success. The primeval story, reduced by the removal of the P section, as easily recognisable here as elsewhere, still contains, however, many duplications and contradictions, and can certainly not be confined to *one* narrative strand. Thus, if we pass over here the narrative of the garden of Eden and the fall, which is very difficult to analyse, in iv, 25 Seth does not appear originally to have been regarded as the brother of Cain, but as the sole son of the first human pair, just as Cain's genealogy in iv, 1, 17a, 18–22,[10] must surely be understood to mean that the whole of later mankind is to be traced back to him. The genealogies of Cain and of Seth are mutually exclusive, and cannot be assigned to the same narrative strand. It is further quite obvious that Noah, the father of Shem, Japheth and Canaan (ix, 21–7) has no place beside the J story of Noah the father of Shem, Ham and Japheth (vi, 5–ix, 19*, x*), in spite of the attempt made by the addition in ix, 18, *and Ham, that is the father of Canaan* to identify them. It is further clear that the Tower of Babel story in xi, 1–9,[11] according to which mankind was divided by direct divine intervention and was split up into a multiplicity of peoples and languages, cannot be united with the table of nations which is made up of P and a second account (J) (x). For according to

[8] Lit., p. 35, n. 2; p. 36, n. 3. Heinisch, *Probleme der biblischen Urgeschichte* (1947); Humbert, *Études sur le récit du paradis et de la chute dans la Genèse* (1940); Rendtorff, 'Genesis viii, 21, und die Urgeschichte des Jahwisten' Kerygma und Dogma 7 (1961), pp. 69–78; von Soden, 'Zu einigen altbabylonischen Dichtungen' Or 26 (1957), pp. 306–20, Pls. XI–XIV; Zimmerli, *I. Mose i–xi. Die Urgeschichte* ([2]1957). Cf. Alfrink, 'La vulgarisation de la science biblique et les documents de l'église' BEThL XII (1959), pp. 65–75; Bea, 'Il problema del Pentateuco e della Storia primordiale' La Civ. Cath. (1948), pp. 116–27; Vosté, 'Epistula Pontificiae Commissionis de Re Biblica: de tempore documentorum Pentateuchi et de genere litterario undecim priorum capitum Geneseos' Bibl 29 (1948), pp. 165–8.

[9] Seierstad, 'Paktstanken og pakten i Genesis xv' TTKi 32 (1961), pp. 10–21. Lit. p. 164, n. 29.

[10] Gabriel, 'Die Kainitengenealogie Gn. iv, 17–24' Bibl 40 (1959), pp. 409–27; Hauret, 'Réflexions pessimistes et optimistes sur Gen iv, 17–24' BEThL XII (1959), pp. 358–65.

[11] Kramer, 'Man's Golden Age: A Parallel to Genesis xi, 1' JAOS 63 (1943), pp. 191–4; Parrot, *La Tour de Babel* (1953), E.T. *The Tower of Babel* (1955).

this latter, mankind, forming a single family in Shem, Ham and Japheth, gradually became divided within itself with the ever-increasing numbers of succeeding generations, so that the many peoples and languages came about of themselves. The question is only whether these sections which do not fit with the remaining material—after the removal of P—are to be regarded as isolated secondary additions or whether they must be described as parts of a strand running parallel to this basic material.

This lack of unity in the J stratum which is noticeable in the primeval history may also be observed elsewhere in this stratum. We have already seen (pp. 187–188) that the main body of the material of xii–xiii, without P and without xii, 10–xiii, 1 (J), finds its sequel in xviii–xix, whereas xii, 10–xiii, 1, is taken up again in xv–xvi* and then again first apparently in xxi, 1–7*. Thus here too there are two series of Yahwistic sections. Furthermore it is very clear that the Yahwistic sections Gen. xxxiv*;[12] xxxv, 5, 21–22ba; xxxviii; xlix, 2–27* do not fit with the J Joseph story, but noticeably disturb it. This is particularly true of xxxviii. Here too the supplementary hypothesis may be invoked, and these sections may be explained as amplifications of the J Joseph story. But against this is the recognition that we are not dealing with unconnected individual passages but clearly with parts of a presentation parallel to the J (and E) narrative. Here too is a presentation like the other, which endeavours to explain, though admittedly in a different manner, how the older brothers—Reuben, Simeon, Levi and Judah lost their right of primogeniture and how the youngest, or next to youngest, Joseph, took their place (p. 197). There is a similar situation in Exod. ii, 23–vi, 1. If we disregard the P material, which amounts to only 2½ verses (ii, 23aβ–5), the section appears, particularly in iii and v, as the combination of two very similar series of narratives, which reveal themselves on closer examination as J and E. But the whole of the material cannot be divided between these two parallel series. There are some sections left which either do not fit in at all or can be fitted in only with difficulty. There is the fragment of the verse ii, 23aα, which, as has long been observed, is directly continued in iv, 19–20a; iii, 21–2; iv, 1–9, 20b–3, 24–6, 30b–1a; and these sections, which have got out of order in the process of compilation, reveal themselves when properly arranged as a third parallel strand to J and E—admittedly fragmentary, but readily restorable. It related how after the death of the Egyptian king (ii, 23aα), Moses received the command from Yahweh to return with his wife and son[13] to Egypt (iv, 19–20a). On the way, evidently in the immediate vicinity of Yahweh's dwelling, Moses, as yet uncircumcised and so exposed to Yahweh's attack, is set upon by Yahweh, but rescued from the danger by his prudent wife (iv, 24–6)[14] [and then being thus equipped as Yahweh's instrument, he is commissioned by God

---

[12] Lehming, 'Zur Überlieferungsgeschichte von Gen. xxxiv' ZAW 70 (1958), pp. 228–50; Speiser, ' "Coming" and "Going" at the "City" Gate' BASOR 144 (1956), pp. 20–3.

[13] בְּנוֹ *his son*, following ii, 22, iv, 25, instead of בָּנָיו *his sons*.

[14] Talmon, 'The "Bloody Husband"' [Hebr., Engl. sum.] Eretz-Israel 3 (1954), pp. 93–6, IV; Blau, 'The ḥatan damim' [Hebr., Engl. sum.] Tarbiz 26 (1956/7), pp. 1–3, I; Ben-Shabbat, 'Notes on J. Blau's Essay "ḥatan damim"' [Hebr., Engl. sum.] Tarbiz 26 (1956/7), p. 213, VII. Cf. p. 44, n. 40; § 126.

with the deliverance of Israel from Egypt. The commission issues in the][15] command to plunder the Egyptians (iii, 21–2). In order that the Israelites may recognise Moses as the one commissioned by Yahweh, the latter empowers him to carry out three signs before the Israelites (iv, 1–9). [In addition he is endowed with the power to do wonders before Pharaoh, and] is given instructions for these. At the same time, he is admittedly told that Pharaoh will not let Israel go in spite of these wonders, and that Moses must therefore threaten him with the slaughter of his first born son by Yahweh (iv, 20b–3). [Moses returns to Egypt], carries out the signs which attest his commission, and gains the people's confidence (iv, 30b, 31a).

We often find this phenomenon again. In addition to the P material, and the parallel series which may be seen to be J and E, there are other sections left which will not fit either P or J and E. It is an important fact that this is also true of the narrative of the events at Sinai-Horeb. This section, more precisely its actual narrative kernel, Exod. xix, 1–xx, 21; xxiii, 20–xxiv, 18; xxxi, 18–xxxiv, 35, is exceptionally difficult to analyse, and we shall therefore not here enter further into the question of its composition. But it appears certain that xxiv, 1–2, 9–11 (Moses and 70 elders with Yahweh), xxiv, 13a, 14–15a (Moses and Joshua on the mountain), and xxxiv, 10–13* (Yahweh's covenant with Israel) do not fit with either J or E (p. 190), and certainly not with P. But these very original and colourful passages do not look at all like amplifications or secondary additions; they appear rather as fragments of another narrative. This assumption is all the easier since both before and after them many traces of a fourth strand running parallel to J, E and P may be observed. xxiv, 1–2, 9–11, 13a, 14–15a, seem to form the central section of this fourth strand which related the manner in which, according to its view, the covenant between Yahweh and Israel came into being. This covenant had here as its content the promise of Yahweh that he would drive out the Canaanites before Israel, and Israel's obligation to guard itself against any association with the Canaanites.

Thus in many places in the Pentateuchal narrative there remains a substantial residuum which strongly resists being assigned to J, E or P, and also does not in the least appear like an amplification of one of these strands or an addition at the time of compilation. It bears a quite special and original stamp. The assumption that we are really dealing here with parts of a fourth narrative strand which runs right through the Pentateuch is favoured by the observation which may readily be made that many of these sections stand out from the three other strands by a certain air of antiquity and crudity, and by this too reveal themselves as being in some way connected. We have seen further that in certain parts of the narrative the sections group themselves naturally into larger connected units, and that between these groups odd elements are repeatedly to be found which may not be incorporated into the structure of J, E and P, but appear reasonably enough to belong with the sections assigned to this fourth strand (pp. 191–3). Thus we may with great confidence gather together as a fourth strand the material which cannot be assigned to the other three narrative

[15] The narrative elements placed in square brackets have fallen out in the process of compilation and are here filled in.

H

sources, in so far as it really makes the impression of belonging to a source and is not simply secondary addition, of which there is certainly no lack (§ 32). In Genesis, the sections which belong here make use of the divine name *Yahweh*. These sections and those which are to be regarded as their sequel in the following books, thus belong to the Yahwistic stratum, which is simply to be divided into two strands just like the Elohistic stratum (E and P). The one with which we are dealing is, as we have seen, particularly crude and archaic, and although a powerful religious spirit also moves strongly through it, it is nevertheless the least touched by clerical and cultic interests. For this reason, we may, for want of a better name, denote it as the 'Lay source' using the siglum L (p. 169).

4. *The dates of origin of the individual narrative strands.* These last points already touch on the question of the date of origin[16] of the individual narrative strands, and we must now turn more particularly to this.

Without questioning the great antiquity of much of their material, we have already indicated (p. 140) that all four narrative strands presuppose Israel as a united ruling people settled in Canaan, and they cannot therefore have come into being before the reign of David. We have also noted that there are to be found hardly any allusions to precise historical events and conditions. Under these circumstances the dating of the strands must be made mainly on the basis of religious outlook and literary history. Such a method of dating can obviously not indicate a precise year or decade, and not even a particular century. At the same time we must also remain aware of the fact that direct lines of development are never found anywhere, and that we must always reckon with times of decline, so that even the broadest suggestions made must still remain very uncertain. But in spite of these points we may nevertheless at least set out a well-founded relative chronology for the sources. L clearly appears as the oldest, and P equally clearly as the youngest. There may be difference of opinion concerning the relative age of the two sources J and E which lie between these, and indeed different views have been put forward and are likely to be put forward again. But that J is the older may claim a greater degree of probability. We should thus have the sequence L, J, E, P.

III. The Four Narrative Strands

§ 28. THE PENTATEUCH SOURCE L

Literature: cf. §§ 5, 18, 19, 22–6.

1. *Its antique flavour.* Roughly the following material may be reckoned to L: Gen. ii, 4b–iii, 24*; iv, 1, 17a, 18–24; vi, 1–4; ix, 21–7; xi, 1–9; xii, 1–4a*, 6–8; xiii, 2, 5, 7–11a, 12bβ–18; xviii–xix; xxv, 1–6, 11b, 21–6a, 29–34; xxvi, 1–2a, 3a, 6–23, 25b–33; xxix, 1–xxx, 24*, 25–43*; xxxi, 1, 3, 19–54*; xxxii, 24b–33; xxxiii, 18–19*; xxxiv; xxxv, 5, 21–22bα; xxxvi, 2b–5*, 9–39*; xxxviii; xlix, 1*,

[16] Rost, 'Zum geschichtlichen Ort der Pentateuchquellen' ZThK 53 (1956), pp. 1–10.

2–7; Exod. i–ii*; iii, 21–2; iv, 1–9, 19–26, 30b–31a; vii, 15b, 17b*, 20aβb; xii, 21–7, 33–9; xiii, 3–16*, 20; xiv*;[1] xv, 20–7;[2] xvi*; xvii, 1a, 8–16; xix, 2–25*; xxiv, 1–2, 9–11, 13a, 14–15a; xxxii, 17–18, 25–9; xxxiii, 3b–4; xxxiv, 10–13*; Num. x, 29–36*; xi, 1–3, 4–35*; xii*; xiii–xiv*; xx, 1–13*, 14–21*; xxi, 1–3, 10–35*;[3] xxv, 1–5*; xxxii*. That L is to be assumed to be the oldest narrative strand is proved primarily by the fact already mentioned that this strand reveals the crudest and most primitive original elements. To the examples already mentioned (pp. 184 f., 191–3) a few more may be added. It appears that the L strand in the primeval history pictured men as nomads, whereas J and P clearly think of them as husbandmen. The genealogy of Cain in iv, 1, 17a, 18–22,[4] which belongs to L, concludes in vv. 21–2 by enumerating the fathers of the three nomadic groups, namely Jabal, the father of those who own cattle, Jubal, the father of the musicians, and Tubal-cain, the father of the smiths. It thus envisages only nomads and knows no other men. To this fits also the fact that the narrative of the building of the tower, which also belongs to L, begins in xi, 2, with the words *Now when they were wandering in the east,* and thus pictures mankind, forming a unit up to that time (xi, 1), as a wandering group of nomads. It is quite clear that in Israel, which became an agricultural people from being a nomadic people, an outline of their history which places nomads at the beginning must be older than one which pictures the first men as husbandmen. The narrative of the building of the tower also appears very archaic by its strongly anthropomorphic conception of God—Yahweh is anxious about his power and so destroys men's proud work. This feature is also to be found in other sections which probably belong to L, namely the fragmentary narrative of the origin of the giants in vi, 1–4, and a verse at the end of the garden of Eden narrative (iii, 22) according to which Yahweh decided to drive men out of paradise because they were otherwise threatening to make themselves completely equal to himself. Quite marked anthropomorphic traits are also to be found in the conception of God in the story, already mentioned, of Yahweh's attack on Moses in Exod. iv, 24–6 (p. 192).

Furthermore, it is an indication of the age and nature of L that, unlike J, it is aware of a disharmony at Sinai. J pictures Israel as departing from Sinai in the liveliest hopes and with its joy unclouded in the prospect of the land which is flowing with milk and honey, and Yahweh as accompanying them in the form in which alone this is possible, namely in the Ark. But L knows of a disharmony with which Israel's sojourn at Sinai[5] came to an end, and this had the result that Israel's departure from Sinai appears rather as a dismissal from the presence of Yahweh than as a joyous march into the land of promise. In this the Ark is evaluated as a very imperfect substitute for Yahweh whose presence is only to be found in the full sense at Sinai. This feature accords with the fact

[1] Speiser, 'An Angelic "Curse": Exodus xiv, 20' JAOS 80 (1960), pp. 198–200.
[2] Lehming, 'Massa und Meriba' ZAW 73 (1961), pp. 71–7.
[3] Noth, 'Num xxi als Glied der "Hexateuch"-Erzählung' ZAW 58 (1940/1), pp. 161–189; Rendtorff, 'Zur Lage von Jaser' ZDPV 76 (1960), pp. 124–35, Pls. 13–16.
[4] Albright, 'Dedan' *Alt-Festschr.* (1953), pp. 1–12; cf. p. 11.
[5] Greta Hort, 'Musil, Madian and the Mountain of the Law' *Jewish Studies Sicher* (1955), pp. 81–93. Lit. p. 197, n. 8; § 126.

that L regards the first men as nomads. For L is no doubt giving expression in this to his enthusiasm for the nomadic ideal. The cultivated land with its sanctuaries represented by holy tent and ark—for L too must have told of the tent and the ark—is only a very imperfect substitute for the true home of Israel and Yahweh, namely the desert with its mountain of God.

2. *Literary form.* From the point of view of form too L is the most primitive of the four narrative works. Whereas in J, E and P we have strictly constructed narrative works, in which not only the individual narratives but also the narrative complexes are linked together, in L the individual narratives follow one another with relatively little connection, and the thread which holds them together is often merely the chronological sequence of the events. A comparison of the stories of Jacob-Esau and Jacob-Laban, as well as that of Jacob and his sons, as they appear on the one hand in L and on the other hand in J and E, may serve to illustrate this point. In L the Jacob-Esau stories and the Jacob-Laban stories stand separately. After Esau has sold his birthright, i.e. his claim to the land of Canaan, to Jacob for a mess of pottage, he goes to Edom and thus passes out of the narrative's field of vision (xxv, 29–34; xxxvi*). This is shown also in the fact that the sections of the genealogy of Esau in ch. xxxvi which belong to L here certainly followed directly on xxv, 29–34. When Jacob returns from Laban to Canaan, he does not meet with Esau at all, so that here no kind of settlement takes place between the two, and indeed, unlike the position in J and E, Jacob's departure from Canaan in L can hardly be thought of as a flight from Esau with whom a settlement has been made in proper legal form. Jacob does not meet with Esau on his return, but with El (xxxii, 24–33).[6] In J and E, however, the Jacob-Laban story is inserted into the middle of the Jacob-Esau story and is thus set in the two halves of the latter, so that the whole presents a higher unity. Jacob deceives Esau and must therefore flee from him (xxvii). He escapes to Laban (xxviii–xxx*). When he returns (xxxi*), Esau advances against him in a warlike attitude—or at any rate in an ambiguous attitude—and Jacob contrives a stratagem to get free of this uncongenial companion and to lead him to withdraw finally into the land of Edom (xxxii–xxxiii*). At this point (xxxiii, 18) the JE material of ch. xxxvi was directly linked.

There is a similar position in the story of Jacob and his sons (p. 192). L presents three narratives which stand separately: xxxiv, xxxv, 5, the crime of Simeon and Levi; xxxv, 21–22abα (in L this certainly stood before xxxiv), Reuben's shameful deed;[7] and xxxviii, the separation of Judah from his brothers. It sums them up in the last words of Jacob in Gen. xlix, 3–7, which may be perhaps completed following Deut. xxxiii, 7: the three eldest sons, who have committed crimes against their father, are cursed; concerning the fourth, who has separated himself from his brothers, the wish is expressed that God will bring

[6] Eissfeldt, 'Non dimittam te, nisi benedixeris mihi' *Mél. Bibl. Robert* (1957), pp. 77–81; Schildenberger, 'Jakobs nächtlicher Kampf mit dem Elohim am Jabok (Gen xxxii, 23–33)' *Misc. Bibl. Ubach* (1954), pp. 69–96; Täubler, 'The First Mention of Israel' PAAJR 12 (1942), pp. 115–20; van Trigt, 'La signification de la lutte de Jacob près du Yabbok, Genèse xxxii, 23–33' OTS 12 (1958), pp. 280–309.

[7] Cf. Iliad IX, 448–57: Phoenix sleeps with the mistress of his father Amyntor, and is hence cursed by the latter.

him back, and the birthright thus taken from the older brother is handed to
Joseph—this must in L have been the sequel of Gen. xlix, 3–7 + Deut. xxxiii, 7.
J and E, on the other hand, have here the Joseph story, which is constructed in
a highly artistic manner and which basically issues in the same point as the much
more primitive parallel narrative of L, yet with the difference that J and E here
at the same time also provide a motive for Israel's migration to Egypt, whereas
L clearly added this feature afterwards and was not able to integrate it into the
narrative we have just outlined.

In yet another direction there is a striking difference between L on the one
hand and J and E on the other, which equally makes clear that L is older than
J and E. In the L narratives the elements of national and tribal history are much
clearer and purer than in J and E, where frequently a more fictional element
prevails and often conceals the background of national and tribal history to such
an extent that it can hardly now be recognised, and the impression is given that
we are dealing not with peoples and tribes but with individuals. The references
—in part simply references rather than narratives—in Gen. xxxv, 21–22abα;
xxxiv; xxxv, 5; xxxviii, to the deeds of the four eldest sons of Jacob which led
to the withdrawal of their birthright, bring the stress on tribal history right into
the foreground and use fictional motifs only so far as it is absolutely necessary
to create a plot. But in the Joseph story of J and E the fictional embroidery is
such that it has almost completely concealed the historical fact which it is meant
to explain, namely how it has come about that the older tribes, which were
once in the lead, had to give up their role to the Joseph tribe. The reader gets
the impression that he is dealing with individuals and not even with Israelites
but with men in general—a too indulgent father, a spoilt youngest child who
has hence become overbearing, and jealous and vengeful elder brothers. It is to
this, as we have seen (pp. 40 f.), that we owe it that these stories possess a vitality
which transcends nations and generations. For it is the purely human interest,
and in this the universal and enduring elements, which are here presented with
such wonderful vividness. Similar to these features of the Joseph story is the
difference between the concise note in L concerning the driving out of the sons
of Abraham's concubine Keturah in Gen. xxv, 1–6,[8] and the Hagar narrative
which parallels it in J in xvi, 4–14, and in E in xxi, 8–21.

3. *Date and place of origin.* In view of all this, it can hardly be doubted that L
is the oldest of the four strands of narrative, and we may ask whether it may
not be even more, namely the first attempt of the kind at all. But though this
cannot be proved, we have no basis for the assumption that L was preceded by
an older narrative work entirely lost to us—at any rate no traces of such a work
have survived. It is, however, extremely difficult to assess the absolute date of
origin of this oldest and probably first sketch. The *terminus a quo*, the reign of
David, has already been mentioned, and since David's life-work, the creation of
the united kingdom, is clearly presupposed as completed, we may specify the
earlier limit more precisely as the end of David's reign. The lower limit cannot
be brought down beyond the disaster to the northern kingdom, namely the year

[8] Philby, *The Land of Midian* (1957); Ryckmans, 'Het Oude Arabië en de Bijbel'
JEOL 14 (1955/6), pp. 73–84, Pls. III–IV. Lit. p. 195, n. 5; § 126.

721 B.C. In fact, this lower limit may be taken further back, and we may say that the appearance of Amos and Hosea must lie after it; at any rate their activity has left no trace in the work. The two centuries between the end of the reign of David, c. 964 B.C. and the appearance of Amos and Hosea, c. 750 B.C. thus mark the period in which the origin of L is most naturally to be placed. A more precise dating is difficult. The narratives which explain the decline of the tribes of Reuben, Simeon and Levi and the isolation of Judah (p. 197) almost certainly refer to events of the premonarchical period, if not of pre-Canaanite times.[9] In their justification of the chief position of Joseph—now broken off in L but certainly to be presupposed here (p. 197)—they do not actually allude to the existence of the northern kingdom, and so we cannot simply assign them to the period after the division of the kingdom, i.e. after 926 B.C. On the other hand, the lack of reference to this event is no conclusive proof that L must have come into being earlier. For the division of the kingdom also plays no part in the sources which certainly came into being after it. To broad circles in the community, at any rate those circles from which our Pentateuchal narrative strands stem, Israel actually remained a unity in spite of its division into two political entities, and this is a fact which makes it appear also relatively irrelevant as to where the individual strands came into existence, whether in the south or the north (below and pp. 200, 203 f.) and certainly makes a definite answer to that question impossible.

We may perhaps endeavour to evaluate, as an argument for a more precise dating of L, the fact that it appears in a special sense to be committed to the nomadic ideal, while it takes up an attitude of reserve or even of rejection towards the land of Canaan with its agricultural life and no doubt also its cultus. The movement which led to the revolution of Jehu, whose prime movers were not merely Elijah and Elisha but also the Rechabites who also took up a negative attitude to agriculture (II Kings x, 15–16), reveals a great enthusiasm for the nomadic ideal, and might therefore have provided the soil in which a work such as L could grow. To this would also fit the fact that just as Elijah goes on a pilgrimage to Yahweh at Horeb when he is despondent, in order there to receive new courage from him (I Kings xix), so too L regards Sinai and not the land of Canaan as the real dwelling of Yahweh, and hence also as the real home of Israel (pp. 195 f.). Admittedly we do not know how far back we must look for the beginnings of this movement. It is attested for us in the middle of the ninth century B.C., and we must certainly reckon with the possibility that it originated already a century earlier as a reaction against the policy of Solomon which was favourable to Canaanite civilisation. On this basis, the century between 950 and 850 B.C. would appear to be suitable for the origin of L. We have already noted that its place of origin cannot be defined with certainty. So far as the stratum of society is concerned in which the compiler of L is to be sought, we must no

[9] Lindblom, 'The Political Background of the Shiloh Oracle' SVT I (1953), pp. 78–87, places the sayings concerning Judah and Reuben in Gen. xlix, 8–12, 3–4 in the period when David was king over Judah, and Eshbaal king over 'Israel'. Cf. also Coppens, 'La bénédiction de Jacob. Son cadre historique à la lumière des parallèles ougaritiques' SVT IV (1957), pp. 97–115; Edelkoort, 'De Siloprofetie' NThSt 23 (1940), pp. 260–76; Eissfeldt, 'Silo und Jerusalem' SVT IV (1957), pp. 138–47. Cf. Lit. p. 229, n. 20; § 126.

doubt think of a member of the priestly class or better of the prophetic. For these were at that time the exclusive bearers of historical tradition and of education. The suggestion that we should look for the compiler of the oldest Pentateuchal narrative work among the descendants of Moses, has been made more than once[10] and is plausible, but cannot be proved or even regarded as probable. However, we shall have to return to this question, as to that of the dating of the oldest Pentateuchal strand, when we come to discuss the possibility that it continues beyond the Pentateuch and the Hexateuch, and perhaps even extends into the books of Kings (pp. 244–8).

§ 29. THE PENTATEUCH SOURCES J AND E

Literature: Davies, 'The Yahwistic Tradition in the Eighth Century Prophets' StOTPr (1950), pp. 37–51; Marie-Louise Henry, *Jahwist und Priesterschrift. Zwei Glaubenszeugnisse des AT* (Arbeiten zur Theologie 3, 1960); Luther, 'Die Persönlichkeit des Jahwisten' in Eduard Meyer, *Die Israeliten und ihre Nachbarstämme* (1906), pp. 105–73; Stoebe, 'Gut und Böse in der Jahwistischen Quelle des Pentateuch' ZAW 65 (1953), pp. 188–204.
Cf. also Literature §§ 22–8, 30–4.

It has already become clear in the characterisation of L just undertaken, where reference has been made to its differences from the strands J and E, that they are later than L. Indeed we have seen that both in content and in form J and E represent a more advanced stage. So we are now only further concerned to specify the exact age of J and E more precisely, and at the same time to describe their peculiarities rather more closely.

1. *J.* The material to be assigned to J is roughly as follows (here as elsewhere no distinction is made between its original compass and any later but relatively insignificant amplifications): Gen. ii, 4b–iii, 24*; iv, 2–16,[1] 17b, 25–6;[2] v, 28 *a son*, 29; vi, 5–ix, 19*,[3] 20; x*; xi, 28–30[4]; xii, 1–4a*, 10–20; xiii, 1; xv*; xvi, 1b–2, 4–14; xxi, 1–7*, 22–34*; xxii*; xxiv*; xxv, 18, 27–8*, xxvi, 2b, 3bα, 24–25a; xxvii*;[5] xxviii, 13–16, 19; xxix, 1–xxx, 24*, 25–43*; xxxi, 19–54*; xxxii, 1–24a*; xxxiii*; xxxvi, 2b–5*, 9–39*; xxxvii, 3–36*; xxxix–l*;[6] Exod. i–ii*; iii*; iv, 18, 29, 31b; v*; vi, 1*; vii–xi*;[7] xii, 29–30, 32; xiii, 21–2; xiv*; xvi*; xvii, 1b–7*;

---

[10] Auerbach (p. 132), pp. 22–33, 98; *Moses* (1953), pp. 7–9; cf. above, p. 138, n. 15.

[1] Abramski, 'The Qenites [Hebr., Engl. sum.] Eretz Israel 3 (1954), pp. 116–24, VI–VII; Castellino, 'Genesis iv, 7' VT 10 (1960), pp. 442–5; Mangan, 'A Discussion of Gen iv, 7' CBQ 6 (1944), pp. 91–3; Sellers, 'Problems in the Story of Cain' Pyatt Memorial Vol. (1953), pp. 53–4.

[2] Horst, 'Die Notiz vom Anfang des Jahwekultes in Genesis iv, 26' *Libertas Christiana, Fr. Delekat zum 65. Geburtstag* (1957) = Beitr. EvTh 26, pp. 68–74. Lit. § 126.

[3] On viii, 21, cf. Rendtorff (p. 191, n. 8).

[4] Gordon, 'Abraham and the Merchants of Ura' JNESt 17 (1958), pp. 28–31; Saggs, 'Ur of the Chaldees. A Problem of Identification' Iraq 22 (1960), pp. 200–9. Lit. § 126.

[5] Eissfeldt, 'Das AT im Lichte der safatenischen Inschriften' ZDMG 104 (1954), pp. 88–118. Cf. above, p. 67, n. 8.

[6] Driver, 'Two Problems in the OT Examined in the Light of Assyriology' Syria 33 (1956), pp. 70–8, see pp. 70–3: Genesis xlvii, 12–17.

[7] Couroyer, 'Un égyptianisme biblique: "Depuis la fondation de l'Égypte" (Exode ix,

xviii*;[8] xix, 2–25*; xx, 18*, 20*;[9] xxiii, 20–33*; xxxiii, 1–3a; xxxiv, 1–28*;
Num. x, 29–36*; xi, 4–35*; xiii–xiv*;[10] xvi*; xx, 14–21*; xxi, 10–35*; xxii–
xxiv*; xxv, 1–5*; xxxii*; Deut. xxxi, 14*, 16*, 23*; xxxiv, 1*, 2–6. Throughout
these J narratives there breathes a spirit of enthusiastic acceptance of agricultural
life, and of national-political power and cultus. Completely characteristic of this
acceptance of the two entities—agriculture and cultus—here bound together in
an inseparable unity, is the cultic decalogue which certainly belongs to J, with
its emphasis on the three harvest festivals (Exod. xxxiv, 18–26).[11] The proud
delight in kingdom and king resounds particularly clearly and strongly in the
Balaam story as J relates it, as well as in many other sayings such as Gen. xii, 3;
xxvii, 29*. Balaam's first word of blessing, Num. xxiv, 3–9, is really a paean on
the glory and fruitfulness of Canaan and on the victorious invincibility of Israel.
His second, Num. xxiv, 15–19, is an equally magnificent song of praise on the
Israelite king. Although in form they are prophetic, they are both in reality
descriptions of present conditions, and the first saying extols Saul, the victor
over Agag (I Sam. xv), and the second looks back on Israel's greatest and most
powerful king, David. It fits well with such a delight in the land, the people, the
king and the cultus that, as we have already mentioned (p. 195), in J Israel's
departure from Sinai is an advance, undertaken joyfully and expectantly, into
the land *which flows with milk and honey* (Exod. xxxiii, 1–3a), and that Yahweh
here himself accompanies his people so as to take up his dwelling in Israel's
land immediately. Such a proud and grateful delight in people, land, cultus and
kingdom, exalted and unshattered, is quite unthinkable after the disaster of 721.
We must therefore in any case place J before this disaster. It remains uncertain
how long before. As we know from Amos' polemic, the middle of the eighth
century B.C. was a time of exalted national hopes and of unclouded delight in
the land, the kingdom and the cultus. J would therefore fit into this period. But
no doubt earlier too there was national optimism in Israel, so that the ninth
century or the end of the tenth century would also be possible for the dating of
J.[12] J does indeed come from just those circles against which, as we have
assumed (p. 198), the opposition expressed in L is directed. Concerning J's
place of origin, the essential points will be made later (pp. 203 f.), by way of
elaboration of what has already been said (p. 198).

2. *E.* To E is to be assigned roughly the following material, again without
specification of the secondary additions preserved in the basic material: Gen.
xv*; xx; xxi, 1–7*, 8–21, 22–34*; xxii*; xxiv*; xxv, 11a, 27–8*; xxvi, 3bβ–5; xxvii*;

---

18)' RB 67 (1960), pp. 42–8; Greta Hort, 'The Plagues of Egypt' ZAW 69 (1957), pp.
84–103; 70 (1958), pp. 48–59. Lit. § 126.

[8] Brekelmans, 'Exodus xviii and the Origins of Yahwism in Israel' OTS 10 (1954),
pp. 215–24; Knierim, 'Exodus xviii und die Neuordnung der mosaischen Gerichtsbarkeit'
ZAW 73 (1961), pp. 146–71.

[9] Greenberg, 'נסה in Exodus xx, 20, and the Purpose of the Sinaitic Theophany'
JBL 79 (1960), pp. 273–6.

[10] Mowinckel, 'Die Gründung von Hebron' *Donum natalicium H. S. Nyberg* (1954),
pp. 185–94 = Orientalia Suecana 4 (1955), pp. 67–76; on xiii, 22.

[11] Auerbach, 'Die Feste im alten Israel' VT 8 (1958), pp. 1–18. Lit. p. 205, n. 7; p. 207,
n. 14; p. 290, n. 38.

[12] Schmökel, 'Zur Datierung der Pentateuchquelle J' ZAW 62 (1950), pp. 319–21.

xxviii, 10–12, 17–18, 20–2; xxix, 1–xxx, 24*; xxxi, 2, 4–18aα, 19–54*; xxxii, 1–24a*; xxxiii*; xxxv, 1–4,[13] 6b–8, 14, 16–20;[14] xxxvi, 2b–5*, 9–39*; xxxvii, 3–36*; xxxix–l*; Exod. i–ii*; iii*; iv, 10–17, 27–8, 30a; v*; vi, 1*; vii–xi*; xii, 31; xiii, 17–19; xiv*; xvii, 1b–7*; xviii*; xix, 2–25*; xx, 18*, 19, 20*, 21, 1–17;[15] xxiii, 20–33*; xxiv, 3–8, 12, 13b, 18b; xxxi, 18b; xxxii, 1–16, 19–24, 30–5; xxxiii, 5–11; Num. xi, 4–35*; xii*; xiii–xiv*; xx, 11b, 14–21*; xxi, 4–9, 10–35*; xxii–xxiv*; xxxii*; Deut. xxxi, 14–18*, 23*; xxxiv, 1*. In spite of some elements, which, like E's Bethel narrative with its pre-Yahwistic traces (see p. 43), make an impression of greater antiquity than the corresponding ones in J, E is as a whole later than J, as has already been stated (p. 184). A few further observations may here be added. As in J, there is also expressed in E a strong Israelite self-consciousness and pride in the people's own special nature. But the difference from J is nevertheless in this respect too very marked. In J the religious and national elements are linked together in a quite natural manner, Israel's possession of the land and her political power are regarded quite simply as Yahweh's gift, and in this respect God and world form a unity, and God's grace is experienced in worldly good fortune. But in E this linkage is very much weakened. It is true that E too relates the promise given to the fathers that Canaan is to come to Israel (Gen. xv, 16; xxvi, 3; xxvii, 28–9*), so that later he can report with gratitude the fulfilment of this promise—for with E it is particularly clear that this strand is continued in the book of Joshua (pp. 250–5). But through his words on this point there echoes something rather like the *to have as if you do not have* of I Cor. vii, 29–31. For it is not the nationalistic and materialistic elements which in the end really matter for Israel, but the fact that God has appointed this people for himself and has separated it for his own possession. This conception, that Israel is an entity taken out of the remaining world of the nations, appointed for the service of the only true God, is expressed very clearly in the beautiful words with which God, according to E, summarises the meaning of the making of the covenant about to be completed on Horeb: *If you will obey me and keep my covenant, you shall be my own possession among all peoples. For all the earth is mine, and you shall be to me a kingdom of priests and a holy nation* (Exod. xix, 5–6).[16] It is a specifically religious goal which is here in view, not a national aim with a religious heightening. So too Balaam's blessing of Israel sounds in E very differently from that in J:

> *Lo, a people dwelling alone   and not reckoning itself among the nations.*
> *Misfortune is not seen in Jacob   nor trouble in Israel.*
> *Yahweh his God is with him   and the shout of a king is in him* (Num. xxiii, 9, 21).

[13] Soggin, 'Zwei umstrittene Stellen aus dem Überlieferungskreis um Schechem' ZAW 73 (1961), pp. 78–87: on I. Gen. xxxv, 1–5, II. Jos viii, 30–5. Cf. p. 159, n. 2.

[14] Habermann, 'The Tomb of Rachel and the Term נפש' [Hebr., Engl. sum.] Tarbiz 25 (1955/6), pp. 363–8, I–II; Muilenburg, 'The Birth of Benjamin' JBL 75 (1956), pp. 194–201; Naor, '"On the Way to Ephrath"' [Hebr.] BIES 22 (1958), pp. 49–54. Lit., p. 545, n. 15; § 126.

[15] On this order, see below, p. 213.

[16] Bauer, 'Könige und Priester, ein heiliges Volk (Ex xix, 6)' BZ 2 (1958), pp. 283–62; Wildberger, *Jahwes Eigentumsvolk* (AThANT 37, 1960). Lit. § 126.

Emphasis is thus laid quite decisively upon Israel's religious heritage, and this is not simply identified with the national heritage, but stands rather in a position of tension with it. This appears quite clearly in what E has to say about the events at Horeb. In the first place, it is characteristic that E's decalogue, the ethical one which is so familiar to us (Exod. xx, 1–17), says nothing about agricultural festivals and apparently deliberately ignores them. More important even than this is the fact that in E—quite unlike J but here in one point like L— the Horeb events echo with a sharp note of dissonance. While Moses is up on the mountain with God, to receive from him the record on stone, written by the finger of God himself, of the covenant already made between God and people— the tablets which begin with the exclusion of other gods and the prohibition of images—the people has already transgressed this covenant by the making of the golden calf. In blazing anger Moses shatters the tablets as soon as he is aware of this transgression, these tablets which God himself has written. This is something quite terrible, a breach which can never again be healed, and which must bring with it dreadful consequences. Moses' attempt at turning away the divine judgement from the people after the destruction of the calf-image and the punishment of the guilty, is unsuccessful. His prayer for this is quite sharply rejected by God: *Now go, lead the people to the place of which I have spoken to you. See, my angel shall go before you, but in the day when I visit, I will visit their sin upon them* (Exod. xxxii, 34). *The place of which I have spoken to you*—with these words spoken almost in a tone of rejection the goal of Israel's wanderings is mentioned, the same goal which J calls the land *which is flowing with milk and honey* (Exod. xxxiii, 3). It fits with this derogatory, or at any rate indifferent, utterance concerning Israel's land that God also says in his already mentioned utterance concerning the meaning of the covenant which is to be concluded: *You have seen how I bore you on eagles' wings and brought you to myself* (Exod. xix, 4). Horeb is thus God's real dwelling, not Canaan.

But the conclusion of the divine threat just quoted from Exod. xxxii, 34: *In the day when I visit, I will visit their sin upon them* is also significant in another respect, in that it makes quite clear what is E's historical viewpoint. Here, with a sinister and gloomy earnestness, there is mention of a fearful punishment which lies in the future. Smaller, temporary punishments such as famine, drought, locusts, wild beasts, earthquakes, disasters in war and the like are clearly not intended. Here it is a total disaster, the end of the people itself. It is the same note which sounds through the threats of Amos:

> *Fallen, no more to rise   is the virgin Israel;*
> *she lies prone on her land   with none to raise her up* (v, 2).
> *The end has come upon my people Israel,*
> *I will never again forgive them* (viii, 2).

It is the same disaster which is here meant—Israel's downfall. The only question is whether the E narrative of Exod. xxxii[17] which ends with this terrible threat

---

[17] Lehming, 'Versuch zu Ex xxxii' VT 10 (1960), pp. 16–50; Lewy, 'The Story of the Golden Calf reanalysed' VT 9 (1959), pp. 318–22; Noth, 'Zur Anfertigung des goldenen Kalbes' VT 9 (1959), pp. 419–22; Petuchowski, 'Nochmals "Zur Anfertigung des 'goldenen Kalbes'"' VT 10 (1960), p. 74.

was written before or after the disaster of 721; i.e., whether it is a real threat like the words of Amos which we have quoted in comparison or whether it is a *vaticinium ex eventu* which is designed to make the disaster which has already taken place intelligible in retrospect and to explain it in terms of the worship of the calf-image. It is nevertheless clear that Israel's fate—whether judged in anticipation or in retrospect—is judged by E exactly as by Amos, Hosea and other prophets. Prophetic influences may also be seen elsewhere in E. Thus it is E and E alone which describes Abraham as a *prophet* (Gen. xx, 7), and it is E too which relates the inspiration of the 70 elders (Num. xi, 14–30*) and makes Moses say on that occasion: *Would that all the people of Yahweh were prophets, and that Yahweh would put his spirit upon them* (verse 29). This liking for prophets fits well with the dating of E in the second half of the eighth century. But admittedly we must not lose sight of the possibility that we ought to go back rather further and place E in the middle of the ninth century. For much as Exod. xxxii, 34, reminds us of Amos v, 2; viii, 2, this threat also reveals great similarity with the proclamation of punishment which, according to I Kings xix, 17–18, Elijah received from the mouth of God at Horeb. The fact that the polemic against the calf image is to be found first in Hosea does not exclude the possibility that it was already condemned in certain circles a century earlier.

3. *Place of origin of J and E.* A firm decision on the place of origin—in the southern or northern kingdom—is here as little possible as it was with L and J (pp. 198 f., 201). It is true that E is generally assigned to the northern kingdom and J to the southern, no doubt also with the idea in mind that J could at the same time be understood as an abbreviation for Judah (the southern kingdom) and E for Ephraim (the northern kingdom). But the grounds adduced for this are not decisive. The fact that according to J it was Judah, and according to E Reuben who in the Joseph story acts as the conscience and the spokesman for his brothers, may simply be due to the technique of the story-teller, and does not necessarily have to be explained as due to the Judaean narrator bringing his tribal hero into the foreground, whereas the Ephraimite, to avoid the prominence given to Judah, transfers this role to Reuben, the eldest of the brothers. Equally indecisive is the argument that J tells of Hebron,[18] a Judaean sanctuary which E passes over, whereas E on the other hand reports in greater detail than J on the north-Israelite sanctuaries of Bethel and Shechem. For, in the first place, it is open to question whether J mentions Hebron at all, or whether the relevant passages are not rather to be regarded as belonging to L or as having been worked over (Gen. xiii, 18; xviii, 1; xxxvii, 14). In the second place, the Bethel narrative in J is at least as detailed as that of E. In the third place, and this is the decisive point, the Pentateuchal narrators definitely did not look at their material and choose it from a narrow particularistic angle, but there was always before them the concept of a united Israel, or at any rate of an Israel which in theory had always remained united, especially since they were dealing with a period long before the division of the kingdom. Thus they utilised the material which seemed to them to be appropriate without considering whether it derived from

---

[18] Mader, *Mambre. Die Ergebnisse der Ausgrabungen im heiligen Bezirk Râmet el-Ḫalîl in Südpalästina 1926–1932* (1957).

their own locality or from the neighbouring kingdom, which in any case was always felt by them to be a real brother. When we are dealing with the question of the origin of the materials, it is important and indeed of the utmost value to establish their precise relationship to their own originally very narrow area. But for the Pentateuchal narrators, these materials have long since lost such a limited association and have become the possession of all Israel. This may best be made clear in the E narrative of the golden calf. Originally, no doubt, this was a story related to the glory of the calf-image of Bethel; the image was made by Aaron. But now, certainly in the southern kingdom, it has become the opposite, and serves to set in its right perspective the apostate origin of this cultic representation, and makes it responsible for the disaster, threatened or already accomplished, to the northern kingdom.[19] But E removes the particularistic element from the story thus formed, and applies guilt and punishment to all Israel.

§ 30. THE PENTATEUCH SOURCE P

Literature: Bruston, 'Le document élohiste et son antiquité' Rev. Théol. de Montauban 4 (1882/3), pp. 13–32, 97–143; Budde, 'Ellä toledoth' ZAW 34 (1914), pp. 241–53; 36 (1916), pp. 1–7; Grelot, 'La dernière étape de la rédaction sacerdotale' VT 6 (1956), pp. 174–89; Hempel, 'Priesterkodex' PW 22 (1954), cols. 1943–67; Humbert, 'Die literarische Zweiheit des Priester-Codex in der Genesis (Kritische Untersuchung der These von von Rad)' ZAW 58 (1940/1), pp. 30–57; Jepsen, 'Zur Chronologie des Priesterkodex' ZAW 47 (1929), pp. 251–5; Kaufmann, 'Probleme der isr.-jüd. Rel.-Gesch.' ZAW 48 (1930), pp. 23–43; 51 (1933), pp. 35–47; Koch, 'Die Eigenart der priesterschriftlichen Sinaigesetzgebung' ZThK 55 (1958), pp. 36–51; *Die Priesterschrift von Exodus xxv bis Leviticus xvi* (FRLANT 71, 1959); Kortleitner, *Quo tempore codex sacerdotalis exstiterit* (1935); Kuschke, 'Die Lagervorstellung der priesterschriftlichen Erzählung' ZAW 63 (1951), pp. 74–105; Löhr, *Untersuchungen zum Hexateuchproblem* I: *Der Priesterkodex in der Genesis* (BZAW 38, 1924); Luther, 'Kāhāl und 'edāh als Hilfsmittel der Quellenscheidung im Priesterkodex und in der Chronik' ZAW 56 (1938), pp. 44–63; Noth (p. 176, n. 31), pp. 180–217; Roth, 'Thèmes majeurs de la Tradition sacerdotale dans le Pentateuque' NRTh 90 (1958), pp. 696–721; Speiser, 'Leviticus and the Critics' *Kaufmann Jub. Vol.* (1960), pp. 29–45; Waterman, 'Some Repercussions from Late Levitical Genealogical Accretions in P and the Chronicler' AJSL 58 (1941), pp. 49–56; Zimmerli, 'Sinaibund und Abrahambund. Ein Beitrag zum Verständnis der Priesterschrift' ThZ 16 (1960), pp. 268–88.

Cf. also Literature §§ 22–6, 35, 126.

It remains now to make a more precise characterisation of the fourth Pentateuchal narrative strand P. We have already indicated which sections are to be allotted to this (pp. 189–9), and it has also been hinted that P in particular has received very many secondary amplifications. In many cases there may well be difference of opinion about their extent. But all critics are agreed that among others, the following sections, practically all of a legal character, are to be denied to the basic content of P: Exod. xii, 15–20, 43–9; xxvii, 20–1; xxx, 1–38;[1]

---

[19] Eissfeldt, 'Lade und Stierbild' ZAW 58 (1940/1), pp. 190–215.
[1] de Langhe, *Het gouden altaar in de Israëlietische eredienst* (1952); 'L'autel d'or du temple de Jérusalem' Bibl 40 (1959), pp. 476–94; Haran, 'The Censer Incense and *Tamid*

xxxi, 1–11; xxxv–xl*; Lev. i–vii;[2] xi–xv;[3] xvii–xxvii; Num. iv; v, 5–vii, 88;[4] xv; xviii, 8–32; xix; xxviii–xxx. Some one or two of these sections, particularly the Holiness Code (Lev. xvii–xxvi), will concern us again. But first we have to deal with the original P[5] alone.

P too is a narrative work[6] and thus forms in fact a parallel to L, J and E. The continuity of what is related is indeed much more strongly brought out than in the other sources. For it is P which has a continuous chronology, beginning with the year of the creation of the world, and so exactly carried through that it serves as the basis of the cosmic periods employed by many Christian groups until quite recently (Anno Mundi 7472 according to the era of Constantinople —Anno Domini 1964) and of the system of dating still normal among Jews (A.M. 5725 = A.D. 1964). This dating of events[7] and of the persons involved gives to the whole the impression or at least the appearance of a structure made with mathematical precision; and this impression is further strengthened by the fact that the work also appears to be sharply marked out into sections. Externally this division is indicated by the superscription placed before individual sections: אֵלֶּה תּוֹלְדוֹת *These are the generations of N.N.* (but in Gen. v, 1, זֶה סֵפֶר תּוֹלְדוֹת *This is the book of the generations*). Only at the first section, the creation narrative of Gen. i, 1–ii, 4a[8] this formula stands not as a superscription but as a colophon (ii, 4a). It has perhaps been added secondarily. Otherwise it stands as a superscription in the following places: Gen. v, 1 (Adam); vi, 9 (Noah); x, 1 (the sons of Noah, Shem, Ham and Japheth); xi, 10 (Shem); xi, 27 (Terah); xxv, 12 (Ishmael); xxv, 19 (Isaac); xxxvi, 1, 9 (Esau); xxxvii, 2 (Jacob), and in addition at Num. iii, 1 (Aaron and Moses).[9] These superscriptions generally mark points at which the presentation which has so far been more comprehensive comes to be restricted to a smaller unit. After a description of the earth and heaven *with all their host*, from v, 1, onwards only one group of

Incense' [Hebr., Engl. sum.] Tarbiz 26 (1956/7), pp. 115–25, I–II; 'The Uses of Incense in the Ancient Israelite Ritual' VT 10 (1960), pp. 113–29, see pp. 124–9. Lit. § 126.

[2] Spiro, 'A Law on the Sharing of Information' PAAJR 28 (1959), pp. 95–101: on Lev. v, 1–6.

[3] Cochrane, 'Biblical Leprosy' BT 12 (1961), pp. 202 f.; Gramberg, ' "Leprosy" and the Bible' BT 11 (1960), pp. 10–23; Nida, 'The Translation of "Leprosy"' BT 11 (1960), pp. 80 f.; Swellengrebel, ' "Leprosy" and the Bible' BT 11 (1960), pp. 69–80; Wallington, "Leprosy" and the Bible' BT 12 (1961), pp. 75–9.

[4] Driver, 'Two Problems in the OT Examined in the Light of Assyriology' Syria 33 (1956), pp. 70–8; pp. 73–7: on Numbers v, 11–28.

[5] Haran, 'The Tabernacle in the Priestly Source' [Hebr.] *Tur-Sinai Jub. Vol.* (1960), pp. 25–42; Segal, 'The Tent of Meeting' [Hebr., Engl. sum.] Tarbiz 27 (1955/6), pp. 231–3, VIII–IX.

[6] Elliger, 'Sinn und Ursprung der priesterlichen Geschichtserzählung' ZThK 49 (1952) pp. 121–43. Lit. § 126.

[7] Auerbach, 'Die babylonische Datierung im Pentateuch und das Alter des Priester-Kodex' VT 2 (1952), pp. 334–42; 'Der Wechsel des Jahres-Anfangs in Juda' VT 9 (1959), pp. 113–21; Kaufmann, 'Der Kalender und das Alter des Priesterkodex' VT 4 (1954), pp. 307–13. Cf. p. 200, n. 11.

[8] Humbert, 'Trois Notes sur Genèse i' NTT 56 (1955), pp. 85–96 = *Opuscules d'un Hébraïsant* (1958), pp. 193–203; Ridderbos, 'Genesis i, 1 und 2' OTS 12 (1958), pp. 214–60. Lit. § 126.

[9] Eissfeldt, 'Biblos geneseōs' *Fascher-Festschr.* (1958), pp. 31–40; 'Toledot' *Klostermann-Festschr.*=TU 77 (1961), pp. 1–8; Holwerda, *Dictaten I: Historia Revelationis Veteris Testamenti* I (1954).

the inhabitants of the earth, namely men, is dealt with. vi, 9 and x, 1, then limit the view to Noah and his sons, and xi, 10, limits it still further, namely to Shem and his descendants. Among these again only one line is to be followed, as is shown by xi, 27, namely that of Terah, which issues in Abraham, Nahor and Haran. Then only Abraham's sons are further considered, first Ishmael (xxv, 12) and then Isaac (xxv, 19). Only Isaac's descendants are, however, to be further examined. So there is no further mention of Ishmael, but only of Esau (xxxvi, 1, 9) and Jacob (xxxvii, 2), but in such a way that here too a narrowing of perspective takes place, and only Jacob and his descendants are further described. Among these the descendants of Aaron and Moses are especially picked out by Num. iii, 1, as being as it were the kernel of Israel. With this, the narrowest circle is reached, and so the formula *These are the generations* comes to an end. Thus it serves to make plain what is passed over more tacitly in the other sources, namely the separate stages of the transition from the history of the world to that of Israel and their final goal.

It is no wonder that a narrative work which is apparently so artistically constructed provided with so many numbers and other quite concrete details, should for a long time have been regarded as absolutely reliable, and that even after the advent of Pentateuchal criticism it should have been regarded as the oldest and most reliable source and so be named as the basic work. As we have seen (pp. 165 f.), it was only in the nineteenth century that scholars—Reuss, Graf, Kuenen and Wellhausen—destroyed this false conception of the age of P and substituted a more appropriate view.

P purports to be a narrative work, but the narrative element is unevenly distributed. Whereas it is in general very thin and often only provides just as much as is absolutely needed to preserve the continuity, it spreads itself very broadly where the narrative issues directly or indirectly in legal precepts. This can be seen in Genesis at the founding of the sabbath (i, 1–ii, 4a),[10] at the issue of the commands to Noah (vi, 5–ix, 19*),[11] at the institution of circumcision (xvii), and at the story of Sarah's burial which establishes the Judaean claim to the cave of Machpelah (xxiii). In the later books it can be seen at the introduction of the feast of Passover and Unleavened Bread (Exod. xii, 1–14),[12] and then above all at the giving of the law at Sinai (Exod. xxv–xxxi, xxxv–xl,[13] Lev. viii etc.). The derivation of customs and practices, and particularly those of a cultic nature, from historical events, is known also to the other sources (e.g. Gen. xxxii, 33 L), but in them narrative is predominant throughout and the laws

[10] Rost, 'Der Schöpfungsbericht der Priesterschrift' CuW 10 (1934), pp. 172–8.
[11] Hulst, '*Kol baśar* in der priesterlichen Fluterzählung' OTS 12 (1958), pp. 26–68.
[12] Gaster, *Passover. Its History and Traditions* (1958); Hertzberg, 'Zum samaritanischen Passah' *Rendtorff-Festschr.* (1958), pp. 130–6; Kraus, 'Zur Geschichte des Passah-Massot-Festes im AT' EvTh 18 (1958), pp. 47–67; Kutsch, 'Erwägungen zur Geschichte der Passafeier und des Massotfestes' ZThK 55 (1958), pp. 1–35; Lauterbach, 'The Date of the Slaughter of the Paschal Lamb' PAAJR 12 (1942), pp. 49–51. Lit. § 126.
[13] Haran, 'The Ark and the Cherubim' IEJ 9 (1959), pp. 30–8, 89–98; 'The Nature of the "'Ohel Mô'ēdh" in Pentateuchal Sources' JSSt 5 (1959), pp. 50–65; 'The Tabernacle in the Priestly Source' [Hebr.] *Tur-Sinai Jub. Vol.* (1960), pp. 27–42; Rost, 'Die Wohnstätte des Zeugnisses' *Baumgärtel-Festschrift* (1959), pp. 158–65; Segal, 'The Tent of Meeting' [Hebr., Engl. sum.] Tarbiz 25 (1955/6), pp. 231–3, VIII–IX. Lit. § 126.

based upon it stand in the background. In P the reverse is the case. Here the legal material actually predominates, and we are almost given the impression that the thin narrative thread is only intended to be something on which this legal material may be hung, or simply serves to bind it together. Here there is, as we have seen (p. 185), a definite point in the spreading of the laws over a long period: they are thus characterised according to their significance and applicability.

But it would be perverse to see the narrative of P merely as a means to an end. P certainly also sets out the history for its own sake, as indeed the inter-weaving of history and law is a characteristic of Israelite-Jewish religion. In the last resort, it is true, its interest is not directed to the past but to the present and future. For the laws, which ostensibly were issued at a particular period in the past, really have their significance for the present and are designed to be authoritative for it. And they are directed to the future even more than to the present. For P is a product of the exilic period, directed towards serving as a legal foundation for the ardently longed-for reconstruction of people and religious community. In this respect it is like the programmatic legal outline at the end of the book of Ezekiel, only that it is projected back into the past and presents its individual sections as having been issued by God in remote antiquity, mostly at Sinai. Such a projection back was nothing new. Sinai, which really was of fundamental importance for the beginnings of Israel's religion, had already been regarded by earlier generations as the point of derivation of the particular law which appeared to them as the divine demand—J as well as E, D and H (§ 35; on L, cf. p. 193). So from what each period relates about Sinai, it is possible in fact to trace the course of the religious history of Israel and Judah. P simply followed this example in setting forth his own sketch of the future as he hoped for it. He presented it as having been revealed by God at Sinai or even earlier, and it was actually in many ways rooted in the past.

In the last stage of this discussion we have already expressed an opinion on the subject of the date of origin of P, namely that it came into existence in the exile, i.e. in the fifth or perhaps already in the sixth century. For this dating, which is very generally agreed, there are two types of argument: 1. those connected with the history of the religion, 2. those connected with literary history. As far as the first is concerned, we may note that the other sources and the book of the covenant (B, § 33) know many cult places; D demands their removal and the centralisation of the cultus in one place; P presupposes this. This places P at the end of the development, and other observations fit with this, observations which show that the cultic ordinances of P are the most developed and hence the latest. Thus, for example, in J and in B (Exod. xxxiv, 18a, 22; xxiii, 15aa, 16) the connections of the three agricultural festivals[14] with nature is quite clear. These connections remain recognisable in D too (Deut. xvi, 3a, 9–11, 13–15), no matter whether the statements made here are original or not, and also in H (Lev. xxiii, 9–12, 15–21*, 39–43*). But in P this point is obscured by the determining of dates according to the calendar (Lev. xxiii, 4–8, 33–6). Admittedly

[14] MacRae, 'The Meaning and Evolution of the Feast of Tabernacles' CBQ 22 (1960), pp. 251–76. Lit. p. 200, n. 11.

such considerations only clarify the relative date of P, by showing that it is later than the other sources. But the arguments from literary history make possible an absolute dating too. The fact is that neither the older historical books, i.e. Judges to Kings, nor the prophets, including Malachi (c. 470 B.C.), reveal any influence of P, whereas Chronicles which was not compiled before 350 B.C. is strongly influenced by P. This cannot be due to chance. We must assume that P came into being not too long before Chronicles, in the fifth, or perhaps already in the sixth century.

Many scholars believe it possible to link P with the person of Ezra, whether by making Ezra the compiler of P or by ascribing to him at any rate the imposition of P upon the Jewish religious community and relating Neh. viii–ix (x) to this event. Whereas the first of these two assumptions remains a mere guess, the second may be shown to have a certain probability, as will be shown in detail when the books of Ezra and Nehemiah are examined (pp. 556–7). In any case we may conclude from the narrative of Neh. viii–ix (x) that P was at that time already combined with the older sources, and thus must have come into existence before what is there related took place, i.e. before 398 B.C. (pp. 257, 553–5).

§31. THE INTERRELATIONSHIP OF THE STRANDS L J E AND P AND THEIR COMBINING

Literature: cf. §§ 22–30, 32–5.

1. *The interrelationship of the strands.* There are thus four narrative strands, L J E and P which lie behind the narrative of the Pentateuch. As the description of them has shown, they run, taking it all in all, parallel to one another, and so the question naturally arises as to whether and how far the later sources are dependent upon the earlier, or whether for all of them there is to be assumed a common basis which has not survived, perhaps to be designated with Noth[1] as G. We noted already in connection with L that it was probably the first to compile an outline of the history extending from the creation of the world to the death of Moses or more probably at least as far as the conquest of Canaan; no traces remain of an older undertaking of the kind. Someone must in any case have made a start, and such an outline was not possible very much earlier than the time assumed for L (p. 140). Israel had first to reach a certain assurance in its political position before it could think of writing an historical work of the kind. But if once such an outline existed, linking Israel's history with that of the world and of mankind, it would exert further influence, and we may therefore reasonably assume that L influenced J, and that one or other of the later outlines will have used the earlier ones as a pattern, though this does not by any means exclude the possibility that each one of them also took up new material, whether it was already shaped in writing, or taken from oral tradition. Dependence may also be of an entirely negative kind and indeed is not infrequently so, so

[1] *Überlieferungsgeschichte des Pentateuch* (1948, ²1960), pp. 40–4.

that the original undergoes transformation and correction. It is not possible to demonstrate dependence or independence in detail, but that we must reckon with both is clear and may be illustrated with a few examples. In the L narrative of Jacob's contest with El (Gen. xxxii, 24–33), it is said in verse 31: *Jacob named the place Peniel: for I have seen Elohim face to face, and yet my life is preserved.* In the J narrative parallel to this (p. 196) of Jacob's meeting with Esau, Jacob says, however, to Esau: *For I have indeed been able to see your face, as one may see the face of Elohim, and you have treated me kindly* (xxxiii, 10). It is clear that there must be a relationship between these two phrases from the L and J narratives, and the relationship must in fact be literary. It can also hardly be doubted that J is dependent. In the place of El in the L story Esau appears in J. It can further hardly be an accident that in the narrative of Jacob's flight from Laban which is clearly made up of two or three parallels combined, the word *steal* (גָּנַב) is used three times, or at any rate twice, in quite different senses. In xxxi, 19, 30 (L) it is said of Rachel and cast as a reproach at Jacob that she has *stolen Laban's teraphim* (גָּנַב). But in xxxi, 20, 26 (E) it is said that Jacob has *stolen* (גָּנַב) *Laban's heart,* i.e. has deceived him, and possibly the reproachful question of Laban to Jacob in verse 27 *Why . . . have you cheated* (גָּנַב) *me?* is to be assigned to a third narrative J. In any case for the actual theft related by L (and J) there is substituted the reproach of *theft of the heart,* that is, of deceit, of secret action, and this is to be understood as a watering down of the older narrative on moral grounds, such as we have observed similarly elsewhere in E (pp. 183–4).

Side by side with such examples of literary dependence of the later sources on the earlier, we may set a wealth of indications which show that the later authors themselves had in their turn more and more new material available which they could incorporate in their presentation. As far as the relationship of J and E to L is concerned, we need only think of the Joseph story in order to recognise this. J and E set out like L to explain the decline of the older tribes and the rise of the younger, and the motif itself may well have been taken over by J and E from L. But they carry it through by quite different means. The material utilised by J and E is quite different from that of L. Elsewhere too quite new material appears in J and E, as in J in the flood narrative, and in J and E in the story of Balaam. P too provides new matter, as in the narrative of the purchase of the cave of Machpelah by Abraham (Gen. xxiii). A very substantial part of this special material in the later sources is doubtless ancient traditional matter, whereas other parts of it, as perhaps the beautiful story of the wooing of Rebekah (Gen. xxiv), may not be due simply to its authors' retelling of a tradition but may actually be an original composition.

2. *The combining of the strands.* The other question outstanding, as to how and when the four narrative strands were brought together, whether they existed separately up to a specific moment and then were combined all at once by a single redactor, or whether this combination took place as the result of several successive redactions, is a question which is better left open until we have discussed the legal sections of the Pentateuch too. We may then survey the origin of the whole Pentateuch (§ 36).

§ 32. AMPLIFICATIONS OF THE NARRATIVE STRANDS

Literature: Bender, 'Das Lied Exodus xv' ZAW 23 (1903), pp. 1–48; Cross and Freedman, 'The Song of Miriam' JNESt 14 (1955), pp. 237–50; Garofalo, 'L'epinicio di Mosè' Bibl 18 (1937), pp. 1–22; Mowinckel, *Offersang og sangoffer* (1951), pp. 131, 169, 175 f., 547, 553, 602, E.T. *The Psalms in Israel's Worship* (1962), I pp. 126, 167, 177, II pp. 247, 259; Rendtorff, 'Sejrshymnen i Exodus xv og dens forhold til tronbestigelssalmerna' DTT 22 (1959), pp. 65–81, 156–71; Rozelaar, 'The Song of the Sea (Exodus xv, 1b–18)' VT 2 (1952), pp. 221–8; Hans Schmidt, 'Das Meerlied. Ex xv, 2–19' ZAW 49 (1931), pp. 59–66; Watts, 'The Song of the Sea—Ex xv' VT 7 (1957), pp. 371–80.

Albright, 'Shinar-Šaṅgar and its Monarch Amraphel' AJSL 40 (1923/4), pp. 125–33; 'The Historical Background of Genesis xiv' JSOR 10 (1926), pp. 231–69; Benzinger, 'Zur Quellenscheidung in Gen xiv' BZAW 41 (1925), pp. 21–7; Böhl, 'Die Könige von Genesis xiv' ZAW 36 (1916), pp. 65–73; 'Tud'alia I, Zeitgenosse Abrahams, um 1650 vChr' ZAW 42 (1924), pp. 148–53; Cornelius 'Genesis xiv' ZAW 72 (1960), pp. 1–7; Del Medico, 'Melchisédech' ZAW 69 (1957), pp. 160–70; Jaritz, 'Wer ist Amraphel in Genesis xiv?' ZAW 70 (1958), pp. 255–6; Jensen, 'Genesis xiv und ein Ausschnitt aus den Res gestae des Aššur-bān-apli' ZA 42 (1934), pp. 232–5; Kroeze, *Genesis Veertien* (Diss. theol. Amsterdam, 1937); Levi della Vida, 'El 'Elyon in Genesis xiv, 18–20' JBL 63 (1944), pp. 1–9; Mayer, 'Die Bedeutung Elams in der Geschichte des Alten Orients' Saeculum 7 (1956), pp. 198–220; Meinhold, *I. Mose xiv* (1911); Rowley, 'Melchizedek and Zadok (Gen xiv and Ps cx)' *Bertholet-Festschr.* (1950), pp. 461–72; Vincent, 'Abraham à Jérusalem' RB 58 (1951), pp. 360–71.

Mowinckel, *Psalmenstudien* V (1924, ²1961), pp. 74–80, 97–129: on Deut. xxvii, 14–29. Cf. also Literature §§ 5, 14, 18, 19, 22, 31, 33–5, 126.

We have repeatedly pointed out (p. 180) that while it is the documentary hypothesis which most readily succeeds in explaining the difficulties of unravelling the composition of our Pentateuchal narrative, everything cannot be done by the application of this hypothesis alone. We must also reckon with a number of amplifications. These are of two kinds, though we cannot always draw a clear dividing line between the two groups. Some of them have been added to the single narrative strands while they were still independent, whereas others were added to the compilation of two or more strands or even to the otherwise completed Pentateuch.

A number of amplifications which are better discussed in connection with their present context, have already been mentioned or will subsequently be mentioned —thus, above all, the Blessing of Jacob (pp. 196, 228 f.) and the Blessing of Moses (pp. 228 f.). With the former it is a matter of an expansion of basic material found in the L strand. With the latter we are dealing with a section which has only been inserted into the narrative context—for the law comes to an end at Deut. xxx and with xxxi the narrative begins again—because there the subject is the imminent death of Moses. This passage therefore ranked as the last words of Moses or could be so understood, just as outside the Pentateuch there are narratives which contain 'last words'. An example of this is the older David narrative which contains the thanksgiving song of David in II Sam. xxii, and his 'pattern of kingship' in xxiii, 1–7 (pp. 278 f.), though we cannot always decide with certainty whether this kind of passage was in the narrative and has been taken up by the compiler or whether it was first inserted secondarily. But the latter is true, for example, of the 'Song of the Sea' put into the mouth of Moses (verse 1a) in Exod. xv, 1b–18, an elaboration of the ancient Hymn of Miriam in xv, 21. This may not derive from the exilic or post-exilic period but may be older. It was hardly placed in the narrative by one of the authors of the sources but was inserted into it secondarily. Cross and Freedman are indeed of the opinion that the song, originating at the latest in the tenth century B.C. and ascribed to Miriam (Exod. xv, 1b–18), was taken up by J in his narrative, whereas E contented himself with mentioning the beginning of the song which served as its title. However, the Song of Moses in Deut. xxxii, 1–43, which is generally adjudged to be a secondary addition, if not perhaps actually composed by the compiler of one of the strands of the Pentateuch (presumably E), was (pp. 226 f.) nevertheless found by him and taken up into his work.

It is not only poetic passages, which could very readily be inserted, which have been taken up secondarily into the narrative. There is no lack of elaborations to the narrative itself, whether a story which stands in the source has been touched up, or that a narrative has been newly added. An example of the first kind is probably to be seen in Gen. xviii, 22b–33, Abraham's prayer to Yahweh that Sodom should be spared even if only ten righteous are to be found in the city, a section which appears more like a secondary extension of the L narrative than as an original component of it. The same is probably true of the beautiful story of Yahweh's appearance before Moses in Exod. xxxiii, 12–23, a story reminiscent of Elijah's meeting with Yahweh in I Kings xix, 9–18. An example of the second kind is to be found in the much discussed and disputed narrative of Gen. xiv. This tells how the Elamite king Chedorlaomer with his confederates fell upon Syria-Palestine, conquered the kings of Sodom and Gomorrah and also took away captive Lot who was at that time living in Sodom; how Abraham pursued the victorious army, defeated it, set Lot free and on his return dedicated a tenth of the booty of war to the priest-king of Salem (Jerusalem). With this narrative it is quite clear that it presupposes the already complete compilation L+J+E+B+D+H+P, and that it has been inserted into it. For it is dependent not only on the L narrative of Lot and Abraham (Gen. xii, 6–8 + xiii, 2, 5, 7–11a, 12bβ–18) and of Sodom (xviii–xix), but also on P with which it has all manner of linguistic peculiarities in common (e.g. רְכוּשׁ *property*). While this fact makes us think of late post-exilic origin for the passage, its content—the invasion of Syria-Palestine in the third millennium by an Elamite-Babylonian army, or in the second millennium B.C. by an Elamite-Mitannian-Hittite army—leads us into very ancient times. Antiquity is also indicated by the names of the peoples conquered who include the Horites (xiv, 6),[1] of whom we know from other sources (Gen. xxxvi, 20–30; Deut. ii, 12, 22) that they lived in the second millennium B.C. This double character of the section may be explained by assuming that a Jew who lived in the late post-exilic period had at his disposal, in addition to our Pentateuch, some information about warlike events in the

---

[1] Eybers, 'Who were the Hivites?' Die Ou. Testamentiese Werkgemeenskap in Suid-Afrika (1959), pp. 6–14; Hrouda, 'Die Churriter als Problem archäologischer Forschung' Archaeologia Geographica 6 (1958), pp. 14–19, Pls. 5–12; on this Parrot, Syria 36 (1959), pp. 326 f.; Speiser, 'The Hurrian Participation' *Cahiers d'Histoire Mondiale* I, 2 (1953). pp. 278–310. Lit. § 126.

remote past, and perhaps a tradition concerning the pre-Israelite priesthood of Jerusalem, and constructed out of these elements a narrative designed to glorify Abraham and the Jerusalem priesthood. In this case, it may be used only with caution as a source of historical information.

The laws too, where the supplementary hypothesis is much more justified than with the narrative, have also, like the narrative, undergone various elaborations, and this must subsequently be discussed in more than one connection (§§ 33–5). We may here simply refer to the dodecalogue of curses in Deut. xxvii, 14–26, a collection of twelve curses against cultic and moral, and in particular also sexual, crimes, which according to their present context were to be pronounced by the Levites on Gerizim or Ebal soon after Israel's crossing of the Jordan. The dodecalogue, which certainly must be connected with cultic cursing ceremonies and is thus not a merely literary formation, is, however, in fact fairly late and probably presupposes P. It evidently always remained the practice in Israel to group cultic and moral precepts or prohibitions in series of ten or twelve members, as in the cultic obligations of Neh. x, 31–40, which represent a decalogue of the time of Nehemiah which at his injunction was taken upon itself by the Jewish community (pp. 69 f., 548 f.).

With this point, we have already turned to the discussion of the laws, and these must now be examined in detail.

IV. THE COLLECTIONS OF LAWS

§ 33. THE BOOK OF THE COVENANT

Literature: Baentsch, *Das Bundesbuch* (1892); Caspari, 'Heimat und soziale Wirkung des at. Bundesbuches' ZDMG 83 (1929), pp. 97–120; Cazelles, 'L'auteur du code de l'alliance' RB 52 (1945), pp. 173–91; *Études sur le Code de l'Alliance* (1946); Kipper, 'De origine mosaica "Libri Foederis"' VD 29 (1951), pp. 77–87, 159–71; Menes, *Die vorexilischen Gesetze Israels* (BZAW 50, 1928); Noth, *Das System der zwölf Stämme Israels* (BWANT 52, 1930), pp. 97–108; Nowack, *Das Bundesbuch* (BZAW 34, 1920), pp. 132–40; Pfeiffer, 'The Transmission of the Book of the Covenant' HThR 24 (1931), pp. 99–109; Thompson, 'The Book of the Covenant Ex xxi–xxiii in the Light of Modern Archaeological Research' ABR 2 (1952), pp. 97–107; Welch, *Deuteronomy. The Framework to the Code* (1932).

Cf. also Literature §§ 4d, 8, 9, 19, 22–32, 34, 35, 126.

1. *Name and contents.* The name Book of the Covenant derives from Exod. xxiv, 7, where it is stated that Moses took the *book of the covenant* (סֵפֶר הַבְּרִית) and read it aloud to the people. Its present context makes it clear that the term Book of the Covenant can in fact only refer to the complex xx, 22–xxiii, 33. The course of the narrative in xx–xxiv is as follows: God speaks the ten words of xx, 2–17 in the ears of the people. The terrified people then say to Moses that henceforth he alone should receive the words of God and hand them on to them; they do not wish to hear God directly nor can they bear to (vv. 18–19). So Moses, after he has pacified the people, goes up nearer to God (vv. 20–1)

and receives from him the instructions of xx, 22–xxiii, 33. After he has received, in xxiv, 1–2, yet another command, not at first carried out, concerning his ascent into the mountain, he imparts to the people *all the words of Yahweh and all the judgments* (אֵת כָּל־דִּבְרֵי יְהוָה וְאֵת כָּל־הַמִּשְׁפָּטִים [xxiv, 3]),writes down *all the words of Yahweh* (כָּל־דִּבְרֵי יְהוָה) as the people declare themselves willing to obey them (verse 4), reads out the *book of the covenant* (סֵפֶר הַבְּרִית) to the people after a solemn sacrificial act (vv. 5–7), and declares, after a renewed pledge by the people accompanied by a ritual of blood sprinkling: *This is the blood of the covenant which Yahweh makes with you on the basis of all these words.* Since the people themselves also heard the decalogue of xx, 2–17, the phrase *all the words of Yahweh and all the judgments* which Moses imparts to the people according to xxiv, 3, and then makes into the basis of the concluding of the covenant, can only refer to the commands which stand in xx, 22–xxiii, 33. To this extent we are justified in applying to this complex the name 'Book of the Covenant'.

This name, which has now become established usage, may stand, and will here be used further, together with the siglum B to represent it. But in reality the reference of xxiv, 7, to the Book of the Covenant is not intended to apply to the complex xx, 22–xxiii, 33, but to the decalogue of xx, 2–17. For it is obvious that the identical expressions *all these words* in xxiv, 8, *all the words of Yahweh* in xxiv, 3,[1] 4, *all the words which Yahweh has spoken* in xxiv, 3, and *all that Yahweh has spoken* in xxiv, 7, refer to the same entity as the expression in xx, 1, *all these words,* namely the decalogue of xx, 2–17. It is thus the decalogue which formed the basis of the covenant concluded in xxiv, 3–8. But this means that originally the people did not themselves actually listen to the decalogue, but first received it imparted to them by Moses who himself had received it alone from Yahweh. xx, 18–21, thus really belongs, not after the decalogue (xx, 2–17) but before it, and its present position is related to the incorporation of the complex xx, 22–xxiii, 33, in the Sinai narrative. By the transposition of xx, 18–21, and xx, 1–17, a place has readily been found for it; and so now it is this complex which appears as the basis of the covenant concluded in xxiv, 3–8, whereas the imparting of the decalogue has been reduced to a mere preliminary, to which no further importance is attached. Other observations, as we shall see (pp. 216–18), confirm this recognition of the secondary insertion of the complex xx, 22–xxiii, 33. But we must first examine somewhat more precisely the content and structure of the Book of the Covenant itself. Within the section xx, 22–xxiii, 33, which we have so far treated as a unity, there stands out, even on a superficial examination, the passage xxi, 1–xxii, 16,[2] as a unit of a particular character. In xxi, 1, it has the title: *And these are the judgments* (מִשְׁפָּטִים) *which you shall set before them,* and it is distinguished by its intelligible arrangement and its generally even style. In the individual units—as for example in the injunction concerning compensation for bodily injury occasioned by quarrels in xxi, 18, 19[3]—the main cases are always introduced by כִּי *when,* and the qualifying

---

[1] *and all the judgments* is a secondary addition.

[2] Diamond, 'An Eye for an Eye' Iraq 19 (1957), pp. 151–5: on xxi, 24; Hoftijzer, 'Ex xxi, 8' VT 7 (1957), pp. 388–91. Lit. § 126.

[3] Fensham, 'Exodus xxi, 18–19, in the Light of Hittite Law § 10' VT 10 (1960), pp. 333–5.

clauses are joined on with אִם *if* (p. 27). Only xxi, 12, 15–17, are formally different, in that here the individual judgements begin with participles (pp. 69 f.), they probably do not originally belong in this context, and vv. 13–14 are in their turn a supplement to verse 12.[4]

The *mishpatim* are preceded in xx, 24–6 (vv. 22–3 are redactional, see p. 218) by ordinances of a cultic nature, namely those which deal with the building of altars,[5] and a compact body of cultic ordinances also follows later in xxiii, (13) 14–19. These latter are very similar to the cultic decalogue of xxxiv, 14–26, and must be somehow related to it (p. 215). The section which stands between the end of the *mishpatim* and the beginning of this group of cultic commands, i.e. xxii, 17–xxiii, 12 (13),[6] contains religious and moral instructions, including also a few which are specifically cultic (xxii, 19, 28–9; xxiii, 10–12 (13)). Finally, xxiii, 20–33, form the conclusion of the law—or more correctly this is how they now appear—holding out the prospect of reward for obedience and punishment for disobedience.

2. *Component parts.* Thus in the so-called Book of the Covenant there is combined a whole mixture of very varied component parts, and it may well be asked whether we are really dealing here with a unity which deserves the name of 'Law book' and not rather with a more accidental collocation of quite disparate elements—in other words a purely literary unit. It is at once clear that xxiii, 20–33, do not originally represent the conclusion of a law book, such as might correspond to Lev. xxvi (pp. 233 f.) or Deut. xxvii–xxx (pp. 230 f.), but are part of a dismissal speech by Yahweh. There is nothing here about following or not following a law, and in particular the law which immediately precedes, and so it is quite unlike Lev. xxvi, Deut. xxvii–xxx (pp. 233 f., 230 f.). Here it is only a matter of obedience or disobedience to the angel who goes with Israel—actually, it is only obedience to him and the reward which follows from this. This may subsequently have been understood in the sense of obedience and disobedience to the law just set forth, but it was not originally so meant. However, the words would be very appropriate as an exhortation given by Yahweh to the people as they depart from Sinai, and no doubt had their original place, as has long been surmised (Smend), at the end of the Sinai narrative, and thus, since we are here concerned only with the older sources and not with P, after xxxiii or xxxiv. With this accords also the fact that xxiii, 20–33, is clearly made up of two parallel speeches, which may be assigned to J and E. But now, if there has been a relatively late displacement, namely only after the combining of J and E which is here presupposed, and so xxiii, 20–33, has been removed from its original intention and has been made artificially into a conclusion of the commandments contained in xx, 22–xxiii, 19, our reasonable doubts concerning the unity of xx, 22–xxiii, 33, are very much strengthened.

[4] Greenberg, 'The Biblical Conception of Asylum' JBL 78 (1959), pp. 125–32. Cf. Lit. p. 220, n. 2; p. 250, n. 11; p. 251, n. 16.

[5] Dussaud, *La Pénétration des Arabes en Syrie avant l'Islam* (1955), pp. 38 f.; Robertson, 'The Altar of Earth (Exodus xx, 24–6)' JJSt 1 (1948), pp. 12–21; Stamm, 'Zum Altargesetz im Bundesbuch' ThZ 1 (1945), pp. 304 f.

[6] Lewy, 'Dating of Covenant Code Sections on Humaneness and Righteousness (Ex. xxii, 20–6; xxiii, 1–9)' VT 7 (1957), pp. 322–6.

If we go further back from xxiii, 20–33, then we note, as already said, the most marked similarity between xxiii, (13) 14–19, and xxxiv, 14–26. These two sections do in fact agree largely in actual wording. The attempt has been made to explain this by assigning one 'decalogue' (xxxiv) to J, and the other (xxiii) to E (e.g. Meinhold),[7] and this, it would appear, would not fit badly with the parallelism which often exists elsewhere between J and E. Above all it would also make it intelligible why the redactor who combined J with E could make J's decalogue (xxxiv) the substitute for that of E (xxiii) (cf. xxxiv, 1, where the second half of the verse *like the first, and I will write upon the tablets the words which stood upon the first tablets which you broke* is a redactional, harmonising addition); whereas if xx is derived from E, there are much greater difficulties in the way of the assumption that xxxiv is to be thought of as the restoration of xx which is in reality quite different. This line of argument is very persuasive and must be seriously considered. But against it we must at once note that the remaining content of E reveals a marked indifference to the cultus which is bound up with agricultural life, and it would therefore be remarkable if E were to have placed agricultural festivals in the centre at the decisive moment for Israel's religion of the giving of the law at Horeb. We have further observed that, notwithstanding the great similarity which otherwise exists between E and J, E does nevertheless undertake marked emendations of the religious and moral attitudes which are presupposed by J (pp. 184 f.). With this would accord well the fact that E has substituted for J's cultic decalogue an ethical decalogue which clearly deliberately passes over the agricultural festivals, just as we may observe that Deuteronomy, which in many respects builds upon E, does not seem originally to have taken account of agricultural festivals in its festival laws (xvi, 1–17). Furthermore, xx, 1–17, and xxiv, 3–8, are linked together by the phrase *all these words* which stands in xx, 1, and is several times repeated in xxiv, 3–8 (p. 213), so that xx, 1–17, does not look like an insertion from another source or a secondary addition not belonging to any source at all, but appears to be an original part of the E narrative to which xxiv, 3–8, certainly belongs. Finally, the expedient of deriving xx, 1–17, from P (Meinhold) is made impossible in that in the P narrative—xix, 1; xxiv, 15b–18a; xxv, 1–xxxi, 17, 18a— which is clearly preserved complete, there is hardly room, in spite of xxv, 16, and xxxi, 18a, for the wording of the decalogue which is evidently here presupposed as already known. So we may leave it with xx, 1–17, derived from E, and must then seek another explanation for the similarity or identity of xxiii, 13–19, and xxxiv, 14–26.

Such an explanation is not far to seek. The fact that the decalogue in xxxiv, 14–26, intended as a substitute for xx, 2–17, deviates so far from the latter and only has something in common with it at the beginning (cf. xx, 3–5,[8] with xxxiv, 14, 17) must very early have been felt to be difficult. The redactor of J and E who carried out the combination, involving probably the identifying of even less similar passages—e.g. the giving of meat (L, J) and of the spirit (E)

---

[7] Meinhold, *Der Dekalog* (1927).
[8] Segert, 'Bis in das dritte und vierte Geschlecht—Ex. xx, 5' CV 1 (1958), pp. 37–9. Lit. § 126.

in Num. xi—might very well have presented these two otherwise so different decalogues as identical in view of their similar openings. But later readers must have felt the need to avoid the difficulty which was found here. So someone has brought it about that the commandments of xxxiv, 14–26, are revealed by God to Moses (xxiii, 13–19) before the making of the covenant which is described in xxiv, 3–8, so that now xxxiv, 14–26, really is the repetition of commandments which have already been issued (xxiii, 13–19) and which had at the same time been made the basis for the concluding of the covenant in xxiv, 3–8. If we ignore small deviations which may be readily understood, xxiii, 13–19, exactly corresponds to xxxiv, 14–26; there are simply omitted in xxiii, 13–19, the commandments which are included in xx, 22–xxiii, 12, namely xxxiv, 17 = xx, 23; xxxiv, 19–20 = xxii, 28–9, and xxxiv, 21 = xxiii, 12. Whoever put xxiii, 13–19, in its present place must then have found the complex xx, 22–xxiii, 12, already in its present position, or else it must be the same hand which put it there.

3. *The interpolating of B.* This large complex too reveals itself to be an insertion. It interrupts the E narrative, in which xxiv, 3–8, is directly linked to xx, 18–21, 1–17. Nor does it find a place either in J, where xxxiv follows directly on the J material of xix; xx, 18*, 20*, or even in L which does not appear to have known of any law issued at Sinai at all (p. 193). We have seen already that to fit with this insertion there has been a transposition in the E narrative and that in xxiv, 3 (E) the words *and all the judgments* have been inserted (p. 213). But other grounds may be advanced for the assumption that Exod. xx, 22–xxiii, 12, was only secondarily inserted in the Sinai narrative. It is clear that both the basic material of Deut. xxvii, 1–8 (in particular vv. 4–7) and also that of Josh. viii, 30–5 (here in particular vv. 30–1) which relate how Moses shortly before his death gave the people the command that they were to erect an altar of unhewn stone to Yahweh on Gerizim[9] after the crossing of the Jordan and how Joshua carried out this command and built such an altar, is to be linked with the altar law which stands at the beginning of the Book of the Covenant (xx, 24–6), and is designed to report the renewal and carrying out of this command. It is striking that out of the Book of the Covenant which has such a wealth of commands, it should be just this which is repeated in Deut. xxvii, 4–7, and it is also quite clear, as is generally agreed, that Josh. viii, 30–5,[10] is inappropriate in its present position. The Israelites have pressed forward only as far as Ai (viii, 1–29). The remainder of central Canaan and the whole of the north is as yet unconquered, and the decisive battles for their control only follow in x and xi. Prior to these battles the erection of an Israelite altar near Shechem is quite impossible. Other explanations do not satisfy, as for example the suggestion that viii, 30–5, represents a tradition deviating from i, 1–viii, 29, and presupposing that Israel's crossing of the Jordan took place not at Jericho but farther north, in about the latitude of Shechem, so that according to this tradition an altar could in fact be erected near Shechem immediately after the crossing. Such a tradition has left no other traces and has to be assumed specially for this par-

[9] So we must read the text in Deut. xxvii, 4, and Josh. viii, 30, instead of *Ebal*, which doubtless derives from anti-Samaritan polemic; cf. Josephus, *Ant.* XIII, 3, 4 (§§ 74–9).
[10] Soggin (p. 201, n. 13).

ticular passage. The solution to the problem is rather to be sought in tracing back both passages, Deut. xxvii, 4–7, and Josh viii, 30–1, to the hand which inserted the Book of the Covenant in its present context. The insertion of the material in the narrative context was not felt to be sufficient; the intention was rather to bind it all the more closely with it by making Moses repeat his instruction for the entry into the land and by making Joshua act accordingly. The impetus to localise the altar, which was to symbolise the bringing into play of the Book of the Covenant, on Mount Gerizim near Shechem was no doubt taken by the redactor from a tradition which is indeed elsewhere attested of a covenant concluded at Shechem (Josh. xxiv; Deut. xxvii, 11–26).

Since the linkages were made when D and P were not yet combined with the older Pentateuchal sources (cf. § 36), and thus Exod. xxv, 1–xxxi, 18a; xxxv–xl, the whole of Lev., Num. i, 1–x, 28, substantial parts of the remainder of Num., Deut. i–xxvi did not yet belong in the Pentateuch, the first link from the end of the Book of the Covenant, or from the narrative of the making of the covenant at Sinai was not so very remote. It remains uncertain why for the second link the quite unsuitable position after Josh. viii, 29, was chosen. We might almost be tempted to believe that the great heap of stones which is mentioned at the end of viii, 29, has attracted to itself the altar of unhewn stones of viii, 30–1. Such a mechanical combination could well be attributed to a redactor. The deriving of the sections Deut. xxvii, 4–7, and Josh. viii, 30–1, from the interpolator of the Book of the Covenant is confirmed by the fact that the interpolator of Deuteronomy, which was also inserted secondarily into the Pentateuchal narrative context, by working over the passages Deut. xxvii, 4–7, and Josh. viii, 30–1, used them in his turn, as links for Deuteronomy.[11] We shall have to deal later with the point (pp. 220–3) that Deuteronomy was really intended to be a substitute for the Book of the Covenant. So it is appropriate that the links which were intended to fit B into the narrative context have now been used to fit in D. That this could happen is evidence to show that the real purpose of Deut. xxvii, 4–7, and Josh. viii, 30–1, had not yet been forgotten.

Thus the whole complex of the Book of the Covenant, xx, 22–xxiii, 33, reveals itself to be secondary. Of xxiii, 20–33, it was possible to show that it is only secondary in its present position, but in its original position after xxxiv, 28. it is originally part of J and E. We have seen that xxiii, 13–19, represents an anticipation of xxxiv, 14–26, and thus is also in content part of the old narrative, namely of J. We may now ask whether it is also possible to say something more precise about the origin and date of xx, 22–xxiii, 12. But first it must be decided whether xx, 22–xxiii, 12, may really be taken as a unity at all. We have seen (p. 214) that we are dealing with a collocation of various elements—cult commandments xx, 22–6, legal precepts xxi, 1–xxii, 16,[12] religious and moral instructions xxii, 17–xxiii, 12. There could nevertheless be here a deeper type of unity, and this does indeed seem to be the case. It is true that the attempts made

[11] Eissfeldt, *Das Lied Moses* (BAL 104, 5, 1958), pp. 43–54.
[12] Falk, 'Exodus xxi, 6' VT 9 (1959), pp. 86–8; Fensham, 'New Light on Exodus xxi, 6 and xxii, 7, from the Laws of Eshnunna' JBL 78 (1959), pp. 160 f.; van Selms, 'The Goring Ox in Babylonian and Biblical Law' ArOr 18, 4 (1950), pp. 321–30. Cf. p. 220, n. 1; § 126.

by, for example, Waterman and Morgenstern to show the presence here, or at least in xxi, 2–xxii, 16 (19), of an artificially ordered structure in decades and pentades (§ 19), have not been successful. In particular, the commands of xxii, 17–xxiii, 12, appear to lack a definite principle of arrangement, or it can no longer be satisfactorily established, though this is in part occasioned by the secondary additions which are certainly present here. But the arranging together of cultic commands, legal precepts, religious and moral instructions with a marked precedence given to the cultic commands does not make this look like a unit which has come into being accidentally as a result of redactional piecing together. This is all the clearer in view of the fact that Deuteronomy and the Holiness Code are constructed in this way too, and in them a variety of instructions of a religious, moral and legal nature are made to follow on a fundamental cultic demand which stands at the beginning (Deut. xii, Lev. xvii). Thus xx, (22) 24–xxiii, 12, disregarding the secondary additions which are certainly present, may properly be understood as a law book deliberately compiled in accordance with a plan, or better as a programmatic legal work.

4. *Date of origin.* We may now ask whether we can say anything concerning the date of origin and the purpose of this programme. Since xx, 22–3, which are at once differentiated by their plural form of address from the singular form 'thou' (used elsewhere with the exception of xxii, 21, and xxiii, 9b, 25aα), are probably an insertion by the interpolator of xx, 24–xxiii, 12 (33), who was seeking to lead on from the decalogue (xx, 1–17) and the impact of its imparting (vv. 18–21) to the law book itself, we may regard the verses 24–6 as the real beginning. It thus begins with the injunction which is clearly a polemical utterance against the elaboration of altar-building and against the confining of the cultus to *one* sanctuary, the injunction to build the altar in simple fashion of earth, and with the explicit statement that Yahweh will appear to the worshipper and bless him everywhere, [13] where by means of a theophany he evokes worship or [14] where he is called upon. It furthermore limits the admission of stone altars by the instruction that the stones used for building an altar must by no means be hewn and that no steps may be made up to the altar. There must, therefore, have grown up in the environment of the compiler of this legal work a tendency to luxurious altar-building and to centralisation of the cultus, and if any one of the many precepts of the Book of the Covenant does bear the impress of its historical setting and so enable us to date it, this is the one.

Now we may point to various occasions in the history of Israel's religion in which a wave of piety clinging to an older hereditary simplicity protested against more elaborate cultic practice dependent upon foreign patterns. The north Israelite movement in the middle of the ninth century, led by Elijah, Elisha and the Rechabites, which led to the revolution of Jehu, is one of these occasions (p. 198). So Morgenstern, for example, has attributed the origin of the *words* (דְּבָרִים), i.e. above all the altar command, to the circles of Elisha, and the more general view that B originated in the northern kingdom has often been put forward (e.g. by Steuernagel*). But we may equally justifiably think of the

[13] בְּכָל־מָקוֹם *at every place*, instead of בְּכָל־הַמָּקוֹם, *at the whole place*.
[14] If instead of אַזְכִּיר, *I cause calling upon*, we read תַּזְכִּיר, *you call upon*.

southern kingdom. Reuss* attributes it to the latter and links it with Jehosha-phat's reform (II Chron. xvii, 7–9), whereas Welch thinks that it was compiled in Kadesh, and Caspari and Cazelles in the area east of Jordan, by Moses or at least in his time. There are thus no unambiguous arguments either for the dating or for the locality to which the Book of the Covenant is to be assigned, and we must therefore be satisfied with the twofold fact that both its legal precepts and also its cultic and ethical commands readily permit the assumption that it came into being in the first centuries after Israel's conquest of the land, and that it must in any case be older than Deuteronomy, compiled in the seventh century and perhaps already at the end of the eighth (p. 232) since the latter presupposes its existence in that it opposes B (pp. 220–3).

5. *The Book of the Covenant and Sinai.* Lastly, we must say a further word as to whether the Book of the Covenant, taken on its own, i.e., xx, 24–xxiii, 12, actually itself claimed to have been revealed at Sinai to Moses and by him to have been revealed to Israel, or whether it ranked without such a claim as an expression of the divine will, presented in the form of a divine address to the people, as it were, unattached to any particular time. Apart from the secondary conclusion xxiii, 20–33 (p. 214), there is in the commands themselves no allusion to the pre-Canaanite situation, such as is so common in the other laws (Deut. xii, 1, 10, 29; Lev. xviii, 3; xix, 23; xxv, 1, 2; xxvi, 46). xx, 22, which clearly connects it with the situation of the events at Sinai (p. 218), does not here come into question since it is secondary, and the same is probably true of the second half of the title referring to the *mishpatim* in xxi, 1, the command to Moses: (*And these are the mishpatim*) *which you are to lay before them.* Thus it is quite possible that B originally had no connection with Sinai. But these considerations, which rest upon a *testimonium e silentio*, are not conclusive. It is also possible that when the Book of the Covenant stood on its own, it had a quite short introduction such as: *Yahweh spoke on Sinai* (*to Israel*) or *Yahweh spoke these words on Sinai and said.*

§ 34. DEUTERONOMY

Literature: Alt, 'Die Heimat des Deuteronomiums' *Kl. Schr.* II (1953), pp. 250–75; Bentzen, *Die josianische Reform und ihre Voraussetzungen* (1926); Berry, 'The Date of Deuteronomy' JBL 59 (1940), pp. 133–9; Breit (§ 3); Dobbie, 'Deuteronomy and the Prophetic Attitude to Sacrifice' SJTh 12 (1959), pp. 68–82; Dumermuth, 'Zur deutero-nomischen Kulttheologie und ihren Voraussetzungen' ZAW 70 (1958), pp. 59–98; Eich-rodt, 'Bahnt sich eine neue Lösung der deuteronomischen Frage an?' NKZ 32 (1921), pp. 41–51, 53–78; Galling, 'Das Gemeindegesetz in Deuteronomium xxiii' *Bertholet-Festschr.* (1950), pp. 176–91; Hospers, *De numerus wisseling in het boek Deuteronomium* (Diss. Utrecht, 1947); Hulst, *Het karakter van den cultus in Deuteronomium* (Diss. Groningen, 1938); 'Der Name "Israel" im Deuteronomium' OTS 9 (1951), pp. 65–106; Kuyper, 'The Book of Deuteronomy' Interpr. 6 (1952), pp. 321–40; Manley, *The Book of the Law. Studies in the Date of Deuteronomy* (1957); Menes (§ 33); Phythian-Adams, 'The Origin and Evolution of Deuteronomy' ChQR 123 (1936/7), pp. 215–47; Puukko, *Das Deuteronomium. Eine literarkritische Untersuchung* (BWAT 5, 1910); von

Rad, *Das Gottesvolk im Deuteronomium* (BWANT 47, 1929); Segal, 'The Book of Deuteronomy' JQR 48 (1957/8), pp. 315–51; Weinfeld, 'The Source of the Idea of Reward in Deuteronomy' [Hebr., Engl. sum.] Tarbiz 30 (1960/1), pp. 8–15, I–II; 'The Dependence of Deuteronomy upon the Wisdom Literature' [Hebr.] *Kaufmann Jub. Vol.* (1960), pp. פס–קה; Wright (p. 16, n. 6).

Cf. also Literature §§ 3, 4d, 8, 9, 19, 22–6, 29–30, 33, 35, 126.

1. *The relationship of D to B.* Our survey of the critical study of D (§ 24) to which we now turn, has shown us that already at an early date it was recognised as a special corpus. Even a superficial reader is aware of this from noting the linguistic usage of the book. No other book reveals such a characteristic style as D. *With thy whole heart and thy whole soul* (vi, 5; xi, 13; xiii, 4 etc.), *the place which Yahweh will choose, to cause his name to dwell there* (xii, 11; xiv, 23; xvi, 2 etc.), *the commands of God which I command you* or the like (iv, 2; xii, 28; xv, 5 etc.)—these and similar expressions are peculiar to D. Our survey of the development of Pentateuchal criticism has also shown that D was in 621 B.C. made the basis for the reform of Josiah, or at any rate played a role in it, and must have come into existence not long before. D is thus the next oldest law book after B. But D does not only follow chronologically upon B, it is also in content determined by B; and this is true in two ways, both in that it took over much from B or alternatively from a source common to both, and so could— though admittedly this would be an exaggeration—even be described as an expansion of B, and also that on the other hand it clearly is in contrast to B and is intended to replace it.

So far as the first point is concerned, we may note that, for example Deut. xv, 12–18, discusses the same situation as Exod. xxi, 2–6,[1] namely the release of a Hebrew slave after a six-year period of service, and this is done in D to a large extent word for word as in B. On the other hand, D appears here as an elaboration of B—or alternatively of the source common to both—bringing more strongly into the foreground the duties of charity and humanity. Deut. xix, 1–13, contains detailed regulations concerning the setting aside of first three cities of refuge for homicides, and then later a further three, though the murderer in the full sense is explicitly excluded from the right of asylum. These regulations resemble in many points the much briefer ones of B in Exod. xxi, 12–14,[2] and may, though not necessarily, be regarded as the elaboration of these and their adaptation to different circumstances. Deut. xxiv, 10–13, like Exod. xxii, 24–6,[3] deals with the consideration which a creditor is to have towards his compatriot who has fallen into debt to him, and in particular towards the poor debtor; and this happens in such a way that either dependence of D upon B or the dependence of both upon a common source is to be assumed.

But what separates D from B is definitely much more important than what links them together, namely their quite opposite attitudes towards the multiplicity of cult places. B explicitly recognises them, D most emphatically rejects

[1] Loretz, 'Ex. xxi, 6; xxii, 8 und angebliche Nuzi-Parallelen' Bibl 41 (1960), pp. 167–75. Cf. p. 217, n. 12.
[2] Dinur, 'The Religious Character of the Cities of Refuge and the Ceremony of Admission into Them' [Hebr., Engl. sum.] Eretz Israel 3 (1954), pp. 135–46, VIII–IX. Lit. p. 214, n. 4; p. 250, n. 11; p. 251, n. 16.   [3] Lit. p. 214, n. 6; p. 675, n. 18.

them. We have seen that it is probable that the opening of B which sanctions the multiplicity of altars is directed against a definite move towards cult-centralisation (p. 218). By contrast it can hardly be doubted that the violent polemic against the multiplicity of cult places which stands at the head of the actual corpus of laws in D, xii–xxvi, and its positive obverse, the energetic demand for the centralisation of the cultus, is directed also against B, and in particular its opening passage. The intention of putting D in the place of B becomes quite clear in the introduction to xii–xxvi, or more correctly in the two introductions: i, 1–5; ix, 8–x, 11;[4] i, 6–iv, 40,[5] and iv, 44–ix, 7; x, 12–xi, 32. For the point of these introductions, with their retrospect of the events which have taken place between Israel's experiences at Horeb and her arrival at her present position in the valley east of Jordan near Beth Peor (iii, 29; iv, 46),[6] is to replace B by D, setting out D as the law which Moses received for himself alone at Horeb from the mouth of God, and which he now wishes to hand on to the people of Israel. As we have seen (pp. 212–14) that is the meaning of the present arrangement of the Sinai narrative in Exod. xx–xxiv, no doubt stemming from the interpolator of B and clearly found there already by the compilers of the two introductions to D, namely that the people did in fact hear the decalogue, but then withdrew in awe, leaving the receiving of the remaining divine communications to Moses alone, and now having these—namely B—spoken to them by Moses.

With the second introduction, iv, 44–ix, 7; x, 12–xi, 32, this purpose becomes quite clear. In its form it is a speech of Moses, or more precisely a loose collection of several homiletical exhortations from his mouth. It begins with the repetition of the decalogue (v, 1–18), and then recalls that the people had requested Moses that he would henceforth alone listen to God and then transmit his commands to them afterwards; and how God explicitly approved this behaviour of the people and summoned Moses now to receive the instructions from his mouth which he was to hand on to the people (v, 19–28). The fact that here retrospect comes to an end and Moses immediately summons the people to obedience to God's command, is due to his having in view naturally not the book made up of Exod. xx, 22–xxiii, 33, i.e. B, but rather the law, D, which he is now to transmit to Israel. This law, which really begins only at xii, 1, does not, however, follow immediately. In v, 29–ix, 7; x, 12–xi, 32, Moses exhorts the people further to faithful obedience, and in these exhortations makes a whole series of scattered allusions to what Israel has experienced since its sojourn in Egypt. These historical examples are certainly intended to strengthen the exhortations too, but the compiler is in them following yet another purpose, namely to make the older Pentateuch narrative in which B is embedded superfluous, or at any rate to correct it and to lead to its being understood in a particular sense.

[4] ix, 8–x, 11, or at any rate the basic material of this section, which ends at x, 11 where i, 6 begins, belongs originally to the first introduction and was only placed in its present position when the two introductions were combined. Cf. below, p. 222.
[5] Lohfink, 'Darstellungskunst und Theologie in Dtn i, 6–iii, 29' Bibl 41 (1960), pp. 105–34; Mørstad, 'Deuteronomium iv, 25–8 og 29–40' NTT 60 (1959), pp. 34–45. Lit. § 126.   [6] Henke, 'Zur Lage von Beth Peor' ZDPV 75 (1959), pp. 155–63, Pls. 3–4.

With the first introduction its real purpose of replacing B by D is not im- mediately recognisable. This is because the opening is now mutilated. It begins in i, 6–7, likewise in the form of a speech of Moses (as indicated already, p. 221, n. 4), with the narrative of the departure from Horeb. This is very remarkable, and the surmise immediately suggests itself that it originally began not with the departure from Horeb but with the events which took place there. This surmise is confirmed. The first introduction began like the second with the imparting of the decalogue, and this beginning is also preserved, as Dillmann observed, incorporated in the second introduction. The passage ix, 25–x, 11, is in fact quite unsuitable in its present position, whereas it would be in place before i, 6, and would here plainly fill a gap. Evidently the redactor who put together the two introductions, desiring to weave them together into a real unity, en- deavoured to remove the duplication in the Horeb narrative, which noticeably disturbed the impression of unity, by amalgamating the first with the second. Originally the first introduction too related how the people heard the decalogue at Horeb, but then besought Moses that he would from then on listen to God alone and subsequently transmit to them God's further instructions; this first introduction is also designed to indicate D as these divine words, first received alone by Moses, and now to be imparted to the people.

It is thus clear that both the actual corpus of law beginning with xii and the two introductory speeches placed before it are intended to put D in the place of B. The introductory speeches do not, however, go so far as to put D actually in the place which B occupies in the narrative of Exod. xx–xxiv, and which it clearly must already have occupied at the date of the two introductions, and so do not present D as actually being published at Horeb. What they do is to present the matter so that Moses at first kept to himself the law which he had received from God at Horeb, and imparted it to the people only shortly before his death. The reason for this procedure is no doubt that the narrative of Exod. xx–xxiv, xxxii–xxxiv, was already so rooted in the popular mind that such a transformation of it would not be possible. All that could be done was that Exod. xx, 22–xxiii, 33, together with the decalogue of Exod. xxxiv, 14–26 was completely absorbed by the decalogue of Exod. xx, 1–17, and the making of the covenant in Exod. xxiv, 3–8, together with the restoration of the tablets in Exod. xxxiv was understood as referring exclusively to it. To achieve this, it was stated in Deut. v, 19, after the imparting of the decalogue, very emphati- cally, that Yahweh spoke only these words to the people and *added nothing to them*. It is possible that the well-known statement in I Kings viii, 9, from the description of the building of the Temple, that nothing but the two stone tablets, the tablets of the covenant, lay in the Ark, was also directed against the Book of the Covenant and not, for example, as has been assumed, against the belief that there were cult stones in the Ark. This attempt at neutralising a law such as the Book of the Covenant and as it were silencing it completely, seems to us not merely remarkable, but also impracticable. But we must bear in mind that the attempt has been successful not only in this case but also in many others. Indeed the evolution of the Pentateuch is marked by the continual neutralising of the older material by the new which comes to be added, in that the older precepts which are allowed to remain, are now quite naturally understood in the light of the newer, or, where that is not possible or necessary, they simply remain unheeded. In essence this process of neutralisation still continues today. For it is only thus that religions which develop further can preserve their ancient records; only thus that Christianity, like Judaism, can hold fast to the Old Testament.

We therefore do not need the assumption made by Kuenen*, namely that the Book of the Covenant, which he ascribes to E, had its original place shortly before the death of Moses, and was driven out of this position by D, though this is an assumption which is certainly worthy of attention and it has indeed been adopted by many scholars. This assumption does in fact raise various difficulties in other respects. In so far as these are connected with the structure and nature of E, they have already been touched upon, at any rate indirectly (pp. 215 f.). We need here only to bring out the further point that, on Kuenen's assumption, the driving out of B from its original position would have had a result which would certainly not be congenial to those responsible for driving it out, namely that B would so to speak have 'fallen up the stairs' and have received a more honourable position than before, actually at Horeb. In actual fact the truth must be that this position was no longer available when the two introductions to D came into being; for otherwise D would certainly have been placed there. So it was necessary to be content with the days shortly before Moses' death and shortly before Israel's crossing of the Jordan, a period which was in fact used also for the setting of other utterances of Moses, his 'Song' (Deut. xxxii) and his 'Blessing' (Deut. xxxiii). It was indeed quite suitable for the purpose (pp. 226-9).

D is thus to be understood as the deposit of a cultic-religious and social-humanitarian movement which is in many respects parallel to that embodied in B, though at decisive points opposed to it. The supporters of this movement we must picture as prophets and priests, and among these no doubt mainly the country priests who are so often commended for special consideration, *the Levites in Israel's gates* (xii, 12, 18; xiv, 27 etc.). Since D is later than B, it reveals itself as influenced by B, occasionally positively, but predominantly negatively. Dependence is expressed in the similarity of formal structure, in that in both the central cultic demand is placed before the other demands, and further in the treatment of many matters which also appear in B. But contrast is shown above all in the rejection of the many sanctuaries and in the desire for centralisation of the cultus which has as its consequence the remoulding of many of the earlier cult-ordinances as prescribed by the so-called 'centralisation laws'. Furthermore the difference between D and B is explained not only in the fact that behind D there stands a quite different personality or a quite different group of men than behind B, and that they are in fact the products of different periods, but also from the fact that the compiler of D had other original materials available to him than did the compiler of B. Just as B added to what may well be his own altar commands a variety of material which had come from elsewhere, so D contains, beside the centralisation laws which are peculiar to it (xii, xiv, 22-29; xv, 19-23; xvi, 1-17, and also probably xvii, 8-13; xxvi, 1-15), much material taken from elsewhere, and it will now be our task to demonstrate this in detail.

2. *The various groups of laws in D.* Even a rapid glance over xii–xxvi shows that in addition to the centralisation laws other regulations group themselves together, recognisable as related by common elements of content or form. This may be seen first in the statutes united in xxi–xxv covering matters of civil law without any reference to the idea of centralisation or to any kind of reform. In form they are all identically constructed in that, utilising the casuistic style (pp. 27–9, 213 f.) the main cases are introduced by כִּי *suppose that* and, in so far as there are such, the subdivisions are introduced by אִם *if*. Furthermore, they do not employ the address to Israel normally used in D; the matter is presented in the form of a report or was so presented in the original form of the material which has now been altered in some parts. To this group belong in particular xxi, 1–9—the atonement for murder committed by an unknown person;[7] xxi, 15–17—the acknowledgement of the firstborn, even if he is not the son of the favourite wife;[8] xxi, 18–21—the stoning of the rebellious son; xxii, 13–21— procedure when a woman is accused of not being a virgin on her entry into marriage; xxii, 22–9—procedure in regard to intercourse with someone else's wife or with a betrothed or unbetrothed girl; xxiv, 1–4—divorce laws;[9] xxv, 5–10—regulations concerning levirate marriage. Although these regulations, similar both in content and form, are now divided up by others of a different kind, we may nevertheless assume that, like the *mishpatim* of B in Exod. xxi, 1– xxii, 16 (pp. 27–9, 213 f.), they too originally formed an independent corpus which the compiler of D found to hand and utilised.

Another small group has the peculiarity that the commands which belong to it—with the sole exception of the regulation in xxii, 5, which is in the style of a report, using the singular form of address—all end with the expression: *For that is an abomination* (תּוֹעֵבָה) *to Yahweh* (*your God*) (or *he is an abomination, or he who does, everyone who does that* or *both of these are abominations* etc. . . .). Here belong xvi, 21–xvii, 1; xviii, 9–12; xxii, 5; xxiii, 19; xxv, 13–16, and per- haps also, although the conclusion is lacking, xxii, 9–12 (cf. also xxiv, 4). We may also assume that this group already lay before the compiler of D, and that he incorporated these laws because they fitted well with his endeavours aimed at the purification of the cultus of Yahweh.

A third group, which is less certainly to be delimited and in part (cf. e.g. xv, 1–18) is related to the first, is formed by the regulations which have been appro- priately called the humanitarian laws. Here we should include xxii, 1–4— exhortations for the care of cattle and property of a compatriot; xxiii, 16–17— the protection of the runaway slave; xxiii, 20–1—prohibition of usury on a compatriot; and the majority of the single regulations in xxiv, 6–xxv, 4. But the 'laws of warfare' too in xx and xxi, 10–14,[10] have been incorporated because

---

[7] Gordon, 'An Akkadian Parallel to Deuteronomy xxi, 1 ff.' RA 33 (1936), pp. 1–6; For an Ugaritic parallel cf. Cazelles, VT 8 (1958), p. 105. Lit. § 126.

[8] Mendelsohn, 'On the preferential Status of the Eldest Son' BASOR 156 (1959), pp. 38–40. Lit. § 126.

[9] Gurewicz, 'Divorce in Jewish Law' Res Judicatae 7 (1956), pp. 357–62; Wambacq, 'De libello repudii' VD 33 (1955), pp. 331–5. Cf. p. 21, n. 15; § 126.

[10] du Buit, 'Quelques contacts bibliques dans les archives royales de Mari' RB 66 (1959), pp. 576–81, cf. pp. 576 f.; Gurewicz, 'The Deuteronomic Provisions for Exemption from

of their humane attitude—or at any rate what has been felt to be their humanity —and not as technical indications for the conduct of war. This is true also of the third 'law of warfare', xxiii, 10–15, which is clearly directed towards the keeping pure of the camp, i.e. of Israel, and has been taken into account for that reason and not actually as a military regulation. This third group is harder to delimit than the others, and so it is less easy to discover how far its component parts already lay before the compiler of D and how far they may not rather come from him. With regard to some regulations, above all those which B also contains (xv, 12–18 = Exod. xxi, 2–6; xxiv, 10–13 = Exod. xxii, 24–6), it is certain or at any rate probable that the compiler of D found them already to hand, but others may very well go back to him or at least to his circle. For it is quite certain that the movement which led to D was inspired by a strongly social and humanitarian, almost social revolutionary impulse.

3. *The original Deuteronomy.* The compiler of D has thus incorporated into his scheme of laws various older materials, actual legal precepts, religious and moral instructions, even some which had no connection or only a very loose one with his main aims of reform. It is therefore not proper to deny such sections to the original Deuteronomy and to reconstruct this as it would appear if only the main demands which are related as being carried out in II Kings xxii–xxiii were to be taken into consideration. B too contains a great deal of material which has nothing whatever to do with its main purpose. On the other hand there cannot for a moment be any doubt that the corpus which we now have in xii–xxvi is not the original Deuteronomy, but that the basic document has here undergone a variety of amplifications and alterations.[11] Thus, simply to mention two sections of fair size, there is a large measure of agreement that xiv, 1–21, and in particular vv. 4–20[12]—the list of clean and unclean animals—and xviii, 15–22—regulations concerning prophecy[13]—are secondary insertions, the first because in vocabulary and style it differs markedly from the remainder of the book and uses the otherwise rare second person plural form of address, the second because of the marked prominence which it gives to the person of Moses, a prominence which in the laws, unlike the framework sections, is quite unique. But even when we have taken out these and various other sections, no clearly ordered or intelligible arrangement appears, and even rearrangements do not alter this fact. Furthermore it is only rarely that we can discover the reasons for this lack of order and can show that the compiler of D fitted together the groups of material which he had before him according to one particular principle or another, and that he inserted his own demands deliberately in this position or that. We have therefore to be content with the statement of the position as it is, without any explanation. It is true that Steuernagel has made it appear probable that in xii not one but three demands for centralisation are present, parallel to

---

Military Service' ABR 6 (1958), pp. 111–21; Herrmann, 'Das Aufgebot aller Kräfte. Zur Interpretation von I K II 96–103 = IV 184–191 und Dtn xx, 5–7' ZAW 70 (1958), pp. 215–20.

[11] Simpson, 'A Study of Deuteronomy xii–xviii' AThR 34 (1952), pp. 247–51.

[12] Cf. p. 31, n. 51.

[13] Teeple, *The Mosaic Eschatological Prophet* (JBL Monograph Series X, 1957).

I

one another, indicated by Steuernagel as D²a, D²b, D²c, and thus separated out: D²a xii, 8–12aα; D²b xii, 1*, 2, 4–7a; D²c xii, 13, 14a, 17–19, 21–3, 26–7, 29–31. But apart from the fact that the material can also be divided up differently, and that it is possible perhaps to manage with only two parallels, this three-strand formation cannot be demonstrated anywhere else in the corpus. Steuernagel himself only finds further matter belonging to D²b in xix, 16–19a; xxii, 23–7, and no further trace at all of D²a. Thus, if Steuernagel's analysis is correct, we have in xii a phenomenon which is restricted to this main demand, in which secondary amplifications are in any case very readily intelligible. In any case the hypothesis that our Deuteronomy was made up by the combination of three editions of the original Deuteronomy would contribute next to nothing to our explanation of the present form of xii–xxvi, and so is in this respect superfluous. Whether it may be better maintained in regard to the framework materials, i.e. to i–xi and xxvii–xxx (xxxiv), must now be examined.

4. *The introduction (i–xi)*. Steuernagel has endeavoured, with great ingenuity, to discover three strands in the introduction (i–xi), two using the plural form of address (D²a and D²b) and the third, D²c, using the singular. But these are in some sections so thin, and the interrelationship of the individual pieces is so uncertain, that even here we cannot really speak of an analysis which is in any degree assured. In the analysis of the conclusion (xxvii–xxx) D²b receives nothing at all; iv, 5–6, 8*, are taken to be the conclusion of D²a; and only D²c receives a relatively detailed concluding section, namely xxvi, 16; xxviii*; xxx, 15, 19b, 20. Decisive for the analysis here too is the distinction between sections using the plural address and those using the singular, though in this case the dearth of plural material makes it impossible to divide it between two strands. Thus we see that in the conclusion only two strands can be demonstrated, and here the assumption of three editions combined is as superfluous as with the main corpus itself. In short, this hypothesis cannot be maintained for the framework sections either. It is indeed certain that parallel strands have been combined, but there are only two of these, not three. In the introduction, i–xi, these may be readily separated from one another, since here the second is simply placed after the first, and only a relatively small part of the first has been incorporated in the second (cf. pp. 221–2). As to xxvii–xxxiv, the analysis is in any case very complicated because here we not only have the two concluding passages but also the older Pentateuchal sources and P, and other additional matter not belonging to any source, such as the Blessing of Moses. Here the two conclusions, corresponding to the double introduction, can only be assuredly separated out with difficulty. We must now examine this question, and hence the analysis of xxvii–xxxiv more closely.

5. *The Song and the Blessing of Moses (xxxii, xxxiii)*. The Song of Moses, xxxii, 1–43, and the Blessing of Moses, xxxiii, may be relatively easily lifted from their context. The former is a psalm. After a retrospect on the history of Israel, filled with experiences of apostasy and sin and hence also of divine discipline and punishment, it proclaims the destruction of Israel's enemies and her glorification. The Song of Moses, Deut. xxxii, 1–43, was generally held to be genuine up till the end of the eighteenth century A.D., but since then it has been dated in a

variety of very different ways.[14] Whereas some still ascribe it to Moses and regard it as a genuine prophecy of the apostasy committed by Israel after her entry into Canaan and of her punishment by Yahweh, the majority see in it a *vaticinium ex eventu*, composed with reference to later times when Israel was oppressed by foreign enemies—Aramaeans in the ninth century, Assyrians in the eighth, Babylonians in the seventh and sixth; yet others, following Sellin's lead, find evidence in it of the contrast between Jews and Samaritans and derive it from the fifth century B.C. We shall have to be satisfied with assessing the song as a *vaticinium ex eventu* put into the mouth of Moses, but we need not accept its dating in so late a period as has been fairly generally thought, during the last hundred years. Since on the one hand the retrospect over Israel's history provided in the song stops at the conquest and the apostasy occasioned by it, and on the other hand the enemies whose execution of the divine judgement is threatened have features which makes it reasonable to think of the Philistines, we may best set the song in the middle of the eleventh century B.C., between the defeat of the Israelites by the Philistines recorded in I Sam. iv and the brilliant victory which Saul gained over them according to I Sam. xiii–xiv. Since in the introduction to the Song of Moses, Deut. xxxi, 14–23, much is reminiscent of E (p. 217, n. 11), we must seriously consider the possibility that E took up this song into his work, finding it already to hand. It was perhaps already attributed to Moses. Since the song in any case at a later date was regarded as a summarising of the Deuteronomic law (p. 217, n. 11), we might go further and say that the song drew the law after it (cf. above, p. 217, n. 11), and thus that the placing of the latter in its present position finds its explanation, or part of its explanation from this fact. In this case priority would be given to the term *song* (שִׁירָה) in xxxi–xxxii, where, as the text now stands, it is remarkable that the two terms *law* (תּוֹרָה) and *song* appear together (תּוֹרָה xxxi, 9, 11, 12, 24, 26; xxxii, 46; שִׁירָה xxxi, 19, 21, 22, 30;[15] xxxii, 44).

xxxiii, however, divides quite clearly into two parts: the psalm-like hymn of vv. 2–5, 26–9 and the collection of sayings concerning the individual Israelite

[14] Albright, 'Some Remarks on the Song of Moses in Deuteronomy xxxii' VT 9 (1959), pp. 339–46; Artom, 'Sul testo di Deuteronomio xxxii, 37–43' RStOr 32 (1957), pp. 285–291; Baumann, 'Das Lied Mose's (Dt xxxii, 1–43) auf seine gedankliche Geschlossenheit untersucht' VT 6 (1956), pp. 414–24; Bellas, 'Τὰ χωρία Δευτ. xxxii, 43, καὶ Ζαχ. xiv, 17' Theologia Athen 13 (1935), pp. 137–45; Budde, *Das Lied Moses* (1920); Cassuto, 'La cantica di Mosè (Deut. xxxii)' Atti XIX Congr. Int. Or. (1938), pp. 480–4; Cornill, *Zur Einleitung in das AT* (1912), pp. 38–42; Dathe, *Disputatio philologico-exegetica in Canticum Mosis Deut. xxxii* (1769); Eissfeldt, *Das Lied Moses* (BAL 104, 5, 1958); Frank, 'The Song of Moses (Dt. xxxii)' [Hebr.] Tarbiz 18 (1946/7), pp. 129–38; Ginsberg, 'The Conclusion of Ha'azinu (Deut. xxxii, 34–43)' [Hebr., Engl. sum.] Tarbiz 24 (1954/5), pp. 1–3, I; Hauri, *Das Moseslied Deuteronomium xxxii* (Diss. theol. Zürich, 1917); Henschke, 'Konjekturen zu Deuteronomium xxxii' [with notes by Hempel] ZAW 52 (1934), pp. 279–82, 289; Kamphausen, *Das Lied Moses* (1862); Klostermann (p. 166, n. 45), (1893), pp. 223–367; Sellin, 'Wann wurde das Moselied Dtn xxxii gedichtet?' ZAW 43 (1925), pp. 161–73; Skehan, 'The Structure of the Song of Moses in Deuteronomy (Deut. xxxii, 1–43)' CBQ 13 (1951), pp. 153–63; 'A Fragment of the "Song of Moses" (Deut. xxxii) from Qumran' BASOR 136 (1954), pp. 12–15; Tur-Sinai, 'Note on Deuteronomy xxxii, 43' [Hebr., Engl. sum.] Tarbiz 24 (1954/5), p. 232, V; Welch, *Deuteronomy. The Framework to the Code* (1932), pp. 141–51; Winter, 'Der Begriff der "Söhne Gottes" im Moselied' ZAW 67 (1955), pp. 40–8. Lit. § 126.

[15] Cf. below, p. 230, n. 21

tribes in vv. 1, 6–25. The hymn begins with an epiphany of Yahweh (vv. 2–3)[16] like that of Judg. v, 4; Hab. iii, 3, and Ps. lxviii, recalls the beginning of his royal rule in Israel (vv. 4–5), and then extols the glory of this God and the security and victoriousness of the people protected by him (vv. 26–9). Since hymns of this kind have a tendency to archaistic expression, a firm decision concerning the age of the psalm is not easy, just as, in the same way, very varied opinions are expressed concerning the date of origin of Ps. lxviii and Hab. iii. The similarity of this psalm to Judg. v shows that taken for itself it could be old and even very ancient indeed.

The collection of sayings concerning the individual tribes in xxxiii, 6–25[17] is certainly pre-exilic, and indeed earlier than the disaster to the northern kingdom, for there is nowhere any hint of this. The sayings presuppose rather that the northern tribes are living in their districts. It is very difficult to say anything more precise, since a number of the sayings are ambiguous, as for example those on Judah and Benjamin, though this is in part due to the corruption or uncertainty of the text. Mowinckel holds[18] that the Blessing of Moses is an imitation or new edition of the Blessing of Jacob, dating from the last third of the seventh century B.C. But we must surely distinguish between the age of the individual sayings and that of their combination. One or two of the sayings certainly go back to the pre-monarchical period, but the collection is later. Starting from the presupposition that the Blessing of Jacob in Gen. xlix belongs to J whereas the Blessing of Moses belongs to E, some have declared that the latter is the younger of the two, and so the attempt has been made to find at least a relative dating. But this presupposition is quite uncertain. In Gen. xlix, as we have seen (pp. 92, 196 f.), some of the sayings are bound up with the L narrative. This applies to the sayings on Reuben, Simeon and Levi (vv. 3–7), as well as to a saying on Judah which has been replaced by the present one (vv. 8–12) but which may perhaps be reconstructed on the basis of Deut. xxxiii, 7, and to a saying on Joseph, also replaced by the present one (vv. 22–6) showing him invested with the rights of the firstborn in the place of the elder brothers. The other sayings have no such relationship with L, and were presumably inserted later, when this narrative connection was forgotten and there was a desire to have a complete series of sayings on all the tribes. At the same time the original Judah and Joseph sayings were replaced from the same motives by ones of a more general nature. But the Blessing of Moses reveals no such connections with the surrounding narrative. Even if we accept the possibility that Deut. xxxiii, 9, has in mind

[16] Blau, 'Zwei dunkle Stellen im Segen Moses (Dt. xxxiii, 2–3, 24–5)' *Kohut Mem. Vol* (1935), pp. 91–108; Nyberg, 'Deuteronomion xxxiii, 2–3' ZDMG 92 (1938), pp. 320–44. Lit. § 126.

[17] Budde, *Der Segen Moses* (1922); Cross and Freedman, 'The Blessing of Moses' JBL 67 (1948), pp. 191–210; Gaster, 'A Qumran Reading of Deuteronomy xxxiii, 10' VT 8 (1958), pp. 217–19; Kittel, *Die Stammessprüche Genesis xlix und Deuteronomium xxxiii traditionsgeschichtlich untersucht* (Diss. Kirchl. Hochsch. Berlin, 1959); Sellin, 'Zu dem Judaspruch im Jaqobssegen Gen. xlix, 8–12 und im Mosesegen Deut xxxiii, 7' ZAW 60 (1944), pp. 57–67; Tournay, 'Le Psaume et les Bénédictions de Moïse' RB 65 (1958), pp. 181–213; Welch (p. 227, n. 14), pp. 116–25. Cf. Walther, 'Scherz und Ernst in der Völker- und Stämmecharakteristik mittellateinischer Verse' AKG 41 (1959), pp. 263–301. Lit. § 126.

[18] ZAW 48 (1930), p. 270, n. 1.

what is related in Exod. xxxii, 25–9, this would not in itself mean recognising an original literary connection between the two passages. The allocating of the two collections of sayings to J and E thus rests simply upon the fact that—with L and J being regarded as a unity—on the one hand we have two older Pentateuchal sources and on the other hand two collections of sayings concerning the individual tribes. Hence it is easy enough to believe that like a whole mass of other parallel materials these also are to be allocated to the two sources. But Deut. xxxiii stands quite alone and in Gen. xlix only the sayings concerning Reuben, Simeon, Levi (Judah and Joseph) are related to the narrative context, whereas the others disturb it, particularly that on Joseph (vv. 22–6) which conflicts with the blessing of Ephraim and Manasseh which is provided in xlviii by both J and E. So we may not regard the two collections as parallels from two parallel narrative strands, but must assume that we are in both cases dealing with individual sections not belonging to the sources, which have been inserted into the Pentateuchal narrative at points which appeared suitable. In the first case, the series of sayings on Reuben, Simeon, Levi (Judah and Joseph), belonging to a particular source, offered an appropriate occasion for inserting the collection of sayings, or rather for completing and modifying the existing series. In the second case, the moment of Moses' death seemed to be an appropriate moment, both for the other last words (the Songs in Deut. xxxii and xxxiii, 2–5, 26–9) and also for this blessing of all the tribes. Gen. xlix and Deut. xxxiii are thus to be understood as isolated series of sayings, of which there were no doubt some others, and perhaps many such, in ancient Israel.

But if we compare the two collections of sayings themselves, it is again very difficult to decide which is the older. Apart from the saying on Joseph, of which at least parts recur in both collections, all the sayings are different, but we can hardly say which in each case is the older and which the younger. At best with the saying on Levi, in which in Gen. xlix, 5–7, there is clearly a reference to the secular tribe connected with Simeon, whereas equally clearly in Deut. xxxiii, 8–11, it is the priestly tribe with its right to manipulate the Urim and Thummim oracle[19] which is referred to, it may be said with probability that Gen. xlix presupposes the older situation. But even this is not absolutely certain. For the quite different assessments of the fate of Levi—Gen. xlix regards the dissolution of the secular tribe as a terrible but self-imposed disaster, whereas Deut. xxxiii extols to the utmost its rebirth as priestly tribe occasioned by this—need not belong to different periods, but might stem from two different social strata. Although an exact dating of the two Blessings is not possible, there is nevertheless much which suggests that that of Gen. xlix derives from an earlier period[20] than does that of Deut. xxxiii. Both, however, are old.

6. *The conclusion (xxvii–xxxiv)*. Deut. xxxiii did not in any case originally belong to Deuteronomy, any more than did the ancient Song of Moses Deut. xxxii, 1–43, taken up by E into his narrative work. This Song, however, belongs

[19] Fahd, 'Une pratique cléromantique à la Ka'ba préislamique' Semitica 8 (1958), pp. 55–79. Lit., p. 72, n. 1.
[20] Vawter, 'The Canaanite Background of Genesis xlix' CBQ 17 (1955), pp. 1–18. Lit., p. 198, n. 9.

inseparably with xxxi, 14–23; xxxii, 44, the narrative of Yahweh's command to Moses and Joshua to write down the Song, and of the carrying out of the command as well as the singing of the Song, so that these verses too are to be assigned to E. There thus remain of Deut. xxvii–xxxiv, only xxvii–xxx; xxxi, 1–13, 24–30; xxxii, 45–52; xxxiv not yet analysed. Of these, xxxi, 2–8; xxxii, 48–52; xxxiv have nothing to do with the Deuteronomic law. They continue the Pentateuchal narrative, in that they tell of the appointment of Joshua as Moses' successor, of the announcement of the imminent death of Moses, and of the death itself. Here, as we have seen (pp. 189, 200 f.), the older Pentateuch sources (xxxiv, 1–6) and P (xxxii, 48–52; xxxiv, 1*, 7–9) have a share in the narrative. In addition, we may also observe Deuteronomic or Deuteronomistic elements (xxxi, 2–8; xxxiv, 10–12), and these make it appear probable that the compiler of the original Deuteronomy or perhaps more probably one or several of its later editors, continued the narrative beyond the instructions of Moses with reference to the law, and certainly included the death of Moses. But, for the moment, we must turn from pursuing this point further, since it is better dealt with in the analysis of the book of Joshua (p. 256), and we must consider rather those component parts of xxvii–xxxii, which are clearly related to the law and represent a sort of concluding passage to it. These are xxvii; xxviii; xxix–xxx; xxxi, 9–13, 24–30;[21] xxxii, 45–7.

We have already discussed (pp. 216–17) the command of Moses to the Israelites in xxvii, 1–8 to erect large stones on Gerizim after crossing the Jordan, and to write the law upon them, and to build an altar according to the prescriptions of Exod. xx, 24–6. xxvii, 11–13 (vv. 9–10 form the beginning of xxviii) tell of Moses' direction that after the crossing of the Jordan six tribes should bless Israel from Gerizim, and six others should curse her from Ebal;[22] and vv. 14–26 contain a dodecalogue of curses to be spoken by the Levites, presumably on Ebal. There then follows in xxvii, 9–10; xxviii[23] a great speech by Moses which proclaims the blessing of Yahweh if the law is obeyed, and his curse if the opposite attitude is taken up; in xxviii, 69, this speech has as its colophon one which might serve as a conclusion to the whole law. But in xxix, 1, Moses gathers the people together again and delivers to them a long closing speech covering xxix–xxx. Here the main part, xxix, 2–xxx, 10, clearly refers back to xxviii in that it brings into relief the terrible seriousness of the threatened curse (xxix, 18–20), and holds out a prospect of divine mercy on the people visited by the curse (xxx, 1–10). xxx, 11–14, then speaks of the fulfilment of the law not being beyond human powers, and vv. 15–20 states in summary that Israel has now to decide for itself between life and death, good fortune and ill fortune, and solemnly implores the people to choose life and good fortune, and thus to be obedient to the law. Following on this, Moses imparted the law to all

[21] In xxxi, 30, שִׁירָה, Song, is a redactional substitution for תּוֹרָה, law
[22] Bülow, 'Der Berg des Fluches' ZDPV 73 (1957), pp. 100–7.
[23] Mørstad, 'Overveielser til Dtn. xxviii' NTT 60 (1959), pp. 224–32; Wenn du der Stimme des Herrn. deines Gottes, gehorchen wirst. Die primären Einführungen zu Dtn. xxviii, 3–6 und 16–19 (1960); Noth, ' "Die mit des Gesetzes Werken umgehen, die sind unter dem Fluch" ' Bulmerincq-Gedenkschr. (1938), pp. 127–45 = Ges. Stud. z. AT (²1960), pp. 155–71.

Israel (xxxi, 1), wrote it down and handed it over to the Levites and elders with the command that it should be read out in the year of release, which takes place every seven years, before all the people at the feast of Tabernacles (xxxi, 9–13). After the completion of the writing down, however, Moses commanded the Levites to preserve the law book in the Ark of the covenant, and proclaimed the law to the whole assembly of the people with strict exhortations to keep it (xxxi, 24–7). In xxxii, 45–7, finally, Moses again directs a warning to Israel, after the completion of the imparting of the law, that they should follow it and so ensure good fortune.

We can thus see that after the removal of the Blessing of Moses in xxxiii, itself old but only much later put in its present position, and of the Song of Moses in xxxii, 1–43, together with its framework xxxi, 14–23; xxxii, 44, which derive from E, and of the narrative xxxi, 2–8; xxxii, 48–52; xxxiv which deals both with the proclaiming of Moses' death[24] and of the installation of Joshua as his successor, the remaining sections of xxvii–xxxiv—xxvii; xxviii; xxix–xxx; xxxi, 1, 9–13, 24–30; xxxii, 45–7—are anything but a completely even narrative in chronological order; in fact they reveal a whole series of repetitions and un-evennesses. Some of these may be explained on the assumption that secondary additions have been made. Of this kind are, in addition to xxvii, 1–8 (p. 230), the sections which tell of the blessing and cursing ceremonies on Gerizim and Ebal, xxvii, 11–13, and xxvii, 14–26, though this does not tell us anything about their age nor about the tradition which is thus attested (p. 212). The speech of Moses in xxix–xxx linked with xxviii is also doubtless secondary, at least as far as xxx, 10. In the same way in xxviii, the unevennesses which may be observed are certainly the result of secondary additions and not due to the existence of two parallel series of blessing and curse which could be regarded as the con-clusions of two editions of Deuteronomy. xxx (11–14) 15–20, on the one hand, and xxxii, 45–7, on the other, could, however, perhaps be most readily under-stood as parallels of this kind. For the two concluding statements in xxx, 15–20, and xxxii, 45–7, are surely not possible side by side, and neither of them really looks like a secondary addition. From this it follows that, as in the introduction i–xi so also in the conclusion, xxvii–xxxii, there are traces to be seen of the two editions of Deuteronomy.

7. *Summary.* If now, leaving aside the secondary additions such as xxxiii and the sections which take the narrative on beyond its conclusion to the law, we survey Deuteronomy once more, we may get the following picture. We have a relatively unified corpus xii–xxvi; this certainly reveals various secondary addi-tions and in xii some which appear to be parallels. It reveals no intelligible prin-ciple of arrangement, but on the other hand provides no basis for the assumption of the combining of parallel bodies of material or of parallel editions of the same corpus. In front of it in i–xi there are two fairly straightforwardly separ-able introductions, and after it in xxvii–xxxii a conclusion made up of passages of very varied character and origin, and this certainly cannot be regarded as the combining of two parallel conclusions, but appears to contain fragments of such

[24] Loewenstamm, 'The Death of Moses' [Hebr., Engl. sum.] Tarbiz 27 (1957/8), pp. 142–57, III–V.

conclusions. It must also be noted that the proclamation of blessing and curse for the fulfilment of the law or the failure to fulfil it in xxviii has no doubt been much expanded secondarily, but reveals no clear traces of parallel speeches, so that xxviii in this respect resembles the corpus of law itself. The explanation which would seem to correspond most readily to this analysis of i–xxxii would be that the original Deuteronomy, containing from the first a conclusion with curses and blessings, underwent two editions which provided it with a framework and added to it a historical introductory speech by Moses—or at any rate one which contains historical allusions—and similarly a concluding word from him. In our book of Deuteronomy we should then have the combination of these two editions.

The original form of Deuteronomy which we have thus inferred corresponds to what we might expect from II Kings xxii–xxiii, the report of the discovery of the law book and of the reform of Josiah started or called for on the basis of it: a law book, claiming to derive from Moses (cf. xxii, 13, *our fathers*), which in addition to the demand for centralisation (xxiii, 9, 21–5) contains also a great variety of other ordinances aimed at purifying the cultus of Yahweh from foreign elements (xxiii, 10–14), and threatens curses if it is not fulfilled (cf. xxii, 16, 19). II Kings xxii–xxiii provides no basis for the assumption that it must also have contained a historical introduction. The claim which it certainly made to derive from Moses does not need to be set out and justified in a lengthy introduction, but may have found its expression in a single sentence, something like i, 1.[25] B and H too have no historical introduction, but begin, forcefully, just as D does at xii, with the cultic demand with which they are most nearly concerned (pp. 218, 233).

8. *D and the political situation of its time*. From all this, we may regard as assured the identification of the original Deuteronomy with the law book discovered in 621 and made the foundation of Josiah's reform or at any rate playing a decisive part in it. We can no longer discover with certainty whether it came into being only at that time or five to ten decades earlier. But in any case it first began to have its effects from the year 621. This is linked with the political circumstances[26] of that time. It could hardly be otherwise, than that the downfall of the Assyrian empire (p. 415), now no longer to be concealed, would have caused a longing for national independence to flare up strongly in the nations held in subjection by it, and so also in Judah. Information such as II Kings xxiii, 15, shows that Josiah decided to win back the ancient northern kingdom, or at least parts of it, not simply twelve years later (vv. 29–30), but already at that time. In his pursuit of this aim of national and political unity and freedom, the aims of this law directed at cultic unity and purity could serve him well, and it was therefore hailed as a welcome support. It is natural to suppose that this book then became well known and so underwent various modifications. Thus the two editions and their combination, which we have thought it proper

[25] On the place names mentioned in i, 1b—some at least do not fit here at all—and among them Tophel, cf. Cazelles, 'Tophel (Deut. i, 1)' VT 9 (1959), pp. 412–15.

[26] Cross and Freedman, 'Josiah's Revolt against Assyria' JNESt 12 (1953), pp. 56–9. Lit., p. 284, n. 14; pp. 296 f., nn. 60–2; p. 348, n. 3; p. 535, n. 17.

to reckon with, may have been formed shortly after 621. Sermons preached as propaganda for the reform could have provided the pattern for much within the framework sections, and in particular for the speeches in iv, 1–40; vi, 1–ix, 7; x, 12–xi, 32. But D also remained the authoritative law for the period of the exile and beyond, and so the editions which we now have may have originated first in the exile. We must return to this question again later (pp. 299–301).

§ 35. THE HOLINESS CODE

Literature: Baentsch, *Das Heiligkeits-Gesetz* (1893); Elliott-Binns, 'Some Problems of the Holiness Code' ZAW 67 (1955), pp. 26–40; Fohrer, *Die Hauptprobleme des Buches Ezechiel* (BZAW 72, 1952), pp. 144–8; Klostermann, 'Beiträge zur Entstehungsgeschichte des Pentateuchs' ZLThK 38 (1877), pp. 401–45 = *Der Pentateuch* I (1893), pp. 368–418: 'Ezechiel und das Heiligkeitsgesetz'; Kornfeld, *Studien zum Heiligkeitsgesetz* (1952); Küchler, *Das Heiligkeitsgesetz. Lev. xvii–xxvi* (Diss. theol. Königsberg, 1929); Morgenstern, 'The Decalogue of the Holiness Code' HUCA 26 (1955), pp. 1–27; Paton, *The Original Form of the Holiness Code. Part I: The Original Form of Leviticus xvii–xix* (Diss. theol. Marburg 1897); Quast, *Analyse des Sündenbewußtseins Israels nach dem Heiligkeitsgesetz* (Diss. theol. Göttingen, 1957); von Rad, *Deuteronomium-Studien* (²1948), pp. 17–24, E.T. *Studies in Deuteronomy* (1953), pp. 25–36: 'Form-criticism of the Holiness Code'; Graf Reventlow, *Das Heiligkeitsgesetz formgeschichtlich untersucht* (WMANT 6, 1961).

Cf. also Literature §§ 4d, e, 8, 9, 19, 22–34.

1. *Name, compass and composition.* From the mass of laws collected in Exod. xxxv to Num. ix, one complex stands out as a special entity, recognisable by particular characteristics of linguistic usage, namely Lev. xvii–xxvi. One of these characteristics is the formula which occurs here particularly frequently: *You are to be holy, for I, Yahweh, your God, am holy* or similarly (xix, 2; xx, 7, 8, 26; xxi, 6, 8, 15, 23; xxii, 9, 16, 32). From this, Klostermann proposed the name 'Holiness Code' (H) for this complex. This name has been generally accepted, and quite properly so, for the feature which gives its particular stamp to this collection is just this: with a very special insistence it holds before the people the idea of holiness in the sense of cultic and ethical cleanness (cf. xx, 25–6).

The collection does not have a title to mark its beginning, but the contents of the command which stands in xvii, 1–9, make it a very suitable opening. This contains the demand that all slaughter of oxen, sheep or goats is to take place exclusively at the altar of Yahweh. We have already seen (p. 221) that D also begins with an instruction dealing with the place of sacrifice, namely the demand that it should be brought only to the one place specified by Yahweh, and B had at the beginning a demand strongly opposed to such centralisation (p. 218). From this point of view, xvii, 1–9, reveals itself directly as the beginning of a particular law book. Its conclusion is, however, very clearly marked. In xxvi, 3–45,[1] Yahweh offers to the people, if they are obedient to the

---

[1] Cf. Noth (p. 230, n. 23).

commands just imparted, the prospect of good fortune and life (vv. 3–13), whereas if they are disobedient, there is a prospect of distress and death (vv. 14–39); though at the same time, like Deut. xxx, 1–10 (p. 230), not without a promise of his mercy if the punishment is accepted with repentance and with a willingness to amend their ways (vv. 40–5). The closing address is followed in verse 46 by a formal colophon: *These are the statutes and ordinances and laws which Yahweh has made between himself and the people of Israel on Mount Sinai by Moses.* Thus Lev. xvii–xxvi stands out clearly as a separate entity, and we may simply raise the question as to whether perhaps some isolated laws standing outside this section and in many respects reminiscent of Lev. xvii–xxvi, actually belong to it, and are to be replaced in their original position. This has in particular been assumed for the short section xi, 43–5, which may have had its original place after xx, 25. The possibility must be admitted, but we cannot be certain, since all the laws which belong in the wider sense to P reveal similarity to one another, and so the existence of a somewhat higher degree of likeness does not automatically justify the assumption that these sections also originally belonged to the same corpus.

If we may with assurance regard Lev. xvii–xxvi as having once constituted an independent corpus, we may also note that there can be recognised in it no clear arrangement or logically ordered sequence, just as was the case with B and D. The demand of xvii, 1–9, concerning the place of slaughter, is followed by the related prohibition of eating blood, and also the prohibition, equally intelligible here, of eating carrion (vv. 10–14, 15–16). In xviii[2] too the arrangement is plain: a general exhortation to keep Yahweh's demands (vv. 1–5), is followed in vv. 6–18 by the prohibition of sexual intercourse with relatives, and in vv. 19–23 by other prohibitions concerning sexual matters, including what does not really belong here but is nevertheless understandable in this context, namely the prohibition of the Molech-sacrifice of children[3] in verse 21. The conclusion (vv. 24–30) is provided by a more general exhortation corresponding to the beginning (vv. 1–5). xix[4] contains a whole series, about thirty in all, of individual commands and prohibitions of a religious and ethical character, substantially identical in part with the ethical decalogue (Exod. xx, 2–17)—so vv. 3–4, 11–12, 30. Others have their parallels in the cultic decalogue of Exod. xxxiv (verse 4, cf. Exod. xxxiv, 17), in B (vv. 33–4, cf. Exod. xxii, 20; xxiii, 9), and in D (verse 9, cf. Deut. xxiv, 19). With such a great variety of material it is clearly possible to arrange it in very varied ways, so that no judgement is possible here on the manner of the arrangement. Nevertheless it is noticeable that among the injunctions which are otherwise couched in the style *Thou shalt (not)* or *You shall (not)* there is also one, vv. 20–2, which appears in the casuistic third person style. Moreover it is noticeable that the observance of the day of rest is twice enjoined, vv. 3 and 30. xx is parallel to xviii in more than one respect, in that in addition to other prohibitions it contains above all those

[2] Cf. p. 70, n. 2.
[3] Cf. p. 70, n. 1.
[4] Maass, 'Die Selbstliebe nach Leviticus xix, 18' *Baumgärtel-Festschr.* (1959), pp. 109–13. Lit. § 126.

concerned with sex, and on these follows in vv. 22–6 a more general exhortation to obedience to Yahweh (like xviii, 24–30). There is a difference as against xviii in that here in xx there are mentioned the punishments which fit each individual crime, though these are missing in xviii. Nevertheless xx is a parallel to xviii and not originally intended as a supplement to it. Within xx itself, there is one prohibition in common with xix (verse 6 = xix, 31). The order is disturbed by the fact that the subject of mediums and soothsayers is twice discussed in different places, vv. 6 and 27, all the more so since verse 27 stands after the general final exhortation, and thus appears belatedly. We may note also that the final exhortation itself is interrupted by a quite concrete instruction (verse 25).

xxi–xxii form a well arranged unit, practically free of unevennesses, and deal with the priests and sacred gifts: xxi, 1–9, the regulations for cleanness to be observed by the priests; vv. 10–15 those for the high priest; vv. 16–24 the bodily imperfections which exclude a man from priestly office; xxii, 1–16, regulations and limitations in regard to the consumption of the sacred gifts; vv. 17–30 the unblemished state of the sacrificial beasts and other regulations concerning the animal sacrifices; vv. 31–3 a general concluding exhortation. Similarly xxiii is a clearly arranged unit, complete in itself in that it is entirely devoted to the festivals and enumerates these in chronological sequence through the year, placing the sabbath at the head. But a closer examination soon reveals, as we have already seen (p. 144), that various hands have been at work on the festival calendar. xxiv contains in vv. 1–9 prescriptions concerning the lamps to be kept burning every night in the 'holy place' in the tent of meeting, and concerning the shew-bread, and in vv. 10–23 details of punishment for blasphemy, murder and the wounding of another person and of cattle. This chapter too contains later additions beside older material, the latter being particularly preserved in vv. 15–22. The situation is similar in xxv,[5] which comprises the regulations for the sabbath years to be held every seven years, and the jubilee years to be held every fifty years, and thus to that extent deals with one type of material. Here the regulations for the sabbath year reveal themselves as the basic material (vv. 1–7, 14, 17–25, 35–40a, 42–3, 47–9, 53, 55), secondarily expanded by the requirements for the jubilee year (the remainder of xxv).

Unevennesses of the kind which have just been pointed out in xxiii–xxv, but which appear also elsewhere in H, may on the whole be explained fairly easily. We are dealing with additions and alterations which were designed to accommodate the older core of H with the laws of P which did not always agree with them. Not infrequently we can point to the passage in our P following which H has been corrected or amplified. Thus for the elaboration of the older festival laws of xxiii, the section in Num. xxviii–xxix, or at any rate a festival calendar corresponding to it, must have been determinative, and the instructions in

[5] Jirku, 'Das israelitische Jobeljahr' *Seeberg-Festschr.* (1929), pp. 169–79; Lewy, 'The Biblical Institution of *derôr* in the Light of Akkadian Documents' Eretz-Israel 5 (1958), pp. 21*–31*: on Lev. xxv, 10 and Jer. xxxiv; North, *Sociology of the Biblical Jubilee* (1954); Rabinowitz, 'A Biblical Parallel to a Legal Formula from Ugarit' VT 8 (1958), p. 95: on xxv, 30; Hans Schmidt, *Das Bodenrecht im Verfassungsentwurf des Esra* (Hallische Universitätsreden 56, 1932); Vitta, 'Il diritto di proprietà presso gli antichi Ebrei' AANL 10 (1955), pp. 538–49: on Ex. xxiii, 10–11, Lev. xxv.

Exod. xxvii, 20–1, for the addition of xxiv, 1–4. We may indeed readily understand that there would be an effort to make the Sinai laws belonging to P in the
broader sense in Exod. xxv–xxxi, xxxv–Num. ix at least to some extent a unity,
and that when H was incorporated or after its incorporation in this law-giving,
it was corrected to fit its context where this seemed necessary. We cannot now
tell whether this was done immediately by the same hand as put H in its present
position, or whether it was done by a later hand, or even whether one or more
hands were concerned in this process of assimilation; nor does it greatly matter.

But when the additions just described have been removed from H, it is still
not a literary unit. xx, 10–26, as we have seen (p. 234) is in large measure a
parallel to xviii, 6–30. Even if we may regard the sequence in xxi–xxv—priests,
sacrifices, festivals, sabbath years (jubilee years)—as being in general no doubt
deliberate and justifiable, it nevertheless remains quite obscure as to why the
regulations in xxiv, 10–23 (p. 235) are in this position; we should expect them
before xxi. Furthermore, the fact already touched on, that a whole series of
injunctions appears in several places in H (xvii, 12 = xix, 26a; xix, 3b = xxvi, 2a;
xix, 27–8 = xxi, 5; xix, 30 = xxvi, 2; xix, 31 = xx, 6; xix, 34 = xxiv, 22, etc.),
can only be explained on the assumption that in H various smaller collections of
laws, containing in part identical or similar regulations, have been united, and
that whoever united them wished to alter their content as little as possible and so
had to let the duplicates stand. This view, that several smaller collections of
laws are united in H, may be regarded as certainly right, and is also quite generally accepted. But there remains uncertainty concerning the number and the
exact limits of the collections here put together. Baentsch distinguishes three
strata: H¹—xviii–xx, xxiii–xxv; H²—xxi–xxii; and H³—xvii, of which admittedly at least the first two in their turn are compositions made up of smaller
collections of laws; and he assumes that these three were put together by the
compiler of xxvi in the form in which we now have it. Bertholet, on the other
hand, reckons with twelve originally independent sections, first put together by
the compiler or redactor of our H. It is hardly possible to arrive at a clear decision,
and indeed recent works on H hardly go into the question, but—so Kornfeld—
only occasionally speak of the double form of certain prohibitions, as for example
the incest prohibitions of xviii and xx, or—so Elliott-Binns—are content with
the more general statement, that H was compiled on the basis of several independent units and collections from various periods, and this probably earlier than D.
If we may not unreasonably assume that the general exhortations to keep the
commands originally stood each at the end of a collection, we should have collections as follows: xvii–xviii marked off by xviii, 24–30; xix by xix, 37; xx by
xx, 22–4, 26 (pp. 234 f.) and xxi–xxii by xxii, 31–3. xxiii has no such general
exhortation at the end, and we might be inclined, since xxiv is to a large extent
later supplement (p. 235) and may therefore be here left aside, to link xxv with
xxiii, and to see in xxiii + xxv an originally independent small collection containing an enumeration of the annual festivals and of the sabbath year. But the
smaller collections thus indicated are not quite unified in themselves, since even
within them duplicates appear (e.g. xix, 3b = xix, 30a).

2. *Date of origin.* If we now inquire into the age of the smaller collections

combined in H, and into the age of H itself, we cannot get a fixed point by placing together the many individual commands reminiscent of the decalogue, the Book of the Covenant, and Deuteronomy. These commands are all, or at any rate for the most part, old or even very old, and furthermore will have been repeated in each generation with greater or less degree of modification of the wording, and in any case with comparatively little concern about the sequence of the sentences. The same is true of the ancient festival laws of xxiii, and of others. But one indication is nevertheless available, pointing to at least somewhat more precisely definable circumstances. In xviii, 21, and xx, 1–5, there is a prohibition of the Molech-sacrifice of children[6] and punishment is prescribed, and in neither case have we any ground for denying the relevant sentences to the original collection. The practice of this child sacrifice is attested for the second half of the eighth century (Ahaz, II Kings xvi, 3) and for the middle of the seventh century (Manasseh, II Kings xxi, 6). In 621 B.C., indeed, Josiah forbade it (II Kings xxiii, 10), but polemic against it continues (Jer. xxxii, 35; cf. vii, 31; xix, 5; Ezek. xvi, 21; xxiii, 37), and this may be explained as meaning that it had revived. The collections which contained xviii, 21, and xx, 1–5, can thus have hardly come into being earlier than the second half of the eighth century, whereas a later dating is possible.

The sections xvii, 1–9, and xxvi, 3–45, which are often adduced to assist in giving a more exact date to H, can in reality do this only very imperfectly, since we cannot decide with certainty either in xvii, 1–9, or in xxvi, 3–45, whether the references here which point to post-deuteronomic and exilic conditions belong to the original content of H or are secondary additions. So far as xvii, 1–9, is concerned, the present wording of the passage clearly presupposes the centralisation of the cultus at one single place. For when verse 4 demands the carrying out of all slaughter—this ranking as sacrifice—before the *tent of revelation*, the *dwelling of Yahweh*, this signifies the recognition of only one sanctuary, though here this is not as in D the place which Yahweh will at some future date choose in the land of promise, but the tent of revelation in the wilderness. But this simply represents the cult place of D projected back into the wilderness, and thus presupposes D and the reform of Josiah. This means that H is later than 621 B.C. But if, with Elliott-Binns, we hold the mention of the *tent of revelation* and of the *dwelling of Yahweh* in xvii, 1–9, to be secondary addition, then the regulations for slaughter given here need not be applied to a single sanctuary. They may then be understood to mean that slaughter for sacrifice is not to be carried out just anywhere in the settlements, but only at the larger pilgrimage sanctuaries which exist in the various districts. If this is so, there is no necessity for dating the section after D, the more so since the conception apparently presupposed by it of regarding all slaughter as sacrifice gives the impression of greater age than the acknowledgement of profane slaughter found in D. The situation in xxvi, 3–45, is similar to that in xvii, 1–9. It is quite clear that the threats expressed here in vv. 14–45 as to what will happen if the law is transgressed can only have received their present form in exilic or post-exilic times, and this is in particular true of vv. 40–5 which speak of the mercifulness of

[6] Cf. p. 70, n. 1, and p. 234.

Yahweh aroused by the penitence of the people in exile. But this does not in itself demand that we should attribute xxvi, 3–45, to so late a date, since the phrases in question may be secondary additions, and the material which remains after they have been removed may very well be of earlier origin.

Under these circumstances it is understandable that scholars today recognise a considerable degree of uncertainty about the dating of H. Whereas many, perhaps the majority, like Fohrer for example, derive H from the exilic period, and thus regard it as later than D, others, as for example Elliott-Binns, place H before D and regard it as having come into being, perhaps in the days of Manasseh, as a product of priests and cult prophets of the Jerusalem Temple who were disposed towards reform. This earlier dating is indeed justified at any rate in that H without any doubt contains ancient material, some very old indeed; and here we must also reckon with the possibility put forward by some scholars that at least part of this material comes from sanctuaries outside Jerusalem— Shechem or Bethel for example. H, as we now have it, though without the additions in Lev. xvii–xxvi influenced by P (pp. 235 f.), no doubt only came into being in the exilic period, and then more probably among the exiles than in the Judaean and Jerusalem homeland. This dating of H is supported above all by its relationship with the exilic prophet Ezekiel, as well as with P, which we must likewise assume to have come into being in the exile. There are so many parallels of content and language between Ezekiel and H that Ezekiel has even been taken for the compiler of H,[7] or it has been assumed that the same earlier originals were utilised by both (Cazelles, Fohrer, Elliott-Binns). We must in fact reckon with this second possibility, and only admit the first in so far as it may be thought to accord with the recognition that H and Ezekiel came into being in roughly the same period and in the same religious environment, and served the same end, namely the building up of a new national community pleasing to God, which, after the hoped-for end of the exile, could begin a new life pleasing to God in the homeland. This aim is also that of P, which also came into being in the exile, though rather later than H. Both of them, though actually directed towards the recovery of the homeland which was desired in the future, are presented as if deriving from the period before the first entry into Canaan and as having been given by God to his people at Sinai.

So far as we can see, H existed at first quite alone, without any historical introduction or conclusion. The claim which it made of having been revealed by God to Moses at Sinai could be seen clearly enough. Apart from the colophon which quite plainly states it (xxvi, 46), it appears in the introductory formula *Yahweh spoke to Moses* (xvii, 1) and in the indication that the commands were intended for the time when Israel would come into Canaan (xviii, 3, 24, 27; xix, 23; xx, 24). In just the same way as D (pp. 220–2, 231 f.), originally standing quite on its own though probably already at this stage provided with a historical introduction and conclusion, was then later inserted into the older Pentateuchal narrative, so too H soon lost its separate existence, and was inserted in a narrative context. We cannot now tell for certain whether it was inserted into P while the latter still stood alone or into the Pentateuch already containing P. Neh. viii, 14–18,

---

[7] Cf. Herrmann, *Ezechiel* (1924), p. XIX.

at any rate presupposes, as we shall see more precisely later (pp. 556–7) that H, or more exactly Lev. xxiii, 33–43, at that time, namely the period of Ezra, already stood in the law book of Moses, by which we are to understand certainly not P still existing on its own, but our Pentateuch. The events which are described in Neh. viii, 14–18, took place in all probability (pp. 554–5) at the beginning of the fourth century B.C. So if H came into existence in the middle of the sixth century, there would be a century and a half available during which it could first be linked with P and then, thus combined, with the older Pentateuch. This is a quite sufficient period of time.

§ 36. THE FORMATION OF THE PENTATEUCH

The analysis has shown that a fairly large number of literary works—or let us say simply books—have been combined in our Pentateuch. Set out in the chronological order which we have ascertained, these are L, J, E, B,[1] D, H, P. There remains the question as to whether we can also establish anything concerning the nature of the process by which these component parts came together, in other words whether they were combined in one redaction, or in successive stages. The first possibility may be excluded immediately; that at least can be said with assurance. For, to mention only some of the reasons, we have seen it probable that the interpolator of B found the combination J + E already in existence (pp. 214 f.) and similarly, that the compilers of the introductions of D knew the course of the Sinai story, though as yet without H and P, and thus presuppose the compilation L + J + E + B (pp. 220 f.). We may thus without any doubt reckon with a process in several stages by which the 'books' preserved in the Pentateuch were brought together, i.e., to use the normal expression, several redactions. For Pentateuchal criticism has become accustomed to use a unified terminology in so far as it denotes as redactors those who brought the material together, in distinction to the compilers or authors of the individual 'documents', 'books' or 'sources'; and the practice is also widespread of differentiating the various redactors by placing next to the abbreviation R for redactor the siglum of the source in raised type to the right of the R. Thus the hand which interpolated B is denoted as R^B, and that which was responsible for the insertion of D is R^D, and so forth. Neither the terminology nor the system of sigla is entirely unambiguous; the former because, for example, the compiler of H already had before him collections fixed in writing, and he combined them, and thus in this respect cannot really be sharply differentiated from a redactor, the latter because a term such as R^D could equally well be understood to mean the one who was responsible for the combining of the two editions of D which are to be assumed (pp. 232 f.), and this term has been so understood. Nevertheless, it seems best to keep to this system. So far as the sigla are concerned, what we have said is sufficient to make it clear in what sense they are used here, and so

---

[1] B itself may be older than L, J and E, and probably is; but as a section of the Pentateuch it is younger than they are (pp. 218 f.).

far as terminology is concerned, there is a distinction, for the most part clearly recognisable, between the author, organically shaping the material, and the redactor working mechanically, at any rate so far as the narrative sources are concerned. We shall therefore do well to keep to the normal terminology and the corresponding sigla.

Thus we must certainly reckon with several redactions taking place one after another, and of these some, like those of R^B and R^D, may be definitely proved (pp. 216–19). In other cases, the situation is less clear. It seems to me, in spite of certain arguments in its favour brought forward by Smend, not certainly provable that J was already combined with L when the author of E wrote his work. It must rather be considered whether perhaps J and E had not already been combined when they were joined with L. Similarly, as we have seen (pp. 238–9), it can hardly be decided with certainty whether H was inserted in P while the latter still existed independently, or whether it was first inserted in the Pentateuch enlarged by the inclusion of P. Furthermore, the date of the individual redactions cannot always be exactly determined, and more often in this we have to be content rather with the general assumption that they took place not long after the origin of the new source. But these questions which we can scarcely answer are not really of very great importance, and we may reasonably enough, since in any case it fits the majority of the redactions, picture the formation of the Pentateuch as a steady joining on of the younger sources in turn to the older body of material, thus assuming as many redactions as are shown by plus signs (+) in the schema $L + J + E + B + D + H + P$, and postulating the activity of an R^J, an R^E, an R^B, an R^D, an R^H, and an R^P. The most important points have already been made (p. 222) concerning the fact that the redactors and their contemporaries always regarded the source which they themselves had joined to the older material as being determinative. They understood the older material from its point of view, or even neutralised this older material and made it ineffective.

In conclusion, we may make this one further point. The stages assumed by Pentateuchal criticism for the formation of the Pentateuch, as they are expressed in the sigla L J E B D H P and R^J R^E R^B R^D R^H R^P are to the same extent hypothetical as that, we may again emphasise, the whole of Pentateuchal criticism is a hypothesis, though admittedly one that rests upon very significant arguments. We must remain aware of this fact. It can only be to the good when, for example Dornseiff in the series of essays 'Antikes zum Alten Testament',[2] untrammelled by this hypothesis, endeavours to solve the Pentateuchal question by a method of his own, resting on observations of the products of Graeco-Roman literature. Little as such works as these have been able to shake the normally accepted Pentateuchal criticism, they nevertheless, quite apart from

---

[2] 1. 'Genesis' ZAW 52 (1934), pp. 57–75 = *Kl. Schr.* I (²1959), pp. 203–46; 2. 'Exodos' ZAW 53 (1935), pp. 153–71 = *Kl. Schr.*, pp. 246–73; 3. 'Levitikon, Arithmoi' ZAW 55 (1937), pp. 127–36 = *Kl. Schr.*, pp. 273–86; 4. 'Die Abfassungszeit (Zeit und Verfasser) des Pentateuchs und die Deuteronomiums- (Deuteronomion-) frage' ZAW 56 (1938), pp. 64–85 = *Kl. Schr.*, pp. 286–329; 'Verworfene Ecksteine' *Curtius-Festschr.* (1957), pp. 61–5; 'Die Verfasser des Pentateuchs' Das Altertum 5 (1959), pp. 205–13. On this see Hempel ZAW 72 (1960), pp. 269 f.

important individual points, have their significance as a warning against too great reliance upon the results of Pentateuchal criticism itself. The important point is indeed, in the last analysis, not this or that individual dissection of the material, but the total outlook. 'Modern' Pentateuchal criticism, now more than 200 years old, put in the place of what was up till then on the whole the determinative flat picture of the Pentateuch, a three-dimensional one. It has enabled us to understand the Pentateuch as an entity which had come into being in the course of a long development covering centuries, indeed a whole millennium. This is its real merit, and this understanding of the material will maintain itself no matter how manifold are the variations which come in the future, just as in previous centuries it has been expressed in very varied ways.

B. THE PROPHETS (נְבִיאִים)

I. THE OLDER HISTORICAL BOOKS (נְבִיאִים רִאשׁוֹנִים FORMER PROPHETS)

§ 37. THE BOOKS OF JOSHUA, JUDGES, SAMUEL AND KINGS CONSIDERED AS PARTS OF A LARGER WHOLE

Literature: Benzinger, *Jahvist und Elohist in den Königsbüchern* (BWANT 27, 1921); Budde, *Die Bücher Richter und Samuel. Ihre Quellen und ihr Aufbau* (1890); Cornill, 'Ein elohistischer Bericht über die Entstehung des israelitischen Königthums in I Samuelis i–xv aufgezeigt' ZKWL 6 (1885), pp. 113–41; 'Zur Quellenkritik der Bücher Samuelis' Königsberger Studien I (1887), pp. 25–89; 'Noch einmal Sauls Königswahl und Verwerfung' ZAW 10 (1890), pp. 96–109; Eissfeldt, *Die Quellen des Richterbuches* (1925); *Die Komposition der Samuelisbücher* (1931); Haney, *The Wrath of God in the Former Prophets* (1960); Hölscher, *Das Buch der Könige, seine Quellen und seine Redaktion* (FRLANT 36, 1923) I, pp. 158–213; Kittel, 'Die pentateuchischen Urkunden in den Büchern Richter und Samuel' ThStKr 65 (1892), pp. 44–71; MacLaurin, *The Hebrew Theocracy in the tenth to the sixth centuries B.C. An Analysis of the Books of Judges, Samuel and Kings* (1959); Simpson, *Composition of the Book of Judges* (1957); Smend, 'JE in den geschichtlichen Büchern des AT' ZAW 39 (1921), pp. 181–217; Wiener, *The Composition of Judges ii, 11 to 1 Kings ii, 46* (1929); Wiese, *Zur Literarkritik des Buches der Richter* (BWANT 40, 1926); Wolff, 'Das Kerygma des deuteronomistischen Geschichtswerkes' ZAW 73 (1961), pp. 35–50.
Cf. also Literature §§ 5, 18, 22–36, 38–41, 126.

1. *Survey of Joshua–II Kings.* The books Joshua to II Kings carry further the narrative which closes in Deut. xxxiv with the death of Moses, continuing it to the showing of favour to the Judaean king Jehoiachin by Evil-merodach in 561 B.C., and thus covering about six and a half centuries if we place the death of Moses at about 1200 B.C. This period is divided into four sections by the division of the narrative material into the four books of Joshua, Judges, Samuel and Kings—a secondary division, as we shall show in a moment,[1] the further division of Sam. and Kings into two books each being even later. These sections

---

[1] Cf. also above, pp. 134–6.

are from the death of Moses to the death of Joshua and Eleazar (Josh. xxiv, 29–33), from there to the beginnings of Samuel (I Sam. i), from there to the last days of David and the beginnings of Solomon (I Kings i–ii), and from there to the favour shown to Jehoiachin (II Kings xxv, 27–30). A closer examination of the actual material reveals immediately, it is true, that these divisions are very imperfect. The death of Joshua and his genealogy are given twice, Josh. xxiv, 29–33, and Judg. ii, 8–10, and between these two statements we find also the notes *And it came to pass after the death of Joshua* in Judg. i, 1, and *And Joshua dismissed* in Judg. ii, 6. Whereas the second half of Josh. gives the impression that the conquest of Canaan by Israel and the allocation of the land to the individual tribes is absolutely complete, we find in Judg. i, 1–ii, 5[2] that this is by no means the case, but that a great deal still remains to be done. The two narratives which tell of the migration of the tribe of Dan (Judg. xvii–xviii) and of the outrage at Gibeah of Benjamin (Judg. xix–xxi), normally designated as 'appendices to the book of Judges', have in reality nothing at all to do with the Judges narratives, and, since they deal with the position of two Israelite tribes which are not yet completely settled or formed, would find their proper place before the narratives of the Judges in iii, 7–xvi, 31, rather than after them. It may easily be seen that the division which is now made between Sam. and Kings breaks the connection between II Sam. xx and its immediate continuation in I Kings i–ii, and it is generally agreed that this is so. The break made between these two closely connected sections is made all the sharper by the fact that II Sam. xxi–xxiv has been inserted between them, itself a complex structure of interwoven narratives, lists and songs.

2. *Is Joshua–II Kings a combination of the continuations of the Pentateuchal sources, or a Deuteronomistic Historical Work?* The books Josh., Judg., Sam., and Kings are thus by no means independent books with intelligible beginnings and endings; nor can we speak of their possessing a clearly ordered structure. Hence, if we are to come to an understanding of their structure and of the history of their formation we must, at any rate at first, disregard the present divisions of the books, and consider the larger complex to which they belong. Although this basic point is unfortunately not always observed, there is nevertheless complete agreement on it between the two main conceptions of the composition of these books, though in the analysis of the books Josh., Judg., Sam., and Kings these views are otherwise diametrically opposed to one another. The first regards the basic material as the combination of the Pentateuchal sources considered as at least in part continuing further. The second denies any connection between Josh.–Kings or rather Deut.–Kings and the Pentateuch, or more properly the Tetrateuch, and treats Deut.–Kings as a historical work, substantially expanded secondarily, compiled in Judah in about 550 B.C. by a Deuteronomistic author from many pieces of material which up till then had existed independently, and

[2] Gurewicz, 'The Bearing of Judges i–ii, 5 on the Authorship of the Book of Judges' ABR 7 (1959), pp. 37–40. On i, 36, הַסֶּלַע, cf. Hammond, 'Petra' BA 23 (1960), pp. 29–32, and on Petra generally Cleveland, 'The Excavation of the Conway High Place (Petra)', AASOR XXXIV–XXXV (1960), pp. 57–78, Pls. 1*–18*; Hammond, 'Excavations in Petra in 1959' BASOR 159 (1960), pp. 26–31. Lit. § 126.

with a variety of supplements of his own. Hölscher, who is perhaps the most
trenchant adherent of the first view, says, on pp. 7 f. of his *Geschichtsschreibung
in Israel* (1952), that 'The five books of Moses and the books of Joshua, Judges,
Samuel and Kings . . . form, as their content shows, in reality a single connected work, which has only subsequently been divided into nine separate
books.' Noth, the real originator of the idea of the Deuteronomistic historical
work (Dtr),[3] declares, on p. 4 of his *Überlieferungsgeschichtliche Studien* I
(1943, [2]1957), that it is proper to disregard at first in the examination of Dtr
the traditional division of the tradition complex of Josh.–Kings, since this is
'in any case a secondary stage in the tradition history'.

3. *The analysis of Joshua–II Kings according to the 'fragment' hypothesis.*
According to Noth, it is the compiler of Dtr who first joined together into one
unit the sections, till then independent, of the books of Josh., Judg., Sam., and
Kings and in addition those of Deut., with the addition of his own elaborations.
In this work insertions were also made later, namely, Josh. xiii–xxii, xxiv;
Judg. i, 1–ii, 5; xiii–xvi; xvii–xxi; II Sam. xxi–xxiv. The compiler of Dtr
found already available Deut. iv, 44–xxx, 20; Josh. ii–xi*, Judg. ii, 6–xii*;
I Sam. i, 1–iv, 1a; iv, 1b–vii, 1; ix, 1–x, 16; x, 27b–xi, 15; xiii, 2–II Sam. ii, 7;
ii, 8–xx, 25; I Kings i–ii; iii, 4–15, 16–28; iv, 1–v, 8, 9–14; vi–vii; viii, 1–13;
ix, 10–14, 15–x, 29; xi, 14–37, the memoranda contained in I xii–II xxiv from
the chronicles of the kings of Israel and the kings of Judah, as well as the Ahijah
narratives of I xi, 29–xiv, 18, the Elijah narratives of I xvii, xix, xxi, II i–ii, the
prophet narratives of I xx, xxii, the Elisha narratives of II iii, 4–viii, 15; xiii,
14–19, the narrative of the anointing of Jehu by a disciple of Elisha in II ix–x,
the Isaiah narratives of II xviii, 17–xx, 19, the account of the finding of the law
in II xxii, 3–xxiii, 3, and the narratives concerning the fall of Jerusalem in
II xxv, 1–26. From the compiler of Dtr himself, however, come Deut. i, 1–iii,
29 (iv, 1–40),[4] i.e. the first of the two introductions to what are by others taken
to be two editions of Deut. (pp. 221–2), Deut. xxxi–xxxiv*, Josh. i; viii, 30–5;
xii; xxiii; Judg. iii, 7–11; I Sam. vii, 2–viii, 22; x, 17–21ba (21bβ–27a); xii,
1–25; I Kings v, 15–32; viii, 14–66; ix, 1–9; xi, 1–13, 38–43; xxi, 21, 22, 24–6,
II Kings x, 28–33; xvii, 7–20; xxi, 1–18; xxiii, 21–7; xxv, 27–30. This historical
work existed on its own for some time, and then, after the older Pentateuchal
sources had been worked into the framework of the P narrative, it was united
with the Pentateuch, or with the Tetrateuch, as we must rather say, since,
according to Noth, P had no narrative of the occupation of the land, and J and E
lost theirs when they were incorporated in P. Of the whole of Deuteronomy,
only xxxiv, 1a, 7–9, which come from P and originally followed directly on
Num. xxvii, 12–23, belongs to a Pentateuch source.

The materials contained in Josh.–Kings exhibit great variety, and actually or
apparently lack, on the one hand, any interconnections among themselves,

---

[3] Herrmann, *Die Bedeutung der Propheten im Geschichtsaufriß des Deuteronomisten,
dargestellt im Rahmen seiner theologischen Leitgedanken* (Diss. theol. Berlin, 1957); Janssen,
Juda in der Exilszeit. Ein Beitrag zur Frage der Entstehung des Judentums (FRLANT 69,
1956), pp. 12–18: 'Das deuteronomistische Geschichtswerk'; Noth, 'Zur Geschichts-
auffassung des Deuteronomisten' Proceedings XXII Congr. Or., Vol. II (1958), pp.
558–66.   [4] Noth ascribes to Dtr only the basic content of iv, 1–40.

while on the other hand they recurrently exhibit basic ideas reminiscent of Deuteronomy. In view of this, we may appreciate Noth's attempt to explain the basic material from Deut. to Kings—considering it as without its later additions —on the assumption that an author influenced by D in the middle of the sixth century B.C. gathered together what were till then independently existing presentations of particular moments of Israel's history, extending from the events at Horeb down to his own time, and compiled them into a historical work, to some extent complete in itself, by the addition of reflections of a historico-theological kind. It is even more intelligible that this analysis of Josh.–Kings or of Deut.–Kings has met with much approval, and has driven into the background the assumption which was formerly very widely accepted, though admittedly not generally approved that Josh.–Kings or Josh.–Sam., or Josh.–Judges, or even Josh. alone represented a combination of the sequels of the Pentateuch sources in a Deuteronomistic edition. For the arguments which point to this assumption are at first somewhat elusive and certainly much less obvious than the very clear multifariousness of Josh.–Kings, which may, so it appears, be better explained on the basis of a 'fragment' hypothesis than of a documentary hypothesis. But the observations which point the other way nevertheless remain weighty, and we must therefore evaluate both the evidence and the attempts which have been built upon it to explain the present form of the books Josh.–Kings. This may appropriately be done by first taking a cursory glance at the history of these attempts.

4. *The analysis of Joshua–II Kings according to the documentary hypothesis.* It has been suggested that J and E—P does not come in for consideration here since it certainly does not continue beyond Josh.—continued not only into Josh., as was earlier generally assumed and as is still assumed today by the majority of those scholars who accept the Pentateuchal documentary hypothesis, but also into Judg.–Sam. or even into Judg.–Kings. This view was indeed put forward or at least hinted at even earlier, though in a rather different form, as for example by Schrader (1869)[5] and Eduard Meyer (1881),[6] and attempts at explaining these books as the result of the combination of two narrative strands, though these were not yet regarded as continuations of the Pentateuch or Hexateuch sources, go considerably further back still (pp. 269–70). But this view first attracted greater support when Cornill and Budde in their works of 1885, 1887 and 1890 had examined it in more detail and given it a sounder basis. The method of dividing the pre-deuteronomic content of Judg.–Kings between J and E which Budde undertook in his later works found considerable approval. For he maintained that 'historical writing in Israel began with the contemporary situation, soon after David, and then, gradually working backwards, eventually took up the traditions concerning the earliest times.'[7] Thus the earliest Yahwist (J^1)—and the position is similar with E—presents the history of Saul and David, a somewhat later one (J^2) the period of the judges,

---

[5] de Wette, *Lehrbuch der hist.-krit. Einl. in die . . . Bücher des AT* ([8]1869)—newly revised by Schrader, pp. 337 f., 349 f.

[6] 'Kritik der Berichte über die Eroberung Palaestinas' ZAW 1 (1881), pp. 117–46.

[7] *Das Buch der Richter* (KHC, 1897), p. XIV.

and other Yahwists, each about a generation later, present the one the period of Moses (J³), another that of the patriarchs (J⁴) and another the primeval period (J⁵). Thus, according to Budde, the J material of Gen.–Kings grew up in a period which extends from the end of the tenth century to towards the end of the eighth, and a similar situation applies to E, except that here the beginning and end of the process are somewhat later. Apart from a whole series of detailed observations, there are two presuppositions decisive here for Budde. The first is that historical writing in Israel, and that means J, must have begun with the period of Israel's glory, the days of David or Solomon, and must first have devoted itself to that period. The second is that the J content of the primeval history in Gen. i–xi, or at any rate substantial sections of it, is unthinkable before the eighth century B.C., since it reveals the influence of prophecy and of Babylonian-Assyrian mythology, both elements which can only then have assumed greater significance in Israel.

There has been no lack of opposition to the attempt to trace the older Penta-teuch or Hexateuch sources through into Kings. Particularly penetrating were the objections raised by Kittel, first in his essay of 1892, and repeated in later works, as for example in his treatment of Judg. and Sam. in the fourth edition of Kautzsch's translation of the Old Testament which appeared in 1922/3.[8] According to him, the basic material of the pre-deuteronomic books of Judg., Sam. and Kings is not made up of the combined continuations of the Hexateuch strands J and E, but consists in a variety of complexes of larger and smaller size: hero stories, royal stories, ark stories, prophet stories and the like. This means that it is the 'fragment' hypothesis and not the documentary hypothesis which is chosen as the guiding thread through the labyrinth of Judg.–Kings. It is true that Kittel does allow a certain weight to the conception which he rejects, in so far as he recognises that some of the hero stories in Judg. (H) and some of the royal stories in Sam. (K) are related to J or to E. He therefore provides them with the sigla HJ HE and KJ KE. Noth's opinion concerning the composition of Judg.–Kings, which has been discussed (pp. 243–4), and Rost's analysis of Sam., which has also already been mentioned (pp. 137–8), carry through further the way indicated by Kittel, though admittedly without laying any par-ticular stress on the point made by him regarding the relationship of some of the narratives from Judg. and Sam. with J and E. On the other hand, Benzinger and Hölscher have not been deterred by this opposition to the tracing of the basic material of Judg.–Kings from J and E, and have set forth a fresh analysis of that kind. Here Benzinger brings down the J narrative to the beginning of the reign of Hezekiah, i.e. to the end of the eighth century B.C., and E to the reign of Josiah, down to about 610 B.C., and regards them both as having also come into being then. Hölscher sees the conclusion of J in I Kings xii, 19, the statement of the lasting breakaway of Israel from the Davidic dynasty, and that of E in II Kings xxv, 27–30, the narrative of the favour shown to Jehoiachin by Evil-merodach in the year 561 B.C., and dates J more than a century after th date of the last event recorded by it, i.e. about 800 B.C., and E after 561 B.C.[9]

[8] *Die Heilige Schrift des AT*, 4th ed. by Bertholet, pp. 367–492.
[9] Cf. below, p. 298.

Whereas Hölscher and Benzinger, following their predecessors, apply the 'new documentary hypothesis' (pp. 164–6) to Judg.–Kings, there has been no lack of attempts to illuminate the composition of these books by means of the 'newest documentary hypothesis'. Bruston himself, the originator of this hypothesis (p. 169), made a start in that he endeavoured to trace the two Yahwists whom he found in the Hexateuch, through Judg.–Kings, and Smend and Eissfeldt have carried these attempts further. So too has Simpson, who finds in the pre-deuteronomic material not only of Judg., but also of I, II Sam. and I Kings i–xiii,[10] the same literary structure as in the pre-deuteronomic Hexateuch, namely J^1, J^2 and E, in which J^2 is a revision of J^1 not a strand parallel to it (p. 170). These scholars have not found much following in this, but there has at the same time been no full discussion of their point of view. Where an attempt at this has been made, as for example by Wiese, it gets no further than the negative statement made on p. 61 of his work of 1926: 'The assumption that two great presentations (J and E) covered the history of Israel from its beginnings (Genesis) until its final collapse (end of II Kings) is an exaggeration of the literary-critical system which is customarily named briefly after Wellhausen.' The position is rather, as we have already indicated, that the view of the books (Deut.) Josh.–Kings, represented especially by Noth, as a compilation, with additions, of many literary complexes till then independent and made by a Deuteronomistic author to be placed in about 550 B.C., has tacitly been put in the place of the older conception, till then at any rate in large measure normative, of the basic material of these books as a combination of the continuation of J and E.

5. *Features common to the two hypotheses.* Although these two views appear to be directly opposed to one another, they nevertheless have two things in common. In the first place, they both assign many sections, some substantial, in Judg.–Kings to a Deuteronomistic hand. What Noth assumes of the compiler of his Dtr corresponds very largely to what the others assign to the assumed Deuteronomistic editions of the basic JE material of these books. Here it is usual to reckon with not one but two editions of the pre-deuteronomistic material, and the attempt is thus made to explain a series of otherwise unintelligible duplicates. Although the phenomena which are here under review may perhaps be explained in another way, this explanation may nevertheless be regarded as the most probable. There is a second point which is held in common both by the analysis which reckons with a basic JE material for the books Josh.–Kings and the combining of two Deuteronomistic editions of this material, and the conception of Deut.–Kings as a Deuteronomistic historical work compiled about 550 B.C. This is the point that both views often assume that the Deuteronomistic redaction omitted on dogmatic grounds many of the older pieces of

---

[10] The analysis of I–II Sam., I Kings i–xiii, which Simpson proposes to make, according to p. 6 of his *Composition of the Book of Judges* (1957), has not yet appeared. But its results are anticipated there: 'The analysis of Judges . . . reveals the same literary structure as that of the Hexateuch . . . the J^1 stratum of material disappears from the narrative shortly after the account of David's transfer of his capital from Hebron to Jerusalem—a fact which favours the date suggested above for that document' viz., 'early in the reign of David' (p. 5).

material available, and that these were only later re-inserted. The sections which Noth regards as secondary (pp. 243–4) are largely identical with those of which Budde, for example, assumes that they originally had no place in the Deuteronomistic treatment of the basic material of Josh.–Kings, but were only later taken up again. If we may say of the first of these two points in common that it rests on conclusive arguments, we can however hardly maintain the second, and must replace it by a better explanation of the position occupied by those sections now in the books of Josh.–Kings which are adjudged to have come into the work secondarily.

6. *The limits of the two hypotheses.* The discussions just set out have made clear, further to what has already been said in § 18, the difficulties which face every analysis of Josh.–Kings or Judg.–Kings. This means that the expositions which follow in §§ 38 to 41 are largely of a hypothetical character, and indeed must be so. But the degree of probability which may be accorded to them nevertheless varies very much with regard to the individual suggestions there put forward. Thus the assumption that J, E and P (or L, J, E and P) continue in Josh., and narrate here the fulfilment of the promises of which they had spoken earlier, has a good deal more to be said for it than the view that P had no narrative of the occupation of the land at all, and that J and E have lost theirs, and so that the narrative of Josh., although it coincides in content fairly closely with what must have stood originally in J and E, may not on any account be used to reconstruct these documents. Further, the material of Judg.–Kings, without its Deuteronomistic sections, at first gives the impression of being a chaotic confusion of many independent pieces just loosely put together, but a closer investigation reveals that many of them are in fact parts of well constructed wholes which may be reconstructed in spite of certain gaps which cannot be filled. This possibility would be excluded if the 'chaos' which now appears to be present in Judg.–Kings had not been preceded by a 'cosmos', and it is thus proper to gather carefully the remnants of connected literary structures and to see whether they fit together; and if this is the case, to restore the contexts to which they once belonged. That there existed such comprehensive narrative works extending from the beginnings of Israel or even of mankind and the world down to the period of the narrator is made probable not only by the detailed observations which must be set out in §§ 38 to 41, but also by a consideration of a more general kind. As has already been suggested on p. 140, all the analogies suggest that Israelite historical writing began when Israel had reached or just passed its zenith, i.e. under or soon after David or Solomon; and that it did not restrict itself to the immediate present or to a section of the past closely connected with it, but presented the whole development of the people from its beginnings, linked with the beginning of the world and of mankind, right down to the contemporary scene. Since L, J and E (or J and E), as we have seen (pp. 194, 200 f.), are to be dated substantially earlier than was often done until recently, i.e.—at any rate this is true for L and J—in the tenth or ninth centuries B.C., there ceases to be any necessity to assume with Budde a gradual development of J and E extending over two centuries or more, or to consider that this development came to an end only in the eighth or seventh centuries B.C. This

is the more evident since we can see that the assumption which was decisive for Budde is untenable, namely that influences of Babylonian myths on the one hand and of 'prophetic' ideas on the other such as appear in many passages which are to be derived from J or E, could not have existed in an earlier period.

§ 38. THE BOOK OF JOSHUA

Literature: (a) Commentaries (i) Series: ATD: Hertzberg (²1959); BOuT: Alfrink (1952); Camb. B: Cooke (1913); CSS: Fernández (1938); Echter-B: Nötscher (1950); HAT: Noth (²1953); HK: Steuernagel (²1923); HS: Schulz (1924); HSAT: Holzinger (1922); IB: Bright, Sizoo (1953); Jerusalem-B: Abel, du Buit (²1958); KeH: Dillmann (²1886); KHC: Holzinger (1901); SAT: Gressmann (²1922); Soncino-B.: Freedman (1950); SZ: Öttli (1893); TU: de Groot (1931).

(ii) Single Commentaries: Kaufman(n), *The Book of Joshua with Commentary and Introduction* [Hebr.] (1959); Roussel (c. i–xii) (1955).

(b) Other literature: Aharoni, *The Settlement of the Israelite Tribes in Upper Galilee* [Hebr.] (1957); 'Problems of the Israelite Conquest in the Light of Archaeological Discoveries' Antiquity and Survival II, 2/3 (1957), pp. 131–50; 'Safed and Upper Galilee' IEJ 8 (1958), pp. 277–83; 'The Northern Boundary of Judah' PEQ 90 (1958), pp. 27–31; 'The Negeb of Judah' IEJ 8 (1958), pp. 26–38, Pls. 12–16; 'The Province-List of Judah' VT 9 (1959), pp. 225–46; Alt, 'Das System der Stammesgrenzen im Buche Josua' *Sellin-Festschr.* (1927), pp. 13–24 = *Kl. Schr.* I, pp. 193–202; 'Josua' BZAW 66 (1936), pp. 13–29 = *Kl. Schr.* I, pp. 176–92; Bach, 'Zur Siedlungsgeschichte des Talkessels von Samaria' ZDPV 74 (1958), pp. 41–54; Bar-Derōmā', *The True Boundaries of the Holy Land according to the Sources* [Hebr.] (1958); Cross and Wright, 'The Boundary and Province Lists of the Kingdom of Judah' JBL 75 (1956), pp. 202–26; Eva Danelius, 'The Boundary of Ephraim and Manasse in the Western Plain' PEQ 89 (1957), pp. 55–67; 90 (1958), pp. 32–43, 122–44; Dornseiff, 'Die antike Mimesis in der altvorderasiatischen Literatur' ZDMG 93 (1939), pp. 296–305 = *Kl. Schr.* I (²1959), pp. 330–9; Eissfeldt, 'Die Eroberung Palästinas durch Altisrael' WdO II, 2 (1955), pp. 158–71; Garstang, *Joshua, Judges* (1931); Goff, 'The Lost Jahwistic Account of the Conquest of Canaan' JBL 53 (1934), pp. 241–9; Jenni, 'Historisch-topographische Untersuchungen zur Grenze zwischen Ephraim und Manasse' ZDPV 74 (1958), pp. 35–40; Kallai (-Kleinmann), 'The Town Lists of Judah, Simeon, Benjamin and Dan' VT 8 (1958), pp. 134–60; *The Northern Boundaries of Judah from the Settlement of the Tribes until the Beginning of the Hasmonaean Period* [Hebr., Engl. sum.] (1960); 'Note on the Town Lists of Judah, Simeon, Benjamin and Dan' VT 11 (1961), pp. 223–7; Karmon, 'Geographical Conditions in the Sharon Plain and their Impact on its Settlement' [Hebr., Engl. sum.] BIES 23 (1959), pp. 111–33, I–III; Kaufman(n), *The Biblical Account of the Conquest of Palestine* (1953); on this cf. Alt, 'Utopien' ThLZ 81 (1956), cols. 521–8; 'Traditions concerning Early Israelite History in Canaan' Scripta Hieros. 8 (1961), pp. 303–34; Malamat, 'External Sources for the Conquest of Palestine' in *Studies in the Book of Joshua* [Hebr.] (1960), pp. 187–219; Margolis, *The Book of Joshua in Greek* I–IV (1931–38); Mazar, 'The Cities of the Territory of Dan' IEJ 10 (1960), pp. 65–77; Möhlenbrink, 'Die Landnahmesagen des Buches Josua' ZAW 56 (1938), pp. 238–68; Mowinckel, *Zur Frage nach dokumentarischen Quellen in Josua xiii–xix* (1946); Noth, 'Überlieferungsgeschichtliches zur zweiten Hälfte des Josuabuches' *Nötscher-Festschr.* (1950), pp. 152–67; Wright, 'The Literary and Historical Problem of Joshua x and Judges i' JNESt 5 (1946), pp. 105–14.

Cf. also Literature §§ 37, 126.

1. *Contents.* The book of Joshua divides naturally into two approximately equal parts, in that i–xii deal with the conquest and xiii–xxiv with the division of the land of Canaan. The first half relates how Joshua made preparations after Moses' death for the crossing of the Jordan (i). The spies in the meantime successfully escaped the danger which threatened them at Jericho to which they had been sent, and brought a report to Joshua (ii).[1] Three days later, the Jordan was crossed to the accompaniment of marvels, while twelve stones were taken from the middle of the Jordan or from its eastern bank and these stones are to be found set up on the western bank or in the middle of Jordan (iii–iv). At the first halting place, Gilgal, the Israelites were circumcised. Here they celebrated the Passover, and here the appearance of a heavenly being made Joshua aware of the sacredness of the place (v).[2] The first fortress which fell into the hands of Israel assisted by miraculous divine action, was Jericho (vi),[3] but the enterprise, seemingly not arduous, against the fortress of Ai, north-west of Jericho, failed because an Israelite named Achan took for himself some of the property plundered in Jericho, against the command of Yahweh. So the enterprise succeeded only after this guilt had been removed from Israel, and the criminal had been executed (vii, 1–viii, 29). On Mount Ebal[4] Joshua erected an altar according to the command of Moses, made sacrifices there, wrote the law of Moses on stones and read it out to the Israelites (viii, 30–5).[5] The Gibeonites, however, terrified by the conquest of Jericho and Ai,[6] by the employment of a stratagem succeeded in getting Joshua to make a treaty with them so that he could not touch them (ix). The Canaanite kings of the southern region, including Japhia of Lachish,[7] marched under the leadership of Adoni-zedek of Jerusalem against Gibeon which had been disloyal to their cause, and were annihilated by Joshua at Gibeon, so that southern Canaan now lay open to Israel (x).[8] Similarly a coalition under the leadership of Jabin of

[1] Graf Reventlow, ' "Sein Blut komme über sein Haupt" ' VT 10 (1960), pp. 311–27: on ii, 19.

[2] George, 'Les récits de Gilgal en Josué v, 2–15' *Mémorial Chaine* (1950), pp. 169–86; Kelso and Baramki, *Excavations at New Testament Jericho and Khirbet En-Nitla* (AASOR XXIX–XXX, 1955); Kraus, 'Gilgal—ein Beitrag zur Kultusgeschichte Israels' VT 1 (1951), pp. 181–99; 'Zur Geschichte des Passah-Massot-Festes im AT' EvTh 18 (1958), pp. 47–67; Muilenburg, 'The Site of Ancient Gilgal' BASOR 140 (1955), pp. 11–27.

[3] Astour, 'Benê-Iamina et Jéricho' Semitica 9 (1959), pp. 5–20; Braidwood, 'Jericho and its Setting in Near Eastern History' Antiquity 31 (1957), pp. 73–81; Garstang, *The Story of Jericho* (²1948); Kathleen M. Kenyon, 'Excavations at Jericho' 1957–8, PEQ 92 (1960), pp. 88–113, Pls. VI–XII; *Jericho* I (1960). Lit. § 126.

[4] Cf. above, p. 216, n. 9.   [5] Cf. above, pp. 216 f.

[6] Judith Marquet-Krause, *Les Fouilles de 'Ay (Et-Tell) 1933–1935* (BAH XLV, 1949); Noth, 'Bethel und Ai' PJB 31 (1935), pp. 7–29. Lit. § 126.

[7] *The Wellcome Archaeological Research Expedition to the Near East Publications: Lachish (Tell ed Duweir)* I (1938), II (1940), III (1953), IV (1958).

[8] Elliger, 'Beeroth und Gibeon' ZDPV 73 (1957), pp. 125–32; Lambert, 'Josué à la bataille de Gabaon' NRTh 76 (1954), pp. 374–91; Pritchard, 'The Water System at Gibeon' BA 19 (1956), pp. 66–75; 'Discovery of the Biblical Gibeon' University Mus. Bull. Philadelphia 21 (1957), pp. 3–26; 22 (1958), pp. 12–24; *Hebrew Inscriptions and Stamps from Gibeon* (1959), on this cf. Avigad, 'Some Notes on the Hebrew Inscriptions from Gibeon' IEJ 9 (1959), pp. 130–3; 'Industry and Trade at Biblical Gibeon' BA 23 (1960), pp. 1, 23–9; 'Gibeon's History in the Light of Excavation' SVT VII (1960), pp. 1–12; ILN 229 (1956), pp. 695–7; 232 (1958), pp. 505–7, 237 (1960), pp. 433–5, 518 f.; 'A Bronze Age Necropolis at Gibeon' BA 24 (1961), pp. 19–24. Lit. p. 251, n. 12; p. 281, n. 45; p. 675, n. 13; § 126.

Hazor[9] of the kings of northern Canaan was broken by Joshua at the waters of Merom,[10] so that the north too was delivered into Israel's power (xi). A list of the Canaanite kings defeated by Israel (xii) concludes the first half of the book.

xiii–xix then relate the allocation of West Jordan to the $9\frac{1}{2}$ tribes and of East Jordan to the $2\frac{1}{2}$ (Reuben, Gad and half Manasseh). Subsequently, in the analysis, we must say something about how that is done (p. 253). In xx there is added to the division of the land the establishing of cities of refuge,[11] and in xxi, cities for the Priests and Levites. Now that the allocation and what is related to it has been disposed of, the $2\frac{1}{2}$ East Jordan tribes are allowed to go, with thanks for the help they have given west of Jordan. They build an altar at first felt to be illegitimate by the other tribes, but then recognised as a simple token of adherence to Yahweh (xxii). Two farewell speeches by Joshua (xxiii, xxiv) conclude the book.

2. *Analysis.* The book of Joshua tells of the fulfilment of the promise, repeatedly made to the fathers, that the land of Canaan should fall to their descendants (Gen. xiii, 14–17; xv, 7, 18; xvii, 8; xxvi, 3–4 etc.), and in this respect it is united in content with the Pentateuch. But there is more to it than this. The individual narrative strands combined in it are also connected in style with the Pentateuch, in other words with the narrative strands there combined. So the joining together of the five books of Moses and the book of Joshua as the 'Hexateuch' is not merely justified, but is indeed essential for the recognition of the present state of the material. Furthermore, the basic observations made with reference to Pentateuchal criticism (§§ 22–36) apply also to the book of Joshua and need not be here repeated. What we do need, however, is the proof that the assumption of the continuation of the Pentateuch sources in the book of Joshua, which follows so readily from general considerations and from

[9] Albright, 'Recent Progress in Palestinian Archaeology: Samaria-Sebaste III and Hazor I' BASOR 150 (1958), pp. 21–5; Avi Yonah, 'Ten Years of Archaeology in Israel' IEJ 8 (1958), pp. 52–65, see pp. 55 f.; Maass, 'Hazor und das Problem der Landnahme' BZAW 77 (1958), pp. 105–17; Malamat, 'Hazor "The Head of all those Kingdoms"' JBL 79 (1960), pp. 12–19; North, 'Hasôr illustrat Megiddo et Jericho' Bibl 37 (1956), pp. 398–9; Yadin, 'Excavations at Hazor' BA 19 (1956), pp. 2–12; 'Further Light on Biblical Hazor. Results of the Second Season, 1956' BA 20 (1957), pp. 33–47; 'Some Aspects of the Material Culture of Northern Israel during the Canaanite and Israelite Periods in the Light of Excavations at Hazor' Antiquity and Survival II, 3/4 (1957), pp. 165–86; 'The Fourth Season of Excavations at Hazor' BA 22 (1959), pp. 1–20; 'Excavations at Hazor, 1955' IEJ 6 (1956), pp. 120–5, Pls. 15–20; 'Excavations at Hazor, 1956' IEJ 7 (1957), pp. 118–23, Pls. 27–32; 'Excavations at Hazor, 1957' IEJ 8 (1958), pp. 1–14, 68, Pls. 1–9; 'Excavations at Hazor, 1958' IEJ 9 (1959), pp. 74–88, Pls. 6–13; 'Three Years of Excavations at Hazor (1955–1957)' BiOr 16 (1959), pp. 1–11, Pls. I–IV; ILN 229 (1956), pp. 951–3, 990–3; 232 (1958), pp. 633–5, 730–3; 234 (1959), pp. 479–81, 527–9; Yadin, etc., *Haẓor I. An Account of the First Season of Excavations, 1955* (1958); *Haẓor II. An Account of the Second Season of Excavations, 1956* (1960); Yeivin, 'The Israelite Settlement in Galilee and the Wars with Jabin of Hazor' *Mél. Bibl. Robert* (1957), pp. 95–104. Lit. § 126.

[10] Tur-Sinai, 'How far extended the Fighting against the Kings of Canaan following the Battle at the Waters of Merom?' [Hebr., Engl. sum.] BIES 24 (1959/60), pp. 33–5, IV–V. Lit. § 126.

[11] Boger, 'The City of Refuge Bezer' [Hebr., Engl. sum.] BIES 22 (1958), pp. 91–4, VII; David, 'Die Bestimmungen über die Asylstädte in Jos. xx' OTS 9 (1951), pp. 30–48; Dinur, 'The Religious Character of the Cities of Refuge and the Ceremony of Admission into Them' [Hebr., Engl. sum.] Eretz-Israel 3 (1954), pp. 135–46, VIII–IX. Literature, p. 251, n. 16.

detailed points which show the relatedness of the book of Joshua with the Pentateuch, really does hold good.

If we begin, as with the Pentateuch, with the entity which is most readily recognised, namely P, this may here too be separated out relatively easily. But this produces a remarkable picture, namely that its linguistic features are only to be detected in a very few places in i–xii, whereas in xiii–xxiv, or more precisely in xiii–xxi, they may be found in large sections. Within i–xii, only the date in iv, 19, together with v, 10–12* and some phrases in ix, 15–27[12] can be regarded as pointers to P. But these passages may equally well stem from the hand of an elaborator writing in the style of P, just as P influence of this kind may also be found in passages which do not themselves belong to P, as for example in Judg. xx (p. 267). In view of the paucity of the P material which can actually be separated out of i–xii, this assumption is more natural than the deriving of these little pieces from P. When we consider xiii–xxi, this assumption may be taken to be a certainty. In actual fact only a small part of xiii, 1–14 may be assigned to P. For this section, apart from a few JE sentences, consists of material which does not belong to the main sources. To this there belongs also the mention of areas which did not immediately fall into the hands of the Israelites, including the five Philistine territories of Gaza, Ashdod, Ashkelon, Gath and Ekron.[13] P begins at xiii, 15–33, with the allocation of East Jordan[14] to the 2½ tribes by Moses, and then links with this in xiv, 1–5*, xv*,[15] xvi*, xvii, 1–11*;[16] xviii, 11–29*; xix*, the allocation of West Jordan to the 9½ tribes, and finally relates the setting aside of the cities of refuge and the Levitical cities (xx–xxi*). Here xiii, 15, which is to be restored following ⑤, has the style of a list, like xiv, 1: *These are the inheritances which Moses gave* etc., and not the style of a narrative. It is very remarkable that there should be a statement of the allocation of East Jordan by Moses after his death has been related by P in

[12] Haran, 'The Gibeonites, the Nethinim and the Sons of Solomon's Servants' VT 11 (1961), pp. 159–69. Lit. p. 249, n. 8; § 126.

[13] Naveh, 'Khirbat al-Muqanna'—Ekron: An Archaeological Survey' IEJ 8 (1958), pp. 87–100, 165–70.

[14] Funk and Richardson, 'The 1958 Sounding at Pella' BA 21 (1958), pp. 82–96; Gese, 'Ammonitische Grenzfestungen zwischen *wādi es-ṣīr* und *nā-'ūr*' ZDPV 74 (1958), pp. 55–64, Pls. 3–4; Hentschke, Ammonitische Grenzfestungen südwestlich von '*ammān*' ZDPV 76 (1960), pp. 103–23, Pls. 11–12; Noth, 'Gilead und Gad' ZDPV 75 (1959), pp. 14–73. Lit. § 126.

[15] Cross, 'A Footnote to Biblical History' BA 19 (1956), pp. 12–17; Cross and Milik, 'Explorations in the Judaean Buqê'ah' BASOR 142 (1956), pp. 5–16; Driver, 'Problems of Interpretation in the Heptateuch' *Mél. Bibl. Robert* (1957), pp. 66–76, see pp. 72–6: IV. On Achsah's Disgust (Jos. xv, 18; Jud. i, 14) and Siserah's Death (Jud. iv, 21); Funk, 'The 1957 Campaign at Beth-zur' BASOR 150 (1958), pp. 1–20; Paul and Nancy Lapp, 'A Comparative Study of a Hellenistic Pottery Group from Beth-zur' BASOR 151 (1958), pp. 16–27; North, 'Three Judean Hills in Josue xv, 9 f.' Bibl 37 (1956), pp. 209–16; Noth, 'Lehrkursus 1954' ZDPV 71 (1955), pp. 1–59, see pp. 42–55; 'Der at. Name der Siedlung auf *chirbet ḳumrān*' ib. pp. 111–23; Sellers, 'The 1957 Campaign at Beth-zur' BA 21 (1958), pp. 71–6; Sellers and Albright, 'The First Campaign of Excavation at Beth-zur' BASOR 43 (1931), pp. 2–13; *The Citadel of Beth-ẓur* (1933). Cf. p. 532, n. 8.

[16] Schunck, 'Ophra, Ephron and Ephraim' VT 11 (1961), pp. 188–200; Simons, 'The Structure and Interpretation of Josh. xvi–xvii' Orient. Neerl. (1948), pp. 190–215; Zaphrir, (Frimorgen), 'Even Three Countries' [Hebr., Engl. sum.] BJPES 14 (1947/9), pp. 93–7, II: on Josh. xvii, 11, Judg. i, 27, I Chron. vii, 29. Lit. § 126.

Deut. xxxiv. The point may, however, be readily explained if in P nothing was related between Deut. xxxiv and Josh. xiii, 15, and so the additional matter follows very soon. The subsequent addition of this material may be explained from the fact that P wished to have the allocation of the whole land, east and west, together, and the reason for this again is that P, as has already often been stressed (pp. 206 f.), does not really offer narrative for its own sake, but a programme of demands concealed in the form of narrative. The enumeration of the areas allocated to the single tribes, which does not by chance begin in the form of a list, is basically the same as is offered at the end of the book of Ezekiel (xlviii, 1–29) in the form of a plan for the allocation of the land, namely a programme for the hoped-for future of Israel now scattered in exile. Thus P concludes with this programme of allocation of land, and with the setting aside of the cities of refuge and the Levitical cities (xx–xxi)[17] which forms an appendix to it. It has no final speech by Joshua, and never did have any such speech. After xxi no further trace of P can be found. Even if there is much in xxii[18] which is reminiscent of P, what we have here is the influence of P's linguistic usage, as in the passages already mentioned in i–xii, but not P itself.

If P is thus absent from the analysis of i–xii, we must then ask how the composition of this first half of the book is to be described. Here we may first leave on one side the sections which clearly go back to a Deuteronomistic hand (see pp. 255–6). The material which remains is anything but unified. In particular the narratives of the crossing of the Jordan (iii–iv) and of the conquest of Jericho give the impression of being much overloaded, and this is not relieved by the assumption of two parallel narratives—quite apart from the impossibility of explaining all the repetitions and contradictions as glosses or annotations or the like. The difficulty is, however, lessened if we endeavour to explain it as a combining of *three* narratives. This may be demonstrated in detail only by minute examination of the text. A few indications of this three-stranded form are, however, quite obvious. The narrative of the preparations undertaken by Joshua for the crossing of the Jordan in i, which is reminiscent of E and so must be derived from E, finds its sequel—so it is generally agreed—after ii in iii, 2. ii, however, the narrative of the spies sent to Jericho,[19] is itself equally clearly made up of two parallel narratives, which may be assigned to L and J. Thus i–iii proves to be a combination of three strands, and these continue through iii–vii. We may here simply draw attention in iii–iv[20] to the narrative

---

[17] Albright (§ 4c); Alt, 'Bemerkungen zu einigen judäischen Ortslisten des AT' ZDPV 68 (1951), pp. 193–210 = *Kl. Schr.* II (1953), pp. 289–305; du Buit, 'Quelques contacts bibliques dans les archives royales de Mari' RB 66 (1959), pp. 576–81, see pp. 577–80; Haran, 'The Levitical Cities: Utopia and Historical Reality' [Hebr., Engl. sum.] Tarbiz 27 (1957/8), pp. 421–39 I–II; 'Studies in the Account of the Levitical Cities' I, JBL 80 (1961), pp. 45–54; II, *ib.* pp. 156–65; Klein, 'The Cities of the Priests and Levites and the Cities of Refuge' [Hebr.] JJPES 3 (1934/5), pp. 81–107; Mazar, 'The Cities of the Priests and the Levites' SVT VII (1960), pp. 193–205. Literature, p. 250, n. 11.

[18] Menes, 'Tempel und Synagoge' ZAW 50 (1932), pp. 268–76.

[19] Abel, 'L'anathème de Jéricho et la Maison de Rahab' RB 57 (1950), pp. 321–30. Cf. p. 249, n. 3.

[20] Alfrink, 'De litteraire compositie van Jos iii en iv' StC 18 (1942), pp. 185–202; Dus, 'Die Analyse zweier Ladeerzählungen des Josuabuches (Jos. iii–iv und vi)' ZAW 72

of the passage of the Jordan to the fact that the taking of twelve stones[21] is ordered three times: iv, 3 *from here* = from the eastern bank (J); iv, 3 *from the middle of Jordan* (L); and iv, 5 from the *middle of the Jordan* (E); and that the setting up of the stones is also dealt with three times: iv, 8 *at the halting place* (L); iv, 9 *in the middle of Jordan* (J); iv, 20 *in Gilgal* (E). From viii onwards the overloading is less, and here the material divides itself without difficulty between two parallel strands, which reveal themselves to be J and E. In i–vii, i.e. up to the conquest of Jericho, including its sequel culminating in the execution of Achan, L, J and E thus run in general parallel to one another; from viii onwards, however, J and E alone appear. This result of the analysis of i–xii in its turn, as we shall see, finds its confirmation and explanation in xiii–xxiv and in the opening of the book of Judges (p. 254) which must here also be taken into account.

In the narrative of the allocation of the land (xiii–xix), without the P material already described, there may in fact be recognised two strands, difficult though the analysis is in detail, i.e. a combination of J and E. In particular xvii, 14–xviii, 10, can only be understood as such a combination. J and E are here as elsewhere very similar to one another, and both differ from P in that the latter treats the 9½ tribes all on a level (xiv, 1–2 etc.), whereas the former first assign their territory to Judah and Joseph and only then take account of the remaining 7 tribes. But J may now be distinguished from E by the following points. According to J, to which appear to belong the sections in Judg. i, 5–7, 10–15, 16b, 19, 23–6, now removed from their original position in order to be combined with the L material in Judg. i, Judah and Joseph, and presumably the other tribes too, have still to fight for their land; but in E it falls to them without a struggle (xi, 23b). Furthermore J mentions gaps in the conquest which E no longer seems to know. In both these points J is related to the L narrative, and thus reveals itself here as elsewhere as standing between L and E.

With vii, as we have seen, all trace of L disappears, and the further narrative is a combination of J and E, if we disregard the P material. In xxiv, the farewell speech of Joshua generally agreed to be from E at least so far as its main material is concerned, there appear to be a few points which suggest that L also makes a contribution. However, these points are too indistinct for it to be possible to base much upon them. It is all the more clear that in Judg. i, 1–ii, 5*, a report on the conquest of Canaan is present which runs parallel to the second half of the book of Joshua, and the question is immediately appropriate as to whether perhaps L, having disappeared at Josh. vii, may not be recognised here. This possibility is all the more worth considering since Judg. i, 1, *And it came to pass after the death of Joshua* places the section i, 1–ii, 5*, in a broader context, and this section joins on precisely where the trace of L in Josh. vii disappeared. In Josh. vii, Israel is still in Jericho, or more exactly, since Jericho has been completely destroyed, in Gilgal, and in Judg. i, 16, the Kenites with the Judaeans break out from the city of palm-trees, i.e. Jericho, while according to ii, 1,

(1960), pp. 107–34; Saydon, 'The Crossing of the Jordan; Jos. chaps iii and iv' CBQ 12 (1950), pp. 194–207.

[21] Seitz, ' "What do these Stones mean?" ' JBL 79 (1960), pp. 247–54.

the angel of Yahweh, in other words probably the Ark, goes up from Gilgal to Bochim near Bethel. We cannot possibly alter the phrase *after the death of Joshua* in Judg. i, 1, into *after the death of Moses.* For Judg. i, 1–ii, 5*, depicts the Israelites as in Gilgal, and thus clearly takes place in West Jordan, and this is a situation which could not on any account be indicated by the reference *after the death of Moses.* The only solution is that here a narrative is presupposed in which Joshua dies in Gilgal, and nothing stands in the way of the assumption that L narrated the matter thus, especially since there are also indications elsewhere that L presents Joshua, not as does J and particularly clearly E (Exod. xxxiii, 11; Num. xi, 28), as a member of the generation following on Moses, but as a contemporary of Moses (Exod. xvii, 8–16, cf. xxxii, 17–18). Thus it is only natural for L to make Joshua die shortly after Moses. If L really has a share in Josh. xxiv, then we should have there the remains of the farewell speech which Joshua gave before his death in Gilgal. That Judg. i, 1–ii, 5*, does belong to L is, however, in any case very probable, and it corresponds excellently with L's relationship to J and E elsewhere that L here with its 'negative account of the conquest', i.e. with the recognition of the incompleteness of the first conquest, is by far the most archaic, and in this case no doubt is also the most credible. That the figure of Joshua has attracted more and more to itself of what cannot really belong to the historical Joshua, simply corresponds to the law, observable everywhere in history, that great men tend to attract material, and this is also confirmed in the Old Testament itself. Thus the victory over Jabin of Hazor in Josh. xi is ascribed to Joshua by E, whereas in Judg. iv, it is apparently assigned by J to Barak, and we can hardly doubt that this latter tradition is to be preferred. We shall have to wait to see whether the results of the excavation of Hazor[22] will contribute anything really decisive to the solution of the historical problems of Judg. iv[23] and Josh. xi.

The analysis of the book of Joshua + Judg. i, 1–ii, 5, thus leads to the separation out of the four strands L, J, E and P. This is of particular importance because it offers a clearer reflection of the conceptions which were held concerning the course of events in the times from which the sources come than could be the case in the material of the Pentateuch which is to a much higher degree legendary. And this shows that the later a source is, the more it is remote from the actual happenings, and pictures them as it was thought they ought to have taken place. According to L, Joshua carries out in West Jordan only one campaign against Jericho. Then he dies and leaves the task of conquest to the tribes working in two groups under the leadership of Judah and Joseph. But these tribes can at first carry out the conquest only very partially, since the fortified cities of the Canaanites offer successful resistance to them. In J and E, Joshua overthrows the Canaanites of the south and north in two great battles after the conquest of Jericho, and he can now himself undertake the allocation of the land. This is carried out—no doubt with an echo of the older point of view of L, where Judah and Joseph undertake the conquest—in such a way that

[22] Cf. p. 250, n. 9.
[23] Zimbalist, 'Kishon and Kishiôn' [Hebr., Engl. sum.] BJPES 13 (1946/7), pp. 28–32 III: on iv, 7, 13.

Judah and Joseph first receive their portion, and then the remainder is allotted
to the remaining seven tribes. Here again are the characteristic differences
between J and E, which make J appear older than E (p. 253). P relates nothing
at all concerning the conquest, no doubt with the idea that the land must fall
without a struggle to the people to whom it should belong according to the will
of God. P prefers to join immediately to the allocation of East Jordan undertaken by Moses, the allocation of West Jordan by *the priest Eleazar, Joshua and
the tribal leaders* (xiv, 1b), in which the decisive influence accorded to the priest
must not be overlooked.

3. *Deuteronomistic editions of the book.* The analysis of the book of Joshua is
not completed with the sorting out of the four narrative strands and their
description. In addition to some larger and smaller isolated insertions which have
the style of P (p. 251), and are therefore relatively late, there is a series of sections
which in their present form are certainly of Deuteronomistic origin, though so
far as their content is concerned they no doubt represent in part older material.
(This is particularly true of the lists of conquered kings and cities in x, 16–43;
xi, 10–xii, 24.) The Deuteronomistic material is in i, 3–9, 12–18; x, 16–43; xi,
10–xii, 24; xxiii etc. It is noteworthy that among these too there are duplicates,
and this is the more significant since, if we again consider the book of Joshua
as including the opening of the book of Judges, we have two conclusions
parallel to one another. Of them the first is almost entirely Deuteronomistic,
while the latter bears at least traces of Deuteronomistic editing: Josh. xxiii
+ Judg. ii, 6–9, for the first, and Josh. xxiv, 1–Judg. ii, 5, for the second. Fairly
generally the position is explained—and indeed it can hardly be explained
differently—as due to the older book of Joshua made up of L + J + E having
undergone two Deuteronomistic editions which have then been combined. The
first of these two editions preserved the material of Josh. xxiv[24] + Judg. i; ii, 1a,
5b, deriving predominantly from E and L and was content to add a few Deuteronomistic expressions, of which that in Judg. ii, 1b–5a, is particularly interesting.
It traces back the incompleteness of the conquest, quite neutrally related by L in
Judg. i, to the sin of Israel, and in this way makes this divergent section serve
the Deuteronomistic bias—a good example of the neutralising of material to
which we have already referred more than once (pp. 222 f., 240). The point is
entirely ignored that there is material in Judg. i which completely contradicts
the presentation of Josh. xiii–xix, and the actual content of the chapter is a
matter of indifference to the Deuteronomistic editor. He uses the narrative
simply as the starting-point of a penitential sermon. The other editor replaced
the farewell speech of Joshua in Josh. xxiv, 1–27, by one of his own, xxiii, and
to this attached immediately the dismissal of the people and the death of Joshua
(Judg. ii, 6–9).

We have already seen, in dealing with Deuteronomy, that it is probable that
its present form is to be explained as the result of the combination of two editions of the original Deuteronomy (p. 232). It is therefore natural to ask whether
the two editions of the book of Joshua which we have just discovered, may not

[24] Wüst, 'Amphiktyonie, Eidgenossenschaft, Symmachie', Historia 3 (1954–5), pp.
129–53. Lit. § 126.

come from the same hands as the two editions of Deuteronomy, and thus may be their sequels. There is much to be said for this assumption. It is also supported by the fact that the narrative of the last hours or days of Moses in Deut. xxxi–xxxiv, which otherwise belongs to the older Hexateuch sources and to P, also reveals a good deal of Deuteronomistic material (see p. 230). It is true that we cannot get complete certainty here, and we shall have to come back to this question more than once in considering the books of Judges, Samuel and Kings (pp. 267, 280, 299 f.).

4. *Separation from the Pentateuch.* A word must be said finally concerning the fact, remarkable in view of the close linkage between the Pentateuch narrative and that of the book of Joshua, that the work was divided and that the book of Joshua now stands as a separate entity beside the Pentateuch. The reason for this is plain enough. Canonical recognition was accorded first to the Torah, the Law, and this comes to an end with the end of the Pentateuch, or strictly speaking a few chapters earlier. But the law-giver, or rather mediator of the law, Moses, belongs most closely with the law, and it is therefore quite natural that the narratives concerning his death were reckoned as belonging to the Torah. It is possible to determine with at least some precision when this separation of the Pentateuch took place. The two Deuteronomistic editions of the book of Joshua must have come into existence not so very long after 621 B.C., even if they were not continuations of the two editions of the original Deuteronomy, and at any rate before the incorporation of P in the Hexateuch. At that stage the separation between the Pentateuch and Joshua had not been made. Nor can it have taken place when P was united with the older material. For P combined its plan for the allocation of the land with the older Hexateuch, and this could hardly have happened if at that time the Torah already formed a separate entity. On the other hand, the emergence of the Samaritan schism already presupposes the division. For the Samaritans, who till then had been associated with the Judaean religious community, took over from this association as their sacred book only the Pentateuch. Admittedly the date of this schism is very uncertain: its dating varies between 400 and 60 B.C.[25]

Other considerations lead to a more precise fixing of the canonising of the Pentateuch. In the first place it is certain that it was not a matter of chance, but was decreed or decided at a definite historical moment. Now we know of such a moment, and its date lies between the two events just mentioned as the upper and lower limits. This is the reorganisation of Judaism on the basis of a divine law carried through at the instigation of a king of Persia, probably Artaxerxes II (404–359) (Ezr. vii, 14). This law, recognised as authoritative by the Persian king with, of course, the co-operation of Jewish experts, is likely to have been the Pentateuch deliberately detached from its sequel in the book of Joshua. For the purpose which the Persian king had in mind this separation must have appeared essential. The book of Joshua also contained, as we have seen, a narrative concerning the allocation of the land to the twelve tribes, and this was

[25] Bright, *A History of Israel* (1959), pp. 391–4; Hölscher, *Gesch. d. isr. u. jüd. Rel.* (1922), pp. 170–3; Noth, *Geschichte Israels* ([5]1961), pp. 317–21, E.T. *History of Israel* ([2]1960), pp. 351–6. Lit. § 126.

certainly understood by the exilic Jews as a programme for the hoped-for future—and was clearly so intended from the outset by P too. The reconstitution of the Jewish religious community by the two men, Nehemiah and Ezra, acting on the commission of the Persian government, signified, however, a deliberate surrender of the hopes of a return of the ancient Davidic kingdom which were still very much alive in the time of Haggai and Zechariah, Zerubbabel and Joshua (pp. 426 f., 433), and a decisive limitation to a community life under Persian authority within narrow bounds.[26] The book of Joshua thus did not fit into the document which was to be the basis of the reconstructed community. Whether we may go further and apply the narrative of Neh. viii–x to the solemn canonising of the Pentateuch may for the moment remain undecided (pp. 556 f.). The limiting of the documents of the covenant to the Pentateuch was in any case undertaken already by Ezra who was committed to the consideration of both Jewish and Persian internal and external interests, and this was done in about 400 B.C.

§ 39. THE BOOK OF JUDGES

Literature: (a) Commentaries (i) Series: ATD: Hertzberg ([2]1959); BOuT: de Fraine (1956); Camb. B: Cooke (1913); EB: Lagrange (1903); Echter-B: Nötscher (1950); EH: Zapletal (1923); HK: Nowack (1902); HS: Schulz (1926); HSAT: Kittel (1922); IB: Myers, Elliott (1953); ICC: Moore ([2]1898 (1949)); Jerusalem-B: Vincent ([2]1958); KeH: Bertheau ([2]1883); KHC: Budde (1897); SAT: Gressmann ([2]1922); Soncino-B: Slotki (1950); SZ: Öttli (1893).

(ii) Single Commentaries: Burney ([2]1920).

(b) Other Literature: Auerbach, 'Untersuchungen zum Richterbuch' ZAW 48 (1930), pp. 286–95; 51 (1933), pp. 47–51; Dornseiff, 'Das Buch Richter' AfO 14 (1941/44), pp. 319–28 = *Kl. Schr*. I ([2]1959), pp. 340–63; Jenni, 'Vom Zeugnis des Richterbuches' ThZ 12 (1956), pp. 257–74; Muntingh, 'The Period of the Judges' OuTWP (1959), pp. 29–34; Oberholzer, 'Geografiese Terme in die Rigtersboek en hulle Vertaling' OuTWP (1959), pp. 35–40; O'Doherty, 'The Literary Problem of Judges i, 1–iii, 6' CBQ 18 (1956), pp. 1–7; Robertson, 'The Period of the Judges' BJRL 30 (1946), pp. 91–114; Rudolph, 'Textkritische Anmerkungen zum Richterbuch' *Eissfeldt-Festschr*. (1947), pp. 199–212; Schreiner, *Septuaginta-Massora des Buches der Richter* (An Bibl 7, 1957); Täubler, *Biblische Studien I: Die Epoche der Richter*, ed. by H.-J. Zobel (1958); van Zyl, 'The Relationship of the Israelite Tribes to the Indigenous Population of Canaan according to the Book of Judges' OuTWP (1959), pp. 51–60; 'The Message Formula in the Book of Judges' OuTWP (1959), pp. 61–4; Vollborn, 'Die Chronologie des Richterbuches' *Baumgärtel-Festschr*. (1959), pp. 192–6.

Cf. also Literature §§ 5, 18, 22–32, 37, 38, 126.

1. *Contents.* We have already seen that i, 1–ii, 9, ought to be assigned to the book of Joshua, and clearly was only taken as the beginning of a new book because it begins in i, 1, with *And it came to pass after the death of Joshua* (pp. 242, 253). But in reality ii, 10–iii, 6, also, apart from the Deuteronomistic survey of the period of the judges in ii, 11–19, belongs to the book of Joshua

[26] Procksch, *Das Bekenntnis im AT* (1936).

K

and not to the book of Judges. For here we are concerned with the motive which led Yahweh not to give complete success to the battles of Joshua or of the first generation of the conquerors, but still to leave in and around Canaan some peoples hostile to Israel. The real judge narratives begin only at iii, 7, and extend to xvi, 31. There then follow, properly denoted as 'appendices' to the book of Judges, two narratives, one concerning the theft of cult objects by the Danites in xvii and xviii, and the other concerning the outrage at Gibeah and its punishment in xix to xxi.[1]

2. *The framework of the Judge-narratives and its religious and theological pragmatism.* The central section iii, 7–xvi, 31, which contains the actual judge-narratives deals with twelve *judges* (שֹׁפְטִים) if we do not include Abimelech, or thirteen if we reckon Deborah as well as Barak. But the narratives concerning them are of very varied length. More detailed treatment is given only to Ehud of Benjamin (iii, 12–30),[2] Deborah of Ephraim and Barak of Naphtali (iv–v), Gideon[3] and Abimelech[4] of Manasseh (vi–ix), Jephthah of Gilead (x, 6–xii, 7)[5] and Samson of Dan (xiii–xvi), and for this reason these are also known as 'major' judges. Concerning Othniel of Kenaz in Judah (iii, 7–11)[6] and Shamgar, who came probably from the Galilean Beth-Anath mentioned in i, 33, and was thus a non-Israelite (iii, 31),[7] we are at least very briefly told which enemy they defeated. But concerning Tola of Issachar (x, 1–2), Jair of Gilead (x, 3–5), Ibzan of Zebulun (xii, 8–10), Elon of Zebulun (xii, 11–12), and Abdon of Ephraim (xii, 13–15), no definite deed is recorded, but, apart from certain notes

[1] Eissfeldt, 'Der geschichtliche Hintergrund der Erzählung von Gibeas Schandtat' *Beer-Festschr.* (1935), pp. 19–40; Sinclair, 'An Archaeological Study of Gibeah (Tell el-fûl)' AASOR XXXIV–XXXV (1960), pp. 1–52, Pls. 1–35. Lit. p. 65, n. 1; § 126.

[2] Galling, 'Erwägungen zum Stelenheiligtum von Hazor' ZDPV 75 (1959), pp. 1–13: on the פְּסִילִים of iii, 19, 26; Kraeling, 'Difficulties in the Story of Ehud' JBL 54 (1935), pp. 205–10. Lit. p. 295, n. 54; § 126.

[3] Alonso-Schökel, 'Heros Gedeon. De genere litterario et historicitate Jdc vi–viii' VD 32 (1954), pp. 3–20, 65–76; Daube, 'Gideon's Few' JJSt 7 (1956), pp. 155–61; Kaufmann, 'The Gideon Stories' [Hebr., Engl. sum.] Tarbiz 30 (1960/1), pp. 139–47, IV–V; Kutsch, 'Gideon's Berufung und Altarbau Jdc vi, 11–24' ThLZ 81 (1956), cols. 75–84; Malamat, 'The War of Gideon and Midian: A Military Approach' PEQ 85 (1953), pp. 61–5; Whitley, 'The Sources of the Gideon Stories' VT 7 (1957), pp. 157–64.

[4] Dossin, 'Une *lectio difficilior* dans Juges ix, 31' OBL (1957), pp. 163–7; Ehrman, 'The Meaning of the Word *torma* (Judges ix, 31)' [Hebr. Engl. sum.] Tarbiz 29 (1959/60), pp. 295, VIII; Gevirtz, 'The Hapax Legomenon רם" (Judg. ix, 31)' JNESt 17 (1958), pp. 59–60; Honeyman, 'The Salting of Shechem' VT 3 (1953), pp. 192–5: on ix, 45; van der Meersch, 'Problema de expugnatione Sichem ab Abimelech (Jud. ix, 22–49)' VD 31 (1953), pp. 335–43; Milik, 'Notes d'épigraphie et de topographie palestiniennes' RB 66 (1959), pp. 550–75, Pls. XIII, XIV, see pp. 560–2: Le sanctuaire de Ba'al Berit à Sichem; Naor, ' "And Abimelech dwelt at Arumah" ' (Jud. ix 41)' [Hebr.] BIES 20 (1950), pp. 16–20. Literature, p. 159, n. 2; § 126.

[5] Albright, 'Notes on Ammonite History' *Miscell. Bibl. Ubach* (1954), pp. 131–6; Mendelsohn, 'The Disinheritance of Jephthah in the Light of Paragraph 27 of the Lipit-Ishtar Code' IEJ 4 (1954), pp. 116–19; Willesen, 'The אפרתי of the Shibboleth Incident' VT 8 (1958), pp. 97–8.

[6] Malamat, 'Cushan Rishathaim and the Decline of the Near East around 1200 B.C.' JNESt 13 (1954), pp. 231–42; Täubler, 'Cushan-Rishathaim' HUCA 20 (1947), pp. 137–42. Lit. § 126.

[7] Alt, *Die Staatenbildung der Israeliten in Palästina* (1930), p. 12, n. 25 = *Kl. Schr.* II (1953), p. 9, n. 3; Milik, 'An unpublished arrow-head with Phoenician Inscription of the 11th–10th Century B.C.' BASOR 143 (1956), pp. 3–6, cf. p. 5, n. 24. Lit. § 126.

with reference to their families, it is simply said that they *judged* Israel and where their graves are to be found. They are therefore called the 'minor' judges. The narratives about the major judges, together with that of Othniel, have this in common, that they all begin with a statement about Israel's sinful actions which have as their consequence the anger of God expressed in terms of permitting hostile attack, and about the cry for help which then moved God to send the judge (iii, 7–9, 11b–15; iv, 1–6; vi, 1–14; x, 6–16; xiii, 1–5). They all close with the statement that the enemy was subjected by the judge in question and that Israel now had so many years' rest (iii, 10b–11a, 30; iv, 23–24 + v, 31b; viii, 28; xii, 7; xv, 20; xvi, 31b). While these introductory and concluding formulae are not always exactly the same and are in fact occasionally missing where it was awkward to introduce them, nevertheless, together with the survey of the period of the judges in ii, 11–19, already mentioned (pp. 257 f.), they give its peculiar stamp to the book of Judges, or more precisely to the middle section which deals with the judges. They set the period of the judges in the framework of a religious and theological pragmatic outlook which shows disaster at the hand of enemies following upon guilt, and divine help following upon the repentance brought about by the distress; and then renewed apostasy, renewed distress etc. in regular succession. But a closer examination readily reveals that this pragmatic outlook is really only externally imposed upon the narratives, without being firmly rooted in them. The narratives certainly tell of distress from enemies and of Israel's prayer for help, of divine hearing and of successful battles fought by the judge sent by God as deliverer. But the idea that the distress was on each occasion brought about by sin, and that after each deliverance the people once again fell back into its sinful action, i.e. apostasy, is quite alien to the majority of the old narratives. It was already applied by E to the Gideon, Jephthah (and Samuel) narratives (p. 262), but otherwise, as we shall see (pp. 266–7), it is of Deuteronomistic origin, and thus was only grafted on to the old narratives relatively late.

The older stories were in fact already linked together in a manner not really appropriate to them before they were set in the Deuteronomistic framework. For the judges are all tribal heroes and by their actions always helped only their own tribes or at most a group of tribes—admittedly a fairly comprehensive one in the case of Deborah and Barak. It follows from this that they only exercised their rule too in this narrower circle. But they have been presented as rulers of all Israel and so at the same time as predecessors of the kings of the united Israelite kingdom. Such a process is quite inevitable, and it is the same with the Hexateuch narratives, which to some extent even more clearly than the judge stories refer originally only to tribes or parts of tribes, or even only to single districts or places, but are now all presented so as to be understood as referring to the prehistory of all Israel. The whole of the tradition has been written down from the point of view of the united kingdom, and from this point of view all the events which remain impressed upon the memory appear as concerning all Israel, as indeed they all did in reality contribute, each in its own way, to the formation of all Israel.

3. *Analysis.* The narratives of the major judges present, however, another

difficulty to our understanding of the material and one which is less easy to resolve. They reveal very largely the same features as the Hexateuch narratives —overloading, repetitions, contradictions, breaks, seams and the like. So we have either to assume small individual additions of all kinds or we may assume the combination of parallel narratives and narrative strands. In other words, are we to apply the supplementary of the documentary hypothesis? Now the assumption that at every point a basic narrative has been elaborated with all kinds of individual additions, glosses, filling in of details, new narrative features etc., just does not satisfy, for example in the Gideon and Abimelech story, and in the Jephthah story. The words, sentences or paragraphs which are felt as overloading or disturbing elements are by no means small isolated pieces but reveal interconnections among themselves. This may be made somewhat more clear in the narrative of Gideon's attack on the Midianite camp in vii, 9–22. Verse 18 shows clearly that here we are dealing with a narrative which only knows of the sounding of trumpets and battle cries as the means of intimidating the enemy, and this story may be recovered more or less complete from vv. 16ab*a*, 17b–19ab*a*, 20a*a*b, 22. But side by side with this are traces of another narrative in which the shattering of jars makes the noise intended to intimidate the enemy, and the hands then set free hold torches and swords.[8] This narrative too, although it has suffered considerable losses when the two were combined, may nevertheless be restored with certainty. In addition, the double mention of the flight of the enemy at the end in vv. 21 and 22 shows quite clearly that we are here dealing with two parallel narratives and not with expansions of *one* basic narrative. The situation is somewhat different in the Samson story,[9] since here only xiii shows signs of a mixture of sources, whereas the narratives of xiv–xv and of xvi make a completely unified impression. Here xiv–xv on the one hand and xvi[10] on the other hand are to be allocated to two Samson narratives, just as in xiii two accounts are now combined, evidently the beginnings of the two strands preserved separately in xiv–xv and xvi. That this is so is shown above all by the similarly worded conclusions of xv and xvi, where we read twice over *And he judged Israel 20 years.*

The narratives concerning the judges which stand in the central section of the book of Judges—those which deal with the minor judges, including Othniel and Shamgar are so short that even if a mixture of sources were present it could not be established—are all combinations of two or even more parallels. This is also true of the section ii, 10–iii, 6, which precedes them, and of the so-called appendix xvii–xxi. In the first section, disregarding the passage ii, 11–19, already noted as Deuteronomistic (pp. 257 f.), there may be recognised at least two different conceptions of the necessity of leaving certain nations unsubjected, and in particular the Philistines.[11] One presents this as a disciplinary punishment imposed by God upon the people because of their sins (ii, 10, 20–2, 23b;

[8] In v. 20 we must certainly read הַחֶרֶב *the sword*, instead of the phrase *the trumpets to blow* (𝔐), which was substituted in order to assimilate the two stories to one another.

[9] Gunkel, 'Simson' *Reden und Aufsätze* (1913), pp. 38–64.

[10] Brunner, 'Das Herz als Sitz des Lebensgeheimnisses' AfO 17 (1954/6), pp. 140 f.: on xvi, 15–18.

[11] Trude Dothan, 'Archaeological Reflections on the Philistine Problem' Antiquity and

iii, 1a, 3–4), while the other sees in it the means chosen by God to make the people proficient in war[12] (ii, 23a; iii, 1b, 2, 5–6). Again, neither of these conceptions looks like an explanation inserted later. The presence here of a more profane and a more spiritual outlook may also be observed occasionally elsewhere in the book of Judges (p. 262). In the two narratives in the appendix, however, that of the Danites in xvii–xviii and that of Gibeah in xix–xxi, there is clear evidence of the existence of a mixture of sources and it may be seen in the fact that in both the narratives it is twice stated concerning their period, and both times with the same variations in the actual wording, that it was a time of lawless behaviour. This is stated in the first narrative on the first occasion with the words: *In those days there was yet no king in Israel; each man did what was right in his own eyes* (xvii, 6), and on the second occasion in a somewhat shorter form: *In those days there was yet no king in Israel* (xviii, 1). In the second narrative, the first formula is to be found in xxi, 25, and in the second in xix, 1. The most illuminating explanation of this is no doubt the assumption that in xvii–xviii and xix–xxi two narrators are concerned in each, and that these are the same two narrators. This assumption is further supported by the lack of unity in the two narratives which may everywhere be detected.

It can hardly be disputed that the majority of the narratives in the book of Judges reveal a mixture of sources, and the question is merely how many strands may be observed in the individual sections. Furthermore, we must ask whether these strands again belong together as parts of narrative sources. So far as the first point is concerned, the analysis can again only be undertaken with a precise examination of every detail; but it is so complicated and difficult, that the enumeration of the verses and parts of verses assigned to the individual strands would be unintelligible without more detailed explanation. The results can therefore here be set out only in general terms. In ii, 10–iii, 6, apart from the Deuteronomistic section ii, 11–19, there seem to be three hands at work, and the same appears to be true of the Gideon and Abimelech story (vi–ix) and of the Jephthah story (x, 6–xii, 7). On the other hand, in the narratives of Ehud (iii, 12–30), of Deborah and Barak (iv–v), of Samson (xiii–xvi), of the theft of the cult objects by the Danites (xvii–xviii),[13] and of the outrage at Gibeah (xix–xxi),[14] only two parallel narratives are recognisable.

The other question, whether the parallels established in the individual narratives reveal themselves as links in continuous chains, must be answered in the affirmative for at least a number of these parallels. We have seen that in the problem dealt with in ii, 10–iii, 6, as to why God did not immediately hand over certain peoples to Israel as a prize, one of the conceptions offered solves the problem in a spiritual manner by explaining that God wished to punish sinful

Survival II 2/3 (1957), pp. 151–64; Wright, 'Philistine Coffins and Mercenaries' BA 22 (1959), pp. 54–66. Lit. § 126.
[12] Cf. p. 134, n. 3.
[13] Bewer, 'The Composition of Judges, chaps. xvii, xviii' AJSL 29 (1912/13), pp. 261–283; Hauret, 'Aux origines du sacerdoce danite, à propos de Jud. xviii, 30–31' *Mél. Bibl. Robert* (1957), pp. 105–13; Mulder, 'De ontstaanstijd van de beide aanhangsels van het boek Richteren (cap. xvii–xxi)' GThT 48 (1948), pp. 99–114.
[14] Bewer, 'The Composition of Judges, Chaps. xx, xxi' AJSL 30 (1913/14), pp. 149–65.

Israel and so restrain it from further sin. In the same way one of the strands in the Gideon-Abimelech story and one in the Jephthah story reveals a spiritual tone, in contrast to that of the parallel narrative, and this spiritual tone is so strong that some scholars have regarded the passages which contain it as not belonging to the sources, but to the hand of a Deuteronomist. But these passages are in fact far too closely bound up with other material in the same context, which is on other grounds clearly assignable to a source, for this to be the case. We are dealing here above all with the sermon of the prophet in vi, 7–10, which stands at the beginning of the Gideon story; with Gideon's rejection of the crown on the grounds that Yahweh is sole ruler in viii, 22–3; with the conception of the Abimelech episode which presents the misfortunes of the Israelites and of Abimelech as a well-deserved punishment for the injustice done to Gideon and his house, which thus at the same time provides an example of the doctrine of retribution, in viii, 33–5; ix, 5b–24, 56–7; and with the double self-abasement of Israel in x, 6–16*, preceding the sending of the deliverer Jephthah. These sections show great similarity one to another, and are, as has long been observed, closely related to E of the Hexateuch, and notably for example to Josh. xxiv*. So, leaving for the moment on one side the question of their connection with E, we may at any rate link together in one strand the passages which belong here from ii, 10–iii, 6, from the Gideon-Abimelech story and from the Jephthah story, leaving open meanwhile the question whether this strand also originally contained narratives concerning other judges, now lost to us, or whether it only consisted of the narratives which have in fact survived.

I Sam. xii, the farewell speech of Samuel, also strongly reminiscent of E and in many respects similar to Josh. xxiv, the farewell speech of Joshua, contains a retrospect on the deeds of kindness which Yahweh has shown to Israel, and among these is mentioned the sending of judges as deliverers from enemy oppression. As examples are mentioned in verse 11—ignoring the corrupted form בְּדָן, perhaps deriving from עַבְדּוֹן (Judg. xii, 13–15) which would then certainly be a secondary addition—Jerubbaal (= Gideon), Jephthah and Samuel. In other words, since Abimelech naturally enough could not appear here, we have exactly the same heroes as are presented in this strand of the book of Judges with its characteristically religious outlook. This can hardly be an accident. We must rather assume that this strand in fact only gave an account of Gideon (= Jerubbaal) and Jephthah as judges, in addition to Samuel who comes later. This accords well with the fact that in the prophetic sermon in vi, 7–10, which precedes the sending of the deliverer Gideon there is mention only of the deliverance of Israel from the power of the Egyptians and the Amorites—for the *oppressors* of verse 9 are clearly the *Amorites* of verse 10—and there is no mention of deliverance from the power of the king of Moab, or of Jabin of Hazor, whose defeats by Ehud and by Deborah and Barak now actually precede the Gideon narrative. The strand to which that prophetic sermon belongs thus clearly did not mention these judges, but only those named in I Sam. xii, 11, and we may therefore affirm that all the narratives of the judges which this strand offered are in fact preserved.

The obvious relationship of this strand with E in the Hexateuch and with the passage I Sam. xii which also reveals the colouring of E, makes it very probable that this is in fact the continuation of the Hexateuch E. We have already seen more than once (pp. 135, 253) that there is no real boundary between the books of Joshua and Judges, and the material at different points which is to be assigned to E does in fact form a coherent whole. In Josh. xxiv, 28–33 = Judg. ii, 6–9, E gives an account of the deaths of Joshua and of Eleazar, and in Judg. ii, 10, it continues: *And all that generation also were gathered to their fathers; and there arose another generation after them.*

This in its turn raises the question whether, after the removal of the E material, the remaining narratives of the book of Judges are to be linked together in one strand or in two, since here and there in the whole work three strands may be recognised and the narratives in which E has no share are for the most part made up of two strands. Further we must ask whether these may be claimed as continuations of the Pentateuch strands L and J which are as yet left without sequel—P certainly did not extend beyond the allocation of the land (pp. 251 f.). Both questions are to be answered in the affirmative. For, as we have already seen (p. 259), when E has been removed, we are certainly not dealing in the remainder with entirely disconnected narratives concerning heroes of various tribes, but with a series of rulers who are conceived of as the predecessors of the kings of the united kingdom, and this in itself represents a bond which holds together the narratives which are admittedly otherwise independent. Once again the question how, after the removal of the E material, the strands remaining in the individual narratives are to be linked together, is one which can only be dealt with by an examination of the text itself, and so here we must be content with indicating that both strands gave information about Ehud (Deborah and Barak), Gideon and Abimelech, Jephthah and Samson, and then further about the Danites (xvii–xviii) and Gibeah (xix–xxi), having first set out approximately the same solution of the problem why God did not give complete success to the first generation of the conquerors (pp. 260 f.). In view of the small amount of what is narrated concerning the minor judges, including Othniel and Shamgar, it is better not to attempt to allocate them to the two series. And here we may add that Alt and others[15] see in the basic material of x, 1–5; xii, 7–15, an authentic tradition concerning the holders of the office of judge which is to be assumed for the pre-monarchical period in Israel. They separate the latter from the leader figures of the hero narratives—with the exception of Jephthah who combines the two in himself—and would regard the term 'judge' as applied only secondarily from the holders of the office of judge to the warrior heroes.

[15] Alt, 'Die Ursprünge des israelitischen Rechts' (1934), pp. 31–3 = *Kl. Schr.* I (1953), pp. 300–2; Fensham, 'The Judges and Ancient Israelite Jurisprudence' OuTWP (1959), pp. 15–22; Grether, 'Die Bezeichnung "Richter" für die charismatischen Helden der vorstaatlichen Zeit' ZAW 57 (1939), pp. 110–21; Hertzberg, 'Die Kleinen Richter' ThLZ 79 (1954), cols. 285–90; Kraus, *Gottesdienst in Israel* (1954), pp. 63–5; *Die prophetische Verkündigung des Rechts in Israel* (ThSt[B] 51, 1957); Noth, 'Das Amt des "Richter Israels" ' *Bertholet-Festschr.* (1950), pp. 404–17; cf. *History of Israel* (²1960), pp. 101 f.; van Selms, 'The Title "Judge" ' OuTWP (1959), pp. 41–50; de Vaux, *Ancient Israel* (1961), pp. 93, 151; Vollborn, 'Der Richter Israels' *Festschr. Rendtorff* (1958), pp. 21–31. Lit. § 126.

The two narrative strands which remain after the removal of the E material also have no proper beginning. The statement made in ii, 23–iii, 6 (pp. 260 f.), that God allowed some undefeated nations to remain in Canaan because he wished to give Israel experience in warfare, quite clearly assumes that there has been some discussion of wars of conquest beforehand. So these two series appear as the continuation of the strands L and J which at any rate do not exclude such a continuation, for they have in fact told of conquest battles and also mentioned gaps in the conquest (p. 254). Which of the two series in the book of Judges is to be linked with the Hexateuch L and which with J can also not on the whole be in doubt, since in the one series many peculiarities recall L, and in the other many recall J.

Thus the Hexateuch narrators L, J and E carried their narrative further, beyond the conquest and division of Canaan, and included at least the period of the judges in their presentation. The material—in addition to hero sagas, traditions concerning the fortunes of tribes (xvii–xviii) and of cities (xix–xxi)—was frequently drawn, as in the Hexateuch, and particularly by L, from oral tradition, which as is shown by the placing of Jair (Num. xxxii, 41) and Jabin of Hazor (Josh. xi, 1–9) at one point in the period of Moses or of Joshua, at another point in the period of the judges (Judg. x, 3–5; iv) (pp. 254, 258), occasionally varies in its chronological setting of events so that their present dating and order cannot be regarded as historical without further examination. Much of the material, like the oldest form of the Gideon and Abimelech stories and the Song of Deborah,[16] L did however already find available in written form. L has hardly combined a particular bias with his presentation. What he did was to present what was available to him, testifying to the deeds of Yahweh and the judges. L's pattern was then followed by J. He tells of substantially the same judges as L and this in itself shows that he is dependent on L. But frequently he tells of something quite different, as for example in the Gideon story where in vii, followed by E, he brings out motives which are impossible before the narrative of viii, 4–21, which belongs almost entirely to L. For whereas, according to vii, Gideon won a complete victory over the Midianites, viii, 4–21 presupposes an attack of the Midianites which has not yet been avenged in which the Midianite kings, who also bear other names here than in vii, 23–viii, 3, have killed Gideon's brothers on Tabor. Thus here we have the same pattern as in the Hexateuch (p. 209). The spring of oral saga had not yet dried up in the time of J; there were other forms of the sagas still in circulation side by side with the already fixed narratives of L.

E too, which, as we have just seen, links closely to J in vii, 9–22, and thus reveals the relationship to J which is often to be observed in the Hexateuch (pp. 189–91), nevertheless also has a good deal of special material. This is certainly only to a very small degree its own creation, and comes rather, as far as the main elements are concerned, from saga material which is still fluid. Nor is it at all astonishing that this should have remained alive so long. For basically it never did come to an end. Rabbinic literature is very rich in elaborations of old sagas and in the invention of new ones. Even if these 'midrashim', measured

---

[16] Lit. p. 100, n. 4.

against the old sagas, often seem rather bloodless and thus reveal themselves as products of the later age, they nevertheless reveal that the fixation of the Biblical books, though already centuries old, could not hinder the process of the further development and the new formation of sagas and legends. How much more lively must it have been while Israel was still settled in the land to which the narratives belong and from whose soil they could derive life and strength! Nevertheless, even here the later formations, i.e. the special material of E, stands out by its more religious flavour from the old basic sagas. The fact that E restricted himself to the relating of the Gideon-Jerubbaal stories and the Jephthah stories may certainly be explained from his religious bias, though this must not be understood to mean something contrasted with the secular. For E the material concerning the period of the judges which was available in L and J and elsewhere was not the kind of material in which he would present the valour—admittedly aroused by Yahweh—of human heroes and the deliverance which his people experienced through them. He directed his aim rather at exhibiting human insufficiency and divine grace. In the alternation of enemy oppression and divine mercy, of which the old judge narratives told, he could present his philosophy of life and his view of history in an emphatic manner. For—and in this he is a predecessor of the Deuteronomist (pp. 266-7)—he represented distress as punishment for sin and deliverance as God's answer to the genuine penitence of the people (vi, 7-10, 25-32; x, 6-16*). For this purpose, the examples of Gideon, Jephthah, and, later, Samuel (I Sam. vii, pp. 270 f.) sufficed. So he left the other judges unmentioned, and in the case of Samson this may have been encouraged by the very crude and hardly religious nature of the story, and in the case of Deborah and Barak by the fact that he had already delivered Jabin of Hazor in Josh. xi into the power of Joshua, whereas according to Judg. iv–v (LJ) he was conquered by (Deborah and) Barak. For in Josh. xi, 1–9, the mention of this king is to be traced to E, whereas J, who introduces him in Judg. iv, no doubt had another name here or perhaps mentioned no name at all. On the other hand, the narrative of Abimelech which does not really fit into the scheme of sin and distress, repentance and grace, offered him a welcome opportunity of presenting vividly the justice of divine retribution (p. 262).

E must have been moved by another special motive for passing over the narratives of the appendix xvii–xxi, which in any case must have presented objections enough to a man of E's stamp and could hardly be transformed into examples of retribution—at least so far as the first of them is concerned. These two narratives, as we have already seen (pp. 260-1), are intended by those who gave them their present form, i.e. L and J, to give a picture of the conditions of the pre-monarchical period, of the 'terrible time'; or perhaps we should say that alongside the desire simply to give an account of that period they have this purpose also in mind. In this way, if they were really written with a forward look to a sequel, they provide a suitable introduction to the narrative of the emergence of the Israelite monarchy, provided that this sequel did in fact present a favourable assessment of the monarchy. We shall see that in the narratives of the origins of the Israelite monarchy in I Sam. i–xv, two other strata are to be observed together with the inclusion of the E stratum in I Sam. xii already noted (p. 262), and these two strata may very readily be understood as the continuations of L and J in the book of Judges. They assess Saul's monarchy as a divine gift of Yahweh (p. 275). The E stratum, however, quite clearly takes a doubtful attitude towards Saul and the monarchy as such, and in fact rejects it. This attitude of E could therefore also help to explain why he passed over the narratives of Judg. xvii–xxi completely.

4. *Deuteronomistic redaction.* Thus the earliest previous stages of our books of Judges which may be clearly depicted are the books of Judges of L, J and E —or, more correctly, since we are not dealing with books with clearly marked beginning and end, nor do they deal simply with judges, three parallel narrative complexes from the 'period of the judges'. With the combination of the L, J and E narratives of the Hexateuch, these three complexes of stories from the period of the judges were also combined, and thus the basic structure of our book of Judges was produced. Later, comparatively little of this was altered, much less at any rate than is generally assumed. The normal conception, represented particularly by Budde, of the formation of the book of Judges also envisages, as has been done here, a pre-deuteronomic book of Judges, different only in that it is thought of as produced by the combination of not three but two sources (J and E). But it reckons with a very deep-rooted interference with the material of this older book, carried out by Deuteronomistic hands. For the Deuteronomistic redaction is supposed not only to have elaborated the religious pragmatism foreshadowed by E, and to have extended it from Gideon and Jephthah also to Othniel, Ehud, Deborah-Barak and Samson—this is clear enough (p. 265)—but above all to have cut out the material which lacked this pragmatism, namely i, 1–ii, 5;[17] ii, 20–iii, 6; ix; xvi; xvii–xxi. These sections of the older book of Judges, still existing at a later date, are then supposed to have been reinserted in the Deuteronomistic book. But this theory of subtraction and reinsertion, working with the idea of the cutting out of substantial pieces of material at one point and their later replacement—a theory, which as we saw (pp. 243, 246 f.), is also accepted by Noth—is here as elsewhere (pp. 270, 280) beset with great difficulties. In this particular case, it ultimately rests only on the fact that in the sections mentioned the religious pragmatism is not expressed or at any rate not so clearly expressed as elsewhere. But this argument falls to the ground as soon as we recognise two points. Firstly, these sections were by their whole nature unsuitable for fitting into the scheme. Secondly, as we have seen (p. 255), when we describe the formation of the Biblical books we must also reckon, here as elsewhere, with a 'neutralising' of the materials which contradicted the bias of the particular redactor or which did not really fit in with it. So also there disappears the necessity, generally felt to be imperative, of denying to the Deuteronomistic and even to the pre-deuteronomic book of Judges the references to the minor judges, and to trace their insertion only to a very late hand. With them the introduction of the religious pragmatic scheme was in fact quite impossible, and they are therefore surely to be regarded as belonging not

[17] Gurewicz, 'The Bearing of Judges i–ii, 5, on the Authorship of the Book of Judges' ABR 7 (1959), pp. 37–40.

merely to the Deuteronomistic book of Judges, but also to the pre-deuteronomic one.

Furthermore, a good deal of what has usually been attributed to the Deuteronomistic or even to later redaction, is to be regarded as in reality older material of the narratives. This also applies to the numbers of years assigned to the duration of enemy oppression and to the rule of the judges (iii, 8, 11, 14, 30; iv, 3; v, 31 etc.). It is entirely natural that when there is an account of a sequence of periods of oppression and of freedom, their duration must also be given. On the other hand, it cannot be denied that these figures, belonging to the sources L, J and E, have been further elaborated by a later hand or by later hands, and have been corrected so as to fit in with the scheme attested by I Kings vi, 1,[18] which assigns 480 years for the period from the Exodus from Egypt to the building of Solomon's Temple.

The part played by the Deuteronomistic redaction in our book of Judges is therefore in the main to be limited to the further elaboration of the religious pragmatism already set forth in E, and it remains only to assess whether we must reckon in this with one or two Deuteronomistic redactors or editors. In the book of Judges itself, apart from the opening i, 1–ii, 9, which has already been analysed from this point of view (pp. 253, 255), there are no clear traces to be found of two Deuteronomistic hands. But in view of the paucity of the material which here in any case comes into consideration, this does not mean very much. In the book of Joshua, with which Judg. i, 1–ii, 9, is to be reckoned, two Deuteronomistic editions are certainly demonstrable. General considerations make it likely that these editions not only follow on from the previous ones of Deuteronomy, but also continue further, presumably down to the time at which they took place, so we may assume that the pre-Deuteronomic book of Judges also underwent two Deuteronomistic editions, which were then combined. They are likely to have been very similar to one another, and from this may be explained the fact that our book of Judges reveals no traces of a double Deuteronomistic redaction. We shall have to come back again to this type of question when we consider the book of Kings (pp. 299–300).

Even after the Deuteronomistic working over, our book of Judges underwent some alterations, of which, however, only the extension of xix–xxi deserves mention. This midrashic extension is in fact not unimportant. It recalls in many respects the manner and style of P, and must therefore come from a hand influenced by it, and thus be fairly late. When the 'stories from the period of the judges', which are not marked off either at the beginning or at the end, were separated off as a separate book cannot be said with certainty. It is likely to have happened only after the separation of the Pentateuch (pp. 255–7).

[18] Chapman, 'Zum Ursprung der chronologischen Angabe I Reg vi, 1' ZAW 53 (1935), pp. 185–9; Rowley, *From Joseph to Joshua* (1950), see Indexes, p. 200.

§ 40. THE BOOKS OF SAMUEL

Literature: (a) Commentaries (i) Series: ATD: Hertzberg ([2]1960); BOuT: van den Born (1956); Camb. B: Kirkpatrick (1930); Cent. B: Kennedy (1904); EB: Dhorme (1910); Echter-B: Rehm (1949); EH: Schulz (1919/20); HK: Nowack (1902); HS: Leimbach (1936); HSAT: Kittel (1922); IB: Caird, Schroeder, Little (1953); ICC: Smith (1912 (1953)); Jerusalem-B: de Vaux ([2]1961); KAT: Caspari (1926); KeH: Thenius-Loehr ([3]1898); KHC: Budde (1902); KV: Goslinga (1956); SAT: Gressmann ([2]1921); Soncino-B: Goldman (1951); SZ: Klostermann (1887); TU: de Groot, I (1934), II (1935).

(ii) Single Commentaries: Segal [Hebr.] (1956).

(b) Other Works: de Boer, *Research into the Text of I Samuel i–xvi* (1938); 'I Samuel xvii. Notes on the Text and the Ancient Versions' OTS 1 (1942), pp. 79–104; 'Research into the Text of 1 Samuel xvii–xxxi' OTS 6 (1949), pp. 1–100; Driver, *Notes on the Hebrew Text of the Books of Samuel* ([2]1913); Hylander, *Der literarische Samuel-Saul-Komplex (I Sam. i–xv). Traditionsgeschichtlich untersucht* (Diss. theol. Uppsala, 1932); Pfeiffer, 'Midrash in the Books of Samuel' *Quantulacumque. Studies Presented to Kirsopp Lake* London (1937), pp. 303–16; Plöger, *Die Prophetengeschichten der Samuel- und Königsbücher* (Diss. theol. Greifswald, 1937); Rehm, *Textkritische Untersuchungen zu den Parallelstellen der Samuel-Königsbücher und der Chronik* (1937); Schildenberger, 'Zur Einleitung in die Samuelbücher' Stud. Anselm. 27–8 (1951), pp. 130–68; Tiktin, *Kritische Untersuchnugen zu den Büchern Samuelis* (FRLANT 33, 1922); Vannutelli, *Libri synoptici Veteris Testamenti seu librorum Regum et Chronicorum loci paralleli* I (1931), II (1934); Vriezen, 'De Compositie van de Samuël-Boeken' Or. Neerl. (1948), pp. 167–89; Wellhausen, *Der Text der Bücher Samuelis untersucht* (1871).

Cf. also Literature §§ 18, 37, 126.

1. *Name and contents.* According to Jewish tradition, deriving from I Chron. xxix, 29–30, the books of Samuel were compiled by Samuel, or by Samuel, Nathan and Gad, and bear the name of their compiler or chief compiler. In actual fact, they were so named because Samuel plays the chief part in them or at least in what is now the first book. The two books originally formed a single unit in the Jewish canon. Hebrew manuscripts and printed editions have only adopted the division into two since 1448, whereas first 𝕲 and subsequently the Vulgate had long preceded them in this. 𝕲 moreover reckons the books of Samuel and Kings as parts of a larger unit and numbers them as the four books of *Kingdoms* (βασιλειῶν), βασιλειῶν α′ = I Sam., βασιλειῶν β′ = II Sam., βασιλειῶν γ′ = I Kings, and βασιλειῶν δ′ = II Kings. This was followed by the Latin translation with its reckoning of Sam. and Kings as four books of kingdoms (Regnorum), though gradually in place of *Regnorum* the name *Regum*, formed on the basis of the Hebrew מְלָכִים *kings*, prevailed.

The division of the book into two is not inappropriate. The principle is here operative which we have already observed (pp. 242 f.) of making the division after the death of a leading individual, in this case after the death of Saul, which is described in I Sam. xxxi. To obtain a rapid survey of the contents, the books may be further divided thus: I i–vii Samuel's childhood and his victory over the Philistines who up till then had heavily oppressed Israel; viii–xv the installation of Saul as king by Samuel at the people's wish and his rejection by Yahweh; xvi–xxxi the relationships between Saul and David, at first friendly and then hostile, and Saul's death in the disastrous battle on mount Gilboa;[1] II i–viii David's rise to power as king of Judah with his residence at Hebron, and then as king of all Israel[2] with his residence in the city of Jerusalem[3] which he conquered; ix–xx, with which I Kings i–ii clearly belong, stories of David's family and in particular of the contests among his sons for the throne, which lead finally, shortly before David's death, to the accession of Solomon. xxi–xxiv now divide II ix–xx from I Kings i–ii and appear as appendices to the history of David. They consist of xxi, 1–14 and xxiv, two narratives concerning a famine and a plague; xxi, 15–22[4] and xxiii, 8–39, two lists of David's heroes with mention of their deeds; xxii and xxiii, 1–7, two songs of David, of which the first reappears in the Psalter as Ps. xviii,[5] and the second is a sort of 'ruler's guide', described by its title as *the last words of David*.

2. *History of criticism.*[6] Even a superficial glance through the books of Samuel reveals that the same features are here present as in the narrative sections of the Hexateuch and of the book of Judges—repetitions and contradictions, breaks and joins, in short a variety of indications of lack of unity. Since the rise of critical work on the OT, indeed already with its originator Eichhorn* (p. 3), such observations have led to attempts at replacing the tradition of the synagogue, recognised to be untrustworthy, by an explanation more suited to these facts. Further detailed research, as examples of which we may note Thenius' Commentary on the Books of Samuel[7] and Wellhausen's revision of the fourth edition of Bleek's *Introduction* (1878),[8] led to the recognition that there are present not merely isolated doublets, but whole parallel strands, and there was also applied to their separation the criterion of historical assessment. Measured by this standard, the complex I i–iii, vii–viii, xii, appeared to be relatively late and valueless, whereas the sections which stand between and follow upon them and which belong much more closely together, i.e. I iv–vi, ix,[9] xi, xiii–xiv,[10] gave the impression of being older and historically more trustworthy. This critical work was brought to a certain conclusion, as we have already suggested (pp. 244 f.), by Budde's commentary of 1902, based on his own previous work, as well as on that of others. Budde divides the narrative material

---

[1] Schelhaas, 'De ondergang van Israëls verworpen koning en de handhaving van het koningschap' GThT 58 (1958), pp. 143–52, 161–70.

[2] Cazelles, review of PRU IV (1956) in VT 8 (1958), pp. 103–6, on p. 104 compares II Sam. ii, 5–7, with the letter of Shuppiluliuma to Niqmad, RŠ 17, 132.

[3] Alt, 'Jerusalems Aufstieg' ZDMG 79 (1925), pp. 1–19 = *Kl. Schr.* III (1959), pp. 243–57; Dinaburg, 'Zion and Jerusalem. Their Role in the Historic Consciousness of Israel' [Hebr., Engl. sum.] Zion 16 (1951), pp. 1–17, I–II; Noth, 'Jerusalem und die israelitische Tradition' OTS 8 (1950), pp. 28–46 = *Ges. Stud.* (²1960), pp. 172–87. Lit. p. 289, n. 33; § 126.

[4] Willesen, 'The Philistine Corps of the Scimitar from Gath' JSSt 3 (1958), pp. 327–35. Lit. § 126.

[5] Cf. p. 104, n. 7.   [6] Cf. also above, pp. 242–8.

[7] *Kommentar zu den Samuelisbüchern* (1842, ²1864, ³1898 by Loehr.).

[8] Cf. p. 166, n. 38.

[9] Bič, 'Saul sucht die Eselinnen (I Sam ix)' VT 7 (1957), pp. 92–7; Stoebe, 'Noch einmal die Eselinnen des *Kiš*' (I Sam ix)' VT 7 (1957), pp. 362–70.

[10] Kline, 'The Ḥa-bi-ru: Kin or Foe of Israel?' WThJ 19 (1956), pp. 1–24: on xiv, 21; Lindblom, 'Ett omstritt ställe i den grekiska bibeln' *Studier Olsson* (1959), pp. 251–61: on xiv, 41–2.

of the books of Samuel into two parallel strands, and assigns these to J and E, i.e. as we have seen (p. 245) to the founders of the J and E 'schools' from which there issued later the J and E narrative strands recognised in the book of Judges and the Hexateuch. But, according to his view, the books of Samuel do not represent the simple addition of J and E. This combination, the pre-deuteronomic book of Samuel, has, like the pre-deuteronomic book of Judges, been subjected to a substantial Deuteronomistic redaction. In the first place into a number of passages which were particularly suitable for it, the favourite Deuteronomistic ideas were introduced, as, for example, I ii, 27–36, with its pointer to the family of Zadok which from the time of Solomon alone had the right to the priesthood in the Jerusalem temple (cf. I Kings ii, 26–7), and II vii, with its pointer to Solomon's temple building (v. 13). Then, large sections which appeared objectionable to the redactor were cut out, i.e. I xv; II ix–xxiv; I Kings i; ii, 1–9, 13–46*, and, partly in connection with this procedure, the separate periods were concluded by comprehensive surveys, i.e. I vii, 13–17, covering the period of the Judges including Samuel, I xiv, 47–51, covering the rule of Saul, and II viii, that of David. The sections excluded by the Deuteronomistic redaction were then, as in the book of Judges, brought back again by a later hand, though to some extent in the wrong place. Thus it has come about, for example, that II xxi, 1–14, xxiv, which really belong before ix, are now very unsuitably placed after II xx, and, with xxi, 15–22; xxii; xxiii, 1–7, 8–39, divide II Sam. xx from its continuation in I Kings i–ii (p. 269).

Budde's conception of these books as the joining of two parallel sources, much curtailed by the Deuteronomistic redaction and subsequently filled out by a later hand, has found much acceptance. But just as since about the beginning of the twentieth century there have been many objections raised to the new documentary hypothesis (pp. 166 f.), so also its application to the books of Samuel has not passed without criticism. Gressmann set up as an alternative a sort of 'fragment' hypothesis, and sought to explain these books as loosely put together from single narratives of larger or smaller size. Here, just as in the analogous phase of Pentateuchal criticism (pp. 166 f.), it is rather a shift of interest which is responsible than a move towards a new answering of the question of the composition of the books. It is the single narratives which here are at the centre of the investigation, and many valuable contributions have been made to their understanding. By contrast, the question of the structure and so the evolution of the book appears as relatively unimportant, and it is thought that everything has been achieved with the analysis of the individual narratives, and that the book can be understood simply as a collocation of many individual narratives. The same may be said of Caspari's commentary on the books of Samuel. Steuernagel* and Rost attempt to explain the composition of the books in a rather different manner. The former in fact assumes for the first book the presence side by side of two strands running in parallel and mutually exclusive. He concedes further that the one, S^a, which covers the main part of I i to II viii, with the exclusion of what is below indicated as the extent of S^b, offers the older and more trustworthy narrative and is likely to have come from the Yahwistic school. The other, S^b (I i, 1–28; ii, 11, 18–21, 26; iii, 1–11, 15–21; iv, 1a; vii,

2–17*; viii, 1–22;[11] x, 17–24; xii*; x, 25b–27a; xv, 1–23, 32–5; xxviii, 3–25*;[12] xxxi, 1–10, 11–13?), strikes in the manner of E a more religious note, and belongs in the Elohistic circle. Neither of these sources goes beyond II viii, but here, apart from some short passages, a third source is met with, namely the family history of David, to which belongs the main part of II ix–xx + I Kings i–ii. Rost, who is not, however, aiming at providing a complete analysis of the two books, completely denies, as we have seen (pp. 137 f.), the existence of narrative strands running parallel to one another, and believes that he can clearly demonstrate in them two narrative works placed not side by side but consecutively, namely the 'Abiathar' source and the 'Succession History' of David. Thus in so far as Rost's partial examination of the material makes it possible to judge, he considers unjustified the tracing of sections lengthwise through the books, and explains them as a series of narrative works, following one upon the other, originally separate, treating quite definite themes and sharply defined. The same is true, as we have seen (p. 243), of Noth. Finally, Smend and Eissfeldt believe that, as in the Heptateuch (pp. 246, 264), the solution of the problem here is to be found in the application of the theory of three sources, and they seek to explain these books as the combination of three parallel strands, which are presumably continuations of the three narrative strands of the Heptateuch— L, J and E.[13]

3. *Analysis.* It thus appears that there is a considerable variety of contributors to the composition of these books, and it will not be easy to explain with even a modicum of clarity a situation which is actually capable of various interpretations. The survey just made of previous analyses does however point to some generally recognised results. One is the separation of the section II ix–xx + I Kings i–ii as a more or less unified entity, while it remains for the moment an open question as to whether this complex should be extended backwards or even further forwards. The other is the recognition that in I vii–xv[14] there are present at least two mutually exclusive presentations of the beginnings of Israelite kingship, and that one of them, to which chs. vii–viii and xii belong, has a marked affinity to the Elohistic sections of the Hexateuch and of the book of Judges, whereas the other is in many respects reminiscent of J.

[11] Stoebe, 'Anmerkungen zu I Sam. viii, 16 und xvi, 20' VT 4 (1954), pp. 177–84.

[12] Trencsényi-Waldapfel, 'Die Hexe von Endor und die griechisch-römische Welt' AcOr[B] 12 (1961), pp. 201–22. Lit. § 126.

[13] On Simpson's analysis, cf. above, p. 246, n. 10.

[14] Beyerlin, 'Das Königscharisma bei Saul' ZAW 73 (1961), pp. 186–201; Buber, 'Das Volksbegehren' *Lohmeyer-Gedenkschr.* (1951), pp. 53–66; 'Die Erzählung von Sauls Königswahl' VT 6 (1956), pp. 113–73; Buccellati, 'Da Saul a David. Le origini della monarchia israelitica alla luce della storiografia contemporanea' Biblia e Oriente 1 (1959), pp. 99–128; Irwin, 'Samuel and the Rise of the Monarchy' AJSL 58 (1941), pp. 113–34; Möhlenbrink, 'Sauls Ammoniterfeldzug und Samuels Beitrag zum Königtum des Saul' ZAW 58 (1940/1), pp. 57–70; Press, 'Der Prophet Samuel. Eine traditionsgeschichtliche Untersuchung' ZAW 56 (1938), pp. 177–225; Robertson, 'Samuel and Saul' BJRL 28 (1944), pp. 175–206 = *The Old Testament Problem* (1950), pp. 105–36; Segal, 'I Samuel x, 7–8' [Hebr.] Tarbiz 22 (1950/1), pp. 124; Weiser, 'I Samuel xv' ZAW 54 (1936), pp. 1–28 = *Ausg. Schr.* (1961), pp. 201–28; 'Samuels "Philister-Sieg"' ZThK 56 (1959), pp. 253–72; 'Samuel und die Vorgeschichte des israelitischen Königtums' ZThK 57 (1960), pp. 141–61; Wildberger, 'Samuel und die Entstehung des israelitischen Königtums' ThZ 13 (1957), pp. 442–69. Lit. § 126.

So far as this last point is concerned, it is in fact quite clear that the sections of I vii–xv which show Elohistic colouring belong together. They must once have been joined in uninterrupted sequence and only lost their interconnection when other material was added to them. xii, Samuel's farewell speech, for example, must at one time have followed directly on the choosing of Saul as king by lot related in x, 17–27*, and this in its turn links back beyond ix, 1–x, 16, to the narrative in viii[15] of how the people brought to Samuel their desire for a king. The question is only whether and how far this strand continues further through the book. Even Steuernagel*, in spite of his reluctance to apply the theory of two sources to the books of Samuel, believed that he could trace this source, his S[b], through to the end of the first book of Samuel, and there can indeed be no doubt that, apart from some small passages and I Sam. xxxi*, the sections which were assigned by him in I xv–xxxi to S[b] (pp. 270 f.) really do belong here. But certain other sections must also be reckoned as belonging to it, namely xvi, 1–13, the anointing of David by Samuel;[16] one strand from the interwoven material of xvi, 14–xxi, 1—a section which can only be unravelled with great difficulty—and particularly here one of the two Goliath narratives[17] combined in xvii; xxi, 11–16, David's remarkable journey to Achish of Gath;[18] xxii, 3–5, David's short stay in Moab; xxiii, 14b–18, David's persecution by Saul and the covenant concluded between David and Jonathan;[19] xxv, 1, David's flight to Paran. These provide an intelligible and fairly compact group of stories, from which at the most small sections have been broken off. We have already seen that one of the narratives which belongs with this strand, namely that concerning Samuel's farewell speech in I xii, quite clearly presupposes in vv. 9–11 the E narrative of the book of Judges, and only this narrative (p. 265), and this can only be explained on the assumption that the same narrator is here engaged as there—in other words, the strand in I Sam. which has Elohistic traits is in reality the continuation of the E of the book of Judges, and hence of the E of the Hexateuch. If this strand may thus be traced with certainty further back, it is nevertheless very difficult to decide whether it may also be found in what follows, namely in II i to I Kings ii. There are some sections here which seem to be superfluous to the main narrative and perhaps derive from a parallel narrative. Among these II vii*, xii, 1–15a*,[20] and I Kings ii, 1–12, 31b–33, 44–5,[21] are strongly reminiscent of E, and could be taken as indications that this strand really does extend beyond I xxviii. It may have been only very sketchy here, as it is also very sketchy in the second half of the first

[15] Mendelsohn, 'Samuel's Denunciation of Kingship in the Light of the Akkadian Documents from Ugarit' BASOR 143 (1956), pp. 17–22.
[16] Goslinga, 'Het geheim der verwachting van Davids koningschap' GThT 57 (1957), pp. 6–21. Lit. p. 279, n. 43.
[17] Donner, 'Zum "Streitlustigen" in Sinuhe B 110' ZÄS 81 (1956), pp. 61 f.; Lanczowski, 'Die Geschichte vom Riesen Goliath und der Kampf Sinuhes mit dem Starken von Retenu' MDAI Kairo 16 (1959), pp. 214–18; Stoebe, 'Die Goliathperikope I Sam. xvii, 1–xviii, 5 und die Textform der Septuaginta' VT 6 (1956), pp. 397–413; de Vaux, 'Les combats singuliers dans l'AT' Bibl 40 (1959), pp. 495–508. Cf. p. 52, n. 61.
[18] Bič, 'La folie de David' RHPhR 37 (1957), pp. 156–62.
[19] Morgenstern, 'David and Jonathan' JBL 78 (1959), pp. 322–5.
[20] Yaron, 'The Coptos Decree and 2 Sam. xii, 14' VT 9 (1959), pp. 89–91.
[21] Yaron, 'A Ramessid Parallel to I K. ii, 33, 44–45' VT 8 (1958), pp. 432 f.

book. On general grounds the probability must be considerable that E, which can hardly have been compiled before the middle of the ninth century (p. 203), carried down the history to its own time or at least near to it. But from I xxviii onwards the position differs from that in the earlier chapters. Up to that point there is a really continuous strand, or, if it is interrupted in short sections, it may easily be completed, whereas from then on there are individual sections which show E's character but no demonstrable connection between them. Hence it is not possible to get beyond a statement of what is possible or probable. When the books of Kings have been discussed, we must come back again to this question more closely (pp. 297–9).

If, at least in I Samuel, an E sequence may be demonstrated almost without gaps, there automatically becomes probable the existence also of an older sequence. E may be recognised, even more clearly in the books of Samuel than previously, as the reshaping into religious form of an older secular presentation, not only in its narrative of the origin of the kingdom, but also elsewhere, e.g. in the replacing of reports concerning David's military service with the Philistines (I xxvii, 1–xxviii, 2; xxix) which present him in an equivocal light, by a narrative which makes him stay only quite a short time in Philistia and shows him secure his speedy discharge by a skilful stratagem (I xxi, 11–16). But if the reshaping of the material presents a continuous strand, it may be assumed that this is also true of the original picture, the more clearly since the original picture admittedly bears the marks of the Yahweh stratum. Thus it is J, or, if L also has a share in it, it includes J, and we should then find here the same relationship of E to J as elsewhere. In fact, the passages which remain in the first book after the removal of the E material not only form a chronological sequence, this itself showing in its turn that there has been a hand at work ordering it, but there are also many links between the individual narratives. Thus the people's desire at the end of the narrative of Saul's victory over the Ammonites, that revenge should be taken on the 'worthless fellows' (xi, 12–13) clearly harks back to x, 26, where it is said that after Saul's election as king there were some who expressed themselves scornfully concerning him. Similarly the rejection of Saul narrated in xiii, 3–15* admittedly presupposes the command of x, 8, which here plays a role. The commonly proposed removal of these two links as secondary additions is quite unjustified. For the verses are in part so firmly integrated into their context, and in part of such individualised nature that their removal is purely arbitrary. But even if we do not wish to recognise these interconnections, it is nevertheless clear with a complex such as I xxvi, xxvii, 1–12*, xxix, 1–11*, xxx, that each narrative in turn presupposes the preceding one, and that the preceding one is directed towards what follows. David, pursued by Saul, eventually goes over to the Philistines in discouragement. When the latter gather for battle against Israel, he wishes to go with them as their liege, but because of the objection of the mistrustful Philistine princes he has to turn back to his Philistine residence. He utilises this opportunity for a blow at the Amalekites which in itself benefits Judah, but, more than this, puts him in a position to send shares of the booty to the elders of Judah and thus to ingratiate himself with his compatriots even though he stands in the service of the national enemy.

If the connection between the individual narratives is not everywhere so clearly visible as here, this is because the material of the first book, even without the E sections, is certainly not unified, but reveals overloadings of various kinds, including doublets standing side by side and parallel narratives interwoven with one another. Of doublets we may mention the generally recognised chapters I xxiv (Engedi)[22] and xxvi (wilderness of Ziph) which relate David's magnanimity towards his pursuer Saul transmitted in the context of the delightful story of David, Nabal and Abigail (xxv),[23] and these are in fact doublets within the Yahweh stratum; for E has a corresponding reference in I xxiii, 14b–18. Furthermore I xix, 11–17 and xx, 1b–xxi, 1,[24] appear to be parallels, in that according to the first story it is Michal[25] who helps David to flight, and according to the second it is Jonathan, whereas according to the E parallel in I xix, 18–24 + xx, 1a, it is Samuel who renders him this service. Similarly, beside E which appears in I xvi, 14–23*, and brings David into contact with Saul by letting him come to his court as an experienced harpist, there appears to be in addition a double account of this event. According to I xiv, 52, and the words in I xvi, 18, 21, *a man of valour, a man of war* (v. 18), *and he became his armour-bearer* (v. 21), which link back to this verse, he was desired by Saul as a valiant warrior. Yet according to the J strand of the Goliath story in I, xvii, 1–xviii, 4, he was quite unknown at court before his victory, and it was this which first opened the way thither for him. A mixture of sources, however, appears to be present within the J material in the Ark narrative in I iv–vi, in the narrative of David's flight to Nob and the extermination of the priesthood there in I xxi, 2–10; xxii, 6–23, and also probably in the account of the objection by the Philistine princes to David's taking part in the battle in I xxix, 1–11. Furthermore, the narratives which deal with Saul's beginnings in I ix–xi;[26] xiii[27]–xiv, clearly fall into two groups. The marvellous story of how Saul goes to seek his father's asses, but finds the kingdom, in ix, 1–x, 16,[28] is continued in I xi, 6a; xiii, 3bα, 4b–5, 7b–15a, and indeed between x, 16, and this sequel there can hardly have been anything else. The narrative of Saul's victory over the Ammonites in xi and that concerning his son's and his own victory over the Philistines which begins before the section xiii, 3–15*, that belongs with ix, 1–x, 16, and continues after it as far as xiv, 46, must therefore be assigned to another strand. But even if one or other of the features mentioned may perhaps be capable of a different explanation than is here given to it, on the whole there can hardly be any doubt that the material of the first book, without the E sec-

---

[22] Aharoni, 'Archaeological Survey of 'Ein-Gedi with an Additional Note by J. Naveh' [Hebr., Engl. sum.] BIES 22 (1958), pp. 27–48, VI–VII, Pls. 10–16.

[23] Driver, 'A Lost Colloquialism in the OT (I Samuel xxv, 6)' JThSt 8 (1957), pp. 272–3; Eissfeldt, *Der Beutel der Lebendigen* (BAL 105, 6, 1960): on I xxv, 29; Malamat, 'Military Rationing in Papyrus Anastasi I and the Bible' *Mél. Bibl. Robert* (1957), pp. 114–21.

[24] Finkelstein, 'An Ignored Haplography in Samuel' JSSt 4 (1959), pp. 356–7: on I xx, 23.

[25] Stoebe, 'David und Mikal' BZAW 77 (1958), pp. 224–43.

[26] On Gibeah in I, x, 26, cf. p. 258, n. 1.

[27] Driver, 'On the Hebr. פצירה (I Samuel xiii, 21)' AfO 15 (1945/51), p. 68. Lit. § 126.

[28] Dornseiff, 'Archilochos von Paros und Saul von Gibea' ThLZ 80 (1955), cols. 499 f.

tions, reveals traces of a double strand over and over again, and is most readily understood as the combination of two parallel strands.

These two parallel strands are related to one another to a large extent like L and J in the Heptateuch, in that L offers the older and cruder narratives, in many cases also historically more credible. Thus the narratives concerning Saul's victories over the Ammonites (I xi) and over the Philistines (I xiii–xiv) are undoubtedly closer to reality than the narrative of J in I ix, 1–x, 16 + xi, 6a + xiii, 3–15*, which ends with Saul's rejection; and of the three parallel narratives concerning David's flight it is the one in which Michal helps him to escape which is clearly the crudest and most archaic, and we may note in passing that it has a contact with L in Genesis in that, like the latter (Gen. xxxi, 19, 21*, 22–3, 27*, 30, 32*, 33*, 34*, 35, 36*), it makes the Teraphim play a significant role in the flight. Thus we may in fact denote these two strands as L and J, and regard them as continuations of the L and J strands which run through the Heptateuch. We have already noted (p. 265) that the two double narratives to be found in the 'appendix' to the book of Judges (xvii–xxi), which may also be allocated to L and J, may be very well understood as introductions to two narratives with a positive view of the monarchy, and this is indeed the case in that L like J in I ix–xiv, regards the monarchy of Saul as a gift of divine grace.

The second book offers a substantially different picture to analysis. We have already seen that of the E stratum there are perhaps a few isolated traces to be discovered, but hardly a connected thread. The Yahweh stratum, however, is substantially unified. II i, the narrative of the effect upon David of the report of the death of Saul and his sons, does, it is true, reveal a few features which may be interpreted as indications of a double strand, and, if this interpretation were correct, this narrative would have to be divided between L and J. But in the main i–viii, apart from vii which has already been discussed (pp. 270, 272 f.), is certainly unified on the whole. The well-constructed narrative is directed towards a clear end. From the anointing of David as king over Judah in Hebron, soon after Saul's death, it passes through the conflict[29] with Eshbaal[30] and Abner, and his anointing as king over all Israel after the assassination of Abner and Eshbaal, and is directed towards his fortifying and cultic adorning of the fortress of Jerusalem planned as his new residence. It ends with a concisely told narrative of David's victories over the Philistines, Moab, Aram,[31] and Edom (viii, 1–15)[32]

---

[29] Eissfeldt, 'Ein gescheiterter Versuch der Wiedervereinigung Israels (II Sam. ii, 12–iii, 1)' NC 3 (1951), pp. 110–27; 'Noch einmal: Ein gescheiterter Versuch der Wiedervereinigung Israels' NC 4 (1952), pp. 55–9; Gordon, 'Belt-Wrestling in the Bible World' HUCA 23, 1 (1950), pp. 131–6, Pls. I–V; Sukenik, ' "Let the young men, I pray thee, arise and play before us" ' JPOS 21 (1948), pp. 110–16.

[30] We must read אִישׁ־בַּעַל (אֶשְׁבַּעַל in I Chron. viii, 33, ix, 39) in II, ii–iv, instead of the form Ish-bosheth (אִישׁ־בֹּשֶׁת) which has been deliberately mutilated.

[31] Malamat, 'The Kingdom of David and Solomon in its Contact with Aram Naharaim' BA 21 (1958), pp. 96–102; Unger, *Israel and the Arameans of Damascus* (1957). Lit. p. 296, n. 57; § 126.

[32] Alt, 'Zu II Samuel viii, 1' ZAW 54 (1936), pp. 149–52; Ap-Thomas, 'A Numerical Poser' JNESt 2 (1943), pp. 198–200: on II Sam. viii, 4; x, 18; I Chr. xviii, 4; xix, 18; Eissfeldt, 'Israelitisch-philistäische Grenzverschiebungen von David bis auf die Assyrerzeit' ZDPV 66 (1943), pp. 115–28 = *Kl.Schr.* II (1963), pp. 453–63.

and a list of the members of David's court (viii, 16–18). This enumeration, which corresponds to the list of the members of Saul's court in I xiv, 49–51, also preceded by a short survey of the king's wars, marks the conclusion of the narrative of the king's reign just as clearly as is the case in I xiv, 49–51, where in fact with xiv, 52, the transition is made to David. The fact that these two closing surveys of the warlike deeds and of the court of the king (wrongly attributed, as has already been suggested, to a Deuteronomistic redactor (p. 270)), are identically constructed, makes it probable that the same source is present in the one place as in the other, viz. L, since xiv, 47–51, is certainly to be assigned to L. Thus L simply related the rise of the two kings, and gave only brief notes concerning their subsequent rule, and this is a completely intelligible procedure which also has its parallels in the judges stories. For there too only the action which forms the basis of the hero's fame is related.

This already establishes the point that the narrative which follows viii, generally recognised as a large coherent passage dealing with the family of David, viz. II ix–xx + I Kings i–ii, the 'Succession Story' (pp. 137–9), cannot be the continuation of ii–vi, viii, but represents a new entity. In fact it stands after viii at too late a point. David's question at the beginning of ix, as to whether anyone survives of the house of Saul, has no meaning after the survey in viii of the whole reign of David, but would perhaps have a suitable place after vi, in that with the taking up of the Ark into Jerusalem the narrative of David's rise to power is at an end, and it is now an appropriate time to do what can be done to heal wounds which have been opened in the conflicts which accompanied his rise. That ix–xx + I Kings i–ii are not the continuation of ii–vi, viii, but rather, though admittedly in a rather special sense, a parallel to it, is also seen in the fact that x, 15–19, relates the same material as viii, 8–13, namely the complete overthrow of Aram, and it is further made probable by the fact that the list of David's officials appears twice, in viii, 16–18, and, with some variations, in xx, 23–6. The only question is whether we are to follow Steuernagel*, Rost, Noth and many others and to see in ix–xx + I Kings i–ii a new source, relating only the events included here, or at any rate mainly these events, if perchance something of the previous material belongs to it or something has been lost before ix. Or are we to assume that this complex is the continuation of one of the sources running through the first book, in which case only J comes in for consideration? For ii–vi, viii belong to L, and features of E are not to be found in the main body of ix–xx + I Kings i–ii. But ix does provide a link to the J strand in the first book in that David's relationship of friendship to Jonathan is especially underlined in both (I xx, 1b–42 + xxi, 1, on the one hand, II ix, 7, on the other), and it has long been observed that the complex reveals a variety of linguistic contacts with the J of the Heptateuch.[33] We must therefore regard these family and court stories of David, which have rightly been praised as a masterpiece or even as *the* masterpiece of Israelite historical writing (p. 50), as the continuation of the J strand noted in the first book. This presupposes that J too related the rise of David to be king over all Israel with his residence in

[33] Klaehn, *Die sprachliche Verwandtschaft der Quelle K der Samuelisbücher mit der Quelle J des Heptateuch* (Diss. theol. Rostock, 1914), cf. also above, p. 245.

Jerusalem, and that this narrative was broken off in favour of that of L. There is nothing to prevent this assumption. A fragment of the J parallel does in fact seem to survive in the verse iv, 4, which disturbs its present context; for this verse also shows the partiality for Jonathan which is characteristic of J. Apart from these points, all that needs to be said about ix–xx + I Kings i–ii has already been said in Part II (pp. 137–42).

It remains only to say a little about the narratives, lists and songs of II xxi–xxiv, properly described as a supplement to the books of Samuel. What first strikes our attention is that here the songs xxii and xxiii, 1–7,[34] which belong together in content as *last words of David*, as the latter is explicitly described, actually stand next to one another. The two narratives, that concerning a famine which broke out in the time of David, and the execution of seven members of Saul's family occasioned by it in xxi, 1–14, and that concerning a plague brought upon Israel as punishment for David's undertaking of a census of the people and the altar of atonement erected to avert this plague in xxiv, 1–25,[35] belong together, but are divided from one another. So too the enumeration of the four descendants of the giants (descendants of Raphah) defeated by David's heroes[36] in xxi, 15–22, and the list of the 'three' and the 'thirty' in xxiii, 8–39,[37] are separated by sections of a different kind. The two narratives are divided by the songs and the lists; the lists are divided by the songs. As the introduction in xxiv, 1, shows: *And Yahweh's anger was again kindled against Israel* the second narrative is the sequel to the first, and the enumeration of the 'sons of Raphah' in xxi, 15–22, and the list of the 'three' and the 'thirty' in xxiii, 8–39, belong closely together in content and form. A sure explanation of this remarkable interlocked effect in the passages can hardly be given. But what is quite clear is that neither the pair of narratives nor the pair of lists is in place between II Sam. xx and I Kings i–ii, and that the pair of songs also does not fit here very well. For I Kings i–ii was originally in all probability the direct continuation of II Sam. xx, and even if that were not the case, we should more naturally think that the sections missing there would be narratives of the same nature as the complexes II Sam. ix–xx and I Kings i–ii, and at most consider it possible for the two 'last words' or one of the two to have stood originally between II Sam. xx and I Kings i–ii. The question then arises as to where these narratives, lists and songs have come from and how they have come into their present position. It would be possible for the two narratives of xxi, 1–14, and xxiv[38] to belong

[34] Johnson, *Sacral Kingship* (1955), pp. 14–17; Mowinckel, ' "Die letzten Worte Davids" II Sam. xxiii, 1–7' ZAW 45 (1927), pp. 30–58; Nyberg, 'Studien zum Religions-kampf im AT' ARW 35 (1938), pp. 329–87, see pp. 377–86.

[35] Speiser, 'Census and Ritual Expiation in Mari and Israel' BASOR 149 (1959), pp. 17–25.

[36] Goldschmid, 'David-Elḥanan' [Hebr., Engl. sum.] BJPES 14 (1947/9), p. 122, IV; Honeyman, 'The Evidence for Regnal Names among the Hebrews' JBL 67 (1948), pp. 13–25, see pp. 23 f.; Pákozdy, "Elḥānān—der frühere Name Davids?' ZAW 68 (1956), pp. 257–9; Schofield, 'Mari and the OT' ET 66 (1954/5), pp. 250–2, see p. 251; Stamm, 'Der Name des Königs David' SVT VII (1960), pp. 165–83; Vogt, "*El haššᵉlōšā lōʼ-bā*" Bibl 40 (1959), pp. 1062 f.

[37] Hull, 'David and the Well of Bethlehem: an Irish Parallel' *Folk-lore* 44 (1933), pp. 214–18: on xxiii, 13–18; Pohl, 'Alalaḫ und AT' Or 28 (1959), pp. 298 f.: on xxiii, 19, 23.

[38] Malamat, 'Doctrines of Causality in Hittite and Biblical Historiography: a Parallel' VT 5 (1955), pp. 1–12; Fuss, 'II. Samuel xxiv' ZAW 74 (1962), pp. 145–64.

to the main strand of II Sam. ix–xx + I Kings i–ii, i.e. to J, and originally simply to have occupied another position within it. xxi, 1–14, might thus be understood as a preparation for ix. It must be so understood if xxi, 7, with its statement that David, when he delivered up the descendants of Saul, spared a son of Jonathan because of his friendship with his father, originally belongs to the narrative and is not, as may be possible, a gloss based upon ix. xxi, 1–14, would then have its original place before ix, and the narrative of the plague (xxiv)[39] which in fact belongs closely with xxi, 1–14, could have followed directly after ix. We may also suggest reasons for the removal of the two narratives from their original position, as for example that a redactor wished to explain the plagues here described as being, together with Absalom's rebellion (II xii, 10–12), the punishment for David's sin against Bathsheba and Uriah, and was hence compelled to place them right at the end of the Absalom story, i.e. after xx (cf. p. 288 on I Kings xi, 1–40). But a firm decision is not possible.

The position is different in regard to the lists of xxi, 15–22; xxiii, 8–39,[40] and the songs of xxii; xxiii, 1–7. First, so far as the lists are concerned, there is really no connection between them, so that each must be assessed on its own. In the first, xxi, 15–22, the opening *And the Philistines had war again with Israel* showed that originally it belonged in a narrative context. We might therefore consider whether it forms the sequel to the narrative in II Sam. v, 17–25, concerning two victories of David over the Philistines; this would indicate that it belonged to L. The shifting of the section to its present position could then be explained as due to a redactor's wish first to carry through to the end the narrative of David's own deeds, before he turned to his heroes. This would also provide a reason for the placing of the list in xxiii, 8–39, in its present position. Originally it could have stood as a part of L after the list of David's court in II Sam. viii, 16–18, assigned to L. These lists are in any case ancient, no matter whether we owe their preservation to the fact that they originally belonged in one of the narrative series which we may establish in Samuel, or whether they at first existed as separate pieces and were only later taken up in the narrative of the books of Samuel. In this connection the fact should also be mentioned that the parallel list to II Sam. xxiii, 8–39, in I Chron. xi, 10–47, is six verses longer, and so enumerates more heroes of David than does the former (p. 532), evidence that even books from a later period such as Chronicles could still produce valuable ancient records (p. 532).

With regard to the two songs, II Sam. xxii and xxiii, 1–7, of which the former reappears in the Psalter as Psalm xviii (pp. 104, 452), it is difficult to decide whether they belonged originally to one of the series of material surmised for the books of Samuel, either composed by the compiler himself, or, what is much more probable, were found by him readily available and taken up into his work. We have already noted that they do not really belong between II Sam. xx

---

[39] It may be noted that in I Chron. xxi, this narrative is placed after the story of the Ammonite war (cf. II Sam. xi–xiii, I Chron. xx, 1–3) and part of the 'giants' tradition (cf. II Sam. xxi, 18–22, I Chron. xx, 4–8). [Translator's note.]

[40] Botterweck, 'Zur Eigenart der chronistischen Davidgeschichte' *Christian-Festschr.* (1956), pp. 12–31 = ThQ 136 (1956), pp. 402–35, cf. pp. 15 = 411 f., on David's heroes; Elliger, 'Die dreissig Helden Davids' PJB 31 (1935), pp. 29–75.

and I Kings i–ii, and thus, since here in the main we have J and in addition also E, can hardly be considered as parts of J and E. No such difficulties would prevent their being assigned to L, and we could even assign both songs to the one narrative work. But, apart from other objections, against this possibility must be set the normal dating of both passages in the late pre-exilic period or even later, a dating based upon substantial grounds. If this late dating is correct, the songs cannot have belonged to a narrative strand which was utilised in the pre-deuteronomic work, but must have been inserted later, perhaps only after its Deuteronomistic edition. But it may be that these two songs, like many other Old Testament songs, and in particular those in the Psalter, are considerably older than is usually assumed, and then they could be assigned to one of the older narrative works, as seems to be the case with the Song of Moses in Deut. xxxii, 1–43 (pp. 226–7).

Thus it appears that the books of Samuel too are to be explained as the combination of three narrative strands, amplified secondarily with various individual passages, the three strands being continuations of the corresponding Heptateuch strands L, J and E, though here as everywhere else it is self-evident that the authors of the strands, even that of L, found available to them material already formed. Thus the L narrative of the fortunes of the Ark, now divided into two parts corresponding to the different moments in time of the narrative (I iv–vi and II vi),[41] must have lain before the author of L as a connected whole. Likewise he certainly found already to hand the lists of members of the court of Saul (I xiv, 49–51) and of David (II viii, 16–18), the undoubtedly genuine funeral dirge of David on Abner in II iii, 33–4, and the lists of the sons born to David in Hebron (II iii, 2–5, including Absalom, son of Maacah the daughter of Talmai, king of Geshur)[42] and in Jerusalem (II v, 13–15, including Solomon); and perhaps likewise the enumeration of the heroic deeds of David's companions (II xxi, 15–22) as well as the lists of the 'three' and the 'thirty' (II xxiii, 8–39). Undoubtedly a number of others of L's narratives were not set down in writing for the first time by him, but were already available in written form and could be taken up into his work with perhaps only slight modifications. This impression is made in particular by the narratives of II ii–vi, viii, which, in contrast to the more legendary stories of the first book which L probably still found as popular tales, must be reckoned to the type of historical writing[43] (p. 50). In the general outline of his presentation, J is dependent, so far as the first book

[41] Bewer, 'The Original Reading of I Sam vi, 19a' JBL 57 (1938), pp. 89–91; Driver, 'The Plague of the Philistines (I Samuel v, 6–vi, 16)' JRAS (1950), pp. 50–2; Dus, 'Der Brauch der Ladewanderung im alten Israel' ThZ 17 (1961), pp. 1–16; Naveh, 'Khirbat al-Muqanna'—Ekron. An Archaeological Survey' IEJ 8 (1958), pp. 87–100, 165–70. Pls. 20–3; Nielsen, 'Some Reflections on the History of the Ark' SVT VII (1960), pp, 61–74; Palache, 'De beteekenis van de muis in I Sam. vi' Op. Min. (1959), pp. 99–100; Porter, 'The Interpretation of II Samuel vi and Psalm cxxxii' JThSt 5 (1954), pp. 161–73; Tur-Sinai, 'The Ark of God at Beit Shemesh (I Sam. vi) and Pereṣ 'Uzza (II Sam. vi, 1; I Chron. xiii)' VT 1 (1951), pp. 275–86; Winton Thomas, 'A Note on וְנוֹדַע לָכֶם, I Samuel vi, 3' JThSt 11 (1960), pp. 52 f. Lit. § 126.
[42] Mazar, 'Geshur and Ma'cah' [Hebr., Engl. sum.] Zion 23/4 (1958/9), pp. 115–23, I; 'Geshur and Maacah' JBL 80 (1961), pp. 16–28.
[43] Goslinga, 'Wanneer is David Koning geworden over geheel Israël?' GThT 56 (1956), pp. 11–16. Lit. p. 272, n. 16.

is concerned, upon that of L, but he too could also derive material from the living source of popular tradition. For while such masterpieces of narrative art as I ix, 1–x, 16, and xxiv were certainly shaped by J, he did not invent the material and was not even inspired by L (xxvi)—this applies to the second example—to the invention of a similar tale, but derived it from popular story-telling. This is even more true of the section II ix–xx + I Kings i–ii, which has no original in L. Here we must certainly reckon with written originals. So far as the funeral dirge of David on the death of Saul and Jonathan (II i, 17–27) is concerned, which was apparently first brought into the narrative context by J, it is quite clear that he found it already in written form. Even E who, as we have seen (pp. 272 f.), for the most part undertakes a reshaping with a religious bias of the L and J presentation, was able to derive further new material from popular tradition, and this not only of a kind which reveals the taste of a relatively late period and stands rather far from historical reality (I xix, 18–24 + xx, 1a; xxi, 11–16) but also narratives which go back to good ancient tradition, such as that concerning Saul's campaign against the Amalekites in I xv, and that concerning his visit to the witch of Endor in I xxviii.

4. *Deuteronomistic redaction*. It has already been said (p. 270) that the books of Samuel when complete as to content though not yet delimited (cf. below) underwent a Deuteronomistic redaction like the books of Joshua and Judges. But this redaction has interfered with the material much more slightly than is usually believed. Apart from other small additions, it is really only I ii, 27–36, and II vii[44] which bear clear marks of Deuteronomistic revision. The first of these shows this especially in the threat which is often but perhaps wrongly interpreted as a *vaticinium ex eventu* referring to the dismissal from office of the priests here envisaged as descendants of Eli (verse 36), brought about by the reform of Josiah. The second shows it in the reference to Solomon's building of the Temple (verse 13). In these circumstances we cannot decide whether, as in Deut., Josh. and Judg. we have also in Sam. two Deuteronomistic editions combined, or only one. It is, however, probable that we should assume two editions, though almost identical and therefore coinciding when they were combined, since Kings again appears most naturally as the combination of two Deuteronomistic editions, and these editions are surely likely to have covered the whole of the period lying between the purported publication of D, i.e. Moses' last days, and its carrying through, i.e. the reform of Josiah (p. 300). The dividing off of the narratives contained in Sam. as a separate book is likely to have taken place, as with Josh. and Judg., in connection with the constituting of the Pentateuch as a separate entity (pp. 256–7).

5. *Historical value*. We have already said what is essential concerning the

[44] Ahlström, 'Profeten Natan och tempelbygget' SEA 25 (1960), pp. 5–22; 'Der Prophet Nathan und der Tempelbau' VT 11 (1961), pp. 113–27; van den Bussche (p. 538, n. 23); McKenzie, 'The Dynastic Oracle: II Sam. vii' Theol. Studies 8 (1947), pp. 187–218; Morenz, 'Ägyptische und davidische Königstitulatur' ZÄS 79 (1954), pp. 73 f.; Mowinckel, 'Natanforjettelsen 2. Sam Kap. vii' SEA 12 (1947), pp. 220–9; Noth, 'David und Israel in 2 Samuel vii' *Mél. Bibl. Robert* (1957), pp. 122–30 = *Ges. Stud. z. AT* (²1960), pp. 334–5; Simon, 'La Prophétie de Nathan et le Temple' RHPhR 32 (1952), pp. 41–58; Widengren (p. 51, n. 59), pp. 59–61: on II Sam. vii. Lit. § 126.

historical worth of the books of Samuel. A short summary will therefore suffice
here. In the first book, the narratives of all three strands have a strongly legendary character, though those in L and J are substantially nearer to the actual
course of events than those of E, which strongly modifies the actual events in
line with certain religious ideas and ethical postulates. But in the second book,
the narratives of L in ii–vi, viii and of J in ix–xx + I Kings i–ii are very reliable,
and we must often assume that originals were here used which go back to eye-
witnesses. E, if indeed the small sections which are reminiscent of his manner
are really to be ascribed to him, here too modifies the events in line with his
religious and ethical pragmatism. The two narratives which stand in the
'appendix' II xxi–xxiv, namely II xxi, 1–14,[45] xxiv are strongly legendary in
character, but still allow the historical events to which they are linked to be
clearly recognised. Even more historically reliable are the lists in II xxi, 15–22;
xxiii, 8–39, in part combined with anecdotes. Of the songs taken up in part by
L and J and in part by later elaborators, David's funeral dirges on Saul and
Jonathan (II i, 17–27)[46] and on Abner (II iii, 33–4) are certainly genuine. Nor
is this completely impossible with the thanksgiving song of David (II xxii) and
with his last words (II xxiii, 1–7). It is, however, more reasonable to assume that
they have simply been put into his mouth, though this may have happened
comparatively early, for they must at any rate derive from the time when at
least the Judaean monarchy still existed. On the other hand, the possibility of
genuineness can hardly be seriously considered with reference to the Song of
Hannah (I ii, 1–10),[47] a psalm belonging to the type of the hymn (pp. 105–9),
though this does not by any means imply that it must have been inserted at a
late date in the Samuel narrative and may not already have been taken up by E.

§ 41. THE BOOKS OF KINGS

Literature: (a) Commentaries: BOuT: van den Born (1958); Cent. B: Skinner (1904);
Echter-B: Rehm (1949); EH: Šanda (1911/12); HK: Kittel (1902); HS: Landersdorfer
(1927); HSAT: Eissfeldt (1922); IB: Snaith, Sockman, Calkins (1954); ICC: Montgomery,
Gehman (1951); Jerusalem-B: de Vaux (²1958); KeH: Thenius-Loehr (³1898); KHC:
Benzinger (1899); SAT: Gressmann (²1921); Soncino-B: Slotki (1950); SZ: Klostermann
(1887).
   (b) Other Works: Aharoni, 'The Chronology of the Kings of Israel and Judah' [Hebr.]
Tarbiz 21 (1949/50), pp. 92–100; Albright, 'The Chronology of the Divided Monarchy of
Israel' BASOR 100 (1945), pp. 16–22; 'Further Light on Synchronisms between Egypt

---

[45] Cazelles, 'David's Monarchy and the Gibeonite Claim' PEQ 87 (1955), pp. 165–75;
Dus, 'Gibeon—eine Kultstätte des Šmš und die Stadt des benjaminitischen Schicksals'
VT 10 (1960), pp. 353–74; Kapelrud, 'King and Fertility. A Discussion of II Sam. xxi,
1–14' NTT 56 (1955), pp. 113–22; 'King David and the Sons of Saul' Suppl. to Numen
IV (1959), pp. 294–301; 'König David und die Söhne des Saul' ZAW 67 (1955), pp.
198–205; Prado, 'El exterminio de la familia de Saul (2 Sam. xxi, 1–14)' Sefarad 14 (1954),
pp. 43–57. Lit. p. 250, n. 9; § 126.
[46] Goslinga, 'Davids Klaaglied over Saul en Jonathan' GThT 50 (1950), pp. 53–70;
Speiser, 'An Analogue to II Sam. i, 21, 'Aqht 1, 44–45' JBL 69 (1950), pp. 377 f.
[47] Bressan, 'Il cantico di Anna' Bibl 32 (1951), pp. 503–21; 33 (1952), pp. 67–89. Lit. § 126.

and Asia in the Period 935–685 B.C.' BASOR 141 (1956), pp. 23–7; Begrich, *Die Chronologie der Könige von Israel und Juda und die Quellen des Rahmens der Königsbücher* (BHTh 3, 1929); Burney, *Notes on the Hebrew Text of the Books of Kings* (1903); Carlier, *La chronologie des rois de Juda et d'Israël* (1953); Hallo, 'From Qarqar to Carchemish: Assyria and Israel in the Light of New Discoveries' BA 23 (1960), pp. 34–61; Jepsen, *Die Quellen des Königsbuches* (1953, [2]1956); Lewy, *Die Chronologie der Könige von Israel und Juda* (1927); van der Meer, *The Chronology of Ancient Western Asia and Egypt* ([3]1963); Mowinckel, 'Die Chronologie der israelitischen und jüdischen Könige AcOr [L] 10 (1932), pp. 161–277; 'Israelittisk-judeisk kongekronologi' NTT 56 (1955), pp. 279–95; Rudolph, 'Zum Text der Königsbücher' ZAW 63 (1951), pp. 201–15; Thiele, 'The Chronology of the Kings of Judah and Israel' JNESt 3 (1944), pp. 137–86, I Pl.; *The Mysterious Numbers of the Hebrew Kings* (1951); ' A Comparison of the Chronological Data of Israel and Judah' VT 4 (1954), pp. 185–95; 'The Question of Coregencies among the Hebrew Kings' *Papers Irwin* (1956), pp. 39–52; New Evidence on the Chronology of the Last Kings of Judah' BASOR 143 (1956), pp. 22–7;[1] Vogelstein, *Biblical Chronology* I (1944); Wevers, 'Double Readings in the Book of Kings' JBL 65 (1946), pp. 307–10; 'A Study in the Hebrew Variants in the Books of Kings' ZAW 61 (1945/48), pp. 43–76; 'A Study in the Textual History of Codex Vaticanus in the Books of Kings' ZAW 64 (1952), pp. 178–89; Winckler, 'Beiträge zur Quellenscheidung der Königsbücher' *At. Untersuchungen* (1892), pp. 1 54. Cf. also Literature §§ 5, 18, 22–32, 37–40, 126.

1. *The framework.* Sufficient has been said already (p. 268) concerning the name and division of these books. They receive their particular stamp from the formulae which introduce and conclude the accounts of the various kings, the so-called framework sections. Already in I ii, 10–12, for David and xi, 41–3; xiv, 19–20, for Solomon and Jeroboam the concluding formula appears, and in iii, 2–3, for Solomon also at any rate a part of the otherwise normal introduction, namely the statement concerning his behaviour in cultic matters. But the full framework appears for the first time for Rehoboam in I xiv, 21–4: *Rehoboam was 41 years old when he became king, and he reigned 17 years in Jerusalem. . . . His mother's name was Naamah the Ammonitess.* [22]*And he*[2] *did what was evil in the sight of Yahweh, and ' he'*[3] *provoked him more than all ' his'*[4] *fathers had done with the sins which they committed.* [23]*They built high places for themselves . . .* etc., and in xiv, 29–31: *Now the rest of the acts of Rehoboam and all that he did, are they not written in the book of the history*[5] *of the kings of Judah . . .* [31]*And Rehoboam slept with his fathers and was buried,*[6] *in the city of David . . . and his son Abijah*[7] *became king in his place.* This framework appears from then on for all the kings of Israel and Judah, except that for the former the age of accession and the name of the queen mother are not given. With some few of the kings the framework or a part of it is missing, but this is always due to the particular nature of their accession or their death. Thus the concluding formula is lacking for the kings Joram and Ahaziah, murdered by Jehu (II ix, 22–8), and the introductory formula for the rebel Jehu (II x, 34–6). Both are missing for Athaliah,[8] because her accession and her death are reported differently in the narrative of II xi. Furthermore, it is natural that the concluding formula should,

---

[1] For further literature on the chronology of the years 626–586 B.C., see below, p. 296 n. 60.

[2] *Judah* is to be omitted, and the 3rd sing. form to be read in place of the 3rd plural.

[3] See previous note.   [4] See previous note.   [5] Literally: *the acts of the days.*

[6] Omit: *with his fathers.*   [7] Masing, 'Abia' CV 2 (1959), pp. 61–70.

[8] Katzenstein, 'Who Were the Parents of Athaliah?' IEJ 5 (1955), pp. 194–7.

be lacking with the kings who were violently deposed by the enemy, Hoshea of Israel (II xvii, 1–6),[9] Jehoahaz of Judah (II xxiii, 31–4), Jehoiachin of Judah (II xxiv, 8–17),[10] who is in addition further mentioned in II xxv, 27–30, and Zedekiah of Judah (II xxiv, 18–xxv, 21).

Of the points mentioned in the introductory formula, there are three that merit special attention. In the first place, there is the synchronism which stands next to the years of the duration of the reign, i.e. the dating of the accession of each Israelite king—with Nadab (I xv, 28) and Elah (I xvi, 10) their death also —according to the year of the then ruling Judaean king, and of the accession of each Judaean king by the year of the then ruling Israelite king. So, for example, we have in I xv, 25: *Nadab ben Jeroboam became king over Israel in the second year of Asa, king of Judah,* and in xv, 1: *In the eighteenth year of king Jeroboam ben Nebat, Abijah became king over Judah.* These synchronistic notes might have been based on a work like the 'Synchronistic History' from the library of Ashurbanipal, which sets together the contemporaneous events of Babylonian and Assyrian history.[11] They frequently do not agree with the absolute figures given for the reigns of the individual kings, and both series conflict at many points with the actual chronology which may be established from Assyrian sources. The reason for these disagreements was at first sought in the unreliability and artificiality of both the biblical series of figures. Subsequently there was a tendency to place trust in the absolute figures for the reigns and to see the errors exclusively or almost exclusively in the synchronistic notes, in that the latter were regarded as the result of later artificial calculation in contrast to the absolute figures thought to rest upon reliable ancient tradition. But the publication of synchronistic combinations of Assyrian and Babylonian kings extending back as far as the beginning of the second millennium,[12] gave a stimulus to further examination of the actual material, with the result that the synchronistic dates in the books of Kings have also proved themselves to be old and basically reliable. If incongruities are present within these dates and they do not fit with the absolute figures, the reason is that both in the absolute and in the synchronistic figure references many errors have crept in, and it is probable that we should also reckon with the possibility suggested by Begrich that several numerical systems were used and so have become confused.

The second point which should be especially dealt with from the framework is the judgement of the individual kings on the basis of whether they permitted the cultus practised outside the Temple of Jerusalem or not. If they did, they

[9] Albright, 'An Ostracon from Calah and the North-Israelite Diaspora' BASOR 149 (1958), pp. 33–6; Borger, 'Das Ende des ägyptischen Feldherren Sib'e=סוא' JNESt 19 (1960), pp. 49–53; Donner, 'Neue Quellen zur Geschichte des Staates Moab in der zweiten Hälfte des 8. Jh. vChr.' MIOF 5 (1957), pp. 155–84, see pp. 164 f.; Maisler, 'The Israelite Exiles at Gozan' [Hebr., Engl. sum.] BJPES 15 (1949/50,) pp. 83–5, III; Malamat, 'The Tell Halâf (Gozan) Texts' [Hebr., Engl. sum.] BJPES 15 (1949/50), pp. 99–102, IV; Segal, 'An Aramaic Ostracon from Nimrud' Iraq 19 (1957), pp. 139–45; Yeivin, 'Who was Šō' the King of Egypt?' VT 2 (1952), pp. 164–8. Lit. § 126.

[10] Noth, 'Die Einnahme von Jerusalem im Jahre 597 vChr' ZDPV 74 (1958), pp. 133–57.

[11] Schmökel, *Geschichte des alten Vorderasien* HdO II, 3 (1957), p. 173. Cf. p. 284, n. 18.

[12] AOT, pp. 333–5, 359–61; ANET, pp. 272–4, 301–3; Schmidtke, *Der Aufbau der babylonischen Chronologie* (1952), pp. 84–90, 90–7.

receive an unfavourable judgement; otherwise they receive a favourable one. The kings of Israel all fall under this condemnation, admittedly somewhat softened in II Kings iii, 2; xvii, 2, for Joram and Hoshea,[13] and so too does a substantial number of the Judaean kings. Unqualified approval is given only to Hezekiah (II xviii, 3–7) and Josiah (II xxii, 2),[14] while with Asa[15] to whom, among other things, there is reckoned as credit the removal of his idolatrous mother from her position of 'Great Lady' (גְּבִירָה)[16] (I xv, 11–15), Jehoshaphat (I xxii, 43–4), Joash (II xii, 3–4), Azariah (II xv, 3–4), and Jotham (II xv, 34–5), it is more or less limited. Hezekiah and Josiah[17] are indeed the only ones who acted really decisively against the cultus on the high places, and therefore correspond fully to the royal ideal of the Deuteronomist.

The standard here applied to the kings of Israel and Judah presupposes the reform of Josiah in the year 621 B.C. and the finding of the law which became its basis, i.e. our Deuteronomy, or rather the original Deuteronomy (see § 34). The compiler of the framework sections, a Deuteronomist, cannot therefore have written before 621 B.C. Now these framework sections so determine the whole structure of the book that their compiler must at the same time be the compiler[18] of our book of Kings. This book in its present form cannot therefore have come into existence before 621 B.C. The last date mentioned in it, that of the pardon of Jehoiachin (II xxv, 27–30), falls in the year 561 B.C. This seems to necessitate the conclusion that our book could not have been written before that year. But we must also reckon with the possibility that a book compiled a longer or shorter time before 561 may have been subsequently amplified and carried further with II xxv, 27–30, or with even larger sections. There is indeed no lack

---

[13] Cf. above, p. 112, n. 36, and Dinaburg, 'פרק בתהלים מזמנו של הושע בן אלה' (=A Psalm from the period of Hoshea ben Elah) in לזכר א.מ. לונץ. =A.M. Lunz Memorial Vol. (Jerusalem, 1928), pp. רסא–רנ =250–61.

[14] Buis, *Josias* (1958); Junge, *Der Wiederaufbau des Heerwesens des Reiches Juda unter Josia* (BWANT 75, 1937); Malamat, 'The Historical Background of the Assassination of Amon, King of Judah' IEJ 3 (1953), pp. 26–9; Procksch, 'König Josia' *Zahn-Festgabe* (1928), pp. 19–53; Yadin, 'The Reorganisation of the Army of Judah under Josiah' [Hebr., Engl. sum.] BJPES 15 (1949/50), pp. 86–98, III–IV. Literature, p. 232, n. 26; pp. 296 f., nn. 60–2.

[15] Janssens, 'Asa ou un caractère sur le trône de Juda' Rev. de l'Univ. de Bruxelles N.S.8 (1955/6), pp. 147–66.

[16] Cazelles, 'Le Mère du Roi-Messie dans l'AT' Academia Mariana Internationalis V (1959), pp. 39–56; Donner, 'Art und Herkunft des Amtes der Königinmutter im AT' *Joh.-Friedrich-Festschr.* (1959), pp. 105–45; Molin, 'Die Stellung der Gebira im Staate Juda' ThZ 10 (1954), pp. 161–75; de Vaux, *Les institutions de l'AT*, I (1958), pp. 180–2, E.T. *Ancient Israel* (1961), pp. 117–19.

[17] Todd, 'The Reforms of Hezekiah and Josiah' SJTh 9 (1956), pp. 288–93. Lit. p. 296, n. 58; § 126.

[18] As we shall show in a moment, we have to reckon with two or even more compilers or editors of the book. More than two are assumed by Jepsen who thinks that the first redactor put together soon after 586 a book made up of a synchronistic chronicle compiled between 705 and 701, and a historical work which came into being about half a century later, adding judgements on the cultic attitude of the kings and references to sources. This was then worked over about 550 by a second redactor, and about 500 B.C. by a third, and later it underwent further isolated additions and modifications. In the discussion which follows, for the sake of simplicity, we shall refer repeatedly to *the compiler*, and this is justified in that of the two compilers the one had in any case a much larger share in the book than the other, and is thus its main compiler.

of indications that the compilation of the book did take place earlier. II xxii, 20, sounds as if it had been written before the death of Josiah, i.e. before 609 B.C. If that really is so, we should have to assume that the real compiler of our book, who was strongly influenced by Josiah's reform and saw in it the really significant event in Israel's history, began his work shortly after, and that at a later date, after 561, a man of kindred spirit continued his book down to 561. But we must also consider the possibility that II xxii, 20, comes from a source utilised by the compiler. The verse may then contribute nothing towards determining the date of origin of our book, and there would apparently be nothing in the way of the assumption that it was compiled not merely after 609 but in fact only after 561. The question of the compiler and his date becomes the more complicated by the fact that we have perhaps to reckon with two compilers or editors (pp. 299–300), quite apart from the possibility of secondary amplifications at the end. The points just considered in relation to II xxii, 20, and II xxv, 27–30, then suggest the dating of one, the main compiler, shortly before 609, and that of the other shortly after 561. But if we consider that we do not need to go so far down for the dating of the second and must in any case regard the reference to the year 561 as being a supplement, we may move the second compiler back a couple of decades and think of him as active shortly after 587; for the disaster of 587 is presupposed several times in our book. Above all, there is concealed in II xxii, 15–20, the account of the oracle of Huldah, side by side with a version written before 587[19] (and indeed before 609), another version which clearly looks back upon the catastrophe. Admittedly not all passages which refer to the exile are to be assigned to the second editor. Some of them are certainly to be assigned to still later hands (pp. 300–1).

Finally, we must say a further word concerning the *sources* mentioned in the concluding formulae of the framework. There are three sources which are referred to here by the compiler: 1. *The Book of the history of Solomon* for Solomon (I xi, 41); 2. *The Book of the history of the kings of Israel* for the Israelite kings, first for Jeroboam I (I xiv, 19) and last for the next to last king, Pekah (II xv, 31. The last king, Hoshea, has in fact no concluding formula); 3. *The Book of the history of the kings of Judah*, first for Rehoboam (I xiv, 29), and last for Jehoiakim (II xxiv, 5. The last two kings, Jehoiachin[20] and Zedekiah, also have no concluding formulae).

With regard to the Book of the history of Solomon,[21] the necessary points will be made subsequently (pp. 286–90). Concerning the nature of the *Books of the history of the Kings of Israel* and *of Judah*, which we must presumably picture as two separate books,[22] we can get a fairly clear impression from some phrases

[19] Auerbach, 'Die Umschaltung vom judäischen auf den babylonischen Kalender' VT 10 (1960), pp. 69–70; 'Wann eroberte Nebukadnezar Jerusalem?' VT 11 (1961), pp. 128–136. Literature, p. 349, n. 7; § 126.

[20] Albright, 'King Joiachin in Exile' BA 5 (1942), pp. 49–55; Böhl, 'Nebukadnezar en Jojachin' NThSt 25 (1942), pp. 121–5 = *Op. Min.* (1953), pp. 423–9, 525; Weidner, 'Jojachin, König von Juda, in babylonischen Keilschrifttexten' *Mélanges Syriens Dussaud* II (1939), pp. 923–35, Pls. I–V. Lit. p. 531, n. 3.

[21] Thieberger, *Le roi Salomon et son temps. Un des carrefours de l'histoire* (1957). Lit. § 126.

[22] Procksch, 'Der hebräische Schreiber und sein Buch' *Kuhnert-Festschr.* (1928), pp.

which appear in the concluding formulae. For many details the compiler refers to these books, saying that more is to be found there on the matter in question. So we find it for Jeroboam I as to *how he waged war and how he ruled* (I xiv, 19); for Zimri,[23] as to *the conspiracy which he made* (I xvi, 20); for Ahab, as to *the ivory house which he built, and all the cities which he built* (I xxii, 39). From this we may conclude that in the *Books of the history of the kings of Israel* and *of Judah* we are dealing with annalistic enumerations of the acts of the individual kings, and not with a narrative work compiled according to a comprehensive plan.[24] These books must have been based upon official records, since the knowledge of so many details can hardly have been preserved elsewhere, but they were themselves not official but private publications, since it is presupposed that they can be consulted by anyone. Where the compiler produces concrete details of the kind just mentioned, he is likely to have taken all of them, or at any rate the majority from these works. An example would be the report in I xv, 16–22, of the attack by the Israelite king Baasha on Asa of Judah, and the expedition of Benhadad, king of Damascus against Baasha which this occasioned.[25] But narratives like those of Elijah (I xvii–xix, xxi) are hardly likely to have been in such books; the compiler must have derived these from elsewhere.

2. *The narratives within the framework.* We might take as the first section within the framework the passage II Sam. ii, 4–I Kings ii, 9, in that II Sam. ii, 4, relates David's accession and I Kings ii, 10–11, brings his reign to a close. However, quite apart from the fact that this section overlaps the second book of Samuel, the introductory formula for Solomon, which perhaps does not actually come from the compiler of the books of Kings but was inserted later, appears only in I iii, 2–3. This is clearly because I ii, 13–46,[26] deals with preliminaries to the claiming of the throne by Solomon and this section is thus an introduction to his reign without really belonging to his reign itself and can just as well be understood as the aftermath of David's reign. David's reign is thus not fixed in so clear a framework as the reigns of the subsequent kings.

The concluding formula which corresponds to the opening reference to Solomon in I iii, 2–3, stands in xi, 41–3, so that here the framework is filled out with iii, (1) 4–xi, 40. The structure of this section, as we now have it, is probably planned thus: iii, 4–15 Solomon's accession sacrifice at Gibeon and Yahweh's promise to bless him with wisdom as a ruler; iii, 16–28, an example of the gift bestowed upon him—the Solomonic judgement; iv, 1–v, 8 (EVV. iv, 28),

1–15, thinks of one work, namely, 'annals deriving from Jerusalem . . . which, in the history of the divided kingdom (932–722) set in parallel the twofold reigns according to the kings of Judah' and 'according to the kings of Israel' (pp. 7–8). Somewhat differently, Lewy, pp. 27–31.

[23] Dhorme, 'Rapport sur les travaux de l'École Archéologique Française de Jérusalem' CRAI (1959), pp. 359–62: '. . . une citadelle dans laquelle le P. de Vaux suggère de reconnaître le donjon dont il est question dans *I Rois xvi*, 18, à propos du suicide de Zimri' (p. 360).

[24] Montgomery, 'Archival Data in the Book of Kings' JBL 53 (1934), pp. 46–52.

[25] Yadin, *Hazor* II (1960), p. 37, n. 217, 1: 'The destruction of Stratum IX, in which the city wall was destroyed, is definitely connected with the campaign of Ben-Hadad, King of Aram, about 885 B.C.' (So Aharoni). Cf. also I (1958), p. 22.

[26] Tsevat, 'Marriage and Monarchical Legitimacy in Ugarit and Israel' JSSt 3 (1958), pp. 237–43: on II Sam. iii, 7; xii, 8; xvi, 21; I Kings ii, 13–25.

Solomon's administration; v, 9–14 (EVV. iv, 29–34), Solomon's learning; v, 15 (EVV. v, 1)–ix, 14, preparations for the building of Temple and palace, the erection of these buildings together with the preparation of the Temple furniture, the dedication of the Temple and the second appearance of Yahweh, the settlement with King Hiram for his deliveries of building material;[27] ix, 15–24, fortifications;[28] ix, 25–x, 29, Solomon's wealth and wisdom (including x, 1–10, 13, the Queen of Sheba); xi, 1–40, Solomon's polygamy and idolatry and the divine punishment brought about by the stirring up of enemies.

We thus clearly have here a certain plan in the arrangement of the material. But it is unlikely that we have this section in the form in which it was produced by the compiler of the book of Kings. It seems to have undergone various dis- locations. Firstly, we find a whole series of repetitions, partly of content, partly in actual wording. v, 6–30 is substantially equivalent to the section x, 23–6 + ix, 10–23,[29] the one standing before the narrative of the building of Temple and palace to which Hiram[30] gave his support, and the other standing after, and iv, 20 + v, 1 (EVV. iv, 21) says approximately the same as v, 4–5 (EVV. iv, 24–5). We can hardly regard a compiler who could freely handle the material which was at his disposal as being responsible for such repetitions. At the most we might assume that the sources which lay before him covered in part the same material and that in combining the remaining material of the sources he simply put together these duplicates. This possibility must be seriously considered. Yet a glance at $\mathfrak{G}$ shows that there is a better explanation to hand. Codex Vaticanus ($\mathfrak{G}^B$, p. 712)[31] and the Lucianic recension ($\mathfrak{G}^{Luc}$, p. 712) offer in fact in iii–xii a text-form which deviates sharply from $\mathfrak{M}$ both in order and content. After ii, 35; ii, 46, and xii, 24, they have large additions— denoted in the editions of Swete (p. 714), Rahlfs (pp. 714–15) and Brooke- McLean (p. 714) as ii, 35 a–o, ii, 46 a–l, and xii, 24 a–z—which in addition to extra material, not indeed very great in extent, beyond $\mathfrak{M}$, contain groups of verses, single verses and parts of verses which in $\mathfrak{M}$ are scattered about over ii–xi, and, at least in part, also stand there in $\mathfrak{G}^B$ and $\mathfrak{G}^{Luc}$, and are thus provided twice in them. Clearly down to the time of origin of $\mathfrak{G}$ (§§ 90, 121) the text of iii–xi was still fluid and various groupings of the material existed. $\mathfrak{G}^B$ and $\mathfrak{G}^{Luc}$ certainly represent a combination of such different text- forms, but our $\mathfrak{M}$ is also to be understood thus. We can hardly go much further than the recognition of this. In any case, a restoration of the original form of iii–xi, i.e. the form as it was created by the compiler of our book, appears to be impossible.

[27] Fensham, 'The Treaty between Solomon and Hiram and the Alalakh Tablets' JBL 79 (1960), pp. 59–60.
[28] Wright, 'A Solomonic City Gate at Gezer' BA 21 (1958), pp. 103 f.; Yadin, 'Solomon's City Wall and Gate at Gezer' [Hebr.] BIES 22 (1958), pp. 115–21; 'New Light on Solomon's Megiddo' BA 23 (1960), pp. 62–8.
[29] On the supply cities of I ix, 19, cf. Yadin, Hazor II (1960), pp. 6–9, Pls. IV–V and frontispiece.
[30] Liver, 'On the Chronology of Hiram King of Tyre' [Hebr., Engl. sum.] BIES 17 (1952/3), pp. 86–94, I.
[31] Hrozný, Die Abweichungen des Codex Vaticanus vom Hebräischen Texte in den Königs- büchern (Diss. phil. Tübingen, 1909).

It is easier, within iii–xi, to determine what comes from the pen of the Deuteronomistic compiler and was not taken by him from elsewhere. iii, 2–3, 14, the main part of viii and of xi, 1–13, are in any case to be put to his account. As far as other sections are concerned, for example v, 17–19, 21, we may hesitate between ascribing them to the compiler and regarding them as older material. As elsewhere the boundaries between Deuteronomistic products and older narratives, particularly those of Elohistic origin or bearing an Elohistic stamp, are not always quite clear (pp. 261–3). For the understanding of the method of the Deuteronomistic compiler, however, the selection which he has made from the available material and the arrangement which he gave to it are of even greater importance than his own contributions. Thus it is characteristic for him that among the buildings the Temple stands right in the forefront (vi, 1–38; vii, 13–51; viii), whereas the palace buildings which were much more comprehensive and also took up twice the time in building (vii, 1, contrast vi, 37–8) are only dealt with in vii, 1–12. It is also characteristic of him that to the account, clearly provided in quite a neutral form in his source, of the admission of foreign women to Solomon's harem and of the cult places built for their benefit, he adds a judgement stigmatising this behaviour of Solomon's as sin and idolatry and presenting it as the basis of external and internal political failures (xi, 1–40). Here he simply places these failures, which at least in part (cf. xi, 21, 25) belong to the beginning of Solomon's reign, at the end of his life, either because the building of cult places for the foreign gods was reported only for Solomon in his old age (xi, 4) or because he believed that he could only impute this idolatry to the king at that period of his life.

As to the source from which the compiler derived the material for his presentation in iii–xi, he tells us himself, for he concludes his information about Solomon in xi, 41, with the remark that *the rest of the history of Solomon and all that he did and his wisdom are written in the book of the history of Solomon.* We must surely understand this reference to mean that the compiler took at least a part of his material from this book and now refers to this source anyone who wishes to know more. It is not thereby claimed that the whole of the material was taken from this book, and the possibility remains open as to whether other sources, as for example the continuation which we may assume of the Octateuch sources beyond the Octateuch (pp. 293, 297), have been utilised, without it being possible to give a firm answer to the question. If we had any justification for thinking of the Book of the history of Solomon as an annalistic enumeration of the deeds of Solomon and of the events of his reign—as we believed it possible to picture the *history of the kings of Israel* and *of Judah* (pp. 286–7)—we should be inclined to derive from another source the narratives which have the character of legend, saga or tale, like the dream at Gibeon (iii, 4–15), the Solomonic judgement (iii, 16–28), and the visit of the Queen of Sheba (x, 1–10, 13). But xi, 41, explicitly states that in this *history of Solomon* there is also information about his *wisdom,* and this must surely prove that the book also contained narratives like iii, 16–28 and x, 1–10, 13. We must therefore picture it as a very varied and disunified collection of quite different materials which it derived in its turn from older sources, and suppose that it derived the lists iv, 1–6; iv, 7–19 + v, 7–8, as well as the notes about the palace buildings (vii, 1–12) and their equipment, and in particular the throne of ivory[32] and gold (x, 18–20), at least indirectly from the court archives. The description of the building of the Temple (vi, 1–38; vii, 13–51)[33] more probably derived from the Temple archives, whereas the narratives which have the nature of saga or tale may perhaps derive from the continuation of the Octateuch strands or from other narrative books, or may possibly have been taken from oral popular tradition.

If we now disregard the various forms in which the text crystallised out after its long period of fluidity (p. 287), it is difficult to decide whether and how far another hand was at work on iii–xi after the compiler of the book of Kings. The section iv, 20–v, 6 (EVV. iv, 26), which contains information about Solomon's daily needs (v, 2–3, EVV. iv, 22–3),[34] about the number of his horses (v, 6, EVV. iv, 26) etc., interrupts in a way which we find intolerable the list in iv, 7–19 + v, 7–8 (EVV. iv, 27–8) of the twelve officers of Solomon, and we are therefore readily inclined to make a second hand responsible for this inelegance because we do not care to attribute it to the compiler himself. But it is quite conceivable that the compiler himself thought it necessary with regard to the deliveries mentioned in v, 7–8 (EVV. iv, 27–8) of food and fodder for the household and stables of the king, to insert first some figures about both (v, 2–3, 6, EVV. iv, 22–3, 26). The position is similar in regard to ix, 26–x, 13, where the information in ix, 26–7 + x, 11–12, which belong together, is interrupted by the story of the visit of the Queen of Sheba in x, 1–10,[35] and even

---

[32] Barnett, *A Catalogue of the Nimrud Ivories with other examples of Ancient Near Eastern Ivories in the British Museum* (1957); J. W. Crowfoot and Grace M. Crowfoot, 'Early Ivories from Samaria' *Samaria-Sebaste* 2 (1938); Mme C. Decamps de Mertzenfeld, *Inventaire Commenté des Ivoires Phéniciens et Apparentés découverts dans le Proche-Orient, Texte et Album* (1954); Giveon, 'Notes on the Nimrud and Palestine Ivories' [Hebr., Engl. sum.] BIES 22 (1958), pp. 55–61, V.

[33] Albright, 'Dunand's New Byblos Volume' BASOR 155 (1959), pp. 31–4, cf. p. 32; Alt, 'Archäologische Fragen zur Baugeschichte von Jerusalem und Samaria in der israelitischen Königszeit' WZ Greifswald 5 (1955/6), pp. 33–42 = *Kl. Schr.* III (1959), pp. 303–25; Avi-Yonah (ed.), *The Book of Jerusalem: Jerusalem, its Natural Conditions, History and Development* I [Hebr.] (1956); Garber, 'Reconstructing Solomon's Temple' BA 14 (1951), pp. 2–24; 'Reconsidering the Reconstruction of Solomon's Temple' JBL 77 (1958), pp. 123–9; on this Albright and Wright, 'Comments on Professor Garber's Article' *ib.* pp. 129–32, and Garber, 'Additional Remarks' *ib.* pp. 132–3; Irwin, 'I Kings vii, 20' JNESt 4 (1945), pp. 53 f.; Kraus, 'Archäologische und topographische Probleme Jerusalems im Lichte der Psalmenexegese' ZDPV 75 (1959), pp. 125–40; Myres, 'King Solomon's Temple and other Buildings and Works of Art' PEQ 80 (1948), pp. 14–41; Parrot, *Le Temple de Jérusalem* (1954); E.T. *The Temple of Jerusalem* (1957); Thomson, 'A Row of Cedar Beams' PEQ 92 (1960), pp. 57–63; de Vaux, *Ancient Israel* (1961), pp. 312–30; Vincent, *Jérusalem de l'AT*, II, III (1956), pp. 373–31: 'Le Temple de Salomon'; 'Le caractère du temple Salomonien' *Mél. Bibl. Robert* (1957), pp. 137–48; Waterman, 'The Damaged "Blueprints" of the Temple of Solomon' JNESt 2 (1943), pp. 284–94; Widengren, 'Aspetti simbolici dei templi e luoghi di culto del Vicino Oriente Antico' Numen 7 (1960), pp. 1–25; Williams, 'Palestinian Temples' Iraq 11 (1949), pp. 77–89, Pl. XXXIII; Yeivin, 'Jachin and Boaz' PEQ 91 (1959), pp. 6–22. Lit. p. 50, n. 52; p. 250, n. 9; p. 269, n. 3; § 126.

[34] Eissfeldt, 'The Alphabetical Cuneiform Texts from Ras Shamra published in *Le Palais Royal d'Ugarit*, Vol. II (1957)' JSSt 5 (1960), pp. 1–49. See pp. 26, 47.

[35] van Beek, 'Frankincense and Myrrh in Ancient South Arabia' JAOS 78 (1958), pp. 141–52; 'Frankincense and Myrrh' BA 23 (1960), pp. 70–95; van Beek and Jamme, 'An

L

more noticeably, the conclusion of this story, x, 13, is separated from its main section x, 1–10, by x, 11–12. But here too this arrangement, which seems to us unsuitable, may be deliberate and depend upon the following considerations. Gold[36] came into the land (1) as a result of the Ophir expedition (ix, 26–7)[37] and (2) by the Queen of Sheba (x, 1–10). The latter, however, according to x, 10, also brought precious stones into the land, and so to the reference to the gold another is added to the effect that that Ophir expedition, in addition to other products, also brought precious stones. Such a principle of arrangement, inelegant as it may appear to us, may equally well have been followed by the compiler himself as by a secondary hand.

Relatively comprehensive too is the material inserted between the closing formula for Solomon and the closing formula for Jeroboam, for whom of course, in view of the revolutionary nature of his accession to the throne, the introductory formula is missing: it covers xii, 1–xiv, 18. The narrative here included in xii, 32–xiii, 32 (33) concerning the threat to the altar at Bethel by a Judaean man of God, is probably a secondary insertion in the book of Kings, and not to be ascribed to the Deuteronomistic compiler. The fact that this legend, perhaps linked with Amos' appearance in Bethel, clearly presupposes Josiah's reform and even in xiii, 2, mentions his name, would not in itself exclude the possibility that it could be derived from the compiler of the book, but xiii, (33) 34, links quite clearly back over xii, 32[38]–xiii, 32 (33), directly to xii, 31, and this marks out the intervening narrative as a secondary insertion. The remaining material could have been taken by our compiler from the *History of the Kings of Israel* mentioned in xiv, 19, but if we are to regard this history, as has appeared probable (p. 286), as a sort of annalistic work, narratives like those of the division of the kingdom in xii, 1–20, and of Ahijah of Shiloh's threat to Jeroboam in xiv, 1–18, hardly seem likely to belong to it. We must therefore derive these narratives from some other material available to the compiler, and here again the possibility must be considered that this could have been the continuation of the narrative work of the Octateuch, if such a continuation may be assumed (pp. 293, 299).

Even more material is to be found between the introductory and concluding formulae for Ahab, i.e. between xvi, 29–30, and xxii, 39–40, and in fact the narratives included here fall into two groups. xx[39] and xxii[40] which form a

Inscribed South Arabian Clay Stamp from Bethel' BASOR 151 (1958), pp. 9–16; Chastel, 'La Légende de la Reine de Saba' RHR 119 (1939), pp. 204–25; 120 (1939), pp. 27–44, 160–74. Lit. § 126.

[36] Rothenberg and others, *Die Wüste Gottes. Entdeckungen auf Sinai* (1961); *God's Wilderness. Discoveries in Sinai* (1961). Lit. § 126.

[37] Liver, 'The Chronology of Tyre at the Beginning of the First Millennium B.C.' IEJ 3 (1953), pp. 113–20; Schreiden, 'Les Entreprises navales du roi Salomon' AIPhHOS 13 (1955), pp. 587–90. Lit. § 126.

[38] Segal, 'Intercalation and the Hebrew Calendar' VT 7 (1957), pp. 250–307, cf. pp. 257–9; 'The Hebrew Festivals and the Calendar' JSSt 6 (1961), pp. 74–94, cf. pp. 76–7. Lit. p. 200, n. 11.

[39] Meek, 'I Kings xx, 1–10' JBL 78 (1959), pp. 73–5; Yadin, 'Some Aspects of the Strategy of Ahab and David (I Kings xx; II Sam. xi)' Bibl 36 (1955), pp. 332–51. Lit. § 126.

[40] Haller, *Charisma und Ekstasis. Die Erzählung von dem Propheten Micha ben Jimla, I Kön, xxii, 1–28a* (Theol. Existenz heute NF 87, 1960).

larger unity as is shown by the dates in xx, 26 (*and at the turn of the year*) and xxii, 1 (*for three years 'he had peace'*[41]. . . *But in the third year . . .*), provide narratives of Ahab's wars with Aram, in which Ahab is regarded with sympathy, described as wise (xx, 4), loving honour (xx, 7–9), magnanimous (xx, 33) and bold (xxii, 35), and is only lightly reproached because, unlike the Judaean Jehoshaphat, he is not susceptible to the truth proclaimed by the genuine prophet of Yahweh (xxii, 8, 18, 26–7). But the other group of narratives, the Elijah[42] narratives of xvii–xix + xxi, are in the strongest opposition to Ahab and his wife Jezebel. Of these narratives, xvii–xviii form a coherent unit somewhat mutilated only at the beginning because of the notes in xvi, 31–3 which go back to the Deuteronomistic compiler. This opens with the beginning of the three year drought and famine (xvii, 1)[43] and closes with its termination (xviii, 41–6). Between the beginning and end of this section stand originally independent narratives now skilfully woven into a sequence: Elijah at the brook Cherith (xvii 2–6),[44] Elijah at the house of the widow of Zarephath (xvii, 7–24), and the divine judgement on Carmel (xviii).[45] There follows on xvii–xviii the narrative of Elijah's pilgrimage to Horeb in xix, 1–18, and here the opening words indicate that it is the continuation of the previous complex *Ahab told Jezebel . . . how he had slain the prophets with the sword.* [2]*Then Jezebel sent . . . to Elijah, saying: . . . I shall see that tomorrow at this time your life will be like the life of one of them.* Since Elijah's resignation, expressed in xix, 4, 14, does not really fit well with the great success just achieved in xviii, it has been asked whether xix, 1–18, originally belongs with xvii–xviii. But the prophet's change of mood is understandable, and xix, 1–18, may thus rank as the original continuation of xvii–xviii.

Another observation is more important and more conclusive. The narrative xix, 1–18 appears to be directed towards a sequel which covers Hazael's wars against Israel, Jehu's revolution and Elisha's activity. At any rate this is suggested by vv. 15–17 where Elijah receives the commission from God to anoint Hazael as king over Aram, Jehu as king over Israel, and Elisha as prophet and so as his successor. Now in II viii, 7–15; ix, 1–12, the anointing of Hazael[46] and Jehu

[41] וַיֵּשֶׁב instead of וַיֵּשְׁבוּ, *they had peace*, following ⅏.

[42] *Élie le prophète* (Les Études Carmélitaines, 35, 36, I (1956), II (1957)); Fohrer, *Elia* (1957); Gunkel, *Elias, Jahve und Baal* (1906); *Meisterwerke hebr. Erzählungskunst I: Geschichten von Elisa* (1922); Keller, 'Wer war Elia?' ThZ 16 (1960), pp. 298–313; Wallace, *Elijah and Elisha* (1957). Lit. n. 45.

[43] Hallevy, 'אליהו התשבי' HUCA 29 (1958), pp. 6–7.

[44] Wenham, 'The Black Arabs of the Jordan Valley' ET 68 (1956/7), p. 121.

[45] Alt, 'Das Gottesurteil auf dem Karmel' *Beer-Festschr.* (1935), pp. 1–18 = *Kl. Schr.* II (²1959), pp. 135–49; Ap-Thomas, 'Elijah on Mount Carmel' PEQ 92 (1960), pp. 146–55; Astour, 'Métamorphose de Baal. Les rivalités commerciales au IXᵉ siècle' Evidences 75 (1959), pp. 35–40; 77 (1959), pp. 54–8; Avi-Yonah, 'Mount Carmel and the God of Baalbek' IEJ 2 (1952), pp. 118–24; Eissfeldt, *Der Gott Karmel* (SAB 1953, 1, 1953); Galling, 'Der Gott Karmel und die Achtung der fremden Götter' *Alt-Festschr.* (1953), pp. 105–25; Junker, 'Der Graben um den Altar des Elias. Eine Untersuchung über die kultische Überlieferung von I Kg xviii, 29–38' Trierer ThZ 69 (1960), pp. 65–74; Peake, 'Elijah and Jezebel. The Conflict with the Tyrian Baal' BJRL 11 (1927), pp. 296–321; Rowley, 'Elijah on Mount Carmel' BJRL 43 (1960/1), pp. 190–219; de Vaux, 'Les prophètes de Baal sur le Mont Carmel' BMB 5 (1941), pp. 7–20. Lit. n. 42.

[46] Yadin, etc., *Hazor* II (1960), p. 37, n. 217, 2: 'The destruction of Stratum VII, following

is ascribed not to Elijah but to Elisha. These sections are thus not the sequel demanded by I xix, 1–18, but a parallel version. Evidently the attempt has been twice made (p. 142) to group around an eminent personage the tremendous events which shook Israel about the middle of the ninth century B.C., namely the prophetic revolutionary movement directed against the dynasty of Ahab because of its favouring of a foreign cult, and the Aramaean wars which pressed so terribly upon Israel. In one of these attempts Elijah stood in the centre, with Elisha only as one of his instruments; in the other it was Elisha himself. The first attempt found expression in I xvii, 1–xix, 18; the second in II viii, 7–15 + ix–x[47] (xi). But both these versions are incomplete. As we have seen (p. 291), the conclusion of the first is missing, and, as we shall see in a moment (p. 293), the beginning of the second. When the two versions were combined, perhaps by the compiler of our book, but more probably by the redactor of one of the works he used, the beginning of the one and the conclusion of the other were evidently utilised, a procedure which can also be observed in other similar cases. We may then ask whether the narrative of Elisha's call in xix, 19–21,[48] is to be reckoned to the first version or the second. Now in xix, 16, Elijah receives a command to *anoint* Elisha as prophet; but in xix, 19–21, nothing is said about an anointing. Instead, Elijah casts his mantle over Elisha and so makes him his disciple. However, the word *anoint* used just before for the appointment of Hazael and Jehu as kings and there intended quite literally may be meant in a figurative sense for the appointment of Elisha, and we may thus confidently regard vv. 19–21 as the sequel to vv. 1–18. But there is a gap between vv. 18 and 19. For the anointing of Hazael and Jehu which is placed in the command of xix, 16, before the call of Elisha must also have preceded it in the carrying out of the command. The omission of this narrative is quite simply explained: it was left out in favour of the parallel in II viii, 7–15; ix, 1–12.

To the series of passages which place Elijah in the centre of the action belongs also the narrative of the judicial murder of Naboth in I xxi.[49] It is now hardly possible to suggest where it originally stood in the series. In 𝕲 it follows immediately upon xix, and the narratives of xx and xxii which belong together (pp. 290 f.) actually stand adjacent to one another. But in 𝔐 it is placed before xxii and thus divides xx from xxii, and this is to be explained on the grounds that the compiler of our book or a later editor wished to make the death of Ahab narrated in xxii follow as directly as possible upon the threat of his death in xxi, 19. To make the link between threat and fulfilment even closer, the same hand added vv. 35bβ, 38 to xxii. On the other hand the conclusion of xxi, vv. 27–29, must be older, for it postpones the threat spoken against Ahab in v. 19 because of his readiness to repent and applies it only to his sons, and thus does not fit with xxii. It does not actually belong to the original content of xxi. It is

which the storehouses fell into disuse, can be related to the campaign of Hazael, King of Aram, about 814 B.C.' (So Aharoni.) Cf. also I (1958), p. 22.

[47] Gunkel, 'Die Revolution des Jehu' Deutsche Rundschau XL (1913), pp. 289–308 = *Meisterwerke hebr. Erzählungskunst* I (1922), pp. 67–94.

[48] Alt, 'Die literarische Herkunft von I Reg. xix, 19–21' ZAW 32 (1912), pp. 123–5.

[49] Alt (p. 300, n. 68); Napier, 'The Omrides of Jezreel' VT 9 (1959), pp. 366–78.

to be ascribed rather to the redactor who combined the two sections I xvii–xix, xxi and II viii, 7–x (xi) which represent different strands (p. 292). The two strands clearly both told of the threat directed against Ahab and of its fulfilment, but in a somewhat divergent manner, as may be seen by I xxi, 19, on the one hand and II ix, 24–6, 30–7, on the other. I xxi, 19, presupposes that the threat will be carried out upon Ahab himself, as was also thought by whoever added vv. 35bβ, 38 to xxii; II ix, 24–6, however, looks back to a form of the threat which was more generally expressed and could be understood to refer to a punishment directed at Ahab's descendants. In other respects too II ix, 24–6, 30–7, does in fact presuppose a somewhat differently formed Naboth story from the one which is preserved from the other strand in I xxi, different above all in the fact that there must have been a narration not only of Naboth's execution but also of that of his sons. From II ix, 24–6, 30–7, we may thus reconstruct the beginning of the second strand in at least one point (p. 292).

To the strand of I xvii–xix + xxi belongs also lastly II i, 2–17, the narrative of the threat by Elijah to king Ahaziah when he consults the oracle of an alien god. Vv. 9–16, which describe graphically how Elijah causes fire from heaven to fall upon two captains sent to arrest him, but spares the third when he begs mercy, are perhaps a later amplification.

It is clear enough that the various narratives which are inserted between I xvi, 29–30 and xxii, 39–40, are not all taken from the *History of the Kings of Israel* cited in xxii, 39, as the source for the period of Ahab, or at least that only a small part of them is so derived. For these narratives belong at least in part to larger bodies of material, and do not fit at all into a work of annalistic character, unless perhaps the latter were in its turn dependent upon narrative works of a different kind and had taken over material from them. We cannot decide for certain what the narrative works may have looked like which were used, even if perhaps only indirectly, by the compiler of our book. We are concerned with three different groups, as we have seen, if we take into consideration also the section II viii, 7–x (xi): the royal stories of xx + xxii, and the two strands which attempt to group the events which stirred up Israel in the second third of the ninth century around the characters of Elijah or Elisha. These may be complexes which were limited to the period of Ahab and its immediate precursors and sequels. But we must also consider the possibility that they were more comprehensive works and so perhaps the continuations of the Octateuch sources. The more secular royal stories would fit well with L, and the Elisha strand would bear more or less the same relationship to the Elijah strand which elsewhere J bears to E. The narrative of II viii, 7–x (xi) which makes political movements control prophetic, has been replaced by a version which stresses prophecy much more fully and thus possesses a religious character, namely I xvii–xix. That, however, may be a matter of chance. The observation just made is by no means sufficient to determine the allocation of the three complexes to L, J and E, and this is emphasised by the fact that, as already indicated (p. 142), we shall meet with a similar relationship of three narratives again later in II xviii, 13–xix, 37[50] (pp. 296, 328 f.), and here their allocation to L, J and E is excluded.

[50] Cf. p. 142, n. 23. On Ararat, cf. Benedict, 'Urartians and Hurrians' JAOS 80 (1960),

Thus a quite large block of narratives, consisting entirely of ones which turn around the person of Elisha, stands in II ii, 1–xiii, 21.[51] However, this block does not belong simply to the reign of one king, but the narratives are divided between the reigns of three kings, those of Joram of Israel (iii, 1–viii, 24), of Jehu of Israel (ix, 1–x, 36),[52] and of Joash of Israel (xiii, 10–xiv, 16), and are inserted between their introductory and concluding formulae. The first of the narratives, however, that of Elijah's ascension, II ii,[53] now stands outside the framework, after the concluding formula for Ahaziah in II i, 17–18, and before the introductory formula for Joram in II iii, 1–3. It remains doubtful whether the usual explanation of this special position for the narrative is right, namely that it does not come from the compiler but was only later inserted in his book. In 𝔊 it stands after iii, 1–3, and thus within Joram's framework, and this may be its original position. Its transposition might then have arisen from the consideration that the prophet Elisha must have taken up his office before king Joram, just as the narrative of his death in xiii, 14–21, also stands at least in some measure outside the framework since the concluding note for Joash which properly belongs after the narrative, namely in II xiv, 15–16, has later been brought forward to II xiii, 12–13, probably so that the prophet should die after the king. The opposite is true of the narrative of Elijah's ascension; its position outside the framework is to be explained, in that it has been brought secondarily into the reign of a king by an introductory formula for Joram in i, 17, being placed in front of it, so that Joram now has two introductory formulae (i, 17, and iii, 1–3), just as Joash has two concluding formulae (xiii, 12–13, and xiv, 15–16).

The Elisha stories within II ii, 1–xiii, 21, are of varied types: legends, sagas and historical narratives (§ 5). The legends present Elisha as leader of prophetic settlements existing in Bethel, Jericho and Gilgal, and presumably derive from these circles. To these belongs the cycle of legends of II ii which culminates in Elijah's ascension and the transfer of his prophetic power to Elisha. So also do II iv, 1–7, 38–41, 42–4; vi, 1–7, the miracles of the ever-replenished oil, of the health-giving meal, of the feeding of a hundred men and of the floating axe, and also that of the secret life-giving power flowing out from Elisha's bones in II xiii, 20–1 (p. 46, n. 43). Of a different kind is the narrative of the woman of Shunem in iv, 8–37 + viii, 1–6, now divided into two parts by the compiler of the book or by someone else because viii, 1–6, takes place seven years later than iv, 8–37, and these seven years are evidently to be filled out by the material standing between iv, 8–37, and viii, 1–6. In this narrative Elisha does not appear surrounded by prophetic disciples, but stands alone having only one helper, Gehazi, with him. His dwelling, or one of his dwellings, seems, according to iv, 25, to be Mount Carmel, and in viii, 1–6, he is evidently already dead (v. 4).

pp. 100–4; Nagel, 'Ein urartäischer Helm aus dem Argisti-Magazin' AfO 19 (1959/60), pp. 144–7.

[51] Heller, 'Drei Wundertaten Elisas' CV 2 (1959), pp. 83–5.

[52] Albright, 'The New Assyro-Tyrian Synchronism and the Chronology of Tyre' AIPhHOS 13 (1955), pp. 1–9.

[53] Galling, 'Der Ehrenname Elisas und die Entrückung Elias' ZThK 53 (1956), pp. 129–48.

Chapter v, the healing of Naaman of his leprosy, presupposes connections on the part of Elisha with the prophetic bands (v. 22), but the story differs from the legends just discussed in iv, 1–7, 38–41, 42–4; vi, 1–7, in that here in ch. v Elisha stands much nearer to the great political events than in those legends, and ch. v thus approaches the type of the historical narrative. The Naaman story has in common with the Shunamite narrative iv, 8–37 + viii, 1–6, the fact that in both Gehazi appears as Elisha's servant, but even so they can hardly belong to the same narrative strand. For according to v, 27, Gehazi became a leper for the rest of his life, and this is clearly not presupposed in viii, 1–6. Nor can ch. v have followed viii, 1–6, since, as we have seen, Elisha is apparently dead in viii, 1–6.

Of yet another kind are the narratives of Elisha's part in Joram's campaign against Mesha of Moab in II iii, 4–27;[54] of the blinding of the Aramaeans in vi, 8–23; of his prophecy that the Aramaeans would suddenly abandon the siege of Samaria in vi, 24–vii, 19; and of the magical actions designed to destroy the Aramaeans which Elisha on his death-bed teaches to king Joash, in xiii, 14–19. Here Elisha is completely involved in higher political activity. In ch. iii admittedly he scornfully punishes Ahab's descendant Joram, but otherwise he is thought of as the helper of Israel, and in vi, 8–23;[55] vi, 24–vii, 19 (in spite of vi, 31–32) completely supports Israel's king and people in the conflict against the hereditary enemy Aram. But these stories in their turn, which are to be assigned to the type of historical narrative, differ among themselves, in that in the narrative of II iii, like the royal stories of I xx, xxii, Elisha is assigned merely a subsidiary role, whereas elsewhere he is the chief character. But even vi, 24–vii, 19, can hardly have belonged to the same context as vi, 8–23. For whereas according to vi, 23, there were no further Aramaean plundering expeditions in the land, vi, 24–vii, 19, actually tells of a siege of Samaria by the Aramaeans. We have already spoken about viii, 7–15, ix, x (pp. 291–2) and have seen that we have here probably the second half of a larger narrative work whose first half has been broken off in favour of a similar version, namely I xvii–xix, xxi. The narrative of xi[56] possibly contains two strands (p. 298). From its content it is clearly of Judaean origin and thus differs from ix–x. It is now linked with ix–x by the cross-reference in xi, 1, to the death of Ahaziah narrated in ix, 27–8, and could originally belong—or at any rate one strand of it—to the same narrative context as ix–x, in that the events in Judah are in fact the direct sequel of Jehu's revolution which concerned primarily the northern kingdom.

The Elisha narratives which the compiler of the book of Kings utilised were thus very varied. Some of them he probably found simply as unrelated narratives one beside another; this is particularly so with the legends. But

[54] Bernhardt, 'Beobachtungen zur Identifizierung moabitischer Ortslagen' ZDPV 76 (1960), pp. 136–58; Murphy, 'Israel and Moab in the Ninth Century B.C.' CBQ 15 (1953) pp. 409–17; Uri, 'De Burcht van Kerak, of de Krak van Moab' Tijdschrift voor Geschiedenis 68 (1955), pp. 213–23; van Zyl, The Moabites. With a Preface by A. van Selms, a Text of the Mesha Inscription, and a Map (1959). Lit. p. 258, n. 2; § 126.

[55] Kaplan, ' "And he Prepared Great Provision for Them" ' [Hebr., Engl. sum.] BIES 17 (1952/3), pp. 49–51, III: on II vi, 23.

[56] Rudolph, 'Die Einheitlichkeit der Erzählung vom Sturz der Atalja', Bertholet-Festschr. (1950), pp. 473–8.

others, for example, especially viii, 7–xi, 20, certainly belonged to larger entities, though we cannot say anything more precise about them. The possibility that we should allocate the Elisha narratives to L, J and E must certainly be considered, but the material here as in other complexes in the book (pp. 286 f., 293) is insufficient for proof. We can in some cases recognise the principles on which these various originals have been arranged, not always very happily. This has already been shown for iv, 8–37 + viii, 1–6 (p. 295). For the placing of vi, 24–vii, 19, before viii, 7–15, we must observe that in vi, 24–vii 19, a certain Benhadad is the protagonist, and in viii, 7–15, a Benhadad is killed. Our compiler, rightly or wrongly, has taken the Benhadad of the first narrative to be the same person as the Benhadad of the second, and therefore had to put the first before the second. But the sequence chosen by the compiler must not be regarded as determinative for the historical evaluation of the narratives.[57] It is more likely that the narratives which depict Elisha's attitude to the king as friendly, i.e. not only xiii, 14–19, but also v; vi, 8–23; vi, 24–vii, 19, have their true historical setting not under Joram the son of Ahab but under Jehu and his sons Jehoahaz and Joash. Elisha stood in opposition to the sons of Ahab.

Another large block of narratives is set between the introductory and concluding formulae for Hezekiah, i.e. between II xviii, 1–3, and xx, 20–21, and for most of these Isaiah stands in the centre so that we may assume that the compiler of our book took this material from a collection of Isaiah legends. Our book of Isaiah cannot be the source. The sections of the book of Kings which here come in question, namely II xviii, 13–xx, 19,[58] have rather been inserted secondarily in the book of Isaiah,[59] which at that time only comprised i–xxxv (p. 328). There is only one passage within xviii, 13–xx, 19, which does not centre upon Isaiah and clearly does not derive from the Isaiah legends, but presumably stood in the *History of the Kings of Israel,* namely xviii, 14–16, the report of Hezekiah's submission to Sennacherib and his payment of heavy tribute to the victor. This, we may note, was not included when xviii, 13–xx, 19, was transferred to the end of the book of Isaiah.

With regard to the last more detailed narratives which the book of Kings offers,[60] the account of Josiah's reform in II xxii–xxiii[61] and that of the catastrophe

[57] Cf. Jepsen, 'Israel und Damaskus' AfO 14 (1941–4), pp. 153–72. Lit. p. 275, n. 31; § 126.

[58] Albright, 'New Light from Egypt on the Chronology and History of Israel and Judah' BASOR 130 (1953), pp. 4–11, see pp. 8–11: The Date of Sennacherib's Second Campaign against Hezekiah; Bright, *History of Israel* (1959), pp. 282–7: The Problem of Sennacherib's Campaigns in Palestine; Haag, 'La Campagne de Sennachérib contre Jérusalem en 701' RB 58 (1951), pp. 348–59; Hintze, 'Eine neue Inschrift vom 19. Jahre König Taharqas' MIOF 7 (1960), pp. 330–3; Horn, Review of Gordon, *The World of the OT* (1958), JBL 78 (1959), pp. 370–2, cf. pp. 371 f.; Janssen, 'Que sait-on actuellement du Pharaon Taharqa?' Bibl 34 (1953), pp. 23–43; Leemans, 'Marduk-apal-iddina II, zijn tijd en zijn geslacht' JEOL 10 (1948), pp. 432–55; Luckenbill, *The Annals of Sennacherib* (OIP 2, 1924); Le Moyne, 'Les deux ambassades de Sennachérib à Jérusalem' *Mél. Bibl. Robert* (1957), pp. 149–53; Orlinsky, 'The Kings-Isaiah Recensions of the Hezekiah Story' JQR 30 (1939/40), pp. 33–49; Vieyra, 'Sennachérib à Ninive' RA 54 (1960), pp. 41–4; Vikentiev, 'Quelques considérations à propos des statues de Taharqa trouvées dans les ruines du palais d'Esarhaddon' Sumer 11 (1955), pp. 111–16. Lit. p. 23, n. 23; p. 284, n. 18, p. 305, n. 10; p. 328, n. 88; § 126.   [59] Differently Jepsen, p. 77.

[60] Albright, 'The Nebuchadnezzar and Neriglissar Chronicles' BASOR 143 (1956),

of 587 in xxv,[62] we may ask whether they derive from the compiler himself or whether he found them, or at least the first of them, already to hand, perhaps in the *History of the Kings of Judah*. A decision on this point depends upon the dating of the compilation of the book (p. 285). But even for the period which the compiler or amplifier (pp. 284 f.) actually lived through or could have lived through, it is not impossible that he utilised accounts made by others, as may be seen from a comparison of xxv, 22–6, with Jer. xl, 7–xli, 18. It is clear that xxv, 22–6, is an extract from the narrative in the book of Jeremiah or of the version which underlies it. We may assume a similar position for II xxii–xxiii, with a greater degree of probability since here there is a notable stylistic difference[63] between the narrative of the finding of the law book and its effects in II xxii, 3–xxiii, 3, 9, 21–5, and the enumeration of individual measures of a cultic and political kind undertaken by Josiah in II xxiii, 4–8, 10–15, 19–20. These latter are surely taken from the *History of the Kings of Judah*.

3. *The pre-deuteronomic book of Kings.* Our book of Kings thus contains a great deal of narrative material, which in all probability cannot have stood in the *History of Solomon*, nor in the *History of the Kings of Israel* and *of Judah*, but must have been derived from elsewhere. We have several times hinted at the possibility (pp. 290, 293) that at least for a part of this material the source might be the postulated continuation of the Octateuch sources, L + J + E, in other words a pre-deuteronomic book of Kings. To this question we must now devote a little more attention. There is no lack of parallels of various kinds, not only of individual narratives but also of narrative complexes, and we have seen that the two or three parallels which have been indicated would not fit badly with the character of the sources L, J and E known to us from the Octateuch. In addition to such parallels there is also a series of narratives and references which have not yet been pointed out, which reveal a mixture of sources and appear to be made up from two narratives. Examples are I xi, 14–22 + 25aβb, the rebellion of the

pp. 28–33; Barnett, 'The Siege of Lachish' IEJ 8 (1958), pp. 161–4, Pls. 30–2; Bengtson, 'Neue Quellen zur Geschichte der neubabylonischen Zeit' Historia 6 (1957), pp. 499–502; Finegan, 'Nebuchadnezzar and Jerusalem' JBR 25 (1957), pp. 203–5; Freedman, 'The Babylonian Chronicle' BA 19 (1956), pp. 50–60; Hyatt, 'New Light on Nebuchadrezzar and Judean History' JBL 75 (1956), pp. 277–84; Kutsch, 'Zur Chronologie der letzten judäischen Könige (Josia bis Zedekia)' ZAW 71 (1959), pp. 270–4; Malamat, 'A New Record of Nebuchadrezzar's Palestinian Campaigns' IEJ 6 (1956), pp. 246–55, Pl. 32; Nötscher, ' "Neue" babylonische Chroniken und AT' BZ 1 (1957), pp. 110–14; Parker and Dubberstein, *Babylonian Chronology 626 B.C.–A.D. 45* (²1956); Tadmor, 'Chronology of the Last Kings of Judah' JNESt 15 (1956), pp. 226–30; Vogt, 'Nova chronica Babylonica de pugna apud Karkemiš et expugnatione Ierusalem' Bibl 37 (1956), pp. 389–97; 'Chronologia exeuntis regni Iuda et exsilii' Bibl 38 (1957), pp. 229–33; 'Die neubabylonische Chronik über die Schlacht bei Karkemisch und die Einnahme von Jerusalem' SVT IV (1957), pp. 67–96; Wiseman, *Chronicles of Chaldaean Kings (626–556 B.C.) in the British Museum* (1956); on this Kraus VT 8 (1958), pp. 109–11. Lit. p. 285, n. 19.

[61] Borger, 'Mesopotamien in den Jahren 629–21 vChr' WZKM 55 (1959), pp. 62–76; Horst, 'Die Kultusreform des Königs Josia (II. Rg. xxii–xxiii)' ZDMG 77 (1923), pp. 220–238; Jepsen, 'Die Reform des Josia' *Baumgärtel-Festschr.* (1959), pp. 97–108. Lit. p. 232, n. 26; p. 284, n. 15.

[62] Malamat 'The Last Wars of the Kingdom of Judah' JNESt 9 (1950), pp. 218–27.

[63] R. Meyer, 'Auffallender Erzählungsstil in einem angeblichen Auszug aus der " Chronik der Könige von Juda" ' *Baumgärtel-Festschr.* (1959), pp. 114–23.

Edomite Hadad; and II xi,[64] the deposing and assassination of Athaliah.[65] These phenomena could be readily explained if we assumed the existence of a pre-deuteronomic book of Kings representing a combination of L, J and E. General considerations make this assumption a very natural one. There is no sharp boundary between the books of Samuel and Kings (p. 135). At least one of the sources which run through II Sam. certainly extends into the book of Kings, and what may be proved for one can at any rate not be stated to be impossible for the others. We should rather expect that if they were compiled after the death of David—and this seems a necessary assumption for all three, L, J and E (pp. 197f., 200, 203)—they would continue their presentation down to their own time.

There are thus good grounds for the view that with the book of Kings also the Deuteronomist did not make a completely new outline, but worked over a book of Kings already available to him, namely the continuation of the narrative works of the Octateuch, and carried it down further beyond the point which it reached. But it is nevertheless not possible to reconstruct this original and then divide it up again into its individual strands. There has been, as we have already noted (pp. 244–6), no lack of attempts at doing this. Beginning from the theory which reckons with only two sources (J and E) for the pre-deuteronomic material, Benzinger and Hölscher have set out to divide the whole of the older material of the books of Kings between J and E. Benzinger believes it possible to trace J as far as II xvii, 3–4, and therefore assumes that J was compiled under Hezekiah, or more correctly—since this is how he seems to picture the process —that the last edition of J was formed under Hezekiah. The latest traces of E, on the other hand, he finds in the account of Josiah's reform in II xxii–xxiii, and so considers that E was concluded not long before the death of Josiah in 609 B.C. As against this, Hölscher thinks that J extended only as far as the division of the kingdom (I xii), and that everything that follows comes from E which he places after 587, except in so far as the material is the product of the Deuteronomistic compiler or is an even later addition. Whereas Benzinger considers that the compiler utilised the annalistic *History of Solomon* and *Histories of the Kings of Israel* and *of Judah* as well as J and E, according to Hölscher he only had J and E in front of him, and it is E which in its turn made use of those annals. Over against these adherents of the two-source theory, Smend has sought to explain the pre-deuteronomic book of Kings as a combination of his three Octateuch sources (J^1 = L, J^2 = J, E), though in this he limits himself to indicating sections which would fit in with L, J and E, clearly motivated by the feeling that it is not in fact possible to trace through the whole course of these strands. He finds the latest trace of L in the oldest Elisha narratives such as II iv, 8–37, that of J in II ix–x, and that of E in II v, vi, 8–23. In addition, in his view, the compiler of our book utilised also the *History of Solomon* and the *History of the Kings of Israel* and *of Judah*, and in particular took from the latter material concerned with the Temple in Jerusalem, namely II xi, xii, 5–17;[66] xxii–

---

[64] Cf. p. 295, n. 56.
[65] Cf. p. 282, n. 8.
[66] Falk, 'Craftsmen and Faith (2 K xii, 15–16, xxii, 5–6)' [Hebr., Engl. sum.] Tarbiz 28 (1958/9), pp. 251–3, I; McKane, 'A Note on 2 Kings xii, 10' ZAW 71 (1959), pp. 260–5. Lit. p. 435, n. 2.

xxiii. Simpson, however, as we have seen (p. 246), believes it possible to trace his J¹, J² and E as far as I Kings xiii.

In these views there is thus agreement only on the point that there was a pre-deuteronomic book of Kings, and that the Octateuch narrative work extended beyond the end of the books of Samuel. It remains in dispute how far it extended, how far the individual strands combined in it extended, and how many such strands are to be assumed. But the division of the kingdom is in any event regarded as included in this, and, if we accept the three-source theory, included in all three sources. Perhaps also, at any rate J and E, or E alone, included the prophetic revolution in the second third of the ninth century and the Aramaean wars of that period. The decision on these questions depends upon the period at which the pre-deuteronomic Pentateuch or Enneateuch strands and their working together into the pre-deuteronomic historical work are dated. The earlier this is placed, the earlier we must place the beginning of the material which was added by the compiler or first redactor of the books of Kings—or whatever else we may choose to call the writer who here comes in question. In spite of many objections to which Jepsen's recently propounded analysis of the book of Kings otherwise gives rise, we may nevertheless follow one of his suggestions and perhaps picture the matter as follows: a synchronistic chronicle of the kings of Israel and Judah compiled towards the end of the eighth century B.C. and extending from David to Hezekiah gave the impetus to the continuation of the pre-deuteronomic historical work, in that the beginnings of this chronicle fitted in with the conclusion of this historical work and further material was added at the end. To illuminate in detail the further development of our book remains impossible, as we have seen. But we may confidently affirm, against Jepsen who assumes with reference to many ancient narratives, like those of I xvii–xxii, as also those of Judg. i and xvii–xxi, that they were first taken up by later redactors, that these materials are much more likely to have been derived from one of the Enneateuch strands, and thus represent parts of the pre-deuteronomic historical work.

4. *The Deuteronomistic compilers* or editors of our book have thus proceeded substantially differently from the editors of the previous books of Joshua, Judges and Samuel, though these latter are connected with the former, and possibly to be identified with them (pp. 255 f., 266 f., 280). The latter, in addition to L + J + E, had little or relatively little material still available, and they therefore had in general to limit themselves to the elaboration of the older narrative with pious speeches or reflections (Josh. xxiii; Judg. ii, 1b–5a, 11–19; I Sam. ii, 27–36*; II vii*). But for the period after David there was available, particularly for the Jerusalem kings, a great deal of material in narratives and reports, and the compilers could therefore choose as they wished. Their own predilections directed them to give a prominence on the one hand to the Jerusalem Temple and on the other hand to the prophets, whereas the actual political events interested them less. So they put in all they could concerning the Temple and the prophets, but made a fairly rigid selection from among the remaining narratives and reports. It did not bother the compilers that in this way the individual kings were treated quite unevenly and that the fullness or brevity

of the accounts often did not correspond with their real significance, as is the case with Omri,[67] the founder of Samaria,[68] dismissed in no more than six verses (I xvi, 23–8). All that mattered was that the Temple and the prophets should be given their due. Under these circumstances it is indeed worth recognising that they did at least provide a continuous narrative and took account of all the kings. Where the reigns which are unprofitable as far as the Temple and the prophets are concerned are mentioned only with the most meagre data, this book is similar to P, in that the latter also admittedly provides a continuous narrative, but only becomes more detailed where it is a matter of imparting legal regulations. It is in any case not surprising that in these circumstances the pre-deuteronomic book of Kings came to be much more concealed than was the case with the pre-deuteronomic Octateuch.

But if the Deuteronomistic compilers of our book worked so differently from the editors of the preceding books, it would appear that we must call in question the otherwise very natural assumption that we are dealing with the same two Deuteronomists who edited in the spirit of Deuteronomy the great pre-deuter-onomic historical work which began with the creation and came down to the seventh century B.C. and into which Deuteronomy itself was inserted. Yet the difference between our book of Kings and the preceding books can be explained —and should be explained—simply from the fact that for the former other sources were available in addition to L, J and E, and further from the fact that the application of the Deuteronomistic standard—permitting the cult at the high places or not—was only relevant from the time of the building of Solomon's Temple, and so it was only from that point on that a more thoroughgoing trans-formation of the pre-deuteronomic book became possible and necessary. We may therefore nevertheless retain the assumption that two Deuteronomistic hands edited the original Deuteronomy and in connection with this worked over the whole of the subsequent history at least as far down as Josiah. Admittedly certainty cannot be attained here (pp. 284–5).

5. *Later alterations*. Even with the Deuteronomistic editing, or if two are to be assumed, with the combination of the two Deuteronomistic editions, the book of Kings was not however finally closed. It did in fact undergo various altera-tions subsequently. Whether these alterations included the reinsertion by a later hand of a number of passages from the older sources which the Deuteronomists had left out—e.g. I ii, 13–46a; xiv, 1–18;[69] xvii, 1–xxii, 38—as is believed by Hölscher, Noth, Jepsen and others following earlier scholars, is as doubtful

[67] Follet, 'Nova quaedam de usu Annalium Shalmaneser III' ad historiam biblicam illustrandam' VD 30 (1952), pp. 227–33; Morgenstern, 'Chronological Data of the Dyn-asty of Omri' JBL 59 (1940), pp. 385–96; Thompson, 'Extra-Biblical Data and the Omri Dynasty' ABR 3 (1953), pp. 24–40; Whitley, 'The Deuteronomic Presentation of the House of Omri' VT 2 (1952), pp. 137–52. Lit. p. 292, n. 49; § 126.

[68] Alt, *Der Stadtstaat Samaria* (BAL 101, 5, 1945) = *Kl. Schr.* III (1959), pp. 258–302; Crowfoot, etc., *Samaria-Sebaste. Report on the Excavations at Samaria* 1931–1935 I (1942), II (1938), III (1958); Parrot, *Samarie, Capitale du Royaume d'Israël* (1955), E.T. *Samaria* (1958); Reisner, etc., *Harvard Excavations at Samaria* I. II (1924); Wright, 'Samaria' BA 22 (1959), pp. 67–78; 'Israelite Samaria and Iron Age Chronology' BASOR 155 (1959), pp. 13–28. Lit. p. 674, n. 11.

[69] On Tirzah xiv, 17 f., cf. p. 490, n. 26.

here as it is in the books of Judges and Samuel (pp. 266, 280). But the book nevertheless did receive additions after the activity of the second editor, or the redactor of the two editions, even though a quite clear distinction is not possible between the work of the second editor, perhaps active only after 587 (pp. 284–5) and these even later supplements. We can mention here only a selection of the larger additions of this kind. The prayer spoken by Solomon at the dedication of the Temple (I viii), which itself comes from the Deuteronomistic compiler, reveals secondary additions (vv. 23–6, 41–51). To these elaborations of the prayer corresponds the divine answer, the theophany of ix, 1–9. We have already referred to the prophetic legends of I xii, 32–xiii, 33, and II i, 9–16, which probably come from a later hand (pp. 290, 293). In addition, the explanation of the downfall of the northern kingdom in II xvii, which certainly has a Deuteronomistic and even a pre-deuteronomic basis, has been later filled out (vv. 7–20, 29–40), and so also has the list of Manasseh's sins (II xxi, 7–15). These additions are in a line with the activity of the compilers; they are all of a religious and theological nature.

II. THE WRITING PROPHETS (נְבִיאִים אַחֲרֹנִים LATTER PROPHETS)

§ 42. GENERAL CONSIDERATIONS CONCERNING THE BOOKS OF ISAIAH, JEREMIAH, EZEKIEL AND THE TWELVE MINOR PROPHETS

Literature: Ayuso, 'Los elementos extrabíblicos de los profetas' EstBíbl 6 (1947) pp. 347–402, 455; Balla, *Die Botschaft der Propheten* (1958); Baumgartner, 'Die Auffassungen des 19. Jh. vom israelitischen Prophetismus' AfK 15 (1922), pp. 21–35 = *Zum AT* (1959), pp. 27–41; Beaucamp, *Sous la main de Dieu.* I: *Le prophétisme et l'élection d'Israël* (1956); Béguerie, Leclerq, Steinmann, *Études sur les Prophètes d'Israël* (1954); Bewer, *The Prophets* (Harper's Annotated Bible, 1955); Birkeland, *Zum hebräischen Traditionswesen. Die Komposition der Prophetischen Bücher des AT* (ANVAO 1938, 1, 1938); Brongers, *De scheppingtradities bij de profeten* (1945); Buber, *The Prophetic Faith* (1949); Chaine, *Introduction à la lecture des Prophètes* ([10]1957); Cornill, *Der israelitische Prophetismus* ([13]1920); Deden, *De messiaanse profetieën* (1947); Duhm, *Israels Propheten* ([2]1922); Engnell, 'Profetia och tradition' SEA 12 (1947), pp. 110–39; 'Profetismens ursprung och upkomst' *Religion och Kultus* (1950), pp. 1–18; Fohrer, 'Neuere Literatur zur at. Prophetie' ThR 19 (1951), pp. 277–346; 20 (1952), pp. 193–271, 295–361; Grönbæk, 'Zur Frage der Eschatologie in der Verkündigung der Gerichtspropheten' SEA 24 (1959), pp. 5–21; Guillaume, *Prophecy and Divination among the Hebrews and other Semites* (1938); Gunkel, *Die Propheten* (1917); Gunneweg, *Mündliche und schriftliche Tradition der vorexilischen Prophetenbücher als Problem der neueren Prophetenforschung* (FRLANT 73, 1959); Gurewicz, 'Prophecy in Israel' ABR 2 (1952), pp. 29–41; Hammershaimb, 'On the Ethics of the OT Prophets' SVT VII (1960), pp. 75–101; Heaton, *The Old Testament Prophets* (1958); Hempel, *Worte der Propheten in neuer Übertragung und mit Erläuterungen* (1949); Henshaw, *The Latter Prophets* (1959); Hentschke, 'Gesetz und Eschatologie in der Verkündigung der Propheten' ZevE 4 (1960), pp. 46–56; Herrmann, 'Die Ursprünge der prophetischen Heilserwartung im AT' ThLZ 83 (1958), cols. 641–3; Heschel, *Die Prophetie* (1936); Hölscher, *Die Propheten* (1914); Jenni, *Die politischen Voraussagen der Propheten* (AThANT 29, 1956); Kraus,

Die prophetische Verkündigung des Rechts in Israel (ThSt[B] 51, 1957); Kuhl, *Israels Propheten* (1956); E.T. *The Prophets of Israel* (1960); de Liagre Böhl, 'Priester und Prophet' NThSt 22 (1939), pp. 298–313 = *Op. Min.* (1953), pp. 50–62, 479 f.; Lindblom, *Profetismen i Israel* (1934); 'Gibt es eine Eschatologie bei den at. Propheten?' StTh 6 (1953), pp. 79–114; Lods, 'Recherches récentes sur le prophétisme israélite' RHR 104 (1931), pp. 279–316; *Les prophètes d'Israël et les débuts du Judaïsme* (1935); E.T. *The Prophets and the Rise of Judaism* (1937); Mattuck, *The Thought of the Prophets* (1953); Micklem, *Prophecy and Eschatology* (1926); Milley, *The Prophets of Israel* (1959); Moriarty, 'The Prophets: Bearers of the Word' The Bridge 3 (1958), pp. 54–83; Mowinckel, *Jesaja-disiplene, Profetien fra Jesaja til Jeremia* (1926); Neher, *L'Essence du Prophétisme* (1955); Paterson, *The Goodly Fellowship of the Prophets* (1949); von Rad, 'Les idées sur le temps et l'histoire en Israël et l'eschatologie des prophètes' *Hommage à W. Vischer* (1960), pp. 198–209; Robinson, 'Neuere Propheten-Forschung' ThR 3 (1931), pp. 75–103; *Prophecy and the Prophets in Ancient Israel* (³1944); Rohland, *Die Bedeutung der Erwählungstraditionen Israels für die Eschatologie der at. Propheten* (Diss. theol. Heidelberg 1956, 1957); Rost, *Israel bei den Propheten* (BWANT 71, 1937); Rowley, 'The Nature of Prophecy in the Light of Recent Study' HThR 38 (1945), pp. 1–38 = *The Servant of the Lord* (1952), pp. 89–128; *Prophecy and Religion in Ancient China and Israel* (1956); Rowley (ed.), *Studies in OT Prophecy, pres. to Th. H. Robinson* (1950); Sarfatti, 'Pious Men, Men of Deeds and the Early Prophets' [Hebr., Engl. sum.] Tarbiz 26 (1956/7), pp. 126–53, II–IV; Scott, *The Relevance of the Prophets* (²1951); Skinner, *Prophecy and Religion* (⁴1936 (1961)); Smith, *The Prophets and their Times*, 2. ed. rev. by Irwin (1941); Steinmann, *Le prophétisme biblique des origines à Osée* (1959); Voegelin, *Order and History. I Israel and Revelation* (1956); Volz, 'Die radikale Ablehnung der Kultreligion durch die at. Propheten' ZSTh 14 (1937), pp. 63–85; *Prophetengestalten des AT* (³1944); Vriezen, 'Prophecy and Eschatology' SVT I (1953), pp. 199–229; Welch, *Kings and Prophets of Israel* (1952); *Prophet and Priest in Old Israel* (²1953); Wolff, 'Hauptprobleme at. Prophetie' EvTh 15 (1955), pp. 446–68; 'Das Geschichtsverständnis der at. Propheten' EvTh 20 (1960), pp. 218–35.

Cf. also Literature §§ 10, 20, 126.

The four books of the 'Former Prophets'—or six if we take into account the division made only later of the books of Samuel and Kings into two each—are, as we have seen, originally parts of a larger complex, eventually made into the Deuteronomistic historical work. They only became separate books relatively late and are therefore primarily to be evaluated as parts of a larger entity. But as far as the 'Latter Prophets' are concerned—the books of Isaiah, Jeremiah, Ezekiel and the twelve minor prophets, transmitted in varying order (p. 383)— the position is quite different, in that at least two of them contain more than one originally independent book. Thus our book of Isaiah, in addition to the sections which are at least in the main concerned with the prophet of the second half of the eighth century B.C. who bears this name (or are regarded as concerned with him), namely i–xxxix, contains also the two complexes xl–lv and lvi–lxvi. These belong to a substantially later date, and, as we shall see, were only secondarily added to Isa. i–xxxix and so came to be ascribed to the eighth-century prophet. A similar situation exists with regard to Zech. ix–xiv. In the Jewish canon, the books of the twelve minor prophets, which were originally independent entities, are reckoned as one book. Thus the 'Latter Prophets' have never represented a literary unit of a higher order. So it may here suffice to mention a selection of the most important literature relevant to the 'writing prophets' and in particular of those works which are concerned with the literary questions which affect them. And we may simply preface the analysis of the individual books which immediately follows with the observation which applies to them all, that with them the position is similar to that which prevails in regard to the Pentateuch and the older historical books. Here too the interest in literary critical questions, which was very lively at the end of the last century and the beginning of the present one, has declined greatly in the last four or five decades, and attention has been directed to other questions—questions of textual criticism, of the history of material and form, historical and psychological questions, not to mention the specifically 'theological' questions. This explains why it is that in what follows in the discussion of literary analysis as it has affected the individual prophetic books, many older works have had to be dealt with, whereas only relatively few works of this kind can be mentioned from the more recent period.

(a) *The Major Prophets*

§ 43. ISAIAH I–XXXIX

Literature: (a) Commentaries (i) Series: ATD; Kaiser ([2]1963) (c. i–xii); Bibelhilfe: Hertzberg ([2]1952); Camb. B: Skinner (1896/98); Cent. B: Whitehouse (1905); EB: Condamin (1905); Echter-B: Ziegler (1948); EH: Feldmann (1925/26); Harper's B: Bewer (1950); HK: Duhm ([4]1922); HS: Fischer, I (1937), II (1939); HSAT: Guthe and Eissfeldt (1922); IB: Scott, Kilpatrick (1956); ICC: Gray, Isa. i–xxvii (1912 (1947)); Jerusalem-B: Auvray, Steinmann ([2]1957); KAT: Procksch, Isa. i–xxxix (1930); KD: Delitzsch ([4]1889); KeH: Dillmann-Kittel ([6]1898); KHC: Marti (1900); SAT: Hans Schmidt ([2]1923); Soncino-B: Slotki (1949); SZ: Orelli ([3]1904); TU: van der Flier, I (1923), II (1926); WC: Wade (1911 (1929)).

(ii) Single Commentaries: Bentzen, I (1943), II (1943); Bratsiotis (1956); Bredenkamp (1887); Cheyne, I ([5]1889), II ([4]1886); Feldmann (1940); Hitzig (1833); Kissane, I (1941), II (1943); Koenig (1926).

(b) Other Works: Anderson, 'Was Isaiah a Scribe?' JBL 79 (1960), pp. 57 f.; Blank, *Prophetic Faith in Isaiah* (1958); Brillet, *Isaïe* (1945); Budde, 'Über die Schranken, die Jesajas prophetischer Botschaft zu setzen sind' ZAW 41 (1923), pp. 154–203; *Jesajas Erleben . . . (Kap. vi, 1–ix, 6)* (1928); 'Zu Jesaja i–v' ZAW 49 (1931), pp. 16–40, 182–211; 50 (1932), pp. 38–72; Cheyne, *Introduction to the Book of Isaiah* (1895); Cornill, 'Die Composition des Buches Jesaja' ZAW 4 (1884), pp. 83–105; Driver, 'Linguistic and Textual Problems: Isaiah i–xxxix' JThSt 38 (1937), pp. 36–50; Dumeste, 'Le message du prophète Isaïe' Vie Spirit. 76 (1947), pp. 748–67; Eaton, 'Commentaries on Isaiah' Theology 60 (1957), pp. 451–5; 'The Origin of the Book of Isaiah' VT 9 (1959), pp. 138–57; Eitan, 'A Contribution to Isaiah Exegesis' HUCA 12/13 (1937/38), pp. 55–88; Fullerton, 'Viewpoints in the Discussion of Isaiah's Hopes for the Future' JBL 41 (1922), pp. 1–101; Giesebrecht, *Beiträge zur Jesajakritik* (1890); Hölscher, 'Jesaja' ThLZ 77 (1952), cols. 683–94; Jennings, *Studies in Isaiah* (1935); D. R. Jones, 'The Traditio of the Oracles of Isaiah of Jerusalem' ZAW 67 (1955), pp. 226–46; Koch, 'La théologie de l'Esprit de Yahvé dans le Livre d'Isaïe' BEThL XII (1959), pp. 419–33; Liebreich, 'The Compilation of the Book of Isaiah' JQR 46 (1955/56), pp. 259/77; 47 (1956/57), pp. 114–38; Loretz, 'Der Glaube des Propheten Isaias an das Gottesreich' ZKTh 82 (1960), pp. 40–73, 149–81; Martin-Achard, 'Sagesse de Dieu et sagesse humaine chez Ésaïe' *Hommage à W. Vischer* (1960), pp. 137–44; Mowinckel, *Profeten Jesaja* (1925); 'Die Komposition des Jesajabuches Kap. i–xxxix' Acta Or [L] 11 (1933), pp. 267–92; 'Komposisjonen av Jesajaboken kap.

i–xxxix' NTT 44 (1943), pp. 159–71; *Jesaja* (1949); Renard, 'Le messianisme dans la première partie du Livre d'Isaïe' BEThL XII (1959), pp. 398–407; Scott, 'The Literary Structure of Isaiah's Oracles' StOTPr (1950), pp. 175–86; Skehan, 'Some Textual Problems in Isaiah' CBQ 22 (1960), pp. 47–55; Steinmann, *Le Prophète Isaïe: sa vie, son œuvre, son temps* (²1955); Stenning, *The Targum of Isaiah* (²1953); Ziegler, 'Zum literarischen Aufbau verschiedener Stücke im Buche des Propheten Isaias' BZ 21 (1933), pp. 131–49, 237–54; *Untersuchungen zur Septuaginta des Buches Isaias* (1934).

Cf. also Literature §§ 42, 44, 45, 104, 115, 126.

1. *Survey of i–lxvi.* Our book of Isaiah divides naturally into three sections: sayings i–xxxv, narratives xxxvi–xxxix, sayings xl–lxvi. Following on hints made by Ibn Ezra (†1167),[1] it was first explicitly recognised by Eichhorn (1783)[2] and Döderlein (1789)[3] that xl–lxvi—at first regarded as a literary unit, 'Deutero-Isaiah' and only later, as we shall see (pp. 341 f.) divided into two units, xl–lv 'Deutero-Isaiah' and lvi–lxvi 'Trito-Isaiah'—could not derive from the prophet Isaiah who was active in the eighth century, but must be attributed to a prophet who appeared in the sixth century. This view has generally come to prevail, in spite of continually renewed denials, recently for example by Allis, *The Unity of Isaiah* (1950), and E. J. Young, *Studies in Isaiah* (1954) and *Who wrote Isaiah?* (1958). The grounds for this dating of xl–lxvi, or more precisely actually only of xl–lv are indeed decisive: the mention of Cyrus, designated in xliv, 28 as (*my*) *Shepherd* (רֹעִי) and in xlv, 1, as (*his*) *anointed* (מְשִׁיחוֹ); Babylon (not Assyria) threatened with downfall in xlvii, 1, xlviii, 14; the peculiarities of linguistic usage and of thought. The presence of xxxvi–xxxix, which, as we have already seen (p. 296), derive from the book of Kings (II Kings xviii, 13–xx, 19) also show that at one time the book of Isaiah must have ended with xxxv. The narratives have clearly been appended at the end of a book. Hence the two main sections (i–xxxix and xl–lxvi) or more properly the three (i–xxxix, xl–lv, lvi–lxvi) must be treated separately.[4]

2. *The personality of Isaiah, and his period of activity.* We must preface the literary analysis of i–xxxix with at least some brief statement, demanded by those chapters, concerning the person and period of Isaiah. Concerning the prophet himself, apart from the name of his father, Amoz (i, 1, אָמוֹץ), who is in no way connected with the prophet Amos (עָמוֹס), we learn only that he was married to a wife who apparently was also prophetically gifted (viii, 3, *prophetess*), and that by this marriage he had at least two children: *A remnant returns* (vii, 3, שְׁאָר יָשׁוּב),[5] and *Speed-spoil-haste-booty* (viii, 3, מַהֵר שָׁלָל חָשׁ בַּז),[6]

[1] Cf. p. 2, n. 4.   [2] *Einleitung ins AT*, III (1783), pp. 76–97.
[3] *Esaias* (³1789), pp. XII–XV (p. XII: 'Non est praetereundum quid de *authentia* vaticiniorum Esaiae, quam nuper in dubitationem pro ingenii sui accumine adduxit Ill. Eichhorn [*Introduct. in V.T., T. III, p. 76*] videatur statuendum'; p. XV: 'Quare consentaneum videtur, orationem vel potius librum posteriorem a Capite XL. ad serius, Esaia, aevum referre, atque sub finem exilii ab anonymo quodam, vel homonymo antiquo vate, compositum profiteri').
[4] Cf. further, § 45, 3.
[5] Blank, 'The Current Misinterpretation of Isaiah's *She'ar Yashub*' JBL 67 (1948), pp. 211–15, cf. also *Prophetic Faith in Isaiah* (1958), ch. ii; Dreyfus, 'La doctrine du reste d'Israël chez le prophète Isaïe' RSPhTh 39 (1955), pp. 361–86; L. Koehler, 'שְׁאָר יָשׁוּב und der nackte Relativsatz' VT 3 (1953), pp. 84 f.; Müller, *Die Vorstellung vom Rest im AT* (Diss. theol. Leipzig, 1939). Lit. § 126.

of which the first was in 734–733, taken by Isaiah to his significant meeting with King Ahaz at the water conduit of the upper pool (vii, 3)[7] and so was then presumably about two to four years old, and the second was born then (viii, 3). So far as we can tell, Isaiah appeared exclusively in Jerusalem, and since, on the evidence of his message, he is seen to be intimately bound up with city and temple, we may assume him to be a Jerusalemite. The widely held view, perhaps in some measure justified by the fact that he can make a request for service to men of importance (viii, 2), that he was of noble birth, perhaps even of royal descent, is however simply a guess. The tradition that he was sawn in two under Manasseh, attested by the Martyrdom of Isaiah ch. v (§ 92), and elsewhere[8] is legendary.

He was called in the year of Uzziah's death, 746[9] (vi), and his last utterance, so far as we know, belongs to the time of Sennacherib's threat to Jerusalem in 701 (xxxvi–xxxvii). The period of his activity is thus the last four and a half decades of the eighth century, the reigns of the Judaean kings Jotham (745– 742), Ahaz (741–726) and Hezekiah (725–697), decades which were filled with the most momentous events, more so than almost any other period of Israelite history. They are reflected in Isaiah's message, and it remains unintelligible without an exact knowledge of contemporary history.[10] The most important events of this period are the Syro-Ephraimite War of 734–733 (vii–viii); the death of Tiglathpileser in 726 (xiv, 28–32?),[11] the rebellion of northern Israel against his successor Shalmaneser V (726–723), which ended in the conquest of Samaria and the destruction of the northern kingdom by his successor Sargon[12] (722–706) in the year 721 (xxviii, 1–4); the attempts undertaken with a greater or lesser degree of energy by Hezekiah, in alliance with other states of Palestine-Syria and with support from Egypt, at throwing off the Assyrian yoke, in particular that of 713–711, which ended with the conquest of Ashdod, the centre of the conspiracy, by Sargon in 711 (xx), and that of 704–701 directed against Sargon's successor (xiv, 28–32?)[13] Sennacherib (705–681) which had as its sequel the terrible visitation of Judah and the serious threat to Jerusalem of the year 701 (xxxvi–xxxvii). It is possible that the book of Isaiah also reflects the fears which Sargon's expedition in 715 against the Arabian eastern coast of the Red

---

[6] Morenz, ' "Eilebeute" ' ThLZ 74 (1949), cols. 697–9; Rignell, 'Das Orakel "Maher-salal Has-bas" Jesaja viii' StTh 10, 1 (1957), pp. 40–52.

[7] Burrows, 'The Conduit of the Upper Pool' ZAW 70 (1958), pp. 221–7. Literature, p. 19, n. 3; p. 52, n. 60; p. 675, n. 15.

[8] Thus in Heb. xi, 37, where the right reading is surely ἐπρίσθησαν, *they were sawn in two*, and not ἐπειράσθησαν, *they were tempted*.

[9] The chronology here set out is not the only one proposed for this period. [Translator's note.]

[10] Alt, 'Das System der assyrischen Provinzen auf dem Boden des Reiches Israel' ZDPV 52 (1929), pp. 220–42 = *Kl. Schr.* II, pp. 188–205; 'Die Territorialgeschichtliche Bedeutung von Sanheribs Eingriff in Palästina' PJB 25 (1930), pp. 80–8 = *Kl. Schr.* II, pp. 242–9; 'Neue assyrische Nachrichten über Palästina' ZDPV 67 (1945), pp. 128–46 = *Kl. Schr.* II pp. 226–41; 'Tiglathpilesers III. erster Feldzug nach Palästina' *Kl. Schr.* II (1953), pp. 150–62; Eissfeldt, 'Ezechiel als Zeuge für Sanheribs Eingriff in Palästina' PJB 27 (1931), pp. 58–66; Rudolph, 'Sanherib in Palästina' PJB 25 (1930), pp. 59–80; Yellin, 'The Mention of Fire in Isaiah and the Downfall of Sennacherib' *Or. Stud. C. E. Pavry* (1933), pp. 501–3. Lit. p. 296, n. 58; § 126.   [11] Cf. pp. 149; 313.

[12] Or by Shalmaneser himself. Cf. BA, 23 (1960), p. 51. [Translator's note.]

[13] Cf. pp. 149; 313.

Sea must also have evoked in Judah; Procksch at any rate would trace x, 5–15, 28–32,[14] to this period.

3. *The structure of i–xxxv.* It is usually thought that i–xxxv is built up on the pattern known to us from the book of Ezekiel (p. 373) and from the book of Jeremiah in the form which is preserved in 𝔊 (pp. 348–9)—namely, threats against his own people, threats against other nations, promises for his own people. Such a view is possible. For i–xii contain in the main threats against Judah and Jerusalem, xiii–xxiii (xxvii) mainly threats against foreign nations, and in xxiv(xxviii)–xxxv xxxiii–xxxv contain promises. Chs. xxviii–xxxii, though sounding in the main a note of threat against his own people, do in fact contain many phrases which speak of promise. But the pattern is certainly by no means so clearly set out here as in the book of Ezekiel and in the Greek form of Jeremiah, and if i–xxxv is really so arranged, then whoever was responsible was not able to set about rearranging the given material with anything like so great freedom as was the case with Ezekiel and Jeremiah. He had rather to be content to force into this pattern material which was already in many respects arranged. Thus the assumption that i–xxxv was constructed according to that pattern does not give us much information by which we may recognise the evolution of the section itself.

Apart from this, the attempts at explaining the present form of i–xxxv move between two extremes. On the one hand, it is assumed that there was a combining of several medium-sized or small collections; on the other hand, that there was a basic collection covering i–xxxv into which complexes and single passages were inserted. Duhm, for example, declared himself in favour of the first assumption, regarding i–xii and xiii–xxiii, as two originally independent collections which he thought could hardly have originated before the second century B.C. More precisely he regarded i–xii as a collection of mainly genuine words against Judah and Jerusalem, and xiii–xxiii as another, of threats against foreign nations, of which a smaller proportion was genuine. He also viewed as originally independent booklets the late apocalypse xxiv–xxvii, and the placing together in xxviii–xxxiii of seven sayings beginning with *Woe* (הוֹי, xxviii, 1; xxix, 1, 15; xxx, 1; xxxi, 1; xxxiii, 1), or *See* (הֵן, xxxii, 1), these latter containing much genuine Isaianic material but compiled only at quite a late date. With regard to the also late eschatological composition xxxiv–xxxv, he leaves it open as to whether it ever existed independently, or whether it was from the outset designed as the conclusion of i–xxxiii. The analysis made by Procksch rests upon the same principle, the assumption of various independent units subsequently combined. He reckons with three originally independent collections, namely the basic material of i, ii–vi; ix, 7–x, 4;[15] xxviii–xxxi (xxxii), compiled by Isaiah himself; the sayings from the period of the Syro-Ephraimite War (vii, 1–ix, 6;[16] xi, 1 ff.) gathered by Isaiah's disciples; and the speeches on the nations

[14] Press, 'Topographical Notes, (a) "Inhabitants of Gebim" (Is. x, 31)' [Hebr., Engl. sum.] BJPES 12 (1945/6), pp. 163, XI.

[15] Kissane, 'The Qumrân Text of Isaiah ix, 7–9 (IQIsᴬ)' BEThL XII (1959), pp. 413–18. Lit. § 126.

[16] Lindblom, *A Study on the Immanuel Section in Isaiah Isa. vii, 1–ix, 6* (Scripta Min. Soc. Litt. Lundensis 1957/8: 4, 1958). Cf. below, p. 310, n. 32.

(x, 5–34; xiv, 24 ff.; xv–xxiii) also put together by his disciples. All three have later undergone various expansions with non-genuine material. At the opposite extreme stand, for example, Budde and Mowinckel. The former sums up his opinion at one point in the statement that 'an original book of Isaiah' has been drastically reshaped 'by rearrangements, excisions and insertions'.[17] The latter, however, has set out a penetrating analysis of i–xxxv (xxxix), and we may properly look rather more closely at this.

Mowinckel, in direct contrast to Duhm, disputes the view that i–xii, xiii–xxiii, xxviii–xxxii, ever existed as independent collections and assumes rather that these subdivisions have come into existence as the result of the working over, expansion and perhaps also dislocation of an older book, which admittedly in its turn had been compiled from three larger and two or three smaller collections. Of these, the first three contained substantially Isaianic material, whereas the other two contained only non-genuine material. These collections are A=vi, 1–viii, 23a, written by Isaiah himself before the crisis of the Syro-Ephraimite War of 733 B.C.; B=i, with the title i, 1, compiled by a disciple of Isaiah in the early period of Manasseh; C=ii, 1 (title=i, 1), 6–22; iii; iv, 1; v, 1–7; ix, 7–20; v, 25–30; x, 1–4; v, 8–24; x, 5–34; xi, 1–9(?); xiv, 24–27 (28–32); xvii; xviii; xx; xxii; xxviii, 1–4, 7–13, 14–22, 23–29; xxix, 1–8, 9–16 (17–24); xxx, 1–17 (18–26?), 27–33; xxxi; xxxii; xxxiii (?) which came into existence in the later Assyrian period or perhaps only in the Neo-Babylonian period, as a collection of the words of Isaiah which were still available and not contained in any other collection. B and C were put together first, and then A was inserted in B+C, this probably only after 587. Later xxxiv–xxxv were added to A+B+C. It was another modification, however, which produced a more marked change in the appearance of A+B+C. This was the incorporation in A+B+C or rather in that part of C which stood within xiii–xxiii+xxx, 6–7, of a collection, deriving from the fourth century, of foreign nation oracles all beginning with the title *Oracle* (מַשָּׂא). This title was then transferred also to the sections belonging to C within xiii–xxiii+xxx, 6–7. In all probability the eschatological poems of xxiv–xxvii were added later still. Thus xiii–xxiii (xxvii) owes to this secondary modification its present appearance of being a self-contained subsection, giving the impression of having once been an independent collection. This is also the case with i–xii. For xi–xii (or xi, 10–xii, 6, if xi, 1–9, really belongs to C), which form the conclusion to i–xii and might therefore suggest that i–xii was once an independent collection, were only inserted late in A+B+C.

These analyses are based in general on the same features—the double title in i, 1, and ii, 1; the interruption of the sayings in i–xii by the 'narratives' of vi–viii; divisions after xii and xxiii (xxvii) suggestive of the ends of books; the מַשָּׂא-titles in xiii–xxiii+xxx 6–7. They reveal various points of resemblance—the view that vi, 1–ix, 6, or vi–viii, form a separate entity; that xi–xii are entirely or substantially non-genuine, xxiv–xxvii and xxxiv–xxxv entirely so. That they lead to such very different results derives from the fact that these features are ambiguous. An analysis which explains everything and satisfies everyone is thus

[17] ZAW 41 (1923), p. 165.

hardly likely ever to be attained. But efforts to reach it nevertheless have their value. For without them the structure of the book would remain quite unintelligible, and much that is of value for the exegesis of the individual sayings and speeches would be lost. For while it is true that every literary unit which can be shown to be independent must be explained primarily from itself (p. 129), it is also quite clear that this book does not, like the Psalter or the book of Proverbs, present a loose collocation of sayings and speeches, poems and narratives whose precise sequence does not matter at all. The book has undergone a long and very complicated history in which, though on the one hand material which belongs together has been separated, on the other hand related material has also remained together. Thus it is clear that the sections ix, 7–20 and v, 25–30, which reveal the same refrain (ix, 11, 16, 20; v, 25) belong together, and the same is true of v, 8–24, and x, 1–4a,[18] which reveals itself as a collection of seven *woes* (v, 8; v, 11; v, 18; v, 20; v, 21; v, 22; x, 1). Since it is the section vi, 1–ix, 6 which separates these two pairs of related material, the separation must somehow be related with the insertion of vi–viii (vi, 1–ix, 6) in another collection— perhaps in the way in which Budde and Mowinckel suggest (p. 307). A separation of related sections by a passage of quite different content, resulting from the literary prehistory of the book is also to be seen in the complex x, 5–34,[19] which is now intended to be a great utterance of woe against Assyria, but in reality represents the placing together of a threat against Assyria (x, 5–15, 24–34) and one against Judah (vv. 16–23), and only becomes intelligible with the separation of these poems belonging to quite different periods.

On the other hand, it can hardly be an accident that vii, a third person narrative concerning Isaiah, and viii, an autobiographical narrative of Isaiah, stand together. They have been placed together because they refer to the same period, namely that of the Syro-Ephraimite War.[20] It is equally not a matter of chance that, apart from vi, 1–ix, 6, the whole content of ii, 1+ii, 6–x, 4+x, 16–23, appears to derive from the early period of Isaiah's activity, whereas the genuine Isaiah sayings which follow—x, 5–15, 24–34;[21] xiv, 24–7, 28–32; xvii, xviii, xx—contain threats against foreign nations, and thus Mowinckel's suggestion of the insertion of a מַשָּׂא-collection represents only the amplification of an already existing complex of foreign nation oracles.

4. *The material in i–xxxv which derives from Isaiah.* The illumination of the process by which the book of Isaiah came into its present form, possible only with the most careful analysis of the book as it now is, in itself an important and rewarding task, is also valuable for the delimitation and explanation of the individual literary units. We now turn to consider these, and here we shall first mention the genuine sections, and then subsequently the remainder, though passing over non-genuine passages which are only small in size. In this the arrangement of the book may be determinative for the enumeration of the passages. For, so far as the genuine sections are concerned, the arrangement is in

---

[18] x, 4b, is not original.

[19] Schelhaas, 'Het verband in Is. x, 5–xii, 6' GThT 50 (1950), pp. 105–20.

[20] Graham, 'Isaiah's part in the Syro-Ephraimitic Crisis' AJSL 50 (1933/4), pp. 201–16. Literature, p. 310, n. 32.

[21] Alonso-Schökel, 'Is. x, 28–32: Análisis estilístico' Bibl 40 (1959), pp. 230–6.

fact substantially chronological, and with the non-genuine sections the date of origin is in general determinable only so approximately that an enumeration of them in chronological order would be impossible.

(a) i, 2–26[22] forms a group of five sayings, probably originally independent, of which only the second, vv. 4–9, may be dated with fair certainty in the year of Sennacherib's attack upon Judah, namely 701 B.C., whereas the remainder, because of their general religious and ethical content, could in fact be placed in any period of Isaiah's activity. i, 2–3[23] is a prophetic judgement saying concerning Israel's ingratitude; i, 4–9, diatribes against the people, remaining impenitent in spite of fearful disasters, and likened to a body bruised all over; i, 10–17, a prophetic Torah-saying (pp. 73–5) against the worthlessness of the cultus; i, 18–20[24] a disputation saying in which Yahweh sets forth just retribution as the principle of his action; i, 21–6, a diatribe in the form of a funeral dirge against the corruption of Jerusalem.

(b) ii, 6–21, is a powerful poem in the form of a diatribe and threat, perhaps the most moving of all Isaiah's sayings. The diatribe is directed against human stubbornness which expresses itself in every conceivable form, and there is threatened the day of judgement of Yahweh which will ruthlessly bring low everything high and exalted, including all the cedars of Lebanon and all the oaks of Bashan (v. 13).[25] Unfortunately the poem is much corrupted with all manner of textual errors, additions and dislocations so that its aesthetic impression is somewhat lessened. But its contents are so powerful that it makes its full impact in spite of its damaged condition. It can hardly be doubted that we have here a poem of the youthful prophet, concerned with especial passion to declare the sole majesty of God, and it is certainly no accident that in this as in other sayings which derive from his early period there is much to remind us of Amos (p. 312). Evidently the youthful prophet modelled himself on this master.

(c) To Isaiah's early period there also belongs the threat in iii, 1–9, which proclaims for Jerusalem and Judah the loss of leadership and the coming of rule by the rabble, the prophetic judgement speech of iii, 12–15,[26] against the nation's leaders—possibly, however, to be treated as a unit with the previous section, the threatening poem against the arrogant daughters of Jerusalem in iii, 16–iv, 1,[27] the parable of the vineyard in v, 1–7,[28] which in content represents a diatribe and threat, and the woes, widely separated by redactional insertions and other accidental changes, to be arranged perhaps, following Budde, as: (i,

---

[22] Rignell, 'Isaiah Chapter i' StTh 11, 2 (1958), pp. 140–58; Robertson, 'Isaiah Chapter i' ZAW 52 (1934), pp. 231–6. Lit. § 126.
[23] Nielsen, 'Ass and Ox in the OT' *Studia Or. I. Pedersen* (1953), pp. 263–74; Ziegler, 'Ochs und Esel an der Krippe. Biblisch-patristische Erwägungen zu Is. i, 3 and Hab. iii, 2 LXX' MThZ 3 (1952), pp. 385–402.
[24] Sjöberg, ' "Om edra synder äro blodröda . . ." ' Till tolkningen av Jes i, 18' SEA 12 (1947), pp. 309–26. Lit. § 126.
[25] Virgulin, 'Il Libano nel libro di Isaia' Riv Bibl 7 (1959), pp. 343–53.
[26] Löw, 'Den historiska bakgrunden till Jes iii, 12a' SEA 9 (1944), pp. 49–53; Weil, 'Exégèse d'Isaïe iii, 1–15' RB 49 (1940), pp. 76–85. Lit. § 126.
[27] Ginsberg, 'Gleanings in First Isaiah' *Kaplan Jub. Vol.* (1953), pp. 245–59: pp. 245 f. on iii, 16–iv, 6. Lit. § 126.
[28] Bentzen, 'Zur Erläuterung von Jes v, 1–7' AfO 4 (1927), pp. 209–10; Junker, 'Die literarische Art von Is. v, 1–7' Bibl 40 (1959), pp. 259–66.

29–31), v, 8–10, 17, 11–13, 22, 14, 18–21;[29] x, 1; v, 23; x, 2–4a; v, 24. These are directed against attitudes which are anti-social, pleasure-seeking, denying God and sophistical, and which like the other sections just mentioned contain many reminiscences of Amos.

(d) There follows in vi the autobiographical account of the call vision[30] experienced in the year of Uzziah's death, i.e. 746 B.C. This originally stood at the beginning of the book, immediately after the title i, 1, or ii, 1 (p. 307).[31] That it is the product of a genuine experience can hardly be doubted. But it is also certain that Isaiah has given to his experience a deliberately artistic form, though whether immediately after or much later cannot be decided. The narrative is built up of three parts. The first (vv. 1–4) describes the majesty of Yahweh enthroned in his Temple-palace; the second (vv. 5–7) relates the purgation of the prophet to prepare him for his call, and the third (vv. 8–13) his commissioning by Yahweh. This commission is mysterious and gloomy. It is to bring about the hardening of the people so that it will come all the more certainly to destruction. Only when the disaster has fallen can reconstruction begin. For a *holy seed* (v. 13) a *remnant*, as it is called elsewhere (vii, 3; x, 20–2; xxviii, 5) is to survive.

(e) This vision narrative is now followed in vii by the account, dated in *the days of Ahaz*, concerning the notable encounter between the king and the prophet accompanied by his son, שְׁאָר יָשׁוּב (*a remnant which returns*). This culminates in the powerful saying (v. 9): *If you will not believe, you will not be established*, and in the Immanuel prophecy[32] (vv. 10–25) (cf. p. 316). It is

---

[29] Dahood, 'Ugaritic *ṭat* and Isaia v, 18' CBQ 22 (1960), pp. 73–5.

[30] Albright, 'The High Place in Ancient Palestine' SVT IV (1957), pp. 242–58; Engnell, *The Call of Isaiah: an Exegetical and Comparative Study* (1949); Hesse, *Das Verstockungsproblem im AT* (BZAW 74, 1955), pp. 21–91; Hvidberg, 'The Masseba and the Holy Seed' NTT 56 (1955), pp. 97–9; Iwry, '*Maṣṣēbāh and Bāmāh* in 1 Q Isaiah^A vi, 13' JBL 76 (1957), pp. 225–32; Jenni, 'Jesajas Berufung in der neueren Forschung' ThZ 15 (1959), pp. 321–39; Whitley, 'The Call and Mission of Isaiah' JNESt 18 (1959), pp. 38–48. Lit. § 126.

[31] Liebreich, 'The Position of Chapter Six in the Book of Isaiah' HUCA 25 (1954), pp. 37–40.

[32] Bird, 'Who is "the Boy" in Isaias vii, 16?' CBQ 6 (1944), pp. 435–43; Blank, 'Immanuel and Which Isaiah?' JNESt 13 (1954), pp. 83–6: cf. also *Prophetic Faith in Isaiah* (1958), ch. ii; Bratcher, 'A Study of Isaiah vii, 14' BT 9 (1958), pp. 97–126; Brunec, 'De sensu "signi" in Is. vii, 14' VD 33 (1955), pp. 257–66, 321–30; 34 (1956), pp. 16–29; Budde, 'Das Immanuelzeichen und die Ahaz-Begegnung Jesaja vii' JBL 52 (1933), pp. 22–54; von Bulmerincq, 'Die Immanuelweissagung (Jes vii) im Lichte der neueren Forschung' Acta et Comment. Univers. Dorpat B 37, 1 (1936), pp. 1–17; Cazelles (p. 284, n. 16); Coppens, 'La Prophétie de la 'Almah' EThL 28 (1952), pp. 648–78; 'La prophétie d'Emmanuël (Is. vii, 14–16)' *L'Attente du Messie* (1954), pp. 39–50; Duncker, ' "Ut sciat reprobare malum et eligere bonum" Is. vii 15B' BEThL XII (1959), pp. 408–12; Fahlgren, 'hā 'almā. En undersökning till Jes. vii' SEA 4 (1939), pp. 13–24; Fohrer, 'Zu Jes vii, 14, im Zusammenhang von Jes vii, 10–22' ZAW 68 (1956), pp. 54–6; Gordon, ' 'Almah in Isaiah vii, 14' JBR 21 (1953), p. 106; Gottwald, 'Immanuel as the Prophet's Son' VT 8 (1958), pp. 36–47; Gross, 'Die Verheißung des Emmanuel (Is. vii, 14)' Bibel u. Kirche 15 (1960), pp. 102–4; Hammershaimb, 'Immanuelstegnet' DTT 8 (1945), pp. 223–44; 'The Immanuel Sign' StTh 3 (1950/1), pp. 124–42; Hansen, 'Immanuel' DTT 3 (1940), pp. 31–47; Hooke, 'The Sign of Immanuel' *The Siege Perilous* (1956), pp. 222–34; Irwin, 'That troublesome *'almah* and Other Matters' Review and Expositor 50 (1953), pp. 337–60; Junker, 'Ursprung und Grundzüge des Messiasbildes bei Isajas' SVT IV (1957), pp. 181–96 = Trierer ThZ 66 (1957), pp. 193–207; Kissane, ' "But-

a biographical account referring to Isaiah in the third person, and although it is often done, we have hardly the right to assimilate vii to vi and viii by changing the third person into the first and hence to regard vii too as originally an auto-biographical account. But at the same time there can hardly be any doubt that the narrative is in all essentials completely trustworthy.[33]

(f) The autobiographical account in viii also belongs in the period of the Syro-Ephraimite War. This relates first (vv. 1–4) how Isaiah was commanded by Yahweh to write upon a large tablet[34] *For Speed-spoil-haste-booty*, and so to name his second son borne to him at this time by the prophetess.[35] He was thus to proclaim that soon *the spoil of Damascus and the booty of Samaria would be carried away*, and that the two cities and lands were soon to be conquered by Tiglathpileser, as the conclusion of v. 4, *before the king of Assyria*, no doubt a gloss, rightly indicates. In vv. 5–10 there follows first a threat (5–8) directed against the people looking furtively to Assyria for help and so to be delivered to Assyrian attack, as well as the proclamation in vv. 9–10[36] of the overthrow of all the apparently dangerous intrigues and warlike preparations by the hostile world of nations—a passage which no doubt derives from Isaiah, not from the time of the Syro-Ephraimite War, but rather from the second half or the last period of the prophet's activity. Then in vv. 11–23, after a divine revelation which makes clear to him the real seriousness of the situation, we have Isaiah's resolve, in sure trust in the future of Zion rooted in Yahweh, to withdraw himself for the time being from his activity among his people which is rushing to its own destruction. Here appears the saying (v. 16): *I will bind up the revelation, 'seal'*[37] *the teaching in my disciples*, and this saying, which may also be

ter and Honey shall he eat" (Is. vii, 15)' Or Bibl Lov I (1957), pp. 169–73; Koehler, 'Zum Verständnis von Jes vii, 14' ZAW 67 (1955), pp. 48–50; Kraeling, 'The Immanuel Prophecy' JBL 50 (1931), pp. 277–97; Moriarty, 'The Emmanuel Prophecies' CBQ 19 (1957), pp. 226–33; Mowinckel, 'Immanuelprofetien Jes. vii. Streiflys fra Ugarit. I.' NTT 42 (1941), pp. 129–57; Palmarini, 'Emmanuelis prophetia et bellum syro-ephraïmiticum (Isaias vii, 10–25)' VD 31 (1953), pp. 321–34; Porúbčan, 'The word '*ôt* in Isaia vii, 14' CBQ 22 (1960), pp. 144–59; Rignell, 'Das Immanuelszeichen. Einige Gesichtspunkte zu Jes. vii' StTh 11, 1 (1957), pp. 99–119; Sæbø, 'Formgeschichtliche Erwägungen zu Jes vii, 3–9' StTh 14, 1 (1960), pp. 53–69; Stamm, 'La prophétie d'Emmanuel' RThPh 32 (1944), pp. 97–123; 'Die Immanuel-Weissagung' VT 4 (1954), pp. 20–33; 'Neuere Arbeiten zum Immanuel-Problem' ZAW 68 (1956), pp. 46–53; Vawter, 'The Ugaritic Use of *ġlmt*' CBQ 14 (1952), pp. 318–22; Vischer, *Die Immanuel-Botschaft im Rahmen des königlichen Zionsfestes* (ThSt [B] 45, 1955); Würthwein, 'Jesaja vii, 1–9' *Heim-Festschr.* (1954), pp. 47–63. Lit. p. 306, n. 16; § 126.

[33] On vii, 6, cf. Albright, 'The Son of Tabeel' BASOR 140 (1955), pp. 34 f.; Donner, 'Neue Quellen zur Geschichte des Staates Moab in der zweiten Hälfte des 8. Jh.vChr' MIOF 5 (1957), pp. 155–84, see p. 171; Mazar, 'Ben Tabal and the House of Tobias' [Hebr., Engl. sum.] Eretz-Israel 4 (1956), pp. 249–51, XVI; 'The Tobiads' IEJ 7 (1957), pp. 137–45, 229–38; Vogt, ' "Filius Ṭāb'ēl" (Is. vii, 6)' Bibl 37 (1956), pp. 263 f.

[34] Instead of גָּדוֹל *large*, we should perhaps read גּוֹרָל *territory allocated by lot* and understand the word usually translated as *tablet*, גִּלְיוֹן rather as a *sheet* (of papyrus); so Galling in ZDPV 56 (1933), pp. 209–18. Cf. Katz, 'Septuagintal Studies in the Mid-Century' *Essays in Honour of C. H. Dodd* (1956), p. 199, n. 3.

[35] Jepsen, 'Die Nebiah in Jes viii, 3' ZAW 72 (1960), pp. 267 f.

[36] Hans Schmidt, 'Jesaia viii, 9 and 10' *Stromata. Festgabe des ak.-theol. Vereins Giessen* (1930), pp. 3–10. Lit. § 126.

[37] חָתוֹם instead of חָתוּם (imperative).

interpreted as Yahweh's command to Isaiah, is often understood to mean that the prophet undertook or received the command to compile a memorial, concerning the revelations received in the situation of the Syro-Ephraimite War, perhaps including his call vision, to justify his attitude in this period. Budde, for example, has repeatedly expressed himself in favour of this interpretation and indicated the memorial writing mentioned in viii, 16 as vi, 1–ix, 6. This view is certainly possible, but it can no more be proved than that xxx, 8 has a similar memorial in view, and that this preserved for us the basic material of xxviii–xxxii (p. 316). It is wiser in making the analysis to disregard such uncertain constructions. In this particular passage (viii, 16), we have probably a figurative expression which states that Isaiah henceforth intends to work, or is permitted to work only in the circle of his disciples.[38]

(g) The poem with refrain, ix, 7–20+v, 25–30, certainly belongs to the early period of Isaiah. It speaks first of four plagues which Yahweh has brought upon Israel in the past; but in spite of their mounting terribleness, the people could not be moved to repentance. It then threatens an evil visitation by the military power *from afar, from the end of the earth* (v, 26), in which the Assyrians are quite clearly intended. Isaiah's dependence upon Amos is here again particularly clear (cf. Amos iv, 6–11).

(h) Also from the early period of Isaiah comes the poem x, 16–23, which, as we have seen (p. 308) is to be detached from x, 5–34. This is now fragmentary as may be seen from the opening word *Therefore* which presupposes a reason for the punishment. The poem contains the threat of a terrible disaster about to fall upon Israel, from which only a small remnant is to be saved. With such contents, it ranks with vi–viii in which too there is repeated reference to a fearful visitation and the deliverance of a remnant.

(i) With the threat to Assyria in x, 5–15, 24–34, there begin the oracles against foreign nations. In vv. 5–14, we have a highly poetic description of the insolent conceit of the Assyrian king, a passage which more than almost any other reveals the great poetic power of Isaiah. This is followed in vv. 15, 24–7, by the consolatory assurance to Judah that Yahweh will bring to an end the raging of Assyria, and in vv. 28–34 by the dramatically presented description of this end. The enemy advancing against Jerusalem from the north is suddenly annihilated at the very moment at which he believes he can overpower the city. The poem certainly comes from the late period of Isaiah, when he had had opportunity to get to know more closely the selfish government of the Assyrians who had at first been regarded by him as the instrument of Yahweh's punishment. He now saw in them, and no longer primarily in Israel, the centre of hostile defiance to God. An exact dating—whether in the period before 711 or in that before 701—is impossible.

(k) In many respects xiv, 24–7, is reminiscent of the poem just dealt with. It now concludes the oracle against Babylon in xiii, 1–xiv, 23, which is certainly non-genuine, and it is a proclamation in the form of an oath sworn by Yahweh, of the destruction of Assyria in Palestine and of the freeing of Israel from the yoke of foreign domination. It may therefore be regarded as genuine, despite

[38] Cf. Eissfeldt, *Der Beutel der Lebendigen* (BAL 105, 6, 1959), pp. 26 f.

various objections which have been made to its being assigned to Isaiah, and may also be placed in Isaiah's late period.

(l) The section which is linked to it, xiv, 28–32,[39] is dated, like vi, 1; vii, 1; and xx, 1. If the traditional text is correct it is *after the year of the death of king Ahaʒ*, i.e. the year 726; but if Bewer is right with his emendation of אָחָז, *Ahaʒ*, to וָאֶחֱזֶה, *then I saw* (p. 149), it probably belongs after the death of Sargon in 705, and has as its content a warning to Philistia not to rejoice over the now broken rod since worse will follow for Philistia, whereas Yahweh's people may be consoled in trust in its God enthroned in Zion. If we keep the text as it is preserved, we may hardly understand the mention of the death of Ahaz to mean that it is he whose death gives an occasion for rejoicing to the land of the Philistines; we must regard the reference simply as a matter of dating. The year of Ahaz' death was also that of Tiglathpileser, and he is the rod at whose breaking Philistia believes she has a right to rejoice. In any case, at that time, whether 726 or 705, Philistia endeavoured by *ambassadors* (v. 32) to persuade Judah to break away from Assyria, but this was rejected by Isaiah.

(m) Most of the sayings gathered in xvii, 1–11,[40] are also genuine. But only the threat of xvii, 1–3, is directed against a foreign power, namely against Damascus, and this must therefore have been uttered before the fall of the Aramaean kingdom, i.e. before 732. Vv. 4–6 and 9–11 on the other hand, contain threats against Israel which is in league with Aram, and these probably derive from about the same period. Vv. 9–11 are of particular interest because here the practice of the cult of Adonis is clearly indicated as the reason for the threatened judgement.

(n) Of a quite different kind is the cry of woe against *the many nations* in xvii, 12–14, threatening them with immediate annihilation, though now they appear to be insuperable. It has been thought that we have here an expression of the eschatological expectation of the destruction of the whole heathen world of nations, often to be found in exilic and post-exilic times and set out in detail in Ezek. xxxviii–xxxix. But the many nations may refer to the multiplicity of peoples represented in the Assyrian army, and there is then no objection to deriving the passage, with its reminiscences of x, 5–15, 24–34; xiv, 24–7, from Isaiah himself.

(o) The saying which follows in xviii is certainly genuine. It begins as a cry of woe against Ethiopia,[41] and then proclaims in highly poetic pictorial language the destruction of Assyria. The saying appears to have been occasioned by the arrival of an Ethiopian embassy at Jerusalem, to win Judah over to an alliance directed against Assyria. The ambassadors are to carry home the report that Yahweh, in the perfection of his own power and without help from outside, will destroy the Assyrians. Since the rule of Egypt by the 25th, Ethiopian,

---

[39] Begrich, 'Jesaja xiv, 28–32. Ein Beitrag zur Chronologie der israelitisch-judäischen Königszeit' ZDMG 86 (1933), pp. 66–79; Bewer, 'The Date in Isa. xiv, 28' AJSL 54 (1937), p. 62; *The Book of Isaiah*, vol. I (1950), p. 44; Irwin, 'The Exposition of Isaiah xiv, 28–32' AJSL 44 (1928), pp. 73–87; Torrey, JBL 57 (1938), p. XII.

[40] Jirku, '*Niṭʿē Naʿamanim* (Jes. xvii, 10c)=*niṭʿē Naʿaman-ma*' VT 7 (1957), pp. 201 f.

[41] Ullendorff, *The Ethiopians. An Introduction to Country and People* (1960). Lit. § 126.

dynasty[42] began in about 715 B.C., the passage cannot have been composed earlier. How much further down we should come cannot be said with certainty. But we should probably think rather of the rebellion against Assyrian overlordship which led to the conquest of Ashdod in 711 than of that which took place in the years after the death of Sargon (705).

(p) A confirmation of this dating may be found in the next certainly genuine section (xx) which is dated immediately after the conquest of Ashdod by one of Sargon's generals (תַּרְתָּן)[43] and contains the threat that the Ethiopians and Egyptians will be led into captivity naked and barefoot, and so *the inhabitants of this island* (*coastland*, v. 6)—which means either the Judaeans or alternatively the Philistines—will find themselves deprived of their associate whom they thought to be so strong, and completely abandoned to the Assyrians. For it is here presupposed that before 711 an alliance had been formed between the Ethiopian dynasty and southern Syria. The threat against Ethiopia is linked to a symbolic action by Isaiah related in narrative form in the third person. At Yahweh's command he has actually gone about naked and barefoot for three years.

(q) xxii, 1–14,[44] though in detail often very difficult to understand, undoubtedly derives from Isaiah. It is a diatribe and threat with the title *Oracle concerning the valley of vision* (v. 1, cf. v. 5),[45] against Jerusalem, the *tumultuous city, full of shoutings* (v. 2), which puts before the eyes of the people, thrilled with premature exultation in view of a rebellion against Assyrian overlordship, the tragic outcome of this freedom movement, as seen in a vision. Again we cannot decide with certainty which attempted rebellion is meant, whether that of 713 or that after 705.

(r) The next section, beginning as a narrative (xxii, 15–25),[46] is a threat and diatribe, which according to the title, now accidentally incorporated in the text itself (v. 15b), is directed *Against Shebna, the steward*.[47] It proclaims to this foreign official his dismissal from his post and from the land, and his replacement by Eliakim, known to us from xxxvi, 22; xxxvii, 2 (where Shebna appears as *secretary*). We cannot be sure whether the passage was put among the foreign oracles because it was directed against a foreigner, or whether there is an even closer connection between it and the preceding section, in that Shebna might be regarded as responsible for the political attitude castigated in xxii, 1–14. In the latter case, it would be traceable to the same period. Since according to xxxvi,

---

[42] Yoyotte, 'Plaidoyer pour l'authenticité du Scarabée historique de Shabako' Bibl 37 (1956), pp. 457–76, Pls. I–III; 'Sur le scarabée historique de Shabako' Bibl 39 (1958), pp. 206–10. Lit. § 126.

[43] Oppenheim, 'The City of Assur in 714 B.C.' JNESt 19 (1960), pp. 133–47; Tadmor, 'Sargon's Campaigns against Ashdod' [Hebr., Engl. sum.] BIES 18 (1953/4), pp. 140–6, III–IV; 'The Campaigns of Sargon II of Assur' JCSt 12 (1958), pp. 22–40, 77–100; ' 'Azeqa in Judah in a Royal Assyrian Inscription' [Hebr., Engl. sum.] BIES 24 (1959/60), pp. 22–32, III–IV. Lit. § 126.   [44] Ginsberg (p. 309, n. 27), pp. 251 f.

[45] Weippert, 'Zum Text von Ps xix, 5, und Jes xxii, 5' ZAW 73 (1961), pp. 97–9. Lit. § 126.   [46] Ginsberg (p. 309, n. 27), pp. 252–7.

[47] Avigad, 'The Epitaph of a Royal Steward from Siloam Village' IEJ 3 (1953), pp. 137–52; 'The Second Tomb-Inscription of the Royal Steward' IEJ 5 (1955), pp. 163–6; Katzenstein, 'The House of Eliakim, a Family of Royal Stewards' [Hebr., Engl. sum.] Eretz-Israel 5 (1958), pp. 108–10, 89*–90*; 'The Royal Steward' IEJ 10 (1960), pp. 149–54.

22; xxxvii, 2, Eliakim is steward in the year 701, the threat against Shebna the steward must be earlier if we may rely upon this piece of information.

(s) xxviii, 1–22, contains almost entirely Isaianic material, but the delimiting of the individual units is often difficult and so more than one interpretation is possible. It is certain that vv. 1–4 represent a unity, a threat and diatribe directed against Samaria, *the proud crown of the drunkards of Ephraim* (v. 1)[48] deriving from the last years of the northern kingdom. But it is uncertain whether after the non-genuine addition in vv. 5–6 the next verses begin a new section with v. 7 or whether they are really loosely linked with vv. 1–4, so that we might assume (so Procksch) that Isaiah took up again later, after 705, his saying from twenty years earlier so as to link on to it (v. 7, *these also*) a threat against the drunken priests and prophets of Jerusalem. It is furthermore uncertain whether then vv. 7–22 are to be regarded as a unity or are to be divided up into smaller units, as vv. 7–8, 9–13,[49] 14–22. But probably we should treat the whole section vv. 7–22[50] as a diatribe and threat directed against the priests and prophets. Occasionally, particularly from v. 14 onwards, it appears that the threat is directed not so much against priests and prophets as against politicians. This may be explained on the grounds that the politicians, threatened by Isaiah with a fearful disaster because of their blasphemous insolence, depend upon these priests and prophets and their visions, and are therefore also involved in a threat which is primarily directed against the latter. We cannot fix the date of vv. 7–22 with certainty, since here ideas are put forward which Isaiah always maintained. The passage would not fit at all badly in the later period, after 713 or 705 in which moreover the sayings gathered in xxviii–xxxi almost all belong, and so we may conveniently place it there.

(t) We should probably say the same about the dating of the surely genuine section xxviii, 23–9[51] which, in the manner of a didactic discussion, demonstrates from the activities of the farmer how Yahweh's attitude always fits purposefully the changes of circumstance, and clearly is intended to reject reproaches made against the way in which the prophet's predictions are alterable or do not come to pass.

(u) With the section xxix, 1–8, beginning as a cry of woe against *Ariel, Ariel, city where David encamped,* we arrive at the passages which contain at one and the same time threat and promise, and these have been interpreted as containing a genuine threat provided with a promise by a later hand.[52] Yet, if for the moment we consider just this example, we should regard both as original and Isaianic. For the idea that Jerusalem and Judah should first come into terrible distress, then be rescued by Yahweh and be able to see their desire upon their enemies destroyed before the gates of Jerusalem, is to be found expressed also

[48] Rost, 'Zu Jesaja xxviii, 1 ff.' ZAW 53 (1935), p. 292.
[49] Hallo, 'Isaiah xxviii, 9–13, and the Ugaritic Abecedaries' JBL 77 (1958), pp. 324–38.
[50] Hooke, 'The Corner Stone of Scripture' *The Siege Perilous* (1956), pp. 235–49; L. Koehler, 'Zwei Fachwörter der Bausprache in Jes. xxviii, 16' ThZ 3 (1947), pp. 390–3; Lindblom, 'Der Eckstein in Jes. xxviii, 16' NTT 56 (1955), pp. 123–32. Lit. § 126.
[51] Liebreich, 'The Parable Taken from the Farmer's Labors in Isaiah xxviii, 23–29' [Hebr., Engl. sum.] Tarbiz 24 (1954/5), pp. 126–8, I–II; Thexton, 'A Note on Isaiah xxviii, 25 and 28' VT 2 (1952), pp. 81–3.
[52] Mowinckel, *Die Komposition*, pp. 282–4.

in other sayings whose genuineness is much less open to doubt (x, 5–15, 24–34; xiv, 24–7; xvii, 12–14). We need hardly reiterate that these are all passages from the later period of Isaiah, from about 713 onwards.

(v) There follow in xxix, 9–12, 13–14, 15, three probably independent diatribes and threats. The first (vv. 9–12), reminiscent of vi, 9–10, sets forth stubbornness as the consequence of sin; the second (vv. 13–14), with an echo of i, 10–17, castigates the externalised piety of the people; the third (v. 15) is a cry of woe upon the politicians who keep their plans secret from Yahweh. The first two sayings could belong to any period of Isaiah. The third has contacts with xxx, 1–5[53] and probably belongs to the same period as this cry of woe directed against the politicians who look furtively towards Egypt, contrary to Yahweh's will, namely in the years 705–701. The next section, entitled *Oracle concerning the Behemoth of the south* (xxx, 6–7), would also fit in these years, if it is genuine, as it seems reasonable to assume. For here, too, at any rate as the text now stands in v. 7, Egypt is depicted as an unreliable and impotent ally. This meaning is obtained whether we keep the original text of v. 7—רַהַב הֵם שָׁבֶת, *Rahab are they. A sitting still*, or emend it to רַהַב הַמָּשְׁבָּת, *Rahab made still*. Egypt is thus compared[54] with Rahab, the mythical primeval monster similar to Behemoth or identical with it, which rages but can do nothing.

(w) There follows in xxx, 8–14[55] a diatribe and threat which moreover proclaims to the people its downfall as punishment for its disobedience to the commands of Yahweh. This begins with the command: *Now go, write it down on a tablet before them, and inscribe it in a record.* It is not clear what is meant by the *it*. From the context it would be most natural to assume that there is a reference to the mysterious name for Egypt just employed, רַהַב הֵם שָׁבֶת, and this is probably the case, the more so since what is here related has an exact parallel in viii, 1–2 (p. 311). Others, as already noted (p. 312) are of the opinion that the command to write *it* down refers to the preparation of a 'memorial writing' similar to that which many assume to be found in vi, 1–ix, 6, a work in which Isaiah was concerned to give an account of his attitude in the years after the death of Sargon. Yet others relate the command to the saying which follows in vv. 9–14 (17).[56]

(x) The diatribe and threat of xxx, 15–17 are intended as the continuation of vv. 8–14, for they are introduced with the word *for*. They set out in opposition to the short-sighted politics of Isaiah's contemporaries who reckon only with human factors, the exhortation reminiscent of vii, 9 (pp. 310 f.): *Discretion and rest is your salvation, in quiet trust is your strength.*[57] But the link with *for* is possibly secondary, and in that case we have a saying which stands on its own, but in any case derives from the same period as the previous one.

(y) The prophecy of salvation concerning the future good fortune of Jeru-

[53] Kuschke, 'Zu Jes. xxx, 1–5' ZAW 64 (1952), pp. 194–5.

[54] Eissfeldt, 'Jeremias Drohorakel gegen Ägypten und gegen Babel' *Rudolph-Festschr.* (1961), pp. 31–7.

[55] Reymond, 'Un tesson pour "ramasser" de l'eau à la mare (Esaie xxx, 14)' VT 7 (1957), pp. 203–7.

[56] Cf. also Galling, *op. cit.* (p. 311, n. 34), p. 213, n. 3.

[57] Keller, 'Das quietistische Element in der Botschaft des Jesaja' ThZ 11 (1955), pp. 81–97.

salem in xxx, 18–26, is certainly non-genuine, even though Procksch would rescue at least some basic element of it for Isaiah. But the threat against Assyria in vv. 27–33[58] is likely to be genuine; it belongs in the series of sayings deriving from Isaiah's later period, proclaiming that Assyria is to be annihilated upon the mountains of Jerusalem.

(z) xxxi, which by its opening *Woe to those who go down to Egypt seeking help* betrays its origin in the period after the death of Sargon, is genuine with the exception of vv. 6–7, and also probably forms a unity. After the threat to these short-sighted politicians with their little faith, vv. 4–5 hold out the prospect of Yahweh's intervention to deliver Jerusalem which is hard pressed by the enemy, and vv. 8–9 underline yet again that Assyria will come to an end by divine action not by the power of men. It is true that other scholars think that the middle section (vv. 4–5) was originally a threat to Jerusalem, and has only become a promise by being worked over, so that not only vv. 6–7 but also vv. 8–9 would be secondary.

(aa) The last saying in the book which may be considered as genuine with at least a high degree of probability, is the summons to be found in xxxii, 9–14 (20), reminiscent of iii, 16–iv, 1, directed towards the *women at ease*, the *complacent daughters* (v. 9), calling them to lament over the disaster about to fall upon Jerusalem and its environs.

5. *The doubtful or non-genuine sections in i–xxxv.* The book of Isaiah i–xxxv, has undergone various amplifications of larger or smaller compass, and in fact these are practically all of the same kind. They are concerned to expand, with elements of promise, the words of Isaiah which are mainly couched in the form of threats. This is done either directly by pronouncing promises for Israel, or indirectly by pronouncing disaster for the other nations and so bringing a message of deliverance for the people itself. To the first group belong xi, 10–16;[59] xiv, 1–2; xxix, 16–24; xxx, 18–26; xxxii, 1–8; and also iv, 2–6,[60] if the passage as a whole is non-genuine and is not merely a saying of Isaiah which has been secondarily expanded. The return of the Diaspora to a homeland now teeming with marvellous fruitfulness, the overthrow of the neighbouring peoples, or peaceful and friendly relationships with them, the rule of a righteous king over righteous subjects cleansed from all sinful stain—such are the main themes of these prophecies of salvation. To these belong also the two songs contained in xii, an eschatological song of thanksgiving (vv. 1–3), and an eschatological hymn (vv. 4–6). Both anticipate the exultant thanksgiving which the people will experience after the fulfilment of the prophecies of salvation.

It is generally recognised that the passages just mentioned do not derive from Isaiah but from a later period, in part indeed from a very much later period. But in regard to three passages opinions differ on the question of genuineness. The first is the proclamation of ii, 2–5, that in the final age Zion, exalted over all the mountains, would be the goal of pilgrimage for all nations and the centre of a

---

[58] Février, 'Essai de reconstitution du sacrifice molek' JA 248 (1960), pp. 167–87: see pp. 181–4; Guillaume, 'Isaiah's Oracle against Assyria (Isaiah xxx, 27–33) in the Light of Archaeology' BSOASt 17, 3 (1955), pp. 413–15.

[59] Ginsberg (p. 309, n. 27), pp. 248–51: 'Inner-Isaian Stratification in xi, 11–16'.

[60] Búda, 'Ṣemaḥ Jahweh' Bibl 20 (1939), pp. 10–26.

universal kingdom of peace. The others are the two Messianic prophecies of ix, 1–6: *The people that wanders in darkness sees a great light . . . For to us a child is born, to us a son is given,* and of xi, 1–9: *There will go out a shoot from Jesse's stump and a branch will bear fruit from his roots.* Since Christianity has seen in these sayings, and particularly in the two Messianic prophecies, the direct proclamation of Jesus Christ, and has prized the prophet Isaiah above all for these prophecies, in addition to the Immanuel prophecy (vii, 14; p. 310), it is understandable that discussion on the question of their genuineness has always been particularly lively.

(a) For ii, 2–4,[61] the decision is relatively easy. This poem occurs not only in the book of Isaiah, but also with insignificant differences in the book of Micah iv, 1–4. Since it cannot be demonstrated that Micah took over the passage from Isaiah, nor that Isaiah took it over from Micah, the most probable assumption is that we have here a passage of anonymous origin which was at one time attributed to Isaiah and at another to Micah. The fact that both in the book of Isaiah and in the book of Micah the poem has been provided with a liturgical saying (ii, 5; iv, 5) calling for the appropriation of its contents by the community, can be quite simply explained as indicating that it was on both occasions taken from a collection of songs intended for the purpose of cultic recitation, or perhaps we should say, in view of the divergences between the liturgical conclusions, from two different collections of this kind. Furthermore, the universalism covering the whole world which this song expresses can hardly be regarded as appropriate either for Isaiah or for Micah, but does fit in the post-exilic period in which various parallels can be found for this poem. It must therefore be denied to Isaiah, a verdict which does not in the least affect its religious content, and indeed it is in every case proper, also in regard to the Messianic prophecies which are discussed next, to accustom oneself to the idea that such sayings carry their value in themselves, quite independently of the period or author from which they derive.

(b) The decision on ix, 1–6, and xi, 1–9,[62] is much more difficult. It is certain that Isaiah, right from the outset (pp. 310 f.), believed in a *remnant*, delivered from the coming disaster. It is further clear that in his later period he proclaimed the destruction of Assyria. That he should have thought of the new people deriving from the *remnant* as being ruled by a member of the Davidic line, is perfectly reconcilable with what has already been said and the Immanuel prophecy too can be so interpreted. So we must immediately recognise that the ideas contained in ix, 1–6[63]—the proclamation of the end of foreign rule and the

[61] Budde, 'Verfasser und Stelle von Mi. iv, 1–4 (Jes. ii, 2–4)' ZDMG 81 (1927), pp. 152–8; von Rad, 'Die Stadt auf dem Berge' EvTh 8 (1948/9), pp. 439–47 = *Ges. Stud. z. AT* (1958), pp. 214–24; Wildberger, 'Die Völkerwallfahrt zum Zion' VT 7 (1957), pp. 62–81. Lit. § 126.

[62] Crook, 'A Suggested Occasion for Isaiah ix, 2–7, and xi, 1–9' JBL 68 (1949), pp. 213–24; 'Did Amos and Micah know Isaiah ix, 2–7, and xi, 1–9?' JBL 73 (1954), pp. 144–51. Lit. § 126.

[63] Ginsberg (p. 309, n. 27), pp. 247 f.: 'The Symbolic Name in ix, 5b'; Jeshurun, 'A Note on Isaiah ix, 5' JBL 53 (1934), pp. 384 f.; McClellan, ' "El Gibbor" ' CBQ 6 (1944), pp. 276–88; Wildberger, 'Die Thronnamen des Messias, Jes ix, 5b' ThZ 16 (1960), pp. 314–32. Lit. § 126.

accession to the throne of a wise and valiant king of the Davidic line, rich in spoils (or eternal) and a bringer of victory—fit without any difficulty into the setting of the other proclamations of Isaiah. This is unaffected by whether we accept the view of Budde and others that the promise here spoken is directed towards the southern kingdom of Judah, or whether, with Alt, we see it as referring to the northern kingdom of Israel[64] or more precisely to those parts of it which were cut off from it in 732 B.C. On the other hand, it is undeniable that the book contains a wealth of non-genuine prophecies of salvation, and hence the fact that the content of ix, 1–6, can be reconciled with the rest of Isaiah's thought-world does not constitute a proof that the passage really does derive from him. Nor can any certain conclusion be drawn from the position which it occupies as to whether or not it is genuine. It is admittedly certain that with its opening: *The people that wanders in darkness sees a great light*, it has been placed here because of its contrast with the darkness which is described at the end of viii, but this motive could equally have influenced Isaiah himself or one of his disciples or someone much later, to insert the passage. Thus a completely certain verdict is not possible, but nevertheless the probability is that ix, 1–6, is genuine.

(c) The situation is quite different in regard to xi, 1–9. If we consider first the position of the passage, we may see that it is apparently placed here by way of contrast to the conclusion of the poem in x, 5–15, 24–34, directed against Assyria. For in x, 33–4, the destruction of Assyria, at the moment at which it appears to have reached its highest point (p. 312), is compared with the stripping of a tree and the rooting out of a wood, even Lebanon, and with this is contrasted the shoot coming out of the stump of Jesse in xi, 1. But it remains quite uncertain who placed it here, and so no argument is available on this basis for a decision concerning the genuineness of xi, 1–9. So far as the contents of the passage are concerned, the description given in vv. 2–5 of the marvellous gifts of the Messiah does not go beyond ix, 1–6, and is thus in that respect assignable to Isaiah. The highly poetic depiction of the state of peace prevailing on Mount Zion, however, in which not only are all conflicts between men at an end but also the native rapacity of the beasts has disappeared and they are all content with vegetable food, uses colours which we do not otherwise find in Isaiah's palette, but which we do find in many pictures of the happy final age deriving from a later date. So here, even though the possibility of tracing this passage to Isaiah is by no means excluded, the balance inclines in favour of regarding it as non-genuine.

(d) To the second group of later additions belongs first the poem in xiii, 2–22, with its title *Oracle concerning Babylon which Isaiah ben-Amoz saw*. In vivid and lively poetry it threatens Babylon with downfall, but appears in vv. 5–16, to have been elaborated secondarily to refer to the proclamation of the Day of Yahweh.[65] It is the Medes (v. 17) who are to bring about the judgement

[64] Alt, 'Jesaja viii, 23–ix, 6. Befreiungsnacht und Krönungstag' *Bertholet-Festchr.* (1950), pp. 29–49 = *Kl. Schr.* II (²1959), pp. 206–25; Cf. Eissfeldt (p. 316, n. 54), pp. 35–7.
[65] Budde, 'Jesaja xiii' BZAW 33 (1918), pp. 55–70; Černý, *The Day of Yahweh and some Relevant Problems* (1948). Lit. p. 392, n. 4; p. 398, n. 14; § 126.

on Babylon, and this in itself shows that the poem belongs in the period not long before 538 and thus cannot derive from Isaiah.

(e) xiv, 4b–21,[66] is introduced by a prosaic prophecy of salvation (xiv, 1–2), reminiscent in many of its expressions of Deutero-Isaiah. The main section is a prophetic dirge (pp. 97–8), indicated in the introduction (vv. 3–4a) as a מָשָׁל, *mocking song*, against the king of Babylon. It is a dirge on the despicable end of the world ruler who is suddenly flung down from his exalted place. It is one of the most sublime products of Hebrew poetry and owes its effectiveness not least to its use of mythological motifs. We cannot decide for certain which king is intended. But it is nevertheless probable that it is a Babylonian king as is indicated by the title and also by the prosaic postscript in vv. 22–3, though the possibility that it refers to an Assyrian king must be seriously considered.[67] Thus the passage is probably to be derived from about the same period as the preceding one. But if the poem is really directed against an Assyrian king, it would be about a century older and could come from Isaiah.

(f) There is a larger composition in xv–xvi,[68] with a title in xv, 1, *Oracle concerning Moab*, and a postscript in xvi, 13–14, to the effect that Yahweh will within three years bring to fulfilment this word spoken earlier concerning Moab. xv, 1–9 and xvi, 6–12, each contains a song of lament concerning the devastation of Moab which has either already taken place or is envisaged as having taken place; and xvi, 1–5, sets out the petition for protection directed to Zion for the fugitive Moabites, and the expression of the certainty that after the removal of the oppressor a righteous ruler will sit on the throne. Unfortunately the text of the last passage is exceptionally badly corrupted, so that a clear interpretation is impossible. Much depends upon whether the words *in the tent of David* in xvi, 5, are regarded as genuine or not. If they are genuine, then the point here would be the coming of the Messianic age, and a share in its blessings would be assured also for Moab. Such an idea can hardly be earlier than the post-exilic period. But the genuineness of the words is too uncertain for them to be made the basis of the interpretation or of the dating of the passage. Since otherwise the passage contains no clear references to any particular period, it is impossible to get further than surmise in regard to its date of origin. Moab often suffered disasters or was threatened with them, and there are thus many occasions in which the composition would fit: the period *c.* 770 B.C. when Jonah ben Amittai prophesied to Jeroboam II that he would also reconquer Moab (cf. II Kings xiv, 25);[69] the tension between Edom and Moab indicated by Amos ii, 1, which could have occasioned the young Isaiah (before 734–733) to prophesy a disaster for Moab

---

[66] Dupont-Sommer, 'Note exégétique sur Isaïe xiv, 16–21' RHR 134 (1948), pp. 72–80.

[67] P. Rost (p. 97, n. 9); Robert and Tricot, *Initiation Biblique* (³1954), p. 151 (Gelin): Sargon.

[68] Donner (p. 283, n. 9); Power, 'The Prophecy of Isaias against Moab (Is. xv, 1–xvi, 5)' Bibl 13 (1932), pp. 435–51. Literature, p. 295, n. 54; § 126.

[69] Ginsberg, 'A Preposition of Interest to Historical Geographers' BASOR 122 (1951), pp. 12–14; Maisler, 'Topographical Researches. 5, Lebo Hamath and the Northern Boundary of Canaan' [Hebr., Engl. sum.] BJPES 12 (1945/6), pp. 91–102, VIII; Noth, 'Studien zu den historisch-geographischen Documenten des Josuabuches' ZDPV 58 (1935), pp. 185–255, see pp. 242–8.

from Edom; the visitation of Moab by Sargon on the occasion of his campaign against north-west Arabia in 715 B.C.; the oppression of Moab by the Arabs pouring in from the desert into the cultivated land in the fifth or even as late as the second century B.C., and so forth. All these events have been regarded as appropriate occasions for this composition (Hitzig, Procksch, Power, Marti, Duhm).

This in itself shows that the assigning of xv and xvi to Isaiah rests upon a very weak foundation. For the passage contains no particular ideas which are characteristic of him and only of him. This is true in particular of the concluding saying xvi, 13–14. Procksch, for example, wishes to understand this as a recapitulation of the immediately preceding promise of xvi, 1–5, treating xvi, 6–12, as not genuine. He would apply it, in view of the *three years* in v. 14 reminiscent of xx, 3, to the time between the beginning of the attempted rebellion against Sargon (713) and its end, the conquest of Ashdod by the Assyrians in 711, and so would ascribe it to Isaiah. But it could equally well stem from a later writer who wished to indicate that the fulfilment of the lament, now understood as a threat, lay in the immediate future, as in xxi, 16–17 in relation to xxi, 13–15 (p. 322). We may possibly regard the same redactor as responsible for this in both cases, perhaps the same man who put together the מַשָּׂא-series (p. 307). The Isaianic origin of xv–xvi is therefore very improbable, and the fact that substantial parts of this section, namely xvi, 6–10, xv, 2–3, 4–7; xvi, 11–12, reappear in Jer. xlviii, 29–38a, and are here ascribed to Jeremiah, strengthens the doubt of their genuineness. Indeed Bardtke claims that the passages common to Isa. xv–xvi and Jer. xlviii are Jeremianic.[70] Oracles against foreign nations were often anonymous material, and when it was a matter of expanding sayings on the subject deriving from the known prophets, could therefore be ascribed at one time to one prophet and at another time to another.

(g) xix,[71] too, with its title *Oracle concerning Egypt*, is hardly genuine. This is quite generally agreed with regard to vv. 16–25, and it is also clear enough that we here have late, in part very late, appendices to vv. 1–15. But the threat too in vv. 1–15 of a fearful judgement about to fall upon Egypt contains in any case nothing that is characteristic of Isaiah, so that the possibility of tracing it to Isaiah and placing it—as Procksch does—in the period when Egypt set itself, as the prophet thought, against the will of Yahweh by its share in the Ashdodite alliance, cannot even be regarded as probable. The proclamation of v. 4, that Yahweh will *sell* Egypt *into the hand of a hard master* and that *a fierce king will reign over them* is not unambiguous, and could be applied to Psammeticus I (c. 660 B.C.), or, more probably, to Cambyses (529–522). So here too we must refrain from giving a more precise date.

(h) xxi, 1–10, bears the title *Oracle concerning the wilderness of the sea*. Here *sea* is probably to be understood as 'the road to the sea', namely to the Persian Gulf, and *the wilderness of the sea* as indicating the Syro-Arabian desert lying to the west of the lower course of the Euphrates, as shown by Dussaud in his

---

[70] ZAW 54 (1936), p. 248 (see below, p. 362, n. 40).
[71] Feuillet, 'Un sommet religieux de l'Ancien Testament. L'oracle d'Isaïe xix (vv. 16–25), sur la conversion de l'Égypte' RSR 39 (1951), pp. 65–87. Lit. § 126.

M

essay 'Sur le chemin de Suse et de Babylone',[72] which is also in other respects significant for the understanding of xxi, 1–17. The content of xxi, 1–10, is the proclamation of the imminent fall of Babylon. In this respect the passage belongs in a series of many similar ones, which are all to be placed in the period just before 538 (xiv, xlvii, Jer. l, 1–li, 58, among others). But this particular one, the description of a visionary experience which revealed to the seer the certainty of the imminent disaster, is nevertheless of particular significance. More than any other, it allows us to see into the inner life of the prophet who here speaks to us, and allows us to learn something about his second ego, here spoken of as *watchman* (v. 6). It is above all to Duhm that we owe the right understanding of this so significant vision description.[73]

The two passages which follow come from the same period, and perhaps from the same visionary, although Procksch wishes to trace them to Isaiah. The first of these (xxi, 11–12) has the title *Oracle concerning Dumah*,[74] and the second (vv. 13–15) *Oracle in the steppe* (in the text of v. 13: *in the steppe*). The former contains the answer, as yet indefinite, to a question from Seir directed to the *watchman*, i.e. the prophet, concerning the end of the night, no doubt meaning the end of Babylonian world rule. The latter contains a summons to the inhabitants of Tema to bring water and food to the caravans of the Dedanite fugitives *from the sword* (from Babylon threatened by the enemy or already taken?). To this summons there has been appended a postscript in vv. 16–17 similar to that in xvi, 13–14 (p. 321), in which the previous passage is understood, no doubt wrongly, as a threat against Kedar, and it is said that it will now quite soon be fulfilled.

(i) Difficulties of a special kind are raised by chapter xxiii[75] with its title *Oracle concerning Tyre*. For whereas in vv. 5 and 8, and then in vv. 15–18, it is certainly *Tyre* which appears as the city with which the threat and subsequently the promise are concerned, in vv. 2 and 12 the reference is rather to *Sidon*. Procksch would explain this by saying that a passage concerning Sidon coming from Isaiah (vv. 1–4, 12–14) was amplified by a passage concerning Tyre from a very much later period, and then, later still, a further Tyre passage (vv. 15–18) was added. Rudolph agrees with Procksch in the assumption that there is a genuine Isaianic basis in xxiii and in the judgement that vv. 15–18 are secondary. But he sees vv. 1–14 as a threat constructed in three strophes (1bβ–4, 6; 7–9, 5; 10–13) uttered by Isaiah in the years of the great Palestinian rebellion against Assyria, between 705 and 701 B.C., directed against Phoenicia generally and in particular against Tyre and Sidon. The attempt to prove the basic material of xxiii as Isaianic deserves careful attention, the more so since a warn-

[72] AIPh 4 (1936), pp. 143–50. Cf. Dhorme, 'Le désert de la mer' RB 31 (1922), pp. 403–6 = *Recueil Dhorme* (1951), pp. 301–4.
[73] Obermann, 'Yahweh's Victory over the Babylonian Pantheon, the Archetype of Is. xxi, 1–10' JBL 48 (1929), pp. 307–28; cf. Scott, 'Isaiah xxi, 1–10: The Inside of a Prophet's Mind' VT 2 (1952), pp. 278–82. Lit. § 126.
[74] Instead of דּוּמָה *Dumah* we should perhaps read אֱדֹם (*Edom* = *Seir* in v. 11). On *Dumah* cf. Dussaud, *La pénétration des Arabes en Syrie avant l'Islam* (1955), pp. 24–7. 121–3, 175; van den Branden, ''Umm'attarsamm, re di Dûmat' Bibbia e Oriente 2 (1960), pp. 41–7; Scheiber (Lit. § 126 on p. 309, n. 23). Lit. p. 523, n. 35; p. 663, n. 5.
[75] Rudolph, 'Jesaja xxiii, 1–14' *Baumgärtel-Festschr.* (1959), pp. 166–74.

ing directed to Phoenicia in those critical years would fit well with Isaiah's other preaching. The only doubtful point is that this attempt is bound up with very radical handling of the text, and particularly that of v. 13 where Rudolph alters the first half to *See Assyria has decreed it (Sidon) for destruction*. Under these circumstances we should probably give preference to the possibility entertained by other scholars, namely that the catastrophe foretold for Sidon refers to the destruction of the city by Artaxerxes III Ochus in 348 B.C. and the misfortune which befalls Tyre refers to the conquest of the island fortress by Alexander the Great in 332 B.C. This is made all the more probable in view of the fact that the events referred to in vv. 15–18, lying about seventy years apart, could well be on the one hand the destruction of Tyre in 332 and on the other hand the recovery of the city's prosperity which began with the grant- ing of autonomous rule by Ptolemy II in 274 B.C. It is in any case a point of importance that we can date the appendix xxiii, 15–18, with virtual certainty. For this allows us to draw some conclusions concerning the age of the מַשָּׂא- collection in xiii–xxiii+xxx, 6–7 (pp. 307–8), and makes it probable that the postscripts in xvi, 13–14, and xxi, 16–17, also refer to this same late period.

(k) xxiv–xxvii[76] stand out from their context as a separate entity. This is en- tirely made up of eschatological prophecies in general terms, in that it begins with the threat of the downfall of the world and ends with the promise of the return of the Jewish Diaspora. But even a rapid survey shows that we have here a composition made up of very varied elements. xxiv, 1–3, 13, 17–23; xxv, 6–8; xxvii, 1, 12–13, are quite clearly prophecy, recognisable as such by their tenses and they also agree with one another in content. Yahweh will destroy the world (xxiv, 1–3) so that only very little survives (xxiv, 13). Escape is impossible, for chaos returns. The powers on high and the kings of the earth are chained and held fast in prison for the future reckoning. But on Zion Yahweh will assume his kingship (xxiv, 17–23). *On this mountain* Yahweh will then prepare for all nations a great feast, will dry all tears and in par- ticular bring to an end the hatred in all the world against his own people (xxv, 6–8). The present rulers of the world he will destroy (xxvii, 1), and the Jewish Diaspora from east and west he will gather to Zion (xxvii, 12–13).

This eschatological prophecy is now interrupted by a series of passages of a different kind, namely songs. xxiv, 4–6, laments that the earth must vanish away because of its own guilt; the disaster, according to xxiv, 7–9, is expressed particularly in the cessation of the enjoyment of wine and of joyous song, and is particularly recognisable in the disconsolate condition of the destroyed

---

[76] Beek, 'Ein Erdbeben wird zum prophetischen Erleben (Jesaja xxiv–xxvii)' ArOr 17' 1 (1949), pp. 31–40; Hylmö, *De s. k. profetiska liturgiernas rytm, stil och komposition·* I Jes xxv, 1–xxvi, 21 (1929); Kessler, *Gott geht es um das Ganze. Jesaja lvi–lxvi und xxiv– xxvii* (Die Botschaft des AT 19, 1960); Lindblom, *Die Jesaja-Apokalypse Jes xxiv–xxvii* (1938), 'Die Jesaja-Apokalypse in der neuen Jesajahandschrift' Bull. Soc. Lettres Lund 1950/1, II (1951), pp. 87–97; Lohmann, 'Die selbständigen lyrischen Abschnitte in Jes xxiv–xxvii' ZAW 37 (1917/18), pp. 1–58; Eduard Meyer, *Ursprung und Anfänge des Christentums* II (1921), pp. 5–8, 174–9; Mulder, *Die Theologie van die Jesaja-Apokalipse* (1954); Rudolph, *Jesaja xxiv–xxvii* (1933); Smend, 'Anmerkungen zu Jes xxiv–xxvii' ZAW 4 (1884), pp. 161–224.

worthless city (xxiv, 10–12). In xxiv, 14–16, there are set in contrast the joyful songs of others—of the whole Jewish world, so it appears—and the expression of the poet's apprehensions that the distress is not yet at an end. xxv, 1–5,[77] is a hymn to Yahweh, who has destroyed *the fortified city*, and similarly the hymn in xxv, 9–12, extols Yahweh as the one who protects *this mountain*, Zion, whereas he abandons Moab to be trodden underfoot and throws to the ground the strongly fortified city. xxvi, 1–6, too, is a hymn: the well-protected city of the Jews, or rather their God who brings them salvation but has thrown down *the lofty city*, is extolled. xxvi, 7–19, contains a prayer, rather like a national lament, asking for the removal of the distress which is oppressing the people and which it cannot avert of itself, and for the restoration to life of dead compatriots.[78] xxvi, 20–1, the divine answer to this, has a prospect of speedy response. xxvii, 2–5,[79] is a song put into the mouth of Yahweh in which he describes the Jewish people as his faithfully guarded vineyard. xxvii, 7–11, finally, a reflective passage, affirms that in contrast to the *fortified city* destroyed by Yahweh, Jacob's sin will be expiated by the setting aside of idolatrous cult objects.

For a whole group of these passages it is clear enough that there is a quite natural and intelligible relationship between them and the surrounding prophecy—whether this connection is original or secondary. This is particularly true of the hymns xxv, 1–5; xxv, 9–12; xxvi, 1–6; xxvii, 2–5, which are eschatological hymns as the introductions to the last three of them reveal: *On that day (it will be said* or *sung).* They thus anticipate the rejoicing at the fulfilment of the prophecies of salvation which have just been uttered. The connection between xxiv, 4–12, 14–16, and its context is less clear. vv. 4–12, which in style are descriptive, do not really continue the threat of vv. 1–3, but they do perhaps indicate the circumstances and events which have provided the occasion for the more far-reaching threat of vv. 1–3. In vv. 14–16 the poet enjoins that there should be a halt called to the premature rejoicing at the destruction, which has already taken place, of the city hostile to the Jews, since the end of the hostile peoples as a whole is not thereby yet confirmed. Thus xxiv, 4–12, 14–16, may be understood as part of the larger context xxiv, 1–23. The prayer of xxvi, 7–19, together with the answer which follows it, shows, however, no literary link with its context, and the same is true of the reflective passage xxvii, 7–11.

Thus xxiv–xxvii is hardly to be regarded as a work built on a unified plan, nor can this be shown to be probable even for xxv–xxvi which Hylmö tried to explain as a prophetic liturgy after the pattern of xxxiii (p. 327). On the other hand, the passage does not merely present a meaningless confusion; the majority of the passages which give the impression of being insertions appear to have been deliberately placed where they now stand. Various ways of explaining this situation have been proposed. Duhm declared that xxiv–xxvii consist

---

[77] Coste, 'Le texte grec d'Isaïe xxv, 1–5' RB 61 (1954), pp. 36–66.

[78] de Savignac, 'La rosée solaire de l'ancienne Égypte' NC 6 (1954), pp. 345–53: on xxvi, 19b; Humbert, 'La rosée tombe en Israël. À propos d'Ésaïe xxvi, 19' ThZ 13 (1957), pp. 487–93.

[79] Robertson, 'Isaiah xxvii, 2–6' ZAW 47 (1929), pp. 197–206. Lit. § 126.

of the combination of an apocalypse comprising roughly the previously mentioned passages of prophecy and a (later) collection of songs which are in the
main concerned with the downfall of a city, and in this he has been followed
by many, including Sellin* and Procksch. Steuernagel*, on the other hand,
assumed the existence of a core of material, to be seen in xxiv, 1–23, which has
been expanded in various stages, eventually to reach the extent which we now
have. Rudolph has sought the solution to the problem in the assumption of
various prophecies and poetic works, ten in number, related in content and
coming for the most part from the same compiler, but nevertheless independent
and even mutually exclusive. Lindblom has followed a similar line, dividing the
basic material of Isa. xxiv–xxvii, into five eschatological songs (xxiv, 1–6,
16aβ–20; xxv, 6–10a; xxvi, 20–1; xxvii, 12–13) and four songs of thanksgiving or
exultation (xxiv, 7–16aα; xxv, 1–5; xxvi, 1–14; xxvii, 2–11) and separating off
xxiv, 21–3; xxv, 10b–12; xxvii, 1; as well as the song of lament in xxvii, 15–19,
as secondary additions.

Scholars are even more at variance with regard to the date of xxiv–xxvii, or
its individual parts. Recently Beek has again claimed the Isaianic origin of
the section, and explains it as having been occasioned by the earthquake mentioned in Amos i, 1, Zech. xiv, 5. But the majority of scholars are agreed that
it does not fit into the pre-exilic period, and must be dated later. The exact
date of its origin is very variously fixed. From the exile onwards down to the
end of the Old Testament development, i.e. the end of the second century B.C.,
every century has been proposed as the period of its composition—the exilic
period by Reuss*, the immediate post-exilic period by Dillmann, the fifth
century by Smend and Lindblom, the fourth by Kuenen†, the time of Alexander or of the first of the Diadochoi by Cheyne, Ed. Meyer, Rudolph and
Mulder, the time of John Hyrcanus (134–104) by Duhm and Marti. Procksch
derives the prophecies from the third century, but the songs from the second
half of the second century, just as Duhm too holds that the songs are later than
the apocalypse. The evidence adduced for fixing the date includes the existence
of a large Jewish Diaspora (xxvii, 12–13), the presence of a developed angelo-
logy (xxiv, 21), and the beginnings of a belief in resurrection (xxvi, 19)[80]—all
arguments which indicate a post-exilic date, but do not make possible a more
precise dating—and more particularly the repeated mention of a destroyed
hostile city and the mention of the exultation which sounds *from the west* in
xxiv, 14. Thus Rudolph and Lindblom both interpret the city as being Babylon,[81]
the former thinking of its conquest by Alexander in 331, the latter of its destruction by Xerxes in 485. Procksch, working especially from the mention of
the *west* in xxiv, 14, sees the conquered city as Carthage, destroyed by the
Romans in 146. Duhm thinks of the destruction of Samaria by John Hyrcanus
in 110, and Mulder interprets the hostile city as being the Moabite Dibon.

The differences in the analysis and in the dating of xxiv–xxvii give a good

[80] Ackroyd, 'Criteria for the Maccabean Dating of OT Literature' VT 3 (1953), pp.
113–32; see pp. 121–5.
[81] Pallis, 'The History of Babylon, 598–593 B.C.' *Studia Or. Pedersen* (1953), pp. 275–94.
Lit. § 126.

impression of the difficulty of arriving at assured conclusions, and remind us
that here as in other cases the main point is an exact knowledge of the actual
material, and that there must be no rigid reliance upon any one possible interpretation. With this warning, it may be said that the analysis is probably to be
sought in the direction indicated by Duhm and others, and that xxiv–xxvii are
to be understood essentially as the combination of an apocalypse foretelling the
end of the world and the breaking in of divine rule on Zion, and of a collection
of 'songs' on the downfall of a hostile city. So far as the date is concerned, it
may perhaps be right to reverse the order of apocalypse and songs suggested
by Duhm and accepted by others, and so to see the songs as older and as having
attracted elaboration by the apocalyptic prophecies. So far as the absolute
dating is concerned it must be said that in view of the three main arguments
mentioned above, the fourth century must probably be regarded as the earliest.
We cannot decide more precisely which period must then be chosen in the two
centuries which remain at our disposal, since the references to the city allow of
various applications and the passage which mentions the west is open to more
than one interpretation. But it may at least be said that the common identification of the city with a great metropolis, such as Babylon, is hardly correct. For
when we read in xxvi, 6, that *the feet of the poor* (i.e. the Jews) *trampled it*, it is
most natural to assume that the Jews at least had some share in its conquest.
We must therefore think of a city in the region of Judah. In xxv, 10, *Moab* is
mentioned as doomed to destruction, and in v. 12 there is a reference to the
destruction of a city which is most naturally to be sought in Moab. Usually, it
is true, xxv, 10–12, or at any rate xxv, 10b–11, is cut out as a secondary addition, and others alter the מוֹאָב, *Moab*, of the text in xxv, 10, into אוֹיֵב,
enemy.[82] But it is very much open to question whether there is any justification for the removal of this one quite concrete reference to the enemy in
xxiv–xxvii, all the more since the presupposition in xxiv, 7–12, that wine plays
a great role for the hostile city would, in view of xvi, 7–10, fit excellently with
Moab. Indeed xv–xvi may in any case be adduced in order to shed light on
xxiv–xxvii. For not only is there recognisable in the latter (xxv, 10) the same
fanatical hatred of the Jews against Moab which appears in the former (xvi, 6),
but in both passages the destruction of the hostile power is set over against a
reference to Zion as refuge (xvi, 1–5 and xxv, 6–8), a place of refuge which
according to xxiv–xxvii is also to be available to the inhabitants of the defeated
city and their land (xxv, 3?). In short, we should perhaps consider xxiv–xxvii,
or in the first place the cycle of songs which it contains, as having been occasioned by a disaster fallen upon Moab and its capital, and then assess the various
possibilities of dating mentioned for xv–xvi, though here in any case only the
later period comes in for consideration. If, as is possible,[83] the references in
xxvii, 1, to the mythical monsters *Leviathan*[84] and *Tannin* are to be understood
as meaning the Seleucid and Ptolemaic kingdoms, then this would make very
probable the dating of the section in the third century B.C.

[82] Torrey, HThR 31 (1938), p. 246.
[83] Eissfeldt (1932) (p. 36, n. 5), pp. 25–7.
[84] Lods, 'La victoire sur Léviatan' CRAI (1943), pp. 283–97.

If the reference to the destroyed city really does refer to a disaster which befell Moab, then xxiv–xxvii may also be set side by side with xxxiv–xxxv, in that in both passages a judgement falling upon a particular people in the environment of Judah, in the one case Moab, in the other Edom, is extended into a world disaster, and provides an occasion for the promises of the glory of the kingdom of Yahweh on Zion. We must not press the comparison further. From the literary point of view xxxiv–xxxv is much more rigidly constructed than xxiv–xxvii, and so far as the date of origin is concerned, xxiv–xxvii is clearly substantially later than xxxiv–xxxv.

(l) xxxiii,[85] as Gunkel has shown, represents a 'prophetic liturgy', that is to say a composition consisting of various literary types (v. 1 cry of woe, v. 2 national lament, vv. 3–6 prophetic utterance, vv. 7–9 national lament, vv. 10–13 oracle, v. 14a prophetic utterance, vv. 14b–16 Torah liturgy, vv. 17–24 prophetic utterance). As a whole it forms a prophecy of the future, namely a prediction of the destruction of the hostile world-power and the proclamation of the final age, in which Jerusalem, freed of sinners and sins, will enjoy a happy existence under the kingship of Yahweh. The enemy whose destruction is foretold is not named. On the other hand the pronouncements about the oppressor are sufficiently concrete to make it clear that the prophet-poet had in mind definite contemporary conditions, and was not just pronouncing an expectation of a theoretical apocalyptic nature, vague as to time and place. The comparison of Jerusalem with a tent which remains always in its place and is not (again) to be pulled down (v. 20) suggests the exile, and v. 21 perhaps the Greek Mediterranean fleet. The expectation of the downfall of the world ruler and of the then rising fortune of Jerusalem first received the developed form in which it here appears only in the exilic and post-exilic period. In view of these considerations it is impossible to assume Isaianic authorship for xxxiii; it must rather be assigned to the post-exilic period. But we cannot decide with certainty whether we should look to the early or the late post-exilic period, in other words, whether the oppressor is to be thought of as the Persians or the Greeks.

(m) xxxiv and xxxv[86] belong together. xxxiv, after an introduction summoning the nations to pay attention (v. 1), describes the imminent final judgement of the nations (vv. 2–4), and then in particular the visitation upon Edom which is destined to be completely devastated (vv. 5–17).[87] xxxv, on the other hand, describes how the desert will become a watered land, fruitful and cultivated, and how the blind will see again, the lame will walk, the deaf will hear; and how a clean and safe road will run through the desert, by which Yahweh's ransomed

[85] Gunkel, 'Jesaia xxxiii, eine prophetische Liturgie' ZAW 42 (1924), pp. 177–208.

[86] Caspari, 'Jesaja xxxiv und xxxv' ZAW 49 (1931), pp. 67–86; Mailland, La "petite apocalypse" d'Isaïe (Diss. theol. Lyon, 1956); Muilenburg, 'The Literary Character of Isaiah xxxiv' JBL 59 (1940), pp. 339–65; Olmstead, 'II Isaiah and Isaiah, chapter xxxv' AJSL 53 (1936/7), pp. 251–3; Pope, 'Isaiah xxxiv in Relation to Isaiah xxxv, xl–lxvi' JBL 71 (1952), pp. 235–43; Torrey, The Second Isaiah (1928), pp. 103–4, 279–304; Wernberg-Møller, 'Two Difficult Passages in the OT' ZAW 69 (1957), pp. 69–73, see pp. 71–3: (b) Isa. xxxv, 4.

[87] Leibel, 'Baqe'a, a Name of a Bird' [Hebr., Engl. sum.] Tarbiz 29 (1959/60), pp. 191, XII: on Isa. xxxiv, 15.

will return home to Zion. This contrast between the destruction of the nations, and particularly Edom, and the glorification of the Jews, is deliberate. It is elaborated with colours which are characteristic of Isaiah xl–lxvi. For this reason Torrey has ascribed xxxiv–xxxv to the compiler of xl–lxvi, and others have followed him in this. But the relationship is more likely to be explained on the grounds that the poet of xxxiv–xxxv has been influenced by xl–lxvi. There can be no thought of the section being genuine. It belongs at the earliest to the end of the sixth century B.C.

6. *The historical appendix xxxvi–xxxix.* We have already observed (p. 304) that xxxvi–xxxix[88] represents a repetition of II Kings xviii, 13–xx, 19, and the reason for this repetition is clear, namely the desire to collect together in one book everything concerned with Isaiah. We cannot ascertain with certainty when the chapters were appended to the book of Isaiah, consisting then only of i–xxxv. Jesus ben Sira, writing in about 190 B.C., as may be seen from Ecclus. xlviii, 22–5, knew not only xxxvi–xxxix but also xl–lxvi as parts of the book. The reference to Hezekiah's payment of tribute to Sennacherib (II Kings xviii, 14–16) was not taken over into the book of Isaiah with the remaining material. On the other hand, apart from unimportant differences, the Isaiah text has a large addition in xxxviii, 9–20, namely the 'Psalm of Hezekiah', an individual song of thanksgiving (pp. 121–4), which has been put into the mouth of Hezekiah on his recovery from his illness, though in reality it is hardly likely to have anything to do with Hezekiah.

There are three legends, of which the first appears in duplicate form, which are here brought together. The first (xxxvi, 1–xxxvii, 9a, 37–8, and xxxvii, 9b–36 respectively) relates how Isaiah prophesied the withdrawal of Sennacherib to the dispirited Hezekiah in the threatening situation of the year 701 B.C. The second (xxxviii) tells how he prophesied to the king as he lay in bed ill, first foretelling his approaching death and then, in response to the king's prayer, the prolonging of his life by fifteen years.[89] The third (xxxix) tells how he prophesied to the king the disaster of 587 when the latter showed himself agreeable to an embassy sent by the Babylonian king Merodach Baladan.[90] The embassy was evidently sent to win Hezekiah over to the support of a rebellion to be undertaken against Assyria. The second narrative must stand with the third before the first, since the events here related clearly belong either to the period before the beginning of the rebellion which ended with the disaster of 701 or to its first stages (cf. xxxviii, 5–6; xxxix, 2). It is difficult to say how far this is linked to historical fact. But the third and first give a picture of Isaiah's attitude which corresponds exactly with what we know of him from his own words. The prophecy of the disaster of 587, as it is pronounced in xxxix, 6–7,

[88] Honor, *Sennacherib's Invasion of Palestine* (1926); Irwin, 'The Attitude of Isaiah in the Crisis of 701' JR 16 (1936), pp. 406–18; Jepsen, *Nabi* (1934), pp. 86–8; Meinhold, *Die Jesajaerzählungen Jesaja xxxvi–xxxix* (1898); Orlinsky, 'The Kings-Isaiah Recensions of the Hezekiah Story' JQR 30 (1939/40), pp. 33–49; Wilhelm Rudolph, 'Sanherib in Palästina' PJB 25 (1930), pp. 59–80. Lit. p. 296, n. 58; p. 305, n. 10.

[11] Iwry (p. 46, n. 44); Yadin (p. 46, n. 44).

[90] Follet, 'Une nouvelle inscription de Merodach-Baladan II' Bibl 35 (1954), pp. 413–28; Gadd, 'Inscribed Barrel Cylinder of Marduk-apla-iddina II' Iraq 15 (1953), pp. 123–34, Pls. IX–X.

admittedly does not belong to history, but to legend. But that Isaiah should have required of the king that he should absolutely refuse to receive the offer of an alliance from Merodach Baladan is quite in line with his rejection of the appeal of Ahaz to Assyria and that of Hezekiah to Egypt later (vii, xviii, xx, xxx, 1–7, xxxi). It is equally to be expected from his repeated prophecies of Assyria's destruction (x, 5–15, 24–34 and others) that in the danger of the year 701 he should have declared Jerusalem to be impregnable. Thus although the legends of xxxvi–xxxvii hardly give a reliable picture of the external events of the year 701—that is to be found rather in the report in II Kings xviii, 14–16, which agrees with the Assyrian annals—they nevertheless give a reliable impression of Isaiah's attitude. So the three prophecies of salvation in xxxvii, 22–35, of which the first represents a mocking song put into the mouth of Yahweh, are likely to be genuine in spite of various objections which have been raised against them, and in any case they may be taken into account when it is a matter of forming a picture of the content of Isaiah's proclamation.

7. *The prophet Isaiah.* i–xxxix, as the analysis has sufficiently shown, have undergone a very varied literary history. The notes which go back to Isaiah and his disciples have been very greatly disturbed as to order, and intermingled with much non-genuine material. But the picture of Isaiah himself, as it shines out of the genuine content of i–xxxix, cannot be obscured by these alterations. On the contrary, we may gain a good impression, and no doubt a correct one, both of the poetic form of his proclamation and of its content. We have had occasion to speak often already of the form, but a final summarising statement must here be made about the content. In the final analysis, Isaiah remained always constant in his message. Enthusiastic claims for the recognition of the sole majesty of Yahweh and a passionate campaign against anything and everything which sets itself against that or attempts to obscure it—these are the characteristics of his proclamation from beginning to end. But in his judgement as to who and what at any given moment constituted the worst and most dangerous opponent of the divine majesty, Isaiah varied, and to a superficial view it might appear as if he finally proclaimed exactly the opposite of what was characteristic of his initial period. This is only apparently true. In reality Isaiah always remained constant in the religious kernel of his message.

Ethical and social disorders, blasphemous and self-sufficient ways of life, piety become shallow and barren in cultic observance, a hankering after foreign customs and cults in city and country—these are the things which at first Isaiah saw as rebellion against the sovereignty of the holy Yahweh. In a fearful annihilating judgement from which only a remnant will escape, Yahweh will bring all this to an end. If at first Isaiah pictures the judgement in various forms— natural catastrophes, civil war, etc.—with the Syro-Ephraimite war the Assyrians come into the forefront as the instrument of judgement, as indeed from that time on his view is primarily directed to the external political events. The experience he then had of failure in his exhortation to desist from all military and political measures, and to accept unconditional trust in Yahweh alone, admittedly at first led him to withdrawal. In 726 we again hear from him, if xiv, 28–32, is to be referred to this year (p. 313), but he only appeared again energetically when it was a matter of averting the attempts at inducing Hezekiah to attempted rebellion against Assyria from 720 onwards, or at any rate from about 713 on. As in 734/733, he again exhorts a sole trust in the help of Yahweh and the avoidance of all military and political measures, and holds the prospect of fearful disasters in front of the stubborn and self-opinionated politicians and the people who follow them. Though we cannot say precisely when the change began, Isaiah's proclamation later does, however, undergo a significant change, or perhaps only a completion, as he gets to know the Assyrians more nearly. The centre of godless insolence is now no longer or at least not primarily his own people, but Assyria. So he proclaims to the latter that it is to be destroyed upon Palestinian soil by Yahweh in the sight of the holy city which it threatens, and there is to blossom a new future on Zion for Judah, i.e. for its *remnant*, the people which it has despised and scorned, enslaved and plundered.

§ 44. ISAIAH XL-LV

Literature: (a) Commentaries: On xl–lxvi, HSAT: Budde (1922); IB: Muilenburg, Coffin (1956); KAT: Volz (1932); SAT: Haller (²1925); Torch B: North (²1964) (on xl–lv). See also commentaries noted in § 43.

(b) Other Works: Begrich, *Studien zu Deuterojesaja* (1938); Behr, *The Writings of Deutero-Isaiah and the Neo-Babylonian Royal Inscriptions* (1937); Bentzen (1948, 1955), (p. 105, n. 9); Blank, 'Studies in Deutero-Isaiah' HUCA 15 (1940), pp. 1–46; de Boer, *Second Isaiah's Message* (OTS 11, 1956); Budde, *Die sogenannten Ebed-Jahwe-Lieder* (1900); Caspari, *Lieder und Gottessprüche der Rückwanderer* (1934); Cazelles, 'Les Poèmes du Serviteur' RSR 43 (1955), pp. 5–55; Coppens, *Nieuw licht over de Ebed-Jahweh-Liederen* (1950); 'Les origines littéraires des Poèmes du Serviteur de Yahvé' Bibl 40 (1959), pp. 248–58; 'Le serviteur de Yahvé. Vers la Solution d'une énigme' BEThL XII (1959), pp. 434–54; Creager, 'The Grace of God in Second Isaiah' *Bibl. Stud. H. C. Alleman* (1960), pp. 123–36; Cross, 'The Council of Yahweh in Second Isaiah' JNESt 12 (1953), pp. 274–7; Driver, 'Linguistic and Textual Problems: Isaiah xl–lxvi' JThSt 36 (1935), pp. 396–406; Eissfeldt, *Der Gottesknecht bei Deuterojesaja (Jes. xl–lv) im Lichte der israelitischen Anschauung von Gemeinschaft und Individuum* (1933), cf. 'The Ebed-Jahwe in Isaiah xl–lv in the Light of the Israelite Conceptions of the Community and the Individual, the Ideal and the Real' ET 44 (1932/3), pp. 261–8; 'Neue Forschungen zum 'Ebed-Jahwe-Problem' ThLZ 68 (1943), cols. 273–80; Elliger, *Deuterojesaja in seinem Verhältnis zu Tritojesaja* (BWANT 63, 1933); Engnell, 'Till frågan om Ebed Jahve-sångerna och den lidande Messias hos "Deuterojesaja"' SEA 10 (1945), pp. 31–65; 'The 'Ebed Yahweh Songs and the Suffering Messiah in "Deutero-Isaiah"' BJRL 31 (1948), pp. 54–93; Fischel, 'Die deuterojesajanischen Gottesknechtslieder in der jüdischen Auslegung' HUCA 18 (1943/44), pp. 53–76; Fischer, *Isaias xl–lv und die Perikopen vom Gottesknecht* (1916); *Wer ist der Ebed . . .?* (1922); Freedman, 'The Slave of Yahweh' Western Watch 10 (1959), pp. 1–19; Glahn and L. Köhler, *Der Prophet der Heimkehr (Jesaja xl–lxvi)* (1934); Vol. I, Glahn, *Die Einheit von Kap. xl–lxvi des Buches Jesaja*; Vol. II, L. Köhler, *Das Buch Jesaja Kap. lvi–lxvi*; Gressmann, 'Die literarische Analyse Deuterojesajas' ZAW 34 (1914), pp. 254–97; *Der Messias* (FRLANT 43, 1929), pp. 285–323; Guillet, 'La polémique contre les idoles et le Serviteur de Yahvé' Bibl 40 (1959), pp. 428–34; Gunkel, *Ein Vorläufer Jesu* (1921); Haag, 'Ebed-Jahwe-Forschung 1948–1958' BZ 3 (1959), pp. 174–204; Haller, 'Die Kyros-Lieder Deuterojesajas' FRLANT 36 (1923), I, pp. 261–77; Hempel, 'Vom irrenden Glauben' ZSTh 7 (1929/30), pp. 631–60; Herntrich, 'Gottes Knecht und Gottes Reich nach Jesaja xl–lv' ZSTh 16 (1939), pp. 132–70; Hyatt, 'The sources of the Suffering Servant Idea' JNESt 3 (1944), pp. 79–86; Junker, 'Ecce Servus Meus (Is. xlii, 1). Der gegenwärtige Stand des Ebed-Jahwe-Problems' Trierer ThSt 1 (1941), pp. 23–43; Kaiser, *Der Königliche Knecht. Eine traditionsgeschichtlich-exegetische Studie über die Ebed-Jahwe-Lieder bei Deuterojesaja* (FRLANT 71, 1959); Kittel, *Jes. liii und der leidende Messias im AT* (1899); *Geschichte des Volkes Israel* III, 1 (1927), pp. 203–57; L. Köhler, *Deuterojesaja (Jesaja xl–lv) stilkritisch untersucht* (BZAW 37, 1923); de Leeuw, 'De koninklijke verklaring van de Ebed-Jahweh-Zangen' EThL 28 (1952), pp. 449–71; 'Le Serviteur de Jahvé, figure royale ou prophetique?' *L'attente du Messie* (1954), pp. 51–6; *De Ebed-Jahwe-profetieën* (1956); R. Levy, *Deutero-Isaiah* (1925); de Liagre Böhl, 'Prophetentum und stellvertretendes Leiden in Assyrien und Israel' *Op. Min.* (1953), pp. 63–80; Lindblom, *The Servant Songs in Deutero-Isaiah* (1951); Lindhagen, 'De tre sista decenniernas Ebed Jahve-forskning' STKv 8 (1932), pp. 350–75; *The Servant Motif in the Old Testament* (1950); 'Ebed Jahve-problemet i svensk exegetic' SEA 18/19 (1955), pp. 32–71; 'The Servant of the Lord' ET 67 (1955/6), pp. 279–88, 300–2; Lofthouse, 'Some Reflections on the "Servant Songs"' JThSt 48 (1947), pp. 169–76; May, 'The Righteous Servant in Second Isaiah's Songs' ZAW 66 (1954), pp. 236–44; Meek, 'Some Passages bearing on the Date of Second Isaiah' HUCA 23, 1 (1950/1), pp. 173–84; van der Merwe, *Pentateuchtradisies in die prediking van Deuterojesaja* (Diss. Theol. Groningen, 1955); Morgenstern, 'Jerusalem—485 B.C.' HUCA 27 (1956), pp. 101–79; 28 (1957), pp. 15–47; 31 (1960), pp. 1–29; 'The Message of Deutero-Isaiah in its Sequential Unfolding' HUCA 29 (1958), pp. 1–67; 30 (1959), pp. 1–102; Mowinckel, *Der Knecht Jahwäs* (1921); 'Die Komposition des deuterojesajanischen Buches' ZAW 49 (1931), pp. 87–112, 242–60; 'Neuere Forschungen zu Deuterojesaja, Tritojesaja und dem ¦Äbäd-Jahwä-Problem' AcOr [L] 16 (1938), pp. 1–40; 'Til uttrykket "Jahvaes tjener", Streiflys fra Ugarit. II' NTT 43 (1942), pp. 24–6; 'Selvstendige enkeltutsagn eller større talenheeter hos Deuterojesaja' DTT 9 (1946), pp. 142–68; *Han som kommer* (1951), pp. 129–73 (E.T. *He that cometh* (1956), pp. 187–257); Mudge, 'The Servant Lord and His Servant People' SJTh 12 (1959), pp. 113–28; North, *The Suffering Servant in Deutero-Isaiah* (1948, ²1956); 'The Suffering Servant: Current Scandinavian Discussions' SJTh 3 (1950), pp. 363–79; 'The Interpretation of Deutero-Isaiah' NTT 56 (1955), pp. 133–45; Pákozdy, *Deuterojesajanische Studien* I (1940), II (1942) [Hungarian with German summary]; Palache, 'The 'Ebed-Jahveh Enigma in Pseudo-Isaiah' *Sinai en Paran. Op. Min.* (1959), pp. 69–98; van der Ploeg, *Les Chants du Serviteur de Jahvé dans la seconde partie du Livre d'Isaïe* (1936); Porúbčan, *Il Patto Nuovo in Is. xl–lxvi* (1959); Press, 'Der Gottesknecht im AT' ZAW 67 (1955), pp. 67–99; Rignell, *A Study of Isaiah Ch. xl–lv* (1956); H. W. Robinson, *The Cross in the Old Testament* (1955), pp. 55–114 (originally published as *The Cross of the Servant* (1926)); Rowley, 'The Suffering Servant and the Davidic Messiah' OTS 8 (1950), pp. 100–36 = *The Servant of the Lord* (1952), pp. 59–88; 'The Servant of the Lord in the Light of Three Decades of Criticism' *The Servant of the Lord* (1952), pp. 1–57; 'The Servant Mission. The Servant Songs and Evangelism' Interpr. 8 (1954), pp. 259–72; Rudolph, 'Der exilische Messias' ZAW 43 (1925), pp. 90–114; Saggs, 'A Lexical Consideration for the Date of Deutero-Isaiah' JThSt 10 (1959), pp. 84–7; Saydon, 'The Literary Structure of Isaias xl–lv and the Servant Songs' Melita Theologica 6 (1953), pp. 1–15; 'The Use of Tenses in Deutero-Isaiah' Bibl 40 (1959), pp. 240–301; Scharbert, 'Stellvertretendes Sühneleiden in den Ebed-Jahwe-Liedern und in altorientalischen Ritualtexten' BZ 2 (1958), pp. 190–213; Sellin, *Serubbabel* (1898); *Der Knecht Gottes bei Deuterojesaja. Studien zur Entstehungsgeschichte der jüdischen Gemeinde nach dem babylonischen Exil I* (1901); *Das Rätsel des deuterojesajanischen Buches* (1908); *Mose* (1922); 'Tritojesaja, Deuterojesaja und das Gottesknechtsproblem' NKZ 41 (1930), pp. 73–93, 145–73; 'Die Lösung des deuterojesajanischen Gottesknechtsrätsels' ZAW 55 (1937), pp. 117–217; Simon, *A Theology of Salvation: A Commentary on Isaiah xl–lv* (1953); Sidney Smith, *Isaiah Chapters xl–lv: Literary Criticism and History* (1944); Snaith, 'The Servant of the Lord in Deutero-Isaiah' StOTPr (1950), pp. 187–200; Staerk, *Die Ebed-Jahwe-Lieder in Jes. xl ff.* (1913); Steinmann, *Le livre de la Consolation d'Israël et les prophètes du retour de l'exil* (1960); Stevenson, 'Successive Phases in the Career of the Babylonian Isaiah' BZAW 66 (1936), pp. 89–96; Stuhlmueller, 'The Theology of Creation in Second Isaias' CBQ 21 (1959), pp. 429–67; Winton Thomas, 'The Sixth Century B.C.: A Creative Epoch in the History of Israel' JSSt 6 (1961), pp. 33–46; Torrey (p. 327, n. 86); Tournay, 'Les Chants du Serviteur dans la Seconde Partie d'Isaïe' RB 59 (1952), pp. 355–84; Treu, 'Anklänge iranischer Motive bei Deuterojesaja' StTh Riga II (1940), pp. 79–95; von Waldow, *Anlass und Hintergrund der Verkündigung des Deuterojesaja* (Diss. theol. Bonn, 1953); Zimmerli, in Zimmerli and Jeremias, *The Servant of God* (1957), pp. 1–42 = ThWNT 5 αἶς θεοῦ (1952 (1954)), pp. 653–72; 'Le nouvel "exode" dans le message des deux grands prophètes de l'exil' *Hommage à W. Vischer* (1960), pp. 216–27.

Cf. also Literature §§ 42, 43, 45, 104, 115, 126.

We have already seen (p. 304) that the chapters Isa. xl–lxvi cannot derive from the Isaiah who was active in the second half of the eighth century, but must be two centuries later in date. But xl–lxvi themselves give rise to various other questions. In the first place we have to decide whether this complex is to be divided into two parts, xl–(lii)lv and (liii)lvi–lxvi, coming from different compilers or from different periods. Further there arises the question of the unity of each of these two parts. We shall first survey the problems and the solutions which have been proposed, and then set out conclusions with regard to them.

1. *The question of the unity of xl–lv: survey of criticism.* The unity of xl–lv has been contested in various ways. The most extreme positions are the admittedly very different views of Caspari and Morgenstern. The former, as the title of his book (published in 1934) shows, sees in Isa. xl–lv not the product of an individual but of a group, and so regards this complex as being the 'Songs and Sayings of the Returning Exiles' (*Lieder und Sprüche der Rückwanderer*). The latter, in his essays on 'Jerusalem—485 B.C.', leaves xl–xlviii or at any rate the basic material of these chapters to the exilic prophet Deutero-Isaiah, but relates xlix–lv, with the exception of the 'Ebed Yahweh songs to the fearful catastrophe which befell Judaism in the year 485 B.C. Otherwise the general practice has been to ascribe the main body of xl–lv to a single poet-prophet, and to trace only isolated sections of it to another hand, or else to assume that we are dealing with one compiler, but with different periods, and perhaps also with different localities, of his activity. So far as this last point is concerned, Kuenen*, Kosters, Kittel and others have derived xl–xlviii from the period before the promulgation of the edict of Cyrus in 538, but have assumed that xlix–lv were, in large measure at least, written after the promulgation of the edict and after the return of the Jews, and indeed as belonging to Palestine in contrast with xl–xlviii compiled in Babylonia. The basis for this division lay in the observation that there is mention of Cyrus[1] and of the imminent conquest of Babylon only in xl–xlviii and not in xlix–lv. In the latter section we find instead that the concerns of the restored Jerusalem religious community are set forth. Others, like Duhm, Marti, Mowinckel and Volz emphasise, however, that these differences between xl–xlviii and xlix–lv are quite insignificant when compared with the elements which they have in common, and so regard

[1] Jenni, 'Die Rolle des Kyros bei Deuterojesaja' ThZ 10 (1954), pp. 241–56; Simcox, 'The Rôle of Cyrus in Deutero-Isaiah' JAOS 57 (1937), pp. 158–71; Simon, 'König Cyrus und die Typologie' Judaica 11 (1955), pp. 83–9.

xl–lv as having been compiled or delivered by Deutero-Isaiah at about the same time and in the same place, whether in Babylonia (Volz), in Palestine (Mowinckel), in Egypt (Marti), or in the region of Lebanon (Duhm). Begrich also undertakes to divide the literary units in xl–lv between two different periods, though he traces them to the same poet-prophet; but these are not set before and after the edict of Cyrus in 538, but comprise the years 553/552 to 547/546 on the one hand, and a short period after 546 ending definitely before 538 on the other hand. To the seven-year period belong the sayings which proclaim in more general terms an eschatological battle of the nations, while the sayings which mention Cyrus belong to the short subsequent period. Thus for Begrich the sayings which are assigned to the first period do not by any means stand only in xl–xlviii, but about half of them are to be found in xlix–lv. Unambiguous references to historical events are thus clearly not present in Isa. xl–lv, apart from the appearance of Cyrus and the impending catastrophe for Babylon. The sections, however, which many scholars assign to someone other than the main compiler of xl–lv, i.e. Deutero-Isaiah, are primarily the ''Ebed-Yahweh songs', and in addition smaller or larger passages outside these songs which are regarded as additions made by the collector of Deutero-Isaiah's sayings, namely one of his disciples, perhaps identical with Trito-Isaiah.

First, the 'Ebed-Yahweh songs. After Duhm, in the first edition of his commentary on Isaiah in 1892, had decisively separated out the poems xlii, 1–4 (7);[2] xlix, 1–6;[3] l, 4–9;[4] lii, 13–liii, 12,[5] and denied them to Deutero-Isaiah, it came to be regarded generally as an irrefutable view that these songs constitute a particular entity, which, whether older or younger than Deutero-Isaiah or coming from himself, nevertheless have in view a different 'Ebed-figure than their context. The reasons put forward for this view have remained the same as those which Duhm put forward: 1. the loose connection of the songs with their context and the possibility of removing them without leaving any gap, and 2. the differences between the statements concerning the 'Ebed in the context on the one hand and in the songs on the other, in that in the former the 'Ebed undoubtedly refers to Israel, and is thus to be understood collectively (xli, 8, 9; xlii, 19; xliii, 10, etc.), whereas in the latter, and particularly in the last song (lii, 13–liii, 12) the term can only be understood as referring to

[2] Marcus, 'The "Plain Meaning" of Isaiah xlii, 1–4' HThR 30 (1937), pp. 249–59.
[3] Bewer, 'Two Notes on Isaiah xlix, 1–6' *Kohut Mem. Vol.* (1935), pp. 86–90; Giblin, 'A Note on the Composition of Isaias xlix, 1–6 (9a)' CBQ 21 (1959), pp. 207–12; Rignell, 'Den s.k. andra Ebed-Jahvesången' STKv 28 (1952), pp. 26–32.
[4] Palmarini, 'Notula Critica in tertium Carmen Servi Jahwe (Is. l, 4)' VD 31 (1953), pp. 209 f.; Rignell, 'Jesaja kap. l' STKv 29 (1953), pp. 108–119.
[5] Albright (p. 310, n. 30), pp. 244–6; Ginsberg, 'The Arm of YHWH in Isaiah li–lxiii and the Text of Isa liii, 10–11' JBL 57 (1958), pp. 152–6; Heller, 'Hiding of the Face. A Study of Is. liii, 3' CV 1 (1958), pp. 263–6; Iwry (p. 310, n. 30); Krinetzki, 'Der Einfluß von Jes lii, 13–liii, 12 par. auf Phil ii, 6–11' ThQ 139 (1959), pp. 157–93, 291–336; Leveen, 'יה' in Isaiah lii, 15' JJSt 7 (1956), pp. 93 f.; Nyberg, 'Smärtornas man. En studie till Jes. lii, 13–liii, 12' SEÅ 7 (1942), pp. 5–82; Rignell, 'Isa. lii, 13–liii, 12' VT 3 (1953), pp. 87–92; Th. H. Robinson, 'Note on the Text and Interpretation of Isaiah liii, 3, 11' ET 71 (1959/60), p. 383; Seeligmann, 'Δεῖξαι αὐτῷ φῶς (Jes liii, 11)' [Hebr., Engl. sum.] Tarbiz 27 (1957/8), pp. 127–41, III; Sonne, 'Isaiah, liii, 10–12' JBL 78 (1959), pp. 335–42; Young, *Isaiah liii* (1952). Lit. § 126.

an individual. It is true that in regard to the more exact definition of the individualistic interpretation there is anything but unanimity of opinion, and with this is connected the fact that the date of composition of the songs too is very differently assessed.

Duhm (1892) thought that the poems referred to a prophetic teacher of the law, and that they originated in about the middle of the fifth century B.C. Sellin at first (1898) referred them to Zerubbabel, then to Jehoiachin (1901), and later still (1922) to Moses. For quite a time it appeared as if the view maintained by Mowinckel in 1921 (already considered in Acts viii, 34), that the 'Ebed of the songs was the prophet himself, had at last solved the problem. For many scholars openly expressed their adherence to this view, including Balla,[6] Gunkel, Haller, Hans Schmidt,[7] and Begrich, whereas others modified it. Thus in 1930 Sellin expressed the view that only the first three songs had been composed by Deutero-Isaiah with reference to himself, whereas the fourth was compiled by his disciple Trito-Isaiah (pp. 341–6) 'as an elegy by the disciple upon his master'. This view leads to a consideration of the part which Trito-Isaiah is assumed by many scholars to have had in xl–lv. In 1933, Elliger sought to support this point of view with the thesis that the first three songs too, deriving from Deutero-Isaiah himself (xlii, 1–4; xlix 1–6; l, 4–9) had been considerably amplified by Trito-Isaiah with references to his master (xlii, 6b; xlix, 7aβ–8aα, 8bαβ; l, 10) and in 1937, Sellin made full use of Elliger's arguments to maintain the position which he had taken up in 1930. Volz too (1932) ascribes only the first three songs to Deutero-Isaiah as a 'piece of autobiography', whereas he regards the fourth as an eschatological song belonging to the fourth or third century. But Mowinckel himself gave up his 1921 thesis in 1931, and expressed the view, at first only tentatively, that the 'Ebed-songs had originated in the circle of Deutero-Isaiah's disciples, and attested a change which had come about here in views concerning the person of the bringer of salvation. For whereas Deutero-Isaiah had regarded Cyrus as this, his disciples had found this unsatisfactory and had so directed their hopes towards the more spiritual character of the 'Ebed, and had given expression to this in the 'Ebed-songs, imitated from the Cyrus songs of Deutero-Isaiah (xliv, 24–xlviii, 22*). With this view Mowinckel approaches the interpretation maintained by Kittel among others. Kittel had explained the 'Ebed of the songs as a martyr from the environment of Deutero-Isaiah, a leader from the latest period of the Babylonian exile, who is at the same time an eschatological figure. A similar view is maintained by Rudolph (1925) and Hempel (1939), of whom the latter (in this like Mowinckel), being inspired by Haller, regards the 'Ebed as the figure of a spiritual saviour, deliberately contrasted with the political deliverer Cyrus with whom at first Deutero-Isaiah's hopes had been associated. The interpretations of, for example, Johann Fischer (1916, 1922, 1939), van der Ploeg (1936), and Cazelles (1955) are of an eschatological kind; according to them, the 'Ebed of the songs is the Messiah.

[6] 'Das Problem des Leides in der Geschichte der israelitisch-jüdischen Religion' FRLANT 36 (1923), I, pp. 214–60, see pp. 245–7.
[7] *Gott und das Leid im AT* (1926), pp. 29–32.

The discussion of the 'Ebed-Yahweh problem has remained a very lively one, as may be seen by reference to the bibliography given on pp. 330–2, which in any case represents only a somewhat arbitrary choice among the literature belonging to this subject. In the last three or four decades, however, it has received a particular stress by reason of the fact that account began to be taken more strongly than previously of the influences of the myth of a yearly dying and rising youthful deity, or of the cult determined by the idea of sacral kingship. The former was done for example by Gressmann (1929), the latter by Engnell (1948). These two explanations are not by any means mutually exclusive nor do they preclude the possibility of the influence of other ideas on the 'Ebed-figure. Thus Engnell lays his emphasis upon the connection of the 'Ebed with the ideology of the sacral kingship expressed in the cultus, and in particular with the notion connected with it of the vicarious suffering and death of the king. Side by side with this he reckons with influences from the myths of Adonis-Tammuz and of Al'iyan Ba'al and Mot. Gressmann includes, together with such mythical elements, recollections of a historical character, namely king Josiah. Moreover, both Gressmann and Engnell see in the 'Ebed a figure expected in the future, and thus present a Messianic interpretation.

Recent treatment of the 'Ebed-problem is indeed everywhere marked by the tendency for the boundaries between the different methods of interpretation to be more and more obscured and for them to merge increasingly in one another. This is primarily true of the various forms of individualistic interpretation, where we may see for example how Coppens (1950) attempts to unite the interpretation of the 'Ebed as a king, rather like the older attempts made by Sellin, with the Messianic interpretation. He sees in the songs traits which point to Jehoiachin and Zedekiah, and yet wishes to understand the resulting picture of the 'Ebed as a prophecy of the Messiah. But it may also be said further that the division between the individual and collective interpretations has become very thin. For the upholders of the collective interpretation, the 'Ebed is Israel, empirical or ideal. Among these may be mentioned Graf Baudissin* (1901), Budde (1900), Kennett,[8] Peake,[9] Smend[10] and Wellhausen,[11] and in the next generation or the next but one Steuernagel* (1912), Hölscher,[12] König (1926), Eissfeldt (1933) and Lods* (1950)—although with some of these there are already many crossings of the boundary between the two types. The interpretations offered by Nyberg (1942), North (1948) and Rowley (1952, 1954), clearly represent combinations of the individual and collective views of the 'Ebed. For Nyberg the 'Ebed is a figure which rises above the boundaries of time and belongs at one and the same time to past, present and future, and at the same time also unites individual traits—recollections of the historical persons of the patriarchs, Moses, David and the prophets, and of the mythical figures of Tammuz and Al'iyan Ba'al—and collective features. So the 'Ebed is seen as an individual figure who also simultaneously represents the whole

[8] *The Servant of the Lord* (1911).
[9] *The Problem of Suffering in the OT* (1904); *The Servant of Yahweh* (1931).
[10] *Lehrbuch der at. Religionsgeschichte* (²1899), pp. 352–60.
[11] *Israelitische und jüdische Geschichte* (⁵1904), pp. 161–2.
[12] *Geschichte der israelitischen und jüdischen Religion* (1922), pp. 122–4.

people Israel. North and Rowley, however, both assume, though admittedly with various differences in detail, that the prophet's conception of the 'Ebed underwent a development, in that he at first regarded the people of Israel as fulfilling the 'Ebed's task, but later considered that it could only be achieved by the vicarious suffering and death of an individual—a development expressed particularly in the difference between the fourth and the three first songs. The views of Nyberg, North and Rowley reveal already that the main point in the discussion has moved from the question as to who the 'Ebed is to the problem of what he signifies, and this becomes particularly clear in Lindblom (1951). In his view, the 'Ebed incorporates an idea, namely that of Israel's ecumenical mission, and the question as to who the 'Ebed is appears to him therefore to be as meaningless as to ask who is indicated by the lost son whose story is told in Luke xv, 11–32. The direction in which present-day discussion of the 'Ebed problem is moving carries with it the realisation that we must resign ourselves to abandoning the illumination of all the factors which contributed to the shaping of the 'Ebed-figure, which was confidently held to be attainable by earlier generations of scholars. But, as may be seen for example in Kaiser's work of 1959, this movement has undoubtedly helped to pave the way for a deeper assessment of the truth incorporated in the figure of the 'Ebed, namely that vicarious suffering by the innocent is man's highest good, a truth which in Jesus' suffering and death is made a reality bringing salvation.

2. *The structure of xl–lv: survey of criticism.* So far as other aspects of the structure of xl–lv are concerned, we may see here Budde and Mowinckel as representatives of two diametrically opposite conceptions. The former considers xl–lv to be a writing by Deutero-Isaiah, from the start intended to be read, built up according to a deliberate plan and revealing a continual progression of thought. The latter, however, sees in xl–lv a quite loose sequence of individual sayings of Deutero-Isaiah, which have been put together by one of his pupils according to the very external principle of catch-words, and thus without any arrangement according to thought or content. Mowinckel assumes that there are 41 such sayings—not including the 'Ebed-poems. Gressmann, L. Köhler and Volz also regard these chapters as consisting of a collection of many individual songs and sayings. Gressmann reckons 49 such units, Köhler 70, Volz (without the 'Ebed-songs) 50. The question as to how we should explain the arrangement of these units as they have come down to us is not expressly dealt with by Gressmann and Köhler, but Volz explains it by saying that Deutero-Isaiah himself put his songs together and arranged them in an order following content and chronology. Robinson has maintained a similar view.[13] On the other hand, Elliger sees in Trito-Isaiah, the disciple of Deutero-Isaiah, the collector of his master's sayings. The latter had only to a small extent put together as larger units his speeches, sayings and songs, so that the disciple had almost everywhere a free hand in their arranging. In this he was guided by principles of content, and, conscious that he was working entirely in the spirit of his master, felt himself justified too in working over what had been left to him and in completing it, and did this not only in respect of the 'Ebed-

[13] 'Baruch's Roll' ZAW 42 (1924), pp. 209–21, see pp. 218–19.

songs (see p. 334). According to Elliger, xlii, 19–23; xlv, 9–10; xlvi, 12–13; xlvii; xlviii, 8b–10, 16b–19; xlix, 22–6; l, 1–3; li, 4–5, 10b, 12–14; lii, 3; liv–lv[14] come from the pen of Trito-Isaiah. Trito-Isaiah is thought to have completed his edition of the words of his master, elaborated with his own additions, even before Babylon was captured by Cyrus.

3. *The unity of xl–lv.* If we now attempt to express an opinion concerning the problems which have just been presented, it is in the first place certain that xl–lv belong in the second half of the sixth century, as Babylon's fortunes began to wane or perhaps had already collapsed, and Cyrus was making himself very widely known by his warlike deeds. The poet-prophet hopes that the fall of the Babylonian world-power, brought about by Cyrus, will mean the freeing of the exiled Jews, their return to Jerusalem, and the rebuilding of the Temple. For it is Yahweh who has called this Cyrus and is making use of him for the benefit of Israel. It is hardly possible to determine exactly the moment to which the poems belong which give expression to such a hope. We are concerned with poetry, and its pronouncements are often ambiguous and allusive, ranging broadly over time and space and casting over events a veil which conceals their reality. Hence the attempts made with great knowledge and penetration by Stevenson and Sidney Smith to define exactly in time the individual phases of the more or less ten-year period of activity of this exilic prophet must, in spite of important points of detail, be regarded on the whole as not really going beyond subjective assessments. We must place these compositions between the beginning of Cyrus' series of victories, in about 550, and the conquest of Babylon in 538, and we must be satisfied with this. The fact that expectations are expressed in xlvi, 1–2; xlvii, in reference to the fate of Babylon which were not in fact fulfilled, makes it reasonable to assume that these utterances at least must belong before the capture of the city. But more than this cannot be said, and we have hardly a right to make a division between xlviii and xlix, and to derive xlix–lv from substantially different conditions than xl–xlviii. Everywhere the same notes are to be heard, except in a few secondary additions like xliv, 12–20—the mockery of the idols, and lii, 3–6—a reflection on the fact that Israel was handed over to its oppressors without any price being paid. The main themes are the turning of Israel's fortune, the return to Jerusalem, the rebuilding of Temple and city, Israel's misfortunes undeserved by her and indeed borne by her as a substitute for other nations, the nations[15] turned towards Zion as the religious centre of the world, conversion to Yahweh as the only God, the creator[16] of heaven and earth and the lord of history. While first one and then another of these ideas comes to the fore, there is however nowhere any clear break to be observed, not even between xlviii and xlix. Actually, the end (lv, 8–13) clearly links back to the beginning (xl, 3–5), in that in both places there is mention of the wonderful return of Israel and of Yahweh to Zion. So too the fact that after

---

[14] Morgenstern, 'Two Prophecies from 520–516 B.C.' HUCA 22 (1949), pp. 365–431: on Isa. lv, 1–5, lx, 1–3, 5–7. Lit. § 126.

[15] Lambert, 'Le livre d'Isaïe parle-t-il des Chinois?' NRTh 75 (1933), pp. 965–72; on xlix, 12 סִינִים.

[16] Rendtorff, 'Die theologische Stellung des Schöpfungsglaubens bei Deuterojesaja' ZThK 51 (1954), pp. 3–13.

xlviii Cyrus, Babylon and the Chaldeans are not again mentioned and that here the poet's thoughts turn rather to the restored fortunes of Jerusalem, is to be explained as due to a certain pattern of thought, but may not be used as a proof that xlix–lv belong to another period or another environment from that of xl–xlviii.

So far as this last point is concerned, namely the home of the poet,[17] here, unlike the fixing of the date, no clear decision is possible. But the most likely assumption is that the prophet belongs among those who looked forward for themselves to the great transformation from the events set in motion by Cyrus' appearance, namely among the exiles. With them he has borne the sad lot of exile, and now feels with them, though very much more intensely, the joy of the anticipation that everything is to change.

4. *The structure of xl–lv.* If we turn now to the question of the structure of xl–lv, there is no doubt that Budde is right in thinking that there is present a certain arrangement according to content and ideas. It cannot be chance that the utterances concerning Cyrus are in general within the complex xliv, 24–xlviii, 22; that the proclamations of Babylon's fall, which in their turn are mostly to be found here, are set in a framework formed by these, and that the other sayings brought together in xliv, 24–xlviii, 22, which are not concerned directly with Cyrus and Babylon, may without any difficulty be understood as echoes of those which explicitly mention Cyrus and Babylon. The fact, too, already mentioned, that the conclusion (lv, 8–13) looks back to the beginning (xl, 3–5), points to a planned arrangement. At the same time, however, it is equally true that we cannot speak of a continuous development of thought or of a logical arrangement everywhere recognisable. Budde has therefore to admit that there are many repetitions and that the boundaries between the sections which he assumes are not sharp, but that the sections merge into one another. In these circumstances the understanding of the sayings depends in the first place upon just this question of the right defining of the smallest individual units. Whether it was Deutero-Isaiah himself or some other who collected his sayings and put them into their present form cannot be decided with certainty. But we shall probably be right in thinking of the latter possibility. At any rate the analogy of the other prophetic books or of most of them makes this likely.

We should probably count in xl–lv about 50 small units—songs and sayings —perhaps more or perhaps less. For a completely certain delimitation of the individual units is not possible since breaks in form and content are also possible within a unit. Thus xl, 1–2;[18] xl, 3–5; xl, 6–8 are certainly at least relatively independent sections. The second begins with the words *A voice calls*, and the third with *A voice says*. Furthermore, the second has in *For the mouth of Yahweh has spoken it*, a clear concluding formula. But in spite of this the three sayings are probably to be thought of as being, from the first, subsections of the larger unit, vv. 1–8. For 'introductions' and 'conclusions' such as *says the Holy One*, *says Yahweh*, appear even in the middle of literary units, and may not therefore

---

[17] Kapelrud, 'Levde Deuterojesaja i Judea?' NTT 61 (1960), pp. 23–7.
[18] Tom, 'Welke is de Zin van het "dubbel ontvangen" uit Jesaja xl, 2?' GThT 59 (1959), pp. 122–3.

automatically be treated as marks of the beginning or end of a unit (so for example xl, 25; xli, 14, 21; xliii, 12). Like xl, 1–8, xl, 12–31 is probably also to be regarded as a connected poem, and is not to be divided for example into four smaller units: xl, 12–16; xl, 17–20; xl, 21–6; xl, 27–31. We may thus be in doubt in many cases concerning the precise limits of the individual sections, but we must nevertheless recognise that it is a necessary pre-condition of the understanding of Deutero-Isaiah that we should separate them out as clearly as possible.

With the delimitation of the units, however, we have already undertaken an important preliminary for defining their form and content, and so for the recognition of the types to which they belong. The poet-prophet employs a very wide variety of types. In addition to the specifically prophetic types—narratives of vision or audition (xl, 3–5, 6[19]–8), sayings of consolation and promise (xl, 1–2; xliii, 1–2[20]) diatribes (xlviii, 1–11), and exhortations (li, 1–8)—he also is fond of using the messenger's saying (xl, 9–11), the disputation (xli),[21] the mocking song (xliv, 9–11; xlvii), and the historical reflection (xliii, 22–8).[22] But in his work a particularly large part is taken up with hymns and hymnlike elaborations of the other types, and this specifically in the two forms, the one in which God describes himself in the first person (xliv, 24–8), and the one in which he is described in the third person (xliv, 23). Thus sometimes Yahweh ascribes to himself qualities or deeds which are to be extolled, and sometimes the poet expresses them concerning him. It is not surprising that the hymn and its opposite the mocking song, together with historical reflection and disputation, play so large a part in his work. These forms are in fact conditioned by the content of his preaching. For he feels himself called to proclaim the unique majesty of his God, and no other type suits this so well as the hymn. This majesty signifies superiority over all other gods, and to present this, the disputation or the mocking song are the right forms. Historical reflection, however, serves to express properly the certainty that Yahweh controls the history of Israel and of mankind.[23] Now this already indicates that Deutero-Isaiah's message differs considerably from that of the older prophets. They themselves, or the God who speaks through them, are characterised above all by tremendous energy of purpose; but in Deutero-Isaiah this energy is subdued partly by contemplative reflection and partly by lyrical feeling, with the effect that the lyrical mood leaves its mark on the whole, and Deutero-Isaiah, more than the other prophets, has become a poet.

We should therefore picture the activity of this prophet as quite different

[19] Miegge, 'Autour d'une exégèse orthodoxe d'Ésaïe xl, 6' *Hommage à W. Vischer* (1960), pp. 165–70; Stoebe, 'Zu Jesaja xl, 6' WuD 2 (1950), pp. 122–8. Lit. § 126.

[20] von Waldow, '. . . *denn ich erlöse dich*'. *Eine Auslegung von Jesaja xliii* (BSt 29, 1960).

[21] Torrey, 'Isaiah xli' HThR 44 (1951), pp. 121–36.

[22] van der Merwe, 'Onverdiende Genade 'n Studie oor Jesaja xliii, 22–28' HTSt 10 (1954), pp. 167–91; 'Die Betekenis van "*m⁰liçē'kā*" (Woordvoerders) in Jes. xliii, 27' HTSt 11 (1955), pp. 169–77.

[23] Bentzen, 'On the Ideas of "the Old" and "the New" in Deutero-Isaiah' StTh 1 (1948/9), pp. 183–7; Elliger, 'Der Begriff "Geschichte" bei Deuterojesaja' *Otto Schmitz-Festschrift* (1953), pp. 26–53; North, 'The "Former Things" and the "New Things" in Deutero-Isaiah' StOTPr (1950), pp. 111–26.

from that of his predecessors. For them either we have actual narratives (e.g Isa. vii) or we may clearly deduce (e.g. Amos v, 2, p. 96) that there were particular motives for their appearance. But xl–lv contain no indications at all of concrete occasions of preaching, nor do they permit any reconstruction of such an occasion. It is therefore very much open to question whether we ought to picture Deutero-Isaiah as a 'speaker' at all. The whole nature of his compositions makes us think more readily of the unseen audience of the writer rather than of a congregation sitting before a speaker. But no certain decision can be made on this; nor would it really assist us in our understanding of the poems.

5. *The 'Ebed Yahweh songs.* We have recognised that xl–lv is a collection of about 50 poems which are certainly at least in part grouped according to the relatedness of their content. In some cases—in particular this is true of 'concluding hymns' like xliv, 23—they are deliberately placed in their present setting. But in general they are quite loosely arranged without any connections with one another. This recognition disposes of the first argument for the excision of the 'Ebed-Yahweh songs, namely that they have no links with what precedes and follows them. There remains only the second argument, that the figure of the 'Ebed which appears in them is not to be interpreted collectively as in the surrounding material, but can only be understood as referring to an individual. But this argument too is open to objection. For it is by no means the case that in the context of the songs, where it is true that the 'Ebed is undoubtedly to be understood as Israel, this 'Ebed is always clearly defined as a collective entity. There are in fact many features in his delineation which only appear to be suitable to an individual: He is addressed as 'thou' (xli, 8–16),[24] he has a right hand (xli, 13), he has eyes and yet cannot see, ears and yet cannot hear (xlii, 19), he was formed by Yahweh in the body of his mother (xliv, 1–2), and so forth. In this respect there is no qualitative distinction between the 'Ebed of the context and the 'Ebed of the songs, but only a quantitative one, in that in the latter more individual characteristics are ascribed to the 'Ebed than in the former. Under these circumstances a *prima facie* case exists for the assumption that the 'Ebed-songs come from Deutero-Isaiah and that the 'Ebed figure appearing in them is to be understood in the same way as the 'Ebed elsewhere in Deutero-Isaiah. If it may be further shown that the conception of the community as a clearly defined individual such as appears in the 'Ebed figure of the songs signifying Israel, entirely corresponds to the manner of Hebrew thinking and may be attested by many other examples, this most natural assumption becomes also the most probable. And in fact there is a whole wealth of evidence available for this, of which we need only mention here the personification of Jerusalem and Samaria in Ezek. xvi and xxiii which goes far beyond that of the 'Ebed of the songs.

The same may be said of the argument often regarded as conclusive against the interpretation of the 'Ebed of the songs as Israel, namely the fact that according to xlix, 5–6, the 'Ebed has a mission to Israel. For this is by no means

[24] Hamlin, 'The Meaning of "Mountains and Hills" in Isa. xli, 14–16' JNESt 13 (1952), pp. 185–90.

a unique case, but lies entirely within the orbit of Hebrew thought on this kind of matter. Hebrew thought traces the people of Israel—as indeed every corporate group—back to a single ancestor. This ancestor—in the case of the people of Israel it is Israel or Jacob, or Isaac and Abraham—does not belong merely to the past, but remains present in the community descended from him. He is in it, but at the same time beyond it. He is identical with it and yet at the same time stands over against it as a sort of ideal entity, the goal and fulfilment of its existence, and can thus make demands upon it, demanding something from it and having a mission to it. The 'Ebed is in fact just this, the ancestor and representative of the people, endowed with the prophetic title of honour, *servant*, and thus thought of as prophet. As such, as was indeed the task and fate of the prophets, for example Jeremiah, he has to work upon the people and to suffer for the people. The 'Ebed of the songs is thus, exactly as in their context, both identical with Israel and at the same time also not identical. He shares in the fate and guilt of empirical Israel and is yet at the same time, as a kind of ideal Israel, an example and saviour for the other nations and for empirical Israel itself. In the 'Ebed figure of the songs, and particularly in the last of them (lii, 13–liii, 12), there is thus simply set forth in a particularly vivid and powerful manner what Deutero-Isaiah also proclaims elsewhere, namely that Israel has had to bear its hard fate for the sake of a high purpose, namely that its God should be recognised and honoured in all the world as the only and true God, not only by all Israelites but by all the world. In other words, Israel has suffered as a substitute for the other nations. Furthermore, it is clear that what has been said above (pp. 335–6) about the timeless significance of the 'Ebed figure, recently especially stressed, remains entirely valid with the application of the figure to Israel which is here maintained.

§ 45. ISAIAH LVI–LXVI

Literature: Abramowski, 'Zum literarischen Problem des Tritojesaja' ThStKr 96/97 (1925), pp. 90–143; Cramer, *Der geschichtliche Hintergrund der Kap. lvi–lxvi im Buch Jes.* (1905); Dahood, 'Some Ambiguous Texts in Isaiah' CBQ 20 (1958), pp. 41–9; Elliger, *Die Einheit des Tritojesaja* (BWANT 45, 1928); 'Der Prophet Tritojesaja' ZAW 49 (1931), pp. 112–41; Gressmann, *Über die Jes lvi–lxvi vorausgesetzten zeitgeschichtlichen Verhältnisse* (1898); Kessler, 'Zur Auslegung von Jesaja lvi–lxvi' ThLZ 81 (1956), cols. 335–8; 'Studien zur religiösen Situation im ersten nachexilischen Jh. und zur Auslegung von Jesaja lvi–lxvi' WZ Halle 6 (1956/7), pp. 41–73; *Gott geht es um das Ganze. Jesaja lvi–lxvi und xxiv–xxvii* (Die Botschaft des AT 19, 1960); Kosters, 'Deutero- en Trito-Jezaja' ThT 30 (1896), pp. 577–623; Littmann, *Über die Abfassungszeit des Tritojesaja* (1899); McCullough, 'A Re-Examination of Isaiah lvi–lxvi' JBL 67 (1948), pp. 27–36; Odeberg, *Trito-Isaiah (Isaiah lvi–lxvi)* (1931); Whitley, *The Exilic Age* (1957); Zillessen, ' "Tritojesaja" und Deuterojesaja' ZAW 26 (1906), pp. 231–76; Zimmerli, 'Zur Sprache Tritojesajas' SThU 20 (1950), pp. 110–22.
    Cf. also Literature §§ 42–4, 58–61, 104, 115, 126

    1. *The separation of lvi–lxvi as an independent entity.* Just as Duhm's commentary on Isaiah of 1892 was epoch-making for the distinguishing of the

'Ebed-Yahweh songs, so it was too for the separation of lvi–lxvi as an independent entity. Duhm ascribed these chapters to a prophet whom he named 'Trito-Isaiah' who lived in Jerusalem in the period shortly before Nehemiah, roughly contemporary with Malachi. He thus regarded them as the work of a single author. The view that lvi–lxvi do not come from Deutero-Isaiah whose words are to be found only in xl–lv, has come to be fairly generally accepted. But not only the dating in about 450 B.C. but also the question of unity have been contested. In fact only Littmann[1] (1899) and Zillessen (1906) have followed Duhm on both points. Sellin (1901) and Elliger (1928 and 1933) adhere to the unity of the chapters, but do not trace them to the time of Malachi, but to that of Haggai and Zechariah (c. 520). Most scholars, however, have abandoned the idea of unity and apportion the poems which can be differentiated in lvi–lxvi to about a dozen different compilers from the period assumed by Duhm, or alternatively—and so particularly by Budde and Volz—to the period from the eighth or seventh centuries down to the third. We may here mention Cheyne (1895), Kosters (1896), Cramer (1905), Budde (1906 and 1922), Abramowski (1925) and Volz (1932) among others. But there is no lack also of scholars who go back behind Duhm and assign lvi–lxvi to the same compiler as xl–lv. König (1926), Torrey (1928) and Glahn (1934) have taken this view. Torrey also includes xxxiv–xxxv (p. 328) and ascribes xxxiv–xxxv, xl–lxvi to an author living about 400 B.C., and Glahn considers that lvi–lxvi were compiled between 536 and 530 B.C. by Deutero-Isaiah or by one of his disciples. That there are many common features both in ideas and in linguistic usage between xl–lv and lvi–lxvi, is however also admitted by those who do not believe in the identity of the compilers of the two sections.

The differences of opinion on this question itself suggests that the arguments adduced to decide it are ambiguous and can hence be applied in opposite ways. Nevertheless the basic points are in fact much firmer than might appear. In the first place, certain passages in lvi–lxvi do reveal great similarity to Deutero-Isaiah, in that they also depict salvation as being very close at hand and describe this event with the same colours which he had employed. This is particularly true of lvi, 1b, 8; lvii, 14–19; lviii, 8–9, 10b–12;[2] lx³–lxii; lxv, 15–25; lxvi, 6–16. But here, as Zimmerli has shown, there is at the same time in the expressions which are reminiscent of Deutero-Isaiah a peculiar note which makes it essential to derive lvi–lxvi from another hand than that of Deutero-Isaiah. Furthermore, there is lacking (pp. 343–5) in the whole section the uniform stamp which xl–lv reveals, and this makes it most improbable that lvi–lxvi come from the same compiler as xl–lv, unless we are to assume that the compiler wrote lvi–lxvi in quite different circumstances from those of xl–lv—a view which hardly differs in result from the assumption of another compiler. The undoubted relationship between lvi–lxvi and xl–lv is therefore probably

[1] Littmann, however, regards lxiii, 7–lxiv, 11, as older than the remaining sections, and assigns it to the period before 520.

[2] Morgenstern, 'Two Prophecies from the Fourth Century B.C. and the Evolution of Yom Kippur' HUCA 24 (1952/3), pp. 1–74: on Isa. lv, 6–13, lviii, 1–12.

[3] Brayley, ' "Yahwe is the Guardian of His Plantation". A Note on Is. lx, 21' Bibl 41 (1960), pp. 275–87. Lit. p. 343, n. 4.

to be explained on the grounds that lvi–lxvi, or at any rate large parts of it, were written in conscious dependence on xl–lv. Indeed Elliger and Sellin consider their Trito-Isaiah to be actually a disciple of Deutero-Isaiah. With a reversal of the relationship of age of the two works to one another, McCullough places lvi–lxvi earlier than xl–lv, considering that this complex was compiled between 587 and 562 by a member of the prophetic group which preserved the Isaianic tradition.

2. *The problem of the unity of lvi–lxvi*. The dependence of lvi–lxvi, or at any rate of substantial parts of it, upon Deutero-Isaiah may thus be regarded as a firmly established fact. But the question still has to be settled whether these chapters derive from one hand, i.e. actually from a Trito-Isaiah, or whether they are to be divided among several compilers. There are certain passages which are particularly reminiscent of Deutero-Isaiah, among them in the first place the three poems with their content of promise which have been combined in lx–lxii (lx,[4] lxi, lxii) and the poems equally containing promise in lvii, 14–19 and lxvi, 6–16. These reveal such strong relationship to one another that we must here at least think in terms of derivation from one poet. The position, however, is somewhat different with the poem lvi, 1–8, which exhorts righteous action and in particular the observance of the sabbath, and promises to all who respond to the exhortation, even to proselytes and eunuchs, a share in Yahweh's salvation and full rights to membership in his cult-community. In this concern for proselytes and eunuchs and in the injunction to sabbath observance new notes are sounded which apparently point to a fairly late period. Even though here too there are some points which are reminiscent of Deutero-Isaiah (vv. 1b, 8), these do not justify our assigning the section to the same poet who appears in lx–lxii; lvii, 14–19; lxvi, 6–16, as imitator of Deutero-Isaiah. For the latter's style has been very widely imitated at very different periods, as may be seen from the example of xxxiv–xxxv. Much the same might be said of the poems lviii, lxv, lxvi, 5 + 17–24.[5] The first exhorts right fasting and promises to the obedient a reward described in Deutero-Isaianic colours (lviii, 8–9, 10b–12); the second and third threaten punishment to the adherents of idolatrous cults, but hold out to those who honour Yahweh the prospect of glowing promises expressed in Deutero-Isaianic terms (lxv, 15–25; lxvi, 18–24). For it is not these promises which are the main theme, but rather the instruction concerning right fasting, and the polemic against idolaters. Again, we may consider the passages which stand in lvi, 9–lvii, 13. These are perhaps to be regarded as forming a larger unit. In lvi, 9–12, we have a diatribe and threat against the self-seeking leaders of the people, in lvii, 1–6, a lament at the disappearance of the righteous and a diatribe against the idolatrous *sons of the sorceress*, in lvii, 7–13, a diatribe and threat against apostate Jerusalem depicted as a harlot. This section contains nothing which in any way recalls the

---

[4] Causse, 'La Vision de la nouvelle Jerusalem (Esaïe lx) et la signification sociologique des assemblées de fête et des pèlerinages dans l'orient sémitique' *Mél. Syriens Dussaud* II (1939), pp. 739–50; Grelot, 'Un parallèle babylonien d'Isaïe lx et du Psaume lxxii' VT 7 (1957), pp. 319–21. Lit. p. 342, n. 3.

[5] Jefferson, 'Notes on the Authorship of Isaiah lxv and lxvi' JBL 68 (1949), pp. 225–30. Lit. § 126.

imitator of Deutero-Isaiah. The same is true of the passages put together in the form of a liturgy in lix. lix, 1–4 (8) is a diatribe against the people murmuring because of Yahweh's inactivity; 9–15a a confession of sin by the people, in the style of a national lament; and 15b–20, a promise of Yahweh's intervention to help. It is also true of the poem in lxiii, 1–6, related to this last section (lix, 15b–20) and reminiscent of vision narratives, on Yahweh's vengeance on Edom. Furthermore it is entirely true of the national lament in lxiii, 7–lxiv, 11, beginning with a hymnic narrative, which stands much nearer to the lament in ch. iii of the book of Lamentations, than to the poems in lvi–lxvi which stem from the imitator of Deutero-Isaiah. Finally there is the quite different rejection of Temple building set out in lxvi, 1–4. Nothing similar is to be found in Deutero-Isaiah or in the sections of lvi–lxvi, which recall him. At the most there may be relationship with the polemics against idolatrous cults in lvii, 1–6,[6] 7–13;[7] lxv; lxvi, 5+17–24.

In view of all this, there is really no good reason for regarding lvi–lxvi as a unity or for deriving it from one and the same author. The stylistic arguments which Elliger has adduced for the unity of lvi–lxvi do not in reality possess the validity which he accords them, especially in view of the fact that he himself has to admit that there are many differences of expression between the individual poems. If we consider the contents of the individual sections, these do not appear to belong to the same period any more than they are products of the same poet. Admittedly the opposite view cannot be proved either. Unlike Isaiah and Deutero-Isaiah, no traces may be found here of allusions to concrete events which would make possible the precise dating of one or another of the sections. The criterion often employed as to whether there is reference (e.g. lvi, 5) or not (e.g. lxiii, 7–lxiv, 11; cf. lxiv, 9, 10) to the new Temple and to the rebuilt walls of Jerusalem for the purpose of dating before or after 520–516 is only a very imperfect substitute and cannot really perform the service expected of it. We are here in the realm of poetry, and poetry often rises above actual conditions and does not permit a prosaic and historical interpretation of its utterances. Altogether uncertain is the dating according to the history of religion and thought, since in the first place we know very little concerning the periods which are here in question, and in the second place phenomena such as externalised worship (lviii) and the honouring of strange gods (lxv, 11) are certainly not limited to one period but may have appeared at different times. Here, as often elsewhere, we have to lay our main stress upon the understanding of the content, and be satisfied with recognising possibilities as far as the dating is concerned.

With this reservation we may, however, say that of the two periods which are open to choice—namely the middle of the fifth century, the time of Malachi, or the last third of the sixth century, the time of Haggai and Zechariah—the latter clearly deserves to be preferred. Both in regard to the tension between Jews who have returned from captivity and those who have remained in the

---

[6] Greenfield, 'The Prepositions *b* . . . *taḥat* . . . in Jes. lvii, 5' ZAW 73 (1961), pp. 226–8; Weise, 'Jesaja lvii, 5 f.' ZAW 72 (1960), pp. 25–32. .

[7] Wernberg–Møller, 'Two Notes' VT 8 (1958), pp. 305–8, see pp. 306 f.: on lvii, 9.

land, and in regard to the hopes for a great change in affairs, lvi–lxvi appear to presuppose the same conditions as do Haggai and Zechariah. But whether all the poems are to be assigned to this period is again open to question. The national lament, lxiii, 7–lxiv, 11,[8] may be decades older, and have been composed shortly after 587. The diatribe and threat against Jerusalem the harlot in lvii, 7–13, reminiscent of Ezek. xvi, xxiii, may be even older than 587, and this could also be assumed for the polemic against alien cults to be found in lvii, 1–6. But alien cults were also definitely practised by the population which remained in the land after 587, so that the passage may be later. The repudiation of a plan of temple building by the representatives of a syncretistic semi-Judaism in lxvi, 1–4, might be referred to an attempt at rebuilding the temple before 538 by those who remained in the land. On the other hand, many scholars would assign to a much later period the polemic against the worshippers of alien deities in lxv (vv. 3–6, 11), even to the fourth or third centuries, since the worship of the deities here named, Gad *Fortune* and Meni *Chance,* if it did not actually originate in the Hellenistic period, at any rate appears to have acquired greater significance then. Indeed behind the Tyche of the Hellenistic and Roman periods there may well be concealed a Semitic deity like Gad or Meni or rather their female counterpart.[9] The poems which come from the imitator of Deutero-Isaiah, lx–lxii; lvii, 14–19; lxvi, 6–16, however, would in any case fit particularly well in the period of Haggai and Zechariah, and would reveal to us the background to the Messianic hopes which they attest.

We cannot get beyond mere possibilities, and so too the question cannot be answered as to how the poems in lvi–lxvi, stemming perhaps from different periods, have come together here. We must simply be satisfied with the fact that collections of disparate prophetic material are also to be found elsewhere, e.g. in Isa. xiii–xxiii and Jer. xlvi–xlix (li) (pp. 306, 362–4). At best we can imagine that it is probable that the book lvi–lxvi in its turn presupposes smaller collections, as for example the booklet lx–lxii, for this separates the similar sections lix, 15b–20, and lxiii, 1–6, which probably originally stood together. The upholders of the unity of lvi–lxvi are not in a better position. They are unable to demonstrate the existence of an arrangement in lvi–lxvi according to chronology or content. They therefore ascribe the collection to a redactor, but cannot indicate the principles upon which he carried out his arranging.

3. *The combination of Isaiah xl–lv, lvi–lxvi, with Isaiah i–xxxix.* It is thus completely clear that Isa. lvi–lxvi does not derive from the Isaiah of the eighth century whose preaching is contained in i–xxxix of his book, any more than does xl–lv. To the question, however, as to how we are to explain the incorporation of these two complexes into the book of Isaiah, and hence their assigning to the prophet of the eighth century, we can give no definite answer. We can only leave open two possibilities, the one reckoning with pure chance, and the other taking into account the relationship of content between i–xxxv

---

[8] Buse, 'The Markan Account of the Baptism of Jesus and Isaiah lxiii' JThSt 7 (1956), pp. 74 f.; Morgenstern, 'Isaiah lxiii, 7–14' HUCA 23, 1 (1950/1), pp. 185–203. Cf. the interpretation offered by L. E. Browne, *Early Judaism* (1920), pp. 70–86, that the poem is 'the plaint of a Samaritan prophet'.

[9] Zimmern, 'Šīmat, Sīma, Tyche, Manāt' Islamica 2 (1927), pp. 574–84.

(xxxix) and xl–lxvi. It is possible that xl–lv and lvi–lxvi as anonymous prophecies came to be written in the same scroll after Isa. i–xxxix, and that gradually these anonymous sections were ascribed to the prophet last named, i.e. Isaiah. (We may perhaps have similar grounds for assuming the coming together of Zech. i–viii and ix–xiv (p. 440).) But the other possibility is more probable. This is the assumption that xl–lv was united with i–xxxv (xxxix), and lvi–lxvi with xl–lv or with i–lv just because similarities of style and content suggested that they were derived from the same author. That there are marked points of relationship between lvi–lxvi and xl–lv has already been repeatedly emphasised (p. 342). But the relationship between i–xxxix and xl–lv is not less great. The pathos of a heroic trust in God is shared by Deutero-Isaiah with Isaiah, and the similarity between the two extends into linguistic usage, as may at any rate be shown by the one example, namely that Isaiah's characteristic description of Yahweh as the *Holy One of Israel* (i, 4; v, 19, etc.) is also common in Deutero-Isaiah (xli, 14, 16, 20, etc.). Under these circumstances, the possibility of explaining the relationship between xl–lv and i–xxxv (xxxix) and between lvi–lxvi and xl–lv in terms of content may be put in the form of the assumption that xl–lxvi stem from prophetic circles which in a special sense regarded themselves as the disciples of Isaiah, and thought themselves called to guard and elaborate what he had left to them. In any case, the evidence of Ecclus. xlviii, 22–5, from about 190 B.C. shows that the book of Isaiah containing i–lxvi was then in existence, and this is confirmed by the Isaiah scrolls which have come to light near Qumrān, written in the second or first centuries B.C. (pp. 681–2). II Chron. xxxvi, 22–3, quotes as Jeremianic the now fulfilled Cyrus promise which clearly depends on Isa. xliv, 28. But it is not possible to decide whether this is to be explained as showing that at the time when this passage was composed, i.e. in the fourth century B.C. (p. 540), there were certain circles in which Isa. xl–lv (lxvi) was attributed not to Isaiah but to Jeremiah, or whether it is the result of an oversight, perhaps a simple scribal error (*Jeremiah* for *Isaiah*).

§ 46. JEREMIAH

Literature: (a) Commentaries (i) Series: ATD: Weiser (⁴1960); BOuT: Wambacq (1957); EB: Condamin (³1936); HAT: Rudolph (²1958); Harper's B: Bewer, I (1951), II (1952); HK: Giesebrecht (²1907); HS: Nötscher (1934); HSAT: Rothstein (1922); IB: Hyatt, Hopper (1956); Jerusalem-B: Gelin (²1959); KAT: Volz (²1928); KeH: Hitzig (²1866); KHC: Duhm (1901); SAT: Hans Schmidt (²1923); SB: Vittonato (1955); Soncino-B: Freedman (1949); SZ: Orelli (³1905); Torch-B: Cunliffe-Jones (1960); TU: van Ravesteijn, I (1925), II (1927); WC: Elliott-Binns (1919).

(ii) Single Commentaries: Æschimann (1959); Cornill (1905); Leslie (1954); Ricciotti (1923).

(b) Other Works: Augustin, 'Baruch und das Buch Jeremia' ZAW 67 (1955), pp. 50–6; Baumgärtel, 'Zu den Gottesnamen in den Büchern Jeremia und Ezechiel' *Rudolph-Festschr.* (1961), pp. 1–29; Baumgartner, *Die Klagegedichte des Jeremia* (BZAW 32, 1917); Beek, *Het twistgesprek van de mens met sijn God* (1946); Bentzen, *Helgen eller Højeforræder?*

Jeremias og hans Folk (1943); Birkeland, 'Grunddrag i profeten Jeremias förkunnelse'
SEA 1 (1936), pp. 31–46; *Jeremia, profet og dikter* (1950); de Boer, *Jeremia's Twijfel.
Rede . . . Leidse Universiteit* (1957); Broughton, 'The Call of Jeremiah. The Relation of
Deut. xviii, 9–22 to the Call and Life of Jeremiah' ABR 6 (1958), pp. 39–46; Driver,
'Linguistic and Textual Problems: Jeremiah' JQR 28 (1937–8), pp. 97–129; Erbt, *Jeremia
und seine Zeit* (1902); Gelin, *Jérémie* (1952); Gordon, *The Rebel Prophet, Studies in the
Personality of Jeremiah* (1931); 'A New Date for Jeremiah' ET 44 (1932/3), pp. 562–5;
Hertzberg, *Prophet und Gott* (BFChrTh 28, 3, 1923); Holladay, *The Root Šûbh in the OT*
(1958); 'Prototype and Copies. A New Approach to the Poetry-Prose Problem in the Book
of Jeremiah' JBL 79 (1960), pp. 351–67; Horst, 'Die Anfänge des Propheten Jeremia'
ZAW 41 (1923), pp. 94–153; Hyatt, 'The Deuteronomic Edition of Jeremiah' Vanderbilt
Studies in the Humanities I (1951), pp. 71–95; *Jeremiah, Prophet of Courage and Hope*
(1958); Kipper, *De restitutione populi Israeli apud prophetam Jeremiam* (1957); L. Koehler,
'Beobachtungen am hebräischen und griechischen Text von Jeremia Kap i–ix' ZAW 29
(1909), pp. 1–39; Krinetzki, 'Jeremiah als Beter' Bibel und Kirche 16 (1961), pp. 74–80;
Lofthouse, *Jeremiah and the New Covenant* (1925); May, 'Towards an Objective Approach
to the Book of Jeremiah: The Biographer' JBL 61 (1942), pp. 139–55; 'Jeremiah's Biographer' JBR 10 (1942), pp. 195–201; 'The Chronology of Jeremiah's Oracles' JNESt
4 (1945), pp. 217–27; Michaud, 'Le témoignage des ostraca de Tell Douweir concernant
le prophète Jérémie' RESBab (1941), pp. 42–60; Miller, *Das Verhältnis Jeremias' und
Hesekiels sprachlich und theologisch untersucht* (1955); Morgan, *Studies in the Prophecy of
Jeremiah* (1955); Mowinckel, *Zur Komposition des Buches Jeremia* (1914); 'Motiver og
stilformer i profeten Jeremias diktning' Edda 26 (1926), pp. 233–320; *Prophecy and Tradition* (1946), pp. 61–5; Neher, *Jérémie* (1960); Rendtorff, 'Zum Gebrauch der Formel
nᵉʾum jahwe im Jeremiabuch' ZAW 66 (1954), pp. 27–37; H. W. Robinson, *The Cross in the
Old Testament* (1955), pp. 115–92 (= *The Cross of Jeremiah* (1925)); T. H. Robinson,
'Baruch's Roll' ZAW 42 (1924), pp. 209–21; 'Jeremiah: the Story of the Book' *The Story
of the Bible* (1938), pp. 719–30; Rudolph, 'Zum Text des Jeremia' ZAW 48 (1930), pp.
272–86; 'Zum Jeremiabuch' ZAW 60 (1944), pp. 85–106; Schwally, 'Die Reden des Buches
Jeremia gegen die Heiden. xxv. xlvi–li' ZAW 8 (1888), pp. 177–217; Skinner, *Prophecy and
Religion. Studies in the Life of Jeremiah* (1922 (1936)); G. A. Smith, *Jeremiah* (⁴1929);
Stade, 'Bermerkungen zum Buche Jeremia' ZAW 12 (1892), pp. 276–308; Steinmann, *Le
Prophète Jérémie: sa vie, son œuvre et son temps* (1952); Stoebe, 'Seelsorge und Mitleiden bei
Jeremia' WuD 4 (1955), pp. 116–34; Tannert, 'Jeremia und Deuterojesaja' ThLZ 83
(1958), cols. 725 f.; Winton Thomas, *The 'Prophet' in the Lachish Ostraca* (1946); 'The
Age of Jeremiah in the Light of Recent Archaeological Discovery' PEQ 82 (1950), pp.
1–15; 'Again "The Prophet" in the Lachish Ostraca' BZAW 77 (1958), pp. 244–9;
Torrey, 'The Background of Jeremiah i–x' JBL 56 (1937), pp. 193–216; Vogt, 'Jeremias-
Literatur' Bibl 35 (1954), pp. 357–65; 'I tempi di Geremia secondo nuovi documenti'
Civ Catt 108 (1957), pp. 28–36; 'La caduta di Garusalemme secondo nuovi documenti'
ib. pp. 267–78; Volz, *Studien zum Text des Jeremia* (BWAT 25, 1920); *Der Prophet Jeremia*
(³1930); Welch, *Jeremiah: His Time and His Work* (1928 (1951)); Wildberger, *Jahwewort
und prophetische Rede bei Jeremia* (Diss. theol. Zürich, 1942).
    Cf. also Literature §§ 20, 42, 47, 69, 126.

1. *The Prophet and his time.* Jeremiah came from Anathoth, situated four
miles north-east of Jerusalem, modern 'Anātā (i, 1; xi, 21, 23; xxix, 27; xxxii,
7–9). His father, Hilkiah, was a priest (i, 1), and so Jeremiah may have been a
descendent of Abiathar who was exiled to Anathoth by Solomon (I Kings ii, 26).
Of his family life we hear otherwise only that at Yahweh's command he had to
abstain from marriage and from founding a family[1] (xvi, 1–2). But in addition
we learn much more from his book about his life and about his personality than

---

[1] Goldman, 'Was Jeremiah married?' ABR 2 (1952), pp. 42–7.

we know about any other prophet. So far as his life is concerned, the narratives which probably stem from his disciple Baruch are a source of the first order (pp. 354–5), but his personality appears in all his compositions and sayings, especially those which are in the style of the individual song of lamentation (pp. 358 f.), and becomes most clear to us in the monologues which have also been termed his confessions (p. 357).

Jeremiah's activity extended like Isaiah's over four decades. He received his call in the thirteenth year of Josiah, i.e. 626 B.C. (i, 2; xxv, 3), and the last words which we have from him come from the time shortly after the conquest of Jerusalem (587), when the remnant of the Jews who had fled to Egypt had also taken Jeremiah there with them (xliv). The external[2] and internal political events of these four decades, so momentous for Judah, are reflected more or less clearly in the book of Jeremiah: the Scythian alarm which shook the Near East at the time of the prophet's call (p. 424), the Reform of Josiah in 621,[3] the short-lived change-over of supremacy in Syria-Palestine from the Assyrians to the Egyptians and the sudden death of the pious Josiah in 609 which was connected with this,[4] the installation first of Jehoahaz by the 'people of the land' as his successor, and then that of Jehoiakim by Pharaoh Necho, the reign of this king filled with all manner of cruelty and evil (608–598), the change-over of supremacy over Syria-Palestine from the Egyptians to the Babylonians and their powerful king Nebuchadrezzar (604–562), the first deportation which affected Jehoiachin the successor of the rebellious Jehoiakim (597), and the rule of the last king Zedekiah (597–587). It is above all, however, the individual stages of the siege and conquest of Jerusalem[5] and the events which immediately followed, culminating in the assassination of Gedaliah[6] and the withdrawal of the Jewish survivors to Egypt, which influenced Jeremiah's preaching and personal fortune most greatly, and hence have found a marked echo in his book.

2. *Survey of the book: its form in* 𝔐 *and* 𝔊. The book as it appears in 𝔐 divides naturally into four sections: (a) i–xxv, mainly prophecies against his own people; (b) xxvi–xlv, mainly narratives concerning Jeremiah; (c) xlvi–li, prophecies against foreign nations; (d) lii, historical appendix = II Kings xxiv, 18–xxv, 21. However, this is not the only final form which the book received. Its shape as it appears in 𝔊 deviates from that in 𝔐. 𝔊 presents the oracles against foreign nations not at the end as 𝔐 does, but in the middle of the book, after xxv, 13 (14 is missing in 𝔊), and furthermore they are in a different order. 𝔐 presents them in the order: Egypt (xlvi, 2–28), Philistines (xlvii, 1–7), Moab (xlviii), Ammonites (xlix, 1–6), Edom (xlix, 7–22), Damascus

---

[2] Nielsen, 'Jeremja og Jojakim' DTT 13 (1950), pp. 129–45; Rost, 'Jeremias Stellungnahme zur Aussenpolitik der Könige Josia und Jojakim' CuW 5 (1929), pp. 69–78.

[3] Cross and Freedman, 'Josiah's Revolt against Assyria' JNESt 12 (1953), pp. 56–8. Lit. p. 284, n. 15; pp. 296 f., nn. 60–2; nn. 4–5 below.

[4] Rowton, 'Jeremiah and the Death of Josiah' JNESt 10 (1951), pp. 128–30.

[5] Ginsberg, 'Judah and the Transjordan States from 734–582 B.C.E.' *Marx Jubilee Vol.* (1950), I, pp. 347–68; Malamat, 'The Last Wars of the Kingdom of Judah' JNESt 9 (1950), pp. 218–27.

[6] de Vaux, 'Le sceau de Godolias, maître du Palais' RB 45 (1936), pp. 96–102; Diringer, 'Seals and Seal Impressions' *Lachish III* (1953), pp. 347 f.

(xlix, 23–7), Kedar (xlix, 28–33), Elam (xlix, 34–9), Babylon (l–li). 𝕲, however, has them in this order: Elam, Egypt, Babylon, Philistines, Edom, Ammonites, Kedar, Damascus, Moab. In other ways too 𝕲 differs from 𝔐; the text
form of 𝕲 is about one-eighth shorter than that of 𝔐. In the main it is single
verses and parts of verses which 𝕲 does not include, but there are also larger
sections missing such as xxxiii, 14–26; xxxix, 4–13; li, 44b–49a; lii, 27b–30. In
part this deficiency may certainly be explained as accidental omission, produced for example by homoioteleuton, as in xxxix, 4–13; li, 44b–49a, and in a
whole series of shorter omissions. Others go back to the efforts of the translator to lighten the text of his original which seemed to him overloaded and
unwieldy, as perhaps xvii, 1–5aα. But there is also no lack of cases where the
explanation is that the relevant passage was not yet in the original, e.g. xxxiii,
14–26. Among the fragments of the Hebrew text of Jeremiah which have come
to light near Qumrān there are texts (alongside some which represent 𝔐 or
an earlier form of it) which attest the shorter form presupposed by 𝕲.

It is quite clear that this form is the result of a planned arrangement. But it
is equally clear that the plan was either upset or not consistently carried through.
Thus i–xxv contain mainly prophecies, but there are also narratives in it, as in
xix, 1–xx, 6, which would be more naturally expected in the section xxvi–xlv.
The latter, however, is interrupted by the passages xxx–xxxi and xxxiii, 1–
xxxiv, 7, which contain prophecies and not narratives. Furthermore, the
chronological arrangement of the narratives which was evidently intended and
also probably at one time carried through, has become disordered. We must
ask whether it is possible to say something more precise about the evolution of
the book and so find an explanation for its present form.

Here we must first consider a narrative which may perhaps give us a significant pointer, namely xxxvi. In the fourth year of Jehoiakim,[7] i.e. 605 B.C.,
we are here told, Jeremiah received the command from Yahweh to write down
on a scroll all the words which he had so far received concerning *Jerusalem*,[8]
Judah and all the nations,[9] so as to place once more before the people the threats
which according to v. 29 culminate in the proclamation of the destruction of
the land by the king of Babylon, and so to move the people to repentance.
Jeremiah dictated all these words to Baruch ben-Neriah, and the latter read this
scroll to the people in the temple on the occasion of a fast held in the fifth year
of Jehoiakim, in the ninth month (December 604). When the king's ministers
assembled in *the secretary's room* (xxxvi, 12)[10] heard of this, they had Baruch
brought to read the scroll before them. Alarmed at its contents, they informed
the king and the latter too had the scroll read to him. But what was read did not
have any effect upon him. Instead, he cut off the columns as they were read and
threw them into the brazier standing before him. Then Jeremiah dictated the
words afresh to Baruch, *and many similar words were added to them* (v. 32).

The Baruch mentioned here appears several times in the book of Jeremiah.

[7] Auerbach, 'Der Wechsel des Jahres-Anfangs in Juda' VT 9 (1959), pp. 113–21.
Lit. p. 285, n. 19; § 126 to p. 285, n. 19.
[8] Reading thus with 𝕲 in v. 2 instead of *Israel*.
[9] It is possible that *and all the nations* is a later addition occasioned by xlvi–li.
[10] Galling, 'Die Halle des Schreibers' PJB 27 (1931), pp. 51–7.

In xxxii, 12, Jeremiah hands over to him a deed of sale. In xliii, 3, the Jews who have fled into the neighbourhood of Bethlehem, after the assassination of Gedaliah, assert that it is Baruch who has instigated Jeremiah to warn them against escaping to Egypt, and in xliii, 6, it is related that the leaders of this company compelled him as well as Jeremiah to accompany them to Egypt. xlv, finally, contains an oracle personally directed to Baruch, and proclaimed to him by Jeremiah in connection with what is related in xxxvi.

All this shows that Baruch must have been very closely associated with Jeremiah, and that at least in the years 605–587 he must have been his constant companion. This inevitably brings the surmise that this Baruch was concerned in the formation of the book, and this not simply as Jeremiah's agent as in xxxvi. Now the book contains many narratives concerning Jeremiah told in the third person, which do not therefore come from the prophet himself. These could have been compiled by Baruch. This assumption is particularly likely for those in xxxvii–xliv which deal with Jeremiah's behaviour during the siege of Jerusalem and after its conquest. For Jeremiah's fortune was at that time Baruch's too, and no one could have been so well informed about Jeremiah's behaviour during this period as he was.

We must therefore ask whether the original scroll mentioned in that narrative and what we have just surmised concerning Baruch's part in the making of the book may still be recognised and defined more precisely.

3. *The original scroll.* First, the original scroll must be considered. The closing comment in xxxvi *and many similar words were added to them* is so indefinite that it does not tell us when this adding took place or for how long it continued. We should therefore first consider only the question of the appearance and content of the scroll burnt by the king, i.e. the real 'original scroll'. Naturally, this can only have contained sayings received up till 605, and furthermore it is probable that it really was concerned only with *sayings* and not also, for example, with narratives. Thus we may exclude all sayings stemming from the period after 605, and the narratives which are not simply introductions to sayings but, like xx, 1–6, really tell us something about Jeremiah's life. Something may also be said on the positive side concerning the nature of the sayings which come in for consideration in this original scroll. They must have been exclusively or at any rate predominantly of a threatening kind and (xxxvi, 29) have contained the proclamation of the destruction of the land by the Babylonians. This latter assumption is confirmed by xxv*. This passage is, like xxxvi, dated in the fourth year of Jehoiakim, and by its retrospect of the previous preaching of Jeremiah in v. 3, reminiscent of xxxvi, 2, and by its reference to *everything written in this book* (v. 13), reveals itself clearly as the introduction or conclusion to the original scroll; and it shows that this scroll contained primarily threats and presented the seventy-year[11] (vv. 11, 12, cf. xxix, 10)

11 Ackroyd, 'Two OT Historical Problems of the Early Persian Period' JNESt 17 (1958), pp. 13–27, see pp. 23–7: The 'Seventy Year' Period; Borger, 'An Additional Remark on P. R. Ackroyd JNESt XVII, 23–7' JNESt 18 (1959), p. 74; Orr, 'The Seventy Years of Babylon' VT 6 (1956), pp. 304–6; Plöger, '"Siebzig Jahre"' *Baumgärtel-Festschr.* (1959), pp. 124–30; Whitley, 'The Term Seventy Years Captivity' VT 4 (1954), pp. 60–72; 'The Seventy Years Desolation' VT 7 (1957), pp. 416–18.

occupation of Judah by Nebuchadrezzar as punishment for its sin and apostasy (vv. 9, 11, 13).

Thus, if the original scroll or more properly its enlarged 'new edition' is contained in the present book—which is by no means certain, but is possible and indeed probable—we should most properly assign to it the sections deriving from the years 626–605 which correspond to the conditions just made clear. Leaving aside xxx–xxxi and xlvi–li which will be discussed elsewhere with a view to determining their age (pp. 361–4), only i–xxv contain utterances from these years. In this section of the book, however, the so-called monologues of Jeremiah (xi, 18–xii, 6; xv, 10–21; xvii, 12–18; xviii, 18–23; xx, 7–18), do not come in question since they hardly fit into a collection of diatribes and threats, and it is as this that we must picture the original scroll. This is also true of the compositions, couched largely in the style of the individual lament or dirge within i–xxv (pp. 358–9), for they do not have the directly threatening character that we should expect judging from xxv*. The same is true of the reflections and the sayings and poems which resemble the *mashal* (p. 359). The compositions which warn, threaten or upbraid (p. 358) more readily come in for consideration, especially those sayings and poems which proclaim the enemy from the north (p. 358). But if we have rightly described xxv* as the conclusion of the original scroll, the most likely assumption is that the scroll contained speeches similar in content and form to this passage. There is no lack of such passages. Indeed, in i–xxv may be found a whole series of passages—mostly marked by being introduced as first-person reports and in this too suitable to dictation going back to Jeremiah himself and corresponding to the first-person form of xxv*—which do all contain direct threats. These are the following passages: i, 2*, 4–10, his call; i, 11–17 (19), two visions, of the almond twig[12] and the cauldron coming from the north;[13] iii, 6–13, a word of Yahweh from the days of Josiah concerning the faithlessness of Judah which far exceeds the guilt of Israel; vii, 1–viii, 3,[14] the great Temple sermon, which falls into three sections: vii, 1–15, a diatribe against false reliance on the temple and a threat of its destruction; vii, 16–20, a diatribe against the cult of the queen of heaven and a threat against Jerusalem; vii, 21–viii, 3, diatribe against sacrifices and against 'Tophet', and a threat of terrible disaster for the inhabitants of Jerusalem; xi, (1) 6–14, a threat against Jerusalem which has broken the covenant; xiii, 1–14,[15] a threat against Israel and Judah, linked with the narrative of the girdle, and a threat to Jerusalem linked to a proverb concerning a wine jar;

[12] Williams, 'Jeremiah's Vision of the Almond Rod' *Papers Irwin* (1956), pp. 90–9; Wood, 'Jeremiah's Figure of the Almond Rod' JBL 61 (1942), pp. 99–103.

[13] Budde, 'Über das erste Kapitel des Buches Jeremia' JBL 40 (1921), pp. 23–37; Irwin, 'The Face of the Pot, Jeremiah i, 13b' AJSL 47 (1931), pp. 288 f.; Lindblom, 'Der Kessel in Jer i, 13 f.' ZAW 68 (1956), pp. 225–7; Michaud, 'La vocation du "prophète des Nations"' *Hommage à W. Vischer* (1960), pp. 157–64; Stade, 'Der "Völkerprophet" Jeremia und der jetzige Text von Jer. Kap, i' ZAW 26 (1906), pp. 97–123.

[14] Eichrodt, 'The Right Interpretation of the OT: a Study of Jeremiah vii, 7–15' Theology Today 7 (1950), pp. 15–25; Fohrer, 'Jeremias Templewort vii, 7–15' ThZ 5 (1949), pp. 401–17; Pákozdy, 'Der Tempelspruch des Jeremia' ZdZ 12 (1958), pp. 372–81; Stone, 'The Temple Sermons of Jeremiah' AJSL 50 (1933/4), pp. 73–92; Strobel, 'Jeremias, Priester ohne Gottesdienst?' BZ 1 (1957), pp. 214–24: on Jer. vii, 21–3.

[15] Balla, 'Jeremia xiii, 1–11' *Heiler-Festschr.* (1942), pp. 83–110; Baumann, 'Der

xvi, 1–13, the command to Jeremiah to take no wife and have no children, and to take no part in rejoicing or sorrow, and a terrible threat to Jerusalem; xvii, 19–27, the prohibition of desecration of the sabbath with a threat to Jerusalem; xviii, 1–12, a threat to Judah connected with the narrative of the potter; one of the two narratives combined in xix, namely xix, 1, 2*, 10, 11a, a threat to Jerusalem connected with the breaking of a jar; xxii, 1–5, a threat directed against the king of Judah, probably Jehoiakim, apparently at the beginning of his reign; xxv* (pp. 350, 364), the conclusion of the original scroll.

In favour of this separating out of the original scroll is the fact that in it are included all the passages which are introduced as first person narratives, in so far as they are concerned with the period before 605, with the sole exception of the introductions ii, 1; xiv, 11, 14; xv, 1. Of these, xiv, 11, 14; xv, 1, probably belong, as we shall show, to a liturgy (p. 356) and are to be understood in that context. ii, 1, might originally have been the introduction to vii, 1–viii, 3, which would then in the original scroll have formed the continuation of i, unless we are also to assign such a passage as ii[16] to the original scroll, or alternatively regard ii, 1–2aα as a late addition. The first person introductions in xxiv, 3, 4; xxvii, 2; xxxii, 6, 26 𝔊; xxxv, 12 𝔊, however, stand in or at the head of passages which are to be assigned to the 'new edition' of the original scroll (p. 353).

The passages here assigned to the original scroll stand out from their context, because of their style for the most part, as was already observed by Cornill and Erbt. They are couched in a prose style akin to the sermon,[17] a style which only occasionally rises to poetic rhythm, and they are often, like similar passages in Ezekiel, reminiscent of the diction of Deuteronomy and the Deuteronomists, as well as that of Deutero- and Trito-Isaiah. For this reason, Duhm denied them in the main to Jeremiah, with the exception of i, and many scholars have followed him in this—including Mowinckel, Hölscher, Horst and Rudolph—though some of them have done so with reserve. Rudolph, for example, does not allow prose style in itself to be evidence of the non-genuineness of a passage, and in addition assumes for at least some of the sections taken to be 'deuteronomistic' that they have a core which stems from Jeremiah himself. But too great significance is in fact being assigned to the stylistic difference, often certainly very great, between these passages and the compositions of Jeremiah, if from this it is concluded without further ado that they come from a different compiler. In reality, in many other prophets we find prose autobiographical accounts side by side with the direct retailing of their utterances in poetic form (p. 147). We should therefore allow these passages to which objection has been taken to belong to Jeremiah, and derive them most naturally from the original scroll. In recent times, Weiser too has firmly maintained their genuineness, though admittedly without assigning them to the original scroll.

linnene Schurz Jer. xiii, 1–11' ZAW 65 (1953), pp. 77–81; de Bondt, 'De linnen gordel uit Jer. xiii, 1–11 GThT 50 (1950), pp. 17–39.

[16] Milgrom, 'The Date of Jeremiah, Chapter ii' JNESt 14 (1955), pp. 65–9. Lit. § 126.

[17] Bright, 'The Date of the Prose Sermons of Jeremiah' JBL 70 (1951), pp. 15–35.

The real original scroll was, as we have seen, later enlarged by the addition of *many like words* (xxxvi, 32). The natural assumption is that in this 'enlarged edition' it was a matter of the addition of passages which were similar to the original content; and this guess is confirmed by xxxvi, 32. We may therefore assign to the new scroll all the first person reports which stem from the period after 605–604, the year of the dictation and of the destruction of the actual original scroll. These passages are: xxiv,[18] the vision of the two baskets of figs, which symbolise on the one hand those deported in 597 with Jehoiachin, and on the other hand those who were then left in Jerusalem; xxvii, the proclamation of the supremacy of Babylonia by a yoke carried by Jeremiah, a parallel to the narrative of xxviii which is to be assigned to 'Baruch'; xxxii, the purchase of the field, undertaken by Jeremiah as a sign that the recovery of Judah and Jerusalem was determined; xxxv, Jeremiah's visit to the Rechabites, and, linked with their loyalty, the castigation of Judah's unfaithfulness. It can be seen that we are here in each case concerned with reports—now somewhat out of order as far as chronology is concerned—concerning significant experiences and actions which it was worthwhile to preserve, like the similar passages of the actual original scroll. The whole work, original scroll and appendix, is thus in fact a memorial, something like a diary, which is quite similar to the related memoranda of Hosea (pp. 387–90) and Isaiah (pp. 310–12), Ezekiel (pp. 374–80) and Zechariah (pp. 431–2). We may reckon with it as a clearly demonstrated entity which at least in very large measure actually goes back to Jeremiah himself. Its genuineness is suspect particularly in the prohibition of the desecration of the sabbath in xvii, 19–27, and in various parts of the Temple sermon in vii, 1–viii, 3.

Other scholars, for example Weiser, hold it to be vain to attempt to rediscover the original scroll mentioned in xxxvi, in our present book of Jeremiah. Yet others, including Rudolph, wish to identify it with the passages, or some of the passages, assigned by Mowinckel to his source A (pp. 355 f.), a collection of sayings and poems such as is described above on pp. 147–50. We must therefore remain aware of the hypothetical character of the points just set out with regard to the original scroll. Nevertheless these points have their validity in so far as the passages so indicated as belonging to the original scroll, or at any rate the majority of them, reveal themselves by features of style and content as a unit of a particular kind. They correspond in fact largely with Mowinckel's source C, which he assumes was compiled in the time of Ezra by a Deuteronomist living in Babylonia or Palestine, who is supposed himself to have compiled the speeches which it contains, with occasional employment of Jeremianic forms of speech. But we have already shown that the fact that the diction of many of these passages is reminiscent of the Deuteronomic sermon-style is not a sufficient ground for denying them to Jeremiah—or at any rate their basic material, since secondary expansions may certainly be demonstrated. Mowinckel's assumption is quite improbable, namely that the compiler of source C originally referred to Jeremiah in the third person, and that it was subsequently altered into the first person. Autobiographical reports, some even in prose style,

[18] Winton Thomas, 'Note on מוּעָדִים in Jeremiah xxiv, 1' JThSt 3 (1952), pp. 47–52.

N

are to be found, as we have seen (pp. 148–9), already in the oldest of the writing prophets. They may therefore also be attributed to Jeremiah, and most naturally assigned to the original scroll. At any rate, they fit it better than any other sections from i–xxv which have been suggested.

4. *The work of Baruch.* If, as it appears, the original scroll may even now be reconstructed, we may ask further whether we can still recognise in the book Baruch's own work,[19] namely the narratives which tell about Jeremiah in the third person. The beginning of this could have consisted in the narrative in xix, 2*, 3–6 (7–9), 11b, 12–15; xx, 1–6, concerning Jeremiah's sufferings as a result of his 'Tophet' sermon, now combined with a first-person report (p. 352). To this undated narrative is linked the story in xxvi[20] which took place at the beginning of the reign of Jehoiakim, which has for a long time[21] been recognised as an account of the attendant circumstances of Jeremiah's 'Temple sermon' in vii, 1–viii, 3. This is followed by the narratives already mentioned, xxxvi (pp. 349–50), and xlv (p. 350), which take place in the fourth year of Jehoiakim. To these may be linked the narratives dated in the fourth year of Zedekiah concerning Jeremiah's clash with Hananiah, his letter to Babylon, and the ceremony of cursing against Babylon committed to Zedekiah's quartermaster in xxviii,[22] xxix, and li, 59–64, as well as the narrative in xxxiv, 8–22,[23] which presupposes the siege of Jerusalem, concerning a vow broken by the Jerusalemites and the threat of punishment consequent upon it. Baruch's narrative work would thus have comprised the following passages: xix, 2*, 3–9, 11b–15 +xx, 1–6; xxvi; xxxvi; xlv; xxviii–xxix; li, 59–64; xxxiv, 8–22; xxxvii–xliv. We cannot now discover for certain why xxxvi, xlv[24] (numbered in 𝕲 as li, 31–5, and standing at the end of Jeremiah's prophecies), and li, 59–64, have lost their original place, and now stand in a chronologically unsuitable position. However, for li, 59–64, there is a likely explanation: the saying of Jeremiah here quoted was applied to the threats set out in l, 1–li, 58, and so the passage was placed after them. The misplacement of xlv may also be explained. xliv contains threats against the Jews living in Egypt. But Baruch also belongs among them (xliii, 3, 6). In order to avert a possible misunderstanding that the curse was also to fall upon Baruch, a redactor removed the oracle favourable to him from its original position, and added it to xliv. Thus Baruch was explicitly excepted from the threats uttered in xliv.[25] xxxvi, finally, could have come into its present position because it was desired to interpret its conclusion with the reference to the adding of many like words to the original scroll, as including all the sayings

[19] Rost, 'Zur Problematik der Jeremiabiographie Baruchs' *Meiser-Festschr.* (1951), pp. 241–5.

[20] Blank, '*Of a Truth the Lord Hath sent me*' (1955): on xxvi, 15.

[21] According to Torrey, JBL 56 (1937), p. 194, this was already put forward by Jacob Alting (1687).

[22] The first half-verse of xxviii, 1, is now in disorder, and is to be restored following 𝕲: *And it came to pass in the fourth year of Zedekiah, king of Judah, in the fifth month.* Differently, H. Schmidt, 'Das Datum der Ereignisse von Jer. xxvii und xxviii' ZAW 39 (1921), pp. 138–44.

[23] David, 'The Manumission of Slaves under Zedekiah' OTS 5 (1948), pp. 63–79.

[24] Weiser, 'Das Gotteswort für Baruch Jer. xlv und die sogenannte Baruchbiographie' *Heim-Festschr.* (1954), pp. 35–46 = *Ausg. Schr.* (1961), pp. 321–9.

[25] Otherwise Weiser.

preceding it in i–xxxv. The assigning of the narratives just mentioned to Baruch follows from the generally accepted and probable assumption, that the man who is mentioned as so closely bound up with the fortunes of Jeremiah, and who appears as his secretary in xxxvi, is likely to have had a share in the book as we have it. Mowinckel contests this view, and regards Baruch simply as a public scribe who in this capacity wrote down the original scroll at Jeremiah's dictation, but does not come in question as the compiler of any part of our book. Yet even according to Rudolph and Weiser, Mowinckel's scepticism is unjustified in regard to the assumption that Baruch wrote down a history of the life, or rather of the sufferings, of his revered master, and that this has been preserved for us as a part of the present book of Jeremiah. In any case, the points which have just been set out retain their significance—as in the case of the original scroll—in that the relevant narratives certainly at one time formed an independent book. They coincide with Mowinckel's source B, which according to him was compiled in Egypt between 580 and 480.

Thus there is much to be said in favour of tracing back to Baruch the biographical narrative work just described. But some scholars would attribute to Baruch an even more extensive part in the formation of the book of Jeremiah. Thus Volz traces back the basic form of i–xlv to Baruch, and assumes that he shaped the three sections of this which may be distinguished clearly in content and form, namely i–xxv, sayings (λόγια); xxvi–xxxvi, narratives as framework for sayings; xxxvii–xlv, a continuous narrative concerning the last years of Jeremiah's life. He believes that Baruch concluded each section with a reference to the dictating of the original scroll, the first in xxv, 1–14 (see p. 351), the second in xxxvi, and the third in xlv. Rudolph considers it possible that it was the compiler of the passages assigned by him, like Mowinckel, to source C (p. 353), who carried out the main redaction of the whole book of Jeremiah, and he endeavours to demonstrate the principles upon which this redactor worked. In reality, we must reckon with a much more complex process for the formation of the book. We can no longer determine with certainty how many hands or stages of editing are to be assumed. We may possibly, however, distinguish with reasonable assurance the individual component parts which were once independent and then brought together in the process of redaction. We have already described two of these, the first person accounts contained in the original scroll and its second edition, and the narratives stemming from Baruch. We may now ask whether it is possible to say something about the origin of the passages which do not fit into these two collections.

In considering this question, we shall first limit ourselves to an examination of i–xxv, namely to the words of Jeremiah which remain over after the separation out of the original scroll, for the most part coinciding with those which Mowinckel assigns to his source A, which like B (cf. above) he considers to stem from Egypt between 580 and 480. These oracles and compositions exist to some extent in smaller groups, arranged from the point of view of subject-matter, and these no doubt existed at one time independently. Three of them are provided with titles, namely xiv, 1–xv, 4, *concerning the drought*, xxi, 11–xxiii, 8, *concerning the court of Judah*; xxiii, 9–40, *concerning the prophets*. Probably, however, there are other small collections concealed in i–xxv, though since they have no titles they cannot be discovered with such a degree of certainty.

5. *Collections with titles in i–xxv.* We may first examine the collections provided with titles in i–xxv. The first of these, xiv, 1–xv, 4, has a title which is corrupt in 𝔐, but may be restored with certainty as: *The word of Yahweh, which came to Jeremiah with reference to the drought.* This passage is strongly reminiscent of Joel i–ii, and just as the latter may be described as a liturgy composed on the occasion of a plague of locusts, so this passage may be regarded as a liturgy occasioned by a drought. Here we cannot exclude the possibility that Jeremiah functioned on such an occasion as a cult-prophet (p. 118), however much this idea goes directly against the earlier common ideas on the relationship of the writing prophets to the cultus. Alternatively his composition may be an imitation of a form which really belonged within the cultus. The description of the distress (xiv, 2–6) is followed by the prayer of the people, couched in the style of a national lament (vv. 7–9), and to this Yahweh gives a negative answer (vv. 10–16) made all the more bitter by a word of the prophet charging the people with guilt (v. 13). There follows a lament by the prophet at the destruction of his people, in the style of a funeral dirge (vv. 17–18), and the people then renews its plea for the averting of the distress, again in the tone of the national lament (vv. 19–22). But they meet with the sharpest denial (xv, 1–4), while Yahweh indicates to Jeremiah, who clearly is thought of as leading the prayer and as intercessor, that any intervention on behalf of the people is useless. We cannot unfortunately say anything concerning the date of this passage.

In xxi, 11–xxiii, 8, there are gathered together threats against the kings of Judah. This group of passages is arranged chronologically, at any rate from xxii, 10, onwards; after a glance back at the death of Josiah, we deal in order with Jehoahaz-Shallum, Jehoiakim, Jehoiachin and Zedekiah, or more correctly with the Messiah contrasted with Zedekiah. It is open to question whether the preceding sayings (xxi, 11–xxii, 9) are in chronological order, especially since xxii, 1–5, is apparently a passage from the first person account (see p. 352) parallel to the oracle of xxi, 11–12. In a general way xxi, 1–10, also belongs to this collection—the narrative concerns an oracle delivered to king Zedekiah and the people during the siege of Jerusalem—in that it too contains a saying directed to a king and has clearly been connected with xxi, 11–xxiii, 8, for this reason. Admittedly it stands too early and would find its correct chronological position only after xxii, 30. This is probably to be explained on the grounds that the interpolator of this passage found xxi, 11–xxiii, 8, already in existence as a complete collection concluding with a prospect of the Messiah, and did not wish to disturb this. So he was unable to insert xxi, 1–10, in the collection before xxiii, 1. To add it at the end, however, was also impossible, since this would have spoiled the effect of the Messianic prospect. There remained only the possibility of placing the passage in front of the section. The date of origin of the majority of the passages in xxi, (1) 11–xxiii, 8, is provided by the fact that they refer to particular kings. The collection as a whole cannot have come into existence before Zedekiah. The individual sayings are certainly genuine. Whether the collection, too, i.e. its basic form at least, goes back to Jeremiah himself or was put together by someone else, cannot now be decided. At least one later hand has certainly contributed to its present form.

The collection of sayings *concerning the prophets* (xxiii, 9–40) cannot be dated with certainty. We know from xxvi–xxix that in the time of Jehoiakim (xxvi, 11) and of Zedekiah (xxvii–xxix), Jeremiah came into sharp conflict with the prophets, and so we might think of assigning the sayings of this collection to that period. But in xxiii, 9–40, we do not find definite reproaches against the prophets which actually point to the situations of xxvi–xxix—i.e. false trust in Egypt, vain resistance to Babylon—and hence we cannot exclude the possibility that these sayings come from an earlier period. At that time too Jeremiah was engaged in conflict against false prophets. We could certainly assume this without precise evidence, and we actually have references to it (ii, 8, 26; v, 13; xviii, 18, etc.). The individual sayings of the collection are genuine, perhaps with the exception of vv. 33–40.[26] Nothing certain can be said about the origin and age of the collection itself.

6. *Other originally independent sections in i–xxv.* We may also relatively easily separate out from i–xxv the monologues or confessions[27] as independent groups, although here titles are entirely lacking. These are unique poems too on account of their poetical value. Here Jeremiah lays before his God his whole personal attitude and opens up a very profound view of his inner life and of the conflict within him between human inclination and prophetic compulsion. These are xi, 18–23; xii, 1–6;[28] xv, 10–21; xvii, 12–18; xviii, 18–23; xx, 7–18. Thus they all stand within xi–xx and so preserve, it would appear, the recollection of a stage when they were even more closely linked together, and belonged to a once independent collection. It is quite improbable that these compositions were distributed among the threats against Judah and Jerusalem by Jeremiah himself, say at the time of the dictation of the original scroll. His disciples too are certainly likely to have kept this small collection at first separate from other words of the master. It would be most natural to suppose that Jeremiah kept these prayers which lay bare his innermost self entirely to himself, and that they first became publicly known after his death. There is not the least ground for doubting their genuineness, even if individual verses or parts of verses are disputed, and the delimitation of the individual sections is at times not quite certain.

The material which still remains in i–xxv after the removal of the monologues as well (ii–vi; viii, 4–x, 25; xii, 7–17; xiii, 15–27; xv, 5–9; xvi, 19–21; xvii, 1–11; xviii, 13–17), has also probably in its turn been put together from

[26] Walker, 'The Masoretic Pointing of Jeremiah's Pun' VT 7 (1957), p. 413; Wernberg-Møller, 'The Pronoun אתמה and Jeremiah's Pun' VT 6 (1956), pp. 315 f.

[27] Behler, *Les confessions de Jérémie* (1959); Blank, 'The Confessions of Jeremiah and the Meaning of Prayer' HUCA 21 (1948), pp. 331–54; Bratsiotis (p. 12); Mihelic, 'Dialogue with God: A Study of Some of Jeremiah's Confessions' Interpretation 14 (1960), pp. 43–50; von Rad, 'Die Konfessionen Jeremias' EvTh 3 (1936), pp. 265–76; Simon, 'The Mysticism of Jeremiah' ChQR 161 (1960), pp. 270–9.

[28] Driver, StOTPr (1950), pp. 59–61: on xii, 5; 'Jeremiah xii, 6' JJSt 5 (1954), pp. 177 f.; Ehrman, ' A Note on בוטח in Jer. xii, 5' JSSt 5 (1960), p. 153; Stummer, 'Bemerkungen zu Jer. xii, 1–6' Stud. Anselm., 27/28 (1951), pp. 264–75. Lit. § 126.

smaller groups of individual passages related in date of origin, content or form. But we lack here any means of defining this more precisely, and must therefore be content merely to give a survey of the various elements in this remaining material. At the beginning are several larger and smaller poems such as ii, 1–13, or ii, 1–19—for the delimitation here as elsewhere is not always quite clear— which are in part combined with a retrospect to the period in the wilderness when there was an unclouded relationship of trust between Yahweh and Israel. They castigate the people's apostasy to the Baals and its political alliances with neighbouring powers which also indicate apostasy from Yahweh. They reveal the marked dependence of Jeremiah upon older prophets, in the first place upon Hosea,[29] and in the second place upon Isaiah. There appear in fact actual verbal echoes of expressions in these two prophets. Thus *the devotion of your youth* in Jer. ii, 2,[30] recalls *the days of her youth* in Hos. ii, 17; and *be appalled, O heavens, at this,* in Jer. ii, 12, recalls *hear, ye heavens,* in Isa. 1, 2, the more so since in both cases the words belong to a context with similar meaning. We should most probably derive these compositions from the period of Jeremiah's beginnings, when in the content and form of his proclamation he was still strongly dependent upon his predecessors, and had not yet come to develop fully his own particular characteristics.

There is also a group of compositions which have in common the fact that they proclaim, with a very vivid description of what is to come, the breaking in of an enemy coming from the north.[31] To these belongs iv, 5–8,[32] beginning with a summons to Zion to flee, then threatening the disaster coming from the north, describing the raging of the enemy pictured as a lion climbing up out of the Jordan thickets, and closing with a summons to lamentation. iv, 11–13; iv, 15–17; v, 10–17;[33] vi, 1–8;[34] viii, 16–17, are poems and sayings with a similar content. It has been thought that the grim and ominous threat of an enemy breaking in from the north was occasioned by the onslaughts of the Scythians (p. 424) which disturbed the Near East shortly after 630, and that later, after 605, Jeremiah applied it to the Babylonians. This is possible, but by no means certain. But we must in any case assign these compositions with their youthful vividness to the early period of Jeremiah.

The threat of the coming disaster is often in Jeremiah expressed in the form of a lament interwoven with motifs from the funeral dirge, or even purely in the funeral dirge form. The danger, which is actually still in the future, is depicted as if already taking place, and now the people or the prophet, or even Yahweh himself, takes up a song of lament or a funeral dirge. Admittedly it is not always possible to differentiate with certainty between those songs which

[29] Gross, *Die literarische Verwandtschaft Jeremias mit Hosea* (Diss. theol. Berlin, 1930); 'Hoseas Einfluss auf Jeremias Anschauungen' NKZ 42 (1931), pp. 241–56, 327–43.
[30] Wiéner, 'Jérémie ii, 2: "Fiançailles ou Épousailles"?' RSR 44 (1956), pp. 403–7.
[31] Childs, 'The Enemy from the North and the Chaos Tradition' JBL 78 (1959), pp. 187–98; Hyatt, 'The Peril from the North in Jeremiah' JBL 59 (1940), pp. 499–513; Lauha, *Zaphon* (1943).
[32] Winton Thomas, 'מלאו in Jeremiah iv, 5: A Military Term' JJSt 3 (1952), pp. 47–52.
[33] Sutcliffe, 'A Note on לא הוא Jer. v, 12' Bibl 41 (1960), pp. 287–90.
[34] On Beth-Haccherem vi, 1, cf. below, p. 545, n. 15.

prophetically anticipate events and those which are composed with reference to a disaster which has already taken place, but the majority of them are clearly of the proleptic nature just described. A moving example of this is in iv, 19–21, where the land, pictured as a person, gives a heart-rending expression to the convulsions and consequent devastations brought about by the raging of the battle, seen as if in a vision. No less moving is the lament which the prophet takes up in viii, 18–23, at his people's downfall, culminating in the lines:

> O that my head were waters　　and my eyes a fountain of tears,
> that I might weep day and night　for the slain of the daughter of my people.

The song in ix, 20–1, prescribed for the mourning women, is a lament actually called a funeral dirge (נְהִי, קִינָה) in ix, 19. These songs of lamentation too, or at any rate those which are such only in form and in reality represent prophecy, are to be assigned to the early period of Jeremiah's activity, and may perhaps be thought to have been occasioned by the Scythian peril.

Finally, there is in i–xxv, a whole series of poems and sayings which for the most part have no special characteristics and could be assigned to another prophet. There are diatribes, exhortations and threats, reflections and sayings and poems akin to the *mashal*. Thus in v, 26–8, we have a diatribe against the deceitful rich, and in v, 30–1, a similar one against lying prophets and priests. viii, 4–9, presents a diatribe and threat against the people persisting in its unnatural impenitent condition. xiii, 15–16, contains a serious exhortation to repentance, while there is yet time, and xiii, 23, is a profound reflection concerning the radical evil in man who is as little able to do good as the Ethiopian can change his skin or the leopard his spots. It is quite impossible to undertake to fix the date of origin of these and similar sayings. We can only recognise quite simply that there are no well-founded objections to their genuineness.

Admittedly the borderline between non-genuine sayings and this last group of Jeremianic sayings is fluid, just because we are here frequently dealing with sayings which could perfectly well be assigned to other prophets. It is obvious that i–xxv contains non-genuine material too, and this is quite generally recognised. Thus x, 1–16, is rightly denied to Jeremiah, containing as it does a composition reminiscent of Deutero-Isaiah on the mockery of idols (vv. 1–5, 8–9) and a hymnic extolling of Yahweh (vv. 6–7, 10–16). The same applies to other passages. With xvii, 5–8,[35] however, a wisdom poem very similar to Ps. i, the position is different. Here we have a picture, in terms of a tree which dries up in the desert and of one which flourishes by the water, of the contrast between the life of the one who trusts in man and the one who relies upon God. The very common doubt concerning Jeremianic origin arises in reality only from the prejudice, essentially long outmoded, that psalm composition is later than Jeremiah, a prejudice which moreover, also for a time caused some scholars to be mistrustful of the genuineness of the monologues and of the compositions of Jeremiah in the style of the lament or the funeral dirge, but which in this respect has long been repudiated.

7. *The composition of i–xxv.* i–xxv represents a composition made up of very

---

[35] Davidson, 'The Interpretation of Jeremiah xvii, 5–8' VT 9 (1959), pp. 202–5.

varied larger and smaller collections, or of parts only of such collections. These have certainly been combined according to definite principles, however much i–xxv gives us in many places the impression of meaningless confusion. Sometimes too we may still recognise these principles, as we have seen in the case of xxi, 1–10 (p. 356). But it is hardly worth while trying to go further. For i–xxv certainly does not present a completely logically formed unity. The general view, or at least one which is very widely held, is that i–xxv are arranged substantially in chronological order; i–vi contain documents from the early period of Josiah 639–621; vii–xx mainly from the period of Jehoiakim 608–598, and xxi–xxiv mainly from the period after 598.[36] This view will not bear close examination. Such an examination reveals that the words in i–vi actually do come in the main from the early period of Jeremiah, but that there are also some passages from a later period, as for example ii, 36–7, a saying which is probably to be brought down to the time after 608, or at least later than 612. It reveals further that the assigning of the sayings in vii–xx to the period of Jehoiakim rests only on the deriving of the temple speech of vii, 1–viii, 3, from the beginning of Jehoiakim's reign, a view which depends upon xxvi, 1. Otherwise, the whole matter is quite undefined. The view upheld by Volz that the passage xi, 1–14 (17),[37] represents a criticism of the overthrow of Josiah's reform by Jehoiakim, is in fact quite uncertain. For if, in spite of the denials of Rudolph and others, the words of *this covenant* mentioned here are to be referred with Rowley and others to Deuteronomy, and hence the passage xi, 1–14 (17), is to be considered as a witness to the view that Jeremiah at first gladly welcomed the reform of Josiah, he may nevertheless soon have expressed his disappointment at the meagre success which it had among the mass of the people. Rothstein too derives the passage from the time of the reform itself. Similarly, the threat to Jeremiah by other inhabitants of his village Anathoth presupposed in xi, 18–xii, 6, can be equally well understood in the earlier period, in the time of Josiah, as in the later. So a chronological arrangement is hardly the basis of the oracles and poems which comprise the material preserved in i–xxv, or at any rate this is not the main principle of arrangement. The placing of the diatribes, exhortations and threatening poems of ii–vi at the beginning, material which actually does belong to Jeremiah's early period, is to be explained rather on the grounds that the book of Jeremiah was to be introduced by a 'sermon' in the form of a summary of the Jeremianic message—just as the book of Isaiah is opened by ch. i. The temple sermon of vii, 1–viii, 3, deriving from the first person account in the original scroll, rounded off this summary appropriately and was therefore placed immediately after ii–vi. The fact that the laments concerning Jeremiah's personal fortunes only begin at xi, 18–xii, 6, is to be explained

[36] So Volz, commentary, p. xliv; Rudolph, commentary, p. xvii.

[37] Cazelles, 'Jérémie et le Deutéronome' RSR 39 (1951), pp. 5–36; Hyatt, 'The Original Text of Jeremiah xi, 15–16' JBL 60 (1941), pp. 57–60; 'Torah in the Book of Jeremiah' JBL 60 (1941), pp. 381–96; Puukko, 'Jeremias Stellung zum Deuteronomium' BWAT 13 (1913), pp. 126–53; Robert, 'Jérémie et la Réforme deutéronomique d'après Jér. xi, 1–14' RSR 31 (1943), pp. 5–16; Rowley, 'The Prophet Jeremiah and the Book of Deuteronomy' StOTPr (1950), pp. 157–74; Schofield, 'The Significance of the Prophets for Dating Deuteronomy' *Studies in History and Religion*, ed. by Payne (1942), pp. 44–60; Smith, 'The Decalogue in the Preaching of Jeremias' CBQ 4 (1942), pp. 197–209.

from the idea that the basic points of Jeremiah's preaching were first to be set out before there should be any expression of the complaints at the hostility directed against him because of this. In short, we are left with the position that it is hardly worth while attempting to get behind the smaller collections recognisable in i–xxv. In any case it is not these which are really important, but the individual sayings, poems and speeches. Only the 'original scroll' deserves greater attention, as a collection.

8. *The 'Booklet of Consolation', xxx–xxxi*. If we now leave i–xxv, we come next in the 'booklet of consolation' in xxx–xxxi[38] to yet another originally independent collection of oracles and poems. Its present position in the middle of the narratives is no doubt to be explained on the grounds that it was brought into association with the narrative of the purchase of the field in xxxii which issues in a prophecy of salvation, and so was placed before this as an introduction. It is certain that it is based upon a core which actually stems from Jeremiah, and this comprises at least the poems of xxxi, 2–22, which in spite of the no doubt original mention of *Zion* in vv. 6, 12 (cf. iii, 11–18, and especially verse 14), clearly refer to the northern kingdom. But it is probable that the poems gathered in xxx, 5–21 (24) are also genuine. They are now (see vv. 4, 6, 8–9) concerned with Israel and Judah, but probably originally referred to the northern kingdom alone like those in xxxi, 2–22. We may leave open the question as to whether the Jeremianic material in xxx–xxxi is to be thought of as a unified composition—so Volz and Rudolph (according to Rudolph it comprises xxx, 5–7, 10–24; xxxi, 2–22,[39] 31–7)—or, as is more usual, as a collection of poems and sayings with similar content. The date of origin of the section is also in dispute. In general it is now associated with the expansionist policy of Josiah, which extended over the territory of the old northern kingdom of Israel (II Kings xxiii, 15–20), whether it is thought, as by Rudolph, that this policy was the presupposition of the hopes here expressed by Jeremiah, or, as by Rost, that the policy was approved by Jeremiah's words. But whether xxx–xxxi are really so strongly conditioned by political events is open to question. There is much which favours placing them at the beginning of Jeremiah's activity. At that time, when Judah was not yet directly drawn into the vortex of the great world-political events, and when as yet even in the internal life of the country no special undertakings were in being, it is most natural to think that Jeremiah pursued the idea of Israel's restoration. Later Judah's own fate lay heavily enough upon his heart. But it is also certain that the booklet contains non-genuine material, in just the same way as xxxii–xxxiii, the narrative of the purchase of the field, now forming in some measure a unity with it, has

---

[38] Devescovi, 'Annotazione sulla dottrina di Geremia circa la nuova alleanza' Riv Bibl 8 (1960), pp. 108–28; Gelin, 'Le sens du mot "Israël" en Jérémie xxx–xxxi' *Mémorial J. Chaine* (1950), pp. 161–8; Goldman, 'The Authorship of Jeremiah Chapter xxxi' ABR 2 (1952), pp. 109–10; Hertzberg, 'Jeremia und das Nordreich Israel' ThLZ 77 (1952), cols. 595–602; Lempp, 'Bund und Bundeserneuerung bei Jeremia' ThLZ 80 (1955), cols. 238–9; Ortmann, *Der Alte und der Neue Bund bei Jeremia* (Diss. theol. Berlin, 1940); Rost, (p. 348, n. 2); *Israel bei den Propheten* (BWANT 71, 1937), pp. 54–71; Sekine, 'Davidsbund und Sinaibund bei Jeremia' VT 9 (1959), pp. 40–57. Lit. § 126.

[39] Ziener, ' "Femina circumdabit virum" (Jer. xxxi, 22), eine Dittographie' BZ 1 (1957), pp. 282 f. Lit. § 126.

also received various secondary elaborations. Non-genuine, probably, are xxxi, 23–30, 35–40, in addition to the present form of the title in xxx, 1–4, and some other smaller sections. Jeremiah's authorship has also not been unquestioned for the beautiful saying concerning the new covenant in xxxi, 31–4, a saying which nevertheless has its own intrinsic value. As far as content is concerned, it certainly could be put into the mouth of Jeremiah. The narrative of xxxii makes it quite certain that in a cheerless contemporary situation, which apparently left no room for hope, he believed in a new age of salvation and also proclaimed it. It also corresponds entirely to the rest of his message that the most precious value of this time of salvation would be a personal communion between the individual man and his God. The booklet can, however, have received its present form only after the catastrophe of 587 which is clearly presupposed in xxxi, 38–40, and it is unlikely that Jeremiah himself was responsible for it.

9. *The oracles against foreign nations, xlvi–li.* When we turn to the collection of oracles against foreign nations in xlvi–li, 58,[40] we can immediately see clearly that the threat against Babylon (l, 1–li, 58)[41] cannot in its present form derive from Jeremiah, in view for example of the mention of the king[42] of the Medes as Babylon's chief enemy. It must come from the years before the conquest of Babylon, or may already presuppose that conquest, and thus belongs with passages such as Isa. xiii, 1–xiv, 23; xxi, 1–10; xl–lv (p. 337). A closer examination reveals that we have here a composition which has incorporated a good deal of alien matter. A whole series of groups of verses, single verses and parts of verses reappear in other places in the Old Testament with the same form of words or a similar form, and priority rests at any rate in most cases with the other passages, or with the original which lies behind both them and l, 1–li, 58. The most important passages which come in question here are as follows (in each case with the corresponding reference in brackets): l, 13 (xlix, 17); l, 16 (Isa. xiii, 14); l, 30 (xlix, 26); l, 40–6 (xlix, 18+vi, 22–4+xlix, 19–21); li, 15–19 (x, 12–16); li, 25–6 (Ezek. xxxv, 3–4); li, 40 (Isa. xxxiv, 5–7). There can be no doubt about the late composition of the present form of l, 1–li, 58. It hardly seems justifiable to go even further and inquire whether there is here any Jeremianic basis at all, or whether the passage is not rather to be explained as a compilation occasioned by the narrative of li, 59–64. In this case, a later writer felt himself bound to reconstruct or rather to invent the exact wording of the threat against Babylon which according to this narrative was at Jeremiah's behest sunk in the Euphrates within sight of the city by Zedekiah's quartermaster. A core of material deriving from Jeremiah himself may, it would appear, be demonstrated in l, 17–20.[43]

[40] Bardtke, 'Jeremia der Fremdvölkerprophet' ZAW 53 (1935), pp. 209–39; 54 (1938), pp. 240–62.

[41] Budde, 'Über die Capitel l and li des Buches Jeremia' JDTh 23 (1878), pp. 428–70, 529–62.

[42] We must read the singular with 𝕲 in li, 11, 28, rather than the plural of 𝔐. Rosenthal, 'Minni-Alemania?' JQR 48 (1957/8), pp. 204–7: on li, 27.

[43] Eissfeldt, 'Jeremias Drohorakel gegen Ägypten und gegen Babel' *Rudolph-Festschr.* (1961), pp. 31–7.

The collection of oracles against foreign nations must thus certainly have come into being a very considerable time after the period of Jeremiah's activity. But this does not by any means suggest that it could not in fact contain some genuine Jeremianic material. We shall have rather to examine each passage with this possibility specially in mind. The threats against Egypt, xlvi, 3–12, 14–24, fit completely into the framework of Jeremiah's preaching which elsewhere too warns against Egypt (ii, 18, 36; xliii, 8–13). Furthermore, they are delivered in a high poetic tone and in this respect too are worthy to be attributed to him. We may therefore acknowledge them as Jeremiah's. So far as the other oracles are concerned, the one against Moab (xlviii, 1–47)[44] and the one against Edom (xlix, 7–22), are now in a form which certainly cannot derive from Jeremiah. xlviii, 1–47, actually has, as we have seen, large sections in common with Isa. xv–xvi (pp. 320–1), and xlix, 7–22 overlaps in part with Obad. 1–10 (p. 402), and in addition contains a whole series of verses which also appear elsewhere in the book of Jeremiah (v. 18=l, 40; vv. 19–21=l, 44–6; v. 22=xlviii, 40–1). In these respects these oracles are like those directed against Babylon, and form a fairly late composition in their present form. But they may nevertheless contain a genuine core. After 587 we could scarcely expect a saying like the one which appears in the Moab oracle in which the Moabite god Chemosh is compared with Bethel, the god of the Israelites,[45] and which says of the latter that he could not prevent the disaster on the northern kingdom (xlviii, 13). For after the downfall of the southern kingdom itself there could hardly be so spiteful and self-righteous an attitude towards the northern kingdom. So far as the other oracles are concerned, we might note that in the one directed against the Philistines (xlvii, 1–7),[46] the phrase in v. 2 *out of the north*, sounds very much like Jeremiah and favours the genuineness of the passage, but it is not conclusive. In the other oracles, a decision for or against is hardly possible.[47] Thus we cannot everywhere decide clearly what in xlvi, 1–li, 58, comes from Jeremiah, and what does not. Certain points are, however, clear: (1) that there is genuine material in this collection; (2) that this genuine material has been amplified by expansion and by the addition of new passages, and (3) that the collection, like Isa. xiii–xxiii and Ezek. xxv–xxxii, is to be considered as a fairly late endeavour to gather together a series of threatening oracles directed against as many as possible of the neighbouring peoples. Volz can hardly be right in the view which he has maintained, namely that the oracles directed against foreign nations, including what he regards as an introduction to them in xxv, 15–38, comprise a book compiled soon after the death of Nebuchadrezzar, i.e. about 560, by a great unknown prophet, 'Deutero-Jeremiah', for this does not take adequate account of the many disparate

---

[44] Irwin, 'An Ancient Biblical Text' AJSL 48 (1932), pp. 184–93; on xlviii, 11. Lit. § 126.

[45] Eissfeldt, 'Der Gott Bethel' ARW 28 (1930), pp. 1–30, cf. pp. 10–12=*Kl. Schr.* I (1962), pp. 206–33, cf. pp. 214–16.

[46] Malamat, 'The Historical Setting of Two Biblical Prophecies on the Nations' IEJ 1 (1950), pp. 149–59, see pp. 154–9 on Jer. xlvii.

[47] North, 'The Oracle against the Ammonites in Jeremiah xlix, 1–6' JBL 65 (1946), pp. 37–43.

elements which are combined in xlvi–li. Nor can Bardtke's assumption be right
—in spite of many individual observations which are of value—that Jeremiah,
who he supposes to have been born only in 635 and to have been called as a
prophet only in 617, considered himself in his early period as concerned with
proclaiming disaster only on foreign nations, and that he pronounced his
threats against the foreign nations at that time and gathered them together in a
collection which comprised the basic material of i, 2, 4–10 (call-pericope);
xxv, 15–17 (cup-pericope); xlvii (against Philistia); xlix, 34–9 (against Elam);
xlvi, 18–24 (against Egypt); xlviii (against Moab); xlix, 1–6 (against Ammon);
xlix, 7, 8, 22, 10, 11 (against Edom); xlix, 23–7 (against Damascus); xlix, 28–33
(against Kedar), and xxv, 27–9 (pericope of the cup of rejection)—all this
before he was changed in about 615 into a prophet who had in the first instance
to proclaim disaster to his own people.

The second half of xxv, i.e. vv. 15–38[48] is somehow connected with the collection of oracles against foreign nations. It contains in vv. 19–26 a list of foreign
nations which is reminiscent of those mentioned in xlvi–li, and 𝔊, which in fact
places the foreign nation oracles after xxv, 13 (pp. 348–9), clearly regarded
xxv, 15–38, as the conclusion of this collection. But originally the passage had
nothing to do with this collection. It is rather the conclusion of the first-person
account dictated in the original scroll—at least this is true of its original core
which is to be limited to vv. 15–17, 27–9 (note here the concluding *Oracle of
Yahweh of hosts*). Indeed in v. 15 we read *Thus said Yahweh to me.* In view of
the relationship of content between xxv, 15–17, 27–9, and the foreign nation
oracles, a later writer thought that the collection should be placed here, before
v. 15. This position it has kept in 𝔊. In 𝔐 at any rate the conclusion of v. 13,
which is similar to xlvi, 1—*what Jeremiah prophesied concerning all nations*—
shows that here too the foreign nation oracles originally followed. Later in the
text tradition attested by 𝔐 they were moved from this position and placed
after xlv, but with vv. 15–38 left where they were. The reason for this move
cannot be established with certainty; we can at most make a guess. Perhaps it
was desired that the book should not close with threats against the Judaean
remnant, as in xliv. Perhaps—and this is the more probable—the threat spoken
against Pharaoh in xliv, 30, attracted to itself the fuller threat against Egypt in
xlvi, and hence, since xlvi was part of the collection, drew with it xlvi–li, and so
resulted in the collection being made to follow xliv—disregarding xlv which
was felt to be merely an appendix to xliv or perhaps did not at that time yet
stand in that position (p. 354). However this may be, there can be no doubt
that 𝔊 has the collection of foreign nation oracles in its original position, or
in an older position, and that in the text-tradition lying behind 𝔐 too it once
stood here.

10. *The historical appendix, lii.* We have already indicated that lii which now
follows on li, 64b, *Thus far are the words of Jeremiah*, is an historical appendix,
which by and large coincides with II Kings xxiv, 18–xxv, 30. It was no doubt
taken from there and placed here, in the same way that II Kings xviii, 13–xx, 19,
was repeated at the end of the book of Isaiah when it finished at xxxv. In

[48] Ringgren, 'Vredens Kalk' SEA 17 (1952), pp. 19–30.

this, the section which deals with Gedaliah (II Kings xxv, 22–6) has been omitted because it was in its turn an extract from Jer. xxxix–xli, and Jer. lii, 28–30, has been added from an unknown source, a valuable note concerning the Judaeans exiled by the Babylonians in the years 598—or rather 597 since *in the seventh year of Nebuchnedrezzar* (v. 28) is probably to be replaced by *in the eighth year of Nebuchadrezzar*—587 and 582. But whereas the repetition of the passage in the book of Isaiah is readily intelligible, namely from the desire to have all the words of Isaiah together (pp. 328–9), the reason for the repetition in the book of Jeremiah is not so obvious, since II Kings xxiv, 18–xxv, 30, not only contains no saying of Jeremiah, but does not even mention him, and is only concerned with Zedekiah, the conquest of Jerusalem, and its consequences and the pardoning of Jehoiachin.[49] Probably the placing of II Kings xxiv, 18–xxv, 30, at the end of the book of Jeremiah was intended to point to the fulfilment of the threats pronounced by Jeremiah against Judah and Jerusalem. But it is also possible that by this means there was to be provided a sort of introduction to the Lamentations of Jeremiah. For the latter, as is shown by their title and by the position after Jeremiah accorded them in 𝔊 (p. 571), were ascribed to Jeremiah (p. 505).

We also appear to have a passage taken from another book in the account of Gedaliah's assassination in xl, 7–xli, 18. It does not mention Jeremiah, and can therefore hardly be ascribed to Baruch or to the compiler of the narratives which we have assigned to Baruch. But since the account is closely bound up with the context, which is a narrative dealing with Jeremiah, it is possible that it was taken up by the compiler of that narrative, in other words by Baruch.

§ 47. EZEKIEL

Literature: (a) Commentaries (i) Series: ATD: Eichrodt (1959–66) BK: Zimmerli (1956 ff.); BOuT: van den Born (1954); Camb. B: Davidson and Streane (1916); Cent. B: Lofthouse (1907); COuT: Aalders, I (1955), II (1957); Echter-B: Ziegler (1948); Harper's B: Bewer (1954); HAT: Bertholet and Galling (1936); Fohrer and Galling (1955); Herder B: Schumpp (1942); HK: Kraetzschmar (1900); HS: Heinisch (1923), HSAT: Rothstein (1922); IB: May, Allen (1956); ICC: Cooke (1936 (1951)); Jerusalem-B: Auvray (²1957); KAT, Herrmann (1924); KeH: Smend (²1880); KHC: Bertholet (1897); KV: Noordtzij I (²1956), II (²1957); Montserrat-B: Augé (1955); SAT: Hans Schmidt (²1923); SBOT: Toy (1904); Soncino-B: Fisch (1950); SZ: Orelli (²1896); TU: Troelstra (1931); WC: Redpath (1907).

(ii) Single Commentaries: Cornill (1886); James Smith (1931); Matthews (1939).

(b) Other Works: Ackroyd, 'Commentaries on Ezekiel' Theology 62 (1959), pp. 97–100; Auvray, 'Le problème historique du Livre d'Ézéchiel' RB 55, (1948) pp. 503–19; 'Remarques sur la langue d'Ézéchiel' BEThL XII (1959), pp. 461–70; Baumgärtel (§ 46); Berry, 'Was Ezekiel in the Exile?' JBL 49 (1930), pp. 83–93; 'The Glory of Yahweh and the Temple' JBL 56 (1937), pp. 115–17; 'The Composition of the Book of Ezekiel' JBL 58 (1939), pp. 163–75; Bewer, 'Textual and Exegetical Notes on the Book of Ezekiel' JBL 72 (1953), pp. 158–68; van den Born, 'De historische situatie van Ezechiels Prophetie' EThL

---

[49] On this, in relation to the adding of Jer. lii, cf. Baltzer, 'Das Ende des Staates Juda und die Messias-Frage' *Festschr. von Rad* (1961), pp. 33–43 on Jer. xxxix, II Kings xxiv–xxv, II Chron. xxxvi.

23 (1947), pp. 159–72; 'Ezechiël—Pseudo-Epigraaf?' StC 28 (1953), pp. 94–104; Bowman, 'Ezekiel and the Zadokite Priesthood' Transact. Glasgow Or. Soc. 16 (1957), pp. 1–14; Broome, 'Ezekiel's Abnormal Personality' JBL 65 (1946), pp. 277–92; Browne, *Ezekiel and Alexander* (1952); Cassuto, 'L'ordinamento del libro di Ezechiele' *Miscell. Mercati*, I (1946), pp. 40–51; Cooke, 'Some Considerations on the Text and Teaching of Ezekiel xl–xlviii' ZAW 42 (1924), pp. 105–15; Dahl, 'Crisis in Ezekiel Research' *Quantulacumque . . . Kirsopp Lake* (1937), pp. 265–84; Delorme, 'Conversion et pardon selon le prophète Ézéchiel' *Mémorial Chaine* (1950), pp. 115–44; Driver, 'Ezekiel: Linguistic and Textual Problems' Bibl 35 (1954), pp. 145–59, 299–312; Dürr, *Die Stellung des Propheten Ezechiel in der israelitisch-jüdischen Apokalyptik* (1923); Eichrodt, *Krisis der Gemeinschaft in Israel* (1953); Elliger (p. 72, n. 2); Ellison, *Ezekiel: The Man and his Message* (1956); Fairbairn, *An Exposition of Ezekiel* (1960); Finegan, 'The Chronology of Ezekiel' JBL 69 (1950), pp. 61–6; Fohrer, 'Die Glossen im Buche Ezechiel' ZAW 63 (1951), pp. 33–53; *Die Hauptprobleme des Buches Ezechiel* (BZAW 72, 1952); 'Das Symptomatische der Ezechielforschung' ThLZ 83 (1958), cols. 241–50; Freedman, 'The Book of Ezekiel' Interpr. 8 (1954), pp. 446–71; Gordis, 'The Book of Ezekiel in Contemporary Criticism', JewRev 4 (1946) pp. 57–77; Greenberg, 'On Ezekiel's Dumbness' JBL 77 (1958), pp. 101–5; Gruenthaner, 'Recent Theories about Ezekiel' CBQ 7 (1945), pp. 438–46; Battersby Harford, *Studies in the Book of Ezekiel* (1935); Herntrich, *Ezechielprobleme* (BZAW 61, 1932); Herrmann, *Ezechielstudien* (BWAT 2, 1908); Hölscher, *Hesekiel. Der Dichter und das Buch* (BZAW 39, 1924); Howie, *The Date and Composition of Ezekiel* (1950); Irwin, *The Problem of Ezekiel* (1943); 'Ezekiel Research since 1943' VT 3 (1953), pp. 54–66; Jahn, *Das Buch Ezechiel auf Grund der Septuaginta hergestellt* (1905); Kessler, *Die innere Einheitlichkeit des Buches Ezechiel* (Berichte d. theol. Sem. d. Brüdergemeinde, H.11, 1926); Kittel, *Geschichte des Volkes Israel*, III, 1 (1927), pp. 144–80; Kuhl, *Die literarische Einheit des Buches Ezekiel* (Diss. theol. Tübingen, 1917); 'Zur Geschichte der Hesekiel-Forschung' ThR 5 (1933), pp. 92–118; 'Neuere Hesekielliteratur' ThR 20 (1952), pp. 1–26; 'Der Schauplatz der Wirksamkeit Hesekiels' ThZ 8 (1952), pp. 401–18; 'Zum Stand der Hesekiel-Forschung' ThR 24 (1956/7), pp. 1–53; Margalioth, 'The Laws of the Priests and of the Sacrifices in Ezekiel' [Hebr.] Tarbiz 22 (1950/1), pp. 21–7; Messel, *Ezechielfragen* (SNVAO, 1945); Noth, 'La catastrophe de Jérusalem en l'an 587 avant Jésus-Christ et sa signification pour Israël' RHPhR 33 (1953), pp. 81–102; = 'Die Katastrophe von Jerusalem im Jahre 587 vChr. und ihre Bedeutung für Israel' *Ges. Stud. z. AT* (²1960), pp. 346–71; Oesterley, 'The Book of Ezekiel: A Survey of Recent Literature' ChQR 116 (1933), pp. 187–200; Orlinsky, 'Where did Ezekiel receive the Call to Prophecy?' BASOR 122 (1951), pp. 34–6; Procksch, 'Die Berufungsvision Hesekiels' BZAW 34 (1920), pp. 141–9; von Rabenau, 'Die Entstehung des Buches Ezechiel in formgeschichtlicher Sicht' WZ Halle 5 (1955/6), pp. 659–94; 'Die Form des Rätsels im Buche Hesekiel' WZ Halle 7 (1957/8), pp. 1055–7; 'Das prophetische Zukunftswort im Buch Hesekiel' *Studien zur Theol. der at. Überlieferungen . . . von Rad* (1961), pp. 61–80; Graf Reventlow, 'Die Völker als Jahwes Zeugen bei Ezechiel' ZAW 71 (1959), pp. 33–43; Robinson, *Two Hebrew Prophets: Studies in Hosea and Ezekiel* (1948), pp. 63–125; Rowley, 'The Book of Ezekiel in Modern Study' BJRL 36 (1953/4), pp. 146–90; Martin Schmidt, *Prophet und Tempel* (1948), pp. 109–71; 'Zur Komposition des Buches Hesekiel' ThZ 6 (1950), pp. 81–98; Seinecke, *Geschichte des Volkes Israel* I (1876), p. 138; II (1884), pp. 1–20; Sellin, *Geschichte des israelitisch-jüdischen Volkes* II (1932), pp. 33–52; Spiegel, 'Ezekiel or Pseudo-Ezekiel?' HThR 24 (1931), pp. 245–321; 'Toward Certainty in Ezekiel' JBL 54 (1935), pp. 145–71; Sprank, *Ezechielstudien* (BWANT 40, 1926); Stamm, 'Nils Messel, Ezechielfragen' ThZ 3 (1947), pp. 304–9; Staudigel, 'Die Begriffe Gerechtigkeit und Leben und das Problem der Gerechtigkeit Gottes bei Ezechiel' ThLZ 83 (1958), cols. 723–5; Steinmann, *Le prophète Ézéchiel et les débuts de l'exil* (1953); Thackeray, 'The Greek Translators of Ezekiel' JThSt 4 (1903), pp. 398–411; Torrey, *Pseudo-Ezekiel and the Original Prophecy* (1930); 'Certainly Pseudo-Ezekiel' JBL 53 (1934), pp. 291–320; 'Notes on Ezekiel' JBL 58 (1939), pp. 69–86; Tsevat, 'The Neo-Assyrian and Neo-Babylonian Vassal Oaths and the Prophet Ezekiel' JBL 78 (1959), pp. 199–204; Vogelstein, 'Nebuchadnezzar's Reconquest of Phoenicia and

Palestine and the Oracles of Ezekiel' HUCA 23, II (1950/1), pp. 197–220; Vogt, 'Textumdeutungen im Buch Ezekiel' BEThL XII (1959), pp. 470–94; Weir, 'Aspects of the Book of Ezekiel' VT 2 (1952), pp. 97–112; Zimmerli (p. 72, n. 2); *Erkenntnis Gottes nach dem Buche Ezechiel* (1954); ' "Leben" und "Tod" im Buche des Propheten Ezechiel' ThZ 13 (1957), pp. 494–508; 'Ezechiel' ThLZ 82 (1957), cols. 333–40; 'Israel im Buche Ezechiel' VT 8 (1958), pp. 74–90; 'Le nouvel "exode" dans le message des deux grands prophètes de l'exil' *Hommage à W. Vischer* (1960), pp. 216–27; Zunz, 'Bibelkritisches II, Ezechiel' ZDMG 27 (1873), pp. 676–89.

Cf. also Literature §§ 10, 20, 42, 126.

1. *The Prophet Ezekiel: the date and place of his activity.* The book which bears the name of Ezekiel tells us the following concerning the person, period and place of activity of Ezekiel ben Buzi. He was a priest (i, 2), he had a wife who was taken from him by death shortly before or during the siege of Jerusalem, i.e. before 587 (xxiv, 18). He lived during his prophetic activity at Tel-abib (i, 1; iii, 15)[1] by the great canal (the *river Chebar*),[2] probably not far from Nippur. Here he had been settled with the exiles of 598 (i, 1). He dates his revelations by the years of this exile, namely the exile of Jehoiachin (i, 2).[3] In the fifth year of this, which was perhaps the thirtieth year of his life—for so some scholars would explain the puzzling thirtieth year[4] of i, 1—i.e. in the year 593—he received his call, and the last date in the book is the 27th year,[5] i.e. 571 (xxix, 17). Ezekiel's activity thus extends over somewhat more than two decades. Living in exile and providing those who were sharing this fate with warning, exhortation and consolation in the questions and distresses which moved them (xiv, 1–11; xx; xxxiii, 10–20), he directed his main attention, however, to the fate of the homeland and of his native city of Jerusalem. His message is primarily concerned with these, i.e. threats before the disaster of 587 (cc. i–xxiv), and subsequently his promises (xxxiii–xlviii). Visionary movements from Babylonia to Jerusalem (cc. viii–xi,[6] xl–xlviii) vividly express this intimate concern with the homeland.

2. *Survey of criticism.* The book of Ezekiel has been so often examined in the past 100 years, and such varied and divergent theories have been proposed concerning its composition, the date and place of its origin, that it is necessary

[1] Löwinger, 'Tel Abib–Til Abūbi (Ezek. iii, 15)' *Ét. Or. Hirschler* (1950), pp. 62–72.
[2] Vogt, 'Der Nehar Kebar: Ez. i' Bibl 39 (1958), pp. 211–16.
[3] Albright, 'The Seal of Eliakim and the Latest Preëxilic History of Judah, with some Observations on Ezekiel' JBL 51 (1932), pp. 77–106; *The Excavation of Tell Beit Mirsim* III (AASOR 21/22, 1943), p. 66, n. 9, Pl. 29, 9.
[4] Berry, 'The Title of Ezekiel (i, 1–3)' JBL 51 (1932), pp. 54–7; Bewer, 'The Text of Ezek i, 1–3' AJSL 50 (1933/4), pp. 96–101; Budde, 'Zum Eingang des Buches Ezechiel' JBL 50 (1931), pp. 20–41; Troelstra, 'De aanhef van Ezechiël' NThSt 16 (1933), pp. 5–16; Tur-Sinai, 'The Double Dating of Ezekiel i, 1' [Hebr.] BIES 23 (1959), pp. 5–7; Whitley, 'The "thirtieth" Year in Ezekiel i, 1' VT 9 (1959), pp. 326–30.
[5] Albright, 'The Assyro-Tyrian Synchronism and the Chronology of Tyre' AIPhHOS 13 (1955), pp. 1–9; Eissfeldt, 'Das Datum der Belagerung von Tyrus durch Nebukadnezar' FuF 9 (1933), pp. 421–2 = *Ras Schamra und Sanchunjaton* (1939), pp. 4–8 = *Kl.Schr.* II (1962), pp. 1–3.
[6] Gaster, 'Ezekiel and the Mysteries' JBL 60 (1941), pp. 289–310; Torczyner, '*Semel ha-qin'ah ha-maqneh*' JBL 65 (1946), pp. 293–302; Virolleaud, 'Contribution à l'étude du vocabulaire de Ras Shamra' GLECS III (1937/40), pp. 73–4, see p. 73; 'On peut se demander si, dans Ezéchiel viii, 3, il ne convient pas de lire *semel ha-'eqn'e* 'idole de lapis', au lieu de *semel haq-qine'ah* 'idole de la jalousie'. Lit. § 126.

to give at least a partial survey of the work done on the book during this period.

At first, the book was regarded as a work compiled by the prophet Ezekiel who had been deported to Babylon in 598, and composed according to a unified plan in the year mentioned in xl, 1, namely 573. Smend in particular (1880) praised the well-ordered and in some measure quite systematic arrangement of the book. He even considered 'that no passage could be removed without endangering the whole structure'.[7] This recognition of the unity of the book was admittedly only possible with the loss of its truth and closeness to reality. The dates were declared to be invented and the prophecies to be *vaticinia ex eventu*. Bertholet (1897), building upon the work of Cornill (1886), then modified Smend's view in that he assumed that Ezekiel at the time when he undertook the compilation of the book twenty-five years after his exile, i.e. in 573, made use of earlier notes and to some extent left these unaltered. But Bertholet held firmly to the view that it was Ezekiel himself who had compiled the book as we have it. Admittedly he imposed a double limitation on this. On the one hand, the text of the book of Ezekiel is in an extremely bad state and must first be corrected in part with the assistance of $\mathfrak{G}$.[8] On the other hand, it cannot be denied that there are passages in the book which stand in very unsuitable positions and can only have been put there secondarily, whether this was done by Ezekiel himself, as in the case of xxxiii, 23–33, or whether we are dealing with later glosses and amplifications, as in the case of xxiv, 22–3, and xxvii, 9b–25a.

Kraetzschmar (1900), however, was very much more aware of the unevenness to be found everywhere in the book—repetitions, dislocations, contradictions and so forth—and he put forward the view that, considering above all the many actual or merely possible doublets (i, 1–3, 13–14; iii, 4–9; iv, 9–17; vii, 1–9,[9] etc.), the book represents the combining of two parallel recensions. Side by side with the material in the form of a first-person account, which forms by far the largest part, there are two passages in which Ezekiel is referred to in the third person (i, 2–3, and xxiv, 24). Kraetzschmar therefore assumed the existence of a first person and a third person recension, of which the latter was probably an extract from the former. A redactor would then have combined these two recensions. This rather artificial theory, which certainly cannot be maintained in its affirming of a third-person recension, was to this extent later modified by Budde* (1906) when he assumed that the book compiled by Ezekiel himself underwent several editions differing among themselves, and that these were later worked together with the aim of producing a unified and standard text-form.

With Kraetzschmar and Budde the idea of a unified book compiled by the prophet himself is at least still in the background. But with Herrmann (1908 and

---

[7] p. XXI.

[8] Danielsmeyer, *Neue Untersuchungen zur Ezechiel-Septuaginta* (Diss. theol. Münster, 1936); Ziegler, 'Die Bedeutung des Chester Beatty-Scheide Papyrus 967 für die Textüberlieferung der Ezechiel-Septuaginta' ZAW 61 (1945/8), pp. 76–94; 'Zur Textgestaltung der Ezechiel-Septuaginta' Bibl 34 (1953), pp. 435–55. Cf. p. 703, n. 12.

[9] Goettsberger, 'Ez. vii, 1–16, textkritisch und exegetisch undersucht' BZ 22 (1934), pp. 195–223.

1924) any belief in such a book was completely denied and the book was explained as being rather a compilation which had come into being gradually, made up of a whole series of individual groups and isolated passages. This, it was supposed, had been put together by Ezekiel in the course of his long activity, and received some few further expansions by later hands. Ezekiel here completely disappears as the creator of a planned and ordered book, but the genuineness of the individual prophecies, poems and speeches is all the more firmly emphasised, and it would almost appear that the price paid for holding firmly to the content is the loss of the formal arrangement.

In contrast to this we now meet with the views of Hölscher (1924). Some older scholars, such as Zunz (1873) and Seinecke (1884) had declared that the book was a pseudepigraphon from the second half of the fifth century, or even from the Maccabaean period. Hölscher declared that a very substantial part of the book, more than half, was not genuine, and he ascribed this to a redactor working in the fifth century. He holds to the assumption that Ezekiel, deported to Babylon in 598, was the author of a series of passages preserved in the book. But only parts of the book are regarded as going back to him, namely i, 4, 28; iii, 1, 8–10, 2, 11–12, 14–16, 24b; iv, 1–2, 9–11; v, 1–2; viii, 1–3, 5–7, 9–17;[10] ix, 1–7, 11; xi, 24–5; xv, 2–5; xvi, 3–12, 15, 24–5; xvii, 1, 4–9; xix, 2–9; xxi, 14, 16, 19–21; xxiii, 2–6, 11, 14–17, 19–20, 22–5, 27; xxiv, 3–5, 16–17; xxvii, 3–9a, 25b–36; xxviii, 12–19; xxix, 3–5; xxx, 21; xxxi, 3–4, 6–8; xxxii, 2, 18–19, 22–4, 26–7. This covers the call vision (i–iii*);[11] the symbolic actions on Jerusalem's fate (iv–v*); the removal to Jerusalem (viii–ix*+xi, 24–5); eight poems on Judah and Jerusalem—the poem on the wood of the vine (xv*), the two harlot poems (xvi* and xxiii*), the eagle poem (xvii*), the lioness poem (xix*), the sword poem (xxi*), the cauldron poem (xxiv, 3–5), and the lament for the dead (xxiv, 16–17); a poem on Tyre (xxvii*); and five on Egypt (xxviii–xxxii*). Except for the call vision, the symbolic actions and the removal to Jerusalem, these are all poetic passages. Some of them were dated from the first. For the dates in i, 1–2; iii, 16; viii, 1; xxvi, 1; xxix, 1; xxx, 20; xxxi, 1; xxxii, 1; xxxii, 17, are in part genuine, unlike the others in xx, 1; xxiv, 1; xxix, 17; xxxiii, 21;[12] xl, 1. The whole of the remaining material, however, all of it prose, comes from the redactor in the fifth century, in so far as it is not even later. It is this redactor who must be considered as the real creator of the book as we have it. He deliberately writes using Ezekiel's name, and includes his own productions among the passages which really come from Ezekiel because he wishes to show that just as the earlier threats against Jerusalem, Tyre and Egypt found their fulfilment, so too his threats against the evil practices and conditions of his time, and also his prophecies of salvation, will be fulfilled. Here there is clearly discernible a prejudice against the Jews who remained in Palestine and a preference for those who were taken into exile, or for all those

[10] Saggs, 'The Branch to the Nose' JThSt 11 (1960), pp. 318–29. Lit. § 126.

[11] Dornseiff, 'Exkurs über Hesekiels Kerube' ZNW 36 (1937), pp. 234–8; Driver, 'Ezekiel's Inaugural Vision' VT 1 (1951), pp. 60–2; Irwin, '*Hashmal*' VT 2 (1952), pp. 169–70; Ridderbos, 'De cherubs in Ezechiëls roepings-visioen' GThT 36 (1935), pp. 509–15, 537–44.

[12] Bewer, 'Das Datum in Hes. xxxiii, 21' ZAW 54 (1936), pp. 114 f.

living in the Diaspora. This Judaism of the dispersion is the guarantee of Jewish hope, and its return home is the necessary precondition of salvation.

Thus with Hölscher we find two ideas set out, the one that the book is a pseudepigraphon, and the other that it reveals a bias in favour of exiled Judaism. These are kept within bounds by Hölscher's assumption that there is a genuine core to the book, but with Torrey (1930) they are set out without any such restraint at all. He sees in the basic material of the book a pseudepigraphon which came into being in about 230 B.C. This was occasioned by the description given in II Kings xxi, 1–17, of Manasseh, and so purports to be a prophecy originating in his thirtieth year (i, 1 = 30th year of Manasseh), i.e. 666 B.C., of these abominations together with the proclaiming of the punishment threatened because of them. Torrey assumes that soon after 230 a revision was undertaken which ascribed this book, up till then regarded as the work of a Jerusalem prophet, to the prophet Ezekiel living in exile, and therefore added the dates which reckon from the exile of Jehoiachin (i, 2, etc.) to those which reckon from the period of Manasseh (i, 1). The reviser was in this guided by the quite unhistorical theory of the books of Chronicles (p. 556) that the restoration of the post-exilic cult-community was not to be attributed to the Jews who remained in the land but to those who returned home from the exile.

The view which Torrey represents, that the book is a quite late pseudepigraphical construction, did not at first have any effect. But the distinguishing of passages which have features strongly suggesting a Palestinian background but no trace of exilic origin, and others which clearly derive from the exile or purport to do so, was taken up at about the same time by James Smith (1931) and by Herntrich (1932). In this discussion, some part was played by a point which had been noted already two centuries earlier, and applied to the illumination of the Ezekiel problem,[13] although by reason of its ambiguity it was not really appropriate to use it. This is the reference in Josephus (Ant. X, 5, 1, § 79) who suggests that two books concerning the destruction of Jerusalem were written by Ezekiel and handed down. Smith searches for these two books of Ezekiel in the book as we have it. In one of them, to which belong all the passages which have a Palestinian stamp—and this means by far the larger part—there is reflected the Palestinian activity of the prophet. In the other (xx, 32–44; xxxvi, 16–32;[14] xxxvii, 11–14), we have the deposit of his earlier activity in exile. He puts back Ezekiel's appearance by a century and more from the normal dating, and places him in the northern kingdom.[15] The dates of the captivity thus refer at least in part to the first deportation of Israel, namely to the year 734 (II Kings xv, 29), and the 30th year of i, 1, indicates the 30th year after the downfall of Samaria, namely 691. Herntrich, on the other hand, adheres to the normal view as to date and place of activity, and sees in the basic material of i–xxxix the work of a prophet active in Jerusalem in the last years of its existence. An exilic redactor who wished to present the Jews deported in 598 as

[13] Rowley, BJRL 36 (1953/4), p. 155, n. 1.
[14] Filson, 'The Omission of Ezek. xii, 26–8, and xxxvi, 23b–38, in Codex 967' JBL 62 (1943), pp. 27–32. Cf. below p. 703, n. 12.
[15] Ezekiel was designated as a pre-exilic prophet belonging to one of the northern tribes by Gaster, The Samaritans (1925), p. 15.

the spiritually leading stratum, then worked over this genuine material, probably about 573 (xl, 1), and for this reason added mainly the datings referring to the exile. Among other things he was responsible for the transformation of viii–xi into a story telling of the visionary removal of the prophet from the exile to Jerusalem. xl–xlviii also goes back to him.

Similar presentations to that of Herntrich have been offered by Battersby Harford (1935), and Berry (1939). Matthews (1939) and Irwin (1943), who have much in common with Hölscher, particularly that they limit the genuine material of the book as he does to the 'poetic' passages which form only a fragment of it, likewise belong with Herntrich at least in that they consider that Ezekiel was active in Jerusalem before 587, and that his words were later worked over from the exilic standpoint by a redactor living in the Babylonian exile. Irwin reckons with an actual deportation of the prophet into the exile. Bertholet (1936), on the other hand, assumes two phases in Ezekiel's activity, of which the first, covering the years 593–586 took place in Jerusalem and is introduced by the vision of the scroll in ii, 3–iii, 9, whereas the second took place in exile in 585, and begins with the throne-chariot vision of i, 4–ii, 2. Likewise, though with many differences in detail, we find that Spiegel (1931), Auvray (1943, 1947), van den Born (1947), Robinson (1948), Kuhl (1952), and Steinmann (1953) all reckon with activity by Ezekiel both in Jerusalem and in the exile, and consider that at any rate the main material of the book represents the deposit of this double activity.

Messel (1945) comes near to Torrey's view of the book as a pseudepigraphon composed centuries after the dates mentioned in the book itself. According to Messel, Ezekiel appeared towards the end of the fifth century among the *golah* returned from exile and then compiled the basic material of i–xxiv and xl–xlviii. Roughly half a century later a redactor re-edited this basic material, added a great variety of additional matter, and projected Ezekiel's activity into the exile. Torrey's view is even more nearly approached by Browne (1952) and van den Born (1954). The former regards the datings in the book as veiled allusions to events of the fourth century, namely a deportation of rebellious Palestinian Jews in 344 to the Caspian Sea, to which late sources[16] give obscure references. The latter considers our book to be the autobiography of an author who belonged to the time of Ezra and Nehemiah and who in theology stood near to the Priestly Code (P), and that it represents a work dependent upon actual or supposed post-exilic biblical texts, worked over in the time of Alexander the Great, the time to which xxxviii–xxxix are said to refer. In contrast to the many works just mentioned which depart very far from the information given in the book of Ezekiel itself concerning the place and date of the prophet's activity, as well as concerning the way in which the book came into being, other scholars adhere to the substantial correctness of this information, and thus regard the book as the deposit of the preaching of Ezekiel, active as a prophet in the exile from 593 onwards. Such are Cooke (1936), Martin Schmidt (1948), Finegan (1950), Howie (1950), Orlinsky (1951), Mullo Weir (1952), Fohrer

---

[16] Eusebius, *Chronicle*, ed. Schoene (1875), II, pp. 112 f., ed. Helm ([2]1956), pp. 121, 363. Cf. Schürer, GJV III ([4]1909), pp. 7 f. (E.T. II, 2 (1898), p. 223).

(1952, 1955), Zimmerli (1956 ff.), and Eichrodt (1959 ff.). It goes without saying that in detail the views of the scholars named diverge in many ways from one another.

3. *The composition of the book.* It is impossible here to discuss the many and very varied solutions of the problem of Ezekiel which have just been mentioned—and only a selection has been given despite the number of names here noted. So far as the period and place of the prophet's activity is concerned, we must be satisfied with the remark that there are no really decisive arguments against the reliability of the tradition which finds expression in many passages in the book (pp. 374–80), particularly with regard to the dating. These show Ezekiel as having been called to be a prophet in the exile in 593 and as having been active there as such until 573 or perhaps somewhat longer. All the hypotheses which have been proposed in place of this labour under much greater difficulties than does the traditional view. But the question of the composition of the book, and in particular of the extent and nature of Ezekiel's share in this, demands a somewhat more detailed discussion. However, we may in this, in view of what has just been said about the reliability of the tradition, ignore those solutions of the Ezekiel problem which treat the book as a pseudepigraphon from later times. The analyses which are left may, in spite of their great differences, be divided into two groups. One group regards the prophet himself as the compiler, if not of the present book, yet of its basic material. The other group traces to the prophet only single sayings or small collections of such sayings, but regards the arrangement of these in a book as having been undertaken by one or more later hands, in whom we may most probably see pupils or disciples of Ezekiel.

The survey given above of the course of Ezekiel study during the last hundred years has shown that the prevailing view at the beginning of this period, that the book was compiled by the prophet himself, has been more and more set aside by the second view. This is that the book is rather a putting together of the many words and smaller collections left behind by the prophet, undertaken only at a later date. It is true that Herrmann assumed that Ezekiel himself undertook this compilation. But in his view the result of this compilation was simply a rather unsystematic setting of pieces one beside the other, or simply an utter confusion, and thus his view does not differ substantially from that which is put forward by others—as for example recently by Fohrer—which denies the prophet any share in the formation of his book as such, and regards this formation as having been undertaken exclusively by later hands, ascribing to Ezekiel only single sayings or at most small collections of sayings. As the first phase of the making of the book out of the individual pieces left by Ezekiel, Fohrer postulates the placing together of sections with related content—containing accounts of ecstatic experiences or symbolic actions or perhaps having the same key words. In his view, the second phase is marked by the arrangement in chronological sequence of the groups which have thus come into existence and been provided with dates. This produced the following eight collections as the basic core of the book: i, 1–iii, 15; iii, 16a+iv, 1–v, 17; viii, 1–xi, 13; xv, 1–xvi, 43+xx, 1–32; xxiv, 1–24; xl, 1–xlviii, 35; xxvi, 1–xxviii, 19; xxix, 1–xxxii,

32. He considers that the remaining collections and single sections were inserted in this core following considerations of chronology or content. A more considerable transformation was then effected by the transposing of the threats directed against foreign nations from the end of the book to the middle, namely after the words of judgement concerning Judah and Jerusalem. Various smaller adjustments followed—transpositions, the dovetailing of originally independent sections, the insertion of new passages to some extent stemming from the revisers themselves, the addition of various glosses—before the book received its present form. This he regards as made up of four parts: i–xxiv, threats against Israel (Judah) and Jerusalem; xxv–xxxii, threats against foreign nations, namely Ammon, Moab, Edom, Philistia, Tyre, Sidon and Egypt; xxxiii, Ezekiel's office of watchman, the standard of divine retribution, the threat against those who remain in the land after the fall of Jerusalem; xxxiv–xlviii, prophecies of salvation for the new Israel, from which xl–xlviii stand out as a special unit, concerned with the vision of the new Temple, the new city of Jerusalem and the new land of Palestine.

Now there can be no doubt that the book of Ezekiel came into being as the result of a process which was long drawn out, and that many hands had a share in it. The earlier assumption that Ezekiel himself compiled the book just as we have it, or at least in its determinative form, has rightly long been abandoned. On the other hand, however, the book clearly contains a framework of passages deriving from the prophet himself, namely those which are couched in first-person form. This reveals itself as a planned entity not only by the datings of its individual sections, in general in correct chronological order—these will be more closely examined in a moment—but also by the fact that the call vision of i, 1–iii, 15, the removal vision of viii–xi, the sharp rejection reported in xx of the plan being considered in the circles of the exiles to build a cult-place in their present settlement, and the vision of Yahweh's re-entry into the renewed Jerusalem Temple in xl–xlviii, all present in a sense a continuous development. For according to i, 1–iii, 15, Jerusalem is the place of the throne-chariot of Yahweh, according to viii–xi Yahweh leaves Jerusalem on his throne-chariot and thus delivers city and Temple over to destruction, in xx the erection of a cult-place in another centre is rejected in view of the expectation of the rebuilding of the Jerusalem Temple in the coming age of salvation, and in xl–xlviii the rebuilding of the Jerusalem Temple is proclaimed. The sequence of the dated sections, and among them in particular the arrangement of these four which refer to the fate of the Temple, can only be ascribed to Ezekiel, provided indeed we are seriously reckoning with the existence of a contribution in first-person style by the prophet to the book and are not tracing the relevant passages to, say, the compiler of a late pseudepigraphon. Even Fohrer indirectly admits this. For when he indicates as a relatively early phase in the evolution of the book the chronological arrangement of the smaller collections which contain dates, he thereby recognises that the dates, which in his opinion do actually derive from the prophet himself, have a considerable significance for the formation of the book. It is of no decisive importance whether we think that Ezekiel wrote the dated sections on single loose sheets, or that they were parts of a connected memoir. The point is rather that the dates as such offer a chrono-logical sequence and at any rate in this present an entity, no matter whether this entity appeared as such in Ezekiel's own notes or not. Furthermore, there is all the less ground for doubting the possibility of the compilation of a sequence of dated first-person accounts by Ezekiel himself, in view of the fact that such first-person accounts appear not first in Zechariah, but already in Hosea, Isaiah and Jeremiah (pp. 147–50). We must therefore examine the indications which point to our book of Ezekiel having been based upon small literary forms which may go back to the prophet himself. This must be done just as carefully as is normal in the case of other prophetic books, as for example with Isaiah and Jeremiah, and just as carefully as the endeavour is made to establish the existence of narrative works of medium or smaller compass comprised in the Pentateuch and in the older historical books, having regard for the particularly complex stratification there.

4. *Traces of an earlier arrangement.* When we come to a closer examination of the dates,[17] we must follow the undoubtedly appropriate principle that these always refer only to the passage which follows directly. We thus get the follow-ing series of dated experiences and speeches of the prophet: the call vision on 5:IV:5 (i, 1–iii, 15);[18] the three actions which symbolise Jerusalem's fate on 12:IV:5 (iii, 16a+iv–v, see pp. 375 f. on iii, 16); the removal vision on 5:VI:6 (viii–xi);[19] the rejection of plans for temple building or the like (p. 376) of 10:V:7 (xx); symbolic action and speeches on the day of the beginning of the siege on 10:X:9 (xxiv);[20] prophecy against Tyre's gloating on 1:?[21]:11 (xxvi); prophecy against the Pharaoh on 12:X:10 (xxix, 1–16); promise to Nebuchad-rezzar of the conquest of Egypt on 1:I:27 (xxix, 17–21); prophecy against Egypt on 7:I:11 (xxx, 20–6); prophecy against the Pharaoh on 1:III:11 (xxxi, 1–18); funeral dirge on the Pharaoh 1:XII:12 (xxxii, 1–16); funeral dirge on the Pharaoh on 15:?[21]:12 (xxxii, 17–32); the opening of Ezekiel's mouth on the day that the news of the conquest of Jerusalem arrived on 5:X:12 (xxxiii, 21–2); and the vision of the new Jerusalem, etc., on 10:?[21]:25 (xl–xlviii).

This series of dated sections as we now have it cannot be in its original form. Apart from the interruption of the series of dates by xxix, 17–21, which is natural enough when an appendix is added, we find in fact two other disloca-tions. In the first place, the oracle against Tyre dated 1:?:11 in xxvi stands too

[17] Dussaud, 'Les dates des prophéties d'Ézéchiel' RHR 76 (1917), pp. 145–64.

[18] Baumann, 'Die Hauptvisionen Hesekiels in ihrem zeitlichen und sachlichen Zusam-menhang untersucht' ZAW 67 (1955), pp. 56–67; Dussaud, 'Les visions d'Ézéchiel' RHR 37 (1898), pp. 301–13; Höhne, *Die Thronwagenvision Hesekiels. Echtheit und Herkunft der Vision Hes i, 4–28, und ihrer einzelnen Züge* (Diss. theol. Erlangen [typescript], 1953), cf. ThLZ 80 (1955), cols. 113 f. Lit. § 126.

[19] Balla, 'Ezechiel viii, 1–ix, 11; xi, 24–5' *Bultmann-Festschr.* (1949), pp. 1–11; Horst, 'Exilsgemeinde und Jerusalem in Ez viii–xi' VT 3 (1953), pp. 337–60; Susumu Jozaki, 'A Study of Ezekiel xi, 14–21' Kwansei Gakuin University Annual Studies 6 (1958), pp. 29–41.

[20] Bauer, 'Hes. xxiv, 17' VT 7 (1957), pp. 91–2; Hempel, 'Eine Vermutung zu Hes xxiv, 15 ff.' ZAW 51 (1933), pp. 312 f.; Kelso, 'Ezekiel's Parable of the Corroded Copper Caldron' JBL 64 (1945), pp. 391–3.

[21] The number of the month has been accidentally omitted here.

early, since the one that follows in xxix, 1–16, directed against the Pharaoh falls in the 10th year. In the second place, the last two sayings concerning Egypt are dated on the 1st and 15th days of the 12th month of the 12th year in xxxii, 1 and xxxii, 17. Admittedly the latter has now no number for the month, but since it follows on 1:XII:12 in xxxii, 1, it must also have had the 12th month. But the date which follows in xxxiii, 21, is 5:X:12. The first unevenness may be explained quite simply. It was desired to have all the oracles directed against Egypt together, and so the oracle against Tyre, which originally stood among them, was taken out and put in front, and this was the more necessary since the appendix in xxix, 17–21, presupposes an earlier mention of Tyre. But the second dislocation seems to make necessary the assumption that in i, 1–2, to xl, 1, there are in reality two series of dates. One of these refers to passages which concern Jerusalem and Israel and extend over the period between the 5th day of the 4th month of the 5th year and the 10th day of an undefined month of the 25th year after the deportation of Jehoiachin. The other series refers to oracles against foreign nations and extends from the 1st day of an undefined month of the 11th year to the 5th day of the 12th month, or, if we take into account the appendix in xxvii, 17–21, to the 1st day of the 1st month of the 27th year of exile. This assumption is at least more probable than the other alternative, not in itself quite impossible, that Ezekiel in his autobiographical account deliberately interrupted the sequence of the passages directed to his own people by the insertion of the threats against foreign nations at any rate the majority of which as far as date is concerned do belong here. Further too in favour of the first assumption is the fact that this is another point which shows the close connection between xxiv and xxxiii.

As Rothstein and Sellin appear to have been the first to note, xxxiii, 21–2, must in fact once have followed directly upon xxiv, 26–7. In the latter passage it is announced that a refugee will arrive bringing the news of the fall of Jerusalem and that Ezekiel will at this moment be released from his dumbness, as it was foretold. In the former passage, xxxiii, 21–2, the refugee actually arrives with his message, and Ezekiel's dumbness immediately ceases. Here then, in addition to the two small sections xxxiii, 1–9, and xxxiii, 10–20, which are not original at this point, it is the oracles against foreign nations which separate xxiv, 26–7, and xxxiii, 21–2. This confirms the conclusion just drawn from the date series that the foreign nation oracles were only secondarily placed in their present position; in other words, that the passages which concern Jerusalem and Israel, just like the oracles directed against foreign nations, once stood alone.

If we wish to get a proper picture of the first series, we must make a further rearrangement, also probably first recognised as necessary by Rothstein and Sellin. We must move the sections iii, 16b–21, 22–7; iv, 4–8 (or the basic material of them) to their original position before xxiv, 26, while retaining the half verse iii, 16a, as the dating of the symbolic actions which follow in iv–v. We may then clearly understand the beginning and end of the first half of this series, which covers Ezekiel's preaching up to the fall of Jerusalem. It comprises at the beginning the call and commission, the arrival in Tel-abib (i, 1–iii, 15) and the command to perform certain actions (iii, 16a; iv–v), and at the end the proclamation of dumbness and of the release from it, and the actual release (iii, 16b–27; iv, 4–8; xxiv, 26–7; xxxiii, 21–2). It is further noteworthy that all the passages of this series concerning Jerusalem and Israel are narratives of quite concrete and significant events. They are not, like the undated passages, speeches which are in some measure undefined as to time and place, introduced only with something like: *The word of Yahweh came to me thus: But you, son of man, speak*, and so merely beginning as narratives. On the opening events just noted there follows in viii–xi the removal from the exile to Jerusalem, in xx the narrative of the rejection of the plans for the building of an exilic temple or the like, and the conclusion, also just noted, of this first half of Ezekiel's activity. The second half is filled out with the vision of the new Jerusalem in xl–xlviii which begins as a narrative.

As far as xx is concerned, this has repeatedly had its genuineness contested. together with its date, for example by Hölscher. We may therefore point especially to the fact that here too we have the narrative of a significant event, namely the rejection of a temple planned by the exiles,[22] or at least of a cultic measure under consideration by them, which Ezekiel judges to endanger the still potentially valid claim to exclusiveness of the Jerusalem Temple. This was naturally an event which the prophet had to preserve in his autobiographical account. But from this a new light is then also shed on chapters xl–xlviii, equally frequently contested. The essentially negative content of xx demands a positive counterpart, and this, already anticipated in xx, 40–44, actually follows in xl–xlviii. We may thus no more doubt the genuineness of the basic material of xl–xlviii[23] than that of the core of xx.

This result is confirmed by an examination of the other material. Outside the passages provided with dates, no narratives appear in the book of Ezekiel concerning significant concrete events. Elsewhere, as has already been hinted, the narrative is only a form, whereas in reality we are dealing with speeches of a fairly general kind, or—as in the case of xiv, 1–11[24]—the narrative is simply the starting-point for such speeches. The sole exception is actually xii, 1–20, an action by Ezekiel symbolising the deportation of people and prince. We can hardly doubt the genuineness of the basic material here, though admittedly it has certainly been expanded secondarily. Thus, if this is not to be taken as an objection to the point just made, we should either have to assume that the

[22] Cf. Menes (p. 252, n. 18), pp. 271–3.

[23] Dean, 'The Date of Ezekiel xl–xliii' AJSL 43 (1926/7), pp. 231–3; Elliger, 'Die großen Tempelsakristeien im Verfassungsentwurf des Ezechiel (xlii, 1 ff.)' Alt-Festschr. (1953), pp. 79–103; Farmer, 'The Geography of Ezekiel's River of Life' BA 19 (1956), pp. 17–22; Gese, *Der Verfassungsentwurf des Ezechiel (Kap. xl–xlviii). Traditionsgeschichtlich untersucht* (1957); Howie, 'The East Gate of Ezekiel's Temple Enclosure and the Solomonic Gateway of Megiddo' BASOR 117 (1950), pp. 13–19; Jeremias, 'Hesekieltempel und Serubbabeltempel' ZAW 52 (1934), pp. 109–112; Lods, 'Les cuisines du temple de Jérusalem' RHR 127 (1944), pp. 30–54; Procksch, 'Fürst und Priester bei Hesekiel' ZAW 58 (1940/1), pp. 99–133; Vincent, 'L'autel des holocaustes et le caractère du temple d'Ézéchiel' Anal. Bolland, 67 (1949), pp. 6–20, 1 Pl.; *Jérusalem de l'AT* II–III (1956), pp. 471–95. Literature, p. 379, n. 43; § 126.

[24] Zimmerli, 'Die Eigenart der prophetischen Rede des Ezechiel. Ein Beitrag zum Problem an Hand von Ez. xiv, 1–11' ZAW 66 (1955), pp. 1–26. Lit. § 126.

dating has accidentally fallen out at the beginning of the passage[25]—and in favour of this assumption is the fact that there is otherwise no date between viii, 1 and xx, 1, and that this forms the largest complex left without any dating —or that the passage originally stood after iv–v. It is in fact very closely related to the three symbolic actions described there, and we may easily find a reason for its misplacement. In viii–xi it is related that Yahweh leaves his city and Temple.[26] It may have seemed inappropriate to a later editor that the people and prince had first left the city, and he removed this objection by transposing xii. However that may be it is nevertheless clear that the dated Jerusalem-Israel passages are reports of actual concrete events, whose preservation the prophet must have regarded as having special value, and in this respect the autobiographical account by Ezekiel is similar to those of Isaiah and Jeremiah, as also to that of Zechariah.

The oracles against foreign nations in xxv–xxxii, which likewise begin as autobiography, also form a self-contained series like the autobiographical accounts and sayings concerning events which affected Jerusalem and Israel. Since here too the principle holds that the dates only refer to the passages which immediately follow upon them, we have this series: a threat against Tyre from 1:?:11 (xxvi, 1–21); a threat against the Pharaoh from 12:X:10 (xxix, 1–16); a supplementary threat against Egypt from 1:I:27 (xxix, 17–21); a threat against the Pharaoh from 7:I:11 (xxx, 20–6); a prophetic funeral dirge on the Pharaoh from 1:III:11 (xxxi); a prophetic funeral dirge on the Pharaoh from 1:XII:12 (xxxii, 1–16),[27] and a prophetic funeral dirge on Egypt from 15:?:12 (xxxii, 17–32). Unlike the series referring to Jerusalem-Israel, there are here no accounts of events but only prophecies and dirges. But these passages, originally arranged in a regular chronological order (p. 374), including the appendix in xxix, 17–21, are, with their dates, all clearly concerned with a quite definite, significant political situation, and in this respect this series of foreign nation oracles also represents the preservation of important events in the form of a diary or memorial.

This series of foreign nation oracles provided with dates is now interrupted by others which are not dated, and which also differ in content from the first series in that they are couched in much more general terms than the others, and do not like these refer to a definite political situation. There stand out among them the four oracles in xxv against the Ammonites, Moabites, Edomites and Philistines, because of their noticeable brevity and colourlessness. As far as these are concerned, we must seriously reckon with the possibility that they do not come from Ezekiel, but, similarly to what we have observed in Isa. xiii–xxiii and Jer. xlvi–li (p. 362), were secondarily added to round off the prophecies of Ezekiel against Tyre and Egypt and make them into a corpus of foreign nation oracles comprising all the neighbouring lands. The chapter

[25] The commentaries of Cooke (p. 398), Hermann (p. 232), and Kraetzschmar (p. 251) assume that the date has fallen out in xxxvii, 1, and this possibility must certainly be seriously considered.

[26] May, 'The Departure of the Glory of Yahweh' JBL 56 (1937), pp. 309–21.

[27] Eissfeldt, 'Schwerterschlagene bei Hesekiel' StOTPr (1950), pp. 73–81; Lods, 'La "mort des incirconcis"' CRAI (1943), pp. 271–83.

has been provided moreover with a formula built on the pattern of the auto-biographical account: *The word of Yahweh came to me thus: Son of Man, direct your face 'against'*[28] *the Ammonites* (xxv, 1–2). It is possible that the prophecy against Sidon in xxviii, 20–6, and one of the oracles directed against Egypt, namely xxx, 1–19, are not genuine. Neither is dated, and they also have fewer concrete features than the others. The remaining undated passages, however, are undoubtedly genuine, apart from secondary elaborations which they too, like the dated oracles, have received as for example in xxvii, 9b (11)–25a (25).[29] These are the prophetic funeral dirge on the commercial city of Tyre, pictured as a splendid merchant ship[30] in xxvii, 1–9a, 25b–36; the threat against the prince of Tyre who thinks himself a god in xxviii, 1–10, and the prophetic funeral dirge on the king of Tyre overthrown from the mountain of the gods in xxviii, 11–19.[31] The only question is how these passages have come into their present position—whether they owe it to Ezekiel or to a later hand. No definite decision can be made. Nevertheless we shall hardly wish without strong reason to admit that Ezekiel himself later watered down his own coherent arrangement, in view of the fact that he evidently wished, by putting together the dated sayings somewhat like a diary and by adding to them the appendix in xxix, 17–21, to preserve the memory of the most important events. We must there-fore probably ascribe to a later hand the insertion of the undated passages. We nevertheless have here in all probability two different collections of foreign nation oracles, the series arranged like a diary and the looser collection of similar passages.

If we now turn again to the part of the book which is concerned with Jeru-salem and Israel, namely i–xxiv and xxxiii–xlviii, we may readily adopt the same explanation for what is now here to be observed, namely that the diary-like series of dated narratives and speeches is interrupted by undated passages. Here too it is more probable that these passages were inserted secondarily by someone else rather than by Ezekiel himself. The passages in question are as follows (omitting those already mentioned (pp. 375–7) and a few smaller sections): vi–vii, the proclamation of a fearful judgement on the mountains of Israel as punishment for idolatrous cult practice; xii, 21–xiv, 11,[32] the proclama-tion of the speedy fulfilment of the prophetic threat of judgement, and new threats against false prophets and prophetesses; xiv, 12–23, God's individual retribution and the reason for the special treatment of Jerusalem;[33] xv, the

---

[28] Reading עַל, following ⑥, rather than *to* with 𝔐.

[29] But see p. 96, n. 7; § 126.

[30] Garrett, 'A Geographical Commentary on Ezekiel xxvii' Geography 24 (1939), pp. 240–9; S. Smith, 'The Ship Tyre' PEQ 85 (1953), pp. 97–110. Lit. § 126.

[31] Barnes, 'Ezekiel's Denunciation of Tyre' JThSt 35 (1934), pp. 50–4; Dus, 'Melek, Ṣōr Melqart?' ArOr 26 (1958), pp. 179–85; Mackay, 'The King of Tyre' ChQR 234 (1934), pp. 239–58; Widengren, *The Ascension of the Apostle and the Heavenly Book* (1950), pp. 94–7.

[32] Brownlee, 'Exorcising the Souls from Ezekiel xiii, 17–23' JBL 69 (1950), pp. 367–73. Lit. § 126.

[33] Barton, 'Danel, a Pre-Israelite Hero of Galilee' JBL 60 (1941), pp. 213–25; Daiches, 'Ezekiel and the Babylonian Account of the Deluge. Notes on Ez. xiv, 12–20' JQR 17 (1905/6), pp. 441–55; Joüon, 'Trois noms de personnages bibliques à la lumière des textes d'Ugarit' Bibl 19 (1938), pp. 280–5; Lewy, 'Nāḫ et Rušpān' *Mél. Syriens Dussaud*, I

allegory of the vine-wood;[34] xvi, Jerusalem the harlot;[35] xvii, the allegory of the eagle;[36] xviii, God's individual retribution; xix, the allegory of the lioness; xxi, the proclamation of a fire breaking out in the south (vv. 1–5), and threats with the sword of God (vv. 6–37);[37] xxii, diatribes and threats against sinful Jerusalem; xxiii, the harlots, Samaria and Jerusalem; xxxiii, 23–9, threat against the people of Jerusalem; xxxiii, 30–3, threat against the exiles; xxxiv, diatribe and threat against the false shepherds of the people, and the promise of a true shepherd,[38] David; xxxv + xxxvi, 1–15,[39] threat against Edom, and promise for the mountains of Israel; xxxvi, 16–38, promise of the purification and sanctification of Israel; xxxvii, 1–14, the vision of the bones of the dead, symbolic of Israel's resurrection;[40] xxxvii, 15–28, promise of the reuniting of Israel and Judah under David;[41] xxxviii–xxxix, the attack by Gog of Magog on Jerusalem, and his destruction;[42] finally a whole series of passages in xl–xlviii which in form or content contradict the purpose set out in the introduction in xl, 1–4, as for example xliii, 13–27,[43] a description of the altar of burnt-offering and of the rites which are to be observed at its dedication. This immediately stands out from its context by the fact that Ezekiel is not led to the altar by the angel; the passage begins directly in descriptive style: *And these are the measurements of the altar.*

The position with the foreign nation oracles was that some of the undated passages were certainly genuine, whereas others were probably not genuine. The idea therefore naturally suggests itself that the undated passages in the Jerusalem-Israel collection are to be assessed similarly. For it is clear, in view of the discoveries made in xxv–xxxii (p. 377), that we cannot adopt Kittel's

(1939), pp. 273–5; Noth, 'Noah, Daniel und Hiob in Ezechiel xiv' VT 1 (1951), pp. 251–60; Spiegel, 'Noah, Daniel and Job, touching on Canaanite Relics in the Legends of the Jews' *L. Ginzberg Jub. Vol.*, Engl. Sect. (1945), pp. 305–55. Cf. p. 523, nn. 38–9.

[34] Baumann, 'Die Weinranke im Walde. Hes. xv, 1–8' ThLZ 80 (1955), cols. 119 f.

[35] Bloch, 'Ézéchiel xvi; exemple parfait du procédé midrashique dans la Bible' CahSi 9 (1955), pp. 193–223; Eissfeldt, 'Ezechiel als Zeuge für Sanheribs Eingriff in Palästina' PJB 27 (1931), pp. 58–66; 'Hesekiel Kap. xvi als Geschichtsquelle' JPOS 16 (1936), pp. 286–92. Lit. § 126.

[36] Alt, 'Psammetich II. in Palästina und in Elephantine' ZAW 30 (1910), pp. 288–97; Foster, 'A Note on Ezekiel xvii, 1–10, and 22–24' VT 8 (1958), pp. 374–9; Greenberg, 'Ezekiel xvii and the Policy of Psammetichus II' JBL 76 (1957), pp. 304–9; Louise Pettibone Smith, 'The Eagle(s) of Ezekiel xvii' JBL 58 (1939), pp. 43–50.

[37] Moran, 'Gen xlix, 10 and its Use in Ez xxi, 32' Bibl 39 (1958), pp. 405–25.

[38] Brownlee, 'Ezekiel's Poetic Indictment of the Shepherds' HThR 51 (1958), pp. 191–203. Lit. § 126.

[39] Morgenstern, 'The Rest of the Nations' JSSt 2 (1957), pp. 225–31.

[40] Riesenfeld, *The Resurrection in Ezekiel xxxvii and in the Dura-Europos Paintings* (1948).

[41] Barnes, 'Two Trees become One: Ezek. xxxvii, 16–17' JThSt 39 (1938), pp. 391–3; Haag, 'Ezechiels Beitrag zur messianischen Theologie' Stud. Anselm 27/28 (1951), pp. 276–85; Hammershaimb, 'Ezekiel's View of the Monarchy' *Studia Or. Pedersen* (1953), pp. 130–40.

[42] Aalders, *Gog en Magog in Ezechiël* (1951); Albright, 'Gog and Magog' JBL 43 (1924), pp. 378–85; Bewer, 'Das Tal der Wanderer in Hesekiel xxxix, 11' ZAW 56 (1938), pp. 123–5; Gerleman, 'Hesekielbokens Gog' SEA 12 (1947), pp. 148–62; Myres, 'Gog and the Danger from the North in Ezekiel' PEFQSt 64 (1932), pp. 213–19.

[43] du Plat Taylor, *Myrton-Pigadhes. A Late Bronze Age Sanctuary in Cyprus* (1957), pp. 103–11, Pl. II; Paul Rost, 'Der Altar Ezechiels, Kap. xliii, 13–17' MAOG 4 (1928/9), pp. 170–4. Literature, p. 376, n. 23.

argument in favour of the genuineness of all or nearly all the passages on the grounds that the autobiographical introductory form cannot be invented and is therefore a certain mark of genuineness. It is more likely that the secondary passages have been assimilated to this peculiarity of the genuine ones, and can therefore not be regarded as genuine without further ado. Thus a clear distinction between genuine and non-genuine is very difficult, the more so since, quite apart from difficulties resulting from corruption of the text, we must often reckon with the possibility of a genuine core which has been very much worked over and hence distorted almost out of all recognition. In xvi and xxiii the original material may still be recognised relatively easily, since here the revision has added extra material at the end, i.e. by the addition of xvi, 44–63, and xxiii, 36–49, rather than by touching up the original. But in the case of xx, which moreover belongs among the dated sections, the genuine material can, as we have seen (p. 376), only be freed from secondary additions with difficulty. The Gog prophecy in xxxviii–xxxix and, as we have indicated, the vision of the new Temple, etc., in xl–xlviii, have also been much elaborated. The same is true of the call vision in i–iii and of the visionary transportation of Ezekiel in viii–xi.

Whereas these are cases of revision of a genuine original, there are also some passages which appear to be entirely secondary. This is particularly the case with some sections of the complexes xxv–xxxii, xxxiv–xxxvii, xl–xlviii, which contain promises for Israel expressed directly or implicitly. We have seen how the books of Isaiah and Jeremiah have also been expanded with a variety of promises of salvation (pp. 317, 361 f.). We cannot, however, doubt that after the disaster of 587 Ezekiel really did change from being a prophet of woe to being one of weal. So these additions do not introduce new features into his actual personality, but simply underline those which are already present and which correspond to the actual historical reality.

We may thus explain the present form of i–xxiv + xxxiii–xlviii as consisting of a gathering together, somewhat in the form of a diary going back to Ezekiel himself, of dated events, expanded by the insertion of further oracular material, largely genuine but sometimes non-genuine. If this is right, then we may perhaps understand from this the numerous doublets, such as xiii, 11–12//xiii, 13–14; xiv, 4–5//xiv, 6–7 (8); xviii, 21–4//xviii, 26–8, 32. These cannot all or even for the most part be understood as Fohrer does as glosses, in other words as simple growth of the text; nor can they be explained as peculiarities of the diction either of Ezekiel or of a redactor. There may have been several collections of speeches, ultimately certainly also going back to Ezekiel, and in the same collection the same theme may have been dealt with more than once. Thus the redactor, who wished to expand the memoir-like collection by the prophet so that it would give a picture of the range and content of his whole proclamation, had before him several treatments of the same topic, which often corresponded closely even in wording. His presentation was made up from these, and it was bound to happen that many duplicates slipped in.

5. *The conclusions to be drawn from the analysis.* We may finally attempt a survey of the analysis of the book of Ezekiel as it has been made possible by

the tracing of the smaller collections which lie behind it. Here we may note first that it appears probable that there were two autobiographical accounts, rather like diaries, compiled by Ezekiel himself. One of these contained the revelations and actions, poems and speeches, which referred to Jerusalem and Israel. The other had the threats against Tyre and Egypt, which strengthened and supported Jerusalem in its anti-Babylonian policy which was contrary to the will of Yahweh. In addition to these memoirs, exactly dated because of their connection with quite definite historical events, Ezekiel also left some other speeches and compositions of more general content, also couched in autobiographical style. We cannot now tell for certain whether we are here dealing with isolated passages or with smaller and larger collections; nor how many such there were. These notes were then combined with the memoirs, probably by someone other than Ezekiel himself. The principle upon which this combination was made can in some places still be recognised, particularly clearly in the case of the poems referring to Tyre and Egypt, where, as was in the nature of the case quite natural, the undated passages were appended to the dated ones. So far as the sections referring to Jerusalem-Israel are concerned, this at least is plain, that the undated sayings containing promises have always been inserted after the point in the memorial which reports the arrival of the news of Jerusalem's fall and the end of Ezekiel's dumbness, i.e. after xxxiii, 22. Indeed the majority of these sayings actually do derive from the period after the conquest of Jerusalem.

The two memoirs were then united, though we cannot say now whether this happened before or only after their expansion with undated passages. The way this happened was that the threats against Tyre and Egypt were inserted between the threats against Jerusalem-Israel and the promises made to them, and now appear as an introduction to the promises. The compilation, which up till then had substantially comprised genuine material, did however receive various expansions by later hands, and these expansions, as in other prophetic books, affected particularly the threats against foreign nations and the promises for the people itself.

6. *The portrait of Ezekiel.* In spite of the touching-up with non-genuine elements, which here as elsewhere have at any rate in part an enduring value in themselves and are not to be set on one side without further concern as mere padding, the book nevertheless gives a clear and accurate picture of Ezekiel. He appears as a visionary seeing great visions reminiscent of the heavenly journeys and travels of the later apocalypses (pp. 621, 622), and as one who carried out strange symbolic actions. He appears also as a superb poet, with a wide range of metaphors, and as a preacher and pastor of souls who tears down as ruthlessly as he builds up again carefully. He appears as what one might almost call a philosopher of religion, brooding over God's dealings with sinners and righteous; and as the architect of the new Temple and of its cultus, concerned equally with the greatest as with the smallest points. In addition to this, it brings us close to the man Ezekiel himself—or 'the son of man',[44] as he is addressed by God (e.g., ii, 3)—who at first seems so strange, hard, even repulsive, but who

[44] Eichrodt, 'Zum Problem des Menschensohns' EvTh 19 (1959), pp. 1–3.

then reveals his sympathetic and sensitive nature, endeavouring to conceal this inner nature beneath a hard outer shell. It is true that the book and the man himself present a mixture of opposites, and there is such a great difference between the powerful feeling of the poems on Tyre and Egypt and the sober reflections on the doctrine of retribution in xviii and xxxiii, that it is quite understandable that it was not thought possible to attribute both to one individual. But, apart from the fact that elaborate allegories like the vine-wood and lioness poems of xv and xix do actually provide a middle term between the two extremes, there is no sufficient ground for denying either the one or the other to Ezekiel, especially in view of the fact that, as we have seen, in earlier prophets too we may observe the presence of sayings which differ considerably in content and style (pp. 148–9). If, following Hölscher, we may mention the two apparently mutually exclusive extremes, Ezekiel is not merely 'the poet with his dazzling imaginative and passionate rhetoric', nor merely 'the formal priestly author and pioneer of legal and ritualistic Judaism'; he is both together, and more besides.

(b) *The Twelve Minor Prophets* (*The Book of the Twelve*)

§ 48. THE BOOK OF THE TWELVE PROPHETS

Literature: (a) Commentaries. (i) Series: ATD: I Weiser (³1959); II Elliger (⁴1959); Bibelhilfe: Jepsen (1938); BK: Wolff, Hosea (1961); BOuT: Deden, Hos-Mic (1953): Nah-Mal (1956); Camb. B: Cheyne, Driver, Lanchester, Davidson, Barnes (1882–1920); Cent. B: Horton, Driver (1904–6); COuT: van Gelderen en Gispen, Hos (1953); Aalders, Ob, Jon (1958); EB: van Hoonacker (1908); Echter-B: Nötscher (1948); *EΠΔ*: Vellas (1947–1950); Erläuterungen zum AT: Procksch, I (1910); II (²1929); Expositor's B: G. A. Smith (1896–8, ²1928); Harper's B: Bewer (1949); HAT: Robinson and Horst (²1954); HK: Nowack (³1922); HS: I Lippl, Theis (1937); II Junker (1938); HSAT: Guthe, Marti, Rothstein, Kautzsch-Bertholet (1923); IB: Mauchline, Phillips, Thompson, Langford, Fosbroke, Lovett, Smart, Scarlett, Wolfe, Bosley, Taylor, Cleland, Thurman, Thomas, Sperry, Speers, Dentan (1956); ICC: Harper, Smith, Ward, Bewer, Mitchell (1905–12 (1948–53)); Jerusalem-B: Osty, Am, Hos (²1958); George, Mic, Zeph, Nah (²1958); Trinquet, Hab, Ob, Joel (²1959); Gelin, Hag, Zech, Mal (³1960); Feuillet, Jon (²1957); KAT: Sellin (²,³1929–30); KeH: Hitzig-Steiner (⁴1881); KHC: Marti (1904); Montserrat-B: Augé (1957); SAT: Gressmann (²1921), Hans Schmidt (²1923), Haller (²1925); Soncino-B: Lehrman, Goldman, Cashdan (²1952); SZ: Orelli (³1908); Torch-B: Knight, Hos (1960); Jon (²1956); Marsh, Am, Mic (1959); TU: Bleeker, Hos-Mic (1932–4); Smit, Nah-Mal, (1926–34); WC: Brown, Edghill, Cooke, Stonehouse, Wade (1906–32).

(ii) Single Commentaries: Wellhausen (³1898); Duhm (Translation 1910); ZAW 31 (1911), pp. 1–43, 81–110, 161–204: Notes on the Twelve Prophets.

(b) Other Literature: Budde, 'Eine folgenschwere Redaktion des Zwölfprophetenbuchs' ZAW 39 (1922), pp. 218–29; Coppens, *Les Douze Petits Prophètes* (1950); Davies, 'The Yahwistic Tradition in the Eighth-Century Prophets' StOTPr (1950), pp. 37–51; Driver, 'Linguistic and Textual Problems: Minor Prophets' JThSt 39 (1938), pp. 154–66, 260–73, 393–405; Ginsberg, 'Notes on the Minor Prophets' [Hebr., Engl. sum.] Eretz-Israel 3 (1954), pp. 83–4, IV; Jepsen, 'Kleine Beiträge zum Zwölfprophetenbuch' ZAW 56 (1938), pp. 85–100; 57 (1939), pp. 242–55; 61 (1945/8), pp. 95–114; Richter, *Erläuterungen zu dunkeln Stellen in den Kleinen Propheten* (BFChTh 18, 3/4, 1914); E. Vogt, 'Fragmenta Prophetarum Minorum Deserti Iuda' Bibl 34 (1953), pp. 423–6; cf. below, pp. 707 f.; Wolfe, 'The Editing of the Book of the Twelve' ZAW 53 (1935), pp. 90–129; Ziegler's works on the Greek of the Minor Prophets (1934–45), noted below on p. 704, n. 13.

Cf. also Literature §§ 42, 49–61, 126.

In his 'Praise of the Fathers' (p. 598) Jesus ben Sira, after naming Isaiah, Jeremiah, Ezekiel and Job, mentions in xlix 10, the Twelve Prophets (שנים עשר הנביאים *ιβ' προφῆται*), and expresses the wish that their bones may *revive again out of their place (grave)*. There is clearly presupposed here the gathering together of the small books Hosea to Malachi into one book, just as in the Jewish canon these books are actually counted as one book (p. 569). In addition to the name provided by this passage in ben Sira—Book of the Twelve Prophets—the book has also commonly been called the 'Minor Prophets' or 'The Book of the Minor Prophets', a title which probably occurs first in Augustine, *De civitate dei*, XVIII, 29 (Prophetae Minores), and which is here explained as referring to the small size of these books by comparison with the books of Isaiah, Jeremiah and Ezekiel, and not in any way as intending to suggest that the prophets whose names are given to these books were themselves of minor importance.

The order of the twelve books differs in 𝕲 from that in 𝔐. In 𝔐 the chronological criterion has clearly been determinative: firstly those books which actually or supposedly belonged to the period of the supremacy of Assyrian power, the second half of the eighth century—Hosea, Joel, Amos, Obadiah, Jonah and Micah—of which Joel (pp. 394 f.), Obadiah (pp. 402 f.) and, so far as the composition of the book is concerned, Jonah (p. 405) are not really of that period; secondly, those which belong to the time of the downfall of Assyrian world-power, the last third of the seventh century—Nahum, Habakkuk and Zephaniah; finally those which may be traced to the beginning of the Persian period, the end of the sixth and the first half of the fifth century—Haggai, Zechariah and Malachi. 𝕲 places the last six books in the same order as 𝔐, but presents the first six in a different order. It appears that this order has been determined for the first five—Hosea, Amos, Micah, Joel and Obadiah—by their length, while the place of Jonah at the end of this group of six, in spite of its exceeding the book of Obadiah in length, is probably designed to take account of the view that this book does not, like the others, provide the words of God and of the prophet, but only a narrative concerning a prophet.

So far as the date of the gathering together of these twelve little books is concerned, it cannot be earlier than the latest of its component parts. Thus, since certain of these, like Joel (pp. 394 f.) and 'Deutero-Zechariah' (pp. 437–40), can hardly have come into existence before the fourth century, or perhaps even the third, the date cannot be before about 300 B.C. The lower limit is provided by the above-mentioned passage in ben Sira at the beginning of the second century, so that we may consider the collection to have come into being as a unit in the course of the third century. Probably the redactor no longer knew the twelve books as independent entities. It is likely that some of them had already, at an earlier time, been gathered into smaller collections, just as smaller collections underlie the books of Isaiah, Jeremiah and Ezekiel. Nothing more precise than this can be said, since the evidence which is relevant here is capable of more than one interpretation.

§49. HOSEA

Literature: Allwohn, *Die Ehe des Propheten Hosea in psychoanalytischer Beleuchtung* (BZAW 44, 1926); Batten, 'Hosea's Message and Marriage' JBL 48 (1929), pp. 257–73; Baumann, ' "Wissen um Gott" bei Hosea als Urform von Theologie?' EvTh 15 (1955), pp. 416–25; Baumgartner, *Kennen Amos und Hosea eine Heilseschatologie?* (Diss. theol. Zürich, 1913); Behler, 'Divini amoris suprema revelatio in antiquo foedere dato (Osee, c. xi)' Angelicum 20 (1943), pp. 102–16; Birkeland, 'Profeten Hosea's forkynnelse' NTT 38 (1937), pp. 277–316; Brillet, *Amos et Osée* (1946); Brown, *The Book of Hosea* (1932); Buck, *Die Liebe Gottes beim Propheten Osee* (1953); Budde, 'Der Schluß des Buches Hosea' *Studies C. H. Toy* (1912), pp. 205–11; 'Der Abschnitt Hosea i–iii' ThStKr 96/7 (1925), pp. 1–89; 'Zu Text und Auslegung des Buches Hosea' I, II, JBL 45 (1926), pp. 280–97; III, JPOS 14 (1934), pp. 1–41; IV, JBL 53 (1934), pp. 118–33; 'Hosea i und iii' ThBl 13 (1934), cols. 337–42; Coppens, 'L'histoire matrimoniale d'Osée' *Nötscher-Festschr.* (1950), pp. 38–45; Crane, 'The Prophecy of Hosea' BS 89 (1932), pp. 480–94; Dumeste, 'Le message du prophète Osée' Vie Spirit. 75 (1946), pp. 710–26; Farr, 'The Concept of Grace in the Book of Hosea' ZAW 70 (1958), pp. 98–107; Fohrer, 'Umkehr und Erlösung beim Propheten Hosea' ThZ 11 (1955), pp. 161–85; Frey, 'Der Aufbau der Gedichte Hoseas' WuD 5 (1957), pp. 9–103; Ginsberg, 'Studies in Hos i–iii' (*Y. Kaufmann Jub. Vol.* (1960), pp. 50–69; Gordis, 'Hosea's Marriage and Message: A New Approach' HUCA 25 (1954), pp. 9–35; Heermann, 'Ehe und Kinder des Propheten Hosea' ZAW 40 (1922), pp. 287–312; Humbert, 'Les trois premiers chapitres d'Osée' RHR 77 (1918), pp. 157–71; 'Osée le prophète bedouin' RHPhR 1 (1921), pp. 97–118; 'La logique de la perspective nomade chez Osée et l'unité d'Osée ii, 4–22' BZAW 41 (1925), pp. 158–66; Lindblom, *Hosea. Literarisch untersucht* (1927); Maly, 'Messianism in Osee' CBQ 19 (1957), pp. 213–25; May, 'An Interpretation of the Names of Hosea's Children' JBL 55 (1936), pp. 285–91; McKenzie, 'Knowledge of God in Hosea' JBL 74 (1955), pp. 22–7; 'Divine Passion in Osee' CBQ 17 (1955), pp. 287–99; North, 'Hosea's Introduction to his Book' VT 8 (1958), pp. 429–32; Nyberg, 'Das textkritische Problem des AT am Hoseabuche demonstriert' ZAW 52 (1934), pp. 241–54; *Studien zum Hoseabuch* (1935); *Hoseaboken* (1941); Östborn, *Yahwe and Baal. Studies in the Book of Hosea and Related Documents* (LUA I 51, 6, 1956); Rieger, *Die Bedeutung der Geschichte für die Verkündigung des Amos und Hosea* (1929); H. W. Robinson, *Two Hebrew Prophets* (1948), pp. 10–61; Th. H. Robinson, 'Die Ehe des Hosea' ThStKr 106 (1934–5), pp. 301–13; Rowley, 'The Marriage of Hosea' BJRL 39 (1956/7), pp. 200–33; Hans Schmidt, 'Die Ehe des Hosea' ZAW 42 (1924), pp. 245–72; Sellin, 'Die geschichtliche Orientierung der Prophetie des Hosea' NKZ 36 (1925), pp. 607–58, 807; Snaith, *Mercy and Sacrifice. A Study of the Book of Hosea* (1953); Tushingham, 'A Reconsideration of Hosea, Chapters i–iii' JNESt 12 (1953), pp. 150–9; Valeton, *Amos en Hosea* (1894); German trans. by Echternacht (1898); Volz, *Die vorexilische Jahweprophetie und der Messias* (1897), pp. 24–40; Vuilleumier, *La tradition cultuelle d'Israël dans la prophétie d'Amos et d'Osée* (Cahiers Théologiques 45, 1960); Waterman, 'Hosea, Chapters i–iii, in Retrospect and Prospect' JNESt 14 (1955), pp. 100–9; Wolfe, *Meet Amos and Hosea* (1945); Wolff, ' "Wissen um Gott" bei Hosea als Urform von Theologie' EvTh 12 (1952/3), pp. 533–54; 'Erkenntnis Gottes im AT' EvTh 15 (1955), pp. 426–31; 'Hoseas geistige Heimat' ThLZ 81 (1956), cols. 83–94.

Cf. also Literature §§ 42, 48, 126.

1. *The date and personality of the prophet.* The superscription in i, 1, names as the period of Hosea's activity the reigns of the kings of Judah, Uzziah (784–746), Jotham (746–742), Ahaz (741–726) and Hezekiah (725–697), and of the king of Israel, Jeroboam II (786–746). There is here no real synchronism, for only the regnal years of Uzziah and Jeroboam overlap, whereas those of the kings of Judah—Jotham, Ahaz and Hezekiah—go beyond this. It may therefore be assumed that the list of kings of Judah has been added secondarily, following the pattern of Isa. i, 1, perhaps in order to depict Hosea as a contemporary of Isaiah. The dating in the period of Jeroboam which then remains is confirmed by i, 4, which presupposes that power was still in the hands of the dynasty of Jehu, which came to an end with the mere six months' reign of Jeroboam's son Zechariah. So far as the lower limit of Hosea's activity is concerned, there is nothing to suggest that he lived on as late as the fall of Samaria, or even its siege. It is, however, probable that the book reflects not only the inner confusion and the murders of kings which followed the death of Jeroboam (vii, 3, 16; viii, 4), but also apparently the Syro-Ephraimite war of 734/733 (v, 8–vi, 6). The dating *in the days of Jeroboam* is thus only approximately correct, and does not exclude the possibility that the prophet was also active after Jeroboam's death. It is possible that the superscription was originally only intended to refer to ch. i.

Hosea was a native of the northern kingdom, or at any rate worked there exclusively. Even if from time to time he looks towards Judah and castigates the evil conditions there too (v, 8–vi, 6), yet in the main his proclamation is entirely concentrated on the situation in the northern kingdom. We have no certain information concerning his actual life, apart from his marriage which must be discussed later. Perhaps, with Cazelles, 'The Problem of the Kings in Os. viii, 4' CBQ 11 (1949), pp. 14–25, we may however deduce from mocking words uttered by the people against him, such as *The prophet is a fool, the man that hath the spirit is mad* (ix, 7), that Hosea, unlike Amos (p. 397) belonged to the prophetic profession. It remains uncertain whether, as Duhm has suggested, he was of priestly family. His membership of the prophetic profession certainly cannot have hindered him in his ruthless condemnation of the evil conditions in both priestly and prophetic circles. On the contrary, it would appear that it was his intimate knowledge of the conditions which really gave his attacks their forcefulness.

2. *The contents and divisions of the book.* The book has fourteen chapters, of which the first three contain a narrative or more correctly (pp. 387–90) two narratives concerning Hosea's marriage with a speech of Yahweh set between them (ii). iv–xiv contain a loose collection of sayings and poems. These are: iv, 1–10,[1] a diatribe and a threat against the sinful priests who set a bad example to the people; iv, 11–19,[2] a diatribe and threat against the people because of its immoral idolatry; v, 1–7, a diatribe and threat against priests, people and royal

---

[1] Junker, 'Textkritische, formkritische und traditionskritische Untersuchung zu Os iv, 1–10' BZ 4 (1960), pp. 165–85. Lit. § 126.
[2] Rost, 'Erwägungen zu Hosea iv, 13 f.' *Bertholet-Festschr.* (1950), pp. 451–60; Zolli, 'Hosea iv, 17–18' ZAW 56 (1938), p. 175.

house because of their idolatry;[3] v, 8–vi, 6,[4] a diatribe and threat against Judah and Israel because of crimes committed there during the Syro-Ephraimite war, together with a proclamation that only sincere repentance can make an impression upon Yahweh and move him to withdraw the punishment which is otherwise unavoidable; vi, 7–11a,[5] a diatribe against Israel, apparently because of its idolatry; vi, 11b–vii, 7, a diatribe against Israel because of the folly of its king-making; vii, 8–16, a diatribe and threat against Israel because of its mania for foreign things; viii, 1–14, a diatribe and threat against Israel because of its cultic and political failures—calf-image and king-making; ix, 1–9, a diatribe and threat against Israel's idolatrous and immoral cultus.

The sayings in iv, 1–ix, 9, assembled apparently without any principle of arrangement, are directed entirely against the idolatrous cult and the political evils of the time. In contrast to this, the remainder of the book (ix, 10–xiv, 10) contains in the main poems which trace the source of Israel's sinfulness in her past by means of historical retrospect. Thus we have in ix, 10–14, *I found Israel üke grapes in the wilderness*, a diatribe and threat against Israel's apostasy at Baal-peor (Num. xxv); ix, 15–17, *All their wickedness began in Gilgal*, a diatribe and threat against the Israelite kingship established at Gilgal (I Sam. xi, 14–15; xiii, 7–15; xv, 10–35);[6] x, 1–8, *Israel harvested the vine*, a diatribe and threat against the failures which began as Israel's prosperity increased, expressed in the form of calf-image and kingship; x, 9–15,[7] *O Israel, thou hast sinned since the days of Gibeah*, a diatribe against Israel's kingship inaugurated at Gibeah, the scene of the outrage of Judg. xix–xxi[8] and the residence of Saul (I Sam. xi, 4), and a threat of terrible distress in warfare as a punishment; xi, 1–11, *When Israel was a child then I loved him*, a diatribe and threat against Israel because of ingratitude towards Yahweh, and a promise of divine mercy; xii, 1–15,[9] *Ephraim compasseth me about with falsehood, and the house of Israel with deceit*, a diatribe and threat against Israel because of its insincere attitude towards Yahweh, already figured in the life and conduct of Jacob; xiii, 1–11 (the opening being corrupt), a diatribe and threat against Israel which to its earlier idolatry has now added the worship of the calf-image; xiii, 12[10]–xiv, 1, *The iniquity of Ephraim is bound up; his sin is laid up in store*, a diatribe against Israel's incorrigibility and a threat of terrible punishment; xiv, 2–9, a call to repentance to Israel and a

[3] Elliger, 'Eine verkannte Kunstform bei Hosea (Zur Einheit von Hos v, 1 f.)' ZAW 69, (1957), pp. 151–60.

[4] Spiegel, 'A Prophetic Attestation of the Decalogue: Hosea vi, 5 with some Observations on Psalms xv and xxiv' HThR 27 (1934), pp. 105–44; Zolli, 'Note on Hosea vi, 6' JQR 31 (1940/1), pp. 79–82. Literature, p. 113, n. 40; p. 391, n. 15.

[5] Torczyner, '"Gilead, a city of them that work iniquity"' [Hebr.] BJPES 11 (1944), pp. 9–16: on vi, 8.

[6] Cf. p. 249, n. 2.

[7] Goshen-Gottstein, '"Ephraim is a well-trained heifer" and Ugaritic *mdl*' Bibl 41 (1960), pp. 64–6; Robertson, 'Textual Criticism of Hosea x, 11' Transact. Glasgow Univ. Or. Soc. 8 (1938), pp. 16 f. Lit. § 126.

[8] Cf. p. 258, n. 1.

[9] Gertner, 'An Attempt at an Interpretation of Hosea xii' VT 10 (1960), pp. 272–84; Jacob, 'La femme et le prophète. À propos d'Osée xii, 13–14' *Hommage à W. Vischer* (1960), pp. 83–7; Vriezen, 'Hosea xii' NThSt 24 (1941), pp. 144–9; 'La tradition de Jacob dans Osée xii' OTS 1 (1942), pp. 64–78. Lit. p. 387, n. 11; § 126.

[10] Vuilleumier-Bessard, 'Osée xiii 12 et les manuscrits' RQ 1 (1958/9), pp. 281–2.

promise of divine grace; xiv, 10, a concluding exhortation that all the words of the book should be taken to heart.

3. *Separation of the individual sayings and poems, and of the non-genuine material in iv, 1–xiv, 10.* In iv, 1–xiv, 10, the text is considerably corrupted in long sections. This makes the understanding of the content difficult and also makes uncertain the separation of the individual units from one another, so that here and there the divisions may be made rather differently from what has just been set out. But on the other hand the section iv, 1–xiv, 10, has come down to us without any considerable secondary material, and particularly without any large-scale additions. The attempts made at one time by Marti and Volz to deny to Hosea all or even a large part of the oracles of salvation, for example xi, 8–11; xiv, 2–9, may be considered to have failed, or are only right in so far as genuine prophecies may have been expanded by a later hand. i–iii make it clear beyond any shadow of doubt, as we shall see in a moment, that Hosea had from the outset a conception of the forgiveness of Israel after punishment, and this he proclaimed. Even the assumption earlier much in favour (cf. Valeton, Nowack, Marti, etc.) that every mention of Judah (in addition to i, 7, and ii, 2, there are iv, 15; v, 5, 10, 12–14; vi, 4, 11; viii, 14; x, 11; xii, 1,[11] 3) was to be traced to secondary alteration or expansion of the original text, is to be limited to the statement that only in a few of these passages is this the case. But that Hosea cannot be denied every mention of Judah is clearly shown by the section v, 8–vi, 6; for here the removal of the name *Judah* destroys the sense of the whole passage. In iv, 1–xiv, 10, however, the following passages at any rate must be regarded as later additions: iv, 3, 9; vii, 10; xiv, 10. In particular, xii appears to have been dislocated by many additions.

4. *The problem of chs. i–iii.* In i–iii the text is far better preserved than in iv, 1–xiv, 10; on the other hand this section provides much more difficult literary and exegetical problems. Both groups of problems belong closely together; it is nevertheless best at first to consider each group on its own. From the literary point of view the question is, whether in i–iii there is to be found a consecutive narrative of Hosea's marriage, now admittedly distorted by omissions and additions but nevertheless one which can be reconstructed, or whether there is a series of independent and in part parallel sections. Budde has expressed himself decisively in favour of the first view, which is only possible by the assimilation of the third-person narrative of ch. i (altering the third-person forms in vv. 2, 3, 4, 6 to the first person) to the first-person narrative of ch. iii, or by the opposite assimilation of ch. iii (altering the first-person forms in vv. 1, 2, 3 to the third person) to ch. i. Budde regards ii, 1–3, as a later substitute for the part of the narrative broken off at this point, in which Hosea discovered the adultery of his wife and drove her away with the divorce formula which is perhaps still preserved in ii, 4, *She is not my wife, and I am not her husband,*[12] and he links ii, 4–iii, 5, to the preceding passage by seeing in the genuine material of ii, 4–25, a description of 'Yahweh's return under the pressure of an

[11] Reines, 'Hosea xii, 1' JJSt 2 (1951), pp. 156 f.; Zolli, 'Il significato di רד e רתת in Osea xii, 1 e xiii, 1' RStOr 32 (1957), pp. 371–4. Literature, p. 386, n. 9; § 126.
[12] Cf. p. 66, n. 4.

undiminished love to the unfaithful one, anticipating the picture of a future complete unity in an indissoluble new bond of love.' On this there then follows in ch. iii the 'summons to Hosea to have a similar sentiment, and his action towards the same goal', just as in ch. i, Yahweh's action, namely the repudiation of Israel, precedes the narrative of the repudiation of Hosea's wife which is to be supplied between i, 9, and ii, 4. The other view is represented by T. H. Robinson (1935 and 1954) among others. Since it is only by emendation of the text that the occurrence of a third-person narrative in ch. i and of a first-person narrative in ch. iii can be obviated, the assumption that ch. iii is a parallel to ch. i seems the most natural, the more so since the link made between chs. i and iii, as for example by Budde's restoration of ch. ii, is very artificial. In principle with a text capable of such very different interpretations, such as we have in Hos. i–iii, an explanation which retains the traditional wording deserves to be preferred to others which involve all manner of alterations of the text. Thus we must keep the 'I' of ch. iii just as firmly as the 'He' of ch. i, and this means that we here have information concerning Hosea's marriage from two different hands, and so to some extent forming parallel narratives. Nor does the designation of ch. iii as a parallel to ch. i need to imply that exactly the same stage in the relationship of Hosea to his wife is described in the one as in the other. It may well be the case that ch. iii represents a second stage, following on that described in ch. i. The *Yet again* of iii, 1, makes this indeed seem probable, and H. W. Robinson regards ch. iii similarly as an autobiographical continuation of the biographical narrative of ch. i. Ch. i then relates the beginning of the marriage partnership, while ch. iii relates how, after an interruption which is here assumed, it was taken up afresh, though at first with certain restrictions: *Many days you are to remain for me, not playing the harlot and not having a husband* (iii, 3). That there should be a third-person narrative for the presentation of one phase of an event, while for another phase a first-person narrative is employed, occurs elsewhere, as for example in the case of Isa. vii–viii (pp. 148 f., 310 f.).

With this interpretation of chs. i and iii, there remains no necessity for bringing ch. ii directly into relation with what is related in chs. i and iii, and the words of Yahweh gathered in ch. ii[13] may then be treated as what on an unprejudiced examination they appear to be, namely a collection of detached sayings, not forming a coherent whole, but all turning upon the same subject, the relationship of Yahweh to Israel, pictured as his wife. The only question is, how far they come from Hosea and how far they represent later additions.

The possibility must be seriously considered whether ii, 23–5, and similarly ii, 1–3, which are fairly generally regarded as not genuine, should be denied to Hosea. In both passages the name of the first son of Hosea, *Jezreel*, which in i, 4, signifies that the blood-guilt of Jezreel, in other words Jehu's murder of Joram and Ahaziah (II Kings ix, 22–7), is to be avenged upon the dynasty of Jehu which is still upon the throne, is used in a quite different sense, as a designation for Israel, and this change of meaning can hardly be attributed to Hosea himself. On the other hand, there is hardly any sufficient reason for

---

[13] Freedman, 'פשתי in Hosea ii, 7' JBL 74 (1955), p. 275.

regarding ii, 16–22 as not genuine, where it is said that the punishment with which Yahweh threatens his wife Israel of taking her out of the cultivated land into the wilderness, will bring Israel to her senses and to self-examination, and so will make possible a new betrothal between her and Yahweh. Hosea does seem to have had in view and to have proclaimed from the start a positive purpose in the catastrophe which he regarded as unavoidable, a purpose which is represented by the possibility of a renewal of the covenant between Yahweh and Israel, broken by Israel's entry into agricultural life and into the Canaanite cultus so closely bound up with it. The narrative of ch. iii also mentions this positive goal in verse 5, and there too it is hardly justifiable to strike out this prospect of future salvation as a secondary addition. Only the words *and David their king* may be secondary.

The second of the two questions indicated above (p. 387) concerns the interpretation of the subject-matter of chs. i–iii, and this has found such very varied answers that it is quite impossible even to list them, let alone to recount them fully and evaluate them. It must suffice to give a very general survey of a selection, and this—if all the detailed variations are disregarded—allows them to be gathered into these three groups. (1) Chs. i–iii are simply an allegory of the relationship of Yahweh to Israel. (2) Chs. i–iii are a narrative of the actual marriage experiences of Hosea. Hosea is forced to undergo the shattering experience of discovering that the woman whom he loves and whom he has married, has become unfaithful to him, and he sees in this, laid upon him as prophet by his God, an *imitatio* of the experiences which Yahweh has had with Israel; he then projects back the experience which he actually had only during the marriage, by saying that Yahweh commanded him to marry a wife who was inclined to unfaithfulness and to receive children from her who were not his own. (3) Chs. i–iii are a report of the marriage undertaken by Hosea at Yahweh's prompting with a woman who was actually involved in unchastity, one who was engaged in the practice of sacred prostitution,[14] herself a temple prostitute. The upholders of the second and third types of interpretation may be still further subdivided in that some of them reckon with only one woman, whereas others think in terms of two different wives of Hosea, one of whom may then have been an innocent girl, the other a temple prostitute.

The interpretation of Hos. i–iii as an allegory prevailed right on into the second half of the nineteenth century, and this view has also found isolated defendants more recently. Thus Gressmann (1921) favoured it, and many of the most recent discussions, for example that of Gordis (1954), at any rate approach very near it. The view that the story deals with Hosea's bitter experience of his wife's unfaithfulness only during the actual marriage, and that this was projected back into the past as a commandment of Yahweh to marry an idolatrous wife, was upheld by Wellhausen and Budde among others, and recently again by Weiser. As a result of a more profound understanding of the nature of the Canaanite cultus, and more particularly of the sacred prostitution bound up with it, an understanding made possible by more recent research, the

---

[14] Asmussen, 'Bemerkungen zur sakralen Prostitution im AT' StTh 11 (1958), pp. 167–92.

view has prevailed increasingly in the last three or four decades that the woman whom Hosea married at Yahweh's command was a temple prostitute—or if we have to reckon with two different women, one of them was such. Hans Schmidt (1924), T. H. Robinson (1935, 1954), Fohrer (1951, 1952), Tushingham (1953) and many others have set out views of this kind.

In view of the number and great variety of the different attempts at solving the problem of Hos. i–iii, it may well seem impossible to arrive at a solution which will be to any extent convincing. But if we adhere to the principle which is always to be recommended when we deal with texts which are capable of many interpretations, of making the understanding of the literary situation the basis for the discussion of the subject-matter, the way is opened for the possibility of a solution of the problem of the content which at least goes so far as to exclude a number of the suggested solutions as *a priori* impossible. Thus if chs. i and iii really represent sections of parallel narratives, in the third and the first person respectively, then it is thereby clear that we are dealing with the personal experience of the prophet, and not with mere allegory. For the presence of two reports, one biographical and one autobiographical, can only be explained if we are dealing with a real event. It would, to say the least, be very strange if an allegory were related in this duplicate form. Thus the discussion of the composition of chs. i–iii supports the view which is in any case the most obvious. We are thus dealing in chs. i and iii with an experience which the prophet himself has undergone. But the further question is whether i, 2, and iii, 1 are to be understood to mean that Hosea, in order to present in plain terms the relationship between Yahweh and Israel, married at Yahweh's command a woman known already as a harlot and an adulteress—perhaps a temple prostitute, or even two such women—or, more probably, he first underwent the painful experience of his wife's unfaithfulness in the marriage and then subsequently recognised the deep symbolic meaning of his experience and interpreted his marriage as deriving from the command of Yahweh. Although it is not possible to make a clear-cut decision on this, the latter appears to be the more probable answer. The description of the woman as *adulterous* in iii, 1, really only fits this conception, and not the description of the woman as a temple prostitute. This also makes it clear that we are dealing with the same woman in chs. i and iii. The sad experience which Hosea underwent with the faithless Gomer in accordance with Yahweh's will, and the love which joins with a desire to educate her so that he takes her to himself again, also at Yahweh's behest, reflect what Israel does to Yahweh in faithless ingratitude, and how Yahweh in spite of this repeatedly shows inexhaustible kindness to Israel. This is in any case the real meaning of Hos. i–iii, and thus it comes about, as indeed the prophet intends, that the only thing which matters, as in the 'Ebed Yahweh songs, and particularly the last of them, Isa. lii, 13–liii, 12, is not who the 'Ebed is, but what he signifies (pp. 335 f., 340 f.).

5. *The composition of the book.* We have seen that iv, 1–xiv, 10, is a collection composed solely of sayings without any kind of biographical or historical addition, whereas i–iii presents a compilation made up of biographical narration, sayings and autobiographical material. Of these three elements of the book, the

autobiographical must naturally go back directly to the prophet, while the biographical material will come from the hand of one of his disciples. As regards the sayings, we cannot say for certain whether they have been collected by the prophet himself or in the circle of his disciples. But what may be said is that this collection was formed relatively early, and if not during the lifetime of the prophet, at least shortly after his death. For there are only very few additions, and this is most easily explained if the collection came into existence and took on a fixed form at an early date. The book as a whole can hardly have been put together by the prophet himself, but was compiled by someone later, without it being possible to fix an exact date.

6. *Hosea—the poet, the prophet and the man.* In spite of its relatively small compass and its frequent serious textual corruption, the book nevertheless gives us a clear picture of Hosea. He is a poet who possesses a wonderfully rich pictorial language, who knows how to present the most fearful and terrible threats (xiii, 7–8) as impressively as the people's prayer of confession occasioned by sincere repentance (vi, 1–3;[15] xiv, 3–4), and the gracious promises of God charged with urgent love (xi, 8–9; xiv, 5–9). He is a prophet who struggles passionately against the immoral cultus of Canaan, and against the foolish internal and external political intrigues, opposing to them the demand for loyal and grateful dependence upon God in simplicity and trust. He condemns the corruption of his people so earnestly that he considers it necessary that she should be removed from her land. This he announces, but regards the disaster only as the unavoidable condition for the healing of the people and for making possible a new fellowship between her and her God. He is a man of deep inward feelings, sensitive and reflective, whose heart is deeply wounded by the faithlessness of the woman he loves. He is nevertheless not embittered by such an experience; by it his eyes are opened to the enormity of human faithlessness and sinfulness which certainly makes serious punishment necessary, but can finally only be overcome by the revealing of an even greater love.

§ 50. JOEL

Literature: Amon, *Die Abfassungszeit des Buches Joel* (Diss. theol. Würzburg, 1942) [typescript]; Baumgartner, 'Joel i und ii' BZAW 34 (1920), pp. 10–19; Budde, ' "Der von Norden" in Joel ii, 20' OLZ 22 (1919), cols. 1–5; 'Der Umschwung in Joel ii' (*ib.* cols. 104–110); Dennefeld, *Les problèmes du livre de Joël* (1926); Holzinger, 'Sprachcharakter und Abfassungszeit des Buches Joel' ZAW 9 (1889), pp. 89–131; Jensen, 'Inledningssporgmaal i Joels bog' DTT 4 (1941), pp. 98–112; Kapelrud, *Joel Studies* (1948); Kritzinger, *Die profesie van Joël* (1935); Merx, *Die Prophetie des Joel und ihre Ausleger* (1879); Rinaldi, *Il libro di Joele* (1938); Sellers, 'Stages of Locust in Joel' AJSL 52 (1935/6), pp. 81–5; Thompson, 'Joel's Locusts in the Light of Near Eastern Parallels' JNESt 14 (1955), pp. 52–5; Treves, 'The Date of Joel' VT 7 (1957), pp. 149–56; Widmer, *Die Kommentare von Raschi, Ibn Esra, Radaq zu Joel. Text, Übersetzung und Erläuterung* (1945).
Cf. also Literature §§ 48, 126.

[15] König, 'Die Auferstehungshoffnung bei Osee vi, 1–3' ZKTh 70 (1948), pp. 94–100; Stamm, 'Eine Erwägung zu Hos. vi, 1–2', ZAW 57 (1939), pp. 266–8.

1. *Contents.* The phrase *The word of Yahweh that came to Joel ben Pethuel* stands at the head of the book of Joel. In 𝔐 the text contains four chapters, whereas in 𝔊 and 𝔙 chs. ii and iii of the Hebrew are combined to form ch. ii. The English versions follow this arrangement, while Luther's translation combines iii and iv of the Hebrew to form ch. iii. The title merely provides the name of the prophet, but gives no information concerning his person or the period to which he belonged. In this case we are entirely dependent upon the results of analysis.

After the description in i, 2–4, of the unparalleled fearfulness of a plague of locusts just experienced, the prophet in vv. 5–14[1] directs especially to the priests the demand that they should mourn and appoint a great day of fasting. In vv. 15–20[2] he puts into their mouths a prayer of lamentation introduced by the words *Alas for the day.* In ii, 1–11, he calls for the trumpet signal to sound the alarm in Zion, since now the locusts, spreading terror and destruction like an army, are penetrating even into the capital. On this there follows, first in the form of a speech of Yahweh, and then of the prophet, the exhortation to repentance, with an expression of the hope of divine mercy (vv. 12–14) and in vv. 15–17 a renewed summons to a general day of repentance and prayer, the prayer to be spoken by the priests (v. 17) again being given here. The prayer—so v. 18 informs us—finds a hearing with Yahweh, and vv. 19–27 provide the wording of God's gracious answer anticipating the driving away of the locusts and the restoration of all the damage occasioned by them. This speech of Yahweh is interrupted by a summons spoken by the prophet to thankful rejoicing in vv. 21–3[3] (24?), which is perhaps to be understood eschatologically, since it anticipates the response of God to the prayer which in the context is proclaimed as if it had only just begun.

Now while chs. i–ii are in general clearly concerned with a plague of locusts, there is in i, 15*; ii, 1b, 2a (10a), 11b, mention of the Day of Yahweh. Here the plague of locusts is understood to be a premonitory sign of the approach of the Day of Yahweh. Chs. iii–iv are then completely concerned with the Day of Yahweh.[4] Ch. iii enumerates the phenomena which will accompany this Day—the endowment of all Israelites with the spirit of prophecy and all kinds of wonderful happenings in the heavens—and makes clear that those who worship Yahweh are to be rescued from this final disaster. Ch. iv describes in several detached passages the judgement which is to be fulfilled upon the heathen nations in the valley of Jehoshaphat, and in contrast to this the security of Zion and the wonderful fertility of the Jewish land, and the watering of the valley of Acacias[5] (Shittim) by a fountain coming out from the temple of Yahweh. Among the heathen nations, Tyre, Sidon and the Philistines are explicitly

---

[1] Frankfort, 'Le כִּי de Joël i, 12' VT 10 (1960), pp. 445–8.

[2] Kapelrud, 'Joel i, 17. Et oversettelsesproblem' NTT 45 (1944), pp. 285–92.

[3] van der Meiden, 'De vertaling van het woord מוֹרֶה in Joël ii, 23' GThT 51 (1951), pp. 136–9. Sellers, 'A Possible OT Reference to the Teacher of Righteousness' IEJ 5 (1955), pp. 93–5: on ii, 21–3. Lit. § 126.

[4] Bourke, 'Le jour de Yahvéh dans Joël' RB 66 (1959), pp. 5–31, 191–212; Largement and Lemaitre, 'Le Jour de Yahweh dans le contexte oriental' BEThL XII (1959), pp. 259–66. Literature, p. 319, n. 65; p. 398, n. 14.

mentioned,[6] and one of the reproaches levelled at them is that they have *sold the people of Judah and Jerusalem to the Greeks* (iv, 6).

2. *The problem of the book.* The decisive question is first whether i–ii and iii–iv are to be understood as prophecy, or rather as a narrative of past events or a description of present ones. If i–ii were prophecy, it would be most natural to attribute the whole book to one hand. But if they are narrative or description, then the book falls into two different parts, and it is not clear at first sight whether they do come from the same author. Earlier the interpretation, represented for example by Merx, was commonly held, that the first part is prophecy. But since the end of the last century the view that it is descriptive has prevailed more and more. Wellhausen, Nowack, Marti, Sellin, Robinson, Weiser and others have advocated it, and it is in fact the most obvious and natural. It does not, however, appear to deal adequately with the verses or parts of verses which speak of the Day of Yahweh (i, 15*; ii, 1b, 2a (10a), 11b), since here it is clear that something future is being prophesied. Duhm, developing the observations of older commentators, tried to explain this fact on the assumption that iii and iv, which deal with the Day of Yahweh, were later added to i–ii with their description of a plague of locusts, and that this addition also occasioned the reinterpretation of i–ii expressed in the additions mentioned in these chapters to a proclamation of the Day of Yahweh.[7] This assumption has found widespread acceptance. Recently Robinson has advocated it and Weiser too at least in that, assigning i–iv to the same prophet, he regards iii–iv as having been added by the prophet when he wrote down the words which he had spoken on the occasion of the plague of locusts, where the pointers to the Day of Yahweh were present from the first. Others, like Kritzinger, Rinaldi and Kapelrud, stress even more strongly that iii–iv and i–ii belong together. Kapelrud indeed, in connection with copious citation of the Ugaritic texts in explaining the book, has given a distinctive note to the discussion of the problem of Joel by describing the basic material of the book, conceived as a liturgy deriving from the cult-prophet Joel, as closely connected with the Enthronement festival of Yahweh on the one hand and with the ancient Near Eastern and Canaanite fertility cult on the other.

Those who have expressed doubts about Duhm's proposed removal of the mention of the Day of Yahweh in i–ii are right in that the sentences here in question are firmly anchored in their contexts, and that the description of a present plague of locusts and the threat of the coming Day of Yahweh need not be by any means mutually exclusive. The plague can from the outset be regarded as the forerunner or as the first phase of the Day of Yahweh, and indicated as such. On the other hand, it is clear that iii–iv are strongly differentiated from i–ii both in style and in content, and it is also indisputable that in iii–iv we have a collection of various utterances concerning the last time,

[5] Milik, 'Notes d'épigraphie et de topographie palestiniennes' RB 66 (1959), pp. 550–75, Pls. XIII, XIV: pp. 553–5 on 'Torrent des Acacias, Joël iv, 18' (EVV iii, 18).

[6] Rinaldi, 'Poenae Phoeniciis et Philistaeis denuntiatae apud Ioel iii, 4–8 (hebr. iv, 4–8)' VD 18 (1938), pp. 268–71. Lit. § 126.

[7] Isa. xiii in its present form is perhaps also to be understood in this way. Cf. Budde, *op. cit* (p. 319, n. 65).

such as are characteristic of the apocalyptic literature and paralleled in Ezek. xxxviii–xxxix or in Zech. xii–xiv. Thus many of those who defend the unity of the book, like Jepsen, reckon at least with apocalyptic amplifications made at a later date. Therefore though we can follow Duhm neither in the excision of the passages in i–ii which mention the Day of Yahweh, nor in assigning the whole content of iii–iv to one or more later hands, he is nevertheless right in considering that the description of the coming and driving away of a plague of locusts, which stems from Joel, and in particular the cultic liturgies which are combined with it, have been written over with the addition of apocalyptic prophecies. The true character of Joel's description of this was for a long time unrecognised. We are left then with the conclusion that Joel's prophecy was really concerned with an ordinary distress of his own time, and that the prospects of final catastrophe which he provides are only intended to emphasise the terribleness of the present distress, and are not there for their own sake.

We have here one of the very rare examples—but hence all the more valuable—of a prophet's concern with the cares and needs of everyday life, and we can see from it that the prophets who otherwise, as proclaimers of the divine will, belong at a higher level, yet also have their part or may have their part in a professional manner in civil life. In this case, we have an example of the duty which falls upon a prophet when there is a plague in the land. It was then his concern, and not that of the priest, to instigate the holding of a day of repentance, but even more it was his concern to receive and transmit the divine answer to the people's prayer. This answer could only be received by a prophet. Thus it is these words of Yahweh mediated by the prophet in ii, 12, 19–20, 25–7, which designate Joel as a prophet and have rightly found for his book a place among the books of the prophets. The basic material of the book gives us information about the part played by an otherwise unknown prophet Joel in the fast day held because of a plague of locusts, and thus gives us in large measure the actual words which Joel then spoke, partly in his own name, and partly in the name of Yahweh.

3. *Date of origin.* Since the writing contains no allusions to precise historical dates, its assignment must on the whole be made in accordance with the development of religion and thought. As far as iii–iv are concerned, these are clear. The hope here expressed of the condemnation of the nations which have attacked Jerusalem in the last times can only be possible in the post-exilic period in the developed form in which it is found here. The exile and the scattering of the Jews throughout the world is moreover clearly presupposed in iv, 2. The mention of the Greeks in iv, 6, shows further that we must go down into the fourth or even the third century B.C. The indication of those points in iii–iv which point to a late date does not completely fix the origin of what goes back to Joel, since the passages here in question may possibly belong to the elaborations which the basic material has certainly undergone. But i–ii, which are undoubtedly genuine, also contain many indications of post-exilic and even late post-exilic origin: the absence of any mention of the royal court in i, 11; ii, 16; the presupposition of the daily burnt-offering in i, 9; ii, 14; the Hebrew containing a relatively large number of Aramaisms. Admittedly Jewish tradi-

tion, which for a long time was determinative in more modern scholarship
and still is so in some circles even today (cf. for example, Theis and Amon),
contradicts this view. For this tradition, as the position of Joel between the
eighth-century prophets Hosea and Amos shows, regards the book as a product
of the earlier period, though we cannot yet discover with certainty on what
grounds this dating was determined.

§ 51. AMOS

Literature: Andrews, 'Hesiod and Amos' JR 23 (1943), pp. 194–205; Bach, 'Gottes-
recht und weltliches Recht in der Verkündigung des Propheten Amos' *Dehn-Festschr.*
(1957), pp. 23–34; Balla, *Die Droh- und Scheltworte des Amos* (1926); Baumann, *Der Aufbau der Amosreden* (1903); Baumgartner (§ 49); Botterweck, 'Zur Authentizität des Buches
Amos' BZ 2 (1958), pp. 161–76; Brillet (§ 49); Budde, 'Zur Geschichte des Buches Amos'
BZAW 27 (1914), pp. 63–77; 'Zu Text und Auslegung des Buches Amos' JBL 43 (1924),
pp. 46–131; 44 (1925), pp. 63–122; Copass, *Amos* (1939); Cramer, *Amos. Versuch einer
theologischen Interpretation* (BWANT 51, 1930); Cripps, *A Critical and Exegetical Commentary on the Book of Amos* (²1955); Dumeste, 'Le message du prophète Amos' Vie Spirit.
74 (1945), pp. 834–52; 75 (1946), pp. 424–37; Gordis, 'The Composition and Structure of
Amos' HThR 33 (1940), pp. 239–51; Hammershaimb, *Amos* (²1958); Irwin, 'The Thinking
of Amos' AJSL 49 (1933), pp. 102–14; Junker, 'Amos, der Mann, den Gott mit unwider-
stehlicher Gewalt zum Propheten macht' Trierer ThZ 65 (1956), pp. 321–8; Kapelrud,
'God as Destroyer in the Preaching of Amos and in the Ancient Near East' JBL 71 (1952),
pp. 33–8; *Central Ideas in Amos* (SNVAO 1956, 4, 1956 (1961)); 'Profeten Amos og hans
yrke' NTT 59 (1958), pp. 76–9; L. Kochler, *Amos* (1917); 'Amos Forschungen von 1917–
1932' ThR 4 (1932), pp. 195–213; Lehming, 'Erwägungen zu Amos' ZThK 55 (1958),
pp. 145–69; Loehr, *Untersuchungen zum Buche Amos* (BZAW 4, 1901); Maag, *Text,
Wortschatz und Begriffswelt des Buches Amos* (1951); Mays, 'Words about the Words of
Amos. Recent Study of the Book of Amos' Interpret. 13 (1959), pp. 259–72; McCullough,
'Some Suggestions about Amos' JBL 72 (1953), pp. 247–54; Morgenstern, 'Amos Studies'
HUCA 11 (1936), pp. 19–140; 12/13 (1937/8), pp. 1–53; 15 (1940), pp. 59–305 (these
studies published 1941 as a book); 32 (1961), pp. 295–350; 'The Universalism of Amos'
Tribute to Leo Baeck (1954), pp. 106–26; Neher, *Amos, Contribution à l'étude du prophétisme*
(1950); Eva Osswald, *Urform und Auslegung im masoretischen Amostext. Ein Beitrag zur
Kritik an der neuren traditionsgeschichtlichen Methode* (Diss. theol. Jena, 1951) (typescript,
cf. ThLZ 80 (1955), col. 179); Rieger (§ 49); Hans Schmidt, *Der Prophet Amos* (1917);
Seierstad, 'Erlebnis und Gehorsam beim Propheten Amos' ZAW 52 (1934), pp. 22–41;
Speier, 'Bemerkungen zu Amos' VT 3 (1953), pp. 305–10; 'Bemerkungen zu Amos II'
Homenaje à Millás-Vallicrosa II (1956), pp. 365–72; van Steenbergen, *Motivation in
Relation to the Message of Amos* (Diss. theol. Univ. of Southern California, Los Angeles,
1953); Stephany, 'Charakter und zeitliche Aufeinanderfolge der Drohsprüche in der
Prophetie des Amos' CuW 7 (1931), pp. 281–9; Susumu Jozaki, 'The Secondary Passages
of the Book of Amos' Kwansei Gakuin University Annual Studies 4 (1956), pp. 25–100;
Valeton (§ 49); Vuilleumier (§ 49); Watts, 'The Origin of the Book of Amos' ET 66
(1954/5), pp. 109–12; *Vision and Prophecy in Amos* (1958); Weiser, *Die Profetie des Amos*
(BZAW 53, 1929); Wolfe (§ 49); Würthwein, 'Amos-Studien' ZAW 62 (1950), pp. 10–52.
Cf. also Literature §§ 48, 49, 126.

1. *The period, place of origin and person of the prophet.* The superscription in
i, 1, indicates that Amos *saw* his words *in the days of Uzziah king of Judah,*

and in the days of Jeroboam . . . king of Israel, two years before the earthquake.
Unfortunately the mention of the earthquake, referred to also in Zech. xiv, 5,[1]
does not help us to arrive at a more exact dating of the activity of Amos or
rather—for it is in this way that the mention of the exact year is primarily to be
understood—of its beginning, since we do not know when it took place. But
even without this, it can be seen that the dating given in the superscription
placing Amos under Uzziah (784–746) and Jeroboam (786–746) is correct.
The period of about forty years thus indicated may be somewhat further limited.
vii, 9, where Amos threatens that Yahweh will arise with the sword against
the house of Jeroboam, confirms the information of the superscription. This
mention of the *house of Jeroboam* does not imply its last member, Zechariah,
who was assassinated after a reign of only six months, as can be seen from other
passages which presuppose that Israel was at the time at the height of her power,
and more particularly had won significant victories over Aram (vi, 13;[2] cf. v,
18; vi, 1). The national pride which echoes in these passages can be most
readily understood about the middle, or alternatively towards the end of the
brilliant reign of Jeroboam (cf. II Kings xiv, 23–9[3]). We must therefore put the
appearance of Amos in about 760–750. It was the time when Aram, its power
broken by Adad-nirari III (810–782), could not be any danger to Israel, and
when on the other hand Assyria itself was not advancing near enough to
threaten her.

The superscription names Tekoa as Amos' home town, and this presumably
means the place which lies about 12½ miles south of Jerusalem, mentioned also
in II Sam. xiv, 2; I Chron. ii, 24; II Chron. xi, 6; the modern Khirbet Tekū'a,
and not, as Hans Schmidt[4] has suggested, a place of the same name, otherwise
unknown, in the northern kingdom. Amos was by profession a shepherd,[5]
which probably means that he was an independent cattle owner rather than a
shepherd looking after cattle belonging to others. In addition, according to
vii, 14, he also grew sycamore figs or was expert—thus the literal meaning of
בּוֹלֵס in vii, 14–in the tending of their fruit.[6] Since sycamore fig trees do not
flourish in Tekoa because it lies too high, we must assume that Amos may have

---

[1] Loewe, 'Zechariah xiv, 5' ET 52 (1940/1), pp. 277–9; *Haẓor* II (p. 250, n. 9), pp. 24–36.

[2] Metzger, 'Lodebar und der *tell-el-mghannije*' ZDPV 76 (1960), pp. 97–102.

[3] Gordon, JBL 70 (1951), pp. 161 f., translates xiv, 28aβ: 'restored Damascus and Hamath from Judah into Israel', identifying Judah here with Sam'al. Lit. § 126.

[4] 'Die Herkunft des Propheten Amos' BZAW 34 (1920), pp. 158–71. Cf. Speier, VT 3 (1953), pp. 305 f.

[5] i, 1. נֹקֵד *tender of small cattle*, vii, 14 בּוֹקֵר *tender of large cattle*. It is scarcely necessary to alter vii, 14, following i, 1, in spite of the mention of *small cattle* in vii, 15, since Amos may in fact have possessed or shepherded small cattle (sheep and goats) and large cattle. In the Ugaritic texts, *nqd* appears as the title of cult servants, cf. I AB VI 54–5, where *rb nqdm*, 'chief of the shepherds' stands in parallel with *rb khnm*, 'chief of the priests' (Montgomery, AThR 18 (1936), p. 254). This does not justify the suggestion made by Bič, 'Der Prophet Amos—ein Haepatoskopos' VT 1 (1951), pp. 293–6, to regard נֹקֵד and בּוֹקֵר in Amos i, 1; vii, 14, as designations of a cultic functionary, and to see in Amos an inspector of the liver; cf. Murtonen, 'The Prophet Amos -a Hepatoscoper?' VT 2 (1952), pp. 170–1.

[6] Keimer, 'Eine Bemerkung zu Amos vii, 14' Bibl 8 (1927), pp. 441–4; 'An Ancient Egyptian Knife in Modern Egypt' *Ancient Egypt* (1928), pp. 65 f.

owned land either in the hill country which runs down to the Mediterranean, or in the valley of the Dead Sea, which may both well have stood in close economic relationship to Tekoa, since the pasture-land of the place extended in those directions. He may have grown the trees there, unless he was in fact a shepherd working in the service of others and also practised the craft of culti-vating sycamore figs from place to place. More important, however, than the positive information concerning Amos' profession is the negative which is underlined by the first information, namely, that he is no *nabi'*, does not belong to the *nabi'*-profession but has another source of livelihood and therefore does not need to live on the profession of *nabi'*. With pride Amos stresses his non-adherence to the profession, and particularly so because it thus becomes all the more clear that it is Yahweh's direct intervention which has led him to make his proclamation (vii, 15).[7]

We learn only little concerning the further course of his life apart from the short narrative of his conflict with the chief priest at Bethel which has just been evaluated (vii, 10–17). It is quite clear that he appeared with his proclamation mainly, probably indeed exclusively, in the northern kingdom. It is possible that he had already travelled in the northern kingdom and had come then to know the prevailing conditions. This could readily be understood if he is to be thought of as a shepherd engaged in the service of others and as a tender of sycamore figs. After his call, he appeared in Bethel, and certainly not only on the occasion described in vii, 10–17, which led to his expulsion. It is more probable that many of his other sayings, particularly the diatribe against the cultus in v, 21–7,[8] were spoken in Bethel, and the fifth vision, in which Amos sees Yahweh standing beside the altar (ix, 1–4) was certainly also experienced there. We may however certainly assume that he also appeared in the capital, and those diatribes and threats which explicitly mention Samaria—iii, 9–11; iv, 1–3; vi, 1–7—are naturally to be thought of as having been spoken there. Admittedly Amos may have acquired the knowledge of the immorality pre-vailing in the capital, presupposed in these sayings, before his call to be a prophet, and may have hurled these accusations against it from a distance. Nothing definite can be said concerning the duration of Amos' activity, but from the book we get the impression that it was only short. After the fulfilment of the task laid upon him by Yahweh, he may have returned to his normal profession.

2. *The different elements in the book.* The book in its present form gives on

[7] Ackroyd, 'Amos vii, 14' ET 68 (1956/7), p. 94; Baumann, 'Eine Einzelheit' ZAW 64, (1952), p. 62; Danell, 'Var Amos verkligen en nabi?' SEA 16 (1951), pp. 7–20; Driver, 'Amos vii, 14' ET 67 (1955/6), pp. 91 f.; Gunneweg, 'Erwägungen zu Amos vii, 14' ZThK 57 (1960), pp. 1–16; Herntrich, 'Das Berufungsbewußtsein des Amos' CuW 9 (1933), pp. 161–76; van Hoonacker, 'Le sens de la protestation d'Amos vii, 14–15' EThL 18 (1941), pp. 65–7; MacCormack, 'Amos vii, 14' ET 67 (1955/6), p. 318; Rowley, 'Was Amos a Nabi?' *Eissfeldt-Festschr.* (1947), pp. 191–8; Stoebe, 'Der Prophet Amos und sein bürgerlicher Beruf' WuD 5 (1957), pp. 160–81; Vogt and Driver, 'Waw explicative in Amos vii, 14' ET 68 (1956/7), pp. 301 f. Lit. § 126.

[8] Hyatt, 'The Translation and Meaning of Amos v, 23–24' ZAW 68 (1956), pp. 17–24; Junker, 'Amos und die "opferlose Mosezeit"' ThGl 27 (1935), pp. 686–95; Speiser, 'Note on Amos v, 26' BASOR 108 (1947), pp. 5 f.; Würthwein, 'Amos v, 21–27' ThLZ 72 (1947), cols. 143–52.

the one hand the impression of good and deliberate arrangement, but on the other hand there is no lack of indications of a still better arrangement of the material, now disturbed. The superscription (i, 1) is followed by an isolated saying (i, 2)[9] placed as a sort of motto probably not to the whole book but only to the first poem, that on the nations. This saying also appears in Joel iv, 16, and in a somewhat different form in Jer. xxv, 30–1, in connection with threats against foreign nations. These are followed in i, 3–ii, 16,[10] by the large poem on the nations, made up of eight strophes, though originally probably only of five (p. 400), which proclaims the punishment of Yahweh upon Damascus, the Philistines, Tyre, Edom, the Ammonites, Moab, Judah, and above all Israel,[11] because of *three transgressions*,[12] *yea four*, committed by them. We then have in iii, 1–v, 6, three sayings or groups of sayings beginning with *Hear this word* (שִׁמְעוּ אֶת־הַדָּבָר הַזֶּה), and in v, 7–vi, 14, three beginning with *Woe* (הוֹי); iii, 1–15; iv, 1–13; v, 1–6; and v, 7–17,[13] *Woe to those who turn justice to wormwood*, v, 18–27, *Woe to those who desire the day of Yahweh*,[14] vi, 1–14, *Woe to those who are at ease in Zion*. A fourth group beginning *Hear this* (שִׁמְעוּ זֹאת), which therefore might have been expected after v, 6, appears in viii, 4–14, but is here quite unsuitable since it divides the fifth vision (ix, 1–4) from the fourth (viii, 1–3). vii, 1–ix, 4, has the narrative of the five visions of Amos (vii, 1–3; vii, 4–6;[15] vii, 7–9;[16] viii, 1–3; ix, 1–4), but only the first three follow one another in direct sequence. Between the third and fourth there is inserted the narrative already mentioned of Amos' conflict with the chief priest of Bethel (vii, 10–17),[17] and between the fourth and fifth, the group of *Hear* sayings just cited. The fifth vision is followed first by a hymnic fragment in ix, 5–6, which is certainly not genuine (p. 400), then in ix, 7–10, a threat which as far as 8b is equally certainly genuine, and finally in ix, 11–15, the concluding promise which is probably to be denied to Amos (pp. 400 f.).

How the present condition of the book is to be explained cannot at every point be made clear. As far as vii, 10–17, is concerned, the reason for its present position is obvious: a redactor has regarded the threatening of Jeroboam with

[9] Bertholet, 'Zu Amos i, 2' *Bonwetsch-Festschr.* (1918), pp. 1–12, where it is described as giving an echo of the experience of his call.

[10] Bentzen, 'The Ritual Background of Amos i, 2–ii, 16' OTS 8 (1950), pp. 85–99; Malamat, 'Amos i, 5, in the Light of the Til Barsip Inscriptions' BASOR 129 (1953), pp. 25–6.

[11] Beek, 'The Religious Background of Amos ii, 6–8' OTS 5 (1948), pp. 132–41; Dürr (p. 66, n. 4), pp. 150–4; Zolli, 'Note Esegetiche (Amos ii, 7a)' RStOr 16 (1936), pp. 178–83. Lit. § 126.

[12] Soper, 'For Three Transgressions and for Four. A New Interpretation of Amos i, 3 etc.' ET 71 (1959/60), pp. 86 f.

[13] הוֹי, *Woe*, is to be supplied at the beginning of v, 7.

[14] Couturier, 'Le Jour de Yahveh dans l'AT' Revue de l'Université d'Ottawa (1954), pp. 193–217; Mowinckel, '"Jahves dag"' NTT 59 (1958), pp. 1–56, 209–29; von Rad, 'The Origin of the Day of Yahweh' JSSt 4 (1959), pp. 97–108. Lit. p. 319, n. 65; p. 392, n. 4; § 126.

[15] Rinaldi, 'Due note ad Amos' RStOr 28 (1953), pp. 149–52: 1. Amos iii, 11b (Vulg.), 2. Amos vii, 4 (Hebr.).

[16] Junker, 'Text und Bedeutung der Vision Amos vii, 7–9' Bibl 17 (1936), pp. 359–64; Mackenzie, 'The Plumb Line (Amos vii, 8)' ET 60 (1949), p. 159.

[17] L. Rost 'Zu Amos vii, 10–17' *Zahn-Festgabe* (1928), pp. 229–36.

the sword which stands at the end of the third vision (vii, 9) as being the same as the threat, similarly worded, which occurs in the narrative vii, 10–11, and has therefore linked the narrative to the third vision, even though it meant separating the third and fourth visions. But we can no longer determine whence the redactor took this narrative, whether it was from another position in the book or from an independent collection of third-person information concerning Amos. The latter is, however, the more probable; at any rate such a procedure finds parallels in the books of Isaiah, Jeremiah and Hosea (pp. 148 f.). It is hardly possible to find a really intelligible explanation for the present position of viii, 4–14. Nor is the placing of the threat in ix, 7–10, easily explained, linked as it is across the non-genuine verses ix, 5–6, to the fifth vision. Perhaps the passage was put in its present position at the same time as viii, 4–14, which means that the fifth vision has been set in the middle of a collection of words of Amos exhibiting many parallels to i–vi, though an intelligible reason for this procedure cannot be discovered, unless it be the desire to provide a sufficient motive for the vision which threatens final annihilation.

It is noteworthy furthermore that the five visions which most probably belong to the beginning of the prophet's activity, perhaps even describe his call, stand not at the beginning of the book but at the end. The reason for this position of the visions is probably the same which has determined the similar situation in the book of Isaiah: the desire to let Yahweh himself speak before a description of the prophet's experience is given, or to let the book begin with a summarising 'sermon' by the prophet (p. 310). Again we cannot decide with certainty whether we should go further and think that the visions once stood at the beginning of the book and were then removed from that position, or that the redactor of the book had before him two independent collections—or if we include the conjectured biographical report, three at least—i.e. the biographical report, the first-person narrative of the visions, and at least one collection of sayings. This latter possibility seems, in view of all that has so far been said about the formation of the prophetic books, to be the more probable.

3. *Amos' share in the composition of the book.* When we ask how far Amos himself had a part in the compilation of the book which bears his name, we must first assign the narratives of the visions to the prophet. Since in the collection of sayings in i–vi the prophet also speaks once in the first person (v, 1), we must also trace back to his actual writing down or dictation if not the collection itself, at least parts of it. This also appears probable because of the poem on the nations, for in so far as this is genuine it certainly comes from Amos, even as regards its form. But these observations do not suffice to prove that individual sections of the book were actually written down or dictated by Amos himself. The book as a whole, in which, as we have seen, there are several component parts, including a third-person narrative, certainly does not go back to Amos himself. Moreover, the collection of sayings which it contains in i–vi has also probably been gathered together by another hand, since the grouping together of several individual sayings into larger speeches beginning with *Hear* and *Woe* (p. 398) has obscured the demarcation of the originally quite independent sayings, and this can hardly be attributed to the prophet himself. In

addition, there is no lack of indications that there were at least two such collections, in part parallel to each other, and this can be more readily explained as due to the shaping of the material by others than on the grounds of Amos' own authorship. There is no need to doubt the genuineness of the individual sayings, or at any rate of the large majority of them. This is guaranteed, if only by the pregnancy of their expression, and their rigid rhythmic form. There are, apart from the poem on the nations, about twenty-five individual sayings which can be differentiated in those parts of the book which contain 'words': iii, 1–2, 3–8,[18] 9–11, 12,[19] 13–15; iv, 1–3, 4–5, 6–12a; v, 1–3, 4–6,[20] 7+10–11, 12, 14–15, 16–17, 18–20, 21–7; vi, 1–7, 8–10, 11, 12, 13–14; viii, 4–7, 9–10, 11–14;[21] ix, 7, 8–10*. By far the majority are threats with or without motive. The best-known example of a literary type which is not specifically prophetic, but taken from another department of life, is the dirge on the death of the maiden Israel in v, 2 (pp. 127–8).

4. *Secondary additions.* The book, like that of Hosea, is comparatively free from secondary additions. Apart from odd verses and parts of verses, there are three more important expansions. First, the poem on the nations in i, 3–ii, 16, has probably been enlarged by the addition of the Tyre strophe (i, 9–10), the Edom strophe, which appears to condemn Edom's attitude after 587 (i, 11–12), and certainly the Judah strophe, which is noteworthy for its very general and Deuteronomic expressions (ii, 4–5). Secondly, at three points in the book, three sections of a hymn have been inserted, namely iv, 13; v, 8–9,[22] and ix, 5–6, though it cannot be said with certainty whether the reason for this insertion was a purely external one, namely that the Amos scroll still had a little space at these points, or whether considerations of content led to this procedure, perhaps the desire to underline the preceding threats by means of a hymn to Yahweh (v, 8–9; ix, 5–6) or to replace them (so it would appear in iv, 13).[23] Finally, we must also regard the concluding promise to the book (ix, 11–15) as an addition, although the position is not so clear here as in the two preceding cases. Sellin's view of ix, 11–15, as the original sequel to vii, 10–17, which gives a strong emphasis to the threat expressed there against the northern kingdom by a promise to the southern kingdom, deserves to be seriously considered. But ix, 11–15, is very similar to other prophecies of salvation which are

[18] Holwerda, *De exegese van Amos iii, 3–8* (1948); Junker, 'Leo rugiit, etc. Eine textkritische und exegetische Untersuchung über Amos iii, 3–8' Trierer ThZ 59 (1950), pp. 4–13; Winton Thomas, 'A Note on נוֹעָדוּ in Amos iii, 3' JThSt 7 (1956), pp. 69 f.

[19] Benson, ' "From the mouth of the lion"; the Messianism of Amos' CBQ 19 (1957), pp. 199–212; Dürr (p. 66, n. 4), p. 150; Rabinowitz, 'The Crux at Amos iii, 12' VT 11 (1961), pp. 228–31; Reider, 'דמשק in Am iii, 12' JBL 67 (1948), pp. 245–8. Lit. § 126.

[20] Hesse, 'Amos v, 4–6, 14 f.' ZAW 68 (1956), pp. 1–17.

[21] Bartina, ' "Vivat Potentia Beer Šeba" (Am viii, 14)' VD 34 (1956), pp. 202–9; Neuberg, 'An Unrecognized Meaning of Hebrew DOR' JNESt 9 (1950), pp. 215–17: on viii, 14. Lit. p. 182, n. 2.

[22] Driver, 'Two Astronomical Passages in the Old Testament' JThSt 4 (1953), pp. 208–12: on Amos v, 8–9, Job xxxviii, 12–15.

[23] Gaster, 'An Ancient Hymn in the Prophecies of Amos' Journal Manchester Eg. Or. Soc. 19 (1935), pp. 23–6; Horst, 'Die Doxologien im Amosbuch' ZAW 47 (1929), pp. 45–54 = *Gottes Recht* (1961), pp. 155–66; Watts, 'An Old Hymn Preserved in the Book of Amos' JNESt 15 (1956), pp. 33–9.

recognised to be late, and the position of the verses at the end of a book, where in other cases too consolatory prophecies are readily added (p. 317), is suspicious. So the matter is better left with Wellhausen's classic statement, which admittedly was applied by him to ix, 8–15; 'Roses and lavender instead of blood and iron . . . Amos . . . means what he says. . . . After he has just before far surpassed all his earlier threats, he cannot suddenly blunt their sharpness, he cannot let milk and honey flow from the cup of Yahweh's wrath at the end. . . . It is a later Jew who has appended this coda, and removed the genuine conclusion, because this sounded too harshly in his ears.'[24]

5. *The portrait of the prophet.* The book of Amos, like that of Hosea, in spite of its extreme brevity, is quite sufficient to give us a picture of the prophet. It shows him as a master of form, who, no doubt following earlier patterns, presents his visionary experiences concisely and vividly, and his diatribes and threats in sharp and pregnant language, but who also has the capacity for producing larger units like the poem on the nations, and the—fragmentary—poem with refrain in iv, 6–12a, on the lack of effect of the punishments with which Israel has been threatened by Yahweh in the past. He also shows himself as a great poet when, as in the dirge on the maiden Israel in v, 2, he takes over into his language motives from non-prophetic types. The fact that in his book diatribes and threats are in a large majority, is bound up with the harsh and relentless content of his message. With an uncompromising radicalism he meets the religiosity of his contemporaries and compatriots who have grown self-sufficient and comfortable. He ruthlessly tears down their illusions: how could Yahweh ever be bound to his people by any kind of natural or physical bonds, so that while punishing her, he could never entirely give her up? He proclaims with sublime monotony that Yahweh measures the nations, even and indeed specially his own, only with the standard of righteousness and morality. He contends with a polemic well nigh blasphemous that even the richest sacrifices and other activities of the cult could not make the slightest impression upon God nor lead him to withdraw his arm when it is held out for an annihilating stroke. He threatens the annihilation of the people as quite unavoidable and though with a bleeding heart, can triumph at the victory of his God expressed in the downfall of his people. For to him God is everything, and Israel nothing.

§ 52. OBADIAH

Literature: Abel, 'L'expédition des Grecs à Pétra en 312 avant J.-C.' RB 46 (1937), pp. 373–91; Bekel, 'Ein vorexilisches Orakel über Edom' ThStKr 80 (1907), pp. 315–43; Bič, 'Ein verkanntes Thronbesteigungsfestorakel im AT' ArOr 19 (1951), pp. 568–78; 'Zur Problematik des Buches Obadjah' SVT I (1953), pp. 11–25; Cannon, 'Israel and Edom. The Oracle of Obadiah' Theology 15 (1927), pp. 129–40, 191–200; Edelkoort, 'De profetie van Obadja' NedThT 1 (1946/7), pp. 276–93; Grimme, 'Der Untergang Edoms' Welt als Geschichte 3 (1937), pp. 452–63; Robinson, 'The Structure of the Book of Obadiah' JThSt 17 (1916), pp. 402–8; Rudolph, 'Obadja' ZAW 49 (1931), pp. 222–31;

---

[24] *Die Kleinen Propheten* ([3]1898), p. 96.

Starcky, 'The Nabateans' BA 18 (1955), pp. 84–106, see p. 86; Theis, *Die Weissagung des Abdias* (1917); Veldcamp, *Het gezicht van Obadja* (1957).

Cf. also Literature p. 242, n. 2; §§ 48, 126.

1. *Contents.* In the title *The Vision of Obadiah. Thus speaks the Lord Yahweh. Concerning Edom*, the words *thus speaks the Lord Yahweh* are probably a secondary addition. This title is followed in verse 1b by an account of a summons by the peoples to themselves, received in ecstatic audition, to go to battle *against her*, that is against Edom. In vv. 2–9, there follows the threat of the complete downfall of Edom, for we must understand the verses thus, and not as a narrative of something which has already taken place, as we shall see in a moment. The reason for this sentence of punishment is given in vv. 10–14 + 15b: Edom gloated over Jerusalem's hard fate—a clear allusion to the disaster of 587—and indeed even added to Jerusalem's sufferings. This is now to be paid back to her (15b). In vv. 15a + 16–21[1], however, the horizon widens. Here there is mention of the day of Yahweh about to break in on all nations, to bring destruction to all peoples, but to mark for Zion the dawn of unclouded good fortune.

2. *The composition and date of origin of the book.* Small as the book is, there are nevertheless very varied views concerning its composition and date of origin. So far as its composition is concerned, we may note simply the two extremes. Robinson sees the booklet as a collection of fragments of poems against Edom from various periods (vv. 1–5, 6–7, 8–11, 12–14, 15–16, 17–18, 19–21), whereas Rudolph and Weiser divide vv. 1–18 into two oracles going back to Obadiah, vv. 1–14 + 15b, and 15a + 16–18, and even consider it possible that the conclusion vv. 19–21, which was in any case added later, may owe its origin to Obadiah. Theis and Edelkoort ascribe the whole booklet to the prophet, placed by Theis in the middle of the ninth century, and by Edelkoort in the middle of the sixth century B.C. As far as the date of origin is concerned, however, opinions vary between the beginning of the ninth century and the fifth century. Sellin, substantially followed by Theis, finds the occasion for this threat against Edom in the conflicts which broke out between Edom and Judah after Edom's break away from Judah in about 850 B.C. (II Kings viii, 20–2). So he dates the basic material of the book, i.e. vv. 1–10, in about 800 B.C. This is for him determined also by the fact that vv. 1–10 reappear substantially in Jer. xlix, 7–22 (p. 363), and on the supposition that this passage in the book of Jeremiah was not a secondary addition there, vv. 1–10 must be older. He could also have brought in as an argument the placing of the book among the prophetic books which belong to the eighth century, for this must certainly be explained on the grounds that the redactor of the Book of the Twelve also dated Obadiah in this early period. The derivation of the book from the fifth century, i.e. from the period when the Arab tribes began to press into the cultivated land more strongly than previously from the steppe lying to the south and east of Palestine, was suggested in all probability first by Wellhausen, and in this he

---

[1] Gray, 'The Diaspora of Israel and Judah in Obadiah v. 20' ZAW 65 (1953), pp. 53–9; Kornfeld, 'Die Jüdische Diaspora in Ab. 20' *Mél. Bibl. Robert* (1957), pp. 180–6.

has been followed by many others. Wellhausen and his followers understand vv. 2–9 not as a threat, but as a narrative or description, and must therefore find a situation in which Edom really was particularly harshly overrun.

Two points seem certain. (1) vv. 2–9 are not a description but a genuine threat; and (2) vv. 11–14+15b, which Sellin admittedly separates from vv. 1–10 and treats as a later addition to the basic material dated in the period about 800 B.C., actually form an indivisible unit with vv. 1–10, in that vv. 2–9 contains the threat and vv. 10–14+15b the reason for it. In vv. 11–14, however, it is quite certain that there is reference to Edom's malicious attitude at the time of Jerusalem's destruction in 587. So vv. 1–10 are thus fixed as not older than this. Since vv. 11–14 give the impression that the sting of Edom's behaviour towards Jerusalem still rankles with the Jews, we must place these verses and hence the whole of vv. 1–14+15b shortly after 587, roughly in the same period to which the oldest poems in the book of Lamentations belong (pp. 503 f.). The identity of a series of verses from Jer. xlix, 7–22, with verses from vv. 1–10 here is no argument against this dating. For the oracle against Edom attributed to Jeremiah in Jer. xlix, 7–22 is certainly not entirely genuine, and the verses which are identical with those in Obadiah's threat can have been added later to the Jeremianic basic material (p. 363). This is what is likely to have happened. Nor does the position of Obadiah in the Book of the Twelve provide an argument to the contrary. We have already seen in the case of the book of Joel that we cannot everywhere rely upon the arrangement in the Book of the Twelve though it was evidently intended to be chronological.

We cannot pronounce so definitely upon vv. 15a+16–21. It is admittedly certain that vv. 15a+16–21 form an independent section which is not connected with what precedes. It is also clear that this section subdivides further into two independent units, vv. 15a+16–18 and vv. 19–21; the second may be differentiated from the first by the fact that it is written in prose. But we can hardly decide definitely whether these two sections—or at least the first of them —are also to be attributed to Obadiah, or whether they belong to a later period. It is possible that Obadiah after a threat against Edom also pronounced a general proclamation of the day of Yahweh, which anyway represents Edom as especially affected. But on the other hand it is certain that older oracles which refer to a concrete event have later been filled out to present a stronger proclamation of the day of Yahweh. It is sufficient to point to Joel (§ 50) and Isa. xiii (pp. 319 f.). It is thus more probable that we should deny vv. 15a+16–18 and 19–21 to the Obadiah who was active just after 587, and attribute them to one or rather two later hands. A more precise dating is hardly possible.

§ 53. JONAH

Literature: Aalders, *The Problem of the Book of Jonah* (1948); Bird, *The Book of Jona* (1938); Blank, ' "Doest Thou Well to be Angry?" A Study in Self-Pity' HUCA 26 (1955), pp. 29–41; Boehme, 'Die Composition des Buches Jona' ZAW 7 (1887), pp. 224–84; Boman, 'Jahve og Elohim i Jonaboken' NTT 37 (1936), pp. 159–64; Childs,

'Jonah. A Study in OT Hermeneutics' SJTh 11 (1958), pp. 53–61; Dijkema, 'Het Boek Jona' NThT 25 (1936), pp. 338–47; Feuillet, 'Les sources du livre de Jonas' RB 54 (1947), pp. 161–86; 'Le sens du livre de Jonas' RB 54 (1947), pp. 340–61; Gemser, 'Die Humor van die OuT' HTSt 8 (1951), pp. 49–63; Goitein, 'Some Observations on Jonah' JPOS 17 (1937), pp. 63–77; Goldman, 'Was the Book of Jonah originally written in Aramaic?' ABR 3 (1953), pp. 49 f.; Haller, *Die Erzählung von dem Propheten Jona* (Theol. Ex. 65, 1958); Hart-Davies, 'The Book of Jonah in the Light of Assyrian Archaeology' Journ. Victoria Institute 69 (1937), pp. 230–49; Heuschen, 'L'interprétation du livre de Jonas' Rev Eccl Liège 35 (1948), pp. 141–59; Jansen, 'Har Jonaboken en enhetlig opbygning og en bestemt hovedtendens?' NTT 37 (1936), pp. 145–58; Komlós, 'Jonah Legends' *Ét. Or. Hirschler* (1950), pp. 41–61; Loretz, 'Herkunft und Sinn der Jona-Erzählung' BZ 5 (1961), pp. 18–29; Mowinckel, 'Efterskrift til pastor Th. Bomans artikkel' NTT 37 (1936), pp. 164–8; Hans Schmidt, *Jona, eine Untersuchung zur vergleichenden Religionsgeschichte* (FRLANT 9, 1907); Snaith, *Notes on the Hebrew Text of Jonah* (1945); Stollberg, *Jona* (Diss. theol. Halle, 1927); Trépanier, 'The Story of Jonas' CBQ 13 (1951), pp. 8–16; Winckler, *Altorient. Forsch.* II, 2 (1900), pp. 260–5.

Cf. also Literature §§ 48, 126.

1. *Contents.* The book of Jonah differs from the other prophetic books in that it does not contain entirely or substantially sayings which the prophet has proclaimed in the name of Yahweh, but a narrative concerning the prophet. It begins entirely in the style of a story: *Now the word of Yahweh came to Jonah ben-Amittai, thus* (i, 1), and it tells how this Jonah endeavoured to avoid Yahweh's command to summon Nineveh to repentance, by attempting to escape by ship from Joppa to Tarshish. To quieten a storm which was raised on his account by the deity and which threatened to wreck the ship (i, 4),[1] he was thrown into the sea by the sailors, and swallowed by a great fish. After he had been in its belly for three days and had uttered a song of thanksgiving (ii, 3–10), he was vomited out on the land (i, 2–ii, 11). He now obeyed the renewed command of Yahweh to preach repentance to Nineveh. The people of Nineveh humbled themselves[2] and so God gave up the punishment he had intended (iii). Jonah was reduced to a mood of despair and God brought home to him the folly of his attitude by making a gourd grow up which gave Jonah shade, and then made it wither away so that Jonah now sat without shade and grieved for the dead plant. Yahweh reproached him for wishing that the plant had been spared; how much more has Yahweh the right to spare the great city which contains so many children and cattle (iv).

2. *The origin of the material.* In II Kings xiv, 25, there is mention of a prophet Jonah ben-Amittai from Gath-hepher,[3] which, according to Josh. xix, 13, is to be sought in the area of the tribe of Zebulun. The passage relates that he proclaimed to Jeroboam II (786–746) the extension of his kingdom again to the size which it had in the time of David. There was thus in actual fact a prophet with this name in the middle of the eighth century. But we may well ask whether

---

[1] Freedman, 'Jonah i, 4b' JBL 77 (1958), pp. 161–2.

[2] Schaumberger, 'Das Bussedikt des Königs von Ninive bei Jonas iii, 7, 8, in keilschriftlicher Beleuchtung' Misc. Bibl. 2 (1934), pp. 123–34; Weidner, 'Das Archiv des Mannu-kî-Aššur' (*Die Inschriften vom Tell Halaf*=AfO Beih. 6 (1940), pp. 8–46. See pp. 13 f., No. 5: Edict of Adadnirari III (810–782) to the governor of Guzâna concerning the holding of a day of repentance.

[3] *ḫirbet eẓ-ẓerrāʿ* near *el-mešhed*, north-east of Nazareth.

the book which is named after him—but which is not attributed to him—has anything more to do with him than using his name. The proclamation pronounced by him in II Kings xiv, 25, has no relationship to the commission which is placed upon him according to the book. However, already during the lifetime of this Jonah or soon after his death, a story may have been told about him which had as its subject his protest, eventually in vain, against a commission by Yahweh, just as something similar was at an early date told with regard to Elijah (I Kings xix, 4–8). Such legendary narratives have this measure of historical content in that the conflict between prophetic compulsion and human desires and abilities—particularly clearly recognisable in Jeremiah (p. 357)—was evidently part of every prophet's experience. Our book has actually *two* such legends as its basis. The one is concerned with Jonah's resistance, eventually broken down by Yahweh, to the commission to summon Nineveh to repentance (i–iii); the other shows how Jonah's dissatisfaction with Yahweh's mercy is led to the point of absurdity by the latter's action (iv). With these legends, or more properly with the first of them, there is interwoven a mythological, fairy-tale motif which is found throughout the world, namely the motif of the swallowing and vomiting out of a man by a great fish, known, for example, in one form of the Perseus saga.

3. *Date of origin. Purpose.* From these materials an unknown compiler has made up a work, our book, and we cannot now discover in detail what he found already to hand and what he himself added to it. We can only say with certainty that the broad universalism and tolerant humanity which give the book its attractive tone, belong to the compiler and his time. While it is possible that such ideas were already hinted at in the material which the compiler found to hand, the belief as it is now stated, that Yahweh's mercy is not limited to Israel, but includes even quite alien people, even the inhabitants of a city hated by Israel, and also includes animals, certainly belongs to the compiler. This determines his period. In the pre-exilic period such far-reaching universalism and such unconditional tolerance are difficult to imagine. We must therefore assign the book to the post-exilic period. With this agrees also the fact that the Assyrian empire and its capital are clearly far away in the past. The various Aramaisms (i, 7, בְּשֶׁלְמִי, *on whose account?*; iii, 2, קְרִיאָה, *proclamation*, etc.) also fit this. Whether, as is often done, the book is to be understood as a counter to the exclusive and particularistic measures taken by Nehemiah and Ezra (pp. 544, 546), may be left an open question. A spirit like that of the compiler can be understood quite apart from this. We can in any case not bring down the dating of the book later than 200 B.C., for it is presupposed by the books of Ecclesiasticus (xlix, 10) and Tobit (xiv, 4, 8) which came into being at the beginning of the second century.

In the Book of the Twelve, the book stands among those which actually or supposedly originated in the eighth century. This corresponds to the fact that the prophet did actually appear in the eighth century. We cannot determine whether this placing of the book is at the same time intended to suggest that the book originated then. In any case, this dating would be no more determinative than it was in the cases of Joel and Obadiah (pp. 395, 402).

4. *The Psalm—ii, 3–10. Problems of literary criticism.* The book has not come down to us in the form in which it left the compiler, but has undergone some few, though insignificant alterations. In the first place, Jonah's prayer (ii, 3–10),[4] a 'song of thanksgiving', like many in the Psalter (pp. 121–4), was added secondarily, and perhaps at the same time there was added verse 2 as introduction to it. We cannot thereby determine whether the psalm is older or younger than the book. It may indeed be older. Furthermore, as Winckler perceived, iv, 5, has been moved from its original position after iii, 4, and in connection with this, iv, 5bα, *and made a booth for himself there and sat under it in the shade,* has been added. Secondary additions are probably also to be found in i, 8aβ, *on whose account this evil has come upon us,* and i, 10bγ, *for he had told them.* But apart from this the book is a unity. Attempts at making a division into sources, as made by Böhme and Hans Schmidt, must be regarded as unsuccessful. Even the interchange between *Yahweh* and *Elohim* hardly justifies a division of the material between two sources. It is true that the phenomenon is remarkable. In i, 1–iii, 3, we have *Yahweh*; in iii, (3) 4–10, *Elohim and ha-Elohim*; in iv, 1–5, *Yahweh*; in iv, 6, *Yahweh Elohim*; in iv, 7–9, *ha-Elohim* and *Elohim*; in iv, 10–11, *Yahweh*. However, the occurrence of *Elohim* in iii, 3, and iii, 4–10, within a section which otherwise uses *Yahweh*, is quite intelligible. For in the expression *Nineveh was a great city for Elohim* in iii, 3, *Elohim* is used adjectivally, as we might speak of a *divinely beautiful city,*[5] and in iii, 4–10, or more strictly iii, 7–9, we are concerned with the relationship to God of the Ninevites, i.e. worshippers of other deities, though in vv. 5 and 10, where the narrator speaks, we should have expected *Yahweh* again. But in iv, 7–9, we ought in any case to have *Yahweh,* and *Yahweh Elohim* in iv, 6, is also inexplicable. A satisfactory explanation of the facts has not yet been given.[6]

§ 54. MICAH

Literature: Beyerlin, *Die Kulttraditionen Israels in der Verkündigung des Propheten Micha* (FRLANT 72, 1959); Bruno, *Micha und der Herrscher aus der Vorzeit* (1923); Budde, 'Das Rätsel von Micha i' ZAW 37 (1917–8), pp. 77–108; 'Micha ii und iii' ZAW 38 (1910/20), pp. 2–22; 'Verfasser und Stelle von Micha iv, 1–4 (Jes. ii, 2–4)' ZDMG 81 (1927), pp. 152–8; Copass and Carlson, *A Study of the Prophet Micah* (1950); Elliger, 'Die Heimat des Propheten Micha' ZDPV 57 (1934), pp. 81–152; Gunkel, 'Der Micha-Schluss' ZS 2 (1924), pp. 145–78; J. Jeremias, 'Moreseth-Gath, die Heimat des Propheten Micha' PJB 29 (1933), pp. 42–53; Lindblom, *Micha, literarisch untersucht* (1929); Milik, 'Fragments d'un Midrash de Michée dans les Manuscripts de Qumrân' RB 59 (1952), pp. 412–18, cf. § 109; Procksch, 'Gat' ZDPV 66 (1943), pp. 174–91, cf. pp. 175–81; Louise Pettibone Smith, 'The Book of Micah' Interpr. 6 (1952), pp. 210–27; Stade, 'Bemerkungen

[4] Johnson, 'Jonah ii, 3–10. A Study in Cultic Phantasy' StOTPr (1950), pp. 82–102 Stenzel, 'Zum Vulgatatext des Canticum Jonae' Bibl 33 (1952), pp. 356–62.
[5] Winton Thomas, 'A Consideration of some unusual ways of expressing the superlative in Hebrew' VT 3 (1953), pp. 209–24: cf. pp. 210–19.
[6] Rosin, *The Lord is God. The Translation of the Divine Names and the Missionary Calling of the Church* (1956), pp. 6–33: 'Function and Interrelation of the Designations of God in the Book of Jonah, Chapter i, Chapters ii–iv.'

über das Buch Micha' ZAW 1 (1881), pp. 161–72; 'Weitere Bemerkungen zu Micha iv, v' ZAW 3 (1883), pp. 1–16; 'Micha ii, 4' ZAW 6 (1886), pp. 122–3; 'Micha i, 2–4 und vii, 7–20, ein Psalm' ZAW 23 (1903), pp. 163–71; Vilnai, 'The Topography of Palestine in the Prophecies of Micah' [Hebr.] BJPES 6 (1939), pp. 127–31.

Cf. also Literature §§ 48, 126.

1. *Date, place of origin, and person of the prophet.* The superscription calls Micah a Morashtite (מֹרַשְׁתִּי) and places him, though this is in a secondary addition, in the days of Jotham (745–742), Ahaz (741–726) and Hezekiah (725–697). Jer. xxvi, 18, also describes him thus and mentions the reign of Hezekiah as the time of his appearance. In Micah i, 14, the home of Micah— for it is evident that that is what is meant—is designated as Moresheth-gath (מוֹרֶשֶׁת גַּת), which is to be sought on the site of *tell ed-jēde*, situated in the Shephelah, the hill country of Judah, twenty-two miles south-west of Jerusalem. Micah was a man of the country, not of the town, and hence it is understandable that he was moved, like Amos who also came from the countryside, by the evils of the capital cities Samaria and Jerusalem. The date given in the title, and confirmed as far as Hezekiah is concerned by Jer. xxvi, 18, fits well with the content of the book in that it shows that Micah began his proclamation before the fall of Samaria, but then turned to Judah and Jerusalem alone (pp. 409 f.). Micah was thus a contemporary of Isaiah, and it is possible and indeed probable that the latter may have exerted some influence upon him. Concerning the personality of Micah, we learn nothing else, not even whether he belonged by profession to the *nebi'im* or not.

2. *Contents and divisions of the book.* The title in i, 1, is followed in vv. 2–7 by a threat against Israel and Judah which begins as the description of Yahweh's appearance for world-judgement (vv. 2–4). Vv. 8–16 contain either the lament over the disaster which the advance of a hostile army has brought on a series of places lying to the south-west and south of Jerusalem, including the home of Micah—or, since i, 8–16, may be so interpreted and has been so understood recently again by Fohrer, the threat of such a disaster couched in the form of a lament. Like Isa. x, 27–34, it makes use of the names of the places affected with a play upon words and ideas. ii, 1–5,[1] then provides a harsh *woe*, reminiscent of Isa. v, 8–10, against the rich who ruthlessly take away from their poorer compatriots both fields and houses. ii, 6–11, a lively dispute between those attacked by the prophet (vv. 6–7) and the prophet himself (vv. 8–11), is perhaps not to be understood as an independent section, but as the continuation of the preceding verses. In any event, Micah here reproaches his opponents with driving others by force out of house and home (vv. 8–9). ii, 12–13, however, is quite different; here the reuniting of scattered Israel is promised, and there is held out the prospect of a great success in war, or—since perhaps the expression used here is intended metaphorically and is to be understood in a more general sense—a new time of great prosperity. In iii, 1–4, there follows again a diatribe and threat directed against the leaders of the people because of their

[1] Alt, 'Micha ii, 1–5. Γῆς ἀναδασμός in Juda' NTT 56 (1955), pp. 13–23 = *Kl. Schr.* III (1959), pp. 373–81; Weil, 'Le chapitre ii de Michée expliqué par Le Premier Livre des Rois, chapitres xx–xxii' RHR 121 (1940), pp. 146–61.

anti-social behaviour. It is introduced by the phrase *And I said*, which looks almost like the remnant of an autobiographical account, but in view of its brevity we can hardly draw further conclusions from it (p. 149). The next section too, vv. 5–8, is a diatribe and threat, introduced by *Thus spoke Yahweh*, perhaps linked back to the *I said* of iii, 1. It is directed against the false prophets, who order their prophecies according to the payment offered to them or refused them; to them Micah opposes himself in justifiable consciousness of his own position (v. 8):

> But I am filled with power² and with justice and with might
> to declare to Jacob his transgression and to Israel his sin.

Vv. 9–12, finally, also provide a diatribe and threat. It is directed against the law-breaking rulers of Jacob, i.e. as v. 10 indicates, of Judah, against the priests who sell their *torah*, and against the prophets who prophesy for money, and it closes with the terrible threat, which as we know from the testimony of Jer. xxvi, 18, had not yet been forgotten more than a century later (v. 12):

> Therefore because of you Zion shall be plowed as a field
> and Jerusalem shall become a heap of ruins and the Temple hill a wooded
> height.³

Whereas i–iii, with the exception of ii, 12–13, contain nothing but threats, iv–v have only promises, or at any rate what appear to be only promises⁴ (see below, on v, 9–14). There are five sections, apart from v, 9–14. The series is opened with the proclamation of iv, 1–5, which, as we have seen (p. 318), is substantially identical with Isa. ii, 2–4. This asserts that at the end of the days the mountain of Yahweh will overtop all other mountains, and will form the centre of the kingdom of peace ruled over by Yahweh and sought out by all the nations. In vv. 6–7 there follows a promise that Yahweh will gather the scattered and will be king over them in Zion. A similar promise is to be found in the section vv. 8–14, which is in detail often very difficult to understand and may be variously interpreted, the only difference being that here the promise is longer delayed in view of the distress caused by the attack of the power of the heathen nations against Jerusalem, a period which is to precede the final victory of Yahweh and Zion. v, 1–5,⁵ is directed to Bethlehem, with its opening—corrected according to 𝕲—*And thou, Beth-ephrath, smallest among the clans of Judah*, and promises that from it there is to come for Israel the ruler and saviour whose origins reach back into remote antiquity. v, 6–8, anticipates in noble metaphorical language that the remnant of Jacob will stand as victor over all nations. The conclusion of v, 9–14, as it now stands, with in v. 14 its mention of the *vengeance* to be fulfilled in *anger and wrath upon the nations*, also contains with its threat against the heathen an indirect promise for Israel. But apart from this it is clearly directed against Israel itself and is in many ways reminiscent of the threats in

---

² The words *with the spirit of Yahweh* are to be omitted as a gloss.
³ The singular is to be read for the plural.
⁴ Crook, 'The Promise in Micah v' JBL 70 (1951), pp. 313–20.
⁵ Fitzmyer, ' לֹ as a Preposition and a Particle in Micah v, 1 f' CBQ 18 (1956), pp. 10–13.

Isa. ii, 6–8. It proclaims that Yahweh will remove from Israel everything connected with military preparations, magic and idolatry.

vi, 1–vii, 6, present yet another complex of sayings, diatribes, exhortations, threats and laments. At the beginning (vi, 1–8)[6] there stands the impressive judgement speech, introduced by vv. 1–2, between Yahweh (vv. 3–5) and Israel (vv. 6–7). This is closed by the prophet, who takes up the word for Yahweh already at the end of verse 5, with the exhortation:

> *He has told you, O man, what is good*
>> *and what does Yahweh require from you*
> *But to do justice and love kindness*
>> *and to walk humbly with your God?*[7]

In vi, 9–16, there follows a diatribe against the city which has become wealthy by the use of false measures and weights, with a threat of its complete destruction. The next passage (vii, 1–6), a song of lamentation reminiscent of Isa. lvii, 1–2, in which the prophet speaks of the terrible corruption of his compatriots, is concerned with similar evils—dishonesty, corruptibility, twisting of justice, faithlessness.

The conclusion of the book is provided by a promise of the exaltation of Zion over the heathen world, in its form a prophetic liturgy (Gunkel) divided into four parts: vv. 7–10 an individual lament or a song of trust; vv. 11–13, a prophecy; vv. 14–17, a prayer like a national lament; vv. 18–20, a prayer like a national lament which begins as a hymn.

Thus, to summarise, the contents and groupings of the material of the book appear as follows: i–iii (without ii, 12–13), threat; iv, 1–v, 8, promise; v, 9–vii, 6, threat; vii, 7–20, promise.[8]

3. *Genuine and non-genuine passages.* The decision is fairly simple with regard to i–iii. With the exception of the verses ii, 12–13, the passages gathered in i–iii are certainly genuine. Admittedly Sellin, following the suggestion made by earlier scholars, regards ii, 12–13, as belonging originally after iv, 6–7, and refers them to the 'gathering of the population of Palestine which took refuge in Jerusalem in 701 in face of the onslaught of the Assyrians . . . and to their marvellous deliverance from the siege by Yahweh.'[9] Hence he regards them as belonging to Micah. Since in i, 6, Samaria is presupposed as still standing, we must assign i, 2–7, to the period before 721. i, 8–16, like Isa. i, 4–9 (p. 309), probably presupposes, however, the devastations brought upon the land of Judah by Sennacherib in 701 B.C., and is therefore to be dated in this period, or, if in fact it is not intended to be a lament on a disaster which has already taken

---

[6] Anderson, 'A Study of Micah vi, 1–8' SJTh 4 (1951), pp. 191–7; Deissler, 'Micha vi, 1–8: Der Rechtsstreit Jahwes mit Israel um das rechte Bundesverhältnis' Trierer ThZ 68 (1959), pp. 229–34.

[7] Hyatt, 'On the Meaning and Origin of Micah vi, 8' AThR 34 (1952), pp. 232–9; Stoebe, 'Und demütig sein vor deinem Gott. Mi vi, 8' WuD 6 (1959), pp. 180–94; Winton Thomas, 'The Root צנע in Hebrew, and the Meaning of קדרנית in Malachi iii, 14' JJSt 1 (1949), pp. 182–8.

[8] Reicke, 'Mik. vii såsom "messiansk" text' SEA 12 (1947), pp. 279–302.

[9] *Kommentar* (²,³1929), pp. 308, 322.

place but the threat of one to come (p. 407), it may be dated somewhat earlier, about 711, but certainly later than 721. The remaining sections contain no clear indication of a particular period. To conclude from the mention of *Jacob* and *Israel* in ii, 7; iii, 1, 9, that the existence of the northern kingdom is here still presupposed, is unsatisfactory, since iii, 9–12, quite clearly shows that the prophet is using the names *Israel* and *Jacob* for Judah. There is thus no need to date these before 721. Moreover, the accusations and threats which are here set out are of such a general character that they could fit into any period; they hardly become more intelligible by being dated in a particular time. At the most, we might perhaps say that the stubborn confidence which is expressed in the saying of iii, 11, *Is not Yahweh in our midst?* is most readily understandable after Hezekiah's reform. But since we do not know the year of this reform (cf. II Kings xviii, 3–7), this does not really help us very much.

It is very difficult to decide about the genuineness of the oracles of salvation in iv, 1–v, 8, and ii, 12–13—for in subject-matter these latter verses belong in the thought-world of iv, 1–v, 8 (p. 409). We must certainly take serious account of the arguments brought forward for their genuineness, earlier by Hans Schmidt and Sellin, and recently by Lippl, Copass and Carlson. The view is based on the necessity of deriving the messianic prophecies from pre-exilic Judah, organised as a monarchy, and the impossibility of assigning them to post-exilic Judaism which was organised as a community and was opposed to dynasties;[10] the similarity of the messianic hopes in Micah to those of his contemporary Isaiah; the relationship between the expectations set forth in ii, 12–13+iv, 6–7, and iv, 8–14, and those expressed in Isa. xxix, 1–8, and the necessity of assigning the former to the same period as the latter, namely most probably to the year 701; and other arguments of the kind. But very powerful reasons militate against these and argue for the non-genuineness and late origin of the passages. In the first place it is a quite indisputable fact—and indeed in many other passages has been accepted without question—that threats like that of iii, 12, have been watered down by secondary addition of promises (pp. 317, 400 f.). It is all the more natural to assume this at least in regard to iv, 1–5, since this passage also appears in the book of Isaiah, and the double occurrence makes it impossible to assign it with certainty to one or other. Or, if we suppose that Micah took it over from Isaiah (so Sellin, and similarly Copass and Carlson), then it cannot be assigned to both. This makes the most natural assumption that which has recently been made again by Robinson and Weiser, that it is an anonymous passage ascribed in the one place to the one prophet, and in the other place to the other (p. 318). Furthermore, there is the fact that according to Jer. xxvi, 18, Micah was clearly known to posterity only as the proclaimer of the terrible threat against the Temple hill in iii, 12, but not for the promise which now follows it.

The other passages certainly contain some material which could be interpreted as belonging to Micah's period, but they do not have to be so understood; and side by side with them there are many ideas and expressions which otherwise appear only or predominantly in passages from a later period. This is true of iv, 6–7, v, 6–8, the promise of the gathering of the Judaean diaspora and

[10] Thus Hans Schmidt, *Der Mythos vom wiederkehrenden König im AT* (²1933), p. 30.

its victory, and of iv, 8–14, the eschatological expectation of the destruction of the heathen nations which have advanced against Jerusalem (p. 394). So far as the specifically messianic prophecy of v, 1–5, is concerned and its similarity to those of Isaiah, we have already seen (pp. 318–19) that the latter are not all undisputed as to their genuineness, and further there can be no doubt at all that the messianic hope, which certainly extends back into the pre-exilic period, was also fostered, indeed was most industriously fostered, in the exilic and post-exilic periods. In these circumstances, the fact that the passages stand in the book of Micah is no more proof that they must come from Micah than that Isa. xi, (1) 10–xii, 6, must be ascribed to Isaiah because they have been preserved for us in the book of Isaiah. We must therefore affirm, though with due caution, that iv, 1–v, 8, are probably not genuine.

We have already said (pp. 408 f.) of v, 9–14, that it resembles Isa. ii, 6–8, and we have hinted that it has perhaps been secondarily transformed from a threat against the people of Israel to being a threat against foreign nations. There is thus no reason for denying the passage to Micah in its original form, unless, keeping the threat against the nations in verse 14, we are to regard it as a deliberately archaising promise of cultic purity to the Jerusalem of the final age, in which case it could then be compared with Zech. xiv, 20–1. But this is not the most natural interpretation, and we may therefore leave the passage to Micah. The same may be said of the judgement speech of Yahweh with his people (vi, 1–8), which has of course its own lasting value. The possibility suggested in verse 7a of the sacrifice of the first-born could well point to the period of Micah, since according to the information in II Kings xvi, 3, xxi, 6, children were at that time offered in Judah as Molech-sacrifices (pp. 69 f., 234). But apart from this, the idea of giving up the most precious and dear possession, the first-born son, was always one that lay near at hand in Israelite religion, which not only knew of human sacrifice from the practices of related neighbouring peoples (II Kings iii, 27), but also always had examples to hand in the record of its own past, whether these were legendary or historical (Gen. xxii, Judg. xi, 34–40).

The diatribe of vi, 9–16, and the lament of vii, 1–6, reveal no features which do not fit with Micah and his time. While the second could in itself fit with any other period, the first, which reproaches the city here castigated with having *observed the statutes of Omri and all the works of the house of Ahab* (v. 16), and says that it is therefore to be delivered up for destruction, seems to have Samaria and not Jerusalem in mind, and thus presupposes the existence of Samaria. It must therefore like i, 2–7 (pp. 409–10) be attributed to the period before 721. It is true that this interpretation is not essential. The *works of the house of Ahab* could here be used quite generally as a typical expression for evils of the worst kind, and so be applied to Jerusalem. In that case the more precise date of the passage cannot be determined, but it may in any case be attributed to Micah.

The passage vii, 7–20, comprising a 'liturgy', a unity made up of the four sections 7–10, 11–13, 14–17, 18–20 (p. 409), is fairly generally regarded as a post-exilic proclamation of salvation, presupposing the destruction of Jerusalem and the exile. This view is taken by even those scholars, such as Weiser, who are otherwise prepared to deny only few parts of the book to Micah. In fact the passage has various features which can be understood as pointing to such a late period—the hope of the rebuilding of the destroyed walls of Jerusalem (גְּדֵרָיִךְ 11), a tremendous influx of people from all the world (12), and the like. But such an interpretation of these passages is not obligatory, and neither Jerusalem nor Zion is explicitly mentioned. 14b contains a very archaic-sounding description of Yahweh as the one *who dwellest alone in the wood, in the midst of Carmel.* Admittedly this is most often altered so as to change שֹׁכְנִי, *(thou) who dwellest,* into שֹׁכְנֵי, *(those) who dwell,* so as to render *who dwell there in the wood, in the midst of Carmel,* or *of the garden land,* in apposition to *thy people, the flock of thy inheritance,* in 14a. But if the text is accepted, then it seems likely that the speakers of the prayer in 14–17, and hence of the whole liturgy 7–20, may be the inhabitants of the northern kingdom of Israel, or of the truncated kingdom of Ephraim which was left after 732, or—and this is the most likely—of the territory of the Assyrian province created after its removal in 722, for to them Carmel was dear and specially familiar as the place of the gracious presence of Yahweh.[11] Since it is clear on other grounds that Micah included the northern kingdom in his message (p. 407), there is no difficulty in assuming that in vii, 7–20, he should have expressed the expectation of a future salvation for this part of Israel. Micah vii, 7–20, might then be placed side by side with the 'Ephraimite booklet of consolation' in Jer. xxx–xxxi, in which Jeremiah gives moving expression to his concern for the fate of members of the former northern kingdom (pp. 361 f.). Thus, in spite of many hesitations, among which is the consideration of the relationship of the passage with some sections of 'Trito-Isaiah', belonging probably to the sixth century B.C., the attributing of the poem vii, 7–20, to Micah must nevertheless be seriously considered.

If the points so far made are correct, and if v, 9–14, or at least the basic material of this passage, vi, 1–8; vi, 9–16; vii, 1–6; vii, 7–20, are really all to be ascribed to Micah, then we should have only ii, 12–13; iv, 1–5; iv, 6–7; iv, 8–14, and v, 1–8, as secondary additions to the material which certainly derives from him. Probably—leaving aside ii, 12–13—iv, 1–5, the promise of the future exaltation and significance of the Temple mount, was added first, to tone down and reverse the terrible threat spoken against it in iii, 12, and this promise may then have drawn the others after it. So we might explain the fact that the main part of the promises stand in the middle of the book, and not, as otherwise usually happens in the prophetic books, at the end. It would then no longer be necessary to follow the view felt to be essential by many scholars, as for example Robinson, to regard the whole of iv, 1–vii, 20, as consisting of additions appended secondarily to the book of Micah which originally finished at iii, 12.

4. *The portrait of the prophet.* If we may finally attempt to present a picture of the prophet Micah, we shall best begin from the clearly genuine words in i–iii, with the exception of ii, 12–13. Here we may recognise Micah as a poet skilled in play upon words (i, 8–16) and as one who does not mince his words

[11] Eissfeldt, *Der Gott Karmel* (SAB 1953, 1, 1953), p. 7, n. 3.

in composing sharp-edged diatribes and threats. These occasionally enable us to recognise dramatically the debate between the prophet and his opponents. So far as their content is concerned, his message is directed, at least in regard to Samaria, against idolatrous elements of the cult, but in the main it is the social oppression of the small man by the leading classes against which his ruthless attacks are directed, and no less against the way in which priests and prophets, greedy for gain, forgetful of their duty and without honour, not only do not protest at this activity of the rich, but even condone it and further it.

If we now also include v, 9–vii, 20, the picture of the poet Micah is filled out in that he is shown to handle also the lament form (vii, 1–6) and further to construct a 'liturgy' (vii, 7–20) made up of elements from various forms. Above all, however, the judgement speech of vi, 1–8, reveals his capacity for broad conceptions, vividly perceived as if in a vision. So far as content is concerned, v, 9–vii, 6, coincides in general with i–iii, except that the judgement speech sets beside the more negatively presented message the positive divine demands—simple justice, and piety in thought and action. vii, 7–20, if really genuine, would further add to the picture of the prophet the sympathetic feature that he, as a child of the southern kingdom, felt like Jeremiah a real concern in the disaster to the north and expressed a confident hope in a new future for the inhabitants of its former territory.

The promises which are to be denied to Micah, ii, 12–13, and iv, 1–v, 8, are valuable testimonies to the hope of coming salvation which enlivened and supported post-exilic Judaism and for Christians v, 1–3, is particularly dear and well-known as the saying which they have learnt to understand as a prophecy of Jesus, thanks to the evangelist Matthew (ii, 5–6):

> *And thou, Bethlehem in Judaea,*
> *art by no means least among the princes of Judah;*
> *For from thee shall come forth for me the ruler,*
> *Who shall be lord over my people Israel.*

§ 55. NAHUM

Literature: Florit, 'Ripercussioni immediate della cadute di Ninive sulla Palestina' Bibl 13 (1932), pp. 399–417; Goslinga, *Nahums godspraak tegen Nineve* (1924); Gunkel, 'Nahum i' ZAW 13 (1893), pp. 223–44; Haldar, *Studies in the Book of Nahum* (1947); Happel, *Der Psalm Nahum (Nahum i)* (1900); *Das Buch des Propheten Nahum erklärt* (1902); Humbert, 'Essai d'analyse de Nahoum i, 2–ii, 3' ZAW 44 (1926), pp. 266–80; 'Nahoum ii, 9' REJ 83 (1927), pp. 74–6; 'La vision de Nahoum ii, 4–11' AfO 5 (1928/9), pp. 14–19; 'Le problème du livre de Nahoum' RHPhR 12 (1932), pp. 1–15; Kleinert, 'Nahum und der Fall Ninives' ThStKr 83 (1910), pp. 501–34; Lods, 'Trois études sur la littérature prophétique' RHPhR 11 (1931), pp. 211–19; Maier, 'Recent Archaeological Light on Nahum' Concordia Theol. Monthly 7 (1936), pp. 692–8; *The Book of Nahum: A Commentary* (1959); on this cf. Wolfe, JBL 78 (1959), pp. 369 f.; Mihelic, 'The Concept of God in the Book of Nahum' Interpr. 2 (1948), pp. 199–208; Smit, *Het boek van den profeet Nahum* (1934).
Cf. also Literature §§ 48, 109.

1. *Contents.* The title: *Oracle of Nineveh. Book of the vision of Nahum the Elkoshite* (i, 1), is followed by an alphabetic psalm, which is a hymn on the epiphany of Yahweh and extends at least as far as v. 9 (with v. 2b placed after v. 9: א–ג, '–n). The surmise that the alphabetic acrostic may extend even further is reasonable, and v. 10 could with a small rearrangement be regarded as a ס (s)-line. But the attempts which have repeatedly been made to restore the complete alphabetic psalm extending as far as ii, 3, or ii, 4, have not led to any assured and recognised results.

From ii, 4, onwards, there is a connected unit, self-contained and readily intelligible, extending to ii, 14. But i, 10–ii, 3, are evidently in disorder. For i, 12–13 (14?) and ii, 1, 3, have as their subject a promise to Judah, whereas i, 10–11 (14?), and ii, 2, contain a threat against the enemy. We should probably therefore regard i, 1–13 (14?)[1] and ii, 1, 3, as a unit, containing a word of promise for Judah, whereas i, 10–11 (14?), and ii, 2, form the beginning of the threat directed against Nineveh continued in ii, 4–14.[1] The word of promise speaks of the destruction of the oppressor and the restoration of Israel. But the threat presents an exalted poetic description, in the most vivid colours, of the hostile attack on Nineveh, a description which, for example in ii, 7, 10, presents the events so vividly that it looks as if it is an eyewitness account or is looking back on events which have already taken place. The opening כִּי עַד, *for till* (i. 10) is perhaps, following iii, 1, to be corrected with Duhm, Sellin, Elliger and others, into הוֹי עִיר, *woe to the city!*

A second cry of woe begins in iii, 1, and it is hardly possible to say with certainty whether ch. iii is to be treated as a unity or whether it is to be divided into three units. iii, 8, where Nineveh is addressed: *Are you any better than No-Amon?* may be understood as a new beginning, though this is not essential. It is more likely that we should regard iii, 18 as marking the beginning of a new unit, the more so since the last word of verse 17, אַיָּם, *where are they?* is to be read with ⅏ as אוֹי, *woe!* or better as אֵיךְ, *ah, how!* and treated as the beginning of the following verse: *Woe* (or *Ah, how*) *your shepherds sleep!* iii, 1–7, threatens the destruction of Nineveh, again with the most vivid and graphic description of the warlike operations leading to the taking of the city, and it presents this as the punishment for her harlotries and magical practices, the source of her successes, in other words for her treacherous political and commercial undertakings. iii, 8–17, is linked to the capture of No-Amon,[2] the Egyptian Thebes, by the Assyrians in 662, and proclaims the same fate for Nineveh: siege and capture of her fortresses by the enemy. iii, 18–19, finally, in form a dirge rather than a national lament, presents the disaster as if it has already taken place: Nineveh's *shepherds and officers* have fallen, and the people is scattered upon the mountains.

2. *The period of the prophet.* Concerning the person of Nahum himself, we know only that he was an Elkoshite. But since the situation of the Elkosh or Alkosh thus indicated is quite unknown, this information does not help us. His

---

[1] Gaster, 'Two Notes on Nahum' JBL 63 (1944), pp. 51 f.: on i, 12; ii, 4.

[2] van Doorslaer, 'No Amon' CBQ 11 (1949), pp. 280–95: No-Amon = the predecessor of Alexandria. Cf. Vulg.: 'Alexandria populorum'. Lit. § 126.

date, however, may be fixed much more definitely: after 662 and before 612. The fall of Egyptian Thebes is quite clearly presupposed, though admittedly this does not allow us to say how far this event lies in the past. If at first we gain the impression that it must have taken place a relatively short time previously, we must nevertheless consider that the fall of this powerful metropolis, whose beauty and glory are well attested even today by the imposing temple ruins and the priceless treasures of its royal graves, is likely to have remained for a long time fresh in the memory. At the lower limit too there is some uncertainty, since it cannot be said with certainty how far we must date the prophet before 612. The star of Assyria and of Nineveh began to wane rapidly after the death of Ashurbanipal (c. 630), and signs of decay were discernible even earlier. It is therefore possible to assume that Nahum's prophecy originated two or even three decades before the disaster to Nineveh in 612. On the other hand, the nearer the end approached, the greater must have been the fever of excitement among the nations which languished under the Assyrian yoke, and we should therefore not remove the prophecy too far from 612. In any event it appears clear that we are dealing with genuine threats belonging before the catastrophe, and not with a triumphant retrospect upon events already in the past. Elliger and Robinson have recently expressed themselves in favour of this view, and Haldar agrees with this view in that he considers that the book originated before the fall of Nineveh. In other respects, however, Haldar goes his own way, for he regards the book as a political propaganda document originating in cult-prophetic circles in about 614, in which the hated enemy is identified with dangerous figures from Sumerian, Babylonian and Ugaritic mythology.

Humbert, Lods and Sellin, however—though differing in detail among themselves—see in Nahum's writing a prophetic liturgy composed by Nahum after the fall of Nineveh (August 612) for the accession (autumnal) festival which fell some two months later. Attractive as is Humbert's view of verse i, 9, readily corrected so as to form a question answered in vv. 2b, 9b, *For what do you praise*[3] *Yahweh? Yahweh is an avenger on his enemies . . .,* we must not build too much upon this uncertain foundation. The verses are clearly intelligible and are evidently to be understood as a prophecy, and so treat Nineveh's downfall as belonging to the future. We may therefore take it that the book is to be dated between 662 and 612. The attempt, made for example by Sellin, to find an argument for a more precise dating from the religious attitude of the book, does not really provide an answer. Sellin thinks that Josiah's reform is clearly presupposed by the book, since we should otherwise have to assume that the prophet would have had a word to say against Judah's sinfulness, whereas soon after the reform which corresponded to prophetic demands such a need would not have been present. But this, it would seem, represents too simplified a history of Israelite religion. The reform does not mark a break for all prophecy or for all prophets. Before and after, the so-called prophets of salvation were the same. In the book of Nahum, in spite of Sellin's protest, we have prophecy in the style of the prophecy of salvation which is contested by

---

[3] Reading תְּשַׁבְּחוּן instead of תְּחַשְּׁבוּן, *do you think?*

Jeremiah and his like, though this does not by any means indicate that the book is religiously of less value. It has its own religious significance, and justice cannot be done to it if it is measured by the standard of the 'prophecy of woe'.

3. *Problems of genuineness.* In general the book appears quite clearly genuine, and it is only with regard to the fragment of the poem in i, 2–9, that we must ask whether it stems from Nahum or not. It is clear enough that in tone it fits in with Nahum's threats, in that it presents Yahweh as the friend of his friends and the enemy of his enemies. But this does not indicate a recognition of its genuineness without any further discussion. For elsewhere too in prophetic writings, in suitable and in unsuitable places, psalms have been inserted second-arily—e.g. in Jonah ii, 3–10 (p. 406), Isa. xii (p. 317). This possibility must also be reckoned with here. But then the question immediately arises as to why only the first half of the alphabetic psalm was inserted. A purely mechanical explanation would be that perhaps there was on the scroll in question only such a small amount of clear space as not to permit the incorporation of the whole psalm. Or perhaps it appeared to the redactor that the *l*-line (v. 9b) or the *n*-line (v. 2b) provided a good opening to the book of Nahum, and so he only incorporated the psalm up to this point. We cannot get beyond a guess in this. Nor can anything precise be said concerning the age of the psalm, if its non-genuineness is presupposed. It may be younger than the book of Nahum, and this is indeed probable, but it is not impossible that it could be older. For the form of the hymn is undoubtedly much older than Nahum (pp. 105–9), particularly with the combination which we have here with its description of a theophany.

§ 56. HABAKKUK

Literature: Bévenot, 'Le Cantique d'Habacuc' RB 42 (1933), pp. 499–525; Brownlee, *The Text of Habakkuk in the Ancient Commentary from Qumran* (JBL Monograph Series XI, 1959); Budde, 'Habakuk' ZDMG 84 (1930), pp. 139–47; 'Zum Text von Habakuk Kap i u. ii' OLZ 34 (1931), cols. 409–11; Cannon, 'The Integrity of Habakkuk cc. i, ii' ZAW 43 (1925), pp. 62–90; Delcor, 'La geste de Yahvé au temps de l'Exode et l'espérance du psalmiste en Habacuc iii' *Misc. Bibl. Ubach* (1954), pp. 287–302; Duhm, *Das Buch Habakuk* (1906); Evans, 'The Song of Habakkuk' BS 112 (1955), pp. 62–7, 164–9; Friedmann, 'L'enigma di Habaquq' Religio 11 (1935), pp. 219–230; Giesebrecht, *Beiträge zur Jesaiakritik* (1890), pp. 196–8; Gruenthaner, 'Chaldeans or Macedonians?' Bibl 8 (1927), pp. 129–60, 257–89; Humbert, *Problèmes du livre d'Habacuc* (1944); Lachmann, *Das Buch Habbakuk. Eine textkritische Studie* (1932); Nielsen, 'The Righteous and the Wicked in Habaqquq' StTh 6 (1953), pp. 54–78; Rothstein, 'Über Habakkuk, Kap. i u. ii' ThStKr 67, (1894), pp. 51–85; Hans Schmidt, 'Ein Psalm im Buche Habakuk' ZAW 62 (1950), pp. 52–63; Stade, 'Habakuk' ZAW 4 (1884), pp. 154–9; Staerk, 'Zu Habakuk i, 5–11. Geschichte oder Mythos?' ZAW 51 (1933), pp. 1–28; Torrey, 'Alexander the Great in the Old Testament Prophecies' BZAW 41 (1925), pp. 281–6; 'The Prophecy of Habakkuk *Kohut Mem. Vol.* (1935), pp. 565–82; Vischer, *Der Prophet Habakuk* (BSt 19, 1958), Walker and Lund, 'The Literary Structure of the Book of Habakkuk' JBL 53 (1934), pp. 355–70.
    Cf. also Literature §§ 48, 126.

1. *Contents.* The title in i, 1: *The oracle which the prophet Habakkuk saw,* is followed in i, 2–4, by a complaint expressed in the tone of the individual song of lament. This is presumably spoken by the prophet, since it is hardly to be understood as made by the people speaking in the first person singular. It is a complaint that *the godless surrounds the righteous* (v. 4), and in i, 5–11, follows the divine proclamation that he will cause *the Chaldeans, that bitter and violent nation* (v. 6) to come, and they are then described in all their warlike valour and ruthlessness. In i, 12, there begins again a complaint in the first person singular, i.e. by the prophet, and the subject of the complaint is here, as in i, 2–4, that God is content to watch inactive while *the godless swallows up the righteous* (v. 13). In ii, 1, a first-person declaration is made—and here it is particularly clear that this is the prophet—that he will *stand upon his watch,* in order to *spy out* what *Yahweh* will *answer to his complaint.* The answer follows in ii, 2–4,[1] introduced by the words *And Yahweh answered me,* to the effect that *the perverse* or *the puffed up*[2] (evidently identical with *the unrighteous* of i, 2–4, and i, 12–17), will come to an end, whereas *the righteous will remain alive.* There follow in ii, 5–20, five, or perhaps rather six (p. 420), cries of woe against a sinner, who is a plunderer, deceitful, violent and idolatrous, and these are concluded in v. 20, with a summons to show awe before Yahweh, this being contrasted with the last woe which castigates the reverencing of idols. The third chapter is introduced with a new title *Prayer of the prophet Habakkuk, in dithyrambic form (?),* and closes with a corresponding colophon in v. 19, *For the choirmaster (musical director) with stringed instruments.* This is thus designated as a psalm, as the superscription and colophon show with their technical musical expressions which cannot be interpreted in detail with any certainty (pp. 453–4). The main part of the psalm at least, i.e. vv. 3–15, is a hymn celebrating Yahweh's epiphany.

2. *Different interpretations and datings of the book.* In spite of its small compass, the book of Habakkuk has been understood and dated in very different ways. There are so many of these that we can only here give a survey of a selection from among them. The first question which arises is whether the oppression of the righteous by the godless of which the prophet complains is to be attributed to a tension within Judah or to a conflict between Judah and an external enemy. Rothstein (1896) thought of the first possibility, and dated the book in about 605, seeing in the righteous the pious Judaeans and in the godless the group of Judaean godless and their representative king Jehoiakim, and considering that the prophet threatens their punishment by the Chaldeans. A similar view has been put forward by Humbert (1941) and Nielsen (1953). The former considers that the book is a liturgy compiled by the Jerusalem cult-prophet Habakkuk for a penitential day held in 602–601 and directed against Jehoiakim. The latter applies it to the replacing of Shallum by Jehoiakim in 608 (II Kings xxiii, 31–xxiv, 6; Jer. xxii, 10–19). Other scholars, and probably the majority of those who have expressed their

---

[1] Stenzel, 'Habakuk ii, 1–4, 5a' Bibl 33 (1952), pp. 506–10; 'Habakkuk ii, 15–16' VT 3 (1953), pp. 97–9.

[2] In v. 4 the corrupt עֻפְּלָה, *she is puffed up,* is to be altered to הָ(עַוָּל) or הַ(עֲמָל) or הָ(גֶּבֶר) or הָ(עָפֵל)

P

views on this problem, agree in holding that the interpretation of the conflict between the righteous and the godless should be seen as referring to the oppression of Judah by an external enemy, but they differ in their identification of this enemy, and hence vary substantially in their dating of the prophet. There is the view that the godless refers to the Assyrians, whose wrongs committed against Judah as against other peoples Yahweh promises to avenge by means of the Chaldeans who are threatening Assyria; hence Habakkuk is to be dated at any rate before the collapse of Assyria, i.e. before 612. This view was put forward very firmly by Budde about thirty years ago (1930, 1931) and in this he has recently (1953) been followed by Mowinckel. Wellhausen and Giesebrecht, however, excising i, 5–11, as a secondary addition, see in i, 2–4, 12–17, a lament concerning the maltreatment of the nations, and in particular of Judah, by the Chaldeans; this carries with it the dating of the prophet in the time of the Chaldean-Neo-Babylonian empire, between 612 and 538 B.C. Sellin takes up a similar position in regard to the interpretation of the godless as the Chaldeans, though without excising i, 5–11. In the first edition of his commentary on the Book of the Twelve in 1922 he had adopted a view close to that of Duhm (see below), but in the new edition of the commentary in 1929–30 he took up this alternative. In his view, the book of Habakkuk, which he regards, as we shall show in a moment, as a connected prophetic liturgy, is concerned with the distress from the Chaldeans which lies heavy upon Judah. It was compiled between the Chaldean attack in 600 attested by II Kings xxiv, 2, and the conquest of Jerusalem in 587. Duhm, on the other hand, dates the book three centuries later (though not going so far as Happel who places it four centuries later, deriving it from the Seleucid period). Duhm finds in it an echo of the victorious campaign of Alexander the Great and of the Macedonians, and bases this view in the main upon the textual correction of i, 6, where he changes *Chaldeans* into *Kittim* = *Greeks*, though also upon various indications in i, 5–11; ii, 15–16; iii, 13, 16, which appear to him to fit especially well with Alexander and the Greeks, as particularly the *eastwards* of i, 9, which in his view presupposes a victorious campaign coming into the Near East from the west. Hence he regards the whole book of Habakkuk, including the psalm, as the work of a visionary living in Palestine, with the exception only of iii, 17–19, which he judges to be a later appendix. It reveals the impression upon him of the victorious campaign of Alexander the Great, and was compiled between the battles of Issus (333) and Arbela (331).

These different interpretations of the godless and the righteous, and the resulting very widely divergent datings of the prophet and his book, are at many points connected with textual emendations, omission of words and phrases, and rearrangement of sections, as well as with particular views concerning the literary structure of the book as a whole. Thus Wellhausen and Giesebrecht, who see the Chaldeans in the godless, omit (cf. above) i, 5–11, because here the Chaldeans are assessed positively. Budde supports his interpretation of the godless as the Assyrians by transposing i, 5–11, after ii, 4, and thus obtains a connected complaint in i, 2–4, 12–17, concerning the raging of the Assyrians, together with the prayer for a divine answer linked to this in ii, 1. He then finds this divine answer in ii, 2–4; i, 5–11; ii, 5. Sellin, on the other hand, sees the book as an artistically constructed prophetic liturgy, built up in this way: i, 2–4, the first prayer of the people—a complaint at the violent assault of the godless; i, 5–11, the first divine answer—all the world must suffer under the Chaldean distress; i, 12–17, the second prayer of the people—a bitter reproach that God permits such insolent action on the part of the godless; ii, 1–5, the second divine answer—the punishment which is his desert will hasten to overtake the godless; ii, 6–20, five woes hurled at the godless world-conqueror by the nations oppressed by him; iii, 1–15, the vision of Yahweh's duel with the world conqueror; iii, 16–19, the closing prayer of the community —side by side with the terror which derives from the fearful content of the vision, the sadness at the lamentable conditions of the present time, it gives expression nevertheless to the sure confidence of a new future for the people, brought about through God's help. In a similar way Humbert considers the liturgy compiled by Habakkuk for the purpose indicated on pp. 417–18 to be constructed as follows: i, 2–4, complaint; i, 5–10, Yahweh's answer; i, 11–17, complaint; ii, 1–5a, Yahweh's answer; ii, 5b–20, five woes; iii, prayer.

As in similar cases, it will be best with the book of Habakkuk, which is clearly open to such varied interpretation, at any rate at first to avoid any emendations of the text, transpositions and the like. This means above all that the one concrete name which the book mentions, the הַכַּשְׂדִּים, the Chaldeans, in i, 6, may neither be excised, nor as Duhm wishes to do, changed for example into הַכִּתִּים, the Kittim. So far as this last point is concerned, it is certainly a remarkable coincidence that the Habakkuk 'Commentary' found in 1947 near Qumrān at the north-west corner of the Dead Sea (§§ 104, 109) says concerning the traditional the Chaldeans that the Kittim are meant. But this 'actualisation' of the traditional כַּשְׂדִּים, which is entirely intelligible in the period of the origin of the 'Commentary'—i.e. the second or first century B.C.—namely, that they are interpreted with reference to the Seleucids or the Romans, nevertheless un-doubtedly presupposes the word כַּשְׂדִּים and thus provides rather an argument against Duhm's correction of the text than one in favour of it. The context in which in i, 6, the Chaldeans are mentioned, hardly permits any other view than that they are summoned by Yahweh as his instrument of punishment, so that they may bring to an end the deeds of the godless complained of in i, 2–4. It remains uncertain who is meant by the godless, whether it is a group within Judah represented as a single figure, or whether it is an external enemy. The first would be quite possible. Isa. vii, 18–20; x, 5–6, and other passages suffic-iently demonstrate that the prophets were familiar with the idea that Yahweh entrusts to other nations the carrying out of punishment upon his own people or upon parts of it. So the interpretation of the godless in this way is justified. On the other hand the description of the godless, which is in any case a personi-fication and hence is the more difficult to define clearly, contains, in spite of this, many features which point rather to a hostile foreign people than to an inner Judaean group, as for example i, 17, and iii, 12, where it is said of him that he slaughters and threshes nations. But if an alien people is to be understood in the figure of the godless, this can only refer to the Assyrians in view of the fact that the Chaldeans are named as carrying out the punishment upon him. With this fits also the observation that the reproach offered to the godless in ii, 17, that he has done violence to Lebanon, agrees strikingly with Isa. xxxvii, 24, in which the Assyrian boasts that he has climbed into the most remote recesses of Lebanon and has felled its loftiest cedars and most precious cypresses. We must therefore interpret the godless as referring to the Assyrian, and this means that Habakkuk is to be placed almost at the same time as Nahum, i.e. at the end of the seventh century when the break-up of the Assyrian power and the consolidation of that of the Chaldeans began to be plain to the world.

A further remark is necessary concerning the literary form of the book. In content it does form a unity, in that all its separate sections have as their subject the downfall of the godless: i, 2–11, complaint and divine answer; i, 12–17, ii, 1–4, repetition of the complaint and of the divine answer; ii, 5–20, five or rather six cries of woe (p. 417); iii, prayer. But whether these passages also comprise *in form* a literary unity, in other words are brought together as a liturgy, is open to question. There is in reality no strength in what appears to be an argument for this view, namely the link between the double complaint and answer in i, 2–ii, 5, with the cries of woe in ii, 6–20—ii, 5, *all nations*, and ii, 6, *all these*, namely the nations mentioned in ii, 5. The position is rather that the double complaint and answer extend probably only as far as ii, 4, and the cries of woe begin with ii, 5, where we should read at the beginning הוֹי בֹּגֵד, *woe to the robber*. These then form a series not of five, but of six woes, and so the connection of *all nations* in v. 5 and *all these* in v. 6, cannot be used as evidence of a literary connection between the first section, i, 2–ii, 4, containing human complaint and divine answer, and the second, the six cries of woe of ii, 5–20. Just as ii, 5–20, is a self-contained section, so also is iii. Even if, as is possible and indeed probable, the statement of iii, 2, that the prophet has heard *the report* of Yahweh and has *seen* his *work*[3] refers back to ii, 2–5, this indicates only a relationship of content and not necessarily a literary relationship between i, 2–ii, 4, and iii. We must therefore regard the book of Habakkuk as a loose collection of a group of songs of lamentation and oracles (i, 2–ii, 4), a series of six cries of woe (ii, 5–20), and the prayer of iii, which all stem from the same prophet Habakkuk, probably a cult-prophet, and originated in approximately the same period.

3. *The Prayer of Habakkuk*. Some more particular discussion is necessary of ch. iii[4] entitled the *prayer of Habakkuk*. In form it is an individual psalm of lamentation, in content a collective psalm (§ 15, 6.9). Since Stade in 1884

---

[3] Cf. p. 421, n. 5.

[4] Albright, 'The Psalm of Habakkuk' StOTPr (1950), pp. 1–18; Cassuto, 'Il capitolo iii di Habaquq e i testi di Ras Shamra' Annuario Studi Ebr. (1935/7), pp. 7–22; Driver, 'Critical Note on Habakkuk iii, 7' JBL 62 (1943), pp. 121 f.; García, 'El Cántico de Habacuc' Cultura Bíblica 5 (1948), pp. 171–4, 254–60; Good, 'The Barberini Greek Version of Habakkuk iii' VT 9 (1959), pp. 11–30; Irwin, 'The Psalm of Habakkuk' JNESt 1 (1942), pp. 10–40; 'The Mythological Background of Habakkuk, Chapter iii' JNESt 15 (1956), pp. 47–50; Mowinckel, 'Zum Psalm des Habakuk' ThZ 9 (1953), pp. 1–23; Stephens, 'The Babylonian Dragon Myth in Habakkuk iii' JBL 43 (1924), pp. 290–3; Zolli, 'Una teofania biblica e la riforma religiosa di Amenofi IV Echenaton' Actes XX. Congr. Int. Orient. (1940), pp. 278–85. Lit. § 126.

declared it to be non-genuine and traced it to the post-exilic period, the passage
has fairly generally been regarded as a late production, as indeed psalmody as
a whole was ascribed only to the post-exilic age (pp. 446–8). For Duhm, who
considered that the whole book of Habakkuk originated only towards the end
of the fourth century, these objections to the genuineness of the poem were not
relevant. So he regarded it, or more precisely vv. 2–16, as being from Habakkuk.
In the same way Sellin, who dates the book three centuries earlier, rejecting the
preconceived notion that psalmody is as a whole a post-exilic product, declared
that ch. iii was genuine and treated it as an original component part of the
liturgy composed by Habakkuk between 600 and 587. But the possibility of
deriving the poem from the prophet who lived in the pre-exilic period is not
bound up with the view of the book as a liturgy. It may quite well be combined
with the suggestion just made that we should understand chapters i–iii as a
loose collection consisting of various independent literary units.

There is much in favour of the view that i–ii and iii derive from the same
author. In the first place the general theme is the same in both: the confident
expectation that Yahweh will soon bring to an end the oppression of his
people by the external enemy. In addition there are also in the language various
points of contact, particularly in the fact that in both (iii, 13, and i, 4, 13), the
enemy is described as *the godless*. Finally, as we have seen, iii, 2, with its
affirmation that the prophet has *heard the report* of Yahweh and has 'seen'[5] his
work and with its prayer that Yahweh will soon bring about what has been
heard and seen, links back clearly to ii, 2–5. These points do not provide
absolute proof of the identity of the compiler of i–ii with that of iii—for the
similarity of the poem to the prophecy could have led a redactor to ascribe the
anonymous poem to Habakkuk and so to append it to his prophecies. But
equally the presence of the liturgical-cultic notes (pp. 453–4) at the beginning
and at the end do not compel the assumption that the passage cannot come
from Habakkuk and that it must have been taken as an anonymous poem from
a collection similar to our book of psalms and have been ascribed secondarily
to Habakkuk. We must certainly reckon with the possibility that Habakkuk
himself from the outset provided these notes to this poem, compiled by him
for cultic use—we have already seen that quite apart from this, there is reason
to see that Habakkuk was in close relation to the Temple cultus, and was thus
a cult-prophet. There are in fact no substantial arguments against deriving the
poem from Habakkuk, and even the fact that the Habakkuk 'Commentary'
from Qumrān limits its 'exposition' to chs. i–ii and leaves ch. iii out of account,
is not a decisive argument. For this does not by any means have to be taken
as indicating that at the time of the composition of the commentary, *c.* 100 B.C.,
ch. iii did not yet belong to the book of Habakkuk. There are many other
possibilities which are to be preferred to this.

The poem is in its main part, as we have already seen, a hymn which celebrates an epiphany of Yahweh for battle against his enemy, depicting this in
mythological colours.[6] It is to be understood as an anticipation of the praise to

---

[5] Reading רָאִיתִי with ⅗ instead of יָרֵאתִי, *I am afraid* in 𝔐.
[6] Cf. the literature on p. 420, n. 4.

be offered for the help of Yahweh, thought of as already having taken place, or better experienced in vision. It is thus an eschatological hymn. Vv. 16–19 also belong to the prayer of Habakkuk, for the colophon stands after v. 19 and not after v. 15. The prophet describes first the terrible effects which were produced in his own body by the vision of Yahweh's battle for the destruction of his enemy (v. 16a). Then, speaking here more in the name of his people than in his own name, he expresses the certainty that Yahweh, in spite of the present desperate condition of the land (v. 17),[7] will nevertheless reveal himself as its saviour.

4. *The personality of Habakkuk and his period.* Habakkuk allows us, more than do other prophets, to see into the inner processes of visionary experience, and we become aware of features similar to those in the anonymous passage in Isa. xxi, 1–10 (pp. 321–2). ii, 1–2, reveals to us how the prophet prepares himself inwardly for the reception of a vision, and how he then receives it, and iii, 16a, gives us a glimpse of the agony, not merely mental but also physical, which is or may be the consequence of a vision. Habakkuk was thus an actual visionary, standing in the service of the Temple cultus, and it is probably no accident that the superscription of his book explicitly gives him the title *nabi'*, which only happens elsewhere with Haggai and Zechariah. Apart from this we know nothing at all about Habakkuk's own person.[8] So far as the date of his writing is concerned, it must have been compiled before 612, the year of the conquest of Nineveh, since it is directed against Assyria and presupposes that its world empire still exists. On the other hand, since the Chaldeans are already visible on the horizon, we must assume that the successful rebellion of the Chaldean Nabopolassar against the Assyrians has already taken place, and thus place the work later than 625. Thus the years 625–612 appear as the period in which Habakkuk is to be dated, roughly the same period which comes into consideration for Nahum.

Habakkuk has another point in common with Nahum. Unlike Amos and Isaiah, they are free of reproaches against their own people, and see all evil on the side of the enemy. Habakkuk thus, like Nahum, belongs among the 'prophets of weal'. But this does not mean depreciating his religious power, any more than it does with Nahum. For what Habakkuk expresses is by no means simply patriotic indignation at the misfortunes suffered at the enemy's hands, but rather the agony of his spirit at the evil which follows from the world rule of an unjust and immoral power. This is basically the same feeling which was expressed 700 years later by the compiler of the Apocalypse of Ezra, who gave to it a more rational form, though not any the less moving, resulting as here from the most profound experience and suffering (§ 99). Nor is it an accident that a greater than Habakkuk, namely Paul, chose a saying from this book to express his new and deeper religious experience—the saying in ii, 4, which

---

[7] It is possible that v. 17 is not original and has been inserted in the psalm so that it could be used in times of scarcity and cattle disease. So Rudolph, *Jesaja xxiv–xxvii* (BWANT 62, 1933), p. 36. Similarly Elliger, p. 51, but differently Mowinckel, p. 20.

[8] On the rôle played by Habakkuk in the apocryphal story of Bel and the Dragon, cf. p. 590, and on the legendary locating of his grave, cf. Beyer, ZDPV 54 (1931), p. 223, and Thomsen, *ib.* 65 (1942), p. 128.

Luther too experienced anew: *the righteous shall live by his faith* (Rom. i, 17; Gal. iii, 11).⁹

§ 57. ZEPHANIAH

Literature: Cornill, 'Die Prophetie Zephanjas' ThStKr 89 (1916), pp. 297–332; Florit, 'Sofonia, Geremia e la cronaca di Gadd' Bibl 15 (1934), pp. 8–31; Gerleman, *Zephanja, textkritisch und literarisch untersucht* (1942); Ginsberg (p. 309, n. 27), pp. 258 f.: Zephaniah's Witness to Isaiah'; Hyatt, 'The Date and Background of Zephaniah' JNESt 7 (1948), pp. 25–9; Nicolsky, 'Pascha im Kulte des jerusalemischen Tempels' ZAW 45 (1927), pp. 174–90, 241–53, esp. pp. 187–90, 243; Schwally, 'Das Buch Ssefanjâ' ZAW 10 (1890), pp. 165–240; Smith and Lacheman, 'The Authorship of the Book of Zephaniah' JNESt 9 (1950), pp. 137–42.
Cf. also Literature § 48.

1. *Contents.* The title (i, 1) traces Zephaniah's genealogy back to his great-great-grandfather, a certain *Hezekiah*, and also says of him that *the word of Yahweh came to him in the days of Josiah ben Amon, king of Judah.* This is followed by the passage vv. 2–18, which has as its subject the proclamation of the day of Yahweh which is especially to come upon Judah and Jerusalem. The passage is now presented as a unit, but it is to be divided into two clearly separate sections (vv. 2–6+8–13, and vv. 7+14–18), by transposing v. 7 to a position before v. 14, and by omitting the words *and it will happen on the day of Yahweh's sacrifice*, which were added at the beginning of v. 8 as a result of the placing of v. 7 before v. 8. If the passage is so divided, vv. 2–6+8–13 contains the threat of a world judgement breaking with terrible force upon Judah and Jerusalem because of their idolatry, their unrighteousness and self-confidence, whereas 7 + 14–18 provides a proclamation of the day of Yahweh in tones of uncanny horror. This latter is familiar from the Latin rendering of this passage:¹ *Dies irae, dies illa solvet saeclum in favilla*, effectively used by Goethe in his 'Faust'.² In ii, 1–3,³ there is linked to this an exhortation, directed particularly to the poor in the land, to *seek Yahweh* and to *seek righteousness*, so that *perhaps you may be hidden on the day of the wrath of Yahweh.* ii, 4–15, however, contains the proclamation of punishment upon the Philistines, Moab and the Ammonites, the Cushites and Assyria. iii, 1–13, returns to Jerusalem. Beginning (vv. 1–4)⁴ as a cry of woe concerning the disobedient city and its sinful leaders and judges, prophets and priests, the poem then provides in vv. 5–7 a prospect of terrible distresses of war breaking out upon other nations, distresses through which Yahweh, though unsuccessfully, sought to

---

⁹ Nygren, ' "Den rättfärdige skall leva av tro." Ur ett bibelords historia genom två och ett halvt årtusende' SvTK 19 (1943), pp. 281–91; 20 (1944), pp. 225 f.
¹ Kulp, 'Der Hymnus Dies irae, dies illa' MGkK 38 (1933), pp. 256–63.
² Part I, ll. 3798–9.
³ Gray, 'A Metaphor from Building in Zephaniah ii, 1' VT 3 (1953), pp. 404–7.
⁴ Elliger, 'Das Ende der "Abendwölfe" ' *Bertholet-Festschr.* (1950), pp. 158–75; on iii, 3; Stenzel, 'Zum Verständnis von Zeph. iii, 3b' VT 1 (1951), pp. 303–5.

warn his people,[5] and it goes on in vv. 8–13 to proclaim the judgement which Yahweh brings upon his own people, which is to lead to the separation of all evildoers, and to the creation of a devout and blessed remnant. The book closes in iii, 14–20, with a summons to Jerusalem to rejoice and exult, anticipating the deliverance of the city, and this turns once more in vv. 18–20 to a promise of deliverance.

2. *Problems of genuineness, and the period of the prophet.* There is no doubt of the genuineness of the basic material of i, 2–ii, 3, in spite of the attempt made by Smith and Lacheman to explain the whole book as a pseudepigraphon compiled in about 200 B.C. Furthermore, it is clear that this passage fits well in the period to which it is assigned in the title, the days of Josiah ben Amon, king of Judah (639–609), and that there is no need to follow Hyatt in placing Zephaniah's activity two or three decades later under Jehoiakim (608–598). The reproaches levelled in i, 4–6, against the worship of Baal, of the host of heaven and of the Ammonite god Milkom,[6] make it possible to fix the dating more exactly, namely before the reform of Josiah, which brought such malpractices to an end, at least for a time (p. 232). It is also possible, though this cannot be proved, that it was the Scythian upheaval which according to Herodotus I, 103–106, swept through Palestine in the years between 630 and 625 (p. 348) which occasioned Zephaniah's prophecy of the day of Yahweh and finds an echo in it. Without the same certainty as with i, 2–ii, 3, we may also affirm for ii, 4–15, or at any rate for the original basic material within this passage, that it derives from Zephaniah. Certainly the threatening of other nations fits well with his proclamation of the day of Yahweh, which means a world judgement, and indeed such a statement is rather to be expected, the more so if the proclamation of the world judgement really was occasioned by the Scythian menace which threatened the whole world. But it must be said on the other hand that with the exception of the saying directed against Assyria (vv. 13–15), the threats do not reveal any features which are directly characteristic of Zephaniah and his time, and we have already several times met with expansions of the prophetic books by oracles of salvation for their own people and threats against foreign nations (p. 317). We must also recall finally that, as we have seen (p. 306), several prophetic books are built up on the pattern, threats against their own people, threats against foreign nations, and promises for their own people, and that it could happen, in accordance with this pattern, that threats against the neighbouring peoples have been inserted secondarily in the middle of this book. No certain decision is, however, possible. We can only point to what is definite and generally recognised, namely that the genuine basic material which may be assumed to be present has undergone later elaboration which in part clearly reveals its post-exilic, or at least exilic, origin. Here belong the beginning and end of v. 7: *The land by the sea[7] shall belong to the remnant of the house of Judah,* and *For Yahweh, their God shall visit them and restore their fortune.* The same is true of vv. 8, 9aab, 10–11.

[5] Schoneveld, 'Zefanja iii, 5b' NThSt 22 (1939), pp. 253–7.
[6] Reading מְלִכֹּם instead of *their king* in 𝔐 (v. 5).
[7] הַיָּם is to be added here following 𝔊.

We are, however, again on firm ground in dealing with the poem on Jerusalem (iii, 1–13), beginning with *Woe* (הוֹי), culminating in the proclamation of a judgement leading to purification. This poem is certainly genuine, and has merely been elaborated in vv. 8–10, so that the foreign nations appear as the object of the judgement and purification. The passage is to be assigned to the same period as i, 2–ii, 3. Nor is it in itself impossible that Zephaniah might have appended to this poem, which closes with a promising prospect of the blessed end-time to break in after the judgement and purification, the summons in vv. 14–17, to rejoicing at this end-time, envisaged as already begun. On the other hand, however, such eschatological songs have often been added later, as we have seen in the case of Isa. xii (p. 317). Perhaps we should therefore deny to Zephaniah not only the oracle of salvation which begins afresh in vv. 18–20, but also vv. 14–17, and regard the latter as an exilic or post-exilic addition.

3. *The genealogy of Zephaniah.* A further word must be added about the genealogy of Zephaniah going back to his great-great-grandfather. Since the mention of a great-great-grandfather is very unusual, it has been thought that the reason was that this ancestor of the prophet was Hezekiah, the well-known king of that name,[8] and that it was because of this important fact that the genealogy was traced back to him. We must admit the possibility of this assumption, but it cannot be proved. Nor can the fact that in i, 8–9, the prophet appears to be familiar with the royal court, be used as a decisive argument for or against this suggestion. For the conditions at the royal court could also be known to others than actual members of the royal family, and furthermore, a protest against the evils which prevail at the court may equally well be attributed to a member of the court as to one who stands outside. For our understanding of the personality and the message of Zephaniah a decision on this point would thus have little significance.

We know nothing otherwise concerning the personality of Zephaniah. His book testifies, however, to his poetic ability and the penetration of his message. So far as the first point is concerned, the lament in i, 10–11, pictured as breaking out on the day of the coming judgement in the separate quarters of Jerusalem, is as perfectly depicted as is the utter desolation of Nineveh in ii, 13–15, and the fact that the *Dies irae* lives on today is not an accident, but rather a proof of the fact that Zephaniah was able to fill the threat of the day of judgement in i, 14–16, with an uncanniness and gloom the impression of which no one can escape. In content, his proclamation is concerned with a sharp protest against the worship of alien deities, against the aping of foreign customs, and against self-confident attitudes which deny God, and on the positive side the exhorting of devout humility and straightforward righteousness (ii, 3; iii, 12–13), which is reminiscent of Micah vi, 8. In short, he gives us a good impression of the purity and depth of the movement which led to the reform of Josiah.

[8] Audet, 'Les Proverbes et Isaïe dans la tradition juive ancienne' Études et Recherches. Cahiers de Théol. et de Philos. 8 (1952), pp. 23–30, cf. p. 25.

§ 58. HAGGAI

Literature: Ackroyd, 'Studies in the Book of Haggai' JJSt 2 (1951), pp. 163–76; 3 (1952), pp. 1–13; 'The Book of Haggai and Zechariah i–viii' *ib.* 3 (1952), pp. 151–6; 'Two OT Historical Problems of the Early Persian Period' JNESt 17 (1958), pp. 13–27; Bentzen, 'Quelques remarques sur le mouvement messianique parmi les Juifs aux environs de l'an 520 avant Jésus-Christ' RHPhR 10 (1930), pp. 493–503; Bloomhardt, 'The Poems of Haggai' HUCA 5 (1928), pp. 153–95; Budde, 'Zum Text der drei letzten kleinen Propheten' ZAW 26 (1906), pp. 1–28; James, 'Thoughts on Haggai and Zechariah', JBL 53 (1934), pp. 229–35; Kittel, *Geschichte des Volkes Israel* III, 2 (1929), pp. 441–57; North, 'Critical Analysis of the Book of Haggai' ZAW 68 (1956), pp. 25–46; Rothstein, *Juden und Samaritaner* (BWAT 3, 1908); Siebeneck, 'The Messianism of Aggeus and Proto-Zacharias' CBQ 19 (1957), pp. 312–28; Waterman, 'The Camouflaged Purge of Three Messianic Conspirators' JNESt 13 (1954), pp. 73–8; Wolff, *Haggai* (BSt 1, 1951).
Cf. also Literature §§ 48, 59, 126.

1. *The period of the prophet and the contents of the book.* The separate sections of this little book are dated exactly. They all fall within the second year of the Persian king Darius (521–485),[1] that is, in the year 520, and they cover the period of four months in that year from the first day of the sixth month (i, 1) to the twenty-fourth day of the ninth month (ii, 10, 20). Concerning the person of the prophet himself, we learn only that he was a *nabi'* (i, 1), a cult-prophet (§ 10, pp. 428–9).

The contents of the book are as follows. In i, 1–11, dated on the first day of the sixth month, the prophet exhorts the governor Zerubbabel[2] and the High Priest Joshua to rebuild the Temple,[3] explaining the prevailing misfortunes culminating in earning wages to put into *a bag with holes* (צְרוֹר נָקוּב, i, 6)[4] as God's answer to the neglect of the rebuilding.[5] In i, 12–15, we are told how Zerubbabel, Joshua and the people responded to the appeal, and that the building was begun on the twenty-fourth day of the sixth month. ii, 1–9, consists of a new prophetic word to Zerubbabel, Joshua and the people, dated on the twenty-first day of the seventh month. This states that the Temple now being built will even surpass the former one in glory, since as a result of an imminent transformation of the world political situation, the treasures of all nations are to flow into it. A third prophetic word follows in ii, 10–19, dated on the twenty-fourth day of the ninth month. First the prophet makes clear

---

[1] Benedict and von Voigtlander, 'Darius' Bisitun Inscription, Babylonian Version, Lines 1–19' JCSt 10 (1956), pp. 1–10; Henning, 'The Murder of the Magi' JRAS (1944), pp. 133–44; Hinz, 'Das erste Jahr des Großkönigs Dareios' ZDMG 92 (1938), pp. 136–73; König, *Der falsche Bardija. Dareios der Große und die Lügenkönige* (1938); Nyberg, 'Das Reich der Achämeniden' *Historia Mundi*, ed. Valjavec, III (1954), pp. 56–115, 505 f., cf. pp. 75–9; Poebel, 'Chronology of Darius' First Year' AJSL 55 (1938), pp. 142–65; 285–314; 'The Duration of the Reign of Smerdis' AJSL 56 (1939), pp. 121–45; Whitcomb, *Darius the Mede* (1958). Lit. p. 543, n. 6; p. 586, n. 6.

[2] Grosheide, 'Zerubbabel' GThT 48 (1948), pp. 51–62, 65–91.

[3] Brand, 'Some Observations on the Second Temple Edifice' [Hebr., Engl. sum.] Tarbiz 29 (1959/60), pp. 210–17, II–III.

[4] Eissfeldt, *Der Beutel der Lebendigen* (BAL, 105, 6, 1960), p. 39; Loewe, 'The Earliest Biblical Allusion to Coined Money?' PEQ 87 (1955), pp. 141–50.

[5] Peter, 'Zu Haggai i, 9' ThZ 7 (1951), pp. 150 f.

to his hearers, by means of a priestly *torah* (pp. 73–4), that whereas uncleanness is contagious, holiness is not, and *so it is with this people, and with this nation*, i.e. they stand unclean before Yahweh, and so it is *with every work of their hands and what they offer there is unclean* (v. 14). ii, 15–19, adds that from this day forward all failure in the crops will come to an end, and instead there will prevail rich blessing in barn and field. The fourth and last saying, also given on the twenty-fourth day of the ninth month (ii, 20–3) promises to Zerubbabel that after the imminent shaking of the heathen powers which now rule the world, he will be made by Yahweh *like a signet ring* (v. 23), i.e. he is to receive the messianic royal dignity.

The book of Haggai is fortunately supplemented by that of his contemporary Zechariah (Zech. i–viii) who began his activity in the eighth month of the second year of Darius, a month before the last divine word received by Haggai; and also by the record of Ezra iii–vi, where in addition to Haggai and Zech. i–viii one or two further sources are utilised which deal with the building of the Temple (pp. 542–3). In Ezra v, 1; vi, 14, Haggai is also mentioned by name, side by side with Zechariah.

2. *Literary problems*. The book offers a number of problems. Most obvious is that of the date in i, 15. Since the note of the year in v. 15b is perhaps to be taken over into ii, 1, as the completion of the note of day and month to be found there, it is just the phrase in v. 15a, *on the twenty-fourth day of the month, in the sixth* (month) which is left rather in the air. Further, the section ii, 10–19, introduced by the date *twenty-fourth day of the ninth month* apparently contains two quite distinct themes, utterly different in content and meaning—the statement based upon the priestly *torah* that *this people and this nation is unclean* in vv. 10–14, and the promise that *Yahweh will bless from this day forward* in vv. 15–19. Rothstein, with reference to Ezra iv, 1–5, has shown that the first saying is concerned with the repudiation of the offer of help in the building of the Temple and of taking part in the Temple cultus, made by the Samaritans, or more probably by the Jews remaining in the land, and this would fit well with the date, twenty-fourth of the ninth month, when the building had been under way for three months, and its successful conclusion could be foreseen. On the other hand, in view of i, 1–11, where the failures in the harvest are traced to the neglect of the building of the Temple, ii, 15–19, should be thought of as having been spoken not on the twenty-fourth of the ninth month when the building had already been under way for a long time, but quite soon after the beginning of the work. It is in fact stated that the day from which Yahweh will bless (v. 19) is also the day that *the foundation of Yahweh's Temple was laid* (v. 18). These two difficulties—that of i, 15a, and ii, 15–19—disappear on Rothstein's suggestion that ii, 15–19, originally stood after i, 15a. It was received and spoken on the twenty-fourth day of the sixth month, three and a half weeks after the call to build the Temple (i, 1–11), when presumably, after the preparatory work undertaken in the meantime (i, 12–14), the foundation stone was laid with due celebration. We have not to look far for the explanation of the movement of this saying from its original place after i, 15a, to ii, 15–19, which then resulted in the insertion of the date, *twenty-fourth of the ninth month,*

in v. 18. This saying, like that of ii, 10–14, is dated on a twenty-fourth day—the one on the twenty-fourth of the sixth month, ii, 10–14, on the twenty-fourth of the ninth—and this fact caused a redactor who did not observe the difference of month to unite the two sections which belong to the twenty-fourth day, with the result that now, including ii, 20–3, all three words belonging to the twenty-fourth day stand together. In doing this, however, as so often happens, he did not work sufficiently carefully and left the date of the section in its original position in i, 15.

In addition, i, 1–11, does not seem to be in order. Vv. 5–11 give the impression of being overloaded, for vv. 5–6 provide a parallel to 7+9–11. Usually this is eased by deletion (of v. 7 or 7b only) and by transposition (v. 8 or v. 7a+8 after v. 11), but the possibility must be considered that we have here the combination of parts of two small collections, namely of a memorial to Haggai, to be discussed in a moment, and of a looser collection of his sayings. At any rate, in Zech. i–viii the quite similar situation seems to demand such an explanation (p. 432). Here in Haggai, i, 1–6+8 must be ascribed to the memorial and i, 7+9–11 to the collection of sayings.

3. *Haggai's share in the formation of the book.* The dated introductions to the individual prophetic words—or more properly divine words—always refer to Haggai in the third person, the interchange between *to* (אֶל), Haggai (ii, 20), and *by the hand of* (בְּיַד־), Haggai (i, 1; ii, 1, 10) being presumably without significance. The narrative of the response to the demand for the rebuilding of the Temple in i, 12, also mentions Haggai in the third person, and likewise the continuation of the narrative concerning the giving of *torah*, where at first Yahweh takes the initiative (ii, 11–12), whereas in ii, 13–14, the prophet appears to act independently. But this is not a real narrative like that in i, 12, but simply the abbreviation of the more elaborate form of ii, 11–12. i, 3, and i, 13, are probably additions. Thus the naming of the prophet in the third person really appears only in the introductions to the words of Yahweh and in the narrative note in i, 12, which relates the sequel to the first word of Yahweh.

It is usually concluded from the fact that the prophet is always referred to here in the third person, that we have an example of a report by someone else. It then has to be added immediately that in view of the very exact and clearly very reliable details of the report, this must go back directly to personal notes of the prophet. But this roundabout procedure seems to be unnecessary. We should rather assume that our book of Haggai—perhaps without the verses which derive from a collection of his sayings—corresponds exactly with the first-person reports which we have seen in Amos, Hosea, Isaiah, Jeremiah and Ezekiel (§§ 51, 49, 43, 46, 47), and which we shall also find in Zechariah (§ 59). It is only that this prophet, in order to enhance the impression of the complete objectivity of his report, has chosen not the first person but the third person form. Concerned as he was in so prominent a way in the beginning and carrying through of the building of the Temple, and seeing his real prophetic work in this, it seemed necessary and natural to him to put together into a report the various stages of his participation. This would indicate that this report was written down very soon after the events, that is to say, after the twenty-fourth of the ninth month of the year 520.

A short note on Haggai's place in the history of Israelite prophecy is included in the section on Zechariah (pp. 433–4).

§ 59. ZECHARIAH I–VIII

Literature: Brunner, 'Aus der Botschaft des Propheten Sacharja' Judaica 15 (1959), pp. 1–11, 129–42; Eichrodt, 'Vom Symbol zum Typos. Ein Beitrag zur Sacharja-Exegese' ThZ 13 (1957), pp. 509–22; Feinberg, 'Exegetical Studies in Zechariah' BS 97 (1940), pp. 189–99, 318–24, 435–47; 98 (1941), pp. 56–68, 169–82, 447–58; 99 (1942), pp. 56–66, 166–79, 332–43, 428–39; 100 (1943), pp. 256–62, 390–6, 513–23; 101 (1944), pp. 76–82, 187–92, 434–45; 102 (1945), pp. 55–73, 417–32; 103 (1946), pp. 28–38, 161–75; van der Flier, 'Zacharja i–viii', ThStKr 79 (1906), pp. 30–49; Galling, 'Die Exilswende in der Sicht des Propheten Sacharja' VT 2 (1952), pp. 18–36; May, 'A Key to the Interpretation of Zechariah's Visions' JBL 57 (1938), pp. 173–84; Rignell, *Die Nachtgesichte des Sacharja* (1950); Rothstein, *Die Nachtgesichte des Sacharja* (BWAT 8, 1910).

Cf. also Literature §§ 48, 58, 60, 126.

1. *The personality and period of the prophet.* Since ix–xiv definitely come from another hand and another period than i–viii, as will be shown more precisely subsequently (§ 60), we are here concerned only with the first half of the book of Zechariah. Its compiler is named in i, 1, as *Zechariah ben Berechiah ben Iddo, the prophet,* and is clearly the same person as the *Zechariah ben (bar) Iddo* mentioned in Ezra v, 1; vi, 14, together with Haggai (p. 427), and probably also the same person as the head of the priestly family of *Iddo* named *Zechariah* in Neh. xii, 16. We must discuss later (p. 435) the explanation of the apparent difference in the citing of his father's name in Zech. i, 1, on the one hand and Ezra v, 1; vi, 14; Neh. xii, 16, on the other. But the passage Neh. xii, 16, deserves special notice, since it shows that Zechariah was of priestly descent. Thus we have here the proof that a prophet who was particularly interested in the Temple and cultus, that is to say a cult-prophet (§ 9. 10), was at the same time a priest, and we may assume that the cult-prophets in general belonged with the priests, or at least that a majority of them did.

The period of our Zechariah is fixed by the dates provided in the book itself even more exactly than by Ezra v, 1; vi, 14; Neh. xii, 16. These dates are as follows: the 8th month of the 2nd year of Darius (i, 1—the note of the day has presumably dropped out); 24.XI.2 (i, 7); 4.XI.4 (vii, 1). Thus Zechariah began his preaching two to three months later than Haggai (Hag. i, 1—1.VI.2), worked for about a month side by side with him (the latest date in Haggai being 24.IX.2 according to ii, 10, 20), and continued to give his prophetic message for two further years. As in the case of Haggai, the building of the Temple plays a large part in Zechariah's prophecy (i, 16; iv, 9; vi, 12, 13), though he does not concentrate upon it to quite such an exclusive degree as does Haggai.

2. *Contents*. The title (i, 1) is followed in i, 2–6, by the oracle, which, in obedience to Yahweh, the prophet delivered first to his contemporaries: an exhortation to repentance with the promise that if they respond, divine grace will not be lacking. In 1, 7–vi, 8, the prophet relates in the first person eight night visions which were granted to him on 24.XI.2. These either contain a promise for the people and its leaders Zerubbabel and Joshua (i, 8–17; ii, 1–4; ii, 5–17; iv, 1–14; vi, 1–8), or declare that the guilt which rests upon people and leaders must be set aside (iii, 1–10; v, 1–4; v, 5–11), and they thus carry on the note which has been sounded in i, 2–6. The eight visions are: i, 8–15 (17), the three (originally probably four) diversely coloured post-horses;[1] ii, 1–4,[2] the four horns and the four smiths; ii, 5–9 (17),[3] the man with the measuring line; iii, 1–7 (10), the cleansing of Joshua the high priest;[4] iv, 1–6aα (6aβb–10a*), 10a*–14, the golden lampstand and the two olive trees which stand beside it;[5] v, 1–4, the flying scroll; v, 5–11,[6] the woman in the ephah carried away from the land by two women with stork's wings; vi, 1–8, the setting out of four chariots with different coloured horses.

In vi, 9–15, introduced by *And the word of Yahweh came unto me, saying*, but without any date, there follows the command to Zechariah to make into a crown[7] silver and gold brought by Jews who have just arrived from Babylon, and to set this upon the head of *Zerubbabel the son of Shealtiel, the governor*,[8] at the same time proclaiming messianic promises to him. vii, 1, contains a further date, 4.XI.4. This date is primarily applicable to the answer to the inquiry brought by men from Bethelsharezer[9] and others to *the priests of the house of Yahweh of hosts and to the prophets*, as to whether fasting should be continued in the fifth month—recalling the burning of the Temple on the

---

[1] Hertzberg, ' "Grüne" Pferde' ZDPV 69 (1953), pp. 177–80; Press, 'Das erste Nachtgesicht des Propheten Sacharja' ZAW 54 (1936), pp. 43–8.

[2] EVV i, 18–21.

[3] EVV ii, 1–5 (13).

[4] Le Bas, 'Zechariah's Enigmatical Contribution to the Corner-Stone' PEQ 82 (1950), pp. 102–22; Galling, 'Das vierte Nachtgesicht des Propheten Sacharja' ZMR 46 (1931), pp. 193–208; Lods, 'Les origines de la figure de Satan, ses fonctions à la cour céleste' *Mél. Syriens Dussaud* II (1939), pp. 649–60; Rüthy, ' "Sieben Augen auf einem Stein" ' ThZ 13 (1957), pp. 523–9; Schärf, *Die Gestalt des Satans im AT* (Diss. theol. Zürich, 1948); Hans Schmidt, 'Das vierte Nachtgesicht des Propheten Sacharja' ZAW 54 (1936), pp. 48–60; Sellin, 'Der Stein des Sacharja' JBL 50 (1931), pp. 242–9; 'Noch einmal der Stein des Sacharja' ZAW 59 (1942/3), pp. 59–77. Lit. § 126.

[5] Boehmer, 'Was bedeutet der goldene Leuchter Sach iv, 2?' BZ 24 (1938/9), pp. 360–4; Frey, 'Der siebenarmige Leuchter und die Ölsöhne' *Bulmerincq-Gedenkschr.* (1938), pp. 20–63; Möhlenbrink, 'Der Leuchter im fünften Nachtgesicht des Sacharja' ZDPV 52 (1929), pp. 257–86; Rost, 'Bemerkungen zu Sacharja iv' ZAW 63 (1952), pp. 216–21; Torrey, 'The Messiah Son of Ephraim' JBL 66 (1947), pp. 253–77, esp. pp. 273–7: on Zech. iv. Lit. § 126.

[6] Marenof, 'Note concerning the Meaning of the Word "ephah", Zechariah v, 5–11' AJSL 48 (1931/2), pp. 264–7; Rost, 'Erwägungen zu Sacharjas 7. Nachtgesicht' ZAW 58 (1940/1), pp. 223–8.

[7] The singular is to be read for the plural 'crowns' in verse 11.

[8] This is to be read in verse 11 instead of *Joshua the son of Jehozadak, the high priest*.

[9] Eissfeldt, 'Der Gott Bethel' ARW 28 (1930), pp. 1–30: cf. pp. 19 f.; Hyatt, 'A Neo-Babylonian Parallel to *Bethel-sar-eṣer*' JBL 56 (1937), pp. 387–94; Kraeling, *Ar. Pap.*, p. 89; Starcky, 'Une tablette araméenne de l'an 34 de Nabuchodonosor' Syria 37 (1960), pp. 99–115, cf. pp. 104 f. Lit. § 126.

seventh day of the fifth month according to II Kings xxv, 8–9. Or it may be applicable to the inquiry itself. But it is now intended to apply to the whole complex of addresses in vii, 4–viii, 23, which provides a great deal more than the answer to that inquiry. vii, 4–14, contains first an exhortation reminiscent of Isa. lviii, to do judgement and righteousness instead of fasting, and to exercise love and mercy. There follow in viii, 1–17, seven promises, each characterised by a special formula as a word of Yahweh (viii, 2, 3, 4, 6, 7, 9, 14), which speak of the new blessing of Jerusalem, the return of the dispersed exiles, and the divine blessing renewed with the beginning of the rebuilding of the Temple —probably this is how the words which are reminiscent of Hag. i, 2–11; ii, 15–19, are to be understood; in any case they are so explained by a note in 9b which may possibly be of secondary origin. Only in viii, 18–19, in a section which also has a special introductory formula, is there a return to the question of fasting, and this is followed by two further promises of a general nature in vv. 20–2 and 23.

3. *Literary problems.* The narrative of the night visions in i, 8–vi, 8, is in the first person. The dating which introduces it in i, 7, does indeed speak of Zechariah in the third person, but since dating and narrative are inseparably linked, we must either assume that i, 7, in so far as the relevant part, namely, the second half of the verse, is genuine and not a later insertion, was originally in first-person form, or rather that Zechariah, like Haggai (p. 428), at the outset spoke of himself in the third person in order to give the impression of greater objectivity. The same is true of i, 1, and vii, 1, the other two dates which are to be found in the book. The book is thus based upon a first-person narrative of Zechariah, similar to the dated autobiographical narrative of Ezekiel (p. 381), and this has preserved the most significant revelations and provided them with an exact dating. To this belonged—more detailed references not being given— i, 1–vi, 8, and vii, 1–3 + viii, 18–19. But—just as in Ezekiel—beside the introductory formulae in the first person provided with dates, there are also some without dating, namely, iv, 8, vi, 9, vii, 4. This may be explained, just as in Ezekiel, as due to the insertion into the dated autobiographical narrative of other sayings which also began as first-person narratives, the insertion having been made more probably by someone other than the prophet himself. In fact the sections introduced by iv, 8; vi, 9; vii, 4, i.e. iv, 8–10a; vi, 9–14; vii, 4–14— can be seen to interrupt the dated memorial, so that iv, 8–10a (together with iv, 6aβ–7) separates 6aα from 10b; vi, 9–14, separates 8 from 15a, and vii, 4–14 (together with viii, 1–17) separates vii, 3, from viii, 18. In the case of iv (6aβ–7), 8–10a, it is generally recognised that these verses interrupt the vision of the lampstand with the two olive trees which stand beside it (iv, 1–6aα, 10b–14), and in vi, 9–14, Rothstein has effectively demonstrated that these verses are an intrusion between vv. 8 and 15a.

The matter is, however, particularly clear in vii, 1–viii, 19, where the answer to the question raised in vii, 3, as to whether fasting should still be observed in the fifth month, is given only in viii, 18–19, with the further point that not only the fast so far observed in the fifth month, but also those in the fourth month (according to Jer. xxxix, 2, the date of the taking of Jerusalem), in the seventh (the date of the murder of Gedaliah according to II Kings xxv, 25; Jer. xli, 1–3) and in the tenth (the beginning of the siege of Jerusalem according to II Kings xxv, 1) are henceforth to be abandoned, and to be converted into days of rejoicing as signs of the now dawning age of salvation. All the intervening material is only loosely and superficially linked to the question (vii, 4–14), or not connected with it at all (viii, 1–17).

These are not, however, the only ways in which Zechariah's dated auto- biographical narrative has been interrupted. It has been amplified also by the addition of further 'words' of which some may be recognised as separate entities by the formula which introduces them *Thus says Yahweh* (viii, 2, 3), while others stand out clearly from their context by reason of their subject- matter. In the first place, a small group of words, which do not belong, has been appended to the third vision (ii, 5–9) in ii, 10–17[10] (a summons to flight from Babylon, a threat against other nations, and a promise that many peoples will join themselves to Yahweh). Furthermore, iii, 8–10, are not a continuation of the fourth vision, but apparently open up a new topic. Thus Hans Schmidt divides iii, 1–10, into two narratives, of which the one (iii, 1–5bα, 6, 7a 8aβ, 9) concerns the legal proceedings against Joshua which end with his installation as high priest, while the other (iii, 5bβ, 8aα, 7b, 8b, 10)[11] concerns the coming of the Messiah, referred to as the 'branch'. It has already been noted that viii, 1–17, together with vii, 4–14, separate vii, 3, from viii, 18, and the introductory formulae in viii, 2, 3, 4, 6, 7, 9, 14, also show clearly that we have here, as in viii, 20–3, a loose collection of independent sayings.

Attempts have been made to incorporate at least some of these sayings in Zechariah's autobiographical narrative by rearrangement, but the more prob- able assumption is that Zechariah's dated memorial, the basis of our book, has had to submit not only to the occasional insertion of other words which begin in the first person, but also—as we have noted in Jeremiah and also in Hosea i–iii (p. 388)—to being interrupted and amplified by other words of Zechariah, collected by himself or in the circle of his disciples, but in any case having no biographical introductory formula.

4. *Zechariah's share in the formation of the book.* There can be no doubt that among the three sections which make up Zech. i–viii—the dated first-person narrative, the other sections which begin in the first person, the sayings which lack a first-person formula—the first two go back to the prophet himself. The more important of these, and also the larger in extent, is the dated memorial. The prophet has here set down the significant revelations which he received in the decisive years from 520 to 518, with indications of when they occurred, revelations which all proclaim the age of salvation and the breaking-in of the messianic kingdom as being near at hand, and, indirectly rather than explicitly, summon to the building of the Temple as the guarantee of this kingdom, while at the same time not omitting exhortation to repentance and to the abandoning of everything unrighteous. The three dates which are mentioned in this memo- rial (VIII.2; 24.XI.2; 4.IX.4) must have been specially important days for the

[10] Vriezen, 'Two Old Cruces' OTS 5 (1948), pp. 80–91, cf. pp. 88–91: on ii, 12.
[11] Lit. p. 430, n. 4.

people concerned in the rebuilding of the Temple and looking for the messianic age with passionate longing, but we are not in a position to say anything more precise about them. Thus we are not able to decide whether Zechariah received the visions included in i, 7–vi, 8, all in one night and wrote them down on the following morning—eight visions, or seven if the fourth, iii, 1–7, did not originally belong to the group, but occupied an independent position, as Elliger and Horst assume—or whether we should follow Galling in regarding i, 7, as containing the date on which the prophet openly proclaimed revelations which he had received earlier over a longer period. As regards the undated sections of the first person material, the prophet must have regarded them as not needing to be incorporated in the memorial because the questions with which they were concerned are not of such decisive importance as the others, unless it be the case that the dates have here dropped out and they are thus to be regarded as parts of the dated memorial, which might readily be assumed for vi, 9–14. As regards the third part of the material, the sayings, we cannot discover how far the prophet himself was concerned in their writing down and preservation, and it is here that there is the greatest degree of possibility that non-genuine material has slipped in. These are for the most part—as in vii, 4–14; viii, 1–17, 20–3—sayings of very general content, which any other prophet could have spoken. But there is no real ground for suspicion of any one of them.

5. *Later insertions.* The book thus appears as a composition made up of the three elements described, but this does not fully explain its present form. A few further insertions were made in it, of which the most important must be mentioned: vi, 9–14, which originally concerned the crowning of Zerubbabel as messianic king, was, as has already been indicated (p. 430, n. 8), later altered, no doubt under the impact of Zerubbabel's failure. The crown was to be placed rather upon the head of the high priest Joshua, so that this action should at the same time offer a prophecy of the future messiah. Jepsen, it is true, believes that the traditional text may be preserved on the assumption that the procedure had this symbolic meaning from the very outset.

6. *The content of the prophecy of Zechariah and Haggai.* The content of their prophecy reveals Zechariah and his contemporary Haggai as true successors of Ezekiel, who was active seventy years before them. Like him they hold strongly to the demands of the older prophets for humility before God and strictly ethical behaviour, and begin the task, for which Ezekiel had sketched the outline, of building the new Temple and creating a new people, depicting—and here they veer away from the old prophetic line—the grace of Yahweh and the coming of the age of salvation as being primarily dependent upon the building of the Temple. Zechariah so far follows in the steps of Ezekiel as to present the chief part of his message in the form of the relating of 'night visions'. They are undoubtedly real experiences, though we unfortunately cannot establish what impressions from the prophet's everyday life or what patterns there were which as elsewhere contributed to the formation of the visionary experience. On the other hand, there can be no doubt that Zechariah worked over these experiences subsequently, and gave them literary form, as was similarly the case with

Ezekiel. Zechariah thus points the way to the later pseudepigraphical apocalyptic writings, which present what they have to say exclusively in the form of visionary experiences (pp. 55–6).

§ 60. ZECHARIAH IX–XIV

Literature: Ackroyd, 'Criteria for the Maccabean Dating of OT Literature' VT 3 (1953), pp. 113–32, cf. pp. 127–31; Cannon, 'Some Notes on Zechariah c. xi' AfO 4 (1927), pp. 139–46; Heller, 'Die letzten Kapitel des Buches Sacharja im Lichte des späteren Judentums' ZAW 45 (1927), pp. 151–5; Jansma, 'Inquiry into the Hebrew Text and the Ancient Versions of Zechariah ix–xiv' OTS 7 (1950), pp. 1–142; Kittel, *Geschichte des Volkes Israel* III, 2 (1929), pp. 690–5; Kraeling, 'The Historical Situation in Zech ix, 1–10' AJSL 41 (1924/5), pp. 24–33; Kremer, *Die Hirtenallegorie im Buche Zacharias auf ihre Messianität hin untersucht* (1930); Stade, 'Deuterozacharja' ZAW 1 (1881), pp. 1–96; 2 (1882), pp. 151–72, 275–309; Staerk, *Untersuchungen über die Komposition und Abfassungszeit von Zach ix–xiv* (1891).
Cf. also Literature §§ 48, 59, 126.

1. *Contents.* After the superscription *Oracle, the Word of Yahweh*, which will be discussed later (p. 440), there follows first in ix, 1–8, a threat against Hadrach, Damascus and Hamath, as well as against Tyre and Sidon, and against the Philistine cities, and then a promise of divine help for Judah. To this is joined the promise of a king of peace for Jerusalem (vv. 9–10), and of strength for victory for Ephraim and Judah (vv. 11–17). There follows a small, presumably independent section, x, 1–2, to the effect that only Yahweh is able to give rain, not the teraphim and the diviners. x, 3–12,[1] threatens the shepherds and the bell-wethers, and promises to the flock, according to verse 6 the house of Judah and the house of Joseph, a return to their land, while Assyria and Egypt are to be laid low. xi, 1–3, proclaims the downfall of the world-power in the picture of the fall of the cedars of Lebanon and of the oaks of Bashan. The contents of the next section, xi, 4–17, are as follows. At the command of Yahweh, the prophet tends the sheep doomed to slaughter with the two staffs *Grace* and *Union*, but, after he has caused three shepherds to disappear (8a), he lays down the shepherd's office and breaks the two staffs. Thereupon Yahweh orders him to take up the implements of a worthless shepherd, as a sign that a worthless shepherd will come, and a woe is uttered against the latter (17).

A new section, chs. xii–xiv, indicated by a further superscription: *Oracle, the Word of Yahweh against Israel* (p. 440), contains first in xii, 1–xiii, 6, an eschatological proclamation as follows. The heathen nations which threaten Jerusalem are destroyed; the house of David and the inhabitants of Jerusalem do penance for one who has been condemned to death, and the land is cleansed from all impurity. In xiii, 7–9, the shepherd of Yahweh together with two-thirds of his sheep is threatened with destruction, while the last third is to be

---

[1] Winton Thomas, 'Zechariah x, 11a' ET 66 (1954/5), pp. 272 f.

purified to be the people of God. Then in ch. xiv, there is a promise of the destruction of the heathen nations which have ranged themselves against Jerusalem, and the glorification which is to be experienced by Jerusalem and the Temple is painted in the most brilliant colours.

2. *History of criticism.* The recognition that ix–xiv cannot come from the author of the first eight chapters of the book, is very ancient. The impetus to such a recognition was not, however, provided by a critical analysis of these chapters, but by the fact that a saying from them, namely that concerning the thirty pieces of silver which according to xi, 12–13,[2] is paid out to the shepherd as his reward, is quoted in Matt. xxvii, 9–10, as a saying of Jeremiah. Since this New Testament witness was given greater credence than the Jewish tradition which attributed ix–xiv to the Zechariah of the first eight chapters, Jeremiah was seen as the author of ix–xi, or ix–xiv. More detailed critical examination of the situation since the beginning of the eighteenth century has made possible a more exact division between ix–xi, and xii–xiv; ix–xi, which apparently presuppose the existence of Ephraim, that is, the northern kingdom, and name Assyria and Egypt as its enemies (ix, 10, 13; x, 6, 7, 10, 11), were now assigned to the period just before 721, while xii–xiv, which only speak of Judah and appear in xii, 11,[3] to look back upon the death of Josiah (609), were assigned to the period between 609 and 587. This view was further developed in two ways. First, Bertholdt in 1814[4] put forward the suggestion that ix–xi were composed by the Zechariah ben Jeberechiah, named as one of the witnesses called in by Isaiah in Isa. viii, 2, and that the two books, i–viii and ix–xi, which belonged to completely different periods, had been brought together because of the identity of the names of their authors. In the process, the two Zechariahs became one, and the father of the first, Iddo, now became the grandfather of the one Zechariah figure. It would follow that the name given in i, 1, as that of the author *Zechariah ben Berechiah ben Iddo* is due to the combination of *Zechariah ben Iddo* and *Zechariah ben Berechiah*, an explanation which appeared to be confirmed by the fact that, as we saw (p. 429), Ezra v, 1; vi, 14 (Neh. xii, 16), actually name the prophet Zechariah, the author of i–viii, who was active between the years 520 and 518, as *Zechariah ben Iddo*. Secondly, Ewald[5] proposed placing the section xiii, 7–9, which appears to be meaningless in its present position, after xi, 17, where it would continue the threat against the shepherd of xi, 17, in a satisfactory manner, and is itself intelligible in this position.

This modified view of ix–xi+xiii, 7–9, belonging before 721, and of xii–xiv before 587 enjoyed great favour for a long time. But it has also met with

---

[2] Eissfeldt, 'Eine Einschmelzstelle am Tempel zu Jerusalem', FuF 13 (1937), pp. 163 f. = *Ras Schamra und Sanchunjaton* (1939), pp. 42–6 = *Kl. Schr.* II (1963), pp. 107–9; Torrey, 'The Foundry of the Second Temple at Jerusalem' JBL 55 (1936), pp. 247–60; 'The Evolution of a Financier in the Ancient Near East' JNESt 2 (1943), pp. 295–301.

[3] Delcor, 'Deux passages difficiles: Zach. xii, 11 et xi, 13' VT 3 (1953), pp. 67–77; Giveon, ' "In the Valley of Megiddon" (Zech. xii, 11)' JJSt 8 (1957), pp. 155–63; Hoftijzer, 'À propos d'une interprétation récente de deux passages difficiles: Zach. xii, 11 et Zach. xi, 13' VT 3 (1953), pp. 407–9.

[4] *Hist.-krit. Einleitung in . . . A. u. N.T.* IV (1814), pp. 1697–1728.

[5] *Die Propheten des Alten Bundes* I (1840), pp. 308–24.

considerable opposition. In so far as this was concerned to hold to the tradition which attributes ix–xiv to the Zechariah who was active about 520, it was not indeed to be regarded as very significant, since, in view of the obvious differences between i–viii and ix–xiv, it was to be judged ineffective from the start. But much more attention was aroused by the views, anticipated by Hugo Grotius[6] and Eichhorn* among others, and impressively argued by Stade in 1881 and 1882, setting ix–xiv in the Greek period, and, more precisely, in the period of the first Diadochoi. Even though Stade's thesis was soon modified in a variety of ways, in that the unity he assumed for the section was broken up and its separate parts assigned to various authors, and in that the setting was sometimes taken back into the fourth century, and sometimes taken down into the Maccabaean period, the view that ix–xiv were not older than i–viii, but came from a later period, has won increasing approval. There has been no lack also of compromises between the older setting of either ix–xiv or ix–xi and the later. Thus Kuenen*, Baudissin*, Steuernagel*, Kraeling and others have assumed for ix–xi a pre-exilic basis which was then worked over in the Greek period. Lastly, we may note that Sellin has attempted in an original manner to combine the view of Bertholdt with the placing of ix–xiv in the Greek period. He treats ix–xiii (regarding ch. xiv as an addition from a period ten years later) as coming from the Maccabaean period, and more precisely from the decade 150–140. But these chapters were written, like the somewhat older book of Daniel (§ 71), as a pseudepigraphical apocalypse and attributed to the Zechariah ben Jeberechiah of Isa. viii, 2. This attempt at explaining the remarkable presence together of features which at any rate apparently belong to the older, pre-exilic period, and of elements which are clearly late, post-exilic, has also found little favour. The view which has come to prevail is rather that ix–xiv should be assigned to the end of the Persian period, or the beginning of the Greek, to the fifth, fourth or third century (Jepsen, Elliger, etc.). Yet Horst has now again seriously raised the possibility, for ix, 1–xi, 3, and Tadmor for ix, 1–11,[7] that in this section there may be a reflection of conditions belonging to the period about 740 or 730. There is, moreover, far-reaching agreement that neither ix–xiv, nor even ix–xi and xii–xiv, are unities, but that they represent collections of smaller units, whose number and extent are admittedly very variously estimated.

This survey of the work so far done on ix–xiv, confusing enough in spite of the omission of many of the dates, may give a conception of the complexity of the problem. The fact is that these chapters contain on the one hand a whole series of very ancient features which point to the pre-exilic period (cf. above), and on the other hand reveal traces of later times (pp. 437–9). Furthermore, certain sections, such as ix, 1–8, xi, 4–17; xii, 1–xiii, 6, contain clear allusions to definite historical events and conditions, but these are nevertheless not sufficiently clear for it to be possible to place them with certainty. They permit rather a whole series of explanations. Finally, the text is in many places uncertain or corrupt, and its restoration may be made in various ways. Thus

[6] Buhl, 'Sacharja' PRE XVII (³1906), pp. 295–304, cf. p. 301. Lit. § 126.
[7] Cf. Lit. § 126 on p. 437, n. 8.

the oscillation between a pre-exilic and a post-exilic dating, and, if a decision has been made as between these, between various periods within the general dating chosen, may be clearly appreciated.

3. *Date of origin.* We may now examine those sections which may be recognised as more or less independent in the endeavour to trace their probable period of origin, and so obtain a basis upon which the dating of the whole complex of Zech. ix–xiv may be assessed. We shall have to follow Elliger in assigning ix, 1–8,[8] to the year 332, if only because of the allusion to be found here (v. 3) to the rampart heaped up by Tyre, and more precisely to the period of this year when Alexander made preparations for the siege of Tyre. The promise of a king bringing salvation to Zion (ix, 9–10),[9] which follows upon this and was perhaps from the very start intended as a conclusion to it, may well belong to about the same period. The proclamation of the restoration of Israel (ix, 11–17)[10] linked to these, in which the phrase *against thy sons, O Greece* (13) can hardly be cut out as a gloss—or even if it may be cut out, nevertheless gives a correct interpretation of the context—breathes a somewhat different spirit from ix, 1–8. For whereas in this section, as we have seen, the destruction of the small states of Syria and Palestine by Alexander is welcomed, ix, 11–17, threatens the new world-rulers, the Greeks, with destruction. Clearly, in the intervening period the Jews have began to feel the pressure of the new rule. Thus ix, 11–17, may be attributed to the end of the fourth century or the beginning of the third. The warning contained in x, 1–2, that prayer for rain should be made to Yahweh and not to the teraphim, gives at first sight an impression of antiquity by its mention of the teraphim as apparently still holding in popular belief a position as living entities, and may have been incorporated in its present context as a quotation, for some reason which we can no longer discern. Elliger's suggestion is, however, also worth considering, that the section should be regarded in an allegorical or symbolical sense as a prayer not for actual rain but for salvation metaphorically conceived as rain, which can only be given by Yahweh and not by the false gods of the later period which are to be understood here in the reference to teraphim. In any case these verses provide no evidence for the dating of Zech. ix–xiv or of one of the smaller collections which seem to underlie this complex. Thus it seems reasonable to assign the units gathered together in ix, 1–x, 2, to about 300 B.C., though it is hardly possible to decide whether we should think of their coming from one or more authors. The references which are clearly present here to an earlier period

---

[8] Cazelles, 'La mission d'Esdras' VT 4 (1954), pp. 113–40, cf. pp. 138 f.; Delcor, 'Les allusions à Alexandre le Grand dans Zach ix, 1–8' VT 1 (1951), pp. 110–24; Elliger, 'Ein Zeugnis aus der jüdischen Gemeinde im Alexanderjahr 332 vChr. Eine territorialgeschichtliche Studie zu Sach ix, 1–8' ZAW 62 (1950), pp. 63–115; 'Sam'al und Ḥamat' ThLZ 72 (1947), cols. 157–8; Malamat, 'The Historical Setting of Two Biblical Prophecies on the Nations' IEJ 1 (1950/1), pp. 149–59, cf. pp. 149–54; Masing, 'Die Proklamation des Tab'alsohnes' *Bulmerincq-Gedenkschr.* (1938), pp. 117–26. Lit. § 126.

[9] Feigin, 'Babylonian Parallels to the Hebrew Phrase "Lowly and Riding upon an Ass" ' [Hebr.] *Studies Moses Schorr* (1944), pp. 227–40; on this, Nougayrol, RA 44 (1950), p. 39, n. 3; Salonen, ArOr 17, II (1949), p. 320 (refs. kindly supplied by Dr. Ernst Kutsch).

[10] Bewer, 'Two suggestions on Prov. xxx, 31 and Zech. ix, 16' JBL 67 (1948), pp. 61–2. Lit. § 126.

(ix, 1, 10, 13, to the existence of the states of Damascus and Ephraim; ix, 5, to the king of Gaza) are then to be explained as archaisms, or as due to the use of older material.

In the section x, 3–12, it is also tempting at first in view of the mention of the *House of Judah* and the *House of Joseph* (v. 6), of *Ephraim* (v. 7) and of *Assyria* (vv. 10, 11), to think of the period before 721 as the period of origin, but the traces of a quite late period are here even more numerous than in the previous poem. Above all, there is in vv. 6–10, a quite clear assumption of the exile and of the existence in both east and west of a large diaspora. The *House of Joseph* and *Ephraim* are therefore to be explained as due to archaic and eschatological language, and *Assyria* and *Egypt* are here to be understood as references to Seleucid Syria and Ptolemaic Egypt, just as in Isa. xix, 23–5, xxvii, 13 (pp. 321, 323–7) and presumably also in the Qumrān War Scroll[11] (§ 107). Against these powers, or one of them, is certainly also directed the prophetic mocking song on the fall of the world-ruler in xi, 1–3. The pictorial language, however, makes difficult if not impossible the discovery of its reference to precise historical events. Thus since in x, 3–xi, 3, the Seleucid and Ptolemaic powers are threatened with downfall, the shepherds and goats threatened in x, 3—if they are in fact original here and v. 3a is not with Elliger to be excised as a secondary addition—must also be understood as referring to the kings of these powers and not to kings of Judah.

The parabolic narrative concerning the shepherds in xi, 4–17,[12] which must primarily be understood on its own, since Ewald's suggestion of treating xiii, 7–9, as its conclusion cannot be proved to be correct, clearly has a reference to quite definite events. But as a result of its parabolic language, the allusions which it contains are capable of many interpretations and may be applied to very different events and personages. The fact that it is also clear that the section has been repeatedly worked over, makes it all the more difficult to get to the sense of the basic material. Thus interpretation of the three shepherds destroyed in one month mentioned in verse 8 (which is moreover textually in many ways unsatisfactory), has oscillated between referring them to Moses, Aaron and Miriam (Jerome), and referring them to Galba, Otho and Vitellius (Calmet). Between these two extremes there stand such explanations as that of Ewald, who sees in the three shepherds of xi, 8, the three kings Zechariah, Shallum and Menahem, who according to II Kings xv, 10, 14, 16–17, followed rapidly one upon the other, and those of Marti and Sellin, of whom the former saw an allusion to the renegade high priests Lysimachus, Jason and Menelaus (Josephus, *Ant.* XII, 5. 1–9. 7; XII, 3. 1–3; XX, 10. 1), while the latter interprets them as meaning the Tobiads Simon, Menelaus and Lysimachus, who were driven out by Onias (Josephus, *Bell. Jud.*, I, 1; cf. II Macc. iii–iv). To this

---

[11] Col. 1, line 2, כתיי אשור, the *Kittim of Assyria*; line 4, הכתיים במצרים, the *Kittim in Egypt*. Cf. below, p. 653.

[12] Brouwer, *Wachter en Herder, een exegetische studië over de herderfiguur in het Oude Testament, inzonderheid in de pericopen Zach xi en xiii, 7–9* (1949); Bruce, 'The Book of Zechariah and the Passion Narrative' BJRL 43 (1960/1), pp. 336–53; Feigin, 'Some Notes on Zechariah xi, 4–17' JBL 44 (1925), pp. 203–213; Rehm, 'Die Hirtenallegorie Zach xi, 4–14' BZ 4 (1960), pp. 186–208.

divergence in the interpretation of the three wicked shepherds there corresponds the variety of interpretation of the good shepherd. It is clear that there is a lack of really decisive evidence, and in this matter we must not be led astray by the fact that since the last quarter of the nineteenth century the view has enjoyed increasing favour that xi, 4–17, is to be interpreted as reflecting events of the period of the Maccabaean rising, as, for example, by Marti and Sellin. For the reason is simply that for this period we have a relative wealth of evidence available, whereas we know practically nothing of the fortunes of the Jewish church-state in the second half of the fourth century and in the third, and so cannot mention any events from this period of about one hundred and fifty years which might find an echo in Zech. xi, 4–17. Since, as we have seen, the appropriate setting for ix, 1–x, 2, is in the last third of the fourth century or the beginning of the third, it is natural to assume about the same period for the origin of xi, 4–17. For this reason too it seems worth while to consider the significant suggestion of Elliger, to regard the separation of the Samaritan religious community from the Jerusalem Temple and its cultus, which began about the end of the fourth century, as providing the historical background for the section xi, 4–17, and to assign it to this period, though admittedly even this view involves many puzzles.

The section xii–xiv contains no indications at all of pre-exilic origin. On the contrary the indications of later origin are particularly numerous. Of such are the expectation which dominates xii, 1–9, of an eschatological onslaught of the heathen nations against Jerusalem which ends with their complete annihilation (cf. p. 313), and the picture provided in xiii, 1–6, of the situation in the last days, when men will be ashamed of the vocation of prophet. But there is clearly an allusion in xii, 10–14,[13] to a concrete event, which appears to be the execution of a criminal. Unfortunately it is again impossible to discover what is intended. As to the interpretations of the man who is killed as being Onias III who was killed in 170 (II Macc. iv, 32–8; Dan. ix, 26), as Sellin has suggested, or as being Simon, murdered in 134 (I Macc. xvi, 11–22) as suggested by Duhm,[14] the same point applies which has already been made concerning the interpretation of the shepherds in xi, 4–17, as denoting figures of the years preceding the Maccabaean rising. They only make the impression they do, because we know practically nothing concerning the fortunes of the Jewish national and religious community during the period between 350 and 200, when events no doubt occurred which could be referred to in xii, 10–14. Thus in this passage we cannot get further than confessing that we do not know, and that, so far as we can see, we are unlikely ever to know. The same is unfortunately true of the threat found in xiii, 7–9, against shepherd and flock, that is to say, against leader and people, which issues in a promise in so far as the catastrophe which is about to fall upon shepherd and flock will bring with it the purification of

[13] Delcor, 'Zach xii, 10' RB 58 (1951), pp. 189–99; 'Zach xii, 11 et xi, 13' VT 3 (1953), pp. 67–77; Levy, 'Secharja xii, 10' MGWJ 81 (1937), pp. 293–6; Torrey, 'The Messiah Son of Ephraim' JBL 66 (1947), pp. 253–77, cf. pp. 272 f.: on xii, 9–11; Tsevat, 'Sociological and Historical Observations on Zechariah xii' [Hebr., Engl. sum.] Tarbiz 25 (1955/6), pp. 111–17, I.
[14] ZAW 31 (1911), pp. 195 f.

one-third of the people to be the people of God. Neither passage offers indications which enable even a moderately certain dating to be discovered.

Ch. xiv[15] offers indications only of a late date of origin, and it is moreover probable that the conceptions of the day of Yahweh which are here gathered together and which are to some extent contradictory, do not come from a single hand, but have been successively added. Indications of a particular period of origin are moreover not to be found.

4. *Summary of results.* If, with a reiterated emphasis on the especially large degree of uncertainty in all the interpretations and settings suggested, we gather together the net result of our exposition of Zech. ix–xiv, there appears to be no real need, if we may deal with this point first, to ascribe xii–xiv to the same author as ix–xi. In xii–xiv there are predominantly general expectations of the eschatological onslaught of the heathen nations and their destruction, and of the good fortune of Jerusalem which will then begin, whereas in ix–xi, apart from the obscure shepherd parable of xi, 4–17, there is concrete prophecy concerned first with the rise and then with the collapse of the Greek-Macedonian world-power (ix, 1–xi, 3). We must therefore regard ix–xi on the one hand and xii–xiv on the other as two separate booklets, and this is confirmed by the fact that each has its separate superscription and that the two superscriptions have at any rate the same opening words: *Oracle, Word of Yahweh.* Since a superscription which begins in exactly the same way also introduces the book of Malachi—so named but really anonymous (p. 441)—the explanation would seem to be that the redactor of the Book of the Twelve appended to the last book which had the name of a known prophet—namely Zechariah—three anonymous collections—namely, Zech. ix–xi, xii–xiv, and Malachi. To each of these he gave the title *Oracle, Word of Yahweh,* or (since this double title is unusual and is either to be explained as an extension of the phrase *Word of Yahweh* by the addition of *Oracle,* or more probably as an explanation of the term *Oracle* by the addition of *Word of Yahweh,* dependent upon Jer. xxiii, 33–40), he placed only one of the two designations in front of them, thus marking the beginning of the individual collections. In the course of time the first two of these collections were added to the prophet whose name was last mentioned, namely Zechariah, while the third, as the result of a misunderstanding of Mal. iii, 1 (p. 441) was attributed to 'Malachi'.

Whether this division of Zech. ix–xiv into two booklets is sufficient may indeed be doubted. There is in fact little relationship between the prophecies of ix, 1–xi, 3, and the parable of xi, 4–17, and we have already seen that ch. xiv is not a unity, but contains elements of diverse origin. Perhaps then we ought to assume not only for ix–xi but also for xii–xiv at least two authors. This is, however, not absolutely necessary, and we may do better to keep to the assumption of one author for each, a Deutero-Zechariah for ix–xi, and a Trito-Zechariah for xii–xiv, of which the first may be assigned to about 300 B.C., and the second to a period a few decades later.

[15] Abel, 'Aṣal dans Zacharie xiv, 5' RB 45 (1936), pp. 385–400; Zolli, 'Note Esegetiche (Zaccaria xiv, 6, 7)' Bibl 20 (1939), pp. 284–7. Lit. § 126.

§ 61. MALACHI

Literature: (a) Commentaries: Bulmerincq, *Der Prophet Maleachi* I (1926), II (1932).

(b) Other Works: Botterweck, 'Mal. i, 2–5, 6–10; ii, 1–9, 10–16; iii, 13–21' Bibel und Leben 1 (1960), pp. 28–38, 100–9, 179–85, 253–60; Budde (cf. § 58); Cameron, 'A Study of Malachi' Transact. Glasgow Univ. Or. Soc. 8 (1938), pp. 9–12; Grimme (cf. § 52); O. Holtzmann, 'Der Prophet Maleachi und der Ursprung des Pharisäerbundes' ARW 29 (1931), pp. 1–21; Levy, 'Der Prophet Maleachi' *Festschr. z. 75 jähr. Bestehen des jüd.-theolog. Seminars der Fraenkelschen Stiftungen* (1929), II, pp. 273–84; Pfeiffer, 'Die Disputationsworte im Buche Maleachi' EvTh 19 (1959), pp. 546–68; Torrey, 'The Prophecy of "Malachi"' JBL 17 (1898), pp. 1–15.

Cf. also Literature §§ 48, 60, 126.

1. *The title of the book and the name of the prophet.* We have just seen (p. 440) that the superscription *Oracle, the Word of Yahweh to Israel by Malachi* is the same, as far as its first part is concerned, as those to be found in Zech. ix, 1, and xii, 1. As far as the second part *by Malachi* is concerned, *mal'ākî* (מַלְאָכִי) is in reality not a proper name, but the noun with possessive suffix (*my*) *messenger* which appears in iii, 1, and it is clear that this expression *my messenger* has only as a result of misunderstanding come to be regarded as the supposed name of the prophet who stands behind the book. In fact, at a later date, the messenger of Yahweh, who according to iii, 1, is to prepare the way for Yahweh, has been identified with the author of the book, and so the phrase *my messenger* has been taken from iii, 1, and placed at the beginning of the book as an indication of authorship. It remains uncertain whether מַלְאָכִי was still regarded as an appellative *my messenger* or was at once understood as a proper name. Certainly at a later stage this latter view became general, and natural, even though 𝔊 with its rendering ἐν χειρὶ ἀγγέλου αὐτοῦ, *by his messenger*, still represents the appellative conception. Bulmerincq's explanation of *mal'ākî* as representing an abbreviated form of the (otherwise unattested) proper name *mal'ākiyyāh* can hardly be right. It is preferable to keep to the normal explanation. Thus we do not know the author of this book by name, any more than we know those of the books Zech. ix–xi and Zech. xii–xiv (p. 440) which immediately precede it.

2. *Contents.* The book is divided in 𝔐 into three chapters, in 𝔊 and 𝔙 and in the English versions, into four, since 𝔐 iii, 19–24, is reckoned as iv, 1–6. It falls into six sections, which are all stylistically similarly constructed, in that they imitate the dialogue form of a spoken debate, and give the word first to Yahweh or to the prophet as his representative, and then follow it with the reply of the people or of the priests, continuing the interchange of speeches between the two sides as required. The first section (i, 2–5) affirms that Yahweh has kept his love for Jacob as against the related people of Edom which has been handed over to destruction.[1] The second section (i, 6–ii, 9) is addressed to the priests, reproaching them that they offer inferior sacrifices to Yahweh and threatening them with a dreadful curse if they continue such behaviour.[2]

[1] Herranz, 'Dilexi Jacob, Esau autem odio habui' Est Bíbl 2 (1941/2), pp. 559–83.
[2] Mariani, 'De sacrificio a Malachia praedicto' Antonianum 9 (1934), pp. 193–242,

The third (ii, 10–16) condemns the fact that Jewish men have divorced their Jewish wives in order to marry foreign women in their place. The fourth (ii, 17–iii 5)[3] makes a reply to those who doubt the reality of divine retribution, to the effect that the day of judgement will soon come. The fifth (iii, 6–12) traces the plagues from which the people are at present suffering—scarcity of crops and locusts—to the fact that the tithe has not been fully paid, and gives full assurance of God's rich blessing when this duty is strictly fulfilled. The sixth (iii, 13–21)[4] protests to the pseudo-God-fearers who doubt the justice of divine retribution that on the day of judgement the truly pious will receive God's reward, whereas the godless are to be destroyed. These six sections of controversy are followed in iii, 22–4, by a further exhortation to obedience to the law of Moses and the proclamation that the prophet Elijah will come before the day of Yahweh.

3. *Literary problems* are hardly present in the book. A suspicion of non-genuineness has only been raised with regard to ii, 11–12, or ii, 11b–13a, and iii, 22–4. As far as ii, 11b–13a, is concerned, the removal of these words which condemn the marriage of foreign women would give a more general character to the reproach made to the people in ii, 10–16, since divorce then would be absolutely condemned here, and not just divorce occasioned by a desire for a foreign wife. Since ii, 11b–13a, fits badly from a structural point of view also in the context of ii, 10–16, it is probable that we have here a later addition. This is certainly true of iii, 22, and iii, 23–4. The appendix iii, 22, equating the message of 'Malachi', and perhaps of the prophets as a whole, with the demands of the Mosaic law, exhorts observance of this law, so that the question of the date when this appendix was added depends upon what is meant by the law—whether D or P or even the Pentateuch as we know it. iii, 23–4, however, are intended to make precise the proclamation in iii, 1, of a heavenly messenger who is to precede Yahweh when he appears for judgement, and to correct this by indicating that Elijah is this messenger.

4. *Date of origin.* The book is assigned by the majority of scholars to the first half of the fifth century, in other words between Haggai-Zechariah (*c.* 520) and Nehemiah-Ezra (*c.* 400). The chief grounds for this dating are on the one hand the existence of the Temple cultus (pp. 441 f.) and on the other hand the fact that in the life of the community and in the cultus those evils have become widespread against which Nehemiah and Ezra subsequently campaigned—namely mixed marriages, and lack of strictness in the fulfilment of cultic duties. This dating also fits with the fact that the influence of the Priestly code is not yet to be discerned, for it is clearly Deuteronomy which ranks as the finally authoritative law, and its language has also in fact influenced Malachi. So even Bulmerincq agrees with the normal dating of the book, at any rate in so far as he considers that its separate sections came into being from 485 onwards, but he admittedly differs from this normal view in regarding Malachi, born

361–82, 451–74; Witzel, 'Dienstinstruktionen an das hethitische Tempelpersonal' Stud. Anselm. 27/8 (1951), pp. 476–85. Lit. § 126.

[3] A. Robinson, 'God the Refiner of Silver' CBQ 11 (1949), pp. 188–90: on iii, 3.

[4] Winton Thomas (p. 409, n. 7) on קָדֹרַנִּית, iii, 14; Vattioni, 'Mal. iii, 20 e un mese del calendario fenicio' Bibl 40 (1959), pp. 1012–15.

about 515 and dying about 445 or earlier, as one of the assistants of Ezra, supposed to have supported him in the preparations for his reform and even accompanying that reform by the latest of his utterances (iii, 6–12, 13–21, 22–4). To Bulmerincq, who here reveals himself as influenced by statements of the Targum and of Jerome, the messenger of iii, 1, is none other than 'the priest and scribe Ezra even now on the way from Babylon to Jerusalem'.[5] This unusual view cannot be maintained, if only because Ezra must be placed after Nehemiah (pp. 552–5), and it is therefore better to abide by the less definite dating of the book. This is to be accepted as correct. It has not been disproved even by Holtzmann's attempt to interpret the covenant of those who fear God mentioned in iii, 16, as the 'synagogue' of the Asidaeans of I Macc. ii, 42, and so to attribute this phrase and hence the book to the first half of the third century.

The situation shortly before Nehemiah and Ezra also suits Malachi in respect of the content of his message. In the demand for humble reverence before God as it is expressed particularly in the majestic expression put into the mouth of Yahweh in i, 14: *I am a great king, and my name is great among the nations,* and in the proclamation of imminent judgement (iii, 1–5) reminiscent, of Zephaniah's *Dies irae* (p. 423), Malachi is completely a prophet in the older sense of the term. But in his stress upon the value of strict fulfilment of cultic duties and on keeping Jewish blood pure (ii, 10–16), he goes further along the road in which Ezekiel, Haggai and Zechariah have preceded him, and is that much removed from an Amos, who demanded judgement, but not cultus, and for whose God the Israelites were no better than the Ethiopians (ix, 7, iii, 1–2).

C. THE WRITINGS (כְּתוּבִים *HAGIOGRAPHA*)

§ 62. THE ORDER OF THE 'WRITINGS'

It will be necessary in the fourth part of this book, which deals with the History of the Canon (pp. 568–70), to show the variations in the order of the books which belong to the third section of the Old Testament canon, the 'Writings'. This is true not only of various differences between the tradition represented by 𝔊 and that attested in 𝔐, but more still in the many differences which appear in this respect within the manuscripts themselves of 𝔐. Thus in Codex L (p. 691) and in Mishael ben 'Uzziel,[1] representing Palestinian tradition, Chronicles stands at the beginning of the 'Writings'; whereas the Babylonian Talmud (Baba Batra 14b) and the Berlin ms. or. qu. 680, which is of Babylonian origin, place Chronicles at the end of the 'Writings', after Ezra-Neh. In addition, the position of Job and Proverbs varies, in that Job sometimes stands before Proverbs and sometimes after. In what follows, the order of the 'Writings'

---

[5] II, p. 336.
[1] Kahle, *The Cairo Geniza* (1947), pp. 66–9; (²1959), pp. 115–18. Cf. below p. 687 (Lipschuetz).

provided by Codex L is taken as determinative, and the only deviation from it is that Chronicles is given its appropriate place (pp. 530–1) before Ezra-Neh.

§ 63. THE PSALTER

Literature: (a) Commentaries (i) Series: ATD: Weiser (⁵1959); E. T. Hartwell (1962); BK: Kraus (²1962); Camb. B: Kirkpatrick (1902); Cent. B: Davison and Davies (1904/6); COuT: I (Ps. i–xli) Ridderbos (1955); II (Ps. xlii–cvi) Ridderbos (1958); Echter-B: Nötscher (1947); HAT: Hans Schmidt (1934); HK: Baethgen (³1904); Gunkel (⁴1926); HS: Herkenne (1936); HSAT: Bertholet (1923); IB: McCullough, Taylor, Sclater, Poteat, Ballard (1955); ICC: Ch. A. and E. G. Briggs (1906/7 (1951, 1952)); Jerusalem-B: Tournay, Schwab, Gelineau, Chifflot (³1958); KAT: Kittel (⁵·⁶1929); KD: Delitzsch (⁴1883, ⁵1894); KeH: Olshausen (1853); KHC: Duhm (²1922); SAT: Staerk (²1920); Soncino-B: Cohen (²1950); SZ: Kessler (²1899); TU: I, II Böhl (1946/7), III Gemser (1949); WC: Barnes (1931).
(ii) Single Commentaries: Bentzen (1940); Bonkamp (1949, ²1956); Calès (⁶1936); Castellino (1955); Eerdmans (1947); Hupfeld-Nowack (³1888); Kissane, I (1953), II (1954); König (1927); Leslie (1949); Oesterley (⁴1953); Peters (1930); Podechard, I (Pss. i–lxxv) (1949); II (Pss. lxxvi–c, cx) (1954); Wutz (1925).
(b) Other Works: Arens, *Die Psalmen im Gottesdienst des Alten Bundes* (Trierer ThSt 11, 1961); Ayuso, 'Los elementos extrabíblicos de Job y del Salterio' Est Bíbl 5 (1946), pp. 429–458; Baumann, 'Struktur-Untersuchungen im Psalter' ZAW 61 (1949), pp. 114–76; 62 (1950), pp. 115–52; Bentzen, *Inledning til de gammeltestamentlige Salmer* (1932); Bloemendaal, *The Headings of the Psalms in the East-Syrian Church* (Diss. theol. Leiden, 1960); Bonnard, *Le Psautier selon Jérémie* (1960); Bonnes, *David et les Psaumes* (Maîtres spirituels 13, 1957); Boson, 'Una divisione logica del Salterio' Stud. Anselm. 27–8 (1951), pp. 195–207; Bout, *Het ʒondebesef in het Boek der Psalmen* (Diss. theol. Leiden, 1952); Braude, *The Midrash on Psalms (Midrash Tehillim). Transl. from the Hebrew and Aramaic* (1959); Budde, *Die schönsten Psalmen* (1915); 'Zum Text der Psalmen' ZAW 35 (1915), pp. 175–195; Buttenwieser, *The Psalms. Chronologically treated* (1938); Calès, 'Publications récentes sur les Psaumes' RSR 26 (1936), pp. 587–600; Castellino, 'Poesia e religione dei Salmi' *Secoli sul Mondo a cura di Giovanni Rinaldi* (²1957), pp. 309–34, 586–7; Clarke, *Analytical Studies in the Psalms* (1949); Coppens, 'Les parallèles du Psautier avec les textes de Ras Shamra Ougarit' Muséon 59 (1946), pp. 113–42; *Het Onsterfelijkheidsgeloof in het Psalmboek* (Med. Ac. van België XIX, 3, 1957); 'Les Psaumes des Ḥasidîm' (*Mél. Bibl. Robert* (1957), pp. 214–24; Cosgrave, 'Recent Studies on the Psalms' Bull. Canad. Soc. Bibl. Stud. 5 (1939), pp. 3–15; Driver, 'Notes on the Psalms' JThSt 36 (1935), pp. 147–56; 43 (1942), pp. 149–60; 44 (1943), pp. 12–32; 'Textual and Linguistic Problems of the Book of Psalms' HThR 29 (1936), pp. 171–95; Drijvers, *Les Psaumes: genres littéraires et thèmes doctrinaux* (1958); Eerdmans, 'Sojourn in the Tent of Jahu' OTS 1 (1942), pp. 1–16; 'Essays on Masoretic Psalms' *ib.*, pp. I–VIII, 105–300; Farndale, *The Psalms in New Light* (1956); Franken, *The Mystical Communion with JHWH in the Book of Psalms* (1954); Frost, 'Asseveration by Thanksgiving' VT 8 (1958), pp. 380–90; Gelin, *Les Pauvres de Yahvé* (1953); Ginsberg, 'Some Emendations in Psalms' HUCA 23, 1 (1950/1), pp. 97–104; Gispen, *Indirecte gegevens voor hat bestaan van den pentateuch in de Psalmen?* (1928); Gunkel, *Ausgewählte Psalmen* (⁴1917); Gunn, *God in the Psalms* (1956); Hauret, 'L'Interprétation des Psaumes selon l'école "Myth and Ritual"' RSR 33 (1959), pp. 321–42; 34 (1960), pp. 1–34; Hempel, 'Neue Literatur zum Studium des Psalters' ZAW 56 (1938), pp. 171–4; Hjelt, 'Die Bedeutung des 'āwen im AT' StOr 1 (1925), pp. 61–8; Holm-Nielsen, 'Den gammeltestamentlige salmetradition' DTT 18 (1955), pp. 135–48, 193–215; 'The Importance of Late Jewish Psalmody for the Understanding of OT Psalmodic Tradition' StTh 14 (1960), pp. 1–53; Hylmö, *De s.k. Vallfartssångerna i Psaltaren* (1925); Jansen, *Die spätjüdische Psalmendichtung* (1937); Junker, 'Einige Rätsel im Urtext der Psalmen' Bibl 30 (1949), pp. 197–212;

Kennett, 'The Historical Background of the Psalms' *OT Essays* (1928), pp. 119–218
Lauha, *Die Geschichtsmotive in den at. Psalmen* (1945); Lindblom, 'Bemerkungen zu den
Psalmen I' ZAW 59 (1942/3), pp. 1–13; Magne, 'Répétitions de mots et exégèse dans
quelques Psaumes et le Pater' Bibl 39 (1958), pp. 177–97; Michel, *Tempora und Satzstellung in den Psalmen* (AETh 1, 1960); Montgomery, 'Recent Developments in the Study of the
Psalter' AThR 16 (1934), pp. 185–98; Mowinckel (§§ 15, 16); Murphy, 'A new Classification
of literary Forms in the Psalms' CBQ 21 (1959), pp. 83–7; Niemeyer, *Het Probleem van de
Rangschikking der Psalmen* (1950); Oesterley, *A Fresh Approach to the Psalms* (1937);
Paterson, *The Praises of Israel: Studies literary and religious in the Psalms* (1950); Peters,
'Senkrechte Doppelschreibung als Fehlerquelle in den Psalmen' BZ 22 (1934), pp. 1–12;
Piatti, *Il libro dei Psalmi* (1955); Pidoux, *Du portique à l'autel. Introduction aux Psaumes*
(1959); 'Quelques allusions au droit d'asile dans les Psaumes' *Hommage à W. Vischer*
(1960), pp. 191–7; Ridderbos, *Psalmen en Cultus* (1958); 'De huidige stand van het onderzoek der Psalmen' GThT 60 (1960), pp. 8–14; Ringgren, *Psaltarens fromhet* (1957), E.T.
(revised ed.) *The faith of the Psalmists* (1963); 'Quelques traits essentiels de la piété des
Psaumes' *Mél. Bibl. Robert* (1957), pp. 205–13; Robert, 'L'exégèse des Psaumes selon les
méthodes de la Formgeschichtliche Schule' *Misc. Bibl. Ubach* (1953), pp. 211–26; Sauer,
Die strafende Vergeltung Gottes in den Psalmen I (Diss. theol. Basel 1957 (1961)); 'I nemici
nei Salmi' Protestantesimo 13 (1958), pp. 201–7; Schönbächler, *Die Stellung der Psalmen
zum at. Opferkult* (1941); Schulz, *Kritisches zum Psalter* (1932); *Psalmenfragen* (1940); Smal,
Die Universalisme in die Psalms (1956); Snaith, 'The triennial Cycle and the Psalter' ZAW
51 (1933), pp. 302–7; *Studies in the Psalter* (1934); *Hymns of the Temple* (1951); Stamm
(§ 15); Steinmann, *Les psaumes* (1951); Tournay, 'Les Psaumes complexes' RB 54 (1947),
pp. 521–42; 56 (1949), pp. 37–60; 'En marge d'une traduction des Psaumes' RB 63 (1956),
pp. 161–81, 496–512; 'Sur quelques rubriques des Psaumes' *Mél. Bibl. Robert* (1957),
pp. 197–204; 'Recherches sur la chronologie des Psaumes' RB 65 (1958), pp. 321–57; 66
(1959), pp. 161–90; Tsevat, *A Study of the Language of the Biblical Psalms* (1955); on this
cf. Mowinckel, NTT 57 (1956), pp. 115–23 and ThLZ 81 (1956), cols. 199–202; Tur-Sinai,
'The Literary Character of the Book of Psalms' OTS 8 (1950), pp. 263–81; Vellas,
'Ἐκλεκτοὶ Ψαλμοί (²1955); Weiser, 'Zur Frage nach den Beziehungen der Psalmen
zum Kult' *Bertholet-Festschr.* (1950), pp. 513–31 = *Ausg. Schr.* (1961), pp. 303–21; Westermann, *Das Loben Gottes in den Psalmen* (²1961); 'Struktur und Geschichte der Klage im
AT' ZAW 66 (1954), pp. 44–80).
    Cf. also Literature §§ 6, 9, 14–16, 32, 126.

1. *The name of the book. The enumeration of the Psalms in* 𝔐 *and in* 𝔊.
The designation of the book among the Jews was סֵפֶר תְּהִלִּים *book of songs*
or simply תְּהִלִּים *songs*. To this corresponds the designation used in the New
Testament (Luke xx, 42, Acts i, 20) βίβλος ψαλμῶν and the title ψαλμοί
which appears in most manuscripts of 𝔊. Our word 'Psalms' derives from this.
But a few manuscripts of 𝔊 have as title the word ψαλτήριον *stringed instrument*, or *collection of songs*. Hence our word 'Psalter'.

    The Psalter contains 150 psalms, but 𝔊 differs from 𝔐 in the enumeration
in that it divides two psalms into two which are treated as units in 𝔐, and
conversely in two cases treats as one what are regarded as two psalms in 𝔐.
Thus Ps. ix and Ps. x 𝔐, and Ps. cxiv and Ps. cxv 𝔐 comprise in each case
one psalm in 𝔊, and Pss. cxvi 𝔐 and cxlvii 𝔐 are then divided into two in 𝔊.
The result is that Pss. i–ix 𝔐 correspond to Pss. i–ix 𝔊, Pss. x–cxiii 𝔐 to
Pss. ix–cxii 𝔊, Pss. cxiv–cxv 𝔐 to Ps. cxiii 𝔊. Ps. cxvi 𝔐 is then divided
into two in 𝔊. Thus Ps. cxvi, 1–9 𝔐 appears as Ps. cxiv 𝔊, and Ps. cxvi,
10–19 𝔐 as Ps. cxv 𝔊. Then Pss. cxvii–cxlvi 𝔐 correspond to Pss. cxvi–
cxlv 𝔊. Ps. cxlvii 𝔐 is also divided into two in 𝔊, so that Ps. cxlvii, 1–11 𝔐

is Ps. cxlvi 𝔊, and Ps. cxlvii, 12–20 𝔐 is Ps. cxlvii 𝔊, and the remainder of the psalms, cxlviii–cl, correspond in enumeration in 𝔐 and 𝔊. The matter may be tabulated as follows:

𝔐	𝔊
i–ix	i–ix (a)
x–cxiii	ix (b)–cxii
cxiv–cxv	cxiii
cxvi, 1–9	cxiv
cxvi, 10–19	cxv
cxvii–cxlvi	cxvi–cxlv
cxlvii, 1–11	cxlvi
cxlvii, 12–20	cxlvii
cxlviii–cl	cxlviii–cl

When a psalm is being referred to in 𝔊, this peculiarity of enumeration for Pss. ix–cxlvii needs to be watched.

The fact that there is at times a difference between 𝔐 and 𝔊 in their view of the extent of a psalm, is a proof that the tradition is in this respect not necessarily reliable—hardly surprising in view of the lack of clear marks to separate the independent units, which also makes so difficult the recognition of the separate sayings in the prophetic books. Thus it is possible that, even where 𝔐 and 𝔊 agree in their view of the extent of a psalm, it may not in fact have been correctly transmitted. We may give just two examples of this: Pss. xlii and xliii, which are reckoned as two poems in both 𝔐 and 𝔊, in reality undoubtedly form one psalm (p. 63). Conversely, Ps. xix, considered as a unity in both 𝔐 and 𝔊 is certainly to be divided into two poems—vv. 2–7, which represents the torso of a hymn to Yahweh as the creator of all things and particularly of the sun, and vv. 8–15, which contains a hymnic praise of the law. Admittedly the latter can hardly have existed independently, but was from the first intended to complete the hymn torso in that it presents the law as much more worthy of praise than the sun (p. 109, n. 23; p. 127).

2. *The age of psalmody.* There has already been a fairly detailed discussion of the psalms in the first part of this book, covering both the cultic poems (§ 15) and the wisdom compositions (§ 16). So far as the former are concerned, it has been shown that their individual types—hymn and song of thanksgiving, collective and individual song of lament, etc.—derive originally from the cultus, but that they have then, in varying measure in the different types, become detached from the cultus and have become spiritual songs. By this indirect route they have again become songs which were utilised in the cultus, though no longer in a cultus of the old Israelite type, tied to particular places and to sacrifice, but in a worship 'in spirit and in truth'. It was in this direction that the postexilic temple cultus increasingly developed, in spite of the increase in sacrificial acts, and this is even more true of the worship of the synagogue.[1] We have further seen that the Israelites took over from the Canaanites their cultic songs, at any rate in large measure, as they did many of their cultic practices, and the

[1] Mowinckel, 'Traditionalism and Personality in the Psalms' HUCA 23, 1 (1950/51), pp. 205–31.

Canaanites in their turn are to be thought of as being in this respect dependent upon Egypt, Babylonia and Asia Minor. The same is true of the wisdom compositions. The beginnings of Israel's cultic and wisdom poetry thus go back as far as the beginnings of Israel's settlement in Canaan, though this certainly does not mean that the specimens of these types of composition preserved in the Psalter and outside it are as old as that. Certain poems in the Psalter definitely belong to the pre-exilic period, even to the early pre-exilic period. This is true not only of the royal songs, but in all probability also of the third and last section of Ps. xxiv which may be considered as the song sung at the feast of the bringing back of the Ark, as it is described in II Sam. vi. The Psalm represents a complex consisting of a hymn (vv. 1–2), a Torah instruction (vv. 3–6), and a song of processional entry (vv. 7–10) (see p. 108). Here only a part and not the whole psalm may be ascribed to David or to his time. Similarly we may also assume that various other psalms or parts of psalms derive from such an early period. In some cases, as for example appears to be the case with Ps. lxxx (p. 112, n. 36), the pre-exilic date of composition may be specified fairly exactly. In other cases, as with the royal songs, we can at least say that they are likely to have originated in the period in which monarchy still actually existed in Israel or Judah.

In that phase of psalm study which now lies half a century and more ago, when by far the greater proportion of the psalms was assigned to the post-exilic period and in only a very few cases was the possibility of greater age entertained, it was customary to describe the Psalter as the 'Hymnbook' of the post-exilic Jewish community. In so far as the Psalter as an entity only came into existence in the post-exilic period, this description is appropriate. But the late origin of the Psalter does not exclude the possibility that some or even many of the psalms may be assumed to be older and perhaps very much older. In the same way recently compiled hymnbooks of Christian communities today contain not a few poems which are centuries or even millennia old. A comparison of the book of Psalms with modern hymnbooks on this basis would be instructive. Only a few indications of its value can be given here. The hymns in the hymnbooks reflect the various periods in the history of Christian piety. Thus the Reformation produced Paulus Speratus' 'Salvation has come to us from grace and sheer kindness':[2] the distress of the Thirty Years' War produced Paul Gerhardt's 'Commit thou all thy griefs';[3] the period of rationalism produced Christian Fürchtegott Gellert's 'If a man says: I love God, but hates his brothers'[4] —to mention these periods alone, without looking at earlier and later ones.

[2] 'Es ist das Heil uns Kommen her von Gnad und lauter Güte.' We might compare the lines in Luther's hymn 'Out of the depths I cry to thee' (translated by Catherine Winkworth),

Our pardon is Thy gift; Thy love
And grace alone avail us.

[3] Translated by John Wesley from 'Befiehl du deine Wege'.

[4] 'So jemand spricht: ich liebe Gott und hasst doch seine Brüder.' We might compare from the same period Joseph Addison's:

The spacious firmament on high,
With all the blue ethereal sky,
And spangled heavens, a shining frame,
Their great Original proclaim.

Much the same is true of the Psalter. Pss. xxix (p. 109) and civ (p. 106), taken over by Israel from its Canaanite environment, sing the greatness and glory of Yahweh, as they appear in nature. Pss. xxiv, 7–10 (p. 108), lxxvi (p. 109), lxxviii (p. 125), lxxxix (p. 112), cxxxii (p. 103) and cxxxvi (p. 121), originating in the time of David or at any rate making use of traditions from that period, stress the significance of the deeds of David, and particularly the significance of his bringing in of the Ark to Jerusalem. Pss. lxxxii (p. 111) and xci (pp. 120, 126), equally stemming from this period, celebrate Yahweh's victory over El, 'Elyon and Shaddai. The period of the Exile is echoed so strongly in Pss. cxxvi (p. 115) and cxxxvii (cf. below) that even two and a half millennia later we are deeply moved when we hear or read them. Again only a selection has been given and no mention made of other periods which with their particular situations are likewise reflected in the Psalter.

Thus, just like our hymnbooks, the Psalter contains material from many centuries, though admittedly older songs have in many ways received new forms. So the question of the age of the songs contained in the Psalter cannot be easily answered, and in particular it is hardly possible to give a firm decision as to whether the majority of the psalms are of pre-exilic or post-exilic origin. It is clear that the Psalter contains songs which originated in the exilic and post-exilic periods: this is demonstrated by Pss. cxxvi and cxxxvii. Pss. cxxii,[5] cxxxiv,[6] and cxxxvii[7] show further that the exiles brought 'Songs of Zion' with them from their homeland and that there must therefore have been such songs in existence there at an earlier period. As far as the Psalter as a whole is concerned, we shall have to be content with the very general statement that it contains, in addition to exilic and post-exilic elements, songs and parts of songs which are old and perhaps very old indeed. This indicates that each individual psalm must be examined with reference to its age, and hence that the fixing of the date of composition of the Psalter depends upon this too, for the Psalter in its present form must be later than the latest of its poems. The question of the dating of the Psalter and of the smaller collections which underlie it will be discussed later (pp. 448–51). We may at this stage simply indicate one further point. In recent Psalm study, there is a tendency, unlike that of Psalm study at about the turn of the last century, to ascribe at least a substantial number of the psalms to the pre-exilic period and even to the early pre-exilic period. This also sheds new light on the phrase לְדָוִד which stands at the head of 73 psalms, whether it is to be understood as meaning (composed) *by David*, or *for David*, or *concerning David*. Although it is not thereby shown to be reliable in all cases, or even in the majority of cases, it nevertheless appears to contain some core of truth. We must return to this point later (pp. 451–3).

3. *Smaller collections.* In § 21 (pp. 152 f.) the division of the Psalter into five books (i–xli,[8] xlii–lxxii, lxxiii–lxxxix, xc–cvi, cvii–cl[9]) has already been men-

[5] Horst, EvTh 16 (1956), p. 53 = *Gottes Recht* (1961), pp. 264 f.

[6] Albright, NTT 56 (1955), pp. 1–12.

[7] Glombitza, NThT 14 (1960), pp. 329–49: on Pss. lxxix, xciv, cxxxvii. Lit. § 126.

[8] Bič, 'Das erste Buch des Psalters. Eine Thronbesteigungsfestliturgie' Suppl. to Numen IV (1958), pp. 316–32; Marschall, *Die 'Gottlosen' des ersten Psalmenbuches* (1929).

[9] Bosniak, *The Commentary of David Kimhi on the Fifth Book of the Psalms cvii–cl* (1954).

tioned, and allusion was also made to the point that smaller collections must underlie the whole book. These smaller collections must now be discussed rather more fully. The position is not like that in the book of Proverbs, where the smaller collections which underlie the book are simply arranged one after the other, and have even kept their titles. In the Psalter, the information available allows of various definitions of the larger of these collections, and admits various possible explanations as to how they were joined together or interwoven. At many points we can hardly go beyond a mere description of the facts, and admit that an assured explanation is not to hand.

Pss. iii–xli clearly represent a collection of poems ascribed to David, for all these psalms bear the title of David with the exception of Pss. (i, ii), x and xxxiii. Pss. i and ii were probably placed at the beginning rather later, perhaps only by the redactor of the Psalter as we have it. They form a sort of prologue enjoining the understanding of the psalms which follow, on the one hand as exhortations to observe the Torah (Ps. i), and on the other hand as testimonies to belief in the Messiah (Ps. ii). Ps. x, which is not really a complete psalm but only the second half of an alphabetic acrostic which comprises Pss. ix (א–כ, '–*k*) and x (ל–ת, *l–t*), and Ps. xxxiii either has lost its title of David in 𝔐 since this appears in 𝔊, or may have been inserted subsequently. Furthermore, xlii–lxxxiii appear as what was once an independent collection, since here and only here the divine name *Elohim* is normally used and not *Yahweh* (*Elohim* appears here 200 times, *Yahweh* only 43, whereas in the remainder of the Psalter *Elohim* appears only 29 times, and *Yahweh* 642). This may certainly be explained as a result of the replacement of *Yahweh*, which originally appeared in these psalms too, by *Elohim*. Pss. lxxxiv–lxxxix, with the exception of lxxxvi which is ascribed to David, are, like large sections of Pss. xlii–lxxxiii, ascribed to guilds of singers, and such an ascription does not appear again after lxxxix. This fact, together with the appearance of the final doxology clearly marking the end of the collection only at the end of Ps. lxxxix, makes it clear that Pss. lxxxiv–lxxxix are also to be reckoned with this collection and are to be regarded as an appendix, though, because they were added later, they remained unaffected by the Elohistic revision of the main section. Finally, we may distinguish in xc–cl four smaller collections, which are in large measure distinguished by the titles of the psalms they comprise, and further by the fact that they all conclude with a series of psalms containing *Give thanks* (הוֹדוּ) or *Hallelujah* (הַלְלוּ־יָהּ or simply הַלְלוּ). Only Pss. cxix and cxxxvii do not fit into this, and these were probably inserted later. The four collections are:

1. Pss. xc–civ, in which the individual psalms have no special features, but which is distinguished by the fact that the majority of the songs of 'Accession to the throne' (pp. 109–11) are gathered together here. This collection is concluded with Pss. cv–cvii.

2. Pss. cviii–cx, *of David*, concluded with Pss. cxi–cxviii, among which Ps. cxv has no *Hallelujah* at the beginning, but is perhaps to be understood, as in 𝔊, as belonging with Ps. cxiv.

3. Pss. cxx–cxxxiv, *Songs of Pilgrimage* (שִׁיר־הַמַּעֲלוֹת; cxxi שִׁיר לַמַּעֲלוֹת),[10]

---

[10] Bratsiotis, Αἱ Ὠιδαι των Αναβαθμων του Ψαλτηριου (²1956); Press, 'Der zeit-

concluded with Pss. cxxxv–cxxxvi.

4. Pss. cxxxviii–cxlv, *of David*, concluded with Pss. cxlvi–cl.

These larger collections are in their turn made up of smaller collections. Thus Pss. xlii–lxxxiii is made up of li–lxxi *of David* (with Ps. lxxii, *of Solomon*, as an appendix); Pss. xlii–xlix, *of the Korahites*; Pss. l+lxxiii–lxxxiii, *of Asaph*. In these smaller collections it is at least in some measure possible to recognise the principles upon which the individual psalms in them have been arranged. This is particularly clearly the case in Pss. xlii–xlix, where psalms are placed together which may be shown to belong together in the same group by the terms which appear in their superscriptions, terms which will be discussed subsequently: Pss. xlii + xliii (one psalm only) and xliv מַשְׂכִּיל,[11] xlv מַשְׂכִּיל שִׁיר, xlvi שִׁיר, xlvii מִזְמוֹר, xlviii שִׁיר מִזְמוֹר, xlix מִזְמוֹר. The position is similar in Pss. li–lxxii: lii–lv מַשְׂכִּיל, lvi–lx מִכְתָּם, lxii–lxiv מִזְמוֹר, lxv–lxviii מִזְמוֹר and שִׁיר, lxix–lxxi without any such term. This arrangement cannot be accidental, and since furthermore we find in Pss. xlii–lxxii two groups of psalms with the heading מַשְׂכִּיל etc., but do not find all the מַשְׂכִּיל etc.psalms gathered into one group, this confirms the conclusion drawn from the indications of 'compiler' that Pss. xlii–xlix on the one hand and Pss. li–lxxii on the other form two separate and once independent collections. In addition to this grouping according to the terms, other considerations will have been determinative, as for example the consideration of similarities of content and form. It is certainly not a matter of chance that in Ps. iii (see v. 6) and iv (see v. 9)[12] we have a morning and an evening poem side by side, and the placing together of Pss. xxxiv[13] and xxxv is probably to be explained as due to the mention of the angel of Yahweh in both (xxxiv, 8, xxxv, 5).

The oldest of the larger collections is probably Pss. (i) iii–xli, and we should probably picture the evolution of the Psalter as arising from the gradual linking of other collections to this, without being able to define precisely the individual stages of this process and its completion, or being able to date it with certainty. The dating of the Psalter as a whole is, as we have seen (p. 448), dependent upon the dating of the latest of the poems included within it, and this is particularly difficult because the psalms which come in for consideration in the first place here, Pss. xliv, lxxiv, lxxix, lxxxiii, are so variously dated. Some scholars date them in the Maccabean period,[14] i.e. in the first half of the second century B.C. (p. 113), whereas others consider them as being several centuries earlier, and important arguments may be adduced in fact for both views. If the earlier dating of these psalms is correct, then there is nothing to hinder the assumption put forward for example by Begrich and Hans Schmidt, that the Psalter was closed

geschichtliche Hintergrund der Wallfahrtspsalmen' ThZ 14 (1958), pp. 401–15.

[11] Gertner (Lit. § 126 on p. 534, n. 16).   [12] Cf. above, p. 120, n. 52.

[13] Couroyer, RB 57 (1950), pp. 174–9; Holm-Nielsen, ThSt 14 (1960), pp. 49–50; Liebreich, HUCA 27 (1956), pp. 181–92; Th. H. Robinson, ET 52 (1940/1), p. 117.

[14] Ackroyd, *The Problem of Maccabean Psalms* (Diss. Cambridge, 1945); 'Criteria for the Maccabean Dating of OT Literature' VT 3 (1953), pp. 113–32; Devreesse, *Le commentaire de Theodore de Mopsueste sur les Psaumes* (i–lxxx) (StT 93, 1939); *Essai sur Theodore de Mopsueste* (StT 141, 1948); Goossens, *Die Frage nach makkabäischen Psalmen* (1914); Hassler, *Commentationes criticae de Psalmis Maccabaicis quos ferunt*, I (1827); II (1832). Lit. § 126.

in the fourth century B.C. Alternatively, it may have been closed only in the middle of the second century B.C. It is hardly possible to come down further than the middle of the second century, since I Maccabees, compiled about 100 B.C. quotes in vii, 17 a phrase from a psalm, namely lxxix, 2–3, and quotes it fairly clearly as holy scripture, and the prologue to Ben Sira written about 117 B.C. appears to presuppose the existence of at least the main part of the third section of the canon, the *Writings* (כְּתוּבִים), of which the Psalms are the chief element. Nevertheless we now know from the evidence of the Qumran discoveries that at about the beginning of the Christian era there were manuscripts in circulation in which the order of the psalms differs in places from the one which is familiar to us (p. 683, n. 17).

4. *Titles and other notes added to the Psalms.*[15] The majority of the psalms are provided with notes, which, as will be seen more clearly in a moment, refer to compilers, mode of composition, musical performance and the like. Normally these appear as titles, but sometimes also in the body of a psalm or at the end.[16] Their textual transmission is very uncertain, since 𝔊 lacks many of the notes of 𝔐, but also has many others, and the Syriac translation in this respect goes entirely its own way. This is evidence that as far as these notes are concerned we are dealing in part at least not with ancient material, but with relatively late additions to the text of the psalms. We must limit this discussion to the notes which appear in 𝔐; these present difficulties enough. For here too, much more even than in the question of the evolution of the Psalter, it is often the case that we can only rarely go beyond a statement of the facts, and have to recognise that there is no satisfactory explanation. Tremendous efforts have been made towards the understanding of these notes—titles, marginal notes and subscriptions, but there are only very few accepted results. Indeed, even at the point of listing what these notes are, uncertainty begins. For with several of them it is possible to be in doubt under which heading they should be placed. Thus they have been variously described as (*a*) indications of compiler, (*b*) name of type of psalm, (*c*) technical musical expression, or (*d*) indication of the cultic situation which is appropriate to the psalm in question. Leaving on one side such borderline cases, we must here limit ourselves to dealing with a selection of these notes, and in the case of those which are normally and probably rightly denoted as indications of compiler examine at least the most important material.

The most important of the names of 'compilers' are those of David,[17] to whom 73 psalms are ascribed, and the *Korahites* and *Asaph*, both of which appear twelve times in the titles. These names are always introduced with the particle לְ, which may mean *by, for,* or *concerning*. There is thus room for various interpretations. The notes *lb'l, lkrt, l'qht* which appear at the top of some of the clay tablets from Ugarit, where the *l* is certainly not followed by the name of the author, but by the name of the hero of the poem—Ba'al, Keret, Aqhat, may lead

---

[15] Guilding, 'Some Obscured Rubrics and Lectionary Allusions in the Psalter' JThSt 3 (1952), pp. 41–55; cf. *The Fourth Gospel and Jewish Worship* (1960); Preuss, 'Die Psalmenüberschriften in Targum und Midrasch' ZAW 71 (1959), pp. 44–54. Lit. § 126.

[16] J. W. Thirtle, *The Titles of the Psalms* (²1905).

[17] Ridderbos, 'Het bindend karakter van het *le Dâwîd* in de opschriften der Psalmen' GThT 52 (1952), pp. 184–92.

us to the assumption that the *l* of these psalm titles is to be understood similarly, and not, as was formerly the predominating view, as *l auctoris*. Nevertheless the traditional interpretation cannot in fact be abandoned, at any rate in the sense that the tradition as we have it regards the names following the *l* as denoting the compiler, or the performers. This latter could be considered for the Korahites and Asaph, and does in fact denote something very little different from the first possibility. In the case of David the point is confirmed by the fact that in thirteen cases there is added to the expression *by David* a note of the occasion on which he is supposed to have composed or recited this psalm (Pss. iii, vii, xviii, xxxiv, li, lii,[18] liv, lvi, lvii, lix, lx, lxiii, cxlii). In one or two cases, as for example with Ps. xviii (pp. 278–9), the possibility does not seem to be quite excluded that we have a composition which really does go back to David. But this is not really the case with the majority of the 73 psalms ascribed to David. Here the ascription to David is rather to be explained on the grounds that later generations, as the books of Chronicles show (I xxii, 2–xxix, 5), regarded him as the originator of their entire cultic organisation, and so also as the composer of their temple songs. In this they were justified in so far as David was in fact a poet by divine favour (p. 94 and cf. Amos vi, 5), and also did much for the cultus (cf. II Sam. vi and pp. 108, 447). It follows from this that the exact dating of some of these psalms, depending almost exclusively on references in the books of Samuel, deserves due attention as being a first attempt at 'introduction' (pp. 1–2), but it cannot be regarded as historical without further discussion.

Just how critically we must regard the ascription *by David* and the indications of occasion given with reference to him in thirteen of the titles, is shown by the fact that those psalms which really seem to derive directly or indirectly from the Davidic period (p. 447) have neither the phrase *by David* nor an indication of occasion by way of explanation. Neither of these types of material depends upon reliable tradition; they are the result of scholarly consideration of 'introduction' which may be as wide of the mark as are modern statements of the same kind.

The same is true of the ascription of Ps. xc to *Moses*, and that of Pss. lxxii and cxxvii to *Solomon*. The note *by the Korahites* (Pss. xlii, xliv–xlix, lxxxiv–lxxxv, lxxxvii–lxxxviii), or *by Heman*, which is apparently identical in content with the former since it denotes the same choir and in Ps. lxxxviii appears side by side with *by the Korahites*, as well as the notes indicating *by Asaph* (Pss. l, lxxiii–lxxxiii), and the third group *by Ethan* (Ps. lxxxix), are all, however, historical in the sense that the psalms so indicated are certainly connected with the guilds of singers known to us from the books of Chronicles, Ezra-Nehemiah, which no doubt in part at least preserve ancient traditions.[19] (For Asaph cf. Ezra ii, 41, II Chron. xxix, 30 etc., for Korah-Heman cf. I Chron. xv, 19, for Ethan cf. I Chron. xv, 19.) It is indeed possible that this connection is not simply that these guilds had to perform the psalms named after them, but also that they were concerned in psalm composition.[20] It is only reasonable to suppose that

---

[18] Scharf, VD 38 (1960), pp. 213–22; Schedl, BZ 5 (1961), pp. 259 f.
[19] Albright, *Archaeology and the Religion of Israel* ([3]1953), pp. 126 f., 210.
[20] On Asaph, cf. Eissfeldt (p. 227, n. 14), pp. 26–41.

psalm composition had a place in the circles of these guilds of singers; perhaps indeed it was chiefly in them that composition took place.

Among the notes which clearly denote the type of a psalm, the majority are plain enough philologically, but the discovery of the precise technical meaning associated with them in particular contexts is nevertheless impossible. מִזְמוֹר (Pss. iii–vi etc.) and שִׁיר (Pss. xlvi, cxx–cxxxiv) both mean *song,* but why Ps. iii and others should be entitled מִזְמוֹר and Pss. xlvi and others שִׁיר is unknown to us. תְּהִלָּה is a *hymn,* a *song of praise,* and would thus be suitable as the term for the psalms which we denote as hymns (§ 15, 3), of which there are a considerable number. In the Psalter itself, which, as we have seen, at a later time bore the title תְּהִלִּים, only one psalm (cxlv)[21] is thus denoted. The position is similar with תְּפִלָּה which means *prayer,* and would be suitable for many psalms, but actually appears as a title only with Pss. xvii, lxxxvi, cii, cxlii, and in lxxii, 20. With מַשְׂכִּיל too we are not really in any doubt about the root meaning: *giving insight, making wise,* but it remains obscure as to what technical sense the word has acquired when it appears in the title of Pss. xxxii, xlii etc. מִכְתָּם (Ps. xvi,[22] lvi–lx, rendered by Luther as 'a golden jewel') and שִׁגָּיוֹן (Ps. vii) are also philologically difficult or at least uncertain.

Among the technical musical notes[23] the commonest are לַמְנַצֵּחַ (Pss. iv, v,[24] vi, viii, ix etc.) and סֶלָה Pss. iii, 3, 9; iv, 5; vii, 6; ix, 17, 21 etc.).[25] The latter must mean something like *interjection* or *interlude,* and would thus indicate a vocal or instrumental resumption or underlining of what has just been performed. Opinions are, however, divided with regard to the first term. It is in the first place uncertain whether the vocalisation of the word in 𝔐 as the Piel participle is correct, or whether we should prefer what is attested in 𝔊, Theodotion and the Targum, probably presupposing the vocalisation מְנַצֵּחַ, indicating an abstract noun. For the former the rendering *to the director, choirmaster, music master* is appropriate and is already found in Aquila and Jerome. The latter has been revived by Mowinckel, for example, in rendering it as *for making to shine,* namely the face of Yahweh, *for making gracious.* Other notes of a technical musical kind are עַל־אַיֶּלֶת הַשַּׁחַר *according to the hind of the dawn* (?) in Ps. xxii, 1,[26] עַל־יוֹנַת אֵלֶם רְחֹקִים *according to the dove of dumbness in the distance* (?) in Ps. lvi, 1, which it has been suggested denote the melody, and עַל־עֲלָמוֹת *according to the maidens' guise* (Ps. xlvi, 1), עַל־הַשְּׁמִינִית, *according to the eighth, the octave* (Ps. vi, 1), which have been interpreted as denoting the tone, though this can be nothing more than a guess.[27]

[21] Liebreich, HUCA 27 (1956), pp. 181–92.

[22] Behler, RB 49 (1940), pp. 240–2; Mowinckel, ThLZ 82 (1957), cols. 649–54. Lit. § 126.

[23] Carl H. Kraeling and Lucetta Mowry, 'Music in the Bible' *Ancient and Oriental Music,* ed. by Egon Wellesz = *The New Oxford History of Music* I (1957), pp. 283–312, 493 f. Lit. § 126.

[24] Irwin, 'Critical Notes on Five Psalms' AJSL 49/50 (1932), pp. 9–20: on Pss. v, vi, vii, xv, xxiv.

[25] Gyllenberg, 'Die Bedeutung des Wortes Sela' ZAW 58 (1940/1), pp. 153–6; Scott, 'The Meaning and Use of *Selah* in the Psalter' Bull. Canad. Soc. Bibl. Stud. 5 (1939), pp. 17–24; Snaith, 'Selah' VT 2 (1952), pp. 43–56.

[26] Jirku, ZAW 65 (1953), pp. 85–6.

[27] May, ' 'Al . . in the Superscriptions of the Psalms' AJSL 58 (1941), pp. 70–83.

Finally, there are the notes, unfortunately not very numerous, which refer to the cultic occasion which is appropriate to the particular psalm. These are of very varied kind and of differing value. Some, such as לְהַזְכִּיר *for the odour offering* (?—cf. אַזְכָּרָה *odour offering* Lev. ii, 2, 9, 16 etc. [RSV *pleasing odour*]) in Ps. xxxviii, 1; lxx, 1, are not clear in meaning; others, such as שִׁיר־חֲנֻכַּת הַבַּיִת *song for the dedication of the temple* in Ps. xxx, and לְיוֹם הַשַּׁבָּת *for the sabbath day* in Ps. xcii are only of value in so far as they show not the original use of the psalm, but only on what festival day it used to be sung at a somewhat fortuitous date rather later.[28] On the other hand the note to Ps. c לְתוֹדָה *for the thank-offering* preserves the original cultic reference of the psalm, and the same is true of the very expressive title of Ps. cii: *prayer of an afflicted man when he is faint and pours out his complaint before Yahweh*; this quite rightly assigns the psalm to the type of individual lament (§ 15. 9).

It is a matter for very great regret that so many of the notes added to the psalms remain quite unintelligible to us, or are at any rate very doubtful in meaning. We could otherwise penetrate much further into the meaning of the songs in question than it is now possible for us to do, and could above all gain a more vivid picture of their use and of the way they were performed with musical accompaniment.

§ 64. JOB

Literature: (a) Commentaries (i) Series: ATD: Weiser (³1959); Bibelhilfe: Hertzberg (1949); BK: Horst (1960); Camb. B: Davidson (1884); Cent. B: Peake (1905); EB: Dhorme (1926); Echter-B: Junker (1951); EH: Peters (1928); HAT: Hölscher (²1952); HK: Budde (²1913); HS: Szczygiel (1931); HSAT: Steuernagel (1923); IB: Terrien, Scherer (1954); ICC: Driver and Gray (1921 (1951)); Jerusalem-B: Larcher (²1957); KD: Delitzsch (²1876); KeH: Dillmann (⁴1891); KHC: Duhm (1897); KV: Kroeze (1960); Montserrat-B: Augé (1959); SAT: Volz (²1921); SBOT: Siegfried (1893); Soncino-B: Reichert (1946); SZ: Volck (1889); Torch-B: Anthony and Miriam Hanson (²1962); TU: Bleeker (²1935); WC: Gibson (1899 (1919)).

(ii) Single Commentaries: Fohrer (1948); Kissane (²1946); Koenig (1929); Merx (1871); Steinmann (1946, 1955); Stier (1954); Tur-Sinai (1957).

(b) Other Works: Ayuso (§ 63); Baumgärtel, *Der Hiobdialog* (BWANT 61, 1933); Beek (§ 46); Beer, *Der Text des Buches Hiob* (1897); Bickell, 'Kritische ˌBearbeitung des Iobdialoges' WZKM 6 (1892), pp. 137–47, 241–57, 327–34; 7 (1893), pp. 1–20, 153–68; Budde, *Beiträge zur Kritik des Buches Hiob* (1876); Buhl, 'Zur Vorgeschichte des Buches Hiob' BZAW 41 (1925), pp. 52–61; Buttenwieser, *The Book of Job* (1922); Caquot, 'Traits royaux dans le personnage de Job' *Hommage à W. Vischer* (1960), pp. 32–45; Margaret B. Crook, *The Cruel God: Job's Search for the Meaning of Suffering* (1959); Dahood, 'Some Northwest-Semitic Words in Job' Bibl 38 (1957), pp. 306–20; 'The Root עוב II in Job' JBL 78 (1959), pp. 303–9; Driver, 'Problems in Job' AJSL 52 (1935/6), pp. 160–70; 'Problems in the Hebrew Text of Job' SVT III (1955), pp. 72–93; Edelkoort, *Het boek Job en het probleem van het lijden* (1946); Eerdmans, *Studies in Job* (1939); Ehrenberg, *Hiob der Existentialist* (1952); Feinberg, 'The Poetic Structure of the Book of Job and the Ugaritic

---

[28] Marie Pierik, *The Psalter in the Temple and the Church* (1957); Liebreich, 'The Hymns of the Levites for the Days of the Week' [Hebr.] Eretz-Israel 3 (1954), pp. 170–3: on Pss. xxiv, xlviii, lxxxii, xciv, lxxxi, xciii, xcii.

Literature' BS 103 (1946), pp. 283–92; Fine, 'The Tradition of a Patient Job' JBL 74 (1955), pp. 28–32; Fohrer, 'Form und Funktion in der Hiobdichtung' ZDMG 109 (1959), pp. 31–49; ' "Nun aber hat mein Auge dich geschaut". Der innere Aufbau des Buches Hiob' ThZ 15 (1959), pp. 1–21; 'Überlieferung und Wandlung der Hioblegende' *Baumgärtel-Festschr.* (1959), pp. 41–62; Foster, 'Is the Book of Job a Translation from an Arabic Original?' AJSL 49 (1932/3), pp. 21–45; Frey, 'Zur Sinndeutung des Leidens im AT' WuD 6 (1959), pp. 45–61; Gese (§ 65); Ginsberg, 'עיונים בספר איוב' 21 'לשוננו (1957), pp. 259–64: on iv, 17–20; vi, 14–23; xvi, 2–9; xxxiii, 1–11; Gordis, 'The Temptation of Job' Judaism 4 (1955), pp. 195–208; Grill, *Zur Kritik der Composition des Buches Hiob* (1890); Hempel, 'Das theologische Problem des Hiob' ZSTh 6 (1929), pp. 621–89; Hertzberg, 'Der Aufbau des Buches Hiob' *Bertholet-Festschr.* (1950), pp. 233–58; Herz, 'Formgeschichtliche Untersuchungen zum Problem des Hiobbuches' WZ Leipzig 3 (1953/4), pp. 157–62; Houtsma, *Textkritische Studien zum AT. I: Das Buch Hiob* (1925); Humbert, 'Le modernisme de Job' SVT III (1955), pp. 150–61; 'À propos du livre de Job' *Opuscules d'un Hébraïsant* (1958), pp. 204–19; Jastrow, *The Book of Job* (1920); Jung, *Antwort auf Hiob* (³1961); Junker, *Jobs Leid, Streit und Sieg* (1948); K. Kautzsch, *Das sogenannte Volksbuch von Hiob und der Ursprung von Hiob Kap. i, ii, xlii, 7–17* (1900); Knight, 'Job' SJTh 9 (1956), pp. 63–76; Koepp, 'Vom Hiobthema' ThLZ 74 (1949), cols. 389–96; Kraeling, *The Book of the Ways of God* (1938); Kuhl, 'Neuere Literarkritik des Buches Hiob' ThR 21 (1953), pp. 163–205, 257–317; 'Vom Hiobbuche und seinen Problemen' ThR 22 (1954), pp. 261–316; Lillie, 'The Religious Significance of the Theophany in the Book of Job' ET 68 (1956/7), pp. 485 f.; Lindblom, 'Die Vergeltung Gottes im Buche Hiob' *Bulmerincq-Gedenkschr.* (1938), pp. 80–97; 'Joblegenden traditionshistoriskt undersökt' SEA 5 (1940), pp. 29–42; *Boken om Job och hans lidande* (1940); *La composition du livre de Job* (1945); Lods, 'Recherches récentes sur le livre de Job' RHPhR 14 (1934), pp. 501–33; Möller, *Sinn und Aufbau des Buches Hiob* (1955); Orlinsky, 'Some Corruptions in the Greek Text of Job' JQR 26 (1935/6), pp. 133–45; Peterson, 'Job och döden' SEA 7 (1942), pp. 83–109; Prado, 'La creación, conservación y gobierno del universo en el libro de Job' Sefarad 11 (1951), pp. 259–88; van Proosdij, *Het boek Job* (1948); Rhodokanakis, 'Das Buch Hiob' WZKM 45 (1938), pp. 169–90; G. Richter, *Erläuterungen zu dunklen Stellen im Buche Hiob* (BWAT 11, 1912); *Textstudien zum Buche Hiob* (BWANT 43, 1927); H. Richter, 'Erwägungen zum Hiobproblem' EvTh 18 (1958), pp. 302–24; *Studien zu Hiob. Der Aufbau des Hiobbuches, dargestellt an den Gattungen des Rechtslebens* (Diss. theol. Leipzig, 1954 (1959)); H. W. Robinson, *The Cross in the OT* (1954), pp. 9–54; Th. H. Robinson, *Job and his Friends* (1954); Rowley, 'The Book of Job and its Meaning' BJRL 41 (1958/9), pp. 167–207; Sarna, 'Epic Substratum in the Prose of Job' JBL 76 (1957), pp. 13–25; Hans Schmidt, *Hiob* (1927); Schmitt, *Leben in den Weisheitsbüchern Job, Sprüche und Jesus Sirach* (1954); Sekine, 'Schöpfung und Erlösung im Buche Hiob' BZAW 77 (1958), pp. 213–23; 'Théodicée dans l'AT' Orient 1 (1960), pp. 23–34; Sellin, *Das Problem des Hiobbuches* (1919); *Das Hiobproblem* (1931); Shapiro, 'The Problem of Evil and the Book of Job' Judaism 5 (1956), pp. 46–52; Spiegel, 'Noah, Danel and Job' *L. Ginzberg Jub. Vol.* I (1945), pp. 305–55; Stange, 'Das Problem Hiobs und seine Lösung' WZ Griefswald 5 (1955/6), pp. 131–4; Stevenson, *The Poem of Job* (²1948); *Critical Notes on the Hebrew Text of the Poem of Job* (1951); Stewart, *The Message of Job* (1959); Sutcliffe, 'Notes on Job, textual and exegetical' Bibl 30 (1949), pp. 66–90; 31 (1950), pp. 365–78; Taylor, 'Theology and Therapy in Job' Th Today 12 (1955/6), pp. 451–62; Terrien, *Job. Poet of Existence* (1957); Thilo, *Das Buch Hiob* (1925); Thompson, 'Out of the Whirlwind. The Sense of Alienation in the Book of Job' Interpr. 14 (1960), pp. 51–63; Torczyner, *Das Buch Hiob. Eine kritische Analyse des überlieferten Hiobtextes* (1920); 'Hiobdichtung und Hiobsage' MGWJ 69 (1925), pp. 234–48; Tur-Sinai, 'Hiob xi und die Sprache der Amarna-Briefe' BiOr 9 (1952), pp. 162 f.; Ulanow, 'Job and his Comforters' The Bridge III (1958/9), pp. 234–68; Vriezen, 'De overwinning van het tragische levensgevoel in Israël' Kernmomenten (1947), pp. 33–48; Westermann, *Der Aufbau des Buches Hiob* (1956); on this cf. Fohrer, VT 7 (1957), pp. 107–11; Wildberger, 'Das Hiobproblem und seine neueste Deutung' Reformatio 3 (1954), pp. 355–63, 439–48; Wutz, *Das Buch Job* (1939);

Ziegler, 'Der textkritische Wert der Septuaginta des Buches Job' Misc Bibl 2 (1934), pp. 277–96.
    Cf. Literature §§ 11, 16, 126.

1. *Contents.* The book opens with a narrative, related in six scenes, four on earth (i, 1–5, 13–22;[1] ii, 7–10, 11–13) and two in heaven (i, 6–12; ii, 1–6), telling of Job's piety and prosperity, the suspicion cast on him by the Satan (p. 430, n. 4) and his trial, the renewed suspicion and renewed trial, and the arrival of his three friends, Eliphaz from Teman, Bildad from Shuach, and Zophar from Naamah. There follow in iii, 1–xlii, 6 speeches which are differentiated in form from the opening and closing narrative in that the narrative is in prose, whereas the speeches are metrically constructed. These are impressively introduced by Job's complaint (iii)[2] which culminates in his cursing of his birth, and there follows in iv–xxvii the dialogue of Job with his friends, for which the last scene of the prologue prepares by telling of the friends' arrival. The dialogue is in three cycles (iv–xiv,[3] xv–xxi, xxii[4]–xxvii). This is followed in xxviii–xxxi by a monologue by Job, in xxxii–xxxvii by speeches of a fourth friend, Elihu the Buzite, and in xxxviii, 1–xl, 2 by a speech of Yahweh. After Job, responding to Yahweh's summons in xl, 2, has answered briefly in xl, 3–5, there follows in xl, 6–xli, 26 a second speech of Yahweh, and in xlii, 1–6 a second answer by Job. We shall have to deal later with the content of all these speeches combined in iii, 1–xlii, 6. xlii, 7–17 contains the concluding narrative, which tells of the burnt offering made by the three friends at Yahweh's behest for their expiation (7–9), the change in Job's fortunes (10), the visit of his relatives and acquaintances (11), the surpassing of his former prosperity (12–15) and his death under divine blessing (16–17).

2. *History of criticism.* There has been much discussion about the literary composition of this book, not only or even primarily from interest in questions of literary criticism in themselves, but for the purpose of understanding the book and its real purpose. This is in the highest degree dependent upon the literary analysis. At the same time it is true that the analysis itself is much more dependent upon the interpretation of the book, based upon intuitive understanding, than is the case with other books, and so to a much greater degree at the mercy of subjective feelings and personal taste. It is therefore no wonder that the results generally recognised are here very small, and will no doubt always remain so.

    There is a relatively large measure of agreement in the judgment upon the opening and closing narrative. It is fairly generally regarded as being an older folk-tale, which the composer of the speeches utilised as a framework for his composition. The main argument adduced for this assumption is that the

---

[1] Ricciotti, ' "Et nu j'y retournerai" ' ZAW 67 (1955), pp. 249–51: on i, 21.
[2] Ullendorff, 'Job iii, 8' VT 11 (1961), pp. 350–1.
[3] Coggan, 'The Meaning of חטא in Job v, 24' Journal of Manchester Eg. Or. Soc. 17 (1932), pp. 53–6; Fullerton, 'On Job, Chapters ix and x' JBL 53 (1934), pp. 321–49; 'Job, Chapters ix and x' AJSL 55 (1938), pp. 225–69; Sarna, 'איתנים Job xii, 19' JBL 74 (1955), pp. 272 f.
[4] Gordis, 'Corporate Personality in Job: A Note on xxii, 29–30' JNES 4 (1945), pp. 54 f.; Sarna, 'A Crux Interpretum in Job xxii, 30 ימלט אי־נקי' ib. 15 (1956), pp. 118 f.

speeches have in view a quite different solution of the problem of Job than does the framework narrative, for the former points to the inner conquest of his suffering by Job, where the latter shows his outward restoration. There is here a possibility, accepted by some scholars, though rejected by others, that the poet or a later writer made alterations in this folk-tale itself, and himself perhaps added the scenes with the Satan (i, 6–12; ii, 1–2) and the visit of the three friends (ii, 11–13), together with the corresponding scene in the epilogue (xlii, 7–9). Thus Batten[5] considers the Satan scenes as secondary, whereas Alt[6] restricts the oldest form of the Job narrative to i and xlii, 11–17. Fohrer[7] thinks that the relatives of Job, who, as he believes, were mentioned in the folk-tale as Job's tempters, have been replaced by the friends or have been pushed into the background, and he regards xxxviii, 1 as the introduction to a pronouncement by Yahweh in favour of Job and against his relatives, such as was found in the folk-tale as may be seen from xlii, 7, but which is now replaced by the speeches of God.

At any rate the majority of scholars—we may mention here only Hempel, Kissane, Irwin,[8] Hölscher and Fohrer[9]—are also agreed in regard to the four Elihu speeches of xxxii–xxxvii (xxxii, 6–xxxiii, 33; xxxiv; xxxv; xxxvi–xxxvii).[10] These do not form an original part of the poem, but were inserted into it at a later stage. The introduction to them, in prose narrative style (xxxii, 1–5), and so too their actual openings (xxxii, 6–22, and xxxiii, 8–11), do, it is true, attempt to link the appearance of Elihu with the preceding dialogue between Job and the three friends. But this attempt, in the view of those who contest the genuineness of these speeches, cannot disguise the fact that Elihu's appearance is not anticipated in the preceding chapters, nor does it have any effect in what follows. It would be just possible to explain the non-mention of Elihu in the opening narrative on the assumption that the poet wished to introduce him at a later stage, namely in xxxii, 1–5; but the fact that he is not taken into account at all in the closing narrative would still remain quite incomprehensible. A second argument is also put forward, namely that the Elihu speeches interrupt what is clearly intended as the direct movement from the speeches of Job (xxix–xxxi) to those of God (xxxviii, 1–xl, 2 and xl, 6–xli, 26). At least it appears that xxxviii, 1–2 (and similarly xl, 6) presuppose that Job has just spoken, and not Elihu. In the third place we must note that there are substantial linguistic differences between xxxii–xxxvii and their context. Finally, the point is stressed that the Elihu speeches with their teleological interpretation of suffering—suffering being designed to bring the one who is tested to self-knowledge and to be to him a source of blessing—directly contradict the poet's purpose, for, as is shown by what follows in xxxviii, 1–xlii, 6 (pp. 458–60), he declares that no theoretical solution of the problem of suffering is possible. The speeches violently disturb the artistic structure of the original book. Admittedly there has been no lack of

[5] 'The Epilogue to the Book of Job' AThR 15 (1933), pp. 125–8.
[6] 'Zur Vorgeschichte des Buches Hiob' ZAW 55 (1937), pp. 265–8.
[7] 'Zur Vorgeschichte und Komposition des Buches Hiob' VT 6 (1956), pp. 249–67.
[8] 'The Elihu Speeches in the Criticism of the Book of Job' JR 17 (1937), pp. 37–47.
[9] 'Die Weisheit des Elihu' AfO 19 (1959/60), pp. 83–94.
[10] Komlós, 'אַף־בְּרִי יַטְרִיחַ עָב' VT 10 (1960), pp. 75–7: on xxxvii, 11.

influential scholars who have defended the originality of the Elihu speeches Among older scholars, we may mention Budde, Cornill*, Wildeboer* and Thilo, among more recent scholars Ridderbos,[11] Dennefeld[12] and Kroeze.[13] One of the older scholars, Cornill, has not only declared that the Elihu speeches mark the 'crowning point of the book of Job', but also that they offer 'the only solution of the problem which the poet could give from his Old Testament standpoint'.[14]

Further, it is also normal to deny to the original poet the beautiful poem in xxviii, which concerns Wisdom to which God alone has access. Here we should probably add before vv. 1 and 7 as the opening of the strophes, the refrain of v. 12 = v. 20, so that the poem would then form four uniformly constructed sections. As it stands, it belongs to the speech of Job which covers xxvi–xxxi, but it is considered by many scholars—we may mention Kraeling, Kissane and Hölscher—to be quite impossible in the mouth of Job. For if Job could at this point have proclaimed this hymn to Wisdom, it would no longer be necessary for God in xxxviii–xli to point him to His wisdom and majesty which surpass all human understanding. It is true that here too there are some who are quite prepared to engage in critical study of the book of Job at other points, but who defend the genuineness and originality of this poem, as for example has been done by König.

There are also points of unevenness in the speeches of God in xxxviii–xli.[15] These seem to indicate additions by a second or third hand, and are generally so explained. In the first place the description of the hippopotamus (בְּהֵמוֹת) in xl, 15–24[16] and that of the crocodile (לִוְיָתָן) in xl, 25–xli, 26 fit very badly into their context. The divine speech in xl, 7–14 which precedes these descriptions calls upon Job himself to do what he has claimed God does not do, namely to carry out a just ordering of the world, and to prove this by holding down all the proud and godless. There follow the descriptions of the hippopotamus and the crocodile which are evidently now to be understood as examples of particular pride and stubbornness, and Job is to demonstrate his capabilities by binding them. But in reality the hippopotamus and the crocodile are here described simply for their own sake, and there is no suggestion that they are examples of particular stubbornness. (It is actually the hippopotamus and the crocodile which are intended here, and not, as for example Hertzberg considers, the mythological monsters of the primeval time, the dragon and the serpent.) Hence many scholars, for example Lindblom and Hölscher, are of the opinion that these two poems were added by a later hand. Others, like Steuernagel and Hertzberg, affirm their genuineness. Similarly disputed is the section concerning the ostrich in xxxix, 13–18, lacking in 𝔊; its genuineness is doubted by Eerd-

[11] 'De redevoeringen van Elihu' GThT 38 (1937), pp. 353–82.
[12] 'Les discours d'Élihou' RB 48 (1939), pp. 163–80.
[13] 'Die Elihureden im Buche Hiob' OTS, 2 (1943), pp. 156–70.
[14] *Einleitung in das Alte Testament* (⁴1913), p. 249.
[15] MacKenzie, 'The Purpose of the Yahwe Speeches in the Book of Job' Bibl 40 (1959), pp. 435–45. Lit. § 126.
[16] Driver, 'Mythical Monsters in the OT' *Studi Or. Levi Della Vida* I (1956), pp. 234–49: on xl, 15–24 (בְּהֵמוֹת) and xl, 25–xli, 26 (לִוְיָתָן).

mans and Hölscher, but is the more firmly defended by others, for example Boehmer.[17]

Furthermore, it is felt by many that it is difficult to understand why God speaks to Job twice *from the storm* (xxxviii, 1 and xl, 6), in two speeches, xxxviii–xl, 2 and xl, 6–14; xlii, 3aα, 4[18] and that Job in response twice acknowledges his submission,[19] in xl, 3–5 and xlii, 1–2, 3aβb, 5–6. Some—for example Dillmann—consider that the two divine speeches and the two acts of submission may in fact be united, arranging the material thus: the speech xxxviii–xl, 2 directs attention to the greatness and wisdom of the creator, expressed in nature, and this leads Job to submit in xl, 3–5. In xl, 6–14; xlii, 3aα, 4 God now summons Job bluntly to take over from him the government of the world, namely the governing of the human world, and to manage it better than God has done. This leads Job to a full recognition of his impotence and helplessness, and brings him to complete submission. But to this it may be objected that the beginning of the second divine speech reads exactly like a completely new beginning, and does not look back upon a divine speech already uttered. The introduction is exactly like that to xxxviii–xl, 2, and this surely means that it is a parallel to the former passage. Thus Siegfried, Fullerton[20] and Lindblom wish to accept only one of the two speeches, namely the first, xxxviii, 1–xl, 2 and only one of the acts of submission, namely again the first, xl, 3–5, and to excise the second in each case, namely xl, 6–14+xlii, 1–6. Against this it may be objected that xl, 6–14+xlii, 1–6 is undoubtedly more closely linked with the main theme of the preceding dialogue than is xxxviii, 1–xl, 5. In xl, 6–14; xlii, 3aα, 4, we are concerned with the great question of the righteous ordering of the fortunes of men, whereas xxxviii, 1–xl, 2 point to God's greatness and wisdom as it appears in nature, in the face of which human power and wisdom must hold its peace. Thus here we have a similar theme dealt with as in the poems on the hippopotamus and the crocodile (xl, 15–xli, 26), and also in the poem on wisdom in xxviii, and, as we have seen, these are generally regarded as secondary. Kraeling, for example, considers xl, 6–14 as the core of the genuine divine speech, which has otherwise been lost. Other scholars—following Bickell we have Budde, Duhm, Steuernagel*, Sellin*, Lods*, Hölscher and others—assume that the insertion of the poems on the hippopotamus and the crocodile (xl, 15–xli, 26) has necessitated dividing into two both the speech of Yahweh and Job's response, thus considering that xxxviii, 1–xl, 2+xl, 6–14; xlii, 3aα, 4 and xl, 3–5 +xlii, 1–2, 3aβb, 5–6 originally formed two units.

Finally, there is no small number of scholars who deny both speeches of God and both responses of Job to the original poem, and presupposing also the non-genuineness of the Elihu speeches, recognise as genuine only the dialogue concerning the problem of suffering, or at any rate its basic material in iii–xxvii, 10+xxix–xxxi. Volz, Baumgärtel and others have expressed this view.

[17] 'Was ist der Sinn von Hiob xxxix, 13–18 an seiner gegenwärtigen Stelle?' ZAW 53 (1935), pp. 289–91.
[18] In xlii, 3aα, 4, the text is not in order. As it stands, it can only be understood as part of the divine speech and not as part of Job's declaration of submission (xlii, 1–2, 3aβb, 5–6).
[19] Kuyper, 'The Repentance of Job' VT 9 (1959), pp. 91–4.
[20] 'The Original Conclusion to the Book of Job' ZAW 42 (1924), pp. 116–35.

Hans Schmidt does not go quite so far. He considers that the poem is quite clearly directed towards the appearance of God in person to Job at the end. But the compiler regarded the terse but significant verses xl, 1–4 as sufficient for this purpose. Later writers developed the theme of xl, 1–4 further in the poetic elaborations of xxxviii–xxxix and xl (5)6–xlii, 6. Eerdmans has put forward a similar view. In recent years, Kuhl has appeared as a particularly determined representative of the view that the original book of Job did not end with any kind of divine speech, but simply with the revelation of God to Job in the thunderstorm. According to Kuhl it is the theophany and this alone which makes Job aware of the reality of God and of his fellowship with him, and so raises him above all question and doubt. Later writers did not understand this solution of the problem, or considered it to be unsatisfactory, and so one of them—a poet but not that of the original work—added the divine speeches, which set out to show man's inability to understand God's mysterious activity, and so to give a solution to the problem of Job which is quite different from that of the original composition.

Thus we may see that, apart for the moment from the closing narrative, the whole of the material which follows on xxxi has been denied to the original work. But this is not the end of the matter. Within iii–xxxi too, where we have already seen the questions raised about the poem contained in xxviii, other very substantial sections have also been declared to be non-genuine. The individual scholars who have expressed such views—Grill, Siegfried, Volz, Jastrow, Fullerton, Baumgärtel, Irwin,[21] Kraeling, Lindblom and many others—differ from one another in detail in their separating out of secondary additions, and the arguments which they bring forward are not always the same. Apart from metrical considerations, which, especially with Irwin, play a large part, the standard by which genuine and non-genuine material is assessed is, however, much the same. Those sections are excised as non-genuine which do not appear to be suitable to the picture of Job, moved in his inmost self at the treatment which he has received from Godand yet holding unshakably both to his innocence and to his confidence in the justice of God—sections, that is, which put in his mouth weak and doleful complaints and a humble and submissive acknowledgement of guilt. The speeches of the friends,[22] however, are only considered to be original in so far as they are concerned with determined attacks upon Job's stubborn and blasphemous self-righteousness, and with the attempt to move him away from this attitude and to bring him to the acknowledgement of his guilt. The theorising elaborations concerning the fate of the godless and concerning the moral ordering of the world which appear scattered among this material are all regarded as later additions. In either case, the motive which has led to the additions is thought to be the desire to lend an appearance of general applicability to the unique case which the original composition set out with such vividness, often going right in the teeth of normal theological opinion. A substantial number of passages suspected of being additions may be removed from

[21] 'An Examination of the Progress of Thought in the Dialogue of Job' JR 13 (1933), pp. 150–64; 'Poetic Structure in the Dialogue of Job' JNESt 5 (1946), pp. 26–39.
[22] Irwin, 'The First Speech of Bildad' ZAW 51 (1933), pp. 205–16.

their present position without the context being in any way disturbed and without the passages themselves losing their meaning. This is true of laments such as iii, 3–12, 20–6;[23] hymns such as v, 9–16; didactic poems concerning the fate of the godless such as viii, 12–19 and xv, 20–35; or the famous great oath of cleansing in xxxi, 1–34, 36, 38–40. This fact appears as a welcome confirmation of the objection which has been taken to them primarily upon grounds of theology and content. These passages are in fact of more general significance and therefore intelligible without any reference to Job's particular case.

The two most notable representatives of this method of approach are Baumgärtel and Kraeling, and we may here conveniently take as an example only the former, who is the more forceful in his views. He arrives at the result that out of the whole book of Job the only original material is the basic matter of the first dialogue and a monologue by Job which follows on this, incompletely preserved in xv–xxxi. To the original dialogue he assigns iv, 1–v, 7,[24] 27; vi, 1–30; viii, 1–11, 20–2; ix, 1–3, 11–23, 32–5; xi, 1–5, 10–20; xiii, 1–19, and to Job's monologue xvi, 6, 9, 12–17, 18–21; xix, 2–29;[25] xxiii, 2–7, 10–17; xxxi, 35, 37. In the dialogue, the friends replied to Job that there is no suffering without guilt (Eliphaz), that Job should ask God for mercy and that he would then again receive from him health and well-being (Bildad), and that God already knows the wicked and that only one way remains open to Job, namely that he should repent (Zophar). But Job sharply rejects his friends' attacks, and holds firm to his certainty that he is in the right over against God and will receive justice. In the monologue he again gives free rein to his indignation at the injustice which he has suffered, but then struggles through more and more to the certainty that God is not his enemy but his friend and will publicly proclaim this, and concludes in a truly regal pride with the expression of confidence that he is nevertheless in the right. The original work is thus 'the cry of a pious man from the despair into which he has been driven in his distress by the constraints which weigh so heavily upon his piety',[26] namely as a result of the doctrine of retribution. 'This pious man engages in an arduous personal struggle with God so far as it is possible at all within these limits; he holds firmly to an enduring trust in God, a trust which is severely put to the test, but not to be destroyed, and calls to him in bold and assured hope.'[27] But in the original work no problem is posed.

Up to this point, we have looked mainly at those who consider that our book of Job is a compilation made up of various elements of different origin. But if

[23] Katz, 'A Psychoanalytic Comment on Job iii, 25' HUCA 29 (1958), pp. 373–83.

[24] Driver, 'On Job v, 5' ThZ 12 (1956), p. 485; Palache, 'Drie Plaatsen uit het Boek Job' *Sinai en Paran. Op. Min.* (1959), pp. 7–14: on iv, 10–12; v, 5; vi, 7.

[25] Sofia Cavaletti, 'Il rotolo dell' Orante' RStOr 32 (1957), pp. 293–9; Loren R. Fisher, 'ŠDYN in Job xix, 29' VT 11 (1961), pp. 342–3; Galling, 'Die Grabinschrift Hiobs' WdO II (1954/9), pp. 3–6; Gehman, 'סֵפֶר, an Inscription, in the Book of Job' JBL 63 (1944), pp. 303–7; Hölscher, 'Hiob xix, 25–7 und Jubil xxiii, 30–1' ZAW 53 (1935), pp. 277–83; Lindblom, ' "Ich weiß, daß mein Erlöser lebt"' StTh Riga 2 (1940), pp. 65–77; Meek, 'Job xix, 25–27' VT 6 (1956), pp. 100–3; Stamm, 'Versuche zur Erklärung von Hiob xix, 24' ThZ 4 (1948), pp. 331–8; Waterman, 'Note on Job xix, 23–7' JBL 69 (1950), pp. 379 f. Lit. § 126.

[26] Baumgärtel, p. 187.   [27] pp. 187–8.

our survey of the history of the study of the book of Job is to be adequate to the facts, we must at least mention a small number of those who have argued in favour of the unity of the book. To this category belong first those scholars who consider the book as coming entirely or almost entirely from the same compiler, as a work not compiled by him all at once, but written down in various stages. Among these we may mention Merx, Sellin, Dhorme and Peters as viewing the formation of the book in this way. This view comes very close to that which considers the book of Job as a collection of several parts deriving from different hands, in that it similarly regards the book as not having been produced all at once. But there have never been lacking those who declared that the book of Job is also in this sense a unity, and have seen in it an artistic literary composition, formed by one author according to a deliberate plan. Most recently, Möller has decisively declared this to be his view.

3. *Analysis*. We may now attempt to assess the critical work which has so far been carried out upon this book, and its results in reducing the book we have to a small fragment of its present content. In doing so we must begin from the point that the book as we have it does not present simply a collection of speeches, but also contains an action, and that this belongs to its real nature. Subsequent elaboration of the speeches and perhaps also of the narrative may be readily understood, but it is very improbable that either one of these two parts is entirely of secondary origin and had no basis at all in the original plan, nor does this correspond with the processes which may be observed elsewhere by which a book is later elaborated. Thus we may take it as established that the narrative framework forms an integral part of the book. Here it matters very little, and can hardly now be established whether the author really did take over an old folk-tale unaltered, or whether he simply found to hand the material of an older story concerned with the righteous Job and himself put it into shape. It is quite clear that he took over the material, and this appears probable if only because of Ezek. xiv, 14, 20 where a righteous man Job is mentioned beside Noah and Daniel, without there being any possibility that there is here a reference to our book of Job. More than this cannot be said. The point which has repeatedly been brought forward in favour of the view that the author took over a folk-tale in the form in which he used it, namely that the narrative framework solves the problem of suffering in a much more external way than do the speeches, is not a decisive argument against assigning the framework to the author. He could perfectly well have deliberately set the matter out on two levels, just as Goethe does in his *Faust* when he clothes the most exalted wisdom and ideas about life in a form which has been borrowed from crude belief in devils and spirits.

But it is not only the framework which is proved to be original on this basis. This is also true of the intervention of God in the debate and of a response of Job making submission. Without this there would be no link at all to the closing narrative. Something must happen before this; it cannot be just talk. After Job, in xl, 3–5; xlii, 1–2, 3aβb, 5–6, has recognised God as infinitely beyond all human understanding, and has thus withdrawn his complaint against him, God recognises that Job's attitude is justified by the reproach which he directs at

Job's friends that they have not spoken rightly of him as has his servant Job (xlii, 7). This is the deeper meaning of the link between the beginning of this closing narrative and Job's recantation; both of them recognise that the other is in the right—Job acknowledges God, but God also acknowledges Job, the latter has thus not deluded himself when he stressed over and over again to his friends that he was in the right and that God was his friend and would show himself to be so. The speech of God and the submission of Job thus equally form an integral part of the book. It is certainly very probable that both of these sections have been elaborated secondarily. But it seems impossible, as has been done by Hans Schmidt and others, to restrict the original content to xl, 1–4, or to cut it down in some similar way. The divine speech would then consist of only a single verse (xl, 2),[28] and would seem to be much too meagre. Nor is it easy to see why after the long speeches by the friends and Job himself, such a single sentence, even if it does come from the mouth of God, would drive Job to recant. But such effectiveness does belong to the speeches of God in xxxviii, 1– xl, 2; xl, 6–14; xlii, 3aα, 4—shortened by the omission of the descriptions of the hippopotamus[29] and the crocodile (xl, 15–xli, 26), which may certainly be regarded as later additions. We must therefore consider that at least the basic material of these speeches is original. We cannot here decide with certainty how the presence of two speeches (xxxviii, 1–xl, 2 and xl, 6–14; xlii, 3aα, 4) and of two recantations by Job (xl, 3–5 and xlii, 1–2, 3aβb, 5–6) is to be explained. Has this two-fold division been brought about only by the insertion of xl, 15– xli, 26, so that originally the two parts of the two speeches belonged together and formed only one speech in each case (xxxviii, 1–xl, 2+xl, 6–14; xlii, 3aα, 4 and xl, 3–5 | xlii, 1–2, 3aβb, 5–6, p. 459)? Or are we to consider either xxxviii, 1–xl, 5 or xl, 6–14+xlii, 1–6 alone as original? Since the insertion of xl, 15– xli, 26 by no means necessitates the division of the divine speech and the recantation, we should probably decide in favour of regarding only one divine speech with a recantation as genuine, and, on the basis of what has already been said (p. 459) this will be xl, 6–14, xlii, 3aα, 4+xlii, 1–2, 3aβb, 5–6. Or perhaps we might picture the matter in this way. There may have been various forms of the book of Job which were later combined. One of these contained the divine speech xxxviii, 1–xl, 2 and the response of Job which follows in xl, 3–5; another contained xl, 6–14 (15–xli, 26), xlii, 3aα, 4 as its divine speech, and xlii, 1–2, 3aβb, 5–6 as Job's response. It is possible that other unevennesses which may be observed in the book as we now have it are to be explained similarly.

So far as the speeches of Job and his friends are concerned, the arguments which have already been brought forward to prove the non-genuineness of the Elihu speeches of xxxii–xxxvii[30] and of the poem on the inaccessibility of Wisdom in xxviii[31] appear to be decisive. It may also be regarded as proved that the

---

[28] Fullerton, 'On the Text and Significance of Job xl, 2' AJSL 49 (1932/3), pp. 197–211; Zimmermann, 'Supplementary Observations on Job xl, 2' AJSL 51 (1934/5), pp. 46 f.

[29] Haas, 'On the Occurrence of the Hippopotamus in the Iron Age of the Coastal Area of Israel' BASOR 132 (1953), pp. 30–4, cf. p. 2.

[30] Esh, 'Job xxxvi, 5a in Tannaitic Tradition' VT 7 (1957), pp. 190 f. Lit. § 126.

[31] Waterman, 'Note on Job xxviii, 4' JBL 71 (1952), pp. 167–70. Lit. § 126.

third cycle of speeches is not in order (xxii–xxvii).[32] Here it is immediately noticeable that only the first two friends, Eliphaz and Bildad, speak, and not the third, Zophar. Furthermore, Bildad's speech (xxv, 1–6) is particularly brief and Job's answer in xxvi–xxvii, which curiously is twice introduced (xxvi, 1 and xxvii, 1), contains arguments which would suit the friends better than Job or at least would suit them equally well, namely xxvi, 5–14; xxvii, 7–10, 13–23. But it is uncertain how this disorder is to be explained. It may be due to the loss or displacement of the Zophar speech, or, if we assume that the poet deliberately excluded Zophar from the third cycle, it may be due to the confusing of the speech of Bildad with that of Job, or, lastly, as Baumgärtel suggests, because the whole third cycle is secondary, put together by using passages from Job's monologue, and that this has itself been further brought into disorder. But the theory that the third cycle is of secondary origin cannot be proved in detail.

Nor can this be done in the case of the second cycle, which is in any case completely in order and is only regarded by Baumgärtel as secondary—put together with the working in of sections of the Job monologue—because here are attributed to Job as to the friends arguments all or most of which have nothing or very little to do with what one might have expected from both sides in this particular situation (pp. 460–1). That a distinction between genuine and non-genuine material cannot be made on this basis, will be shown in a moment in reference to certain detailed points in the first cycle.

Baumgärtel recognises the basic material of the first cycle as genuine, but he reduces even this to about half its present compass by cutting out everything which is of a general character and does not apply to Job's particular case. This includes, among other passages, the laments iii, 3–12, 13–19, 20–6; vii, 1–10; vii, 12–21; ix, 25–31; x, 1–22; xiii, 23–7; xiv, 1–22, and the hymns v, 9–16; ix, 4–10;[33] xii, 7–10;[34] xii, 13–25. But the hymnic sections v, 9–16 and xii, 13–25 are well and truly linked with their context. In v, 8 which, as Baumgärtel claims with a reference to Torczyner, does not have to be removed from its present position because of its similarity to xiii, 3, and is judged to be an original part of Job's speech, Eliphaz exhorts Job to commit his cause to God, and in v, 17 he extols as fortunate the one who allows himself to be set right by God. The intervening hymnic statements about God, couched mainly in participial style, are entirely in place. Similarly xii, 13–25 fits perfectly in its present position. For here, with the exception of verse 22 which has long been regarded as doubtful, we are concerned with the working of divine omnipotence which so arbitrarily destroys, and such blasphemous words can only be regarded as Job's and must be assigned to him. Moreover, so far as the hymns are concerned, we may simply point out further that not only in Ben Sira (p. 598), but also in the Egyptian Insinger papyrus[35] belonging to the first half of the first century A.D.,

[32] Barton, 'The Composition of Job xxiv–xxx' JBL 30 (1911), pp. 66–77; Pfeiffer*, p. 671; Tournay, 'L'ordre primitif des chapitres xxiv–xxviii du Livre de Job' RB 64 (1957), pp. 321–34. Lit. § 126.
[33] Driver, 'Two Astronomical Passages in the OT' JThSt 7 (1956), pp. 1–11: on ix, 9 and xxxviii, 31–2.
[34] de Guglielmo, 'Job xii, 7–9 and the Knowability of God' CBQ 6 (1944), pp. 476–82.
[35] Boeser, *Transkription und Übersetzung des Papyrus Insinger* (Oudheidkund. Mededeel.

wisdom poetry continually passes over into the hymnic style,[36] and it is quite impossible to excise all these hymns and hymn-like sections as secondary. Nor can it be shown to be probable that the laments and similar passages in Job—as in iii and xiv, 1–22[37]—are to be denied to the original composition. The grounds adduced for this are that they picture Job, who appears in the sections which are alone considered to be genuine as rebellious and raging against God in the conviction of his innocence, as sensitive and sorrowful and conscious of guilt; this, it is thought, would suit any other suffering person as well as Job. But in reality this shows once again how the Jewish individual is bound up with the collective unit, and, from a literary point of view, shows the adherence to the literary type. When the Jew utters a lament, he does so in traditional forms, and if a poet wishes to present a sufferer, he puts into his mouth the conventional laments. This also makes it clear that there is no necessity to deny to the original composition Job's lament at his lost fortunes in xxix–xxx or his great oath of cleansing in xxxi.

Thus we cannot distinguish between genuine and non-genuine by judging whether, in his own words or in those of his friends, it is Job's particular situation which is kept precisely in mind or not. We must rather allow to the poet a wider range and assume that he is always keeping the situation in mind and especially taking account of it in Job's reverent submission of himself before God and of the recognition of his attitude by God, bound up with the repudiation of the attitude of the friends. He may nevertheless sometimes give free rein to poetic licence, and so attribute more general traits to Job in his sufferings and to the friends who address him and accuse him, and put into their mouths words of a more general kind, which would also be suitable in other situations and with other characters. So with reference to iii–xxxi, we hardly need to assume with Peters and others, that the passages which reveal these more general features are 'separate elaborations' by the poet, 'perhaps even some deriving from the earlier period of his life'.[38] But this does not mean that everything in iii–xxvii, xxix–xxxi is really original. We should in fact remove a variety of secondary additions, in so far as we may not be dealing with variants from parallel editions of the book of Job (p. 463). But—and this is the point of the observations just made—the non-genuineness can only be established in each individual case by a consideration of the text itself. There is no general principle, and there is in any case no basis for the assumption that the non-genuine material in iii–xxxi exceeds the genuine material or that it has at some points completely concealed it. Even the pessimism of Torczyner and Buttenwieser with regard to the present arrangement of the book, and their attempt to restore the original and meaningful order, are unjustified, and, apart from

uit 's Rijksmuseum van Oudheden te Leiden, NR III, 1, 1922); Botti und Volten, 'Florentiner-Fragmente des Pap. Insinger' AcOr [H] 25 (1960), pp. 29–42, Pls. I–II; Lexa, *Papyrus Insinger*, I. II (1926); Spiegelberg, Beiträge zur Erklärung des Pap. Insinger' OLZ 31 (1928), cols. 1025–37. Lit. § 126 on p. 83, n. 3.

[36] Cols. 31, 3–32, 24 *et passim*.

[37] Orlinsky, 'The Hebrew and Greek Texts of Job xiv, 12' JQR 28 (1937/8), pp. 57–68.

[38] Peters, p. 47*.

individual points which are of value, they result rather in a hindrance than a help to its understanding.

It remains uncertain to whom and to what period we should attribute the sections which are to be denied to the original composition. We must consider the possibility, already mentioned more than once (p. 462), that they go back to the poet himself, on the assumption that he continued to concern himself with the subject of the work and so subsequently incorporated his sketches, whether earlier or later, in the main work. But here as elsewhere the more likely assumption is that later hands have been actively at work on the book, and have added the sections which disturb the course of the original work.

4. *The purpose of the work.* The book of Job deals with a situation of distress which may affect any man, and it does so in a way which touches every heart. It is therefore readily intelligible that this book—just like Ecclesiastes (§68)—has often been related to contemporary philosophical viewpoints and has been claimed as illustrating them. This is true of the works by Jung and Ehrenberg mentioned on pp. 454 f. Indirectly such discussions may contribute to a deeper understanding of the book, and so must be taken into account. But the determinative point for the historical and critical assessment of the purpose of the book, or more properly of the original composition which underlies it, can only be an unprejudiced exegesis of the passages which are recognised as belonging to it. The work itself gives the following indications of its nature and purpose. After the exposition provided in the introductory narrative (i–ii) and a moving lament by Job (iii), there begins in ch. iv the debate in three cycles (iv–xiv, xv–xxi, xxii–xxvii) between the friends and Job (iv–xxvii). Although there are many repetitions, both in the speeches of the friends and in Job's words, and so there is no strict progression of thought, we may nevertheless discern a deliberate structure, and this in three respects: (*a*) the friends represent—as does Job himself in the last resort, though admittedly with an opposite result—the current doctrine of retribution, that suffering is punishment for sin and that hence Job himself, suffering particularly severely, must have sinned particularly seriously. They may be distinguished from one another in that Eliphaz as the eldest sets forth this conviction with caution and with the utmost consideration of Job's feelings, whereas Zophar as the youngest rushes in as if wielding a cudgel, while Bildad treads a middle path. (*b*) The friends' accusations become increasingly clear. (*c*) Job at first discusses the issue with his friends, but then increasingly abandons the polemic against them to turn directly towards and against God, and this in such a way that his passionate reproaches against God are more and more accompanied by a longing for him as the ultimate salvation, and by a trust in him as the true and only friend. After reproach and the expression of yearning and trust have reached their climax in xxix–xxxi, God in xxxviii, 1–xl, 2 and xl, 6–14; xlii, 3aα, 4 (or probably only in the second of these two speeches, xl, 6–14; xlii, 3aα, 4), sets before Job the madness of his insolence by pointing him to the mystery of natural occurrences which surpass all human insight and ability, and (or alternatively) summons him to undertake the ordering of the world, and in particular to overthrow the godless and unrighteous and so to remove from the world the scandal which arises from the good

fortune of the godless. Job now recognises his impotence and the folly of his complaints, and admits the madness of his reproaches (xl, 3–5 and (or) xlii, 1–2, 3aβb, 5–6). But God also recognises the justice of Job's position (xlii, 7–9) and there follows the closing narrative which tells of Job's restoration (xlii, 10–17).[39] Thus it is not a theoretical solution to the problem of suffering which the original book offers, but rather we are shown how the pious man, who suffers in spite of being bound by belief in retribution, is able to overcome his suffering in practice. This he does by casting himself with ever-growing trust into the arms of God, who threatens his ethical self by decreeing undeserved suffering and so appears as his enemy. Although an explanation of his suffering remains denied to him, he is nevertheless acknowledged by this God as he maintains his own moral position.

5. *The presuppositions of the work.* In this question the first point to be emphasised is that this work must have been born of an intense personal experience, which must be pictured as being as great as the capacity of the poet to set it forth.

> Though in their mortal anguish men are dumb,
> To me a God hath given to tell my grief—[40]

the author of Job must have experienced this even more deeply than the author of those words. For the ultimate source of his poetic skill lies in the depth and intensity of his sense of being possessed by God. But in addition to what the poet himself contributed, there were also external influences which were determinative for his work, influences both in regard to its religious content and in regard to its literary form. The most important presupposition so far as content is concerned is the fact that the question as to why the godless so often prosper while the pious suffer, was being repeatedly discussed in the period of Jewish religious history which immediately preceded the date of this book, namely, as we shall see in a moment (p. 470), in the fifth and fourth centuries B.C. So long as the individual felt himself to be less an individual than a member of a community, the contradiction between the belief in God's just retribution and the realities of life was not felt so sharply. If the individual pious man did not receive the reward due to him, or the appropriate punishment did not befall the individual godless man, men could console themselves with the thought that the community to which they both belonged would receive the reward or the punishment. But when, particularly as a result of the preaching of Ezekiel (xviii; xxxiii, 10–20), the doctrine of retribution was atomised, and it was expected that the rewarding of the good and the punishment of the evil would take place within the short span of time, so easily surveyed, which belongs to each individual, the observation forced itself upon men that the realities of life frequently did not correspond with the belief, but actually sharply contradicted it again and again. From this there resulted for the pious a deep distress of spirit,

---

[39] van Dijk, 'La découverte de la culture littéraire sumérienne et sa signification pour l'histoire de l'antiquité orientale' Or Bibl Lov 1 (1957), pp. 5–28, cf. pp. 15 f.: on xlii, 11.
[40] 'Und wenn der Mensch in seiner Qual verstummt, gab mir ein Gott, zu sagen, was ich leide' (Goethe, *Tasso* 11.3432–3, transl. Anna Swanwick (1850)—quoted by Goethe as the motto to the second part of his *Trilogie der Leidenschaft* [1827]).

which often caused deeper suffering to sensitive and receptive minds than all merely external distress (cf. Pss. xlix, lxxiii). Thus the book of Job presupposes both the doctrine of retribution and the distress which arises for the pious from its conflict with what really happens. Job as well as his friends adhere to this doctrine, but with the significant difference that the latter force reality within the bounds of the doctrine and hence do not feel anything of the contradiction between them, whereas Job comes to feel the tension intensely and with the utmost distress, and yet does not in the process lose his belief in God, a belief which is theoretically inseparable from the doctrine of retribution. Job is in fact only strengthened in belief, and so in practice by his piety overcomes the theory of retribution.

In addition to these religious presuppositions, we must note certain literary points. We have already seen that the poet was dependent upon an older narrative. But the speeches too presuppose earlier patterns and models. We should probably distinguish two different types. On the one hand we have the disputes and contests of wits of the wise at courts or in the 'schools'—attested for example in I Kings x, 1–10, 13—which, as may be seen from an Egyptian parallel, the 'literary dispute'[41] from the time of Rameses II (1292–25), could also include the mockery of the opponent.[42] On the other hand we have the speeches of the contending parties in law suits.[43] But it is not only these two types which have exerted influence upon this work. As we have already seen, it makes considerable use of other forms, namely the hymn and the individual lament.

In addition to this dependence of the book of Job on the literary types just mentioned, there exists also at least the possibility that it was influenced by certain actual non-Israelite models. There is in fact no lack of ancient works which are concerned with the testing of a hero or a pious man by all manner of misfortune, his trials and his restoration to his former fortunate state. Many of these works are older than the book of Job, so that we could entertain the possibility that it was influenced by them. Whether this really happened is another question. In no case can it be proved or be shown to be even probable, and so all we can do here is to mention a selection of these non-Israelite works which have been assumed to have served the book of Job as a model, or which have been considered in this connection. From the Indian area we should mention the poem of the king Yuddhisthira who valiantly overcame the suffering brought upon him as the result of unlucky play at dice, in spite of his wife's discouraging attitude.[44] The book of Job has for a long time between compared with works

---

[41] Erman, *Die Literatur der Ägypter* (1923), pp. 270–94; E.T. (1927), pp. 214–34; AOT, pp. 101–5; ANET, pp. 475–9.

[42] von Rad, 'Hiob xxxviii und die altägyptische Weisheit' SVT III (1955), pp. 293–301 = *Ges. Stud. z. AT* (1958), pp. 262–71.

[43] L. Köhler, *Hebrew Man* (1956), pp. 158–63.

[44] Holstijn, 'Een "arische" Jobeïde' NThSt 22 (1939), pp. 52–60. [Cf. also in A. and M. Hanson, *Job*, p. 9, a reference to the legend of king Harischandra. The Harischandra legend is related in the Markandeya Purana (I, 7, 12), which seems in its oldest form to belong to about A.D. 300. Cf. Pargiter's translation in *Bibliotheca Indica* (1885–1905), quoted in Winternitz, *A History of Indian Literature*, vol. I (Calcutta, 1927), p. 559. Cf. also J. Muir's summary in *Original Sanskrit Texts*, vol. I (London, 1872), pp. 379 ff.   (I am indebted to Professor A. T. Hanson for these references. P.R.A.)]

of Greek thought,[45] but more recently Aeschylus' *Prometheus Bound* in particular has frequently been compared,[46] and this not simply by the noting of similarities and differences, more or less independently of the question of literary relationships between them, but also with the aim of proving direct influence of Aeschylus' *Prometheus* on the book of Job.[47] Among the various Egyptian works which have been considered as models for the book of Job, the one most worth noting is the 'Dispute of a man weary of life with his soul'.[48] But there are much closer connections between the book of Job and three Babylonian works and one Sumerian work, and here it is not only that there are similarities in detail, but that they may also be compared with Job as a whole. These are the poems 'I will praise the lord of wisdom' (*ludlul bēl nēmeqi*),[49] 'The Babylonian Ecclesiastes',[50] 'The righteous sufferer'[51] and 'Man and his god'.[52] Although, as we have seen, in no one of these cases can the dependence of the book of Job upon the relevant non-Israelite work be shown, yet these parallels do at least demonstrate that in the centuries before the period of its author, thoughtful and pious men in many places not only experienced trials like his, but also like him made the attempt to give artistic expression to their experiences of suffering. The comparison of the book of Job with these non-Israelite parallels, real or supposed, shows however at the same time that the former as a poetic work of art and as a testimony to genuine piety rises far above them all.[53]

[45] Fries, *Das philosophische Gespräch von Hiob bis Platon* (1904); Paulus, 'Le thème du Juste Souffrant dans la pensée grecque et israélite' RHR 121 (1940), pp. 18–66.
[46] Irwin, 'Job and Prometheus' JR 30 (1950), pp. 90–108; Lindblom, 'Job and Prometheus, a Comparative Study' *Dragma Nilsson* (1939), pp. 280–7; May, 'Prometheus and Job' AThR 34 (1952), pp. 240–6.
[47] Alvárez de Miranda, 'Jób y Prometeo' Anthologia Annua 2 (1954), pp. 207–37; Gans, *De invloed van Aeschylus' Prometheus op het boek Job*, see Kuhl in ThR 21 (1953), p. 306.
[48] Erman (p. 468, n. 41), pp. 122–30 (E.T. pp. 86–92); AOT, pp. 25–8; ANET, pp. 405–7; DOTT, pp. 162–7; de Buck, 'Inhoud en achterground van het gesprek van hen levensmoede met zijn ziel' Kernmomenten (1947), pp. 19–32; R. Faulkner, 'The Man Who Was Tired of Life' JEA 42 (1956), pp. 21–40; T. E. Peet, *A Comparative Study of the Literatures of Egypt, Palestine, and Mesopotamia* (1931), pp. 114–17; Gertrud Thausing, 'Betrachtungen zum "Lebensmüden"' *Junker-Festschr.* I=MDAI Cairo 15 (1957), pp. 262–7. Lit. § 126.
[49] AOT, pp. 273–81; ANET, pp. 434–7; Landersdorfer, *Eine babylonische Quelle für das Buch Hiob?* (1911); Leichty, 'Two New Fragments of Ludlul Bēl Nēmeqi' Or 28 (1959), pp. 361–63; Williams, 'Notes on Some Akkadian Wisdom Texts' JCSt 6 (1952), pp. 1–7; 'Theodicy in the Ancient East' Canadian JTh 2 (1956), pp. 14–26.
[50] DOTT, pp. 97–103; Dhorme, 'Ecclésiaste ou Job?' RB 32 (1923), pp. 5–27 = *Recueil Ed. Dhorme* (1951), pp. 685–709; Ebeling, *Ein babylonischer Kohelet* (1922); Landsberger, 'Die babylonische Theodizee' ZA 43 (1936), pp. 32–76.
[51] Lambert, 'The Literary Structure, Background and Ideas of the Babylonian "Poem of the Righteous Sufferer"' A XXIV IOK (1959), pp. 145–8; Lambert and Gurney, 'The Sultantepe Tablets III. The Poem of the Righteous Sufferer' An St 4 (1954), pp. 65–99; Nougayrol, 'Une version ancienne du "Juste Souffrant"' RB 59 (1952), pp. 239–50, Pls. VII–VIII; von Soden, 'Zu einigen altbabylonischen Dichtungen' Or 26 (1957), pp. 306–20, Pls. XI–XIV, pp. 315–19: 'Zum altbabylonischen Gedicht vom schuldlos Leidenden'. Lit. § 126.
[52] Kramer, '"Man and his God". A Sumerian Variation on the "Job" Motif' SVT III (1955), pp. 170–82; cf. BASOR 88 (1942), p. 182; Schmökel, 'Hiob in Sumer' FuF 30 (1956), pp. 74–6.
[53] Kuschke, 'Altbabylonische Texte zum Thema "Der leidende Gerechte"' ThLZ 81 (1956), cols. 69–76; Stamm, 'Die Theodizee in Babylon und Israel' JEOL 9 (1944), pp. 99–107; *Das Leiden des Unschuldigen in Babylon und Israel* (1946).

6. *The locality and date of the author.* The fact that the scene of the poem is set in the steppe country lying to the east or south-east of Palestine, where Uz (i, 1), Teman (ii, 11), Shuach (ii, 11) and Naamah (ii, 11) are to be sought, strongly suggests that the poet himself lived in this area; and indeed the tribes which lived in this area, the Edomites, are in fact elsewhere famed as guardians of 'wisdom' (Obad. 8; cf. also pp. 86, 475 f.). But since we may with certainty assume that the folk-tale utilised by the work had its setting in the east, perhaps in the area of Safa,[54] this must be the explanation of why the author set his hero there. It gives us then no information about his own home. The fact that the poems concerning the hippopotamus and the crocodile (xl, 15–xli, 26) presuppose acquaintance with Egypt, has been thought to suggest that the poet lived in Egypt, perhaps in Alexandria, where there was indeed from about 300 B.C. onwards a rich flourishing of Jewish intellectual and literary activity. But the poems, as we have seen, are probably secondary, and could therefore at most serve indirectly as an argument for the place of origin of the author, in that we must recognise it as most easily to be explained that a work which had arisen in Egypt should be amplified by material which certainly originated there. But there is no certainty here, and it can certainly not be excluded that the author actually lived in Palestine.

The date too of the work can only be determined very approximately. The inner struggle which is presupposed by the work, arising out of the conflict between the theory of retribution and the reality of life, assumed its acute form, so far as we know, only in the post-exilic period. Thus, in spite of Pfeiffer* who dates the book or at any rate its basic material in about 600, we should probably think of the post-exilic period, and perhaps most probably of the later period rather than the earlier, i.e. in about the fourth century. The language of the book fits in with this, for it often reveals an Aramaic colouring, or more precisely, as some scholars think it right to assume,[55] an Edomitic-Aramaic, or Arabic-Aramaic colouring. Ben Sira presupposes the existence of the book, and says of *Job the prophet* that *he fulfilled all the ways of righteousness* (xlix, 9 Hebr. text).

§ 65. THE PROVERBS OF SOLOMON

Literature: (a) Commentaries: BOuT: van der Ploeg (1952); Camb. B: Perowne (1916); Cent. B: Martin (1908); Echter-B: Hamp (1949); HAT: Gemser (²1963); HK: Frankenberg (1898); HS: Wiesmann (1923); HSAT: Steuernagel (1923); IB: Fritsch, Schloerb (1955); ICC: Toy (1899, 1948); Jerusalem-B: Duesberg et Auvray (²1957); KD: Delitzsch (1873); KeH: Nowack (²1883); KHC: Wildeboer (1897); SAT: Volz (²1921); Soncino-B: Cohen (²1952); SZ: Strack (²1899); TU: Gemser, I (1929) II (1931); WC: Oesterley (1929).

(b) Other Works: Ayuso, 'Los elementos extrabíblicos de los Sapienciales' Est Bíbl 6 (1947), pp. 187–223; Bauckmann, 'Die Proverbien und die Sprüche des Jesus Sirach'

[54] Eissfeldt, 'Das Alte Testament im Lichte der safatenischen Inschriften' ZDMG 104 (1954), pp. 88–118, esp. pp. 109, 116.
[55] Pfeiffer, 'Edomitic Wisdom' ZAW 44 (1926), pp. 13–25; *Introduction*, p. 680; Foster, AJSL 49 (1932–33), pp. 21–45.

ZAW 72 (1960), pp. 33–63; Dornseiff, 'Hesiods Werke und Tage und das alte Morgenland' Philologus 89 (1934), pp. 397–415 = *Kl. Schr. I* (²1959), pp. 72–95; Driver, 'Problems in the Hebrew Text of Proverbs' Bibl 32 (1951), pp. 173–97; Drubbel, 'Le conflit entre la Sagesse profane et la Sagesse religieuse' Bibl 17 (1936), pp. 45–70, 407–28; *Les Livres sapientiaux d'Israël dans leurs sources préexiliques* (1936); Dürr (1932) (p.86, n.10); Gaspar, *Social Ideas in the Wisdom Literature of the OT* (1947); Gese, *Lehre und Wirklichkeit in der alten Weisheit. Studien zu den Sprüchen Salomos und zu dem Buche Hiob* (1958); Gispen, *De wijze in Israël* (1956); Gordis, 'The Social Background of Wisdom Literature' HUCA 18 (1943/4), pp. 77–118; Harkness, *Les sources de la morale occidentale* (1957); Kaminka, 'Septuaginta und Targum zu Proverbia' HUCA 8/9 (1931/2), pp. 169–91; Kroeze, *Paraphrase van het boek Spreuken* (1950); Kuhn, *Beiträge zur Erklärung des Salomonischen Spruchbuches* (1931); Mihalik, *Das mosaische Gesetz als Quelle des salomonischen Spruchbuches* (Diss. theol. Wien, 1946; cf. ThLZ 79 (1954), col. 190); Power, *The Proverbs of Solomon* (1949); Ranston, *The OT Wisdom Books and their Teaching* (1930); Ringgren, *Word and Wisdom* (1947); Ruttenberg, 'Proverb-Clusters in the Book of Proverbs' [Hebr., Engl. sum.] Tarbiz 26 (1956/7), pp. 328–9, IX; Rylaarsdam, *Revelation in Jewish Wisdom Literature* (1946); Skehan, 'A Single Editor for the Whole Book of Proverbs' CBQ 10 (1948), pp. 115–30; Story, 'The Book of Proverbs and Northwest Semitic Literature' JBL 64 (1945), pp. 319–337; Winton Thomas, 'Notes on some Passages in the Book of Proverbs' JThSt 38 (1937), pp. 400–3; 'Textual and Philological Notes on some Passages in the Book of Proverbs' SVT III (1955), pp. 280–92; du Toit, *Bijbelse en Babilonies-Assiriese Spreuken* (1942); Toombs, 'O.T. Theology and the Wisdom Literature' JBR 23 (1955), pp. 193–6; Torczyner, מִשְׁלֵי שְׁלֹמֹה (1947); Wallis, 'Zu den Spruchsammlungen Prov. x, 1–xxii, 16 und xxv–xxix' ThLZ 85 (1960), pp. 147–8; Yanouver, 'Studies in the Book of Proverbs' [Hebr.] Tarbiz 22 (1950/1), pp. 202–16.

See also Literature §§ 11, 16, 64, 126.

1. *Title and composition of the book.* The Book of the Proverbs of Solomon has in the Hebrew text (i, 1) the title מִשְׁלֵי שְׁלֹמֹה בֶן־דָּוִד מֶלֶךְ יִשְׂרָאֵל *The proverbs of Solomon ben-David, king of Israel.* It is hence referred to as the *Proverbs of Solomon* (מִשְׁלֵי שְׁלֹמֹה)[1] or simply מִשְׁלֵי *Proverbs*, in Greek as παροιμίαι Σολομῶντος or παροιμίαι, and in Latin as *liber proverbiorum (Salomonis)* or *proverbia.* This book bears the marks of its origin more plainly than other Old Testament books. Its separate sections have in fact special titles, which reveal that the passages which now follow them once formed separate collections. Even i, 1, which now appears as the title of the whole book, was probably originally only the title for i, 2–ix, 18, the first part of the book. The next title, מִשְׁלֵי שְׁלֹמֹה *Proverbs of Solomon*, appears at x, 1, and refers to x, 1–xxii, 16. The third, דִּבְרֵי חֲכָמִים *Words of the wise*, has come now into the first verse (xxii, 17) of the collection which it introduces, but, as 𝔊 shows, it belongs before this verse; it refers to xxii, 17–xxiv, 22. As a heading to xxiv, 23–34, marking off this passage too as an originally independent collection, there stands the title גַּם־אֵלֶּה לַחֲכָמִים *Also these of the wise.* The fifth collection (xxv–xxix) is introduced by a longer title, which must be considered further at a later stage: *These too are the proverbs of Solomon, which the men of Hezekiah, king of Judah, collected* (xxv, 1). There follows in chapter xxx a further collection, the sixth, with the title: *The words of Agur ben-Jakeh the Massaite,*[2] and

---

[1] Vargha, 'De titulo משלי שלמה (Prov. i, 1)' Antonianum 11 (1936), pp. 219–22.

[2] Reading הַמַּשָּׂאִי instead of *the oracle* 𝔐. Albright, 'The Biblical Tribe of Massa' and Some Congeners' *Studi Or. Levi Della Vida* I (1956), pp. 1–14.

the last collection (xxxi) has the title: *The words of Lemuel, the king of Massa, which his mother taught him.*

This last title now also covers the 'Praise of the virtuous housewife', a poem whose 22 verses begin with the letters of the alphabet in turn (xxxi, 10–31). But this is originally an independent poem, and has presumably only been put in this position and ascribed to the mother of Lemuel because in verse 3³ the latter had warned her son of improper relations with women, and a later editor felt the need to set something positive over against this negative utterance. In 𝔊 the poem actually stands in a different place. Here xxxi, 1–9 and xxxi, 10–31 are divided by the fifth collection, xxv, 1–xxxix, 27 described as *Proverbs of Solomon*, so that it is Solomon who here proclaims the praise of the virtuous wife and manager. The fourth collection too (xxiv, 23–34) stands in a different position in 𝔊 from the one it occupies in 𝔐, namely between xxx, 1–14 and xxx, 15–33, and these differences between 𝔐 and 𝔊 confirm what is admittedly in any case quite clear, namely that the book is made up of several smaller collections which may be variously arranged.

Some of these collections, and particularly the second (x, 1–xxii, 16), are in their turn made up of even smaller collections. We find in them—especially in x, 1–xxii, 16—a whole series of verses and half-verses which occur more than once. Thus x, 1 =xv, 20; x, 2b=xi, 4b; x, 6b=x, 11b; x, 8b=x, 10b; x, 13b =xix, 29b, and this can surely only be explained on the assumption that the redactor of x, 1–xxii, 16 combined two or more collections which to some extent contained the same proverbial material. Nothing can, however, now be discovered concerning the nature and extent of these smallest collections.

2. *The nature of the seven collections united in the book, and their date of composition.* The larger collections all have their own particular character. The first (i, 1–ix, 18)⁴ begins with a longer introduction (i, 1–6) and owes its character to the fact that alongside a few isolated sayings consisting mostly of two verses (i, 7–9; iii, 1–12, 19–20; ix, 7–12) and smallish proverbial poems (iii, 13–18,⁵ 21–6, 27–30, 31–5; vi, 1–5, 6–11,⁶ 12–15, 16–19), it contains wisdom poems of greater length. In these it is sometimes a father (teacher) who addresses his son (pupil) and gives him exhortations (i, 10–19; ii, 1–22; iv, 1–27 etc.), and sometimes Wisdom personified is introduced as speaking and commending herself (i, 20–33; viii;⁷ ix⁸), at one point contrasted with Dame Folly

---

³ Dahood, Th St [USA] 15 (1954), pp. 627–31. Lit. § 126.
⁴ Boström, *Proverbiastudien. Die Weisheit und das fremde Weib in Spr.* i–ix (1935); Humbert, 'La "femme étrangère" du livre des Proverbes' RES (1937), pp. 49–64; 'Les adjectifs "zār" et "nŏkrī" et la "femme étrangère" des Proverbes Bibliques' *Mél. Syriens Dussaud*, I (1939), pp. 259–66=*Opuscules d'un Hébraïsant* (1958), pp. 111–18; Robert, 'Les attaches littéraires bibliques de Proverbes i–iv RB 43 (1934), pp. 42–68, 172–204, 374–84; 44 (1935), pp. 344–65, 502–25. Lit. § 126.
⁵ Marcus, 'The Tree of Life in Proverbs' JBL 62 (1943), pp. 117–20: on iii, 18; xi, 30; xiii, 12; xv, 4.
⁶ Rabin, 'מעט חבק ידים לשכב (Proverbs vi, 10; xxiv, 33)' JJSt 1 (1949), pp. 197 f.
⁷ Albright, 'The Refrain "and God saw ki tôb"' *Mél. Bibl. Robert* (1957), pp. 22–6, pp. 23 f.: on viii, 22; Bauer, '"Initium viarum suarum"—Primitiae potentiae Dei (Prov. viii, 22)' VD 35 (1957), pp. 222–7; 'Encore une fois Proverbes viii, 22' VT 8 (1958), pp. 91–2; Donner, 'Die religionsgeschichtlichen Ursprünge von Prov. Sal. viii' ZÄS 82 (1957), pp. 8–18; Grollenberg, 'À propos de Prov. viii, 6 et xvii, 27' RB 59 (1952),

(ix). Among the exhortations given by the father to his son, there stand out the warnings against relations with strange women (v, 1–23; vi, 20–35; vii, 1–27). The poems which deal with this theme in v, 1–23 and vi, 20–35 are separated by vi, 1–19 which contains a series of shorter poems warning against giving pledges, idleness, treachery and other things which God hates. Similar dislocations can also be observed elsewhere, so that this collection too can be seen to have undergone various literary changes.

The long passages which are characteristic of this collection—ch. ii is in reality composed of a single sentence—make it evident beyond all doubt that the collection i, 1–ix, 18 is the latest. This argument from form is confirmed by a consideration of the content, for the manner in which wisdom and folly are here personified probably betrays Greek influence, just as it is possible that the long sentences too are to be explained as due to the influence of the Greek language on the Hebrew. We should therefore regard the collection i, 1–ix, 18, and probably at any rate the larger part of the smaller sections which it comprises, as being fairly late, and date them not before the fourth century or even the third. To come further down is impossible because Jesus ben Sira (xlvii, 17) in about 190 B.C. ascribes to Solomon not only the types mentioned in I Kings v, 12—שִׁיר and מָשָׁל, song and proverb—but also חִידָה and מְלִיצָה, riddle and hard question, and the mention of these types must surely presuppose Prov. i, 6. If we determine the age of i, 1–ix, 18, the latest of the collections incorporated in the book of Proverbs, we determine at the same time the age of the whole book. It cannot have come into being before the fourth century.

In marked contrast to i, 1–ix, 18, the collection x, 1–xxii, 16[9] consists of nothing but single proverbs, 375 in number, without any continuity. They are sometimes arranged according to content—similarity of subject-matter—as apparently in ch. x, where proverbs are often arranged in twos (vv. 2–3, 4–5, 6–7), and in xvi, 12–15 where sayings concerning the king are gathered. In other cases they appear to be grouped in accordance with their formal similarity, as in xi, 9–12 where four sayings beginning with b stand together (cf. p. 87). But in general no principle of arrangement can be established, and we are simply left with the individual sayings. With considerable variations and with occasional repetitions, they are concerned with the different behaviour and condition of

pp. 40–3; Kraus, *Die Verkündigung der Weisheit: Eine Auslegung des Kapitels Sprüche* viii (1951); de Savignac, 'Note sur le sens du verset viii, 22 des Proverbes' VT 4 (1954), pp. 429–32; Scott, 'Wisdom in Creation: The '*Amôn* of Proverbs viii, 30' VT 10 (1960), pp. 213–23; Stecher, 'Die persönliche Weisheit in den Proverbien Kap. viii' ZKTh 75 (1953/54), pp. 411–51; Waser, 'A Brief Study of the Relationship between the Eighth Chapter of Proverbs and the Prologue of St. John's Gospel' *MacDonald Presentation Vol.* (1933), pp. 425–54. Lit. § 126.

[8] Skehan, 'The Seven Columns of Wisdom's House in Prov. ix, 1' CBQ 9 (1947), pp. 190–8; Staerk, 'Die sieben Säulen der Welt und des Hauses der Weisheit' ZNW 35 (1936), pp. 232–61; Winton Thomas, 'Note on בַּל־יָדְעָה in Proverbs ix, 13' JThSt 4 (1953), pp. 23 f.

[9] Couroyer, 'Une coutume égyptienne? (Proverbes xvii, 10)' RB 57 (1950), pp. 331–5; Dahood, 'Immortality in Proverbs xii, 28' Bibl 41 (1960), pp. 176–87; Driver, 'Proverbs xix, 26' ThZ 11 (1955), pp. 373 f.; Robert, 'Le Yahvisme de Prov. x, 1–xxii, 16, xxv–xxix' *Mémorial Lagrange* (1940), pp. 163–82; Wolfson, 'Notes on Prov xxii, 10 and Psalms of Solomon xvii, 48 [xvii, 43]' JQR 37 (1946/7), p. 86. Lit. § 126.

the wise and the foolish, the godless and the pious, and so forth. Here we may note that in the sayings collected in x–xv, the different nature of these two groups of men is almost always contrasted in one and the same sentence, so that the sayings are in the form of contrasting parallelism, whereas in xvi, 1–xxii, 16 this form appears relatively rarely. x, 1–xxii, 16 does not really provide us with any special indications to reveal its date of origin. The Aramaisms which are to be found here as in the other parts of the book (xiv, 34 חֶסֶד *reproach*; xvii, 10 נָחַת *to descend*; xviii, 24 רָעַע *to break*; xix, 20 קַבֵּל *to receive*, etc.) make it clear that the collection can hardly be traced to the pre-exilic period, but they do not give us any information about the age of the individual sayings, nor of the smaller collections probably united in x, 1–xxii, 16. We can confidently assume that older, pre-exilic material is also preserved in x, 1–xxii, 16. How far back we may go has already been suggested in the first part of this book (§§ 11 and 21. 2).

The third collection (xxii, 17–xxiv, 22) contains twenty-nine or thirty proverbial poems, which consist for the most part of two or three verses. In each of these the first (or the first two) very often contains an exhortation to all manner of good conduct, or a warning against all manner of bad conduct, while the second or third verse, introduced by כִּי *for* or by פֶּן *lest*, describes the consequences of the good or bad action (e.g. xxii, 22–3, 24–5, 26–7; xxiii, 4–5, 10–11, 13–14, 15–16, 17–18, 19–21, 26–8; xxiv, 1–2, 15–16, 17–18, 19–20, 21–2). The remainder of the material consists of somewhat larger poems and of single-verse sayings (e.g. xxii, 28; xxiv, 7). The pattern for this collection, or at least for xxii, 17–xxiii, 12, was provided by the Egyptian Wisdom Teaching of Amen-em-ope, probably composed in about 1000 B.C.[10] Out of the eleven sayings in this section ten are borrowed, sometimes word for word, from Amen-em-ope. The Egyptian wisdom book, however, has perhaps also determined the whole collection in that it comprises thirty *houses* (chapters), and the Old Testament collection also was intended to contain thirty sayings (and in fact does so approximately), according to the statement of the compiler in xxii, 20: *Do I not*

---

[10] AOT, pp. 38–46; ANET, pp. 421–4; DOTT, pp. 172–91, Pl. 9; Aalders, *Bijbelse Spreuken en de onderwijzing van Amen-em-Ope* (1934); Alt, 'Zur literarischen Analyse der Weisheit des Amenemope' SVT III (1955), pp. 16–25; Brunet, 'Proverbes xxii, 17–xxiv, 22 et la possibilité d'une source égyptienne' Sciences ecclésiastiques 1 (1948), pp. 19–40; Budge, *Facsimiles of Egyptian Hieratic Papyri in the British Museum*, Second Series (1923), Pls. 1–14; *The Teaching of Amen-em-apt* (1924); Drioton, 'Sur la Sagesse d'Aménémopé' *Mél. Bibl. Robert* (1957), pp. 254–80; 'Le Livre des Proverbes et la Sagesse d'Aménémopé' BEThL XII (1959), pp. 229–41; Erman, 'Das Weisheitsbuch des Amen-em-ope' OLZ 27 (1924), cols. 241–52; 'Eine ägyptische Quelle der Sprüche Salomos' SAB XV (1924), pp. 86–93, Pls. VI–VII; Gressmann, 'Die neugefundene Lehre des Amen-em-ope und die vorexilische Spruchdichtung Israels' ZAW 42 (1924), pp. 272–96; Keimer, 'The Wisdom of Amen-em-ope and the Proverbs of Solomon' AJSL 43 (1926/7), pp. 8–21; Lange, *Das Weisheitsbuch des Amenemope* (Danske Vidensk. Selskab. Hist.-filol. Medd. XI, 2, 1925); Möller, *Kritische Beiträge zur angeblichen Abhängigkeit der Sprüche Salomos xxii, 17–xxiv, 22 von der ägyptischen Lehre des Amen-em-ope* (Nach dem Gesetz und Zeugnis (1932), special offprint, 32 pp.); Morenz, 'Eine weitere Spur der Weisheit Amenemopes in der Bibel' ZÄS 84 (1959), pp. 79–80; Oesterley, 'The "Teaching of Amen-em-ope" and the OT' ZAW 45 (1927), pp. 9–24; *The Wisdom of Egypt & the OT in the light of the newly discovered 'Teaching of Amen-em-ope'* (1927); van Wijngaarden, *Het boek der wijsheid van Amen-Em-Ope* (1930). Lit. § 126.

write for you thirty[11] *with admonition and wisdom?* It is true that in content only about a third of the thirty sayings correspond to the thirty chapters of Amen-em-ope. The other two-thirds present Israelite material or have been derived from elsewhere, as for example, xxiii, 13–14 from the Teaching of Ahikar.[12] But in form, in the placing together of thirty sayings or saying-poems, the redactor does actually appear to follow the Egyptian pattern. It is true that there are some who believe that instead of Amen-em-ope being the source, it itself derived material from Proverbs, directly or indirectly. Thus in recent years (1959–62), Drioton has urged the assumption that Amen-em-ope translated into Egyptian a Hebrew book of wisdom which had come into being in a Jewish-Egyptian settlement. The relationship between the book of Proverbs and the Teaching of Amen-em-ope would then be explained on the assumption that the compiler of the book of Proverbs took over a good deal of material from that (lost) Hebrew wisdom book. But the arguments for the priority of Amen-em-ope are stronger than those which are used to maintain its dependence upon a Hebrew original, and so we must abide by the assumption that Amen-em-ope provided the pattern for the compiler of Prov. xxii, 17–xxiv, 22 or xxii, 17–xxiii, 12. The fact that we can here show with certainty the literary dependence of a section of the book of Proverbs on Egyptian wisdom literature, and at the same time must date not only the Egyptian original but also its imitation by an Israelite at a fairly early period, and certainly in the pre-exilic period, confirms the suggestion made earlier (§ 11) that wisdom literature in Israel is not simply a product of the later period.

The second collection *Of the wise* (xxiv, 23–34) contains five sayings, each comprising 2–4 verses, which are directed against partiality and laziness. This collection contains nothing which points to a particular time of origin.

The collection xxv[13]–xxix comes, according to its title (xxv, 1), from the *Men of Hezekiah*. This again comprises short sayings, mostly of one verse, 128 in number in a total of 139 verses; only a few, as in xxv, 4–5; xxvi, 18–19, extend over two verses. In general, they are pronouncements, and only relatively rarely, as in xxv, 6–10, exhortations. xxv–xxvii[14] prefer the form of a comparison, i.e. parabolic parallelism, whereas xxviii–xxix,[15] like x–xv, prefer antithetic parallelism. According to the title, which may be accepted as reliable, the collection xxv–xxix stems from the period around 700 B.C.

The Words of Agur ben-Jakeh, the Massaite (xxx),[16] i.e. a member of the Arab tribe of Massa (Gen. xxv, 14) to which Lemuel, king of Massa (xxxi, 1)

---

[11] The traditional text שִׁלְשׁוֹם (*Kᵉtīb*) or שָׁלִשִׁים (*Qᵉrē*) would mean *the day before yesterday* or *officers*. We should therefore, with Erman and Gressmann, read שְׁלוֹשִׁים *thirty*.

[12] Col. VI, line 82: AOT, p. 457; ANET, p. 428; DOTT, pp. 272, 274 f. On Ahikar cf. p. 52, n. 64.

[13] Hoekstra, 'Wat is de betekenis van Proverbia xxv, 23?' Vox Theologica 24 (1953/4), pp. 138–43; Morenz, 'Feurige Kohlen auf dem Haupt' ThLZ 78 (1953), cols. 187–92: on xxv, 22; van der Ploeg, 'Prov. xxv, 23' VT 3 (1953), pp. 189–91; van der Ploeg and Hoekstra, 'Het raadsel van Spreuken xxv, 23' Vox Theologica 24 (1953/4), pp. 174–7.

[14] Harris, 'A Mention of Pottery Glazing in Proverbs' JAOS 60 (1940), pp. 268 f.: on xxvi, 23.

[15] Winton Thomas, 'The Interpretation of Proverbs xxix, 5' ET 59 (1947/8), p. 112.

[16] Torrey, 'Proverbs, Chapter xxx' JBL 73 (1954), pp. 93–6. Lit. § 126.

also belongs, begin (vv. 1–4) with a monologue which makes very much the same point as becomes clear to Job by God's speech to him (Job xl, 4–5; xlii, 2–6), namely that God is incomprehensible to man, and that silence and resignation are therefore appropriate to him. Since the second passage too (vv. 5–6) is also reminiscent of Job (xl, 5; xlii, 6), and similarly the conclusion, though admittedly this cannot be interpreted with certainty (vv. 32–3, cf. Job xl, 4 *hand on mouth*), Agur appears as a wise man who takes up the position to which Job could only come as the result of a struggle. The third saying too, a prayer to God for protection from riches and poverty (vv. 7–9, cf. I Kings iii, 11), is religious in nature. The fourth (v. 10) is a social injunction. There follow six numerical sayings—vv. 11–14 is also such a numerical saying (pp. 85 f.), with a phrase missing at the beginning, which might be supplied from Prov. vi, 16 with a different numeral. These are vv. 11–14, 15–16, 18–19 (20),[17] 21–3, 24–8, 29–31.[18] The series is now interrupted by two single sayings, probably inserted later—vv. 17 and 20. The collection contains nothing which points to a particular period of origin.

The Words of Lemuel, the King of Massa, which his mother taught him (xxxi), finally, contain in turn a warning against dissipation with women (vv. 2–3), against wine (vv. 4–7), and an exhortation to help those who are in need (vv. 8–9). There then follows the praise of the virtuous housewife (vv. 10–31),[19] probably added later (p. 472). There are no indications of date.

3. *Solomon's part in the book.* We have very varied collections, stemming from different periods and different lands, making up the book, and the material contained in them in individual sayings is even more widely diverse in its origin, belonging to the most diverse periods and peoples. It is very possible that one or another of the sayings does come from Solomon, or was perhaps collected by him, and the possibility cannot be excluded that one or another of the quite small collections which are presupposed by the larger ones in the book, actually goes back to him. This is all that can be said about Solomon's direct part in the book. For the rest, the tradition that he is the compiler of this book, as of Ecclesiastes and Wisdom, may be explained from the fact, quite correctly attested by I Kings v, 9–14; x, 1–10, 13, 23–4, that Solomon cultivated wisdom poetry at his court, or at any rate cultivated a particular kind of such poetry (p. 85).

4. *The content of the proverbs.* Finally, so far as concerns the contents of the sayings and wisdom poems which make up the book, consisting as they do of general truths about life and specific commands and prohibitions, warnings against evil and exhortations to right action, they cover the whole realm of life in all its vicissitudes—government and civil life, trade and justice, crafts and agriculture, family and slaves, work and holiday, joy and sorrow. There is also concern with the attitude of man towards God, and this indeed not infrequently, just as the book itself opens with the beautiful saying: *The fear of God is the*

[17] Sutcliffe, 'The Meaning of Proverbs xxx, 18–20' Irish ThQ 27 (1960), pp. 125–31.
[18] Bewer (p. 437, n. 10).
[19] Crook, 'The Marriageable Maiden of Prov. xxxi, 10–31' JNESt 13 (1954), pp. 137–40; Driver, 'On a Passage in the Baal Epic (IV AB III 24) and Proverbs xxxi, 21' BASOR 105 (1947), p. 11.

beginning of wisdom (i, 7). But the piety here commended is of a general human character, and the specifically Israelite contribution is in the background. The basis for the commendation of wisdom and piety is on the one hand purely secular and rational, the unfortunate consequences of foolish and impious action being vividly painted and the reward of right action emphatically inculcated. On the other hand the point is made that it is Yahweh on whose blessing alone everything depends, while all man's effort by himself alone is in vain (x, 22). But these are not in the last resort different points of view. For the blessings of salvation which are envisaged by the Proverbs of Solomon and the remaining books of the Wisdom literature, and especially Jesus ben Sira, are entirely this-worldly and of a material kind. A happy life in good health, with delight in children and grandchildren, in prosperity or at least with a sufficiency, until the term is reached which is in any case set to human life—such is God's reward for right action, and at the same time the fruit of one's own achievements, just as poverty and distress are at one and the same time a matter of personal responsibility and of divine punishment. Even if there is a sharp contrast between the morality and religion depicted in the Proverbs and in the other wisdom books, and the lofty appeal of the prophets to the will, and the emotional depth of the psalms, that morality and religion nevertheless conceals values which have also preserved their significance to later generations and will continue to do so. And this is not least the result of the picturesque form of the sayings, combining in so happy a manner profound depths of experience and childlike simplicity.

§ 66. THE BOOK OF RUTH

Literature: (a) Commentaries (i) Series: ATD: Hertzberg (²1959); BK: Gerleman (1960); BOuT: de Fraine (1956); Camb. B: Cooke (1913); Echter-B: Fischer (1950); HAT: Haller (1940); HK: Nowack (1902); HS: Schulz (1926); HSAT: Kautzsch-Bertholet (1923); IB: Smith, Cleland (1953); Jerusalem-B: Vincent (²1958); KAT: Rudolph (²1962); KeH: Bertheau (²1883); KHC: Bertholet (1898); SAT: Gressmann (²1922); Soncino-B: Slotki (²1952); SZ: Oettli (1889); Torch-B: Knight (²1956); TU: Smith (1930); UAHC Bettan, (1950).

(ii) Single Commentaries: Joüon (²1953); Slaughter (1954).

(b) Other Works: Abramowski, 'Eine spätsyrische Überlieferung des Buches Ruth' *Bulmerincq-Gedenkschr.* (1938), pp. 7–19; Cannon, 'The Book of Ruth' Theology 16 (1928), pp. 310–19; Elena M. Cassin, *L'adoption à Nuzi* (1938); Margaret B. Crook, 'The Book of Ruth—A New Solution' JBR 16 (1948), pp. 155–60; David, 'The Date of the Book of Ruth' OTS 1 (1942), pp. 55–63; Feigin, 'Some Cases of Adoption in Israel' JBL 30 (1931), pp. 186–200; Fueter, *Das Buch Ruth* (1955); Glanzman, 'The Origin and Date of the Book of Ruth' CBQ 21 (1959), pp. 201–7; Gunkel, 'Ruth' *Reden und Aufsätze* (1913), pp. 65–92; Gurewicz, 'Some Reflections on the Book of Ruth' ABR 5 (1956), pp. 45–57, 175; Humbert, 'Art et leçon de l'Histoire de Ruth' RThPh 26 (1938), pp. 257–86 = *Opuscules d'un Hébraïsant* (1958), pp. 83–110; Jepsen, 'Das Buch Ruth' ThStKr 108 (1937/38), pp. 416–28; L. Köhler, 'Die Adoptionsform von Rt iv, 16' ZAW 29 (1909), pp. 312–14; 'Ruth' SThZ 37 (1920), pp. 3–14; Loretz, 'The Theme of the Ruth Story' CBQ 22 (1960), pp. 391–9; van Maanen, *Het boek Ruth en zijn perspectieven* (1952); Myers, *The Linguistic and Literary Form of the Book of Ruth* (1955); Reinach, 'Fossiles juridiques' Revue Archéologique V, 35 (1932), pp. 83–96; Robertson, 'The Plot of the Book of Ruth' BJRL 32

(1950), pp. 207–28; Sierra, 'Il libro di Ruth' RStOr 32 (1957), pp. 357–69; Sperber, 'Wiederherstellung einer griechischen Textgestalt des Buches Ruth' MGWJ 81 (1937), pp. 55–65; Staples, 'The Book of Ruth' AJSL 53 (1936/37), pp. 145–57; Thornhill, 'The Greek Text of the Book of Ruth' VT 3 (1953), pp. 236–49; Vellas, 'The Book of Ruth and its Purpose' Theologia, Athens, 25 (1954), pp. 201–10; Vis, 'Enkele opmerkingen over den stijl in het boek Ruth' NThT 28 (1939), pp. 44–54.
    Cf. also Literature §§ 39, 126.

1. *Contents.* The book begins with the phrase: *And it came to pass in the days when the judges judged,* and for this reason it was placed, in Ⓖ and in other versions, after the book of Judges (pp. 568–70). Otherwise it stands among the five Megilloth (p. 570), being the festal scroll for the feast of Weeks, i.e. the wheat harvest. It tells of a famine which compelled the Bethlehemite Elimelech to migrate to Moab with his wife Naomi and his two sons Mahlon and Chilion. After their father's death, the two sons took Moabite wives, the one Orpah, the other Ruth. But soon afterwards, the two sons died, and so Naomi was left alone in a strange land with her two daughters-in-law. After the famine had come to an end in her homeland, Naomi decided to return, but she encouraged her two daughters-in-law to remain in Moab. Orpah submitted to this request after an initial resistance, but Ruth refused with the familiar and beautiful words (i, 16); *Where you go I will go . . .* and accompanied her mother-in-law to Bethlehem. When they arrived and Naomi was greeted by her name (נָעֳמִי =*my pleasantness*), she refused this name and said that in view of her bitter fortune she should better be called Mara (מָרָה—*the bitter one*) (ch. i).

    It was the time of the barley harvest, and so Ruth went into the fields to glean, to keep herself and her mother-in-law alive. It so happened that she came straightway into the field of Boaz, a relative of her dead father-in-law. He had heard of her devotion to her mother-in-law and therefore treated her with especial kindness and saw that she was able to glean particularly plentifully. When she went home after the first day's gleaning, she learnt from her mother-in-law that Boaz was her relative and גֹּאֵל *redeemer* (pp. 482 f.), and so followed her advice and kept to Boaz' fields the whole period of the harvest (ii).[1]

    In order to lead Boaz to take Ruth to wife, Naomi advised her to put on her best clothes and lay herself at the feet of Boaz who was occupied with the threshing on the threshing floor, when he had stretched himself out to sleep in the open at the end of the day's work, and so to offer herself to him. Ruth followed this advice and met with the desired success.[2] But, as Boaz tells her when he finds her lying at his feet, there is another person who stands before him in the right of redemption (iii).

    On the next morning early, Boaz went to the gate of his city, the place of judgement, and there persuaded the one who had the next right of redemption to give up his right. Boaz then declared himself in the proper legal manner, and prepared to carry out the right of redemption, namely to buy the field belonging to Naomi and to marry Ruth. He then took Ruth home and she became the

[1] Staples, 'Notes on Ruth ii, 20 and iii, 12' AJSL 54 (1937), pp. 62–5; Stinespring, 'Note on Ruth ii, 19' JNESt 3 (1944), p. 101; Zimolong, 'Zu Rut ii, 7' ZAW 58 (1940/41), pp. 156–8.   [2] May, 'Ruth's Visit to the High Place at Bethlehem' JRAS (1939), pp. 75–8.

mother of a son. This son was adopted by Naomi. *And the women of the neighbourhood gave him a name, saying, 'A son has been born to Naomi.' They named
him Obed; he was the father of Jesse, the father of David* (iv, 1–17).

There follows in iv, 18–22, with its own title *Now these are the descendants of
Perez*, the genealogy of David, which is traced back through Jesse, Obed, Boaz
and so to Perez (the son of Judah, cf. Gen. xxxviii).[3]

2. *The secondary character of iv, 17b–22.* It may be regarded as generally
recognised that the genealogy of David in iv, 18–22 does not originally belong
here, but has been added secondarily, following I Chron. ii, 4–15 or derived
from the same source from which this latter passage comes. But we must also
go a step or two further and remove as an addition not only the end of iv, 17:
he was the father of Jesse, the father of David, but also the words which precede:
they named him Obed, and hence assume that originally another name stood here
which was removed when the addition was made. Verse 17a raises difficulties
both in form and in content. As far as its form is concerned, it is noteworthy
that the explanation of the name introduced by לֵאמֹר *saying* precedes the
name-giving itself. It is true that the giving of the explanation before the name
itself is to be found not infrequently (Gen. xxix, 33, 34, 35; xxx, 6, 8, 11, 13, 18,
20, 23; xxxviii, 29 etc.), but in these cases the explanation is never introduced
by *saying*. What we find is rather that it is narrated that *he (they) said* such and
such, and after the content of this saying, which gives the reason for the name,
the name-giving follows, often introduced by עַל־כֵּן *therefore.* Thus in
Gen. xxix, 34, we read: *And again she conceived and bore a son, and said: Now
this time my husband will adhere to me, because I have borne him three sons.
Therefore she named[4] his name Levi (adherent).* Where elsewhere the name is
introduced by *saying* (Gen. v, 29; xxx, 24; Judg. vi, 32; I Sam. iv, 21), the actual
name-giving precedes, as is indeed alone intelligible, since the phrase *saying*
refers back to it. Thus in Gen. xxx, 24: *And she called his name Joseph (may he
add one), saying: May Yahweh add to me another son.* Where elsewhere, as in
the passage just cited, the actual name appears, we have in the passage in Ruth,
simply the indefinite שֵׁם *name;* there then follows the explanation introduced
by *saying*, and only then do we get the name itself: *And the women of the neighbourhood gave him a name, saying: 'A son has been born to Naomi.' They named
him Obed.* The difficulty in the content is that there is no kind of relationship,
such as appears in the examples mentioned above, between the explanation
A son has been born to Naomi (the pleasant) and the name *Obed (servant, worshipper).* We should have expected, as was already observed by Peters,[5] as a name
for the son something like בֶּן־נֹעַם *(ben-no'am), son of pleasantness, the
pleasant one. A son is born to the pleasant one* would then provide the explanation
for the name *the pleasant one,* and this would provide a reasonable connection
between the name and its explanation.

Since iv, 17 thus raises difficulties of form and content, we may assume that
the text is not here in order, but has undergone secondary alterations. We have

[3] Dijkema, 'Ruth iv, 17–22' NThT 24 (1935), pp. 111–18.
[4] Reading קָרְאָה following ⅁ instead of *he named* (𝔐).
[5] ThRv 13 (1914), p. 449; cf. also Gunkel, p. 84.

already indicated in what way the restoration of the original text is to be sought. Nor can there be any doubt what it is that has led to the substitution of the indefinite *name* for the name *ben-nō'am* and to the addition of *Obed* as the proper name for the child. It was the desire to make the child into the grandfather of David. Tradition gave his name as Obed. So Ruth's child, adopted by Naomi, was given the name *Obed* with the removal of the name *ben-nō'am* which originally stood in the narrative. In other words, the Ruth narrative had originally nothing at all to do with David, but has only secondarily been made into a narrative concerning David's ancestors.

The recognition of this makes irrelevant all the arguments which have otherwise been adduced to explain the Ruth narrative as part of the family history of David. The reference in I Sam. xxii, 3 to David's having gone to Moab after his breach with Saul, and to his having brought his aged parents into security with the king of Moab, gives no more basis for postulating connections of kinship between the house of David and Moab than does David's flight to Achish of Gath suggest that we may conclude kinship between his family and the Philistines (I Sam. xxi, 11–16; xxvii). The wish expressed to Boaz in iv, 12 concerning his marriage with Ruth: *and may your house be like the house of Perez, whom Tamar bore to Judah* in fact proves by the very fact that there is no mention in connection with Perez of any special relationship to Boaz that the Perez genealogy does not belong to the original material of the book, rather than proving the reverse. But we may well assume that the mention of Perez in this wish was the reason (or one of the reasons) for the addition of the Perez genealogy. We need then only to explain the identity of the name of our Boaz with the one which appears in the genealogy in I Chron. ii, 4–15, or which appeared in the original utilised both by that genealogy and by the appendix iv, 18–22. Probably I Chron. ii, 4–15, or the material upon which it is based, already presupposes the relating of the Ruth narrative to David. For the possibility that the identity of the names is a matter of chance, and that the Boaz of David's genealogy has nothing to do with the Boaz of the Ruth narrative is no more probable than the alternative, namely that the Boaz of the Ruth narrative derives from David's genealogy. In this latter case, we should expect that either at the first mention of Elimelech (i, 2) or at that of Boaz (ii, 1) there would have been a reference to their membership of the family of David. Since later substitution of Boaz for another name is improbable, we are left only with the assumption that the figures of the Ruth narrative were subsequently made into ancestors of David. The fact that the story actually dealt with people of Bethlehem made this assumption easy, and since the narrative took place in the days of the judges, Boaz and Ruth could readily be understood as the great-grandparents of David. Such a process is not isolated. In fact it often happens that legendary or fictional narratives are secondarily applied to historical personalities. Thus at the end of the ⑮ text, Job is identified with the Edomite king Jobab of Gen. xxxvi, 33 (here too by means of a list), and other traditions link Job with other persons and events of Biblical history.[6]

3. *The book of Ruth as a short story (Novelle).* The story of Ruth, which, as

[6] Peters, *Das Buch Job* (EH) (1928), p. 16*; Stevenson, *The Poem of Job* (1947), pp. 73–86.

we have now shown, is to be separated from its connection with the family of David, is seen to be a folk-tale, or better a short story which has been woven out of a folk-tale, which undoubtedly in its locality and period—Bethlehem, Moab, the time of the judges—is linked with historical events, but is otherwise pure fiction. If Myers is right, then in its original form it actually had a poetic structure. The persons who appear in it are hardly likely to be historical. The names of the two sons of Elimelech, Mahlon and Chilion, were evidently invented for the narrative, for, in spite of the objections made by Rudolph against the generally accepted explanation, they are certainly meaningful names (*maḥlôn* = *weakness* and *kilyôn* = *consumption*). As far as the names of the two Moabitesses are concerned, Orpah and Ruth, the interpretation very often similarly given—'*orpāh* = *the unfaithful* and *rût* = *the companion, friend*—is admittedly less certain. It is probable that we have here genuine women's names, though their interpretation remains uncertain and they do not appear outside this book. In any case Boaz and Elimelech are normal names, which admittedly only occur here in the Old Testament, and in their form they fit perfectly well in the period of the judges. They were probably chosen because of their archaic flavour by the writer of the narrative, who lived, as we shall see in a moment, very much later. Naomi too is a woman's name of the normal kind, though also not otherwise attested. The writer is therefore unlikely to have invented it. But it is probable that the choice of this name for the woman who stands beside Ruth in the centre of the narrative is deliberate. In it the narrator could make clear the change in the fortunes of its bearer—the *pleasant one* who is *not-pleasant* but *bitter*, the adoptive mother of the *pleasant one* (i, 20; iv, 17). Staples' view that all the names which appear in the book have reference to the fertility cult is no more probable than his assertion that the book, which in his view reveals many other motifs belonging to this cult, is intended to depict the transition from sorrow to joy in the course of the world's life, and to present the birth of a child as the sign of a more fortunate age.

4. *The chief personages.* The theme of this little book is the fortunes of two women, mother-in-law and daughter-in-law, who are severely visited, the one by the death of her husband and her two sons, the other by the loss of her husband and by childlessness, and who withstand the test nobly. The one is more concerned for her daughter-in-law than for her personal well-being and so at the same time remains faithful to her husband's family, while the other values the human bonds which bind her to her mother-in-law more highly than her own people and religion and the prospect of a second marriage. Both women have to be regarded as the heroines of the idyllic narrative, for the one would be nothing without the other. Naomi, though characteristically the Hebrew story does not explicitly say so, may be recognised as a woman who is worthy of the affection of her daughter-in-law. It is she who induces Ruth to offer herself to Boaz. Without her motherly care and her sense of the family, the story could not have come to so happy an ending. But only Ruth and not Naomi is still physically in a position to become a mother, and it is she who wins the heart of Boaz by her loyalty and industry as by her courage and behaviour in a delicate moment. Thus Ruth contributes what is essential to the happy

R

ending, namely her body and her heart, while Naomi shows her daughter-in-law how to use these gifts skilfully for the attainment of the goal. Since Naomi is naturally much more closely bound up with the family of her husband than Ruth who has only just come from an alien environment, and indeed has only come over to the people and religion of Israel for Naomi's sake, it is quite understandable that Ruth's son ranks as Naomi's son and is named after her. In the fact that she willingly allows this to happen, Ruth again shows herself as the ready and obedient servant of her mother-in-law.

Thus the two women belong together and cannot be separated. Beside them there appears Boaz as the kindly, wise farmer, respectable and pious. The setting in which these characters are placed is the life of the farming community; the harvest in the fields and the threshing on the threshing floor. The chief characters are drawn with feeling; they are noble and generous and so were considered worthy—at a later stage as we have seen—to be taken up into the ancestry of David. So too there is an idyllic charm in the pictures of harvest and threshing, and it is no wonder that the Jews made the book into the scroll for the harvest festival (pp. 478, 570), and that well beyond Judaism the farmer and any who love the life of the land have a particular affection for the book of Ruth.

5. *The religious content of the narrative.* We should not overlook the religious content of the narrative, which is certainly not stressed but is not for that reason any the less strong. Yahweh is the protector of the widow, and he is a God who does not allow loyalty to go unrewarded. Ruth has chosen Yahweh as her God (i, 16). It is this God, *under whose wings she has come to take refuge* (ii, 12), who, as Boaz expresses it, will reward her for her faithfulness towards her mother-in-law (ii, 12). It is Yahweh who, according to the testimony of the women of the neighbourhood (iv, 14), has taken Naomi into his care after having earlier saddened her, as she has felt (i, 20–1). This feature, that God after the endurance of suffering and trial by the one afflicted, then restores what he has taken, is shared by this story with the folk-tale (pp. 456 f., 462) of Job, and in this respect this book may be set beside the Job narrative.

6. *The legal institution of 'redemption'.* These features of the book—its religious content, the nobility of its characters and the charm of farming life—are features which are independent of change. But side by side with them we must note the institution of 'redemption' which is tied to a particular time and to particular legal practice, and is woven into the course of the story as a fascinating motif increasing the tension. We are here concerned with the custom—admittedly it cannot now be understood clearly in every detail—related to the Levirate marriage (i.e. marriage by a brother-in-law), in which it is the duty of the nearest relative of a childless widow or of one who lacks any male descendant, to marry her along with the purchase of her property, to count the son who results from the union as the son of the dead husband of his wife and then to entrust to this son the property of the dead man. There is frequent reference in the Old Testament to the duty of Levirate marriage (Gen. xxxviii; Deut. xxv, 5–10), and we also have frequent reference to the duty of the next of kin to buy the land which would otherwise be lost to the family (Lev. xxv, 25; Jer. xxxii),

but the combination of Levirate marriage and the duty of redemption appears only here.[7]

7. *The date of the book.* This may be fixed with reasonable certainty in the post-exilic period. The note in iv, 7 according to which it was *in former times* the custom to pull off one's shoe and hand it to the other party in a contract on the occasion of a redemption or exchange, in confirmation of the legal proceedings, makes it quite clear that there is a considerable period between that of the narrator and that of the story he is telling. It can hardly be used as a proof that the book is substantially later than Deut. xxv, 5–10 on the grounds that the practice here mentioned is evidently no longer in use at the time of the compilation of the book of Ruth and hence appears to have been completely misunderstood. In actual fact the practice in Deut. xxv, 5–10 is admittedly similar to that mentioned in Ruth iv, 7, but is not identical with it, and the latter cannot therefore be explained as due to a misunderstanding of the former. Nor, as has also often happened, may it be concluded from the fact that the narrator reports a mixed marriage and so evidently looks with favour on the foreign woman (ii, 10), that we have here an explicit protest against the rigorous measures against mixed marriages which were carried out by Nehemiah and Ezra (Ezr. x; Neh. xiii, 23–7), so that the book is then to be dated at about this time or a little later. For it is hardly possible to speak of a pronounced bias in the story. We may only say that the breadth of outlook towards another nation which appears here as in the book of Jonah is more readily intelligible in a later than in an earlier period. Used thus, this argument does also lead to the post-exilic period, and that we should there go down to about the fourth century follows also from the many Aramaisms which the book has, such as לָהֵן *therefore* (i, 13) and קִיֵּם *to settle, confirm* (iv, 7).

§ 67. THE SONG OF SONGS

Literature: (a) Commentaries (i) Series: ATD:Ringgren (^{5}1962); Camb. B: Harper (1902); COuT: Aalders (1952); EB: Pouget et Guitton (^{5}1957); Echter-B: Fischer (1950); HAT Haller (1940); HK: Siegfried (1898); HS: Miller (1927); HSAT: Budde (1923); IB: Meek, Kerr (1956); Jerusalem-B: Robert (^{3}1958); KD: Delitzsch (1875); KeH: Hitzig (1855);

[7] Brongers, 'Enkele opmerkingen over het verband tussen lossing en leviraat in Ruth iv' NedThT 2 (1947/8), pp. 1–7; Burrows, *The Basis of Israelite Marriage* (1938); 'Levirate Marriage in Israel' JBL 59 (1940), pp. 23–33; 'The Marriage of Boaz and Ruth' JBL 59 (1940), pp. 445–54; 'The Ancient Oriental Background of Hebrew Levirate Marriage' BASOR 77 (1940), pp. 2–15; P. Cruveilhier, 'Le lévirat chez les Hébreux et chez les Assyriens' RB 34 (1925), pp. 524–46; David, *Vorm en weʒen van de huwelijkssluiting naar de Oud-oostersche rechtsopvatting* (1934); *Het huwelijk van Ruth* (1941); Dronkert, *Het huwelijk in het OT* (1957); Lacheman, 'Note on Ruth iv, 7–8' JBL 56 (1937), pp. 53–6; Mittelmann, *Der altisraelitische Levirat* (1934); Neufeld, *Ancient Hebrew Marriage Laws* (1944); Puukko, 'Die Leviratsehe in den altorientalischen Gesetzen' ArOr 17, II (1949), pp. 296–9; Rowley, 'The Marriage of Ruth' HThR 40 (1947), pp. 77–99 = *The Servant of the Lord and other Essays* (1952), pp. 161–86; Schoneveld, *De betekenis van de lossing in het boek Ruth* (1956); Speiser, 'Of Shoes and Shekels' BASOR 77 (1940), pp. 15–20; Vriezen, 'Two Old Cruces' OTS 5 (1948), pp. 80–91, pp. 80–8: on iv, 5. Lit. § 126.

KHC: Budde (1898); SAT: Staerk (²1920); Soncino-B: Lehrman (²1952); SZ: Oettli (1889); Torch-B: Knight (1955); TU: Gemser (1931); UAHC Bettan (1950).

(ii) Single Commentaries: Bea (1953); Buzy (³1953); Ewald (1826); Gordis (1954); Halter [Hebr.] (1959); Hengstenberg (1853); Kalt (1933); Rothstein (1893); Ruffenach (²1932).

(b) Other Works: de Ambroggi, *Il Cantico. Dramma d'amore sacro* (1952); Audet, 'Le sens du Cantique des Cantiques' RB 62 (1955), pp. 197–221; 'The Meaning of the Canticle of Canticles' ThD 5 (1957), pp. 88–92; Bentzen, 'Remarks on the Canonisation of the Song of Solomon' *Studia Or. Pedersen* (1953), pp. 41–7; Budde, 'Was ist das Hohelied?' PJ 78 (1894), pp. 92–117; Buzy, 'Un chef-d'œuvre de poésie pure: le Cantique des Cantiques' *Mémorial Lagrange* (1940), pp. 147–62; 'La composition littéraire du Cantique des Cantiques' RB 49 (1940), pp. 169–94; 'L'allégorie matrimoniale de Jahvé et d'Israël et le Cantique des Cantiques' RB 52 (1945), pp. 77–90; 'Le Cantique des Cantiques' L'Année Théologique 8 (1947), pp. 1–17; 'Le Cantique des Cantiques: exégèse allégorique ou parabolique?' RSR 39 (1951), pp. 99–114; Chouraqui, *Le Cantique des Cantiques* (1953); Curley, 'The Lady of the Canticle' AER 133 (1955), pp. 289–99; Driver, 'Hebrew Notes on "Song of Songs" and "Lamentations"' *Bertholet-Festschr.* (1950), pp. 134–46; Dubarle, 'L'amour humain dans le Cantique des Cantiques' RB 61 (1954), pp. 67–8; 'Le Cantique des Cantiques' RSPhTh 38 (1954), pp. 92–102; Feuillet, 'Le Cantique des Cantiques et la tradition biblique' NRTh 74 (1952), pp. 706–33; *Le Cantique des Cantiques* (1953); 'La formule d'appartenance mutuelle ii 16 et les interprétations divergentes du Cantique des Cantiques' RB 68 (1961), pp. 5–38; Frings, *Die Anfänge der europäischen Liebesdichtung im 11. und 12. Jahrhundert* (SAM 1960, 2); Gaster, 'What "The Song of Songs" means' Commentary 13 (1952), pp. 316–22; Gebhardt, *Das Lied der Lieder* (1931); Geslin, *L'amour selon la nature et dans le monde de la grâce. Le Cantique des Cantiques* (1939); Gordis, 'A Wedding Song for Solomon' JBL 63 (1944), pp. 263–70; Hamp, 'Zur Textkritik am Hohenlied' BZ 1 (1957), pp. 197–214; Harbsmaier, *Das Hohelied der Liebe* (BSt 3, 1952); Haupt, *Biblische Liebeslieder* (1907); Herder, *Lieder der Liebe* (1778); Horst, 'Die Formen des althebräischen Liebesliedes' *Littmann-Festschr.* (1935), pp. 43–54; Krauss, 'Die "Landschaft" im biblischen Hohenliede' MGWJ 78 (1934), pp. 81–97; 'Die Rechtslage im biblischen Hohenliede' MGWJ 80 (1936), pp. 330–9; 'The Archaeological Background of some Passages in the Song of Songs' JQR 32 (1941/42), pp. 115–37; 33 (1942/43), pp. 17–27; 35 (1944/45), pp. 59–78; Kuhl, 'Das Hohelied und seine Deutung' ThR 9 (1937), pp. 137–67; Kuhn, *Erklärung des Hohen Liedes* (1926); Landsberger, 'Poetic Units within the Song of Songs' JBL 73 (1954), pp. 203–16; Langerbeck, *Gregorii Nysseni in Canticum Canticorum* (1960); Lys, 'Le plus beau chant de la création' EtThR 33 (1958), pp. 87–117; Margolis, Montgomery, Hyde, Edgerton, Meek, Schoff, *The Song of Songs. A Symposium* (1924); Murphy, 'The Structure of the Canticle of Canticles' CBQ 11 (1939), pp. 381–91; 'Recent Literature on the Canticle of Canticles' CBQ 16 (1954), pp. 1–11; *The Book of Ecclesiastes and the Canticle of Canticles with a Commentary* (1961); Oesterley, *The Song of Songs* (1936); van der Oudenrijn, 'Vom Sinne des Hohen Liedes' Divus Thomas, Freiburg 31 (1953), pp. 257–80; 'Scholia in locos quosdam cantici canticorum' Bibl 35 (1954), pp. 268–70; Piatti, 'Il Cantico dei Cantici alla luce del libro di Geremia' Divus Thomas, Piacenza 56 (1953), pp. 18–38, 179–210; Ringgren, 'Hohes Lied und hieros gamos' ZAW 65 (1953), pp. 300–2; 'Hieros gamos i Egypten, Sumer och Israel' Religion och Bibel 18 (1960), pp. 23–51; Robert, 'Le genre littéraire du Cantique des Cantiques' RB 52 (1945), pp. 192–213; 'La déscription de l'Époux et de l'Épouse dans Cant. v, 11–15 et vii, 2–6' *Mélanges Podechard* (1945), pp. 211–23; 'Les appendices du Cantique des Cantiques (viii, 8–14)' RB 55 (1948), pp. 161–83; Rowley, 'The Interpretation of the Song of Songs' JThSt 38 (1937), pp. 337–63; 'The Riddle of the Song of Songs' Baptist Quart. 8 (1937), pp. 411–16; 'The Song of Songs: an Examination of Recent Theory' JRAS (1938), pp. 251–76; 'The Interpretation of the Song of Songs' *The Servant of the Lord* (1952), pp. 187–234; Rudolph, 'Das Hohe Lied im Kanon' ZAW 59 (1942/43), pp. 189–99; 'Die literarische Form des Hohen Lieds' Nachrichten der Gießener Hochschulgesellschaft 17 (1948), pp. 5–13; Schmökel, 'Zur kultischen Deutung des Hohenliedes' ZAW 64 (1952), pp. 148–55; *Heilige Hochzeit und Hoheslied* (1956); on this cf. Horst,

ThLZ 83 (1958), cols. 184–6; Segert, 'Die Versform des Hohenliedes' *Charisteria Rypka* (1956), pp. 285–99; Snaith, 'The Song of Songs: the Dances of the Virgins' AJSL 50 (1933/34), pp. 129–42; Thilo, *Das Hohelied* (1921); Torczyner, שִׁיר הַשִּׁירִים (1942/43); Vaccari, 'Il Cantico dei Cantici nelle recenti pubblicazioni' Bibl 9 (1928), pp. 443–57; Waterman, *The Song of Songs. Translated and Interpreted as a Dramatic Poem* (1948); Wetzstein, 'Die syrische Dreschtafel' Ztschr. f. Ethnologie 5 (1873), pp. 270–302; Wittekindt, *Das Hohe Lied und seine Beziehungen zum Istarkult* (1927); Wutz, *Das Hohelied* (1940); Zolli, 'In margine al Cantico dei Cantici' Bibl 21 (1940), pp. 273–82; 'Visionen der Liebe im Hohenlied' WZKM 51 (1948), pp. 34–7.

Cf. also Literature §§ 12, 126.

1. *The name of the book. Its traditional interpretation and ascription to Solomon.* The book has the title שִׁיר הַשִּׁירִים אֲשֶׁר לִשְׁלֹמֹה *The Song of Songs of Solomon*, where the genitive expression *Song of Songs* is used in the superlative sense and describes the song as the most beautiful. The Greek and Latin translations rendered the name quite literally as ᾆσμα ᾀσμάτων ὅ ἐστιν τῷ Σαλωμών and *canticum canticorum* (*Salomonis*), or abbreviated to ᾆσμα and *canticum*. Since Luther, the normal name for the book in German has been 'Hoheslied' (the noble or sublime song), a free rendering but conveying the right meaning.

The fact that the Song of Songs was taken into the canon, and its use as festal scroll at Passover (p. 570), are due probably to the allegorical interpretation of its chief characters. The lover, king Solomon, is interpreted as Yahweh, and the beloved, the Shulammite,[1] as Israel. But the fact that in the second century A.D. the book had still to struggle for the recognition of its canonicity (p. 568), and that according to Tosephta Sanhedrin 12, 10[2] and other passages in Rabbinic literature, Rabbi Akiba (†A.D. 137) cursed those who used to sing passages from the Song of Songs in the wine-shops[3]—evidently still understanding it in its literal sense[4]—shows on what an insecure foundation the allegorical interpretation rests. Nor is the ascription of the song to Solomon which appears in the title any more secure. In all probability it is to be explained from the fact that on the one hand Solomon is mentioned several times (i, 5; iii, 7, 9, 11; viii, 11), and on the other hand there is mention in I Kings v, 12 of 1005 songs by Solomon. Thus it was easy to assume that this song, which actually mentions Solomon, must be one of the 1005 and indeed the most beautiful of them. Furthermore, as Audet has convincingly shown, it is members of the class of the *Wise* (חֲכָמִים) to whom we owe the collection of the songs which are gathered together in this book, and for them the ascription to Solomon, their patron, was quite natural. In any case, since the tradition which we possess on the matter gives rise to some doubts, the meaning and the date of origin of the poems must be discovered from the analysis of the book itself.

2. *The form of the book.* The right understanding of the book depends to a most marked degree on our conception of its form. Three different opinions

[1] Goodspeed, 'The Shulammite' AJSL 50 (1933/4), pp. 102–4; Rowley, 'The Meaning of "The Shulammite" ' AJSL 56 (1939), pp. 84–91.
[2] Zuckermandel, p. 433.
[3] Mechilta on Exod. xv, 2 (Hoffmann, p. 60), cf. Benoit, 'Rabbi Aqiba ben Joseph, sage et héros du judaïsme' RB 54 (1947), pp. 54–89, cf. p. 68. Lit. p. 680, n. 1.
[4] Cf. also the Mishna tractate Sanhedrin 3, 1.

have been put forward: (a) the Song of Songs is a unified lyrical poem, (b) it is a drama, (c) it presents a quite loosely assembled collection of single love songs.

The view is maintained by Thilo, Bea and others that the Song of Songs is a carefully arranged composition, leading from inclination and longing on the part of the lover (i, 2–8)[5] through the bridal period and betrothal to married life (vii, 12–viii, 14), or, as Bea thinks, regarding the love-relationship between man and woman as a parable of God's relationship to his people, leading from God's choice of his people to its full fellowship with him. This view has in its favour the fact that the book has come down to us as a continuous text and not, like the Psalms, as a collection of individual songs clearly separated from one another. But this is an unsatisfactory argument. For in other places too, we find that a work transmitted as a continuous text in reality comprises a multiplicity of quite separate units. This is true, for example, in the prophetic books where long sections clearly present a collocation of many separate sayings; but this is only in part clearly indicated by titles and colophons, introductions and conclusions. In the case of this book, the changes of person and situation, of mood and idea, are so great that the conception of the book as a unified composition can only be maintained by subjecting it to excessively ruthless treatment.

Its interpretation as a drama has been put forward in many varied ways. It has been viewed as a sort of opera—Origen († 254)[6] had already put forward a view something of this kind—and this has been maintained with great differences in detail by Delitzsch, Ewald, Oettli and Rothstein. On the other hand, Gebhardt, assuming that at the time of the book's origin, namely the third century B.C. (p. 490), the mime, which was widespread among the Greek neighbours of Palestine, had exerted an influence on the Jews also, interpreted the song as a mime, i.e. as a play in which instead of several people being engaged there is only one, who characterises the various personages by variation in voice and indicates the action by gestures. Waterman interprets the basic material of the book as a play in which several actors appear and which moreover represents a historical event, namely the rejection of Solomon's wooing of Abishag of Shunem (I Kings i, 1–2; ii, 13–25) and her loyal adherence to her peasant lover; a work stemming from northern Israel and later worked over in the southern kingdom and dislocated. But any one of these interpretations of the Song of Songs as a drama comes to grief on the impossibility of demonstrating the marks of a connected and meaningful action in the text itself, and there is also the more general objection that elsewhere in the Old Testament there are no traces of dramatic poetry and that this type of work evidently did not suit the Jewish spirit.

Justice is best done to the text by the interpretation of the book as a collection of disconnected songs. Among the Church Fathers, this view is already found in Theodore of Mopsuestia († 428).[7] It was maintained by Herder and Goethe

---

[5] Gaster, 'Canticles i, 4' ET 72 (1960/1), p. 195. Lit. § 126.

[6] Daniélou (p. 709, n. 51), p. 285; Lawson, *Origen, The Song of Songs. Commentary and Homilies. Translated and Annotated* (1957); Urbach, 'Rabbinic Exegesis and Origenes' Commentaries on the Song of Songs and Jewish-Christian polemics' [Hebr., Engl. Sum.] Tarbiz 30 (1960/1), pp. 148–70, V–VI.

[7] Lusseau, 'Le Cantique des Cantiques' in Robert et Feuillet, *Introduction à la Bible* I (²1959), pp. 655–66, cf. p. 659.

in the period when a feeling for folk-literature revived, and it was Reuss* who first put it forward in a work of Old Testament introduction. This view then received substantial confirmation from the fact that love-songs and marriage-customs of the last century in Syria and Palestine were collected and set beside the Song of Songs. Such study was begun by J. G. Wetzstein, who, in about the middle of the nineteenth century was for many years Prussian consul in Damascus. Of his observations, the following are particularly relevant: on the day before the marriage, the bride dances a sword dance to the rhythm of a song sung by one of the bystanders, a song which describes her adornment and her bodily beauty (*wasf*). During the week which follows on the bridal night, the young couple are fêted as king and queen; a threshing board set up on the threshing floor serves as a throne. During this 'royal week' various songs are sung, including yet another *wasf* on the young couple. The application of these observations to the understanding of the Song of Songs as a collection of such songs sung at wedding festivities was then carried out pre-eminently by Budde.

It is clear that a group of songs, like for example iii, 6–11[8] 'The royal throne of Solomon and king Solomon', first becomes clear and intelligible when placed side by side with these Syrian wedding songs. We may from this imagine that in Israel too bridegroom and bride were fêted as king and queen, and here the bridegroom was thought of as the king who was the most famous because of his splendour and his reputation for love, namely Solomon, and the bride as the Shunammite of I Kings i–ii,[9] who did not actually become queen but was the fairest maiden in all Israel and the nurse of king David. In addition, we hear of a wedding week in Gen. xxix, 27; Judg. xiv, 12, 17 (cf. Isa. lxi, 10), and in Sota 9, 14 it is mentioned that the crowning of the bridegroom continued until the time when Jerusalem was threatened by Vespasian (A.D. 69) and that of the bride until the invasion by Quietus (A.D. 117). The descriptive poem indicated by Wetzstein, the *wasf*, corresponds exactly to the description of the maiden by her lover in iv, 1–7,[10] the description of the lover by the maiden in v, 10–16, and the description of the (dancing?) maiden by the bystanders in vii, 1–6.

Thus we may assume that one group of the songs now gathered in the Song of Songs was composed for wedding festivities of the kind described, and was recited at them. But others have no reference to this kind of situation, but are simply love songs expressing the longing of the man for the woman, of the woman for the man, and the joy of their union. Here the man's love is often expressed with the metaphor of pasturing, and the beauty of the woman with that of the garden or vineyard, or of a richly laden table, but in such a way that metaphor and content are interwoven. Thus we find it in the short poem of i, 7–8: *Tell me, you whom my soul loves, where you pasture your flock* or in the dialogue of the lovers as they rest in the open air, i, 9–17. Such love songs too, though they have no direct reference to the marriage, may be recited at wedding

[8] Krauss, 'Der richtige Sinn von "Schrecken in der Nacht" HL iii, 8' *Gaster Anniversary Vol.* (1936), pp. 323–30.

[9] Waterman, 'Some Historical and Literary Consequences of Probable Displacement in I Kings i–ii' JAOS 60 (1940), pp. 383–90.

[10] Eissfeldt, *Der Beutel der Lebendigen* (BAL 105, 6, 1960), pp. 20 f. on iv, 7 and vi, 6; Isserlin, 'Song of Songs iv, 4: An Archaeological Note' PEQ 90 (1958), pp. 59 f. Pl. VI.

festivities and are likely to be so used, and so in this way we may perhaps understand the book as being a collection of wedding poetry. However, the reference of the love songs just mentioned to the wedding is a loose one, and it would be doing violence to them to seek to explain them precisely from wedding festivities. And the attempt everywhere here to discover married love or at any rate the love of bride and bridegroom is vain, and would be to confine to the sphere of narrow and middle-class legitimacy, songs which extol love as a powerful force, often outspokenly, while always profoundly and inwardly. Nor would it be any more correct to argue the opposite view, namely that here free love is boldly proclaimed in contrast to marriage. The best commentary on these songs is provided by similar songs, on the one hand from ancient Egypt[11] or Babylonia,[12] or also ancient Greece,[13] and on the other hand from the modern orient, as they have been collected by Dalman,[14] Littmann,[15] Jacob,[16] Musil,[17] Stephan,[18] Linder[19] and others.

3. *Contents.* This discussion of the form of the poems has to a large extent already anticipated what has to be said about content. The allegorical application[20] to Yahweh and Israel, attested for the first century A.D. by IV Ezra (II Esdras) v, 23–30, was taken over by the early church, simply with the substitution of Christ for Yahweh, and the church or the individual pious soul for Israel. In this modified form, often weakened by there being no denial that the reference of the song is really to the love between man and woman, but that this physical love at the same time is understood to be a pattern of the love between Christ and the church or the soul, the allegorical interpretation continues down to the present time. Among Catholic theologians, who, as a glance at the literature on pp. 483–5 and n. 20 below shows, are particularly actively concerned with this book, it remains as much in favour as ever. But even here, it does not by any

[11] ANET, pp. 467–9; AOT, pp. 30 f.; DOTT, pp. 187–91; Gardiner, *The Library of A. Chester Beatty. Description of a Hieratic Papyrus with a Mythological Story, Love Songs and Other Miscellaneous Texts. The Chester Beatty Papyrus No. 1* (1931); Hermann, 'Beiträge zur Erklärung der ägyptischen Liebesdichtung' *Ägyptolog. Stud.*, ed. by Firchow (1955), pp. 118–39; *Altägyptische Liebesdichtung* (1959); Hurd, *World's Oldest Love Poem. Hieroglyphic Text (Louvre C 100)* (1954); Schott, *Altägyptische Liebeslieder* (1950); Suys, 'Les chants d'amour du Pap. Chester Beatty I' Bibl 13 (1932), pp. 209–27.

[12] Lambert, 'Divine Love Lyrics from Babylon' JSSt 4 (1959), pp. 1–15; Meek, 'Babylonian Parallels to the Song of Songs' JBL 43 (1924), pp. 245–52. Cf. Held, 'A Faithful Lover in an Old Babylonian Dialogue' JCSt 15 (1961), pp. 1–26; von Soden, 'Ein Zwiegespräch Ḫammurabis mit einer Frau' ZA 49 (1950), pp. 151–94, Pls. 15–16. Lit. § 126.

[13] Dornseiff, 'Ägyptische Liebeslieder, Hoheslied, Sappho, Theokrit' ZDMG 90 (1936), pp. 589–601 = *Kl. Schr.* I (²1959), pp. 189–202.

[14] *Palästinischer Diwan* (1901).

[15] *Neuarabische Volkspoesie* (1902).

[16] *Das Hohelied, auf arabische und andere Parallelen untersucht* (1902).

[17] *Arabia Petraea* III (1908).

[18] 'Modern Palestinian Parallels to the Song of Songs' JPOS 2 (1922), pp. 199–278, ٢٢–١.

[19] *Palästinische Volksgesänge* I (1952), II (1955), ed. by Ringgren. See here I, pp. 82–110: Ringgren, 'Die Volksdichtung und das Hohelied'.

[20] Lerch, 'Zur Geschichte der Auslegung des Hohenliedes' ZThK 54 (1957), pp. 257–77; Ohly, *Hohelied-Studien. Grundzüge einer Geschichte der Hoheliedauslegung des Abendlandes bis um 1200* (1958); Parente, 'The Canticle of Canticles in Mystical Theology' CBQ 6 (1944), pp. 142–58; Tournay, 'Les chariots d'Aminadab (Cant. vi, 12): Israël, peuple théophore' VT 9 (1959), pp. 288–309; Vulliaud, *Le Cantique après la tradition juive* (1925).

means enjoy exclusive acceptance. Significant Catholic writers such as Dubarle and Audet have expressed themselves rather as in favour of the understanding of the Song of Songs as a collection of songs, concerned with the relationship of love between man and woman, which is prized as one of the great gifts of the creator. In this way, without the devious route of allegorical interpretation, it may have found its way into the canon, like the 'Praise of the virtuous housewife' in Prov. xxxi, 10–31.

More serious consideration than that given to the allegorical and parabolic interpretation of the Song must be devoted to the question as to whether it may not be in origin of mythological and cultic character. At an earlier period, stimulated by Winckler, Erbt[21] put forward such a view, and more recently it has been defended by Ebeling,[22] Meek[23] and Wittekind. According to Wittekind, the Song of Songs represents the cycle of cult songs of a festival of Tammuz-[24] Shalman and Ishtar-Shulammite, which was celebrated in the time of king Manasseh in the Temple at Jerusalem, and which bequeathed many of its features to the Passover festival, so that the use of the book as the festal scroll at the Passover may be understood on the basis of these points of contact. Deeper insight has recently been gained into the great significance of mythical ideas concerning the Sacred Marriage and of cultic practices corresponding to these ideas in the ancient orient, as well as the recognition of the close connections in intellectual and religious life between Canaan and Israel and their environment. Such considerations have recently led Schmökel in particular to seek to explain the book in the light of this complex of mythical and cultic ideas. However, a closer examination of such attempts at interpretation hardly leads to anything more than the probability, certainly worthy of notice and indeed in other ways significant, that in Israel, as elsewhere in the world, the language of lovers has been influenced by mythical and cultic diction, in so far as this has as its subject the love relationship between god and goddess, or between human beings who represent them, just as it is also true that myth has made borrowings from erotic poetry. The consideration of the relationship between love-poetry and religious diction may appropriately make more intelligible the fact—certainly in other respects so remarkable—namely that a collection of quite realistic love songs could be applied to the relationship between Yahweh and Israel and so be taken up in the canon.

We may therefore leave the matter at this point. Here in the Song of Songs we have profane love songs and wedding songs, as they are to be found in all the world and always will be. It remains in many cases uncertain how the individual songs are to be separated from one another and how many there are of them. But the division of a whole series of passages is reasonably certain, and

[21] *Die Hebräer* (1906), pp. 196–202.
[22] 'Aus den Keilschrifttexten aus Assur religiösen Inhalts' MDOG 58 (1917), pp. 22–50, esp. pp. 48–50; cf. ZDMG 78 (1924), pp. LXVIII f.
[23] 'Canticles and the Tammuz Cult' AJSL 39 (1922/3), pp. 1–14.
[24] *Compte Rendu de la III. Rencontre Assyriologique Internationale* (1954), pp. 18–41, Pls. IV–VII: Moortgat, 'Der Bilderzyklus des Tammuz'; pp. 41–67: Falkenstein, 'Tammūz'; pp. 67–9: Otten, 'Boğazköy-Texte zu der Vorstellung vom verschwundenen und wiederkehrenden Gott; pp. 69–74: Kraus, discussion of Moortgat, *Tammuz. Der Unsterblichkeitsglaube in der altorientalischen Bildkunst* (1949).

the right assumption is that there are about 25—Gordis finds 28. A principle of arrangement is only observable here and there, for sometimes the order seems to be based upon catchwords. Thus the consecutive passages iv, 8;[25] iv, 9–11; iv, 12–v, 1; v, 2–vi, 3 all have the word *Lebanon*, and in viii, 1–4 and viii, 5–7 *the mother* is twice mentioned. Since there are a few repetitions (ii, 17a = iv, 6a; ii, 17b = viii, 14; ii, 6–7 = viii, 3–4), we should probably consider whether here—as in other cases (p. 472)—at least two smaller collections which in part contained the same songs, have been combined. Audet reckons with two recensions of songs which came into being in the time of Solomon or even somewhat earlier. Of these, the one, which reflects the life of the shepherd and the farmer, he thinks was handed on orally in the northern kingdom, while the other, with its allusions to life at the royal court and to an urban environment, flourished in the southern kingdom, until in the post-exilic age they were combined by a 'wise man', and provided with the epilogue viii, 6b–7 as well as with the appendices in viii, 8–14. It is certainly right to observe that the book mentions geographical locations both of North Israel (*Lebanon* iii, 9; iv, 8 etc., *Tirzah* vi, 4)[26] as also of Judah (*Jerusalem* ii, 7; iii, 5 etc.), and furthermore, that, as we shall see more precisely in a moment, the collection as we have it comes from the post-exilic period.

4. *Date and place of origin*. These may be determined with reasonable certainty from linguistic indications. There is, in fact, a whole series of Aramaisms, as for example the frequent use of the relative particle שֶׁ in connection with עַד *until* (i, 12; ii, 7 etc.). This in itself already points to a fairly late date, and the occurrence of the Persian loan-word פַּרְדֵּס *park* in iv, 13,[27] which has come over into English as *paradise*, necessitates going down into the Persian period at least. אַפִּרְיוֹן in iii, 9 which is probably borrowed from the Greek (φορεῖον *palanquin*) and not, as Gordis proposes, from the Sanskrit (*paryanka palanquin*) nor, with Widengren,[28] from the Iranian (*upari-yana palanquin*), brings us down further into the Greek period. Hence we must suppose that the book came into being during the third century B.C. in the area which at that time was occupied by the Jewish religious and national community, i.e. in Jerusalem and its environs. But this only means that the form in which the songs have come down to us is so late. The assumption is by no means thereby excluded that older material, indeed even very much older material, underlies them. For in love poetry too tradition plays a particularly notable part. As in the case of the psalms (pp. 446–8, 450f.), we should reckon with the possibility —indeed the probability—that these love songs are at least in large part substantially older than the collection which we now have, and they also have in com-

[25] Bertholet, 'Zur Stelle Hohes Lied iv, 8' BZAW 33 (1918), pp. 47–53; Boehmer, 'Welchen Sinn hat HL iv, 8?' MGWJ 80 (1936), pp. 449–53.
[26] Jochims, 'Thirza und die Ausgrabungen auf dem *tell el-fâr'a*' ZDPV 76 (1960), pp. 73–96, Pls. 8–10; de Vaux, 'Fouilles à Tell el-Fâr'ah, près Naplouse' RB 54 (1947), pp. 394–433, 573–89; 55 (1948), pp. 544–80; 56 (1949), pp. 102–38; 58 (1951), pp. 393–430, 566–90; 59 (1952), pp. 551–83; 62 (1955), pp. 541–89; 64 (1957), pp. 552–80; 68 (1961), pp. 557–92; 'The Excavations at Tell El-Far'ah and the Site of Ancient Tirzah' PEQ 88 (1956), pp. 125–40, Pls. XXIII–XXVI. Lit. § 126.
[27] Jepsen, 'Pardes' ZDPV 74 (1958), pp. 65–8.
[28] *Sakrales Königtum im Alten Testament und im Judentum* (1955), p. 112. Lit. § 126.

mon with the psalms that they reveal many Canaanite or other ancient oriental elements.

§ 68. ECCLESIASTES (KOHELETH)

Literature: (a) Commentaries (i) Series: ATD: Zimmerli (1962); BOuT: van der Ploeg (1953); Camb. B: Lukyn-Williams (1922); COuT: Aalders (1948); EB: Podechard (1912); Echter-B: Nötscher (1948) HAT: Galling (²1964); HK: Siegfried (1898); HS: Allgeier (1925); HSAT: Budde (1923); IB: Rankin, Atkins (1956); ICC: Barton (1908 (1948)); Jerusalem-B: Pautrel (³1958); KAT: Hertzberg (²1963); KD: Delitzsch (1875); KeH: Hitzig-Nowack (²1883); KHC: Wildeboer (1898); SAT: Volz (²1922); Soncino-B: Reichert, (²1952); SZ: Volck (1889); Torch-B: Jones (1961); TU: Gemser (1931); UAHC Bettan (1950).

(ii) Single Commentaries: Bea (1950); Bentzen (1942); Bickell (1884. 1886); Bratsiotis (1951); Gordis (²1955); P. Haupt (1905); Kuhn (BZAW 43, 1926); Odeberg (1929); Phrilingos (1951); Power (1952); Steinmann (1955); Zapletal (²1911).

(b) Other Works: de Ausejo, 'El género literario del Ecclesiastés' Est Bíbl 6 (1947), p. 451; 7 (1948), pp. 369–406; Bertram, 'Hebräischer und griechischer Qohelet' ZAW 64 (1952), pp. 26–49; Blieffert, *Weltanschauung und Gottesglaube im Buche Kohelet* (Diss. theol. Rostock, 1938); Bottéro, 'L'Ecclésiaste et le problème du Mal' NC 7/9 (1955/57), pp. 133–9; Buzy, 'La notion du bonheur dans l'Ecclésiaste' RB 43 (1934), pp. 494–511; 'Les auteurs de l'Ecclésiaste' (L'Année Théologique 11 (1950), pp. 317–36; Cazelles, 'Conjonctions de subordination dans la langue de Qohelet' GLECS 8 (1957/60), pp. 21–2; Dahood, 'Qoheleth and Recent Discoveries' Bibl 39 (1958), pp. 302–18; Dornseiff, 'Das Buch Prediger' ZDMG 89 (1935), pp. 243–9; Driver, 'Problems and Solutions' VT 4 (1954), pp. 225–45; Ebeling, *Ein babylonischer Kohelet* (1922); Eichrodt, 'Vorsehungsglaube und Theodizee im AT' *Procksch-Festschr.* (1934), pp. 45–70; Forman, 'The Pessimism of Ecclesiastes' JSSt 3 (1958), pp. 336–43; 'Koheleth's Use of Genesis' JSSt 5 (1960), pp. 256–63; Galling, 'Kohelet-Studien' ZAW 50 (1932), pp. 276–99; 'Stand und Aufgabe der Kohelet-Forschung' ThR 6 (1934), pp. 355–73; *Die Krise der Aufklärung in Israel* (1952); 'Prediger' RE 22 (1954), cols. 1827–31; Ginsberg, *Studies in Koheleth* (1950); 'Supplementary Studies in Koheleth' PAAJR 21 (1952), pp. 35–62; 'The Structure and Contents of the Book of Kohelet' SVT III (1955), pp. 138–49; Gordis, 'Quotations in Wisdom Literature' JQR 30 (1939/40), pp. 123–47; 'Was Kohelet a Phoenician?' JBL 74 (1955), pp. 103–114; 'Qoheleth and Qumran—a Study of Style' Bibl 41 (1960), pp. 395–410; Hertzberg, 'Palästinische Bezüge im Buche Kohelet' ZDPV 73 (1957), pp. 113–24 = *Baumgärtel-Festschr.* (1959), pp. 63–73; Humbert (§ 11); Kleinert, 'Sind im Buche Koheleth außerhebräische Einflüsse anzuerkennen?' ThStKr 56 (1883), pp. 761–82; 'Zur religions- und kulturgeschichtlichen Stellung des Buches Koheleth' ThStKr 82 (1909), pp. 493–529; Lauha, 'Die Krise des religiösen Glaubens bei Kohelet' SVT III (1955), pp. 183–91; Levy, *Das Buch Qoheleth, ein Beitrag zur Geschichte des Sadduzäismus* (1912); Luder, 'Gott und Welt nach dem Prediger Salomo' SThU 28 (1958), pp. 105–14; MacDonald, *The Hebrew Philosophical Genius* (1936), Chap. V; Miller, 'Aufbau und Grundproblem des Predigers' *Miscell. Bibl.* 2 (1934), pp. 104–22; Muilenburg, 'A Qoheleth Scroll from Qumran' BASOR 135 (1954), pp. 20–8; Murphy, 'The "Pensées" of Coheleth' CBQ 17 (1955), pp. 304–14; Neher, *Notes sur Qohélét* (1951); Pedersen, 'Scepticisme israélite' RHPhR 10 (1930), pp. 317–70; Pfeiffer, 'The Peculiar Skepticism of Ecclesiastes' JBL 53 (1934), pp. 100–9; Ranston, *Ecclesiastes and the Early Greek Wisdom Literature* (1925); Reines, 'Koheleth on Wisdom and Wealth' JJSt 5 (1954), pp. 80–4; Rowley, 'The Problems of Ecclesiastes' JQR 42 (1951/52), pp. 87–90; Rudolph, *Vom Buch Kohelet* (1959); Sæbø, 'Til Forståelse av Qohælæth' TTKi 27 (1956), pp. 20–34; Schunck, 'Drei Seleukiden im Buche Kohelet?' VT 9 (1959), pp. 192–201; Smith, 'A Critical Evaluation of the Book of Ecclesiastes' JBR 21 (1953), pp. 100–5; Staples, '"Profit" in Ecclesiastes' JNESt 4 (1945), pp. 87–96; 'Vanity of Vanities' Canadian JTh 1 (1955), pp. 141–56; Vriezen, 'Prediker en de achtergrond van sijn wijzheid' NedThT 1 (1946/47), pp. 3–14, 65–84; 'De overwinning van het tragische lebensgevoel in Israël' Kernmomenten (1947), pp. 33–48; Weill, 'Le livre du "Désespéré". Le sens, l'intention et la composition de l'ouvrage' Bull. Inst. Franç. Arch. Or. 45 (1947), pp. 89–154; Windel, *Luther als Exeget des Predigers Salomo* (1897); Zimmerli, *Die Weisheit des Predigers Salomo* (1936). Cf. also Literature §§ 11, 16, 64, 65, 126.

1. *The name of the book. The words of Koheleth ben-David, king in Jerusalem* stands as the title of the book, and following this title the book is briefly termed קֹהֶלֶת *Koheleth*,[1] rendered by the versions as ἐκκλησιάστης, *concionator*, '*The Preacher*', with sometimes the addition of the name *Salomonis, Solomon* as a substitute for the *ben-David* of the title, explaining it by the name of that son of David who in fact alone can be meant here. The naming of the compiler as Koheleth is to be found in i, 2, 12; vii, 27; xii, 8, 9, 10 in addition to its occurrence in the title, and twice among these (vii, 27;[2] xii, 8) with the article. It is remarkable that a man should be indicated with a feminine participial form —which might be translated something like *the one (fem.) who collects*—and it is probably to be explained on the grounds that the word denotes primarily an activity or an office, and has then been secondarily transferred to the holder of the office. There is an exact parallel to this development of meaning in the masculine proper names preserved in Ezra ii, 55, 57—הַסֹּפֶרֶת and פֹּרֶכֶת הַצְּבָיִם. Originally these were plainly descriptions of offices, namely the *office of scribe* and the *office of tending gazelles*, and they have then become descriptions of the holders of these offices and could even be used as proper names.[3] The situation is probably the same with מְבַשֶּׂרֶת Isa. xl, 9, which is to be interpreted with Mowinckel[4] as *company of those who give good news*. The word קֹהֶלֶת, derived from the familiar word קָהָל, *assembly, community*, thus means in the first place the activity or the *office of leading the assembly* or *of speaking in the assembly*, and has then come to be used also for *the leader of the assembly* or *the speaker in the assembly*. Ginsberg, however, who, as we shall see (p. 496) regards the book as a translation into Hebrew of an Aramaic original, sees in קֹהֶלֶת an error of translation, arising from the misunderstanding of the Aramaic masculine participle קָהְלָא, in the emphatic state, *the one who calls together*, as if it were a feminine participle in the absolute state.

The replacement of the proper name of Solomon by the description 'speaker' is to be explained as designed to show Solomon in this way as the speaker κατ' ἐξοχήν, a master of words in the very highest sense. This is quite in line with the later elaboration of the figure of Solomon, as it may be seen elsewhere. The king, who according to I Kings iii, 16–28; v, 9–14; x, 1–10+13, 24 is endowed with great wisdom, poetic skill and readiness of wit, has gathered more and more characteristics of this kind, on the principle of 'To him that hath, shall more be given'. It is therefore no wonder that the gift of speech should not be lacking, and particularly so if, as is indeed possible in view of the actual period

---

[1] Barag, ' מה היא "קהלת"?' Tarbiz 21 (1949/50), pp. 101–5; Tur-Sinai, 'ל "מה היא קתלה?"' Tarbiz 21 (1949/50), p. 208. Lit. § 126.

[2] We should here read אָמַר הַקֹּהֶלֶת instead of אָמְרָה קֹהֶלֶת of 𝔐.

[3] Hans Bauer, ZAW 48 (1930), p. 80.   [4] *Religion und Kultus* (1953), p. 109.

of the book's composition (pp. 496–7), we may set the elaboration of this feature in the Greek period with its high prizing of rhetoric, and may assume that this ideal is reflected in the description of Solomon as orator. It is probable that this description also presupposes the existence of legendary narratives concerning Solomon as orator. In any case such an assumption would give a more illuminating and intelligible basis for the application of the title of Koheleth to Solomon than is sometimes adduced as an explanation, namely that in I Kings viii, 1, 55 the verb *to collect* (הִקְהִיל) and the substantive *assembly* (קָהָל) are used in connection with him.

In view of all this, the description of Solomon as Koheleth may be readily understood. So, in spite of xii, 9–11 (see below), there are no grounds for excising as secondary additions those utterances which mention Koheleth as king—i, 12, 16; ii, 7, 9 in addition to the title. Nor is there any ground for defining this מֶלֶךְ with Levy as 'head of a school', or with Ginsberg, vocalising as מֹלֶךְ, as 'man of wealth', 'man of property', and so to surmise that Koheleth was at first thought of simply as a wisdom teacher or a wealthy man, and only subsequently was equated with king Solomon. We should assume rather that in the third century B.C.—for that is probably the date of the book's composition (see p. 497)—a wise man, knowledgeable about life and experienced in the ways of the world, put forward his reflections on the world and on life under the name of Koheleth-Solomon, following in this a custom well known in Egypt and imitated elsewhere too in the Old Testament (Prov. xxxi, 1) of putting one's wisdom teaching into the mouth of a king of the past. Since the compiler not only makes Koheleth speak in the first person (i, 12–18) but also refers to him in the third (i, 2), the title i, 1 and the colophon xii, 9–11, which refer to him in the third person, are to be ascribed to the compiler and not to a later hand. The Egyptian royal teachings likewise have such titles and colophons, as for example in that of Amenemhet for his son.[5] So far as the colophon is concerned, Amenemhet, towards the end of his exhortation, draws attention to the acts of his period of rule. The compiler of Ecclesiastes, however, who, as the choice of the name Koheleth itself shows, is anxious to emphasise with regard to his king that he was wise, concludes by praising him as the teacher of the people and the creator of many sayings, with certainly also a reference to the Old Testament book of the Proverbs of Solomon (§ 65). In these circumstances, we should also feel doubt about the normal interpretation of the *one shepherd*, by whom, according to xii, 11, *the words of the wise are given*,[6] as meaning God, and ask whether by the shepherd is not meant rather the king, i.e. Koheleth, as indeed the naming of the king as shepherd, though rare in Egyptian,[7] is very common in Accadian and also in the Old Testament.

2. *The structure of the book.* The book with its twelve chapters presents a loose collocation of a series of reflections in first person style (i, 12–18; ii, 1–13),

[5] ANET, pp. 418 f.; Erman, *Literatur der Ägypter* (1923), pp. 106–9, E.T. (1927), pp. 72–4.
[6] Galling, 'The Scepter of Wisdom. A Note on the Gold Sheath of Zendjirli and Ecclesiastes xii, 11' BASOR 119 (1950), pp. 15–18; Pautrel, ' "Data sunt a pastore uno" ' RSR 41 (1953), pp. 406–10.
[7] Erman-Ranke, *Ägypten* (1923), p. 525, n. 4; Dieter Müller, 'Der gute Hirte. Ein Beitrag zur Geschichte ägyptischer Bildrede' ZÄS 86 (1961), pp. 126–44.

of exhortations addressed to a second person (iv, 17⁸–v, 8; vii, 9–14; xi, 1–6⁹ etc.), of generally applicable reflections (i, 2–11; iii, 1–8; vii, 1–8 etc.), and of individual wisdom sayings (ix, 17–x, 20).[10] The individual units cannot, however always be clearly separated from one another. Some, it is true, like i, 2–11; i, 12–18; iii, 1–8; xi, 9–xii, 8, stand out easily. But in other cases the boundaries are indistinct. Thus iii, 14–15 [11] may be understood standing alone, but may also be perfectly well linked with iii, 1–13 or with iii, 16–22[12] as a unit. It is similarly open to question whether iv, 1–6 should be treated as a unit or would be better divided into two sections (iv, 1–3 and iv, 4–6). ix, 17–x, 20 is in any case a very loose collocation of individual sayings which for the most part could equally well stand in the book of the Proverbs of Solomon. From this fact, namely that the division of the units is at many points so uncertain, there arises the variation in the counting of the sections among the different interpreters of the book. Hertzberg counts 12, though at many points dividing these into subdivisions. Budde counts 23, while he too subdivides some into smaller sections. Galling counts 37.

There is no logical and steadily progressive line of thought in the book. But it is certainly not a meaningless confusion. *All is vanity* is deliberately placed at the beginning (i, 2), and equally deliberately *Rejoice, O young man, in your youth* (xi, 9–xii, 8)[13] at the end. The former presents the conclusion, again and again repeated, to which all Koheleth's reflections and brooding lead, and the latter is the practical consequence repeatedly drawn from it. On the other hand no illuminating reason can be found to explain why the collection of sayings is put precisely at ix, 17–x, 20, for the section could equally well occupy any other position in the book. The book is thus a loose collocation of reflections, aphorisms and exhortations, often suggesting the style of a diary, and this not only suggests that the attempts which have repeatedly been made, as for example by Bickell, to obtain a better arrangement and a clearer sequence of thought by rearrangements and excisions, are *a priori* wide of the mark, but also makes one mistrustful of the equally frequent endeavours, made recently by Bea and Ginsberg, to demonstrate that the book is arranged according to plan.

3. *Contents*. The book is pervaded by a spirit of sceptical rationalism and tired resignation. All human effort is vain and meaningless. *All is vanity* is said no fewer than twenty times (i, 2, 14; ii, 1, 11, etc.).[14] Everything repeats itself without any meaning (i, 2–11) *and there is nothing new under the sun*.[15] The

---

[8] Joh. Schmidt, 'Koh. iv, 17' ZAW 58 (1940/41), pp. 279 f.

[9] Kruse, ' "Da partem septem necnon et octo" ' VD 27 (1949), pp. 164–9.

[10] Leahy, 'The Meaning of Qoh x, 15' Irish ThQ 18 (1951), pp. 288–90; Staerk, 'Zur Exegese von Koh. x, 20 und xi, 1' ZAW 59 (1942/3), pp. 216–18; Winton Thomas, 'A Note on בְּמַדָּע in Eccl. x, 20' JThSt 50 (1949), p. 127. Lit. § 126.

[11] Galling, 'Das Rätsel der Zeit im Urteil Kohelets (Koh. iii, 1–15)' ZThK 58 (1961), pp. 1–15.

[12] Irwin, 'Eccles. iii, 18' AJSL 56 (1939), pp. 298 f.; 'A Rejoinder' *ib.* 58 (1941), pp. 100 f.

[13] Ginsberg, 'Kohelet xii, 4 in the Light of Ugaritic' Syria 33 (1956), pp. 99–101; Leahy, 'The Meaning of Eccl. xii, 1–5' Irish ThQ 19 (1952), pp. 297–300.

[14] Staples, 'The "Vanity" of Ecclesiastes' JNESt 2 (1943), pp. 95–104. Lit. § 126.

[15] Friedrich, 'Altpersisches und Elamisches' Or 18 (1949), pp. 1–29, cf. pp. 28 f.; Ginsberg, in a review of Harris, *A Grammar of the Phoenician Language*, JBL 56 (1937), pp. 138–43, cf. p. 142; Lévy, 'Rien de nouveau sous le soleil' NC 5 (1953), pp. 326–8.

gathering of wisdom means the gathering of sorrow (i, 12–18).[16] Wealth too, with all its potentialities for the happy enjoyment of life, is vain, for its possessor must in the end leave it to another who is not worthy of it (ii, 4–11, 18–23). Likewise woman is in the last resort only a source of bitter disappointment (vii, 25–8). Even to strive for righteousness is meaningless, since the fate of the righteous is no different from that of the wicked (viii, 14). Above all it is the same fate in death, which affects every man equally, which makes all effort appear in vain (ii, 12–17; iii, 19–22). The *Wise*, among whom Koheleth himself belongs and to whom he is explicitly assigned in the epilogue in xii, 9–11, have, it is true, preserved their optimism with all the breadth of their experience of life, and they represent the view that the inadequacies of the world, which are all too well known to them, rest upon human guilt, and so may be evaded by the wise man who avoids such guilt. But in Koheleth this bald optimism of the schools is overturned into the most profound pessimism, and to him it is indeed the most diabolical delight to draw out this superficial outlook of the class of the wise to its logically absurd conclusion and to show that things turn out just as badly for the wise as for the fools (ii, 19, 21; ix, 11–12). There are, however, two limits to this pessimism which like mildew brings into decay whatever of faith and hope and love may stir in the heart of Koheleth. On the one hand there is the summons, directed to himself and to others, to enjoy life all the more determinedly in view of its brevity and meaninglessness, to enjoy it so long as 'our little lamp burns', and this summons preserves Koheleth from sinking back into blank despair (ix, 1–10).[17] On the other hand, in spite of everything, he never breaks entirely away from his faith in God (ii, 24; iii, 11, 13, 14).[18] Where the first of these, namely that the thought of the impermanence and meaninglessness of human life is felt to be an urge to enjoyment of life, whether more crude or more refined, is a phenomenon which is to be found throughout the world,[19] the second clearly reveals his Jewish heritage. So the book reveals itself as an expression of the clash between world-weary resignation and Jewish faith in God. Faith in God is not entirely broken by this clash, but nevertheless does not give its possessor the power to overcome the experiences which oppress him and the outlooks which confuse him, but remains there—as it has been expressed—like a remnant of childhood faith which has survived into adult manhood—still of some value, but without dynamic. If we want to measure the difference between a genuine and living certainty of God and a faith in God which has been pushed right to the fringe of a philosophy of life, then we must place Koheleth side by side with Job.

[16] Gordis, 'Ecclesiastes i, 17—its Text and Interpretation' JBL 56 (1937), pp. 323–30.

[17] Pfeiffer, 'Hebrew and Greek Sense of Tragedy' *Joshua Bloch Mem. Vol.* (1960), pp. 54–64, cf. pp. 62–4.

[18] Herrmann, 'Zu Kohelet iii, 14' WZ Leipzig 3 (1953/4), pp. 293–5.

[19] Cf. the Egyptian harpist's song (AOT, pp. 28–9; ANET, p. 467); the grave inscription from the Ptolemaic period discussed by Erman, 'Zwei Grabsteine griechischer Zeit' *Sachau-Festschr.* (1915), pp. 102–12, cf. pp. 107–11, and by Spiegelberg, 'Die demotische Literatur' ZDMG 85 (1931), pp. 147–71, cf. pp. 167 f.; the Gilgamesh Epic col. III (AOT, p. 194; ANET, pp. 74 f.); Theognis (Diehl, *Anthologia Lyrica Graeca,* Fasc. 2 (³1950 (1955)), pp. 1–81), lines 567–70, 753–6. Jacoby, 'Theognis' SAB (1931), pp. 90–180 =*Kl. Philol. Schr.* I (1961), pp. 345–455; Lesky, *Geschichte der griechischen Literatur* (1957/8) pp. 159–63. Cf. also above p. 89; Lit. § 126.

4. *Historical setting.* In this description of the contents of the book, we have to some extent already indicated its historical setting. Such a tired philosophy of life is only possible in the last stages of the Old Testament development, and in so far as we may have to reckon with influences on Koheleth from outside (as must indeed be seriously considered (pp. 498–9)), we can only take into account a period when Judaism, as a result of its inner development, was ready for the receiving of such influences. Such a dating of the work in the late post-exilic period, on the basis of its place in the history of Old Testament thought, fits excellently with its linguistic character. For, among all the books of the Old Testament, it is the most affected by Aramaisms. בְּטֵל *to cease from working* (xii, 3), זְמָן *time* (iii, 1) for example, are pure Aramaic words, and as in the vocabulary so too in the formation of words and in constructions the Aramaising character of the language is everywhere noticeable. This goes so far that Burkitt[20] in 1921 put forward a suggestion that the book might be a translation of an Aramaic original, and this has recently been maintained by Zimmermann,[21] Torrey,[22] Ginsberg[23] and others. The arguments put forward in support of this view are certainly deserving of attention and in particular instances are quite striking, but they are nevertheless no more sufficient for the proof of the thesis than are the undoubted Aramaisms in the New Testament gospels a reliable support for the assertion that they are translations of Aramaic originals.[24] The position in both cases is rather to be explained on the grounds that many Aramaic elements have penetrated the diction of the compiler, living in an environment in which Aramaic was spoken, and have thus given to the Hebrew in the one case and to the Greek in the other an Aramaic colouring. Gordis[25] and others have expressed themselves as opposed to the view that the book of Koheleth is a translation of an Aramaic original. How cautious one must in any case be in the assessment of isolated linguistic features is shown also by the fact that Dahood[26] has been able to trace contacts with Canaanite and Phoenician, and Gordon[27] has seen some north-Israelite peculiarities.

However the linguistic question may be decided in this respect, it remains clear that Koheleth originated only in the post-exilic period. It is difficult to determine the date more exactly. The passages which are brought into play for this purpose, in so far as they really do have actual historical events in view, may be applied to various events and circumstances, and in other cases there is no question of allusion to historical events, but only the use of typical, stereotyped examples. Thus iv, 13–16[28] and x, 16, where in the one case the replacement of

[20] 'Is Ecclesiastes a Translation?' JThSt 23 (1922), pp. 22–8.
[21] 'The Aramaic Provenance of Qohelet' JQR 36 (1945/6), pp. 17–45; 'The Question of Hebrew in Qohelet' *ib.* 40 (1949/50), pp. 79–102.
[22] 'The Question of the Original Language of Ḳohelet' JQR 39 (1948/9), pp. 151–60.
[23] See pp. 491, 493.
[24] Cf. Littmann, 'Torreys Buch über die vier Evangelien' ZNW 34 (1935), pp. 20–34; Black, *An Aramaic Approach to the Gospels and Acts* (1946, ²1954).
[25] 'The Original Language of Qohelet' JQR 37 (1946/7), pp. 67–84; 'The Translation Theory of Qohelet Re-examined' *ib.* 40 (1949/50), pp. 103–16; 'Koheleth—Hebrew or Aramaic?' JBL 71 (1952), pp. 93–109.
[26] 'Canaanite-Phoenician Influence in Qoheleth' Bibl 33 (1952), pp. 30–52, 191–221; 'The Language of Qoheleth' CBQ 14 (1952), pp. 227–32.
[27] 'North Israelite Influence on Postexilic Hebrew' IEJ 5 (1955), pp. 85–8.

an elderly king by a young one is extolled as a welcome event, whereas in the other case a woe appears to be pronounced over *the land whose king is a child*, have been thought to allude to the year 204 B.C. when the five-year-old Ptolemy V Epiphanes came to the throne of Egypt. But in x, 16, it is, to say the least, open to question whether the word used here really does mean *child* and not rather *slave*, and in iv, 13–16 we have in reality just one of the many examples to show that everything is really vain and ephemeral. Even the vigorous young man from among the people who amid the tremendous jubilation of the crowd has taken the place of a king who has become senile, will soon lose his popularity and stand alone. It is thus a typical case which cannot be used for the exact dating of the work. Other examples of passages which have been similarly utilised are no better. So it is, for example, with the passage in ix, 13–16 which, if we leave on one side older interpretations with reference to biblical events, has been seen by Sellin*, in dependence upon Friedländer[29] as an allusion to Archimedes' defence of his home town of Syracuse besieged by the Romans and their conquest of it in 212, but by Dornseiff, who here follows Spinner,[30] as an allusion to the quarrel which broke out between the ten Athenian generals and Miltiades before the battle of Marathon in 490, and its consequences. We shall have to be satisfied with the dating arrived at as a result of considering the thought of the work. It may be made a little more precise in that the book can hardly have originated later than the third century. For after the passionate zeal of the Jews for their religion had been newly stirred by the religious policy of Antiochus IV Epiphanes (175–163), it is difficult to think that a book could have come into being which runs so counter to the activist spirit which from then on inspires Judaism. It must rather, already before the outbreak of conflict on the part of the Jews against the Hellenisation and levelling out of their religion, have commanded such respect that it could not then have been excluded. With such a dating of the book at the latest in the third century B.C. agrees the fact that among the rich treasures in leather scrolls from Qumran Cave 4 (see pp. 638–44) substantial fragments were also found of a Hebrew text of Koheleth, which are dated both by their editor Muilenburg and by Cross[31] in the first half of the second century B.C.

5. *Place of origin.* In regard to the place of origin of the work we must also beware of making too definite a judgement. Some scholars, and so particularly Kleinert, have thought of Alexandria. This city was indeed in the third century a centre of flourishing intellectual life and of rich literary activity on the part of the Jews. In addition, it has been thought possible to see in the book definite references to Alexandria, or at least to a sea-port and centre of trade, as for example in the allusion to trade undertakings at sea in xi, 1.[32] Others, like

[28] Irwin, 'Eccles. iv, 13–16' JNESt 3 (1944), pp. 255–7; Torrey, 'The Problem of Ecclesiastes iv, 13–16' VT 2 (1952), pp. 175–7.
[29] *Griechische Philosophie im Alten Testament. Eine Einleitung in die Psalmen- und Weisheitsliteratur* (1904), pp. 151–7.
[30] *Herkunft, Entstehung und antike Umwelt des hebräischen Volkes* (1933), p. 465.
[31] Cross, 'The Oldest Manuscripts from Qumran' JBL 74 (1955), pp. 147–72, cf. pp. 153, 162; RB 63 (1956), p. 58. Cf. Lit. p. 683, n. 18.
[32] Stoute, 'Bread upon the Waters' BS 107 (1950), pp. 222–6.

Hertzberg and Galling, consider, on the other hand, in part by reference to certain metaphors and expressions as in xi, 4; xii, 2, which are supposed to be only suitable to Palestine with its clouds and rain—unlike Egypt—that a Palestinian origin is indicated, whereas Gordon[33] thinks that the book originated in the eastern Jewish diaspora. A definite decision is hardly possible.

6. *Foreign influences.* A more important question is the one already touched upon (p. 496), as to whether and how far foreign influences have had an effect upon Koheleth, and what these foreign influences might be; or whether his attitude can be explained entirely from within Judaism. At an earlier stage, before the evaluation of the results for Old Testament study of the researches in Egyptology and Assyriology, which really began only towards the end of the nineteenth century, it was almost exclusively a question of Greek influences (cf. E. Pfleiderer[34] among others), and attempts were made to discover in the book the ideas of just about all the Greek schools of philosophy, and especially of Heraclitus, the Stoics and the Epicureans. More recently, however, in view of the influence of Egyptian literature on the Old Testament which has been clearly demonstrated in other places, it has been Egyptian features in the book which have been investigated (Humbert, Galling)—Babylonian and Assyrian influence hardly comes into question here, especially since neither 'The Babylonian Koheleth'[35] nor 'The Babylonian pessimistic dialogue between master and slave'[36] reveal any parallels to Koheleth. It is true that other scholars have at the same time endeavoured to support the assumption of Greek influence with new arguments. Thus Allgeier has attempted to show the relationships between Koheleth and the diatribes of the Cynics and Stoics, and Ranston its relationships to the gnomic literature of the Greeks, and particularly to Theognis.[37] Corré,[38] altering the traditional text at ii, 3 from בַּיַּיִן *with wine* to כְּיָוָן *like the Greeks,* even makes Koheleth say of himself that he endeavoured to appear uncircumcised like the Greeks, and so followed Greek wisdom. Dornseiff considers the possibility that what appear as borrowings from the Greek world of thought, and have often been taken to be such, are at least in part ideas which Greece itself had in fact adopted from the east. Van der Ploeg, on the other hand, contents himself with the observation that Koheleth and the Judaism of his time could no more withdraw itself from the influence of its environment, which was Hellenism, than could its contemporaries in general.

The influencing of Koheleth by the Greek spirit appears thus likely enough, and its language also reveals words and expressions which may with at least some probability be regarded as Graecisms—so, for example, עָשָׂה טוֹב εὖ πράττειν *to enjoy oneself* in iii, 12 and מִקְרֶה τύχη *chance* in ii, 14; iii, 19; ix, 2, 3. It is very difficult here to decide how far particular schools of thought

---

[33] See above, p. 496, n. 27.
[34] *Die Philosophie des Heraklit von Ephesus im Lichte der Mysterienidee* (1886), pp. 255–288, 348–52.
[35] AOT, pp. 287–91; ANET, pp. 438–40; DOTT, pp. 97–103. Cf. above, p. 469.
[36] AOT, pp. 284–7; ANET, pp. 437 f. Cf. Speiser, 'The Case of the Obliging Servant' JCSt 8 (1954), pp. 98–105.
[37] Cf. above, p. 495 n. 19.
[38] 'A reference to Epispasm in Koheleth' VT 4 (1954), pp. 416–18.

or particular writings have influenced Koheleth, but it is certain that there is nothing more than casual contact. The position is the reverse in regard to Koheleth's contacts with Egypt, for here we can point to a series of quite definite influences, though it is less proper to speak of an influence of the Egyptian spirit. Egyptian beliefs and customs appear to be presupposed in the mention of the *sacred oath* in viii, 2,[39] and in the funeral customs alluded to in viii, 10.[40] Above all there is the statement of Koheleth, which has always been felt to be remarkable, that *I, Koheleth, was king over Israel in Jerusalem* (i, 12). This sounds as if Solomon-Koheleth had abdicated from the throne during his lifetime and was now looking back upon his rule. This contradicts the familiar historical facts, but may be readily explained from Egypt. For here it is the established style that the publishers of wisdom teachings, viziers or kings, impart them only towards the end of their life to recipients who are called to positions of high honour,[41] and the phrase *I was king* appears to be simply a transference of this Egyptian form to the Hebrew work. In view of the marked dependence upon Egypt which has moreover been clearly established for a number of other passages of Hebrew wisdom literature (see pp. 474–5), it is no matter for surprise that the same should be true of this book which also belongs to that literature.

7. *Additions to the work*. In view of the character of the book as a loose collocation of aphorisms, it lacks a clear development of thought and reveals unevennesses and disjointedness, contradictions and repetitions. But it is quite clear that we should not conclude from this without further ado, as has been done particularly by Siegfried and Podechard, that several hands have been concerned in the book or that several 'sources' have been here interwoven. It is, however, by no means impossible that here and there explanatory phrases have been inserted. This is indeed a very probable supposition. The book did raise serious difficulties for Jewish piety, as may be seen by the disputes which arose around the question of its canonicity (see p. 568). It is therefore no wonder that the effort was made to make it conform in some measure to normal religious thought, and for this reason to strengthen its injunctions to faith in God and also to insert extra expressions of this kind. ii, 26; iii, 17; vii, 18b, 26b; viii, 5, 12b, 13a*a*; xi, 9b; xii, 7b may perhaps represent later adjustments of this kind, for in a number of cases, if they are removed, the line of thought becomes clearer and the context more intelligible.

The conclusion is also an addition by a later hand—hardly xii, 9–11 (p. 493), but surely xii, 12–14. Here we seem to have two different additions, added one after the other, v. 12 and vv. 13–14. The one (v. 12) complains of too much writing of books and too zealous study, and probably in this is less concerned to demand a generally applicable moderation in such matters as to warn against the propagating and study of teachings other than those of the master Koheleth —it thus enjoins *iurare in verba magistri*. The other (vv. 13–14) indicates the

---

[39] Irwin, 'Ecclesiastes viii, 2–9' JNESt 4 (1945), pp. 130 f.
[40] Reines, 'Koheleth viii, 10' JJSt 5 (1954), pp. 86–7.
[41] Cf. the Teachings of Ptah-hotep (AOT, p. 33; ANET, pp. 412–14) and of Amenemhet (ANET, pp. 418–19). Cf. above, p. 83, n. 3.

fear of God which is aware of divine judgement as the one point which in the end alone matters.

§ 69. LAMENTATIONS

Literature: (a) Commentaries (i) Series: ADT: Weiser (²1962); BK: Kraus (²1960); BOuT: Wambacq (1957); Cent. B: Peake (1910); Echter-B: Nötscher (1947); HAT: Haller (1940); HK: Loehr (²1906); HS: Paffrath (1932); HSAT: Loehr (1923); IB: Meek, Merrill (1956); Jerusalem-B: Gelin (²1959); KAT: Rudolph (²1962); KeH: Thenius (1855); KHC: Budde (1898); LBC: Kuist (1960); SAT: Staerk (²1920); Schmidt (²1923); Soncino-B: Goldman (²1952); SZ: Oettli (1889); Torch-B: Knight (1955); TU: Smit (1930); UAHC: Bettan (1950).

(ii) Single Commentaries: Wiesmann (1954).

(b) Other Works: Driver (§ 67); Gottwald, *Studies in the Book of Lamentations* (1954); Janssen, *Juda in der Exilszeit* (FRLANT 69, 1956), pp. 9–12; 'Das Buch der Threni'; Loehr, 'Der Sprachgebrauch des Buches der Klagelieder' ZAW 14 (1894), pp. 31–50; 'Sind Thr. iv und v makkabäisch?' (*ib.*, pp. 51–9); 'Threni iii und die jeremianische Autorschaft des Buches der Klagelieder' ZAW 24 (1904), pp. 1–16; 'Alphabetische und alphabetisierende Lieder im AT' ZAW 25 (1905), pp. 173–98; May (p. 377, n. 26) and on this Baumgartner, ThR 13 (1941), p. 161; Nötscher, 'Schicksal und Freiheit' Bibl 40 (1959), pp. 446–62, cf. pp. 459–62; Noth, 'La catastrophe de Jérusalem en l'an 587 avant Jésus-Christ et sa signification pour Israël' RHPhR 33 (1953), pp. 81–102 = 'Die Katastrophe von Jerusalem im Jahre 587 vChr und ihre Bedeutung für Israel' *Ges. Stud. z. AT* (²1960), pp. 346–71; Rinaldi, *Le Lamentazioni* (1953); Robinson, 'Notes on the Text of Lamentations' ZAW 51 (1933), pp. 255–9; Rudolph, 'Der Text der Klagelieder' ZAW 56 (1938), pp. 101–122; van der Straeten,' La Métrique des Lamentations' *Mélanges de Philologie Orientale* (Liège, 1932), pp. 193–201; Thureau-Dangin,'Une lamentation sur la dévastation du temple d'Ištar' RA 33 (1936), pp. 103–11; Westermann, *Jeremia und Klagelieder* (1956); Wiesmann, 'Die literarische Art der Klagelieder des Jeremias' ThQ 110 (1929), pp. 381–428; 'Der geschichtliche Hintergrund des Büchleins der Klagelieder' BZ 23 (1935/6), pp. 20–43; 'Der Verfasser der Klagelieder ein Augenzeuge?' Bibl 17 (1936), pp. 71–84.

Cf. also Literature §§ 15, 46, 126.

1. *The name of the book*. In Hebrew manuscripts and printed editions the book is normally given the title אֵיכָה, from the opening word of chs. i, ii, iv, אֵיכָה *Ah, how!*, the characteristic opening of the funeral dirge (p. 94). But according to Rabbinic references such as the Talmud passage bab. Baba Batra 15a, the older name was rather קִינוֹת *funeral dirges* (pp. 94–8). This corresponds to the title given to the book in the Greek, Latin and English translations—θρῆνοι, *lamentationes*, Lamentations, except that here, at least usually, there is added Ἰερεμίου, *Jeremiae prophetae*, of Jeremiah, or the like, and thus the ascription of the poems to Jeremiah, which must be considered further at a later stage (p. 505), is expressed in the title too. In consequence, as will be seen later (p. 569), the book is placed immediately after the book of Jeremiah.

2. *Structure and contents*. The book is divided into five independent poems which coincide with its five chapters. The first four are alphabetic acrostics. In the first, second and third there are three verses to each letter, though the first and second have only the first verse of each group of three beginning with the

appropriate letter, and the other two verses in the group may begin with any letter, whereas the third poem has each of the three lines of each group beginning with the same letter. In the fourth poem, there are only two verses to each letter, with the first of these beginning with the appropriate letter while the second is not so determined. Ch. v is not an alphabetic acrostic, but is linked with the alphabetic structure in that it contains 22 verses corresponding to the number of the letters of the alphabet (p. 569). In addition, the first poem differs from the second, third and fourth in that it follows the normal order of the letters of the alphabet—with ע ' before פ *p*, whereas the others put the verses beginning with פ before those beginning with ע. This shows that the first poem comes from a compiler different from that of the second to fourth, or else that it has had a different transmission from them.

The alphabetic acrostic structure of the first four poems means, as in the case of the alphabetic psalms ix+x, xxv, xxxiv, xxxvii, cxi, cxii, cxix, cxlv, that they have an even looser order of thought than is in any case commonly true of Hebrew poetry. It is therefore no matter for surprise that the presentation of ideas does not run smoothly on, but gives the impression of leaping from one point to another, and sheds first one light and then another on the matter which is being sung or rather lamented. The subject-matter with which all five poems are concerned, even the third (pp. 502–3), is the fall of Jerusalem in 587 and the disconsolate condition of the city arising from this. The second and fourth poems contain in this respect the most concrete references to the catastrophe. In ii, 7 we hear the echo of the noise of the conquerors who have broken into the Temple. ii, 9 describes very vividly the destruction of the gates. In iv, 17 there is reference to the moment during the siege when it was believed possible to reckon on Egyptian help (Jer. xxxvii, 5), and iv, 19–20 picture the pursuit and capture of those who escaped with the king from the besieged city (II Kings xxv, 4–7). The fifth song, however, laments over the terrible consequences of the disaster (vv. 2–9). The other poems are less vivid and employ stereotyped metaphors and phrases for the description of the distress, as for example the picture of captivity in the pit, and of being overwhelmed by water (iii, 53–4).

3. *Literary type.* The interpretation of the poems is in large measure dependent upon the understanding of their literary type. Poems 1, 2 and 4 are, as their opening word אֵיכָה *Ah, how!* shows, funeral dirges, and in fact political funeral dirges in which it is a political entity, Jerusalem, which is lamented over as dead (p. 95). The third poem is in form an individual song of lamentation (pp. 115–20) and the fifth is a national song of lamentation (pp. 111–14). But in none of them does the type appear in its pure form. They all reveal influences from other types, mixture of styles, and the recognition of this is just as important as the recognition of the type itself.

The first poem begins in vv. 1–11 as a funeral dirge, and describes how disconsolate is the condition of the city, referred to in the third person, how great is the difference between its present distress and its former prosperity; how its inhabitants are deported and now its streets lie there forsaken, while the enemies triumph, and so forth. In vv. 9c and 11c, the style of the funeral dirge is already abandoned, in that here Jerusalem is introduced as speaker: *O Yahweh see my affliction!* Vv. 12–16[1] are completely in the style of the individual song of lamentation. In first person forms, Jerusalem laments its terrible affliction, sometimes with a very marked personification (v. 13 *fire in my bones*), and sometimes with it being hardly possible to conceal the fact that it is a city which is speaking (v. 15 *my princes, my young men*). V. 17, again in the style of the funeral dirge, reintroduces Jerusalem in the third person, but from v. 18 to the end (v. 22), Jerusalem herself again speaks in the style of the lament, and the poem concludes, entirely in accord with this type, with a prayer that she may be heard (v. 21a *Hear*[2]), and with cursing of the enemies (v. 21c *Bring thou*[3]).

The second poem is also a funeral dirge, and up to v. 10 lament is made concerning Jerusalem that Yahweh has punished her so severely that her elders and her maidens mourn (v. 10). In vv. 11–12 the poet himself, however, takes up the word, and states how deeply he is moved by the fate of his city, and particularly by the terrible fate of the little children. He continues to speak (vv. 13–22) as, addressing the city of Jerusalem, he bewails her fate (vv. 13–17), summons her to cry to Yahweh (vv. 18–19), and puts into her mouth the words of the prayer (vv. 20–2).

The third poem, however, is different in nature, for it is an individual song of lamentation (vv. 1–39), with a short transition to the national song of lamentation (vv. 40–7). Then, perhaps interrupted by v. 48 which possibly introduces the poet as speaker, it runs on into the individual song of lamentation again (vv. 49–66). More precisely, vv. 1–18 present laments of all kinds, such as are characteristic of the individual song of lamentation. V. 19 is a prayer, and this then moves over in vv. 20–39 into the expression of trust (vv. 20–4), and into reflection on the meaning of suffering (vv. 25–39). With v. 40 there appears in place of the first person singular the first person plural form, evidently occasioned by the fact that the next three lines have to begin with **נ** *n* and that this may most readily be achieved by the use of first person plural forms beginning with **נ** *n*. The plural forms continue to v. 47. Vv. 40–7 contain first, in vv. 40–2, the speakers' summons to themselves to repentance, and this then runs on into a renewed lament in vv. 43–7. V. 48, which was probably originally followed by v. 51, contains a lament, again in the singular. It is usual to see in the 'I' of this verse the poet himself, because it bewails the *downfall of the daughter of my people*. But from v. 52 onwards, or probably already from v. 49 onwards, the 'I' certainly does not refer to the poet, but to the unfortunate(s). Thus in v. 48 too, in spite of the differentiation between the 'I' and the 'daughter of my people', which are then in reality one and the same, the 'I' will be the unfortunate. This remarkable dissection is to be found elsewhere too, for example in the 'Ebed-Yahweh poems (pp. 340–1) and in the song of lament and consolation for Jerusalem which appears in the second part of the book of Baruch (iv, 9b–16, 17–29. Cf. p. 593). The lament extends to v. 54, and there follows in vv. 55 ff. the expression of the certainty of being heard, and this in the form of the narration of the deliverance (to v. 62) derived from the song of thanksgiving

---

[1] Freehof, 'Note on Lam. i, 14' JQR 38 (1947/48), pp. 343 f.

[2] Reading שְׁמַע instead of *they have heard* 𝔐.

[3] Reading הָבֵא instead of *thou hast brought* 𝔐.

(pp. 121–4). This then passes over into the request itself and the cursing of the enemies (vv. 63–6).

In spite of the fact that the poem is in large measure in the style of the individual song of lamentation, there ought never to have been any doubt that it was composed from the first with reference to the disaster to Jerusalem. Even the fact that it begins *I am the man*, whereas elsewhere Jerusalem is normally referred to in the feminine as the city, does not provide an argument against this. For on the one hand the change over to '*We*' (vv. 40–7) can only be understood if the poet had from the outset a plural entity in mind, Jerusalem or Judah, and on the other hand the placing of the third poem with the others which clearly apply to the disaster to Jerusalem, represents at the very least the oldest commentary upon the poem that we have. There is no reason for trusting this oldest commentary less than later explanations and modern feelings. If the strong personification of Jerusalem and most of all its equation with a man is very difficult for us to appreciate, we must simply remember that the Israelites felt quite differently in this respect. Thus in the first poem, which clearly refers to Jerusalem, in the midst of elements which fit the city there is also one which pictures Jerusalem as a sick body (i, 13; cf. Isa. i, 5–6), and this is the same picture which appears here in iii, 4. The beginning of the third poem, *I am the man*, is thus clearly to be understood as implying that a suffering figure is presupposed as well known,[4] and here Jerusalem says of itself: '*I am this sufferer.*' In favour of this interpretation is also the threefold underlining of the 'I' at the beginning.

The fourth song is another funeral dirge, and keeps to this style as far as v. 16 in that here Jerusalem or Judah is referred to in the third person. But vv. 17–20 are in the first person plural in the style of the national song of lamentation, and in vv. 21–2 Edom and Zion are addressed by the poet, in that the cup of wrath is held in prospect for Edom too, whereas Zion appears as one who has sufficiently atoned.

The fifth poem is a pure national song of lamentation, which describes in moving words, in prayer and lament, the terrible distress of those who have remained behind in Jerusalem and Judah, and lays this distress before God. It begins (v. 1) with the prayer to Yahweh that he will look at the distress, describes the distress itself in vv. 2–18, and closes, after a hymnic statement about Yahweh (v. 19), with the prayer to him that he would change Jerusalem's fortunes (vv. 20–2).

4. *Date of composition.* As far as the date of composition of the poems is concerned, we may say that they must all have originated after 587. Since the second, fourth and fifth poems contain vivid recollections of the disaster itself, or vividly describe the terrible distress brought about by it, we must not bring them down too far from 587, and in any case we must suppose them to have been composed before 538, the year which again brought new hopes. The first and third poems are less colourful, but since they too know nothing of hope of an improvement in the situation, it will be most natural to place them before 538,

---

[4] Cf. Vermès, 'Quelques Traditions de la Communauté de Qumrân' CahSi 9 (1955), pp. 25–58, cf. p. 57.

unless we are to assume, which is certainly not impossible, that these poems were composed after 538 for a festival held as a memorial to the fall of Jerusalem (cf. Zech. vii, 1–3+viii, 18–19). The dates of composition suggested by Sellin* for the single poems are listed below. Rudolph assigns the first to the year 598, the second and fourth to 587, the third and fifth to a time shortly after the disaster of that year, whereas Gottwald assigns all five to the exilic period, and at the same time ascribes the first four to the same poet.

5. *Place of composition.* Nothing certain can be ascertained as to the place of their composition, whether it was in Palestine or in the Exile. On the one hand, the condition of Jerusalem lying desolate after 587 is so vividly described that it seems essential to think of a poet who is actually in the land (ii, 10; v, 4, 8, 18).[5] On the other hand, emphasis is laid upon those moments of the disaster which must also be unforgettable particularly for the exiles (ii, 7, 12, 14, 20, 21; iv, 3–4, 10, 17–20). We must also bear in mind that, as the example of Ezekiel shows especially, the exiles were often in thought in Jerusalem and were also continually kept informed of the conditions there, so that in fact an exile too could vividly describe the situation in the desolate city of Jerusalem. Again, the fact that the second and fourth poems appear to be dependent upon the language of Ezekiel,[6] does not argue conclusively for a compiler living in the Exile. Ezekiel's message was certainly very soon known among those who were left in the land. We must therefore be content not to have any certain answer to the question as to where the poet—or poets, since we must assume more than one—was living. Sellin* believed, it is true, that he could give a more precise answer. According to him, the second and fourth poems were composed at the beginning of the Exile in Babylonia, and the first was composed there towards its end, whereas the fifth was composed between 550 and 520 in Jerusalem, and the third, probably likewise of Palestinian origin, is probably to be assigned to the fifth century. Rudolph, on the other hand, regards Palestine as the place of origin of all five poems.

6. *The occasion of the poems.* The occasion for the composition of the poems is clear, for they were all composed in recollection of the fall of Jerusalem. But it can hardly be decided with certainty whether they are expressions of personal distress at the disaster which were then taken into use at festivals of mourning, or whether they were from the first composed with a view to use at such mourning festivals, for recitation at them. The genuineness of the feeling which is expressed in them does, however, make the first possibility seem the more probable. Without suggesting that there is any historical connection between the two, we may make a comparison between these poems and Sumerian laments about 1,000 years older, namely those on Ibbisin of Ur,[7] and on the downfall of Ur[8] and of Accad.[9]

[5] Buccellati, 'Gli Israeliti di Palestina al tempo dell'esilio Bibbia e Oriente 2 (1960), pp. 199–210.

[6] Löhr, 'Der Sprachgebrauch des Buches der Klagelieder' ZAW 14 (1894), pp. 31–50.

[7] Falkenstein, 'Die Ibbīsîn-Klage' WdO 1 (1947/52), pp. 377–84; Falkenstein and von Soden, *Sumerische und akkadische Hymnen und Gebete* (1953), pp. 189–92, 376.

[8] Falkenstein and von Soden (see previous note), pp. 192–213, 376 f.; ANET, pp. 455–63. Lit. § 126.

[9] Falkenstein and von Soden (see previous note), pp. 187–9, 376; Güterbock (1934) p. 50, n. 56), pp. 24–37.

7. *The poet himself.* It would be an idle task to endeavour to discover the actual poet or poets. We have to be content with the moving beauty of the poems themselves. The tradition, attested already by 𝕲, is that Jeremiah composed them, and this tradition has again and again found learned and eloquent advocates, most recently in Wiesmann. But they do not fit at all with the picture which we get of Jeremiah from his book. The historical Jeremiah who had proclaimed the coming disaster as the will of Yahweh (xxxvii, 6–10), would, if he had remained in the land, have exhorted humble acceptance of what had happened in accordance with the divine will, and loyal obedience to the Babylonian authorities (xxix, xlii, 7–22), and at the same time he would have envisaged a new time of salvation (cf. xxxii), but he would hardly have lamented as is done in the poems. On the other hand, we can readily understand how Jeremiah, the prophet who lived through the disaster in all its stages and outwardly as well as inwardly suffered most intensely in it, should have appeared to later generations as the compiler of these laments on the fall of Jerusalem. It is immaterial whether the statement in II Chron. xxxv, 25, that Jeremiah composed a lament on Josiah and that this poem was written *in the laments* (עַל־הַקִּינוֹת), is historical or not.

8. *The origin of the collection.* As regards the origin of the collection, we can only say that it was certainly occasioned by a practical need, the need namely to have together the songs sung at the festival of remembrance for the destruction of Jerusalem. It remains uncertain when and where the collection came into being. But we should certainly think of Jerusalem, and, so far as date is concerned, it is hardly necessary to come down further than the fifth century B.C.

§ 70. ESTHER

Literature: (a) Commentaries (i) Series: ATD: Ringgren (²1962); Echter-B: Stummer (1950); HAT: Würthwein (1964); HK: Siegfried (1901); HS: Schildenberger (1941); HSAT: Steuernagel (1923); IB: Anderson, Lichtenberger (1954); ICC: Paton (1908); Jerusalem-B: Barucq (²1959); KeH: Bertheau-Ryssel (²1887); KHC: Wildeboer (1898); KV: Aalders (1947); Montserrat-B: Girbau (1960); SAT: Haller (²1925); Soncino-B:Goldman (²1952); SZ: Oettli (1889); Torch B: Knight (1955); TU: Smit (1930); UAHC: Bettan (1950).

(ii) Single Commentaries: Scholz (1892).

(b) Other Works: Bickerman, 'The Colophon of the Greek Book of Esther' JBL 63 (1944), pp. 339–62; 'Notes on the Greek Book of Esther' PAAJR 20 (1950), pp. 101–33; Christian, 'Zur Herkunft des Purim-Festes' *Nötscher-Festschr.* (1950), pp. 33–7; Driver, 'Problems and Solutions' VT 4 (1954), pp. 225–45, cf. pp. 235–8; Erbt, *Die Purimsage in der Bibel* (1900); Gaster, *Purim and Hanukkah in Custom and Tradition* (1950); Gunkel, *Esther* (1916, 1958); Haupt, *Purim* (1906); Hinz, 'Zu den altpersischen Inschriften von Susa' ZDMG 95 (1941), pp. 222–57; Hoschander, *The Book of Esther in the Light of History* (1923); Jampel, *Das Buch Esther auf seine Geschichtlichkeit kritisch untersucht* (1907); de Menasce, 'Observations sur l'inscription de Xerxès à Persépolis' RB 52 (1944), pp. 124–32; Moreau, 'Un nouveau témoin du texte latin du livre d'Esther' NC3 (1951), p. 398; Morris, 'The Purpose of the Book of Esther' ET 42 (1930/31), pp. 124–8; Motzo, 'La storia del testo di Ester' Ric Rel 3 (1927), pp. 205–8; 'Il testo di Ester in Guiseppe' StMSR 4 (1928), pp. 84–105; *La versione latina di Ester secondo i LXX* (1928); 'I testi greci di Ester' StMSR 6 (1930), pp. 223–31; Ringgren, 'Esther and Purim' SEA 20 (1956), pp. 5–24; Rudolph, 'Text-kritisches zum Estherbuch' VT 4 (1954), pp. 89–90; Ruth Stiehl, 'Das Buch Esther' WZKM 53 (1956), pp. 4–22; 'Esther, Judith und Daniel' in Altheim and Stiehl, *Die aramäische Sprache unter den Achaimeniden*, fasc. II (1960), pp. 195–213; Striedl, 'Unter-suchungen zur Syntax und Stilistik des hebräischen Buches Esther' ZAW 55 (1937), pp. 73–108; Torrey, Review of Vol. III, 1 of the Brooke-McLean-Thackeray LXX, JBL 61 (1942), pp. 130–6; 'The Older Book of Esther' HThR 37 (1944), pp. 1–40; Ungnad 'Keilinschriftliche Beiträge zum Buch Esra und Ester 'ZAW 58 (1940/41), pp. 240–4 59 (1942/43), p. 219; Winter, 'Qumran and the Book of Esther' The Jewish Chronicle No. 4602 (July 5, 1957), p. 16.

Cf. also Literature §§ 84, 126.

1. *Contents.* Since Vashti, the wife of Ahasuerus (Xerxes 485–465), refuses to appear at a feast held by the king in his palace at Susa, she is degraded from her position of honour (ch. i).[1] To find a new wife, the king sends out officers[2] to gather to his palace the most beautiful maidens from the whole realm, among them the Jewess Esther, the adopted daughter of one Mordecai who had been exiled in 598 with Jehoiachin by Nebuchadnezzar. It is she, the most beautiful, who becomes queen, without the king knowing anything of her Jewish blood. At about the same time as she is made queen, Mordecai rescues the king's life by the discovery of a conspiracy (ii). The vizier Haman, who stands in high favour with the king, resolves, in order to gain revenge on Mordecai whom he hates, to destroy all the Jews who live in the Persian empire, and the day is determined by lot (פּוּר *pûr*) as the thirteenth day of the twelfth month, i.e. Adar (February–March). The king grants him the necessary powers (iii). When Esther is informed by Mordecai of the destruction which threatens her people, Esther resolves, in spite of the risk to her life which this involves, to go un-bidden into the king's presence, to request from him deliverance for her people (iv). The king receives his wife graciously, and at her request comes with Haman to a banquet which she arranges, and then agrees that they will both come to the banquet which the queen has planned for the following day. On his return from the first banquet, Haman is again provoked by Mordecai's refusal to show him reverence. He therefore resolves to ask the king the next morning for the execution of Mordecai, and has gallows erected ready for this (v). During the night which follows, the king is reminded of the great kindness which Mordecai had shown him some time before, and so when Haman appears in the palace to make his request early the following day, the king lays on him the duty of showing to Mordecai in his name the highest honours (vi).

On the evening of the second banquet, the queen implores the king to spare her own life and the lives of her people, and points out Haman who is also present as the originator of the scheme of destruction. While the king has gone out into the garden for a moment, Haman throws himself upon the queen's couch, imploring mercy. The king, when he comes in again and sees Haman lying before the queen, believes that he was attempting to ravish her, and as a

[1] Duchesne-Guillemin, 'Les noms des eunuques d'Assuerus' Muséon 66 (1953), pp. 105–108: on i, 10; Gaster, 'Esther i, 22' JBL 69 (1950), p. 381; Klíma, 'Iranische Miszellen' ArOr 26 (1958), pp. 603–16, cf. pp. 614 f. on i, 3.

[2] Klíma, 'Pāqīd-διδάσκαλος' ArOr 23 (1955), p. 481.

punishment has him hanged on the gallows intended for Mordecai. Esther inherits Haman's possessions, and Mordecai his office (vii, 1–viii, 2). At Esther's renewed request, the king has an edict put forth which permits the Jews to cut down on the thirteenth of Adar all who rise against them (viii, 3–17). On the thirteenth of Adar, the Jews kill 510 men in Susa, and 300 men on the fourteenth of Adar which at Esther's request is also granted to them for Susa itself. In the remainder of the empire, however, 75,000 were killed by the Jews on the thirteenth of Adar. As a result, the fifteenth of Adar is decreed as a feast day for the Jews in Susa, and for those in the provinces, the fourteenth. Mordecai and Esther write letters to the whole of Jewry to enjoin upon them the duty of observing the feast of Purim (ix). Further information concerning Ahasuerus and Mordecai is to be found in the Chronicle of the kings of Media and Persia (x).

2. *The type of narrative which the book presents.* The book contains a whole series of historical inaccuracies and inexactitudes. If Mordecai was deported in 598 by Nebuchadnezzar, he was over a hundred years old during the reign of Xerxes (485–465). But this is clearly not the view of the narrator, for he thinks rather that Xerxes is the next successor or one of the next successors of Nebuchadnezzar on the throne of the empire. In the same way as in the book of Daniel, the historical perspective has here been foreshortened (p. 521). The personalities who stand in the centre of the narrative, all of them in high and prominent positions, are, with the exception of the king himself, unknown to us in the sources which we have for Persian history. Furthermore, many of the features of the narrative bear the mark of legend or fiction, and appear also in other literatures. Thus the motif of the king wishing to show off his wife appears in the story of Candaules and Gyges in Herodotus I, 8–13. On the other hand it is clear that the compiler knew something about the governmental organisation of the Persian empire and about the lay-out of the royal palace at Susa. It is also clear that he has taken from a historical event the details with which he has depicted the tension between pagans and Jews leading to the institution of a festival, however much he has exaggerated this so that it has become a grotesque fantasy. We usually call a prose work which is thus based upon a historical foundation a historical novel,[3] and the name does in fact excellently characterise the nature of the Esther narrative.

This judgement concerning the book is generally accepted. But no final decision has yet been reached concerning either the ultimate source of the legendary and fictional motifs, or the historical event which is presupposed by the narrative. So far as the first point is concerned, Jensen[4] and Zimmern[5] have assumed a two-fold mythical basis for the narrative, namely on the one hand a myth of the overcoming of the Elamite gods Human-Haman and Mashti-Vashti

---

[3] Altheim, *Roman und Dekadenz* (1951); *Der unbesiegte Gott* (1957), pp. 67–77: 'Der Roman: Heliodor von Emesa'; Lesky, *Geschichte der griechischen Literatur* (1957/58), pp. 776–88: 'Prosaroman und Epistolographie'; Szepessy, 'Die Aithiopika des Heliodoros und der griechische sophistische Liebesroman' AcAnt [B] 5 (1957), pp. 241–59; Tarn, *The Greeks in Bactria and India* ([2]1951), pp. 463 f.

[4] 'Elamitische Eigennamen. Ein Beitrag zur Erklärung der elamitischen Inschriften' WKZM 6 (1892), pp. 47–70, 209–26. Lit. § 126.

[5] Schrader, *Die Keilinschriften und das AT* ([3]1903), pp. 514–20.

by the Babylonian Marduk-Mordecai and Ishtar-Esther, and on the other hand the well-known myth of the conquest of the power of chaos, here symbolised by Haman, by the creator god Marduk-Mordecai. This suggestion is by no means certain, since Mordecai, for example, need not be the name of a god, but could be regarded as a shortened form of a personal theophoric name containing the divine name Marduk,[6] and, as far as Esther is concerned, this name may be readily explained from the Persian as 'star',[7] and this would make it a normal woman's name. But if the names are not divine names but ordinary personal names, then we are not dealing with myth but with legend or fiction or perhaps saga, and the experiences related about the various personages—the exaltation of an unknown Jewish girl to be Persian queen, the promotion of a Jew to the position of vizier, etc.—are to be judged exactly like the stories of Daniel in Dan. i–vi or of Zerubbabel in III Esdras iii–iv (pp. 575–6). It is clear that in the Jewish eastern diaspora there was a great love for stories of the success of Jews at the court, and also of the ill-will and envy to which they were exposed. Like all such narratives, they are not simply fancies, but are linked to actual events, as for example the glorious career of Nehemiah at the court of Artaxerxes I (pp. 544–5). They do, however, brighten reality with a legendary glow.

3. *The feast of Purim*. The narrative turns upon the feast of Purim, and forms its festal legend. It was this from the outset and not by secondary application, and it has remained so to the present day (pp. 511–12). According to iii, 7, Haman determined by the *pûr* (פּוּר) the day appropriate for the extermination of the Jews, and in ix, 20–32 the celebration of the day by the Jews is explicitly based on the fact that the day fixed by the *pûr* as the day on which destruction was to be for the Jews has been changed into a day of destruction for their enemies (ix, 24, 26). In view of the total character of the book, it is, however, very unlikely that this was the real origin of the feast and of its name. It is, however, the case that *pûr*, which as a foreign word is translated in iii, 7; ix, 24, 26 by the Hebrew גּוֹרָל *lot*, actually means *lot* in Accadian.[8] In the events, therefore, which gave rise to this festival, it is probable that the use of lots played a part, and the fact that the narrative uses a non-Hebrew word, namely *pûr*, strongly suggests that in this festival there is at least some part played by non-Jewish elements and that we are perhaps dealing with a festival borrowed by the Jews of the eastern diaspora from their Babylonian and Persian environment.

The narrative names Susa[9] as the place of origin of the festival and of the measures which brought about its celebration. This was the capital of the Persian

---

[6] On the name of Mordecai cf. Driver, *Aramaic Documents from the Fifth Century B.C.* (1954), p. 20, n. 2; abridged and revised ed. (1957), p. 56; Ungnad, ZAW 58 (1940/41), pp. 243 f.; 59 (1942/43), p. 219: a text from Borsippa (?) mentioning a Mardukâ as an official of Darius I or Xerxes in Susa.

[7] Yahuda, 'The Meaning of the Name Esther' JRAS (1946), pp. 174–8.

[8] Bea, 'De origine vocis פּוּר' Bibl 21 (1940), pp. 198 f.; Lewy, 'Old Assyrian *puru'um* and *pūrum*' RHA 5 (1939), pp. 116–24; Schröder, *Keilschrifttexte aus Assur verschiedenen Inhalts* (1920), No. 2, 125–7 et passim; cf. Dürr, OLZ 38 (1935), col. 297; Stephens, *Votive and Historical Texts from Babylonia and Assyria* (1937), No. 73; cf. Albright, BASOR 67 (1937), p. 37.

[9] Ghirshman, *Cinq Campagnes de fouilles à Suse 1946–51* (1952).

empire and at the same time the centre of the eastern Jewish diaspora. The most natural assumption under these circumstances is undoubtedly that the festival actually did originate in the eastern Jewish diaspora and probably in Susa itself. This would invalidate the attempt at explaining the personages and situations of the book as merely ciphers and as a stage-setting for the real meaning. Thus it has been suggested that Ahasuerus is really Ptolemy Euergetes II (170–164 and 145–117), Esther his queen Cleopatra III who was friendly to the Jews, and Haman the party at the Ptolemaic court hostile to the Jews;[10] or that Ahasuerus stands for the pretender to the Syrian throne Alexander Balas (153/0 to 145), Esther for the daughter of Ptolemy VI Philometor, who was friendly to the Jews, namely Cleopatra the wife of Balas, and Haman for Nicanor, known from the books of Maccabees as a relentless enemy of the Jews (I Macc. vii, 26–50; II Macc. xv, 1–36);[11] or that Xerxes stands for Herod the Great (40–4 B.C.)[12] and Vashti for Mariamne, his wife from the Maccabean family who was later executed by him.[13] But, as has already been indicated, the feature of the narrative which shows the festival and its name as derived from the opponents of the Jews, is probably to be interpreted as meaning that it was at first a pagan festival, then taken over by the Jews. Three of the possibilities here suggested are deserving of mention: (1) the suggestion made by Zimmern and Jensen in connection with their explanation of the narrative as myth (pp. 507 f.) that the festival derives from the Babylonian New Year festival or from the Babylonian and Persian Sakaia festival; (2) Gunkel's suggestion[14] that the Jewish feast of Purim is an imitation of the Persian festival occasioned by the murder of the Magi (Magophonia) which Herodotus relates in III, 68–79; and 3) the equating, suggested by Lewy[15] who takes up and elaborates earlier surmises, of the feast of Purim with the Persian festival of New Year and All Souls, *Farvardīgān*. These are, however, nothing more than suggestions.[16]

Since we have hardly any information at all about the conditions in the eastern Jewish diaspora in the period which here comes in question, namely from the fourth to second centuries B.C., it is hardly surprising that we can give no further information about a festival which came into being there at that time. It could even be the case that, as the story here tells—though admittedly with enormous exaggeration and misrepresentation of the actual situation and events —it was the removal, quite unhoped for and so the more thankfully received, of a terrible danger which threatened the Jews in Susa and perhaps more exten- sively, which occasioned the festival, and that this then developed into a festival observed by the whole of the eastern Jewish diaspora. In the development, at one and the same time the cause and the result of this enlargement of its signifi- cance, the legend connected with it was elaborated with all manner of legendary

[10] So Willrich, Judaica (1900), pp. 1–28.
[11] So Haupt, *Purim* (1906).
[12] See below, p. 623, n. 1; p. 643, nn. 16–17.
[13] So Lévy, 'La répudiation de Vasti' *Actes XXI Congr. Intern. Orient* ([1948] 1949), pp. 114 f.
[14] Esther (1916, 1958), p. 115; RGG II (²1928), col. 379.
[15] 'The Feast of the 14th Day of Adar' HUCA 14 (1939), pp. 127–51.
[16] Doniach, *Purim or the Feast of Esther. An Historical Study* (1933).

and fictional elements. At any rate, the assumption here made of the danger of a pogrom facing the Jews in Susa does not in itself raise any difficulties. For if we had not had the chance find of the Elephantine Papyri (p. 23, n. 24; p. 24, n. 27) to illuminate so vividly the conditions on the Nile island of Elephantine towards the end of the fifth century B.C., how could we have possibly known of the hostility to the Jews there at that time? The date of origin of the festival cannot be determined with so much certainty as its place. The narrative traces it to the period of Persian rule, and this may be right. We certainly should not think of the time of Xerxes' rule, for this, as ch. i shows, already lies in the mists of antiquity, shrouded in legend. But the latest period of Persian rule, i.e. about the middle of the fourth century, could very well be considered as the time of the festival's origin. Admittedly if the festival and the book are to be dated so early, we should have to assume that both remained at first restricted to the eastern diaspora since they first became known in Palestine in the second century B.C.

The assumption is a possible one. The interpretation of the book and the festival as a reflection of the religious struggles of the Maccabean period, recently revived by Pfeiffer*, is hardly credible. But the assumption that it was these struggles which first made the Jewish community of Palestine, which had up till then existed with comparatively little molestation, ready and willing to accept a festival shot through with fanatical hatred against its enemies, is unobjectionable. But if it seems improbable that a book which had come into being in the eastern diaspora together with the festival which forms its central point could have remained unknown to Palestinian Judaism for two centuries, then we should have to bring down its dating towards the end of the second century B.C., in other words close to the time of the origin of the Greek translation of the book (§ 85), though this leaves open the possibility that it had used older material, which is probable. Ruth Stiehl has recently produced significant arguments for the dating of the book between roughly 165 and 145 B.C. In any case, Ben Sira writing in about 190 B.C. in his 'Praise of the Fathers' (xliv–xlix) does not mention Esther and Mordecai, whereas II Maccabees, compiled in about 50 B.C. clearly presupposes that the Purim feast was known and celebrated in the west. It designates Nicanor day as lying one day before the day of Mordecai (xv, 36). Whether the book and festival underwent alterations when taken over by Palestinian Judaism, and how far these went, can hardly now be established. Nevertheless, as Steuernagel* has shown, there are important grounds for assuming this, in that the date of the feast of Purim has been assimilated to that of Nicanor day.

4. *The appendix ix, 20–x, 3.* ix, 19, which is probably to be completed from 𝔊, with its statement introduced by *Therefore . . . celebrate . . .*, to the effect that the Jews in the open country celebrate the feast on the fourteenth of Adar whereas those in the cities celebrate on the fifteenth, forms a good conclusion. There are differences in form and content between this verse and ix, 20–32, in form in that the language in ix, 20–32 is much more stilted and clumsy than in the previous passages, and in content in that according to ix, 20–32 no distinction is made between the Jews of the country and of the town, but that the

celebration is prescribed for them all on the fourteenth and fifteenth of Adar.[17] For these reasons, we should probably agree with Bertheau, Steuernagel*, Pfeiffer*, Bentzen* and others in regarding ix, 20–32 as a later appendix designed to justify a practice which has been altered in the meantime. With ix, 20–32, we must also exclude the concluding remarks about Ahasuerus and Mordecai in x, which in their chronicle style do not conform well with the fictional style of the Esther narrative.[18] Here x, 2 refers to the *Book of the history of the kings of Media and Persia* as the source for further information concerning Ahasuerus and Mordecai. This sounds just like the well-known references to the *Book of the history of the kings of Israel* or *of Judah* in the books of Kings (pp. 285–6), and the reference in Esther may well be regarded as an artificial imitation of that, and the *Book of the history of the kings of Media and Persia* may be nothing but a fiction. We must nevertheless reckon with the possibility that there really was such a book, of midrashic kind, compiled by Jews and containing beside historical information all manner of legends and sagas, and in particular concerned with the experiences of Jews at the Persian court (p. 508).

5. *The additions to the book of Esther.* The appendix in ix, 20–x, 3, which is relatively old and in any case was already present at the time of 𝕲 in about the middle of the first century B.C., must be distinguished from the expansions of the narrative which are normally described as the Additions to Esther. The book actually enjoyed tremendous popularity among the Jews and so was not only translated frequently into Aramaic and Greek, but also underwent various expansions mainly designed to give to the book, which is for the most part purely profane, a stronger religious note. These additions will be discussed in more detail in Part IV (§ 85).

6. *Assessment of the book.* In the assessment of the book, we must distinguish between its aesthetic and its ethical and religious value. As a narrative it deserves full recognition. The varied motifs are drawn together into a relatively coherent unity, and are so arranged that the reader, who is naturally thought of as being on the Jewish side, is kept in an ever-increasing state of tension, and at last breathes a sigh of relief when the change of fortune takes place. Likewise the delineation of the chief personages, and in particular of Esther and Haman, is highly successful. But as part of a collection of sacred scriptures this book makes a very strange impression, for it is purely secular, never mentions God at all, but only once (iv, 14) alludes to him timidly with the phrase *from another quarter*. The fact that in spite of all the objections which would militate against its acceptance, it was nevertheless taken into the canon (p. 568), is in the last resort to be explained from the close connection between Jewish religion and the Jewish national spirit. A book which was so closely bound up with the national spirit, and which indeed the people itself regarded as a source of its power, could not be excluded by the religion which was bound up with it. This we can understand. But Christianity, extending as it does over all peoples and races, has neither occasion nor justification for holding on

---

[17] On the two feast days cf. Bickermann (§ 79), p. 242.
[18] Daube, 'The Last Chapter of Esther' JQR 37 (1946/47), pp. 139–47.

to it.[19] For Christianity Luther's remark should be determinative, a remark made with reference to II Maccabees and Esther in his Table Talk: 'I am so hostile to this book and to Esther that I could wish that they did not exist at all, for they Judaize too greatly and have much pagan impropriety.'[20]

§ 71. DANIEL

Literature: (a) Commentaries (i) Series: ATD: Porteous (1962); Botschaft des AT: Kessler ([2]1955); BOuT: Nelis (1954); Camb. B: Driver (1900); Cent. B: Charles (1913); Connaître la Bible: Steinmann (1961); Echter-B: Nötscher (1948); HAT: Bentzen ([2]1952); HK: Behrmann (1894); Harper's B: Bewer (1955); HS: Goettsberger (1928); HSAT: Marti (1923); IB: Jeffery, Kennedy (1956); ICC: Montgomery ([2]1949); Jerusalem-B: de Menasce ([2]1958); KeH: Hitzig (1850); KHC: Marti (1901); SAT: Haller ([2]1925); Soncino-B: Slotki (1951); SZ: Meinhold (1889); Torch-B: Heaton (1956); TU: Obbink (1932).

(ii) Single Commentaries: Bevan (1892); Charles (1929); Leupold (1949); Linder (1939); Rinaldi (1947); Steinmann (1950); Young (1949).

(b) Other Works: Abel, 'L'ère des Séleucides' RB 47 (1938), pp. 198–213; Aymard, 'Autour de l'avènement d'Antiochos IV' Historia 2 (1953), pp. 49–73, Pl. I; 'Du nouveau sur la chronologie des Séleucides' Rev Ét Anc 57 (1955), pp. 102–12; Baumgartner, *Das Buch Daniel* (1926); 'Neues keilschriftliches Material zum Buche Daniel?' ZAW 44 (1926), pp. 38–56; 'Das Aramäische im Buche Daniel' ZAW 45 (1927), pp. 81–133 = *Zum AT* (1959), pp. 68–123; 'Ein Vierteljahrhundert Danielforschung' ThR 11 (1939), pp. 59–83, 125–44, 201–28; 'Zu den vier Reichen von Daniel ii' ThZ 1 (1945), pp. 17–22; 'Herodots babylonische und assyrische Nachrichten' ArOr 18, 1/2 (1950), pp. 69–106 = *Zum AT* (1959), pp. 282–331; Beek, *Das Daniel-Buch. Sein historischer Hintergrund und seine literarische Entwicklung* (Diss. theol. Leiden, 1935); Bengtson, 'Neue Seleukidenlisten' Historia 4 (1955), pp. 113–14; Bonacker and Volz, 'Eine Wittenberger Weltkarte aus dem Jahr 1529' Die Erde 8 (1956), pp. 154–70 with 8 illustrations; Boutflower, *In and around the Book of Daniel* (1923); *Dadda-'Idri or the Aramaic of the Book of Daniel* (1931); Brownlee, 'The Servant of the Lord in the Qumran Scrolls' BASOR 132 (1953), pp. 8–15; 135 (1954), pp. 33–8, cf. 132, pp. 12–15: 'The Suffering Servant in the Book of Daniel'; Brunet, 'The Book of Daniel' ThD 5 (1957), pp. 58–63; Cavaignac, 'Sur deux dates de l'Antiochus le Grand' RA 50 (1956), pp. 73–84; Dougherty, *Nabonidus and Belshazzar* (1929); Eissfeldt, 'Daniels und seiner drei Gefährten Laufbahn im babylonischen, medischen und persischen Dienst' ZAW 72 (1960), pp. 134–48; Gadd, 'The Harran Inscriptions of Nabonidus' AnSt 8 (1958), pp. 35–92, Pls. I–XVI; 'The Kingdom of Nabuna'id in Arabia' A XXIV IOK (1959), pp. 132–4; von Gall, *Die Einheitlichkeit des Buches Daniel* (Diss. theol. Gießen, 1895); Ginsberg, *Studies in Daniel* (1948); 'The Oldest Interpretation of the Suffering Servant' VT 3 (1953), pp. 400–4; 'The Composition of the Book of Daniel' VT 4 (1954), pp. 246–75; Gross, 'Weltreich und Gottesvolk. Eine theologische Studie zum Buch Daniel' EvTh 16 (1956), pp. 241–51; Gruenthaner, 'The Four Empires of Daniel' CBQ 8 (1946), pp. 72–82, 201–12; Hertlein, *Der Daniel der Römerzeit* (1908); Hoelscher, 'Die Entstehung des Buches Daniel' ThStKr 92 (1919), pp. 113–38; van Hoonacker, 'L'historiographie du livre de Daniel' Muséon 44 (1931), pp. 169–76; Hospers, *Twee problemen betreffende het Aramees van het boek Daniel* (1948); Jepsen, 'Bermerkungen zum Danielbuch' VT 11 (1961), pp. 386–91; Junker, *Untersuchungen über literarische und exegetische Probleme des Buches Daniel* (1932); Kincaid, 'A Persian Prince—Antiochus Epiphanes' Or. Studies

---

[19] Anderson, 'The Place of the Book of Esther in the Christian Bible' JR 30 (1950), pp. 32–43.

[20] Weimar Edition (*Tischreden* vol. 1, 1912), p. 208. Cf. E.T. by W. Hazlitt, *Table Talk* (1909), p. 11.

C. E. Pavry (1933), pp. 209–19; Koch, 'Die Weltreiche im Danielbuch' ThLZ 85 (1960), cols. 829–32; Kolbe, *Beiträge zur syrischen und jüdischen Geschichte* (BWAT 35, 1926), pp. 150–67; Kruse, 'Compositio libri Danielis et idea Filii Hominis' VD 37 (1959), pp. 147–61, 193–211; de Lagarde, Review of Havet, *La modernité des prophètes* (1891), GGA (1891), pp. 497–520; Manni, 'A proposito di una nuova lina babilonese di re ellenistici' Rivista de Filologia 84 (1956), pp. 273–8; Meinhold, *Die Composition des Buches Daniel* (1884); *Beiträge zur Erklärung des Buches Daniel* (1888); Eduard Meyer, *Ursprung und Anfänge des Christentums* II (1922), pp. 184–99; Milik, '"Prière de Nabonide"' RB 63 (1956), pp. 407–15, Pl. I; Möller, *Der Prophet Daniel* (1934); Nelis, 'De vier wereldrijken in het boek Daniël' Bijdragen 15 (1954), pp. 349–62; Noth, 'Zur Komposition des Buches Daniel' ThStKr 98/99 (1926), pp. 143–63; *Das Geschichtsverständnis der at. Apokalyptik* (1954) = *Ges. Stud. z. AT* (²1960), pp. 248–73; Oschwald, *Le livre de Daniel* (1958); Reuter, *Beiträge zur Beurteilung des Königs Antiochos Epiphanes* (Diss. theol. Münster, 1938); Rhodes, 'The Book of Daniel' Interpret. 6 (1952), pp. 436–50; Rowley, *The Aramaic of the OT* (1929); 'The Bilingual Problem of Daniel' ZAW 50 (1932), pp. 256–68; 'Early Aramaic Dialects and the Book of Daniel' JRAS (1933), pp. 777–805; *Darius the Mede and the Four World Empires in the Book of Daniel* (1935, ²1959); 'Some Problems in the Book of Daniel' ET 47 (1935/36), pp. 216–20; 'The Unity of the Book of Daniel' HUCA 23, 1 (1950/1), pp. 233–73) = *The Servant of the Lord* (1952), pp. 235–68; 'The Composition of the Book of Daniel' VT 5 (1955), pp. 272–6; Sachs and Wiseman, 'A Babylonian King List of the Hellenistic Period' Iraq 16 (1954), pp. 202–11, Pls. LII–LIII; Schaumberger (§ 78); Scott, 'I Daniel, the Original Apocalypse' AJSL 47 (1930–31), pp. 289–96; Skeat, *The Reigns of the Ptolemies* (²1954); von Soden, 'Eine babylonische Volksüberlieferung von Nabonid in den Danielerzählungen' ZAW 53 (1935), pp. 81–9; Stevenson, 'The Identification of the Four Kingdoms of the Book of Daniel' Transact. Glasgow Or. Soc. 7 (1934/35), pp. 4–8; Ruth Stiehl (p. 38, n. 23); Swain, 'The Theory of the Four Monarchies' Classical Philology 35 (1940), pp. 1–21; Thilo, *Die Chronologie des Danielbuches* (1926); Torrey, 'Notes on the Aramaic Part of Daniel' Transactions of the Connecticut Academy 15 (1909), pp. 241–82; Vogt, 'Catalogus Cuneiformis Regum Seleucidarum' Bibl 36 (1955), pp. 261 f.; Volz 'Beiträge zu Melanchthons und Calvins Auslegung des Propheten Daniel' ZKG 67 (1956), pp. 93–118; Welch, *Visions of the End* (²1958); Whitcomb, *Darius the Mede. A Study in Historical Identification* (1959); Wolski, 'The Decay of the Iranian Empire of the Seleucids and the Chronology of the Parthian Beginnings' Berytus XII, 1 (1956/57), pp. 35–52; Young, *The Messianic Prophecies of Daniel* (1954); Zimmermann, 'The Aramaic Origin of Daniel viii–xii' JBL 57 (1938), pp. 255–72; 'Some Verses in Daniel in the Light of a Translation Hypothesis' JBL 58 (1939), pp. 349–54; 'Hebrew Translation in Daniel' JQR 51 (1960/61), pp. 198–208.

Cf. also Literature §§ 78, 79, 84, 126.

1. *Contents*. The book tells of experiences and visions of a Jew named Daniel, who was deported from Jerusalem in the third year of Jehoiakim, 605 B.C., by Nebuchadnezzar with others of his compatriots, and was trained at the Babylonian court together with his three friends Hananiah, Mishael and Azariah (i).[1] Daniel is able to divine and then to interpret a dream which Nebuchadnezzar has in the second year of his rule, thus giving an astonishing proof of his wisdom. He is for this reason honoured by the king. At Daniel's own request, the king, however, transfers to his three friends the government of the province of Babylonia which is made over to him (ii).[2] Ch. iii, 1–30 is concerned with

---

[1] Stone, 'A Note on Daniel i, 3' ABR 7 (1959), pp. 69–71.
[2] Altheim, *Weltgeschichte Asiens im griechischen Zeitalter*, II (1948), pp. 180 f.; Baumgartner, 'Zum Traumerraten in Daniel ii' AfO 4 (1927), pp. 17–19; Ehrlich, *Der Traum im AT* (1953), pp. 90–113; Löwinger, 'Nebuchadneccár álma Dániel könyvében' [Nebuchadnezzar's Dream in the Book of Daniel] *Semitic Studies Immanuel Löw* (1947), pp. 109–

these three, for they have refused when commanded by the king, to give honour to a statue erected by him. They are therefore thrown into a furnace, but saved in miraculous fashion.[3] iii, 31–iv, 34 relates, in the form of a letter sent by Nebuchadnezzar to all his subjects, how Daniel interpreted to the king a dream which foretold his temporary madness, and how this interpretation was fulfilled. v, 1–vi, 1[4] is concerned with the appearance of a miraculous writing on the wall of the hall in which Belshazzar was holding a lavish banquet, its reading and interpretation by Daniel and the immediate fulfilment of the interpretation,[5] namely that Belshazzar was killed and succeeded by the *sixty-two year old*[6] *Mede Darius*.[7] vi, 2–29 tells of Daniel's miraculous deliverance from the lions' den,[8] into which king Darius (I, 521–485 B.C.) had had him thrown as a punishment for disobeying the prohibition which he had issued, forbidding that for a period of thirty days any prayer or request should be offered to any god or man other than the king.

In these first six chapters, Daniel is referred to in the third person, while besides him and his three friends there appears all the time as chief personage the king then ruling. A common feature of these chapters, or more strictly of ii, iii, iv and vi, in addition to other points, is that they conclude with an acknowledgement by the king of the sole majesty of the Jewish God. In iii, 33; iv, 31–4;[9] vi, 27–8, this is done in a hymn in a naturally rhythmic form.

Chs. vii–xii present, in first person form—with only the introduction of the first and fourth visions containing references to Daniel in the third person (vii, 1–2a; x, 1)—an account of four visions by Daniel. In the first year of Belshazzar he had a vision of four beasts and of the 'Son of Man', interpreted with reference to the downfall of four world empires and the establishment of the final kingdom of the Jews, a vision which contains as an appendix a note of the term of the raging of the last king of the fourth world empire as being *a time and times and half a time*, i.e. three and a half years (vii, 25) (ch. vii).[10]

120; 'Nebuchadnezzar's Dream in the Book of Daniel' *Goldziher Mem. Vol.*, I (1948), pp. 336–52. Lit. § 126.

[3] Alexander, 'New Light on the Fiery Furnace' JBL 69 (1950), pp. 375 f.; Sanders, 'The Burning Fiery Furnace' Theology 58 (1955), pp. 340–5.

[4] Emerton, 'The Participles in Daniel v, 12' ZAW 72 (1960), pp. 262 f.

[5] Alt, 'Zur Menetekel-Inschrift' VT 4 (1954), pp. 303–5; Bauer, 'Menetekel' *Vierter deutscher Münzforschertag zu Halle (Saale)* (1925), pp. 27–30; Eissfeldt, 'Die Menetekel-Inschrift und ihre Deutung' ZAW 63 (1951), pp. 105–14; Kraeling, 'The Handwriting on the Wall' JBL 63 (1944), pp. 11–18; Melkman, 'Daniël v' NThT 28 (1939), pp. 143–50; Rowley, 'The Historicity of the Fifth Chapter of Daniel' JThSt 32 (1930/31), pp. 12–31.

[6] Galling, 'Die 62 Jahre des Meders Darius in Dan. vi, 1' ZAW 66 (1954), p. 152.

[7] Dandamaev, 'About the Dynasty of Achaemenids' [Russian] Palestinskij sbornik 5 (68) (1960), pp. 3–21.

[8] Bentzen, 'Daniel vi. Ein Versuch zur Vorgeschichte der Märtyrerlegende' *Bertholet-Festschrift* (1950), pp. 58–64; Elena Cassin, 'Daniel dans la "fosse" aux lions' RHR 139 (1951), pp. 129–61.   [9] Nober, 'Notulae lexicales' VD 38 (1960), pp. 35–7: on iv, 33 יְבַעֹון.

[10] Caquot, 'Sur les quatre bêtes de *Daniel* vii' Semitica 5 (1955), pp. 5–13; Coppens and Dequeker, *Le fils de l'homme et les Saints du Très-Haut en Dan. vii* (²1961); Frank, 'The Description of the "Bear" in Dn vii, 5' CBQ 21 (1959), pp. 505–7; Haller, 'Das Alter von Daniel vii' ThStKr 93 (1920/21), pp. 83–7; Noth, 'Die Heiligen des Höchsten' NTT 56 (1955), pp. 146–61 = *Ges. Stud. z. AT* (²1960), pp. 274–90; Waterman, 'A Gloss on Darius the Mede in Daniel vii, 5' JBL 65 (1946), pp. 59–61. Cf. also below, p. 518, n. 21; p. 524, n. 40; p. 526, n. 47; Lit. § 126.

In the third year of Belshazzar, Daniel, transported in vision to Susa, sees by the river Ulai a two-horned ram which is thrust down by a he-goat which attacks from the west. The great horn of the victorious he-goat then falls away, and four other horns arise in its place. From one of these there shoots up a horn, small at first, which becomes very powerful and makes a violent attack on the supreme God and his cultus. The angel Gabriel interprets the ram with the two horns as meaning the kings of Media and Persia, the he-goat as the kings of Greece, the one great horn as the first Greek king, the four horns which replace it as four kings which replace him, and the horn which is small at first, as an insolent king who will arise at the end of the days, who will set himself against the supreme God but will then be suddenly destroyed. The desecration of the cultus is here to last 2,300 evenings and mornings (viii, 14), i.e. 1,150 days = three and a half years (ch. viii).[11] *In the first year of Darius, the son of Xerxes, of Median descent,* Daniel is anxious to understand the 70 years prophesied by Jeremiah (xxv, 11–12; xxix, 10) as the duration of Jerusalem's destruction, and brings his anxiety in prayer before God. He receives the revelation that the 70 years signify 70 weeks of years, i.e. 490 years, and at the same time he learns how this period of time is to be fulfilled, and in particular the fact that the last distress of Jerusalem, the removal of the cultus, will last a half week of years (ch. ix).[12]

In the third year of Cyrus (538–529), Daniel experiences his last vision (x–xii). An angel, who has freed himself for a short time from the protecting angel of the Persian empire[13] who is opposed to him, tells Daniel that after Cyrus three more Persian kings will arise and then a Greek king will establish a powerful empire which will, however, soon fall into four parts. The kings of two of these part kingdoms, the king of the south and the king of the north, are continually at war. The last king of the north will then desecrate the sanctuary of the supreme God and will cruelly persecute his adherents. But when he has reached the apex of his power, he will suddenly be destroyed *between the sea and the glorious holy mountain* (xi, 45). In the distress, Michael will assist Daniel's people, and *everyone whose name is written in the book* shall be saved (xii, 1). Many shall rise from the dead, and the wise shall shine like the shining of the firmament (xii, 2–3).[14] Daniel receives the command to keep secret the revelation which he has received *until the time of the end,* together with the information that *Many shall run to and fro, and knowledge shall increase* (xii, 4).[15] He then learns further that the fulfilment of the prophecy will occupy *a time and times*

---

[11] Krauss, 'Some Remarks on Daniel viii, 5 ff.' HUCA 15 (1940), pp. 305–11. Lit. § 126.

[12] Duca, *Le LXX Settimane di Daniele e le date Messianiche* (1951); Lagrange, 'Les Prophéties messianiques de Daniel' RB 39 (1930), pp. 179–98; Lambert, 'Une exégèse arithmétique du chapitre ix de Daniel' NRTh 74 (1952), pp. 409–17; Szydelski, 'De recto sensu vaticinii Danielis 70 hebdomadum' Collectanea Theologica 19 (1938), pp. 59–114; Torrey, 'The Messiah Son of Ephraim' JBL 66 (1947), pp. 253–77, cf. pp. 268–72: Daniel ix, 24–7; Vogt, '70 anni exsilii' Bibl 38 (1957), p. 236.

[13] Bertholet, 'Der Schutzengel Persiens' Or. *Studies Pavry* (1933), pp. 34–40.

[14] Alfrink, 'L'idée de Résurrection d'après Dan. xii, 1–2' Bibl 40 (1959), pp. 355–71; Kossen, 'De oorsprong van de voorstelling der opstanding uit de doden in Dan xii, 2' Ned ThT 10 (1956), pp. 296–301.

[15] Winton Thomas, 'Note on יְשֹׁטְטוּ in Daniel xii, 4' JThSt 6 (1955), p. 226.

and half a time (three and a half years) (xii, 5–7). At the very end, the period still outstanding after the beginning of the desecration of the cultus is given as 1,290 days (xii, 11) and 1,335 days (xii, 12).

Just as in i–vi the narrative occcasionally rises to poetic rhythm, this happens again in vii–xii. In ix and x–xii the whole of the interpretation given to Daniel by the angel is in rhythmic form: ix, 24–7; xi, 2–xii, 3. In viii the interpretation is poetic at least from the moment when it comes to speak of the last heathen king (viii, 23–6). In vii not only is the whole interpretation poetic, but so too is the conclusion of the vision narrative which describes the appearance of the ancient of days and of the judgement court, and the appearance of the 'Son of Man'. The exalted subject-matter demands and receives an exalted form.

2. *The language of the book*. This book shares with the book of Ezra the remarkable feature that it is written partly in Hebrew and partly in Aramaic. i, 1–ii, 4a is in Hebrew, ii, 4b–vii, 28 in Aramaic, and viii, 1–xii, 13 again in Hebrew. The many attempts which have been made to explain this fact may be divided into four groups. (1) There are those who assume the accidental loss of a part of the Hebrew original and its filling out from an Aramaic translation, or who suggest a similar mechanical explanation. (b) There are those who regard Aramaic as the original language of the whole book of Daniel, and its sections in Hebrew, i, 1–ii, 4a, viii–xii as translations from the Aramaic, and only the prayer of Daniel ix, 4–20[16] (p. 529), which is fairly generally regarded as a secondary addition, as being originally in Hebrew. (c) There are those who consider that the author had definite reasons for using the two languages. (d) There are those who regard i–vi as an older, Aramaic book, which was then filled out by the visions of which only the opening (vii) was written in Aramaic, the remainder (viii–xii) in Hebrew. Because of this Hebrew section, the book then had its opening (i, 1–ii, 4a) translated into Hebrew. The first explanation is that adopted for example by Bevan and Goettsberger. Zimmermann and Ginsberg in particular have argued emphatically in favour of the second. The third admits of many variations and has been put forward in very different forms, so that here we must restrict ourselves to the mention of the most recent statements pointing in this direction, namely those of Rowley and Gordon. Rowley assumes that ii–vi was compiled in Aramaic in the Maccabean period. Somewhat later, the same author added vii, also written in Aramaic. But he then discovered that the Hebrew language was more suitable for the visions which were directed less to the ordinary people than to the educated, and so he used Hebrew for the visions of viii–xii. When he later wished to publish the narratives and the visions together, a work which was thus compiled partly in Aramaic and partly in Hebrew, he rewrote the beginning of ii in Hebrew and placed it as i, 1–ii, 4a in front of the whole. Gordon[17] considers that the compiler of our book of Daniel possibly or even probably followed a pattern which may be seen elsewhere. This is the scheme which may be denoted as ABA, found for example in the Code of Hammurabi where the prologue (A)

---

[16] Wambacq, 'Les prières de Baruch (i, 15–ii, 19) et de Daniel (ix, 5–19)' Bibl 40 (1959), pp. 463–75.
[17] *Introduction to OT Times* (1953), pp. 72 f.; *The World of the OT* (1958), pp. 83 f.

and epilogue (A) are poetic, whereas the laws (B) which stand between are in prose, or in the book of Job which begins and ends with prose narratives (A–A), whereas the intervening material is poetry (B). So in the book of Daniel, he thinks the compiler deliberately began in Hebrew (A) and concluded in Hebrew (A), but used Aramaic for the intervening part. The fourth view is attractive to those scholars—as for example Sellin*, Hölscher, Montgomery, Bentzen and many others—who regard the book of Daniel not as the work of one author, but as the combination of an older corpus (i–vi) with the second half of the book (vii–xii) which originated in the Maccabean period. This will become clearer when we have considered the theories put forward to explain the composition of the book, and so we shall have to return later to the question of the change of language (pp. 527–8).

3. *History of criticism.* The claim which the book itself makes—or more properly the claim of its second half which is in the first person—that it was composed by Daniel, who was deported to Babylon in 605 B.C., was accepted by Synagogue and Church as correct. But it has often been questioned, and so already by the Neo-Platonist Porphyry († c. A.D. 304) who in the twelfth book of his polemical work 'Against the Christians' indicated the second century B.C. as the actual date of the book's composition and described the greater part of its 'prophecies' as *vaticinia ex eventu.*[18] Since the end of the eighteenth century, this later dating has become an assured position of scholarship, in spite of the repeated attempts—as for example by Möller (1934), Linder (1939), and Young (1949)—at proving the correctness of the tradition of Synagogue and Church. Opinions differ only as to whether the whole book is to be ascribed to *one* author who lived in the time of the persecution of Jewish religion by Antiochus IV Epiphanes (175–163), i.e. between 167 and 163, or whether it must be assumed that only the second half comes from this period, while the first part is about a century older. In favour of the first view, the point is made—a point generally recognised—that the book as we have it does at first sight give the impression of unity, but the second view is favoured by the fact that in i–vi nothing points specifically to the period of Antiochus IV, whereas in vii–xii there are everywhere quite unmistakable references to his measures directed against the Jewish cultus (vii, 8, 25; viii, 11–14, 24–6; ix, 27; xi, 31–6),[19] Eichhorn* in 1824 decided in favour of this second view. More than half a century later (1884, 1888), Meinhold put forward very much the same view: ii, 24b–vi, 29 come from the period around 300 B.C., and vii is a later appendix to this; i, 1–ii, 4a

[18] von Harnack, *Porphyrius, 'Gegen die Christen'* (AAB 1916, No. 1), pp. 67–74 = Fragm. 43, 44. Fragment 43A, from the prologue of Jerome's Commentary on Daniel, begins thus: Contra prophetam Danielem XII. librum scripsit Porphyrius, nolens eum ab ipso, cuius inscriptus est nomine, esse compositum, sed a quodam qui temporibus Antiochi, qui appellatus est Epiphanes, fuerit in Judaea, et non tam Danielem ventura dixisse, quam illum narrasse praeterita. denique quidquid usque ad Antiochum dixerit, veram historiam continere; si quid autem ultra opinatus sit, quia futura nescierit, esse mentitum. Cf. Archer, *Jerome's Commentary on Daniel* (1958). Lit. § 126.

[19] Aalders, 'De "Gruwel der Verwoesting"' GThT 60 (1960), pp. 1–5; Beek, '"De Gruwel der Verwoesting"' NThT 29 (1940), pp. 237–52; Cotter, 'The Abomination of Desolation' Canadian JTh 4 (1957), pp. 159–64; Rigaux, 'Βδέλυγμα τῆς ἐρημώσεως' (Mc xiii, 14; Mt xxiv, 15)' Bibl 40 (1959), pp. 675–83; Rowley, 'Menelaus and the Abomination of Desolation' *Studia Or. I. Pedersen* (1953), pp. 303–15.

and viii–xii were, however, first added in the Maccabean period to the older work consisting of ii–vi and vii.

Against this von Gall argued for the unity of the book, and ascribed it, with the exception of the secondary addition of Daniel's prayer in ix, 4–20, to the Maccabean period. Marti and Charles followed him substantially. On the other hand, Gunkel,[20] working more from considerations of content than of literary structure, pointed out that at least in vii an ancient myth provided the basis of the material, and Sellin* described i–vii as a biography of Daniel deriving from the third century which was completed in the time of Antiochus IV Epiphanes with small additions such as ii, 33, 43, 45; vii, 8, 20–1, 24–5, and expanded by the addition of viii–xii. Hölscher elaborated his own views from these two: i–vi represent an Aramaic collection of legends deriving from the third century, of which the opening, i, 1–ii, 4a was secondarily translated into Hebrew. In the third century already the collection was extended by the addition of vii. In the time of Antiochus IV, viii–xii were added, and ii and vii annotated so as to make possible the application of the dream in ii and the vision in vii to Antiochus IV, i.e. ii, 41–3*; vii, 7bβ, 8,[21] 11a, 20–2, 24–5. Later still ix, 4–20 and xii, 11–12 were added. Similarly Haller, Montgomery (the latter with reference only to i–vi), and Noth, regard i–vii as pre-Maccabean, though Haller regards vii as the oldest part of the book, belonging to as early as the end of the fourth century, while Noth takes the same view with regard to ii and vii. In this Noth goes further than Hölscher had done in the excision of elements in vii which do not belong to the original material. He regards also vv. 9–10, 13–14,[22] 18, 27 as later additions, i.e. the setting up of the court of judgement and the appearance of the Son of Man, together with the interpretation of these elements in the vision.

Modern scholarship is far from being agreed as to whether Dan. i–xii is a literary unity, deriving from an author active between 167 and 163, or whether it must be assigned to at least two different hands, of which the one compiled (i, 1–ii, 4a) ii, 4b–vi (vii) in the third century, the other (vii) viii–xii in about 165. This divergence of view may be clearly seen in the lively discussion of this question between Ginsberg and Rowley.[23] Ginsberg, if we ignore secondary additions, sees at least five different hands at work in the book; he traces i–vi to an author writing between 292 and 261, vii belongs to 175–67, viii and x–xii are assigned to two further authors to be dated in 166 or 165, and ix to a somewhat later period. Rowley, however, regards the book, apart from some few secondary additions, as a unified work composed by one author, using older material, during the period of Antiochus IV Epiphanes' persecution of the Jewish religion. Of the arguments which Rowley brings forward in favour of his view and against that of Ginsberg, there are two which deserve special

[20] *Schöpfung und Chaos* (1895, 1921), pp. 323–35 *et passim*.

[21] Morenz, 'Das Tier mit den Hörnern, ein Beitrag zu Dan. vii, 7 f.' ZAW 63 (1951), pp. 151–4.

[22] Scott, ' "Behold, He Cometh with Clouds" ' NTS 5 (1958), pp. 127–32.

[23] Cf., in addition to the publications of these two scholars mentioned on pp. 512–3, Rowley's review of Ginsberg, *Studies in Daniel* in JBL 68 (1949), pp. 173–7; Ginsberg's reply *ib.*, pp. 402–7; and Rowley's further reply *ib.* 69 (1950), pp. 201–3.

mention: (i) the emphasis on the fact that the historically inaccurate assumptions that Belshazzar was king and that a Mede, Darius, ascended the throne as successor to this last king of Babylon, are to be found in both halves of the book (vi, i, ix, 1); (ii) the indication that the dating of the first half of the book, with or without vii, in about the middle of the third century or even earlier, is only possible if certain phrases are excised from ii and vii; these phrases do not give the impression of being secondary additions but appear to be quite firmly linked with their context. The excision is thus quite arbitrary. It must be said at the outset that this divergence in the assessment of the formation of the book of Daniel may be explained largely on the grounds that both Rowley and Ginsberg occasionally derive precise verdicts from very imprecise evidence. They are trying to discover more than can here be discovered, and so go against a basic principle which they both recognise as binding (a basic principle moreover which has often been ignored in other contexts in Old Testament scholarship with disastrous results). For in VT 4 (1954), p. 271, Ginsberg declares that 'beyond a certain point it is a mistake to insist upon defining inexact thinking exactly', and Rowley readily agrees in VT 5 (1955), p. 276.

In general, as the account just given indicates, an older basis has been assumed only for i–vi or i–vii. But Junker extends the search for older originals also into viii–xii, and here finds a good deal which he thinks must be older, and which would even fit particularly well in the exilic period in which Daniel is supposed to have lived and prophesied. On a different basis Eerdmans[24] believes it possible to show the probable origin of ii and vii in the exilic period. He does not interpret the four parts of the image in ii and the four beasts in vii as is usually done (pp. 519–22) with reference to four successive world empires—the Babylonian, the Median, the Persian and the Macedonian-Greek—but with reference to the last four Babylonian kings (ii) and the four kingdoms conquered by Cyrus: Egypt, Media, Lydia and Babylonia (vii). A view of the narrative of Nebuchadnezzar's dream (ii) similar to that put forward by Eerdmans has been held by other scholars. Thus according to Löwinger this dream, representing a historical reality and occasioned by Nebuchadnezzar's anxiety about the succession, is to be understood as a retrospect of the Assyrian kings Sargon (gold), Sennacherib (silver), Esarhaddon (bronze), Ashurbanipal and Shamashshumukin (iron and clay). The interpretation of the dream by Daniel constitutes a warning to Nebuchadnezzar, to the effect that he should not appoint two kings, Evil-merodach and Neriglissar, as his successors and so weaken the power of the Babylonian empire just as the appointment by Esarhaddon of two successors, Ashurbanipal and Shamashshumukin, over the Assyrian empire proved disastrous. Here we find scholarship moving back towards the tradition of Synagogue and Church, in that the book of Daniel, or at any rate its basic material, is ascribed to the exilic period. Kruse assumes a basic work dating from the exilic period, which underwent two elaborations, the one in about 300 B.C., the other in 164 B.C.

Enough has been said with regard to the theories concerning the composition and date of origin of the book. But a word must be added concerning the history

---

[24] *De Godsdienst van Israël* II (1930), pp. 49–55; *The Religion of Israel* (1947), pp. 222–7 .

of the interpretation of the book, and in particular of the four empires of ii and vii. The New Testament applied the book's description of the tribulations which should precede the breaking in of the kingdom of God to contemporary events[25] or interpreted it eschatologically (Mark xiii; II Thess. ii, 4). So there followed quite naturally the interpretation of the fourth empire in Daniel as referring to the empire which existed in New Testament times, namely the Roman empire.[26] On this basis, exegesis in the Church, taking the visions to be genuine prophecies of the exilic Daniel, regarded the first empire as the Babylonian, the second as the Persian, the third as the Greek, and the fourth as the Roman, and this scheme has, as is well known, dominated the writing of history down to modern times.[27] But when the book came to be dated between 167 and 163, this carried with it at the same time the recognition that only the proclamation of the imminent coming of the end-time was genuine prophecy. Otherwise the book provides *vaticinium ex eventu* and the description of the distress preceding the end refers to the violent activity of Antiochus IV, and so the historical outlook does not extend beyond the Seleucid period and the interpretation of the fourth kingdom as applying to the Romans was no longer valid. The fourth and last empire must refer to the Greeks, and this meant that since in ii, 38 the reference of the first empire was clearly to the Babylonians, the second and third had to be referred to the Medes and Persians. This became the normal interpretation of the four empires in scholarly circles. Admittedly the older interpretation in the Church did not entirely die out even in critical circles in so far as Lagarde and Hertlein still applied the fourth empire to the Romans, and since they did not believe in a genuine prophecy here, found it necessary to date i–vii, or parts of it, towards the end of the first century A.D.

4. *Date of composition of the book.* If we are to arrive at any kind of firm view amid this confusing wealth of possibilities, it is desirable first to get quite clear just what can be assuredly discovered. This is the date of composition of the book as we now have it, ignoring for the moment some later additions such as ix, 4–20. It can be clearly proved that the book derives from the period between the return of Antiochus IV from his second campaign against Egypt (167) and his death in April 163.[28] For whereas in xi, 29–39 the second campaign is so exactly 'prophesied' that we here clearly have *vaticinium ex eventu*, the genuine prophecy which begins in xi, 40 with *At the time of the end* concerning the king's death, does not accord with the actual course of events. Whether it is possible to narrow down even further the period during which the book could have been composed, and say that it must have been written between the rededication of the Temple celebrated in December 164 and the death of the king, depends upon whether the period of three and a half years envisaged in vii–xii as the duration of the desecration of the Temple is regarded as genuine prophecy or as *vati-*

[25] Hölscher, 'Der Ursprung der Apokalypse Mrk. xiii' ThBl 12 (1933), cols. 193–202.
[26] Cf. also IV Ezra xii, 11. Josephus, *Ant.* X, xi, 7 (§ 276) presents Daniel as predicting the persecution of the Jewish people both by Antiochus IV Epiphanes and by the Romans.
[27] W. Goez, *Translatio Imperii* (1958), pp. 366–77: 'Translatio Imperii und die Auslegung des Buches Daniel'.
[28] Cuadrado Maseda, 'Un viejo problema histórico-exegético: la muerte de Antioco IV' Cultura Bíblica 14 (1957), pp. 23–33. Lit. § 126.

cinium ex eventu. If it is the latter, then the period which is actually available for the origin of the book is narrowed down to a few months. But it is by no means certain that this is so. It is possible that vii, viii, ix and x–xii are not all of one piece, but were written in different stages of the religious persecution. So the 1,150 days of viii, 14, differing from the 1,290 days in xii, 11, and again from the 1,335 days of xii, 12, may most readily be explained on the assumption that the prophecy has been fitted to the actual course of events, and, as it became necessary, the moment of the end was further postponed. As far as xii, 11–12 is concerned, we are very probably dealing with secondary additions, not by the compiler himself. But it is only to be supposed that he too commented on the changing course of events with his four visions in vii–xii.

We may leave the matter there, with the broader period 167–163 in mind. This dating is then supported by a whole series of further observations. The fact that the book was not included in the canon of the prophets (p. 565) shows already that it can only have been composed very late. This is confirmed by the fact that Ben Sira, writing in about 190, does not mention it in his Praise of the Fathers (xliv–l) whereas I Maccabees, compiled probably in about 100 B.C., has in ii, 59–60 a reference to it, more precisely to i, iii and vi. Furthermore, at Qumrān, fragments of several leather or papyrus scrolls have come to light, probably written in the first century B.C., with the Hebrew and Aramaic text of Daniel[29] (p. 683). It is further confirmed by the fact that the author in the prophecy of x–xii, which is really a restrospect up to xi, 39, gives only very incomplete and often incorrect information about the sixth, fifth and fourth centuries, but from the end of the fourth century onwards, down to about 164, he is able to introduce many details, and increasingly so as we approach the period around 164. Among the errors with regard to the earlier period are the following: the assumption of a deportation in the third year of Jehoiakim (605) in i, 1;[30] the view (v) that Belshazzar, as son and successor of Nebuchadnezzar, was the last king of Babylon, whereas in reality three kings succeeded Nebuchadnezzar, of whom the last, Nabonidus, was the father of the crown prince Belshazzar who did not actually come to the throne,[31] though he was appointed by his father as regent before the latter's departure to Arabia;[32] the information in vi, 1 that, instead of the Persian Cyrus, it was the Mede Darius who was the successor to the last Babylonian king, and the further information that Darius was the son of Xerxes (ix, 1) and that Cyrus was his successor (vi, 29; x, 1), whereas in fact the historical order was Cyrus (Cambyses), Darius, Xerxes: the presupposition (xi, 2, cf. Ezra iv–vi and on this p. 551) that there were altogether only four kings of Persia, i.e. only Artaxerxes in addition to those already mentioned, whereas in reality nine Persian kings reigned.[33] On the

[29] Barthélemy and Milik, *Qumran Cave I* (1955), pp. 150–2, Nos. 71–2; Baillet, RB 63 (1956), p. 55; Cross, *ib.* p. 58.

[30] Nelis, 'Note sur la date de la sujétion de Joiaqim par Nabuchodonosor' RB 61 (1954), pp. 387–91. Cf. also Wiseman, *Chronicles of Chaldaean Kings* (1956).

[31] Rowley, 'The Belshazzar of Daniel and of History' Exp. IX, 2 (1924), pp. 182–95, 255–72.

[32] The defamatory 'Verse account of Nabonidus' (ANET, pp. 312–15; DOTT, pp. 89–91), Col. II. Cf. p. 523, nn. 35–6; Lit. § 126.

[33] Torrey, ' "Medes and Persians" ' JAOS 66 (1946), pp. 1–15.

other hand, xi, 3–39 present a very detailed narrative of the history from Alexander the Great onwards, and from verse 21, i.e. from the accession of Antiochus IV in the year 175, it becomes particularly accurate. Finally, it is generally agreed that the language of the book bears clear indications of a quite late period, and it also contains not only a large number of Persian foreign words,[34] but also Greek words, names of musical instruments in iii, 5.

The dating of the book between 167 and 163 carries with it also the interpretation of the four empires in ii and vii as referring to the Babylonians, the Medes, the Persians and the Greeks. In x–xii, so far as heathen empires are concerned, the writer's view hardly extends beyond the empire of Alexander the Great as it had been divided into the kingdoms of the Diadochi, the Ptolemies and the Seleucids. Before this only the Persian is mentioned here (xi, 2), naturally enough since the vision purports to have been received in the third year of Cyrus the Persian king (x, 1). The vision of viii, dated in the third year of Belshazzar, however, explicitly mentions in addition to the king of Greece symbolised by the he-goat, the *Kings of Media and Persia*, representing these two combined kingdoms by the one symbol of the ram because in any case they belonged closely together, while making it clear that they really are two kingdoms by providing the ram with two horns (viii, 3, 20). The vision of vii, assigned to the first year of Belshazzar, which, unlike that of viii envisages a few years yet of Babylonian rule, must also take account of this, and so represents it by the first beast which precedes the Median, Persian and Greek empires which are represented by the other three beasts. The same is true of ii, dated in the second year of Nebuchadnezzar, where, as has already been seen, vv. 37–8 make clear that the head of the statue refers to Nebuchadnezzar, and this (against Eerdmans) not as a person but as representative of the Babylonian empire. Passages such as vi, 1 and vi, 29 show further that the book also differentiates between the Medes and the Persians outside the visions.

5. *The prehistory of the book.* The dating of the book as we have it at the beginning of the Maccabean period by no means excludes the possibility that it contains older material. It is on the contrary clear that older and even much older material lies behind each of the halves of the book, and the question can only be how far the literary form in which this material existed earlier has also been preserved in the book and can be recovered by the excision of the later additions made by the compiler of the book as we have it.

Since the narratives of i–vi take place at the Babylonian and Persian courts, and contain much that well reflects the conditions there—e.g. in i the training of the pages, in ii, 2; iii, 2 *et passim* the titles of officials, in vi, 2–3 the division of the empire into satrapies and the appointment of three ministers—the most likely assumption is that their material does go back to the Persian period. We also know at least some of this narrative material in an older form. That the enemy penetrated into Babylon without it being noticed by the inhabitants who were celebrating a festival (v) is also related by Herodotus I, 191 and Xenophon, *Cyropaedia* VII, 5, 15, and the history of Nebuchadnezzar's madness appears in another form, apparently independent of the Daniel narrative, in Eusebius,

---

[34] Nyberg, 'Ein iranisches Wort im Buche Daniel' MO 25 (1931), pp. 178–204: פטיש iii, 21.

Praeparatio Evangelica IX, 41. Furthermore, von Soden believes that it is possible to prove that the Babylonian tradition concerning Nabonidus,[35] namely what is preserved about him in the 'verse lampoon'[36] is a source of many of the features of the narratives in Dan. ii–v, now transferred to Nebuchadnezzar and Belshazzar. The discovery of the 'Prayer of Nabonidus' (p. 663) in one of the Qumran caves has confirmed this belief. Furthermore, Berossus[37] relates that Artaxerxes II (405–359 B.C.) erected statues of Anaïtis in Babylon, Susa and Ecbatana and ordered his subjects to worship them. In the book itself, however, all these materials are grouped around a Jewish exile named Daniel and his three friends. Who this Daniel really was, cannot be clearly made out. Generally he is linked with the Daniel who is mentioned as particularly righteous in Ezek. xiv, 14, 20, apparently as a figure of remote antiquity, together with Noah and Job, and as particularly wise in Ezek. xxviii, 3. This does seem very probable, especially if side by side with the narratives of the canonical book, we also take into account the apocryphal story of Susanna (§ 84) which fills out the picture of Daniel the wise as the canonical book depicts him by showing that he was an extremely clever judge.

Among the texts belonging to the middle of the second millennium B.C. which have come to light since 1929 in the north Syrian centre of Ras Shamra-Ugarit, there is also a fairly detailed and relatively well-preserved narrative concerning king Dan'el[38] who appears here as the guardian of the rights of widow and orphan. This has further strengthened the tendency to relate the Daniel of the book with the figure mentioned in Ezek. xiv, 14, 20; xxviii, 3, which in its turn is certainly connected with the Ugaritic Dan'el and has thus been taken over by Israel from the Canaanite-Phoenician area.[39] Nevertheless it remains remarkable that unlike Ezek. xiv, 14, 20; xxviii, 3, where, as we have seen,

---

[35] Amusin, 'Das Qumranfragment des "Gebets" des babylonischen Königs Nabonid' [Russ.] *Vestnik drewnej istorii* 4 (66) (1958), pp. 104–17; Dhorme 'La mère de Nabonide' *RA* 41 (1947), pp. 1–21 = *Recueil Dhorme* (1951), pp. 325–50; Freedmann, 'The Prayer of Nabonidus' *BASOR* 145 (1957), pp. 31–2; Genouillac, 'Nabonide' *RA* 22 (1925), pp. 71–83; Gevarjahu, 'The Qumran Fragments of the Prayer of Nabonid' *Studies in the Dead Sea Scrolls* [Hebr.] (1957), pp. 12–23; Lewy, 'The Late Assyro-Babylonian Cult of the Moon and its Culmination at the Time of Nabonidus' *HUCA* 19 (1945/46), pp. 405–89; de Liagre Böhl, 'Die Tochter des Königs Naboned' *Symbolae Koschaker* (1939), pp. 151–78 = *Op. Min.* (1953), pp. 174–87, 490–3; R. Meyer, 'Das Qumränfragment "Gebet des Nabonid"' *ThLZ* 85 (1960), cols. 831–4; Moran, 'Notes on the New Nabonidus Inscriptions' *Or* 28 (1959), pp. 130–40; Philby, *The Land of Midian* (1957), p. 89; Pohl, 'Die neuen Nabonid-stelen aus Ḥarran' *Or* 28 (1959), pp. 214 f.; Berta Segall, 'The Arts and King Nabonidus' *AJA* 59 (1955), pp. 315–18, Pl. 93; Sidney Smith, *Isaiah Chapters XL–LV* (1944); Vogt, 'Precatio Regis Nabonid in Pia Narratione Iudaica' *Bibl* 37 (1956), pp. 532–4; 'Novae inscriptiones Nabonidi' *Bibl* 40 (1959), pp. 88–102. Cf. above, p. 521; below, p. 663; Lit. § 126.   [36] ANET, pp. 312–15; DOTT, pp. 89–91.

[37] Schnabel, *Berossos und die babylonisch-hellenistische Literatur* (1923), p. 275, Fragment 56.

[38] Aistleitner, *Die mythologischen und kultischen Texte aus Ras Schamra* (1959), pp. 65–82; Driver, *Canaanite Myths and Legends* (1956), pp. 5–8, 48–66; Gordon, *Ugaritic Literature* (1949), pp. 84–103; *Ugaritic Manual* (1955), pp. 179–84; Herdner, 'La Légende Cananéenne d'Aqhat d'après les travaux récents' *Syria* 26 (1949), pp. 1–16; Virolleaud, *La Légende Phénicienne de Danel* (1936); ANET, pp. 149–55; DOTT, pp. 124–8.

[39] Mariani, *Danel, 'il Patriarca Sapiente', nella Bibbia, nella tradizione, nella leggenda* (1945); Noth, 'Noah, Daniel und Hiob in Ezechiel xiv' *VT* 1 (1951), pp. 251–60; Spiegel, 'Noah, Daniel and Job' *Louis Ginzberg Jubilee Vol.* I (1945), pp. 305–55. Lit. p. 378, n. 33.

Daniel appears to belong to remote antiquity, our Daniel is assigned to the end of Babylonian and the beginning of Persian world rule, i.e. to the sixth century B.C. Since not only the names of Daniel's three companions (Neh. viii, 4; x, 3, 24) but also his own name (Ezra viii, 2; Neh. x, 7) are attested for this later period, or more precisely for the fifth century, the possibility must at any rate be entertained that our narrative is attached to a Daniel of the eastern Jewish diaspora of the sixth or fifth centuries. Admittedly, we should have to add at once that this character has been completely overlaid with an abundantly rich mass of legendary and fictional matter which has evidently also made use of that ancient Canaanite-Phoenician Dan'el material and that it is hence impossible now to make historical statements about him. It is uncertain whether these narratives, coming from such a variety of sources, though all now grouped around Daniel and his friends, had been united into a collection and formed an independent literary unit before the compilation in about 165 B.C. of the book as we now have it. Many scholars assume this, and claim that, unlike vii–xii, i–vi do not reveal unambiguous references to Antiochus IV Epiphanes and his fight against the Jews, but do appear to contain allusions to Alexander and the first Diadochi. On these grounds, they date the collection about the middle of the third century B.C. At that time, a Jew, living presumably in the eastern diaspora, collected the group of stories in i–vi, which till then had been in circulation as single narratives, though without being able entirely to remove the traces of their original independence. Such a trace is seen above all in the fact that iii, 1–30 is concerned only with the three companions of Daniel and not with Daniel himself. But in reality, the story of the deliverance of the three companions of Daniel from the furnace is the continuation of the conclusion of ch. ii, and is a preparation for the story of the rescue of Daniel from the lions' den in ch. vi. The fact that Daniel declines the high political office which is offered him by Nebuchadnezzar, and that his three companions are at his suggestion invested with this office (ii, 48 f.), has as its consequence that only the latter, but not Daniel, have their faith put to the test by the command laid upon all the officials of the province of Babylon to worship the statue erected by Nebuchadnezzar. But Daniel does not escape such a test of faith. As ch. vi relates, he was later brought into a quite similar trial and acquitted himself just as brilliantly as his friends had done. Thus i–vi reveals itself to be a skilfully constructed unity, and since, as will be shown later (p. 527), vii–xii is in form and content very similar to i–vi, we must ascribe it to the compiler of the whole book in about 165 B.C.

As with the narratives of i–vi, so too the visions of vii–xii, and particularly those of vii and viii, are based upon older material. Among the four beasts of vii, the fourth is clearly of mythological origin, even if it can hardly be the chaos monster which has here served as pattern, as Gunkel thought, but rather the figure of Typhon[40] belonging to northern Syria, i.e. the realm of the Seleucid power which it symbolises, or one of those monsters with which, according to the Ugaritic texts, Ba'al had to contend,[41] strongly supported by his sister 'Anat.

[40] Eissfeldt, *Baal Zaphon* (1932), pp. 25–7.
[41] Aistleitner (p. 523, n. 38), pp. 11–54; Driver (p. 523, n. 38), pp. 72–120; Gordon

The representation of Persia as a ram, and Syria-Greece as an ibex or he-goat in viii may be explained, as Cumont[42] has shown, from the astronomical geography which is here presupposed, by which each land is under the aegis of one of the signs of the zodiac. Furthermore, the conception of the *ancient of days*, whose *raiment was white as snow and the hair of his head like pure wool* in vii, 9 can hardly have grown up within the religion of Yahweh, but was derived from elsewhere, more probably from northern Syrian mythology[43] than from the Iranian-Babylonian religion.[44] From the latter, however, may have come the conception of guardian angels which according to xi assist the separate peoples, and the same may perhaps be assumed for the figure of the 'Son of Man' of which more must be said later (p. 526). For the many historical details which are alluded to in xi,[45] the author must have had written materials available to him, probably of non-Jewish origin, at least so far as he is concerned with events which lay before his own time, i.e. about up to the accession of Seleucus IV Philopator (187–175)[46] in xi, 20. The prophecy of the destruction of Antiochus IV near Jerusalem in xi, 45—here at least we have one assuredly native Jewish piece of tradition—is clearly dependent upon the expectation that the heathen world-power would be shattered before the gates of Jerusalem, an expectation which at any rate at a date later than Ezek. xxxviii–xxxix (Gog of Magog) became a firm eschatological doctrine. In short, there is no doubt whatever that the visions of vii–xii are largely based upon older and even much older elements, and they only become fully intelligible when their prehistory is illuminated.

It is a quite different question as to whether in vii–xii we must reckon with an older literary form which has been preserved, i.e. whether, as is often thought for i–vi, we should reckon here with a pre-Maccabean book of Daniel. This is, indeed, assumed by Junker and some others for viii–xii. But the assumption hardly requires disproving, since when the elements which come clearly from the Maccabean compiler are removed there is hardly anything left. In vii there

(p. 523, n. 38) (1949), pp. 9–56; Kapelrud, *Baal in the Ras Shamra Texts* (1952), pp. 98–109; Obermann, *Ugaritic Mythology* (1948), pp. 56–71; ANET, pp. 129–42; DOTT, pp. 128–33.

[42] 'La plus ancienne géographie astrologique' Klio 9 (1909), pp. 263–73; Mouterde, 'L'astrologie à Héliopolis. Jupiter Heliopolitanus rex et regulus' BMB 13 (1956), pp. 7–21, Pl. I; on this Nober, VD 36 (1958), pp. 370–4. Lit. § 126.

[43] The head of the Ugaritic pantheon, the god El, is in any case an aged god, and his description as 'b šnm perhaps means: 'father of years'. Cf. Eissfeldt, *El im ugaritischen Pantheon* (1951); Pope, *El in the Ugaritic Texts* (1955).

[44] Gressmann, *Messias* (1929), pp. 343–73; cf. p. 526, n. 47.

[45] Badian, 'Rom und Antiochus der Große. Eine Studie über den kalten Krieg' Die Welt als Geschichte 20 (1960), pp. 203–5 [transl. by Katharina Hartmeyer]; Bengtson, *Griechische Geschichte von den Anfängen bis in die römische Kaiserzeit* (²1960); Cloché, 'La coalition de 315–11 av. J.-C. contre Antigone le Borgne' CRAI (1957), pp. 130–9; Holleaux, *Études d'épigraphie et d'histoire Grecques* I–V (1938–57); Magie, 'The "Agreement" between Philip V and Antiochus III for the Partition of the Egyptian Empire' Journal of Roman Studies 29 (1939), pp. 32–44; Schachermeyr, *Griechische Geschichte* (1960); Schalit, 'The letter of Antiochus III to Zeuxis regarding the establishment of Jewish military colonies in Phrygia and Lydia (Josephus Ant XII, § 148–53)' JQR 50 (1959/60), pp. 289–318; Seyrig, 'Antiquités Syriennes 67: Monnaies contremarquées en Syrie' Syria 35 (1958), pp. 187–97, Pl. XVII; Zambelli, 'L'ascesa al trono di Antioco IV Epifane di Siria' Rivista de Filologia 88 (1960), pp. 363–89. Lit. § 126.

[46] Barton, 'The Composition of the Book of Daniel' JBL 17 (1898), pp. 62–86, esp. p. 76.

are certainly some unevennesses the most important of which is the fact that the request for the interpretation of what has been seen (vv. 20–2) enumerates more features than appear in the vision itself (v. 8). But a pre-Maccabean form of the vision cannot be demonstrated, for, as Ginsberg emphatically says, even the basic material of vii, unlike ii which derives from an earlier period, can only have originated in the reign of Antiochus Epiphanes. In particular, both the group of verses which refer to Antiochus IV (vii, 7bβ, 8, 20aβb, 24b–25) and also those which are concerned with the Ancient of Days, the judgement scene and the 'Son of Man' (vv. 9–10, 13–14, 18, 22, 26–7), may be regarded as being just as original as their context. For the fact that the description of the fourth beast is more detailed than that of the first three corresponds exactly with the mode of presentation in xi, 2–45, where the Persian kings are merely named, whereas the Seleucid Diadochi are treated in detail, and particularly Antiochus IV the last of them. The fact that the description of the appearance of the Ancient of Days, of the judgement scene and the 'Son of Man' takes on a rhythmic form, has parallels in the other visions, as we have seen (p. 516). Finally, the possibility, which cannot be denied though it is by no means proved, that not only in the conception of the Ancient of Days, but also in that of the 'Son of Man' foreign influence, perhaps Parsee, has been operative,[47] does not contribute anything to the question of the originality of vv. 9–10, 13–14 together with vv. 26–7, the interpretation which belongs with it. We must therefore regard vii as a vision composed by the compiler of the visions in viii–xii, speaking of four world empires represented as beasts and of the rule of the Jews seen as a human figure, just as in ii there is a contrast drawn between the four heathen empires symbolised by the differing materials of the individual parts of the statue and the kingdom of the Jews represented by a quite different kind of symbol, namely the stone which is detached by no human hand from the mountain and then grows to be a world-mountain (vv. 34–5, 44–5). This does not exclude the possibility that vii contains secondary elaborations. Thus v. 11a is certainly an addition, whereas v. 12 which fits well after v. 11b may be original. Further-

[47] Leo Baeck, 'Der "Menschensohn"' in Leo Baeck, *Aus drei Jahrtausenden* ([2]1958), pp. 187–98; Emerton, 'The Origin of the Son of Man Imagery' JThSt 9 (1958), pp. 225–42; Feuillet, 'Le Fils de l'homme de Daniel et la tradition biblique' RB 60 (1953), pp. 170–202, 321–46; von Gall, Βασιλεία τοῦ Θεοῦ (1926), pp. 266–9, 412–13; Higgins, 'Son of Man-*Forschung* since "The Teaching of Jesus"' NT *Essays Manson* (1959), pp. 119–35; Kraeling, 'Some Babylonian and Iranian Mythology in the Seventh Chapter of Daniel' *Or. Stud. C. E. Pavry* (1933), pp. 228–31; Manson, 'The Son of Man in Daniel, Enoch, and the Gospels' BJRL 32 (1949/50), pp. 171–93; Moe, 'Der Menschensohn und der Urmensch' StTh 14, 2 (1960), pp. 119–29; Morgenstern, 'The "Son of Man" of Daniel vii, 13 ff. A New Interpretation' JBL 80 (1961), pp. 65–77; Mowinckel, *Han som kommer* (1951), pp. 226–93, E.T. *He that Cometh* (1956), pp. 346–450; Otto, *Reich Gottes und Menschensohn* ([3]1954), E.T. *The Kingdom of God and the Son of Man* (1938); Muilenburg, 'The Son of Man in Daniel and the Ethiopic Apocalypse of Enoch' JBL 79 (1960), pp. 197–209; Parker, 'The Meaning of "Son of Man"' JBL 60 (1941), pp. 151–7; Procksch, 'Der Menschensohn als Gottessohn' CuW 3 (1927), pp. 425–43, 473–81; 'Christus im Alten Testament' NKZ 44 (1933), pp. 57–83; Rost, 'Zur Deutung des Menschensohnes in Daniel vii' *Fascher-Festschr.* (1958), pp. 41–3; Sjöberg, Människosonen och Israel i Dan vii' Religion och Bibel 7 (1948), pp. 1–16; 'Uttrycket "Människoson" i Gamla Testamentet' SvTK 26 (1950), pp. 35–44; *Der verborgene Menschensohn in den Evangelien* (1955), pp. 41–98: 'Der verborgene Messias im Judentum'; Young, *Daniel's Vision of the Son of Man* (1958). Cf. Literature p. 51, n. 59; p. 102, n. 1; p. 105, n. 9; p. 110, nn. 28–9; p. 514, n. 10. § 126.

more, v. 21, which in form too does not fit into its context and would belong better in the description of the vision after v. 8, is an addition, whereas the conclusion of v. 20 which likewise refers to a feature not mentioned in the description of the vision, may nevertheless be original.

6. *The formation of the book of Daniel.* After all this, we may picture the formation of the book of Daniel as follows. A Jew of Jerusalem, unknown to us by name, made use of two groups of material, and formed the book out of them some time after 167 B.C. On the one hand, he had older narratives which told of the fortunes of Daniel and his three companions at the Babylonian, Median and Persian courts, and which included accounts of Daniel's marvellous gift for interpreting dreams, and in particular how he was able to relate a dream of Nebuchadnezzar and interpret it with reference to the end of the heathen world empires and their replacement by the rule of God. On the other hand, he had historical surveys beginning as *vaticinia ex eventu* and issuing in genuine prophecy, making use of mythological elements and Old Testament pronouncements. In using this, he arranged his material in two parallel series. In i–vi he told of what befell Daniel and his three companions under Nebuchadnezzar, Belshazzar, Darius and Cyrus, and, with the omission of Nebuchadnezzar whose dream (ii), interpreted by Daniel, corresponds in content to the visions of vii–xii, he then tells of the visions which Daniel received under Belshazzar, Darius and Cyrus. In both halves of his book, the compiler is assuring both himself and his contemporaries of consolation and strength in the bitter struggle of faith. In i–vi this is done by showing that faithful adherence to the ancestral religion is in the end rewarded by God in that he saves those who are under attack because of their faithfulness, though no direct allusion is made to the acute danger of the time, the threat to Judaism by Antiochus IV. In vii–xii, however, there is quite explicit reference to this, a clear indication is given of the imminent end of this terrible distress, and thus the courage to resist is strengthened. Even if the oppression were to last longer than is here prophesied, it remains true that the victory will belong to God and not to Antiochus Epiphanes. The believer may be sure of this, even if he does not see the fulfilment of the promise; he may go to his rest and wait for the resurrection, a certainty which an angel promises to Daniel in xii, 13 and which we may suppose the compiler of the book—probably to be thought of as advanced in years—applied especially to himself.

We may return now to the question already touched on (pp. 516–17), namely that of the change of language: i, 1–ii, 4a in Hebrew, ii, 4b–vii, 28 in Aramaic, viii, 1–xii, 13 in Hebrew. If the assumption is correct that Daniel i–xii is a unified work, compiled according to plan by one author on the basis of a variety of older material, then the view often held that the change of language is to be explained on the basis of the literary prehistory of the book is no longer tenable. It cannot be the case that a cycle of stories mainly in Aramaic and a collection of visions mainly in Hebrew were combined. We have really no other alternative than to regard the compiler of the book himself as responsible for its double language, as indeed many scholars have supposed (p. 516). Various surmises can be made as to the reasons which could have led him so to construct the book.

The suggestion could be made—and this is one which has not previously been considered—that the compiler took as his model books like Ezra and Nehemiah which, though otherwise written in Hebrew, quote the documents which they offer in the Aramaic original. Admittedly the problem does not solve itself in this way any more than it does in any other. For even if we could perhaps explain why the stories of ii, 4b–vi, 29 were accorded higher value as 'documents' than that of i, 1–ii, 4a, so that the former were compiled in Aramaic whereas the latter is in Hebrew, we should still be left with the puzzle as to what could have led to the distinction between the vision of vii, compiled in the Aramaic language of the 'documents', and the three visions in Hebrew of viii–xii. An explanation of the double language which is entirely satisfactory has not yet been proposed by anyone.

7. *The purpose of the book.* The author's purpose in compiling the book was to encourage his compatriots in their terrible sufferings under the tyranny of Antiochus, so that they would remain faithful to their religion. The legends which he adduced in i–vi showed, on the one hand, how faithful adherence to Jewish religion and custom can bring the pious into temporary distress, but that such faithfulness would in the end be rewarded by God in that he rescues those who are devoted to him from the distress, even if only at the very last moment (i, iii, vi). On the other hand, they showed that God alone is powerful; he may for a certain time allow earthly powers to arise, but in the end he triumphs over them and compels them to acknowledge him as the only power (ii, iii, iv, v, vi). In the visions in vii–xii, the author wished to persuade those who were suffering with him of the certainty that everything which they had to bear was not the result of blind chance, but had been predetermined by God long ago. He indicated the limit set to this, for the time of suffering would now soon be at an end and the day was near at hand when God would shatter the power of the tyrant and himself enter upon his rule of the world, which signified at the same time the rule of his holy ones, the Jews. With this message of encouragement, the author linked one of consolation. In xii, 2–3, the first clear mention of the belief in the resurrection in the Old Testament, he promises to the Jews who have died, and in particular the pious martyrs, that they will awake to eternal life and so will have a share in the kingdom of the final age.

8. *The book of Daniel as an apocalypse.* The confident faith that God is the lord of history, and the triumphant certainty that God will quite soon reveal his royal power and bring low all heathen powers, but will glorify those who acknowledge him, the Jews faithful to the Law, stands in a line with older prophecy and has a power which is timeless and still inspires today. It is indeed possible that the author, like the older prophets, found the glow of his faith repeatedly rekindled by estatic visionary experiences, and that it is this experience which Rembrandt detected and reproduced in the mysterious chiaroscuro of the Berlin *Vision of Daniel,* his representation of the vision of a two-horned ram threatened by a he-goat, as related in ch. viii. But what distinguishes the author from the prophets appears nevertheless to be greater than what links him to them. Two points may be mentioned. On the one hand there is the marked element of erudition, which very nearly stifles the basic visionary ex-

perience, if it really is an experience and the vision is not a mere literary form. On the other hand there is the anonymity which hides itself behind the name of a legendary character of the past. Both points are characteristic of apocalyptic of which the book of Daniel presents the first developed example. Though the combination of prophecy and learning was already hinted at in Ezekiel and Zechariah (pp. 381 f., 433 f.), anonymity is first clearly employed here. The age of a prophecy conscious of direct call by God was now over. It was looked back to as a closed period having normative significance, and if one had something like its message to proclaim, this was presented under the aegis of a name belonging to that bygone age. But this was not all. The older prophets were everywhere taken as models, as for example in the explanation of the vision by an angel in viii, 15–27. This is clearly imitated in all its circumstantial detail—Daniel falls to the ground and is lifted up again by the angel, he is addressed as 'Man (Son of Man)'—from Ezekiel (i, 1–ii, 2, viii, 17) and Zechariah (iv, 1–14). But there is more to it even than this. The prophetic writings were taken to be a source of knowledge of the future and the attempt was made, by means of learned interpretation, to arrive at their true meaning, as Daniel does in ix, 1–3, 24–7 with the seventy years of Jer. xxv, 11–12, xxix, 10. Here too it also becomes clear that apocalyptic is closely associated with erudition.

9. *Expansions and additions.* As has already been suggested, Daniel's prayer in ix, 4–20 represents a later addition, recognisable as such by the fact, among others, that, except for the quotation from the book of Jeremiah in ix, 2, the divine name Yahweh only appears in this prayer in the book of Daniel. It has also already been hinted that xii, 11–12 are probably secondary additions. But in addition to these, the book of Daniel has also received 'Additions' which like those of the book of Esther are preserved for us in the Greek translation and so are reckoned among the Apocrypha. They will therefore be discussed at a later stage (§ 84).

§ 72. THE BOOKS OF CHRONICLES

Literature: (a) Commentaries: ATD: Galling (1954 (1958)); BOuT: van den Born (1960); Camb. B: Elmslie (²1916); Cent. B: Harvey-Jellie (1906); Echter-B: Rehm (1949); HAT: Rudolph (1955); HK: Kittel (1902); HS: Goettsberger (1939); HSAT: Rothstein (1923); IB: Elmslie (1954); ICC: Curtis and Madsen (1910 (1952)); Jerusalem-B: Cazelles (³1961); KAT: Rothstein and Hänel, I (1927); KeH: Bertheau (²1873); KHC: Benzinger (1901); Montserrat-B: Ubach (1958); SAT: Haller (²1925); Soncino-B: Slotki (1951); SZ: Oettli (1889); TU: van Selms, I (1939) II (1947).

(b) Other Works: Albright, 'The Date and Personality of the Chronicler' JBL 40 (1921), pp. 104–24; Asmussen, 'Priesterkodex und Chronik in ihrem Verhältnis zueinander' ThStKr 79 (1906), pp. 165–79; Bea, 'Neuere Arbeiten zum Problem der biblischen Chronikbücher' Bibl 22 (1941), pp. 46–58; Bentzen, 'Sirach, der Chronist und Nehemia' StTh 3 (1950/51), pp. 158–61; Botterweck, 'Zur Eigenart der chronistischen Davidgeschichte *Christian-Festschr.* (1956), pp. 12–31 = ThQ 136 (1956), pp. 402–34; Brunet, 'Le Chroniste et ses sources' RB 60 (1953), pp. 481–508; 61 (1954), pp. 349–86; 'La théologie du Chroniste.

Théocratie et messianisme' BEThL XII (1959), pp. 384–97; Budde, 'Vermutungen zum "Midrasch des Buches der Könige"' ZAW 12 (1892), pp. 37–51; van der Bussche, *Het Probleem van Kronieken* (1950); Gerleman, *Studies in the Septuagint* II: *Chronicles* (LUA 43, 3, 1947); *Synoptic Studies in the OT* (LUA 44, 5, 1948); Grintz, 'Aspects of the History of the High Priesthood' (Hebrew, Engl. summary) Zion 23/24 (1958/59), pp. 124–40, I–II; Grosheide, 'De dateering van de Boeken der Kronieken' GThT 36 (1935), pp. 170–82; Hänel, 'Das Recht des Opferschlachtens in der chronistischen Literatur' ZAW 55 (1937) pp. 46–67; Janssen, *Juda in der Exilszeit* (FRLANT 69, 1956), pp. 118–21: 'Die Entstehung des chronistischen Bildes von dem Lande Juda in der Exilszeit (II Chr. xxxvi, 20 ff.)'; E. Junge, *Der Wiederaufbau des Heerwesens des Reiches Juda unter Josia* (BWANT 75, 1937); Klein, 'Kleine Beiträge zur Erklärung der Chronik' MGWJ 80 (1936), pp. 195–206; Kugler, *Von Moses bis Paulus* (1922), pp. 234–300; Luther, 'Kāhāl und 'edāh als Hilfsmittel der Quellenscheidung im Priesterkodex und in der Chronik' ZAW 56 (1938), pp. 44–63; Mosiman, *Eine Zusammenstellung und Vergleichung der Paralleltexte der Chronik und der älteren Bücher des AT* (Diss. phil. Halle, 1907); Mowinckel, 'Erwägungen zum chronistischen Geschichtswerk' ThLZ 85 (1960), cols. 1–8; Noordtzij, 'Les intentions du Chroniste' RB 49 (1940), pp. 161–8; Noth, *Überlieferungsgeschichtliche Studien*, I (1943 (1957)), pp. 110–80; von Rad, *Das Geschichtsbild des chronistischen Werkes* (BWANT 54, 1930); 'Die levitische Predigt in den Büchern der Chronik' *Procksch-Festschr.* (1934), pp. 113–24 = *Ges. Stud. z. AT* (1958), pp. 248–61; Rehm, *Textkritische Untersuchungen zu den Parallelstellen der Samuel-Königsbücher und der Chronik* (1937); Rudolph, 'Problems of the Books of Chronicles' VT 4 (1954), pp. 401–9; Segert, 'Textkritische Erwägungen in margine des Kommentars zu den Chronikbüchern von W. Rudolph' ArOr 25 (1957), pp. 671–5; Torrey, 'The Apparatus of the Textual Criticism of Chronicles-Ezra-Nehemiah' *Studies W. R. Harper*, II (1908), pp. 55–111; *The Chronicler's History of Israel. Chronicles-Ezra-Nehemiah Restored to its Original Form* (1954); Vannutelli, *Libri Synoptici Veteris Testamenti seu Librorum Regum et Chronicorum loci paralleli*, I (1931) II (1934); Welch, *The Work of the Chronicler. Its Purpose and its Date* (1939); Wellhausen, *Prolegomena zur Geschichte Israels* (²1905), pp. 165–223; E.T. *Prolegomena to the History of Ancient Israel* (1885, reissue 1957), pp. 171–227; Zimmermann, 'Chronicles as a Partially Translated Book' JQR 42 (1951/52), pp. 265–82, 387–412.
Cf. also Literature §§ 73, 126.

1. *Name, compass, contents and purpose.* In the Hebrew texts this work at first formed one book with the title דִּבְרֵי הַיָּמִים (סֵפֶר), (*Book of*) *the daily events* (*annals*). From Jerome's († 420) suggestion (*chronicon totius divinae historiae*), it has acquired the name of 'Chronicles'. 𝔊 calls it Παραλειπόμενα i.e. *the things passed over*, or *left out* (i.e. in Sam. and Kings), and divides it into two books Παραλειπομένων α' β', a division which was then taken over in the other translations and has since 1448 come also into the Hebrew texts.

The work of the Chronicler originally, however, comprised not only the two books of Chronicles, but also the books of Ezra and Nehemiah, and thus presented the history of the kingdom of Judah, in other words of the kingdom of God, from Adam to its re-founding by Nehemiah and Ezra. The books of Ezra and Nehemiah are seen to be the conclusion of the work not only by the similarity of language and of thought—love of the Temple and its cultus, and in particular of the Levites and singers—but especially by the fact that it relates the restoration of those treasures whose loss is related in II Chron. xxxvi, 1–21. In addition, the conclusion of II Chron. (xxxvi, 22–3) agrees almost word for word with the opening of Ezra (i, 1–3), so that the point at which the division was made is clearly recognisable. The reason for the division has been seen, and probably rightly, in the fact that Ezra-Neh. became canonical before Chron., for their contents did not appear in the older books which had already become canonical, whereas those of Chron. did. When later Chron. too became canonical, Ezra-Neh. still kept its prior place so that now, quite inappropriately, the last quarter of the once much larger work stands before its first three quarters. The fact that when Chronicles was taken up into the canon, it did not end precisely where the already canonical book of Ezra-Neh. began is to be explained on the grounds that it was desired to bring the book to an end not at the disaster to Jerusalem (II xxxvi, 17–21) but with an event encouraging new hopes, namely the issue of Cyrus' decree.[1] Similarly, the books of Kings do not end with the narrative of the conquest of Jerusalem, but likewise with a ray of hope, the report of the release of Jehoiachin from prison (II xxv, 27–30). In II Macc. ii, 13,[2] where there is a reference to a library ($\beta\iota\beta\lambda\iota o\theta\eta\kappa\eta$) gathered by Nehemiah and perhaps identical with Chron.-Ezra-Neh., and in the Babylonian Talmud, Baba Batra 15a where there is mention of the part which Ezra and Nehemiah had in our books of Chron. Ezra and Neh., there is perhaps preserved a recollection of the fact that the whole work belongs together.

The whole work may be divided into the following sections: (1) I i–ix, the prehistory of the kingdom of Judah from Adam to Saul, simply in the form of lists, in which, however, the genealogies in part go far beyond David,[3] in some places perhaps as a result of later elaboration; (2) I x–xxix,[4] Saul's death and David; (3) II i–ix, Solomon;[5] (4) II x–xxxvi, from the 'apostasy of the ten tribes' to the Edict of Cyrus; (5) Ezra i–vi, the re-founding of the religious community by Zerubbabel and Joshua; (6) Ezra vii to Neh. xiii, the consolidation of the new community by Ezra and Nehemiah. The aim of the whole work is, however, to prove that in contrast with the godless northern kingdom, it is only the southern kingdom Judah, with its Davidic dynasty and its Jerusalem Temple, which is the true Israel, the legitimate bearer of the divine rule which is actualised in the kingdom of David, and that it is only the community of Jews who returned from the Exile, and not the religious community of the Samaritans, which was in the process of coming into being at the time of the Chronicler, which faithfully maintains and continues this tradition.

2. *The Chronicler's sources.* The sources of the books of Ezra-Neh. will be discussed later (pp. 542–51). In I II Chron. the Chronicler has provided a parallel to Gen.–II Kings, and so has also largely used the books Gen.–Kings as source. Large sections of I II Chron. coincide word for word,[6] or very nearly

---

[1] Rost, 'Erwägungen zum Kyroserlaß' *Rudolf-Festschr.* (1961), pp. 301–7.
[2] Cf. on this Rengstorf, *Ḥirbet Qumrân und die Bibliothek vom Toten Meer* (1960), pp. 29, 61.
[3] Rothstein, *Die Genealogie des Konigs Jojachin und seiner Nachkommen* (*I Chron. iii, 17–24*) (1902). Cf. p. 285, n. 20.
[4] Rogers, 'The Use of ראש in an Oath' JBL 74 (1955), p. 272 on I xii, 20.
[5] Février, 'Paralipomena Punica' (continued) Cahiers de Byrsa 7 (1957), pp. 119–24, Pl. I: on II iii, 14. Lit. § 126.
[6] According to Milik, *Dix ans de Découvertes dans le Désert de Juda* (1957), p. 25 (E.T. *Ten Years of Discovery in the Wilderness of Judaea* (1959), p. 25), the text of Chron., in so far as it runs parallel to I II Sam. depends upon a text form which has close affinities with one which has been found at Qumrân, viz. 4 Q Samᵃ. (cf. p. 683, n. 13). Lit. § 126.

so, with the corresponding sections of Gen.–II Kings. The lists in I i–ix are to a large extent worked up from material in these books, and in I x–II xxxvi, the Chronicler follows in general the material of I Sam. xxxi–II Kings xxv. But he leaves out nearly all information relevant to the northern kingdom, and in the case of certain kings, notably David and Solomon, he suppresses a certain amount of material which might shed an unfavourable light upon them. On the other hand, Chronicles contains a variety of material which is not to be found in Gen.–Kings, but which cannot be due to the Chronicler's own invention—unlike certain other material which must be examined shortly (pp. 535–8). He must have derived this from an earlier source. To this belong many passages in the lists in I i–ix, the list of David's heroes in I xi, 10–47 which is six verses longer than II Sam. xxiii, 8–39a, the notes about the building and equipment of fortresses by Rehoboam in II xi, 5–12[7] and about his wives and children in vv. 18–23, the information about Uzziah's successes against the Philistines in II xxvi, 6 and his building of fortifications and cisterns in vv. 9–10,[8] as well as other material. It is therefore clear that there were available to the Chronicler sources going beyond the compass of our books of Samuel and Kings. These sources, if we may follow the indications of what has just been mentioned, were evidently similar to Sam. and Kings, and must in particular have included such information as is presupposed by the concluding formulae of the framework passages in Kings to be the content of the Annals of the Kings of Israel and of Judah. We could thus indicate the position as follows: at least so far as Judah was concerned, these Annals[9] or the sources upon which they were based[10] were still available to the Chronicler.

In this matter we are not dependent upon mere reconstruction, for the Chronicler himself, just like the compiler of the book of Kings, at the end of his statements about the individual kings of Judah, normally indicates one or more books in which further information may be found concerning them, and in Chron., just as in Kings, it is likely that the work or works referred to has provided at least a part of the material utilised by the Chronicler. It is hardly correct to assume, as Noth, Galling, Torrey, and others would do, that we are dealing in these references with a purely literary imitation of the indications of sources in the book of Kings, not to be taken seriously but like that in Esther x,2 (p. 511). The works cited fall into two groups. To one group belong those for which no compiler is mentioned but where it is simply said that they deal with kings; to the other group belong those in which prophets and seers appear as authors. As far as the first group is concerned, the following titles appear: *The book of the kings of Israel and Judah* (סֵפֶר מַלְכֵי יִשְׂרָאֵל וִיהוּדָה) in II xxvii, 7; xxxv, 27; xxxvi, 8; cf. I ix, 1;[11] *The book of the kings of Judah and Israel* (סֵפֶר הַמְּלָכִים לִיהוּדָה וְיִשְׂרָאֵל, II xvi, 11 סֵפֶר מַלְכֵי יְהוּדָה וְיִשְׂרָאֵל) in II xvi, 11; xxv, 26; xxviii, 26; xxxii, 32; *The book of the kings of Israel*

---

[7] Kraus, 'Chirbet el-chōch' ZDPV 72 (1956), pp. 152–62, Pls. 5–7: on xi, 6. Lit. § 126.
[8] 'Chronique archéologique' RB 63 (1956), pp. 68–100, cf. pp. 74–6: El-Bouquei'ah; Vogt, 'Varia' Bibl 37 (1956), pp. 265 f., cf. p. 266. Cf. above, p. 251, n. 15.
[9] Noth, *Überlieferungsgeschichtliche Studien* I (1943, 1957), pp. 139–43.
[10] Begrich, *Die Chronologie der Könige von Israel und Juda* (1929), pp. 208–9.
[11] Cf. next note.

(סֵפֶר מַלְכֵי יִשְׂרָאֵל) in II xx, 34, cf. I ix, 1;[12] *The words (affairs) of the kings of Israel* (דִּבְרֵי מַלְכֵי יִשְׂרָאֵל) in II xxxiii, 18; and *Midrash of the book of the Kings* (מִדְרַשׁ סֵפֶר הַמְּלָכִים) in II xxiv, 27.[13] In spite of the differences in the titles, it is quite certain that the same work is mentioned in all five cases. This is clear from one consideration alone, namely that the name *Israel* used alone in the title in II xx, 34 and xxxiii, 18 naturally includes Judah, and so is the same as *Israel and Judah* in the other cases. II xx, 34 deals with Jehoshaphat, and xxxiii, 18 with Manasseh, both kings of Judah. The books in the second group, ascribed to prophets, are designated as דִּבְרִים *words* (I xxix, 29; II ix, 29; xii, 15; xx, 34; xxxiii, 19) or as נְבוּאָה *prophecy* (II ix, 29), or חָזוֹן, חֲזוֹת *vision* (II ix, 29; xxxii, 32) or as מִדְרָשׁ *Midrash* (II xiii, 22); or it is stated that the prophet *has written them* (כָּתַב II xxvi, 22). Samuel, Nathan and Gad appear as authors for the history of David (I xxix, 29), Nathan, Ahijah and Jeddi for Solomon (II ix, 29), Shemaiah and Iddo for Rehoboam (II xii, 15), Iddo for Abijah (II xiii, 22), Jehu for Jehoshaphat (II xx, 34), Isaiah for Uzziah (II xxvi, 22), Isaiah for Hezekiah (II xxxii, 32) and *his seers*[14] for Manasseh (II xxxiii, 19).

From this it appears that, in addition to the Midrash of the Kings—for so we may now name the work which has been described in view of its name in II xxiv, 27—the Chronicler also made use of a whole series of prophetic writings. But in actual fact these are likely, in part at least, to coincide with the Midrash of the Kings. This is completely clear for the words of Jehu ben-Hanani mentioned in II xx, 34 as a source for Jehoshaphat. It is said of these words that they were *recorded in the book of the Kings of Israel*. It is also probable in the case of the writings of Samuel (I xxix, 29), Nathan (I xxix, 29; II ix, 29), Gad (I xxix, 29), Ahijah (II ix, 29), Jeddi (II ix, 29), Shemaiah (II xii, 15) and Iddo (II xii, 15; xiii, 22), mentioned at the end of the narratives of David, Solomon, Rehoboam and Abijah, for in the case of these kings the *Midrash of the Kings* is not cited, but the books of Sam. and Kings show them as being closely associated with these prophets so that it can readily be understood that the relevant sections of Sam. and Kings, or of the *Midrash of the Kings* dependent upon them, could be attributed to these prophets. This is the more likely in view of the fact that the older historical books were in any case thought to have been written by prophets, and hence were called 'Former Prophets' (p. 566). Furthermore, all those who are named by the Chronicler as compilers of prophetic writings appear in Sam. and Kings,[15] so that the identification of the books ascribed to them with the relevant sections of Sam. and

[12] 𝔐 here reads: *So all Israel was enrolled by its genealogies; and see, these are written in the Book of the Kings of Israel, and Judah was taken into exile in Babylon because of their unfaithfulness.* 𝔊 𝔓 𝔗 link *and Judah* with the previous words: *in the Book of the Kings of Israel and Judah.* Cf. Rudolph's commentary *ad loc.*

[13] Since סֵפֶר is not rendered in 𝔊, and in II xiii, 22 מִדְרָשׁ stands alone, סֵפֶר is probably a gloss on מִדְרָשׁ, and the title in II xxiv, 27 would then originally have read: *Midrash of the Kings* (cf. p. 534).

[14] Reading חֹזָיו instead of חוֹזַי, either a proper name or meaning *my seers*.

[15] On Iddo (עִדּוֹ), in II xii, 15; xiii, 22 and Jeddi (יֶעְדִּי or יֶעְדּוֹ) in II ix, 29 cf. Budde, ZAW 12 (1892), pp. 49–51; Noth, *Überlieferungsgeschichtliche Studien* I (1943, 1957), p. 134.

Kings is very natural. However, no proof can be offered that all the sources which the Chronicler describes as writings of the prophets were actually only parts of Sam. and Kings or of the Midrash based upon it. II xxxiii, 18–19 can be so understood as to mean that *the words of the seers* and *the words of the kings of Israel* were in front of the Chronicler. It is in any case clear that the Chronicler knew the prophetic books from Isaiah to Malachi; the quotations from Isa. vii, 9 in II xx, 20 and from Zech. iv, 10 in II vi, 9 prove this without doubt.

We must thus concede the possibility that the Chronicler utilised other sources beside the Midrash[16] of the kings, among them perhaps writings by or about prophets. But his main source was certainly that Midrash, and we must now attempt to get as clear a picture as possible of it. We must first consider the name itself. It is very much open to question whether the normal view is correct that here מִדְרָשׁ is already to be understood in the sense of a learned and edifying elaboration and expansion of the biblical histories, and so conclude that at least some of the narratives of this kind in Chron. do not stem from the Chronicler but were already to be found in the Midrash which he abridged. מִדְרָשׁ means *research, study* and then probably also *essay, work*. Hence מִדְרָשׁ הַמְּלָכִים, as we should probably read the text (p. 533, n. 13), is *an essay, work, book concerning the kings*. ⑤ renders the word as βιβλίον in II xii, 22, and as γραφή in II xxiv, 27. It will therefore be best if at first we simply use the word *Midrash* in the title in the sense of *book*, and get a picture of its contents in other ways.

We have already seen that the books of Chronicles on the one hand represent an extract from Gen.–Kings, and on the other hand offer material going beyond Gen.–Kings. The extracts from the older historical work are likely to have been taken by the Chronicler from the Midrash and not from the older historical work Gen.–Kings itself as we have it, and so it is from this source that there certainly comes some of the information which Chron. has in excess of Gen.–Kings. Frequently in the references to the Midrash there is an indication of its containing something which is not in Gen.–Kings, as in the case of the mention in II xxiv, 27 of Joash's sons, divine oracles, and founding of the Temple; in II xxvii, 7 of Jotham's wars; and in II xxxiii, 18 of Manasseh's prayer. The Midrash may thus be seen to be a new edition of the older historical work, enlarged with a variety of new material but perhaps at the same time abbreviated at other points. If the Midrash is the only or at any rate the main source for the Chronicler, then there already belonged to it the information mentioned earlier (p. 532) which Chron. contains in excess of Sam.–Kings, and probably also much of what we must consider in a moment as the Chronicler's special material. In any case we must picture the Midrash as a compilation which has gathered all sorts of material, a work not all of one piece but containing contradictions and repetitions. In these circumstances it is quite evident that it will be difficult for us to distinguish in Chron. between what was taken from the

---

[16] Renée Bloch, 'Écriture et tradition dans le Judaïsme. Aperçus sur l'origine du Midrash' Cah Si 8 (1954), pp. 9–34; Zeitlin, 'Midrash: A Historical Study' JQR 44 (1953), pp. 21–36. Lit. § 126.

Midrash and from any other sources on the one hand and the Chronicler's own compositions on the other.

So far as the historical value of the Midrash is concerned, we may leave on one side the material treated earlier which it has in common with Gen.–Kings and also the material which is to be considered in a moment as the Chronicler's own special material. It will suffice to say a word about the information which goes beyond Gen.–Kings of the kind mentioned on p. 532. These passages, for example the account of Josiah's clash with Pharaoh Necho in II xxxv, 20–5,[17] are to a large extent trustworthy and fill out, particularly in regard to the kings of Judah, the information given in Kings. In the lists in I i–ix there is also concealed valuable ancient material.[18]

3. *The Chronicler's own material*. We must now consider the Chronicler's own material. This is estimated by Noth as making up very nearly half the extent of our books of Chronicles, and Torrey says of it (1954, p. XI) that it reveals the Chronicler as a quite significant narrator, almost unique in the Old Testament in his inventiveness and vividness. We must recognise that it cannot be separated precisely from the content of the Midrash nor from the additions which the book underwent even after the work of its main compiler, additions which Galling assigns in large measure to his second Chronicler, a character whom he believes it possible to indicate as a clear personality. So we must at first use the term 'Chronicler' in the broader sense, and then later narrow it down at least in some degree (pp. 539–40). Even a superficial examination of the book enables us to pick out three features as characteristic, particularly if it is measured against the books of Sam. and Kings which so often run parallel to it: (1) the arrangement and correction of the events according to the religious pragmatism of retributive doctrine,[19] (2) a religious conception of history which reckons with direct divine intervention in events and limits human action to prayer and song, and (3) the marked predilection for Temple and cultus, for Levites and cultic music.

So far as the first point is concerned, we may regard as relatively unimportant the information given in I x, 13–14 that Saul had to fall in battle against the Philistines because he had not heeded Yahweh's word and had consulted a spirit of a dead man instead of Yahweh. Here it was simply a matter of making what had taken place intelligible in retrospect, and this had already happened

---

[17] Couroyer, 'Le litige entre Josias et Nechao' RB 55 (1948), pp. 388–96. Cf. Lit. p. 232, n. 26; p. 284, n. 14; pp. 296 f., nn. 60–2.

[18] Abel, 'Une mention biblique de Birzeit' RB 46 (1937), pp. 217–24: I vii, 30–32; Alt, 'Bemerkungen zu einigen jüdäischen Ortslisten des AT' ZDPV 68 (1951), pp. 193–210 = *Kl. Schr.* II, pp. 289–305, cf. pp. 199–206 or 294–301: I vi, 39–66; Lefèvre, 'Note d'exégèse sur les généalogies des Qehatites' RSR 37 (1950), pp. 287–92: I vi, 7–13, 18–23; Mazar, 'Gath and Gittaim' IEJ 4 (1954), pp. 227–38: I vii, 20–2; viii, 13; Möhlenbrink, 'Die levitischen Überlieferungen des AT' ZAW 52 (1934), pp. 184–231, pp. 197–205: I v, 27–vi, 38; Noth, 'Eine siedlungsgeographische Liste in I Chr. ii und iv' ZDPV 55 (1932), pp. 97–124; Talmon, 'המה הקינים הבאים מחמת אבי בית־רכב"' I Chron. ii, 55' IEJ 10 (1960), pp. 174–80; Waterman, 'Some Repercussions from Late Levitical Genealogical Accretions in P and the Chronicler' AJSL 58 (1941), pp. 49–56. Cf. pp. 24–5, Lit. §§ 40, 126.

[19] Cf. Eissfeldt, 'Zur Kompositionstechnik des Pseudo-Philonischen Liber Antiquitatum Biblicarum' NTT 56 (1955), pp. 53–71.

in I Sam. (xiii, 7b–15a; xv). II xii, 1–12 is more serious, for here in justification of the attack of Pharaoh Shishak, related in I Kings xiv, 25–8, it is said (xii, 1) that Rehoboam had fallen away from Yahweh, and then, still with the retributive scheme in mind, to give a moral basis for the historical fact of the continued and not unprosperous reign of Rehoboam, it is said that the king humbled himself before God because of the exhortation of the prophet Shemaiah, and so received the assurance from Yahweh that the visitation by the Egyptians would only be of short duration. Various misfortunes—illness, loss of shipping, violent death, defeat by enemies—are similarly explained in the cases of Asa (II xvi, 7–12), Jehoshaphat (II xx, 35–7), Joash (II xxiv, 17–25), Amaziah (II xxv, 14–28), and Uzziah (II xxvi, 16–23), as due to sins of all kinds, among which crimes against prophets (II xvi, 10; xxiv, 20–1; xxv, 16) and priests (II xxvi, 16–20) are especially serious. How such a view of history can distort the actual events may be seen particularly clearly in what is said of Manasseh. According to II Kings xxi there was no good to be said of him at all, but plenty of evil. According to II Chron. xxxiii, however, Manasseh's apostate behaviour was limited to the early part of his reign. Later, when he had been taken away as prisoner by the Assyrians *to Babylon*, he humbled himself and was pardoned by Yahweh. Hence he could return to Jerusalem and rule for a further substantial period—altogether twenty-five years (v. 1)—and achieve much. Here what had to be morally justified was the return from a journey made by Manasseh to the Assyrian king—no doubt historical but clearly improperly interpreted by the Chronicler—and the fact of his relatively long and successful reign. The conforming of events to his scheme of retribution is sometimes pushed so far by the Chronicler that in the case of some kings, as for example Asa (II xiii, 23; xv, 10, 19; xvi, 1, 12) or Josiah, he can even mark off to the exact year the phases of their reigns viewed as being determined by their religious and moral behaviour—cult-reform, peace and good fortune, apostasy from Yahweh, war and defeat, sickness and death. Though no doubt this is all done in good faith, these chronological notes, which by their exactness give at first the impression of reliability, prejudice the recognition of the actual course of events. Thus the dates given in II xxxiv, 1–xxxv, 19 for Josiah's cult-reforming measures are treated by some scholars as trustworthy, and have been made the basis for a reconstruction of the events, as by Oestreicher (in his work noted above on p. 172, pp. 60–5).

Miraculous interventions in events by God are described in the narratives of Abijah's victory over Jeroboam (II xiii, 13–20) and of Asa's victory over the Ethiopians (II xiv, 8–14). The Chronicler's conception of history with its ignoring of realities is even more clearly expressed in what he has to relate about Jehoshaphat's great victory over the Moabites, Ammonites and Meunites[20] following on his judicial reform[21] (II xx, 1–30).[22] When news comes of the enemies' attack, a great day of prayer is held in the Temple at Jerusalem at

[20] So in v. 1 with 𝔊 instead of the second *Ammonites*.
[21] Albright, 'The Judicial Reform of Jehoshaphat' *Alex. Marx. Jub. Vol.* I (1950), pp. 61–82.
[22] Noth, 'Eine palästinische Lokalüberlieferung in 2 Chr. xx' ZDPV 67 (1945), pp. 45–71.

which Jehoshaphat utters a prayer to the effect that only God can punish the invaders and so can help (vv. 1–13). A Levite, filled with Yahweh's spirit, proclaims that Yahweh will be with the Judaeans and that they do not need to fight at all (vv. 14–17). On the following morning, Jehoshaphat takes up his position with his army near Tekoa, exhorts them yet again to trust in Yahweh alone, and commands singers to go before the army in sacred attire and to begin a song of thanksgiving. They have hardly begun the song when a mysterious mutual slaughter, brought about by God, begins among the enemy troops, and when the Judaeans arrive, every one of their enemies lies dead upon the ground. The gathering of the booty lasts three days. On the fourth day the Judaeans gather in the *valley of blessing* and *there bless Yahweh*, and the return march to Jerusalem ends in a procession to the Temple accompanied by the music of harps, zithers and flutes (vv. 20–30). So what actually happens is that Yahweh intervenes as *deus ex machina*, while men have nothing to do but pray and sing.

With this, we have already moved on to the third feature which gives the Chronicler's own material its particular stamp, namely his pronounced love for everything cultic, and particularly for cultic singing and the Levites. This may be seen for example in the differences in the Ark narrative as compared with II Sam. v–vi. Now David fetches the Ark from Kiriath-Jearim first and only then begins the building of his palace, and this building may only be begun by David before the final bringing in of the Ark because Yahweh has made known, by the killing of one of the men conducting the Ark, that the Ark should at first still remain outside the residence (I xiii, 1–xiv, 1). Furthermore, the final bringing in (I xv–xvi) takes place with the utmost cultic splendour, far exceeding what is described in II Sam. vi, 12b–19. This love for Temple and cultus is, however, expressed most emphatically by what is said concerning David's preparations for the building of the Temple (I xxii–xxix, a passage of which the main part clearly appears to be later elaboration, so that it is here not the Chronicler so much as one or more of the elaborators who followed in his steps). Everything is here prepared down to the smallest detail. The building materials are acquired, the orders of priests, Levites and singers arranged, and even a complete model of the buildings prepared. It is indeed only because of Yahweh's explicit command that David gave up his dearest wish of building the Temple, but he prepared for it the more zealously and lays it the more urgently upon the heart of his son Solomon.

In fact, David's reign is altogether filled up with his concern for cultic matters. Not very much remains of the picture of David as he is presented to us in the books of Samuel—the bold man of war who can win the hearts of his companions in war and bind them to him, the skilled politician who with all his inward attachment to the cultus nevertheless is able to make it serve his political ends, a man worthy of love, though strongly sensual and also cruel, a loving, lenient though weak husband and father, and a worshipper of Yahweh filled with a deep fatalistically inclined piety. In place of this, it is true, a new feature has appeared, in that with the mention of David there are Messianic overtones, and his figure is seen as a pledge of the Davidic covenant, still valid in the period of the Chronicler and after (cf. I xvii).[23] With this marked interest in Temple and cultus, there appears an especial predilection for the Levites and their rights, which becomes particularly clear when it necessarily leads to the correction of the older narratives which served as a basis, because these did not do justice to the claims of the Levites (claims which at that time did not exist). Thus in I vi, 12–13, 18, unlike I Sam. i, 1, Samuel is made a Levite because according to the law (Num. i, 50–3; iii–iv) only a Levite could come in contact with the Ark. In I xv, 2 David explicitly ordains, with an appeal to the will of Yahweh as expressed in that law, that only Levites may carry the Ark. Very characteristic too is the transformation of the narrative concerning the removal of Athaliah from the throne and her assassination (II Kings xi, cf. II Chron. xxii, 10–xxiii, 21). Now, though admittedly not quite consistently, the soldiers of II Kings xi are replaced by priests and Levites, because, as is explicitly stated by Jehoiada, the leader of the conspiracy, in xxiii, 6, the Temple may be entered only by priests and Levites. Among the larger circle of Levites it is in particular the singers who are nearest the Chronicler's heart. He expends great care in the putting together of their genealogy (I vi, 16–32; xv, 16–21; xxv[24]) and where it is possible he brings singers on to the stage and even introduces their songs as well (I xvi, 4–36; II xx, 19, 21; xxix, 25–30; xxxi, 2).

4. *The historical setting and the value of the Chronicler's special material.* With the first two of the elements just described, the assessment and correction of history according to the scheme of retribution and the conception of history as including God's direct intervention in events, we are dealing with tendencies which are characteristic of Israelite religion from an early stage. The Elohistic narratives of the judges (pp. 264–6) and then their Deuteronomic elaboration (pp. 266–7), and the Deuteronomic book of Kings (pp. 283–5) reveal a similar scheme, and this religious conception of history, remote from reality, is ultimately only a cruder and weaker form of the heroic confidence in faith of an Isaiah, as expressed in his word to king Ahaz: *If you do not believe, you will not abide* (Isa. vii, 9). On the basis of these two points, it is not possible to give a more exact dating in terms of century or decade. But it is different with the third point, the marked prominence given to cultus, Levites and singers. For here it may be clearly recognised by what standard the Chronicler has assessed history, just as was the case in regard to the compiler of the book of Kings. There the book of Deuteronomy provided the standard; here with the Chronicler it is clearly the Pentateuch, already containing the Priestly code which gives it its particular stamp, that is regarded as the norm of action. This may be seen quite clearly from the correcting of the earlier material in reference to the Levites which we have already considered, made with a view to the P-laws, and it is confirmed by a whole series of other observations. Thus in II i, 3 the fact reported in I Kings iii, 4–15 that Solomon sacrificed in Gibeon is excused on the grounds that the Tent of Meeting was in Gibeon at that time, just as earlier

[23] van den Bussche, 'Le texte de la prophétie de Nathan sur la dynastie Davidique' EThL 24 (1948), pp. 354–94, esp. p. 382.

[24] Begrich, BHK (³1937), p. 1368; Torczyner, 'A Psalm by the Sons of Heman' JBL 68 (1949), pp. 247–9, where he claims that the last nine names in I xxv, 4 are in reality the beginning of a song ascribed to one of the sons of Heman.

David's sacrifice on the threshing floor of Ornan (II Sam. xxiv, 25) was justified on the grounds that David, dismayed by the appearance of the angel, could not first have gone to Gibeon (I xxi, 26–xxii, 1). Furthermore, the narratives of Hezekiah's and Josiah's Passover festivals (II xxx, 13–27; xxxv, 1–19) and Hezekiah's measures concerning cultic gifts (II xxxi, 4–16), clearly presuppose the relevant P prescriptions (Exod. xii*, Num. xviii). The earlier view which treated P alone as determinative for the Chronicler was exaggerated, and this has been rightly corrected by von Rad and Noth in that the Chronicler clearly considered the whole Pentateuch as binding and not least D within it. Yet it is clear that for him the Pentateuch owes its peculiar character to P, and the view that the book of Kings presents the history as if D had been operative since Israel's entry into Canaan, while the Chronicler measures the past by the standard of P, does to that extent retain its validity.

Admittedly this is not the whole story. The cultic institutions which the Chronicler regards as ideal and as normative only coincide in part with those which are prescribed in the Pentateuch, and significant measures concerning the Levites and singers find no basis there. Here we clearly have tendencies from the Chronicler's own period and environment which are acquiring validity and are legitimated not as in P by being traced back to Moses, but by being traced back to David. Side by side with P's lawgiver, Moses, David as orderer of cult and cult music has a somewhat independent position. Clearly in the measures undertaken by David which are not sanctioned by the Pentateuch, expression is being given to cultic movements of the Chronicler's own time, and this is the more easily to be understood since the Chronicler in all probability is to be sought in the circles of those who were the bearers of this new movement, the Levites and singers. But the fact that David has been made into the originator of the measures here in view is to be explained on the basis of the high esteem which David enjoyed in the circles of the Levitical singers. The one who had in actual fact done much for cultic singing (p. 452), has now become the patron of the cult singers, and so there are attributed to him the institutions which these circles were aiming at or had already achieved.

This brings us to the question as to whether the Chronicler's own material has historical value, and if so how far. So far as the transformation of the older history after the pattern of P is concerned, and the measures attributed to David just mentioned, these represent a distortion of the earlier period and in this respect are irrelevant as sources for the historian. On the other hand, for the Chronicler's own period, the fourth century, and, since the term 'Chronicler' may here too include the later additions (p. 540), also for the third and probably also for the second centuries (p. 540), they are of very great value, the more so since otherwise we have practically no information available for this period. The same is true of the scheme of retribution and the religious conception of history, for they give us some idea of the philosophy of life and of history which developed in the later post-exilic period in circles which were very remote from the real events and therefore had no longer any understanding of the past history of their people, when it still possessed a powerful political life of its own and claimed as its own a religion suited to this political condition. However, the narratives which belong in this category are, in part at least, not entirely valueless for our knowledge of the earlier periods. They are formed here and there from old and reliable material, probably taken from the *Midrash of the Kings*. Thus the information about Manasseh's prayer and his being heard are certainly historically valueless, but the note in the context, preserved only here, about his journey to the Assyrian king (II xxxiii, 11–13, p. 536) appears nevertheless to be trustworthy.

5. *The period of composition of Chronicles. Later additions.* The recognition that the Chronicler presupposes that P is already combined with the older Pentateuch, and thus the completed Pentateuch, and the fact that the Chronicler carries down his presentation, which also includes our books of Ezra and Nehemiah (pp. 530–1), to beyond 398 B.C., the *terminus a quo* for the book is fixed: it must be after 398 (pp. 554–5). It is reasonable to assume that he did not write so very long after this, since he would otherwise presumably have carried his narrative further. On the other hand the fact that the Chronicler had no longer any clear picture of the chronological order of Nehemiah and Ezra and so could wrongly place the latter before the former (p. 554), is most readily explained if he compiled his work two or three generations after Ezra's appearance. We may thus picture him as active in the middle or in the second half of the fourth century B.C. He ended his story with an event which lay by then 50 or more years back, the appearance of Ezra, but the explanation of this is that nothing had happened since this decisive event in the consolidation of the Jewish religious community, which could be in any way set beside it.

But the book as we now have it was not what the Chronicler then compiled. His work has been further substantially enlarged and variously altered at a later date, as we have seen (p. 535). In particular, it is the catalogues in I i–ix and the lists in I xxiii–xxvii which have received the substantial additions which are in part to be understood as deposits from contemporary conditions. Whether these expansions are at any rate mainly to be ascribed, as Galling believes, to one elaborator, the 'second Chronicler', or are to be assigned to several hands, can hardly be decided definitely. But it is certain that these expansions extend down to the beginning of the second century B.C., for I xxiv[25] for example apparently came into being only then. The first external witness available to us of the existence of the Chronicles is the 'Praise of the Fathers' (Ecclus. xliv–l) compiled in about 190 B.C., which in xlvii, 2–11 (particularly vv. 8–10) clearly presupposes in its statements about David the picture drawn of David in Chronicles,[26] and the second witness is the use of II ii, 2–15 𝔊 by the Jewish historian Eupolemos[27] writing in about 157 B.C.

[25] Annie Jaubert, 'Le calendrier des Jubilés' VT 7 (1957), pp. 35–61, cf. pp. 47 f. on xxiv, 7–18; Winter, 'Twenty-Six Priestly Courses' VT 6 (1956), pp. 215–17. Lit. § 126.
[26] Cf. Ackroyd, 'Criteria for the Maccabean Dating of Old Testament Literature' VT 3 (1953), pp. 113–32: cf. p. 116.
[27] W. von Christ, *Geschichte der griechischen Literatur*, 6th ed. by W. Schmid II, 1 (1920), pp. 589 f.; Dalbert, 'Die Theologie der hellenistisch-jüdischen Missionsliteratur' ThF 4 (1954), pp. 35–42; Lesky, *Geschichte der Griechischen Literatur* (1957/58), p. 728; Schürer, GJV III (⁴1909), pp. 474–7, E. T. *History of the Jewish People* II, 3 (1897), pp. 203–6. Lit. § 126.

§ 73. EZRA AND NEHEMIAH

Literature: (a) Commentaries (i) Series: ATD: Galling (1954, 1958); BOuT: de Fraine (1961); Camb. B: Ryle (1893); Echter-B: Rehm (1950); HAT: Rudolph (1949); HK: Siegfried (1901); HS: Schneider (⁴1959); HSAT: Hölscher (1923); IB: Bowman, Gilkey (1954); ICC: Batten (1913 (1949)); Jerusalem-B: Gelin (1953); KeH: Bertheau-Ryssel (²1887); KHC: Bertholet (1902); Montserrat-B: Ubach (1958); SAT: Haller (²1925); Soncino-B: Slotki (1951); SZ: Oettli (1889); TU: van Selms (1935).

(ii) Single Commentaries: Fernández (1950); Zêr Kābôd (1948) [Hebrew].

(b) Other Works: Ahlemann, 'Zur Esra-Quelle' ZAW 59 (1942/43), pp. 77–98; Albright, 'A Brief History of Judah from the Days of Josiah to Alexander the Great' BA 9 (1946), pp. 1–16; *The Biblical Period* (Reprinted from *The Jews; Their History, Culture and Religion,* ed. by L. Finkelstein, 1949) (1950), pp. 45–55, 62–5; *The Bible after Twenty Years of Archaeology (1932 to 1952)* (Reprinted from Religion in Life 21 (1952), pp. 537–50, (1954), p. 547; *Recent Discoveries in Bible Lands* (1955), pp. 101–6; Allgeier, 'Beobachtungen am Septuagintatext der Bücher Esdras und Nehemias' Bibl 22 (1941), pp. 227–51; Bentzen, 'Sirach, der Chronist und Nehemia' StTh 3 (1950/51), pp. 158–61; Bewer, *Der Text des Buches Ezra* (FRLANT 31, 1922); Bright, *A History of Israel* (1959), pp. 356–86: 'The Reforms of Nehemiah and Ezra'; 'The Date of Ezra's Mission to Jerusalem' *Kaufmann Jub. Vol.* (1960), pp. 70–87; Cazelles, 'La mission d'Esdras' VT 4 (1954), pp. 113–40; Geissler, *Die literarischen Beziehungen der Esramemoiren* (Programm Chemnitz, 1899); Gotthard, *Der Text des Buches Nehemia* (1932–56); 2. ed.: fasc. 1 (1958); Granild, *Ezrabogens literære genesis undersøgt med særlight henblick paa et efterkronistik indgreb* (1949); Grosheide, 'Een geschrift van Tabeël?' GThT 50 (1950), pp. 71–9; 'Twee edicten van Cyrus ten gunste van de Joden (Ezra i, 2–4 en vi, 3–5)' GThT 54 (1954), pp. 1–12; 'Juda als onderdeel van het Perzische Rijk' GThT 54 (1954), pp. 65–76; 'Ezra, de Schriftgeleerde' GThT 56 (1956), pp. 84–8; Johannesen, *Studier over Esras og Nehemjas Historie* (1946); Kapelrud, *The Question of Authorship in the Ezra-Narrative* (1944); Kittel, *Geschichte des Volkes Israel,* III 2 (1929), pp. 330–441, 519–662; Koopmans, 'Het eerste aramese gedeelte in Ezra (iv, 7–vi, 19)' GThT 55 (1955), pp. 142–60; Kosters, *Het Herstel van Israël in het Perzische Tijdvak* (1893) (German transl. by Basedow, 1895); Kugler, *Von Moses bis Paulus* (1922), pp. 201–33, 289–300; Eduard Meyer, *Die Entstehung des Judenthums* (1896); Mowinckel, *Ezra den Skriftlærde* (1916); *Statholderen Nehemia* (1916); ' "Ich" und "Er" in der Ezrageschichte' *Rudolph-Festschr.* (1961), pp. 211–33; Noth, *Überlieferungsgeschichtliche Studien* I (1943 (1957)), pp. 110–180; Nyberg, 'Das Reich der Achämeniden' *Historia Mundi* III (1954), pp. 56–115, cf. pp. 66–110; Pavlovský, 'Ad chronologiam Esdrae vii' VD 33 (1955), pp. 280–4; 'Die Chronologie der Tätigkeit Esdras. Versuch einer neuen Lösung' Bibl 38 (1957), pp. 275–305, 428–56; Schaeder, *Iranische Beiträge* I (1930); *Esra, der Schreiber* (1930); Sellin, *Geschichte des israelitisch-jüdischen Volkes* II (1932), pp. 134–63; Smend, 'Die Listen der Bücher Esra und Nehemia' *Programm zur Rektoratsfeier der Universität Basel* (1881); Torrey, *The Composition and Historical Value of Ezra-Nehemiah* (1896); *Ezra Studies* (1910); Tuland, 'Hanani-Hananiah' JBL 77 (1958), pp. 157–61; ' "Uššayyā" and 'Uššarnâ': A Clarification of Terms, Date and Text' JNESt 17 (1958), pp. 269–275; Welch, *Postexilic Judaism* (1935); Wellhausen, 'Die Rückkehr der Juden aus dem babylonischen Exil' NGG (1895), pp. 166–86; review of Eduard Meyer, *Entstehung des Judenthums,* in GGA (1896), pp. 606–8.

Cf. also Literature §§ 58, 59, 70, 72, 77, 126.

1. *Name and contents.* The books of Ezra and Nehemiah, as has been shown in more detail in the discussion of the books of Chronicles (pp. 530–1), originally formed one large historical work together with the latter, and were only later separated from them. After the separation, they were first, even in 𝕲,

counted as one book, but soon in 𝔊 and then also in the Latin translations the division into two became normal, resulting naturally from the title which appears at Neh. i, 1: *The words of Nehemiah ben-Hacaliah.* The division is first attested in Origen († 254), and Jerome († 420) presupposes it as normal both among Greeks and Latins. Since 1448 the division has also come into Hebrew texts. In the latter the two sections are normally entitled Ezra and Nehemiah, as is the case in the English translation. But the designation of the books is different in 𝔊 and 𝔅. In 𝔊, where Ἔσδρας α΄ is the name of the apocryphal book of Ezra to be discussed later (§ 77), our book of Ezra is designated as Ἔσδρας β΄ and our book of Nehemiah as Ἔσδρας γ΄, while for the Ezra apocalypse, which will also be considered later (§ 99), no Greek title Ἔσδρας δ΄ is attested but only Ἔσδρας ὁ προφήτης and Ἔσδρα ἀποκάλυψις. The situation is different in 𝔅. Here Esdras I denotes our Ezra, Esdras II our book of Nehemiah, while for the apocryphal Ezra (Ἔσδρας α΄) the title Esdras III is used, and for the apocalypse Esdras IV.

Ezra-Nehemiah may thus be treated as a unit, or more correctly the conclusion of a larger unit. It falls into two unequal halves: Ezra i–vi deals with the period from Cyrus' Edict (538) down to the completion of the second Temple (516),[1] and Ezra vii–Neh. xiii covers the reforms of Ezra and Nehemiah, from the seventh year of an Artaxerxes to the thirty-second year of an Artaxerxes, with the question remaining open as to whether we are dealing with the first (465–424) or second (404–359) king of this name—for the third (359–338) hardly comes seriously into consideration.

2. *The Chronicler's contribution and his sources.* The Chronicler, the compiler of the comprehensive historical work covering the two books of Chronicles and the book of Ezra and Nehemiah (pp. 530–1), reveals here the same techniques as in Chronicles. Large, normally word for word extracts from the sources available to him are enriched with additions from his own pen, additions which are nearly always concerned with the Temple and cultus and music (Ezra iii*, Neh. xii, 27–30, 33–6, 41–7). It is true that there are lacking here the very frequent references to sources found in Chronicles (pp. 532–5), we can perhaps only compare with them the rather different indications in Neh. i, 1 (pp. 542, 544), vii, 5 (p. 550), xii, 23 (p. 550). That sources were utilised is as clear here as it was in the previous work, and the sections extracted from the sources may be distinguished with reasonable certainty from the passages which derive from the Chronicler's own hand. The Chronicler's own work is to be found substantially in Ezra iii*; vi, 19–22; vii, 1–11; Neh. xii, 27–43*, in addition to the prayers which may be his in Ezra ix, 6–15; Neh. ix, 6–37.[2] In addition, he seems in Neh. viii–ix to have rewritten in his own style the sources which were available to him for the events here narrated, though with considerable dependence upon their wording. The rest of the material consists of excerpts from sources.

We may now go through these in order, leaving on one side for the moment

[1] Andersen, 'Who built the Second Temple?' ABR 6 (1958), pp. 1–35.
[2] Liebreich, 'The Impact of Nehemiah ix, 5–37 on the Liturgy of the Synagogue' HUCA 32 (1961), pp. 227–37.

the numerous lists. In i, 1–iv, 5 we may leave aside for the moment the passages i, 2–4;[3] i, 8–11a;[4] ii[5] which in any case derive from older originals. It can hardly be decided with certainty whether this section is the Chronicler's own work or whether it was taken by him from a source and enriched with additions of his own, particularly in iii. In spite of the objections raised by Schaeder, Noth, Rudolph and others, we must probably regard it as derived from a source. The next section, iv, 6–vi, 18, stands out, however, quite clearly as an Aramaic source available to him, shortened by him at the beginning (vv. 6–7), and with its opening translated into Hebrew (v. 5). In an account supported by documents, it is concerned with presenting the difficulties with which the people of Jerusalem had to contend in the attempts which they made to rebuild the Temple and the city walls under Darius I[6] (521–485), Xerxes (485–465)[7] and Artaxerxes I (465–424)[8]—only this Artaxerxes can be intended here. The events are, it is true, not in the correct order, for what happened under Xerxes and Artaxerxes (iv, 6–23) now precedes what belongs in the reign of Darius I (iv, 24–vi, 18). But in the source, as we shall see (pp. 551–2), the narrative followed the chronological order of the events, i.e. iv, 24–vi, 18 stood before iv, 6–23. It must here be observed that the source postulated for i, 1–iv, 5 overlaps substantially in material this extract from a source in iv, 6–vi, 18, or more precisely its second half iv, 24–vi, 18.

The next large piece of source material begins at vii, 11 or vii, 12 and is preceded in vii, 1–10 by an introduction which comes from the Chronicler himself, an introduction which is at many points parallel with the source-extract itself. At vii, 8–9 we have already reached the point to which the source brings us again in viii, 32, the moment of Ezra's arrival in Jerusalem, according to vii, 8–9 (cf. viii, 31) *on the first day of the fifth month in the seventh year of Artaxerxes.* So far as the source-extract itself is concerned, beginning at vii, 11 or vii, 12 and extending at least as far as ix, 1–5, it derives substantially from the Memoirs of Ezra. Ezra here speaks everywhere in the first person singular (vii, 28; viii, 15–17, 21–9; ix, 1–5) or uses the plural so as to include his companions on the journey (vii, 27; viii, 17–18, 21–3, 31–2), and there is no sufficient ground for regarding this first person form as artificial. There is no need, with

[3] Bickerman, 'The Edict of Cyrus in Ezra i' JBL 65 (1946), pp. 249–75; Ginsberg, 'Ezra i, 4' JBL 79 (1960), pp. 167–9.
[4] Galling, 'Der Tempelschatz nach Berichten und Urkunden im Buche Esra' ZDPV 60 (1937), pp. 177–83.
[5] Cf. p. 550.
[6] Benedict and von Voigtlander, 'Darius' Bisitun Inscription, Babylonian Version, Lines 1–19' JCSt 10 (1956), pp. 1–10; Cameron, 'The Old Persian Text of the Bisitun Inscription' JCSt 5 (1951), pp. 47–54; P. J. Junge, *Dareios I., König der Perser* (1944); Parker, 'Darius and His Egyptian Campaign' AJSL 58 (1941), pp. 373–7; Erich F. Schmidt, *Persepolis* I (1953), II (1957); on this Hinz, ZDMG 104 (1954), pp. 490–2; 108 (1958), pp. 126–32. Cf. Lit. §§ 58, 59, and especially p. 426, n. 1; p. 586, n. 6. Lit. § 126.
[7] Morgenstern, 'Jerusalem—485 B.C.' HUCA 27 (1956), pp. 101–79; 28 (1957), pp. 15–47; 31 (1960), pp. 1–29, links the allusions in Ezra iv, 6 to difficulties which the Jews experienced under Xerxes, with the rebellion of the Jews which he assumes for the year 485 B.C. and with the disastrous consequences of this. Cf. also Morgenstern, 'The message of Deutero-Isaiah in its sequential unfolding' HUCA 29 (1958), pp. 1–67; 30 (1959), pp. 1–102.
[8] Galling, 'Kronzeugen des Artaxerxes? Eine Interpretation von Esra iv 9f.' ZAW 63 (1952), pp. 66–74.

Mowinckel, to trace this usage to an unknown Jew, naïvely pious, an eyewitness indeed of the events, but not understanding their real significance, who gave a very muddled picture of them in his edifying description. Nor need we ascribe it to the Chronicler himself, as is done with many differences in detail by Torrey, Hölscher, Noth, Kapelrud and others, and then to present Ezra as a completely unhistorical character, a transposition into religious terms of the secular figure of Nehemiah. We may ascribe the basic material of vii, 11–ix, 5 [9] to Ezra himself. Whether this is also true of the prayer in ix, 6–15 is difficult to decide. The possibility may be conceded, but on the other hand such prayers were often readily inserted later, as we have already seen in the case of Dan. ix, 4–20 (p. 529) and as we shall see again in the 'Additions' to Daniel and Esther (§§ 84, 85). The confidence with which Schaeder claims this prayer, as well as that in Neh. ix, 6–37, for the historical Ezra, is hardly justifiable in either case.

Whereas ix, 1–5, the introduction to the narrative about the setting aside of mixed marriages, is taken from the Ezra Memoirs, in the narrative itself there is no use of first person forms, whether singular or plural, by Ezra himself. Everywhere reference is made to him in the third person (x, 1, 2, 5, 6, 10, 16). On the other hand, the Chronicler's own style does not appear clearly anywhere here, so that we cannot follow Noth and ascribe it to his hand. Budde* attempted to explain the situation by assuming that there is here an extract from the Ezra Memoirs, in which the first person forms have simply been replaced by third person forms, and Rudolph takes a similar view. But the more natural assumption is that the Chronicler, in addition to Ezra's own account, had at his disposal another source for the carrying out of the divorce procedure, and that in this case he preferred it. It is possible that he also took from it the lists in x, 18–44.

With Neh. i, 1 we begin the Nehemiah Memoirs, which extend right through our book of Nehemiah and are easily recognisable. In i, 1a they also have a special title, namely *The words of Nehemiah ben-Hacaliah*. According to Galling, it was not the Chronicler, writing in about 300, but only the 'Second Chronicler' (p. 535), the elaborator of the work who is to be placed about a century later, who took up the Nehemiah Memoirs which till then had circulated as an independent work, so as to interweave the activities of the governor Nehemiah and the ecclesiastical commissioner Ezra. It is true, as we shall see more clearly below (p. 552), that this interweaving does not correspond to the historical facts, and represents a reconstruction of events. But there is hardly any real necessity for denying the Memoirs to the original Chronicler and for ascribing them only to a later elaborator. We may thus regard the Chronicler himself as responsible for seeking to bring about the linking of the characters of Ezra and Nehemiah by the uniting of the Ezra Memorial and the Nehemiah Memoirs. In any case, Neh. i, 1b–vii, 5 belongs almost entirely to Nehemiah's Memoirs. Nehemiah begins his account with his receiving of the news of the ruined condition of the walls of Jerusalem, dated *in the month of Chislev* (November–December), *in the*

[9] Fruhstorfer, 'Ein alttestamentliches Konkordat (Esr. vii, viii)' Stud. Anselm. 27/28, (1951), pp. 178–86.

twentieth year (i, 1), and with the permission granted to him by the king *in the month of Nisan* (March–April), *in the twentieth year of Artaxerxes* (ii, 1) to go to Jerusalem (i, 1–ii, 8).[10] He tells of his arrival in Jerusalem, of the beginning of the building of the walls, and of the hostility of the governors of the provinces of Samaria, Ammon and Arabia (or Idumaea),[11] namely Sanballat,[12] Tobiah and Geshem[13] (ii, 9–20). He enumerates the persons, groups and localities which took part in the building of the walls (iii, 1–32),[14] including Beth-haccherem, (iii, 14) mentioned in Jer. vi, 1 and probably to be identified with Ramat Rahel,[15] tells of the mockery of the undertaking by Sanballat and Tobiah (iii, 33–8),[16] and even of violent attempts at hindering it and of measures taken as a result (iv). He tells of the carrying out of a generous measure for the release of debts in favour of the lower classes (v, 1–13),[17] of his own disinterested behaviour throughout his twelve years of office (v, 14–19), of renewed trickery by his colleagues in the neighbouring areas (vi, 1–14, 17–19), and of the completion, in spite of all this, of the building of the walls in fifty-two days (vi, 15–16). He tells finally of the appointment of a city governor and of preparations for increasing the population of the sparsely populated city (vii, 1–5), and gives a list which was found during these preparations, the list of those who returned with Zerubbabel, which is also to be found in Ezra ii (vii, 6–72).

At this point, Nehemiah's first person narrative breaks off for the moment, and what follows in viii–x has nothing to do with the theme of vii, 1–5 (72), the fortifying and securing of Jerusalem. It is the narrative of a great assembly of the people, held *on the first day of the seventh month* (viii, 2, no year is indicated), at which Ezra reads from the *lawbook of Moses* (viii, 1), supported by

[10] Jepsen, 'Pardes' ZDPV 74 (1958), pp. 65–8: on ii, 8.

[11] Alt, 'Judas Nachbarn zur Zeit Nehemias' PJB 27 (1931), pp. 66–74 = *Kl. Schr.* II, pp. 338–45; 'Die Rolle Samarias bei der Entstehung des Judentums' *Procksch-Festschr.* (1934), pp. 5–28 = *Kl. Schr.* II, pp. 316–37; 'Zur Geschichte der Grenze zwischen Judäa und Samaria' PJB 31 (1935), pp. 94–111 = *Kl. Schr.* II, pp. 346–62.

[12] Rowley, 'Sanballat and the Samaritan Temple' BJRL 38 (1955/56), pp. 166–98 = *Men of God* (1963), pp. 246–76; 'Sanballat et le temple samaritain' OBL 1 (1957), pp. 175–91; Torrey, 'Sanballat "The Horonite"' JBL 47 (1928), pp. 380–9.

[13] Albright, 'Dedan' *Alt-Festschrift* (1953), pp. 1–12, see p. 4 and cf. BASOR 139 (1955), p. 19; Cross, 'Geshem the Arabian, Enemy of Nehemiah' BA 18 (1955), pp. 46 f.; Rabinowitz, 'Aramaic Inscriptions of the Fifth Century B.C.E. from a North-Arab Shrine in Egypt' JNES 15 (1956), pp. 1–9, Pls. I–VII; G. E. Wright, 'Judaean Lachish' BA 18 (1955), pp. 9–17, see pp. 16 f.

[14] Alt, 'Das Taltor von Jerusalem' PJB 24 (1928), pp. 74–98 = *Kl.Schr.* III, pp. 326–47; Avi-Yonah, 'The Walls of Nehemiah' IEJ 4 (1954), pp. 239–48; Burrows, 'Nehemiah iii, 1–32 as a Source for the Topography of Ancient Jerusalem' AASOR 14 (1934), pp. 115–40; 'Nehemiah's Tour of Inspection' BASOR 64 (1936), pp. 11–21; Simons, *Jerusalem in the Old Testament* (1952), pp. 437–58; Vincent, *Jérusalem de l'Ancien Testament* I (1954), pp. 237–59.

[15] Aharoni, 'Excavations at Ramath Rahel 1954: Preliminary Report' IEJ 6 (1956), pp. 102, 111, 137–57, Pls. 9–14, 21–4; 'Ramat Rahel' IEJ 9 (1959), pp. 272–4; 10 (1960), pp. 261 f.; 11 (1961), p. 84; 'The Second Season of Excavations at Ramat Rahel' [Hebrew, Engl. summary] BIES 24 (1960), pp. 73–119, I–II, 8 Pls.; 'Ramat Rahel', Part I ILN 239 (1960), pp. 1096–98; 239 (1960), pp. 1140–42; Grintz, 'Jehoezer—unknown high priest?' JQR 50 (1960), pp. 338–45; Kutscher, פחזא and its Cognates' [Hebrew, Engl. summary] Tarbiz 30 (1960/1), pp. 112–19, I–II. Cf. p. 201, n. 14; p. 358; p. 675, n. 14; § 126.

[16] Burrows, 'The Origin of Neh. iii 33–37' AJSL 52 (1935/36), pp. 235–44.

[17] Neufeld, 'The Rate of Interest and the Text of Nehemiah v, 11' JQR 44 (1953/54), pp. 194–204. Lit. § 126.

T

the Levites (viii, 1–12).[18] It then tells of a meeting of the heads of families held on the *second day* (viii, 13) which resolves on the celebration of the feast of booths during the current *seventh month* (viii, 14) on the basis of a command *written in the law* (viii, 14) and of the feast itself which lasts for eight days (viii, 15–18). It also tells of a great day of penitence and prayer held *on the twenty-fourth day of this month* (ix, 1), with a long prayer spoken by the Levites (according to 𝔊 by Ezra) (ix),[19] to which there is directly linked in ch. x a document in the first person plural with an enumeration of all the cultic activities undertaken by the whole people. The theme of vii, 1–5 (72) reappears only in **xi, 1–2,** in a report on the carrying out of the measures designed to repopulate Jerusalem, and although the first person singular form does not appear here with reference to Nehemiah, the verses must nevertheless derive, at least as far as their content is concerned, from the Memoirs of Nehemiah. After a series of lists has been given on which comment must be made at a later stage (pp. 549–51), we then have xii, 27–43,[20] the account of the dedication of the walls, which clearly links with vii, 1–5 (72) and xi, 1–2. Here again there appears at once the first person singular for Nehemiah, first in xii, 31. The passage thus derives from his Memoirs, though only its basic material since there are certain points which go back to the hand of the Chronicler.

From Nehemiah's Memoirs comes, lastly, the basic material of xii, 44–xiii, 31, where the first person singular form appears throughout—first in xiii, 6–7 and last in xiii, 31. Nehemiah here describes a number of cultic measures which he carried through after he had returned from a journey to the king undertaken *in the thirty-second year of Artaxerxes.*[21] These measures included the recovery for its original cultic purpose of a room in the Temple occupied by the governor of the province of Ammon (xiii, 4–9), provision for the regular delivery of the tithes (xiii, 10–14), the securing of the sabbath rest (xiii, 15–22), measures against mixed marriages (xiii, 23–7), and (xiii, 24) against the displacing of the Judaean language (יְהוּדִית) by that of Ashdod (אַשְׁדּוֹדִית),[22] the expulsion of a son of the high priest who was son-in-law to the governor of the province of Samaria (xiii, 28–30a), and the regulating of the service of priests and Levites and of the delivery of firewood and firstfruits (xiii, 30b–31). With the formula *Remember me, O my God, for good* which Nehemiah has frequently inserted into his Memoirs (v, 19; xiii, 14, 22), the book closes, and this is clearly also the end of the Memoirs. The formula is reminiscent of the open-

---

[18] On the frequently discussed word מִפֹרָשׁ in viii, 8, cf. Bowman, 'Samaritan Studies' BJRL 40 (1957/8), pp. 298–327, cf. pp. 316–19; Franz Altheim and Ruth Stiehl (p. 38, n. 23), pp. 1–16; Gertner (§ 126 on p. 534, n. 16).

[19] Rehm, 'Nehemias ix' BZ 1 (1957), pp. 59–69; Welch, 'The Source of Nehemiah ix' ZAW 47 (1929), pp. 130–7.

[20] Burrows, 'The Topography of Nehemiah xii, 31–43' JBL 54 (1935), pp. 29–39.

[21] Cf. the absence of two or three years' duration of Arsam from his Egyptian satrapy (411/10–408 B.C.): Cowley, *Ar. Pap.*, No. 30; Driver, *Aramaic Documents of the Fifth Century B.C.* (1954), p. 5 *et passim;* Abridged and Revised Edition (1957), pp. 12 *et passim;* Kraeling, *Ar. Pap.*, p. 105 *et passim.*

[22] Del Medico, 'Asdod et l'Asdodien' *Actes V Congrès Internat. Sciences Onomastiques,* Vol. I (Salamanca 1958), Separ. 13 pp.; Milik, *Dix ans de Découvertes dans le Désert de Juda* (1957), p. 89, E.T. *Ten Years of Discovery in the Wilderness of Judaea* (1959), p. 131. Lit. § 126.

ings of Aramaic votive and memorial inscriptions,[23] and shows that Nehemiah's autobiography is intended as an offering to God.

Nehemiah's Memoirs, which form the basic material of i, 1–vii, 5 +xi, 1–2 +xii, 27–xiii, 31, are a self-contained document of very marked individuality. It is all the more remarkable that the Chronicler, or perhaps some later editor, should not have allowed it to retain its impressiveness as a complete entity but has disturbed it by inserting extracts from other sources. We must look again at viii–x. In viii–ix, which must be examined by themselves, Ezra is the chief personage in everything (viii, 1, 2, 4, 5, 6, 9, 13; ix, 6 ⑮). Nehemiah appears only in viii, 9, but here *Nehemiah, i.e. the governor and* is clearly a gloss and is agreed to be such, so that in fact Ezra alone dominates the story. This in itself makes it probable that viii–ix now stands in the wrong position and really belongs with what is related in Ezra vii–x. This is confirmed by a consideration of the dating of the section and a comparison of it with the dates in Ezra vii–x, for in spite of Noth's criticism, the dating gives a clear impression of originality and genuineness and is not to be rejected. The events described in Neh. viii–ix take place on the first (viii, 2), second (viii, 13), fifteenth to twenty-second (viii, 18) and twenty-fourth (ix, 1) days of the seventh month. Since the year is not indicated, we should be obliged, with the passage in its present context, to look at the last-mentioned year. This would be the twentieth year of Artaxerxes (ii, 1), and from Nisan, the first month, mentioned there, up to viii, 2, six months would have elapsed. Since vi, 15 places the completion of the walls at the twenty-fifth day of Elul, the sixth month, and since the events of viii–x, also according to their present position, purport to have taken place before the dedication of the walls (xii, 27–43), the period of six days between vi, 15 and viii, 2 is quite adequate. But it is not easy to understand why the dedication festival is held at least a month after the completion of the walls (vi, 15; ix, 1), and why in the meantime so many other measures are undertaken and also that a great festival is even celebrated, quite apart from the difficulty already indicated that Nehemiah is not mentioned in viii–ix. But if we connect viii–ix with Ezra vii–x, then the passage not only fits in well as far as its content is concerned, but it also fits as regards its dates.

In Ezra vii, 7–9 (viii, 31–2), the day of Ezra's arrival in Jerusalem is given as the first day of the fifth month of the seventh year of an Artaxerxes, and for the various stages of the divorce proceedings there are given the twentieth day of the ninth month (x, 9), the first day of the tenth (x, 16), and the first day of the first (x, 17), which may be taken to be the seventh (to eighth) year of Artaxerxes. Stylistic unevenness in vii, 7–9 make it seem possible that some alteration has been made here. But this does not justify in any way the removal of the date given here as a secondary addition, as is done by Noth and Galling. Nor does it justify the assumption which Galling makes in connection with this, that the elaborator, his 'Second Chronicler', wished with his seventh year to provide a link to the last-mentioned sixth year (vi, 15: *the sixth year of the reign of Darius the king*) and hence to underline still further the Chronicler's view that the constituting of the community followed directly upon the completion of the

[23] Lidzbarski, *Handbuch der nordsemitischen Epigraphik* (1898), pp. 165–9.

Temple. We should rather give the same credence to the date, with its day, month and year in vii, 7–9, as well as to the indications of day and month in x, 9, 16, 17. With the present arrangement of the book of Ezra-Neh., in which Ezra ix–x follows directly on Ezra vii–viii, nothing takes place between the arrival in Jerusalem on the first day of the fifth month and the beginning of the divorce proceedings on the twentieth day of the ninth. This is very odd. For Ezra had come with a definite commission, precisely prescribed in the king's firman in vii, 11–26, namely that he should *make inquiries about the situation in Judah and Jerusalem according to the law of your God, which is in your hand* (vii, 14, cf. vv. 25–6).[24] The beginning of ix, 1 *And when I had completed this* presupposes, furthermore, that something has happened previously, and naturally something more than the delivery of the sacred gifts which he had brought and the handing over of his letter of authorisation to the Persian authorities, to which alone there is reference just before (viii, 32–6). Neh. viii–ix takes place on the first, second, fifteenth to twenty-second and twenty-fourth days of the seventh month, and thus fits excellently into the period between Ezra viii, 32–6 (the beginning of the fifth month) and ix, 1 (x, 9) (the middle of the tenth), the more so since Neh. viii–ix does actually tell of measures which were carried out on the basis of a law read by Ezra and clearly brought with him (viii, 1—*to bring*). Furthermore, the divorce measures of Ezra ix–x link on very well too with Neh. viii–ix, in that here the law is made known which according to the indications given by Ezra in Ezra ix, 1–2 is contradicted by the attitude of the people. Indeed, this complaint itself demands that there should have been some mention previously of a norm against which their attitude can be measured. In short, it appears clear that Neh. viii–ix has its right position, both as regards content and date, between Ezra viii, 36 and ix, 1.

A further question is whether Neh. viii–ix also belongs from a literary point of view to Ezra vii–x, and forms part of the Ezra Memoirs. Since Ezra nowhere here speaks in the first person, but is always referred to in the third (viii, 2, 4 *et passim*), this assumption is less likely and it would seem that we should trace this section to another source which was available to the Chronicler in addition to the Memoirs, as at Ezra x. But the abandonment of the first person form of the Ezra Memoirs may be connected with the insertion of the passage in the Nehemiah Memoirs. And since in Neh. viii–ix the Chronicler's own style is in any case markedly visible, there would seem here to be more probability in the assumption which was rejected for Ezra x, namely that the Chronicler did actually extract the substance of Neh. viii–ix from the Ezra Memoirs, but himself gave it its present form, perhaps with the addition of the prayer of ix, 6–37, and in doing so substituted for the first person reference to Ezra, the third person form.

The declaration of obligations in Neh. x now follows, as we have seen, directly upon the long prayer of ix, 6–37 spoken by the Levites or by Ezra on the twenty-fourth day of the ninth month (ix, 1), and appears to fit well in this position. After the introduction of the law brought by Ezra, prepared for in Neh. viii, 1–12, has been interrupted by the celebration of the feast of booths

24 Falk, 'Ezra vii, 26' VT 9 (1959), pp. 88 f.

(viii, 13–18), it is now taken up again (ix) with the holding of a day of penitence, already shown to be appropriate in viii, 9–10, and it is sealed by the declaration of the people pledging itself to the various cultic actions (x). Ezra ix–x would then stand after what is related in Neh. x, and this, it would appear, is also made appropriate by the fact that the people has specifically in Neh. x, 31 pledged itself to the avoidance of mixed marriages, and so the intimation of the existence of mixed marriages made by Ezra in Ezra ix, 1–2 may be understood as occasioned by Neh. x, 31. On the other hand, however, in spite of Rudolph's opposite opinion, the connection between Neh. x and ix is very poor. x, 1 begins with the statement *Because of all this we pledge ourselves,* and this can scarcely refer back to the prayer which immediately precedes, nor to the narrative which precedes it in ix, 1–5 of the holding of a day of penitence. It presupposes rather something like a statement, also in the first person plural, of the necessity of far-reaching measures. Furthermore, there is nowhere in ch. x a reference to a pledge made to obey a newly introduced law, but only to the carrying out of certain definite individual actions, ten in number, with reference to a long recognised law (x, 30), which is clearly Deuteronomy. Finally, and this is decisive, Ezra is not mentioned at all, whereas *Nehemiah the governor* (x, 3) appears at the head of those who set their seal to this declaration. Since it further appears that the cultic actions mentioned in x, 31–40 correspond very largely with the measures carried through by Nehemiah in xiii, 4–31, we should link ch. x with these measures and assume that in connection with them, perhaps at their conclusion to ensure their continued observance, Nehemiah urged the people to make the formal declaration of ch. x, just as, according to ch. v, in a similar way he compelled them to desist from making demands upon their poorer compatriots. It does not automatically follow from this that the assumption made by Bertholet and Schaeder is correct, namely that Neh. x comes from the Nehemiah Memoirs. It may well be that the document came to the Chronicler from elsewhere, perhaps from the Temple archives. But it seems certain that we should recognise what took place in Neh. x as Nehemiah's own action.

The view that Neh. x is the continuation of viii–ix and comes from Ezra's Memoirs, is at least in this degree on the right track in that viii–ix do actually point forward to a continuation similar to what is in ch. x, namely to the account of the formal acceptance by the people of the law brought by Ezra. Thus the Chronicler has evidently here used the technique which can so often be observed in compilers (pp. 292, 390), of weaving together two parallel or similar presentations by taking from one of them the first half and from the other the second half, and so constructs an event whose separate stages are historical but which as a whole is without real foundation.

Finally we must examine the lists. A number of them probably belonged originally to the sources in which they now stand. Thus Ezra viii, 1–14, the list of those who returned with Ezra, belongs to the Ezra Memorial; Ezra x, 18–44, the list of those who had contracted mixed marriages, to the source which is to be assumed for Ezra x (p. 548), and Neh. iii, the list of those who took part in the building of the walls, to the Nehemiah Memoirs. Or they may have been taken by the Chronicler from some other reliable tradition, derived by him perhaps from the Temple archives. It is hardly possible to come to a decision with regard to the list of those who signed the document pledging obedience in Neh. x, 2–28[25] since the passage is in a state of such confusion that it can only be unravelled with difficulty. It may belong to the source which is otherwise to be recognised in ch. x, or, since vv. 2–28 can be taken out as an insertion, to a source which runs parallel to this. Alternatively, it may be an artificial construction gathered out of Ezra ii and other lists, as for example that in Neh. xii, 1–9, 10–11, 12–26, with which it has much in common. xi, 3–19 (24), the list of the heads of the province living in Jerusalem, has a parallel in I Chron. ix, 2–18 which must go back to the same original as the one here. Whether this original is, as we might expect from Neh. xi, 1–2, an enumeration of those who were settled in Jerusalem by Nehemiah, is possible, but cannot be proved. The list of Jewish settlements in the countryside in xi, 20 (25)–36,[26] however, certainly does not fit into the period of Nehemiah, since the area which it presupposes as Jewish exceeds what belongs to his time. The list probably derives from a later period, and was perhaps composed by the Chronicler himself, though a pre-exilic origin is not absolutely impossible. The lists of priests and Levites in xii, 1–26 depend at least in part upon reliable sources, as may be seen from the reference in the list of Levites in xii, 23–6 to a *book of annals* (xii, 23), evidently the Temple chronicle. But in their present form they stem from the Chronicler or more probably from a later hand. We may note further that the inelegant accumulation of lists from xi, 3–xii, 26, which cuts off xi, 1–2 from its sequel in xii, 27–43, is to be explained on the grounds that the mention of the populating of Jerusalem and of the cities of the land in xi, 1–2, which perhaps originally referred to a list which should follow, made easy the insertion of catalogues of persons and places.

The most difficult problem in reference to the lists is, however, the double occurrence of the catalogue of *the people of the province who came up out of the captivity of the exiles . . . with Zerubbabel* etc. in Ezra ii and Neh. vii, 6–72.[27] In Ezra ii it stands in its appropriate historical position, and in Neh. vii, 5 it is given by Nehemiah because, according to the verses vii, 4–5 which derive from his Memoirs, when he was preparing for the registration of the population necessary for filling up Jerusalem he *found the book of the genealogy* (reading הַתְיַחֵשׂ instead of הַיַחֵשׂ) *of those who came up earlier and found written in it: These are the people of the province* etc. From a purely literary point of view the double occurrence of this list may undoubtedly be most readily explained if the Chronicler already found it in two places in the sources which he used, once here in the Nehemiah Memoirs, and then also in the source which we assumed he had used (p. 543) for Ezra i, 1–iv, 5. Torrey has objected that the list is

[25] Ibáñez Arana, 'Sobre la colocación original de Neh. x' Est Bibl 10 (1951), pp. 379–402; Jepsen, 'Nehemia x' ZAW 66 (1954), pp. 87–106.

[26] Alt, 'Bemerkungen zu einigen judäischen Ortslisten des AT' ZDPV 68 (1951), pp. 193–210 = *Kl. Schr.* II, pp. 289–305.

[27] Allrik, 'The Lists of Zerubbabel (Nehemiah vii and Ezra ii) and the Hebrew Numeral Notation' BASOR 136 (1954), pp. 21–7; Galling, 'The "Gōlā-List" according to Ezra ii// Nehemiah vii' JBL 70 (1951), pp. 149–58; 'Von Naboned zu Darius' ZDPV 69 (1953), pp. 42–64; 70 (1954), pp. 4–32; Wilkie, 'Nabonidus and the Later Jewish Exiles' JThSt 2 (1951), pp. 36–44.

simply an invention of the Chronicler. Other scholars, including Kosters, Wellhausen, Hölscher, Pfeiffer*, Albright, Ahlemann and Bright, have regarded it as a survey of the population of the province of Judah in the time of Nehemiah or of Ezra. But in spite of these objections, the list may be regarded as genuine, and represent the enumeration of the returned exiles in various stages between about 538 and 515, or perhaps (with Galling) as the list of the Temple community (Ezra v, 3f.) which at the satrap Tattenai's request was laid before him soon after 520. So the assumption that the Chronicler did find the list in both places meets with no difficulties. If, however, we are to think that he himself chose to set out the list twice without such an external inducement, then it can only have been that he found the list in the context of the Nehemiah Memoirs and left it there, and that he had already placed this list at the point where it belongs historically, namely between Ezra i and iii. The list is firmly rooted in the Nehemiah Memoirs. Although, unfortunately, the Memoirs are not at this point given in their entirety, we may nevertheless see how important the discovery of this list was for Nehemiah. For it ends at vii, 72a, where the text is to be emended from III Esdras v, 46: *So the priests and the Levites and some of the layfolk settled in Jerusalem, but the singers and gatekeepers and servants and the rest of Israel in their cities.* Thus it gives Nehemiah the right to restore the situation as it had formerly been—for in the meantime it had evidently become less favourable so far as the occupation of Jerusalem was concerned—by transferring some of those who lived outside into Jerusalem and so carrying through the policy of synoecism which he considered necessary (cf. xi, 1–2).

3. *The order of the Chronicler's sources.* We must say just a little more about the order of the sources as the Chronicler found it. We have already noted that the first half of the Aramaic extract (Ezra iv, 6–23) is in the wrong position chronologically, and ought to follow the second half, namely iv, 24–vi, 18 (22). This remarkable state of affairs must probably be explained on the grounds that the Chronicler utilised two main sources for Ezra i–vi, of which one was in Hebrew (i, 1–iv, 5) and the other in Aramaic (iv, 6–vi, 18). In this second source, iv, 6–23 stood after iv, 24–vi, 18 so that the correct order of the Persian kings—(Cyrus), Darius, Xerxes, Artaxerxes—was preserved. But the Chronicler here regarded the order of subject-matter as more important. He wished to put together the successful attempts made by the enemies of the Jews at hindering them, whether they referred to the Temple or the city walls, and so to the story told in the Hebrew source in iv, 1–5 of the hindering of the building of the Temple under Cyrus and Darius, he linked first from the Aramaic source the narrative of the hindering of the building of the walls under Xerxes and Artaxerxes (iv, 6–23), before he gave its information about the successful averting of the attempts made under Darius at interrupting the Temple building which had again been begun (iv, 24–vi, 18). If it is thought that the Chronicler did not do this, then we must ascribe the transposition to a later hand, perhaps as a result of a desire for having to hand a really detailed account of the sins of the hated Samaritans.[28]

[28] M. Gaster, *The Samaritans* (1925); Montgomery, *The Samaritans* (1907).

The very remarkable division of the Nehemiah Memoirs (between vii on the one hand and xi, 1–2 on the other) by the section Neh. viii–ix taken from the Ezra Memoirs and the passage in ch. x which belongs in content to the end of Nehemiah's activity, must next be considered. Rudolph assumes that we have here a secondary dislocation of the order which the Chronicler set out: Ezra i–viii; Neh. vii, 72b–viii, 18; Ezra ix, 1–x, 44; Neh. ix, 1–x, 40; i, 1–vii, 72a; xi, 1–xiii, 31, a dislocation which was occasioned by the similarity of the original ending of Ezra viii to the end of Neh. vii, 6–72a. If we do not accept this, then the dislocation may well be explained from the Chronicler's desire to make Ezra and Nehemiah active together in the two great events—the introduction of the law and the dedication of the walls—and it was only proper that the religious action should precede the profane. Hence he first put together the two cultic events of Neh. viii–ix and Neh. x, and made them into one action brought about by Ezra and Nehemiah together, and placed this after the repair of the walls but before their dedication. In doing this, he made a small alteration in the text to make Nehemiah take part in the introduction of the law (viii, 9) and Ezra in the dedication of the walls (xii, 36).

4. *Date of composition. Additions.* If Ezra-Nehemiah originally formed the conclusion of the great work of the Chronicler (pp. 530–1), then the determination of the date of origin of I II Chron. as the middle or second half of the fourth century (p. 540) also fixes the date of Ezra-Nehemiah. It is true that, like Chronicles, Ezra-Nehemiah has also received a whole series of later additions, particularly of lists; and it may perhaps be the case that some alterations, which in the foregoing discussion have been ascribed to the 'Chronicler', may in reality be the work of a later writer. But in this a clear distinction can hardly be made, and it is also possible that the Chronicler himself did not find all the sources mentioned in the discussion in isolated form, but in part already combined, so that it was not the Chronicler himself but his predecessors who may have been responsible for their remarkable arrangement. Here too firm conclusions cannot now be drawn, since the arguments which are adduced in attempting to arrive at them are ambiguous and do not provide actual proof.

5. *The significance of the analysis for the historical evaluation of the books.* The effort to understand the composition of Ezra-Nehemiah is in the first instance a literary task. But just as in every other case the sketching of the course of history depends upon the most careful analysis of the traditions which are available, i.e. upon the critical study of the sources, so here too this point is particularly clear. A picture derived from the traditional arrangement of the book of Ezra-Nehemiah of the events linked with the names of Ezra and Nehemiah will be quite different from one which corresponds to the sifting and arranging of the source material which we have here undertaken. But even agreement about the literary analysis of Ezra-Neh. by no means implies agreement also on the verdict which is given upon the historical value of the books or upon the chronology of the events which they describe. The most disputed issue is still the chronological order of the two chief personages, Ezra and Nehemiah, and here much depends upon the answer to the question as to which Artaxerxes it

was who commissioned them, Artaxerxes I (465–424) or Artaxerxes II (404–359). For Nehemiah we can, indeed, only think of Artaxerxes I, since the Elephantine paypri compel us to date his contemporary Sanballat, the governor of Samaria, in the reign of this king. Thus the year of Nehemiah's mission to Jerusalem given in Neh. i, 1 as the twentieth year of Artaxerxes, and of his leave given in xiii, 6 as the thirty-second year, are respectively 445 and 432. Nehemiah's activity is thus fixed in the period from 445 to 432 B.C., or until after 432. Scholars are practically unanimous in regarding Artaxerxes I as the king who comes in question for Nehemiah. Torrey is one of the exceptions, and he considers that Nehemiah was commissioned by Artaxerxes II, and supports his view by pointing out that in Ezra iv, 7, 8, 11, 23; vi, 14, where it is clear that Artaxerxes I is intended, the name is spelt with שׁ *š*, but in Neh. ii, 1; v, 14; xiii, 6, as Ezra vii, 1, 7, 11, 12, 21; viii, 1 it is spelt with ס *s*, and from this he concludes that the Artaxerxes of Ezra vii–viii and Neh. is different from the one mentioned in Ezra iv and vi, the former being Artaxerxes II and the latter Artaxerxes I. But if we may, in spite of this exception, regard the placing of Nehemiah in the reign of Artaxerxes I as fairly generally agreed, opinions differ very widely indeed as to which king of this name is to be understood in the Artaxerxes mentioned in Ezra vii and viii, and so which actual year is implied by the seventh year of this king mentioned in Ezra vii, 7. Many scholars (p. 554) decide in favour of Artaxerxes I, and so fix the seventh year of Artaxerxes in Ezra vii, 7 as 458, and indeed the order of the material as it now stands in the book of Ezra-Neh. can hardly be understood otherwise. But although this appears to fit, it cannot be disputed that the Elephantine papyri[29] make it probable that Ezra should be dated about two generations later than Sanballat, who was Nehemiah's contemporary.

Among the detailed arguments which point to this dating, we may here mention one. Ezra x, 6 relates that on the evening of the first day after his action directed against mixed marriages, Ezra withdrew into the Temple room of Jehohanan ben-Eliashib and spent the night there. This Jehohanan is in all probability the grandson of the high priest Eliashib who was approximately contemporary with Sanballat and Nehemiah. This necessitates placing the activity of Ezra in Jerusalem about half a century after that of Nehemiah, in other words fairly exactly at the point demanded by the mention of the seventh year in Ezra vii, 7 if this is referred to Artaxerxes II, i.e. 398 B.C. This dating of Ezra, put forward by van Hoonacker as early as 1880[30] and from 1890 onwards supported in a series of publications[31] has found considerable support, and particularly in recent years a relatively large number of scholars has accepted it,

---

[29] AOT, pp. 450–62; ANET, pp. 491–2; DOTT, pp. 256–69; Cowley, *Ar. Pap.* (1923); Kraeling, 'New Light on the Elephantine Colony' BA 15 (1952), pp. 50–67 = BA Reader (1961), pp. 128–44; *Ar. Pap.* (1953); Eduard Meyer, *Der Papyrusfund von Elephantine* (³1912). Cf. p. 23, n. 24; p. 24, n. 27; p. 26, n. 33.
[30] Cf. Cazelles, VT 4 (1954), p. 114, n. 3.
[31] 'Néhémie et Esdras, nouvelle hypothèse sur la chronologie de l'époque de la restauration' Muséon 9 (1890), pp. 151–84, 317–51, 389–401; *Néhémie en l'an 20 d'Artaxerx`s I, Esdras en l'an 7 d'Artaxerxès II* (1892); *Nouvelles études sur la restauration juive après l'exil de Babylone* (1896); 'La succession chronologique Néhémie-Esdras' RB 32 (1923), pp. 481–494; 33 (1924), pp. 33–64.

including Rowley (1948),[32] Snaith (1952),[33] Kraeling (1952 and 1953), Cazelles (1954). But, as has already been said, there have been others who place Ezra's appearance in Jerusalem before that of Nehemiah, with Scott,[34] Wright,[35] Fernández and Jepsen, or who place him in the period when Nehemiah was absent on leave from Jerusalem, i.e. roughly between 432 and 426. This latter solution, or one similar to it, has been accepted by various scholars following the lead of Albright—Rudolph in his commentary of 1949, Pavlovský in his discussion of 1957, and Bright in his *History of Israel* (1959) and in his contribution to the *Kaufmann Jubilee Volume* (1960). Pavlovský dates Nehemiah's first period of office in Jerusalem in 445–433 and his second in 430; he considers that in 430 Nehemiah was accompanied by Ezra and that Ezra's independent activity in Jerusalem began in 428 and lasted for some years. Admittedly those who adopt this view have to reckon with a corruption of the original numeral in Ezra vii, 7, replacing the seven of the text by 37[36] or some similar figure (the thirty-seventh year of Artaxerxes I = 428 B.C.), and this does not encourage belief in its correctness.

Thus for the dating of Ezra there really remains only the choice between 458 and 398. Tradition favours the first view. Its testimony may not be lightly disregarded. For the assumption that succeeding generations correctly preserved the chronological order of the two men, Ezra and Nehemiah, who were so important for them, is much more natural than the supposition of an error. On the other hand, it must be observed that the identity of name of the two kings Artaxerxes, I and II, could have led relatively quickly to their being identified. If reports were to hand from the seventh year of an Artaxerxes, and others from the twentieth and thirty-second year, their arrangement by the Chronicler in the order indicated by the figures is just as easy to understand as that Kraeling 2,300 years later, according to the statement made in his *Ar. Pap.* p. 111, at first assigned the Brooklyn Museum papyri dated from the first, third, fourth, fourteenth, sixteenth, twenty-eighth, thirty-first and thirty-eighth years of an Artaxerxes all to Artaxerxes I, and only later recognised that those from the first, third and fourth years were to be assigned to Artaxerxes II. Such a confusion may be attributed also to the Chronicler, who is to be dated in about 350 (p. 540), a half century after Ezra's assumed arrival in Jerusalem in 398. Thus we may grant that the assumption that Ezra, commissioned by Artaxerxes II, appeared in Jerusalem in 398, has greater probability than his dating under Artaxerxes I. This probability is still further strengthened by the information

---

[32] 'The Chronological Order of Ezra and Nehemiah' *Goldziher Mem. Vol.* I (1948), pp. 117–49 = *The Servant of the Lord, and other Essays on the O.T.* (1952), pp. 131–59; 'Nehemiah's Mission and its Background' BJRL 37 (1954–55), pp. 528–61 = *Men of God* (1963), pp. 211–45.

[33] 'The Date of Ezra's Arrival in Jerusalem' ZAW 63 (1952), pp. 53–66.

[34] 'Nehemiah-Ezra?' ET 58 (1946/47), pp. 263–7.

[35] *The Date of Ezra's Coming to Jerusalem* (1947, ²1958); *The Building of the Second Temple* (1958). On this cf. Rowley JSSt 3 (1958), pp. 398–401.

[36] בִּשְׁנַת־שֶׁבַע וּשְׁלֹשִׁים instead of לְאַרְתַּחְשַׁסְתְּא. Bright (1959, p. 386; 1960, p. 85) explains the traditional reading as due to haplography in that of three successive words beginning with שׁ, one, the last, has fallen out. But in reality וּשְׁלֹשִׁים does not begin with שׁ, any more than does בִּשְׁנַת.

gained from the Brooklyn papyri to the effect that the Persian rule over Egypt did not break up by 404, as was formerly assumed, but only in 400 or 399, and by the natural inference from this, which Cazelles has put forward, that the Persians, with the loss of their Egyptian bulwark, would have to lay very great stress upon the procuring of ordered conditions in Palestine, and so just at that time, 398 B.C., entrusted Ezra with a task directed towards that end.

6. *The historical value of the individual sources.* Something must now be said about the historical value of the individual sources themselves, without taking into account the way they are now linked together, in so far as they have not so far been considered, as has been done with the lists. It is quite clear that the two Memorials, that of Nehemiah and that of Ezra, as documents which come from the influential personalities themselves, are very valuable. They represent historical sources of the first order, provided we exercise a little caution in regard to the tendency which is at any rate clear with Nehemiah not to hide his own light under a bushel but to stigmatize the neighbouring governors as envious and slanderous associates and even to reprimand the Jewish aristocracy for their lack of community spirit. The events which these documents relate are highly significant, and it is no less important that they give us lifelike portraits of two Jews from the second half of the fifth and the beginning of the fourth centuries. One, Nehemiah, is a rich courtier and administrator, filled with loyalty to the religion and national life of his fathers, suspicious and skilful, harsh towards himself and towards other people, and not entirely without vanity. The other, Ezra, is a theologian filled with deep, though narrow piety and with warm love for his own people, a love which does not shrink from ruthlessness of action.[37] But both of them were determined to accept the consequences of what they recognised to be a clear necessity for the Jews, that they must give up the idea of independent national life, and so they sought to build up the Jewish community again under the protection of Persian rule. In spite of Torrey's arguments to the contrary, with his doubting of the existence of a Memorial composed by Nehemiah and his ascribing of the passages which are normally assigned to Nehemiah, rather to the Chronicler, who based his work upon sources unknown to us, we may see in the basic material of Neh. i–vii, x–xiii an account which comes from Nehemiah himself and which is for this reason alone in large measure reliable. Much the same is true, though here the position is not so clear, of the passages in the books of Ezra-Neh. which, though now admittedly somewhat out of order, purport to be an autobiographical account by Ezra and indeed are to be taken as such, namely Ezra vii–x, Neh. viii–ix or at least their basic material.

Valuable historical sources are also to be seen in the account of the divorce measures in Ezra x and the Aramaic documents in Ezra iv, (6) 8–16, 17–22; v, 6–17; vi, 3–12,[38] the latter at least genuine so far as their basic material is concerned. It is true above all, though again with the proviso just made, that the

---

[37] Bentzen, 'Ezras Persönlichkeit' StTh 2 (1949/50), pp. 95–8.

[38] Galling, 'Kyrosedikt und Tempelbau' OLZ 40 (1937), cols. 473–8; Rundgren, 'Über einen juristischen Terminus bei Esra vi, 6' ZAW 70 (1958), pp. 209–15; de Vaux, 'Les Décrets de Cyrus et de Darius sur la reconstruction du Temple' RB 46 (1937), pp. 29–57. Cf. p. 556, nn. 41–2.

royal firman given to Ezra in vii, 12–26[39] is genuine. The objections raised above all by Wellhausen, both against the other documents and particularly against this last one, are based upon the idea that so detailed a concern with the peculiarities and special wishes of Judaism and so intimate a knowledge of it, could not be attributed to the Persian king. But these objections have lost their force by reason of the recognition which was originally made by Eduard Meyer and further elaborated by Schaeder, that the Persian government clearly had Jews as advisers and that Ezra, *the scribe of the law of the God of heaven* (Ezra vii, 12), i.e. 'secretary, adviser for questions of the Jewish religion' at that time occupied this office and possibly himself composed the firman. The point is further confirmed by the many indications, recently gathered together by Cazelles, of the religio-political measures of the Persian government which are concerned with the same consideration for non-Persian cults as is the firman of Ezra vii, 12–19 (26).

The most difficult decision concerns the historical value of Ezra i, 1–iv, 5. The question must here be left open as to whether the Chronicler used a source for this section and if he did, how far he made use of it, or whether he narrated for himself the events from the edict of Cyrus to the beginning of the reign of Darius, while making use of the documents of v, 11–vi, 12 and of the books of Haggai and Zechariah (p. 543). It is certain that the information concerning the celebration of the autumnal festival immediately after the arrival of the returned exiles in 538, concerning the appointment of Levites in accordance with the law, and concerning the musical arrangements at the laying of the foundation stone etc. in iii, 4–13, comes from the Chronicler and is unhistorical. But the laying of the foundation stone of the Temple in the second year of Cyrus is by no means historically impossible. Even the report of attempts at hindering the work by *the adversaries of Judah and Benjamin* in iv, 1–5 may contain genuine recollections, quite apart from the fact that the interest of Cyrus in the re-founding of the Jerusalem religious community, attested also by Ezra vi, 3–5[40] is certainly historical. Thus, even if we abandon the actual wording of i, 2–4, there is no good reason to follow Torrey[41] and others, and to declare the tradition of the reconstituting of the Jewish religious and national community by the returned exiles between 538 and 520 as a quite incredible theory put forward by the Chronicler, and then to allow this scepticism to influence further the assessment of other books such as Ezekiel (p. 370).[42]

7. *Ezra's law.* Finally, we may consider the question as to what is to be understood by the law which Ezra brought with him and of which Neh.

[39] Nober, 'Lexicalia irano-biblica' VD 36 (1957), pp. 102–5; 'El significado de la palabra aramea *'āsparnā* en Esdras' Est Bíbl 16 (1957), pp. 394–401; 'אַדְרַזְדָּא (Esdras vii, 23)' BZ 2 (1958), pp. 134–8; 'De nuevo su . . . *āsparnā*' Est Bibl 19 (1960), pp. 111 f.; Rundgren, 'Zur Bedeutung von *šršw*, Esra vii, 26' VT 7 (1957), pp. 400–4. Lit. § 126.
[40] Cf. p. 555, n. 38.
[41] 'The Chronicler's History of the Return under Cyrus' AJSL 37 (1920/21), pp. 81–100; *The Chronicler's History of Israel* (1954), pp. XXIV–XXVIII.
[42] Liver, 'Return from Babylon, its Time and Scope' [Hebrew, Engl. summary] Eretz-Israel 5 (1958), pp. 114–19, 90*

viii–ix appears to recount the introduction. This is a question which has an important part to play in the history of Pentateuchal criticism and the attempt at its solution has contributed to the right dating of P (pp. 239, 257). In the first place, we must here leave out of account ch. x which has formerly been used in the consideration of this law, being understood as a narrative of the formal pledge to accept the law, for it probably has nothing to do with the events of viii–ix, but refers to measures undertaken by Nehemiah and not by Ezra (p. 548). Nor can we simply draw conclusions from what is related about the festival of booths in viii–ix concerning the law which underlay this festival, since here the Ezra Memoirs are undoubtedly not preserved in their original form, but with a strong admixture of additions by the Chronicler. Other considerations have, however, made it seem probable that it was the Hexateuch amplified by the addition of P but shortened by the omission of the book of Joshua which at that time, namely in 398, must have acquired authority in Judaism (pp. 208, 257). With this now fits the fact that whereas Nehemiah's reforms in large measure presuppose the Deuteronomic law which belonged in Palestine, for Ezra it was requirements belonging to P, whether its basic material or its elaborations, which appear to have been authoritative. Thus Ezra evidently made the basis of his reform the laws of P which originated in the Exile, standing in the line of Ezekiel, or more probably a complex which included this law and was definitely determined by it, namely our Pentateuch.[43] Thus, just as II Kings xxiii, 21–3 may be taken as a pointer to D which appears then and then only (Deut. xvi, 1–8*), so Neh. viii, 14–18 may be taken as evidence that Ezra in 398 introduced as the basic law of Judaism not P alone, but probably the older Pentateuch amplified by the addition of P.

[43] Cf. Grelot, 'Études sur le "Papyrus Pascal" d'Éléphantine' VT 4 (1954), pp. 349–84; 'Le Papyrus pascal d'Éléphantine et le problème du Pentateuque' VT 5 (1955), pp. 250–65.

PART FOUR

THE CANON

I. The History of the Canon

Literature: Aalders, *Oud-Testamentische Kanoniek* (1952); Bardtke, *Die Handschriften-funde am Toten Meer mit einer kurzen Einführung in die Text- und Kanonsgeschichte des AT* (²1953); Buhl, *Kanon und Text des AT* (1891); Budde, *Der Kanon des AT* (1900); Christie, 'The Jamnia Period in Jewish History' JThSt 26 (1925), pp. 347–64; Diem, *Das Problem des Schriftkanons* (Th St [B] 32, 1952); von Dobschütz, 'The Abandonment of the Canonical Idea' AJTh 19 (1915), pp. 416–29; Duhm, *Die Entstehung des AT* (²1909); Eberharter, *Der Kanon des AT zur Zeit des Ben Sira* (ATA III, 3, 1911); Filson, *Which Books belong in the Bible? A Study of the Canon* (1957); Flack, Metzger and others, *The Text, Canon and Principal Versions of the Bible* (1956); Hänel, *Der Schriftbegriff Jesu* (1919); Haran, 'Problems of the Canonization of Scripture' [Hebr., English summary] Tarbiz 25 (1955/56), pp. 245–71, I–III; Hölscher, *Kanonisch und Apokryph* (1905); F. Horst, 'Das AT als Heilige Schrift und als Kanon' ThBl 11 (1932), cols. 161–73; Jeiteles, 'Die Bibel im babylonischen Talmud' Jahrb. d. Jüdisch-Literar. Ges. 21 (1930), pp. 1–18; Jepsen, 'Kanon und Text des AT' ThLZ 74 (1949), cols. 65–74; 'Zur Kanongeschichte des AT' ZAW 71 (1959), pp. 114–136; Kamenezki, 'Der Biblische Kanon' in Soloweitschik, *Vom Buch, das tausend Jahre wuchs* (1932), pp. 170–80; van Kasteren, 'Le canon juif vers le commencement de notre ère' RB 5 (1896), pp. 408–15, 575–94; Katz, 'The OT Canon in Palestine and Alexandria' ZNW 47 (1956), pp. 191–217; 49 (1958), p. 223; König, *Kanon und Apokryphen* (1917); Leenhardt, '"Sola Scriptura" ou: Écriture et tradition' EtThR 36 (1961), pp. 5–46; Leipoldt and Morenz, *Heilige Schriften* (1953); Lindblom, *Kanon och Apokryfer* (1920); Lods, 'Tradition et canon des Écritures' EtThR 36 (1961), pp. 47–59; Mehl, 'Essai de socio-phénoménologie de la tradition' EtThR 36 (1961), pp. 83–100; Mensching, *Das Heilige Wort* (1937); Merk, Ruwet et al., *De S. Scriptura in universum* (⁶1951); Michaéli, 'À propos du Canon de l'AT' EtThR 36 (1961), pp. 61–8; Moffatt, 'The Sacred Book in Religion' JBL 53 (1934), pp. 1–12; Morenz, 'Entstehung und Wesen der Buchreligion' ThLZ 75 (1950), cols. 709–16; Mullen, *The Canon of the OT* (1893); Obbink, 'Over de plaats van het Heilige boek in de religie' Vox Theologica 23 (1952/53), pp. 3–12; Östborn, *Cult and Canon. A Study in the Canonisation of the OT* (1950); H. W. Robinson, 'Canonicity and Inspiration' ET 47 (1935/36), pp. 119–23; L. Rost, 'Zur Geschichte des Kanons bei den Nestorianern' ZNW 27 (1928), pp. 103–6; Ryle, *The Canon of the OT* (²1909); Schelkle, 'Heilige Schrift und Wort Gottes' ThQ 138 (1958), pp. 257–74; W. R. Smith, *The OT in the Jewish Church* (²1892); Staerk, 'Der Schrift- und Kanonbegriff der jüdischen Bibel' ZSTh 6 (1929), pp. 101–19; Sundberg, 'The OT in the Early Church. A Study in Canon' HThR 51 (1958), pp. 205–26; Swete, *An Introduction to the OT in Greek*, revised by Ottley (1914), pp. 1–28, 197–288; Torrey, 'The Aramaic Period of the Nascent Christian Church' ZNW 44 (1952/53), pp. 205–23; Vellas, 'Die Heilige Schrift in der griechisch-orthodoxen Kirche' *Die orthodoxe Kirche in griechischer Sicht* (1959), pp. 121–40; Wildeboer, *Het ontstaan van den Kanon des Ouden Verbonds* (1891, ⁴1098); English transl. by B. W. Bacon (1891); 'De vóór-Thalmudische Joodsche Kanon' ThSt 15 (1897), pp. 159–77; 16 (1898), pp. 194–205; 17 (1899), pp. 185–95; Zarb, *De historia canonis utriusque Testamenti* (1934); Zeitlin, *An Historical Study of the Canonization of the Hebrew Scriptures* (1933). Lit. § 126.

§74. NAME AND PREHISTORY

1. *Name.* The word 'Canon' has several meanings, but in its application to the Old Testament and to the Bible as a whole it describes them as a book which derives from divine revelation and provides the normative rule for the faith and life of the religious man. In this sense, the word 'Canon'[1] appears first in Christian fathers of the fourth century. Older than this there is the description of the Old Testament as 'Sacred Scripture(s)' or 'Scripture(s)', a description not identical in meaning with Canon but probably identical in its practical application. This appears already in the New Testament[2] and is to be found likewise in Philo,[3] Josephus[4] and the Mishna.[5] In this last there is occasionally added to this name (כִּתְבֵי הַקֹּדֶשׁ) the expression *defiling the hands* (מְטַמְּאִים אֶת־הַיָּדַיִם)[6] which means that the touching of these books, which by their very nature carry holiness, demands the washing away of this holy substance.

2. *Prehistory.* It was only in the second century A.D., as we shall see (p. 568), that the formation of the Old Testament canon came to an end. But its prehistory begins centuries or even millennia earlier. Its starting-point is the belief that particular utterances of men are in reality the word of God and as such can claim for themselves especial authority. In Israel there are six different kinds of words which rank as divine words (though neither they nor their names may be sharply differentiated): the *judgment* (מִשְׁפָּט, pp. 26–9) of the lawgiver and judge, the *word* (דָּבָר, pp. 69–70) which appears as command or prohibition from the proclaimer of the divine will, the *directive* (תּוֹרָה, pp. 73–5) of the priest, the *saying* (דָּבָר, pp. 76–80) of the prophet, the *song* (שִׁיר, pp. 87–8) of the singer, and the *proverb* (מָשָׁל, pp. 81–7) of the wise. We are here at first dealing with oral utterances bound up with the course of events so that they are lost with the time to which they belong. A newer revelation may also directly make an older one invalid. But particular words of this kind in the course of time take on lasting validity and are written down. This process begins with the utterances which concern profane and sacral law, i.e. the *judgment*, the *word* and the *directive* which gradually merge into the *law* (תּוֹרָה) in the narrower sense. But the other kinds of divine words are gradually associated with it. Thus it is said concerning the collection of *judgments* to be found in Exod. xxi, 2–xxii, 16, that God commanded Moses to lay them before the people for their acceptance (xxi, 1), and concerning the

---

[1] Oppel, Κανών. *Zur Bedeutungsgeschichte des Wortes und seiner lateinischen Entsprechungen (regula-norma)* (1937); Wenger, *Canon in den römischen Rechtsquellen und in den Papyri* (SAW 220 (1942), second monograph).

[2] ἱερὰ γράμματα II Tim. iii, 15, γραφαί Matt. xxi, 42. See further W. Bauer, *Griechisch-Deutsches Wörterbuch zu den Schriften des NT* ([5]1958), *s.v.* ἱερός, γράμμα, γραφή, βίβλος, κανών, νόμος (Engl. Tr. by W. F. Arndt and F. W. Gingrich from ed. 4, 1952 [1957]) and TWNT I (1933), pp. 613–20: βίβλος, βιβλίον (Schrenk), pp. 742–73: γράφω, γράφη etc. (Schrenk); III (1938), pp. 221–30: ἱερός (Schrenk); pp. 600–6: κανών (Beyer); IV (1942), pp. 1016–77; νόμος (Kleinknecht, Gutbrod), Engl. transl. *Law* (1962), esp. pp. 79 f.

[3] *De Vita Mosis* I § 23; II § 290 etc.   [4] *Ant.* XX 12, 1 § 261 etc.

[5] Yadaim 3, 5; Shabbat 16, 1.   [6] Yadaim 3, 5.

words of the two decalogues it is related that they were written upon tablets at Yahweh's dictation or even by Yahweh himself (Exod. xxxiv, 28; xxiv, 12; xxxi, 18; xxxii, 15–16). It is said, however, of Deuteronomy, which contains *judgments*, *words* and *directives* that it was to be set down in a holy place and to be protected in all circumstances from additions or omissions (Deut. xxxi, 26; iv, 2; xiii, 1). These legendary accounts without doubt contain genuine recollections of old beliefs and customs, perhaps very ancient ones.

The laws even when fixed in writing are still bound up with the course of events, and must give place when a new law claims divine authority and so finds acceptance. The formation of the Pentateuch, as we have seen (see § 36), is in large measure to be understood as due to the replacement of older bodies of law by newer ones, and though the old ones are not completely done away with, yet they are now interpreted in accordance with whatever is the most recent expression of the divine will (see pp. 220–3).

The introduction of Deuteronomy marks a particularly important stage in this process. It falls in a period when human reason was beginning to compete with divine inspiration as the power to create law, and was begun at the precise moment of history when such an undertaking could coincide completely with the political, social and intellectual movements of the time, and so could be carried through as a national action of the first importance (pp. 171–3). Hence this event was bound to have a much greater significance for the period that followed than had been the case with earlier codes. But the introduction of D does not by any means represent the completing of the formation of the canon. Subsequently other schemes of law deriving from divine inspiration were set up, of which H, Ezck. xl–xlviii and P have come down to us. P embodying H was then incorporated in the older Pentateuch, till then dominated by D, and so in its turn gave its stamp to the whole work. With the introduction of the Pentateuch thus constructed the formation of the canonical law was substantially at an end. No new corpus of law was united with it, but the older form was simply expanded along the line indicated by the normative P.

More strongly even than the law, the prophetic saying was bound up in the course of events, for it was concerned with the ever-changing conditions in the life of the people. The saying of one prophet was not seldom directed against that of another, and Hos. i, 4–5 (p. 388) is a classic example of the correction of an earlier prophetic revelation (II Kings ix, 1–12) by a later. Nevertheless the consciousness of having proclaimed a word of God which stood above the changes of events developed early in the prophets, as their memorials show (pp. 148–50), and so already at an early stage there was something like a succession in the prophetic message (Jer. xxvi, 18; p. 410). But here too the authority of the divine word from the past was subject to that of the present, and not *vice versa*. To confirm his message a prophet might well cite a word from an earlier man of God, though, as Hos. i, 4–5 shows, the determining factor was the revelation which he himself had received. Gradually too the spring of prophetic inspiration dried up. From Deutero-Isaiah onwards we find in the prophetic books an increasing number of references to earlier prophets, which clearly arise from the consciousness that the great classical period of prophecy is over.[7] Finally, in about the third or second century, the prophetic charisma comes completely to an end, as is shown by I Macc. iv, 46 and other passages, and it makes way for apocalyptic erudition in which the writings of the older prophets become simply the normative rule for their prophecies or even provide methods of calculating the future (Dan. ix, 2). Thus are fulfilled the necessary conditions for the formation of a collection of prophetic writings enjoying canonical validity.

Songs and wisdom sayings do not make the same claim as do law and prophetic word to derive from divine revelation, and it therefore appears at first difficult to understand how they too ultimately attained canonical status. But in the last resort every phenomenon which goes beyond man's everyday experience appears as a divine inspiration and is so used, and this is particularly true of the song and the wisdom saying.[8] The very names for these types and the names of those responsible for them are such as to make very clear the divine dynamic which is operative in them. We have considered this in regard to the song (p. 87) and similarly in regard to the proverb (p. 82). With regard to the song, we must add that we are here primarily concerned with the cultic song. This, as has become clear to us repeatedly (pp. 108–11), had its setting in the earlier period among prophets, the cult-prophets, so that the later singers and Levites are their successors, and with the songs which they uttered and to a large extent also composed (pp. 452 f.), they acquired something of their predecessors' position of honour. It is true that we cannot here trace the consciousness that creative power deriving from divine activity came to an end at a specific period. This cannot be shown either for the song or for wisdom poetry, and both of them did in fact live on vigorously into the post-canonical period. However, a real decline in power is observable here too, but the fact that, as we shall see (pp. 563–4), in the case of songs and wisdom poetry canonical status was accorded only to actual or supposed products of an earlier period was due not to that but to the transference to this sphere of the limitation which had become natural in the case of law and prophecy.

§ 75. THE FORMATION OF THE CANON

1. *The traditional view of the formation of the canon.* Before we can set out the actual historical formation of the canon, we must briefly consider the traditional conception of its origin, a conception which was dominant until the nineteenth century and still today finds adherents here and there. Strictly speaking, it is hardly possible here to speak of a process of formation at all. For the canon is seen as a work which goes back to the direct intervention of God, to his inspiration, and in its formation the human compilers or authors of the separate books are really active as nothing more than merely mechanically

[7] Isa. xlviii, 3; Zech. i, 4; vii, 7 etc.
[8] Cf. Grapow, 'Die Einleitung der Lehre des Königs Amenemhet' ZÄS 79 (1954), pp. 97–9, and Deut. xxxii, 2 לְקַחִי?—*the teaching revealed to me.*

operating tools. However, this divine creative activity is seen as appearing in a chronological sequence, and the view that it is really only a matter of mechanical writing down at divine dictation has never been carried through to its logical conclusion. We may thus speak here of a history of the formation of the canon.

A significant witness to the beginnings of the traditional view is the passage in Josephus' writing from about A.D. 95, *Contra Apionem* I, 8,[1] a passage which will be mentioned again later (pp. 567 f.). In his endeavour to show that the historical tradition of the Jews comprised in the Old Testament is particularly reliable, Josephus stresses that the Jews do not possess a large number of books which contradict one another, but twenty-two which are completely reliable and have preserved their original form and suffered no additions or mutilations. Five of them—the Pentateuch—were written by Moses. The next thirteen books,[2] covering the period from the death of Moses down to Artaxerxes *who was king of the Persians after Xerxes* (i.e. Artaxerxes I, 465–424), were compiled by the prophets who followed Moses (pp. 302 f., 533), and the last four[3] contained cultic songs and rules for life. *From Artaxerxes, however, down to our time*—so the passage continues—*everything has been written down, but the same reliability is not accorded to these writings as to the writings before them because there was then no longer a reliable succession of prophets.* Here Moses is thought of as the earliest author of part of the canon, and as the lower limit for the completion of the canon the period of Artaxerxes I is explicitly fixed. With this agrees the statement in the Baraitha[4] bab. Baba Batra 14b–15a, according to which Moses wrote the Pentateuch and Job, Joshua wrote Josh. and Deut. xxxiv, 5–12 (p. 158), Samuel wrote Sam., Judg. and Ruth, David wrote the Psalms, Jeremiah wrote Jer., Kings and Lam., Hezekiah and his associates wrote Isa., Prov., Songs and Eccl., the men of the great synagogue (p. 564) wrote Ezek., the Twelve, Dan. and Esther, and lastly Ezra wrote Ezra-Neh. and the genealogies in Chron.[5] Here too the canon contains no writing composed before Moses and none after the time of Artaxerxes.

According to these pieces of information, Ezra appears as the compiler of the latest of the books of the canon, but otherwise no special significance is ascribed to him in regard to its formation. But the most characteristic feature of the traditional view is that it traces back the canon as a whole to Ezra. The oldest witness to this view is in a narrative, roughly contemporary with the Josephus passage, at the end of the book of IV Ezra (xiv, 18–48). According to this, Ezra is described as receiving his visions in the thirtieth year after the fall

---

[1] §§ 38–42; cf. also *Ant.* X § 35.

[2] The thirteen are: Josh., Judg. + Ruth, Sam., Kings, Isa., Jer. + Lam., Ezek., the Twelve, Job, Dan., Esther, Ezra + Neh., Chron. With regard to their order we can only say that it is hardly likely to be that just given, but probably placed Job among the historical books, Chron.-Ezra-Neh. after Kings, Dan. before or after Ezek., and perhaps the Twelve before Isa.

[3] The four are: Pss., Prov., Songs, Eccl., i.e. David's Psalter and the three books of teaching ascribed to Solomon.

[4] Baraitha *the* (teaching) *to be found outside* is the designation of a tradition not taken up into the official Mishna but deriving from the same period, i.e. up to A.D. 200.

[5] Audet, 'Les Proverbes et Isaïe dans la tradition juive ancienne' Cahiers de Théol. et de Philos. 8 (1952), pp. 23–30; Dalman, *Traditio rabbinorum veterrima de librorum Veteris Testamenti ordine atque origine* (1891).

of Jerusalem, i.e. 557 B.C. When he complained that the law was burnt and now no one would know God's deeds and plans for the future, he received the commission to prepare many writing tablets[6] and to provide himself with assistants, and then, endowed by God with miraculous knowledge, in forty days dictated ninety-four books to his assistants. The first twenty-four he published, but the seventy others, which are intended only for the wise, he withheld. While these latter refer to the apocalypses, the twenty-four[7] coincide with our canonical books. According to this it is Ezra to whom the creation or rather the re-creation of the canon goes back.

This conception of the origin of the canon, more or less modified, remained normative for the early and mediaeval church. It even resisted the criticism of humanism and the Reformation, for though it had to exchange its colouring of legend and mystery for one of reason and learning, it nevertheless retained its central point, the derivation of the closed canon from Ezra. It was a Jewish scholar, Elias Levita, who in 1538 expressed the derivation of the canon from Ezra in its new form, the form which remained normative for Jews and Christians for two centuries: '... the twenty-four books were not then joined together. Now they [Ezra and his associates] have joined them together, and divided them into three parts ... and arranged the Prophets and Hagiographa not in the order in which they have been put by our Rabbins of blessed memory, in Baba Bathra.' So writes Levita in the third foreword to his book *Massoreth ha-Massoreth* which appeared in 1538.[8] For Levita the associates of Ezra are identical with the *men of the great assembly* (*synagogue*) (אַנְשֵׁי כְנֶסֶת הַגְּדוֹלָה) referred to in Baba Bathra. This is usually thought to be a legendary association, whose existence was supposed on the basis of Neh. viii–x, but according to Bickerman it is to be regarded as referring simply to those exiles who were *gathered* (כָּנַס *to gather*, Ezek. xxii, 21; xxxix, 28) by Zerubbabel and Ezra from the Diaspora and returned to the homeland.[9] Scholars of such standing as Buxtorf the Elder († 1629) and Hottinger († 1667), Leusden († 1699) and Carpzov († 1767) took over Levita's view of the formation of the canon and elaborated it further. It required all the force of the criticism which came from the philosophy of enlightenment and rationalism (pp. 2–3) to shake this firmly-rooted doctrine and to replace it by a view which corresponds to historical reality.

2. *The actual process.* The actual process of the formation of the canon has already been made clear in the indications given in § 74 and in many remarks

---

[6] The first Arabic translation has here رقوق, *ruqūq, parchments.*

[7] On the enumeration see pp. 568–70.

[8] Ginsburg, *The Massoreth ha-Massoreth of Elias Levita* (1867), p. 120; cf. Eissfeldt, *Der Beutel der Lebendigen* (BAL 105, 6, 1960), pp. 38–40. Lit. § 126.

[9] Bickerman, '"Viri magnae congregationis"' RB 55 (1948), pp. 397-402; Dhorme, 'Le texte hébreu de l'AT' RHPhR 35 (1955), pp. 129–44; Englander, 'The Men of the Great Synagogue' HUCA Jubilee-Vol. (1925), pp. 145–69; Finkelstein, 'The Maxim of the Anshe Keneset Ha-Gedolah' JBL 59 (1940), pp. 455–69; *The Pharisees and the Men of the Great Synagogue* [Hebr., Engl. summary] (1950); Hoenig, *The Great Sanhedrin* (1953); Kuenen, *Over de mannen der groote Synagoge* (1876), German transl. in Budde, *Gesammelte Abhandlungen zur Biblischen Wissenschaft von Dr. Abraham Kuenen* (1894), pp. 125–60; Moore, *Judaism* I (1927), pp. 29–36; III (1930), pp. 6–15.

which have been made in Part III (pp. 232 f., 556 f., etc.), and we need only draw out the most significant points. The formation of the canon began, as we saw, from the law, and here the most important moments are the introduction of D in the year 621 and of the Pentateuch enlarged by the incorporation of P in the year 398. A rigid fixing of the extent or of the text of the law was, it is true, by no means yet provided by what happened in 398, but its main contents were determined so that occasional later additions and alterations (pp. 204, 212) only affected it superficially. The validity of the norm introduced in 398 is attested in Chronicles, compiled about 350, which regards this norm as determinative also for the earlier period and accordingly modified its description of that period (pp. 538 f.). It is attested further by the Pentateuch being taken over as sacred scripture by the Samaritan community (p. 256) which broke away from the Jewish religious community probably about 300 B.C., and also by the translation of the Pentateuch into Greek which is to be placed in about the middle of the third century B.C., the 'Septuagint', which owes its origin to the need of the Greek-speaking Jews of Alexandria to have their sacred scripture in the Greek which had become their mother tongue (§ 90). The name for this part of the canon was *Law* (תּוֹרָה), because since ancient times it had belonged to certain of its parts (pp. 30, 73 f.).

The second part, the *Prophets* (נְבִיאִים, pp. 302, 566), must have been more or less closed by about 200 B.C. so far as the number of books which belong to it is concerned. In about 190 Jesus ben Sira in his 'Praise of the fathers' mentions the Twelve Prophets after Isaiah, Jeremiah and Ezekiel (xlviii, 22–xlix, 12), and thus proves that he knew these too as a coherent and closed book. This fits with the fact that the book of Daniel, which originated in about 164, did not find a place permanently in this part of the canon, but had to be content with a place in the third part (p. 521), and that the Qumrān community's (§ 104) own collection of sacred scriptures appears to coincide with that which is mentioned in the 'Praise of the fathers' (cf. p. 567, n. 11) and apparently did not include Dan., if we may judge from the use for this book of scrolls of a smaller size and made of less valuable material—papyrus instead of leather.[10] This is further confirmed by the fact that the grandson of Ben Sira, writing in about 117 B.C., who translated his grandfather's work into Greek, says in the prologue to the translation with reference to his grandfather that before he compiled his own book he had devoted himself to the study of *the law and the prophets and the remainder of the books which have come down from the fathers*. And the grandson asks pardon for any deviations in his translation from the original text on the grounds that a certain difference between original and translation also exists in the case of the law and the prophets and the remaining books. Here too we cannot actually say that at that time, i.e. about 200 B.C., the extent and the text of the books reckoned in the prophetic canon was already completely fixed. But apart from Dan. no new book has since then succeeded in getting into this part of the canon, and this book could not maintain its place there but found its final position among the *Writings*. The name *Prophets* (נְבִיאִים) for this part of the

[10] Barthélemy and Milik, *Qumran Cave I* (1955), p. 150; Milik, 'Elenchus textuum ex Caverna Maris Mortui' VD 30 (1952), pp. 34–45, 101–9, see p. 38.

canon was provided by the derivation of its individual writings from prophets. The distinction between *earlier* (רִאשׁוֹנִים) and *later* (אַחֲרֹנִים) *Prophets*, is attested only from about the eighth century A.D. It is not certain whether the terms *earlier* and *later* are here meant in a temporal or spatial sense—i.e. whether the prophetic compilers of Josh.-Kings are being described as earlier than Isa., Jer., Ezek. and the Twelve, or whether they are being described as the first books in the order of the canonical books, standing before the others.

With our mention of what the grandson of Ben Sira has to say about his grandfather's studies and about the translation of the law, the prophets and the other writings, we have already arrived at the third part of the canon (pp. 443 f.). Ben Sira's grandson calls the writings which belong to this part of the canon, then only in process of formation, simply *books* (βιβλία). Elsewhere they are designated as *Writings* (כְּתוּבִים) or as *Hagiographa*, with a narrowing of what is in itself a more comprehensive term. We can hardly decide whether the term is to be understood as meaning *Other Writings, Other Hagiographa,* in the same way that Ben Sira's grandson speaks of the other traditional books (τὰ ἄλλα πάτρια βιβλία), or whether it is to be explained as meaning that the books which were coming together as the third part of the canon are to be differentiated from the books of the *Torah* and the *Prophets* which were read out in the Synagogue worship, because, in large measure at least, they were only written. But it is certain that the use in worship of the *Torah* and the *Prophets* contributed substantially to the canonical evaluating of these books, and to that extent gave them an advantage over the majority of the *Writings*. Among these it could only be the Psalms which were sung in worship which could compete with the *Torah* and the *Prophets*. Indeed they did gain canonical status first among the *Writings* and their name was also used as a comprehensive title for the third division of the canon (p. 567). As far as the other *Writings* are concerned, even if we cannot actually know, we can largely guess at the motives which determined their canonical evaluation.

We have already seen (pp. 560–1) that songs and wisdom poetry were regarded as ultimately inspired by God. In this way, in addition to the Psalms, the way was eased for Prov. and Eccl. to reach a position of particular honour, and Lam. and Songs too, being also songs, could make a claim on that basis. In addition, so far as the wisdom books were concerned, there was the further point that they were traced back to Solomon, and for the two collections of poems that they were traced back to Jeremiah and Solomon respectively. Furthermore, Lam. was certainly used from an early date at cultic celebrations, namely at the fast held as a memorial to the destruction of Jerusalem (pp. 504–5). As the scroll of the feast of Purim, Esther was from the start particularly valued at least in the eastern diaspora (p. 509). Ruth is set in the period of the judges and was probably very early associated with the already canonical book of Judges. In addition, at any rate in its present form (pp. 479–80), it tells of David's ancestors, and so occasionally occupies a position before the Psalter which is ascribed to David. Daniel, it is true, could not maintain its position in the prophetic canon, but nevertheless enjoyed in large measure the high valuation which was given to the prophetic books. The book of Ezra-Neh., which as a part of the Chronicler's work, had at one time belonged with the 'Former Prophets', was able to tell of important events affecting the law and so at a later stage retained something of its position of honour. It may also have been because of its valuing of law and cultus (see pp. 537–8) that Chronicles, which originally belonged with Ezra-Neh. but was at first separated from its sequel as being of less importance and so was not taken up into the canon, subsequently found its way back into the present collection. Thus, though in regard to the details we cannot come beyond surmises, we can already see the grounds which were determinative in the formation of the third part of the canonical books of the Hebrew Bible.

The references by Ben Sira's grandson indicate, however, only the beginnings of this third group.[11] It was two centuries before it was finally closed. By about A.D. 100 finality was reached at least in regard to the selection of books to be accepted, though not yet in regard to their order. This is proved by the references in Josephus[12] and IV Ezra (pp. 563–4) to the effect that there are 22 (so Josephus) or 24 (so IV Ezra) particularly sacred writings. Both enumerations presuppose the compass of the canon as we now have it, including its third section. The information which is available to us for the period between these two points—117 B.C. and A.D. 100—gives us a glimpse into the way things moved. There are valuable indications in Philo, *De vita contemplativa* § 25 and Luke xxiv, 44, which belong to the middle or the second half of the first century A.D. Philo reports concerning the Therapeutae that they took with them into their cells only *laws and words prophesied by prophets and psalms and the other writings by which knowledge and piety may be increased and perfected* (νόμους καὶ λόγια θεσπιθέντα διὰ προφητῶν καὶ ὕμνους καὶ τὰ ἄλλα οἷς ἐπιστήμη καὶ εὐσέβεια συναύξονται καὶ τελειοῦνται). In the Lucan passage, the risen Jesus says to his disciples that everything must be fulfilled which is written concerning him in the *law of Moses and the prophets and the psalms*. Thus in both passages the canon with its three parts is clearly presupposed, and the only special point is that the third part, described by Philo as *psalms and the other writings* whereas Luke xxiv, 44 names it as *the psalms* from its most notable writing, is not more exactly defined as to content. The attempt has been made to prove from Matt. xxiii, 35 (Luke xi, 50 f.) that it was at that time substantially the same as now, for here Jesus holds out before the Jews as guilt which must still be atoned *all the righteous blood shed on earth, from the blood of innocent Abel to the blood of Zechariah the son of Barachiah whom you murdered between the Sanctuary and the altar*. It is thought that this presupposes the arrangement of the canon with Genesis as the first book, with its story of Cain and Abel (Gen. iv, 1–16), and Chronicles as the last with the narrative of the murder of Zechariah by Joash (II xxiv, 20–1). But another

---

[11] According to Rabinowitz 'The Qumran Authors' *spr hhgw/y'* JNESt 20 (1961), pp. 109–14, the work mentioned as ספר ההגו/י several times in the Damascus Document (§ 106) and in the Manual of Discipline (§ 105) from Qumrān, and understood by him as a Book of Meditation or Study presupposes the same stage in the formation of the canon as does the Prologue to Ben Sira. Cf. above, p. 565.

[12] Fell, 'Der Bibelkanon des Flavius Josephus' BZ 7 (1909), pp. 1–16, 113–22, 235–44. Cf. above, p. 563, nn. 1–2. Lit. § 126.

interpretation of the incident mentioned in Matt. xxiii, 35, Luke xi, 50 f., is possible. It may refer to the murder of Zechariah the son of Bareis (Ζαχαρίας υἱὸς Βάρεις [Βαρισκαίου Βαρούχου]) which happened in the Temple in Jerusalem during the first Jewish revolt against Rome (66–70), as related by Josephus, *Bell. Jud.* IV 5, 4 (§§ 334–44). These passages in Matt. and Luke cannot therefore be regarded as providing sure evidence that in the time of Jesus Chronicles already occupied the last place in the canon.[13] Even if this were the case, it would not necessarily prove that the New Testament knew all the books of the third part of the canon and recognised them as all of equal worth. Indeed, this does not seem to have been the case. At any rate, apart from Ezra-Neh. which hardly appears to be relevant to the point, the only books which are never quoted in the New Testament are Songs, Eccl. and Esther—with Eccl. the point is not quite certain—and it was just these books, together with others, including Prov. and even Ezek., which still had to struggle for recognition in Jewish circles in the first and second centuries A.D., or at any rate had to defend themselves against attacks on their position as sacred writings.

A substantial contribution to the ultimate removal of such objections was made by a synod held in about A.D. 100 in Jamnia (Jabne), some 12 miles south of Jaffa, and the centre of Jewish intellectual life between A.D. 70 and 135. Though unfortunately we know otherwise very little about this synod, it is at least clear that it regarded its task as the securing of the Jewish heritage, and that in this it succeeded. The syncretistic movements of apocalyptic threatened the historical heritage of Judaism from within. The nature and significance of these movements have had new light shed upon them by the finds of texts of Qumrān (§ 104). From outside, the threat came from Christianity, now becoming a danger. These threats from within and without necessitated at that time in particular the formation of a normative canon of sacred scriptures which would make it possible for Judaism to concentrate upon the real sources of its inward strength and to secure this against all attempts at destroying it. So now what had come into being as a result of gradual growth was formally declared binding and for this purpose was also undergirded with a dogmatic theory. Among the writings inherited from the fathers certain were regarded as valid. As the passage from Josephus cited on p. 563 and other passages from rabbinic literature show, these were first the law which was clothed with a unique dignity and at all times has formed the canon within the canon, and in addition those writings which stemmed from the period between Moses (Deut. xviii, 15; Ecclus. xlvi, 1) and Artaxerxes I, regarded as the period which alone was filled with the movement of the prophetic spirit. In actual fact all the canonical books did originate in this period, or, if not, were ascribed to it.

3. *The enumeration and arrangement of the books of the canon.* We normally reckon 39 books to the Old Testament—five books of Moses, Josh., Judg., two

---

13 Baeck, 'Secharja ben Berechja' in Baeck, *Aus drei Jahrtausenden* (²1958), pp. 215–21; Blank, 'The Death of Zechariah in Rabbinic Literature' HUCA 12/13 (1937/38), pp. 327–346; Klostermann, *Das Matthäusevangelium* (³1938), pp. 189 f.; Eduard Meyer, *Ursprung und Anfänge des Christentums*, I (1921), pp. 234–38; Rudolf Meyer, *Der Prophet aus Galiläa. Studie zum Jesusbild der drei ersten Evangelien* (1940), pp. 48–50; Wellhausen, *Einleitung in die drei ersten Evangelien* (²1911), pp. 118–23. Lit. § 126.

books of Sam., two books of Kings, Isa., Jer., Ezek., twelve books of Minor Prophets, Pss., Job, Prov., five Megilloth, Dan., Ezra, Neh., two books of Chron. But two different methods of counting them have come down to us from within Judaism, making totals of 22 and 24. The former, as we have seen (p. 563), is presupposed by Josephus, and is to be found among many church fathers who are clearly describing Jewish practice, viz. Melito, Origen, Eusebius, Cyril of Jerusalem, Epiphanius, Jerome and Augustine.[14] The number 22 is arrived at by counting as one book each not only Sam., Kings, the twelve Minor Prophets, Ezra+Neh., Chron., but also Judg.+Ruth and Jer.+Lam., and thus 17 may be subtracted from our 39. The reckoning as 24 differs from this by counting Ruth and Lam. as separate books, and so reaches this total. This reckoning may be inferred from IV Ezra xiv, 18–48, as we have also already seen (pp. 563 f.). The opinions of scholars differ, however, as to which method of counting is to be regarded as original. Some, including particularly Strack,[15] prefer the number 24, while others, among whom in addition to C. F. Schmid[16] and Kuenen[17] we should particularly mention Zahn,[18] prefer the number 22. The supporters of the number 24 consider the reckoning as 22 probably to derive from Alexandrian Judaism and regard it as a device based upon fitting the number of the books to that of the letters of the alphabet, whereas the other scholars regard the number 24 as artificial and unrealistic. We cannot exclude the possibility that both systems of counting were seriously used. But since there are indications that the counting of Judg.+Ruth and Jer.+Lam. as making up one book each is original, corresponding to their being contained in one scroll each, and that Ruth and Lam. only later received the rank of separate books, we should probably regard the enumeration of the books of the Old Testament as 22 as being the older.

The passages from the prologue by Ben Sira's grandson, from Philo's *De vita contemplativa*, Luke xxiv, 44 and bab. Baba Batra 14b–15a (p. 567) show that the division of the three parts of the canon was firmly fixed at a fairly early date. For the first part, the order of the books, the five books of Moses, follows from the nature of the material. But in this matter of order the situation is different in the second part. The former prophets, it is true, always stand in the order Josh., Judg., Sam., Kings, and this is also obvious since here, as in the Pentateuch, the order corresponds to the chronological sequence of the events described. It is possible that the recollection that Gen.–Kings had once formed a great historical work (pp. 134–6) still had its effects. But for the latter prophets the tradition varies in regard to the order. The passage bab. Baba Batra 14b, which clearly represents the practice current among the Jews of the eastern diaspora, puts them in the order: Jer., Ezek., Isa., and the Twelve, whereas the Masora (see p. 680) from Palestine has the order with which we are

---

[14] Schultz, 'Augustine and the Old Testament Canon' BS 112 (1955), pp. 225–34.
[15] 'Kanon des Alten Testaments' PRE IX (³1901), pp. 741–68, see pp. 752, 756–9.
[16] *Historia antiqua et vindicatio canonis sacri Veteris Novique Testamenti libris II comprehensa* (1775), I, pp. 220–78.
[17] *Historisch-kritisch Onderzoek naar het ontstaan en de verzameling van de Boeken des Ouden Verbonds* III (1865), pp. 394–450.
[18] *Geschichte des Neutestamentlichen Kanons* II, 1 (1890), pp. 143–343.

familiar: Isa., Jer., Ezek., the Twelve, a difference which is perhaps to be explained on the grounds that the Masora regarded the chronological order as determinative, whereas the order in Baba Bathra takes account of the fact that Isa. is as a book later than Jer. and Ezek., which would in fact correspond precisely to what was arrived at from an analysis of the books. The tradition concerning the order of the individual books in the third part of the canon is of almost bewildering complexity, again in large measure conditioned by the differences between Babylonian Jewish and Palestinian Jewish learning. We must here be content with the note that very often Pss., Job, Prov. or Pss., Prov., Job (pp. 443 f.) stand at the beginning and Ezra-Neh. Chron. at the end, but that Chron. also can take the first place (pp. 443 f.), and further that the placing together of the five Megilloth first appears regularly from the sixth century A.D. onwards. These Megilloth are the five scrolls read at the main feasts of the Jewish ecclesiastical year, Songs for Passover, Ruth for the Feast of Weeks or Harvest, Lam. for the fasts held in remembrance of the destruction of Jerusalem, Eccl. for Booths and Esther for Purim. The order in which they correspond to their use in the ecclesiastical year, as they have just been given, first became the established usage, however, from the twelfth century.[19]

4. *The tradition represented by 𝕲 and by the Qumrān documents*. The form of the canon as fixed by the decisions at Jamnia, as we have just described it, is not, however, the only one of which we know. In the tradition represented in 𝕲 and also by the Qumrān documents, there is preserved a form of canon which is to be regarded as an expression of the stage of development lying before the pronouncements of Jamnia, and so as less rigid than was then produced. In fact it takes not one but several forms, for the manuscripts of 𝕲 represent great variety both in the number of the Old Testament books which they include and in their order, and in this they undoubtedly perpetuate older Jewish tradition. In detail, the form of canon embodied in 𝕲, which may be regarded as a single form if we ignore its varieties, is related to the Jamnia form in that it agrees in regard to the first part, the *Torah*, but differs from it substantially in the arrangement and number of the books belonging to the second and third parts, the *Prophets* and the *Writings*. The arrangement of the books here is clearly determined by the principle that there stand first the historical books which deal with the past, then the poetic and didactic writings, understood as being in a special sense books of edification and instruction for contemporary life, and the prophetic writings directed towards the future provide the ending. This means that Josh. to Kings remain in the same order, and Ruth, which in the canon of Jamnia was incorporated in the third part, the 'Writings', here occupies its ancient position after the book of Judges. But from Kings onwards the arrangement takes on a completely different complexion. Chron., Ezra-Neh. and

[19] On the order of the books of the OT cf. Audet, 'A Hebrew-Aramaic List of Books of the OT in Greek Transcription' JThSt 1 (1950), pp. 135–54; Ben-Zvi, 'The Codex of Ben Asher' Textus 1 (1961), pp. 1–16, 12 Pls., see pp. 2f.; Swete, *Introduction to the OT in Greek*, rev. by Ottley (1914), p. 200: 'Order of the Books in Jewish Lists'; Torrey, 'Ein griechisch transkribiertes und interpretiertes hebräisch-aramäisches Verzeichnis der Bücher des AT aus dem 1. Jh. nChr' ThLZ 77 (1952), cols. 249–54; Yellin, 'The "Crown" of Damaskus' Mizraḥ u-Maʿarav 1 (1919), pp. 23–127.

Esther,[20] which as historical books now belong to the first group, follow immediately on Kings. The poetic books Pss., Prov., Eccl., Songs, Job, follow, and as a third group, again having its own special order, the prophets, namely Hos., Amos., Micah, Joel, Obad., Jonah, Nahum, Hab., Zeph., Hag., Zech., Mal., Isa., Jer.+Lam., Ezek., Dan. We have already noted (pp. 268, 530, 541 f.) that ᴳ divides into two the books of Sam., Kings, Chron., and Ezra-Neh., which 𝔐 keeps as units. The English versions of the Old Testament contain the same books as 𝔐, but follow ᴳ in the arrangement of the books in groups— law, history, poetry, prophecy—with some differences in the order of the last two groups.

II. APOCRYPHA AND PSEUDEPIGRAPHA

§ 76. GENERAL CONSIDERATIONS

Literature: The Greek texts of the Apocrypha are all to be found in Fritzsche, *Libri apocryphi Veteris Testamenti* (1871)—a critical text; in Swete's edition of ᴳ (the text of codex B and sometimes of A, p. 714); in Rahlfs' edition of ᴳ—a critical text (p. 714). In the edition of Brooke-McLean-Thackeray (p. 714), there have so far appeared of the Apocrypha III Esdras, Jdth., Tob., and in the Göttingen edition (p. 714), I Macc. (Kappler, 1936), II Macc. (Hanhart, 1959), III Macc. (Hanhart, 1960), Susanna, Bel and the Dragon (Ziegler, 1954), Bar. and Ep. Jer. (Ziegler, 1956), Odes[1] (Rahlfs, 1931), and Wisd. (Ziegler, 1962). For the Pseudepigrapha, the editions of the texts are mentioned for each book in the appropriate paragraph.

Bonsirven, *La Bible apocryphe en marge de l'AT. Textes choisis et traduits* (1953); *Die apokryphe Bibel am Rande des AT* (1959); Charles, *The Apocrypha and Pseudepigrapha of the Old Testament, in English . . . edited in Conjunction with many Scholars*, 2 vols. (1913 (1963)); Fritzsche and Grimm, *Kurzgefaßtes exegetisches Handbuch zu den Apokryphen des AT* (1851–1860); Hammershaimb et al., *De gammeltestamentige Pseudepigrafer* (from 1953); Hartum, הַסְּפָרִים הַחִיצוֹנִים (from 1958); Kahana, הַסְּפָרִים הַחִיצוֹנִים ([2]1956); Kautzsch, *Die Apokryphen und Pseudepigraphen des AT in Verbindung mit anderen übersetzt und herausgegeben* (2 vols., 1900, reprint 1921, 1962); Riessler, *Altjüdisches Schrifttum ausserhalb der Bibel übers. u. erl.* (1928); Zeitlin et al., *Jewish Apocryphal Literature* (from 1950); Zöckler, *Die Apokryphen des AT nebst einem Anhang über die Pseudepigraphenliteratur* (1891).

Beek, *Nationale en Transcendente Motieven in de Joodse Apokalyptiek* (1941); *Inleiding in de Joodse Apokalyptiek van het Oud- en Nieuwtestamentische tijdvak* (1950); Bloch, *On the Apocalyptic in Judaism* (1952); Bousset, *Die Religion des Judentums im späthellenistischen Zeitalter* (3rd ed. by Gressmann, 1926), pp. 6–52; Braun, *Griechischer Roman und hellenistische Geschichtschreibung* (1934); Brockington, *A Critical Introduction to the Apocrypha* (1961); Burkitt, *Jewish and Christian Apocalypses* (1914); Grace Edwards, 'The Exodus and Apocalyptic' in *Papers for Andrew Irwin* (1956), pp. 27–38; Fohrer, 'Die Struktur der at. Eschatologie' ThLZ 85 (1960), cols. 401–20; Freedman, 'History and Eschatology' Interpret. 14 (1960), pp. 143–54; Friedlaender, *Pirḳê de Rabbi Eliezer* (1916), pp. XXI–LIII; on this cf. Annie Jaubert, VT 7 (1957), p. 39; Frost, *OT Apocalyptic* (1952); Gaster, *Studies*

---

[20] So far as the more recent editions of ᴳ are concerned (p. 714), that of Swete, following Codex B, places Esther in the second group, among the didactic books, whereas those of Brooke-McLean-Thackeray and Rahlfs, following the majority of manuscripts, have the order given above, Chron., Ezra-Neh., Esther, and this is also to be preserved in the Göttingen edition as is shown by the plan which has been drawn up.

[1] On 'Odes' (Cantica) cf. § 83 below.

and Texts in Folklore, Magic, Medieval Romance, Hebrew Apocrypha and Samaritan Archaeology, I–III (1925–28); L. Ginzberg, 'Some Observations on the Attitude of the Synagogue towards the Apocalyptic-Eschatological Writings' JBL 41 (1922), pp. 115–36; Goodspeed, *The Story of the Apocrypha* (1939); Hooke, 'The Myth and Ritual Pattern in Jewish and Christian Apocalyptic' in *The Labyrinth* (1935), pp. 211–33, 3 Pls. = *The Siege Perilous* (1956), pp. 124–43; Hughes, *The Ethics of Jewish Apocryphal Literature* (1909); Hurwitz, *Die Gestalt des sterbenden Messias. Religionspsychologische Aspekte der jüdischen Apokalyptik* (1958); Kiessling, *Der Hellenismus in der deutschen Forschung* (1956); Kipper, 'Escatologia na Literatura Apócrifa do AT' RCuBíbl 3 (1959), pp. 84–110; Lagrange, *Le Judaïsme avant Jésus-Christ* (1931); Lesky, *Geschichte der Griechischen Literatur* (1957/58), pp. 725–32; Mayer, *Die biblische Vorstellung vom Weltenbrand. Eine Untersuchung über die Beziehungen zwischen Parsismus und Judentum* (Bonner Or. St. 4, 1956), on this cf. Nober, Bibl 39 (1958), pp. 100–6; Metzger, *An Introduction to the Apocrypha* (1957); on this cf. Baumgartner, Gnomon 30 (1958), pp. 231 f.; Moore, *Judaism in the First Centuries of the Christian Era*, Vol. I (1927), pp. 125–216, Vol. III (1930), pp. 40–60; Oesterley, *Introduction to the Books of the Apocrypha* (1935 (1953)); on this cf. Katz, ThLZ 63 (1938), cols. 394 f.; Pfeiffer, *History of NT Times. With an Introduction to the Apocrypha* (1949 (1954)); Plöger, *Theokratie und Eschatologie* (WMANT 2, 1960); Reicke, 'Official and Pietistic Elements of Jewish Apocalypticism' JBL 79 (1960), pp. 137–50; Roessler, *Gesetz und Geschichte in der spätjüdischen Apokalyptik* (WMANT 3, 1959); Rowley, *The Relevance of Apocalyptic* (^{2}1947, ^{3}1963); *Jewish Apocalyptic and the Dead Sea Scrolls* (1957); Russell, *Between the Testaments* (1960); Schürer, GJV III (^{4}1909), pp. 188–716, E.T. (1897) II, 3; Stählin, 'Die Hellenistisch-Jüdische Litteratur' in Christ, *Geschichte der Griechischen Litteratur*, II 1 (^{6}1920), pp. 535–656; Torrey, *The Apocryphal Literature* (1945); Vawter, 'Apocalyptic: Its Relation to Prophecy' CBQ 22 (1960), pp. 33–46; Welch, *Visions of the End* (1923 (1959)); Widengren, 'Quelques rapports entre Juifs et Iraniens à l'époque des Parthes' SVT IV (1957), pp. 197–241. Pls. II–V; *Iranisch-semitische Kulturbegegnung in parthischer Zeit* (AFLNW 70, 1960); Zeitlin, 'Jewish Apocryphal Literature' JQR 40 (1949/50), pp. 223–50. Lit. § 126.

More important than the peculiarities of ⅏ in the arrangement of the books which belong to the second and third parts of the canon of Jamnia (considered on pp. 570–1), is the fact that the collection provided by ⅏ in the three divisions which correspond to those two parts of the canon, namely the historical, the poetic-didactic and prophetic writings, contains more books than are in the Jamnia canon. These are the writings described by the names 'Apocrypha' and 'Pseudepigrapha' which we must define more precisely in a moment (p. 573), or at least some of them, for here the individual manuscripts of ⅏ differ in the selection they offer. This difference between the compass of the Hebrew Old Testament as determined by the decision of Jamnia and the more comprehensive collection of Sacred writings of the Old Testament as represented by ⅏ and its daughter translations (p. 713) led in Christian councils of the following period to lively discussions as to which form of the canon was to be regarded as authoritative. The Greek Church, after initial hesitations, eventually at the Synod of Jerusalem in 1672,[2] accorded canonical recognition to four books of ⅏ beyond those of the Jamnia canon (pp. 570 f.), namely Wisd., Ecclus., Tob., and Jdth. In the Roman Catholic Church, the Council of Trent in 1546[3] recognised

[2] Mulert, *Konfessionskunde* (^{2}1937), p. 114; (^{3}ed. by Schott, 1956), p. 146.
[3] Duncker, 'De singulis S. Scripturae libris controversis in Concilio Tridentino' Stud. Anselm. 27/28 (1951), pp. 66–93; 'The Canon of the Old Testament at the Council of Trent' CBQ 15 (1953), pp. 277–99; García de la Fuente, 'El Canon bíblico en el Concilio de Trento según Jerónimo Seripando' Ciudad de Dios 169 (1956), pp. 35–72.

the following books as canonical: the Additions to Dan. and Esther, Bar. and Ep. Jer., I II Macc., Jdth., Tob., Ecclus., Wisd. The Books III and IV Ezra and Man. were, however, added as appendix to the New Testament. Protestantism has on the other hand considered as authoritative only the writings contained in the Hebrew canon, and accorded to the others a lesser value. In this the Lutheran Church was more liberal than the Reformed. The former followed Luther[4] who in his first complete Bible translation in 1534, included the books of Jdth., Wisd., Tob., Ecclus., Bar., Ep. Jer., I II Macc., Additions to Esther and Dan., Man., with the heading: 'Apocrypha, that is books which are not held to be equal to holy scripture and yet are profitable and good to read.' The Reformed Church, which at first treated the Apocrypha similarly in their Bible translations, subsequently left them out.

The books which we normally describe as 'Apocrypha'—a name probably first used in this sense by Carlstadt (p. 2)—do not exhaust the number of writings prized as edifying by certain groups within Judaism and then by Christian communities, and hence reckoned in the broader sense as belonging to the Old Testament. The name 'Apocrypha' actually covers only those among them which were taken up into the Greek and Latin Bible. Oriental Church communities—Syriac, Coptic, Armenian, Ethiopic and others—knew other such writings and held them in esteem. These are for the most part preserved not in their original Hebrew or Aramaic or even Greek form, but only in the languages of these Church communities, but in some cases fragments of them in their original language have become known again recently among the Qumrān discoveries (§ 104). These are usually known by the name 'Pseudepigrapha' and this name is so used here. It is true that it is not really completely appropriate. For on the one hand this name only fits some of the writings for which it is used, namely those which, like Enoch, are actually in circulation 'under a false name', and thus wrongly claim to have been compiled by a man of God of the Old Testament. On the other hand the name could be applied to certain books of the canon and of its appendix the Apocrypha, as for example Dan., Bar., Ep. Jer., Wisd., which purport to derive from Daniel, Baruch, Jeremiah and Solomon respectively, but in fact were composed centuries later by unknown authors. The number of writings called 'Pseudepigrapha' in the sense here used is very large, particularly if we include many which are preserved only fragmentarily or are even known only from their titles, and it has been substantially increased by the Qumrān discoveries (§ 104). It is thus clear that in what follows only a small selection of them can be considered. This selection coincides, in the order of treatment also, with those which are provided in Kautzsch's *Aopkryphen und Pseudepigraphen des Alten Testaments* (1900, new ed. 1921),[5] but adds the apocryphal and pseudepigraphical writings which have come to light in the caves near Qumrān.

[4] Hirsch, *Drei Kapitel zu Luthers Lehre vom Gewissen* (Lutherstudien I, 1954).

[5] The edition mentioned in the literature to § 76 by Charles provides in English translation those of Kautzsch together with 1. The Mishna Tractate פִּרְקֵי אָבוֹת *Sayings of the Fathers* (Herford), 2. The Story of Ahikar (see above, p. 52, n. 64) (Harris, Lewis, Conybeare), 3. Fragments of a Zadokite Work (Charles), i.e. the Damascus Document which is discussed in § 106 below.

(a) *Apocrypha*

§ 77. III ESDRAS (I ESDRAS)

Literature: Charles: S. A. Cook, I, pp. 1–58; Fritzsche-Grimm: Fritzsche; HAT Rudolph (1949); Kahana: Kahana (²1956); Kautzsch: Guthe I, pp. 1–23; Riessler, pp. 247–254. 1281 f.; Zöckler, pp. 155–61.

Allrik, '1 Esdras according to Codex B and Codex A as appearing in Zerubbabel's List in 1 Esdras v, 8–23' ZAW 66 (1954), pp. 272–92; Bayer, *Das III. Buch Esdras und sein Verhältnis zu den Büchern Esra-Nehemia* (BSt XVI, 1, 1911); Shalit, 'Κοίλη Συρία from Mid-Fourth Century to the Beginning of the Third Century B.C.' Scripta Hierosolymitana, I (1954), pp. 64–77; Tedesche, *A Critical Edition of I Esdras* (Diss. phil. Yale Univ, 1928); Torrey, 'The Nature and Origin of "First Esdras" ' AJSL 23 (1906/07), pp. 116–41; 'A Revised View of First Esdras', *Louis Ginzberg Jub. Vol.*, I (1945), pp. 395–410; Walde, *Die Esdrasbücher der Septuaginta. Ihr gegenseitiges Verhältnis untersucht* (BSt XVIII, 4: 1913).

Cf. also Literature §§ 72, 73.

The book of III Esdras (𝔊 ῎Εσδρας α', p. 542) has been preserved only in Greek and in an old Latin translation made from the Greek. It does not really represent a new book, but only a translation of the conclusion of Chron., of the canonical book of Ezra, and of a small part of Neh., enlarged by the addition of one longer passage (iii, 1–v, 3) and two smaller passages (i, 21–2 and v, 4–6). Thus i, 1–20, 23–55 = II Chron. xxxv, 1–xxxvi, 21; ii, 1–11 = Ezra i, 1–11; ii, 12–26 = Ezra iv, 7–24; v, 7–71 = Ezra ii, 1–iv, 5; vi, 1–ix, 36 = Ezra v, 1–x, 44; ix, 37–55 = Neh. vii, 72–viii, 13aα.

The content of i, 1–ii, 14 is Josiah's celebration of the Passover and his death, the last kings of Jerusalem and the conquest of the city with the destruction of the Temple, the issue of Cyrus' edict and the first return under Sanabassar. There follows in ii, 15–26 the narrative of the hindering of the building of the wall and of the Temple (the Temple is explicitly mentioned in vv. 17, 19), which, here with a clear misunderstanding of the chronological order of the Persian kings (p. 551), is designed to explain why the building of the Temple which had been ordered by Cyrus, was at a standstill until the second year of Darius. To this is linked the long extra section iii, 1–v, 3,[1] the contest between the three pages before Darius, which in its present context, is evidently intended to show how it came about that it was granted to Zerubbabel to take up again the building of the Temple which had been at a standstill since the time of Cyrus. v, 4–vii, 15 describes the return home of the exiles under Zerubbabel, the reconstructing of the altar, the laying of the Temple foundation stone, a new interruption to the work, its resumption and happy completion with the celebration of the Passover associated with it. viii, 1–ix, 36 relates Ezra's arrival and action against mixed marriages. To this is joined the narrative of Ezra's

[1] Rudolph, 'Der Wettstreit der Leibwächter des Darius 3 Esra iii, 1–v, 6' ZAW 61 (1949), pp. 176–90; Rundgren, 'Zur Bedeutung von ΟΙΚΌΓΕΝΗΣ in III Esr. iii, 1' Eranos 55 (1957), pp. 145–52; Schalit, 'The Date and Place of the Story about the Three Bodyguards of the King in the Apocryphal Book of Ezra' [Hebr.] BJPES 13 (1946/47), pp. 119–28; Torrey, 'The Story of the Three Youths' AJSL 23 (1906/7), pp. 177–201.

reading out of the law on the first day of the seventh month in ix, 37–55, and the sequel breaks off in the middle of the sentence: *And there were gathered together*.

The impression which is given by the present conclusion of the book that something has here been lost, is probably wrong, for the words *And they were gathered together* probably represent a secondary addition indicating that the sequel is to be found elsewhere, namely in Neh. viii, 13 ff., and the book originally ended with *because they were inspired by the words which they had been taught*. Nor is anything missing at the beginning of the book. It appears rather as if the author or compiler of this book wished to give an extract from the history of the Jewish Temple, beginning with the last great Passover held by Josiah before the destruction of the Temple, then emphasising Zerubbabel's service to the rebuilding of the Temple, and closing with the restoration of the cultus by Ezra.

There is disagreement as to how the arrangement of the material made by the compiler of the book is to be explained—whether the compiler himself altered the order given in the canonical Ezra-Neh., or whether he had in front of him a Zerubbabel-Ezra book which had not yet been united with the Memoirs of Nehemiah. In favour of the first possibility there is the fact that the compiler arbitrarily altered the passage Ezra i–v which he certainly had before him in the form in which it appears in the canonical book of Ezra, and we may therefore ascribe to him the linking of Neh. vii, 72–viii, 13aa to Ezra x, 44. As an argument in favour of the other possibility, it is claimed by Mowinckel, Hölscher and others that Josephus seems to presuppose a tradition in which the combining of the Zerubbabel-Ezra narrative with the Nehemiah narrative was not yet known. In *Ant.* XI 1–5, 5 he tells of Cyrus, Zerubbabel, and Ezra, and then in 5, 6–8 of Nehemiah. But Josephus clearly presupposes III Esdras and is dependent upon it. Even less can the argument be used in favour of the second possibility that in III Esdras there is preserved the original connection of Neh. vii, 72–viii, 13aa. The original order is not Ezra vii–x, Neh. vii, 72–ix, but Neh. viii–ix had their original place between Ezra viii and ix–x (p. 548). The connection of Neh. vii, 72–viii, 13aa with Ezra x in III Esdras thus proves rather that the compiler knew and used our Ezra-Neh. What is certain is that III Esdras provides a better translation of the relevant Hebrew and Aramaic section of (II Chron.) Ezra and Neh. than that of the canonical Ezra-Neh. which derives from the translator of Chronicles and is by some held to be the translation of Theodotion (§ 122). Whether the redactor of III Esdras himself translated the appropriate sections of Chron.-Ezra-Neh., or used a translation available to him, can hardly be decided with any certainty. The first possibility seems the more probable.

The insertion in iii, 1–v, 3, probably originally written in Greek, and hardly likely to be a translation from Aramaic, relates how on the occasion of a contest between three pages of Darius the first extolled wine as the most powerful, the second the king, the third, *that is Zerubbabel* (iv, 13), women (iv, 14–32) and then the truth (iv, 33–41);[2] The king accords the victory to Zerubbabel and the

---

[2] Ryan, ' "Magna est Veritas, et praevalebit" ' AER 135 (1956), pp. 116–24. Lit. § 126.

latter asks for and receives as his reward the restoration of the Temple vessels and permission to rebuild the Jerusalem Temple. It then tells how the heads of families assigned to this task go joyfully to Jerusalem under the protection of an escort of cavalry provided for them by Darius. As with several of the Additions to Dan. and Esther (see §§ 84, 85), we have here in this expansion of the narrative of Chron.-Ezra material which is not originally Jewish, but Persian, secondarily transferred to a Jewish hero. The narrative has for the most part been left in its original form, with only the introduction of a few allusions to Old Testament passages in the hero's speech (thus iv, 40a = Dan. ii, 37; iv, 59 f. = Dan. ii, 22–3) and thus he is characterised as a Jew. But the transfer itself has been made by alterations from iv, 43 onwards and by its completion so that instead of the different reward envisaged in iii, 5–7; iv, 42, it is now the rebuilding of Jerusalem etc. which is requested. It is hardly possible to decide whether the other feature which is hardly original, namely that the third page extols not one but two things as most powerful, first women and then truth, belongs to the adaptation of the narrative to Jewish thought or whether it came in at an earlier stage in the development of the material. But it is clear that the Judaising of the story must be older than its uniting with i–ii. For iv, 43–6 can only be understood to mean that Cyrus had decreed that the Temple vessels should be sent back to Jerusalem, but had not actually sent them himself, and that it was Darius who for the first time was to order the rebuilding of the Temple and to send back the vessels. But this contradicts the information in ii, 1–14 according to which both were carried out by Cyrus. The words *that is Zerubbabel* in iv, 13, which even in form give the impression of being a secondary addition, appear to have been inserted only after the uniting of iii, 1–v, 3 and i–ii, and the same is probably true of the phrase *him and all who were with him* in iv, 47, which assigns to the hero in addition the role of leader of the returning exiles. Both additions certainly come from the author or redactor of the book; and to him is also credited the passage v, 4–6, with which he leads over from iii, 1–v, 3 into the Ezra text which was in front of him (v, 7–71 = Ezra ii, 1–iv, 5).

The *terminus a quo* for the book is the existence of the book of Daniel (cf. above), i.e. 165 B.C., the *terminus ad quem* its use by Josephus, i.e. A.D. 90. The text shows in vocabulary and style of translation the natural Greek which is found also in books which were translated early; so we must probably date the book in the second century B.C.

§ 78. THE FIRST BOOK OF MACCABEES

Literature: (a) Commentaries (i) Series: Charles: Oesterley I, pp. 59–124; Clamer-B: Grandclaudon (1951); EB: Abel (1949); Echter-B: Schötz (1948); Fritzsche-Grimm: Grimm; Hartum: Hartum (1958); HS: Bévenot (1931); Jerusalem-B: Abel et Starcky (³1961); Jew Apocr Lit: Tedesche, Zeitlin (1950); Kahana: Kahana (²1956); Kautzsch: Kautzsch I, pp. 24–81; Sa Bi: Laconi (1960); Zöckler, pp. 27–89.
(ii) Single Commentaries: Dancy (1954); Gutberlet (1920).

(b) Other Works: Aalen, *Die Begriffe 'Licht' und 'Finsternis' im Alten Testament, im Spätjudentum und im Rabbinismus* (1951), pp. 130–50: 'Das Chanukkafest'; Abel, 'Topographie des campagnes machabéenes' RB 32 (1923), pp. 495–521; 33 (1924), pp. 201–17, 371–87; 34 (1925), pp. 194–216; 35 (1926), pp. 206–22, 510–33; Ayuso, 'Los elementos extrabíblicos de los Macabeos y apéndices de AT' Est Bíbl 7 (1948), pp. 147–66; E. R. Bevan, 'Syria and the Jews' *Cambridge Ancient History* VIII (1930), pp. 495–533; Bévenot, 'The Armenian Text of Maccabees' JPOS 14 (1934), pp. 268–83; Bi(c)kerman(n), *Die Makkabäer* (1935); *Der Gott der Makkabäer* (1937); 'Un document relatif à la persécution d'Antiochos IV Épiphane' RHR 115 (1937), pp. 188–223; 'Une question d'authenticité: Les privilèges juifs' AIPhHOS 13 (1955), pp. 11–34; de Bruyne, 'Le Texte grec des deux premiers livres des Machabées RB 31 (1922), pp. 31–54; de Bruyne et Sodar, *Les anciennes traductions latines des Machabées* (1932); Ettelson, *The Integrity of I Maccabees* (1925); Farmer, *Maccabees, Zealots, and Josephus* (1956); Heinemann, 'Wer veranlaßte den Glaubenszwang der Makkabäerzeit?' MGWJ 46 (1938), pp. 145–72; Holleaux, 'La mort d'Antiochos IV Epiphanès' Rev Ét Anc 18 (1916), pp. 77–102; Kahrstedt, *Syrische Territorien in hellenistischer Zeit* (AGG, XIX 2, 1926); Kolbe, *Beiträge zur syrischen und jüdischen Geschichte. Kritische Untersuchungen zur Seleukidenliste und zu den beiden ersten Makkabäerbüchern* (BWAT 35, 1926); Lévy, 'Les deux Livres des Maccabées et le Livre hébraïque des Hasmonéens' Semitica 5 (1955), pp. 15–36; Mazar, 'The Tobiads' IEJ 7 (1957), pp. 137–45, 229–38; Mejía, 'Posibles contactos entre los manuscritos de Qumran y los Libros de los Macabeos' RQ 1 (1958/59), pp. 51–72; 'Contribución de Qumrân a la exégesis de los Libros de los Macabeos' BEThL XIII (1959), pp. 20–7; Eduard Meyer, *Ursprung und Anfänge des Christentums* II (1921), pp. 121–278, 454–62; Momigliano, *Prime linee di storia della tradizione maccabaica* (1930); Niese, *Kritik der beiden Makkabäerbücher* (1900); North, 'Maccabean Sabbath Years' Bibl 34 (1953), pp. 501–15; Plöger, 'Die makkabäischen Burgen' ZDPV 71 (1955), pp. 141–72; 'Die Feldzüge der Seleukiden gegen den Makkabäer Judas' ZDPV 74 (1958), pp. 158–88; Renaud, 'La loi et les lois dans les livres des Maccabées' RB 68 (1961), pp. 39–67; Rongy, 'L'historicité du premier livre des Macchabées' Rev Eccl Liège 30 (1938/39), pp. 230–44; Sachs and Wiseman (§71); Schaumberger, 'Die neue Seleukiden-Liste BM 35603 und die makkabaische Chronologie' Bibl 36 (1955), pp. 423–35; Schlatter, *Jason von Kyrene. Ein Beitrag zu seiner Wiederherstellung* (1891); Schunck, *Die Quellen des I. und II. Makkabäerbuches* (1954); Simons, *Jerusalem in the Old Testament* (1952), pp. 131–57: 'Millo and Akra'; Stein, 'The Liturgy of Hanukkah and the first two Books of Maccabees' JJSt 5 (1954), pp. 100–106, 148–55; Tcherikover, *Hellenistic Civilization and the Jews*, translated by S. Applebaum (1959); Vincent, *Jérusalem de l'Ancien Testament*, I (1954) pp. 175–92; 'Acra'; Vogt (§ 71); Wellhausen, 'Über den geschichtlichen Wert des zweiten Makkabäerbuchs im Verhältnis zum ersten' NGG (1905), pp. 117–63; Willrich, *Urkundenfälschung in der hellenistisch-jüdischen Literatur* (FRLANT 38, 1924); Zeitlin, 'The Tobias Family and the Hasmoneans' PAAJR 4 (1932/33), pp. 169–223.

Cf. also Literature §§ 71, 76, 79, 126.

The first book of Maccabees comprises sixteen chapters. Its Hebrew name is preserved for us only in a transcription Σ(φ)αρ βηθ Σαβαναιελ *Book of the House of Sabanaiel*, which goes back to Origen. It is textually uncertain and its second half has not yet been explained.[1] It tells quite briefly of Alexander's victorious campaigns in the east, of the division of his great empire between the Diadochi and their successors (i, 1–9), then going on to deal in more detail with the plundering of the treasures and ornaments of the Jerusalem Temple (including the precious curtain, τό καταπέτασμα i, 22)[2] by Antiochus IV and his struggle against the Jewish religion (i, 10–64). The theme proper begins in ii,

[1] Abel (1949), pp. IV–V; Abel et Starcky (1961), pp. 7–8.
[2] Cf. Pelletier, 'Le "Voile" du temple de Jérusalem est-il devenu la "Portière" du temple d'Olympie?' Syria 32 (1955), pp. 289–307. Lit. § 126.

U

namely the description of the heroic struggles of the Maccabees for the freedom of religion and people. First there is information about Mattathias of Modein who by the murder of a Jew who was prepared to make heathen sacrifice and of the officer who had summoned him to offer it gave the signal for a general rising (ii). Then it tells of his sons Judas Maccabeus (iii, 1–ix, 22),[3] Jonathan (ix, 23–xii, 53) and Simon (xiii, 1–xvi, 18) who not only won back the Temple and rededicated it[4] (iv, 36–61) and gained complete freedom of religious observance (vi, 55–63), but also created a strong Jewish state extending over a wide area (xiv, 25–49). Finally, it tells quite briefly of John Hyrcanus[5] (xvi, 19–24). The book thus covers the period from 333 or 175 to 134 or rather to 103.

The originality of certain passages has been particularly contested, namely xiv–xvi, because they are not reproduced by Josephus[6] who follows the presentation of I Macc. up to xiii; viii, the making of a covenant between Judas and the Romans,[7] x, 22–47, Demetrius' offer of friendship to Jonathan, xii, 1–23, the renewal of the covenant with Romans and Spartans by Jonathan;[8] and xv, 15–24, the letter of the Romans offering protection to the Jews. But the disputing of the originality of these passages is hardly justifiable. They are likely rather to have belonged to the book from the first, as indeed it is hardly possible to make any objections against their historical reliability.

For the first half of the book, i–vii or more properly up to the narrative of Judas' death in ix, which runs parallel to the main part of II Macc. the compiler of I Macc. is thought by Schlatter and Kolbe to have used as a source the work of Jason of Cyrene which is explicitly cited in II Macc. (§ 79), or to have used it together with other source material. But this surmise is hardly correct. We should rather explain the narrative features which are common to I Macc. i–ix and II Macc. as resulting from the fact that the compiler of I Macc. and Jason of Cyrene used largely the same sources, namely, in addition to oral tradition which must certainly be allowed for, a Seleucid Chronicle, an account of the deeds of Judas, and documents from Jerusalem archives. In any case the use of the originals which were available is made here in a very different spirit from that in II Macc., quite apart from the fact that I Macc. is certainly the translation of a Hebrew original into Greek,[9] whereas II Macc., with the exception of the two letters in i, 1–ii, 18 which are to be taken as translations from the Hebrew,

[3] Burney, 'An Acrostic Poem in Praise of Judas Maccabaeus (I Macc. iii, 1–9)' JThSt 21 (1920), pp. 319–25.

[4] Rankin, The Origins of the Festival of Hanukkah (1930); 'The Festival of Hanukkah' in Hooke, The Labyrinth (1935), pp. 159–209.

[5] Stern, 'The Relations between Judea and Rome during the Rule of John Hyrcanus' [Hebrew, Engl. summary] Zion 26 (1961), pp. 1–22, I.

[6] Bell. I 1, 1–2, 3; Ant. XII 5, 1–XIII 7, 4.

[7] Bammel, 'Die Neuordnung des Pompeius und das römisch-jüdische Bündnis' ZDPV 75 (1959), pp. 76–82; Täubler, Studien zur Entwicklungsgeschichte des römischen Reiches. I: Die Staatsverträge und Vertragsverhältnisse (1913), pp. 239–54: 'Der Vertrag mit den Juden 161'.

[8] Dornseiff, 'Echtheitsfragen II. I. Sparta Bruder in Abraham' Würzburger Jahrbücher für die Altertumswissenschaft 1 (1946), pp. 128–32; Schüller, 'Some Problems connected with the supposed Common Ancestry of Jews and Spartans and their Relations during the last Three Centuries B.C.' JSSt 1 (1956), pp. 257–68. Lit. § 126.

[9] Torrey, 'Three Troublesome Proper Names in First Maccabees' JBL 53 (1934) pp. 31–3.

was not only originally composed in Greek but is profoundly influenced by the spirit of Hellenistic 'pathetic historiography'. Whereas we find in the latter a pronounced interest in cultic matters and an often crude superstition, the author of I Macc. shows understanding for the affairs of the nation and for political matters, and paints as the participants real people, certainly pious but at the same time conscious of their own strength and responsibility. It is hardly surprising that it has been said that the relationship of I Macc. to II Macc. is like that of Sam. and Kings to Chron. But in spite of this difference between the two presentations, it would be an error to regard only I Macc. as trustworthy[10] and to set II Macc. on one side as a misrepresentation of history in religious terms, just as it would be equally perverse to follow Niese and give the preference in all cases to II Macc. We shall have rather to follow the recommendation made by Wellhausen and others and proceed on an eclectic principle, considering in each case which of the two, I Macc. or II Macc., offers the more trustworthy presentation.

The date of composition of I Macc. is limited upwards by its statement at the end (xvi, 23–4) that the other deeds of Hyrcanus (134–103) are written in the *annals of his high priesthood*. For this note presupposes if not the death of Hyrcanus at least the passing of a substantial part of his period of office. I Macc. can thus hardly have been composed before the last or next to last decade of the second century B.C. Its translation into Greek seems to have been made not long after. As place of origin Palestine, and in fact Jerusalem, is most probable.

In regard to the Greek text of I Macc., which, as has been said, represents the translation of a lost Hebrew original, it may further be worth noting that the Vulgate here, as in II Macc., has the Old Latin translation (§§ 123, 124), which was made from an older and better Greek text than the Greek manuscripts now available to us can offer, and is therefore of value in textual criticism.

§ 79. THE SECOND BOOK OF MACCABEES

Literature: (a) Commentaries (i) Series: Charles: Moffatt, I, pp. 125–54; Clamer-B: Grand-claudon (1951); EB: Abel (1949); Echter-B: Schötz (1948); Fritzsche-Grimm: Grimm; Hartum: Hartum (1958); HS: Bévenot (1931); Jerusalem-B: Abel et Starcky (³1961); Jew Apocr Lit: Tedesche, Zeitlin (1954); Kahana: Kahana (²1956); Kautzsch: Kamphausen, I, pp. 81–119; SaBi: Laconi (1960); Zöckler, pp. 90–139.

(ii) Single Commentaries: Gutberlet (1927).

(b) Other Works: Bickermann, 'Ein jüdischer Festbrief vom Jahre 124 vChr (II Macc i, 1–9)' ZNW 32 (1933), pp. 233–54; de Bruyne, 'Le Texte grec du deuxième livre des Macchabées' RB 39 (1930), pp. 503–19; Cavaignac, 'Remarques sur le deuxième livre des "Macchabées"' RHR 130 (1945), pp. 42–58; Luis Gil, 'Sobre el estilo del Libro Secundo de los Macabeos' Emerita. Revista de linguistica y filologia classica 26 (1958), pp. 11–32; Kappler, *De memoria alterius libri Maccabaeorum* (Diss. phil. Gött. 1929); Katz, 'The Text of 2 Maccabees reconsidered' ZNW 51 (1960), pp. 10–30; 'Eleazar's Martyrdom in 2 Maccabees: The Latin Evidence for a Point of the Story' StP IV (1961), pp. 118–24; Laqueur, *Kritische Untersuchungen zum zweiten Makkabäerbuch* (1904); Lévy, 'Notes

[10] Mölleken, 'Geschichtsklitterung im I. Makkabäerbuch' ZAW 65 (1953), pp. 205–28.

d'histoire hellénistique sur le second livre des Maccabées' AIPhHOS 10 (1950), pp. 681–99; Manson, 'Martyrs and Martyrdom' BJRL 39 (1956/57), pp. 463–84; Marchel, 'De resurrectione et retributione statim post mortem secundum 2 Mach comparandum cum 4 Mach' VD 34 (1956), pp. 327–41; Mugler, 'Remarques sur le second livre des Maccabées' RHPhR 11 (1931), pp. 419–23; Surkau, *Martyrien in jüdischer und frühchristlicher Zeit* (FRLANT 54, 1938), pp. 9–29; Torrey, 'The Letters prefixed to Second Maccabees' JAOS 60 (1940), pp. 119–50.

Cf. also Literature §§ 71, 76, 78, 126.

At the beginning of II Macc. are two letters from the Palestinian Jews to the Egyptian Jews with the demand that they too should celebrate the festival of the rededication of the Jerusalem Temple (i, 1–9, 10–ii, 18). Only then do we get the prologue (ii, 19–32) in which the author tells us that his book is a summary (ἐπιτομή ii, 26, 28) of the work in five books of Jason of Cyrene, a personage otherwise unknown to us, but probably a contemporary of the author of I Macc. (p. 578). Then follows the narrative first of the miraculous punishment of Heliodorus who had been sent to Jerusalem to plunder the Temple treasures by Seleucus (IV, 187–175 : iii),[1] then of the expulsion of the pious high priest Onias by his brother Jason who was friendly to Hellenism, and of his expulsion by Menelaus and of the murder of Onias instigated by Menelaus (iv).[2] With ch. v, II Macc. has thus reached the point with which I Macc. begins at i, 10, after the short introduction of i, 1–9, and v–xv run by and large parallel to I Macc. i–vii, extending thus as far as Judas' victory over Nicanor (160) and to the institution of Nicanor Day, dedicated to the remembrance of this victory.

In the parallel passages I Macc. i–vii and II Macc. v–xv, leaving aside the special material which each book offers, we may note that I Macc. iv, 26–vii, 50 and II Macc. ix–xii differ from one another substantially in that I Macc. relates the victory of Judas over Lysias (iv, 26–35), the rededication of the Temple (iv, 36–61), the battles against neighbouring peoples hostile to the Jews (v)[3] and the death of Antiochus IV Epiphanes (vi, 1–17) in this order, whereas II Macc. arranges the events thus: the death of Epiphanes (ix),[4] the rededication of the Temple (x, 1–8), the victory over Lysias (xi, 1–15 (38)), battles against neighbouring peoples (xii). It is fairly generally agreed that the events actually took place in the order given in I Macc. But very divergent answers have been given to the question how the rearrangement in II Macc. is to be explained and who undertook it, whether perhaps Jason of Cyrene himself or his summariser or even a still later reviser. It is probable that it is connected with the extension of the summary by the two letters which are placed in front of it, i, 1–9 and i, 10–ii, 18—which cannot be ascribed to the summariser who certainly began his work with the prologue ii, 19–32, but must be the work of a later hand. These two letters are first a summons directed in 143 B.C. from the Jews in Jerusalem and Judaea to the Jews in Egypt to celebrate with them the

---

[1] Bickerman, 'Héliodore au Temple de Jérusalem' AIPhHOS 7 (1939/44), pp. 5–40; Plöger, 'Hyrkan im Ostjordanland' ZDPV 71 (1955), pp. 70–81, esp. pp. 78–81.
[2] Stern, 'The Death of Onias III' [Hebrew, Engl. summary] Zion 25 (1960), pp. 1–16, I.
[3] Galling, 'Judäa, Galiläa und der Osten im Jahre 164/3 v. Chr.' PJB 36 (1940), pp. 43–77.
[4] Dagut, 'II Maccabees and the Death of Antiochus IV Epiphanes' JBL 72 (1953), pp. 149–57.

festival of the rededication of the Temple, and second a forgery ascribed to Judas with similar content, belonging to about 60 B.C. They both clearly presuppose that the rededication of the Temple followed on the death of Antiochus IV. So the reviser who put these two letters in front of the summary of Jason of Cyrene fitted the order of these two events, correctly related by the summary as by I Macc., to the order presupposed in the two letters, and thus moved ch. ix, which in the summary stood after x, 1–8, to its present position. This rearrangement carried with it the displacing of the narratives of Judas' victory over Lysias (xi) and of his battles against the neighbouring peoples (xii).

We have already mentioned the other differences between I Macc. and II Macc. (pp. 578 f.), and also the fact that the latter book has in any case a not inconsiderable historical value. As an indication of its superstition we may refer to the crudity of the miraculous punishments brought upon Heliodorus (iii) and Antiochus (ix), and as an indication of its attitude, actually reminiscent of Pharisaism, there is the characteristic story of a faithfulness to the law which does not shrink from martyrdom, as it is revealed by Eleazar, the seven brothers and their mother (vi, 18–vii, 42), and furthermore the confident belief in the resurrection which supports the mother and her sons (vii, 14, 23–36)[5] as well as Razis in his death agony when he was driven to suicide by Nicanor (xiv, 37–46).

So far as the date of the book's composition is concerned, we must place Jason of Cyrene, whose historical work formed its basis, probably like I Macc. towards the end of the second century B.C., and the summariser about a generation or two later. The reviser of the summary, however, to whom we must ascribe, as we saw on pp. 580–1, the addition of the two letters in i, 1–ii, 18 as well as the rearrangement of material connected with them, can hardly be thought to have been active earlier than the second half of the first century B.C., since the second of the letters which he placed before the summary appears to have originated in about 60 B.C. II Macc. thus received its present form only then. The locality of both summariser and reviser is probably Alexandria.

So far as the original language and text of II Macc. are concerned, it has already been observed on p. 578 that apart from the two letters in i, 1–ii, 18 for which a Hebrew original is to be presupposed, the book was originally composed in Greek, and furthermore, that the Old Latin translation preserved in the Vulgate (p. 579) has particular significance.

§ 80. THE THIRD BOOK OF MACCABEES

Literature: (a) Commentaries: Charles: Emmet, I, pp. 155–73; Fritzsche-Grimm: Grimm; Hartum: Hartum (1958); Jew Apocr Lit: Hadas (1953); Kahana: Gaster (²1956); Kautzsch: Kautzsch, I, pp. 119–35; Riessler, pp. 682–99, 1312–1313; Zöckler, pp. 140–54.

(b) Other Works: Cohen, *Judaica et Aegyptiaca. De Maccabaeorum Libro III, Quaestiones Historicae* (1941); Emmet, *The Third and Fourth Book of Maccabees* (1918); Hadas,

[5] Bückers, 'Das "Ewige Leben" in 2 Makk vii, 36' Bibl 21 (1940), pp. 406–12.

'III Maccabees and Greek Romance' Review of Religion 13 (1949), pp. 155–62; Jesi, 'Notes sur l'édit Dionysiaque de Ptolémée IV Philopator' JNESt 15 (1956), pp. 236–40; Lévy, 'Ptolémée Lathyre et les Juifs' HUCA 23, 2 (1950/51), pp. 127–36; Moreau, 'Le troisième Livre des Maccabées' Chronique d'Égypte 16 (1941), pp. 111–22; Tracy, 'III Maccabees and Pseudo-Aristeas' Yale Classical Studies 1 (1928), pp. 241–52; Willrich, 'Der historische Kern des III. Makkabäerbuches' Hermes 39 (1904), pp. 244–58.
    Cf. also Literature §§ 76, 126.

This book is quite wrongly called a Book of Maccabees, for it has nothing at all to do with the Maccabees. It relates rather, in seven chapters, how Ptolemy IV Philopator (221–204), after his victory at Raphia in 217 over Antiochus III, the Great (223–187), wished to enter the Temple at Jerusalem, but was prevented by a divine miracle of punishment (i, 1–ii, 24). It relates then how he endeavoured to lead the Egyptian Jews in Alexandria into idolatry, and because they resisted resolved to have them trampled to death by elephants on the race course, but in the moment of greatest danger they were three times miraculously delivered (ii, 25–vi, 21). So now, at the expense of the entirely altered king, they instituted from the eighth to the fourteenth of Epiphi (July 3–9) a joyful festival to be celebrated year by year, and also received a letter of protection from the king which allowed them at the same time to destroy their apostate compatriots, and how in another Egyptian city, Ptolemais, they also instituted a festival of joy and thanksgiving (vi, 22–vii, 23).

Apart from the introduction (i, 1–7), for which the author must have had available information concerning the battle at Raphia, the book is entirely of a legendary character. The narrative of the miracle which brought punishment upon Ptolemy is very similar to what is said in II Macc. iii about Heliodorus, and Josephus in *Contra Apion*. II 5 (§§ 53–5) ascribes to Ptolemy Physcon (146–117) the plan to have the Jews trampled to death by elephants and his repentant withdrawal from it, and, just like III Macc., derives from this event a Jewish festival of the Alexandrian Jews. The events related can thus make no claim to reliability. But the book nevertheless has historical value for its reflection of the widespread anti-Jewish feelings which existed in the last two or three pre-Christian centuries, in Egypt just as in the east (pp. 509–10). Furthermore, we must give credence to the information that the Alexandrian Jews knew a festival similar to Purim which had arisen in the eastern diaspora, a festival which like that was celebrated as a memorial to deliverance from a great danger. If it were not for the difference of date, one might almost assume that we have here the Purim festival adapted to Egyptian circumstances.

The book with its somewhat bombastic style was certainly written originally in Greek, and probably in Alexandria. Its date of composition is probably the end of the first century B.C. At any rate we must place it before A.D. 70 since it clearly presupposes the undamaged condition of the Jerusalem Temple. Hadas assigns the book to the years 25–24 B.C., when the civil rights of Egyptian Jewry were threatened, and ascribes it to an Alexandrian Jew who decked out in the form of fiction dim recollections of an event which lay in the more remote past.

§ 81. THE BOOK OF TOBIT

Literature: (a) Commentaries: Charles: Simpson, I, pp. 174–241; Clamer-B: Clamer (1949); Echter-B: Stummer (1950); EH: Schumpp (1933); Fritzsche-Grimm: Fritzsche; Herder-B: Bückers (1953); HS: Miller (1940); Jerusalem-B: Pautrel (²1957); Jew Apocr Lit: Zimmermann (1958); Kahana: Heller (²1956); Kautzsch: Löhr, I, pp. 135–47; Montserrat-B: Estradé e Girbau (1960); Zöckler, pp. 162–84.

(b) Other Works: Franz Altheim and Ruth Stiehl, 'Aḥīḳar und Tobit' (§ 70), pp. 182–95; Beek, 'Het Boek Tobit en de "Mēt Miswāh" ' *Pro Regno Pro Sanctuario van der Leeuw* (1950), pp. 19–29; Bévenot, 'The Primitive Book of Tobit' BS 83 (1926), pp. 55–84; Glasson, 'The Main Source of Tobit' ZAW 71 (1959), pp. 275–7; Huet, 'Le conte du "mort reconnaissant" et le livre de Tobie' RHR 71 (1915), pp. 1–29; Liljeblad, *Die Tobiasgeschichte und andere Märchen mit toten Helfern* (1927); Johannes Müller, 'Beiträge zur Erklärung und Kritik des Buches Tobit' BZAW 13 (1908), pp. 1–53; Margarete Plath, 'Zum Buch Tobit' ThStKr 74 (1901), pp. 377–414; Prado, 'La indole literaria del libro de Tobit' Sefarad 7 (1947), pp. 373–94; 'Historia, enseñanzas y poesia en el Libro de Tobit' Sefarad 9 (1949), pp. 27–51; Rist, 'The God of Abraham, Isaac and Jacob' JBL 57 (1938), pp. 289–303, cf. pp. 295–7; Rosenthal, *Vier apokryphische Bücher aus der Zeit und Schule R. Akiba's* (1885), pp. 104–50; Schulte, *Beiträge zur Erklärung und Textkritik des Buches Tobias* (1914); Sereni, 'Il libro di Tobit' Ric Rel 4 (1928), pp. 43–55, 97–117, 420–39; 5 (1929), pp. 35–49; Torrey, ' "Nineveh" in the Book of Tobit' JBL 41 (1922), pp. 237–45; Zeitz, 'Der Äsoproman und seine Geschichte' Aegyptus 16 (1936), pp. 225–56.

Cf. also Literature §§ 11, 76, 126.

The book of Tobit relates in its fourteen chapters how Tobit, a pious man of Naphtali deported to Nineveh in 721 B.C., came there to wealth and was able to deposit a substantial sum of money with a compatriot named Gabael in Rages in Media. After many vicissitudes arising out of his pious custom of burying dead compatriots, blinded and quite impoverished, he remained pious and prayed to God for help (i, 1–iii, 6). Things were also going badly for the Jewess Sarah, the daughter of Raguel, in Ecbatana, for she had already lost seven husbands, killed by the demon Asmodeus on their wedding night. She too prayed to God and he resolved to help both of them through the agency of the angel Raphael (iii, 7–17). One day Tobit sent his son Tobias to Media to fetch the money which he had deposited with Gabael in Rages, and sent him off with good advice (iv), including the exhortation that he should accumulate for himself a *treasure of good works* (iv, 9).[1] Raphael, recognised neither by the father nor by the son, went with him as travelling companion (v). When they reached the Tigris, Tobias, at Raphael's command, caught a great fish and cut out of it for later use its heart, liver and gall. The heart and the liver he was to burn in the bridal night with Sarah, who was to be his wife, so as to frighten away Asmodeus (vi). Tobias married Sarah and thanks to the remedy provided for him by Raphael, did actually remain safe from the machinations of the demon (vii–viii). Meanwhile Raphael fetched the money from Gabael and also brought the latter to the wedding festival (ix). After the wedding, Tobias returned with Sarah and Raphael to his parents who had long been awaiting him. Tobias healed his father, who came to meet him, from his blindness by rubbing the gall of the fish on his

---

[1] Widengren (§ 76), p. 216.

eyes (x–xi). When Tobit and Tobias wished to pay Raphael his wages, he made himself known to them. Tobit then pronounced a prayer of thanksgiving in which he also prophesied the disaster to Jerusalem in 587 and its subsequent glorification (xii–xiii). At the age of 158 years and now at the threshold of death, he exhorted his son to leave Nineveh and to flee to Media since the punishment prophesied by the prophet Jonah for Nineveh was about to take place. When his mother Anna had also died and had been buried beside his father, Tobias went to Ecbatana, buried his parents-in-law there and survived the downfall of Nineveh (xiv).

The story is richly ornamented with fine speeches (iv, xii, 6–15), prayers (iii, 1–6, 11–15; ix, 15–17; xiii), and wisdom sayings (iv, 13–19; xii, 6–10). It purports to relate the fortunes of an Israelite deported in 721, but in reality gives a vivid and clearly realistic picture of the conditions in the eastern Jewish diaspora in about 200 B.C. (p. 585). It is thus largely of a legendary, fictional character. For in the main it can be seen, as was suggested already by Simrock[2] in 1856, as a variant of the very widely known 'tale of the grateful dead man' —known for example in Andersen's *Travelling Companion* of 1855.[3] In its Armenian form it runs somewhat as follows: A wealthy merchant purchases a maltreated corpse from the creditors of the dead man and buries it. Later he falls into poverty and distress. On the advice of an unknown servant he marries the only daughter of a wealthy man who lives in his town. Five husbands she has had have already died on their wedding night. On the wedding night a snake creeping out of the bride's mouth attempts to kill the merchant, but the servant hurries in, tramples on it and then reveals himself as the dead man whose corpse the merchant had treated so reverently. It is clear that there is a connection between the material of this story and the narrative of the book of Tobit. In the latter, it is simply that the hero of the story has split into two characters, father and son, and the angel[4] has taken the place of the dead man. Furthermore, the narrative has been influenced also by the story of the wise Ahikar,[5] who is mentioned in xiv, 10 and in i, 21–2; ii, 10; xi, 17 appears as Tobit's nephew.

The narrator has, however, filled this alien material with the spirit of Jewish legal piety. The characters are simply patterns of Jewish piety, devoted to God, reverent to their parents and to their dead compatriots, just and merciful, modest and chaste. So throughout the story there is a delightful air of good sound family feeling which is reminiscent of the most beautiful of the Genesis narratives (p. 40). The ideas about angels and demons, borrowed from Parseeism, as the alien name *Asmodi*[6] still shows clearly, have been completely adapted to Jewish thinking and do not conflict with belief in God.

[2] *Der gute Gerhard und die dankbaren Todten* (1856), pp. 131–2.
[3] Glasson, however, considers that the author of the book is primarily dependent upon a form of the legend of Admetus similar to that preserved in Apollodorus. He also, like Rosenmann, *Studien zum Buche Tobit* (1894), finds in Tobit's dog (xi, 9) a reminiscence of that of Odysseus.
[4] Pautrel et Lefèbvre, 'Trois textes de Tobie sur Raphaël' RSR 39 (1951), pp. 115–24.
[5] Cf. p. 52, n. 64.
[6] Duchesne-Guillemin, *Ormazd et Ahriman* (1953), p. 84; Haupt, 'Asmodeus' JBL 40 (1921), pp. 174–8; Widengren (1957) (§ 76), pp. 215 f.

It is thus no wonder that the book has enjoyed the greatest popularity in Judaism and then subsequently in Christendom too. This is shown by the fact that the Greek text has survived in three recensions, the first being represented above all by Vaticanus and Alexandrinus, the second by Sinaiticus,[7] and the third by the minuscules 44, 106, 107, 610. The original language was, however, certainly Semitic, and probably Aramaic rather than Hebrew.[8] Among the Qumrān fragments (p. 641) small pieces have been found of both a Hebrew and an Aramaic text of Tobit[9] and are preserved in the Palestine Museum in Jerusalem, awaiting publication.[10]

The locality in which the book is set, the eastern diaspora, is probably also its place of origin, even though its composition in Palestine is not impossible. So far as date is concerned, it must probably be placed before the Maccabean rising. In any case it cannot possibly be brought down later than 20 B.C., since xiv, 5 *they will rebuild the Temple, though not like the former one* could hardly have been written after the rebuilding of the Temple by Herod.

§ 82. THE BOOK OF JUDITH

Literature: (a) Commentaries (i) Series: Charles: Cowley, I, pp. 242–67; Clamer-B: Soubigou (1949); Montserrat-B: Estradé e Girbau (1960); Echter-B: Stummer (1950); Fritzsche-Grimm: Fritzsche; Herder-B: Bückers (1953); HS: Miller (1940); Jerusalem-B: Barucq ([2]1959); Kahana: Simon ([2]1956); Kautzsch: Löhr, I, pp. 147–64; Sa Bi: Priero (1959); Zöckler, pp. 185–213.

(ii) Single Commentaries: Grintz, *The Book of Judith. A Reconstruction of the Original Hebrew Text with Introduction, Commentary, Appendices and Indices* [Hebrew] (1957); Scholz, *Commentar über das Buch Judith und über Bel und Drache* ([2]1896).

(b) Other Works: Bentzen, 'Der Hedammu-Mythus, das Judithbuch und ähnliches' Ar Or 18, 3 (1950), pp. 1–2; Brunner, *Der Nabuchodonosor des Buches Judith* (1940, [2]1959); Colunga, 'El género literario de Judit' Ciencia Tomista 74 (1948), pp. 98–125; Dubarle, 'Les textes divers du Livre de Judith. À propos d'un ouvrage récent'[1] VT 8 (1958), pp. 344–373; 'La mention de Judith dans la littérature ancienne, juive et chrétienne' RB 66 (1959), pp. 514–49; 'Rectification: Sur un text hébreu de Judith' VT 11 (1961), pp. 86–7; Lewy, 'Enthält Judith i–iv Trümmer einer Chronik zur Geschichte Nebukadnezars und seiner Feldzüge von 597 und 591?' ZDMG 81 (1927), pp. LII–LIV; Carl Meyer, 'Zur Entstehungsgeschichte des Buches Judith' Bibl 3 (1922), pp. 193–203; Rengstorf, 'Die Stadt der Mörder (Matth. xxii, 7)' BZNW 26 (1960), pp. 106–29, cf. pp. 108–9, 116–17; Schwartz, 'Un fragment Grec du Livre de Judith' RB 53 (1946), pp. 534–7, Pl. VII; Ruth Stiehl

---

[7] Saydon, 'Some Mistranslations in the Codex Sinaiticus of the Book of Tobit' Bibl 33 (1952), pp. 363–5.

[8] Joüon, 'Quelques hébraïsmes du Codex Sinaiticus de Tobie' Bibl 4 (1923), pp. 168–74.

[9] Burrows, *More Light on the Dead Sea Scrolls* (1958), pp. 35, 177 f.; Dupont-Sommer, *Les écrits esséniens découverts près de la Mer Morte* (1959), pp. 308 f.; E.T. *The Essene Writings from Qumran* (1961), p. 296; Milik, RB 63 (1956), p. 60; *Dix ans de Découvertes dans le Désert de Juda* (1957), p. 29; E.T. *Ten Years of Discovery in the Wilderness of Judaea* (1959), pp. 31 f.; Sutcliffe, *The Monks of Qumran* (1960), p. 13. Lit. § 126.

[10] According to Milik, RB 63 (1956), p. 60, the name of the father here appears as טובי, and that of the son as טוביה.

[1] On the above-mentioned commentary by Grintz, cf. also the review by Martin, Bibl 41, (1960), pp. 436 f.

(§ 70); Steinmann, *Lecture de Judith* (1953); Stummer, *Geographie des Buches Judith* (1947); de Vuippens, *Darius I, le Nabuchodonosor du livre de Judith* (1927).

Cf. also Literature §§ 76, 126.

The book of Judith contains sixteen chapters and relates how Nebuchadnezzar's general Holofernes punished the disobedient western part of the empire, Syria, Arabia and Palestine (i–iii), and in spite of the warning given him by an Ammonite Achior[2] of whom he asked advice, prepared to attack the Israelites who had just returned from the Exile (iv–vi). He besieged Bethulia,[3] probably to be sought at Qabatiya near Dothan (Gen. xxxvii, 17; II Kings vi, 13),[4] which prevented his further advance to the south and towards Jerusalem, and by seizing the well brought the city into the greatest distress (vii). The decision had already been made to surrender the city to the enemy in five days' time when the rich and pious widow Judith offered to get help for the city (viii). After a prayer (ix) she betook herself, beautifully adorned, into the enemy camp (x). She was successful in winning Holofernes' trust and at the same time in arousing his passion. When he hoped after a banquet to enjoy her, she cut off his head and returned to Bethulia with it (xi–xiii). The Ammonite Achior, at the sight of Holofernes' head, was converted to Judaism; the enemies, discouraged by the loss of their general, were totally defeated. Judith, honoured by all the people and also by the high priest, began a hymn[5] and a great festival of thanksgiving was held in Jerusalem. Judith, who in spite of many offers had remained a widow and had given further proofs of her piety in the law, died at the ripe old age of 105 years (xiv–xvi).

This story, with its fanatical nationalism and religious passion, related in a highly poetic tone, can make no claim to be historical. It can be seen how little the author knew history from the fact that he makes Nebuchadnezzar (604–562) king of the Assyrians with his residence in Nineveh which had been destroyed in 612, and shows him still ruling even after the restoration of the Jewish religious community (520–516). But some historical events are apparently nevertheless reflected in the book, and in this respect the book resembles in its problems the narrative of Gen. xiv (pp. 211–12). Like this story it appears to describe reliably the route of armies marching from east to west or south-west. Brunner, whom Hinz[6] is also inclined to follow, postulates a military action against Syria and Egypt undertaken on behalf of the usurper Aracha who, according to the Behistun inscription was involved in the 'revolt of the Magians' in 522 B.C.[7] and gave himself out to be Nebuchadnezzar. But this is less probable than the campaigns of Artaxerxes III Ochus (359–338) against Phoenicia and Egypt in about 350 B.C., for in these there took part the generals Orophernes and

---

[2] Cazelles, 'Le personnage d'Achior dans le livre de Judith' RSR 39 (1951), pp. 125–37.
[3] Dussaud, 'Samarie au temps d'Achab' Syria 6 (1925), pp. 314–38. Pls. XLII, XLIII; 7 (1926), pp. 9–29, cf. 7, p. 21; Steuernagel, 'Bethulia' ZDPV 66 (1943), pp. 232–45.
[4] Free, 'The First, Second, Third, Fourth, Fifth, Sixth, Seventh Season at Dothan' BASOR 131 (1953), pp. 16–20; 135 (1954), pp. 14–20; 139 (1955), pp. 3–9; 143 (1956), pp. 11–17; 152 (1958), pp. 10–18; 156 (1959), pp. 22–9; 160 (1960), pp. 6–13. Lit. § 126.
[5] Jansen, 'La composition du chant de Judith' AcOr[L] 15 (1937), pp. 63–71.
[6] 'Zur Behistun-Inschrift des Dareios' ZDMG 96 (1942), pp. 326–49, see p. 326.
[7] Cf. above, p. 426, n. 1; p. 543, n. 6.

Bagoas, both of whom are mentioned in the book, Bagoas admittedly only in a subordinate position (xii, 11). But the narrator can hardly have had at his disposal anything more than confused information about these events, and possibly a list of the areas and cities which were then involved in the common sufferings. So far as the main point, the action of Judith, is concerned, we cannot decide with certainty whether there is here the recollection of a heroic action by a resolute Jewish woman comparable with the Jael of the Song of Deborah,[8] or whether we have the use of a legendary narrative type. The former possibility seems to be the more likely. In any case the narrative, if the events of 350 do underlie it, must have been written down a substantial time after them. For the national and religious fervour and the spirit of scrupulous zeal for the law place the book in the period of the Maccabean rising. Since ii–iv appear to presuppose that Galilee and the Sea coast (ii, 28 Jamnia and Ashdod) are not yet united with Judaea, the reign of Alexander Jannaeus (102–76)[9] would mark the lower limit.

The narrator is thus to be set in about the middle of the second century B.C., roughly contemporary with that of Esther (§ 70), and he has produced from the material available to him a historical novel marked by the most intense national and religious fervour. The superiority of the Jewish people over all others is strongly emphasised, though admittedly with the limitation that it may only claim this privileged position and inviolability if it remains faithful to God's law; then it may be quite sure of divine protection (v, ix). Judith herself is drawn as a model of the piety of the law: modest and benevolent, scrupulously careful in the keeping of the laws of purity and of food, her undertaking accompanied at every point with pious prayer, whether at the beginning (ix), at the most crucial moment (xiii, 4–5) or in its successful accomplishment (xvi, 2–18).

The Greek text is available in four recensions—the Textus Receptus, Codices 19 and 108, Codex 58, Codices 106 and 107. The oldest witness to it is to be found on an ostracon containing parts of xv, 1–7 from the second half of the third century A.D., which was found in Cairo in 1946 and published in the same year by Schwartz. The book certainly goes back to a lost Hebrew original.[10] The midrashic Hebrew elaborations of the Judith narrative which have come down to us,[11] are, however, unlikely to be directly derived from this original.

---

[8] Bruns, 'Judith or Jael?' CBQ 16 (1954), pp. 12–14; 'The Genealogy of Judith' CBQ 18 (1956), pp. 19–22.

[9] Kanael, 'Notes on Alexander Jannaeus' Campaigns in the Coastal Region' [Hebrew, Engl. summary] Tarbiz 24 (1954/55), pp. 9–15, III. Lit. § 126.

[10] Zimmermann, 'Aids for the Recovery of the Hebrew Original of Judith' JBL 57 (1938), pp. 67–74.

[11] Gaster, 'An Unknown Hebrew Version of the History of Judith' PSBA 16 (1893/94), pp. 156–63; Jellinek, בית המדרש I (1853), pp. 130–1; II (1854), pp. 12–22; Wünsche, *Aus Israels Lehrhallen. Kleine Midraschim zur späteren legendarischen Literatur des AT*, II (1908), pp. 164–85.

§ 83. THE PRAYER OF MANASSEH (ORATIO MANASSIS)

Literature: (a) Commentaries: Charles: Ryle I, pp. 612–24; Fritzsche-Grimm: Fritzsche; Kahana: Artom (²1956); Kautzsch: Ryssel, I, pp. 165–71; Riessler, pp. 348f. (1921); Zöckler, pp. 236–8.

(b) Other Works: Nau, 'Un Extrait de la Didascalie: La Prière de Manassé' Rev. de l'Orient Chrét. 13 (1908), pp. 134–41; Schneider, 'Der Vulgata-Text der Oratio Manasse' BZ 4 (1960), pp. 277–82; Volz, 'Zur Überlieferung des Gebetes Manasses' ZKG 70 (1959), pp. 293–307; Widengren, 'Hieros gamos och underjordsvistelse' Religion och Bibel 7 (1948), pp. 17–46, cf. pp. 37–46; Wilkins, 'The Prayer of Manasseh' Hermathena 16 (1911), pp. 167–78.

Cf. also Literature §§ 76, 126.

Most of the Greek manuscripts add, as an appendix to the Psalms, the Odes (Cantica)—not to be confused with the Odes of Solomon (p. 611, n. 2)—a collection of up to fourteen songs, which for the most part are extracted from the Old Testament, like Exod. xv, 1–19, Deut. xxxii, 1–43, and which like the Psalms were regularly used in worship. Among them is to be found in the Codex Alexandrinus (A), and so also in Swete (p. 714) as No. 8, and in the Göttingen LXX edition (p. 714) and in Ralhfs (p. 714) as No. 12, the Προσευχὴ Μανασσῆ, an individual song of lamentation (pp. 115–20) in which Manasseh, after a hymnic invocation of God (vv. 1–7), confesses his sins (vv. 8–12), prays for forgiveness (v. 13), expresses his confidence that he will be heard (v. 14) and offers his thanks (v. 15). The prayer is occasioned by the narrative in II Chron. xxxiii, 12–13 which tells of Manasseh's prayer of repentance and his being heard, and particularly by xxxiii, 18–19, where the Chronicler mentions this prayer as actually being among the sources available to him. The text which is preserved in 𝕲 is however not the translation of the prayer cited by the Chronicler, but a free composition, clearly originally composed in Greek, by a Jew from a fairly late period, probably already in Christian times. In addition to its occurrence in the manuscripts of 𝕲, it is to be found also in the Syriac Didascalia[1] from the third century and in the later revised form of this, the Apostolic Constitutions.[2] This is the earliest evidence of its existence.

§ 84. THE ADDITIONS TO DANIEL

Literature: (a) Commentaries (i) Series: BOuT: Nelis (1954); Charles: Bennett, Kay and Davies, I, pp. 625–64; Fritzsche-Grimm: Fritzsche; Kahana: Heller (²1956); Kautzsch: Rothstein, I, pp. 172–93; Zöckler, pp. 214–21, 231–35.

(ii) Single Commentaries: Scholz, *Commentar über das Buch Esther mit seinen Zusätzen und über Susanna* (1892); *Commentar über das Buch Judith und über Bel und Drache* (²1896).

Other Works: Baumgartner, 'Susanna. Die Geschichte einer Legende' ARW 24 (1926), pp. 259–80 = *Zum AT* (1959), pp. 42–66; 'Der weise Knabe und die des Ehebruchs beschul-

---

[1] Achelis and Flemming, *Die syrische Didaskalia* (1904), pp. 36–7.
[2] Funk, *Didascalia et constitutiones apostolorum* I (1905), pp. 84–9.

digte Frau' ARW 27 (1929), pp. 187–8 = *Zum AT* (1959), pp. 66–7; Forderer, 'Der Schild des Achilleus und der Lobgesang im Feuerofen' StG 8 (1955), pp. 294–301; Heller, 'Die Susannaerzählung: ein Märchen' ZAW 54 (1936), pp. 281–7; Julius, *Die griechischen Danielzusätze* (1901); Katz, 'The Text of 2 Maccabees Reconsidered' ZNW 51 (1960), pp. 10–30, cf. pp. 27–30 Appendix: 'πρεσβυτέριον in I Tim. iv, 14 and Susanna 50'; Kuhl, *Die drei Männer im Feuer* (1930); I. L[évi], 'L'histoire "de Suzanne et les deux vieillards" dans la littérature juive' REJ 95 (1933), pp. 157–71; MacKenzie, 'The Meaning of the Susanna Story' Canadian JTh 3 (1957), pp. 211–18; Zimmermann, 'The Story of Susanna and its Original Language' JQR 48 (1957/58), pp. 237–41; 'Bel and the Dragon' VT 8 (1958), pp. 438–40.

Cf. also Literature §§ 76, 126.

In 𝔊 and in 'Theodotion' (§ 122), there is found before Dan. iii, 24 𝔐, forming iii, 24–5, a short prose introduction to two extra passages which appear then as iii, 26–45 and iii, 52–90—the Prayer of Azariah and the Song of the Three Young Men in the Furnace. They are separated from one another by a further short passage of prose (iii, 46–51) which describes the tremendous heat of the fire streaming out of the furnace, the burning of the Chaldeans standing by, and the preservation of the three by an angel. Then with iii, 91 f. = iii, 24 f. 𝔐 the text rejoins the narrative of the canonical book. Since iii, 24 f. 𝔐 corresponds to iii, 46–51 𝔊 in content though not in length, some scholars regard iii, 46–51 𝔊 as an elaboration of iii, 24 f. 𝔐, whereas others suspect that there is an omission in 𝔐.

In 𝔊, after the canonical book, but before it in Theodotion, is to be found the story of Susanna, the beautiful God-fearing wife of a Babylonian Jew named Joakim, who is falsely accused of adultery by two Jewish elders whom she has spurned, but is saved by the skilful interrogation conducted by the wise Daniel, who is introduced without prior mention, not only in Theodotion but even in 𝔊, as *Daniel who was still very young* (v. 45).

This is followed by the double narrative of Bel and the Dragon (in Theodotion this follows the canonical Daniel), which again introduces Daniel anew (v. 2), here more clearly in 𝔊 than in Theodotion. Daniel proves to the king (in Theodotion identified as Cyrus) that it is not the statue representing Bel which eats the food placed before it, but the priests, and so brings about the destruction of the image by the king. Then Daniel kills the live dragon which is worshipped by the Babylonians, and does so, as he promises the king, without any weapons but by means of cakes made of pitch, fat and hair which are thrown into the dragon's mouth and cause him to burst. When the people rise against the king because of the destruction of the statue of Bel and the killing of the dragon, he gives up Daniel who is thrown into the lions' den. But Daniel, provided with food by Habakkuk who is miraculously carried to Babylon, remains unharmed by the lions. 𝔊 gives as title to this double narrative the words: *From the prophecy of Habakkuk, the son of Jesus, of the tribe of Levi.*

The Prayer of Azariah and the Song of the Three Young Men are not to be regarded as further elaborations of the canonical narrative, like the Prayer of Manasseh (§ 83) or the prayers of Esther and Mordecai (§ 85). We have here texts which a redactor found ready to hand, at least in large measure, and he inserted them in what he thought to be suitable places, though in reality, at least so far as the Prayer of Azariah is concerned, the position is very unsuitable. The Prayer of Azariah is a national song of lamentation in first person plural form. Even its form is unsuitable in the mouth of Azariah, but its contents even more so. For the song contains also the confession of transgression of the law (vv. 29–30). But Azariah and his friends have just been cast into the furnace because of their loyal adherence to the religion of the law. The Song of the Three Young Men may be divided into three sections: vv. 52–56 the introduction to a song of thanksgiving, elaborated with hymnic motives; vv. 57–88a the main section, a hymn like Ps. cxlviii, with the first half of each verse invoking to the praise of God first the works and angels of the Lord (vv. 57–8), then the heavens (vv. 59–73), then the earth (vv. 74–82), then Israel (vv. 83–7) and then, clearly inserted by the redactor into the text he was using, Hananiah, Azariah and Mishael (v. 88a). The second half of each verse is the same: *Sing praise to him and highly exalt him for ever*. Vv. 88b–90 form the conclusion of a song of thanksgiving, probably in part (vv. 89–90) taken from Ps. cxxxvi (vv. 1–2). Probably both the 'Prayer' and the 'Song' are translations of Hebrew originals. But any indications which might enable us to date the two poems are entirely lacking.

The Susanna narrative belongs to the group of biblical stories which were originally of profane origin, but have been taken over by Judaism from its environment (p. 576).[1] More precisely, we have here two narrative motifs, the one of the accusation of the innocent woman and the other of the wise young judge. Their transference to the biblical Daniel was very easy on the one hand because he, like his Ugaritic namesake who is perhaps identical with him (pp. 523 f.), was thought to be particularly righteous and wise (cf. Ezek. xiv, 14, 20, xxviii, 3, p. 378, n. 33), and on the other hand because his name means *My judge is God* or perhaps *Judge of God*. But as in the other cases, the alien material has been completely saturated in the spirit of Judaism. Whether there was a Semitic original—Hebrew or Aramaic—cannot be decided with certainty, nor can any precise indications be given of the date of composition.

The narratives of Bel and the Dragon are designed to make mock of heathen religion. The device adopted by Daniel in the first, the scattering of ashes on the floor so as to show up the footsteps, is a motif which appears elsewhere in story and legend. Behind the second, in addition to an element taken from the legend of Habakkuk, there may well be a Babylonian saga, an earlier form of which may perhaps be seen on an Assyrian cylinder-seal.[2] Here again, with this double narrative we cannot give any definite answer to the questions whether there was a Semitic original or to what date it is to be assigned.

---

[1] Blümel, 'Drei Weihreliefs an die Nymphen' Deutsche Beiträge zur Altertumswissenschaft 12/13 (1960), pp. 23–8. Plate I reproduces the nymph-relief from Mycale belonging to about 250 B.C. Blümel comments: 'It is the famous theme of Susanna in the bath in an ancient classical form.'

[2] Jastrow, *Bildermappe zur Rel. Bab. u. Ass.* (1912), Pl. 198.

§ 85. THE ADDITIONS TO ESTHER

Literature: (a) Commentaries (i) Series: Charles: Gregg, I, pp. 665–84; Echter-B: Stummer (1950); Fritzsche-Grimm: Fritzsche; Herder-B: Bückers (1953); HS: Schildenberger (1941); Jerusalem-B: Barucq (1952); Kahana: Stein (²1956); Kautzsch: Ryssel, I, pp. 193–212; Zöckler, pp. 222–9.

(ii) Single Commentaries: Scholz, *Commentar über das Buch Esther mit seinen Zusätzen und über Susanne* (1892).

(b) Other Works: Jacob, 'Das Buch Esther bei den LXX' ZAW 10 (1890), pp. 241–98; Marcus, 'Dositheus, Priest and Levite' JBL 64 (1945), pp. 269–71.

Cf. also Literature §§ 70, 76.

The 𝕲 text of the book of Esther, apart from some smaller additions, includes a series of passages in excess of 𝔐. In the editions of Swete and Brooke-McLean (p. 714) they are marked with capital Roman letters and with verse numbers added, while in the edition of Rahlfs they are indicated with the addition of small letters to the appropriate verse numbers of the canonical book of Esther, and, as in the Codex Vaticanus, are placed at the points in the Hebrew text which are indicated by Rahlfs' enumeration. They are as follows: (1) A 1–11 =i, 1^{a-l}, the dream of Mordecai;[1] (2) A 12–17=i, 1^{m-r}, the discovery by Mordecai of the first conspiracy directed against Artaxerxes; (3) B 1–7=iii, 13^{a-g}, the edict of Artaxerxes concerning the destruction of the Jews; (4) C 1–11 =iv, 17^{a-i}, Mordecai's prayer for the saving of the Jews; (5) C 12–30=iv, 17^{k-z}, Esther's prayer; (6) D 1–16=v, 1, 1^{a-f}, 2, 2^{a-b}, Esther's reception by the king; (7) E 1–24=viii, 12^{a-x}, Artaxerxes' edict for the protection of the Jews; (8) F 1–10=x, 3^{a-k}, the interpretation of Mordecai's dream; (9) F 11 =x, 3^{l}, the date of the bringing of the Greek translation of the book of Esther to Egypt. Jerome (§ 124) collected these additions at the end of the canonical book, so that in the Vulgate they appear as chapters xi–xvi. Luther presents them, separated from the canonical book, in seven chapters among the Apocrypha, and the same is true of the older English versions. The RSV preserves the enumeration of the chapters xi–xvi but indicates by cross reference where the different passages belong in the canonical book.

Among these additions, the only real expansions of the canonical narrative are (1), (8) and (9). (2) is a parallel to ii, 19–23; vi, 3. (3), beginning: *The copy of this letter, however, read as follows,* is a further expansion of iii, 6–13, and hence appropriately stands in 𝕲 after iii, 13. (4), Mordecai's prayer, is similar, a further expansion of iv, 16–17, and so appropriately stands after iv, 17, and the same is true of (5), Esther's prayer, which links directly to the preceding one. (6) is an elaboration of v, 1–2, and also a substitute for it; hence it appears in its place. (7), beginning: *The following is a copy of the letter,* is intended to supply the actual wording of the edict for the protection of the Jews mentioned in viii, 9–12, and hence stands rightly after viii, 12.

Thus we have additions of three kinds. The first group, consisting of prayers, are designed to deepen the religious content of the book; the second, providing

---

[1] Ehrlich, 'Der Traum des Mardochai' ZRGG 7 (1955), pp. 69–74.

the wording of the edicts mentioned in the narrative, are to strengthen its trust-worthiness; the third group, however, Mordecai's dream and its interpretation, and the discovery of the conspiracy, are simply the result of a desire for further story-telling. The question arises as to whether these passages were originally written in Hebrew and were actually before the translator of the book, or whether they are additions made only in Greek. The answer should probably be that B and E were written originally in Greek, but that ACD and F presuppose a Hebrew or Aramaic original. In any case they are relatively old. For according to the colophon (F 11 =x, 3[1]) the translation, made by a Jerusalemite named Lysimachus, was brought to Egypt in the fourth year of Ptolemy and Cleo-patra, i.e. since Ptolemy XII must be meant, in the year 78–77 B.C. So at that date the additions which form an integral part of the Greek translation were already in existence. In E 10, 14 (xvi, 10, 14), Haman, the enemy of the Jews, is described as 'a Macedonian', i.e. as one who wishes to make the Persians subject to the Macedonians (Seleucids), whereas Mordecai and the Jews appear as friends of the Persians. As Altheim[2] and Ruth Stiehl[3] have shown, this can most easily be explained from the period before the rise of the Arsacid ruler Mithridates, i.e. before 130 B.C., and thus the Additions are probably to be dated not much later than the book of Esther itself, about the middle of the second century B.C. But the process of expanding the Esther narrative which was so much a favourite, by no means came to an end with these additions; later still various legends grew up around it. Josephus too (*Ant.* XI 6=Addition B) used the book including the Additions.

§ 86. THE BOOK OF BARUCH

Literature: (a) Commentaries (i) Series: BOuT: Wambacq (1957); Charles: Whitehouse, I, pp. 569–95; CSS: Knabenbauer (1891); Echter-B: Hamp (1950); Fritzsche-Grimm: Fritzsche; Herder-B: Schneider (1954); HS: Kalt (1932); Jerusalem-B: Gelin ([2]1959); Kahana: Kahana ([2]1956); Kautzsch: Rothstein, I, pp. 213–25; Zöckler, pp. 239–49.
(ii) Single Commentaries: Kneucker, *Das Buch Baruch* (1879).
(b) Other Works: Harwell, *The Principal Version of Baruch* (Diss. phil. Yale Univ., 1915); Herbst, *Das apokryphische Buch Baruch, aus dem Griechischen ins Hebräische über-tragen* (Programm Hildesheim, 1886); Pesch, 'Die Abhängigkeit des 11. salomonischen Psalms vom letzten Kapitel des Buches Baruch' ZAW 67 (1955), pp. 251–63; Stoderl, *Zur Echtheitsfrage von Baruch* i–iii, 8 (1922); Thackeray, *The Septuagint and Jewish Worship* ([2]1923), pp. 80–111; Wambacq, 'Les prières de Baruch (i, 15–ii, 19) et de Daniel (ix, 5–19)' Bibl 40 (1959), pp. 463–75; 'L'unité littéraire de Baruch i–iii, 8' BEThL XII (1959), pp. 455–60.
Cf. also Literature §§ 46, 69, 76, 87, 100, 101, 121, 123, 124.

Baruch, the friend of Jeremiah and sharer in his fortunes, who wrote down at least the original scroll for Jeremiah at his dictation (pp. 349–54), enjoyed great favour in later Judaism as the supposed author of various writings. This book

---

[2] 'Arsakiden und Sassaniden' *Historia Mundi* IV (1956), pp. 516–41, cf. p. 524.
[3] 'Esther, Judith und Daniel' (§ 70) pp. 210–13.

is one of them. The title states that it was written by Baruch in Babylon after the capture of Jerusalem by the Chaldeans. There follows in i, 3–14 the story of how Jehoiachin (Jeconiah) and the other exiles with Baruch who had been settled in Babylonia at the river Sud,[1] after he had read them the book, collected money and sent it with the book to Jerusalem. The money was sent so that from it the expenses of sacrifices for king Nebuchadnezzar and for the exiles living under his protection might be defrayed, and the book so that it might be read in the Temple on festal days. The main part of the book begins at i, 15 and consists of two parts: (1) the great confessional prayer, in the style of a national song of lamentation, in i, 15–iii, 8, and (2) two poems, iii, 9–iv, 4 and iv, 5–v, 9. The first of these, a didactic poem, is ornamented with hymnic motifs and is reminiscent of Prov. i–ix and Job xxviii; it summons Israel, addressed in the second person singular, to return to the source of its good fortune, namely wisdom, which is to be identified with the Law. The second, a chain of poems built up into a larger unit, contains songs of consolation at the beginning and end, in which the poet, or even God himself, speaks encouragingly to Israel-Jerusalem (iv, 5–9a; iv, 30–5; iv, 36–v, 4; v, 5–9), and in the middle are songs of lamentation in which Jerusalem herself speaks and expresses her distress (iv, 9b–16, iv, 17–29). These latter, in spite of their expression of hope for a speedy return of her children which lights up Jerusalem's complaint, are reminiscent of 'The Lamentations of Jeremiah', while the former are reminiscent of Deutero-Isaiah. The two main sections, i, 15–iii, 8 on the one hand and iii, 9–v, 9 on the other, have no connection with one another, but are simply placed side by side and each must therefore be understood for itself.

The prayer of repentance in i, 15–iii, 8 contains many reminiscences of the style of Jeremiah (e.g. ii, 23//Jer. vii, 34), but is particularly closely related to Daniel's prayer in Dan. ix, 4–19 and may indeed be described as an expanded form of this prayer; it thus certainly goes back to a Hebrew original. Since Daniel's prayer is secondary in the book of Daniel, as we have seen (p. 529), we may not date this passage very early, and in any case hardly before the first century B.C. On the other hand, the statement made in ii, 21–6 that the disaster came upon Judah and Jerusalem because their inhabitants did not submit themselves to the king of Babylon, does not need to be interpreted as an allusion to the revolt against the Romans (p. 594), which would necessitate dating the passage after A.D. 70. We should probably think of a somewhat earlier date, and in favour of this it may also be noted that in ii, 17 belief in the resurrection is apparently not yet presupposed. It is probable that the poems in iii, 9–v, 9 were also originally composed in Hebrew. So far as their date is concerned, we have at least for iv, 5–v, 9 a point of contact in that a passage from this (v, 5–9) is practically identical in wording with Ps. Sol. xi, 2–7, and, as has been shown by Pesch, probably served as a model for the psalm passage. Since the Psalms of Solomon are to be dated about the middle of the first century B.C. (p. 613), a date in the first half of this century would seem probable.

The ascribing of the prayer of repentance and of the poems to Baruch may be

[1] Bewer, 'The River Sud in the Book of Baruch' JBL 43 (1924), pp. 226 f.

explained from the fact that Baruch, together with Jeremiah, was the only one of those directly involved in the disaster to Jerusalem in 587 who left written material behind, and hence could easily be thought to be the author of writings which were concerned with this disaster. Just as there were ascribed to Jeremiah the Letter of Jeremiah (§ 87) and the Lamentations (§ 69), so other passages which dealt with the disaster were ascribed to Baruch. At the end of the Syriac Apocalypse of Baruch (lxxviii–lxxxvi, cf. § 100), there is a long letter directed by him to the nine and a half tribes exiled by the Assyrians. In the book of Baruch it is the prayer of repentance and the poems, both of which clearly bewail the distress of the Exile, which are ascribed to him. It followed naturally from this that Baruch, who in actual fact according to the evidence of Jer. xliii, 6 was taken to Egypt, had here to be transposed to Babylon (i, 1) because the prayer of repentance demanded an exilic situation (iii, 8) and the poems could also be understood similarly (iii, 10). It can no longer be discovered which of the two passages was first ascribed to Baruch by the prefixing of i, 1–2, whether it was the prayer of repentance or the poems. If the phrase *in Babylon* in i, 1 was really occasioned by iii, 8, it would be the prayer of repentance to which this superscription first referred. But the poem also begins (iii, 10) with the question to Israel as to how it has come about that she is in the land of the enemy, and so *in Babylon* in i, 1 could equally have been occasioned by that. But it is possible that this phrase *in Babylon* was first inserted in i, 1 with reference to i, 3–14. This passage is in any case a later insertion, for it not only separates i, 15 from i, 2 to which it was intended to be the direct sequel, but it also pre- supposes a quite different situation from that in i, 1–2 and the rest of the book with this title. It does not like the latter presuppose the period after the disaster of 587 (i, 2), but (i, 7, 10) the time after Jehoiachin's deportation (598) when the Temple was in existence and the sacrificial cultus was still in being (verse 10). We cannot fix with certainty the date of the passage i, 3–14 or of the Hebrew original which may reasonably be assumed for it. It has been suggested that Baruch's summons to the people of Jerusalem to offer sacrifices and to pray for Nebuchadnezzar (vv. 10–12) is really a protest against the discontinuance of the sacrifices for the Roman emperor which took place in A.D. 66 according to Josephus, *Bellum* II 17, 2–4. But this assumption is by no means necessary. The summons to sacrifices for Nebuchadnezzar may be understood quite simply as an imitation of the letter of Jeremiah to the exiles of 598 (Jer. xxix, 5–7), as indeed the passages ascribed to Baruch reveal echoes of Jeremiah.

§ 87. THE LETTER OF JEREMIAH (EPISTULA JEREMIAE)

Literature: (a) Commentaries: BOuT: Wambacq (1957); Charles: Ball, I, pp. 596–611; Fritzsche-Grimm: Fritzsche; HS: Kalt (1932); Kahana: Artom (²1956); Kautzsch: Rothstein, I, pp. 226–229; Zöckler, pp. 250–4.

(b) Other Works: Artom, 'L'origine, la data e gli scopi dell' Epistola di Geremia' Annuario Studi Ebr. 1 (1935), pp. 49–74; Baars, 'Two Palestinian Syriac Texts identified as Parts of the Epistle of Jeremy' VT 11 (1961), pp. 77–81; Naumann, *Untersuchungen über den apokryphen Jeremiasbrief* (BZAW 25, 1913); Thackeray, *Some Aspects of the Greek OT* (1927), pp. 53–64.

Cf. also Literature §§ 46, 69, 76, 86, 100, 101, 121, 123, 124.

The Letter of Jeremiah[1] is placed by 𝔊 after Jer.+Bar.+Lam., but in the Vulgate (p. 718) and in Luther and the older English Versions it is linked with the book of Baruch and counted as its sixth chapter. (The R.S.V. indicates this enumeration but prints the letter separately.) It purports, according to its superscription, to be directed by Jeremiah to those exiled by Nebuchadnezzar to Babylon, and contains in its 72 verses a warning against worshipping heathen idols, and the proof that they are not gods, but dead matter. The details mentioned in the course of the polemic, such as processions of gods (vv. 3–5), and sacred prostitution (vv. 42–3),[2] make it seem probable that the author has Babylonian cult practices in mind. It may therefore be assumed that here a Jew living in Babylonia is castigating and mocking the cultus of his environment, and contrasting with it the worship of his own, the true God (vv. 5–6). It is also clear that Jeremiah's letter to the exiles of 598 (xxix) and the mockery of idols which is in Jer. x, 1–16 put into the mouth of Jeremiah, though certainly not actually his, have led the author to put his ideas into the form of a letter sent by Jeremiah to the exiles. Furthermore, the author is dependent upon Deutero-Isaiah's magnificent satire on the makers and worshippers of idols (Isa. xliv, 9–20).

The letter survives in Greek[3] but appears to be based upon a Hebrew original. If II Macc. ii, 2, which speaks of a warning given by Jeremiah against golden and silver idols, presupposes this letter, then we should have evidence that it already existed about the middle of the first century B.C. But even without this it seems probable that the letter should be dated not later than the second century B.C. Artom believes that there was a Hebrew original and that this was composed in Babylonia in about 400 B.C.

§ 88. THE WISDOM OF JESUS BEN SIRA (ECCLESIASTICUS)

Literature: (a) Editions: Lévi, *L'Ecclésiastique ou la Sagesse de Jésus, fils de Sira. Texte original hébreu édité, traduit et commenté,* I (1898), II (1901); *The Hebrew Text of the Book of Ecclesiasticus, edited with brief Notes and a selected Glossary* (1904 (1951)); Marcus, *The*

---

[1] A new Jeremiah apocryphon preserved in Arabic and written in Syriac characters (Garshuni), was published in 1927 by Mingana: 'Woodbrooke Studies, Editions and Translations of Christian Documents in Syriac and Garshuni' by A. Mingana, with Introduction by J. Rendel Harris. I. "A New Jeremiah Apocryphon"' BJRL 11 (1927), pp. 329–42, 352–437; Mingana, *Woodbrooke Studies* I (1927), pp. 125–38, 148–233; Marmorstein, 'Die Quellen des neuen Jeremia-Apocryphons' ZNW 27 (1928), pp. 327–37; Vitti, 'Apocryphum Ieremiae nuper detectum' VD 8 (1928), pp. 316–20. Cf. also below, p. 665.

[2] Baumgartner, 'Herodots babylonische und assyrische Nachrichten' ArOr 18 1/2 (1950), pp. 69–106 = *Zum AT* (1959), pp. 282–331, cf. pp. 81–3 = 296–8.

[3] Papyrus fragments of the Greek text have come to light in Qumrān Cave 7. Cf. de Vaux, RB 63 (1956), p. 572; Dupont-Sommer, *Les écrits esséniens découverts près de la Mer Morte* (1959), p. 310; E.T. *The Essene Writings from Qumran* (1961), p. 297; Sutcliffe, *The Monks of Qumran* (1960), p. 12. Cf. p. 707, n. 46. Lit. § 126.

Newly Discovered Original Hebrew of Ben Sira (1931); Peters, *Der jüngst wiederaufgefundene hebräische Text des Buches Ecclesiasticus* (1902, ²1905); Segal, ספר בן סרה השלם (²1959); Smend, *Die Weisheit des Jesus Sirach. Hebräisch und deutsch. Mit einem hebräischen Glossar* (1906); *Die Weisheit des Jesus Sirach erklärt* (1906); *Griechisch-Syrisch-Hebräischer Index zur Weisheit des Jesus Sirach* (1907); Strack, *Die Sprüche Jesus', des Sohnes Sirachs* (1903).

(b) Commentaries: Charles: Box and Oesterley, I, pp. 268–517; CSS: Knabenbauer (1902); Echter-B: Hamp (1951); EH: Peters (1913); Fritzsche-Grimm: Fritzsche; HS: Eberharter (1925); Herder-B: Schilling (1956); Jerusalem-B: Duesberg and Auvray (²1958); Kahana: Kahana (²1956); Kautzsch: Ryssel, I, pp. 230–475; SAT: Volz (²1921); Zöckler, pp. 255–354.

(c) Other Works: Auvray, 'Notes sur le Prologue de l'Ecclésiastique' *Mél. Bibl. Robert* (1957), pp. 281–7; Baumgartner, 'Die literarischen Gattungen in der Weisheit des Jesus Sirach' ZAW 34 (1914), pp. 161–98; Bauckmann (§ 65); de Bruyne, 'Le prologue, le titre et la finale de l'Ecclésiastique' ZAW 47 (1929), pp. 257–63; Carmignac, 'Les rapports entre l'Ecclésiastique et Qumrân' RQ 3 (1961/62), pp. 209–18; Driver, 'Hebrew Notes on the "Wisdom of Jesus ben Sirach"' JBL 53 (1934), pp. 273–90; 'Ecclesiasticus: A New Fragment of the Hebrew Text' ET 49 (1937/38), pp. 37 f.; Forster, 'The Date of Ecclesiasticus' AThR 41 (1959), pp. 1–9; Ginsberg, 'The original Hebrew of Ben Sira xii, 10–14' JBL 74 (1955), pp. 93–5; Jacob, 'L'histoire d'Israël vue par Ben Sira' *Mél. Bibl. Robert* (1957), pp. 288–94; Kahle, 'The Age of the Scrolls' VT 1 (1951), pp. 38–48, cf. pp. 46–8; 'Zu den Handschriftenfunden in Höhlen beim Toten Meer' Das Altertum 3 (1957), pp. 34–46, cf. pp. 43 f.; *The Cairo Geniza* (²1959), pp. 8–13; Kaiser, 'Die Begründung der Sittlichkeit im Buche Jesus Sirach' ZThK 55 (1958), pp. 51–63; Kuhn, 'Beiträge zur Erklärung des Buches Jesus Sira' ZAW 47 (1929), pp. 289–96; 48 (1930), pp. 100–21; Lehmann, 'Ben Sira and the Qumran Literature' RQ 3 (1961/62), pp. 103–16; Lévi, 'Un nouveau fragment de Ben Sira' REJ 92 (1932), pp. 136–45; Marcus, 'A Fifth Manuscript of Ben Sira' JQR 21 (1930/31), pp. 223–40; Margoliouth, *The Origin of the 'Original Hebrew' of Ecclesiasticus* (1899); 'The Date of Ben Sira' *Gaster Annivers. Vol.* (1936), pp. 403–8; Michaelis, 'Das Buch Jesus Sirach als typischer Ausdruck für das Gottesverhältnis des nachalttestamentlichen Menschen' ThLZ 83 (1958), cols. 601–8; Nöldeke, 'Bemerkungen zum hebräischen Ben Sīrā' ZAW 20 (1900), pp. 81–94; Roth, 'Ecclesiasticus in the Synagogue Service' JBL 71 (1952), pp. 171–8; Schirmann, 'A New Leaf from the Hebrew "Ecclesiasticus" (Ben Sira)' [Hebrew, Engl. summary] Tarbiz 27 (1958/59), pp. 440–3, I. 2 Pls.; 'Some Additional Leaves from Ecclesiasticus in Hebrew' [Hebrew, Engl. summary] Tarbiz 29 (1959/60), pp. 125–34, II–III; Segal, 'The Evolution of the Hebrew Text of Ben Sira' JQR 25 (1934/35), pp. 91–149; ' "Additional Leaves from Ecclesiasticus in Hebrew" ' [Hebrew, Engl. summary] Tarbiz 29 (1959/60), pp. 313–23, I–II; Siebeneck, 'May their Bones return to Life! Sirach's Praise of the Fathers' CBQ 21 (1959), pp. 411–28; Storr, 'Bedenken gegen die Echtheit des hebräischen Jesus Sirach' ThQ 106 (1925), pp. 203–31; Taylor, *The Originality of the Hebrew Text of Ben Sira in the Light of the Vocabulary and the Versions* (1910); Torrey, 'The Hebrew of the Geniza Sirach' *Alex. Marx Jub. Vol.* (1950), pp. 585–602; Trinquet, 'Les liens "Sadocites" de l'écrit de Damas, des manuscrits de la Mer Morte et de l'Ecclésiastique' VT 1 (1951), pp. 287–92; Vattioni, 'Nuovi fogli ebraici dell' Ecclesiastico' Riv Bibl 8 (1960), pp. 169–79; Vogt, 'Novum Folium Hebr Sir xv, 1–xvi, 7 MS B' Bibl 40 (1959), pp. 1060–62; 'Novi Textus Hebraici Libri Sira' Bibl 41 (1960), pp. 184–90; Winter, 'Ben Sira and the Teaching of "Two Ways"' VT 5 (1955), pp. 315–18; Ziegler, 'Zum Wortschatz des griechischen Sirach' BZAW 77 (1958), pp. 274–87; 'Die hexaplarische Bearbeitung des griechischen Sirach' BZ 4 (1960), pp. 174–85.

Cf. also Literature §§ 11, 21, 64, 65, 68, 72, 76, 89, 126.

The book of Jesus ben Sira is known also by its Latin title (*Liber*) *Ecclesiasticus*, a title which, since Rufinus (A.D. 345–410) has usually been explained as indicating that among the books read in the Church but not included in the canon, he regarded this as the most important, i.e. simply as the *book of the*

Church. But in reality this title is probably connected with the fact that this book was set beside the book of Ecclesiastes (§ 68), and so was provided with a similar title, *Ecclesiasticus*, a form derived from *Ecclesiastes*, the latinised form of ἐκκλησιαστής which is in its turn the Greek translation of קֹהֶלֶת.[1]

We are here in the fortunate position—unlike any other book in the Old Testament, including the apocrypha and pseudepigrapha—that we have information concerning both the author of the original Hebrew text and also concerning the one who made the Greek translation. In the colophon to the main section, which extends as far as l, 26 (l, 27–9),[2] Jesus ben-Eleazer ben-Sira (יֵשׁוּעַ בֶּן־אֶלְעָזָר בֶּן־סִירָא) is explicitly named as the author, and the appendix (li, 1–30) contains two further colophons, evidently deriving from two different recensions of the text, which mention the same name.[3] The translator, moreover, in his prologue, indicates his grandfather (πάππος) Jesus as the author of the original, and says of him that, after zealous study of the sacred scriptures (p. 565), he in his turn thought it necessary to write a book to exhort good manners, wisdom, and life according to the law.

Concerning himself the translator[4] tells us that he came to Egypt in the thirty-eighth year of king Euergetes—Ptolemy Physcon VII Euergetes II (170–164 and 145–117) is meant—i.e. in 132 B.C., stayed there during the king's reign and then translated his grandfather's work into Greek for the Greek-speaking Jews of Egypt. Thus he made this translation after 117. Indirectly these references to the grandson tell us a little more about the grandfather. The grandson clearly came from Palestine to Egypt and brought his grandfather's book from there with him. So the grandfather lived and wrote in Palestine, probably in Jerusalem, and the contents of the book fit well with this assumption. So far as his date is concerned, since the grandson probably came to Egypt as a young man, we must go back about 60 years from 132 to arrive at the grandfather's period of life and activity. We should thus arrive at about 190, and this is confirmed by the fact that in ch. l Ben Sira praises the rule of a high priest Simon, and probably has in mind Simon II who was in office in about 190 and was the father of Onias III who was deposed by Antiochus IV in about 173.[5]

In literary character the book belongs like the book of Proverbs to the class of wisdom books, and like Proverbs contains all kinds of exhortations and promises, statements of experience and rules of life, and the like, put together in any sort of order, but in such a way that sayings which refer to the same topic are frequently brought together: ii, 1–18 exhortations to patience in suffering; iii, 1–16[6] exhortations to respect for parents and its rewards; iv, 1–10 exhortations to support the poor and oppressed; xxx, 21–4; xxxiii, 13b (EVV. xxx, 21–25)[7]

---

[1] de Bruyne, pp. 260–2; Hamp, Review of the 2nd German edition of this present work, BZ 3 (1959), pp. 107–12, cf. p. 111.

[2] Enumeration of chapters and verses following Smend.

[3] On the text, cf. Smend's explanation.

[4] Cadbury, 'The Grandson of Ben Sira' HThR 48 (1955), pp. 219–25 = BT 7 (1956), pp. 77–81.   [5] Josephus, *Ant.* XII 4, 10 (§§ 223–5); cf. p. 580, n. 2.

[6] J. Bauer, 'Des Vaters Segen . . ., Der Fluch der Mütter' Bibel und Liturgie 23 (1955/56), pp. 295 f.: on iii, 9.

[7] Winton Thomas, 'The LXX's Rendering of שְׁנוֹת לֵב טוֹב in Ecclus. xxxiii, 13' VT 10 (1960), p. 456.

warning against anxiety and care; xxx, 28–32 (EVV xxxiii, 19–23), exhortations to preserve one's self-respect and independence until death; xxx, 33–40 (EVV. xxxiii, 24–31) exhortations to right behaviour towards slaves; xxxiv, 12–xxxv, 13 (EVV. xxxi, 12–xxxii, 13) exhortations to mannerly behaviour at banquets; xxxvii, 27–xxxviii, 23 exhortations to moderate conduct, to consultation of the doctor, and to prayer and sacrifice in illness, as well as to right behaviour in cases of mourning. Alongside such groups of sayings there are, as in many parts of the book of Proverbs, in Job and Ecclesiastes (pp. 472 f., 464, 493 f.), poems on wisdom: i, 1–20, iv, 11–19, xiv, 20–xv, 8, one of which is an alphabetic acrostic, to be found in the appendix, li, 13–29. Unlike Proverbs, but like the book of Job and the papyrus Insinger (p. 464), the book contains a series of poems of a different kind: hymns about God and the perfection and splendour of his works such as xvii, 1–14;[8] xxxix, 12–35; xlii, 15–xliii, 33; li (1)–(16);[9] prayers in the form of national songs of lamentation such as xxxiii, 1–13a[10] +xxxvi, 16b–22; thanksgiving songs such as li, 1–12. Special attention should be drawn to three further passages: (1) 'Praise of the Fathers' (xliv, 1–xlix, 16)[11] already frequently mentioned, a poetic retrospect on Israel's great men, beginning at xliv, 16, after the introduction in xliv, 1–15, with Enoch and closing in xlix, 13 with Nehemiah, and then in xlix, 14–16 again emphasising Enoch and Joseph, Shem and Seth, but above all Adam whose glory exceeds all beings; (2) the description of the high priest Simon which follows directly on this, and in particular his appearance on the great Day of Atonement (l, 1–24), which concludes in vv. 22–4 with an expression of thanks to God and a wish for blessing for the readers and for Simon—the original of the hymn 'Now thank we all our God'; (3) the praise of the scribe and the wise, whose profession is exalted far above all others, in xxxviii, 24–xxxix, 11,[12] which evidently reflects the author's ideal in life.

In its religious and ethical contents the book has much in common with the book of Proverbs, as indeed all the productions of wisdom poetry, as receptacles for traditional material centuries old, are often very similar to one another. We need not therefore repeat here what was said with regard to Proverbs. But this book has also a special stamp expressing the character of its author. Much more strongly than in Prov. or than in Eccl. the universal and general human interest recedes behind the specifically Jewish. Wisdom for our author is not identical with the fear of God as such, but with the Jewish law in particular.[13] His whole love is for the religion of the law and its cultic forms of expression (xxxii, 1–13 [EVV. xxxv, 1–11]; xlv, 6–26; l, 1–24), and he knows well

---

[8] de Fraine, 'Het Loflied op de menselijke waardigheid in Sir xvii, 1–14' Bijdragen 11 (1959), pp. 10–23.
[9] The Hymn li (1)–(16), which includes among the righteous deeds of Yahweh a thanksgiving for the election of the sons of Zadok, is lacking in the Greek translation: cf. Kahle (1957), pp. 39, 43 f. Vargha, 'De psalmo hebraico Ecclesiastici c. li' Antonianum 10 (1935), pp. 3–10.
[10] Driver, 'Ben Sira xxxiii, 4' JJSt 5 (1954), p. 177.
[11] Maertens, L'éloge des Pères (Ecclésiastique xliv–l) (1956); Siebeneck, 'May their Bones Return to Life! Sirach's Praise of the Fathers' CBQ 21 (1959), pp. 411–28.
[12] Skehan, 'They shall not be found in parables' CBQ 23 (1961), p. 40: on xxxviii, 33.
[13] Liebermann, 'Ben-Sira à la lumière de Yerouchalmi' REJ 97 (1934), pp. 50–7.

how to unite this positive piety with the demands of an enlightened wisdom (xxxviii, 1–15). He too came into contact with Greek culture and learning to which the Jerusalem Jewish community had at that time laid itself open in considerable measure, but it did not make him hesitant about his ancestral faith, as it did so many of his contemporaries, but rather strengthened him in it. Compositions like the Praise of the Fathers and the Praise of Simon clearly make a deliberate contrast between the new ideal which has come from outside and that which was inherited from the fathers.

So far as the transmission of the text is concerned, we have the Greek text of 𝔊, which in its turn served as basis for many daughter translations and among them the particularly important Old Latin; and also the Syriac translation, made direct from the Hebrew text, but occasionally dependent upon 𝔊. In addition we have available for about two thirds of the Hebrew text, fragments from five Hebrew manuscripts dating from the ninth, tenth and eleventh centuries. Like so many other literary treasures (pp. 649 f., 689) they came to light from 1896 onwards in the Geniza of the Synagogue of Ezra in Cairo,[14] and have gradually been published.[15] The value of the text attested by these Geniza fragments is admittedly much in dispute, and the doubts expressed concerning its genuineness soon after its discovery, for example by Margoliouth (1899), were later taken up again vigorously by Torrey (1950) and Ginsberg (1955), who see in it a late and worthless re-translation of the Syriac version. On the other hand Kahle (1947, 1951, 1959), and following him Trinquet (1951) and others, recently put forward the suggestion that the text of the Hebrew Ben Sira in the manuscripts found in the Cairo Geniza goes back, like that of the 'Damascus Document' (§ 106), to the Qumrān community, and this would make its great age and reliability very probable. It is reported by Baillet in RB 63 (1956), p. 54[16] that among the fragments which have come to light in Qumrān Cave II there are also two pieces of the Hebrew text of Ben Sira, one of which comprises Ecclus. vi, 20–31, and agrees almost exactly with the text of the Cairo Geniza.[17] Though the significance of this discovery can only be assessed properly when the two fragments have been published, it may nevertheless be affirmed already that this discovery sheds a new light on the problem of the genuineness of the manuscripts of the Hebrew text of Ben Sira discovered in the Cairo Geniza.

---

[14] Goitein, 'L'état actuel de la recherche sur les documents de la Geniza du Caire' REJ 118 (1959/60), pp. 9–27. Lit. § 126.

[15] Cowley and Neubauer, *The Original Hebrew of a Portion of Ecclesiasticus (xxxix, 15 to xlix, 11)* ... (1897); Schechter and Taylor, *The Wisdom of Ben Sira. Portions of the Book Ecclesiasticus from Hebrew Manuscripts in the Cairo Geniza Collection* (1899).

[16] Burrows, *More Light on the Dead Sea Scrolls* (1958), pp. 35, 177 f.; Dupont-Sommer, *Les écrits Esséniens découverts près de la Mer Morte* (1959), p. 309; E.T. *The Essene Writings from Qumran* (1961), p. 296; Sutcliffe, *The Monks of Qumran* (1960), p. 13.

[17] Milik, *Dix ans de découvertes dans le Désert de Juda* (1957), p. 29; E.T. *Ten Years of Discovery in the Wilderness of Judaea* (1959), pp. 31 f. Lit. § 126.

§ 89. THE WISDOM OF SOLOMON (SAPIENTIA SALOMONIS)

Literature: (a) Commentaries: BOuT: Drubbel (1957); Charles: Holmes, I, pp. 518–68; Echter-B: Fischer (1950); Fritzsche-Grimm: Grimm; EH: Heinisch (1912); Herder-B; Kalt (1938); HS: Feldmann (1926); Jerusalem-B: Osty (²1957); Kahana: Stein (²1956), Jew Apocr Lit: Reider (1957); Kautzsch: Siegfried, I, pp. 476–507; Zöckler, pp. 355–95.

(b) Other Works: Blakeney, *The Praises of Wisdom; being Part I of the Book of Wisdom* (1937); Delcor (§ 126); Dulière, 'Antinoüs et le Livre de la Sagesse' ZRGG 11 (1959), pp. 201–27; Dupont-Sommer, 'Les "impies" du Livre de la sagesse sont-ils des Épicuriens?' RHR 111 (1935), pp. 90–109; Eising, 'Die theologische Geschichtsbetrachtung im Weisheitsbuch' Suppl. Vol. I of NTA (1951), pp. 28–40; 'Die Weisheitslehren und die Götterbilder' Bibl 40 (1959), pp. 393–408; Emerton, *The Peshiṭta of the Wisdom of Solomon* (StPb 2, 1959); Fichtner, 'Die Stellung der Sapientia Salomonis in der Literatur- und Geistesgeschichte ihrer Zeit' ZNW 36 (1938), pp. 113–32; 'Der AT-Text der Sapientia Salomonis' ZAW 57 (1939), pp. 155–92; Finan, 'Hellenistic Humanism in the Book of Wisdom' Irish ThQ 27 (1960), pp. 30–48; Focke, *Die Entstehung der Weisheit Salomos* (FRLANT 22, 1913); Gärtner, *Komposition und Wortwahl des Buches der Weisheit* (Diss. phil. Würzburg, 1912); Heinemann, *Poseidonios' metaphysische Schriften* I (1921), pp. 136–53: 'Die griechische Quelle des Buches der Weisheit'; 'Synkrisis oder äußere Analogie in der "Weisheit Salomos"' ThZ 4 (1948), pp. 241–51; Kuhn, 'Beiträge zur Erklärung des Buches der Weisheit' ZNW 28 (1929), pp. 334–41; 'Exegetische und textkritische Anmerkungen zum Buche der Weisheit' ThStKr 103 (1931), pp. 445–52; Lange, 'The Wisdom of Solomon and Plato' JBL 55 (1936), pp. 293–302; Macdonald, *The Hebrew Philosophical Genius* (1936); Motzo, 'L'età e l'autore della Sapienza' RicRel 2 (1926), pp. 39–44; Pfleiderer (p. 498, n. 34), pp. 289–352, 356–65; Philonenko, 'Le Maître de justice et la Sagesse de Salomon' ThZ 14 (1958), pp. 81–8; des Places, 'Un emprunt de la "Sagesse" aux "Lois" de Platon?' Bibl 40 (1959), pp. 1016 f.; Purinton, 'Translation Greek in the Wisdom of Solomon' JBL 47 (1928), pp. 276–304; Risberg, 'Textkritische und exegetische Anmerkungen zur Weisheit Salomons' ZAW 33 (1913), pp. 206–21; Siebeneck, 'The Midrash of Wisdom x–xix' CBQ 22 (1960), pp. 176–82; Speiser, 'The Hebrew Origin of the First Part of the Book of Wisdom' JQR 14 (1923/24), pp. 455–82; Stein, 'Ein jüdisch-hellenistischer Midrasch über den Auszug aus Ägypten' MGWJ 42 (1934), pp. 558–75; Thyen, *Der Stil der Jüdisch-Hellenistischen Homilie* (1955), pp. 26–7; Vellas, Η επιδρασις της Ελληνικης φιλοσοφιας επι του βιβλιου της σοφιας Σολομωντος (1961); Weber, 'Die Composition der Weisheit Salomo's' ZWTh 47 (1904), pp. 145–69: 'Vier Aufsätze über die Unsterblichkeit, die Seelenlehre, Heimat und Zeitalter, den Auferstehungsglauben der Weisheit Salomos' *ib.* 48 (1905), pp. 409–44; 51 (1909), pp. 314–32; 53 (1911), pp. 322–45; 54 (1912), pp. 205–39; Williams, 'Armenian Variants in the Book of Wisdom' JThSt 7 (1956), pp. 243–6; Ziener, *Die theologische Begriffssprache im Buche der Weisheit* (BBB 11, 1956); 'Die Verwendung der Schrift im Buche der Weisheit' Trierer ThZ 66 (1957), pp. 138–51; 'Johannesevangelium und urchristliche Passafeier' BZ 2 (1958), pp. 263–74, cf. pp. 266–70: 'Weisheitsbuch und Johannesevangelium'.

Cf. also Literature §§ 11, 16, 21, 64, 65, 68, 76, 88, 126.

The nineteen chapters of this book fall into three sections, of which the first (i–v) is written entirely in verses whose lines are parallel, the second (vi–ix) and the beginning of the third (x–xii, 18) are in general also in poetry, but contain occasional passages of prose, while the remainder of the third (xii, 19–xix, 22) is almost entirely in prose, which only occasionally takes on poetic tones. The first part is concerned with the superiority of the pious and wise to the godless; the second is a song of praise on wisdom, beginning as an exhortation to kings to seek for it (vi, 1–11) and closing in a prayer for it (ix); the third describes the miracles of wisdom, how they were revealed in Israel's history from Adam[1] up to Israel's entry into the holy land. This theme is interrupted in xiii–xv by a discourse on the folly of idolatry.

The book belongs to the wisdom literature, and like Prov. and Eccl. is ascribed to Solomon,[2] and indeed, as is shown by viii, 10–11; ix, 7–8, 12, it was written from the outset as a pseudepigraphon under his name. It is also like Eccl. in that Solomon sometimes appears in the first person (vi–ix) and addresses others (i, 1; vi), but sometimes he himself is completely in the background and as it were allows the real author to speak (i, 2–v, 23; x–xix). In Jesus ben Sira we found that the individual sayings became less important than the poems on wisdom; the book of Wisdom has no such sayings, but only poems[3] or discourses, though it is true that the characteristic form of the sayings, the *parallelismus membrorum*, is at first preserved, but then becomes less strictly observed and is finally abandoned entirely. This development in Jewish wisdom writing, going far beyond Prov., Job, Eccl., Ecclus., in itself shows the effects of foreign, namely Greek, stylistic influences. These influences appear clearly in individual features of the style, as for example the chain-like series of statements in vi, 17–20, reminiscent of Rom. v, 3–5. But more than this, the whole book, and in particular its second more prosaic half, is written entirely in the bombastic and pathetic style of the Hellenistic age, and Jerome was right when he said that even the style of the book 'stinks'[4] of Greek eloquence.

The contents correspond to the form. The thoroughly Jewish core is decked out with all manner of features borrowed from Greece, or more properly from the syncretism of Hellenistic, Egyptian and Oriental ideas—mediated according to Heinemann through Posidonius (135–51 B.C.)—and these have occasionally even affected the core of thought itself. To these external features belongs the apparent imitation of the language of the Mysteries when the author in ii, 22 speaks of God's secrets, which are not recognised by the godless,[5] and in viii, 4 calls wisdom the *initiate in the knowledge of God*; so too when in viii, 7 he praises wisdom as the teacher of the four cardinal virtues σωφροσύνη, φρόνησις, δικαιοσύνη, ἀνδρεία—*self-control, prudence, justice and courage*. But when in viii, 20 belief is expressed in the pre-existence of the soul, this, together with the statement in ix, 15 that the body represents a burden to the soul, shows more than the taking over of Hellenistic externals. For here is the pessimistic dualism which is reminiscent of some passages from the Qumrān writings, particularly in the Manual of Discipline and the Hymn Scroll,[6] and in both cases is likely to be of Iranian origin, and this is in process of basically transforming Judaism or at any rate giving it a new note. In fact the religion of the author is thoroughly

---

[1] Camps, 'Midraš sobre la história de les plagues' *Misc. Bibl. Ubach* (1953), pp. 97–113; Dupont-Sommer, 'Adam, "Père du Monde", dans la "Sagesse de Salomon" (x, 1–2)' RHR 119 (1939), pp. 182–203.

[2] Skehan, *The Literary Relationship between the Book of Wisdom and the Protocanonical Wisdom Books of the O.T.* (1938).

[3] Peters, 'Ein hebräischer alphabetischer Psalm in der Weisheit Salomons Kap. ix' BZ 14 (1917), pp. 1–14.   [4] 'ipse stilus Graecam eloquentiam redolet'.

[5] Weisengoff, 'The Impious of Wisdom ii' CBQ 11 (1949), pp. 40–65.

[6] Dubarle, 'Une source du livre de la Sagesse?' RSPhTh 37 (1953), pp. 425–43; cf. below §§ 105, 108.

directed towards the other world[7] and in its underestimating of the values of this world it differs sharply from the older Jewish religion for which the possessions of this world were religious possessions because they were the signs of God's pleasure and his reward for good and honest action. For the author even life itself is no longer the highest of all goods, and childlessness may for him in some circumstances be a better fortune than many children (iii–iv).

As a result of these considerations, the position of the book within the history of thought and also its place of origin can to some extent be determined. The second and first centuries B.C. mark the classical period of this kind of Jewish learning and literature, influenced both in form and content by oriental and Hellenistic thought. Its typical representative, though differing from the author of this book in many respects, may be considered to be Philo (c. 25 B.C. to A.D. 40); its classical locality is Alexandria. Thus we must consider the first century B.C. as the period and Alexandria as the setting of the book. We cannot decide with certainty whether Paul knew and used it. There are not infrequent echoes of it in his letters (xi, 22; xii, 12–18 similar to Rom. ix, 19–23; xii, 8, 10, 11a, 20a similar to Rom. ix, 22 etc.), but they may be explained as due to the common training of Paul and of the author of the book. According to Dulière, the book contains in xiv, 15 an allusion to the death of Hadrian's favourite Antinous[8] in about A.D. 130, and cannot therefore have come into being, at any rate in its present form, before that date.

The purpose which the author had in mind in this book was clearly the defence of Jewish belief in God, using the tools of Hellenistic learning, and this in two directions, namely against compatriots who had become apostates, and against his heathen environment. The godless who are contrasted with the righteous in i–v are clearly Jews (cf. ii, 16; iii, 16; v, 6–7);[9] they abandon themselves to lighthearted enjoyment of life and in their brazen behaviour, not shrinking even from infringements of the law, they feel the quiet, sincere life of the righteous as an irksome reproach. The description of the folly of idolatry in xiii–xv and the proof of the difference between the fortunes of Egyptians and Israelites in xvi–xix,[10] however, are intended, at any rate secondarily, to reveal to heathens the superiority of Judaism and to win them over to it.

It is generally recognized that the book is a unity in at least the sense that its Greek text comes from one hand. But some scholars consider it possible that the first part—i–v or i–ix or i–xi, 1 (the division varies)—had a Hebrew original and was translated into Greek by the author of the remainder. However, the arguments adduced for this view are hardly valid. The Vulgate text (§ 124) of the book is particularly valuable[11] because it is taken from the Old Latin

---

[7] Bückers, *Die Unsterblichkeitslehre des Weisheitsbuches* (1938); Dupont-Sommer, 'De l'immortalité astrale dans la "Sagesse de Salomon"' REG 62 (1949), pp. 80–7; Schütz, *Les idées eschatologiques du Livre de la Sagesse* (1935).

[8] Kübler, *Antinoupolis* (1914), pp. 7–8, 21–3, 1 Pl. Lit. § 126.

[9] Suggs, 'Wisdom of Solomon ii, 10–v: A Homily Based on the Fourth Servant Song' JBL 76 (1957), pp. 26–33.

[10] Cabaniss, 'Wisdom xviii, 14 f.: An Early Christmas Text' VigChr 10 (1956), pp. 97–102.

[11] de Bruyne, 'Étude sur le texte latin de la Sagesse' Rev Bénédict 41 (1929), pp. 101–33; Ziegler, 'Zur griechischen Vorlage der Vetus Latina in der Sapientia Salomonis' *Junker-Festschr.* (1961), pp. 275–91. Cf. below, p. 717. Lit. § 126.

translation (§ 123). In Khirbet Mird (p. 640) a fragment, as yet unpublished, of the Greek text of Wisdom has come to light.[12]

(b) Pseudepigrapha

§ 90. THE LETTER OF ARISTEAS

Literature: (a) Text: Thackeray in Swete, *Introduction to the OT* (²1914), pp. 531–606; Wendland, *Aristeae Epistula* (1900).

(b) Commentaries: Charles: Andrews, II, pp. 83–122; Jew Apocr Lit: Hadas (1951); Kahana: Kahana (²1956); Kautzsch: Wendland, II, pp. 1–31; Riessler, pp. 193–233, 1277–79.

(c) Other Works: Franz Altheim and Ruth Stiehl, 'Alexander the Great and the Avesta' East and West 8 (1957), pp. 123–35, cf. pp. 125–7; 'Μεταγραφή' Philologia Sacra (1958), pp. 9–48; Bickermann, 'Zur Datierung des Pseudo-Aristeas' ZNW 29 (1930), pp. 280–98; Dornseiff, *Echtheitsfragen antik-griechischer Literatur* (1939), pp. 69 f.; Février, *La date, la composition et les sources de la Lettre d'Aristée à Philocrate* (1925); Herrmann and Baumgärtel, *Beiträge zur Entstehungsgeschichte der Septuaginta* (BWAT 30, 1923), pp. 39–80; Jellicoe, 'St. Luke and the "Seventy (-Two)" ' NTS 6 (1959/60), pp. 319–21; 'St. Luke and the Letter of Aristeas' JBL 80 (1961), pp. 149–55; Kahle, *The Cairo Geniza* (1947), pp. 132–7; (²1959), pp. 209–14; 'The Greek Bible and the Gospels. Fragments from the Judaean Desert' StEv = TU 73 (1959), pp. 613–21; Meecham, *The Oldest Version of the Bible* (1932); *The Letter of Aristeas* (1935); Momigliano, 'Per la data e la caratteristica della lettera di Aristea' Aegyptus 12 (1932), pp. 161–72; Orlinsky, Review of Hadas, *Aristeas to Philocrates* (1951) Crozer Quarterly 29 (1952), pp. 201–5; Stählin, 'Josephus und der Aristeasbrief' ThStKr 102 (1930), pp. 324–31; Stricker, *De Brief van Aristeas* (VAA 62, 4, 1956); Tcherikover, 'The Ideology of the Letter of Aristeas' HThR 51 (1958), pp. 59–85; *Corpus Papyrorum Judaicarum*, I (1957), pp. 1–47; Thackeray (§ 87), pp. 17–31; Tracy (§ 80); Tramontano, *La lettera di Aristea a Filocrate* (1931); Willrich, *Urkundenfälschung in der hellenistisch-jüdischen Literatur* (FRLANT 38, 1924), pp. 86–91; Zuntz, 'Zum Aristeas-Text' Philologus 102 (1958), pp. 240–6; 'Aristeas Studies I: "The Seven Banquets" ' JSSt 4 (1959), pp. 21–36; 'II: "Aristeas on the Translation of the Torah" ' JSSt 4 (1959), pp. 109–26.

Cf. also Literature §§ 76, 121, 122, 126.

The 'Letter' directed by Aristeas to his brother Philocrates describes itself more correctly in §§ 1 and 322 as a διήγησις narrative. It purports to be an account written down already within the reign of Ptolemy II Philadelphus (285–246), concerning the journey Aristeas made to Jerusalem to fetch the Jewish Pentateuch and men who would be able to prepare a transcription (μεταγραφή) and a translation (ἑρμηνεία) into Greek. Ptolemy II wished, when attention was drawn to the point by the director of the royal library, Demetrius Phalereus, to have in his library the Jewish Torah in Greek transcription[1] and translation. To obtain the original text for this, he sent his two courtiers Aristeas and Andreas to Jerusalem. A fairly concise account is given of the main subject: the suggestion made by Demetrius, the first negotiations by letter with the high priest Eleazar, the selection of six times twelve qualified

---

[12] Burrows, *More Light on the Dead Sea Scrolls* (1958), pp. 33 f. Cf. p. 704, n. 22.
[1] Cf. below, pp. 605, 702, 711 f.

men (six from each tribe), departure from Jerusalem, arrival in Alexandria, reception at court, the making of the transcription and the translation, carried out by the 72 being brought together in a building put at their disposal on the island or peninsula of the Pharos, and there by examination in common of the work prepared by each one of them, arriving within 72 days at a unified result, accepted by them all and then confirmed by representatives of the Jewish community of Alexandria. The insertions are more detailed: the release of the Jews who are living in Egypt as slaves (§§ 12–27),[2] the description of the gifts made by the king to Eleazar (§§ 51–82), the description of Jerusalem (§§ 83–120), the conversation of Aristeas and Andreas with Eleazar concerning the deep spiritual meaning of the Jewish food laws (§§ 121–171), the conversation at table between the king and the 72 on all manner of ethical and religious questions, and in particular those which are concerned with the government of a people—a sort of pattern for rulers (§§ 187–300), designed to set out the superiority of Jewish wisdom to Greek philosophy, recognised by the Greek philosophers themselves.

The letter is undoubtedly a fabrication. It was certainly not written before the end of the second century B.C. as has been shown by Bickermann from the evidence of certain exactly datable documentary formulae and titles, such as χαίρειν καὶ ἐρρῶσθαι greeting and health (§ 35), ἐὰν οὖν φαίνηται if it seem good (§ 32), τῶν ἀρχισωματοφυλάκων of the chief of the bodyguards (§ 40). Hadas dates the letter in about 130 B.C.; Orlinsky considers it to be about forty years older. The author is to be sought among the educated Jews of Alexandria, familiar with the Egyptian court. There can be no doubt as to what he was aiming at in the work which he then wrote. He is endeavouring to demonstrate the reliability of the Greek Pentateuch which at that time was regarded as standard by the Jews of Alexandria, and at the same time to show the tremendous superiority of Jewish wisdom, identical with the Law, to all Greek learning. He does this, just as other Jews of Alexandria also did at that time, by permitting the Jews whom he introduces to dispute with Greek philosophers and other educated non-Jews in meal-time discussions as did the Sophists. And he shows them demonstrating their superiority. Furthermore, for this purpose he makes use of historical sources. The references to the settlement of Jews in Egypt (§§ 12–27) contain much credible detail. He uses a writing composed in the third century B.C. entitled 'Concerning kingship' (Περὶ βασιλείας),[3] and that genre of travel description which sees the political ideal of Greek philosophy actualised among foreign peoples. In the description of Jerusalem, which so often goes beyond reality and gets lost in Utopianism, the influence of this literary genre is clearly discernible. But above all, the author builds upon the tradition, which he clearly presupposes as well-known, that the Torah was transcribed and translated into Greek at the command of Ptolemy II, though certainly not without elaborating this in his turn, presumably in the direction of substantially exaggerating the part which the king and the court had in the matter.

It is conceivable that in the first half of the third pre-Christian century a

---

[2] Schubart, 'Aristeas § 23' Aegyptus 31 (1951), pp. 148–9.
[3] Tarn, *The Greeks in Bactria and India* (1938), pp. 414–36.

librarian concerned for the completion of the collection of treasured scrolls under his care, took the trouble to obtain a transcription[4] and a translation into Greek of the Hebrew Torah, and that he obtained the king's assistance in this. This is made the more likely in view of its being certain that at that time the Alexandrian Jews possessed a transcription of the Torah into Greek and also a Greek translation of it, and that this served the same purpose for them as was served by the Targums (§ 119) for the Aramaic-speaking Jews of Palestine. But the tracing back of the Greek translation of the Torah, together with its transcription, to the initiative of a Demetrius Phalereus and his king may equally be an invented idea designed to shed greater glory upon such a translation. So both Kahle and Katz (pp. 708–9), in their reconstructions of the beginnings of the translation, make no use of this motif. But for the rest they go very different ways. According to Kahle, Alexandrian Jewry in the latter half of the second century B.C. had available a considerable number of what he believes, from his interpretation of § 30 of the Letter, to be Greek Pentateuch 'Targums', differing substantially from one another. They wished to set these aside by means of a standard translation. This Letter provides the legend which then soon came into existence explaining that this translation went back to the suggestion of a famous Greek scholar and clearly was produced with divine aid, a legend which provided suitable propaganda for the new translation beside which the older ones were still maintaining themselves. By contrast with this, Katz points out that the language of the Greek Pentateuch points to the early third century B.C.[5] and that from the middle of the second century B.C. there have come two papyrus fragments with the Greek text of Deuteronomy, in part damaged (pp. 706 f.), and he concludes from this that the 𝕲 translation of the Pentateuch must be a century and a half older than Kahle supposes and that the variants presupposed by §30 of the Letter are to be explained as due to corruption of this translation.[6] How far, moreover, the information of the Letter is reliable, can hardly be ascertained. It may be correct that the Pharos island was the setting of a translators' commission, but the number 72—which rounded off as 70 gave its name to the translation, i.e. 'That of the Septuaginta' and then simply 'Septuaginta' (LXX)—is certainly fictional. So also the claim that the translators were Palestinian Jews must be corrected since it was rather Jews of Alexandria who made the translation.

This work enjoyed great popularity among Jews and Christians as a witness to the making of 𝕲 of the Pentateuch and the high honour in which it was held, and so to the making of 𝕲 altogether. Josephus reproduces it in detail (*Ant.* XII 2, §§ 11–118), and many Church Fathers did the same, while enhancing its

---

[4] Morenz, 'Das Koptische' HdO I, I, 1 (1959), pp. 90–104. Cf. pp. 91 f. 'We meet with transcriptions of Egyptian words into Greek script for the first time in works of the second or even of the third century B.C.' Cf. p. 702, n. 1. Lit. § 126.

[5] Cf. Wackernagel, 'Die griechische Sprache' *Kultur der Gegenwart*, Part I, Section VIII (³1924), pp. 371–97, cf. p. 388.

[6] In reality the phrase ἀμελέστερον δὲ καὶ οὐχ ὡς ὑπάρχει σεσήμανται *copied somewhat carelessly and not corresponding to the original* in § 30 does not refer to variants in the Greek Pentateuch which could be due to the presence of different translations or to the corruption of an original translation. It refers to defective and ambiguous vocalisation of the Hebrew text.

miraculous features.[7] So a relatively large number of manuscripts of the Greek text has come down to us.

§ 91. THE BOOK OF JUBILEES

Literature: (a) Text: Ethiopic: Dillmann, *Liber Jubilaeorum, aethiopice* (1859); Charles, *The Ethiopic Version of the Hebrew Book of Jubilees* (1895); Latin: Ceriani, *Monumenta Sacra et Profana* I 1 (1861), pp. 9–54, 63 f.; Rönsch, *Das Buch der Jubiläen oder die Kleine Genesis* (1874).

(b) Commentaries: Charles: Charles, II, pp. 1–82; Hammershaimb: Noack (1958); Kahana: Goldman (²1956); Kautzsch: Littmann, II, pp. 31–119; Riessler, pp. 539–666, 1304–11.

(c) Other Works: Albeck, *Das Buch der Jubiläen und die Halacha* (Beilage zum Jahresbericht der Hochschule für die Wissenschaft des Judentums in Berlin, 1930); on this cf. Finkelstein, MGWJ 76 (1932), pp. 525–34; Baumgarten, 'The Beginning of the Day in the Calendar of Jubilees' JBL 77 (1958), pp. 355–60; 78 (1959), p. 157; Bohn, 'Die Bedeutung des Buches der Jubiläen' ThStKr 73 (1900), pp. 167–84; Büchler, 'Studies in the Book of Jubilees' REJ 82 (1926), pp. 253–74; 'Traces des idées et des coutumes hellénistiques dans le Livre des Jubilés' REJ 89 (1930), pp. 321–48; Finkelstein, 'The Book of Jubilees and the Rabbinic Halaka' HThR 16 (1923), pp. 39–61; 'The Date of the Book of Jubilees' HThR 36 (1943), pp. 19–24; van Goudoever, *Biblical Calendars* (1959); Annie Jaubert, 'Le calendrier des Jubilés et de la secte de Qumrân. Ses origines bibliques' VT 3 (1953), pp. 250–264; *La date de la Cène. Calendrier biblique et liturgie chrétienne* (1957); 'Le calendrier des Jubilés et les jours liturgiques de la semaine' VT 7 (1957), pp. 35–61; Klein, 'Palästinisches im Jubiläenbuch' ZDPV 57 (1934), pp. 7–27; Kutsch, 'Der Kalender des Jubiläenbuches und das A und NT' VT 11 (1961), pp. 31–41; Leach, 'A Possible Method of Intercalation for the Calendar of the Book of Jubilees' VT 7 (1957), pp. 392–7; Morgenstern, 'The Calendar of the Book of Jubilees, its Origin and its Character' VT 5 (1955), pp. 34–76; Noack, 'Qumran and the Book of Jubilees' SEA 22/23 (1957/58), pp. 191–207; Rowley, 'Criteria for the Dating of Jubilees' JQR 36 (1945/46), pp. 183–7; Segal, 'The Hebrew Festivals and the Calendar' JSSt 6 (1961), pp. 74–94; Testuz, *Les idées religieuses du Livre des Jubilés* (1960); Wiesenberg, 'The Jubilee of Jubilees' RQ 3 (1961/2), pp. 3–40; Zeitlin, 'The Book of Jubilees, its Character and its Significance' JQR 30 (1939/40), pp. 1–32; 'The Book of Jubilees' JQR 35 (1944/45), pp. 12–16; 'Criteria for the Dating of Jubilees' JQR 36 (1945/46), pp. 187–9; 'The Book of "Jubilees" and the Pentateuch' JQR 48 (1957/58), pp. 218–35; 'The Beginning of the Day in the Calendar of Jubilees' JBL 78 (1959), pp. 153–6.

Cf. also Literature §§ 76, 126.

The Book of Jubilees is so entitled because it divides the course of the world into 'Jubilees', the Jubilee periods of Lev. xxv (49 years), which in their turn are subdivided each into seven weeks of years consisting each of seven solar years of 364 days.[1] It is also named 'Little Genesis' because it runs parallel to Genesis, though falling much below it in value. It reproduces the essential content of Gen. i to Exod. xii by relating that this story was imparted to Moses at God's command by an angel on Sinai so that it might be written down. Quite

---

[7] For an example of a story of this kind, perhaps going back to Origen and criticised by Porphyry in his work Κατὰ Χριστιανούς, cf. Franz Altheim and Ruth Stiehl, 'Neue Bruchstücke aus Porphyrius' Κατὰ Χριστιανούς' Gedenkschr. Georg Rohde (1961), pp. 23-38 = Altheim, *Geschichte der Hunnen* III (1961), pp. 110–25.

[1] Vogt, 'Antiquum Kalendarium Sacerdotale' Bibl 36 (1955), pp. 403–8.

large sections are simple reproductions of Gen. i–Exod. xii. But there are a few deviations in the arrangement of the material from the biblical order. Thus Gen. xxxviii stands between xli and xlii. But more significant are the elaborations of the material with both narrative and legal material, i.e. haggadic and halachic expansions. Examples of haggada are xi, 16–24 where Abraham at the age of fourteen years arrives at the pure knowledge of God and at the same time makes a practical discovery which makes it possible when ploughing to set the seed so deep in the earth that the birds can no longer steal it. Another such passage is xxiii, 19–31 where there is put into the mouth of Abraham an eschatological prospect of the disaster which will come upon Israel because of her wickedness, and of the age of salvation to come after her repentance. So far as halachic expansion is concerned, in ch. ii the short conclusion of the creation narrative in Gen. ii, 1–4a, following on the institution of the Sabbath, is elaborated quite substantially in ii, 17–33, and the book ends with a renewed inculcation of the sabbath command likewise going into great detail (l, 6–13).[2] In iii, 8 the conclusion is drawn from the fact that Adam and Eve were created in the first Seven (week), but that Eve was only shown to Adam in the second, that the mother has to remain unclean seven days at the birth of a male child, but twice seven, i.e. fourteen days, at the birth of a female child; so a basis is given for the law of Lev. xii, 1–8. According to xv, 1–2, Abraham celebrates the feast of the firstfruits of the grain harvest (Lev. xxiii, 10–14) and according to xvi, 20–31 the feast of booths (Lev. xxiii, 39–43), exactly in accordance with the Law. In the last words which Abraham directs in ch. xxi to Isaac before his death, there are to be found in addition to the general warning against idolatry and disobedience to God, quite specific injunctions also about the offering of sacrifices, about the kinds of wood to be used for the burnt offering, and about washings and such like (vv. 6–20). In short, the patriarchs appear here as pedantic observers of the Law, and very frequently actions are related concerning them which are prescribed only by rabbinic elaboration of the Law but not by the biblical Law itself, as for example in the case of Abraham the procession around the altar at the feast of booths (xvi, 31).

In all this, Israel's peculiar position and her duty to keep herself from contact with everything unclean and heathen, is most emphatically inculcated (xv, 31–2; xxii, 16–20; xxx, 7–17), and it is possible that the introduction of a solar year of 364 days too, ordered in vi, 29–38 in connection with the Flood, is designed to separate the Jews from an environment in which other time systems are utilised.

These elaborations of the Law and the efforts to keep Israel separate from everything unclean, breathe the same spirit which marks the writings of the Qumrān community (§§ 104–12) and the Damascus Document which is also connected with that community (§ 106); and these writings and the book of Jubilees have also many other points in common.[3] So, for example, the Manual of Discipline like this book declares the same solar year to be normative. We must therefore regard this book as deriving from this community, in spite of

---

[2] Liebreich, 'Jubilees l, 9' JQR 44 (1953/54), p. 169.
[3] Molin, *Die Söhne des Lichtes. Zeit und Stellung der Handschriften vom Toten Meer* (1954), pp. 96 f., 109, 116, 160–2. Cf. also literature in next footnote.

the objections raised by Noack, and the fact that among the Qumrān dis-coveries there are also fragments of nine manuscripts of the original Hebrew of the book,[4] confirms this. So far as the date of its composition is concerned, the *terminus a quo* is provided by the reference in iv, 17–19 to older sections of the book of Enoch (pp. 619–20), to be dated *c.* 170 B.C.; and the *terminus ad quem* by the repeated quotations from it in the Damascus Document (p. 652) which probably was written between 140 and 50 B.C. Thus about 100 B.C. would appear to be the date of its composition.[5] Zeitlin and Albright,[6] it is true, date the book much earlier, the former in the fifth century, and the latter in the third century B.C., but the arguments which they adduce are hardly sufficient in view of the grounds upon which the later dating is based. The dating of the book in about 100 B.C. does not by any means exclude the possibility, however, that older traditions are embodied in it. In fact the very much more detailed geographical notes as compared with the parallels in Gen. to Exod. xii and as compared with the Old Testament as a whole, reflect older tradition.[7] Similarly, elaborations both here in v, 1–14 and in Enoch vi–xi, of the narrative fragment concerning the fall of the angels in Gen. vi, 1–4 are not simply freely invented extensions of Gen. vi, 1–4, but also represent the reproduction of older mythological tradi-tion.

The book is completely preserved in an Ethiopic translation found in Abys-sinia in the middle of the nineteenth century, and in 1861 Ceriani published fragments of a Latin translation[8] which covers about one third of the whole. Both the Ethiopic and Latin translations go back to a Greek translation of the Hebrew original, of which, as has been mentioned, there are now available frag-ments of several manuscripts.

[4] Baillet, RB 63 (1956), p. 54; Barthélemy and Milik, *Qumran Cave I* (1955), pp. 82–4, Nos. 17–18, Pl. XVI: 'Livre des Jubilés'; Burrows, *More Light on the Dead Sea Scrolls* (1958), pp. 178 f., 374–8, 407 f. etc.; Dupont-Sommer, *Les écrits esséniens découverts près de la Mer Morte* (1959), p. 310; E.T. *The Essene Writings from Qumran* (1961), p. 298; Milik, RB 63 (1956), p. 60; *Dix ans de Découvertes dans le Désert de Juda* (1957), pp. 29 f.; E.T. *Ten Years of Discovery in the Wilderness of Judaea* (1959), p. 32; Sukenik, מגילות גנוזות מתוך גניזה סקירה שנייה (1950), p. 53; Sutcliffe, *The Monks of Qumran* (1960), pp. 13 f., 112 f.; Torrey, 'A Hebrew Fragment of Jubilees' JBL 71 (1952), pp. 39–41; de Vaux, 'La grotte des manuscrits hébreux' RB 56 (1949) pp. 586–609, Pls. XIII–XVIII, cf. pp. 602–5, Pl. XVIa: 'Un fragment du Livre des Jubilés en hébreu.' Cf. below, pp. 641, 664. Lit. § 126.

[5] Cf. also R. Meyer, 'Levitische Emanzipationsbestrebungen in nachexilischer Zeit' OLZ 41 (1938), cols. 721–8.

[6] *From the Stone Age to Christianity* ([2]1946), pp. 266 f.

[7] Herrmann, *Die Erdkarte der Urbibel* (1931), pp. 17–26; Hölscher, *Drei Erdkarten* (1949), pp. 57–73: 'Die Karte des Jubiläenbuches'; Stechow, 'Zur Kenntnis Inner-Afrikas in antiker Zeit' Petermanns Geogr. Mitt. 98 (1954), pp. 25 f.; Uhden, 'Die Erdkreis-gliederung der Hebräer nach dem Buche der Jubiläen' ZS 9 (1933/34), pp. 210–33.

[8] On the question of the existence of a Syriac translation, cf. Tisserant, 'Fragments syriaques du Livre des Jubilés' RB 30 (1921), pp. 55–86, 206–32 = *Recueil Cardinal Eugène Tisserant* (1955), II, pp. 25–87.

§ 92. THE MARTYRDOM AND ASCENSION OF ISAIAH
(MARTYRIUM ET ASCENSIO ISAIAE)

Literature: (a) Text: Charles: *The Ascension of Isaiah translated from the Ethiopic Version, which, together with the new Greek Fragment, the Latin Versions, and the Latin Translation of the Slavonic, is here published in full* (1900); Dillmann, *Ascensio Isaiae Aethiopice et Latine* (1877); Tisserant, *L'Ascension d'Isaïe. Traduction de la version éthiopienne avec les principales variantes des versions grecque, latines et slave avec introduction et notes* (1909).

(b) Commentaries: Box, *The Apocalypse of Abraham and the Ascension of Isaiah* (1919); Charles: Charles, II, pp. 155–62; Flemming-Duensing, 'Die Himmelfahrt des Jesaja' in Hennecke, *Neutestamentliche Apokryphen* (²1924), pp. 298 f., 303–14; Hammershaimb: Hammershaimb (1958); Kautzsch: Beer, II, pp. 119–27; Riessler, pp. 481–4, 1300–1.

(c) Other Works: Bosse, 'Zur Erklärung der Apokalypse der Asc. Jesaiae' ZNW 10 (1909), pp. 320–3; Burch, 'The Literary Unity of the Ascensio Isaiae' JThSt 20 (1919), pp. 17–23; 'Material for the Interpretation of the Ascensio Isaiae' JThSt 21 (1920), pp. 249–285; Flusser, 'The Apocryphal Book of Ascensio Isaiae and the Dead Sea Sect' IEJ 3 (1953), pp. 30–47; on this van der Ploeg BiOr 11 (1954), pp. 154 f.; Galling, 'Jesaia-Adonis' OLZ 33 (1930), cols. 98–102; Surkau (§ 79), pp. 30–3; Lüdtke, 'Beiträge zu slavischen Apokryphen' ZAW 31 (1911), pp. 218–35, cf. pp. 222–6: 'Zur Ascensio Isaiae'; Schoeps, *Die jüdischen Prophetenmorde* (1943), pp. 6 f.

Cf. also Literature §§ 76, 126.

A collection of three writings concerning the prophet Isaiah, two complete and one fragmentary, has come down to us in an Ethiopic translation from the fifth to seventh centuries A.D., and in fragments of Greek, Latin, Coptic[1] and Old Slavonic translations. These cover in i–v* the Martyrdom of Isaiah, iii, 13–iv, 18 the fragment of a Vision of Isaiah, and vi–xi the Ascension of Isaiah.

i, 1–2a, 6b–13a, ii, 1–iii, 12+v, 1b–14 is of Jewish origin and presupposes a Hebrew original. It is linked to the note in II Kings xxi, 1–18, that Manasseh favoured all manner of idolatry and shed much innocent blood, and relates how Isaiah, who had already foretold to Hezekiah the apostasy of Manasseh and his own martyrdom, had fled with a small band of adherents to a lonely mountain in the wilderness, but as the result of the slander of a lying prophet named Belchira was arrested there by Manasseh and sawn in two. The legendary story motif of the sawing in two is perhaps to be explained as the taking over of an Iranian legendary motif, or, more probably, the transfer of a motif from the Adonis myth to Isaiah. It is probable that Heb. xi, 37 alludes to this legend (p. 305), and Origen († 254) certainly knew it. But it must be older and come roughly from the period to which belong also the legends of the martyrdom of Eleazar and of the seven brothers together with their mother (II Macc. vi, 18–vii, 42), i.e. the beginning of the first century B.C. This kind of martyr legend no doubt goes back to the period of the persecution of Jewish religion by Antiochus Epiphanes. Flusser ascribes the Martyrdom of Isaiah to the Qumrān community and interprets it as a typological presentation of the figure of the 'Teacher of Righteousness' which played so great a part in the writings of the

---

[1] Lefort, 'Coptica Lovaniensia' Muséon 50 (1937), pp. 5–52; 51 (1938), pp. 1–32, see 51 (1938), pp. 24–30; 'Fragments d'Apocryphes en copte-akhmîmique' Muséon 52 (1939), pp. 1–10, see pp. 7–10; cf. also below, p. 713, n. 73.

Qumrān community (§§ 106, 108, 109), and there is no doubt that this legend has much in common with the Qumrān writings.

The fragment in iii, 13–iv, 18 contains a prospect, ascribed to Isaiah, of the coming of Jesus, the founding of the Church, the appearance of Belial and the final judgement. It is a Christian work and may have been composed about A.D. 100.

vi–xi, the Ascension or Vision of Isaiah, describes Isaiah's visionary ascent through the seven heavens to the throne of the Most High, where he hears the command of the Most High to Christ to go down to earth, and then sees the latter born, crucified and risen again. This little work is likewise Christian in origin and probably comes from the second century A.D.

These three sections were later, probably not before the third or fourth century, combined by a Christian hand and linked together by the expansion of ch. i and by other insertions. It is possible that there were two stages of redaction, first the combining of the Martyrdom with iii, 13–iv, 18, and then the combining of the expanded Martyrdom with the Ascension.

§ 93. THE PSALMS OF SOLOMON

Literature: (a) Text: Greek: Fritzsche (p. 571), pp. 569–89; von Gebhardt, Ψαλμοὶ Σολομῶντος (1895); Swete (p. 714), III (²1899), pp. 765–87; Rahlfs (p. 714), II (1935 (1959)), pp. 471–89; Syriac: Harris and Mingana, *The Odes and Psalms of Solomon*, 2 vols. (1916, 1920); Retranslation in Hebrew: Frankenberg, *Die Datierung der Psalmen Salomos* (1896), pp. 66–97.

(b) Commentaries: Charles: Gray, II, pp. 625–52; Kahana: Stein (²1956); Kautzsch: Kittel, II, pp. 127–48; Riessler, pp. 881–902, 1323 f.; Ryle and James, *Psalms of the Pharisees* (1891).

(c) Other Works: Aberbach, 'The Historical Allusions of Chapters iv, xi and xiii of the Psalms of Solomon' JQR 41 (1950/51), pp. 379–96; Baars, 'An Additional Fragment of the Syriac Version of the Psalms of Solomon' VT 11 (1961), pp. 222–3; Begrich, 'Der Text der Psalmen Salomos' ZNW 38 (1939), pp. 131–64; Braun, 'Vom Erbarmen Gottes über den Gerechten. Zur Theologie der Psalmen Salomos' ZNW 43 (1910/51), pp. 1–54; Holm-Nielsen (§ 63); Jansen, *Die spätjüdische Psalmendichtung: ihr Entstehungskreis und ihr 'Sitz im Leben'* (SNVAO, 1937, 3); Kuhn, *Die älteste Textgestalt der Psalmen Salomos* (BWANT 73, 1937); Lagrange, *Le Judaïsme avant Jésus-Christ* (1931), pp. 149–63; Lietzmann, *Geschichte der alten Kirche*, I (1932, ³1953), pp. 12–16; Eduard Meyer, *Ursprung und Anfänge des Christentums* II (1921), pp. 315–19; O'Dell, 'The Religious Background of the Psalms of Solomon' RQ 3 (1961/62), pp. 241–57; Pesch (§ 86); Viteau, *Les Psaumes de Salomon. Introduction, texte Grec et traduction, avec les principales variantes de la version Syriaque par Fr. Martin* (1911); Wellhausen, *Die Pharisäer und die Sadduzäer* (1874, ²1924), pp. 131–64.

Cf. also Literature §§ 14–16, 63, 76, 126.

In early Christian lists of canon there is often mention of ψαλμοὶ Σολομῶντος, sometimes recognised as sacred scripture and sometimes not. The collection of psalms itself has, however, disappeared, and was only rediscovered at the beginning of the seventeenth century. We now possess it in eight Greek manuscripts[1] and in addition in a Syriac translation made from the Greek. The original was undoubtedly in Hebrew.

The collection comprises eighteen psalms which are in some respects similar to the canonical psalms, but also have characteristic peculiarities of their own. The main types of the Psalter—hymn (ii, 30, 33–7; iii, 1–2), collective and individual songs of lamentation (ii, 19–25; vii; viii, 22–34; xvi, 6–15), song of thanksgiving (xiii, 1–4; xv, 1–6; xvi, 1–5), didactic poem (iii, 3–12; vi)—are to be found here too, a proof of how vigorous these types were.[2] Even the technical musical terms known from the Psalter (p. 453) *for the musical director* (εἰς νῖκος = לַמְנַצֵּחַ viii, 1), and *Selah* (διάψαλμα = סֶלָה xvii, 31; xviii, 10), are to be found, probably to be taken as indicating that these psalms too were used in the cult. The difference between these psalms and those of the Psalter consists however in the fact that the types are much more markedly intermingled here than in the Psalter, and that the reflective element has been enormously developed. Ps. Sol. ii begins like a national song of lamentation with a historical retrospect (vv. 1–14), gives space to reflection (vv. 15–18), again takes up the retrospect (vv. 19–21), passes over from this in vv. 22–5 to a prayer in the style of the individual song of lamentation, turns back to historical narrative (vv. 26–7), goes on into reflection (vv. 28–9), hymn (v. 30)

---

[1] Five of them place the Psalms of Solomon between Wisd. and Ecclus., one of them after these books, and two of them after the Odes mentioned on p. 588; cf. Swete, III, pp. xvi f.

[2] This is revealed not only in the 'Thanksgiving Hymns' (הוֹדָיוֹת) which were discovered in 1947 near Qumrān and published in 1955 (to be considered later in § 108), but also in the five apocryphal psalms preserved in Syriac, discussed by Noth in ZAW 48 (1930), pp. 1–23, by Delcor, 'Cinq nouveaux psaumes esséniens' RQ 1 (1958/59), pp. 85–102, and by Philonenko, 'L'Origine essénienne des cinq Psaumes syriaques de David' Semitica 9 (1959), pp. 35–48. Of these at least Nos. 2, 3 and 4, and perhaps also No. 5, go back to a Hebrew original and were probably composed in the pre-Christian period. No. 2 is a mixture of hymn and wisdom poem, No. 3 an individual song of thanksgiving, No. 4 an individual song of lamentation, and No. 5 an individual song of thanksgiving with hymnic elements. The same is true of the 'Odes of Solomon', coming from Christian gnostic circles of the second century A.D., written in Greek but, apart from the recent discovery of the Greek text of No. 11 (cf. Testuz, *Papyrus Bodmer* X–XII (1959): XI 'Onzième Ode de Salomon'), preserved only in Syriac or Coptic translation, for here too there is much which can immediately be seen to be imitation of the types in the Psalter. Ode 5 is a song of trust, Ode 16 a hymn, Ode 25 a song of thanksgiving, and so forth. Cf. Walter Bauer, *Die Oden Salomos* [Syr. (Copt.) Text with German transl.] (KlT 64, 1933); Bernard, *The Odes of Solomon. Ed. with Introduction and Notes* (TSt 8, 1912); Gressmann, 'Die Oden Salomos' in Hennecke, *Nt. Apokryphen* (²1924), pp. 437–72; Grimme, *Die Oden Salomos. Syrisch-Hebräisch-Deutsch* (1911); Harris and Mingana, *The Odes and Psalms of Solomon* (1916, 1920); cf. also Abramowski, 'Der Christus der Salomooden' ZNW 35 (1936), pp. 44–69; Baumgartner, 'Das trennende Schwert. Oden Salomos xxviii, 4' *Bertholet-Festschr.* (1950), pp. 50–7 = *Zum AT* (1959), pp. 274–81; Carmignac, 'Les affinités qumrâniennes de la onzième Ode de Salomon' RQ 3 (1961/62), pp. 71–102; Fabbri, 'El enigma de la xxivᵃ oda de Salomon' Ciencia y Fe 16 (1960), pp. 383–98; Frankenberg, *Das Verständnis der Oden Salomos* (BZAW 21, 1911); Grant, 'The Odes of Solomon and the Church of Antioch' JBL 63 (1944), pp. 363–77; Gressmann, 'Die Oden Salomos' Intern. Wochenschr. f. Wiss., Kunst u. Techn. 5 (1911), cols. 897–908, 949–58; Gunkel, 'Die Oden Salomos' *Reden u. Aufsätze* (1913), pp. 163–92; G. Kittel, *Die Oden Salomos überarbeitet oder einheitlich?* (BWAT 16, 1914); Schoeps, 'Habakuk-Kommentar und Oden Salomos' ZRGG 3 (1951), pp. 328–31; Segelberg, 'Evangelium Veritatis. A Confirmation Homily and its Relations to the Odes of Solomon' Or Suec 8 (1959), pp. 3–42; de Zwaan, 'The Edessene Origin of the Odes of Solomon' *Quantulacumque Kirsopp Lake* (1937), pp. 285–302. Cf. §§ 108, 126.

and expression of trust (v. 31), and finally (vv. 32–7) in a sort of hymnic introduction, summons the great ones of the earth to reverence before God, and his pious ones to his praise. Pss. Sol. viii and xv, furthermore, are good examples of the way in which the reflective element overlays the other types.

A whole group of these poems (iii, v, vi, vii, ix, x, xii, xiv, xv, xvi) are out-pourings of a pious heart, expressed in fairly general terms and relatively colourless. They are particularly concerned with the contrasts between the pious and the sinners. These are by nature timeless and hardly permit a more precise dating. But others allude quite clearly to particular events, and may thus be dated and so make possible a dating of the whole work which is at least reasonably correct. Ps. Sol. viii undoubtedly refers to the capture of Jerusalem by Pompey[3] and the dethronement of the Hasmonean dynasty (63 B.C.). It is true that the poet also feels this event to be a divine visitation of his people, but his satisfaction at the overthrow of the godless and immoral Hasmoneans is much srtonger, as also at the killing of the leaders who had influenced them and the captivity of their sons and daughters (vv. 20–1). Ps. Sol. ii[4] also looks back with satisfaction on the fall of the Hasmoneans and their supporters (vv. 1–18). But the judgement on what has taken place is somewhat different from that in Ps. Sol. viii. In the meantime, the poet has come to feel how terribly heavily the hand of the Romans weighs upon the Jews and upon Jerusalem, and with a change of viewpoint rather like that which came over Isaiah's prophecy with reference to the Assyrians (p. 312), he has come to see that the Romans did not act out of zeal for God's cause, but according to their own desires (vv. 19–25). Thus he has heard with double satisfaction of the death of Pompey who was murdered in 48 B.C. near the Egyptian city of Casios near Pelusium (vv. 26–37).[5] It is possible that xvii, 7 also refers to Pompey, for here it is said that God has cast down the *godless* of verse 5, i.e. the Hasmoneans, and has removed their seed from the land, *in that a foreigner came up against them who was not of our race.* But it is more probable that the foreigner, who, as it appears from the sequel, enjoyed a long period of rule, refers to Herod (40 or 37–4 B.C.).[6] In that case we must date this psalm after 37 B.C. From these two psalms we may also date the others and assign them to the period between 63 and about 30 B.C., without its being necessary to assert that they all come from one poet. Several poets may have contributed to them, but they certainly all come from the same period.

Usually these psalms are explained in relation to the opposition characteristic of this period between the Pharisees and the Sadducees, and so Ps. Sol. iv, for example, is interpreted as a Pharisaic curse against a Sadducean hypocrite. But although it is true that Pss. Sol. ii, viii and xvii reflect the position which was taken up by the Pharisees towards the political events of that period, the attitude of the other psalms cannot be regarded as characteristic of that one group alone, nor can the nature of the godless against whom they are directed be limited to the behaviour of the Sadducees. We have rather a type of piety which may be

---

[3] Abel, 'Le siège de Jérusalem par Pompée' RB 54 (1947), pp. 243–55. Lit. § 126.

[4] Dölger, 'Zum zweiten Salomonischen Psalm. Der versiegelte Halsriemen der Kriegsge-fangenen' Antike und Christentum 1 (1929), pp. 291–4.

[5] Eissfeldt (p. 36, n. 5), p. 40.

[6] Cf. below, p. 623, n. 1.

demonstrated everywhere, expressed here in positive and negative terms. Pharisaism was certainly of this kind, but not Pharisaism alone. The belief in resurrection (iii, 12; xiii, 11; xiv, 9–10) and the doctrine of free will (ix, 4), as set forth in these psalms, are certainly characteristic of the Pharisees in contrast to the Sadducees, but they are here mentioned without any polemic directed against the latter, and may therefore hardly be used as an argument to prove that these psalms must be understood from the contrast between Pharisees and Sadducees. Nor is it proved by the intense Messianic hope[7] which is expressed in Pss. Sol. xvii and xviii.[8] For the yearning expectation of a legitimate king from the Davidic line, well-pleasing to God, bound up with urgent prayer for its speedy realisation, is not specifically Pharisaic. Voices have been raised in protest against interpreting all the poems as Pharisaic attacks on the Sadducees, and Lagrange wished to apply Ps. Sol. iv actually to a Pharisee designated as a hypocrite. Whether this is the right interpretation of the psalm is doubtful, occasioned as it is by the picture which the New Testament draws of the Pharisees. But it is worth noting as a warning against too great confidence in tracing these poems to Pharisaic circles, the more so since the Psalms of Solomon show many points of contact with the Qumrān texts (§ 108), and this shows that ideas which were formerly regarded as belonging exclusively to the Pharisees were evidently accepted in other circles too, and particularly in the Qumrān community which belongs in the broader sense to the Essenes.

Thus these poems are likely to have been composed between 63 and 30 B.C., and certainly in Palestine. The individual poems, unlike for example Wisd. vi–ix (p.601), nowhere make the claim that they were written by Solomon, and we must therefore assume that it was only the collection as a whole which was ascribed to Solomon, no doubt because they could not be taken up into the Davidic Psalter which had long been closed, and so were ascribed to David's son since he ranked as the next most famous song-writer (I Kings v, 12).

§ 94. THE FOURTH BOOK OF MACCABEES

Literature: (a) Text: Fritzsche (p. 571), pp. 351–86; Swete (p. 714), III (²1899), pp. 729–762; Rahlfs (p. 714), I, pp. 1157–84.

(b) Commentaries: Charles: Townshend, II, pp. 653–85; Fritzsche-Grimm: Grimm; Jew Apocr Lit: Hadas (1953); Kahana: Schur (²1956); Kautzsch: Deissmann, II, pp. 149–77; Riessler, pp. 700–28, 1313–14; Dupont-Sommer (1939).

(c) Other Works: Bickermann, 'The Date of Fourth Maccabees' *Louis Ginzberg Jubilee Vol.*, I (1945), pp. 105–12; Dörrie, *Passio SS. Machabaeorum. Die antike lateinische Übers. des IV. Makkabäerbuches* (AGA III, 22, 1938); Freudenthal, *Die Flavius Josephus beigelegte Schrift Über die Herrschaft der Vernunft . . ., eine Predigt aus dem ersten nachchristl. Jahrh.* (1869); Gelin, 'Les origines bibliques de l'idée de martyre' *Lumière et Vie* 36 (1958), pp. 123–9; Günther, 'Zeuge und Märtyrer' ZNW 47 (1956), pp. 145–61; Heinemann,

---

[7] Sjöberg, *Der Verborgene Menschensohn in den Evangelien* (1955), pp. 41–98: 'Der verborgene Messias im Judentum.'

[8] Manson, 'Miscellanea Apocalyptica' JThSt 46 (1945), pp. 41–5, see pp. 41 f.: Ps. Sol. xviii, 6.

Poseidonios' metaphysische Schriften, I (1921), pp. 154–9: 'Die Quelle des vierten Makkabäerbuches'; Lauer, 'Eusebes Logismos in IV Macc.' JJSt 6 (1955), pp. 170 f.; Norden, *Die antike Kunstprosa* I (1889, ²1909 (1958)), pp. 416–20, *21* (2nd ed. *17*); Surkau (§ 79), pp. 14–29; Thyen (§ 89), pp. 12–14; Wifstrand, 'Martyr' SvTK 34 (1958), pp. 262–9; Winckler, 'Das vierte Makkabäerbuch' Altorientalische Forschungen, 3. Reihe I 1 (1902), pp. 79–89; Zeitlin, 'The Legend of the Ten Martyrs and its Apocalyptic Origin' JQR 36 (1945/46), pp. 1–16.
    Cf. also Literature §§ 76, 78, 79, 89, 126.

The description of this work as IV Macc.—probably not original—is misleading because it gives the impression that we have here a narrative work like I, II and III Macc. But in fact the book is a diatribe, a philosophical treatise in the form of a speech, on the theme that reason is mistress of the passions. So the original title of the work is likely to have been περὶ αὐτοκράτορος λογισμοῦ. The theme, following out the programme indicated in the prologue of i, 1–12, is at first set forth in philosophical dogmatic form (i, 13–iii, 18), though here it is true that there is reference to examples from biblical history—Joseph (ii, 2–3), Moses (ii, 17), Jacob (ii, 19), David (iii, 6–18). But the real proof from history begins only after iii, 19. After an introduction which relates the beginning of the persecution of Jewish religion by Antiochus IV Epiphanes (iii, 20–iv, 26; cf. II Macc. iii, 1–40; iv, 7–vi, 11), the martydom of Eleazar (II Macc. vi, 18–31) and that of the seven brothers (II Macc. vii) and finally that of their mother (II Macc. vii) are introduced in v, 1–xvii, 6 to demonstrate the truth of the thesis by these steadfast martyrs. The conclusion is made up of a consideration of the great value of such martyrdom (xvii, 7–xviii, 24), proposing in xvii, 9–10 an epitaph suitable for the martyrs and adding in xviii, 6–19 a speech by the mother to her sons. It is because of these historical examples taken from II Macc., that the book received the name IV Macc., and it has indeed a certain right to it.

The book is characterised by the combination of Greek form and Jewish content. The Greek element is, however, by no means limited to the literary form of the diatribe. The book also reveals influences of Greek thought, and more precisely of Stoic philosophy. Its theme—reason as the ruler over the passions—is a Stoic principle. The four cardinal virtues φρόνησις, δικαιοσύνη, ἀνδρεία, σωφροσύνη (i, 18) and the ἀπάθεια (viii, 9, 18; xii, 4) shown by the martyrs are also Stoic. But in the last resort even these philosophical concepts are only a matter of form. The substance of the book is Jewish through and through. The real point is the preservation of the Jewish Law, and the power by which that is possible is not that Stoic virtue at all, but obedience to God. This is shown already in iii, 15 where it is the throught of God's judgement which restrains David from drinking the water which has been fetched by his people at the risk of their lives. Obedience to the Law is given by Eleazar (v, 16) and the seven brothers (ix, 2) as the reason for their refusal to eat pork, and the mother explains that her sons are under an obligation because of piety (xvi, 17) and because of God (xvi, 19) to endure all tortures. The strength of the author's link with his own people appears again in the thought that the martyrs are suffering vicariously for their people, for the atonement of its sins and for its purification (i, 11; vi, 29; xvii, 21–2). The belief too, which at first appears more Greek than Jewish, in the immortality of pious souls, as expressed in xiv, 6; xviii, 23, is wholly conformed to Jewish religion. At first sight it might appear paradoxical that it should be just these Jewish martyrs who are invoked as witnesses to a principle of Greek philosophy, martyrs who gave their lives in the rejection of a religious policy which would favour Hellenism. Yet a closer examination shows that the author has permitted no compromise with the spiritual forces with which for those martyrs there was absolutely no compromise possible, but that he too is working, though with different means, for the same goal for which they died.

But if it is true that the author is completely a Jew who only uses Greek elements in order to underline the more emphatically by that means the eternal significance of what is Jewish, and if too his knowledge of Greek philosophy does not go really deep, then we must seek him in all probability where such a contact between Jewish and Greek ways is best attested, namely in Alexandria, though Antioch could also be his home, as has been suggested recently by Dupont-Sommer and Hadas, following suggestions made by earlier scholars. So far as date of composition is concerned, since the book presupposes the existence of II Macc., it cannot be earlier than the middle of the first century B.C. The possibility certainly exists that it ought to be dated up to 100 or 150 years later; Bickerman dates it in about A.D. 53, Hadas about 40, and Dupont-Sommer as late as 117/118. The book was undoubtedly originally written in Greek. It is preserved in a group of manuscripts of 𝕲, and also in many of the manuscripts of Josephus, and thus, certainly wrongly, was thought to be by Josephus. The Passio SS. Machabaeorum, published by Dörrie in 1938 is a free Latin rendering of the Greek text of the book, deriving from Christian circles towards the end of the fourth century.

§ 95. THE SIBYLLINE ORACLES

Literature: (a) Text: Alexandre, *Oracula Sibyllina* (1841–56, ²1869); Geffcken, *Oracula Sibyllina* (1902); Kurfess, *Sibyllinische Weissagungen. Urtext und Übersetzung* (1951); Rzach, *Oracula Sibyllina* (1891).

(b) Commentaries: Charles: Lanchester, II, pp. 368–406; Geffcken in Hennecke, *Neutest. Apokr.* (²1924), pp. 399–422; Kahana: Reider (²1956); Kautzsch: Blass, II, pp. 177–217; Riessler, pp. 1014–45, 1326–28.

(c) Other Works: Aalen (§ 78), pp. 218–23; Bauer, 'Oracula Sibyllina I 323ab' ZNW 47 (1956), pp. 284 f.; Dornseiff, *Verschmähtes zu Vergil, Horaz und Properz* (SAL 97, 6, 1951), pp. 44–85; Geffcken, *Komposition und Entstehungszeit der Oracula Sibyllina* (1902); Hoffmann, *Wandel und Herkunft der sibyllinischen Bücher in Rom* (Diss. phil. Leipzig, 1933); Holzinger, *Erklärungen zu einigen der umstrittenen Stellen der Offenbarung Johannis und der Sibyllinischen Orakel* (SAW 216, 3, 1936); Jeanmaire, *La Sibylle et le retour de l'âge d'or* (1939); Kerényi, 'Das persische Millennium im Mahābhārata, bei der Sibylle und Vergil' Klio 29 (1936), pp. 1–35; Kurfess, 'Das Mahngedicht des sogenannten Phokylides im zweiten Buch der Oracula Sibyllina' ZNW 38 (1939), pp. 171–81; 'Oracula Sibyllina I/II' ZNW 40 (1941), pp. 151–65; 'Zu den Oracula Sibyllina' *Dold-Festschrift* (1952), pp. 75–83; 'Wie sind die Fragmente der Oracula Sibyllina einzuordnen?' Aevum 26 (1952), pp. 228–235; 'Vergils vierte Ekloge und die Oracula Sibyllina' HJ 73 (1954), pp. 120–7; 'Oracula

Sibyllina XI (IX)–XIV (XII) nicht christlich, sondern jüdisch' ZRGG 7 (1955), pp. 270–2; 'Horaz und die Sibyllinen' ZRGG 8 (1956), pp. 253–6; 'Rowley, 'The Interpretation and Date of Sibylline Oracles III 388–400' ZAW 44 (1926), pp. 324–7; Youtie, 'Sambathis' HThR 37 (1944), pp. 209–18.

Cf. also Literature § 76.

There is a remarkable parallel to Israelite prophecy with its development into Jewish apocalyptic. This is the sibylline prophecy, which came from the orient to the Greeks, and, at first deriving from genuinely charismatic inspiration, gradually became the subject of learned and rational reflection and produced a large body of sibylline literature in the form of hexameters. In this a particular point of parallel to Jewish apocalyptic is noteworthy, namely that very early, apparently earlier than in Judaism so that in this Judaism must be thought of as being dependent upon the sibylline literature, fictitious prophecies were ascribed to an original sibyl purporting to belong to the remote antiquity of the pre-Homeric age, though in reality they were *vaticinia ex eventu*, and so there came into being 'a kind of Greek history in future form'.[1] This literary type, like so many others, was taken up by the Jews in the second century B.C. and used by them as a medium of Jewish propaganda, with the sibyl actually made into a daughter-in-law of Noah (III, 826). To this sibyl are attributed praises of pious Israel, warnings against heathen idolatry and threats against the enemies of the Jews, and she was made to prophesy Jewish history either instead of or alongside Greek, issuing in the appearance of the Messiah.[2] Later this genre was also taken over by Christians, and they created new sibylline oracles and worked over old ones from their own point of view. In about the sixth century A.D. these oracles, heathen, Jewish and Christian, were united in a collection of which twelve books have survived, viz. I–VIII and XI–XIV. Books VI, VII, VIII[3] and XIII are Christian. The remainder are Jewish or at least contain Jewish matter. The largest amount of Jewish material is to be found in III, IV and V.

In Book III, based upon a Babylonian or Persian sibyl prophesying Alexander, the Jewish revision is clearly recognisable in the glorification of the Jewish people (vv. 218–47, 573–600 *et passim*) and in the descriptions of the Messianic age (vv. 619–22, 652–60, 702–31). Since vv. 192–3, 318, 608 indicate as turning-point a seventh kingdom of Egypt with a king who is Greek by descent, namely Ptolemy VII Physcon (170–164 and 145–117), Book III must have come into being then. But later a great deal was added, as for example vv. 36–92 where there is allusion in v. 52 to the second triumvirate (43 B.C.) and in v. 75 to Cleopatra († 30 B.C.). The third Book certainly came from Egypt.

Book IV, which presupposes in vv. 130–6 the outbreak of Vesuvius in 79 A.D. and in vv. 137–9 the idea of Nero's return and so his death in A.D. 68, can only have been written towards the end of the first century A.D.; nothing can be determined about its place of origin.

[1] Geffcken, *Neut. Apokr.* p. 400.
[2] Sjöberg (p. 613, n. 7).
[3] Jeanmaire, 'Le règne de la Femme des derniers jours et le rajeunissement du monde. Quelques remarques sur le texte de "Oracula Sibyllina" VIII 190–212' AIPhHOS 4 (1936), pp. 297–304.

In Book V, vv. 1–51 even carry us beyond Hadrian (117–138) and his three successors (138–180), and thus show that the work cannot have been in the form in which we have it before the end of the second century A.D. But the lament spoken in vv. 397–413 at the destruction of the Temple of Jerusalem nevertheless proves that its basis is older. It is likely to have been composed soon after the destruction of Jerusalem (A.D. 70) and certainly in Egypt.

§ 96. THE ETHIOPIC BOOK OF ENOCH

Literature: (a) Text: Ethiopic: Charles, *The Ethiopic Version of the Book of Enoch . . . together with the fragmentary Greek and Latin Versions* (1906); Dillmann, *Liber Henoch aethiopice* (1851); Flemming, *Das Buch Henoch. Äthiopischer Text* (1902); Greek: Radermacher, *Das Buch Henoch, herausgegeben . . . von Flemming und Radermacher* (1901), pp. 18–60, 113–14; Swete (p. 714), III², pp. 789–809.

(b) Commentaries: Charles: Charles, II, pp. 163–281; Hammershaimb: Hammershaimb (1956); Kahana: Kahana und Feitlowitz (²1956); Kautzsch: Beer, II, pp. 217–310; Riessler, pp. 355–451, 1291–97.

(c) Other Works: Agourides, Ἐνὼχ ἤτοι ὁ χαρακτὴρ τῆς περὶ τῶν ἐσχάτων διδακαλίας τοῦ βιβλίου τοῦ Ἐνώχ (1955); van Andel, *De structuur van de Henochtraditie en het NT* (StTh Rheno-Traiectina II, 1955); Bietenhard, 'Die "konsequente Eschatologie", das Buch Henoch und Qumran' Kirchenblatt f.d. ref. Schweiz 115 (1959), pp. 274–6; Black, 'The Eschatology of the Similitudes of Enoch' JThSt 3 (1952), pp. 1–10; Bonner, *The Last Chapters of Enoch in Greek* (1937); Burkitt, 'Robert Henry Charles 1855–1931' Proc. British Ac. 17 (1931), pp. 437–45; Dix, 'The Enochic Pentateuch' JThSt 27 (1926), pp. 29–42; Grelot, 'La géographie mythique d'Hénoch et ses sources orientales' RB 65 (1958), pp. 33–69; 'La légende d'Hénoch dans les apocryphes et dans la Bible, origine et signification' RSR 46 (1958), pp. 5–26, 181–210; 'L'eschatologie des Esséniens et le livre d'Hénoch' RQ 1 (1958/59), pp. 113–31; Gry, *Les paraboles d'Hénoch et leur messianisme* (1910); Jeremias, 'Ein neuer Textfund: das Henochfragment der Chester-Beatty-Papyri' ThBl 18 (1939), cols. 145 f.; Kaplan, 'Angels in the Book of Enoch' AThR 12 (1929/30), pp. 423–37; 'The Pharisaic Character and the Date of the Book of Enoch' *ib.* pp. 531–7; 'Versions and Readings in the Book of Enoch' AJSL 50 (1933/34), pp. 171–7; Kuhn, 'Beiträge zur Erklärung des Buches Henoch' ZAW 39 (1921), pp. 240–75; Lods, 'La chute des anges' RHPhR 7 (1927), pp. 295–315; Messel, *Der Menschensohn in den Bilderreden des Henoch* (BZAW 35, 1922); Mowinckel, 'Henokskikkelsen i senjødisk apokalyptikk' NTT 41 (1940), pp. 206–36; *Han som kommer* (1951), pp. 226–93: 'Menneskesønnen'; E.T. *He that Cometh* (1956), pp. 346–455: 'The Son of Man'; Otto, *Reich Gottes und Menschensohn* (²1940, ³1954), pp. 132–70, 310–26; E.T. of ed. 1 (1934) *The Kingdom of God and the Son of Man* (1938), pp. 176–218, 388–92; Pedersen, 'Zur Erklärung der eschatologischen Visionen Henochs' Islamica 2 (1926), pp. 416–29; N. Schmidt, 'The Apocalypse of Noah and the Parables of Enoch' *Or. Stud. Paul Haupt* (1926), pp. 111–23; Sjöberg, 'Känner 1 Henok och 4 Esra tanken på den lidande Människosonen?' SEA 5 (1940), pp. 163–83; *Der Menschensohn im äthiopischen Henochbuch* (1946); 'Der verborgene Messias im Judentum' (p. 613, n. 7); Stier, 'Zur Komposition und Literarkritik der Bilderreden des äthiopischen Henoch' *Littmann-Festschr.* (1935), pp. 70–88; Torrey, 'Notes on the Greek Text of Enoch' JAOS 62 (1942), pp. 52–60; Ullendorff, 'An Aramaic "Vorlage" of the Ethiopic Text of Enoch?' *Atti del convegno internazionale di Studi Etiopici* (1960), pp. 259–268; Vitti, 'Ultime critiche su Enoc etiopico' Bibl 12 (1931), pp. 316–25; Völter (§ 99); Welch, 'A Zealot Pamphlet' Exp 25 (1923), pp. 273–87; Zimmermann, 'The Bilingual Character of I Enoch' JBL 61 (1942), pp. 159–72; Zuntz, 'Notes on the Greek Enoch' JBL

61 (1942), pp. 193–204; 'Enoch and the Last Judgment (ch. cii, 1–3)' JThSt 45 (1944), pp. 161–70.
    Cf. also Literature §§ 76, 97, 126.

The Book of Enoch, denoted as Ethiopic because of the manner of its being handed down—a matter to be discussed subsequently (p. 622)—is an apocalyptic compilation. It may be divided into the following parts: (1) i–v, introductory speech by Enoch: proclamation of world judgement; (2) vi–xxxvi, angelological matter: vi–xi the fall of the angels, the birth of the giants, the proclamation by Noah of the punishment of the angels, xii–xvi proclamation by Enoch of the punishment of the angels, xvii–xix and xx–xxxvi two partly parallel narratives concerning visionary journeys by Enoch through the world and the underworld; (3) xxxvii–lxxi, Messianic matter: xxxvii, an introduction to the Similitudes which follow in xxxviii–lxix, consisting of xxxviii–xliv concerning the dwelling of the righteous and the activities of the angels, xlv–lvii concerning the Messiah and his judgement, lviii–lxix concerning the judgement by the Son of Man, lxx–lxxi Enoch's ascension and appointment as Son of Man;[1] (4) lxxii–lxxxii, astronomical and calendar matter: lxxii–lxxx+lxxxii, 4b–20 concerning sun, moon, intercalary days, stars, compass directions etc., lxxxi, 1–lxxxii, 4a (probably the conclusion of xx–xxxvi) the end of Enoch's journeys; (5) lxxxiii–xc, historical matter: lxxxiii–lxxxiv a dream vision concerning the coming flood, lxxxv–xc a dream vision of world history which describes the Jews with the symbol of domestic animals, and the heathen with the symbol of wild animals, from Adam indicated by the white bull to the white buffalo with large black horns, which represents the Messiah;[2] (6) xci–cv, the book of admonition: xci, 1–11, 18–19, Enoch's admonition to his children, summoning them to walk in righteousness, xciii, 1–14+xci, 12–17 (this being the correct order, the leaves having been misplaced) the apocalypse of the ten weeks which presents the whole course of world history to judgement and the age of salvation in ten weeks (according to Thorndike,[3] this is a secret history of the community of the new covenant up to the point at which it settled at Qumrān); xcii+xciv–cv an indication of the punishment of the sinners and the reward of the righteous, and an exhortation to the righteous to endure; (7) cvi–cviii, the conclusion of the book: cvi–cvii miracles at the birth of Noah, cviii Enoch's exhortation to the pious to endure.
    Some of the main sections just indicated were originally independent books and may still be recognised as such by their titles. Thus the main body of xxxvii–lxxi has a title at xxxvii, 1–2, and lxxii–lxxxii at lxxii, 1. From the last main section (cvi–cviii), cviii stands out as a separate entity by reason of its special title (cviii, 1). Another group of passages may be seen to have belonged together at one time by the fact that in them it is Lamech and Noah and not Enoch as elsewhere who stand at the centre. These are vi–xi, xxxix, 1–2a,

[1] Cf. p. 526, n. 47.
[2] Torrey, 'The Messiah Son of Ephraim' JBL 66 (1947), pp. 253–77, cf. pp. 266–8.
[3] 'The Apocalypse of Weeks and the Qumran Sect' RQ 3 (1961/62), pp. 163–84: on xciii, 1–10+xci, 12–17.

liv, 7–lv, 2; lx; lxv, 1–lxix, 25; cvi–cvii. These passages probably come, at least in part, from the book of Noah or the book of Lamech, mentioned in Jub. x, 13, xxi, 10 and elsewhere and belonging to the first half of the second century B.C. It is mentioned in a Greek list of apocryphal and pseudepigraphical books (Λάμεχ).[4] In some further cases the sections which originally belonged together may be recognised by the fact that they presuppose the same historical situation or have the same linguistic usage and the same range of thought.

When all these points are taken into account, we may say the following concerning the composition of the book of Enoch and the age of its component parts. The impression of greatest age is given by the Ten Weeks Apocalypse of xciii + xci, 12–17, since the last week of the world history which clearly already lies behind the author, namely the seventh—the last age begins with the eighth —does not yet include the Maccabean rising. It therefore comes from about 170 B.C., being thus somewhat older than the book of Daniel. There follows the apocalypse with animal symbols of lxxxv–xc. It is clear that the Maccabees are intended in the lambs or goat-kids with horns mentioned in xc, 9–16. But opinions differ as to whether reference is here made only to Judas († 160) and John Hyrcanus (134–103), or to Alexander Jannaeus (103–76) as well. In the former case, the apocalypse would have to be dated under John Hyrcanus,[5] in the latter case, under Alexander Jannaeus.[6] The section of admonitions in xci–cv—omitting the Ten Weeks Apocalypse—contains a contrast between the righteous and the godless, interpreted as referring to the conflict between Pharisees and Sadducees, and hence they have been dated in the period of Alexander Jannaeus (103–76) because at that time this conflict was particularly marked. The same is true of the Similitudes of xxxvii–lxxi. The interpretation of the righteous and godless mentioned in xci–cv and xxxvii–lxxi as signifying the Pharisees and the Sadducees is admittedly very uncertain, the more so since, as we shall see,[7] the book of Enoch clearly derives from the Qumrān community, whose writings have much to say about righteous and godless, but are not in this concerned so much with the tension between two groups within the Judaism of the time as with the conflict of mythological cosmic entities. Thus the dating of the sections xci–cv and xxxvii–lxxi in the first quarter of the first century B.C. can hardly be based on this. But since in lvi, 5–6 it is probably the Parthians and not the Romans who are mentioned as enemies of the Jews, thus indicating a date earlier than 63 B.C., it does seem as if this period is the most likely for xxxvii–lxxi and so also for xci–cv. To the same period there may also be assigned the introductory speech in i–v, the dream vision of the flood in lxxxiii–lxxxiv, and Enoch's last admonition in cviii. The mainly cosmological section xii–xxxvi* + lxxxi, 1–lxxxii, 4a and the astronomical book lxxii–lxxxii* are by their very nature difficult to date. Since, however, the book of Jubilees, written towards the end of the second century B.C. (p. 608), appears in iv, 17–19

---

[4] Schürer, GJV III (⁴1909), pp. 358 f., E.T. (1897) II, 3, pp. 126 f.

[5] Stern, 'The Relations between Judea and Rome during the Rule of John Hyrcanus' [Hebr., Engl. summary] Zion 26 (1961), pp. 1–22, I.

[6] Torrey, 'Alexander Jannaeus and the Archangel Michael' VT 4 (1954), pp. 208–11; Zeitlin, 'Queen Salome and King Jannaeus Alexander' JQR 51 (1961/62), pp. 1–33.

[7] pp. 621, 641, 661 f.

to presuppose just these sections of the book of Enoch, we may hardly date them later than 150, and probably they should be dated earlier.

This dating of the Messianic vision-speeches xxxvii–lxxi in the first third of the first pre-Christian century is not accepted by Milik. His view is based on the evidence from Qumrān. Whereas fragments have been found of other sections of the book of Enoch, none have been found from xxxvii–lxxi. In connection with this, he sheds new light on both the process by which the whole book came into being and on its date of origin. According to him, xxxvii–lxxi come from a Jewish Christian of the second century A.D. who wished to present his ideas concerning the Messiah and the Son of Man under the authority of the patriarch Enoch. It was the author of xxxvii–lxxi, who, having in mind the pattern of the Mosaic Pentateuch, the five books of Moses, and the Davidic Pentateuch, the five books into which the Psalter is divided, created an Enoch Pentateuch, made up of the four older main sections of the book—vi–xxxvi, lxxii–lxxxii, lxxxiii–xc, xci–cv—together with the fifth section xxxvii–lxxi which he himself added to these. In this way, the book received its present form. In this case, the book of Enoch, so far as its nature and date are concerned, would need to be set beside the Testaments of the Twelve Patriarchs, at least if, as we shall see (pp. 634–5), the view of de Jonge and others is right that this book was compiled by a Christian in about A.D. 200, making use of older Jewish elements.

The passages now combined in the book of Enoch differ much from one another not only in date of origin but also in content. The apocalypses of animal symbols (lxxxv–xc) and of Ten Weeks (xciii+xci, 12–17) present visions which provide first in the form of prophecy a retrospect of the period lying between the supposed author, Enoch—in lxxxv–xc the retrospect actually begins with Adam—and the real author who belongs to the second century B.C., and then a prospect of the last age (pp. 618–19). Such eschatological prevision is to be found also in the other parts of the book, as in i–v, x–xi, xlv–lvii. In particular the admonitions of xci–cv, cviii are bound up with a prospect of the fortunes of the sinners and of the righteous. But side by side with this is all manner of cosmogony and cosmology, astronomy and calendar matters which the visionary comes to see and hear during his journeys through the underworld, the earth and the heavens (xvii–xxxvi+lxxxi, i–lxxxii, 4a; xli, 3–xliv, 1; lxxii–lxxxii). Though this is not without points of contact with the older prophetic literature (I Kings xxii, 16–23), there is nevertheless here clearly a preponderance of non-Jewish material. A confusion of elements of Chaldean, Iranian, Egyptian and Greek learning is here displayed to the reader, and offers fascinating though difficult problems to anyone who wishes to discover the origin of the individual elements. The idea of the heavenly journey is probably Egyptian rather than Iranian; the astronomical learning is mainly Chaldean, and the idea of the regularity of natural phenomena is Greek. In view of the rich variety of these alien elements it is understandable enough that Judaism, when it had to fight for its very existence and was aware that its endurance would be possible only by the inspiration of its own powers, excluded the whole of the apocalyptic literature from its canon with the exception of the book of Daniel which had already been accepted (pp. 565, 566). It is at the same time intelligible that such a person as Mani[8] should have been attracted by the peculiar cosmology and anthropology of this book and should have made use of it.[9]

It is around the figure of Enoch that all the writings incorporated in the book have gathered themselves. It was he who was considered worthy to receive all these visions and to experience all these miraculous journeyings. The fact that Enoch attained in later Judaism this great significance as a visionary is to be explained from the terse statements which are made about him in Gen. v, 22, 24, namely that he *walked with God*, and that *God took (translated) him*. Though the first statement may well originally have been intended only as a witness to especial piety, at a later stage it came to be understood with reference to his secret knowledge, as may be seen from Ecclus. xliv, 16, and the idea of heavenly journeys in vision could easily be attached to the word *take, translate* (לָקַח). This fuller interpretation of Gen. v, 22, 24 was however assisted or perhaps even occasioned by the fact that Enoch as the seventh patriarch of mankind corresponds to the seventh Babylonian primeval king Enmeduranna[10] and by the 365 years of his life clearly reveals connections with the sun; he has thus had transferred to him many further features from the portrait of Enmeduranna, the originator of soothsayers and augurs, and the recipient of divine revelations, particularly from the sun god.[11]

In the search for the real authors of the works united in the book of Enoch, attention was earlier drawn to lxxxiii, 2, according to which Enoch received two visions before his marriage, so that celibacy appears as the ideal of perfection, and the suggestion was made that in addition to Pharisees among whom the authors were sought in the first place, Essenes too might have had some share in the work. This suggestion has since been confirmed by the fact that the writings which have come to light near Qumrān belonging to the group which was settled there and resembled the Essenes, have much in common with the book of Enoch, and that among the texts found there, in addition to fragments of other apocalypses similar to this work (pp. 661–3), there are also fragments of ten manuscripts of the Hebrew and Aramaic text of the book or of the material on which it was based.[12]

---

[8] Henning, 'Ein manichäisches Henochbuch' SAB (1934), pp. 27–35.

[9] Böhlig, 'Aus den manichäischen "Kephalaia des Lehrers"' WZ Halle 5 (1955/56), pp. 1067–84, cf. p. 1067; 'Christliche Wurzeln im Manichäismus' Bulletin de la Société d'Archéologie Copte 15 (1960), pp. 41–61, cf. p. 55.

[10] AOT, pp. 147–50; ANET, pp. 265 f.; Zimmern, 'Die altbabylonischen vor- (und nach-) sintflutlichen Könige nach neuen Quellen' ZDMG 78 (1924), pp. 19–35.

[11] Cf. Jansen, *Die Henochgestalt. Eine vergleichende religionsgeschichtliche Untersuchung* (1939). [Comparison may also be made with the king Etana, mentioned in the Sumerian king list, who was said to have been carried up to heaven. 'The Sumerian myth relates that Etana tried to reach the upper heavens against the will of the gods, and failed miserably' *Views of the Biblical World* ed. by M. Avi-Yonah and A. Malamat, I (1959), p. 29 (originally published in Hebrew as פני עולם המקרא), where a cylinder-seal from the third millennium B.C. in the Staatliche Museen, Berlin, is reproduced depicting this ascent to heaven on eagles' wings. P.R.A.]

[12] Barthélemy and Milik, *Qumran Cave I* (1955), pp. 84–6 No. 19 Pl. XVI: 'Livre de Noé'; Burrows, *More Light on the Dead Sea Scrolls* (1958), pp. 180, 347, 407 etc.; Dupont-Sommer, *Les écrits esséniens découverts près de la Mer Morte* (1959), pp. 310–13. E.T. pp. 298–300; Milik, 'The Dead Sea Scrolls Fragment of the Book of Enoch' Bibl 32 (1951), pp. 393–400; RB 63 (1956), p. 60; *Dix ans de découvertes dans le Désert de Juda* (1957),

The book of Enoch which we have been discussing is known as the Ethiopic Book[13] because it only exists in complete form in Ethiopic, whereas only parts of its Hebrew or Aramaic original are preserved in translations into Greek[14] and Latin. This Ethiopic translation was rediscovered in 1773, and we now possess almost thirty manuscripts of it. The Ethiopic text goes back to a Greek translation, which in its turn presupposes a Hebrew or perhaps an Aramaic original. The book at first enjoyed great popularity among the Christians, and is indeed quoted (i, 9) in the Epistle of Jude (vv. 14–15). But it was rejected by the Church as it had been earlier by the Synagogue, and thus is explained the fact that it was preserved entire only in the language of a marginal Christian community.

§ 97. THE SLAVONIC BOOK OF ENOCH

Literature: (a) Text: Slavonic: Novaković, Starine, Zagreb, 16 (1884), pp. 67–81; Vaillant, *Le Livre des Secrets d'Hénoch. Texte slave et traduction française* (1952); Bonwetsch, *Di Bücher der Geheimnisse Henochs* (TU 44, 1922 [German translation]).

(b) Commentaries: Charles: Forbes and Charles, II, pp. 425–569; Kahana: Kahana (²1956); Kautzsch: Beer, II, p. 218, n. a; Riessler, pp. 425–73, 1297–98.

(c) Other Works: Burkitt (§ 96), pp. 442 f.; Charles, 'The Date and Place of Writing of the Slavonic Enoch' JThSt 22 (1921), pp. 161–3; Förster, 'Adams Erschaffung und Namengebung' ARW 11 (1908), pp. 477–529; Fotheringham, 'The Date and Place of Writing of the Slavonic Enoch' JThSt 20 (1919), p. 252; 'The Easter Calendar and the Slavonic Enoch' JThSt 23 (1922), pp. 49–56; Gry, 'Quelques noms d'anges et d'êtres mystérieux en II Hénoch' RB 49 (1940), pp. 195–204; Lake, 'The Date of the Slavonic Enoch' HThR 16 (1923), pp. 397 f.; Maunder, 'The Date and Place of Writing of the Slavonic Book of Enoch' The Observatory 41 (1918), pp. 309–16; Otto (§ 96); N. Schmidt, 'The Two Recensions of Slavonic Enoch' JAOS 41 (1921), pp. 307–12.

Cf. also Literature §§ 76, 96, 126.

The Slavonic book of Enoch is to be distinguished from the Ethiopic. It is the translation into Slavonic of a book originally written in Greek (xxx, 13 gives an explanation of the name Adam by an acrostic possible only in Greek). It is dependent upon the other and older Enoch book, but must be assessed as an independent form of the traditions linked to the Enoch figure. The first part (i–xxi) is cosmological and tells of Enoch's journeys through the heavens. The second part too (xxii–xxxviii) at first has cosmological content, but then turns to historical matter. Enoch receives in the highest heaven revelations concerning

pp. 30 f.; E.T. *Ten Years of Discovery in the Wilderness of Judaea* (1959), pp. 33 f.; 'Hénoch au pays des aromates (ch. xxvii à xxxii). Fragments araméens de la grotte 4 de Qumran' RB 65 (1958), pp. 70–7. Pl. I; Sutcliffe, *The Monks of Qumran* (1960), p. 14. Lit. § 126.

[13] For this book there is also used the title 'I (1) Enoch' and for the Slavonic Book of Enoch discussed in § 97 'II (2) Enoch'. By 'III (3) Enoch' is meant the Hebrew apocalypse, written probably in the second half of the third century A.D., which Odeberg published under this title: *3 Enoch or The Hebrew Book of Enoch. Edited and translated for the first time with introduction, commentary, and critical notes* (1928); cf. Bultmann's review in ThLZ 62 (1937), cols. 449–53.

[14] On Lods' works (published 1892 and 1893) on the large fragment of the Greek translation discovered by Grébaut in Akhmîm, cf. Bayet, 'Notice sur la vie et les travaux de M. Adolphe Lods' CRAI (1957), pp. 315–27, cf. p. 316.

creation and concerning the history of mankind as far as the flood. In the third part (xxxix–lxvi) Enoch links to the imparting of the revelations he has just received admonitions for his sons. The book closes with an account of Enoch's ascension (lxvii) and a survey of his life (lxviii).

In the form in which we have the book it is undoubtedly of Christian origin and hardly datable before the seventh century A.D. But it appears to rest upon an older Jewish original. In li, 4, for example, the visiting of the Temple three times in the year is enjoined, and in lix, 1–2; lxi, 4; lxii, 1 the sacrificial cultus is presupposed as still existing. This makes it probable that the original came into being before A.D. 70. The most likely place of origin is Alexandria, but in any case it comes from the Greek-speaking Jewish diaspora.

§ 98. THE ASSUMPTION OF MOSES (ASSUMPTIO MOSIS)

Literature: (a) Text: Latin: Ceriani, *Monumenta Sacra et Profana* I, 1 (1861), pp. 9–13; 55–64; Fritzsche (p. 571), pp. 700–30; Clemen, *Die Himmelfahrt des Mose* (Kl T 10, 1904), Hilgenfeld, *Messias Judaeorum* (1869), pp. 435–68: retranslation into Greek.

(b) Commentaries: Charles: Charles, II, pp. 407–24; Kahana: Kahana (²1956); Kautzsch: Clemen, II, pp. 311–31; Riessler, pp. 485–95, 1301–3.

(c) Other Works: Hölscher, 'Über die Entstehungszeit der "Himmelfahrt Moses"' ZNW 17 (1916), pp. 108–27, 149–58; Kuhn, 'Zur Assumptio Mosis' ZAW 43 (1925), pp. 124–9; Lattey, 'The Messianic Expectation in "The Assumption of Moses"' CBQ 4 (1942), pp. 9–21; 'Vicarious Solidarity in the OT' VT 1 (1951), pp. 267–74, cf. pp. 273 f.; Rosenthal (§ 81), pp. 13–38; Stauffer, 'Probleme der Priestertradition' ThLZ 81 (1956), cols. 135–50, cf. cols. 141 f.; Wallace, 'The Semitic Origin of the Assumption of Moses' ThZ 11 (1955), pp. 321–8; Zeitlin, 'The Assumption of Moses and the Revolt of Bar Kokba' JQR 38 (1947/48), pp. 1–45.

Cf. also Literature §§ 76, 126.

The book of the Assumption of Moses as we have it is introduced in ch. i by the prophecy to Joshua of Moses' death and closes in xi–xii with Joshua's refusal to enter into Moses' heritage and his encouragement by Moses. But the Epistle of Jude speaks in verse 9 of a quarrel which the archangel Michael had to fight out with Satan for Moses' body and there is here clearly an allusion to this book. The narrative must therefore after xii have told of Moses' assumption— hence its name—and then of the struggle for his body. This conclusion is lost.

Between the framework passages there is an apocalypse. Moses reveals to Joshua the coming history of his people from the entry into Canaan, through the division of the kingdom, the destruction of Jerusalem, the rebuilding of the religious community etc., to the dawn of the blessed last age. In this, we find in vi, 1 mention of godless kings who are also high priests, and in vi, 2–6 mention of an insolent king from a non-priestly family with a period of rule of 34 years who will punish these high priest-kings as they deserve. This clearly points to king Herod[1] (37–4 = 34 years) and those whom he punishes are the Has-

[1] Busch, *The Five Herods* (1958); Minkin, *Herod, King of the Jews* (²1959); Mosbech, 'Herodes den Store' DTT 16 (1953), pp. 193–202; Perowne, *The Life and Times of Herod the Great* (1955); *The Later Herods* (1958); Pritchard, *The Excavations at Herodian Jericho*

moneans. Of the sons of this king it is said in vi, 7–8 that they will reign only a short time and that cohorts and the powerful king of the west will attack their territory. This last point clearly refers to the intervention by the Roman emperor which became necessary after Herod's death: the dispatch of the procurator Sabinus and the expedition of the legate Varus.[2] The prophecy then loses its concrete character. *From then on the times will come to an end* is said in vii, 1, and there follow prophecies of the appearance of hypocritical pious men (vii), a terrible persecution of the Jewish religion by a powerful king (viii), the appearance of a certain Taxo[3] of the tribe of Levi, who with his seven sons is ready for a martyr's death for religion (ix), and the dawn of the reign of God (x).[4] It is clear that in viii–ix, as elsewhere, for example in Mark xiii (p. 520, n. 25), events of the Maccabean period are presented as typical precursors of the final age.

By the mention of Herod and the prophecy which was not fulfilled, that his sons' reigns would be of short duration, as well as by the reference to the events of the year 4 B.C., the date of origin of the work is fixed fairly exactly. It must have been composed about 4 B.C. or not long after—Lattey places it shortly before A.D. 30—and probably in Palestine. The dating of it in the second century A.D. by Hölscher and Zeitlin can hardly be maintained. Much in it reminds us of the Qumrān community, including the prophecy of Taxo, whose name goes back, via the Greek τάξων, to the Hebrew מְחֹקֵק understood as 'regulator, supervisor' in Num. xxi, 18 and has parallels in the writings of the Qumrān community, particularly in the מחוקק of the Damascus Document (§ 106) which originated in this community. It had already been suggested earlier that this work was to be ascribed to the circles of the Essenes.

The book has survived only in a Latin translation made from the Greek, but the original was Hebrew or Aramaic.

§ 99. IV EZRA (II ESDRAS)

Literature: (a) Text: Latin: Fritzsche (p. 571), pp. 590–639; Retranslation into Greek: Hilgenfeld, *Messias Judaeorum* (1869), pp. 36–113; all texts, with those in oriental languages translated into German or Latin, together with indications of the editions of the originals in Violet, *Die Esra-Apokalypse (IV Esra)* I (1910); on this cf. Blake, 'The Georgian Version of Fourth Esdras from the Jerusalem Manuscript' HThR 19 (1926), pp. 299–375; 'The Georgian Text of Fourth Esdras from the Athos Manuscript' HThR 22 (1929), pp. 57–105.

1951 (AASOR 32/33, 1958); Schalit, הורדוס המלך האיש ופעלו (English title: *King Herod, Portrait of a Ruler*), 1960; Willrich, *Das Haus des Herodes zwischen Jerusalem und Rom* (1929). Lit. § 126.

[2] Josephus, *Ant.* XVII 10; *Bellum* II 3–6.

[3] Delcor, 'Contribution à l'étude de la législation des Sectaires de Damas et de Qumrân. IV. Le Meḥoqeq du Document de Damas et Taxo dans l' "Assomption de Moïse" ix' RB 62 (1955), pp. 60–6; Mowinckel, 'The Hebrew Equivalent of Taxo in Ass. Mos. ix' SVT 1 (1953), pp. 88–96; Rowley, 'The Figure of "Taxo" in the Assumption of Moses' JBL 64 (1945), pp. 141–3; Torrey, ' "Taxo" in the Assumption of Moses' JBL 62 (1943), pp. 1–7; ' "Taxo" once more' JBL 64 (1945), pp. 395–7. Lit. § 126.

[4] Manson (p. 613, n. 8), pp. 42–5: Ass. Mos. x, 10.

(b) Commentaries: Charles: Box, pp. 542–824; Hammershaimb: Noack (1953); Kahana: Kahana (²1956); Kautzsch: Gunkel, II, pp. 331–401; Riessler, pp. 255–309, 1282–85; Violet, *Die Apokalypsen des Esra und des Baruch in deutscher Gestalt* (1924); WC: Oesterley (1933).

(c) Other Works: Bloch, 'Was there a Greek Version of the Apocalypse of Ezra?' JQR 46 (1955/56), pp. 309–20; 'The Ezra-Apocalypse, was it written in Hebrew, Greek or Aramaic?' JQR 48 (1957/58), pp. 279–84; 'Some Christological Interpolations in the Ezra-Apocalypse' HThR 51 (1958), pp. 87–94; Box, *The Ezra-Apocalypse* (1912); Gry, *Les dires prophétiques d'Esdras (IVᵉ d'Esdras)*, I, II (1938); 'La "Mort du Messie" en IV Esdras, vii, 29 [iii, v, 4]' *Mémorial Lagrange* (1940), pp. 133–9; Kabisch, *Das vierte Buch Esra auf seine Quellen untersucht* (1889); Kaminka, 'Beiträge zur Erklärung der Esra-Apokalypse und zur Rekonstruktion ihres hebräischen Urtextes' MGWJ 76 (1932), pp. 121–38, 206–12, 494–511, 604–7; 77 (1933), pp. 339–55; Keulers, *Die eschatologische Lehre des vierten Esrabuches* (1922); Metzger, 'The "Lost" Section of II Esdras (=IV Ezra)' JBL 76 (1957), pp. 153–6; Montefiore, *IV Ezra. A Study in the Development of Universalism* (1929); Mundle, 'Das religiöse Problem des IV. Esrabuches' ZAW 47 (1929), pp. 222–49; Rosenthal (§ 81), pp. 39–71; Schiefer, *Die religiösen und ethischen Anschauungen des IV. Ezrabuches im Zusammenhang dargestellt* (1901); Schütz, *Die Offenbarung des Johannes und Kaiser Domitian* (FRLANT 50, 1933), pp. 40–4; Sigwalt, 'Die Chronologie des 4. Buches Esdras' BZ 9 (1911), pp. 146–8; Sjöberg (§ 96) (1940); Torrey, 'The Messiah Son of Ephraim' JBL 66 (1947), pp. 253–77, cf. pp. 259–63: on vii, 28–31; Völter, 'Die Gesichte vom Adler und vom Menschen im 4. Esra nebst Bemerkungen über die Menschensohn-Stellen in den Bilderreden Henochs' NThT 7 (1919), pp. 241–73; Wellhausen, 'Zur apokalyptischen Literatur' *Skizzen u. Vorarb.* 6 (1899), pp. 215–49; Zimmermann, 'Underlying Documents of IV Ezra' JQR 51 (1960/61), pp. 107–34.
Cf. also Literature §§ 76, 100.

The book of IV Ezra (on the name cf. p. 542) contains seven visions which Ezra is supposed to have had in Babylon in the thirtieth year after the fall of Jerusalem, i.e. 557 B.C. Leaving on one side the Christian V Ezra¹ which forms i–ii and the likewise Christian VI Ezra² which forms xv–xvi³ we may indicate these visions, following the chapter and verse divisions of the Vulgate, as follows: (1) iii, 1–v, 19; (2) v, 20–vi, 34; (3) vi, 35–ix, 25; (4) ix, 26–x, 59; (5) x, 60–xii, 51; (6) xiii, 1–58; (7) xiv, 1–48. In the first vision, Ezra lays before God the question why Zion which was no worse than the other peoples, and in particular no worse than her despotic ruler Babylon, has been destroyed, and he receives from the angel Uriel the answer that the human mind cannot grasp the activities of God, but that the coming aeon, now near at hand, will bring the solution. The second vision starts from the similar question why God should have abandoned to the other nations his only people, actually chosen by himself, and the answer is roughly the same: there is no solution. In connection with this there is discussion of the age of creation, now approaching its end. In the third vision Ezra raises the question why Israel does not actually possess the earth which was nevertheless made for her sake, and receives the answer that Israel's part lies in the coming aeon and that this can only be reached through this evil world. In connection with this, there is mentioned the fact, which greatly troubles Ezra, that only so few men will be saved

---

¹ Weinel, 'Das fünfte Buch Esra. Das sechste Buch Esra' in Hennecke, *Neutestamentliche Apokryphen* (²1924), pp. 390–4, 394–9. Lit. § 126.
² Cf. previous note.
³ On xv, 28–39, cf. Altheim and Stiehl, *Asien und Rom* (1952), p. 17.

into the coming aeon, whereas the majority, though also God's creatures, are sinners and go to destruction. The answer is that the sinners are themselves responsible and Ezra should be content with himself belonging among the blessed. In the fourth vision Ezra sees Zion as a mourning wife and then in her place all at once a great city—symbol of the people now humiliated but approaching a glorious future. In the fifth vision there appears to him rising up out of the sea an eagle which disappears in the face of a lion coming out of the forest—a symbol of the fourth world empire which will disappear before the Messiah. In the sixth vision Ezra sees a man rise out of the sea who destroys by the fiery breath of his mouth an army which rushes against him, but then he summons to himself another peaceful army. This is the Messiah, the saviour of the world, who will destroy the united heathen powers, but will protect the ten tribes of Israel. In the seventh vision, finally, Ezra's imminent translation is prophesied to him. He then restores the sacred scriptures which were destroyed at the fall of Jerusalem; filled with divine spirit he prepares 94 books with the help of five scribes, of which twenty-four, the canonical books (pp. 563 f.), are intended for publication, whereas the remaining seventy, the apocalypses, are to be kept secret and only made accessible to the wise. The book closes with the translation of Ezra (xiv, 49–50).

The placing of the visionary in the thirtieth year after the destruction of Jerusalem in 587 is clearly a fiction. The book certainly does frequently refer to a destruction of the city, but not to that of 587 B.C., but to that of A.D. 70. The visions quite clearly reveal the terrible inner distress weighing upon the Jews at that time. But it is characteristic of the book that problems of a general human kind are continually bound up with the Jewish question and these are discussed in a profound manner. In the last resort the problem of the book is not simply Israel's distress but that of all mankind, arising out of the conflict between belief in retribution and belief in God, a conflict which is always being observed anew and which has continually to be borne. The candour with which the author discusses this question often reminds us of Job, and there is also no lack of contacts in the content. But the difference between the two is nevertheless greater than what they have in common. IV Ezra has an outlook into the coming aeon and so possesses, as Job did not, a theoretical solution to the problem, though admittedly it still rests here upon hope. Jewish religion had in the meantime developed from a religion of this world into an otherworldly religion.

It is clear that the book was written after A.D. 70; we need only ask, how long afterwards. It has been suggested that the thirtieth year of iii, 1 should be interpreted so as to mean that we should place the standpoint of the author thirty years after the disaster, i.e. in A.D. 100. But this is improbable. The number is more probably an imitation of Ezek. i, 1. On the other hand, the eagle vision of x, 60–xii, 51 which indicates Vespasian, Titus and Domitian as the last Roman emperors, makes possible a fairly certain dating of the book, namely under Domitian (81–96) or rather, soon after his death. Its place of origin can hardly be decided, unless it be that Babylon has been deliberately chosen as a pseudonym for Rome, as in the apocalypse of John in the New Testament (xiv, 8; xvi, 19; xvii, 5; xviii, 10) and that we should look for the author there.

We do not know who the author was, but we can get a profound insight into his mind. He is a man highly endowed with visionary capacity, and gifted with a strong power for poetic creativity; his tender and sensitive heart suffers almost to breaking-point under his people's distress and in addition the afflictions of all mankind have taken hold of him. *For you have come far short of being able to love my creation more than I love it* (viii, 47) is the answer which God gives to the visionary when he asks how he could abandon to destruction his own laboriously formed creatures. But it is in reality the author himself who ascribes to his God the love which goes beyond all human compassion, and so makes clear the overflowing richness of his own love encompassing mankind and creation.

The book is preserved in Latin, Syriac, Ethiopic, Arabic, Armenian, Sahidic and Georgian translations, which all go back in the last resort to a Hebrew original. The richness of the transmission shows the favour this apocalypse enjoyed among Christians, though rejected by the Jews.

§ 100. THE SYRIAC APOCALYPSE OF BARUCH

Literature: (a) Text: Syriac: Ceriani, *Monumenta Sacra et Profana* V 2 (1871), pp. 113–80; Kmosko in *Patrologia syriaca accur. Graffin* I 2 (1907), pp. 1056–66, cols. 1068–1306; Latin translation: Fritzsche (p. 571), pp. 654–99; Greek fragments in Charles II, pp. 487–90.

(b) Commentaries: Charles: Charles, II, pp. 470–526; Kahana: Kahana (²1956); Kautzsch: Ryssel, II, pp. 404–46; Riessler, pp. 55–113, 1270–72; Violet (§ 99) (1924).

(c) Other Works: Gry, 'La date de la fin des temps, selon les révélations ou les calculs du Pseudo-Philon et de Baruch (Apocalypse syriaque)' RB 48 (1939), pp. 337–56; 'La ruine du temple par Titus. Quelques traditions juives plus anciennes et primitives à la base de *Pesikta Rabbathi* XXVI' RB 55 (1948), pp. 215–26; Rosenthal (§ 81), pp. 72–103; Sigwalt, 'Die Chronologie der syrischen Baruchapokalypse' BZ 9 (1911), pp. 397–8; Vallisoleto, 'Christologia in Apocalypsi Baruch Syriaca' VD 11 (1931), pp. 212–21; Zimmermann, 'Textual Observations on the Apocalypse of Baruch' JThSt 40 (1939), pp. 151–6.

Cf. also Literature §§ 76, 99, 101, 126.

The book falls like IV Ezra into seven sections. The first, §§ 1–12, begins with the prophecy to Baruch in the 25th year of Jehoiachin's life, i.e. (cf. II Kings xxiv, 8) the year 591, of the coming destruction of Jerusalem, and then relates how the angels, and not the enemies, will destroy the walls and so make possible the penetration by the enemies; and how Jeremiah goes to Babylon while Baruch remains on the heap of ruins of Jerusalem. Then the revelations proper begin.

In §§ 13–20, Baruch receives the answer to his complaint at Zion's fate, that Zion is first being punished for her purgation, but that later the other nations too, who have up till now enjoyed good, are to be punished. The coming aeon will solve the problems raised by the good fortune of the godless and the transitory existence of those who are nevertheless appointed as rulers of the world. This aeon is coming soon, and then everything which has been will seem as vanity.

In §§ 21–34, in response to Baruch's prayer that God's glory will soon appear and make an end to this life of vanity and impermanence, the answer is that this world must first run its appointed time, but that the end will soon come and that Baruch is to be preserved till that moment of time. There follow revelations concerning the twelve divisions of the coming woes, concerning their extension over the whole world sparing only the holy land, and concerning the appearance of the Messiah[1] who brings in the blessed final age and after whose return to heaven a general resurrection of the dead will take place. Finally Baruch tells the people that Zion after its rebuilding will be once more destroyed, to be rebuilt again only in the final age, but then for ever.

In §§ 35–46 there follows a night vision. There is a great forest standing in a plain enclosed within high mountains. Opposite it is a vine under which a spring flows out. The spring becomes a torrent and destroys the forest, leaving only a single cedar behind. When this too has been cast down, the vine reproaches it for its wickedness and greed for power, and proclaims its downfall. It is then burnt up. But the vine grows up, surrounded by unfading blossoms. The meaning is that the forest represents the four world empires, the spring and the vine the rule of the Messiah which will bring to an end the fourth world empire. The cedar is the last ruler of the fourth world empire who will be killed by the Messiah on Zion whereas the rule of the Messiah will last till the end of this world. This final age is intended for the members of the covenant people who are faithful to the Law, including those who have only at a late date joined themselves to it. Baruch exhorts the elders to a firm hope in that which is imperishable and to holding fast to wisdom and law.

In §§ 47–52 Baruch, after a long prayer for the saving of his people, receives the answer that the last woe will be terrible, and at his further question about the bodily nature of those who have risen from the dead he is informed that at first they will have their former bodily form. But after the judgement, the godless will be changed into hideous forms and will come to the place of torment, whereas the righteous will put on a heavenly garment of light and be taken up among the angels.

§§ 53–76 contain another vision. A cloud travels in haste over the earth, filled with black and white water and with lightning at its upper edge; it allows black and white water to fall alternately six times, and then again particularly dark water mingled with fire—thus thirteen downfalls of water altogether—and finally it is thrown down to the earth by the lightning. The lightning takes possession of the whole earth, and twelve rivers flow up out of the sea and become subject to it. In response to Baruch's request, expressed in the form of a lengthy prayer, he receives the following explanation from the angel Ramael. The cloud is the period of the world as planned by God, the first black water representing Adam's transgression, the fall of the angels and the flood. The bright water which follows is Abraham and his son and grandson with their faithfulness to the Law, their belief in the judgement, and their hope of a new world. The further black waters are the sinners in Israel's history like Manasseh; the bright waters are the righteous like Josiah. The twelfth bright water is the rebuilding of Jerusalem, but the last black water is a terrible final disaster from

[1] Torrey, 'The Messiah Son of Ephraim' JBL 66 (1947), pp. 253–77, see pp. 263–6. Cf. Literature on p. 439, n. 13; p. 632, n. 3.

which only the holy land is excepted. The fourteenth bright water—not mentioned in the vision, so that there must here be assumed an incongruity between the vision and the interpretation, or less probably, *water* must be regarded as a textual error for *lightning* and so corrected—is the Messiah, with whom the blessed final age will dawn. Baruch then receives the command to climb to the top of a mountain and there await the arrival of the Messiah. But he is first to instruct the people.

In §§ 77–87 Baruch exhorts the small company which has remained with him in Jerusalem to faithfulness to the Law, and writes a letter to the exiles in Babylon and to the nine and a half tribes. This letter is included in the text. It is concerned with the disaster to Jerusalem, the nearness of judgement on the heathen, and an exhortation to readiness to repent in view of the imminent end. The letter closes with the exhortation that its recipients should read it aloud in their assemblies, particularly on fast days.

Like the Ezra apocalypse, this Baruch apocalypse has as its special characteristic the extension of the Jewish problem which is raised by the destruction of Jerusalem in A.D. 70—this is clearly presupposed—to the general human issue of the serious problems which are raised by sin and suffering and the transitoriness of life. But in contrast to IV Ezra, the tone here is much less pessimistic. Though this aeon is imperfect, yet the imminent new aeon will be all the more glorious. The contrast is clearly to be explained from the fact that the apocalyptist in Baruch stands far behind IV Ezra both in the profundity of his meditations and in the sensitiveness of his feelings.

The relationship between the two books is so close that it may be assumed that there are literary links between them. Baruch gives the impression of much less originality than IV Ezra, so that we may judge Baruch to be the one that is dependent on the other. But here and there it appears as if Baruch is engaged in polemic against his model. The precise determination of the nature and measure of Baruch's dependence is very difficult because both appear to have taken over a good deal from the *Antiquitates Biblicae* of Pseudo-Philo, an allegorising interpretation of the history of Israel,[2] or at any rate from one of the sources of this work. Pseudo-Philo was recovered from oblivion in 1898 by L. Cohn[3] and made available again in 1917 by M. R. James in English translation,[4] in 1928 by P. Riessler in German,[5] and in 1949 by G. Kisch in its Latin text,[6] based upon a lost Greek translation made at the end of the first century A.D. from the

---

[2] Eissfeldt, 'Zur Kompositionstechnik des Pseudo-Philonischen Liber Antiquitatum Biblicarum' NTT 56 (1955), pp. 53–71. Lit. § 126.

[3] 'An Apocryphal Work ascribed to Philo of Alexandria' JQR 10 (1898/9), pp. 277–332.

[4] *The Biblical Antiquities of Philo, now first translated from the Old Latin Version* (1917).

[5] *Altjüdisches Schrifttum ausserhalb der Bibel übersetzt und erläutert* (1928), pp. 735–861, 1315–18.

[6] *Pseudo-Philo's Liber Antiquitatum Biblicarum* (1949). Cf. Kisch, 'The Editio Princeps of Pseudo-Philo's Liber Antiquitatum Biblicarum' *Alex. Marx. Jub. Vol.* I (1950), pp. 425–46; 'A Note of the New Edition of Pseudo-Philo's Biblical Antiquities' Historia Judaica 12 (1950), pp. 153–8; 'Pseudo-Philo's "Liber Antiquitatum Biblicarum", Postlegomena to the New Edition' HUCA 23, 2 (1950/51), pp. 81–93, with one plate; Spiro, 'Samaritans, Tobiads and Judahites in Pseudo-Philo' PAAJR 20 (1951), pp. 279–355; 'Pseudo-Philo's Saul and the Rabbis' Messiah ben Ephraim' *ib.* 21 (1952), pp. 119–37; 'The Ascension of Phinehas' *ib.* 22 (1953), pp. 91–114.

likewise lost Hebrew original. The dependence of the Baruch apocalypse on IV Ezra provides a *terminus a quo* for determining its date of origin, viz. A.D. 100. Since it (lxi, 7) is quoted in the Epistle of Barnabas (xi, 9) written between 130 and 140, 130 is the *terminus ad quem*. With this agrees the fact that the book does not appear to presuppose the outcome of the final Jewish revolt (132–135).

The book is preserved entire in Syriac, and there are also a few fragments of a Greek translation. The original was probably Hebrew or perhaps Aramaic.

§ 101. THE GREEK APOCALYPSE OF BARUCH

Literature: (a) Text: Greek: M. R. James, *Apocrypha anecdota* II (1897), pp. LI–LXXI, 84–94, with an English translation of the Slavonic text, pp. 95–102; Slavonic: Novakovič, Starine, Zagreb, 18 (1886), pp. 203–9; German translation: Bonwetsch, 'Das Slavisch erhaltene Baruch-Buch' NGG (1896), pp. 91–101.

(b) Commentaries: Charles: Hughes, II, pp. 527–41; Kahana: Artom (²1956); Kautzsch: Ryssel, II, pp. 446–57; Riessler, pp. 40–54, 1269–70.

(c) Other Works: Lüdtke, 'Beiträge zu slavischen Apokryphen' ZAW 31 (1911), pp. 218–35, cf. pp. 219–22: 'Apokalypse des Baruch'.

Cf. also Literature §§ 76, 99, 100.

The book begins with a complaint by Baruch that God has abandoned his city of Jerusalem to Nebuchadnezzar. An angel answers him saying that he should not be anxious about the deliverance of Jerusalem, for God is now going to show him his secrets (i). Then, without there being anything further about the fate of Jerusalem, a description is given of how the angel leads Baruch through the different heavens, as far as the fifth (ii–xvi). The book closes (xvii) with the narrative of Baruch's return and expression of thanksgiving. Thus ch. i is an introduction, otherwise ignored, to a book which is for the rest entirely cosmological. It differs from other writings of the kind by the delicate poetic atmosphere which makes it a very pleasing work. vi–viii are worthy of special mention. Here the visionary, now sojourning in the third heaven, describes the ride of a man of the sun sitting on a chariot moved by forty angels and accompanied by the phoenix which catches the burning rays of the sun with its gigantic wings.

The book contains many points of contact with Greek ideas (the sun-chariot, the phoenix in vi–viii,[1] the moon as a woman in a chariot drawn by deer and lambs in ix) and also has a strong gnostic element. It is of Jewish origin, but has been worked over by a Christian hand, as may be seen in ch. iv with its reference to the use of wine as God's (Christ's) blood at the Last Supper. Origen († 254), mentions in *De principiis* II 3, 6 a book of Baruch which tells of seven heavens, and thus had this apocalypse before him in a somewhat different, probably more original, form. The date of this original form may be assumed to be the second

---

[1] Hubaux and Leroy, *Le mythe du phénix dans les littératures grecque et latine* (1939), p. 260 index under 'Baruch'.

century or perhaps only the beginning of the third century A.D. Since the Syriac Apocalypse of Baruch (*c.* 130) is presupposed by it, it must in any case be dated after 130.

Apart from the Greek text published in 1897, we also possess a Slavonic translation which gives only extracts from it.

§ 102. THE TESTAMENTS OF THE XII PATRIARCHS

Literature: (a) Text: Greek: Charles, *The Greek Versions of the Testaments of the Twelve Patriarchs, edited from nine MSS. together with the Variants of the Armenian and Slavonic Versions and some Hebrew Fragments* (1908 (1960)); Armenian: '*Schatz alter und neuer Väter*', I. *Nichtkanonische Schriften des AT* (1896), ed. by Sargis Josepheantz; cf. Preuschen, 'Die armenische Übersetzung der zwölf Patriarchen' ZNW 1 (1900), pp. 106–40; Slavonic: Tichonrawow, *Pamjatniki otretčennoj russkoj literatury*, I (1863), pp. 96–232. The readings of the Armenian and Slavonic translations are given in Charles' edition.

(b) Commentaries: Charles: Charles, II, pp. 282–367; Kahana: Ostersetzer (^{2}1956); Kautzsch: Schnapp, II, pp. 458–88, 492–506; Kautzsch II, pp. 489–92 (Naphtali taken from the Chronicles of Jerahmeel); Riessler, pp. 1149–1250, 1335–38.

(c) Other Works: Aalen (§ 78), pp. 231–2; Aschermann, *Die paränetischen Formen der 'Testamente der zwölf Patriarchen'* [Diss. theol. Berlin 1955] (cf. ThLZ 81, (1956), cols. 480 f.); Bammel, ''$Aρχιερεὺς προφητεύων$' ThLZ 79 (1954), cols. 351–6; Beasley-Murray, 'The two Messiahs in the Testaments of the Twelve Patriarchs' JThSt 48 (1947), pp. 1–12; Bickerman, 'The Date of the Testaments of the Twelve Patriarchs' JBL 69 (1950), pp. 245–60; Bousset, 'Die Testamente der 12 Patriarchen' ZNW 1 (1900), pp. 141–175, 187–209; Braun, *History and Romance in Graeco-Oriental Literature* (1938), pp. 44–95; Chevallier, *L'esprit et le messie dans le Bas-Judaïsme et le NT* (1958); on this cf. Leipoldt, ThLZ 85 (1960), cols. 39 f.; Dupont-Sommer, 'Le testament de Lévi (xvii–xviii) et la secte Juive de l'Alliance' Semitica 4 (1951/52), pp. 33–53; Eisler, 'Barakhel Sohn & Cie, Reedereigesellschaft in Tanis' ZDMG 78 (1924), pp. 61–3; Eppel, *Le Piétisme juif dans les Testaments des douze Patriarches* (1930); Grelot, 'Le Testament araméen de Lévi est-il traduit de l'hébreu?' REJ 14 (1955), pp. 91–9; 'Notes sur le Testament araméen de Lévi' RB 63 (1956), pp. 391–406; Hunkin, 'The Testaments of the Twelve Patriarchs' JThSt 16 (1915), pp. 80–97; de Jonge, *The Testaments of the Twelve Patriarchs* (1953); 'The Testaments of the Twelve Patriarchs and the NT' StEv = TU 73 (1959), pp. 546–56; 'Christian Influence in the Testaments of the Twelve Patriarchs' NT 4 (1960), pp. 182–235; Leivestad, 'Tendensen i De Tolv Patriarkers Testamenter' NTT 55 (1954), pp. 103–23; Liver, 'The Doctrine of the Two Messiahs in Sectarian Literature in the Time of the Second Commonwealth' HThR 52 (1959), pp. 149–85; Messel, 'Über die textkritisch begründete Ausscheidung vermeintlicher christlicher Interpolationen in den Testamenten der zwölf Patriarchen' BZAW 33 (1918), pp. 355–74; A. Meyer, *Das Rätsel des Jacobus-Briefes* (1930), pp. 179–94: 'Die Testamente der 12 Patriarchen'; R. Meyer (p. 608, n. 5); Munch, 'The Spirits in the Testaments of the Twelve Patriarchs' AcOr[L] 13 (1935), pp. 257–63; Otzen, 'Die neugefundenen hebräischen Sektenschriften und die Testamente der zwölf Patriarchen' StTh 7 (1954), pp. 125–57; Philonenko, 'Le "Testament de Job" et les Thérapeutes' Semitica 8 (1958), pp. 41–53; *Les interpolations chrétiennes des Testaments des Douze Patriarches et les Manuscrits de Qoumrân* (Cahiers de RHPhR 35, 1960); Rabin, 'The "Teacher of Righteousness" in the "Testaments of the Twelve Patriarchs"?' JJSt 3 (1952), pp. 127–8; Schnapp, *Die Testamente der zwölf Patriarchen untersucht* (1884); Schubert, 'Die Messiaslehre in den Testamenten der 12 Patriarchen im Lichte der Texte von Chirbet Qumran' A XXIV IOK (1959), pp. 197–8; Segal, 'The Descent of the Messianic King in the Testaments of the Twelve Patriarchs' [Hebr.] Tarbiz 21 (1949/50), pp. 129–36; Thyen (§ 89), pp. 25–6;

van der Woude, *Die messianischen Vorstellungen der Gemeinde von Qumrân* (1957), pp. 190–216: 'Die messianischen Vorstellungen der Zwölf Patriarchen'.
Cf. also Literature §§ 76, 126.

The Testaments of the XII Patriarchs, whose textual transmission is described on p. 636, are a collection of the last words with which the twelve sons of Jacob took their leave, just before their death, from their sons, thus being in form an imitation of the Blessing of Jacob in Gen. xlix. But their content is quite different. They do not contain as does the Blessing of Jacob the prediction of the fortunes of the individual tribes or a description of their areas of settlement, but parenetic exhortations[1] which are linked in each case to a characteristic deed of the son of Jacob in question. In the process many haggadic elements are inserted, in part reminiscent of the further elaborations of the biblical stories such as are found in Jubilees and in the *Antiquitates Biblicae* (p. 629). Reuben, looking back with shame upon his action against Bilhah (Gen. xxxv, 22; xlix, 4), warns his sons of immorality and of all the dangers which issue from women. Simeon, according to the interpretation of Gen. xlii, 24, had urged Joseph's death particularly from envy and jealousy, and so had to endure as the divine punishment for this, that he was retained in bonds in Egypt. So he warns his sons against envy. Levi[2] relates how after he had been translated to the seventh heaven and had there received his priesthood, he took vengeance on Shechem because of Dinah (Gen. xxxiv), and then in a second vision was provided with the priestly robes by seven men in white garments. After some information about his further experiences (marriage and children), he exhorts his sons to reverence for the Law and to wisdom, and relates that he has learnt from the writings of Enoch that later his descendants would disgrace their office until at last a Messianic[3] priest will lead in the blessed final age.

Judah,[4] partly in connection with Genesis narratives, and particularly Gen. xxxviii, and partly in connection with traditions otherwise unknown to us, but presupposed also in Jub. xxxiv, tells of his courageous actions and of his relations with the Canaanite woman Bessue and with Tamar, occasioned by youthful passion and wine-drinking. He warns his sons against wine, women and avarice, exhorts them to subordinate themselves to Levi, and gives a prospect of Israel's future fortunes: the division of the kingdom, the Exile, the return, the appearance of a Messianic ruler from Judah who will, however, be subordinate to Levi. Issachar, described on the basis of the 𝔊 text of Gen. xlix, 15 *he became a countryman* as the pattern of the unpretentious, simple countryman, strict in morals and pious, exhorts his sons to be like him. Zebulun is described, though there is no basis for this in Gen., as the one of Joseph's brothers who was particularly sympathetic towards him, and in general always exercised

---

[1] von Rad, 'Die Vorgeschichte der Gattung von I Kor. xiii, 4–7' *Alt-Festschr.* (1953), pp. 153–68 = *Ges. Stud. ₹ AT* (1958), pp. 281–96.
[2] Schwartz, 'Du Testament de Lévi au Discours véritable de Celse' RHPhR 40 (1960), pp. 126–45.
[3] Kuhn, 'Die beiden Messias Aarons und Israels' ThLZ 79 (1954), cols. 760–1; Sjöberg (p. 613, n. 7); cf. Literature on p. 631; cf. p. 651.
[4] Schubert, 'Testamentum Juda xxiv im Lichte der Texte von Chirbet Qumran' WZKM 53 (1957), pp. 227–36.

charity, in accordance with a tradition which is likewise unknown to us. So he exhorts his sons to charitable behaviour, and finally gives a prospect of the coming fortunes of Israel. Dan, according to a tradition not known to us, was like Simeon particularly angry with Joseph, and then learnt that anger and lies are in reality the source of all human wickedness. So he warns his sons against these vices. Naphtali, described in Gen. xlix, 21 as *a hind let loose* (or *stretched out*) *who gives beautiful words,* and thus, for so the phrase is apparently understood here, as a figure of outward and inward harmony of disposition, exhorts his sons to pure, pious and kindly behaviour corresponding to the harmonious ordering of the cosmos. Gad, as he relates according to a tradition not contained in Gen., had shown particularly burning hatred against Joseph and thus learnt the harmfulness of hatred. So he warns his sons against hatred and exhorts them to love of their brethren and neighbours. Asher in accordance with his name interpreted as *straight, true,* summons his sons to straightforward kindness. Joseph relates, with all manner of haggadic elaboration of the Genesis narrative, how his chastity was in Egypt subjected to the severest tests, but that he overcame the temptations, and he exhorts his sons to chastity. Benjamin, the youngest brother and full brother of Joseph, did not act against him; he expresses the desire that he should no longer be called *ravenous wolf* (Gen. xlix, 27a), but a worker for the Lord who *divides the spoil* (Gen. xlix, 27b). He encourages his sons to a right and pure way of thinking and sets Joseph before them in this as a pattern.

The exhortations are in part based upon a dualism which has some Iranian elements, and on the prospect of resurrection and judgement. The fact that they enjoin love of God and of neighbour, peacebleness and gentleness, chastity and moderation, shows that the author of the book belongs to ascetic and pietistic circles. Lagrange[5] thought that these should be indicated more precisely as Essenes, whereas Eppel was inclined to think of North Palestinian or Syro-Phoenician 'quiet in the land' from the beginning of the second century B.C. and to see in them the precursors of the Galilean disciples of Jesus. The discovery of the Qumrān texts (§ 104) has shed new light on the date and origin of these 'Testaments', as it has done on so many other questions. It makes it probable that we should regard them, or more precisely the basic material of some or all of them, as deriving from the Qumrān community which flourished between the beginning of the second century B.C. and A.D. 70. There is thus a new explanation at the same time for the similarity which has long been observed and is indeed obvious, between many features of this book and Christian ideas and customs. At least a part of what the two have in common is to be explained not as due to the Christian authorship of the work nor to the assumption of Christian interpolations in an older Jewish original, but rather as due to the relationship between the 'Essene' community of Qumrān and Christianity, though this does not exclude the existence of what are manifestly Christian interpolations particularly in Reuben vi, Simeon vii, Levi ii, iv, viii,[6] xiv, xvi–xviii. Bickerman,

[5] *Le Judaïsme* (1931), pp. 122–30.
[6] Jansen, 'The Consecration in the Eighth Chapter of Testamentum Lev' Numen Suppl. 4 (1958), pp. 356–66.

Dupont-Sommer and the majority of those who have treated the book in the light of the Qumrān writings, favour this solution of the main problem which the Testaments present, and thus repeat, though admittedly with the support of weighty new arguments, the judgement of the book which was held by the first editor of the Greek text, J. E. Grabe (1694) and renewed two centuries later by Schnapp (1884).

But at the same time there is no lack of scholars whose views are worthy of note, who are in favour of a more radical presentation of the view which held the field during the two centuries lying between Grabe and Schnapp. This is the view that the book was compiled by a Christian writer, using older Jewish material, in about A.D. 200. Thus de Jonge, after careful examination of the manuscript transmission of the Testaments, endeavours to prove that the structure of the book as a whole and of its component parts is most readily understandable if it is ascribed to a Christian author to be dated between A.D. 190 and 255. This author made use of two individual Testaments—the Testament of Levi and the Testament of Naphtali, about which something further must be said in a moment (p. 636)—an older haggadic work also used by the book of Jubilees, and in addition Hellenistic fictional motifs in Judaised form, and so himself composed the book as we have it in order to present in the life histories of the twelve sons of Jacob the ideals of the Christian way of life. Milik expressed a similar view, first in RB 62 (1955), pp. 405 f. For him it seemed of particular significance that just as roughly sixty-five years ago in the Geniza of the Ezra Synagogue at Cairo[7] Aramaic fragments came to light of the Testament of Levi, regarded as being an older part of the Testaments as we now have them, so too recently such fragments have been found in two Qumrān caves.[8] By contrast, no trace had been found of a Jewish original of other sections of the Testaments. In view of the wealth and variety of the texts discovered at Qumrān, he believed it proper to deduce from this fact that we may regard it as quite definite that the book did not originate in Palestine in the pre-Christian period. He therefore assumed, like de Jonge, that a Christian author took as pattern the Testament of Levi which he modified in some points, and in this manner constructed the eleven remaining Testaments of the book.

Milik has adhered to this view in spite of the fact that a fragment, this time in Hebrew, has now been found at Qumrān from another Testament, namely that of Naphtali, presenting a more elaborate form of XII Test. Napht. i, 6–12.[9]

[7] Cowley and Charles, 'An Early Source of the Testament of the Patriarchs' JQR 19 (1906/7), pp. 566–83; Kahle, 'Zu den Handschriftenfunden in Höhlen beim Toten Meer' Das Altertum 3 (1957), pp. 34–46, cf. p. 44; *The Cairo Geniza* (²1959), p. 27; Lévi, 'Notes (Encore un mot) sur le texte araméen du Testament de Lévi récemment découvert' REJ 54 (1907), pp. 166–80; 55 (1907), pp. 285–7.

[8] Barthélemy and Milik, *Qumran Cave I* (1955), pp. 87–91, Pl. XVII; Milik, 'Le Testament de Lévi en araméen. Fragment de la grotte 4 de Qumrân' RB 62 (1955), pp. 298–406, Pl. IV; Starcky, RB 63 (1956), p. 66.

[9] Burrows, *More Light on the Dead Sea Scrolls* (1958), pp. 179 f., 282–4, 336 f., 408 f., etc.; Dupont-Sommer, *Les écrits esséniens découverts près de la Mer Morte* (1959), pp. 313–318; E.T. *The Essene Writings from Qumran* (1961), pp. 301–5; Milik, '"Prière de Nabonid"' RB 63 (1956), pp. 407–15, Pl. I, cf. p. 407 n. 1; *Dix ans de découvertes dans le Désert de Juda* (1957), pp. 31 f.; *Ten Years of Discovery in the Wilderness of Judaea* (1959), pp. 34 f.; Sutcliffe, *The Monks of Qumran* (1960), p. 14.

In *Dix Ans de découvertes* (1957), p. 32, *Ten Years of Discovery* (1959), pp. 34 f., repeating the interpretation he had already made in RB 63 (1956), p. 407, n. 1, he explains, after a reference to the recently discovered Hebrew Testament of Naphtali: 'Accordingly, we would be willing to ascribe to the *Testaments of the Twelve Patriarchs* an origin analogous to that of the Book of Enoch. A Jew or Jewish-Christian of the first or second century, using and adapting such Testaments as were already in circulation would have completed an analogous set of Testaments for all the Twelve Patriarchs.' Burrows, *More Light* (1958), pp. 179 f. is inclined to agree with Milik, and this seems also to be true of Sutcliffe, *The Monks* (1960), p. 44. Dupont-Sommer, however, in *Les écrits esséniens* (1959), pp. 313–18, *Essene Writings* (1961), pp. 301–5 declares firmly that the whole book, comprising Testaments of all twelve patriarchs, originated in the Qumrān community in about B.C. 100, and argues this mainly by pointing out that the Damascus Document (§ 106), composed probably in the first century B.C., contains 'numerous parallels, not only to the Testaments of Levi (the French text has Judah by mistake on p. 317) and Naphtali, but also to those of Reuben, Simeon, Judah, Zebulun, Dan, Gad, Asher, Joseph and Benjamin'.

A clear decision on this problem is made the more difficult by the fact that a clear division can hardly be made between Christian revision of a Jewish original by a Christian 'redactor' on the one hand, and the use by a Christian 'author' of older Jewish material on the other. The more precise dating of the book and its sources is also hindered by the fact that, as is conceded also by those who reckon with an older Jewish original, we must assume for this already at the Jewish stage of its evolution a variety of expansions and alterations, and it thus can hardly be clearly decided whether the references to definite historical personalities belong to the basic material of the book or to one of its later elaborations. These references are in any case often ambiguous. There have been found allusions to Hyrcanus (134–103) in Test. Lev. viii, or to Alexander Jannaeus (102–76) in Test. Lev. x, xiv–xvi; Test. Dan. v. But with a full recognition of the difficulties which stand in the way of the dating of the book, we may nevertheless say that the grounds for regarding it as deriving from the Qumrān community are stronger than the arguments which are put forward in favour of it being regarded as the work of a Christian author. Here the primary point is its unmistakeable relationship to some of the Qumrān writings and in particular to the Damascus Document (§ 106) which belongs among them, as may be seen from the work of Otzen (1954) or from the list of allusions to the Testaments in this work given by Rabin *The Zadokite Documents* (1954), p. 83. If the work is ascribed to the Qumrān community, its date is also fixed in that it must have come into existence in the period of that community's flourishing, namely the period between about 200 B.C. and A.D. 70. Bickerman believes it is possible to place it tentatively in the first quarter of the second century B.C., and thus to ascribe it to a contemporary of Jesus ben Sira. This may be right for the basic material of the book, but only for that. For as we have seen we are dealing in this book with a work which was already considerably expanded and modified in the Jewish stages of its evolution.

The book is preserved in ten Greek manuscripts, and in addition in an Armenian and an Old Slavonic translation of the Greek text. The original text of its older Jewish original, the existence of which is to be assumed with a high degree of probability as we have seen, belonging so far as its basic material is concerned to the second century B.C., was certainly Hebrew or Aramaic. The Hebrew Test. Napht.[10] contained in the Chronicles of Jerahmeel and published by Gaster, is, however, hardly likely to be a part of the original text, but rather a late Jewish revision of the Greek transmission which we possess. In addition to the Test. Levi in this book, we have also Aramaic and Greek fragments of another Test. Levi,[11] as well as references to a Syriac translation of it. This was perhaps originally written in Hebrew, and has contacts with the Test. Levi in the book we are considering, but is more extensive, and, since it presupposes the existence of the Temple cultus, must have originated before A.D. 70. This dating fits the point already mentioned that in addition to the fragments written in about A.D. 1000 found more than sixty years ago in the Ezra Synagogue at Cairo, there are now other such fragments which have come to light in Qumrān caves (p. 634).

§ 103. THE LIFE OF ADAM AND EVE (VITA ADAE ET EVAE. APOCALYPSIS MOSIS)

Literature: (a) Text: Latin: Wilhelm Meyer, 'Vita Adae et Evae' AAM 14, 3 (1878), pp. 185–250; Greek: von Tischendorf, 'Apocalypsis Mosis' in *Apocalypses Apocryphae* (1866), pp. X–XII, 1–23; Ceriani, *Monumenta Sacra et Profana*, V 1 (1868), pp. 19–24.

(b) Commentaries: Charles: Wells, II, pp. 123–54; Kahana: Haak (²1956); Kautzsch: Fuchs, II, pp. 506–28; Riessler, pp. 668–81, 1311 f.

(c) Other Works: James, *The Lost Apocrypha of the OT* (1920), pp. 1–8; Mozley, 'The "Vita Adae"' JThSt 30 (1929), pp. 121–49.

Cf. also Literature §§ 76, 126.

Poetic fancy has attached a variety of haggadic narratives to the personages of the parents of mankind, Adam and Eve, and we therefore have a very rich literature of the 'Life of Adam and Eve' as it may be comprehensively designated. Most of the books which belong here are Christian, as for example the 'Book of Adam and Eve'[1] preserved only in Ethiopic and Arabic translations, but at least for the basic material of the two oldest examples of this type we must assume Jewish origin and probably also a Hebrew original text. These are the two works: (1) the Life of Adam and Eve (Vita Adae et Evae), preserved in a Latin translation made from the Greek, and (2) the Greek work which runs

---

[10] Gaster, 'The Hebrew Text of One of the Testaments of the Twelve Patriarchs' Proc. Soc. Bibl. Arch. 16 (1893/94), pp. 33–49 (pp. 83–6 by Marshall), 109–17; Gaster, *Studies and Texts* I (1925/28), pp. 69–85. English translation also in Charles, *Testaments of the XII Patriarchs* (1908), pp. 221–7.

[11] Given by Charles (see previous note), pp. 228–35.

[1] Dillmann, *Das christliche Adambuch des Morgenlandes* (1853); Annie Jaubert, 'Le calendrier des Jubilés et les jours liturgiques de la semaine' VT 7 (1957), pp. 35–61, cf. pp. 52–5. Even this 'Book of Adam and Eve' is not entirely free of Jewish elements.

parallel to this, very often in actual wording, described inappropriately as the Apocalypse of Moses by von Tischendorf. The narrative contained in these two works is as follows: Adam and Eve do penance because of their fall, but Eve is interrupted by a new deception by Satan (only in Vita i–xvii); the birth of Cain and Abel, Abel's death, the birth of Seth and the remaining children (Vita xviii–xxiv, Apoc. Mos. i–v); Adam has a vision in which his death is proclaimed to him, and relates it to his son Seth (only in Vita xxv–xxiv); Adam falls ill, and Eve and Seth try in vain to get the oil of life which flows in Paradise from the tree of mercy (Vita xxx–xliv, Apoc. Mos. v–xiv); Eve relates the fall (only in Apoc. Mos. xv–xxx); Adam's death (Vita xlv–xlvi, Apoc. Mos. xxxi–xxxii); the prayer of the angels for pardon for Adam (only in Apoc. Mos. xxxiii–xxxvi); God has mercy on Adam (Vita xlvi–xlvii, Apoc. Mos. xxxvii); the prayer of the angels for the burial of Adam's body (only in Apoc. Mos. xxxviii–xxxix); the burial of Adam and Abel in Paradise, Eve's death and burial (Vita xlviii–li, Apoc. Mos. xl–xliii).

The narrative is unusually charming and delicate. The motif that the trees of Paradise lose their leaves at the moment when Eve eats the forbidden fruit, but break out again when God enters Paradise on his cherub chariot accompanied by the angels' songs of praise (Apoc. Mos. xxii), is highly poetic. To this delicacy of presentation there corresponds the ascetic tone which is echoed here and there, as in the penance which Adam and Eve impose upon themselves by undertaking to stand 40 or 37 days in the Jordan or in the Tigris (Vita i–xi).

We can hardly decide where the work which underlies these two writings was composed. So far as date of origin is concerned, it is usual to think, since the existence of the Herodian Temple seems to be presupposed, of the time between Herod's building of the Temple (20 B.C.) and the destruction of Jerusalem (A.D. 70).

III. APOCRYPHAL AND PSEUDEPIGRAPHICAL WRITINGS AMONG THE QUMRĀN TEXTS

§ 104. A SURVEY OF THE DISCOVERIES OF TEXTS MADE IN THE WILDERNESS OF JUDAEA SINCE 1947

Literature: (a) Texts: Barthélemy and Milik (with Contributions by de Vaux, Crowfoot, Plenderleith, Harding), *Qumran Cave I* (*Discoveries in the Judaean Desert* I, 1955); Benoit, Milik, de Vaux, *Les Grottes de Murabba'ât* (*Discoveries in the Judaean Desert* II, 1960); Burrows with the assistance of Trever and Brownlee, *The Dead Sea Scrolls of St. Mark's Monastery*. Vol. I: *The Isaiah Manuscript and the Habakkuk Commentary* (1950); Vol. II, Fasc. 2: *The Manual of Discipline* (1951); Sukenik, מגילות גנוזות מתוך גניזה קדומה שנמצאה במדבר יהודה [*Hidden Scrolls. From an ancient Geniza discovered in the Wilderness of Judaea*] I (1948) II (1950); אוצר המגילות הגנוזות שבידי האוניברסיטה העברית [*The Collection of hidden scrolls in the possession of the Hebrew University*] (1955); edition with English text: *The Dead Sea Scrolls of the Hebrew University* (1955).

(b) Other Works: (i) Bardtke, *Die Handschriftenfunde am Toten Meer* I. *Mit einer kurzen*

Einführung in die Text- und Kanonsgeschichte des AT (²1953); *Die Handschriftenfunde am Toten Meer* II. *Die Sekte von Qumrān* (1958, ²1961); Burrows, *The Dead Sea Scrolls. With Translation* (1956); *More Light on the Dead Sea Scrolls. With Translation of Important Recent Discoveries* (1958); Carmignac et Guilbert, *Les Textes de Qumrân. Traduits et Annotés*, I (1961); Dupont-Sommer, *Les écrits esséniens découverts près de la Mer Morte* (1959); E.T. *The Essene writings from Qumran* (1961); Gaster, *The Scriptures of the Dead Sea Sect. In English Translation with Introduction and Notes* (1957); Habermann, *Megilloth Midbar Yehuda. The Scrolls from the Judean Desert* [Hebr., Engl. summary] (1959); Maier, *Die Texte vom Toten Meer*, I, II (1960); Sutcliffe, *The Monks of Qumran as Depicted in the Dead Sea Scrolls with Translations in English* (1960).

(ii) Benoit, Baillet, Milik, Cross, Skehan, Allegro, Strugnell, Starcky, Hunzinger, 'Le travail d'édition des fragments manuscrits de Qumrân' RB 63 (1956), pp. 49–67; 'Editing the Manuscript Fragments from Qumran' BA 19 (1956), pp. 75–96; Cross, *The Ancient Library of Qumrân and Modern Biblical Studies* (1958); Harding, 'Recent Discoveries in Jordan' PEQ 90 (1958), pp. 7–18, esp. pp. 15–17: 'Khirbet Qumran'; *The Antiquities of Jordan* (1959), pp. 185–98, Pls. 29–31: 'Khirbat Qumran'; Hunzinger, 'Aus der Arbeit an den unveröffentlichten Texten von Qumran' ThLZ 85 (1960), cols. 151–2; Milik, 'Le travail d'édition des manuscrits du Désert de Juda' SVT IV (1957), pp. 17–26, esp. pp. 17–21; *Dix ans de découvertes dans le Désert de Juda* (1957); *Ten Years of Discovery in the Wilderness of Judaea* (1959).

(c) Bibliography: Burchard, *Bibliographie zu den Handschriften vom Toten Meer* (BZAW 76, 1957 (1959)); 'Bibliographie' RQ 1 (1958/59), pp. 149–60, 309–20, 461–79, 547–626; 2 (1959/60), pp. 117–51, 299–312; Habermann, 'Bibliography for Study of the Dead Sea Scrolls' [Hebr.] Beth Mikra I (1956/57), pp. 116–21; III (1958), pp. 103–11; IV (1959), pp. 91–5; V (1960), pp. 89–93; Nober, 'Elenchus Bibliographicus' Bibl 30 (1949), Nos. 592–609; 33 (1952), Nos. 571–625; 34 (1953), Nos. 880–927; 35 (1954), Nos. 1044–1121; 36 (1955), Nos. 874–945; 37 (1956), Nos. 644–731; 38 (1957), Nos. 784–939; 39 (1958), Nos. 690–1119; 40 (1959), Nos. 1090–1309, 607–66; 41 (1960), Nos. 919–1045; 42 (1961), Nos. 710–98; 43 (1962), Nos. 789–872; La Sor, 'Bibliography' RQ 2 (1959/60), pp. 459–72, 587–601; 3 (1961/62), pp. 149–60, 313–20, 467–80, 593–602; Stier, IZBG 1 (1951/52), Nos. 992–1123, 2206–88; 2 (1953/54), Nos. 1095–1208; 3 (1954/55), Nos. 1105–92; 4 (1955/56), Nos. 873–1003; 5 (1956/57), Nos. 971–1106; 6 (1958/59), Nos. 1344–1507; 7 (1960/61), Nos. 1177–1295).

Cf. also Literature § 126.

In 1947[1] two Bedouin belonging to the tribe of Taʿāmire[2] which inhabits the locality, came by chance upon a clay jar with leather scrolls written one in Aramaic and six in Hebrew, in a cave, now counted as Cave I, near Khirbet (ruins) Qumrān[3] which lies on the north-west shore of the Dead Sea, six miles south of Jericho, in Jordan territory. Since then new chance finds and systematic searches both there and in other parts of the Wilderness of Judaea have brought to light further similar manuscripts and fragments of manuscripts in large quantities. By far the majority of these come from eleven caves in the neighbourhood of Qumrān. Because of this, the term 'Qumrān scrolls' is generally used, as in this present book, to include the texts found elsewhere in the Wilderness of Judaea. The remainder came to light in caves in the Jordanian

[1] Brownlee, 'Muhammed ed-Deeb's Own Story of His Scroll Discovery' JNESt 16 (1957), pp. 236–9, Pl. XXXVI; Trever, 'When was Qumran Cave I discovered?' RQ 3 (1961/62), pp. 135–41. Lit. § 126.

[2] Couroyer, 'Histoire d'une tribu semi-nomade de Palestine' RB 58 (1951), pp. 75–91.

[3] Probably the site of the 'city of salt' (עִיר הַמֶּלַח) mentioned in Josh. xv, 62. Cf. Cross, *The Ancient Library of Qumran* (1958), p. 39, and above, p. 251, n. 15. Lit. § 126.

Wadi Murabba'āt[4] which flows into the Dead Sea about twelve miles south of Qumrān; in caves in some of the valleys in Israeli territory, running down to the Dead Sea between Masada in the south and Engedi in the north, notably in the Naḥal Ṣe'elîm (Wādi Seyāl), the Naḥal Mishmar (Wādi Maḥras) and the Naḥal Ḥeber (Wādi Ḥabra),[5] and at Khirbet (ruins) Mird situated about six miles south-west of Qumrān, also in Jordan territory. Among the texts found in the Wādi Murabba'āt and in the caves in the valleys between Masada and Engedi, there are some that are biblical—Hebrew fragments of the books of Gen., Exod., Num., Deut., Isa., XII Prophets and Psalms (pp. 681–3), and fragments of a Greek translation of the XII Prophets (p. 707). There are also other Hebrew, Aramaic, Nabataean, Greek, Latin and Arabic texts and fragments of various kinds. But more important still, alongside contemporary coins, weapons, household articles, jewellery and skulls, are the Hebrew, Aramaic, Nabataean, Greek and Latin documents from the period of the second Jewish revolt, namely from the years A.D. 132–135, including letters written by or at the command of the leader of this revolt, Ben-Koseba (Bar-cocheba) and a writing addressed to him.[6]

[4] *Les Grottes de Murabba'ât* (§ 104) (1961).

[5] Avigad, Aharoni, Bar-Adon, Yadin et al., 'The Expedition to the Judean Desert, 1960' IEJ 11 (1961), pp. 1–72, 24 Pls.; 'Judean Desert Caves' IEJ 11 (1961), pp. 77–81; Yadin, 'New Discoveries in the Judean Desert' BA 24 (1961), pp. 34–50; 'More on the Letters of Bar Kochba' BA 24 (1961), pp. 86–95. It is now established that the texts found in the summer of 1952, and offered to the archaeological museum in Jerusalem by their Bedouin finders without the place of their discovery being revealed, actually came from some of the caves investigated in 1960 and 1961 by Israeli archaeologists. Cf. IEJ 11 (1961), pp. 11, 24, 81. Lit. § 126.

[6] Abramson and Ginsberg, 'On the Aramaic Deed of Sale of the Third Year of the Second Jewish Revolt' BASOR 136 (1954), pp. 17–19; Avigad et al. (cf. above, n. 5) IEJ 11 (1961), pp. 1–72, 24 Pls.; pp. 77–81; Bardtke, 'Bemerkungen zu den beiden Texten aus dem Bar Kochba-Aufstand' ThLZ 79 (1954), cols. 295–304; Birnbaum, 'A Fragment in an Unknown Script' PEQ 84 (1952), pp. 118–20; 'An Unknown Aramaic Cursive' PEQ 85 (1953), pp. 23–41, Pl. XXXIV; 'Bar Kokhba and Akiba' PEQ 86 (1954), pp. 23–32; 'The Beth Mashku Document' PEQ 87 (1955), pp. 21–33, Pl. I; 'The Negeb Script' VT 6 (1956), pp. 337–71, Pl. I; 'The Kephar Bebhayu Conveyance' PEQ 89 (1957), pp. 108–32, Pl. XXIV; 'The Kephar Bebhayu Marriage Deed' JAOS 78 (1958), pp. 12–18; *The Bar Menasheh Marriage Deed. Its Relation with other Jewish Marriage Deeds* (PIHAN XIII, 1962); Cross, 'La lettre de Simon ben Kosba' RB 63 (1956), pp. 45–8; Ginsberg, 'Notes on the Two Published Letters to Jeshua Ben Galgolah' BASOR 131 (1953), pp. 25–7; Lacheman, 'The so-called Bar Kokba Letter' JQR 44 (1953/54), pp. 285–90; Lehmann and Stern, 'A Legal Certificate from Bar Kochba's Days' VT 3 (1953), pp. 391–6; Marcus, 'A Note on the Bar Kokeba Letter from Murabba'at' JNESt 13 (1954), p. 51; Milik, 'Une lettre de Siméon Bar Kokheba' RB 60 (1953), pp. 276–94, Pl. XIV; 'Une inscription et une lettre en araméen christo-palestinien' RB 60 (1953), pp. 526–39, Pls. XVIII, XIX; 'Un contrat juif de l'an 134 après J.-C.' RB 61 (1954), pp. 182–90, Pl. IV; 'Note additionnelle sur le contrat juif de l'an 134 après Jésus Christ' RB 62 (1955), pp. 253 f.; 'Deux documents inédits du Désert de Juda' Bibl 38 (1957), pp. 245–68, Pls. I–IV, cf. pp. 255–68, Pls. II–IV; 'Le travail d'édition des manuscrits du Désert de Juda' SVT IV (1957), pp. 17–26, cf. pp. 17–21; I. Rabinowitz, 'A Hebrew Letter of the Second Century from Beth Mashko' BASOR 131 (1953), pp. 21–4; J. J. Rabinowitz, 'Some Notes on an Aramaic Contract from the Dead Sea Region' BASOR 136 (1954), pp. 15 f.; 'Note sur la lettre de Bar Kokheba' RB 61 (1954), pp. 191 f.; 'A Clue to the Nabatean Contract from the Dead Sea Region' BASOR 139 (1955), pp. 11–14; 'A Legal Formula in Egyptian. Egyptian-Aramaic and Murabba'at Documents' BASOR 145 (1957), pp. 33 f.; 'Some Notes on an Aramaic Deed of Sale from the Judean Desert' Bibl 39 (1958), pp. 486–7; Rubinstein, 'The Appellation "Galileans" in Ben Kosebha's Letter to Ben Galgola' JJSt 6 (1955), pp. 26–34; Sonne, 'The Newly Discovered Bar Kokeba Letters' PAAJR 23 (1954), pp. 75–108; Starcky, 'Un contrat nabatéen

The position is similar with the discoveries at Mird.[7] These include some fragments in Greek and in Christian Aramaic (Syro-Palestinian)[8] of New Testament books, a Greek fragment of Wisd. (§ 89), and a Christian-Aramaic fragment of the book of Joshua. But the main body of the material consists of Christian-Aramaic, Greek, Syriac and Arabic documents of the fifth to eighth centuries, above all letters, but including a Greek fragment of Euripides' *Andromache*. The texts which belong directly or indirectly to the Old Testament, with which we are alone here concerned, come in the main from the region of Qumrān.

The texts and text fragments from the finds at Qumrān and the other sites, belonging in this broader sense to the Old Testament field, may be divided into four groups: (1) Hebrew or Aramaic texts of canonical books of the Old Testament,[9] together with Greek texts of its apocrypha and pseudepigrapha; (2) fragments of Greek or Syro-Palestinian translations of Hebrew books of the Old Testament; (3) Hebrew and Aramaic texts of apocryphal and pseudepigraphical writings of the Old Testament otherwise surviving only in Greek or other languages in translation; (4) new, hitherto unknown writings of an apocryphal or pseudepigraphical kind. These last may be subdivided—though the division cannot be made completely strictly: on the one hand are those

sur Papyrus' RB 61 (1954), pp. 161–81, Pls. I–III; Teicher, 'Documents of the Bar Kochba Period' JJSt 4 (1953), pp. 132–4; 'Are the Bar Kokhba Documents Genuine?' JJSt 5 (1954), pp. 39 f.; Toombs, 'Barcosiba and Qumran' NTSt 4 (1957/58), pp. 65–71; de Vaux, 'Les Grottes de Murabba'at et leurs Documents. Rapport préliminaire' RB 60 (1953), pp. 245–67, Pls. VIII–XI; 'Quelques textes hébreux de Murabba'at' RB 60 (1953), pp. 268–75, Pls. XII–XIII; Yadin (p. 639, n. 5), BA 24 (1961), pp. 34–50, 86–95; Yaron, 'Note on the Judaean Deed of Sale of a Field' BASOR 150 (1958), pp. 26–8; Yeivin, 'Some Notes on the Documents from Wadi Murabba'at dating from the Days of Bar-Kôkh'bâ' 'Atiqot 1 (1955), pp. 95–108, Pl. VIII. Lit. § 126.

[7] de Langhe, 'Oude Handschriften in den Woestijn van Juda' Onze Alma Mater 7 Aflev. 4 (1953), pp. 14–19, cf. pp. 18 f.; 'De Leuvense Expeditie naar de Woestijn van Juda' Onze Alma Mater 8 Aflev. 1 (1954), pp. 3–5; 'De Koperen Rol en een nieuwe tocht naar de woestijn van Juda' Onze Alma Mater 14 Aflev. 3 (1960), pp. 1–9; de Vaux, 'Fouille au Khirbet Qumran' RB 60 (1953), pp. 83–106, Pls. II–VII, where the 'Wady en-Nâr' mentioned on p. 85 denotes Mird; G. R. H. Wright, 'The Archaeological Remains at El Mird in the Wilderness of Judaea, with an Appendix, "The Monastery of Kastellion" by J. T. Milik' Bibl 42 (1961), pp. 1–27, Pls. I–XII, Figs. 1–6. Lit. § 126.

[8] Black, *A Christian Palestinian Syriac Horologion* (1954); 'Die Erforschung der Muttersprache Jesu' ThLZ 82 (1957), cols. 653–67; 'The Recovery of the Language of Jesus' NTSt 3 (1956/57), pp. 305–13; Baumstark, 'Das Problem des christl.-palästin. Pentateuchtextes' Or Christ 10 (1936), pp. 201–24; Cantineau, 'Quelle langue parlait le peuple en Palestine au Ier siècle de notre ère?' Semitica 5 (1955), pp. 99–101; Duensing, *Nachlese christlich-palästinisch–aramäischer Fragmente* (NGAW 1955, No. 5 (1956)); Eiss, 'Zur gegenwärtigen aramaistischen Forschung' EvTh 16 (1956), pp. 170–81; Kahle, 'Das zur Zeit Jesu in Palästina gesprochene Aramäisch' ThR 17 (1949), pp. 201–16 = *Opera Minora* (1956), pp. 79–95; 'Das palästinische Pentateuchtargum und das zur Zeit Jesu gesprochene Aramäisch' ZNW 49 (1958), pp. 100–16; *The Cairo Geniza* ([2]1959), pp. 191–208; Kutscher, 'Studies in Galilean Aramaic' [Hebr.] Tarbiz 21 (1949/50), pp. 192–205; 22 (1950/51), pp. 53–63, 185–92; 'Das zur Zeit Jesu gesprochene Aramäisch' ZNW 51 (1960), pp. 46–54; on this cf. Kahle, 'Das zur Zeit Jesu gesprochene Aramäisch: Erwiderung' *ib.*, p. 55; Milik (see p. 639, n. 6), RB 60 (1953), pp. 536–9, Pls. XVIII–XIX; Rosenthal, *Die Aramaistische Forschung seit Th. Nöldeke's Veröffentlichungen* (1939), pp. 144–59: 'Das Christlich-Palästinensische'; Vermès, 'La littérature rabbinique et le Nouveau Testament' Cahiers Sioniens 9 (1955), pp. 97–123, cf. pp. 98–102: 'L'araméen palestinien et le langage des Évangiles'. Lit. p. 679, n. 30; p. 701, n. 8; § 126.   [9] Cf. above, p. 567, n. 11.

which, as we shall see (pp. 642 f.), are directly concerned with the religious community which recognised the Qumrān buildings as their centre, with the ordinances controlling its organisation and the values which determined its inner nature, and on the other hand those which are similar to already known apocrypha and pseudepigrapha and at any rate indirectly reflect the beliefs and hopes which characterised this community.

To the first group belong above all the two Isaiah scrolls which came to light in 1947 in cave 1. The one provides the complete Hebrew text of this prophetic book, while the other contains at any rate about a third of it. There are fragments of about a dozen further scrolls of Isaiah, found later in other caves according to the information given by Muilenburg in BASOR 135 (1954), p. 28 and confirmed by Skehan in RB 63 (1956), p. 59; Hebrew fragments of all the books of the Old Testament with the exception of Esther, and Aramaic fragments of the Aramaic sections of the book of Daniel. Among this material we often have fragments of several scrolls for the same biblical book. There is also the Greek fragment of the Wisdom of Solomon found at Mird. To the second group belong sections of the Greek translation of Lev., Num., and of the XII Prophets (p. 707), as well as the fragment of a Syro-Palestinian translation of Joshua. To the third group belong the Hebrew or Aramaic fragments of the books of Jubilees, Enoch and the Testaments of the XII Patriarchs, or of the earlier forms of these books, as well as one Hebrew and two Aramaic fragments of Tobit. For the fourth group, the following may be listed, in addition to a series of Hebrew and Aramaic text fragments not yet identified: (a) writings which clearly belong to the Qumrān community, which will be described more closely in a moment, such as the Manual of Discipline, the Damascus Document, the War Scroll, the Hymn Scroll and other similar psalm-like compositions; (b) explanations of Old Testament books, applying them to the contemporary situation, namely as prophecies of the external events and inner movements of the period of origin of these 'Commentaries'. Such are the relatively well preserved 'pesher'—this (פשר pešer) being the word used in them for 'interpretation' or 'explanation'[10]—to Habakkuk, as well as fragments of such commentaries on Isa., Micah, Nahum, Zeph., and other biblical writings, and 'florilegia' made up of Old Testament verses and passages which express or seem to express Messianic hopes; (c) apocalypses like the book of Baruch (§ 86) or the Letter of Jeremiah (§ 87); (d) apocalypses like the book of Enoch which tell of secret revelations to biblical characters of remote antiquity or contain eschatological expectations in other forms; (e) books which like Jubilees further elaborate the narrative of one or more biblical books as well as the laws which they provide, and are thus of a haggadic or halachic nature; (f) writings which consist primarily of parenetic, edifying content, and as such may be placed alongside the Testaments of the XII Patriarchs or the wisdom books of the Old Testament; (g) documents whose literary type cannot be determined with certainty, as is the case with many fragments of leather and papyrus, and is particularly true of the copper scroll whose text is still the subject of very varied interpretations (pp. 648, 655f.).

[10] Cf. above, p. 514, n. 5. Gertner (Lit. § 126 on p. 534, n. 16).

Y

The writings which belong to the first and second of the four groups just mentioned, and in particular the two Isaiah scrolls and fragments of a Hebrew text of Samuel which is close to the LXX on the one hand, and the fragments of the Greek Lev., Num., and Twelve Prophets on the other, are of great significance for textual criticism. They must therefore, in so far as this has not already been done in Part III in the analysis of the individual books (pp. 419, 497, 521), be considered in Part V which deals with the history of the text, together with other text discoveries (§ 115) to be mentioned there. Much the same is true of the Hebrew and Aramaic original texts allocated to the third group, original texts of apocrypha and pseudepigrapha hitherto only known in translation, these have therefore been mentioned already in the discussion of these books in Part IV (pp. 585, 599, 608, 621). But the various writings placed in the fourth group will be described somewhat more closely in what follows.

But before this is undertaken, a few remarks of a more general kind are necessary, and these are relevant in part also for the writings belonging to the first three groups. Something must first be said about the origin and date of these writings. The first years which followed on the making known of the discoveries which had been made in the spring of 1947 near Qumrān, two miles northwards from ‘Ain (spring) el-Feshkha[11]—by which name they were at first often described—were full of lively discussions concerning the age of these writings, both in regard to the date of the composition of their originals and the date of the copies surviving in the scrolls which have been preserved. During this time the dates differed widely, for some thought of the third or second centuries B.C., while others of the first centuries A.D. or even of the Middle Ages. But the systematic investigation, begun in 1951 and completed in 1958, of the Qumrān ruins, and of the surrounding area, both close to Qumrān and further afield including the remains of buildings at ‘Ain el-Feshkha,[12] has put an end to such discussions, or has at least made them no longer significant. It is true that we cannot yet regard as certainly proved the duration at first assigned as a result of this investigation to the monastery-like buildings of Qumrān, namely of two centuries from 130 B.C. to A.D. 68 with an interruption extending over the last three pre-Christian decades. But nevertheless it is clearly established that the buildings and the caves in their vicinity served as the centre of an Essene-like religious community[13] during the last two centuries B.C. and the first century A.D.; and further that the written scrolls hidden in some of the neighbouring caves not only belonged to this community but were also at least for the most part composed or at least copied in it. Since the community may already have existed a few decades before it settled in and around Qumrān and may already then have possessed scrolls of its own, it is possible that some of the scrolls

[11] Farmer, 'The Geography of Ezekiel's River of Life' BA 19 (1956), pp. 17–22.

[12] Cf. the reports of the excavations by de Vaux in RB 60 (1953), pp. 83–106, 540–61, Pls. II–VII, XX–XXIV; 61 (1954), pp. 206–36, Pls. V–XII; 63 (1956), pp. 533–76, Pls. III–XIII; 66 (1959), pp. 225–55, Pls. I–XII; and in the Annual of the Department of Antiquities of Jordan 4/5 (1960), pp. 7–11: 'Excavations at 'Ain Feshkhah'; and de Vaux, *L'archéologie et les manuscrits de la Mer Morte* (Schweich Lectures 1959) (1961). Cf. Lit. § 126.

[13] Adam, *Antike Berichte über die Essener* (Kl T 182, 1961); Wagner, *Die Essener in der wissenschaftlichen Diskussion vom Ausgang des 18. bis zum Beginn des 20. Jahrhunderts* (BZAW 79, 1960). Cf. Lit. § 126.

which have been found at Qumrān may derive from this earlier period and have then been brought to Qumrān. The majority of them, however, will belong to the period during which the community had Qumrān as its centre, and thus they will have been composed or copied there between 130 B.C. and A.D. 68. Thus the period of origin may be narrowed to about two centuries. On this point the majority of the experts is now substantially agreed.

Nevertheless there are still those who hold a different opinion. Zeitlin still holds unmoved to the view which he has been putting forward since 1948, that the Qumrān writings are mediaeval forgeries.[14] Others too go their own way, and here we may simply describe in a little more detail the work of two or three scholars in order to indicate the nature of their disagreement with the majority view, and not concern ourselves further with others who, like del Medico,[15] have their own individual view of the matter. Mention may be made of Driver and Roth,[16] and of Rengstorf. The former two, while differing in regard to details, are in agreement on the main issue, and so here an account of the views of Roth will be sufficient. According to Roth, the Qumrān writings derive from a Zealot community[17] which, without having any connection with the previous inhabitants, occupied the Qumrān buildings in the year A.D. 6 and controlled it down to the year A.D. 73, the year of the collapse of the resistance offered to the Romans by the Zealots in Masada, or perhaps for a few years after that. They compiled their writings there, including the songs of thanksgiving (§ 108) composed in reference to the Judas of Galilee referred to in Acts v, 37 or perhaps even composed by him, and the War Scroll (§ 107) composed between A.D. 66 and 73. Rengstorf, on the other hand, sees in the Qumrān buildings not the centre of an Essene type community, but an outpost of the Jerusalem Temple. He therefore ascribes the scrolls found in the caves near Qumrān not to the supposed 'monastic' community, but to the Jerusalem Temple. For him the crucial point is that these scrolls reflect all the spiritual forces which inspired Judaism between 200 B.C. and A.D. 100, and that such a breadth of concern can be attributed to the priestly Temple administration, but not to a sectarian community which was concerned only with its own life and which more or less turned its back on its environment.

Those who accept the majority view still differ in their views as to the decade or half century in the period between 130 or perhaps 170 B.C. and A.D. 68 in which the individual scrolls were composed or written down. Nor is it likely that agreement can be reached on this point since there appear to be no absolutely reliable palaeographical criteria, and clear references to particular historical

[14] Cf. his contributions to the subject in JQR 39–52 (1948/49–1961/62). Lit. § 126.

[15] L'énigme des manuscrits de la Mer Morte (1957); Le mythe des Esséniens (1958).

[16] Roth, The Judean Scrolls. Their Date and Purpose. With Arguments and Evidences by G. R. Driver (1958); 'The Jewish Revolt Against the Romans (66–73) in the Light of the Dead Sea Scrolls' PEQ 90 (1958), pp. 104–21; The Historical Background of the Dead Sea Scrolls (1958); 'The Zealots in the War of 66–73' JSSt 4 (1959), pp. 332–55; 'The Subject Matter of Qumran Exegesis' VT 10 (1960), pp. 51–68. For a critical discussion of Roth's views cf. Rowley, 'The Qumran Sectaries and the Zealots' VT 9 (1959), pp. 379–92; 'The Qumran Sectaries' VT 10 (1960), pp. 227–9. Cf. Lit. § 126.

[17] Hengel, Die Zeloten. Untersuchungen zur jüdischen Freiheitsbewegung in der Zeit von Herodes I. bis 70 n. Chr. (1961). Cf. Lit. § 126.

events are few in number and are even so capable of more than one interpretation (pp. 659–60). We shall here have to be content with the recognition that the majority of the scrolls which are to be described somewhat more fully in what follows, derive from the second or first century B.C. or from the first seven decades A.D. But we must still reckon with the possibility that some of them are older, for it is clear that the composition of a substantial number of the works found in these scrolls, and primarily here that of the books of Isaiah and of the majority of the other biblical books, took place several centuries before the preparation of the Qumrān scrolls which actually contain these works and which are themselves to be dated between 130 B.C. and A.D. 68.

Nor must it be forgotten, as we attempt to give a survey of the writings found near Qumrān and in other places in the Wilderness of Judaea belonging to the realm of the Old Testament, that of the manuscript treasures which have so far been secured, whether by publication or collected for treatment in the Palestine Archaeological Museum or in other places in Jerusalem, so far only a relatively small selection has been made known or even examined in a preliminary way as to its content. This is made very clear by the detailed reports which have been made by the group of scholars entrusted with the arrangement and publication of the text fragments which have come to light in Caves 2 to 6, in their statement in RB 63 (1956), pp. 49–67=BA 19 (1956), pp. 75–96[18] on the stage which their work has reached, as also from those in IEJ[19] and BA by archaeologists concerned with the investigation of the caves in Israeli territory, and from isolated publications of texts made by such scholars in JBL, RB, SVT VII, ZAW and elsewhere. Finally it must be recognised that the examination of the new texts is only in its beginnings. So far we have hardly come beyond the stage of linguistic explanation leading to an appropriate translation. Other tasks which they set for research—the consideration of their place within the history of intellectual, religious, economic and social life—still await solution, and this is also particularly true of critical literary analysis and the understanding of their literary types. So far as the former is concerned, we have clearly, for example, in the Manual of Discipline (§ 105) and the Damascus Document (§ 106) which, as we shall see, is closely connected with it, writings which are not compact, constructed according to a unified plan, but are compilations. So far as the second point is concerned, it was at once seen when samples of the 'Thanksgiving hymns' were made known, that they are to be set beside definite types of songs in the Psalter. But more precise investigations of these two matters, made very much more difficult by the fragmentary condition of the scrolls which here come in for consideration, have yet to be made. So our survey of the new texts which are here relevant must be restricted largely to an indication of their content and an approximate description of their literary character. Only in the few cases where the situation forces upon the student observations of a literary or form-critical kind will these be indicated.

[18] Cf. section (b) (ii) of the literature to § 104, p. 638.
[19] Cf. above, p. 639, n. 5.

§ 105. THE MANUAL OF DISCIPLINE

Literature: The Dead Sea Scrolls of St. Mark's Monastery (§ 104) II, 2 (1951): 'The Manual of Discipline'; *Qumran Cave I* (§ 104), pp. 107–30, Nos. 28 (Titre de la Règle de la Communauté [1 QS]), 28a (Règle de la Congrégation [1 QSa]), 28b (Recueil des Bénédictions [1 QSb]), Pls. XXII–XXIX.

Bardtke (§ 104) (1953), pp. 86–110; (1958), pp. 283–8; Burrows (§ 104) (1956), pp. 371–89; (1958), pp. 393–8; Carmignac and Guilbert (§ 104), I, pp. 9–80 (Guilbert); Dupont-Sommer (§ 104) (1959), pp. 88–127; (1961), pp. 68–109; Gaster (§ 104) (1957), pp. 49–69, 103–8, 97–101, 113–15, 285–8; Habermann (§ 104) (1959), pp. 59–70, 160–4; Maier (§ 104) (1960) I, pp. 21–45, 173–9; II, pp. 9–39, 154–61; Sutcliffe (§ 104) (1960), pp. 149–71, 203; Wernberg-Møller, *The Manual of Discipline, translated and annotated with an Introduction* (1957). Cf. Literature §§ 104, 106.

The work here under consideration has been given various titles: Manual of Discipline, as here, 'Sektenrolle' (Sectarian Scroll), 'Règle de la Communauté', 'Manuale disciplinae' and the like. It was earlier designated by the siglum DSD (DS=Dead Sea; D=Discipline), but now by the siglum 1QS (1Q=from Qumrān Cave 1; S=סרך *serek*, *rule*).[1] This description is not quite clear since this name was first applied to the main part of the work here in question (1QS) found in 1947 in the first Qumrān cave and published in 1951. It was not then imagined that further parts of this work—including, apart from one fragment which contains its title, two larger sections which have their own superscriptions—would turn up in the course of negotiations in 1950. These were published in 1955 (QC I). The title [סר]ך היחד ומן preserved on the fragment and clearly placed on the outside of the scroll agrees with the opening of

---

[1] The earlier system generally used to denote the writings from Qumrān employed sigla which consisted of a combination of DS (=Dead Sea) and an abbreviation of the name of the relevant biblical book (DSIsᵃ=the first, complete Isaiah Scroll; DSIsᵇ=the second, incomplete Isaiah Scroll) or, for the writings which for the most part lacked any traditional name, an abbreviation of the (English) title given to them (DSD: D=Manual of Discipline; DSW: W=War (of the Sons of Light). This has in the meantime been replaced by sigla which indicate first the cave of the discovery, and then for biblical books a shortened form of their name (1QIsᵃ=first Isaiah scroll from Qumrān Cave 1; 1QIsᵇ=second Isaiah scroll from Qumrān Cave 1; 1QJub=fragments of the book of Jubilees from Qumrān Cave 1), and for non-Biblical books an abbreviation of a Hebrew title suitable to them (1QS, 1QSᵃ, 1QSᵇ=סרך היחד *serek ha-yaḥad*, *rule of the community*, the main body and two pieces which appeared later of the Manual of Discipline from Qumrān Cave 1, namely הסרך לכל עדת ישראל *hasserek lᵉkol 'ᵃdat yiśrā'ēl* '*The rule for the whole community of Israel*' and דברי ברכה *dibrê bᵉrākāh*, *words of blessing* or *blessings*. 1QM=מלחמות בני אור *milḥāmôt bᵉnê 'ôr* or *wars of the sons of light*, the war scroll from Qumrān Cave 1; 1QH=הודיות *hôdāyôt*, *songs of thanksgiving*, the hymn scroll from Qumrān Cave 1). For the 'commentaries' on biblical books, there is placed before the indication of the book in question a letter p, the abbreviation of פשר *pešer* *interpretation* (p. 641): 1QpHab=the 'Commentary' on Habakkuk from Qumrān Cave 1. Other abbreviations quoted subsequently have been similarly constructed. In connection with this change of sigla, the siglum CDC = Cairo Damascus Covenant formerly in use for the Damascus Document has been replaced by CD =Cairo Document (the fragments of the Damascus Document which came from the Ezra Synagogue in Cairo), 4QD and 6QD (the pieces of this document found in Qumrān Caves 4 and 6).

A complete list of the sigla to be used for the Qumrān writings may be found in *Qumran Cave I*, pp. 46–7; Burchard (§ 104) (1957 (1959)), pp. 114–18; Dupont-Sommer (§ 104) (1959), p. 431; (1961), p. 421; Sutcliffe (§ 104) (1960), pp. 268–72. Cf. Lit. § 126.

the work, which, according to Carmignac[2] should run לְ[מַשְׂכִּיל . . . לְאַנ] שִׁים לחיו [סֵפֶר סְ[רֶךְ היחד *For the instructor . . . for the men, his brethren, the book of the rule of the community,* or at least it agrees in so far as in both there is reference to the *Rule of the Community*. It remains, however, uncertain whether this name refers to the whole of the scroll, including the *Rule for the whole congregation of Israel* and the *Blessings,* or whether it refers only to the main section without these two. There is therefore an element of uncertainty about the title *Rule of the Community* (1QS) in so far as it may be used in a narrower and in a broader sense. What is meant at any given point is not left in doubt since the two sigla 1QS[a] and 1QS[b] are available for the two appendices. But in view of this we may continue to use the designations 'Manual of Discipline' and the like, which were given to the main section which first became known, as the name for the whole work, and extend them also to the copies of the work which, as is indicated below (p. 648), have come to light later in cave 4.

So far as the content of the copy of this work from cave 1 is concerned, its main section comprises eleven columns (I–XI) and begins by mentioning in I, 1–18[3] the chief duties of those who enter the community, including *to seek God . . . to do what is good and right before him . . . to love all the children of light according to their share in God's decree and to hate all the children of darkness according to their guilt in God's wrath.* In I, 18–III, 12 we have very detailed prescriptions concerning the ceremonies which are to be carried out on admission into the community. III, 13–IV, 26 contains teachings filled with the belief in a cosmic dualism between good and evil as it is to be brought to *the children of light* by the *instructor*. God, so we read here, *has created the spirits of the light and of the darkness,* and *until now the spirits of truth and of wickedness struggle in the hearts of men.* Then follows V, 1–VI, 23[4] introduced by: וזה הסרך לאנשי הַיַחַד המתנדבים לשוב מכול רע *And this is the rule for the men of the community who have shown themselves ready to repent of all evil,* and consisting of prescriptions concerning the common life of the members of the community, concerning their mealtimes and deliberations and the like, in which there is everywhere given prior place to the priests. VI, 24–IX, 11, beginning with: ואלה המשפטים אשר ישפטו בם במדרש יחד על פי הדברים *And these are the iudgments according to which decisions are to be made at the examination of the community according to the particular cases,* contains directives concerning punishments for lighter and more serious crimes of which the members of the community may have made themselves guilty. Lighter crimes are punished by short-term exclusion from the community together with curtailment of provisions: for example hot tempered or disdainful attitude towards a brother. For the denial of the basic principles of the community or for blasphemy there was

---

[2] 'Conjecture sur la première ligne de la Règle de la Communauté' RQ 2 (1959/60), pp. 85–7.

[3] In references to passages from the Qumrān writings, capital Roman numerals indicate the columns, Arabic numerals the lines. The two codex fragments of the Damascus Document (§ 106) from the Geniza of the Ezra Synagogue in Cairo and published by Schechter are, however, cited according to pages and lines.

[4] Mowinckel, 'Mitteilungen zu zwei Qumran-Miszellen' ZAW 73 (1961), pp. 297–9: on IQ H III, 9 f. and IQS VI, 16, 18, 22.

permanent exclusion or the death penalty. These directives, so the section concludes in IX, 10–11, have been valid since the founding of the community and are to remain valid *until the coming of the prophet and of the anointed ones of Aaron and Israel* (עד בוא נביא ומשיחי אהרון וישראל). IX, 12–XI, 8 begins with: אלה החוקים למשכיל להתהלך בם *These are the precepts for the instructor that he may walk in them* and repeats it in IX, 21: ואלה תכוני הדרך למשכיל בעתים האלה *And these are the directives on the way for the instructor in these times*. It provides a kind of summary of the commandments which precede, and takes on a poetic tone with its demand for the praises[5] which are appropriate to be offered to God at particular times of the day, the month and the year (IX, 26). In X, 6 (or at any rate in X, 8) it makes the *instructor,* who has hitherto been referred to in the third person, speak in the first person and make known his will that God should be praised. X, 9–XI, 21 begins with: אזמרה בדעת וכול נגינתי לכבוד אל *I will play with understanding and all my playing on the strings is to the honour of God* and closes with a reflection on the vanity of man. It represents simply a psalm in the first person singular or perhaps more probably a collection of psalm-like passages placed together in the form of a liturgy.

The section 1QSᵃ (p. 646) comprises two relatively well-preserved columns, described at the beginning, as we have seen, as *rule for the whole congregation of Israel at the end of the days*. It describes this community in I, 1–5, first as the elect who follow the instructions of the Zadokite priests and their associates and do not go the evil way of the remainder of the people. In I, 6–25aᵏ[6] it mentions the directives for the admission to the ranks and offices of the community, and in I, 25b–II, 10 the conditions which are determinative for taking part in the assemblies which are granted full juristic, political and military powers. In II, 11–22 it states the order of precedence which applies in these assemblies and at the sacred meals. This *rule of the congregation* thus has much in common with the *rule of the community* which it follows, but it is nevertheless improbable that the *congregation of Israel* here referred to indicates the same entity as the *community* whose affairs are there regulated. They differ from one another among other points by the fact that the *community* appears to have nothing to do with military affairs, whereas these play a large part for the *congregation*. It almost appears as if the *rule of the community* is to be valid for the world as it then was, whereas the *rule for the whole congregation of Israel,* of which it is expressly stated that it is compiled for the end of the days, was intended to regulate the behaviour of the congregation in the expected final age. Much the same will have to be said of the 'War Scroll' (pp. 653–4).

As far as the *words of blessing* or *benedictions* (1QSᵇ) are concerned, we unfortunately have to leave open the question as to the order in which the material originally stood since the sequence of the five pieces of columns which are all that survive cannot be fixed with certainty. Probably the passage had at the beginning words of blessing concerning all the members of the congregation (I, 1–20), and these were followed by blessings on the high priest (I, 21–III, 21),

---

[5] Cf. Talmon, 'The "Manual of Benedictions" ' RQ 2 (1959/60), pp. 475–500.
[6] Borgen, ' "At the Age of Twenty" in 1QSa' RQ 3 (1961/62), pp. 267–77.

the priests (III, 22–V, 19) and the princes of the congregation (V, 20–9). By way of indicating the nature of these benedictions, we may quote here the relatively well-preserved beginning of the blessing which applies to the *sons of Zadok, the priests*—omitting any note of the small gaps in the text: *May the Lord bless thee from his holy dwelling and set thee as a glorious ornament among* [26]*the holy ones and renew for thee the covenant of thy eternal priesthood and give thee thy place in the holy* [27]*dwelling and direct by thy deeds all those of high rank and by the utterance of thy lips all princes* [28]*of the peoples, give to thee as an inheritance the firstlings of all delicacies and bless through thee the purposes of all flesh* (III, 25–8).

In addition to the copy of the Manual of Discipline from cave 1 which we have just considered, there are also available, according to Milik's report in RB 63 (1956), pp. 60 f.; 64 (1957), p. 586; *Ten Years of Discovery in the Wilderness of Judaea* (1959), p. 37, fragments from cave 4 of nearly a dozen other copies of this work. So far as it is possible to judge, taking into account their extent and the state in which they have survived, they agree fairly closely with the text of that copy. Two of them, however, contain a shorter and probably older form of its column V beginning: מדרש למשכיל על אנשי התורה המתנדבים *Teaching of the instructor to the men of the law who have shown themselves ready.*

Some scholars consider that the Copper Scroll discovered in 1952 in Qumrān Cave 3 actually contains a list of the various treasures belonging to the Qumrān community and hidden here and there in the land because of a danger which was threatening. If this is correct, the Copper Scroll also refers directly to the affairs of this community, and it would then be proper to discuss it in connection with the examination of the Manual of Discipline. Others, however, take the view that this is a list of Temple treasures and that as such it has nothing whatever to do with the Qumrān community. But in fact this scroll is probably of a quite different nature and for this reason it will be discussed subsequently in the appropriate context (pp. 665–6).

The same is true of a number of other works whose nature, partly because of their bad state of preservation, can be variously assessed. The alternatives here are as follows: they may be ordinances for the actual cultus or they may be apocalyptic elaborations of the hoped-for final age, two possibilities which are in fact not quite mutually exclusive in so far as the Qumrān community could not actually take part in the Temple cultus and probably also did not wish to do so. The cultic ordinances, therefore, which they handed down and perhaps elaborated further were in any case directed to the future in which it was hoped that there would be a rehabilitation of a legitimate Temple cultus accessible to all the pious. Among these works may be mentioned first the fragments found in cave 4 (Milik, RB 63 (1956), p. 69; *Ten Years of Discovery* (1959), pp. 41, 107–13) from several copies of a work described as Mishmaroth, *watches*, in view of the fact that it contains precise details for the duties of the individual priestly families, with mention of years, beginnings of the months, sabbaths, weeks, and feasts, and with a synchronistic comparison of the two calendars presupposed as being in use, namely the solar calendar with 364 days and the lunar calendar with 354. In addition there belong here the fragments which have come to light in cave 6 of a priestly genealogy (Baillet, RB 63 (1956), p. 55; QC III, pp. 126 f.). These works, as has been suggested above, may be equally well assigned to the apocalypses as to the ordinances determinative for the Qumrān community. This is not, however, the case with the description of the New Jerusalem and other works similar to it which will be considered in § 110 among the 'Apocalypses'.

§ 106. THE DAMASCUS DOCUMENT

Literature: (a) Text: Schechter, *Documents of Jewish Sectaries,* Vol. I: *Fragments of a Zadokite Work* (1910); Lévi, 'Document relatif à la "Communauté des Fils de Sadoc" ' REJ 65 (1913), pp. 24–31; Rost, *Die Damaskusschrift, neubearbeitet* (Kl T 167, 1933); Zeitlin, *The Zadokite Fragments. Facsimile of the Manuscripts in the Cairo Geniza Collection in the Possession of the University Library, Cambridge, England* (JQR, Monograph Series I, 1952); Rabin, *The Zadokite Documents* (²1958).

(b) Translation: Bardtke (§ 104) (1958), pp. 259–76; Burrows (§ 104) (1956), pp. 349–64; Charles, *Fragments of a Zadokite Work* (1912) = *The Apocrypha and Pseudepigrapha of the OT* II (1913), pp. 785–834; Dupont-Sommer (§ 104) (1959), pp. 129–78; (1961), pp. 114–63; Gaster (§ 104) (1957), pp. 71–94, 108–113; Habermann (§ 104) (1959), pp. 77–88; Maier (§ 104) (1960) I, pp. 46–70; II, pp. 40–62; Riessler (§ 76) (1928), pp. 920–41, 1323–25; Staerk, *Die jüdische Gemeinde des Neuen Bundes in Damaskus. Übersetzung der von Schechter veröffentlichten Geniza-Texte mit Noten* (BFChrTh 27, 3, 1922); Sutcliffe (§ 104) (1960), pp. 132–48; Vellas, *Τα εβραϊκα χειρογραφα της κοινοτητος της Δαμασκου* (1961).

Cf. also Literature §§ 104, 105.

The main part of the document (CD)[1] generally known as the 'Damascus Document', the 'Zadokite Work', 'The Writing of the Community of the New Covenant in the land of Damascus' or the like, was discovered towards the end of the nineteenth century in two fragments of manuscripts from the Geniza, that is the storeroom or lumber-room, of the Ezra Synagogue in Cairo. The two run in part parallel to one another, and in part thus fill in one another's gaps, and they belong respectively to the ninth to tenth centuries, and to the eleventh to twelfth. They were published in 1910 by Schechter under the title 'Fragments of a Zadokite Work', and, as may be seen from the rich literature on the subject, of which only a small selection is given below,[2] gave rise at that time to lively discussions as to their origin and date. But though this discovery was made half

---

[1] Cf. above, p. 645, n. 1.
[2] Eisler, 'The Sadoqite Book of the New Covenant. Its Date and Origin' *Occident and Orient [Gaster Anniversary Volume]* (1936), pp. 110–43; Ginzberg, *Eine unbekannte jüdische Sekte,* Part I (1922); Gressmann, 'Eine neuentdeckte jüdische Schrift aus der Zeit Jesu Christi' Internat. Wochenschrift für Wiss., Kunst und Technik 5 (1911), cols. 257–66; Hvidberg, *Menigheden af den Nye Pagt i Damaskus* (1928); 'Die 390 Jahre der sogen. Damaskusschrift' ZAW 51 (1933), pp. 309–11; Ed. Meyer, *Die Gemeinde des Neuen Bundes im Lande Damaskus: eine jüdische Schrift aus der Seleukidenzeit* (AAB 1919, 6, 1919); Moore, 'The Covenanters of Damaskus: a Hitherto Unknown Jewish Sect' HThR 4 (1911), pp. 330–77; Preisker, 'Zum Streit um die Geniza-Texte der jüdischen Gemeinde des Neuen Bundes in Damaskus' ThStKr 98/99 (1926), pp. 295–318; Bo Reicke, *The Jewish 'Damascus Documents' and the New Testament* (SyBU 6, 1946); Schousboe, *La secte juive de l'Alliance Nouvelle au Pays de Damas et le Christianisme Naissant* (1942).

a century before the beginning of the Qumrān finds, this work, just as much as the 'Manual of Discipline', the 'Habakkuk Commentary' and other works, belongs among the products of the Qumrān community and must therefore be treated here with them. These fragments from the Cairo Geniza have the closest points of contact with a number of the scrolls which have now come to light near Qumrān, as for example in the fact that in both the opposing figures of the Teacher of Righteousness[3] and the Prophet of Lies play a great part. But quite apart from this, remnants of at least eight copies of this work have now been found in caves 4, 5 (Milik, RB 63 (1956), p. 61; *Ten Years of Discovery* (1959), p. 38) and 6 (Baillet, RB 63 (1956), pp. 55, 513–23, Pl. II). So the suggestion[4] which was made soon after the discovery of the Qumrān scrolls, in view of the relationship between the main part of the Damascus Document published in 1910 and some of these scrolls, that this work too belonged to the products of the Qumrān community and must have come into existence like its other writings between about 150 B.C. and A.D. 68, has become a certainty. It also makes very probable[5] the assumption that 'Damascus' in the Damascus Document is a secret name for Qumrān suggested by Amos v, 26, 27. At the same time there is resolved the dispute which went on in a lively manner during the first three decades after Schechter's publication concerning the dating of the Damascus Document. Datings ranged from the second century B.C. to the eighth century A.D., and the matter is now settled in favour of those who maintained the greater age of the work.

The larger fragment from the Cairo Geniza, text A, contains eight sheets written on both sides, i.e. sixteen pages. After a summons directed to *all who know righteousness* to pay attention and to take heed *to the deeds of God who will bring all flesh to responsibility and will execute judgment on all those who blaspheme him* (p. 1, lines 1–2), it has a retrospect on the origin of the congregation of the New Covenant. 390 years after God has given Israel into the hand of Nebuchadnezzar, so we read, he has visited her. *Then there sprouted from Israel and Aaron the root of a plant . . . and they recognized that they were sinful men, and they were like blind men . . . 20 years, and God took heed of their doings . . . and raised up for them a Teacher of Righteousness*[6] (מורה צדק) *to lead them in the way of his heart,* while *the man of mockery* (איש הלצון) *. . . gave Israel water of lies to drink and led them astray in a trackless waste* (p. 1, lines 7–15). On p. 2, lines 2–13 there follow first expositions in more general terms concerning the contrast between the pious man chosen by God and the godless who is rejected by him; then on p. 2, line 14 to p. 8, line 21 a survey of the history of Israel which stands under the sign of that contrast, beginning with the fall of the angels and the flood and ending with the emigration of the congregation of the New Covenant to Damascus, or more correctly with a prospect of the final age. On p. 4, lines 2–4 it emphasises *The priests, they are those ready for repentance in*

---

[3] See above, p. 392, n. 3; p. 651; p. 659. Lit. § 126.

[4] Bo Reicke, 'Die Ta'āmire-Schriften und die Damaskus-Fragmente' StTh 2 (1949/50), pp. 45–70.

[5] Cross, *The Ancient Library of Qumrân* (1958), pp. 59 f., n. 46; Sutcliffe, *The Monks of Qumran* (1960), pp. 10 etc.

[6] Weingreen, 'The Title Môrēh Ṣeḏeḳ' JSSt 6 (1961), pp. 162–74. Lit. § 126.

Israel, who leave the land of Judah, and the Levites, they are those who join them-
selves to them, and the sons of Zadok, they are the elect of Israel, those who are named
by name, who remain firm at the end of the days. And on p. 6, line 5, it names as the
foremost guardians of the Law *those ready for repentance in Israel who have left the*
land of Judah and have migrated to the land of Damascus; p. 6, line 7 interprets the
staff of a ruler (מחוקק) of Num. xxi, 18 and p. 7, lines 18–19 the star coming
out from Jacob of Num. xxiv, 17 as referring to the *Teacher of the Law* (דורש
התורה) *who has come to Damascus.* P. 8, lines 11–12 indicates *the chief of the*
kings of Yawan as the instrument of punishment chosen by God for the carrying
out of his wrath on the godless.

Some isolated legal precepts appear already in pp. 1–8 of text A, but the main
body of them appears only in pp. 9–16. There is here a varied succession of
precepts concerning taking of oaths, giving witness, the office of judge, the
keeping holy of the sabbath, the duties of the overseer of the camp, the keeping
of the festivals mentioned in the *book of the time division according to its jubilees*
and its weeks (p. 16, lines 3–4), i.e. in the book of Jubilees (§ 91), and other such
material.

Text B consists of a leaf written on both sides, i.e. two pages. In its first half
(p. 1, lines 1–34a), it runs in some measure parallel to p. 7, line 5–p. 8, line 21
of text A, but in its second half (p. 1, line 34b–p. 2, line 34) it goes beyond text A.
Here we have a discussion first of the terrible fate of the betrayers of the *New*
Covenant in the land of Damascus (בברית החדשה בארץ דמשק), and then of the
fortunate lot of the pious who are ready to repent. But since in text A, p. 8,
line 21, the beginning of the threat which applies to the betrayer is preserved,
it may be affirmed with certainty that text A likewise contained this threat
and probably also the promise which follows it in text B.

We should mention particularly, from the special material in text B, the
sentence on p. 2, lines 13–15 *And from the day when the Teacher of the community*
(or *the unique teacher* (?), יורה היחיד) *was taken away to the destruction of all*
the men of war who went with the man of the lie, there are about forty years. This
gives us a vivid example of the eschatological tension in the Damascus community, for, as p. 1, line 35–p. 2, line 1 shows, the here expected end of the
adherents of the man of the lie coincides with the appearance of the *Messiah*
from Aaron and from Israel (משיח מאהרן ומישראל). In addition, these forty years,
together with the 390 and 20 years mentioned in text A, p. 1, lines 5–6, 10,
have played an important role in the discussion of the date of origin of the work
and the history of the community from which it derives. Of the fragmentary
copies of the Damascus Document found, as was noted on p. 650, in Qumrān
caves 4, 5 and 6, two from cave 4 are sufficiently well preserved for it to be possible to say something about the relationship between their text and that of the
pages which came from the Cairo Geniza. In general the text of cave 4 agrees
with codex A from the Geniza; but it amplifies it at the beginning and end, and
also adds in the main section some precepts which are there missing. According to
Milik, *Ten Years of Discovery* (1959), pp. 151 f., the fragments of the Damascus
Document from cave 4 together with the pages deriving from the Cairo Geniza
provide a reliable basis for the reconstruction of the original form of this work.

It is clear enough that the Damascus Document has much in common with the Manual of Discipline. The only question is how these common features are to be explained, and that means how we are to think of the mutual relationship as regards age and dependence of the two *rules*. We are still a long way from an assured answer to this question. The variety of views concerning the point is such that we cannot here give a survey of them, and so it must suffice to mention three recent expressions of opinion. Butler[7] rightly explains why it is that there is so much hesitation in giving a clear answer to the question. It is because the two works are clearly not in themselves unities, but contain elements of differing age. He considers that the Damascus Document attests a stage of development in the Qumrān community earlier than that attested by the Manual of Discipline. Rowley's view[8] is similar to this. On the other hand, Guilbert[9] holds to the view which has hitherto been predominant, namely that the Manual of Discipline is to be dated earlier than the Damascus Document.

§ 107. THE WAR SCROLL

Literature: (a) Text: *The Dead Sea Scrolls of the Hebrew University* (§ 104), pp. 35–6, Pls. 16–34: 'The War of the Sons of Light with the Sons of Darkness'; on this cf. Milik, RB 62 (1955), pp. 597–601; *Qumran Cave I* (§ 104), pp. 135 f., No. 33, Pl. XXXI: 'La Guerre des Fils de Lumière contre les Fils des Ténèbres (1 QM); Yadin, מגילת מלחמת בני אור בבני חשך (²1957).

(b) Other Works: Bardtke (§ 104) (1958), pp. 215–33; Brongers, *De Rol van de Strijd* (*De Handschriften van de Dode Zee in Nederlandse Vertaling*) (1960); Burrows (§ 104) (1956), pp. 390–9; Carmignac, *La Règle de la Guerre des Fils de Lumière contre les Fils de Ténèbres* (1958); 'Concordance hébraïque de la "Règle de la Guerre" ' RQ 1 (1958/59), pp. 7–50; Carmignac and Guilbert (§ 104), I, pp. 81–125 (Carmignac); Dupont-Sommer (§ 104) (1959), pp. 175–211; 1961, pp. 164–97; Gaster (§ 104) (1957), pp. 261–84, 293–8; Habermann (§ 104) (1959), pp. 95–108; Maier (§ 104) (1960), I, pp. 123–48; II, pp. 111–36; van der Ploeg, *Le Rouleau de la Guerre. Traduit et annoté avec une introduction* (1959); Sutcliffe (§ 104) (1960), pp. 204–33; Yadin, *The Scroll of the War of the Sons of Light against the Sons of Darkness. Edited with Commentary and Introduction.* Translated from the Hebrew by Batya and Chaim Rabin (1962).

Cf. Literature § 104.

This scroll consists of 19 or 20 columns and is relatively undamaged. Its first complete word is המלחמה *the war*, to be filled out to something like [וזה סרך לסדר] המלחמה (*This is the rule for the ordering*) of the war, or [וזה ספר סרך] המלחמה (*And this is the book of the rule of*) the war. It goes on to mention the attack of the sons of light on the sons of darkness, and hence is known as the scroll or writing of the war of the sons of light against the sons of darkness, or simply as the War Scroll (1QM, p. 645, n. 1). In I, 1–10 it names

[7] 'The Chronological Sequence of the Scrolls of Qumran Cave One' RQ 2 (1959/60), pp. 533–9.
[8] 'Some Traces of the History of the Qumran Sect' ThZ 13 (1957), pp. 530–40, cf. p. 539; 'The Qumran Sect and Christian Origins' BJRL 44 (1961/2), pp. 111–56, cf. p. 138. Lit. § 126.
[9] Carmignac and Guilbert, *Les Textes de Qumrân*, I (1961), p. 15.

the groups which belong to the two opposing parties. Since these lines unfortunately have some gaps and so the understanding of the already ambiguous
text is made more difficult, the statements made have been variously interpreted.
But at any rate there are named as the sons of light the Levites, Judaeans and
Benjaminites, while as the sons of darkness there appear the army of Belial, the
host of Edom, Moab, of the Ammonites, the army of the inhabitants of Philistia,
the hosts of the Kittim of Assyria and the breakers of the covenant who support
these groups, i.e. apostate Jews. The book gives precisely worked out military
arrangements for the struggle reckoned as lasting 40 years between the two
groups, in which at first the sons of light will be three times victorious, and then
the sons of darkness will three times get the upper hand, but on the seventh
occasion the victory will fall to the sons of light (I, 11–16). Here in a remarkable
mingling of sober technical military precepts and of utopian and eschatological
religious ideas, a very significant role is assigned to the priests with their songs
and prayers. In II, 1–16 there follow injunctions for the uninterrupted carrying
on of the altar service and a precise survey of the measures necessary for preparation for the war, as well as of the order of the battles against the individual
enemies. Directions concerning the war trumpets (III, 1–11), the standards
(III, 13–V, 2), the weapons (V, 3–14), the order of the battle lines, the duties
of the individual sections of troops as well as the age and purity of their members
(V, 16–VII, 7), the duties of the priests and the significance of the various
trumpet signals given by them (VII, 9–IX, 9), the tactical manœuvres of troops
specially armed and standing under the protection of the archangel (IX, 10–18)
all follow. X, 1–XIV, 1 has prayers and exhortations which, it appears, the high
priest is to speak before the beginning of the battle, while XIV, 2–18 contains a
prayer due to be spoken after the victory. Instructions concerning prayers and
addresses by the high priest and the other priests are also to be found in XV, 1–
XVI, 1, and likewise the conclusion of the scroll, XVI, 3–XIX, 13 is concerned
with the priests' share in the battle, for here there is detail of further trumpet
signals which they are to give, and new prayers and addresses which they are
to pronounce.

In spite of many features which this War Scroll has in common with the other
Qumrān writings, particularly the Manual of Discipline, the Damascus Document, the Hymn Scroll and the Habakkuk Commentary, it differs from them in
the fact that it anticipates the victory of the good cause over the evil not as they
do entirely or primarily as a result of God's intervention, but regarding as essential the very determined and energetic co-operation of men for the attainment of
this goal. The difference may be explained on the grounds that this War Scroll
came into being outside the more quietistically inclined Qumrān community, or
that it came into being at a definite stage of its history when it was especially
activistic in outlook. But such an assumption is by no means necessary, either
in the one form or the other. The peculiarity of the War Scroll may rather be
due to the fact that the eschatological tension with which the whole Qumrān
community was imbued had reached a particularly high level in one of its
members or in one such group, and could only express itself in warlike pictures
such as this scroll offers. It is natural then to assume that its author—or authors

if we should think of a group work—had been in military service before his entry into the Qumrān community, and brought with him his very detailed technical military knowledge. Hans Bardtke, in a lecture delivered in 1959 to the Old Testament Congress in Oxford and since published,[1] has compared this War Scroll with the section dealing with Israelite warfare in a Hebrew codex written in about A.D. 1600, but certainly using older originals, perhaps very much older material. He has in this made a contribution to the better understanding of this remarkable military manual.

The high regard which this 'Book of War' must have enjoyed in the Qumrān community is shown by the information given by Milik in RB 62 (1955), p. 598 and by Hunzinger in RB 63 (1956), p. 67, that in addition to the copy found in 1947 in the Qumrān cave 1, of which we have just considered the contents, fragments have been found in cave 4 of four further copies of this work and these were published in 1957 by Hunzinger.[2] Fragments of an apocryphal work, which, according to Baillet in RB 63 (1956), p. 54, is reminiscent of the War Scroll, have come to light in cave 2.

§ 108. THE HYMN SCROLL AND SIMILAR COLLECTIONS OF SONGS AND PRAYERS

Literature: (i) Text: *The Dead Sea Scrolls of the Hebrew University* (§ 104), pp. 37–9, Pls. 35–58: 'The Thanksgiving Scroll'; on this cf. Milik, RB 62 (1955), p. 601; *Qumran Cave I* (§ 104), pp. 132–4, Nos. 30–1, Pl. XXX: 'Textes liturgiques?'; pp. 136–8, No. 35, Pl. XXXI: 'Recueil de Cantiques d'action de grâces (1 QH)'; pp. 138–41, No. 36, Pl. XXXII: 'Recueil d'Hymnes'; pp. 141–3, Nos. 37–40, Pls. XXXII, XXXIII: 'Compositions Hymniques(?)'.

(ii) Other Works: Bardtke (§ 104) (1958), pp. 233–58; Burrows (§ 104) (1956), pp. 400–15; Carmignac, 'Remarques sur le texte des Hymnes de Qumran' Bibl 39 (1958), pp. 139–55; 'Compléments au texte des Hymnes de Qumrân' RQ 2 (1959/60), pp. 267–76, 549–67; Carmignac and Guilbert (§ 104) I, pp. 127–280 (Carmignac); Dupont-Sommer, 'Le Livre des Hymnes découverts près de la Mer Morte (1 QH)' Semitica 7 (1957); (§ 104) (1959), pp. 217–66; (1961), pp. 198–254; Gaster (§ 104) (1957), pp. 131–97, 201–17; Habermann (§ 104) (1959), pp. 115–44; Holm-Nielsen, *Hodayot. Psalms from Qumran* (Acta Theologica Danica 2, 1960); Licht, *The Thanksgiving Scroll. Text, Introduction, Commentary and Glossary* [Hebr.], (1957); Maier (§ 104) (1960) I, pp. 71–122; II, pp. 111–36; Mansoor, *The Thanksgiving Hymns. Translated and Annotated with an Introduction* (Studies on the Texts of the Desert of Juda III, 1961); van Selms, *De Rol der Lofprijzingen vertaald en toegelicht* (1957); Sutcliffe (§ 104) (1960), pp. 184–203; van der Woude, *De Dankpsalmen* (1957). Cf. Literature § 104.

The manuscript as we now have it consists of 18 incomplete and in part badly damaged columns, together with a number of small fragments. It was probably originally divided into two scrolls. Since the individual poems which

[1] 'Eine der Kriegsrolle von Qumrān verwandte Literaturgattung im Codex XXVIII der Leipziger Sammlung' SVT VII (1960), pp. 292–308.
[2] 'Fragmente einer älteren Fassung des Buches Milḥamā aus Höhle 4 von Qumrān' ZAW 68 (1957), pp. 131–51.

it contains, some 30 to 40 in number,[1] for the most part begin with אודכה אדוני *I thank thee, Lord,* or with ברוך אתה אדוני *Praised be thou, O Lord,* it is normally called the 'Thanksgiving Scroll', but in view of the nature and content of the poems, it might also be called the 'Scroll of songs of confession of faith'. It is in many respects reminiscent of the Old Testament Psalter. Like the latter it is a collection of religious songs, and the poems which it contains reveal great similarity to the psalms, and in particular to those which belong to the three types, individual song of lamentation, individual song of thanksgiving, and hymn. They in fact repeat many expressions and sentences from such psalms. It can scarcely be doubted that we have utterances from one or several members of the Qumrān community. The dualistic contrast between God and Belial, between the children of light and the children of darkness, as well as the strongly marked consciousness of living in the final age or at any rate shortly before its arrival—features which are characteristic of the other Qumrān writings—also give their stamp to this scroll. The poems are characterised by fervent thanks that the one who is praying has been chosen by God and graciously preserved by him from all the persecutions, often very menacing, of the godless; by moving testimonies to the exalted majesty of God on the one hand and to the impermanence and sinfulness of man on the other, as well as by touching confessions of trustful faith in an eternal salvation. This gives them a peculiar charm, as may be seen, for example, in II, 20–30 which begins:

> [20] *I thank thee, Lord*
> *that thou hast set my soul in the bundle of the living[2]*
> *and hast protected me from all the slings of the pit;*

or in II, 31–8, which opens with the lines:

> [31] *I thank thee, Lord,*
> *that thine eye has watched over my soul*
> *and that thou hast saved me from the zeal of the liar,*
> *that [32]out of the band of the blasphemers thou hast delivered*
> *the soul of the poor man, whom they wished to bring to an end;*

or III,[3] 19–36, of which the first third (lines 19–24) runs as follows:

> [19]*I thank thee, Lord,*
> *that thou hast delivered my soul from the pit*
> *and from the hell of destruction,*
> *[20]hast led me up to an eternal height.*
> *So I may walk in an unlimited plain*
> *and know, that there is hope for him,*
> *whom [21]thou has made out of dust for eternal fellowship.*

---

[1] On the original order of the poems and on their metrical structure, cf. Carmignac in Carmignac and Guilbert (§ 104), I (1961), pp. 127–282, and especially pp. 281 f. where he contrasts his own arrangement of the poems with that given by Sukenik in his edition (§ 104).

[2] Eissfeldt, *Der Beutel der Lebendigen* (BAL 105, 6, 1960).

[3] On III, 9 f., see above, p. 646, n. 4.

> *The perverse spirit thou hast cleansed from much sin,*
>   *that he may enter into the place* [22]*with the host of holy ones*
>   *and come into fellowship with the community of the heavenly ones.*
> *An eternal lot thou hast cast for man with the spirits* [23]*of knowledge,*
>   *that he may extol thy name in the community with rejoicing*
>   *and relate thy wonders before all thy works.*
> *But I, a product* [24]*of clay, what am I?*
>   *Kneaded with water; what am I worth and what power is mine?*

or IV, 5–V, 4 where we read a passage reminiscent of Christian ideas of God's gracious mercy:

> [34]*I said:*
>   *Through my transgression I have set myself far from thy covenant.*
> *But at the remembrance of the power of thy hand*
>   [35]*together with the immeasurable nature of thy mercy*
>   *I arose and stood upright.*
> *And my spirit gained firmness before attack*
>   [36]*for I support myself upon thy grace and the immeasurable nature of thy*
>   *mercy.*
> *For thou forgivest sin*
>   *and cleansest man from guilt by thy righteousness.*

It appears as if the poems bear the marks of a definite personality, and it has hence been thought that it is the 'Teacher of Righteousness' mentioned in other Qumrān writings, the founder of the community, who is here speaking. The possibility of this assumption cannot be disputed. But perhaps the 'I' of these poems is at least in most cases not in reality a single personality, but a collective entity, the Qumrān community as a whole, so that the question concerning the 'I' of the Psalms (p. 115) reappears in these poems.[4]

This collection of poems enjoyed great popularity in the Qumrān community. This is revealed by the fact that, as is reported by Milik in RB 62 (1955), p. 601, and by Strugnell in RB 63 (1956), p. 64, among the texts which have come to light in cave 4 there are fragments of no fewer than six copies of this collection. These texts do not all have the poems in the same order as in that from cave 1, and they thus provide a parallel to the copies of the biblical Psalter found in Qumrān caves 4 and 11[5] where there are deviations from the order of the individual poems in the Psalter (Baillet, RB 63 (1956), p. 55; Hunzinger, ThLZ 85 (1960), col. 151). In addition, there were also in the Qumrān community various other collections of poems. Remains of such collections have been published in *Qumran Cave I*, pp. 138–43, Nos 36–40, Pls XXXII–XXXIII, and similar finds in caves 3 and 4 are mentioned by Baillet and Strugnell in RB 63 (1956), pp. 54 f., 64. In addition, Allegro reports in RB 63 (1956), pp. 63, 65, on fragments from cave 4 of liturgical laments over Jerusalem reminiscent of the book of Lamentations (§ 69); and he and Strugnell, *ib.*, pp. 63, 65, mention

---

[4] Mowinckel, 'Jeg'et i Qumran salmene' NTT 62 (1961), pp. 28–46.
[5] Cf. Sanders, Lit. § 126 (on p. 683, n. 17).

fragments of a scroll containing 'Psalms of Joshua'. Strugnell (*ib.*, p. 65) also mentions, in addition to other hymnic works, a collection of poems which are not concerned, as is elsewhere the case, with the individual pious man, but with the people Israel, and present retrospects of its history. He has also published[6] and discussed two larger sections of another work surviving in fragments of at least four scrolls from cave 4. He calls this 'The Angelic Liturgy from Qumrân, 4Q—Rule of the Songs for the Sabbath sacrifice', following the opening of a characteristic passage in it: *From the instructor.*[7] *The Song of the Sabbath sacrifice for the seventh Sabbath on the 16th of the 2nd month. Praise God all ye angels!* It is concerned with angels and heavens to a greater extent than the other Qumrân writings. Fragments have also survived of a whole series of other liturgical works: from cave 4, formulae for the morning and evening prayer and directions for the cleansing ritual (Hunzinger RB 63 (1956), p. 67; ThLZ 85 (1960), col. 152); from caves 1 and 4 the liturgy of the 'Three Tongues of Fire' (QC I, pp. 130–2, No. 29, Pl. XXX; Strugnell, RB 63 (1956), p. 64); from cave 4, a formula for the baptismal rite (Strugnell, RB 63 (1956), p. 64); from cave 1, one for the Day of Atonement[8] and apparently also for other festivals such as the Feast of Weeks (QC I, pp. 136, 152–5, Nos. 34, 34[bis] Pl. XXXI).[9] Baillet[10] (1961) has published substantial sections of columns I–VII of one of the liturgical collections which have come to light in cave 4, namely the דברי המארות *Words of the luminaries (Stars)*—so the title which has been preserved.[11]

§ 109. THE HABAKKUK 'COMMENTARY' AND SIMILAR 'COMMENTARIES'

Literature: The Dead Sea Scrolls of St. Mark's Monastery I (§ 104), pp. XIX–XXI, Pls. LV–LXI: 'The Habakkuk Commentary'; *Qumran Cave I* (§ 104), pp. 77–80, No. 14, Pl. XV: 'Commentaire de Michée'; pp. 81–2, No. 16, Pl. XV; 'Commentaire de Psaumes'; p. 80, No. 15, Pl. XV: 'Commentaire de Sophonie; Bardtke (§ 104) (1953), pp. 125–31; Brownlee, *The Text of Habakkuk in the Ancient Commentary from Qumran* (JBL, Monograph. Ser. 11, 1959); Burrows (§ 104) (1956), pp. 365–70; Cantera Ortiz de Urbina, *El Comentario de Habacuc de Qumran* (1960); Dupont-Sommer (§ 104) (1959), pp. 270–80; (1961), pp. 258–68; Elliger, *Studien zum Habakuk-Kommentar vom Toten Meer* (1953); Gaster (§ 104) (1957), pp. 235–41, 249–53; Habermann (§ 104) (1959), pp. 37–49; Maier

---

[6] Strugnell, 'The Angelic Liturgy at Qumrân—4Q Serek Šîrôt 'Olat Haššabbāt' SVT VII (1960), pp. 318–45, 1 Pl.; Dupont-Sommer (§ 104) (1961), pp. 329–35. Lit. § 126.

[7] Strugnell renders 'sage' and compares RB 63 (1956), p. 61.

[8] Lehmann ' "Yom Kippur" in Qumran' RQ 3 (1961/62), pp. 117–24.

[9] Bardtke (§ 104) (1958), pp. 288–9; Burrows (§ 104) (1958), p. 399; Dupont-Sommer (§ 104) (1959), p. 346; (1961), pp. 335–6; Gaster (§ 104), pp. 289–90, 298; Habermann (§ 104) (1959), pp. 163–4.

[10] 'Un recueil Liturgique de Qumrân Grotte 4: "Les paroles des luminaires" ' RB 68 (1961), pp. 195–250, Pls. XXIV–XXVIII. Lit. § 126.

[11] According to Talmon, 'The "Manual of Benedictions" of the Sect of the Judaean Desert' RQ 2 (1959/60), pp. 475–500, the benedictions found in several Qumrân scrolls belong to a collection of daily and festal prayers arranged in calendar order.

(§ 104) (1960) I, pp. 149–56; II, pp. 137–51; Schoeps (p. 611, n. 2); Segert, 'Zur Habakuk-Rolle aus dem Fund vom Toten Meer' ArOr 21 (1953), pp. 218–39; 22 (1954), pp. 99–113, 444–59; 23 (1955), pp. 178–83, 364–73, 575–619; Sutcliffe (§ 104) (1960), pp. 172–8; van 't Land and van der Woude, *De Habakukrol van 'Ain Fašḥa. Tekst en vertaling* (1954); van der Woude, *Bijbelcommentaren en Bijbelse verhalen. De Handschriften van de Dode Zee in Nederlandse vertaling* (1958); Vellas, *Τα Υπομνημα εις το βιβλιον του Αββακουμ* (1958). Cf. Literature §§ 104, 126.

The actualisation of individual passages from Old Testament books and particularly those of a prophetic and apocalyptic nature, that is to say the interpretation of statements which in their context apply to their contemporary situation so as to relate them to conditions and ideas which are determinative for the later readers, appears already in some canonical and extracanonical books of the Old Testament. Thus Dan. ix understands the 70 years, mentioned in Jer. xxv, 11–12; xxix, 10 to indicate the length of the Babylonian exile, as meaning weeks of years, i.e. 490 years, and as referring to his own time, i.e. *c.* 165 B.C., and the books of Enoch, Jubilees and Test. XII Patriarchs contain many similar examples. But it is only with the Qumrān discoveries that we have come to know works which set out to actualise whole biblical books or groups of related passages from them, and do this by adding to the individual words or sentences or sections of these books an interpretation, often introduced by פשר *pešer,* פשרו *pišrô, interpretation, its interpretation,* applying these statements to the contemporary situation. This kind of work is described as 'Commentary' or as 'Midrash'[1] or even as 'Pesher', which has the advantage that this word is used by these works themselves, admittedly not as a title but at any rate as the technical term for the interpretation of the text in question. In addition to the well-preserved scroll of the Habakkuk Commentary (1QpHab) found in 1947 in cave 1, a whole series of larger and smaller fragments of such commentaries have since come to light in the same cave and in other caves (Allegro, Baillet, Skehan in RB 63 (1956), pp. 62–3, 54, 59). This shows what favour this type of work must have enjoyed in the Qumrān community, though it cannot be clearly decided whether these are authoritative expositions, deriving perhaps from the *true teacher* or private works of an edifying character.[2]

The Commentary on Habakkuk contains thirteen columns. Out of the three chapters in the book of Habakkuk it deals with only the first two headed at i, 1 with *The oracle which Habakkuk the prophet saw,* and thus leaves out of consideration the third chapter, *The prayer of the prophet Habakkuk* (iii, 1). It must remain uncertain whether the Commentary originally covered the whole book of Habakkuk and has lost its last third, the interpretation of Hab. iii, or whether the commentator himself refrained from interpreting Hab. iii because it seemed to him less suitable for the purpose than Hab. i–ii, or whether he had a book of Habakkuk containing only i–ii (pp. 420–1). The nature of the commentary will be most clearly seen if we give three samples from it, the first two from the beginning, and the third from the end. (No note is here made of gaps in the text as it occurs in the scroll where these can be filled in with certainty.) On i, 5 it

---

[1] Cf. above, p. 534, n. 16. Lit. § 126.
[2] So van der Ploeg, *Bijbelverklaring te Qumrān* (MAA 23 No. 8, 1960).

appears that the text which the commentator had before him read not, as in 𝔐 בגוים *among the nations*, but בוגדים *betrayers*. The text here is concerned with a terrible work of Yahweh which appears unbelievable and is near at hand. The explanation is added: *The interpretation of this word refers to the betrayers with the man of the lie* (איש הכזב)—*for they have not believed the words of the true teacher* (מורה הצדקה) *from the mouth of God—and to the betrayers of the new covenant* (II, 1–4). In i, 6, the prophecy of the coming of *the Chaldeans* (הַכַּשְׂדִּים) *that bitter and hasty nation* receives this explanation: *Its interpretation refers to the Kittim* (הכתיאים), *who are swift and heroes in battle* etc. (II, 10–13). Both these interpretations bring into the Habakkuk text matters which affect the period of the commentator. The first speaks of the contrast between the *man of the lie* and the *true teacher* which dominates the thought of the Qumrān community; the second mentions the appearance of the Kittim who were then throwing the world into anguish and unquiet, whether they are to be understood as the Seleucids or the Romans.[3] The explanation of ii, 20: *Silence before him all the world* is: *Its interpretation refers to all the peoples which serve stone and wood, and on the day of judgement God will destroy all worshippers of idols and the godless from the earth* (XIII, 1–4), this provides evidence of the eschatological tension which, as we have seen repeatedly, filled the Qumrān community.

'Commentaries' on other books of the Old Testament or on individual sections from them have already been published[4] for Isa.,[5] Hos.,[6] Mic.,[7] Nah.,[8]

---

[3] Roth, 'The Era of the Habakkuk Commentary' VT 11 (1961), pp. 451–5.

[4] Allegro (RB 63 (1956), p. 62) indicates that the Psalm-commentary found in Cave 4, which is concerned mainly with Ps. xxxvii, also deals with the opening of Ps. xlv. I. Rabinowitz, 'The Existence of a hitherto unknown Interpretation of Psalm cvii among the Dead Sea Scrolls' BA 14 (1951), pp. 50–2, believes that he can prove the existence of a commentary also on Ps. cvii among the Qumrān texts, seeing as a commentary the work QC I, pp. 100–1, No. 25, Pl. XX, assigned tentatively on p. 661 to the apocalypses. But this is hardly likely to be correct.

[5] Allegro, 'Further Messianic References in Qumran Literature' JBL 75 (1956), pp. 174–87, Pls. 1–4, cf. pp. 177–82, Pls. 2–3; 'More Isaiah Commentaries from Qumran's Fourth Cave' JBL 77 (1958), pp. 215–21, Pls. 1–3.
   Bardtke (§ 104) (1958), pp. 299–300; Burrows (§ 104) (1958), pp. 403–4; Dupont-Sommer (§ 104) (1959), pp. 286–8; (1961), pp. 274–6; Gaster (§ 104) (1957), pp. 345–8; Habermann (§ 104) (1959), pp. 150–1; Maier (§ 104) (1960), I, pp. 186–9; II, pp. 166–7. Lit. § 126.

[6] Allegro, 'Further Light on the History of the Qumran Sect' JBL 75 (1956), pp. 89–95, Pls. 1–4, cf. p. 93, Pl. 2; 'A Recently Discovered Fragment of a Commentary on Hosea from Qumran's Fourth Cave' JBL 78 (1959), pp. 142–7, Pl. 1; cf. Testuz, 'Deux fragments inédits des manuscrits de la Mer Morte' Semitica 5 (1955), pp. 37–8, 1 Pl., cf. p. 37, Fig. 2.
   Dupont-Sommer (§ 104) (1959), p. 289; (1961), pp. 276–8; Maier (§ 104) (1960), I, pp. 189–90; II, p. 167. Lit. § 126.

[7] QC I, pp. 77–80, No. 15, Pl. XV.
   Bardtke (§ 104) (1958), pp. 293–4; Burrows (§ 104) (1958), p. 404; Dupont-Sommer (§ 104) (1959), p. 289; (1961), p. 278; Gaster (§ 104) (1957), pp. 229, 247; Habermann (§ 104) (1959), pp. 151–3; Maier (§ 104) (1960) I, pp. 166–7; II, p. 153; Sutcliffe (§ 104) (1960), p. 179. Lit. § 126.

[8] Allegro, 'Further Light on the History of the Qumran Sect' JBL 75 (1956), pp. 89–95, Pls. 1–4, cf. pp. 90–3, Pl. 1; Cross, *The Ancient Library of Qumrân* (1958), pp. 91–4.
   Bardtke (§ 104) (1958), pp. 297–8; Burrows (§ 104) (1958), p. 404; Dupont-Sommer (§ 104) (1959), pp. 280–2; (1961), pp. 268–70; Gaster (§ 104) (1957), pp. 231, 248–9; Habermann (§ 104) (1959), p. 153; Sutcliffe (§ 104) (1960), pp. 180–1. Lit. § 126.

Zeph.,[9] and on Psalms xxxvii,[10] lvii,[11] lxviii.[11] The fragments discovered in several cases belong to more than one manuscript of the same commentary. Sometimes, as with Ps. lvii and Ps. lxviii, the fragments are very small and hardly make it possible to get an idea of the nature of the commentary; but relatively large sections of others have survived. This is true of the Commentary on Nahum (4QpNahum) of which the surviving fragments even allow the supposition that it contains allusions to the conflicts beginning in about 90 B.C. between Demetrius Eukairus and Alexander Jannaeus,[12] related by Josephus in *Ant.* XIII 14, 1–2 and *Bell.* I 4, 4–6. Even with the commentaries which have survived in a very fragmentary state, the pieces which we have are sufficient to establish that they too expounded the relevant biblical text in the light of the thought patterns of the Qumrān community, as does the Commentary on Habakkuk. Even the lamentably small scraps of the Micah Commentary (1QpMicah) fortunately allow us to recognise that the two entities mentioned in Micah i, 5, *Jacob-Samaria* and *Judah-Jerusalem*, are interpreted, the former as meaning the *speaker of lies* (מטיף הכזב) and the latter the *teacher of righteousness* (מורה הצדק) The fragments of the interpretation of Ps lxviii (1QpPs 68) not only contain three times the word פשרו *pišrô*, *its interpretation*, but also the name [כ]תיאים *Kittim*, and thus an expression in the Psalm, apparently *beast of the reeds* (v. 31), was clearly interpreted as referring to the Kittim. The fragment of the Zephaniah Commentary (1QpZeph), which contains parts of Zeph. i, 18–ii, 2 and of the interpretation of this passage, at least makes it clear that here too the interpretation was introduced with פשר *pešer*, *interpretation* and probably sought to indicate the people addressed in the Habakkuk text as the inhabitants of Judah.

With these commentaries we may place three fragmentary writings from cave 4 which apply certain passages or groups of passages from the Old Testament to the contemporary situation of the Qumrān community or to the future which it was awaiting, giving them or appearing to give them messianic interpretation. These are the 'Patriarchal Blessings',[13] the 'Florilegium'[14] and

[9] QC I, p. 80, No. 15, Pl. XV.
Bardtke (§ 104) (1958), p. 294; Dupont-Sommer (§ 104) (1959), p. 289; (1961), p. 278; Habermann (§ 104) (1959), p. 154. Lit. § 126.
[10] Allegro, 'A New Discovered Fragment of a Commentary on Psalm xxxvii from Qumran' PEQ 86 (1954), pp. 69–75, Pl. XVIII; 'Further Light on the History of the Qumran Sect' JBL 75 (1956), pp. 89–95, Pls. 1–4, cf. pp. 94–5, Pls. 3–4; Cross, *The Ancient Library of Qumrân* (1958), pp. 117 f.
Bardtke (§ 104) (1958), pp. 295–7; Burrows (§ 104) (1958), pp. 401–3; Dupont-Sommer (§ 104) (1959), pp. 282–5; (1961), pp. 270–3; Gaster (§ 104) (1957), pp. 243–5, 253–4; Habermann (§ 104) (1959), pp. 154–6; Sutcliffe (§ 104) (1960), pp. 182–3. Lit. § 126.
[11] QC I, pp. 81–2, No. 16, Pl. XV.
Bardtke (§ 104) (1958), p. 295. Lit. § 126.
[12] According to Milik, 'Le travail d'édition des manuscrits du Désert de Juda' SVT IV (1957), pp. 17–26, see p. 26, and Cross, *The Ancient Library of Qumrân* (1958), p. 92, Hyrcanus (הרקנוס) and Aemilius Scaurus (אמליוס), the Syrian governor in 62 B.C., are mentioned in a Mishmaroth text (pp. 648, 668) from Cave 4.
[13] Allegro, 'Further Messianic References in Qumran Literature' JBL 75 (1956), pp. 174–87, Pls. 1–4, cf. pp. 174–6, Pl. 1, I.
Bardtke (§ 104) (1958), p. 298; Burrows (§ 104) (1958), p. 401; Dupont-Sommer (§ 104) (1959), p. 328; (1961), pp. 314–15; Gaster (§ 104) (1957), p. 35; Habermann (§ 104) (1959), p. 149; Maier (§ 104) (1960), I, pp. 182–3; II, p. 164. Lit. § 126.

the 'Testimonia'.[15] So far as the published sections of these permit a pronouncement, they actualise (1) Gen. xlix, (2) II Sam. vii, 10b–14a, Ps. i, 1; ii, 1–2, and
(3) Deut. v, 28–9; xviii, 18–19; Num. xxiv, 15–17; Deut. xxxiii, 8–11 together
with Josh. vi, 26 or rather the Qumrān elaboration of Josh. vi, 26 undertaken
in the already mentioned 'Psalms of Joshua' (p. 657). In a broader sense, there
may also be assigned to this group of writings the collocation of passages from
the book of Isaiah (xl, 1–4; xli, 8–9; xlix, 13–17; lii, 1–3; liv, 4–10)
from cave 4, described by Allegro (RB 63 (1956), p. 63) as the Tanḥumim
Scroll from the description תנחומים *consolations* contained in one of these
extracts.

§ 110. THE APOCALYPSES

Literature: Qumran Cave I (§ 104), pp. 84–6, No. 19, Pl. XVI: 'Livre de Noé'; pp. 99–
100, No. 24, Pl. XX: 'Apocryphe Araméen'; pp. 100–1, No. 25, Pl. XX: 'Une prophétie
apocryphe (?)'; pp. 102–7, No. 27, Pls. XXI, XXII: 'Livre des Mystères'; pp. 134–5, No. 32,
Pl. XXXI: 'Déscription de la Jérusalem Nouvelle' (?).
    Cf. Literature § 104.

Although the Qumrān discoveries have so far provided us only with fragments of apocalyptic writings, the present position nevertheless makes it clear
that writings of this kind were much read in the Qumrān community. It is
further made very probable that at least some of these writings were also written
there. Among the remains of apocalypses found in Qumrān caves belong first
of all the fragments from Cave 1, published in QC I, pp. 84–6, No. 19, Pl. XVI
as 'Livre de Noé', fragments of the Book of Noah mentioned in Jub. x, 13;
xxi, 10 and elsewhere, one of the sources of the Ethiopic Enoch. If the order
suggested in QC I, p. 84 is correct, these fragments contain the following:
(1) a description of the depravity of mankind, (2) the entrance of the four
archangels, (3) the birth of Noah, (4) a song (by Methuselah?). Passages corresponding to the first two of these sections are to be found in Enoch vi–x, and
to the third in Enoch cvi, whereas the fourth finds no echo in the book of Enoch
as we have it. Fragments of a work in Aramaic similar to the Book of Noah have
been found in Cave 6 (Baillet, RB 63 (1956), p. 55).

---

[14] Allegro, 'Further Messianic References in Qumran Literature' JBL 75 (1956), pp. 174–
187, Pls. 1–4, cf. pp. 176–7, Pl. 1, II; 'Fragments of a Qumran Scroll of Eschatological
Midrāšîm' JBL 77 (1958), pp. 350–4, 1 Pl.
    Bardtke (§ 104) (1958), pp. 298–9; Burrows (§ 104) (1958), p. 410; Dupont-Sommer
(§ 104) (1959), pp. 325–7; (1961), pp. 310–14; Gaster (§ 104) (1957), pp. 351–2, 355–6;
Habermann (§ 104) (1959), p. 149; Maier (§ 104) (1960), I, pp. 185–6; II, pp. 165–6.
    Flusser, 'Two Notes on the Midrash on 2 Sam. vii' IEJ 9 (1959), pp. 99–109; Lane, 'A
New Commentary Structure in 4 Q Florilegium' JBL 78 (1959), pp. 343–6; Yadin, 'A
Midrash on 2 Sam. vii and Pss. i–iii (4 Q Florilegium)' IEJ 9 (1959), pp. 95–8. Lit. § 126.
[15] Allegro, 'Further Messianic References in Qumran Literature' JBL 75 (1956), pp. 174–
187, Pls. 1–4, cf. pp. 182–7, Pl. 4.
    Bardtke (§ 104) (1958), pp. 300–1; Burrows (§ 104) (1958), p. 400; Dupont-Sommer
(§ 104) (1959), pp. 329–30; (1961), pp. 315–19; Maier (§ 104) (1960), I, pp. 183–5; II, p. 165.
    Prigent, 'Quelques testimonia' ThZ 15 (1959), pp. 419–30; Treves, 'On the Meaning of
the Qumran Testimonia' RQ 2 (1959/60), pp. 569–71. Lit. § 126.

Also belonging to an apocalypse related to the book of Enoch are the eight Aramaic fragments of scrolls published in QC I, pp. 99–100, No. 24, Pl. XX. These speak of *clouds, thunderclaps, darknesses* and other natural phenomena and are thus reminiscent of Enoch ii, 3; xxiv, 2; xxvi, 1; lx, 20–1; lxix, 22–4. On the other hand it cannot be clearly decided whether the 14 Hebrew fragments, published in the same book on pp. 100–1, No. 25, Pl. XX, are remnants of a prophetic-apocalyptic writing or belong to another literary genre (pp. 648 f.). But it seems probable that we have here an utterance deriving from a prophet or ascribed to one, from the alternation which is to be found here as in many prophetic writings between the I of the author and the I of Yahweh. And with this there agree further the references to historical and geographical matters— *Samaria, Judah, Zion,* the *Shephelah.* According to the reports of Baillet (RB 63 (1956), p. 55), Milik (*ib.*, p. 61) and Starcky (*ib.*, p. 66), there have also come to light in caves 6 and 4 numerous fragments of apocalypses in Hebrew or Aramaic, related to the book of Enoch.

Another work which appears to be an apocalyptic pseudepigraphon is the one of which two columns, fragmentary but relatively well preserved, have come from cave 1 and pieces of two or even four copies from cave 4. The latter are indicated by Milik, RB 63 (1956), p. 61. The former are reproduced and explained in QC I, pp. 102–7, No. 27, Pls. XXI and XXII.[1] From the frequent occurrence in these fragments of the word ר *secret,* this work has been given there the title '*Book of Secrets*' (1QMyst; Myst=Mysteries). The book contains prospects of the certain and speedy coming of the *future secret* (רז נהיה I, 3), and in addition, reflections like those in Enoch xciv–ciii concerning the lot of the pious and the godless, and discussions reminiscent of IV Ezra of problems of life which are insoluble in this aeon and for this reason make the breaking in of the future secret necessary and certain. *Do not all nations hate injustice? And yet it is set in motion by them all. Does not there echo from the mouth of all nations the praise of truth? But is there a lip or a tongue which holds fast to it? What nation has pleasure in being oppressed by a stronger people? But where is there a people which has not oppressed its neighbour? Who has pleasure in being unjustly robbed of his livelihood? But where is there a people which has not unrighteously robbed another of its livelihood?* (I, 8–12). Remnants of an Aramaic book evidently similar to this Hebrew book of secrets have come to light, also in Cave 4, according to the note by Starcky in RB 63 (1956), p. 66.

To this group of apocalyptic literature we may also, in spite of the alternative possibility mentioned above (p. 648), assign an Aramaic work which evidently enjoyed great popularity. For, apart from the fragments already published from Caves 1 and 2,[2] several copies of it have also been found in Caves 4 and 5, according to QC I, p. 134 and RB 63 (1956), p. 66 (Starcky) and p. 55 (Milik). The words *pillar-base, pillars, door, wall, court, altar, sacrifice, priest* on the one hand, and *I saw that they should enter the Temple, that they should bring the bread*

---

[1] Bardtke (§ 104) (1958), p. 292; Burrows (§ 104) (1958), p. 398; Dupont-Sommer (§ 104) (1959), pp. 342–3; (1961), pp. 326–8; Gaster (§ 104) (1957), p. 291; Habermann (§104) (1959), pp. 157–9; Maier (§ 104) (1960), I, pp. 171–2; II, p. 153. Lit. § 126.
[2] Baillet, 'Fragments araméens de Qumrân 2. Description de la Jérusalem Nouvelle' RB 62 (1955), pp. 222–45, Pls. II–III.

on the other hand, make it probable that we have here a work which, like Ezek. xl–xlviii, described the new Jerusalem in a vision, and particularly its Temple and the cultus to be observed in it. It has probably been rightly described by the editors of the fragments from Caves 1 and 2 as 'Description of the New Jerusalem'. A similar apocalyptic work has also come to light in Cave 11 (Harding, PEQ 90 (1958), p. 17).

To the apocalyptic literature must also be assigned the Aramaic work, certainly deriving from the Qumrān community, of which a fragment has come into the possession of Michael Testuz,[3] though without its place of discovery being known. This clearly provides a glimpse of the longed-for final age, of which it is said: *All the righteous survive . . . and no lie shall thenceforth again be found.* The fragmentary work from Cave 4, with its title: *Words of the book which Michael spoke to the angels* (Starcky, RB 63 (1956), p. 66), must also be of an apocalyptic character. This may also be assumed for the fragments, likewise from Cave 4, of the 'Apocalypse of the Jubilees' which reveals some similarities to the Testament of Levi in the Testaments of the XII Patriarchs (§ 102) (Strugnell, RB 63 (1956), p. 65).

Finally, it must be noted that not only have passages from the biblical book of Daniel come to light at Qumrān, as mentioned on p. 521, and p. 683, but fragments also of a cycle of Daniel narratives similar to this book. Milik was able to report in 1956[4] that in Cave 4 fragments had been found of three Aramaic manuscripts containing a narrative like one of those in the book of Daniel. Here too Daniel offers a survey of world history, and first a retrospect extending from the Flood and the building of the tower of Babel, touching on Israel's Exodus from Egypt, and down to the exile of the Jews in 587 B.C. Then there is a prospect of the rule of four world empires and of the final age. To the Daniel cycle belongs also an Aramaic work, surviving in five fragments from Cave 4,[5] described as 'Prayer of Nabonidus' from its title, which as a result of several gaps in the text may at some points be variously interpreted: *The words of the prayer which Nabonai, king of Assyria and Babylon, the Great King, prayed when he was afflicted with an evil leprosy at the command of the Most High God in the city of Teiman[6]*—though the actual words of the prayer have not been preserved. This is an autobiographical statement by the king which begins immediately after the title just quoted—though again here uncertain at some points because of lacunae in the text: *I was afflicted with an evil leprosy for seven years, and dwelt far from men. But when I confessed my transgression and my sin to God, he forgave it. A seer, a Jew among the exiles in Babylon, instructed me in writing that I should give heed and great honour to the name of the Most High God.* Subsequently the work certainly related how he was healed by this God.

---

[3] Testuz, 'Deux Fragments inédites des manuscrits de la Mer Morte' Semitica 5 (1955), pp. 37–8, 1 Pl., cf. p. 38, Fig. 1.

[4] ' "Prière de Nabonide" et autres écrits d'un cycle de Daniel. Fragments araméens de Qumrân 4' RB 63 (1956), pp. 407–15, Pl. I, cf. pp. 411–15.

[5] Milik, RB 63 (1956), pp. 407–11, Pl. I; Ten Years of Discovery (1959), pp. 36 f.

Bardtke (§ 104) (1958), p. 301; Burrows (§ 104) (1958), p. 400; Dupont-Sommer (§ 104) (1959), pp. 337–8; (1961), pp. 321–5; Rudolf Meyer, 'Das Qumranfragment "Gebet des Nabonid" ' ThLZ 85 (1960), cols. 831–4. Cf. above, p. 523, n. 35. Lit. § 126.

[6] de Vaux, ' "Lévites" minéens et lévites israélites' *Junker-Festschr.*, (1961), pp. 265–73.

§ III. HAGGADIC NARRATIVE WORKS

Literature: Avigad and Yadin, *A Genesis Apocryphon from the Wilderness of Judaea* (1956); *Qumran Cave I* (§ 104), pp. 86 f. No. 20, Pl. XVII: 'Apocalypse de Lamech'; pp. 91–7, No. 22, Pls. XVIII and XIX: 'Dires de Moïse'; pp. 97–8, No. 23, Pl. XIX: 'Apocryphes en Araméen'.

Bardtke (§ 104) (1958), pp. 276–83; Burrows (§ 104), pp. 387–93; Dupont-Sommer (§ 104) (1959), pp. 297–306; (1961), pp. 284–94; Gaster (§ 104) (1957), pp. 330–43; Maier (§ 104) (1960) I, pp. 157–65; II, pp. 152–3.

Cf. Literature §§ 104, 126.

The seventh of the scrolls found in 1947 near Qumrān (p. 638) could not at first be unrolled, unlike the two texts of Isaiah, the Habakkuk Commentary, the Manual of Discipline, the Thanksgiving Hymns, and the War Scroll. From some scraps which had broken off and which suggested its nature, it was provisionally thought to be an apocalypse of Lamech, and so entitled. Eventually it was successfully unrolled, and it was then possible to reproduce in facsimile, in transcription into printed Hebrew letters and in English translation, columns II and XIX–XXII out of the twenty-two columns which are preserved in part only in fragments, whereas the content only of the remainder could be given at first. The work is an Aramaic translation or paraphrase of Genesis somewhat like a Targum, which, after the fashion of the book of Jubilees (§ 91), elaborates the biblical narrative with various motifs from other sources. Thus in Gen. xii it adds a description of Sarah's beauty, in Gen. xiii, 14–18[1] detailed topographical references, in Gen. xiv new place names and personal names. To the haggadic narrative works there belongs also the work similar to the book of Jubilees of which, according to Strugnell's report (RB 63 (1956), p. 65), fragments have come to light in Qumrān Cave 4, though the question must for the moment remain open as to whether we have here a source of the book of Jubilees or a later recension of it, or simply a similar work which argues in favour of a calendar deviating from that of the book of Jubilees. Likewise the Aramaic genealogy provided with chronological notes and carried through to the period of the judges, also found in Cave 4 according to Starcky (RB 63 (1956), p. 66), is probably to be included here.

Forty-nine fragments from Qumrān Cave 1, apparently from six columns which make up the beginning of a scroll, belong to a Hebrew work which, in *Qumran Cave I*, pp. 91–7, has been called 'The Words of Moses' (1QDM; DM = דברי משה *dibrê mōšeh, words of Moses*) or 'Little Deuteronomy' on the analogy of the name 'Little Genesis' for Jubilees; for it contains a speech by Moses and stands to Deuteronomy in roughly the same relationship as does the book of Jubilees to Genesis.[2] *In the fortieth year after the emigration of the Israelites from Egypt, in the eleventh month, on the first day of the month,* so we are here told, God summons Moses to mount Nebo and commands him to publish the

---

[1] de Langhe, 'La terre promise et le paradis d'après l'Apocryphe de la Genèse' *Scrinium Lovaniense van Cauwenbergh* (1961), pp. 126–35.

[2] Bardtke (§ 104) (1958), pp. 289–91; Dupont-Sommer (§ 104) (1959), pp. 320–3; (1961), pp. 307–10; Gaster (§ 104) (1957), pp. 225–7; Maier (§ 104) (1960), I, pp. 168–70; II, p. 153. Lit. § 126.

Law which has been given to him on Sinai, and at the same time foretells to him that the people will not keep the commands of the Law and so will be visited by the punishments threatened in it (I, 1–11). Moses commands Eleazar and Joshua to make known the Law to the people (I, 12). Moses exhorts the people to keep the Law and summons them to choose wise men for themselves who can explain the Law to them and to their children (II, 1–12). There then begins the matter with which the work is clearly primarily concerned, namely a very detailed instruction concerning the observance of the festivals. III, 1–7 deal with the sabbath year, and III, 8–12; IV, 1–12, so far as they can be understood, with the great Day of Atonement. The Hebrew word שׁ[בועות] *weeks* on fragment 41 may refer to the Feast of Weeks and would then be evidence that this work also enjoined the celebration of other festivals. It is possible too, as is suggested in QC I, p. 91, that it concluded with the narrative of Moses' death and ascension.

QC I, pp. 97–8, No. 23, Pl. XIX deals with 31 small Aramaic fragments. Here there appears an enumeration of *200 asses, 200 wild asses, 200 sheep* and *200 goats* reminiscent of the meeting of Jacob and Esau in Gen. xxxiii, and likewise the expression *On the fourth . . . he crossed the river* which echoes Gen. xxxii, 23–4. So (p. 97) the possibility is considered that we here have an apocryphal history of the patriarchs, perhaps even the 'Wars of the Patriarchs', one of the sources of the book of Jubilees (Jub. xxxiv, 1–9) and of the Testaments of the XII Patriarchs (Test. Judah iii–vii).

Among the haggadic narrative works we should perhaps also include the Pseudo-Jeremianic work which has echoes of the other books ascribed to Jeremiah or Baruch (see §§ 69, 86, 87, 100, 101) though not identical with any of them. Fragments of this, according to Strugnell (RB 63 (1956), p. 65), have appeared in Cave 4. The same applies to the 'pseudo-historical' Aramaic work which as may be recognised from the fragments likewise from Cave 4 to which Starcky refers in RB 63 (1956) p. 66, takes place in the Persian period and thus is reminiscent of the books of Esther and Daniel.

Lastly, the famous and much disputed Copper Scroll, mentioned briefly already on p. 648, must also probably be reckoned with the haggadic narrative works. This scroll, discovered in Cave 3 in 1952, contains 12 columns with impressed Hebrew letters, about 3,000 in number, and is about 2·40 metres long and 30 cms. high. When it was hidden, it was divided into two part rolls about 180 and 60 cms. long and was found in this condition. The greatest possible difficulties stood in the way of its elucidation, in the first place technical difficulties, and then problems of content and explanation. In view of its very corroded condition, it proved to be quite impossible to unroll the scroll so that it was possible only to recognise the letters which appeared on the reverse sides of the upper layers of each of the two part rolls, though even at this stage[3] this led to the suggestion that the scroll might contain 'a description of the places in which the treasures of the Essene community, its articles of value and its transportable goods were hidden'.[4] When, as the result of a superb piece of

[3] Kuhn, 'Les rouleaux de cuivre de Qumrân' RB 61 (1954), pp. 193–205.
[4] Kuhn (see previous note), p. 204.

technical skill,[5] the two part rolls were successfully sawn up into strips without any substantial damage to the writing on them, and it was then possible to read the text, it did in fact appear that it really contained an enumeration[6] of articles of value—6000 talents, i.e. 200 tons, of gold and silver, and great quantities of precious spices among other items—with a note of the sixty places in which they were hidden, apparently between Carmel in the north and the Wilderness of Judaea in the south[7] and particularly numerous in and around Jerusalem. But a very lively discussion then began as to whether we really have here an inventory of hidden treasures—belonging to the Essene community of Qumrān itself,[8] or to the Jerusalem Temple[9]—or whether we have a product of popular fancy of a fairy-tale quality,[10] somewhat like the story in II Macc. ii, 4–8 which relates how Jeremiah, after the destruction of the Jerusalem Temple in 587 B.C., at the divine command hid the holy tent, the ark and the incense altar in a cave in Mount Nebo, or like the one in the Syriac Apocalypse of Baruch vi, 7–10, according to which on the command of an angel the earth opened before the fall of Jerusalem and received precious cult objects, or the saga presupposed in Josephus *Ant.* XVIII 4, 1 (§§ 85–7) to the effect that Moses hid cult objects on Gerizim. It will in any case be wise to wait before making a final judgement on the nature and purpose of this remarkable copper scroll till its full publication can be considered.[11]

It is probable that the future will bring us information about other haggadic narrative works from the Qumrān library if confirmation is forthcoming of the assumption which has been tentatively put forward in regard to some of the fragments that they are pieces of writings of this nature. This is the case with

[5] Baker, 'Notes on the Opening of the "Bronze" Scrolls from Qumran' BJRL 39 (1956/57), pp. 45–56, Figs. 1–4.

[6] Ullendorff, 'The Greek Letters of the Copper Scroll' VT 11 (1961), pp. 227–8.

[7] Allegro, who considers that the Mount Gerizim mentioned in XII, 4, really means Mount Cypros near Jericho, thinks that the region covered by the hiding places is more limited in size.

[8] Allegro, *The Dead Sea Scrolls* (1956), p. 184; Dupont-Sommer, 'Les rouleaux de cuivre trouvés à Qoumrân' RHR 151 (1957), pp. 22–36, 142–4; *Les écrits esséniens* (1959), pp. 393–404; E.T. *The Essene Writings from Qumran* (1961), pp. 379–93.

[9] Allegro, *The Treasure of the Copper Scroll* (1960), (cf. on this Driver, JSSt 6 (1961), pp. 275–8; Nötscher, BZ 5 (1961), pp. 292–7; de Vaux, RB 68 (1961), pp. 146 f.); 'The Copper Scroll of Qumran: A Story of Hidden Treasure in a Dead Sea Scroll' ILN 238 (1961), pp. 16–19; Kuhn, 'Bericht über neue Qumranfunde und über die Öffnung der Kupferrollen' ThLZ 81 (1956), cols 541–6; 'Zum heutigen Stand der Qumrānforschung' ThLZ 85 (1960), cols. 649–58, cf. cols. 650–1; de Langhe, 'De Koperen Rol en een nieuwe tocht naar de woestijn van Juda' Onze Alma Mater 14 (1960), pp. 1–9; Rabin, The Jewish Chronicle No. 4, 547 (15 June 1956), p. 19; Rengstorf, *Ḥirbet Qumrân und die Bibliothek vom Toten Meer* (1960), pp. 26–8, 34, 40; Roth, 'A New Solution to the Mystery of the Scrolls' Commentary 24 (1957), p. 323. Cf. also Lit. § 126.

[10] Jeremias, 'The Copper Scroll from Qumran' ET 71 (1959/60), pp. 227 f.; Jeremias and Milik, 'Remarques sur le rouleau de cuivre de Qumrân' RB 67 (1960), pp. 220–3; Milik, 'The Copper Document from Cave III, Qumran' BA 19 (1956), pp. 60–4; 'Le rouleau de cuivre de Qumrân (3 Q 15)' RB 66 (1959), pp. 321–57; 'Notes d'épigraphie et de topographie Palestiniennes' RB 66 (1959), pp. 550–75, Pls. XIII, XIV; 'The Copper Document from Cave III of Qumran. Translation and Commentary' Annual Department Antiqu. Jordan 4/5 (1960), pp. 137–45; Mowinckel, 'The Copper Scroll—an Apocryphon?' JBL 76 (1957), pp. 261–5; Silbermann, 'A Note on the Copper Scroll' VT 10 (1960), pp. 77–9.

[11] It has now appeared in de Vaux, Baillet and Milik, *Les 'Petites Grottes' de Qumrān* (*Discoveries in the Judaean Desert of Jordan* III) (1962). Lit. § 126.

the remains of biblical paraphrases of the books of Gen., Exod. and Sam. from Cave 4 to which attention is drawn by Allegro in RB 63 (1956), p. 63, as also with the translation of the book of Job into Aramaic (cf. § 119), Targumic in character, from Cave 11, mentioned by Harding in PEQ 90 (1958), p. 17.

§ 112. PARENETIC AND DIDACTIC WRITINGS. JURIDICAL AND ASTROLOGICAL WORKS

Literature: Qumran Cave I, pp. 101 f., No. 26, Pl. XX: 'Un apocryphe'. Cf. also Literature § 104.

The fragments published in *Qumran Cave I*, pp. 101 f., No. 26, Pl. XX appear to come from a Hebrew work containing exhortations after the nature of the Deuteronomic admonitions and of the wisdom teachings, or like the Testaments of the XII Patriarchs. These may be supplemented, according to Strugnell in RB 63 (1956), p. 64, by fragments of fair size of a scroll from Cave 4. This work admittedly differs from the wisdom literature which is entirely without eschatological elements, by the fact that it knows of the *future secret* which we have already met in the 'Book of the Secrets' (p. 662). But with a work which has come into being in the Qumrān community or perhaps was merely revised there, as this work seems to have been, we should hardly expect anything else. The eschatological spirit which infused this community must also have penetrated into literary types which originally would have been hostile rather than friendly to the reception of such ideas. Whether four further scrolls of which fragments have been found in Cave 4 are identical with this work or represent a separate wisdom book merely similar to it, must, according to Strugnell, RB 63 (1956), p. 64, for the moment remain uncertain. In regard to the four or five fragmentary scrolls with didactic content from Cave 4, it is, according to Strugnell (RB 63 (1956), pp. 64–5), at any rate for the present not possible to decide whether they are independent books of a didactic kind or sayings or groups of sayings incorporated in books of a quite different nature, just as Jub. and Test. XII Patr. contain such insertions.

To a parenetic, didactic work there belong also the fragments from Cave 4 which, as Starcky indicates in RB 63 (1956), p. 67, on the one hand extol as fortunate those who fulfil the divine commands (אשרי *Happy the one who . . .*), and on the other hand depict the punishments which threaten the irreligious.

Pieces of juridical writing—with which moreover some sections of the Manual of Discipline (§ 105) and of the Damascus Document (§ 106) may be reckoned —have been found in Cave 4. There are ordinances for the way of life of the members of the community, and judgements upon criminals among them with mention of their names and a note of the crimes imputed to them (Strugnell, RB 63 (1956), p. 65; Milik, pp. 61–2).[1]

---

[1] Allegro, 'An Unpublished Fragment of Essene Halakha (4 Q Ordinances)' JSSt 6 (1961), pp. 71–3, 1 Pl. Lit. § 126.

Lastly, we may note that there is no lack at Qumrān of fragments of works of an astronomical and astrological nature which are characteristically written in part with special letters or in secret alphabets (Milik, RB 63 (1956), p. 61; Allegro, p. 64). The title of one of the scrolls which apparently belongs to this class has survived: מדרש ספר משה *Midrash*[2] *of the book of Moses* (p. 61); another[3] has the designation written in square script: [דברי] משכיל אשר דבר לכול בני שחר *words of the instructor which he spoke to all the sons of the dawn,* and then in cipher האזינו *Hearken.* We have already noted (p. 648) that the 'Mishmaroth', the writings which regulate the service of the priestly families, give us at the same time information about the two calendars in use in the Qumrān community.

[2] Cf. above, p. 534, n. 16; Gertner (Lit. § 126 on p. 534, n. 16).
[3] Milik, RB 63 (1956), p. 61; Dupont-Sommer (§ 104) (1961), p. 338.

PART FIVE

THE TEXT

Literature: Ap-Thomas, *A Primer of OT Text Criticism* (1947); Buhl, *Kanon und Text des AT* (1891); Bruce, *The English Bible: a History of Translation* (1961); Cross, *The Ancient Library of Qumrân* (1958), pp. 120–45: 'The OT in Qumrân'; Coppens, *La Critique du Texte Hébreu de l'AT* (²1950); 'La critique textuelle de l'AT. Solutions anciennes et données nouvelles' EThL 36 (1960), pp. 466–75; Geiger, *Urschrift und Übersetzungen der Bibel* (1857 (²1928 by Kahle); Herklots, *How the Bible Came to Us: Its Texts and Versions* (1959); Kahle, *The Cairo Geniza* (²1959); *Der hebräische Bibeltext seit Franz Delitzsch* (1962); Kenyon, *Our Bible and the Ancient Manuscripts*, rev. by A. W. Adams (⁵1958); Noth, *Die Welt des AT* (³1957), pp. 237–90, 295–6. Pls. 2, 3A, (⁴1962); E.T. *The OT World* (1965); Orlinsky, 'Jewish Scholarship and Christian Translations of the Hebrew Bible' Yearbook 63. The Central Conference of American Rabbis (1953), pp. 235–52; 'The Textual Criticism of the OT' *Essays Albright* (1961), pp. 113–32; Paret, *Die Bibel. Ihre Überlieferung in Druck und Schrift* (²1950, ³1963); on this Katz, VT 4 (1954), pp. 222 f.; Price, *The Ancestry of our English Bible*, rev. by Irwin and Wilkgren (³1956); Rabin (ed.) Textus, Annual of the Hebrew University Bible Project I (1960), II (1962), III (1963); Roberts, *The OT Text and Versions* (1951); on this Katz, ThLZ 76 (1951), cols. 535–9; H. W. Robinson, *The Bible in its Ancient and English Versions* (²1954); Rypins, *The Book of Thirty Centuries: An Introduction to Modern Study of the Bible* (1951); Soisalon-Soininen, *Van han Testamentin alkuteksti* (1953); Winton Thomas, 'The Textual Criticism of the OT' OTMSt (1951), pp. 238–63; Vandervorst, *Introduction aux textes hébreu et grec de l'AT* (1935); Willoughby, *The Study of the Bible Today and Tomorrow* (1947); Würthwein, *Der Text des AT. Eine Einführung in die Biblia Hebraica von Rudolf Kittel* (²1963); *The Text of the OT: An Introduction to Kittel-Kahle's Biblia Hebraica*, translated by Ackroyd (1957).

I. The Prehistory of the Text Forms which have Survived

§ 113. GENERAL CONSIDERATIONS

The formation of the Old Testament is not completed with the making of the Palestinian canon closed in about 150 B.C., even if we now again restrict our consideration to this and leave entirely on one side the development of the text of the apocrypha and pseudepigrapha. This latter differs for each individual book, as has been here and there indicated in §§ 77–103. The text of the Old Testament still in fact remained fluid. It is true that the consonantal text, as may be seen from the evidence of the Hebrew biblical texts among the Qumrân discoveries, in particular the two Isaiah scrolls discovered in 1947 in Cave 1 and published in 1950 and 1955, had reached by and large even two or three centuries before A.D. 150 the form which appears in the complete manuscripts of the Hebrew Old Testament which are available to us from the ninth and tenth centuries A.D. onwards, though side by side with this there were also at first variant text forms in circulation (p. 684). But the vocalisation only

669

received its final form much later. At first transmitted only orally, it began to be made more definitive in the last century B.C. and the first century A.D., partly by the use of certain consonantal signs to indicate vowels—ו *w* for *o*, י *y* for *i*—and partly by transcriptions of the Hebrew sounds into Greek. From the sixth century A.D. onwards, it began to be fixed by various systems of pointing, until one of them, the Tiberian, gained the upper hand in about A.D. 900, i.e. roughly at the time from which the oldest more or less complete manuscripts of the Hebrew Old Testament derive, and so brought to an end the history of the vocalisation of the text (pp. 687–91).

Between the oldest sections of the Old Testament, which, like the Song of Deborah for example, could have been written down in the twelfth century B.C., and the Hebrew manuscripts of substantial parts of the Old Testament which are available to us, there lie at any rate about 1,000 years, and if we consider the oldest vocalised manuscripts, this gap is lengthened by more than half a millennium. Of course, for the later books of the Old Testament, the interval is shorter between their first writing down and the copies of them which we have, and for the book of Daniel it is even possible that the fragments of it found near Qumrān (p. 521) belong to a copy roughly contemporary with its composition. But for the majority of the books and sections of books in the Old Testament, there is between their composition and the first copies which we have a larger interval, varying between 1,000 and 100 years. During this interval of between one and ten centuries, the books must have been often copied, some of them very often, and it is therefore inevitable that accidentally or deliberately they have been altered to a greater or lesser extent. Since we unfortunately lack any traditions here, we can make no precise statements; it is nevertheless of some use to consider the possibilities of error since this points the way to an explanation and so to the correction of obvious mistakes.

§ 114. BOOKS AND WRITING

1. Books.

Literature: Birt, *Das Antike Buchwesen in seinem Verhältnis zur Literatur* (1882 (1959)); Bland, *A History of Book Illustration. The Illuminated Manuscript and the Printed Book* (1958); Blau, *Studien zum althebräischen Buchwesen* (1902); Bruce, *The Books and the Parchments* (1950); Brunner, 'Ägyptisches Schreibmaterial' HdO I 1, 1 (1959), pp. 59–61; Cernỳ, *Paper and Books in Ancient Egypt* (1952); Diringer, *The Hand-Produced Book* (1953); *The Illuminated Book: its History and Production* (1958); Funke, *Buchkunde. Ein Überblick über die Geschichte des Buch- und Schriftwesens* (1959); Gurney and Finkelstein, *The Sultantepe Tablets* I (1957); on this cf. Lambert, RA 53 (1959), pp. 119–38 and Erica Reiner, JNESt 19 (1960), pp. 23–35; Rivkah Harris, 'The Archive of the Sin Temple in Khafajah (Tutub)' JCSt 9 (1955), pp. 31–58, 59–88, 91–120; Ibscher, 'Der Kodex' Jahrbuch der Einbandkunst 4 (1937), pp. 3–15; Kampman, *Archieven en Bibliotheken in het Nabije Oosten* (1942); Katz, 'The Early Christians' Use of Codices instead of Rolls' JThSt 46 (1945), pp. 63–5; Kenyon, *Books and Readers in Ancient Greece and Rome* (²1951); Klaffenbach, *Bemerkungen zum griechischen Urkundenwesen* (SBA 1960, 6, 1960); Kramer, 'Langdon's Historical and Religious Texts from the Temple Library of Nippur' JAOS 60 (1940), pp. 234–57; Krauss,

Talmudische Archäologie III (1912), pp. 131–98; Lambert, 'Les archives de Urabba, fils de Bazig' RA 54 (1960), pp. 113–30; Milkau, *Handbuch der Bibliothekswissenschaft,* 2nd ed. by Leyh: I. *Schrift und Buch* (1952); III. *Geschichte der Bibliotheken* (1955/57); on this cf. Otten, OLZ 50 (1955), cols. 501–3; Otten, 'Bibliotheken im Alten Orient' Das Altertum 1 (1955), pp. 68–81); Papritz, 'Archive in Altmesopotamien. Theorie und Tataschen' Archivalische Zeitschrift 55 (1959), pp. 11–50; Pohl, 'Bibliotheken und Archive im alten Orient' Or 25 (1956), pp. 105–9; Roberts, 'The Christian Books and the Greek Papyri' JThSt 50 (1949), pp. 155–68; Sanders, 'The Beginning of the Modern Book' The University of Michigan QR (1938), pp. 95–111; Schubart, *Das Buch bei den Griechen und Römern* (1921 (1961)); 'Das antike Buch' Die Antike 14 (1938), pp. 171–95; Schwank, 'Lederrollen oder Papyruskodices?' Erbe und Auftrag 37 (1961), pp. 146–51; van der Falk, 'On the Editions of Books in Antiquity' Vigilae Christianae 11 (1957), pp. 1–10; Weidner, 'Die Bibliothek Tiglatpilesers I' AfO 16 (1952/53), pp. 197–215; 'Amts- und Privatarchive aus mittelassyrischer Zeit' *Christian-Festschr.* (1956), pp. 111–18; 'Der Kanzler Salmanassars I' AfO 19 (1959/60), pp. 33–9; Weitemeyer, *Babylonske og Assyriske Arkiver og Biblioteker* (1955); 'Archive and Library Technique in Ancient Mesopotamia' Libri. International Library Review 6 (1956), pp. 217–38; Wendel, 'Die Übertragung der griechischen Literatur aus der Papyrusrolle in den Pergamentkodex' FuF 18 (1942), pp. 272 f.; *Die griechisch-römische Buchbeschreibung verglichen mit der des Vorderen Orients* (1949).

Cf. also Literature p. 48, n. 48; § 126.

If we want to get a clear picture of the unsatisfactoriness of the transmission of our texts, we must first try to get an impression of the appearance of an Israelite book. Unfortunately we are very badly informed with regard to the Israelite making of books, particularly as regards the earliest periods. We do not actually know whether books were scratched with a hard pointed stylus on tablets of stone and clay, metal and wood—as is clearly attested for records of all kinds and as indeed we might expect (Exod. xxxi, 18; xxxiv, 1; I Macc. viii, 22; xiv, 18, 26, 48)—or whether they were written with pen and ink on soft materials, papyrus and leather. It is quite certain that Israel knew the custom of inscribing words on hard tablets with a stylus. We need only refer to Jer. xvii, 1, where it is said that *Judah's sin is written with a pen of iron, with a point of diamond it is engraved on the tablet of their heart.* But the oldest and at the same time only passage which gives us any information about Israelite books, the narrative concerning Jeremiah's original scroll (pp. 349–50), presupposes the scroll book (Jer. xxxvi, 2 מְגִלַּת־סֵפֶר) as the normal book-form. Other passages confirm this. Ezekiel (ii, 9–10) receives his revelations in the form of a scroll written on the front and on the back, and the poet-prophet of Isa. xxxiv–xxxv proclaims among the signs of the final judgement that the heaven will be rolled up like a book (Isa. xxxiv, 4). Jer. xxxvi, 18 also mentions the material with which writing was done on the scroll, namely ink (דְּיוֹ), and shows further that the scroll was divided into columns (דֶּלֶת) (xxxvi, 23). So far as concerns the material from which the scrolls mentioned in Jer. xxxvi and elsewhere were made, it was certainly predominantly papyrus. In any case at an early date papyrus was exported by Egypt to Syria and no doubt also to Palestine, taking it via Gebal which just because of its importing and exporting of papyrus was later named by the Greeks Byblos the *papyrus city.*[1] The account

[1] Rosén, 'Note on Βύβλος' VT 1 (1951), p. 306; Thierry, 'Gebál, Byblos, Bible; Paper' VT 1 (1951), pp. 130 f. Lit. § 126.

written in about 1100 B.C. by the Egyptian Wen-Amon[2] mentions in fact that in payment for a delivery of timber there was delivered to the prince of Byblos among other things 500 rolls of papyrus.[3] What was normal in about 1100 B.C. had certainly already happened at an earlier date, so that when Israel entered Canaan papyrus was already known there as a writing material alongside the clay tablet.

But it is certain that among the Israelites, even from an early date, scrolls made of skins were in use. Official writings at the court, such as the annals kept there, and significant legal and cultic corpora such as the Mishpatim of the Book of the Covenant (p. 145), and the original Deuteronomy (p. 173), may perhaps be better thought of as having been written on durable skin than on easily damaged papyrus. In any case, at a later date skin or parchment was generally regarded as the normal and obligatory material for Torah scrolls. The Letter of Aristeas (pp. 603–6) says that the Torah brought from Jerusalem was written upon animal skins (§ 176 διφθέραι) with golden writing in Jewish letters, and rabbinic information provides more detailed indication as to what skins might be used for Torah scrolls.[4] It is possible and indeed probable that Ezra who came to Jerusalem from the centre of the Persian empire in which according to Diodorus II 32, 4 βασιλικαί διφθέραι royal (document-) animal skins were in use,[5] brought his Torah in the form of a leather scroll, and that, even if this had not been done earlier, from this time onwards Jewish practice was to write the Torah on leather or parchment scrolls. So the Biblical texts found near Qumrān, which belong roughly to the first century B.C., are for the most part leather scrolls or parts of such. So far as the copies of the books are concerned which are used for reading in worship, this custom has been faithfully adhered to until the present day. For privately owned manuscripts of the Old Testament and its individual books, the codex form came into use from the second century A.D. onwards, and the majority of the manuscripts we possess are codices on parchment, leather or paper.

Now if we may think of the books and sections of books of the Old Testament as being written on papyrus, leather or parchment, then there are certain definite ways in which the text may be damaged and become illegible. Pieces could easily be torn from the thin papyrus, and leather and parchment were exposed to the risk of destruction by mice and insects. The ink, made from lampblack and other substances, could easily be blurred or even completely washed out. The saying *habent sua fata libelli* is quite definitely relevant to the transmission of the books of the Old Testament right through the centuries which preceded the appearance of its first manuscripts.

---

[2] AOT, pp. 75–7; ANET, pp. 25–9. Cf. Literature p. 52, n. 61.

[3] II, 41; cf. Clemen, *Lukians Schrift über die Syrische Göttin* (1938), pp. 8 f., 33 f.; Gressmann, 'Die Reliquien der kuhköpfigen Göttin in Byblos' *Hahn-Festschrift* (1917), pp. 250–68; Herrmann, 'Isis in Byblos' ZÄS 87 (1957), pp. 48–55. Lit. § 126.

[4] jer. Megilla I, 9 (71d); Bardtke, 'Der Traktat der Schreiber (Sopherim). In Auswahl übersetzt' WZ Leipzig 3 (1953/54), pp. 13–31, see pp. 14–15.

[5] Cf. the letters of the Persian satrap Arsam, written on leather, published by Driver, *Aramaic Documents of the Fifth Century B.C.* (1954. Abridged and revised ed. 1957).

2. Writing

Literature: Franz Altheim and Ruth Stiehl, 'Die zweite (aramäische) Inschrift von Mcḫet'a' FuF 35 (1961), pp. 172–8; Hans Bauer, *Der Ursprung des Alphabets* (1937); Birnbaum, *The Hebrew Scripts*, Fasc. 1–2 (1954/55); Bivar, 'A Rosette *phialē* Inscribed in Aramaic' BSOASt 24 (1961), pp. 189–99, Pls. I–II; Elizabeth Bowman, 'A Note on the Development of Egyptian Writing' JNESt 19 (1960), pp. 46–8; van den Branden, 'Anciennes inscriptions sémitiques' BiOr 17 (1960), pp. 218–22, Pl. III; Cohen, *L'Écriture* (1953); *La grande invention de l'écriture et son évolution*, I–III (1956/58); Cook and Woodhead, 'The Diffusion of the Greek Alphabet' AJA 63 (1959), pp. 175–8; Cross, 'The Evolution of the Proto-Canaanite Alphabet' BASOR 134 (1954), pp. 15–24; 'A Ugaritic Abecedary and the origins of the Proto-Canaanite Alphabet' BASOR 160 (1960), pp. 21–6; 'The Development of the Jewish Scripts' *Essays Albright* (1961), pp. 133–202; Cross and Freedman, *Early Hebrew Orthography. A Study of the Epigraphic Evidence* (1952); Cross and Milik, 'A Typological Study of the el Khadr Javelin- and Arrow-Heads' Ann. Departm. Ant. Jordan 3 (1956), pp. 15–23; Diringer, *Le iscrizioni antico ebraiche palestinesi* (1934); 'The Palestinian Inscriptions and the Origin of the Alphabet' JAOS 63 (1943), pp. 24–30, 176–8; 'Early Hebrew Script versus Square Hebrew Script' *Essays S. A. Cook* (1950), pp. 35–49; 'The Early Hebrew Book Hand' PEQ 82 (1950), pp. 16–24; 'Early Hebrew Writing' BA 13 (1950), pp. 74–95; *The Alphabet* (³1952); 'Problems of the Present Day on the Origin of the Phoenician Alphabet' Cahiers d'Histoire Mondiale 4 (1957/58), pp. 40–58; 'Inscriptions. A. Early Canaanite' *Lachish IV Text* (1958), pp. 127–31 and illustrations in IV Plates (1958); *The Story of the Aleph Beth* (1958); Doblhofer, *Zeichen und Wunder. Die Entzifferung verschollener Schriften und Sprachen* (1957); *Le déchiffrement des écritures* (1959); Dougherty, 'Writing upon Parchment and Papyrus among the Babylonians and Assyrians' JAOS 48 (1928), pp. 109–35; Driver, 'Seals and Tombstones' Ann. Departm. Ant. Jordan 2 (1953), pp. 62–5; *Semitic Writing from Pictograph to Alphabet* (²1954); Février, *Histoire de l'Écriture* (²1959); Flight, 'The Present State of Studies in the History of Writing in the Near East' *The Haverford Symposium* (1938), pp. 111–35; Friedrich, 'Schriftsysteme und Schrifterfindungen im alten Orient und bei modernen Naturvölkern' ArOr 19 (1951), pp. 245–59, Pls. XI–XIX; 'Die Parallel-Entwicklung der drei alten Schrift-Urschöpfungen' AnBibl 12 (1959), pp. 95–101, Pls. XIV–XVII; Gelb, *A Study of Writing. The Foundations of Grammatology* (1952); Georgiev, 'L'origine minoenne de l'alphabet phénicien' ArOr 20 (1952), pp. 487–95; Grumach, 'Zur Herkunft des altsemitischen Alphabets' *Leo Baeck-Festschr.* (1938), pp. 161–74; Honeyman, 'Semitic Epigraphy and Hebrew Philology' OTMSt (1951), pp. 264–82; Hooke, 'The Early History of Writing' Antiquity 11 (1937), pp. 261–77, Pls. I–VII = *The Siege Perilous. Essays in Biblical Anthropology and Kindred Subjects* (1956), pp. 153–72; Istrine, 'L'Écriture, sa classification, sa terminologie et les régularités de son développement' Cahiers d'Histoire Mondiale 4 (1957/58), pp. 15–39; Iwry, 'New Evidence for Belomancy in Ancient Palestine and Phoenicia' JAOS 81 (1961), pp. 27–34; Jeffery, *The Local Scripts of Archaic Greece* (1961); Jensen, *Die Schrift in Vergangenheit und Gegenwart* (²1958); Martin, 'A Preliminary Report after Re-Examination of the Byblian Inscriptions' Or 30 (1961), pp. 46–78, Pls. VI–XV; Mercer, *The Origin of Writing and our Alphabet* (1959); Michaud, *Sur la pierre et l'argile. Inscriptions hébraïques et AT* (CAB 10, 1958); 'Une nouvelle lettre en paléo-hébraïque' VT 10 (1960), pp. 453–5; Miltner, 'Wesen und Geburt der Schrift' *Historia Mundi* III (1954), pp. 27–41, 505; Moriarty, 'Early Evidence of Alphabetic Writing' CBQ 13 (1951), pp. 135–45; Moscati, *L'epigrafia ebraica antica 1935–1950* (1951); *Stato e problemi dell' epigrafia ebraica antica* (1952); Saydon, 'Paleography of the OT and its Bearing upon Textual and Literary Criticism of the OT' Melita Theologica 3 (1950), pp. 5–22; Schott, 'Die Erfindung der ägyptischen Schrift; das Schriftsystem und seine Durchbildung; Abhängigkeit und Einwirkung' HdO I 1, 1 (1959), pp. 18–21, 21–31, 32–6; Segert, 'Charakter des westsemitischen Alphabets' ArOr 26 (1958), pp. 243–7; 'Noch zum Charakter der westsemitischen Schrift' ArOr 26 (1958), pp. 657–9; Sixdenier, 'Remarques sur la paléographie samaritaine' JA 248

(1960), pp. 189–97, Pl. I; Tibón, 'Nuevas Investigaciones en la Prehistoria de Alfabeto' Memorias y Revista de la Academia Nacional de Ciencias 57 (Mexico, 1955), pp. 245–348; Weidmüller, 'Wie alt ist unser Alphabet?' Börsenblatt für den deutschen Buchhandel, Frankfurt a. M., No. 88 (4 Nov. 1958), pp. 1429–32; 'Warum A-B-C?' ib., No. 94 (24 Nov. 1959), pp. 1609–13; 'Phönikische Buchstaben—ägyptische Bildzeichen' ib., No. 39 (17 May 1960), pp. 733–9; No. 46 (10 June 1960), pp. 985–91.

Cf. also Literature § 126.

So far as the script is concerned in which we must picture the books of the Old Testament as having been written, it has become clear that at any rate from the middle of the second millennium B.C. the use of the Phoenician alphabetic script was very widespread. This is shown by various texts discovered in the last half century. On the one hand there are those written in Old Canaanite-Old Phoenician alphabetic script, for example the inscription found in Byblos on the sarcophagus of Ahiram[6] belonging to the end of the second pre-Christian millennium, and on the other hand the texts on clay tablets in cuneiform alphabetic script, excavated since 1929 in Ras Shamra,[7] the ancient Ugarit, and belonging to the fourteenth century B.C. The inscriptions give direct evidence, while the Ras Shamra tablets provide indirect evidence in that the cuneiform alphabet which they employ almost certainly presupposes the Phoenician alphabet. This has been transposed into a cuneiform alphabet not following the form of its letters but its principles.[8] Nor is there lacking evidence from Palestine to show that here already in the pre-Israelite period, and at any rate from the middle of the second millennium B.C. onwards, an alphabetic script related to the Phoenician one just mentioned was in use. It may therefore be regarded as proved that the Israelites found this script already present when they entered Canaan, and that they took it over. The earliest Israelite documents, or at any rate those which come from Palestine after it had become Israelite, written in this Old Hebrew script, are: the farmers' calendar from Gezer[9] written on a limestone tablet, dated by most scholars between 1100 and 900 B.C., but by Wirgin towards the end of the eighth century B.C.; the ostraca (potsherds) from Samaria belonging to the first, or perhaps more probably the second,[10] half of the eighth century B.C. with invoices of deliveries of wine and oil to the Israelite royal court;[11]

[6] AOT, p. 440; AOB, figs. 665, 666; ANET, p. 504; ANEP, figs. 456–60.

[7] Jacob, *Ras Shamra-Ugarit et l'Ancien Testament* (1960).

[8] J. Friedrich, *Entzifferung verschollener Schriften und Sprachen* (1954), pp. 42 f., 69–72; E.T. *Extinct Languages* by F. Gaynor (1962), pp. 48 f., 83–6.

[9] AOT, p. 444; AOB, fig. 609; ANET, p. 320; ANEP, fig. 272; DOTT, pp. 201–3, Pl. 11; Garbini, 'Note sul "calendario" di Gezer' Annali dell' Instituto Universitario Orientale di Napoli. N.S. VI (1957), pp. 123–30; Honeyman, 'The Syntax of the Gezer Calendar' JRAS (1953), pp. 53–8; Rahtjen, 'A Note concerning the Form of the Gezer Tablet' PEQ 93 (1961), pp. 70–2; Wirgin, 'The Calendar Tablet from Gezer' Eretz-Israel 6 (1960), pp. 9*–12*. Lit. § 126.

[10] In the second of Yadin's works mentioned in the next note, he links the Samaria ostraca with Menahem's payment of tribute to Tiglath-pileser V in 738 B.C., mentioned in II Kings xv, 19–20, and demonstrates that this dating corresponds to the stratigraphic evidence, since the ostraca belong to Stratum IV. Lit. § 126.

[11] Albright, *Recent Discoveries in Bible Lands* (1955), pp. 42, 95 f.; Birnbaum, 'Ostraca. The Material in Palaeo-Hebrew Script' *Samaria-Sebaste*, III (1957), pp. 11–25, Pls. I–II; Galling, 'Ein Ostrakon aus Samaria als Rechtsquelle' ZDPV 77 (1961), pp. 173–85, Pl. 9; Hempel, 'Die Ausgrabungen in Samaria' ZAW 43 (1925), pp. 147–50; Jirku, 'Das In-

the jar stamps with royal marks or indications of ownership or place of origin, belonging to the eighth, seventh, sixth and fourth centuries B.C., which have come to light in many places,[12] most recently in El-Jib (Gibeon)[13] and Ramat Raḥel (Beth-Haccherem);[14] the account in the tunnel of Siloam from about 700 B.C. which relates how this was made;[15] a long series of seal legends beginning at about this date or perhaps somewhat earlier,[16] including the words on the beautiful seal of *Shemaʻ servant of Jeroboam*;[17] in addition to these, we may mention the ostracon recently found at 'Meṣad Ḥašabyahu', between Jaffa and Ashdod, belonging to the end of the seventh century B.C., containing a complaint by an unknown individual directed to his lord the prince (אדני השר) on account of his wrong treatment by Ḥašabyahu,[18] and the ostraca from the year 588 B.C. containing reports rendered to the military commander of the Judaean fortress of Lachish.[19] These last are not literary monuments but in their

schriften-Material der amerikanischen Ausgrabungen in Samarien' OLZ 28 (1925), cols. 273–81; Noth, 'Das Krongut der israelitischen Könige und seine Verwaltung' ZDPV 50 (1927), pp. 211–44; O'Doherty, 'The Date of the Ostraca of Samaria' CBQ 15 (1953), pp. 24–9; Parrot, *Samarie. Capitale du Royaume d'Israël* (1955), pp. 54–8; E.T. by S. H. Hooke, *Samaria, The Capital of the Kingdom of Israel* (1958), pp. 72–8; Reisner, Fisher, Lyon, *Harvard Excavations at Samaria* I (1924), pp. 227–46; II (1924), Pl. 55; Yadin, 'Recipients or Owners. A Note on the Samaria Ostraca' IEJ 9 (1959), pp. 184–7; 'Ancient Judaean Weights and the Date of the Samaria Ostraca' Studia Hieros. VIII (1960), pp. 9–25. Cf. Lit. p. 300, n. 68. Cf. Franz Altheim and Ruth Stiehl, 'Aramäisches aus Iran' WZ Leipzig 5 (1955/56), pp. 341–8, see pp. 341–3; 'Ostraka aus Nisā' *Supplementum Aramaicum* (1957), pp. 54–63; Sznycer, 'Ostraca d'époque Parthe trouvés à Nisa (U.R.S.S.)' Semitica 5 (1955), pp. 65–98. Lit. § 126.
[12] BRL, cols. 337–40; DOTT, pp. 220–1; Aharoni, 'Some More *YHWD* Stamps' IEJ 9 (1959), pp. 55–6, Pl. 4 D; Avigad, 'A New Class of *Yehud* Stamps' IEJ 7 (1957), pp. 146–53; '*Yehûd* or *Haʻir?*' BASOR 158 (1960), pp. 23–7; Diringer, 'The Royal Jar-Handle Stamps' BA 12 (1949), pp. 70–86; Lapp, 'The Royal Seals from Judah' BASOR 158 (1960), pp. 11–12. Lit. § 126.
[13] Pritchard, 'Inscribed Jar Handles from Gibeon' A XXIV IOK (1959), p. 213; *Hebrew Inscriptions and Stamps from Gibeon* (1959); 'More Inscribed Jar Handles from el-Jib' BASOR 160 (1960), pp. 2–6. Lit. p. 249, n. 8.
[14] Aharoni, 'Hebrew Jar-Stamps from Ramat-Raḥel' [Hebr., Engl. summary] Eretz-Israel 6 (1960), pp. 56–60, 28*, Pl. VII, 3–6. Lit. p. 545, n. 15; § 126.
[15] AOT, p. 445; AOB, fig. 607; ANET, p. 321; ANEP, figs. 275, 744; DOTT, pp. 209–11, Pl. 11; Stoebe, 'Überlegungen zur Siloahinschrift' ZDPV 71 (1955), pp. 124–40. Cf. p. 19; p. 52, n. 60; p. 305, n. 7.
[16] AOB, figs. 575–9; ANEP, figs. 276–8; DOTT, pp. 218–26, Pl. 13; Avigad, 'Some Unpublished Ancient Seals' [Hebr., Engl. summary] BIES 25 (1961), pp. 239–44, II, Pl. ה, 1–6; Galling, BRL, cols. 481–90; 'Beschriftete Bildsiegel des ersten Jt.s vChr vornehmlich aus Syrien und Palästina' ZDPV 64 (1941), pp. 121–202, Pls. 5–12; Giveon, 'Two New Hebrew Seals and Their Iconographic Background' PEQ 93 (1961), pp. 38–52, Pls. III–IV; Hammond, 'An Ammonitic Stamp from Amman' BASOR 160 (1960), pp. 6–15; Landes, 'The Material Civilisation of the Ammonites' BA 24 (1961), pp. 66–86, see pp. 81–5: 'Ammonite Written Materials'; Reifenberg, *Ancient Hebrew Seals* (1950); Yadin, 'A Hebrew Seal from Tell Jemmeh' [Hebr., Engl. summary] Eretz-Israel 6 (1960), pp. 53–5, 28*. Lit. § 126.
[17] AOB, fig. 578; ANEP, fig. 276; DOTT, Pl. 13; Galling, No. 17; Yeivin, 'The Date of The Seal "Belonging to Shemaʻ (the) Servant (of) Jeroboam"' JNESt 19 (1960), pp. 205–212; 'The Date of the Seal of "Shemaʻ Servant of Jeroboam"' [Hebr., Engl. summary] Eretz-Israel 6 (1960), pp. 47–52. 28*, Pl. VII, 2.
[18] Michaud, 'Une nouvelle lettre en paleohébraïque' VT 10 (1960), pp. 453–5; Naveh, 'A Hebrew Letter from the Seventh Century B.C.' IEJ 10 (1960), pp. 129–39, Pls. 17, 18; Vogt, 'Ostracon Hebr. saec. 7 A.C.' Bibl 41 (1960), pp. 183–4. Cf. §§ 4b, 126.
[19] ANET, pp. 321 f.; ANEP, fig. 279; DOTT, pp. 212–15, Pl. 12; Cross, 'Lachish Letter

diction they have much in common with passages of the Old Testament which derive from that period, for example, with many parts of the book of Jeremiah. There is as yet no literary evidence for the period before 1000 B.C. for the use of the Old Canaanite or Old Hebrew script by Israel, but there can be no doubt that the Israelites did in fact after their entry into Canaan compose their writings and books in this script, and that the *lad* (or *servant*=town scribe?) *of the men of Succoth,* who according to Judg. viii, 14[20] had to write down for Gideon in about 1100 the leaders and elders of this city, actually used it.

The Old Hebrew script is a purely consonantal script[21] consisting of 22 signs, in which the consonants *w* and *y* are only occasionally used as indications of the vowels $\bar{o}$, $\bar{u}$ and $\bar{\imath}$, $\bar{e}$ and the consonants *h* and ' as indications of $\bar{a}$. As a result two or more readings are possible with many words, and an interpretation different from the intention of the author can arise. Furthermore, some signs in this script are so like one another that interchanges and miswritings must have appeared very often: thus for example $\triangleleft$ *b* and $\triangleleft$ *r*, $\equiv$ *h* and $\Box$ *ḥ*, $\vee\!\!\vee$ *m* and $\vee$ *n*. In fact a number of obvious textual errors in the Old Testament may be most readily explained on the assumption that letters in the Old Hebrew script have been confused with one another, which means that such errors go back to the period when this script was being used in the composition and writing down of the books.

The Old Hebrew script continued to be used among the Jews until well into the post-exilic period. In the wording of seals and coins it always remained in use; even the coins from the last Jewish revolt (A.D. 132–135) have it.[22] But in the copying of the sacred books also, and particularly of the Torah, the Old Hebrew script continued to be used for a time even though elsewhere it had already been replaced by the Square script which will be considered in a moment. This persistence of the Old script is shown not only by the fact that the Samaritans, when they separated from the Jewish religious community, probably towards the end of the fourth century B.C. (p. 256), took over the Torah, which

IV' BASOR 144 (1956), pp. 24–6; Diringer, 'Ostraca' *Lachish* III (1953), Text, pp. 331–9; Plates, Nos. 48A, 48B; Michaud, 'Les ostraca de Lakiš conservés à Londres' Syria 34 (1957), pp. 39–60; Torczyner, 'The Lachish Letters' *Lachish* I (1938); Yeivin, 'Der historische Hintergrund der Lachis-Briefe' [Hebr.] in מחקרים בתולדות ישראל וארצו ישראל (1960), pp. 294–301.

[20] Leveen, 'The Meaning of וַיִּכְתֹּב in Judges viii, 14' JRAS (1948), pp. 61–2.

[21] Cf. the table of scripts in AOB fig. 606; ANEP fig. 286.

[22] DOTT, pp. 231–5, Pl. 14; Banks, *Coins of Bible Days* (1955); Hill, *A Catalogue of the Greek Coins in the British Museum: Palaestine* (1914); Kadman, *Corpus Nummorum Palaestinensium*, I (1956); II (1957); III (1960); 'The Hebrew Coin Script. A Study in the Epigraphy and Palaeography of Ancient Jewish Coins' [Hebr., English summary] Eretz-Israel 6 (1960), pp. 94–103, 30*–31*, Pl. XXIII; 'Numismatic Research in Israel and the Neighbouring Countries in the Last two Years' IEJ 11 (1961), p. 84; Kadman et al., *Numismatic Studies and Researches*, I (1954); II (1958); Kindler, 'Coins as Documents for Israel's Ancient History' Antiquity and Survival II, 2/3 (1957), pp. 225–36; Kindler and Bernheim, *Thesaurus of Judean Coins from the 4th Century B.C. to the 3rd Century A.D.* [Hebr., Engl. summary] (1958); Rahmani, 'The Coins from Naḥal Seelim and Naḥal Hardof' IEJ 11 (1961), pp. 63–4, Pl. 10 C–G; Reifenberg, *Ancient Jewish Coins* (³1963); *Israel's History in Coins from the Maccabees to the Roman Conquest* (1953); Wirgin and Mandel, *The History of Coins and Symbols in Ancient Israel* (1958); on this cf. Kirschner, 'New Views in Jewish Numismatics' [Hebr., Engl. summary] Eretz-Israel 6 (1960), pp. 115–21, 34*–35*. Lit. § 126.

they recognised as authoritative, in the Old Hebrew script, but also by the discovery among the Qumrān texts of fragments of several biblical scrolls containing Old Hebrew writing, particularly sections of Gen., Exod., Lev., Num., Deut., Job.[23] Side by side with this script, called by the Jews כְּתָב עִבְרִי *Hebrew script,* there gradually gained in significance the form of script named by them כְּתָב מְרֻבָּע *Square script* or כְּתָב אַשּׁוּרִי *Assyrian script.* The first name refers to its square form, the second to its origin from the Syriac-Aramaic language area where the older form of script, also here used at first, had developed into square-shaped letters. In secular use this script had probably come into use soon after the exile. The earliest Jewish inscription which we have in the Square script is that from 'Araq el-Emir in Transjordan,[24] probably from the fourth or even from the fifth or sixth century B.C.[25] It cannot be discovered with certainty from what date the sacred books were written in the new script or were transcribed into it. According to the tradition, it was Ezra who introduced the new script,[26] and this tradition is likely to be correct in so far as it suggests that this innovation was actually introduced in the time of Ezra, about 400 B.C. The biblical texts found near Qumrān, written in the period from the second century B.C. to the first century A.D., apart from the few exceptions already mentioned above, are written in the Square script,[27] and so also is the Nash Papyrus[28] which contains the decalogue and the Shema' prayer and belongs roughly to the same period as the Qumrān texts. Certainly in the time of Jesus the Pentateuch was written in the Square script. For when Jesus says in Matt. v, 18 that no iota or dot will pass away from the Law before the fulfilment of the Messianic prophecies, this can only refer to the Square script, since in this, but not in the old script, the iota (*yodh*) is the smallest letter.

The Square script too gives rise to many errors. Since, like the older script,

[23] *Qumran Cave I* (§ 104), pp. 51–4, No. 3, Pls. VIII, IX; Baillet, RB 63 (1956), p. 55; Harding, 'Recent Discoveries in Jordan' PEQ 90 (1958), pp. 7–18, see p. 17; Hunzinger, ThLZ 85 (1960), cols. 151–2; Skehan, 'Exodus in the Samaritan Recension from Qumran' JBL 74 (1955), pp. 182–7, with one plate; RB 63 (1956), p. 58.

[24] AOB, fig. 608; Albright (p. 647, n. 11) (1955), pp. 107 f.; Finkelstein, 'The Tobiads' HThR 36 (1943), pp. 31–3; Mazar, 'The Tobiads' IEJ 7 (1957), pp. 137–45, 229–38, see pp. 141 f., 229; McCown, 'The 'Araq el-Emir and the Tobiads' BA 20 (1957), pp. 63–76; Plöger, 'Hyrkan im Ostjordanland' ZDPV 71 (1955), pp. 70–81; Vincent, 'La date des épigraphes d''Arâq el-Émîr' JPOS 3 (1923), pp. 55–68; *Jérusalem de l'AT.* II–III (1956), pp. 464–6; Watzinger, *Denkmäler Palästinas*, II (1935), pp. 13–17, Pl. 22. Lit. § 126.

[25] Mazar explicitly states that the inscription from 'Araq el-Emir is one of the oldest examples of the Square script, and regards it as older than the ostraca from Tell el-Kheleifeh (Ezion-Geber), assigned to the sixth and fifth centuries B.C. On the latter, cf. Glueck, 'Ostraca from Elath' BASOR 80 (1940), pp. 3–10; 82 (1941), pp. 3–11, and Albright, 'Ostracon No. 6043 from Ezion-Geber' BASOR 82 (1941), pp. 11–15; Cross, 'The Development of the Jewish Scripts' *Essays Albright* (1961), pp. 133–202, assigns the inscription to the end of the fourth century or the beginning of the third century B.C. (p. 191).

[26] bab. Sanhedrin 21b.

[27] Cf. J. Fischer, *Das Alphabet der LXX- Vorlage im Pentateuch* (ATA, X, 2, 1924); *Zur Septuaginta-Vorlage im Pentateuch* (BZAW 42, 1926); *In welcher Schrift lag das Buch Isaias den LXX vor?* (BZAW 56, 1930).

[28] Cook, 'A Pre-Massoretic Biblical Papyrus' PSBA 25 (1903), pp. 34–56 with two plates; Albright, 'A Biblical Fragment from the Maccabaean Age: The Nash Papyrus' JBL 56 (1937), pp. 145–76; 'On the Date of the Scrolls from 'Ain Feshkha and the Nash Papyrus' BASOR 115 (1949), pp. 10–19; Birnbaum, 'The Date of the Cave Scrolls' BASOR 115 (1949), pp. 20–2.

it only contains consonants, and only indicates certain vowels by the use of the four consonants *w* and *y*, *h* and *'* employed as *matres lectionis* (pp. 670, 676), there are the same sources of error here as in the older script. There are also new ones, since here too certain letters resemble one another closely and invite confusion, as ב *b* and כ *k*, ד *d* and ר *r*, י *y* and ו *w*. In fact many textual errors are to be explained as due to confusion of letters in this script.

II. THE MASORETIC TEXT (𝔐)

Literature: Albrecht, 'Die sogenannten Sonderbarkeiten des masoretischen Textes' ZAW 39 (1921), pp. 160–9; Bamberger, 'Die Bedeutung der Qeri-Kethib' Jb. Jüd.-Lit. Ges. 15 (1923), pp. 217–65; 21 (1930), pp. 39–88; Bardtke, 'Der Traktat der Schreiber (Sopherim)' WZ Leipzig 3 (1953/54), pp. 13–31; Blank, 'A Hebrew Bible Ms. in the Hebrew Union College Library' HUCA 8/9 (1931/32), pp. 229–55; Blau, *Masoretische Untersuchungen* (1891); 'Massoretic Studies' JQR 8 (1896), pp. 343–59; 9 (1897), pp. 122–44, 471–90; Dhorme, 'Le texte hébreu de l'AT' RHPhR 35 (1955), pp. 129–44 = Cahiers de RHPhR 34 (1955), pp. 129–44; Edelmann, 'Zur Geschichte der Masora' *Kahle-Festschr.* (1935), pp. 15–18; *Corpus Codicum Hebraicorum Medii Aevi* (1956–1959);[29] Ehrentreu, *Untersuchungen über die Massora, ihre geschichtliche Entwicklung und ihren Geist* (1925); Eissfeldt, 'Zeilenfüllung' VT 2 (1952), pp. 87–92; Gertner, 'The Masorah and the Levites' VT 10 (1960), pp. 241–84; Ginsburg, *The Massorah compiled from Manuscripts* I–IV (1880/1905); *Introduction to the Massoretico-Critical Edition of the Hebrew Bible* (1897); Gordis, *The Biblical Text in the Making. A Study of the Kethib-Qere* (1937); on this cf. Orlinsky, JAOS 60 (1940), pp. 30–45; 'The Origin of the Masoretic Text in the Light of Rabbinic Literature and the DSS' [Hebr., Engl. summary] Tarbiz 27 (1957/58), pp. 444–69, III–IV; on this cf. Zeitlin, JQR 49 (1958/59), pp. 161–3; Jeremias, 'Ein Anhalt für die Datierung der masoretischen Redaktion?' ZAW 67 (1955), pp. 289 f.; Kahle, *Der masoretische Text des AT nach der Überlieferung der babylonischen Juden* (1902); *Masoreten des Ostens* (BWAT 15, 1913); 'Untersuchungen zur Geschichte des Pentateuchtextes' ThStKr 88 (1915), pp. 399–439 = *Op. Min.* (1956), pp. 3–37; §§ 6–9 in Bauer-Leander, *Historische Grammatik der hebräischen Sprache des AT* (1922 (1961)), pp. 71–162; *Masoreten des Westens* (BWAT 33, 1927/30); 'Die hebräischen Bibelhandschriften aus Babylonien' ZAW 46 (1928), pp. 113–37, Pls. 1–70; 'Der at. Bibeltext' ThR 5 (1933), pp. 227–38 = *Op. Min.* (1956), pp. 68–78; 'Treatise on the Oldest Manuscripts of the Bible' in Goldschmidt, *The Earliest Editions of the Hebrew Bible* (1950), pp. 41–60; 'Ivan Engnell's Text och Tradition' *Nötscher-Festschr.* (1950), pp. 129–36; 'The Hebrew Ben Asher Bible Manuscript' VT 1 (1951), pp. 161–7; 'The Ben Asher Text of the Hebrew Bible' *Donum Natalicium H.S. Nyberg* (1954), pp. 161–70 = Or Suec 4 (1955), pp. 43–52; *Der hebräische Bibeltext seit Franz Delitzsch* (1961); 'Pre-Masoretic Hebrew' Annual Leeds Or. Soc. 2 (1961), pp. 6–10; de Lagarde, *Anmerkungen zur griechischen Übersetzung der Proverbien* (1863), pp. 1–2; *Materialien zur Kritik und Geschichte des Pentateuchs* I (1867), pp. XII, 230 f.; Lieberman, *Hellenism in Jewish Palestine* (1950), pp. 38–43: 'The inverted Nun'; Morgenstern, 'The Loss of Words at the Ends of Lines in Manuscripts of Biblical Poetry' HUCA 25 (1954), pp. 41–83; Roberts, 'The Divergences in the Pre-Tiberian Masoretic Text' JJSt 1 (1949), pp. 147–55; Rothmüller, *Masoretische Eigentümlichkeiten in der Schrift* (1927); Seeligmann, 'Indications of Editional Alteration in the Massoretic Text and the Septuagint' VT 11 (1961), pp. 201–21; Sperber, 'Problems of the Masora' HUCA 17 (1942/43), pp. 293–394, 3 Pls.; Teicher, 'The Ben Asher Bible Manuscripts' JJSt 2 (1950/51), pp. 17–25; Weingreen, 'Rabbinic-Type Glosses in the OT' JSSt 2 (1957), pp. 149–62; Wellhausen, 'Versuch einer Rückwälzung der Textgeschichte' in Bleek, *Einleitung in das AT* (⁴1878), pp. 611–43.

Cf. also Literature § 126.

[29] Cf. p. 690, n. 4.

Since, so long as Hebrew and Aramaic were living languages,[30] probably till the middle of the first millennium A.D., the Hebrew and Aramaic texts of the Bible were preserved only in consonantal form and vowel signs were only then added to this text, we must consider first the history of the consonantal text, and then that of the vocalisation. It is true that the dividing line between vocalised and unvocalised texts is not quite clear, for, as we have seen (pp. 670, 676, 678), the consonantal text uses some consonants also to indicate particular vowels. But each of these two phases in the development of the Hebrew and Aramaic Bible text has its particular problems. So we shall consider first the consonantal text and then the pointing which provides vowel signs for it. The references to literature, apart from some few overlaps, are so arranged that the works which deal with the text as a whole, consonants and vowels, have been placed above, before the next two sections 115 and 116 which deal respectively with the consonantal text and the pointing, publications referring to the Qumrān texts which only have consonants have been placed in § 115, and those which deal with vocalisation in § 116.

§ 115. THE CONSONANTAL TEXT

Literature: (a) Editions of texts: Burrows, *The Isaiah Manuscript and the Habakkuk Commentary* (1950); Sukenik, *The Dead Sea Scrolls* (1955), pp. 30–4, Pls. 1–15: 'The Second Scroll of Isaiah (DSIs^b)'; Barthélemy and Milik, *Qumran Cave I* (*Discoveries in the Judaean Desert* I) (1955), pp. 49–76, 150–2 Nos. 1–13, 71–2 Pls. VIII–XIV; Benoit, Milik, de Vaux, *Les Grottes de Murabba'at* (*Discoveries in the Judaean Desert* II) (1960), pp. 75–86, 181–205 Nos. 1–5, 88, Pls. XIX–XXIV, LVI–LXXIII; Baillet, Milik, de Vaux, *Les 'Petites Grottes' de Qumran* (*Discoveries in the Judaean Desert of Jordan* III) (1962), pp. 48–77, 94–5, 105–16, 142, 143, 147–61, 169–78 Pls. X–XV, XVIII, XX–XXIII, XXX–XXXIV, XXXVI–XXXVIII.

(b) Other Works: Albright, 'New Light on Early Recensions of the Hebrew Bible' BASOR 140 (1955), pp. 27–33; Beegle, 'The Meaning of the Qumran Scrolls for Translators of the Bible' BT 8 (1957), pp. 1–8; Bič, 'Die Glaubwürdigkeit des masoretischen Textes und des der Septuaginta im Licht der Qumranfunde' CV 3 (1960), pp. 158–72; Birnbaum, *The Qumrân* (*Dead Sea*) *Scrolls and Palaeography* (BASOR Suppl Stud 13/14, 1952); Cross, 'A Report of the Biblical Fragments of Cave Four in Wâdî Qumrân' BASOR 141 (1956), pp. 9–13; Delcor, 'Des diverses manières d'écrire le tétragramm sacré dans les anciens documents hébraïques' RHR 147 (1955), pp. 145–73; Goshen-Gottstein, *Text and Language in Bible and Qumran* (1960); Greenberg, 'The Stabilization of the Text of the Hebrew Bible, reviewed in the Light of the Biblical Materials from the Judean Desert' JAOS 76 (1956), pp. 157–67; Hempel, 'Vorläufige Mitteilungen über die am Nordwestende des Toten Meeres gefundenen hebräischen Handschriften' NAG (1949), pp. 411–38; 'Randbemerkungen zu Qumran I' ZAW 67 (1955), pp. 131–9, see pp. 134–7; Kahle, 'The Karaites and the Manuscripts from the Cave' VT 3 (1953), pp. 82–4; Mansoor, 'The Thanksgiving Hymns and the Masoretic Text' RQ 3 (1961/62), pp. 259–66, 387–94; Martin, *The Scribal Character of the Dead Sea Scrolls*, I–II (1958); R. Meyer, 'Das Problem der Dialektmischung in den hebräischen Texten von Chirbet Qumran' VT 7 (1957), pp. 139–48; 'Spuren eines semitischen Präsens-Futur in den Texten von Chirbet Qumran'

[30] Birkeland, *The Language of Jesus* (ANVAO 1954, No. 1); Cantineau, 'Quelle langue parlait le peuple en Palestine au 1er siècle de notre ère?' Semitica 5 (1955), pp. 99–101; cf. above, p. 640, n. 8.

BZAW 77 (1958), pp. 118–28; 'Bemerkungen zu den hebräischen Aussprachetraditionen von Chirbet Qumrān' ZAW 70 (1958), pp. 39–48; Morag, 'The Independent Pronouns of the Third Person Singular in the DSS [Hebr., Engl. summary] Eretz-Israel 3 (1954), pp. 166–9, X; Mowinckel, 'Håndskriftfunnet ved Dødehavet og dets betydning for tekst-historien' NTT 52 (1951), pp. 145–77; North, 'Textual Variants in the Hebrew Bible significant for Critical Analysis' JQR 47 (1956/57), pp. 77–80; Orlinsky, 'Notes on the Present State of the Textual Criticism of the Judean Biblical Cave Scrolls' Papers Irwin (1956), pp. 117–31; van der Ploeg, 'Bijbeltekst en theologie in de teksten van Qumrân' Vox theologica 27 (1956), pp. 33–45; Rabin, 'The Dead Sea Scrolls and the History of the OT Text' JThSt 6 (1955), pp. 174–82; Skehan, 'The Qumran Manuscripts and Textual Criticism' SVT IV (1957), pp. 148–60, 1 Pl.; 'Qumran and the Present State of OT Studies: The Masoretic Text' JBL 78 (1959), pp. 21–5; Teicher, 'Method in Hebrew Palaeography' JJSt 2 (1950/51), pp. 200–2; Trever, 'Some Comments on the Palaeography of the Dead Sea Scrolls' JJSt 2 (1950/51), pp. 195–9; Tur-Sinai, 'The Development of the Letters and the Date of the Dead Sea Scrolls' [Hebr.] BIES 16 (1951), pp. 5–13; Wernberg-Møller, 'Pronouns and Suffixes in the Scrolls and the Masoretic Text' JBL 76 (1957), pp. 44–9.

Cf. also Literature on p. 678 and §§ 116, 125, 126.

It is customary to designate the canonical text as the Masoretic text (𝔐) because it was preserved and secured against every possibility of corruption by Jewish scholars of the second half of the first millennium A.D. known as 'Masoretes' from the Aramaic root מְסַר to transmit, hand down, thus trans-mitters, the successors of the older scribes (סֹפְרִים). Such learned work to secure the text is attested in the Mishna, for example in the utterance of Akiba[1] preserved in Pirke Aboth 3, 13 מָסֹרֶת סְיָג לַתּוֹרָה (scrupulous) transmission (of the text)—a hedge for the Torah; or in the notes on matters of textual criticism and grammar in Pesaḥim 9, 2 and Sota 5, 5, i.e. in about A.D. 200. Already several centuries earlier stress was laid upon the exact transmission of the text, as is shown by the Letter of Aristeas (pp. 603–6) and the passage earlier discussed from Josephus' work Contra Apionem (p. 563). It is shown too by various measures designed to protect the text concerning which the Qumrān texts give us information. But at first this was simply a matter of the establishing of the text for particular areas, larger or smaller, or for the sphere of influence of par-ticular schools of learning. Even within these spheres various other text-forms continued to exist side by side with the one which ranked as authoritative or which was claiming such authority. This is attested by the Samaritan text (§ 118), as well as by the Hebrew originals which are to be inferred for the Peshitta (§ 120) and the Septuagint (𝔊, § 121), which deviate in considerable measure from the Masoretic text. It is also attested by the other isolated wit-nesses to the text, such as the Nash Papyrus (p. 677), the Hebrew texts found in the Phylacteries,[2] the variants in the Codex Severus,[3] and the Cairo Geniza

[1] Ehrhardt, 'The Birth of the Synagogue and R. Akiba' StTh 9 (1956), pp. 86–111. Lit. p. 485, n. 3.

[2] QC I, pp. 72–6, No. 13, Pl. XIV; GM, pp. 80–5, No. 4, Pls. XXII–XXIV; Aharoni, IEJ 11(1961), pp. 22–3, Pl. 11 B. C.; Bowman, 'Phylacteries' TU 73 (1959), pp. 523–38; Haber-mann, 'The Phylacteries in Ancient Times' [Hebr.] Eretz-Israel 3 (1954), pp. 174–7; Kuhn, Phylakterien aus Höhle 4 von Qumran (AAH 1957, 1, 1957); Schneider, 'Der Dekalog in den Phylakterien von Qumrân' BZ 3 (1959), pp. 18–31. Cf. Lit. § 126.

[3] Epstein, 'Ein von Titus nach Rom gebrachter Pentateuch-Commentar und seine Varianten' MGWJ 34 (1885), pp. 337–51; Rengstorf, Ḥirbet Qumrân (1960), pp. 32, 66–7;

fragments.[4] The point is even more clearly emphasised by the numerous Hebrew Bible manuscripts which have recently come to light near Qumrān and elsewhere in the Wilderness of Judaea, belonging to the second and first centuries B.C. and to the first two centuries A.D. This is true both of the complete texts or those which are preserved in large sections such as the Isaiah and Habakkuk scrolls edited by Burrows, and the second Isaiah scroll published by Sukenik, and also of the almost immeasurable wealth of larger and smaller fragments of practically all the books of the Old Testament. Systematic publication was begun for Qumrān in 1955 by Barthélemy and Milik (*Qumran Cave I*) and for Murabbaʿat by Benoit, Milik and de Vaux in 1961 (*Les Grottes de Murabbaʿât*). As is shown by the detailed reports given by those who are concerned in the work in RB 63 (1956), pp. 49–67, and by the publication of numerous fragments which they and others (including Israeli scholars in IEJ 11 (1961), pp. 22–3, 40) have already undertaken, this is to be continued rapidly on a planned system.

Since the two Isaiah scrolls which were discovered in Cave I were published relatively quickly, it is natural that particular attention has been paid to their significance for textual criticism and that the fragments of further scrolls of Isaiah which have been found more recently in other caves have also been taken into account in the discussion.[5] The Habakkuk Commentary[6] and the other

Segal, 'The Promulgation of the Authoritative Text of the Hebrew Bible' JBL 72 (1953), pp. 35–47, see pp. 45–7.

[4] Hempel, *Der textkritische Wert des Konsonantentextes von Kairener Genizafragmenten in Cambridge und Oxford zum Deuteronomium* (NAWG 1959, 10, 1959).

[5] Franz Altheim and Ruth Stiehl, *Das erste Auftreten der Hunnen. Das Alter der Jesajarolle. Neue Urkunden aus Dura-Europos* (1953); Bardtke, 'Die Parascheneinteilung in der Jesajarolle I von Qumrân' *Dornseiff-Festschr.* (1953), pp. 33–75; Barthélemy, 'Le grand rouleau d'Isaïe trouvé près de la Mer Morte' RB 57 (1950), pp. 530–49; Beegle, 'Proper Names in the New Isaiah Scroll' BASOR 123 (1951), pp. 26–30; 'Ligatures with Waw and Yodh in the Dead Sea Isaiah Scroll' BASOR 129 (1953), pp. 11–14; Birnbaum, 'The Date of the Isaiah Scroll' BASOR 113 (1949), pp. 33–45; 'The Date of the Incomplete Isaiah Scroll from Qumrân' PEQ 92 (1960), pp. 19–26; Brønno, 'The Isaiah Scroll DSIa and the Greek Transliterations of Hebrew' ZDMG 106 (1956), pp. 252–8; Brownlee, 'The Manuscripts of Isaiah from which DSIa was copied' BASOR 127 (1952), pp. 16–21; Burrows, 'Variant Readings in the Isaiah Manuscript' BASOR 111 (1948), pp. 16–24; 113 (1949), pp. 24–32; '*Waw* and *Yodh* in the Isaiah Dea Sea Scroll' BASOR 124 (1951), pp. 18–20; Byington, 'יהוה and אדני' JBL 76 (1957), pp. 58–9; Cavaletti, 'גואים nel manoscritto del deserto di Giuda' RStOr 25 (1950), pp. 27–9; Eissfeldt, *Variae Lectiones Rotulorum Manu Scriptorum Anno 1947 prope Mare Mortuum repertorum ad Jes i–lxvi et Hab i–ii pertinentes* (1951); Goldman, 'The Isaiah MSS of the Dead Sea Scrolls' ABR 1 (1951), pp. 1–22; Goshen-Gottstein, 'Bemerkungen zu Eissfeldt's Variae Lectiones der Jesaiah-Rolle' Bibl 34 (1953), pp. 212–21; 'Die Jesaia-Rolle im Lichte von Peschitta und Targum' B bl 35 (1954), pp. 51–71; 'Die Jesajah-Rolle und das Problem der hebräischen Bibelhandschriften' Bibl 35 (1954), pp. 429–42; Guillaume, 'Les manuscrits hébreux' RB 59 (1952), pp. 182–6; 'Some Readings in the Dead Sea Scrolls of Isaiah' JBL 76 (1957), pp. 40–3; Gundry, 'למטלים 1 Q Isaiah a 1, 6 and Mark xiv, 65' RQ 2 (1959/60), pp. 559–567; Hempel, 'Beobachtungen an der "syrischen" Jesajarolle' ZDMG 101 (1951), pp. 138–173; Iwry, 'Maṣṣēbāh and Bāmāh in 1 Q IsaiahA vi, 13' JBL 76 (1957), pp. 225–32; 'The Qumrân IsaiahA and the End of the Dial of Ahaz' BASOR 147 (1957), pp. 27–33; James, *A Critical Examination of the Text of Isaiah based on the Dead Sea Scroll of Isaiah* (Boston University Graduate School 1959) [Microfilm]; Kissane, 'The Qumrân Text of Isaiah ix, 7–9 (1 Q Isᵃ)' BEThL XII (1959), pp. 413–18; Kuhl, 'Schreibereigentümlichkeiten. Bemerkungen zur Jesajarolle (DSIa)' VT 2 (1952), pp. 307–33; Kutscher, *The Language and Linguistic Background of the Complete Isaiah Scroll* [Hebr.] (1959); Lange, 'El Texto del

commentaries on biblical books similar to it have also been given considerable attention from the point of view of their significance for the text of the books which they expound. Furthermore, fragments have been published of about half the books of the Old Testament, either in the Qumrān caves or in other places in the Wilderness of Judaea—Gen.,[7] Exod.,[8] Lev.,[9] Num.,[10] Deut.,[11]

Nuovo Rollo de Isaias Comparado con el Texto Masorético' Revista de Teologia 5 (1955), pp. 19–25; 6 (1955), pp. 21–6; 7 (1955), pp. 29–33; Lehmann, 'A Third Dead Sea Scroll of Isaiah' JJSt 4 (1953), pp. 38–40; Leveen, 'The Orthography of the Hebrew Scroll of Isaiah A' P XXII CO, II (1957), pp. 577–83; Levi della Vida, 'Nota a RStOr XXV, 27–9' RStOr 26 (1951), pp. 39 f.; Lindblom, 'Deuterojesaja i den nyfunna Jesaja-handskriften från Palestina' SvTK 26 (1950), pp. 302–14; 'Die Jesaja-Apokalypse in der neuen Jesajahandschrift' Bull. Soc. Lettres Lund (1950/51), pp. 87–97; 'Die Ebed-Jahwe-Orakel in der neuentdeckten Jesajahandschrift (DSIa)' ZAW 63 (1951), pp. 235–48; Löfgren, 'Zur Charakteristik des "vormasoretischen" Jesajatextes' Donum Natalicium Nyberg (1954), pp. 171–84 = Or Suec 4 (1955), pp. 53–66; Loewinger, 'New Corrections to the Variae Lectionis of O. Eissfeldt' VT 4 (1954), pp. 80–7; 'Remnants of a Hebrew Dialekt in 1Q Is^a' Essays in Memory E. L. Sukenik (1961), pp. 141–61; Martin, The Dead Sea Scroll of Isaiah (1954); 'The Use of Second Person Singular Suffixes in IQIs^a' Muséon 70 (1957), pp. 127–44; Mowinckel, 'Det eldste kjente gammeltestamentlige Bibelhåndskrift' NTT 52 (1951), pp. 252–6; Noth, 'Eine Bemerkung zur Jesajarolle vom Toten Meer' VT 1 (1951), pp. 224–6; Orlinsky, 'Studies in the St. Mark's Isaiah Scroll' I. JBL 69 (1950), pp. 149–66; II. JNESt 11 (1952), pp. 153–6; III. JJSt 2 (1950/51), pp. 151–4; IV. JQR 43 (1952/53), pp. 329–40; V. IEJ 4 (1954), pp. 5–8; VI. HUCA 25 (1954), pp. 85–92; VII. [Hebr., Engl. summary] Tarbiz 24 (1954/55), pp. 4–8, I–III; 'Photography and Paleography in the Textual Criticism of St. Mark's Isaiah Scroll xliii, 19' BASOR 123 (1951), pp. 33–5; Penna, 'La Volgata e il Manoscritto 1 Q Is^a' Bibl 38 (1957), pp. 381–95; Reider and Brownlee, 'On MSHTY in the Qumran Scrolls' BASOR 134 (1954), pp. 27–8; Roberts, 'The Second Isaiah Scroll from Qumrân (1 Q Isb)' BJRL 42 (1959/60), pp. 132–44; Th. H. Robinson, 'New Light on the Text and Interpretation of the OT Supplied by Recent Discoveries' ZAW 73 (1961), pp. 265–9; Rubinstein, 'Isaiah lii, 14 – מָשְׁחַת – and the DSIa Variant' Bibl 35 (1954), pp. 475–9; 'Formal Agreement of Parallel Clauses in the Isaiah Scroll' VT 4 (1954), pp. 316–21; 'Some Aspects of Luzzatto's Commentary on Isaiah in the Light of DSIa' [Hebr., Engl. summary] Melilah 5 (1955), pp. 31–43, III; 'The Theological Aspect of Some Variant Readings in the Isaiah Scroll' JJSt 6 (1955), pp. 187–200; 'Conditional Constructions in the Isaiah Scroll (DSIa)' VT 6 (1956), pp. 69–79; 'A Kethib-Qere Problem in the Light of the Isaiah Scroll' JSSt 4 (1959), pp. 127–33; Seeligmann, 'ΔΕΙΞΑΙ ΑΥΤΩΙ ΦΩΣ' [Hebr., Engl. summary] Tarbiz 27 (1957/58), pp. 127–41, III; Skehan, 'The Text of Isaias at Qumran' CBQ 17 (1955), pp. 158–63; Solá Solé, 'Una tendencia lingüística en el manuscrito de Isaias (DSIa) de Khirbet-Qumran' Sefarad 13 (1953), pp. 61–71; Sonne, 'The X-Sign in the Isaiah Scroll' VT 4 (1954), pp. 90–4; Talmon, 'On the Variant Readings in 1 Q Isaiah^a' [Hebr.] Publications of the Israel Society for Biblical Research 1 (1954/55), pp. 147–56; Trever, 'Isaiah xliii, 19 according to the First Isaiah Scroll (DSIa)' BASOR 121 (1951), pp. 13–16; 'Some Corrections Regarding Isaiah xliii, 19 in the Isaiah Scroll' BASOR 126 (1952), pp. 26 f.; Vaccari, 'De nonnullis lectionibus voluminis Isaiae nuper ad Mare Mortuum reperti' Stud. Anselm. 27/28 (1951), pp. 254–63; Wernberg-Møller, 'Studies in the Defective Spellings in the Isaiah-Scroll of St Mark's Monastery' JSSt 3 (1958), pp. 244–64; Ziegler, 'Die Vorlage der Isaias-Septuaginta und die erste Isaias-Rolle von Qumran (1 Q Is^a)' JBL 78 (1959), pp. 34–59; Zolli, 'L'apporto del Ms. DSIa all' esegesi del libro d'Isaia' Antonianum, Rom, 26 (1951), pp. 295–306; 'Il Canto dei Morti Risorti e il Ms. DSIa in Is xxvi, 18' Sefarad 12 (1952), pp. 375–8. Cf. Lit. § 126.

[6] Brownlee, The Text of Habakkuk in the Ancient Commentary from Qumran (JBL Mon. Ser. XI, 1959); Cantera Ortiz de Urbina, El comentario de Habacuc de Qumran (Textos y estudios del Seminario filologico Cardenal Cisneros, 1960); Díez-Macho, 'El texto biblico del comentario de Habacuc de Qumran' Junker-Festschr. (1961), pp. 59–64; Ratzaby, 'Remarks Concerning the Distinction between Waw and Yodh in the Habakkuk Scroll' JQR 41 (1950/51), pp. 155–7.

[7] QC I, pp. 49–50, No. 1, Pl. VIII; GM, pp. 75–7, No. 1, Pl. XIX.

[8] QC I, pp. 50–1, No. 2, Pl. VIII; GM, pp. 77–8, No. 1, Pl. XX; pp. 81–3, No. 4, Pl.

Judg.,[12] Sam.,[13] Isa.,[14] Ezek.,[15] the Book of the Twelve Prophets,[16] Psalms,[17] Eccl.,[18] and Dan.[19] The number and size of the fragments differ widely from book to book. For Sam., several chapters are available, whereas for Deut. and Hos. only verses or parts of verses, and in the latter case they have for the most part little value for textual criticism. It does, however, happen that even quite small fragments of scrolls are really valuable for textual criticism. The fragment which contains a few words of Deut. xxxii is of very great importance since in verse 8, instead of the word יִשְׂרָאֵל found in 𝔐, it reads אֵל; this justifies the emendation, first proposed a long time ago, of יִשְׂרָאֵל to אֵל on the basis of the LXX rendering θεοῦ. Various pieces of information about many as yet unpublished fragments, both large and small, are to be found in the reports mentioned in the third section of the literature to § 104 and also in other publications, for example, in Cross, *The Ancient Library of Qumrân* (1958), as well as in his essay 'The Development of the Jewish Scripts' in the Essays presented to Albright for his seventieth birthday, pp. 133–202. Here may be found the information, mentioned on p. 349, that fragments have been found at Qumrān of two editions of the Hebrew book of Jeremiah, corresponding to the

XXIII; Aharoni, IEJ 11 (1961), pp. 22 f.; Cross, *The Ancient Library of Qumrân* (1958), pp. 33–4, 143–4; Skehan, 'Exodus in the Samaritan Recension from Qumran' JBL 74 (1955), pp. 182–7, 1 Pl.; de Vaux, 'Quelques textes Hébreux de Murabba'at. I. Fragment de l'Exode' RB 60 (1953), pp. 268–75, Pl. XIIa; Wernberg-Møller, 'The Exodus Fragment from Massada' VT 10 (1960), pp. 229–30.

[9] QC I, pp. 51–3, No. 3, Pl. VIII; Birnbaum, 'The Leviticus Fragments from the Cave' BASOR 118 (1950), pp. 20–7; Cross, *The Ancient Library of Qumrân* (1958), p. 25; Yeivin, 'The Date and Attribution of the Leviticus Fragments from the Cache in the Judaean Desert' BASOR 118 (1950), pp. 28–30.

[10] QC I, p. 53, No. 3, Pl. IX; GM, p. 78, No. 1, Pl. XXI; Cross, RB 63 (1956), p. 56; *The Ancient Library of Qumrân* (1958), pp. 32, 38–9, 143–4.

[11] QC I, pp. 54–62, Nos. 4, 5, Pls. IX, X; GM, pp. 78–9, No. 2, Pl. XXI; pp. 83–5, No. 4, Pl. XXIV; Albright, 'Some Remarks on the Song of Moses in Deuteronomy xxxii' VT 9 (1959), pp. 339–46; Artom, 'Sul testo di Deuteronomio, xxxii, 37–43' RStOr 32 (1957), pp. 285–91; Gaster, 'A Qumran Reading on Deuteronomy xxxiii, 10' VT 8 (1958), pp. 217–219; Cf. p. 227, n. 14; p. 228, n. 17. Lit. § 126. [12] QC I, pp. 62–4, No. 6, Pl. XI.

[13] QC I, pp. 64–5, No. 7, Pl. XI; Cross, 'A New Qumran Biblical Fragment related to the Original Hebrew underlying the Septuagint' BASOR 132 (1953), pp. 15 26; 'The Oldest Manuscripts from Qumran' JBL 74 (1955), pp. 147–72, Fig. 6; *The Ancient Library of Qumrân* (1958), pp. 31–3, 133–4, 140–3; Eybers, 'Notes on the Text of Samuel found in Qumran Cave 4' (*Die Ou Testamentiese Werkgemeenskap in Suid-Afrika, Studies in the Book of Samuel*) (1960), pp. 1–17; Hempel, 'Ein textgeschichtlich bedeutsamer Fund' ZAW 65 (1954), pp. 296–8; Maass, 'Zu den Qumran-Varianten der Bücher Samuel' ThLZ 81 (1956), cols. 337–40. On I II Kings, cf. Baillet, RB 63 (1956), p. 55.

[14] p. 681, n. 5; GM, pp. 79–80, No. 3, Pl. XXII. On Jeremiah cf. above, p. 349. Lit. § 126.

[15] QC I, p. 68 f., No. 9, Pl. XII. Lit. § 126.

[16] GM, pp. 181–205, No. 88, Pls. LVI–LXXIII; Testuz, 'Deux fragments inédits des manuscrits de la Mer Morte' Semitica 5 (1955), pp. 37–8. Pl. I, see p. 37. Pl. I, Fig. 2: Hos. xiii, 15b, xiv, 1a, xiv, 3–6. Lit. § 126.

[17] QC I, pp. 69–72, Nos. 10–12, Pl. XIII; Cross, *The Ancient Library of Qumrân* (1958), p. 25; Hunzinger, ThLZ 85 (1960), cols. 151–2; Milik, 'Deux documents inédits du Désert de Juda' Bibl 38 (1957), pp. 245–68, Pls. I–IV, see pp. 245–55, Pl. I: Psaumes xxxi, 24 f. +xxxiii, 1–18, xxxv, 4–20; Yadin, IEJ 11 (1961), p. 40; BA 24 (1961), p. 44; 'Finding Bar Kochba's Despatches' ILN 239 (1961), pp. 772–5, see p. 772. On Job, cf. below, p. 696. Lit. § 126.

[18] Dahood, 'Qoheleth and Recent Discoveries' Bibl 39 (1958), pp. 302–18, see pp. 303–6. Muilenburg, 'A Qoheleth Scroll from Qumran' BASOR 135 (1954), pp. 20–8.

[19] QC I, pp. 150–2, Nos. 71–2.

fuller text of 𝔐 and to the shorter text which lies behind the Greek translation.

From the great wealth of new insights into the development of the Hebrew text of the Bible which these discoveries make possible, we can here pick out only three observations. (1) In the first place, the two Isaiah scrolls, of which the first, complete one deviates from the Masoretic text substantially more than the second, incomplete one, show us the beginnings of the development which was to issue in the suppression of various popular texts in circulation by a standard text. The same is true of the text of the Habakkuk Commentary. (2) In the second place, we may note the piece of a leather scroll found in 1952 in Qumrān cave 4 and published by Cross in 1953 as 'a fragment related to the original Hebrew underlying the Septuagint'. (According to RB 63 (1956), pp. 56 f., other fragments purchased in the meantime from their Bedouin finders have filled in considerable gaps in the scroll.) This piece contains the Hebrew text, not without gaps, of I Sam. i, 22–ii, 25, and it shows that at the time of its writing, probably in the first century B.C., there was in existence a text-form of the book of Samuel which stands considerably nearer to 𝔊 than to 𝔐. It thus sheds a new light on the question of the 'Protoseptuagint' (p. 709), as well as on the history of the Hebrew text of the Bible, at the same time providing a wonderful justification of the restoration of the text of the books of Samuel undertaken by Wellhausen in 1871 mainly on the basis of 𝔊. (3) In the third place, some Qumrān manuscripts are close to the Samaritan, so that now this text-form too may be traced back into the first century B.C. Quite apart therefore from the manuscripts which do not fit into any of the three groups just mentioned—and there is no lack of such in Qumrān—we thus have for the first century B.C., and perhaps even for the second and third centuries B.C., evidence of three forms of the Hebrew text of the Bible, of which the first represents the preliminary stage of 𝔐, the second is the precursor of the original Hebrew of 𝔊, and the third developed into the Samaritan. The stage in the development of the Hebrew text of the Bible which thus becomes recognisable, is similar in some measure to the stage in the history of the text of 𝔊 to be discussed later (pp. 705–12), a stage characterised by the existence side by side of several recensions as well as of isolated textual witnesses which do not fit into any of the groups. The similarity is to be seen also in the fact that the illumination of this situation, at first appearing so chaotic, belongs among the most important tasks imposed upon scholarship by the new material which has come to light in both fields.

With all the diversity of the text-forms in circulation at the time, there were thus already in the first century B.C. efforts at replacing them by a normative text. But considerable time was yet to elapse before these efforts were successful in reaching the goal of the establishment of a text recognised by the whole of Jewry. However, the basic form of 𝔐 was already in existence about A.D. 100, and from that time on gradually prevailed in the course of a continuous struggle with other text-forms still in circulation. The situation was indeed that at that time, much more strongly than previously, the need was felt for a single authoritative text-form. The same motive which led to the fixing of the canon (p. 568) also provided the impulse for the establishing of the text, primarily of the Torah, down to the smallest detail: there was need of an absolutely reliable basis for belief and action. Rabbi Akiba († A.D. 135)[20] may be regarded, if not as the originator, yet as the first outstanding representative of the kind of biblical exegesis which laid stress upon the letter, and so made necessary the securing of the text down to the smallest detail. Whereas up till the beginning of the Christian era, as the evidence of the Qumrān discoveries shows, there existed a great variety of text-forms, the translations made in the second and third centuries A.D., those of Aquila, Theodotion and Symmachus, show that the text then already had approximately the form in which we now have it. Admittedly only approximately, for there was not a complete lack of variants, and even Aquila and Symmachus presuppose here and there a text deviating from 𝔐. Thus the fixation of the text was only in process of emerging, and the theory adopted by many scholars[21] and particularly by Lagarde, that in about A.D. 130 one codex of the Old Testament was established as the normative archetype and subsequently copied over and over again with all its peculiarities —*literae majusculae, literae minusculae, literae suspensae* etc. (p. 686)—can no longer be maintained in this form. It must be replaced by the assumption that the established text which we have, already at that time in existence in its main characteristics, and indeed already existing two centuries earlier (p. 684), prevailed only after conflict with other text-forms circulating with it, and eventually replaced these completely.

This textual tradition was at first handed down orally. Later the Masoretes began to write down their traditions, putting their notes between the lines of the text and on its margins at both sides and at top and bottom, or collecting them in independent compilations. Numerical information concerning the frequency of the occurrence of individual words and forms in the relevant book or in the Old Testament as a whole, references to peculiarities of writing and other points which will be later specially mentioned (p. 686), form the content of these notes. At the ends of the individual books there are also indications which cover the whole book: the number of words and sentences, the middle word, and so on. The Masora of Aaron ben Moshe ben Asher (pp. 689 90), printed in Kittel's *Biblia Hebraica* from the third edition onwards (begun in 1929 and finished in 1937), gives the reader an impression of the nature of Masoretic learning, and the list of Masoretic technical terms provided with this edition makes it relatively easy to penetrate further into this world of thought which seems so strange and is otherwise difficult of access. The effort to do so is well rewarding. For these notes not only have great significance for the history of Hebrew grammar, but it is also possible to extract from them much that is relevant to the history of the text.

Among the Masoretic notes, the following may be selected as significant for the history of the text and so also at least for the most part significant also for textual criticism: the demand for peculiar writing of individual words such as בראשית in Gen. i, 1 with an unusually large ב at the beginning, and in ii, 4

[20] Cf. p. 485, n. 3; p. 680, n. 1.
[21] Rosenmüller, 1797 and 1834 (cf. Stade ZAW 4 (1884), pp. 302 f.; Preuschen, ZAW 9 (1889), p. 303); Sommer, 1846 (cf. Cornill, ZAW 12 (1892), p. 309).

בהבראם with an unusually small ה, or מ'שה in Judg. xviii, 30 with a raised נ. It may be that in part we have here a pedantic adherence to chance peculiarities of one manuscript which was regarded as providing the normative pattern (pp. 684 f.). But in many cases the peculiar method of writing is of value for the history of the text. Thus the raising of the נ in Judg. xviii, 30 certainly preserves the recollection that the name was originally משה *Moses* and not מנשה *Manasseh*, and that the נ was added in order to release Moses from the disgrace of being the founder of a priesthood outside Jerusalem. In about twenty places, the Masora indicates a reading as תקון סכרים *a correction of the scribes*. The best-known example is in Gen. xviii, 22b, where the original text *and Yahweh remained standing before Abraham* has been corrected to the present text *and Abraham remained standing before Yahweh*, because *to stand before* may be understood as 'to serve' and it was felt to be blasphemous to think that Yahweh should have served Abraham.

Here the alteration has been made on dogmatic grounds, and this is true for most of the other changes. It is very important to note that at any rate a few such alterations of the older text are explicitly attested as such. For this justifies the assumption that in other passages where a corruption of the text must be postulated on internal grounds, even though there is no Masoretic note to indicate it or no other external witness available, in actual fact such a corruption is present. It was the merit above all of Abraham Geiger that he drew attention to the possibility of such tendentious alterations. In fifteen places in the Old Testament, points, called *puncta extraordinaria*, are placed over single letters and words to express doubt as to the correctness of the reading or even to cut out the letters and words in question altogether. An example is וַיִּשָּׁקֵהוּ *and he kissed him* in Gen. xxxiii, 4, where the dots placed over the word indicate that it is wrong; in fact there is nothing corresponding to it in ⅁. Moreover, the scribe of the complete Isaiah scroll from Qumrān was already making use of such *puncta extraordinaria* for purposes similar to those of the Masoretes, as for example in col. X, 23; XXIX, 3, 10. The most frequent and best known of the Masoretic notes is Qere *to be read* and Kethib *what is written*, i.e. the indication that a word is to be read differently from what is written in the text. So for example, instead of what was written in the text at I Sam. v, 6, 12—עפלים *swelling of the anus*—which was felt to be objectionable, we are to read טחרים *haemorrhoids*. Here too we have a kind of dogmatic alteration, and the same is true, if we may here for the moment anticipate a case which involves pointing, with what is termed *Qere perpetuum* because it is not specially noted on each occasion, namely the writing of יהוה with the vowels of אֲדֹנָי *the Lord* as יְהֹוָה (or perhaps with the vowels of שְׁמָא *the name* as יְהֹוָה).[22] But in other cases with the Qere, alterations are suggested which are made on exegetical or grammatical grounds or perhaps also rest upon the comparison of several

---

[22] Alfrink, 'Die Aussprache von שְׁמָא für יְהֹוָה' ThZ 5 (1949), pp. 72–3; Katz, Reply to this, *ib.*, pp. 73–4; Kahle, *The Cairo Geniza* (1947), pp. 172 f. (differently in 2nd ed. (1959), p. 162); Katz, 'Zur Aussprache von יְהֹוָה' ThZ 4 (1948), pp. 467–9; 'יְהֹוָה=JᴱJĀ, יהיה= JĀJĀ?' VT 4 (1954), pp. 428 f.

manuscripts. All in all, this provides us with a confusing mass of small detail, some of it trivial; but not a little of it deserves serious consideration.

Important schools in which this Masoretic learning was cultivated existed in Palestine and in Babylonia. In the former, the centre was at Tiberias; in the latter primarily at Nehardea and Sura. The text handed down and provided with Masora by these was not always entirely uniform. In particular the text and Masora of the Babylonian schools, the Orientals (מְדִנְחָאֵי) differed from those of the Tiberian school, the Occidentals (מַעַרְבָאֵי), and this not only in the pronunciation which was at first transmitted only orally, but also in regard to the consonantal text. Though some of the differences are unimportant, there are also some which are of significance. In Kittel's *Biblia Hebraica* from the third edition onwards the readings of the Orientals have been introduced by Kahle exactly from the manuscripts in which they occur, and the reader, by looking through the *apparatus criticus*, can easily gain insight into the variants which are here in question.

§ 116. THE POINTING OF THE TEXT

Literature: Ben-David, 'The Differences between Ben Asher and Ben Naftali' [Hebr., Eng. summary] Tarbiz 26 (1956/57), pp. 384–409, IV–V; Ben-Ḥayyim, *Studies in the Traditions of the Hebrew Language* (1954); Breuer, *The Punctuation of the Bible by means of the Masoretic Accents* [Hebr.] (1958); on this cf. Perath, BiOr 17 (1960), pp. 75 f.; Cohen, 'Die Bedeutung der verschiedenen Punktationssysteme für die Aussprache des Hebräischen' MGWJ 80 (1936), pp. 390–7; Díaz Esteban, 'Notas sobre la Masora' Sefarad 14 (1954), pp. 315–21; 'The Sefer Oklah w'Oklah as a source of not registered Bible textual variants' ZAW 70 (1958), pp. 250–3; Díez Macho, 'Tres nuevos manuscritos bíblicos "palestinenses" ' Est Bíbl 13 (1954), pp. 247–65; 'Un manuscrito hebreo protomasorético y nueva teoría acerca de los llamados mss Ben Naftalí' Est Bíbl 15 (1956), pp. 187–222, 4 Pls.; 'Nuevos manuscritos importantes, bíblicos o litúrgicos, en hebreo o arameo' Sefarad 16 (1956), pp. 1–22; 'Un manuscrito "Palestinense" en la Biblioteca Nacional de Estrasburgo' Sefarad 17 (1957), pp. 11–17; 'Un manuscrito yemení de la biblia babilónica' Sefarad 17 (1957), pp. 237–79; 'Fragmento del texto hebreo y arameo del libro de Números' Sefarad 17 (1957), pp. 386–8; 'Importants manuscrits hébreux et araméens aux Etats-Unis' SVT IV (1957), pp. 27–46; 'Otros dos manuscritos "palestinenses" de Salmos' Sefarad 18 (1958), pp. 254–271; 'Un especimen de ms. bíblico babilónico en papel' Bibl 40 (1959), pp. 171–6; 'A New Fragment of Isaiah with Babylonian Pointing' Textus 1 (1960), pp. 132–43; Dotan, *Was Ben-Asher really a Karaite?* [Hebr.] (1957); Edelmann, *Corpus Codicum Hebraicorum Medii Aevi* (1956–59); cf. below, p. 690, n. 4; Kahle, 'Die überlieferte Aussprache des Hebräischen und die Punktation der Masoreten' ZAW 39 (1921), pp. 230–9 = *Op. Min.* (1956), pp. 38–47; 'Die Punktation der Masoreten' BZAW 41 (1925), pp. 167–72 = *Op. Min* (1956), pp. 48–53; 'The Ben Asher Text of the Hebrew Bible' *Donum Natalicium Nyberg* (1954), pp. 161–170 = Or Suec 4 (1955), pp. 43–52; 'The Massoretic Text of the Bible and the Pronunciation of Hebrew' JJSt 7 (1956), pp. 133–53; 'Die Aussprache des Hebräischen in Palästina vor der Zeit der tiberischen Masoreten' VT 10 (1960), pp. 375–85; L. Koehler, 'Bemerkungen zur Schreibung und Aussprache der Tiberischen Masora' HUCA 23, 1 (1950/51), pp. 137–55; Leander, 'Bemerkungen zur palästinischen Überlieferung des Hebräischen' ZAW 54 (1936), pp. 91–9; Lipschütz, *Ben Ašer—Ben Naftali. Der Bibeltext der tiberischen Masoreten. Eine Abhandlung des Mischael ben 'Uẓẓiel, veröffentlicht und untersucht* (Diss. phil. Bonn, 1935); R. Meyer, 'Die Bedeutung der linearen Vokalisation für die hebräische Sprachgeschichte' WZ Leipzig 3 (1953/54), pp. 85–94;

'Bemerkungen zu den hebr. Aussprachetraditionen von Chirbet Qumrān' ZAW 70 (1958), pp. 39–48; Mordell, 'The Beginning and Development of Hebrew Punctuation' JQR 24 (1933/34), pp. 137–49; Orlinsky, 'The Origin of the Kethib-qere system: a New Approach' SVT VII (1960), pp. 184–93; Pérez Castro, 'Bemerkungen zu zwei verschiedenen Entwick-lungsstufen in der Überlieferung des hebräischen Bibeltextes' ZDMG 105 (1955), pp. 45*–46;* '¿Ben Ašer—Ben Naftali? Números 13–15 en cinco manuscritos a la luz de Mišael ben 'Uzziel' Homenaje a Millás-Vallicrosa, II (1956), pp. 141–8; 'Corregido y correcto. El MS 19 a (Leningrado) frente al MS Or 4445 (Londres) y al Códice de los Profetas de El Cairo' Sefarad 15 (1955), pp. 3–30; Prijs, 'Über Ben Naftali-Bibelhandschriften und ihre paläogra-phischen Besonderheiten' ZAW 69 (1957), pp. 171–84, 2 Pls.; Roberts, 'The Emergence of the Tiberian Masoretic Text' JThSt 49 (1948), pp. 8–16; Scheiber, 'Unknown Leaves from שאלות עתיקות' HUCA 27 (1956), pp. 291–303, cf. p. 293; Speiser (p. 711, n. 64); Wutz, 'Abweichende Vokalisationsüberlieferung im hebr. Text' BZ 21 (1933), pp. 9–21; Yeivin, 'A Biblical Fragment with Tiberian Non-Masoretic Vocalisation' [Hebr., Engl. summary] Tarbiz 29 (1959/60), pp. 345–56, III–IV; 'Fragment of a Masoretic Treatise' Textus 1 (1960), pp. 185–208, 2 Pls.; 'A Unique Combination of Accents' Textus 1 (1960), pp. 209–10.
    Cf. also Literature on p. 678 and §§ 115, 125, 126.

In the area in which the Canaanite-Phoenician and Old Hebrew script were in use, the practice is early attested of expressing at least some vowels in this script, otherwise limited to the expression of consonants, by the use of particu-lar consonants, especially suitable for the purpose by reason of their 'half-vowel' character (p. 676). This practice was also followed in the writing down of the books of the Old Testament. The biblical scrolls and fragments of scrolls from Qumrān and from various other places in the Wilderness of Judaea all show the use of such *matres lectionis*, particularly frequently in the com-plete Isaiah scroll. This method of indicating vowels then survived as a sup-plement to the newer method when the various systems of pointing which we are about to discuss provided new means of indicating the vowels. There was another method of determining in writing the vocalisation of the biblical books, though admittedly it was restricted to Greek-speaking Jewry. This was the transcription of the text into Greek letters, of which an example is the second column (Secunda) of Origen's Hexapla (pp. 709–10). But measures of this kind could only fulfil very incompletely the purpose for which they were intended. So from the sixth century onwards, and perhaps even from the fifth, first the Babylonian Jews and soon afterwards the Palestinian Jews began to insert vocalisation signs and accents in the manuscripts of the Bible which had up till then contained simply the consonantal text. In both areas the development took place in two stages. The older Babylonian system of vocalisation—we shall from now on limit our discussion to vocalisation and leave on one side the accents which are less significant for our purpose—was constructed in connec-tion with that of the Eastern Syrians. It was replaced in the ninth century by the complicated system which had come into existence towards the end of the eighth century, probably connected with the rise of the Karaite sect. For the Karaite sect which, as its name בְּנֵי מִקְרָא or קָרָאִים *adherents of the Bible* shows, based its teaching exclusively on scripture, had to lay the greatest possible stress upon the exact establishing of the text. In Palestine also a distinction may be made between an older and simpler system of vocalisation, and a later more elaborate one, and here too it is probable that the older one, called *the pointing of the land of Israel* was felt to be unsatisfactory in connection with the rise of the Karaites and was replaced by the newer system, known as the *Tiberian pointing*.

It is easy to understand that the attempt at fixing in writing as exactly as possible the pronunciation of the consonantal text which had hitherto been transmitted only orally, would inevitably lead to new differences between the various schools. Here again the greatest differences were between the Babylonian and Palestinian schools. But the Tiberian pointing, together with its Masora, soon succeeded in dislodging the Babylonian and remained sole master of the field. But even the exponents of the Palestinian tradition were not at one among themselves. It was particularly the two main authorities from the families of ben Naphtali and ben Asher, flourishing probably in the first half of the tenth century, which struggled for supremacy, and it was only towards the end of the twelfth century that Maimonides brought about a decision in favour of the ben Asher text. But this did not mean the complete disappearance of the text and Masora of ben Naphtali. A relatively large amount of it survived, so that by far the majority of our manuscripts of the Bible contain a mixed text from ben Asher and ben Naphtali. In the fourteenth century the assimilation of the manuscripts to one another, which up till then still deviated in small details, was complete, and from then on the manuscripts contain in general the same text form, the *textus receptus*.

As just indicated, the development of the system of pointing may be traced in the fragments of pointed Hebrew manuscripts which have come down to us since the sixth or perhaps the fifth century A.D., for the most part from the Geniza of the Ezra Synagogue in Cairo (p. 599), and also in the complete pointed manuscripts of the whole Old Testament or of its books and groups of books, which extend back to the end of the ninth century A.D. The Babylonian pointed fragments were published by Kahle in his two works mentioned on p. 678, *Masoreten des Ostens* (1913) and 'Die hebräischen Bibelhandschriften aus Babylonien' (1928); and those with Palestinian vocalisation in his *Masoreten des Westens* (1927–30). In the manuscripts of the whole Old Testament or of large parts of it, however, available to us from the end of the tenth century, there are to be found the later more complicated systems, Babylonian on the one hand and Tiberian on the other, the latter revealing the existence side by side of two systems, namely those put forward by the two rival families of scholars, ben Asher and ben Naphtali. This may be made clear by a brief description of some of the manuscripts, enumerated in order of age. The Codex of the Prophets[1] belonging to the Karaite synagogue in Cairo and written in 895 by Moshe ben Asher, the next-to-last member of the great Asher family of scholars, contains the 'Former' and the 'Latter' prophets (pp. 302 f., 566), i.e. Josh. to Mal., and has a ben Asher text. The Petersburg Codex of the Prophets,[2] prepared in

[1] Kahle, 'Zu den Handschriftenfunden in Höhlen beim Toten Meer' Das Altertum 3 (1957), pp. 34–46, cf. p. 46, n. 1.

[2] Strack, *Prophetarum posteriorum Codex Babylonicus Petropolitanus* (1876)—facsimile edition.

916 and containing Isa., Jer., Ezek., and the Twelve Prophets, generally employs the Babylonian pointing signs, but reveals both in the principles of pointing and in the Masora the influence of Tiberias. The Codex of Aaron ben Moshe ben Asher, the last member of the Asher family, provided in the first half of the tenth century with pointing and Masora, represents the ben Asher text.[3] According to a tradition, which is not undisputed, it was preserved at first in Jerusalem, then in Cairo, later in Aleppo, and now apparently in Israeli Jerusalem. It is still sometimes named the Aleppo Codex. The London Codex of the Pentateuch, Ms.Or. 4445, coming from about the same period as this Aleppo Codex and frequently citing in its margin 'the great teacher ben Asher', has readings which are cited as being those of Aaron ben Asher's earlier period in a book by Mishael ben 'Uzziel which will be considered in a moment.

The ben Asher text is also to be found in the Codex Leningradensis which goes back to the year 1008. It was not actually written by Aaron ben Moshe ben Asher himself, but represents a reliable copy of the Bible texts which derived from him, and, as we shall see (p. 691), was for this reason made the basis of Kittel's *Biblia Hebraica* from the third edition onwards. The Codex of the Prophets from the year 1105,[4] named 'Reuchlinianus' from its earlier owner Reuchlin and preserved in Karlsruhe, and the Codex in the British Museum (Add. 21161) containing parts of the 'Prophets' and the 'Writings' and written in about 1150, both, however, provide largely ben Naphtali readings. This is also true, though in differing degree, of the three manuscripts formerly in Erfurt but now in the Berlin State Library: Erfurtensis 1 (fourteenth century), Erfurtensis 2 (thirteenth century), and Erfurtensis 3 (probably eleventh century). With regard to the differences in regard to the text of the Bible between ben Asher and ben Naphtali we are informed not only in the manuscripts which attest them but also by a work compiled in the tenth century by Mishael ben 'Uzziel, edited by Lipschütz, which deals with the differences between the two schools. The great collections of variants made by Kennicott and de Rossi,[5]

---

[3] Cf. below, p. 691.

[4] *Corpus Codicum Hebraicorum Medii Aevi. Redigendum Curavit R. Edelmann, Pars II: The Pre-Masoretic Bible. Codex Reuchlinianus. Codices Palatini I. II.* Published . . . by A. Sperber (1956/59); on this cf. R. Meyer, VT 11 (1961), pp. 474–86; Hempel, 'Fragmente einer dem Cod. Reuchlinianus (Durlach 55) verwandten Handschrift des hebräischen Pentateuch aus Niedersachsen' NGW (1937), pp. 227–37, Pl. 1; Morag, 'The Vocalization of Codex Reuchlinianus: Is the "Pre-Masoretic" Bible Pre-Masoretic?' JSSt 4 (1959), pp. 216–37; Sperber, *A Grammar of Masoretic Hebrew, a General Introduction to the Pre-Masoretic Bible* (1959); on this cf. R. Meyer, VT 11 (1961), pp. 474–86. Lit. § 126.

[5] Kennicott, *Vetus Testamentum Hebraicum cum variis lectionibus* I, II (1776/80), containing only variations in the consonantal text, and de Rossi, *Variae lectiones Veteris Testamenti* (1784/88), taking account also of the pointing. On Kennicott, cf. Gese, 'Die hebräischen Bibelhandschriften zum Dodekapropheton nach der Variantensammlung des Kennicott' ZAW 69 (1957), pp. 59–69. Cf. also Aptowitzer, *Das Schriftwort in der rabbinischen Literatur* (SAW 153, 6, 1906); (160, 7, 1908); Jahresber. d. Israel. Theol. Lehranstalt in Wien 18 (1911), pp. 1–173; 22 (1915), pp. 1–82, who shows that in Rabbis of the eighth and tenth centuries, and even in those of the twelfth, Bible quotations appear which deviate from our consonantal text, and thus presuppose manuscripts with a text which does not everywhere agree with 𝔐. Fischer, 'Die hebräischen Bibelzitate des Scholastikers Odo' Bibl 15 (1934), pp. 50–93; 'Einige Proben aus den hebräischen Bibelzitaten des Scholastikers Odo' BZAW 66 (1936), pp. 198–206. (But cf. also A. Landgraf in fasc. 14 of *Spicilegium Sacrum Lovaniense* (Écrits Théologiques de l'École d'Abélard), esp. pp. xlv–xlvi, xlix–liv;

however, still indispensable although in many respects outdated, are of little
value for the clarification of the history of the pointing because in general the
compilers could only make use of later manuscripts representing the *textus
receptus*. In addition, Kennicott's work only takes account of the consonantal
text and not the pointing.

Printed editions began in 1477, at first of single books and then from 1488
of the whole Old Testament. They used only late manuscripts and so these
printed texts too embody the *textus receptus*, with which, in so far as it is given
at all, the Masora gathered from quite disparate material does not fit in many
cases. This is true, to mention only a few editions, of the Old Testament printed
at Brescia in 1494 which Luther used; of the Second Rabbinic Bible, produced
in 1524–25 by Daniel Bomberg in Venice, under the supervision of Jacob ben
Chayyim and so quite properly termed the 'Bombergiana'. This did for the first
time provide with the text a Masora collected from several manuscripts and in
some measure conforming to the text. It is also true of the Hebrew text of the
Antwerp, Paris and London polyglots (§ 117). Ginsberg's editions of 1894
(1896) and 1926 too, as well as the first two editions of Kittel's *Biblia Hebraica*
(1906, 1909), provide the *textus receptus*. On the other hand, the First Rabbinic
Bible, prepared by Felix Pratensis and published by Daniel Bomberg in Venice
in 1516–17[6] and the Complutensian Polyglot (p. 694) edited[7] by Alfonso de
Zamora, Pablo Coronel and other notable scholars, which appeared in 1514–17
in Alcalá provide a Hebrew text based in large measure on critical examination
of manuscripts, and thus represent a significant first stage in the scientific treatment of the Hebrew text of the Bible. A decisive break with the *textus receptus*
was, however, only ventured upon with the third edition of Kittel's *Biblia
Hebraica*. It was completed in 1937 and has since been several times republished
—the twelfth printing appeared in 1961—with the correction of errors and the
insertion of the variants of the relevant Qumrān scrolls in the *apparatus criticus*
to Isa. and Hab. Here is printed the text of Codex B 19A of the Public Library
of Leningrad belonging to the year 1008 (L). This is a careful copy of the model
codex of ben Asher from the middle of the tenth century, formerly preserved in
the Sephardim synagogue in Aleppo. Thus the text-form provided in Kittel's
Biblia Hebraica since 1937 is three to four centuries older than that provided in
the previous printed editions. In addition, its Masora really corresponds to the
text, so that the two form a unity.

The edition of the text published in 1958 by the British and Foreign Bible
Society in London, prepared by Snaith, rests primarily upon the manuscripts
Or 2626–2628 and Or 2375 now in the British Museum and upon the 'Shem-Tob
Bible' belonging to the Sassoon family. These, like Leningradensis used by
Kahle as the basis for the 3rd edition of Kittel's *Biblia Hebraica*, stand in the

R. Loewe, 'Mediaeval Christian Hebraists of England' Trans. Jewish Hist. Soc. of England
17 (1953), pp. 245 f.).
   [6] Kahle, 'Felix Pratensis—à Prato, Felix. Der Herausgeber der Ersten Rabbinerbibel,
Venedig 1516/17' WdO 1 (1947/52), pp. 32–6.
   [7] Kahle, 'Zwei durch Humanisten besorgte, dem Papst gewidmete Ausgaben der
Hebräischen Bibel' *Essays Leo Baeck* (1954), pp. 50–74 with three plates = *Op. Min.*
(1956), pp. 128–50.

ben Asher tradition. Thus Snaith's edition, though working from a different starting-point, provides a text substantially agreeing with that of Kahle.[8] Snaith's edition has no critical apparatus. On the other hand, a very detailed apparatus is planned for the projected edition of the Hebrew Old Testament[9] by the Hebrew University in Jerusalem. This edition is to be based[10] on the Aleppo Codex.[11] The *apparatus criticus* is to take account of the other ben Asher codices, of pre-masoretic and non-masoretic traditions such as the Qumrān texts and the ancient translations, and will thus make possible for the reader an overall picture of the history of the development of the Hebrew Bible in all its forms.[12]

For the rest, we may simply note the following points with regard to the form of the text as we now have it. The division of the biblical writings into sections according to the meaning,[13] called *parashoth* (פָּרָשָׁה), and the division into verses (פָּסוּק), at first in a very uneven fashion, are attested by some passages in the Mishna, e.g. *Megillah* 4, 4, for the Mishnaic period, i.e. *circa* A.D. 200. The former may now be traced back several centuries further by means of the Qumrān texts. For these texts contain a division of the text into *parashoth*, not, it is true, identical with the one which is in the Masoretic text, but related to it and no doubt historically connected with it. Furthermore, we may well assume that at least some of the works were divided into such sections immediately on their composition. Larger sections were at first marked by a beginning being made on a new line or by the omission of a complete line; smaller sections by leaving some clear space within a line. The larger sections were therefore called *open* (פְּתוּחָה), the smaller *closed* (סְתוּמָה) *parashoth*. At a later stage, only a small space was left clear in both cases, and a פ was written before the larger sections, and a ס before the smaller. Thus a פ stands before Gen. i, 6–8, and a ס before Gen. iii, 16 (p. 129). The division into chapters to which we are accustomed was first taken over into a Hebrew manuscript from the Vulgate in the fourteenth century, and in printed editions it

---

[8] Anon., 'A New Edition of the Hebrew OT' BT 10 (1959), pp. 110–12; Kahle, *Cairo Geniza* (²1959), pp. 138–41; Snaith, 'New Edition of the Hebrew Bible' VT 7 (1957), pp. 207–8; Winton Thomas, 'A New Hebrew Bible' ET 70 (1958/59), pp. 234 f.

[9] Anon., 'A Brief Report on the Hebrew University Bible Project' Textus. Annual of the Hebrew University Bible Project 1 (1960), pp. 210–11. Lit. § 126.

[10] Ben-Zvi, "כתר התורה" של בן אשר שנכתב בארץ־ישראל אור מוצל מאש' Sinai 43 (1958), pp. 5–13; 'The Codex of Ben Asher' Textus 1 (1960), pp. 1–16, 12 Pls.; Dotan, 'האמנם היה בן־אשר קראי?' Sinai 41 (1957/8), pp. 280–312, 350–62; Goshen-Gottstein, 'The Authenticity of the Aleppo Codex' Textus 1 (1960), pp. 17–58; Loewinger, 'The Aleppo Codex and the Ben Asher Tradition' Textus 1 (1960), pp. 59–111. Cf. Lit. § 126.

[11] Cf. above, p. 690.

[12] On the edition of the Hebrew Old Testament which appeared in Jerusalem in 1953 under the name of Cassuto, cf. Kahle, 'The New Hebrew Bible, Jerusalem 1953' VT 3 (1953), pp. 416–20; Simon, 'The Jerusalem Bible' VT 4 (1954), pp. 109 f., Teicher, 'The Jerusalem Bible' The Jewish Chronicle (23 April 1954). The publishing firm הוצאת קורן 'The Ḳoren Publishers' in Jerusalem is producing an edition of the Hebrew Old Testament prepared by D. Goldschmidt, A. M. Haberman and M. Medan, laying particular stress on the correct typographic reproduction of the text.

[13] Cf. the 'division of the tablets in the Babylonian epics according to criteria depending upon the actual content of the material' (Gössmann, *Das Era-Epos* (1956), pp. 4 f.).

appears from Bomberg's First Rabbinic Bible of 1516–17 onwards. The counting of the verses within the chapter divisions was first carried through in 1563
for an edition of the Psalter, and for the whole Old Testament first in 1571.

III. Non-masoretic Forms of the Text

§ 117. GENERAL CONSIDERATIONS. TRANSLATIONS. POLYGLOTS

Literature: Blau, 'Zum Hebräisch der Übersetzer des AT' VT 6 (1956), pp. 97–9;
Delitzsch, *Studien zur Entstehungsgeschichte der Polyglottenbibel des Cardinals Ximenes*
(1871); *Complutensische Varianten zu dem at. Texte* (1878); *Fortgesetzte Studien zur Entstehungsgeschichte der Complutensischen Polyglotte* (1886); Grant, *Translating the Bible* (1961);
Kahle, 'The Hebrew Text of the Complutensian Polyglot' *Homenaje a Millás-Vallicrosa* I
(1954), pp. 741–51; Millás Vallicrosa, 'Restos de una Biblia Hebraica manuscrita en Gerona'
Sefarad 13 (1953), pp. 356–8; Rico, *La Políglota de Alcalá* (1917); Tasker, 'The Complutensian Polyglot' ChQR 154 (1953), pp. 197–210; Ziegler, 'Der griechische Dodekapro-
pheton-Text der Complutenser Polyglotte' Bibl 25 (1944), pp. 297–310.
Cf. also Literature §§ 115, 116, 118–26.

𝔐 is not the only form of the text which has come down to us. There are
others available, some direct—the relevant Qumrān scolls (§§ 104–12, 115) and
the Samaritan Pentateuch—others indirect, namely translations of the Old
Testament, including 𝔊, which by retranslation into Hebrew provide us with
forms of the text which run parallel to 𝔐 and quite often deviate from it. The
Qumrān scrolls, the Samaritan and the translations (Versions) present in their
turn a whole host of problems in textual criticism and ideally we should first
solve all these problems and establish their own text quite firmly before an
attempt was made at making use of them for emendation of 𝔐. But the attainment of this goal is very far distant and is often held to be impossible. In any
case these forms of the text may nevertheless be used for the emendation of 𝔐,
and indeed in many cases with results which are clearly unambiguous and correct. So we may here leave on one side the exposition of the problems of textual
criticism which relate to the texts of the Qumrān scrolls, the Samaritan and the
Versions, the more properly since their discussion, if it were to be in any degree
useful, would take up a great deal of space, whereas a brief summary can more
readily give rise to misunderstandings than contribute to the clarification of the
position. A good deal has already been said about the significance of the Qumrān
writings for textual criticism. What follows simply mentions a limited but
sufficiently comprehensive selection of the almost boundless range of relevant
literature, and a few remarks will be added about the origin, transmission and
editions of the remaining non-Masoretic forms of the text, though admittedly
it will be necessary frequently to refer back to the discussion of the Qumrān texts.
A great part of the material which will be discussed in §§ 118–24 is printed
in the four great Polyglots of the sixteenth and seventeenth centuries, and in
some cases the texts of these still provide the only or the best edition. The

Complutensian, printed in 1514–17 in Alcalá, the Roman Complutum, contains 𝔐, Targum Onkelos to the Pentateuch (§ 119), 𝔊 and the Vulgate (𝔅). The Antwerp Polyglot of 1569–72 reprints the contents of the Complutensian, but provides not only a Targum to the Pentateuch, but also to almost all the other books of the Old Testament. The Paris Polyglot[1] of 1629–45 adds to the content of the Antwerp edition the Samaritan Pentateuch plus its Targum, and in addition the Peshiṭta and an Arabic translation. The London Polyglot of 1654–57 (69), finally, supplements the printing of improved texts of the Paris Polyglot with fragments of the Vetus Latina, with the Targum Pseudo-Jonathan and the fragmentary Targum to the Pentateuch, and with Ethiopic and Persian translations of parts of the Old Testament. It also adds collections of variants and reached its climax in 1669 with the *Lexicon heptaglottum* (Hebrew, Chaldee (Aramaic), Syriac, Samaritan, Ethiopic, Arabic and Persian) by Edmund Castellus. Of the Madrid Polyglot, projected in 1947 by the Spanish Consejo Superior de Investigationes Científicas,[2] there have appeared so far the Prooemium,[3] the Psalterium Visigothicum-Mozarabicum[4] and the Psalterium Hieronymi de Hebraica veritate interpretatum.[5]

§ 118. THE SAMARITAN PENTATEUCH

Literature: (a) Text: Frh. von Gall, *Der hebräische Pentateuch der Samaritaner* (1914/18, ²1963).

(b) Other Works: Baillet, 'Un nouveau Fragment du Pentateuque samaritain' RB 67 (1960), pp. 49–57, Pls. I–II; Ben-Zvi, 'The Book of Abisha' [Hebr., Engl. summary] Eretz-Israel 5 (1958), pp. 240–52, 97*; Bowman, 'Samaritan Studies' BJRL 40 (1957/58), pp. 298–327; 'The Importance of Samaritan Researches' Annual Leeds Un. Or. Soc. 1 (1958/59), pp. 43–54; 'An interesting Leningrad Samaritan Manuscript' Abr-Nahrain 1 (1961), pp. 73–8; Gaster, *The Samaritans* (1925); Hempel, 'Innermasoretische Bestätigungen des Samaritanus' ZAW 52 (1934), pp. 254–74; Kahle, 'Aus der Geschichte der ältesten hebräischen Bibelhandschrift' BZAW 33 (1918), pp. 247–60; 'The Abisha' Scroll of the Samaritans' *Studia Or. Pedersen* (1953), pp. 188–92; Montgomery, *The Samaritans* (1907); Pérez Castro, 'El Séfer Abiša'' Sefarad 13 (1953), pp. 119–29; 'El criptograma del Séfer Abisá' Sefarad 19 (1959), pp. 384–91; *Séfer Abiša'* (1959); 'Das Kryptogramm des Sefer Abischa'' SVT VII (1960), pp. 52–60; Petermann, *Versuch einer hebräischen Formenlehre nach der Aussprache der heutigen Samaritaner* (AKML V, 1, 1868), pp. 219–326: 'Varianten zu dem Pentateuch nach den Samaritanern'; Robertson, 'Notes and Extracts from the Semitic MSS. in the John Rylands Library. 1. Concerning the Abisha Scroll' BJRL 19 (1935), pp. 412–37; '3. Samaritan Pentateuch MSS. with a Description of two Codices' BJRL 21 (1937), pp. 224–72, 3 Pls.; *Catalogue of the Samaritan Manuscripts in the John Rylands Library, Manchester* (1938); 'The Ancient Scroll of the Samaritans' *Gaster Centenary Publication* (1958), pp. 1–7; Talmon, 'Observations on the Samaritan Pentateuch Version' [Hebr.] Tarbiz 22 (1950/51), pp. 124–8; 'The Samaritan Pentateuch' JJSt 2 (1951), pp. 144–150; *Selections from the Pentateuch in the Samaritan Version* (1956/57); Vaccari, 'Due codici del Pentateuco Samaritano' Bibl 21 (1940), pp. 241–6.

Cf. also Literature §§ 115, 116, 126.

[1] Auvray, 'Jean Morin (1591–1659)' RB 66 (1959), pp. 397–414, see pp. 401–5.
[2] Ayuso, 'Una nueva Políglotta española' Cult Bíbl 5 (1948), pp. 226–30.
[3] *Biblia Polyglotta Matritensia cura et studio T. Ayuso Maraʒuela: Prooemium* (1957). Lit. § 126.   [4] VII, 21 (1957).   [5] VIII, 21 (1960).

When the independent Samaritan religious community was founded (p. 256), the Torah was taken over from the Jews. This has subsequently had its own fortunes in transmission, largely without any influence from the Jewish Torah, and thus to this extent represents a form of the text which, if the year A.D. 100 is assumed to be determinative for the origin of 𝔐, is 400 years older than this, and is roughly related to it in the same way as is the text of the complete Isaiah scroll (pp. 641, 684) found near Qumrān. In about 6,000 cases in Kittel's *Biblia Hebraica* the Samaritan, indicated by the siglum 𝔰𝔲 (a Samaritan ש), deviates from 𝔐. Among its many manuscripts, mention may be made of the Abiša' scroll edited by Pérez Castro in 1959, the basis of which goes back to the eleventh century A.D., and the fragment of a parchment codex published by Baillet in 1960, containing Gen. xliii, 20–xliv, 8 and deriving from the thirteenth or fourteenth century. By far the greater part of these variants are orthographical—a more plentiful use of *matres lectionis* and the like—but there is also no lack of differences in substance. Thus in Gen. v and xi, 10–32, the lists of the primeval ancestors and of the descendants of Shem, the figures given by 𝔰𝔲 as the years of their births and of their lives, differ substantially from those of 𝔐, and in Deut. xxvii, 4 𝔰𝔲 has *Geriẓim* instead of *Ebal* in 𝔐. Here, in both cases, we may hesitate to decide which tradition is the more original—even in the latter case. For it is possible that the Samaritans altered *Ebal*, if that was original, into *Geriẓim* because they wished to see their sacred mountain (John iv, 20–4) mentioned here. But it is equally possible and indeed more probable that the Jews out of hatred for the Samaritans changed *Geriẓim* in the text into *Ebal*.[1] In 2,000 of the cases mentioned 𝔰𝔲 agrees with 𝔊 against 𝔐, and this in itself shows that in 𝔰𝔲 and 𝔊 a common text-form appears which deviates from 𝔐. We have already noted (p. 684) that some Qumrān manuscripts stand very near to the text-form of the Samaritan and make possible the tracing back of this text into about the first century B.C.

For the Hebrew Pentateuch of the Samaritans it is at present necessary to use the edition of von Gall, now half a century old. But a new edition is to come from Pérez Castro. In addition we possess translations of it into Greek,[2] into Samaritan Aramaic[3] and into Arabic.[4] These are not without significance for the recovery of the oldest text of the Hebrew Pentateuch of the Samaritans.

---

[1] See above, p. 216, n. 9.

[2] Glaue and Rahlfs, *Fragmente einer griechischen Übersetzung des samaritanischen Pentateuchs* (Mitt. Septuaginta-Untern. Gött. Ges. Wiss. I, 2, 1911).

[3] Peterman and Vollers, *Pentateuchus Samaritanus* (1872/91), and cf. on this Brockelmann, HdO III (1954), p. 143; Goldberg, *Das Samaritanische Pentateuchtargum* (Diss. phil. Bonn, 1935); Kahle, *Textkritische und lexikalische Bemerkungen zum samaritanischen Pentateuchtargum* (Diss. phil. Halle, 1898); Kohn, ZDMG 47 (1893), pp. 626–97; Ramón Díaz, 'Ediciones del Targum Samaritano' Est Bíbl 15 (1956), pp. 105–8.

[4] Cowley, *The Samaritan Liturgy*, I–II (1909), cf. II, pp. XXIII–XXIV; Kahle, *Die arabischen Bibelübersetzungen* (1904), pp. X–XIII; *The Cairo Geniza* (²1959), pp. 53–5; Katten, *Untersuchungen zu Saadja's arab. Pentateuchübersetzung* (Diss. phil. Giessen, 1924); Robertson, 'The Relationship of the Arabic Translation of the Samaritan Pentateuch to that of Saadya' *Saadya Studies* (1943), pp. 166–76; Skoss, *Saadia Gaon, The Earliest Hebrew Grammarian* (1955); cf. p. 714, n. 75.

§ 119. THE TARGUMS

Literature: (a) Text: Berliner, *Targum Onkelos,* I–II (1884); Dalman, *Grammatik des jüd. pal. Aramäisch* (²1905 (1960)), pp. XIV–XV, 11–16, 27–35; *Aramäische Dialektproben* (²1927 (1960)), pp. VI–VII, 6–14; Ginsburger, *Das Fragmententhargum (Thargum jeruschalmi zum Pentateuch)* (1899); *Pseudo-Jonathan (Thargum Jonathan ben Usiël zum Pentateuch)* (1903); Kahle, *Masoreten des Westens* II (BWANT 50, 1930), pp. 1*–13*, 1–65; Lagarde, *Prophetae chaldaice* [= Targum Jonathan] (1872); *Hagiographa chaldaice* (1873); Merx, *Chrestomathia Targumica* (1888); Praetorius, *Das Targum zu Josua in jemenischer Überlieferung* (1899); *Targum zum Buch der Richter in jemenischer Überlieferung* (1900); Sperber, *The Bible in Aramaic:* Vol. I *The Pentateuch according to Targum Onkelos* (1959) (on this cf. Winton Thomas JSSt 5 (1960), pp. 286–8); Vol. II *The Former Prophets according to Targum Jonathan* (1959) (on this cf. Winton Thomas, JSSt 5 (1960), pp. 430 f.); Vol. III *The Latter Prophets according to Targum Jonathan* (1962); Vol. IV *General Conclusions* (in preparation); Stenning, *The Targum of Isaiah* (²1953).

(b) Other Works: Baars, 'A Targum on Exod. xv, 7–21' VT 11 (1961), pp. 340–2; Baumstark, 'Neue orientalistische Probleme biblischer Textgeschichte' ZDMG 89 (1935), pp. 89–118; Black, *A Christian Palestinian Syriac Horologion* (1954); *An Aramaic Approach to the Gospels and Acts* (²1954); 'Die Erforschung der Muttersprache Jesu' ThLZ 82 (1957), cols. 653–68; Brockelmann, HdO III (1953), pp. 141–3; Churgin, 'The Targum and the Septuagint' AJSL 50 (1933/34), pp. 41–65; *The Targum to the Hagiographa* [Hebr.] (1945); Grelot, 'Les Targums du Pentateuque. Étude comparative d'après Genèse iv, 3–16' Semitica 9 (1959), pp. 59–88; Hamp, *Der Begriff 'Wort' in den Aramäischen Bibelübersetzungen* (1938); Kahle, 'Das zur Zeit Jesu in Palästina gesprochene Aramäisch' ThR 17 (1949), pp. 201–16 = *Op. Min.* (1956), pp. 79–95; 'The Targums' [Hebr.] Melilah 3/4 (1950), pp. 70–6; Komlós, 'ביאורים בתרגום אונקלוס' Beth Miqra 3 (1958), pp. 60–2; 'שני ביאורים בתרגומים בענין הגמול' Beth Miqra 4 (1959), pp. 70–1; Kosmala "Mt xxvi, 52–a quotation from the Targum' NT 4 (1960), pp. 3–5; Le Déault, 'Le Targum de Gen. xxii, 8 et I Ptr. i, 20' RSR 49 (1961), pp. 103–6; Peters, 'Targum und Praevulgata des Pentateuchs' Or Chr 9 (1934), pp. 49–54; Speier, 'Beiträge zu den Targumim' SThU 20 (1950), pp. 52–61; Sperber, 'Specimen of a Targum Edition' *L. Ginzberg Jub. Vol.* I (1945), pp. 293–303; Stummer, 'Beiträge zum Problem "Hieronymus und die Targumim"' Bibl 18 (1937), pp. 174–81; 'Zur Stilgeschichte der alten Bibelübersetzungen' ZAW 61 (1945/48), pp. 195–231; Wikgren, 'The Targums and the NT' JR 24 (1944), pp. 79–95; Zuntz, 'On the Opening Sentence of Melito's Paschal Homily' HThR 36 (1943), pp. 299–315.

Cf. also Literature on p. 678; §§ 117, 120–4, 126.

Already in pre-Christian times the replacement of Hebrew by the Aramaic vernacular made it essential that in the Synagogue services the Hebrew text, during or after its reading, should be translated into Aramaic, verse by verse, by a מְתֻרְגְּמָן *dragoman, interpreter,* if the faithful were to understand at all what was read. This was done by free oral rendering; reciting of the translation, the targum (תַּרְגּוּם), was forbidden. But this prohibition did not exclude its writing down, and indeed by the time of Jesus it is clear that there were written Targums. The Babylonian Talmud (Shabbat 115a) mentions an Aramaic Targum to Job. In Qumrān Cave 11 such a Targum has come to light (p. 698),[1] and the reference in Job xli, 17b to a Συριακή βίβλος, as source for the material in the LXX which is not to be found in the Hebrew text, is certainly to such a

---

[1] Harding, PEQ 90 (1958), p. 17; Hunzinger, ThLZ 85 (1960), col. 151. Lit. § 126.

Targum.[2] Though the Targums which derive from the pre-Christian period were only given the edited form in which we have them some centuries later, long passages of the text actually go back to the period of their origin and to this extent represent likewise a text-form older than 𝔐. This has been clearly shown by Kahle in *The Cairo Geniza* ([2]1959), pp. 202 f. for the paraphrase of Deut. xxxiii, 11 given by the Targum Pseudo-Jonathan. It is true that in the use of the Targums for the emendation of 𝔐 the greatest caution must be exercised, for they are not by any means literal translations, but in many ways represent paraphrases, akin to commentaries, of the Hebrew original. The Aramaic 'Genesis Apocryphon' (p. 664) found in Qumrān Cave 1 could also be described as a Targum to Genesis. In so far as the Targums are paraphrases, they may obviously not be used as evidence for a text-form which deviates from 𝔐. We possess Targums to all the books of the Old Testament with the exception of Dan. and Ezra-Neh., and in some cases we have several. They are admittedly of differing value. The most important are the Targums of Onkelos to the Pentateuch[3] and of Jonathan ben-'Uzziel to the Prophets;[4] these are in reality compilations, and hardly works to be attributed to a single author, and furthermore there is the possibility that the names of the Greek translators later discussed (§ 122), Aquila and Theodotion—transformed into Onkelos and Jonathan—have been erroneously associated with these two Targums.[5] They are of Palestinian origin, but were edited in the fifth century A.D. in Babylonia and are for this reason known as Babylonian. Significant also are two Jerusalem Targums to the Pentateuch, of which the first, known as Jerusalem I or Pseudo-Jonathan,[6] is complete, while the second, Jerusalem II, exists only in fragmentary form and is therefore known as the Fragment-Targum. There are also Targums to the *Kethubim* (Writings),[7] which admittedly do not form a unified work but are of very varied character.

[2] Cf. Cross, *The Ancient Library of Qumrān* (1958), p. 26.

[3] Barnstein, *The Targum of Onkelos to Genesis* (Diss. phil. Heidelberg, 1896); Brederek, *Konkordanz zum Targum Onkelos* (BZAW 9, 1906); Díez Macho, ''Onqelos Manuscript with Babylonian transliterated Vocalization in the Vatican Library' VT 8 (1958), pp. 113–33; 'Un manuscrito babilonico de Onqelos en el que se confunden los timbres vocalicos Pataḥ y Qamez' Sefarad 19 (1959), pp. 273–82; Hammer, 'The Onkelos Targum' Interpret. 3 (1949), pp. 174–83; Kasowski, אוֹצַר הַתַּרְגּוֹם אוּנקלוֹס [*Konkordanz zum Targum Onkelos*] (1940); Komlós, 'קו אופיני אחד בשיטת תרגום אונקלוס' *Tur-Sinai-Festschr.* (1960), pp. 116–20; Silverstone, *Aquila and Onkelos* (1931); Sperber, 'The Targum Onkelos in its Relation to the Masoretic Hebrew Text' PAAJR 6 (1935), pp. 309–51. Lit. § 126.

[4] Brownlee, 'The Habakkuk Midrash and the Targum of Jonathan' JJSt 7 (1956), pp. 169–86; Churgin, *Targum Jonathan to the Prophets* (1928); Delekat, 'Ein Septuagintatargum' VT 8 (1958), pp. 225–52; Komlós, 'אופיו של התרגום הארמי למלאכי' *Karl-Festchr.* (1960), pp. 163–70; Melamed, 'The Targum Yehonathan and an Arabic Tafsir of the Song of Deborah' [Hebr.] Eretz-Israel 3 (1954), pp. 198–206; Louise Pettibone Smith, 'The Prophetic Targum as a Guide and Defence for the Higher Critic' JBL 52 (1933), pp. 121–30; Sperber, 'Zur Textgestalt des Prophetentargums' ZAW 44 (1926), pp. 175 f.; 'Zur Sprache des Prophetentargums' ZAW 45 (1927), pp. 267–88; Wieder, 'The Habakkuk Scroll and the Targum' JJSt 4 (1953), pp. 14–18.

[5] Cf. Talmud bab. Megillah 3a; jerus. Megillah 1, 9 (71c); jerus. Qiddušin 1, 1 (59a).

[6] Bernhardt, 'Zu Eigenart und Alter der messianisch-eschatologischen Zusätze im Targum Jeruschalmi I' *Fascher-Festschr.* (1958), pp. 68–83; Marmorstein, *Studien zum Pseudo-Jonathan-Targum*, I (Diss. phil. Heidelberg, 1905); Olmstead, 'Could an Aramaic Gospel be written?' JNESt 1 (1942), pp. 41–70.

[7] Saarisalo, 'The Targum to the Book of Ruth' StOr 2 (1928), pp. 88–104.

Of very much greater importance is material providing evidence of an older Palestinian Targum,[8] the publication of which was begun by Paul Kahle in 1930. The first material came from the Ezra Synagogue of the old city of Cairo, but further material has come from various sources, including the Vatican Library. This provides the clearest possible confirmation of what had long been supposed, namely that the Targums handed down to us through the centuries must have been preceded by older Targums which had, for the most part, come into existence in Palestine. Most of the questions which have been raised by these new Targum discoveries are still awaiting an answer, but it is nevertheless already clear that these texts throw an entirely new light on the origin and development of the Targums.

It has already been noted (p. 696) that Qumrān Cave 11 has produced a fragment of a Targum to Job.[9] To this must be added the fact that remains of a Targum to Lev. (xvi, 12–15, 18–21) have been discovered in Cave 4.[10]

Just as new light has been shed on the textual history of the Samaritan and of the Septuagint by the Qumrān discoveries, so too there are not lacking connections between Qumrān texts on the one hand and readings in the Targums and Peshiṭta on the other, and some of the works mentioned on pp. 681–3, for example Gottstein's study 'Die Jesaia-Rolle im Lichte von Peschitta und Targum', attempt to utilise this fact for the solution of the problems of the Targum and of the Peshiṭta.

[8] Renée Bloch, 'Note sur l'utilisation des fragments de la Guéniza du Caïre pour l'étude du Targum palestinien' REJ 14 (1955), pp. 1–35; Boccaccio, 'Integer textus targum Hierosolymitani primum inventus in codice Vaticano' Bibl 38 (1957), pp. 237–9; Díez Macho, 'Un importante manuscrito targúmico en la Biblioteca Vaticana' *Homenaje a Millás-Vallicrosa* I (1954), pp. 375–463; 'Nuevos fragmentos del Targum palestinense' Sefarad 15 (1955), pp. 31–9, 4 Pls.; 'Un nuovo Targum a los profetas' Est Bíbl 15 (1956), pp. 287–95; 'Una copia de todo al Targum jerosolimitano en la Vaticana' Est Bíbl 15 (1956), pp. 446 f.; 'Una copia completa del targum palestinense al Pentateuco en la Biblioteca Vaticana' Sefarad 17 (1957), pp. 119–21, Pl. I; 'Un segundo fragmento del Targum Palestinense a los Profetas' Bibl 39 (1958), pp. 198–205; 'En torno a la datacion del Targum Palestinense' Sefarad 20 (1960), pp. 3–16; 'The recently discovered Palestinian Targum: its Antiquity and Relationship with the other Targums' SVT VII (1960), pp. 222–45; Fuste Ara, 'El fragmento targúmico T.-S. de la Biblioteca Universitaria de Cambridge' Est Bíbl 15 (1956), pp. 85–94; Kahle, *Masoreten des Westens* II (BWANT 50, 1930), pp. 1*–13*, 1–65; 'Das palästinische Pentateuchtargum und das zur Zeit Jesu gesprochene Aramäisch' ZNW 49 (1958), pp. 100–16; *Cairo Geniza* (²1959), pp. 191–208; Komlós, 'כתבי יד של תרגומים' in ספר יבל סיני (1959), pp. 466–81; Marmorstein, 'Einige vorläufige Bemerkungen zu den neuentdeckten Fragmenten des jerusalemischen (palästinensischen) Targums' ZAW 49 (1931), pp. 231–42; Peters, 'Vom palästinischen Targum und seiner Geschichte' Heil. Land 2 (1940), pp. 9–22; Rámon Díaz, 'Dos notas sobre el Targum palestinense' Sefarad 19 (1959), pp. 133–6; Schelbert, 'Exodus xxii, 4 im palästinischen Targum' VT 8 (1958), pp. 253–63; Teicher, 'A Sixth Century Fragment of the Palestinian Targum?' VT 1 (1951), pp. 125–9; Winter, 'Eine vollständige Handschrift des Palästinischen Targums aufgefunden' ZNW 48 (1957), p. 192; Wohl, *Das Palästinische Pentateuch-Targum* (Diss. phil. Bonn, 1935). Cf. Lit. § 126.

[9] Harding, PEQ 90 (1958), p. 17; Hunzinger, ThLZ 85 (1960), col. 151.

[10] Milik, *Ten Years of Discovery in the Wilderness of Judaea* (1959), p. 31; Rengstorf, *Ḥirbet Qumrân* (1960), pp. 19 f., 25. Lit. § 126.

§ 120. THE PESHIṬṬA AND OTHER OLD SYRIAC TRANSLATIONS

Literature: (a) Text: *Vetus Testamentum Syriace,* ed. S. Lee (London 1823 (1824)); *Vetus Testamentum Syriace et Neosyriace* (Urmia 1852); *Translatio Syra Pescitto Veteris Testamenti ex Codice Ambrosiano sec. fere VI Photolithographice edita curante et adnotante A. M. Ceriani* (1876–1883); *Biblia Sacra juxta versionem simplicem, quae dicitur Pschitta* (3 vols.) (Mosul 1887–1891, ³1951 (Beyrouth)).

(b) Other Works: Allgeier, 'Cod. Phillipps 1388 in Berlin und seine Bedeutung für die Geschichte der Pešitta' OrChr 7 (1932), pp. 1–15; Baars (§ 93); Baumstark, *Geschichte der syrischen Literatur* (1922), pp. 18–19, 23–5 etc.; 'Wege zum Judentum des nt. Zeitalter's Bonner Zeitschr. Theol. Seels. 4 (1927), pp. 24–34; 'Pěšiṭṭā und palästinensisches Targum' BZ 19 (1931), pp. 257–70; 'Das Problem der Bibelzitate in der syrischen Übersetzungsf literatur' OrChr 8 (1933), pp. 208–25; 'Neue orientalistische Probleme biblischer Textgeschichte' ZDMG 89 (1935), pp. 89–118; HdO III (1954), pp. 170–7; Black, 'Rabbula o- Edessa and the Peshitta' BJRL 33 (1951/52), pp. 203–10; Bloch, 'The Printed Text of the Peshitta OT' AJSL 37 (1920/21), pp. 136–44; de Boer, 'A Description of the Sinai Syriac Ms. 35' VT 9 (1959), pp. 408–12; 'OT Peshiṭṭa. A Request' VT 10 (1960), p. 110; Burkitt, *Early Eastern Christianity* (1904), pp. 39–78: 'The Bible in Syriac'; Chabot, *Littérature syriaque* (Littératures chrétiennes de l'Orient, 1935); (Goshen-)Gottstein, 'A List of some Uncatalogued Syriac Biblical Manuscripts' BJRL 37 (1954/55), pp. 429–45; 'Eine Cambridger Syrohexaplahandschrift' Muséon 67 (1954), pp. 291–6; 'Neue Syrohexaplafragmente' Bibl 37 (1956), pp. 162–83; 'Prolegomena to a Critical Edition of the Peshitta' in *Text and Language in Bible and Qumran* (1960), pp. 163–204 = Scripta Hieros. VIII (1960), pp. 26–67; Haefeli, *Die Peschitta des AT mit Rücksicht auf ihre textkritische Bearbeitung und Herausgabe* (1927); Heller, *Untersuchungen über die Peschîttâ zur gesamten hebräischen Bibel* I (1911); Kahle, *The Cairo Geniza* (²1959), pp. 265–313; Mercati, '"Eine Cambridger Syrohexaplahandschrift"' Bibl 36 (1955), pp. 227 f.; van der Ploeg, 'Recente Pešiṭṭa-Studies (sinds 1927)', JEOL 9/10 (1945/48), pp. 392–9; Rahlfs, 'Beiträge zur Textkritik der Peschita, ZAW 9 (1889), pp. 161–210; Schneider, 'Wenig beachtete Rezensionen der Peschitta' ZAW 62 (1950), pp. 168–99; Sperber, 'Peschitta und Onkelos' Kohut Mem. Vol. (1935)' pp. 554–64; Sprey, 'משבה-ܡܫܒܗ' VT 7 (1957), pp. 408–10; Vööbus, 'The Oldest Extant Traces of the Syriac Peshitta' Muséon 63 (1950), pp. 191–204; 'New Data concerning the Philoxenian Version' *Miscell. Kundzinš* (1953), pp. 169–86; 'Das Alter der Peschitta' OrChr 38 (1954), pp. 1–10; 'Der Einfluß des altpalästinischen Targums in der Textgeschichte der Peschitta des AT' Muséon 68 (1955), pp. 215–18; Vosté 'La Pešiṭṭā de Mossoul et la revision catholique des anciennes versions orientales de la Bible' *Miscell. Mercati*, I (1946), pp. 59–94; 'Projet d'une édition critico-ecclésiastique de la Pešiṭṭā sous Léon XIII' Bibl 28 (1947), pp. 281–6; 'Les deux versions syriaques de la Bible d'après Mar Išoʻdad de Merw (c. 850)' Bibl 33 (1952), pp. 235 f.; Wilcox, 'Some Recent Contributions to the Problem of Peshitta Origins' Abr-Nahrain 1 (1961), pp. 62–7; Wood, 'A Syriac Masora' Transact. Glasgow Un. Or. Soc. 14 (1953), pp. 35–42.

Cf. also Literature on p. 669, and §§ 117–19, 121, 126.

Peshitta [*pᵉšiṭṭā, the simple* (i.e. translation)] is the name given to the Syriac translation of the Hebrew Old Testament and the Greek New Testament made probably about the middle or at the beginning of the second century A.D. It was made in Eastern Aramaic by the Syriac Church of Edessa soon after its formation, perhaps making use of older Jewish translations of the Old Testament or of individual parts of it. Even its original form did not exhibit a uniform type of translation, and it subsequently was subjected to various influences from 𝔊 and also from the Targums. Its separate sections are therefore of very varied value. Side by side with faithful translation from the Hebrew, we find renderings aiming at good Syriac style; passages quite free of the influence of 𝕲 appear beside others which have clearly been revised in accordance with 𝕲. Whereas Job is only dependent upon the Hebrew original, the translation of the Psalms is most strongly influenced by 𝕲. Chronicles, which like the apocrypha, was at first left untranslated because not regarded as canonical, was translated later in dependence upon a Targum. In short, a uniform evaluation of the whole Peshitta is impossible. The position differs with the individual books, as may be seen in the works mentioned in the footnotes dealing with the Psalms,[1] Chronicles,[2] the Apocrypha,[3] the Pentateuch,[4] Samuel,[5] Isaiah,[6] and Ruth.[7] This peculiarity of the Peshitta must be carefully taken into account before it is used for the emendation of 𝔐. In addition, as already hinted on p. 698, we must now also take account of the connections between Peshitta and Qumrān readings for clarification of the evolution of the Peshitta.

The division of the Syrian Christians in the middle of the fifth century into the East Syrian Nestorians and the West Syrian Jacobites carried with it the formation of two different text-forms of the Peshitta, a West Syrian and an East Syrian. The former is to be found in the Codex Ambrosianus mentioned on p. 699, and this is followed in Lee's edition, whereas the editions of Urmia and Mosul are based upon the East Syrian text-form.

The Syrian Melkites who remained linked to the Church of the Roman Empire, and sections of the Jacobites who were their neighbours, were led in the fifth and sixth centuries by the desire to conform their Bible to the one which was standard for the eastern part of the Imperial Church, namely the Septuagint, to make Syriac Bible translations of their own, representing a sort of mixture of Peshitta and Septuagint Text. Here belongs the 'Philoxenian', influenced by

[1] Barnes, *The Peshitta Psalter according to the West Syrian Text edited with an Apparatus Criticus* (1904); Bloemendaal, *The Headings of the Psalms in the East-Syrian Church* (1960); Penna, 'I titoli del Salterio siriaco e S. Girolamo' Bibl 40 (1959), pp. 177–87; Peters, 'Pešitta-Psalter und Psalmentargum' Muséon 52 (1939), pp. 275–96; Schneider, 'Biblische Oden im syro-hexaplarischen Psalter' Bibl 40 (1959), pp. 199–209; Vogel, 'Studien zum Pešiṭta-Psalter' Bibl 32 (1951), pp. 32–56, 198–231, 336–63, 481–502.

[2] Barnes, *An Apparatus Criticus to Chronicles in the Peshitta Version* (1897).

[3] Lagarde, *Libri Veteris Testamenti apocryphi syriace* (1861); Lebram, 'Die Peschitta zu Tobit vii, 11–xiv, 15' ZAW 69 (1957), pp. 185–211; McHardy, 'Ben-Ze'eb's Edition of the Peshitta Text of Ecclesiasticus' ZAW 61 (1945/48), pp. 193 f.; Emerton, *The Peshitta of the Wisdom of Solomon* (St Pb II, 1959); on this cf. Black, JSSt 6 (1961), pp. 270–1; Vosté, 'La version syro-hexaplaire de la Sagesse' Bibl 30 (1949), pp. 213–17.

[4] Baumstark, 'Ps.-Jonathan zu Dtn xxxiv, 6 und die Pentateuchzitate Afrahats' ZAW 59 (1943), pp. 99–111; Hänel, *Die außermasoretischen Übereinstimmungen zwischen der Septuaginta und der Peschittha in der Genesis* (BZAW 20, 1911); Peters, 'Peschittha und Targumim des Pentateuchs' Muséon 48 (1935), pp. 1–54; Tonneau, 'Texte syriaque de la Genèse. L'Hexaémeron' Muséon 59 (1946), pp. 333–44; Vööbus, *Peschitta und Targumim des Pentateuchs* (1958); on this cf. Goshen-Gottstein, JSSt 6 (1961), pp. 266–70.

[5] Englert, *The Peshitto of Second Samuel* (1949); Peters, 'Zur Herkunft der Pešiṭta von 1. Sam.' Bibl 22 (1941), pp. 25–34.

[6] Delekat, 'Die syrolukianische Übersetzung des Buches Jesaja und das Postulat einer at. Vetus Syra' ZAW 69 (1957), pp. 21–54; 'Die Peschitta zu Jesaja zwischen Targum und Septuaginta' Bibl 38 (1957), pp. 185–99, 321–35; Diettrich, *Ein Apparatus criticus zur Pešitto zum Propheten Jesaja* (BZAW 8, 1905).

[7] Abramowski, 'Eine spätsyrische Überlieferung des Buches Ruth' *Bulmerincq-Gedenkschr.* (1938), pp. 7–19.

the Lucianic recension of the Septuagint, which was made at the instigation of
Bishop Philoxenus of Mabbug in Northern Syria by his suffragan Polycarp;
and further the translation made by Paul of Tella of the Septuagint text of
the Hexapla, the 'Syro-Hexaplar' which is in part preserved in the Codex
Ambrosianus C.313 Inf. which we shall have to mention again below on
p. 711. The Syro-Palestinian Melkite Church, however, made for itself a
Bible translation in Palestinian Syriac,[8] likewise influenced by the hexaplaric
text, of which at least fragments have come down to us. As we have seen
(p. 640), the small number of these fragments has now been somewhat aug-
mented by others found at Khirbet el-Mird.

§ 121. THE SEPTUAGINT

Literature: (a) Text: Brooke-McLean-Thackeray-Manson, *The OT in Greek*; Rahlfs,
Septuaginta. Id est VT Graece iuxta LXX Interpretes; Societas Litterarum Gottingensis,
Septuaginta. Vetus Testamentum Graece; Swete, *The OT in Greek according to the Septuagint.*
(For further details concerning these editions, cf. below, p. 714.)

(b) Other Works: Bertram, 'Zur Septuaginta-Forschung' ThR 3 (1931), pp. 283–96; 5
(1933), pp. 173–86; 10 (1938), pp. 69–80, 133–59; Bickerman, 'Some Notes on the Transmission of the Septuagint' *Alex. Marx Jub. Vol.*, I (1950), pp. 149–78; Brockington,
'Septuagint and Targum' ZAW 66 (1954), pp. 80–6; Bruce, 'The OT in Greek' BT 4
(1953), pp. 129–135, 156–62; Devreesse, *Introduction à l'étude des manuscrits grecs* (1954);
Dörrie, 'Zur Geschichte der Septuaginta im Jahrhundert Konstantins' ZNW 39 (1940),
pp. 57–110; Gehman, 'Some Types of Errors of Transmission in the LXX' VT 3 (1953),
pp. 397–400; Gerleman, *Synoptic Studies in the OT* (LUA 44, 5, 1948); Giannakopoulos,
'Ἡ παλαιὰ Διαθήκη κατὰ τοὺς Ο' I–IX (1955–1957); Haag, 'Probleme der griechischen
Bibel' Schweizer Kirchenzeitung 123 (1955), pp. 520–2, 534 f.; Hautsch, 'Septuaginta'
RE, IIA (1923), cols. 1586–1621; Herrmann and Baumgärtel (1923) (§ 90); Hunger, 'Ein
neues Septuaginta-Fragment in der Österreichischen Nationalbibliothek' AAW 93 (1957),
pp. 188–99; Jouassard, 'Requête d'un patrologue aux biblistes touchant les Septante' StP I
(1957), pp. 307–27; Kahle (1915), (p. 678); 'Die Septuaginta. Prinzipielle Erwägungen'
Eissfeldt-Festschr. (1947), pp. 161–80; 'Problems of the Septuagint' StP I (1957), pp. 328–
338; 'The Greek Bible and the Gospels. Fragments from the Judaean Desert' StEv (1959),
pp. 613–21; *The Cairo Geniza* (²1959), pp. 209–64; 'The Greek Bible Manuscripts used by
Origen' JBL 79 (1960), pp. 111–18; Katz, 'Notes on the Septuagint' JThSt 47 (1946),
pp. 30–3, 166–9; 48 (1947), pp. 194–6; 'Das Problem des Urtextes der Septuaginta' ThZ 5
(1949), pp. 1–24; 'The Recovery of the Original Septuagint' *Actes du Iᵉʳ Congr. de la Fédér.
Internat. des Assoc. d'Études Classiques* (1951), pp. 165–82; 'Septuagintal Studies in the
Mid-Century' *Essays C. H. Dodd* (1956), pp. 176–208; 'Zur Übersetzungstechnik der
Septuaginta' WdO II 3 (1956), pp. 267–73; Kenyon, *Recent Developments in the Textual
Criticism of the Greek Bible* (1933); *Our Bible and the Ancient Manuscripts*, rev. by Adams
(⁵1958); Mercati, 'Note di letteratura biblica' RB 50 (1941), pp. 5–15; Moir, 'Two Septua-
gint Palimpsest Fragments' JThSt 8 (1957), pp. 1–11, Pls. I–II; Nestle, *Septuagin astudien*
I–VI (1886–1911); Orlinsky, 'On the Present State of Proto-Septuagint Studies' JAOS 61
(1941), pp. 81–91 = AOS Offprint Ser. 13, 1942; 'The Septuagint—its Use in Textual

---

[8] Baars, 'A Palestinian Syriac text of the book of Lamentations' VT 10 (1960), pp. 224–7;
Baumstark, 'Das Problem des christlich-palästinischen Pentateuchtextes' OrChr 10 (1935),
pp. 201–24; Delekat, 'Die syropalästinische Übersetzung der Paulusbriefe und die Peschitta'
NTSt 3 (1957), pp. 223–33; 'Die syropalästinische Jesaja-Übersetzung' ZAW 71 (1959),
pp. 165–201. Cf. above, p. 640, n. 8.

Criticism' BA 9 (1946), pp. 21–34; 'Current Progress and Problems in Septuaginta Research' in *The Study of the Bible Today and Tomorrow* (1947), pp. 144–61; *The Septuagint. The Oldest Translation of the Bible* (1949); 'Margolis' Work in the Septuagint' in *Max Leopold Margolis, Scholar and Teacher* (1952), pp. 33–44; 'Jewish Biblical Scholarship in America' JQR 45 (1954/55), pp. 374–412, cf. pp. 392–8: 'Margolis'; 'Qumran and the Present State of OT Text Studies: The Septuagint Text' JBL 78 (1959), pp. 26–33; Ottley, *A Handbook to the Septuagint* (1920); Prijs, *Jüdische Tradition in der Septuaginta* (1948); Procksch, *Studien zur Geschichte der Septuaginta. Die Propheten* (1910); on this cf. Rahlfs, GGA (1910), pp. 694–705; 'Tetraplarische Studien' ZAW 53 (1935), pp. 240–69; 54 (1936), pp. 61–90; Rahlfs, *Paul de Lagardes wissenschaftliches Lebenswerk* (Mitt. Sept.-Untern, d. Gött. Ges. d. Wiss. IV, 1, 1928), pp. 66–86: 'Die-Septuaginta-Arbeit seit 1866'; Rowley, 'The Proto-Septuagint Question' JQR 33 (1942/43), pp. 497–9; Seeligmann, 'Problemen en Perspectieven in het moderne Septuaginta-Onderzoek' JEOL 6/8 (1943), pp. 359–90°, 763–6; Sperber, 'The NT and the Septuaginta' [Hebr.] Tarbiz 6 (1934/35), pp. 1–29; 'Probleme einer Edition der Septuaginta' *Kahle-Festschr.* (1935), pp. 39–46; 'NT and Septuagint' JBL 59 (1940), pp. 193–293; Stegmüller, *Berliner Septuagintafragmente* (1939); on this cf. Hempel, ThLZ 65 (1940), cols. 122 f.; Swete, *Introduction to the OT in Greek* (²1914); Thackeray (§ 87); Trencsényi-Waldapfel, 'Défense de la version des Septante contre l'accusation d'apanthropie' *Et. Or. Hirschler* (1950), pp. 122–36; Wevers, 'Septuaginta-Forschungen. I. Ausgaben und Texte; II. Die Septuaginta als Übersetzungsurkunde' ThR 22 (1954), pp. 85–138, 171–90; Wutz, *Die Transkriptionen von der Septuaginta bis Hieronymus* (1933); *Systematische Wege von der Septuaginta zum hebräischen Urtext* (1937); on this cf. Kahle, ZDMG 92 (1938), pp. 276–86.
    Cf. also Literature § 126.

Much more significant than the translations of the Old Testament into other Semitic dialects such as have just been mentioned, is its translation into Greek in the Septuagint, whose beginnings, as we have already seen, stretch back into the third century B.C. The occasion for this we have already considered (§ 90). But to what was said there we must now add that the translation of the Hebrew text into Greek was not the first and only way by which to make the Torah and the remaining sacred books accessible to Greek speaking Jews. Wutz has made it seem probable that Greek transcriptions, i.e. the reproduction of the Hebrew with Greek letters, if they did not precede the translation into Greek, at least ran parallel to it. In the period which is relevant, namely the fourth, third and second centuries B.C., there is considerable evidence of the reproduction of non-Greek texts in Greek letters within the area influenced by the spread of Greek culture, and, for example, from North Africa of Punic texts in Greek transcription.[1] The transcription of the Hebrew text of the Bible in Greek letters in the second column of Origen's Hexapla, to which reference must subsequently be made (pp. 709–12), is thus not by any means an innovation. There already existed a long tradition of such a practice, extending back, as we know from the testimony of the Letter of Aristeas (§ 90), into the second and even the third centuries B.C.

---

[1] Berthier et Charlier, *Le sanctuaire punique d'El Hofra à Constantine* (1955), pp. 167 f., Pl. XXVIII A, cf. esp. pp. 168 f., 172; Février, 'Les découvertes d'épigraphiques puniques et néopuniques depuis la guerre' *Stud. Or. Levi della Vida*, I (1956), pp. 274–86, cf. pp. 283 f.; Friedrich, 'Punische Studien' ZDMG 107 (1957), pp. 282–98, cf. pp. 282–90: 'Eine punische Weihung in griechischer Schrift'. Cf. also Literature on p. 605, n. 4 and § 90.

The books of the Old Testament were translated gradually, as may be seen from two facts. On the one hand the grandson of Ben Sira, according to the evidence of the prologue he wrote (pp. 565–7, 597), already had before him in about 117 B.C. translations of the Law, the Prophets and the remaining books. On the other hand, it may be seen from the fact that the 𝔊 text of some books of the Old Testament, for example Isa. and Psalms, clearly presupposes the translation of the Pentateuch and is dependent upon it. But with few exceptions (pp. 575, 592, 597) we know nothing at all about the persons, period and method of working of the individual translators, and are here entirely dependent upon investigation of the individual books of 𝔊 itself. This shows that the nature and value of the translation in the individual books varies greatly. The footnotes contain a selection of the relevant literature on the Pentateuch,[2] Gen.,[3] Exod.,[4] Deut.,[5] Josh.,[6] Judg.,[7] Sam.,[8] Kings,[9] Isa.,[10] Jer.,[11] Ezek.,[12] the Book of

---

[2] Fritsch, *The Anti-Anthropomorphisms of the Greek Pentateuch* (1943); on this cf. Orlinsky, Crozer Q 21 (1944), pp. 156–60 and Manson, JThSt 46 (1945), pp. 78–80; Gooding, *Recensions of the Septuagint Pentateuch* (1955).

[3] Gehman, 'Hebraisms of the Old Greek Version of Genesis' VT 3 (1953), pp. 141–8.

[4] Gooding, *The Account of the Tabernacle. Translation and Textual Problems of the Greek Exodus* (1959); on this cf. Katz, ThLZ 85 (1960), cols. 350–5.

[5] Ziegler, 'Zur Septuaginta-Vorlage im Deuteronomium' ZAW 72 (1960), pp. 237–62; Hempel, 'Zur Septuaginta-Vorlage im Deuteronomium. Eine Entgegnung auf ZAW 1960, 237 ff.' ZAW 73 (1961), pp. 87–96.

[6] Margolis, 'The Grouping of the Codices in the Greek Joshua' JQR 1 (1910/11), pp. 259–63; 'Specimen of a New Edition of the Greek Joshua' *Stud. Israel Abrahams* (1927), pp. 307–23; *The Book of Joshua in Greek*, Parts I–IV (1931–38); Pretzl, 'Die griechischen Handschriftengruppen im Buche Josue untersucht' Bibl 9 (1928), pp. 377–427; 'Der hexaplarische und tetraplarische Septuagintatext des Origenes in den Büchern Josua und Richter' ByZ 30 (1929/30), pp. 262–8.

[7] Pretzl, 'Septuagintaprobleme im Buch der Richter' Bibl 7 (1926), pp. 233–69, 353–83; Schreiner, *Septuaginta-Massora des Buches der Richter* (An Bibl 7, 1957); Soisalon-Soininen, *Die Textformen der Septuaginta-Übersetzung des Richterbuches* (Ann. Ac. Sc. Fennicae B 72, 1, 1951); on this cf. Katz, ThLZ 77 (1952), cols. 154–8 and Lambert, VT 2 (1952), pp. 184–9. Cf. Lit. § 126.

[8] de Boer (§ 40); Gehman, 'Exegetical Methods employed by the Greek Translator of I Samuel' JAOS 70 (1950), pp. 292–6; Wevers, 'Exegetical Principles Underlying the Greek Text of 2 Sam xi, 2–1 Kings ii, 11' CBQ 15 (1953), pp. 30–45.

[9] Wevers, 'Exegetical Principles Underlying the Septuagint of 1 Kings ii, 12–xxi, 43' OTS 8 (1950), pp. 300–22; 'Principles of Interpretation guiding the Fourth Translator of the Book of the Kingdoms' CBQ 14 (1952), pp. 40–56.

[10] Delekat, 'Die syrolukianische Übersetzung des Buches Jesaja und das Postulat einer at. Vetus Syra' ZAW 69 (1957), pp. 21–54; 'Die Peschitta zu Jesaja zwischen Targum und Septuaginta' Bibl 38 (1957), pp. 185–199, 321–35; 'Ein Septuaginta-Targum' VT 8 (1958), pp. 225–52; Fritsch, 'The Concept of God in the Greek Translation of Isaiah' *Bibl. Stud. H. C. Alleman* (1960), pp. 155–69; Hurwitz, 'The Septuagint of Isaiah xxxvi–xxxix in Relation to that of i–xxxv, xl–lv' HUCA 28 (1957), pp. 75–84; Orlinsky, 'The Treatment of Anthropomorphisms and Anthropopathisms in the Septuagint of Isaiah' HUCA 27 (1956), pp. 193–200; Ottley, *The Book of Isaiah according to the Septuagint* (²1909); Seeligmann, *The Septuagint Version of Isaiah* (1948); Ziegler, *Untersuchungen zur Septuaginta des Buches Isaias* (1934); 'Die Vorlage der Isaias-Septuaginta (LXX) und die erste Isaias-Rolle von Qumran (1 Q Isᵃ)' JBL 78 (1959), pp. 34–59.

[11] Baumgärtel (1961) (§ 46); Ziegler, 'Die Septuaginta Hieronymi im Buch des Propheten Jeremias' *Dold-Festschr.* (1952), pp. 13–24; *Beiträge zur Ieremias-Septuaginta* (NAG 1958, No. 2, 1958).

[12] Filson (p. 370, n. 14); Gehman, 'The Relation between the Hebrew Text of Ezekiel and ·hat of the John H. Scheide Papyri' JAOS 58 (1938), pp. 92–102; 'The Relations between ·he Text of the John H. Scheide Papyri and that of the other Greek MSS of Ezekiel' JBL 57

the Twelve,[13] Hab.,[14] Psalms,[15] Job,[16] Prov.,[17] Ruth,[18] Eccl.,[19] Dan.,[20] Chron.,[21] Ezra-Neh.,[22] Ecclus.[23] Some indication may be given for some of these of the results which are generally agreed. The translation of the Pentateuch is good, that of Isaiah of little use. That of Daniel is almost a paraphrase rather than a translation, and in fact in general 𝕲 is in many respects more a witness to the exegesis of the Hebrew text reflecting Egyptian conditions and very Greek in spirit,[24] rather than a testimony to the text itself. In regard to its grammar and

(1938), pp. 281–7; Katz, 'Zur Textgestaltung der Ezechiel-Septuaginta' Bibl 35 (1954), pp. 29–39; Payne, 'The Relationship of the Chester Beatty Papyri of Ezekiel to Codex Vaticanus' JBL 68 (1949), pp. 251–65; Turner, 'The Greek Translators of Ezekiel' JThSt 7 (1956), pp. 12–24; Wevers, 'Evidence of the Text of the John H. Scheide Papyri for the Translation of the Status Constructus in Ezekiel' JBL 70 (1951), pp. 211–16; Ziegler (p. 368, n. 8).

[13] Ziegler, *Die Einheit der Septuaginta zum Zwölfprophetenbuch* (Programm Braunsberg, 1934); 'Beiträge zum griechischen Dodekapropheton' NAG (1943), pp. 345–412; 'Studien zur Verwertung der Septuaginta im Zwölfprophetenbuch' ZAW 60 (1944), pp. 107–31; (1944) (§ 117); 'Der Text der Aldina im Dodekapropheton' Bibl 26 (1945), pp. 37–51.

[14] Good, 'The Barberini Greek Version of Habakkuk iii' VT 9 (1959), pp. 11–30.

[15] Flashar, 'Exegetische Studien zum Septuagintapsalter' ZAW 32 (1912), pp. 81–116, 161–89, 241–68; Soffer, 'The Treatment of Anthropomorphisms and Anthropopathisms in the Septuaginta of Psalms' HUCA 28 (1957), pp. 85–108; Wikgren, 'Two Ostraca Fragments of the Septuagint Psalter' JNESt 5 (1946), pp. 181–4.

[16] Gard, 'The Concept of the Future Life according to the Greek Translator of the Book of Job' JBL 73 (1954), pp. 137–43; Gerleman, *Studies in the Septuagint*. I. *Book of Job* (LUA 43, 2, 1946); Orlinsky, 'Studies in the Septuagint of the Book of Job' HUCA 28 (1957), pp. 53–74; 29 (1958), pp. 229–71; 30 (1959), pp. 153–67; 32 (1961), pp. 239–68; 33 (1962), pp. 119–51; Ziegler, 'Der textkritische Wert der Septuaginta des Buches Job' Misc. Bibl. 2 (1934), pp. 277–96.

[17] Fritsch, 'The Treatment of the Hexaplaric Signs in the Syro-Hexapla of Proverbs' JBL 72 (1953), pp. 169–81; Gerleman, 'The Septuagint Proverbs as a Hellenistic Document' OTS 8 (1950), pp. 15–27; 'Religion och moral i Septuagintas Proverbia-översättning' SvTK 26 (1950), pp. 222–32; *Studies in the Septuagint*. III: *Proverbs* (LUA 52, 3, 1956); Kaminka (§ 65); Zuntz, 'Der Antinoe Papyrus der Proverbia und das Prophetologion' ZAW 68 (1956), pp. 124–84; on this cf. Katz, 'Frühe hebraisierende Rezensionen der Septuaginta und die Hexapla' ZAW 69 (1957), pp. 77–84.

[18] Rahlfs, *Studie über den griechischen Text des Buches Ruth* (1922); *Das Buch Ruth griechisch, als Probe einer kritischen Handausgabe der Septuaginta* (1922); Thornhill, 'The Greek Text of the Book of Ruth: a Grouping of Manuscripts according to Origen's Hexapla' VT 3 (1953), pp. 236–49.

[19] Bertram, 'Hebräischer und griechischer Qohelet' ZAW 64 (1952), pp. 26–49.

[20] Ziegler, 'Der Bibeltext im Daniel-Kommentar des Hippolyt von Rom' NAG (1952), pp. 165–99.

[21] Gerleman, *Studies in the Septuagint*. II: *Chronicles* (LUA 43, 3, 1946); Rogers, *The Old Greek Version of Chronicles* (Diss. Princeton, 1954; Ann. Arbor Univ. Microfilm, 1954).

[22] Allgeier, 'Beobachtungen am Septuagintatext der Bücher Esdras und Nehemias' Bibl 22 (1941), pp. 227–51.

[23] Ziegler, 'Hat Lukian den griechischen Sirach rezensiert?' Bibl 40 (1959), pp. 210–29 =StBiblOr I (1959), pp. 76–95; 'Die hexaplarische Bearbeitung des griechischen Sirach' BZ 4 (1960), pp. 174–85. On Wisd. cf. p. 602. Lit. § 126.

[24] Bertram, 'Die religiöse Umdeutung altorientalischer Lebensweisheit in der griechischen Übersetzung des AT' ZAW 54 (1936), pp. 153–67; ''*IKANOΣ* in den griechischen Übersetzungen des AT als Wiedergabe von *schaddaj*' ZAW 70 (1958), pp. 20–31; 'Zur Prägung der biblischen Gottesvorstellung in der griechischen Übersetzung des AT. Die Wiedergabe von *schadad* und *schaddaj* im Griechischen' WdO II, 5/6 (1959), pp. 502–13; Bickerman, 'Two Legal Interpretations of the Septuagint' Rev. Internat. des Droits de l'Antiquité 3 (1956), pp. 81–104; Descamps, 'La justice de Dieu dans la Bible grecque' Studia Hellenistica V (1948), pp. 69–92; Marcus, 'Jewish and Greek Elements in the Septuagint' *L. Ginzberg Jub. Vol.* I (1945), pp. 227–45. Cf. also Lit. § 126.

lexical content it reveals many peculiarities in which it deviates from classical Greek.[25] Thus when the translation of 𝕲 is utilised for the emendation of evident errors in 𝔐, care must be taken to distinguish between the different books. Whereas, for example the translation of 𝕲 for Sam. can be of real use, this is much less the case with the Minor Prophets and the Psalms. It must further be noted that for some of the books we must reckon either certainly or possibly with more than one translator.

From the period before Origen († 254), much of whose edition of 𝕲 (pp. 709–12) has survived, only a small amount of material was available at the beginning of the twentieth century as evidence for the translation of 𝕲. Apart from quotations in Jewish Hellenistic writers such as Eupolemus (p. 540) from the second century B.C., and Aristeas from the first half of the first century B.C. (Job),[26] and also the Jewish imprecations from Rhenaia, the neighbouring islands to Delos,[27] composed in about 100 B.C., there were only available the passages quoted from it from a century to three centuries later in Philo, Josephus, the New Testament and the Apostolic Fathers. Here, however, we have only small isolated passages which can only be used with the greatest caution for the reconstruction of the earlier history of the transmission of the text of 𝕲. For with some of the witnesses just mentioned, as for example Philo,[28] it is possible and indeed probable that at least some of the citations of 𝕲 to be found in the writings which have come down to us from them do not go back in this form to the authors themselves, but received it only at a later stage. But in the last thirty years older fragments, some of them very old, of the translation of 𝕲 have come to light and been published,[29] first fairly comprehensive passages from the fourth, third and second centuries A.D., and then smaller passages from the second century B.C. From the second century A.D. come the Antinoopolis[30] Papyrus No. 7 containing

[25] Brønno, 'Some Nominal Types in the Septuagint. Contributions to Pre-Masoretic Grammar' Classica et Mediaevalia 3 (1940), pp. 180–213; Gehman, 'The Hebraic Character of Septuaginta Greek' VT 1 (1951), pp. 81–90; Johannessohn, *Der Gebrauch der Präpositionen in der Septuaginta* (Mitt. Sept.-Untern. Gött. Ges. Wiss. III, 3, 1926); 'Das biblische καὶ ἐγένετο und seine Geschichte' Zeitschr. f. vgl. Sprachforschung 53 (1925), pp. 161–212; 'Der Wahrnehmungssatz bei den Verben des Sehens in der hebr. und griech. Bibel' *ib.*, 64 (1937), pp. 145–260; 'Das biblische καὶ ἰδού in der Erzählung samt seiner hebr. Vorlage' *ib.*, 66 (1939), pp. 145–95; 67 (1940), pp. 30–84; 'Die biblische Einführungsformel καὶ ἔσται' ZAW 59 (1943), pp. 129–84; Martin, 'Some Syntactical Criteria of Translation Greek' VT 10 (1960), pp. 295–310; Watson, 'Some Observations on the Use of δίκαιος in the Septuagint' JBL 79 (1960), pp. 255–66.

[26] Schürer, GJV III (⁴1909), pp. 427, 469, 480: E.T. II, 3 (1897), pp. 162, 203 f., 208 f.

[27] Deissmann, *Licht vom Osten* (⁴1923), pp. 351–62, E.T. *Light from the Ancient East* (1910), pp. 423–35; Schürer, GJV III (⁴1909), pp. 57, 142, 427.

[28] Kahle, 'Untersuchungen zur Geschichte des Pentateuchtextes' ThStKr 88 (1915), pp. 399–439 = *Op. Min.* (1956), pp. 3–37, cf. pp. 418–23 (pp. 18–23); 'Die im August 1952 entdeckte Lederrolle mit dem griechischen Text der kleinen Propheten und das Problem der Septuaginta' ThLZ 76 (1954), cols. 81–94 = [Engl.] *Op. Min.* (1956), pp. 113–28, cf. cols. 90–2 (pp. 124–6); *The Cairo Geniza* (²1959), pp. 247–9; Katz, 'A Fresh Aquila Fragment, recovered from Philo' JThSt 47 (1946), pp. 30–3; *Philo's Bible. The Aberrant Text of Bible Quotations in some Philonic Writings and its Place in the Textual History of the Greek Bible* (1950); Schröder, *De Philonis Alexandrini Vetere Testamento* (Diss. phil. Greifswald, 1907).

[29] Bell, *Recent Discoveries of Biblical Papyri* (1937); 'Evidences of Christianity in Egypt during the Roman Period' HThR 37 (1944), pp. 185–208, cf. pp. 199–203.

[30] Roberts, *The Antinoopolis Papyri*, Part I (1950); on this cf. Bell, JThSt 2 (1951), pp. 202–6; Barns and Zilliacus, *The Antinoopolis Papyri*, Part II (1960).

parts of Pss. lxxxii and lxxxiii,[31] and a papyrus fragment in a similar hand in the Bodleian Library containing Ps. xlix, 20–1, 3, 17–21.[32] From the third century A.D. there is the Antinoopolis Papyrus No. 8[33] containing relatively large fragments of Prov., and smaller fragments of Wisd. and Ecclus., and in addition the sheet of papyrus counted as Antinoopolis Papyrus No. 9[34] which is from Prov. Also from the third century A.D. come the fragments of a manuscript of Genesis and the Twelve Prophets, which was published in New York in 1927 by Sanders and Carl Schmidt under the title *The Minor Prophets in the Freer Collection and the Berlin Fragment of Genesis*, and a Bodmer Papyrus containing Pss. xxxiii and xxxiv.[35] The two sheets of parchment of Ezek., described as Antinoopolis Papyrus No. 10[36] belong to the fourth century A.D. Mostly from the third century, but also from the fourth and second centuries A.D., are the remains of eleven codices which probably came from a Christian Church or Monastery library in the Fayyum; these are known, from the name of the owner of the bulk of them, as the Chester Beatty Papyri.[37] They were made available for scientific study by Kenyon, *The Chester Beatty Biblical Papyri* I–VIII (London, 1933–41) and by Johnson, Gehman and Kase, *The John H. Scheide Biblical Papyri: Ezekiel* (Princeton, 1938). So far as the Old Testament is concerned, the Beatty and Scheide papyri comprise larger or smaller sections of Gen., Num., Deut., Isa., Jer., Ezek., Esther, Dan., Ecclus., Enoch.[38] Among them the Daniel fragment, covering about a third of the book of Daniel, is particularly valuable because it provides the text of 𝔊, for which up till that time the only evidence available, apart from the Syro-hexaplar (p. 701) was one single codex Chisianus (Codex Chigi). Elsewhere this rendering has been replaced by the translation of Theodotion (p. 716) or 'Proto-Theodotion'.[39]

The papyrus fragment Fuad 266[40] containing the Greek text of Deut. xxxi, 36–xxxii, 7 and published by Waddell, 'The Tetragrammaton in the LXX'[41] probably belongs to the middle of the second century B.C. This is also worthy of note because twice in the middle of the Greek text it has the Hebrew divine

[31] *Ant. Pap.*, Part I, pp. 1–2, Pl. I. Cf. Lit. § 126.

[32] Barns and Kilpatrick, 'A New Psalms Fragment' PBA 43 (1957), pp. 229–32, Pl. X.

[33] *Ant. Pap.*, Part I, pp. 2–17, Pl. I; Zuntz (cf. above, p. 704, n. 17).

[34] *Ant. Pap.*, Part I, pp. 18–19 (parts of Prov. ii–iii).

[35] *Papyrus Bodmer VII–IX. Épitre de Jude, Les deux épîtres de Pierre, Psaumes xxxiii et xxxiv. Manuscrit du IIIᵉ siècle. Édition préparée par M. Testuz* (1959).

[36] *Ant. Pap.*, Part I, pp. 19–23 (parts of Ezek. xxxiii–xxxiv).

[37] Allgeier, *Die Chester Beatty-Papyri zum Pentateuch. Untersuchungen zur älteren Überlieferungsgeschichte der Septuaginta* (1938); 'Die Bedeutung der Chester-Beatty-Papyri für die Septuagintaforschung' FuF 15 (1939), pp. 20–2.

[38] Photographs are now available of some of the papyri containing these books, in *The Chester Beatty Biblical Papyri. Descriptions and Texts of twelve Manuscripts on Papyrus of the Greek Bible*. Fasc. V Numbers and Deuteronomy, Fasc. VI Isaiah, Jeremiah, Ecclesiasticus, Plates (1958).

[39] Ziegler, *Susanna. Daniel. Bel et Draco* (Septuaginta . . . Soc. Litt. Gottingensis XVI, 2, 1954), pp. 28 f., 61 f.

[40] In *New World Translation of the Christian Greek Scriptures* (1950), pp. 13–14, a few further fragments of Papyrus Fuad 266 have been published which also contain the tetragrammaton. Cf. Vaccari, 'Papiro Fuad, Inv. 266. Analisi critica dei Frammenti publicati in: New World Translation of the Christian Greek Scriptures. Brooklyn (N.Y.), 1950, p. 13s.' StP I (1957), pp. 339–42, and Kahle, *Cairo Geniza* (²1959), pp. 218 f.

[41] JThS 45 (1944), pp. 158–61.

name written in an old form of the Square script.[42] Probably about as old is the Papyrus Greek 458 of the John Rylands Library in Manchester, published by Roberts, 'Two Biblical Papyri in the John Rylands Library'.[43] This consists of six fragments carefully removed from a mummy wrapping, and it contains parts of Deut. xxiii, 24–xxiv, 3; xxv, 1–3; xxvi, 12, 17–19; xxviii, 31–3. In spite of its small compass[44] it offers several particularly noteworthy readings.[45]

These remnants of a pre-Christian Jewish translation of the Hebrew Old Testament into Greek have now been increased in number as a result of the discoveries in the Wilderness of Judaea in the last decade. Fragments of three such manuscripts have come from Cave 4,[46] namely a papyrus scroll containing parts of Lev. ii–v (4QLXX Lev^b), a leather scroll containing pieces of Lev. xxvi, 2–16 (4Q LXX Lev^a), and a leather scroll containing fragments of Num. iii, 30–iv, 14 (4Q LXX Num). All three probably date from the second century B.C. At any rate they witness to a Jewish translation of the Hebrew Old Testament into Greek, as may further be recognised in the case of 4Q LXX Lev^b from the fact that here for the divine name $IA\Omega$ is used, not $Kύριος$. The fourth witness to a Jewish translation of the Old Testament into Greek from the pre-Christian period is provided by the substantial fragments of a leather scroll containing the Twelve Prophets.[47] The larger part of this was found by members of the Ta'āmire tribe in 1952; the remaining, smaller part, by Israeli scholars in 1960 in a cave in the Heber valley (p. 639). This scroll is perhaps somewhat later than the three found in Cave 4 just mentioned, and probably comes from

[42] Cf. also Papyrus Fuad 203 containing a few words of 𝔊, from the end of the first or beginning of the second century A.D. This has been published by Benoit, 'Fragment d'une prière contres les esprits impurs?' RB 58 (1951), pp. 549–65; and described as a formula for threatening or cursing and considered in relation to its significance for the problem of 𝔊 by Katz, 'Papyrus Fuad 203 und die Septuaginta' ThZ 9 (1953), pp. 228–31.

[43] BJRL 20 (1936), pp. 219–44, with two plates: 1. A Ptolemaic Papyrus of Deuteronomy. P. Ryl. Gr. 458 (pp. 219–36, one plate); 2. Fragment of a Testimony Book. P. Ryl. Gr. 460 (pp. 237–44, one plate).

[44] Because of its small compass, the divine name does not appear in it. But it may nevertheless be regarded as certain that 458, like Pap. 266, did not read $κύριος$ but יהוה. It must remain uncertain whether this tetragrammaton was written in the Square script or in old Hebrew characters (pp. 676–7).

[45] Allgeier, 'Dt. xxv, 1–3 im Manchester-Papyrus (PRG 458)' Bibl 19 (1938), pp. 1–18; Caspari, 'Papyrus-Streifen des vorchristlichen Pentateuch' ThStKr 107 (1936), pp. 347–353; Hempel, 'Zum griechischen Deuteronomiumtext des II. Jahrhunderts a. C.' ZAW 55 (1937), pp. 115–27; Hofbauer, 'Zu den Textfamilien der Septuaginta im Deuteronomium' ZKTh 62 (1938), pp. 385–9; Opitz and Schaeder, 'Zum Septuaginta-Papyrus Rylands Greek 458' ZNW 35 (1936), pp. 115–17; Vaccari, 'Fragmentum biblicum saeculi II ante Christum' Bibl 17 (1936), pp. 501–4.

[46] Cross, The Ancient Library of Qumrân (1958), p. 21; Skehan, 'The Qumran Manuscripts and Textual Criticism' SVT IV (1957), pp. 148–60, 1 Pl., cf. pp. 155–60 and plate; Kahle, Cairo Geniza (²1959), pp. 223–6. According to de Vaux, RB 63 (1956), p. 572, a few Greek papyrus fragments of Exod. and Ep. Jer. have come to light in Cave 7. These are now published in Discoveries in the Judaean Desert III (1962), pp. 142 f., Pl. XXX. Cf. above, p. 595, n. 3.

[47] Barthélemy, 'Redécouverte d'un chaînon manquant de l'histoire de la Septante' RB 60 (1953), pp. 18–29, Pl. I; Kahle, 'Die im August 1952 entdeckte Lederrolle mit dem griechischen Text der kleinen Propheten' ThLZ 79 (1954), cols. 81–94 = Op. Min. (1956), pp. 113–28: 'A Leather Scroll of the Greek Minor Prophets and the Problem of the Septuagint'; Cairo Geniza (²1959), pp. 225–8; V[ogt], 'Fragmenta Prophetarum Minorum Deserti Juda' Bibl 34 (1953), pp. 423–6. Cf. above, p. 383.

the end of the first century B.C. But it exceeds the others in significance because so much of it is preserved. In his essay in 1953 Barthélemy could report that parts of the books of Micah, Jonah, Nah., Hab., Zeph. and Zech. were preserved. Since then, as Kahle (*Cairo Geniza* (²1959), p. 226) indicates, on information given by G. Vermès, further sections have come to light, and to this must now be added the fortunate discovery by Israeli scholars of parts of the book of Jonah.[48] The complete publication of the scroll is still to come, but it has already been evaluated in detail, by Barthélemy,[49] Kahle[49] and others.[50]

Barthélemy's assessment of the fragments of the Greek Minor Prophets just mentioned arrives at results quite different from those of Kahle. Since this difference is connected with differences concerning the nature of the translation of ᵹ as such, we must here briefly consider the question which is at issue, merely setting out the main issues and leaving on one side all the other points which are connected with it. As the title of his study shows, Barthélemy values these fragments as a testimony to a stage in the evolution of the translation of ᵹ not hitherto attested. He sees them as evidence of a sporadic revision of the text of ᵹ in accordance with 𝔐 undertaken by a Jew in the first century A.D. This revised text was, he thinks, then taken over by Aquila, Symmachus and probably also Theodotion, to whom reference must be made again shortly (§ 122), for their new translations of the Hebrew text, so that they are to be regarded not as innovators but as continuers of a process already begun. Kahle is also of the opinion that the Greek text of these fragments is of Jewish origin; this may be seen simply from the evidence of the Hebrew letters used in it for the writing of the divine name. But he sees in this text not a recension of the older translation of ᵹ, but the rendering of a popular Hebrew text. Many such existed before the reorganisation of Judaism necessitated by the disaster of A.D. 70, and the Samaritan Pentateuch (§ 118), as well as the texts attested by the complete Isaiah scroll and the Habakkuk Commentary from Qumrān Cave 1 (pp. 681–2), must also be understood as such. The history of ᵹ does not begin for Kahle with an original text which in the course of time has undergone corruptions and recensions. In his view the various Targum-like translations of Hebrew popular texts into Greek mark the beginning (see § 90), and these were only in the course of time assimilated to the *textus receptus* of the Jews. The triumph of a definite text-form of ᵹ thus stands at the end, not at the beginning of the development, and to this extent it is a utopian ideal to endeavour to restore the original text of ᵹ. Thus Kahle finds his conception of the evolution of ᵹ confirmed by the Greek fragments of the Minor Prophets discovered in 1952, whereas Barthélemy regards it as a welcome support for the view maintained by Katz and others, following de Lagarde and Rahlfs. This reckons in the individual books or in groups of books and parts of books of the Old Testament with only *one* Greek translation, its corruption and the suppression of these

[48] IEJ 11 (1961), p. 78; cf. above, p. 639.
[49] Cf. above, p. 707, n. 46.
[50] Katz, 'Justin's OT Quotations and the Greek Dodekapropheton Scroll' StP I (1957), pp. 343–53; Segert, 'Recké zlomky dvanácti proroku z Judské poušte' Listy filologické 5 (1957), pp. 31–4 with summary: 'De prophetarum minorum fragmentis graecis in Iudaico deserto repertis', pp. 34–5.

corrupted forms by a revision undertaken already before Origen (p. 708), largely consisting in the assimilation of it to the Hebrew text regarded by the Jews as normative.

It is difficult to make a clear decision between these two opposing views because the variant material available, which must be controlled if a decision is to be made, is so comprehensive and at the same time so diffuse and ambiguous that it defies any attempt at arranging it systematically. The position here is similar to that which we saw in the literary analysis of the books Josh. to Kings, where (§ 37) two theories, the documentary hypothesis and the fragment-hypothesis, each introducing weighty arguments, lay claim to being able to solve the problems which these books pose. The difficulties here are, however, much greater because not only is the mass of evidence brought forward on both sides much more comprehensive and difficult to take into full account, but it is also much less uniform, much more diffuse than in Josh. to Kings, and so resists even more strongly being forced into the pattern of a particular theory. Perhaps the same is true here as was true in the analysis of the books Josh. to Kings as to whether the victory should be accorded in the contest to the documentary hypothesis or the fragment-hypothesis. Some of the questions which here pose themselves may be answered better from the one side, others more clearly from the other. So in the contrast between the two theories which claim to offer the right solution to the problem of the Septuagint, the 'Targum' hypothesis and the 'Recension' hypothesis, perhaps the relation between them ought to be considered in reality not in terms of contrast but in terms of complement. It may in any case be readily acknowledged on all sides that as Kahle says (*The Cairo Geniza* ([2]1959), p. 264) the next and urgent task of Septuagint research is 'a careful collection and investigation of all the remains and traces of earlier versions of the Greek Bible which differed from the Christian standard text'. This may well be a point of agreement, since Gooding, who in general stands nearer to Katz than to Kahle expresses himself in the same sense on p. 5 of his work mentioned above on p. 703, n. 2. He affirms: 'Since this vast amount of textual evidence is the only material we have from which to reconstruct a history of the text, and since theories are only required to interpret the facts presented by the evidence, a thorough, painstaking examination of all the evidence is at the moment the prime necessity.'

A milestone in the development of the text of the Septuagint is marked by the work of Origen, born in 185, probably in Alexandria, and engaged as teacher there from 203/204 in the catechetical school, and from 232 at the theological school at Caesarea in Palestine. He attempted to produce an edition of it based on a scientific foundation,[51] which should provide the Christian Church with a reliable translation of the Hebrew Old Testament to facilitate its discussions with Judaism. Such an edition seemed to him all the more needful since at the time not only were various text-forms being used by Christians, but in the meantime new, more literal, Jewish translations of the original Hebrew into Greek had come into being, above all those of Aquila, Theodotion and Symmachus, which we shall discuss shortly (pp. 715–16). So Origen, as we learn from him-

---

[51] Daniélou, 'Origène comme exégète de la Bible' StP I (1957), pp. 280–90. Cf. Lit. § 126.

self,[52] from Eusebius[53] and from others,[54] produced in the years 240–245 two magnificent works, the Tetrapla (τὰ τετραπλᾶ)[55] and the Hexapla (τὰ ἑξαπλᾶ), namely, the 'fourfold' and the 'sixfold' works. The former set out side by side with 𝔊 the translations of Aquila, Symmachus and Theodotion; the latter, and more significant work, added to this the original text in Hebrew letters (Column 1) and in transcription in Greek letters (Column 2, 'Secunda'), and here and there Origen also took account of other Greek translations as well, probably of Jewish origin[56] like those of Aquila, Symmachus and Theodotion, namely the Quinta,[57] the Sexta and the Septima.[58] The central interest of Origen lay in the fifth column of the Hexapla, 𝔊, whose relationship to the Hebrew text which he regarded as normative was to be demonstrated. For this purpose he made use of the critical signs which were then normal, devised about the middle of the second century B.C. by the Alexandrian philologian Aristarchus and named after him: the obelos, the asterisk and the metobelos. Where 𝔊 contained matter in excess of the Hebrew, this was marked by an obelos (÷) placed first; where there was an omission, normally filled in from Theodotion, by an asterisk (*) placed first, and then the end of the plus or the minus was shown by a metobelos (✓), often omitted in the manuscripts.[59] By these and similar measures the position was reached that the fifth column contained implicitly a recension of 𝔊 conformed to the Hebrew text. It remains an open question whether the fifth column of the Hexapla was itself intended to be a critical edition made with the use of the 'hexaplaric' symbols, or whether Origen simply used it as a preliminary for an independent edition of 𝔊 and supplied this with variants and critical marks.

Until recently it appeared self-evident that the fifth column of the Hexapla was itself such a critical edition of 𝔊. But in 1958, the palimpsest—of which more must be said directly—containing the 'Mercati fragments' was published in photographic reproduction. Here the column containing 𝔊 is the fourth and not the fifth, since what elsewhere appears as the first column, namely the text in Hebrew letters, is missing. It now appears that 𝔊 has no critical marks, and perhaps therefore opinions have now to be revised and we must assume that in addition to this 𝔊 column of the Hexapla without critical marks there was also

[52] Commentary on Matthew to xix, 14 [ed. Klostermann I (1937), pp. 387 f.]; *Epist. ad Africanum* 5 (Migne PGr XI, cols. 59–62). Cf. Mercati, 'D'alcuni frammenti esaplari sulla Vᵃ e VIᵃ edizione greca della Bibbia' *Note di Letteratura Biblica e Cristiana Antica*=Studi e Testi 5 (1901), pp. 28–46.

[53] *Hist. eccl.* VI, 16 (ed. Schwartz, pp. 552–5). Cf. Mercati, 'Sul testo e sul senso di Eusebio H.e. VI 16' Studi e Testi 5 (1901), pp. 47–60; Schwartz, 'Zur Geschichte der Hexapla' NGG (1903 [1904]), pp. 693–700.

[54] Epiphanius, *De mensuris et ponderibus* 7 and 19 (Migne PGr XLIII, cols. 247–8, 267–70); Jerome, Commentary on Titus iii, 9 (Migne PL XVI, cols. 629–32).

[55] Orlinsky, 'Origen's Tetrapla a Scholarly Fiction?' *World Congress of Jewish Studies* [Summer 1947] (1952), pp. 173–82.

[56] Kahle, 'The Greek Bible Manuscripts used by Origen' JBL 79 (1960), pp. 111–18.

[57] Barthélemy, 'Quinta ou Version selon les Hébreux?' ThZ 10 (1960), pp. 342–53.

[58] Orlinsky, 'The Columnar Order of the Hexapla' JQR 27 (1936/37), pp. 117–29.

[59] Soisalon-Soininen, *Der Charakter der asterisierten Zusätze in der Septuaginta* (Ann. Ac. Sc. Fennicae. B 114, 1959); on this cf. Gooding, Gnomon 30 (1961), pp. 143–8, and Kahle, ThLZ 84 (1959), cols. 743–5; Ziegler, *Isaias* (1939), pp. 53–60: 'Die kritischen Zeichen des Origenes'. Lit. § 126.

a critical edition of ⑥ made by Origen on the basis of this work, and that only the latter was provided with obelos, asterisk and metobelos. At any rate, Paul Kahle, in his review of the work by Soisalon-Soisinen[60] mentioned on p. 710, n. 59, seriously entertains 'the possibility that the Hexapla may have been only the basis for Origen's text-critical work and that the collection of important Jewish biblical texts which it contained really simply provided him with the material for his undertaking'. He considers it to be certain 'that neither in the Hexapla nor in the Tetrapla were diacritical marks to be found in the Septuagint column'. At the same time he draws attention to the fact that the divine name is given in all five columns of the palmpsest in the form of the tetragrammaton (יהוה) written in Hebrew square characters. From this he draws the virtually inevitable conclusion that the Greek Bible texts drawn together in the Hexapla— including ⑥—must all be translations of Jewish origin. Segert,[61] in his review of Mercati's work mentioned below (p. 712, n. 65), has expressed views similar to those of Kahle, while Franz Altheim and Ruth Stiehl in 'Prophyrios und Origenes' Hexapla',[62] though admitting that independent texts of the LXX with diacritical marks were in circulation, set up substantial arguments against the view that the LXX column of the Hexapla did not contain such marks.

Large sections of this fifth column of the Hexapla, or, if we should actually assume its existence, of the critical edition of ⑥ prepared by Origen on the basis of the Hexapla, have survived indirectly in the Syriac translation made in 616–617 by Paul of Tella. Of this, at least the Writings and the Prophets have come down to us in the valuable Codex syrohexaplaris Ambrosianus C.313 Inf. already mentioned above on p. 701. In addition various remains of the fifth column of the Hexapla, or of the critical edition of ⑥ by Origen based upon it, have survived in Greek manuscripts of the Old Testament (among which the minuscule 88 is in this respect of particular importance), as well as in the commentaries on biblical books by the early Fathers and in other places. What was known up to the time was collected by Field in *Origenis Hexaplorum quae supersunt* (1875–76). Since that date a good deal more has been added. The most important recent find was that made by Mercati in 1895 of remains of a copy of the Hexapla covering 110 verses of the Psalms containing the second, third, fourth, fifth and sixth columns, in a palmpsest in the Bibliotheca Ambrosiana in Milan.[63] The preliminary reports of the discovery then issued gave new impetus to Hexapla research and directed attention particularly to the significance of the transcription of the Hebrew text in the second column.[64] The

[60] ThLZ 84 (1959), cols. 743–5.   [61] ArOr 29 (1961), pp. 85–7.

[62] Altheim, *Geschichte der Hunnen* V (1962), pp. 100–9.

[63] Ceriani, 'Frammenti esaplari palinsesti dei salmi nel testo originale scoperti dal dott. ab. G. Mercati' R. Ist. Lombardo di Scienze e Lett., Rendinc. II, 29 (1896), pp. 406–8; Klostermann, 'Die Mailänder Fragmente der Hexapla' ZAW 16 (1896), pp. 334–7; Mercati, 'D'un palimpsesto Ambrosiano contenente i salmi esapli' Atti Acad. Scienze Torino 31 (1895), pp. 655–76.

[64] Franz Altheim and Ruth Stiehl (§ 90); Brønno, 'Studien über hebräische Morphologie und Vokalismus auf Grundlage der Mercatischen Fragmente der zweiten Kolumne der Hexapla' (1943); Chabot, 'À propos des Hexaples' JA IX, 17 (1901), pp. 349 f.; Eissfeldt, 'Zur textkritischen Auswertung der Mercatischen Hexapla-Fragmente' WdO 1 (1947/52), pp. 93–7; Emerton, 'The Purpose of the Second Column of the Hexapla' JThSt 7 (1956), pp. 79–87; Halévy, 'L'origine de la transcription du texte Hébreu en caractères grecs dans

publication of the whole of the fragment[65] begun in 1958 will certainly give a new stimulus to research.

Origen's work did not, however, bring about any uniformity in the text of 𝔊, but merely increased the multiplicity of text-forms, for the often copied fifth column or separate edition now appeared beside the other text-forms but was unable to replace them. So after a short period new ecclesiastical revisions of the text became necessary. Eusebius of Caesarea († 339) and Pamphilus († 309) were responsible for gaining recognition in Palestine for the text of Origen's fifth column or edition as standard text. In Syria and Asia Minor the text-form prepared by the presbyter Lucian[66] in Antioch († 311) enjoyed great respect, and in Egypt, according to Jerome's *In Evangelistas ad Damasum praefatio*,[67] the recension of a certain Hesychius was widely used. Careful analysis of the textual evidence leads to the recognition of further recensions. Thus Rahlfs in his works on the book of Ruth mentioned on p. 704 showed the existence of a recension of unknown origin which he designated with the siglum *R* (=Recension), as well as a further recension dependent upon this and attested in the Catenae, i.e. the chain-like commentaries representing compilations of exegetical comments by various Church Fathers, and hence designated as *C*. He was also able to demonstrate these two in Judges and Kings.

With our mention of these recensions which came into existence in about A.D. 300, we are already approaching the period from which complete or nearly complete manuscripts of 𝔊 have come down to us. The oldest codices, containing the whole Old and New Testaments apart from small gaps, are Vaticanus (B)[68] and Sinaiticus (S or א)[69] belonging to the fourth century, and the Codex

les Hexaples d'Origine' JA IX, 17 (1901), pp. 335–41; Haupert, 'The Transcription Theory of the Septuagint' JBL 53 (1934), pp. 251–5; Heller, *Untersuchung zur Septuaginta* I: *Die Tychsen-Wutzsche Transkriptionstheorie* (1932); Janssens, 'Het Hebreeuws van de tweede kolom van Origenes' Hexapla' JEOL 15 (1957/58), pp. 103–11; Mercati, 'Il problema della colonna II dell' Esaplo' Bibl 28 (1947), pp. 1–30, 173–215; Pretzl, 'Die Aussprache des Hebräischen nach der zweiten Kolumne der Hexapla des Origenes' BZ 20 (1932), pp. 4–22; Speiser, 'The Pronunciation of Hebrew according to (based chiefly on) the Transliterations in the Hexapla' JQR 16 (1925/26), pp. 343–82; 23 (1932/33), pp. 233–65; 24 (1933/34), pp. 9–46; Staples, 'The Second Column of Origen's Hexapla' JAOS 59 (1939), pp. 71–80; Vogt, 'Accentus hebraicus secundum Hexapla' Bibl 41 (1960), pp. 79–81; Wutz, *Die Psalmen textkritisch untersucht* (1925); *Die Transkriptionen von der Septuaginta bis zu Hieronymus* (BWANT 34, 1933); *Systematische Wege von der Septuaginta zum hebräischen Text* (1937); on this cf. Kahle, ZDMG 92 (1938), pp. 276–86. Cf. Lit. §§ 90, 126.

[65] *Psalterii Hexapli Reliquiae. Cura et Studio Iohannis Card. Mercati. Pars Prima. Codex Rescriptus Bybliothecae Ambrosianae O 39 SVP. Phototypice Expressus et Transcriptus* (1958).

[66] Förster, 'Gerechtigkeit für Lucian und den antiochenischen Text' MPTh 45 (1956), pp. 267–72; Hautsch, 'Der Lukiantext des Oktateuch' NGG (1909), pp. 518–43; de Lagarde, *Librorum V.T. canonicorum pars prior* (1883); Mercati, 'Di alcune testimonianze antiche sulle cure bibliche di San Luciano' Bibl 24 (1943), pp. 1–17; Moore, 'The Antiochian Recension of the LXX' AJSL 29 (1912/13), pp. 37–62; Rahlfs, *Lucians Rezension der Königsbücher* (1911); Sperber, 'The Problems of the Septuagint Recensions' JBL 54 (1935), pp. 73–92; Ziegler, 'Hat Lukian den griechischen Sirach rezensiert?' Bibl 40 (1959), pp. 210–29 =StBiOr I (1959), pp. 76–95. Lit. § 126.

[67] Migne, PL XXIX, cols. 557–62, see col. 559.

[68] *Codices e Vaticanis selecti phototypice expressi* IV (*Bibliorum SS. Graecorum Codex Vaticanus gr. 1209*) (1904–7); Rahlfs, 'Alter und Heimat der vaticanischen Bibelhandschrift' NGGW (1909), pp. 72–9; Sperber, 'The Codex Vaticanus B' *Miscell. Mercati* I (1946), pp. 1–18.

Alexandrinus (A)[70] and Codex Ephraemi Syri rescriptus (C),[71] likewise containing the whole Bible, belonging to the fifth century. The most comprehensive collection of variants in the Old Testament text of 𝔊, namely of variants from 311 manuscripts, is still, however, the five volume work of Holmes and Parsons which appeared in Oxford in 1798–1827: *Vetus Testamentum Graecum cum Variis Lectionibus*. Yet Rahlfs, *Verzeichnis der griechischen Handschriften des Alten Testaments* (1914) could count approximately 2,000, and in the meantime more still have been added.

But this by no means exhausts the material which is available for the reconstruction of the text of 𝔊. For the quotations in the Church Fathers offer many more variants, and others may be gathered from the many daughter translations of 𝔊, of which the most important, apart from the Vetus Latina,[72] are the Coptic,[73] Ethiopic[74] and Arabic.[75]

[69] H. and K. Lake, *Codex Sinaiticus . . . reproduced in Facsimile from Photographs*, New Testament (1911), Old Testament (1922); Lauch, 'Etwas vom Codex Sinaiticus' WZ Leipzig 3 (1953/54), pp. 23–9, 125–6; 'Hundert Jahre Codex Sinaiticus' Zeichen der Zeit 13 (1959), pp. 141 f.; Milne and Skeat, *Scribes and Correctors of the Codex Sinaiticus* (1938); *The Codex Sinaiticus and the Codex Alexandrinus* (1938, ²1955); Tindall, *Contributions to the Statistical Study of the Codex Sinaiticus* (1961). Cf. Lit. § 126.

[70] *The Codex Alexandrinus (Royal MS ID V–VIII) in reduced Photographic Facsimile*, Parts I–III (1909–36); Skeat, 'The Provenance of the Codex Alexandrinus' JThSt 6 (1955), pp. 233–5. Cf. Lit. § 126.

[71] Tischendorf, *Codex Ephraimi Syri rescriptus, Fragmenta Novi Testamenti* (1843); *Fragmenta Veteris Testamenti* (1845): facsimile edition. Cf. Lit. § 126.

[72] Cf. pp. 716–18.

[73] Baumstark, *Die christlichen Literaturen des Orients* I (1911), pp. 106–29; Kammerer, *A Coptic Bibliography* (1950); on this cf. Vergote, BiOr 13 (1956), pp. 134 f.; Leipoldt, 'Geschichte der koptischen Literatur' *Gesch. d. christl. Litt. des Orients* (1907 (²1909)), pp. 131–83; Morenz, 'Die koptische Literatur' HdO I, 2 (1952), pp. 207–19; 'Das Koptische' HdO I 1, 1 (1959), pp. 90–104; Simon, 'Bibliographie copte 1–14' in Or 18 (1949)—31 (1962). Auster, Böhlig, Ibscher, Kiessig, 'Zur Umkonservierung des Papyruskodex Ms. Or. Oct. 987' Zentralblatt für Bibliothekswesen 73 (1959), pp. 356–74; Böhlig, *Untersuchungen über die koptischen Proverbientexte* (1936); *Der achmimische Proverbientext nach Ms. Berol. Orient. Oct. 987. I: Text und Rekonstruktion der sahidischen Vorlage* (1958); 'Zur Berliner achmimischen Proverbienhandschrift' ZÄS 83 (1958), pp. 1–3; Léon Dieu, 'Le texte coptesahidique des Livres de Samuel' Muséon 59 (1946), pp. 445–52; Donadoni, 'Una Pergamena Saidica dei ΘΡΗΝΟΙ di Geremia' ArOr 20 (1952), pp. 400–6; 'Un Frammento della Versione Copta del "Libro di Enoch"' AcOr[H] 25 (1960), pp. 197–202; Grossouw, 'De koptische Bijbelvertalingen' StC 9 (1932/33), pp. 325–53; 'De Apocriefen van het O. en N. Testament in de Koptische Letterkunde' StC 10 (1933/34), pp. 434–46; 11 (1934/35), pp. 19–36; 'Un fragment sahidique d'Osée ii, 9–v, 1' Muséon 47 (1934), pp. 185–204, 1 Pl.; *The Coptic Versions of the Minor Prophets. A contribution to the study of the Septuagint* (1938); Hallock, 'The Coptic OT' AJSL 49 (1932/33), pp. 325–35; Ibscher, 'Das neue Chiffonbezugverfahren für Papyrusrestaurierung als Ergänzung der traditionellen Methode' Bull. de la Soc. d. Archéol. Copte 15 (1960), pp. 93–100, Pls. I–II; Kahle, *Bala'izah: Coptic Texts from Deir el-Bala'izah in Upper Egypt* (1954), I, pp. 293–402, Nos. 1–25; Kasser, *Papyrus Bodmer XVI, Exode i–xv, 21–Copte sahidique* (1961); Lefort, 'Coptica Lovaniensia' Muséon 50 (1937), pp. 5–52; 51 (1938), pp. 1–32; 'Fragments d'apocryphes en copte-akhmîmique' Muséon 42 (1939), pp. 1–10; 'Fragments bibliques en dialecte akhmîmique' Muséon 66 (1953), pp. 1–30; Payne, 'The Sahidic Coptic Text of I Samuel' JBL 72 (1953), pp. 51–62; Petersen, 'The Biblical Scholar's Concern with Coptic Studies' CBQ 23 (1961), pp. 241–9; Rahlfs, *Die Berliner Handschrift des Sahidischen Psalters* (1901); Schleifer, *Sahidische Bibel-Fragmente aus dem Brit. Museum zu London* I–III (SAW 162, 6; 164, 6; 173, 5, 1909–1914); Tattam, *Prophetae majores, in dialecto linguae aegyptiacae memphitica seu coptica*, I (1852); Till, 'Saidische Fragmente des AT' Muséon 50 (1937), pp. 175–237; 'Kleine koptische Bibelfragmente' Bibl 20 (1939), pp. 241–63; 'Papyrussammlung der

Among more modern editions of 𝔊 we must mention the three-volume edition by Swete (1887–94; I ([4]1909), II–III ([3]1905, 1907)); the four-volume edition by Brooke, McLean, Thackeray and Manson (from 1906); the edition, to appear in sixteen volumes, by the Göttinger Akademie der Wissenschaften (from 1931), and the handy edition by Rahlfs which first appeared in 1935 ([6]1959). The first and fourth of these are complete. The second reaches as far as Tobit, and of the third, the following volumes are complete: X, *Psalmi cum Odis* (Rahlfs, 1931); IX, 1, *Maccabaeorum liber I* (Kappler, 1936); XIV, *Isaias* (Zieg,er, 1939);[76] XIII, *Duodecim Prophetae* (Ziegler, 1943); XVI, 1, *Ezechiel* (Zieg,er, 1952); XVI, 2, *Susanna. Daniel. Bel et Draco* (Ziegler, 1954); and XV, *Ierem ias, Baruch, Threni, Epistula Ieremiae* (Ziegler, 1957); IX, 2, *Macc. liber II* (Hanhart, 1959); IX, 3, *Macc. liber III* (Hanhart, 1960); and XII, 1, *Sap. Sal.* (Ziegler, 1962). The first of these editions and the second [I, 1–4: *Genesis to Judges and Ruth* (1906–17); II, 1–4: *I Sam. to III Esdras, Ezra, Neh.* (1927–35); III, 1: *Esther, Judith, Tobit* (1940)] are prepared according to the same principle in that they print one codex, namely B or, if it has gaps, another codex, normally A, and in the apparatus indicate the variants of other manuscripts and other witnesses to the text—a few only in Swete, and a very large number in Brooke, McLean, Thackeray and Manson. The Göttingen edition, however, endeavours by considering the whole of the available material, to get to the oldest form of the text that can be reached and provides this, while setting out in the apparatus the readings of the individual textual groups or of individual manuscripts in so far as they can stand as representatives of the

Nationalbibliothek in Wien. Katalog der koptischen Bibelbruchstücke. Die Pergamente' ZNW 39 (1940), pp. 1–57; 'Coptic Biblical Texts Published after Vaschalde's List' BJRL 42 (1959/60), pp. 220–40; Vaschalde, 'Ce qui a été publié des versions coptes de la Bible' RB 28 (1919), pp. 220–43, 513–31; 29 (1920), pp. 91–106, 241–58; 30 (1921), pp. 237–46; 31 (1922), pp. 81–8, 234–58; Muséon 43 (1930), pp. 409–31; 45 (1932), pp. 117–56; 46 (1933), pp. 299–313; Worrell, *The Coptic Manuscripts in the Freer Collection* (1923); *The Proverbs of Solomon in Sahidic Coptic According to the Chicago Manuscript* (OIP 11, 1931); Ziegler, 'Beiträge zur koptischen Dodekapropheton-Übersetzung' Bibl 25 (1944), pp. 105–142. Cf. Lit. § 126.

[74] Cerulli, *Storia della letteratura Etiopica* (1956); Guidi, *Storia della letteratura etiopica* (1932); Harden, *An Introduction to Ethiopic Christian Literature* (1926); Littmann, 'Geschichte der äthiopischen Litteratur' *Gesch. d. christl. Litt. des Orients* (1907, [2]1909), pp. 187–270.

Bachmann, *Dodekapropheton Aethiopum oder die Zwölf Kleinen Propheten der äthiopischen Bibelübersetzung* (1892); *Inedita Aethiopica* (1893); *Die Klagelieder Jeremiae in der äthiopischen Bibelübersetzung* (1893); Boyd, *The Text of the Ethiopic Version of the Octateuch* (1905); *The Octateuch in Ethiopic*, I: *Genesis* (1909); II: *Exodus and Leviticus* (1911); Dillmann, *Octateuchus Aethiopicus* (1853/55); *VT Aethiopici Libri Apocryphi* (1894); Gleave, *The Ethiopic Version of the Song of Songs* (1951); Heider, *Die äthiopische Bibelübersetzung. Ihre Herkunft, Art, Geschichte und ihr Wert für die at. und nt. Wissenschaft*, fasc. 1 (1902); Löfgren, *Die äthiopische Übersetzung des Propheten Daniel* (1927); *Jona, Nahum, Habakuk, Zephanja, Haggai, Sacharja und Maleachi äthiopisch* (1930); Mercer, *The Ethiopic Text of the Book of Ecclesiastes* (1931); Schäfers, *Die äthiopische Übersetzung des Propheten Jeremia* (1912).

[75] Edelmann, 'Features in Arabic Translation of the Pentateuch' [Hebr.] Melilah 5 (1955), pp. 45–50; Graf, *Geschichte der christlichen arabischen Literatur* I (1944 (1953)), pp. 85–297; Margulies, Baron, Lauterbach, Schreier (ed.), *Saadia b. Yusuf al-Faiyumi, Arabische Psalmenübersetzung und Commentar* (1884–1904); Spiegel (ed.), *Arabische Danielversion* (1906). Cf. above, p. 695, n. 4, and Lit. § 126.

[76] Jobannessohn, 'Die Göttinger Septuaginta' ThLZ 65 (1940), cols. 289–96.

groups. The small edition by Rahlfs is based upon a similar principle, but it limits itself in general to the assessment of the three most important manuscripts, Vaticanus (B), Sinaiticus (S) and Alexandrinus (A).

§ 122. THE TRANSLATIONS OF AQUILA, THEODOTION AND SYMMACHUS

Literature: Abrahams, *Aquila's Greek Version of the Hebrew Bible* (1919); Burkitt, *Fragments of the Books of Kings according to the Translation of Aquila* (1897); *Early Eastern Christianity* (1904); Cannon, 'Jerome and Symmachus. Some Points in the Vulgate Translation of Koheleth' ZAW 45 (1927), pp. 191–9; Field, *Origenis Hexaplorum quae supersunt sive Veterum Interpretum Graecorum in totum VT Fragmenta,* I (1875); II (1876); Mercati, *Psalterii Hexapli Reliquiae.* Pars Prima (1958); Katz, 'A Fresh Aquila Fragment, recovered from Philo' JThSt 47 (1946), pp. 30–3; *Philo's Bible* (cf. above, p. 705, n. 28); Katz and Ziegler, 'Ein Aquila-Index in Vorbereitung' VT 8 (1958), pp. 264–85; Krauss, 'Two Hitherto Unknown Bible Versions in Greek' BJRL 27 (1942/43), pp. 97–105; Liebreich, 'Notes on the Greek Version of Symmachus' JBL 63 (1944), pp. 397–403; Möhle, 'Ein neuer Fund zahlreicher Stücke aus den Jesajaübersetzungen des Akylas, Symmachos und Theodotion' ZAW 52 (1934), pp. 176–83; Rahlfs, 'Über Theodotion-Lesarten im NT und Aquila-Lesarten bei Justin' ZNW 20 (1921), pp. 182–99; Reider, *Prolegomena to a Greek-Hebrew and Hebrew-Greek Index to Aquila* (1916); Rüger, 'Vier Aquila-Glossen in einem hebräischen Proverbien-Fragment aus der Kairo-Geniza' ZNW 50 (1959), pp. 275–7; Schoeps, 'Aus frühchristlicher Zeit' in *Religionsgeschichtliche Untersuchungen* (1950), pp. 82–119; Silverstone, *Aquila and Onkelos* (1931); Swete (p. 570, n. 19), pp. 29–58; Taylor, *Hebrew-Greek Cairo Genizah Palimpsests* (1900); Norman Walker, 'The Writing of the Divine Name in Aquila and the Ben Asher Text' VT 3 (1953), pp. 103 f.; on this cf. Katz, VT 4 (1954), pp. 428 f.; Ziegler, 'Textkritische Notizen zu den jüngeren griechischen Übersetzungen des Buches Isaias' NGG (1939), pp. 75–102; *Die jüngeren griechischen Übersetzungen als Vorlagen der Vulgata in den prophetischen Schriften* (Programm Braunsberg, 1943/44); on this cf. Johannessohn, ThLZ 73 (1948), cols. 145–52.

Cf. also Literature §§ 117–21, 123–4.

Since 𝔊, because of its use among Christians and because of its marked deviations from 𝔐, came more and more into disfavour among the Jews in the course of the first century, the need was felt among them for a new translation, adhering as closely as possible to the Hebrew text (a text which was by no means at every point identical with 𝔐). The translation of Aquila—certainly, like those of Theodotion and Symmachus, making use of older such attempts (p. 708)—which came into being in about A.D. 130 was designed to meet this need; it can in fact hardly be excelled for its painful exactness and in its endeavour to reproduce every peculiarity of the original. The tradition that Aquila was a pupil of Akiba has in it at least this much of truth that he worked entirely in the spirit in which Akiba worked, valuing even the smallest detail of the text. Two examples may suffice to illustrate this mode of translating: he renders לֵאמֹר, literally *to say* but used as the introduction to direct speech and therefore translated in 𝔊 with λέγων or ὅτι, by τῷ λέγειν, and the accusative particle אֵת, which in form looks identical to the preposition אֵת *with*, by σύν, though this is not then followed by a dative. It is no wonder that this translation enjoyed great popularity among the Jews. We possess only fragments of it, of which the most important are those which were found over sixty years ago in the Geniza of the Ezra Synagogue in Cairo and published soon after by Burkitt.

Somewhat later, but still within the second century, Theodotion's translation came into existence. In contrast to that of Aquila, this laid stress upon an intelligible Greek, but otherwise is less a fresh translation than a revision of 𝕲 undertaken with as great a dependence as possible upon 𝔐. This rendering found much approval among Christians, and in some places replaced the older 𝕲, so possibly in Ezra-Neh. (pp. 575, 589) and certainly in Dan., where, as has already been indicated above (p. 706), we actually have a 'Proto-Theodotion'.

Beyond this, we have fragments or reports of a whole series of other Jewish translations of 𝔐 into Greek, for example, as we have already seen in the treatment of Origen's Hexapla, the Quinta, Sexta and Septima (p. 710). But special mention need only be made of that of Symmachus, from the beginning of the third century, this attempts to unite literal reproduction of the original text with good Greek, and was used for preference not only by Lucian (p. 712), but also by Jerome in his Vulgate (§ 124).

§ 123. THE OLD LATIN (VETUS LATINA)

Literature: (a) Text: Sabatier, *Bibliorum Sacrorum latinae versiones antiquae* (1739–49, ²1751); *Vetus Latina, Die Reste der altlateinischen Bibel nach Petrus Sabatier neu gesammelt und hrsg. von der Erzabtei Beuron*, I. *Verzeichnisse der Sigel* (1949); II. *Gen* (1954); XXVI. *Epist. Cath., Apok.*, Fasc. 1 (1956); 2 (1958); 3 (1960); *Texte und Arbeiten, hrsg. von der Erzabtei Beuron.* 1. Abt.: *Beiträge zur Ergründung des älteren lateinischen christlichen Schrifttums und Gottesdienstes,* 1/2–49/50 (1917–1958); *Beihefte der Texte und Arbeiten* 1–3 (1941–1957); *Vetus Latina. Gemeinnützige Stiftung.* 1.–11. *Arbeitsbericht* (1951/52–1962); *Aus der Geschichte der lateinischen Bibel.* Fasc. 1 (1957); 2 (1958); 3 (1961).

(b) Other Works: Allgeier, *Die altlateinischen Psalterien* (1928); 'Lehrreiche Fehler in den altlateinischen Psalterien' BZ 18 (1929), pp. 271–93; Ayuso Marazuela, 'Una importante colección de notas marginales de la "Vetus Latina Hispana" ' Est Bíbl 9 (1950), pp. 329–76; 'Origen español del Códice Lugdunense de la Vetus Latina' Est Bíbl 12 (1953), pp. 377–95; *La Vetus Latina Hispana*, I (1953); 'Origen del códice Ottoboniano del Eptateuco' *Misc. Bibl. Ubach* (1954), pp. 115–29; 'El salterio latino en la actualidad' Sefarad 15 (1955), pp. 395–409; 'El Salterio de Gregorio de Elvira y la Vetus Latina hispana' Bibl 40 (1959), pp. 135–59; Belsheim, *Palimpsestus Vindobonensis. Antiquissimi V.T. translationis latinae fragmenta* (1885); Billen, *The Old Latin Texts of the Heptateuch* (1927); 'The Old Latin Version of Judges' JThSt 43 (1942), pp. 140–9; Bischoff, 'Neue Materialien zum Bestand und zur Geschichte der altlateinischen Bibelübersetzungen' *Miscell. Mercati*, I (1946), pp. 407–36; on this cf. Baars, VT 8 (1958), p. 425; Burkitt, *The Old Latin and the Itala* (1896); 'Saint Augustine's Bible and the Itala' JThSt 11 (1910), pp. 258–68; 'Itala Problems' *Miscell. Amelli* (1920), pp. 25–41; Cantera Ortiz de Urbina, 'En torno a la "Vetus Latina Hispana" ' Sefarad 15 (1955), pp. 171–9; Denk, *Der neue Sabatier und sein wissenschaftliches Programm* (1914); von Dobschütz, 'A Collection of Old Latin Bible Quotations: Somnium Neronis' JThSt 16 (1915), pp. 1–27; Dold, *Konstanzer altlateinische Propheten- und Evangelienbruchstücke mit Glossen* (TuA Beuron 7–9, 1923); *Neue St. Galler vorhieronymianische Propheten-Fragmente* (TuA Beuron 31, 1940); 'Was ein Vers der Vetus Latina uns nicht alles lehren kann' Münchener ThZ 5 (1954), pp. 273–5: on Isa. liii, 7; 'Versuchte Neu- und Erstergänzungen zu den altlateinischen Texten in Cod. CLM 6225 der Bayr.

Staatsbibliothek' Bibl 37 (1956), pp. 39–58; B. Fischer, 'Lukian-Lesarten in der Vetus Latina der vier Königsbücher' Stud. Anselm. 27/28 (1951), pp. 169–77; Gamber, *Sakramentartypen* (TuA Beuron 49/50, 1958); Knauer, *Psalmenzitate in Augustins Konfessionen* (1955); König, 'Die Bedeutung der Vetus Latina' Saeculum 4 (1953), pp. 267–73; Kusch, 'Die Beuroner Vetus Latina und ihre Bedeutung für die Altertumswissenschaft' FuF 29 (1955), pp. 46–57; Lagrange, 'De quelques opinions sur l'ancien psautier latin' RB 41 (1932), pp. 161–86; S. Muñoz Iglesias, 'La "Vetus Latina Hispana"' Est Bíbl 14 (1955), pp. 67–71; Ranke, *Par palimpsestorum Wirceburgensium. Antiquissimae VT Testamenti Versionis latinae fragmenta* (1871); Robert, *Pentateuchi versio latina antiquissima e codice Lugdunensi* (1881); *Heptateuchi partis posterioris versio latina antiquissima e codice Lugdunensi* (1900); Rönsch, *Itala und Vulgata* (²1875); Schäfer, *Die altlateinische Bibel* (Bonner Akad. Reden 17, 1957); Schildenberger, 'Arbeit an der Lateinischen Bibel' Benediktinische Monatsschrift 17 (1935), pp. 401–8; 'Bericht über die spanische Forschungsreise der Herren P. Alban Dold und P. Johannes Schildenberger' Span. Forsch. der Görresgesellschaft I, 5 (1935), pp. 97–107; *Die altlateinischen Texte des Proverbien-Buches*, Part I: *Die alte afrikanische Textgestalt* (TuA Beuron 32/33, 1941); 'Die Itala des hl. Augustinus' Dold-Festschr. (1952), pp. 84–102; Schneider, 'Der altlateinische Palimpsest-Psalter in Cod. Vat. lat. 5359' Bibl 19 (1938), pp. 361–82; *Die altlateinischen biblischen Cantica* (TuA Beuron 29/30, 1938); Stenzel, 'Zur Frühgeschichte der lateinischen Bibel' ThRev 49 (1953), cols. 97–103; 'Die Konstanzer und St. Galler Fragmente zum altlateinischen Dodekapropheton' Sacris Erudiri 5 (1953), pp. 27–85; 'Altlateinische Canticatexte im Dodekapropheton' ZNW 46 (1955), pp. 31–60; 'Das Zwölfprophetenbuch im Würzburger Palimpsestcodex (cod. membr. No. 64) und seine Textgestalt in Väterzitaten' Sacris Erudiri 7 (1955), pp. 5–34; Ulecia, 'Un intéressant lectionnaire latin gothique inconnu' BEThL XII (1959), pp. 208–15; Vercellone, *Variae Lectiones Vulgatae latinae Bibliorum editionis*, I–II (1860–1864); Weber, *Les anciennes versions latines du deuxième livre des Paralipomènes* (1945); *Le Psautier Romain et les autres anciens Psautiers Latins* (1953); Ziegler, *Antike und moderne lateinische Psalmenübersetzungen* (SAM 1960, Fasc. 3); 'Altlateinische Psalterien' BZ 5 (1961), pp. 94–115.

Cf. also Literature §§ 117–22, 124–6.

Among the daughter translations of the Septuagint, the most important is the Old Latin, the Vetus Latina, above all because it presupposes a form of the Septuagint antecedent to the recensions undertaken in the third and fourth centuries (p. 712) and so may contribute to the reconstruction of this stage of the development of 𝔊. It is attested from the second and third centuries onwards in North Africa, Southern Gaul and Italy as being used by the Latin-speaking Christian communities which lived in these parts of the Roman empire. But possibly it is based upon an older Latin translation deriving from Jews in these areas, covering either the whole Old Testament or at least some of its books. It is now designated by the comprehensive name Vetus Latina and must be so designated since it has not yet proved possible in regard to the Old Testament to make out whether the many textual variants which occur, go back to different translations—one in North Africa (Afra) and one in Italy (Itala) roughly as in the New Testament—or whether they are to be explained as due to recensions of one translation undertaken more or less deliberately. From the beginning of the fifth century, apart from the books of I and II Macc., Baruch, the Letter of Jeremiah, Ecclesiasticus, and the Wisdom of Solomon (pp. 579, 599, 602 f.), which were not revised by Jerome because he did not regard them as canonical, and therefore were taken up into the Vulgate with their Old Latin text, the Vulgate more and more took the place of the Vetus Latina (§ 124). So only parts of it remain, on the one hand in the Bible quotations of older Latin

Church Fathers such as Cyprian († 258), and on the other hand in manuscripts some of which preserve the text in its pure form while others have it mixed with that of the Vulgate. The Latin translation of the Psalms, which is known as the 'Psalterium Romanum' because of its use in the Roman liturgy, is to be regarded as a witness to the Vetus Latina, though it was formerly assumed that Jerome in A.D. 382 began with this his revision of the Vetus Latina. The critical examination and arrangement of all the surviving parts of the Vetus Latina—coming right down into mediaeval records and early German, Flemish, English and other Bible translations—has been undertaken in the new 'Sabatier'.

§ 124. THE VULGATE

Literature: (a) Text: *Biblia Sacra secundum Vulgatam Clementinam* (1922); *Biblia Sacra iuxta latinam vulgatam versionem ad codicum fidem, cura et studio Monachorum Abbatiae Pont. S. Hieronymi in Urbe O.S.B. edita,* I–XI (1926–1957); *Biblia Sacra Vulgatae Editionis Sixti V Pont. Max. iussu recognita et Clementis VIII auctoritate edita. Editio emendatissima apparatu critico instructa cura et studio Monachorum Abbatiae Pont. S. Hieronymi in Urbe O.S.B.* (1959); Colunga y Turrado, *Biblia Vulgata Latina* (1953); Gramatica, *Bibliorum Sacrorum iuxta Vulgatam Clementinam Nova editio* (1951); Hetzenauer, *Biblia Sacra Vulgatae editionis* (1906); Nolli, *Biblia Sacra Vulgatae editionis iuxta Papae Clementis VIII Decretum. Latine* (1955); *Collectanea Biblica Latina cura et studio monachorum S. Benedicti,* I–XIII (1912–1959).

(b) Other Works: Allgeier, 'Der Brief an Sunnia und Fretela und seine Bedeutung für die Textherstellung der Vulgata' Bibl 11 (1930), pp. 86–107; 'Die mittelalterliche Überlieferung des Psalterium iuxta Hebraeos von Hieronymus und semitische Kenntnisse im Abendland' OrChr 3/4 (1930), pp. 200–31; *Die Psalmen der Vulgata* (1940); 'Lateinische Psalmen-übersetzung in alter und neuer Zeit' Freiburger Universitätsreden 2 (1948), pp. 7–21; Amann, *Die Vulgata Sixtina von 1590* (1912); Bardy, 'Saint Jérôme et ses maîtres hébreux' Revue Bénédictine 46 (1934), pp. 145–64; Berger, *Histoire de la Vulgate* (1893); de Bruyne, 'La critique de la Vulgate' Revue Bénédictine 36 (1924), pp. 137–64; 'La reconstitution du psautier hexaplaire latin' *ib.,* 41 (1929), pp. 297–324; 'Le problème du psautier romain' *ib.* 42 (1930), pp. 101–26; von Dobschütz, *Studien zur Textkritik der Vulgata* (1894); Gordon, 'Rabbinic Exegesis in the Vulgate of Proverbs' JBL 49 (1930), pp. 384–416; Johannessohn, 'Zur Entstehung der Ausdrucksweise der lateinischen Vulgata aus den jüngeren griechischen at. Übersetzungen' ZNW 44 (1952/53), pp. 90–102; Landgraf, 'Die Schriftzitate in der Scholastik um die Wende des 12. zum 13. Jh.' Bibl 18 (1937), pp. 74–94; Marks, *Der textkritische Wert des Psalterium Hieronymi juxta Hebraeos* (1956); Penna, 'La Volgata e il Manuscritto 1 QIsᵃ' Bibl 38 (1957), pp. 381–95; Salmon, 'Il testo e l'interpretazione dei Salmi al tempo di S. Girolamo e di S. Agostino' RivBibl 2 (1954), pp. 97–118; Salmon (ed.), *Richesses et déficiences des anciens Psautiers Latins* (Coll. Bibl. Lat. 13, 1959); Scarpat, *Il Liber Psalmorum e il Psalterium Gallicanum* (1950); Schneider, 'Der Vulgata-Text der Oratio Manasse eine Rezension des Robertus Stephanus' BZ 4 (1960), pp. 277–82; Smit, *De Vulgaat, Geschiedenis en Herziening van de Latijnse Bibelvertaling* (1948); Stummer, 'Die lateinische Bibel vor Hieronymus und das Judentum' ThGl 19 (1927), pp. 184–99; *Einführung in die lateinische Bibel* (1928); 'Einige Beobachtungen über die Arbeitsweise des Hieronymus bei der Übersetzung des AT aus der Hebraica Veritas' Bibl 10 (1929), pp. 3–30; 'Die Landeskenntnis des Hieronymus und ihr Einfluß auf die Vulgata' Heil. Land 80 (1936), pp. 65–76; 'Hauptprobleme der Erforschung der at. Vulgata' BZAW 66 (1936), pp. 233–9; 'Beiträge zu dem Problem "Hieronymus und die Targumim"' Bibl 18 (1937), pp. 174–81; 'Griechisch-römische Bildung und christliche Theologie in der Vulgata des

Hieronymus' ZAW 58 (1940/41), pp. 251–69; 'Zur Stilgeschichte der alten Bibelüberset-zungen' ZAW 61 (1945/48), pp. 195–231; 'Die Vulgata zum Canticum Annae' Mün-chener ThZ 1 (1950), pp. 10–19; 'Beiträge zur Exegese der Vulgata' ZAW 62 (1950), pp. 152–67; 'Secura mens quasi iuge convivium (Prov. xv, 15b)' Münchener ThZ 4 (1953), pp. 37–45; Sutcliffe, 'St. Jerome's Hebrew Manuscripts' Bibl 29 (1948), pp. 195–204; Weber, *Sancti Hieronymi Psalterium iuxta Hebraeos* (1954); Zorell, *Psalterium ex hebraeo Latinum* (²1939).

Cf. also Literature §§ 117–23, 126.

Jerome's Latin rendering, later called the 'Vulgate'[1] represents a translation from the Hebrew, and, though late, it still belongs before 𝔐 finally became abso-lutely fixed. When Jerome was commissioned by Pope Damasus in 382 to make a revision of the Vetus Latina, he at first went through the text following 𝔊. This work of Jerome's is lost apart from the so-called Psalterium Gallicanum, a revision of the Vetus Latina on the basis of Origen's recension of 𝔊, and a similar revision of Job. From 386 on, Jerome[2] lived in Bethlehem, and so in the years 390–405 he translated the Old Testament from the Hebrew, the *Hebraica veritas*. At first this rendering was generally repudiated, but, from the beginning of the seventh century, this translation from the Hebrew prevailed in ecclesiasti-cal use, apart from the Psalter, the Psalterium iuxta Hebraeos, where it was the Psalterium Gallicanum which remained normal. In 1546 it was declared[3] by the Council of Trent (Tridentine) as *textus auctoritate plenus*, that is to say 'authori-tative in matters of faith and life'[4] and it was promulgated as the official Latin text by Sixtus V (1590: Sixtina) and Clement VIII (1592, 1593, 1598: Clementina). A revised text of the Vulgate, taking account of the wealth of manuscript material, is now being provided by the magnificent edition of the Papal Com-mission on the Vulgate,[5] of which so far ten volumes have appeared (Gen.–Psalms). For the Psalms and Canticles (p. 588), Pius XII introduced a new Latin translation in 1945;[6] this takes critical account not only of the Vulgate but also of the original text and of the other ancient translations.

[1] Allgeier, 'Authentisch auf dem Konzil von Trient' Histor. Jahrb. Goerres-Ges. 60 (1941), pp. 142–58; 'Haec vetus et vulgata editio' Bibl 29 (1948), pp. 353–90; Sutcliffe, 'The Name "Vulgate"', *ib.* pp. 345–52.

[2] Steinmann, *Hieronymus Ausleger der Bibel. Weg und Werk eines Kirchenvaters* (1961).

[3] Sutcliffe, 'The Council of Trent and the *Authentia* of the Vulgate' JThSt 49 (1948), pp. 35–42.

[4] Stummer, *Einführung in die lateinische Bibel* (1928), p. 172.

[5] Lietzmann, 'Die neue römische Vulgata' ThLZ 65 (1940), cols. 225–30; Stummer, 'Die neue römische Ausgabe der Vulgata zur Genesis' ZAW 45 (1927), pp. 141–50.

[6] *Liber Psalmorum cum Canticis Breviarii Romani. Nova e textibus primigeniis interpretatio latina cum notis criticis et exegeticis* (1945, ²1957); Allgeier (1948) (see p. 718); Bea, *Die neue lateinische Psalmenübersetzung* (1949); Cooper, 'Jerome's "Hebrew Psalter" and the New Latin Version' JBL 69 (1950), pp. 233–44; Scarpat, *Il Liber Psalmorum e il Psalterium Gallicanum* (1950); Ziegler, 'Das neue lateinische Psalterium' ZAW 63 (1952), pp. 1–15.

§ 125. THE EVALUATION OF THE EVIDENCE FOR TEXTUAL CRITICISM. CONJECTURAL EMENDATION

Literature: Begrich, 'Zur Frage der at. Textkritik' OLZ 42 (1939), cols. 473–83; Bewer, *Der Text des Buches Eʒra. Beiträge ʒu seiner Wiederherstellung* (FRLANT 31, 1922); Coppens, 'Notes philologiques sur le texte Hébreu de l'AT' Muséon 44 (1931), pp. 177–98; 47 (1934), pp. 259–63; 48 (1935), pp. 113–44; Cornill, *Das Buch des Propheten Eʒechiel* (1886), Dahood, 'The Value of Ugaritic for Textual Criticism' Bibl 40 (1959), pp. 160–70 = SBO I (1959), pp. 26–36; Delitzsch, *Die Lese- und Schreibfehler im AT* (1920); Driver, 'Hebrew Notes' JRAS (1944), pp. 165–71; 'Hebrew Studies' JRAS (1948), pp. 164–76; 'Hebrew Notes' VT 1 (1951), pp. 241–50; 'L'Interprétation du texte masorétique à la lumière de la lexicographie hébraïque' EThL 26 (1950), pp. 337–53; 'Glosses in the Hebrew Text of the OT' OrBiblLov I (1957), pp. 123–61; 'Abbreviations in the Masoretic Text' Textus 1 (1960), pp. 112–31; Ehrlich, *Randglossen ʒur hebräischen Bibel* I–VII (1908–1914); Gelin, 'La question des "relectures" bibliques à l'intérieur d'une tradition vivante' BEThL XII (1959), pp. 303–15; Hulst, in co-operation with other scholars, *Helps for Translators*, I. *OT Translation Problems. A Treatment of Difficult Passages in the Masoretic Text* (1960); Junker, 'Konsonantenumstellung als Fehlerquelle und textkritisches Hilfsmittel im MT' BZAW 66 (1936), pp. 162–74; Kennedy, *An Aid to the Textual Criticism of the OT* (1928); Mowinckel, 'Et bibeloversettelsproblem' NTT 60 (1959), pp. 65–86; Nober, 'Elenchus emendationum 1' Bibl 34 (1953), pp. 125–31; North, 'Textual Variants in the Hebrew Bible significant for Critical Analysis' JQR 47 (1956/57), pp. 77–80; Nyberg, 'Das textkritische Problem des AT am Hoseabuche demonstriert' ZAW 52 (1934), pp. 241–54; *Studien ʒum Hoseabuche. Zugleich ein Beitrag ʒur Klärung des Problems der at. Textkritik* (1935); Perles, *Analekten ʒur Textkritik des AT*, I (1905); II (1922); 'Nachträge zu meinen Analekten I u. II' Veröffentlichungen der Alexander Kohut Memorial Foundation 7 (1933), pp. 194–203; Reider, 'The Present State of Textual Criticism of the OT' HUCA 7 (1930), pp. 285–315; Robertson, *The Text of the OT and the Methods of Textual Criticism* (1939); 'Points of Interest in the Masoretic Text' JNESt 2 (1943), pp. 35–9; Rodd, 'Modern Issues in Biblical Study: Rediscovered Hebrew Meanings' ET 71 (1959/60), pp. 131–4; Schildenberger, Textumstellungen und ihre Begründung' *Mél. Bibl. Robert* (1957), pp. 241–53; 'Parallelstellen als Ursache von Textveränderungen' Bibl 40 (1959), pp. 188–98 = SBO I (1959), pp. 54–64; Seeligmann, 'Researches into the Criticism of the Masoretic Text of the Bible' [Hebr., Engl. summary] Tarbiz 25 (1955/56), pp. 118–39, I–II; Segert, 'Die Schreibfehler in den ugaritischen literarischen Keilschrifttexten im Anschluß an das textkritische Hilfsbuch von Friedrich Delitzsch klassifiziert' BZAW 77 (1958), pp. 193–212; Sperber, 'Biblical Hebrew' PAAJR 18 (1948/49), pp. 301–82; Talmon, 'Double Readings in the Massoretic Text' Textus 1 (1960), pp. 144–84; 'Synonymous Readings in the Textual Traditions of the OT' Scripta Hieros. VIII (1961), pp. 335–83; '1 Sam. xv 32b—A Case of Conflated Readings?' VT 11 (1961), pp. 456–7; Vaccari, 'Scrittura fenicia-samaritana nella Bibbia ebraica' Bibl 19 (1938), pp. 188–201; 'Le radici תרץ e פרץ nell' ebraico biblico' *ib.*, pp. 308–314; 'De textu' *Institutiones Biblicae scholis accomodatae* I (⁶1951) pp. 233–362, 12 Pls.; 'Parole rovesciate e critiche errate nella Bibbia ebraica' *Stud. Or. Levi Della Vida*, II (1956), pp. 553–66; Vogt, *Critica Textus VT Hebraici et Graeci. In usum privatum auditorum* (1951); Volz, 'Ein Arbeitsplan für die Textkritik des AT' ZAW 54 (1936), pp. 110–13; Waterman, 'The Authentication of Conjectural Glosses' JBL 56 (1937), pp. 253–9; Wellhausen, *Der Text der Bücher Samuelis untersucht* (1871); Wutz, 'Beiträge zur Technik alter Textkritik' BZ 22 (1934), pp. 16–29.
Cf. also Literature on p. 678; §§ 115–24, 126.

A general rule for the evaluation for text-critical purposes of the Qumrān scrolls, the Samaritan and the Versions cannot be given. But the reader who is familiar with Hebrew, Greek and Latin may relatively rapidly and simply gain an insight into the methods which have here to be employed and the results which can follow, if he works through a few pages of the apparatus in Kittel's *Biblia Hebraica* (p. 691), referring to the list of abbreviations given there and making use of Würthwein's book mentioned on p. 669. It is true that he must not forget that the apparatus of this edition of the Bible, with the exception of some few parts, is now thirty to forty years old and so is in many respects outmoded, and that in particular the methodical evaluation of the textual material from Qumrān and from other places in the Wilderness of Judaea—an undertaking already planned and under way—will bring with it a basic transformation of the apparatus. Quite apart from this, it is in any case essential, if an independent judgement is to be reached, for the various witnesses to the text themselves to be examined, the Qumrān scrolls, the Samaritan, the 𝕲 and the other ancient Versions, since the precise meaning of the passage in question can only be fully understood with a consideration of its wider context; words or groups of words taken out of their context often give rise to misunderstandings. Kittel's edition is thus by no means intended to make the examination of the individual textual witnesses superfluous, but only to facilitate the approach to them and to encourage and prepare the way for more detailed consideration of them. Older books, such as Wellhausen's *Text der Bücher Samuelis*, Cornill's *Ezekiel*, and Bewer's *Text des Buches Ezra*[1] on the one hand, and on the other hand works of the kind mentioned on pp. 679–84 dealing with the text-critical evaluation of the Qumrān scrolls, may do good service as models and pointers to a more thorough text-critical activity. The periodical 'Textus', as has been indicated above on p. 692, n. 9, is designed to assist in the preparation of the critical edition of the Hebrew Old Testament planned by the Hebrew University in Jerusalem. From this too we may expect to gain much towards the evaluation of the material which is available for the investigation of the Old Testament text.

Beside this evaluation of the external witnesses to the text there will always be a place of great importance for free conjecture. But it must be done methodically, with the most careful consideration of the possibilities indicated by the history of the transmission of the text, and must also be kept free of the error of imagining that it is here possible to obtain many results which will stand the test of time. It repeatedly happens that the adducing of new words from the other Semitic languages or from new archaeological discoveries brings it about that a word which was hitherto regarded as corrupt and unintelligible now appears to be completely meaningful and so the conjectures suggested for it are seen to be superfluous and false. Delitzsch's book may serve well to give training in methodical conjectural emendation. Collections of conjectures, which are admittedly in part made in dependence upon external witnesses to the text, may be found in the books by Ehrlich and Perles. Many articles on textual criticism in periodicals provide similar material, as for example those of G. R. Driver. Some of these at least have been mentioned on p. 720, and others in the bibliographical notes to the individual books of the Old Testament.

---

[1] Cf. also S. R. Driver, *Notes on the Hebrew Text of the Books of Samuel* ([2]1913), and Burney, *Notes on the Hebrew Text of the Books of Kings* (1903).

§ 126. ADDITIONAL LITERATURE AND NOTES

§ 1. THE NATURE OF THE UNDERTAKING

Albright and Freedman, 'The Continuing Revolution in Biblical Research' JBR 31 (1963), pp. 110–13; Alonso-Schökel, *Probleme der biblischen Forschung in Vergangenheit und Gegenwart*, translated from the Spanish by Reinhard (1961); Baumgartner, 'Zum 100. Geburtstag von Hermann Gunkel' SVT IX (1963), pp. 1–18; Braun, *The Work of Père Lagrange*, adapted from the French by Murphy (1963); Bright, 'Modern Study of OT Literature' *Essays Albright* (1961), pp. 13–31; Carmino de Catanzaro, 'Some Trends and Issues in OT Studies' AThR 44 (1962), pp. 251–63; Dubarle, 'Bulletin de théologie biblique: Ancien Testament' RScPhTh 46 (1962), pp. 153–93; Duncker, 'Biblical Criticism' CBQ 25 (1963), pp. 22–33; Freedman, 'On Method in Biblical Studies. The Old Testament' Interpret. 17 (1963), pp. 308–18; Hallo, 'New Viewpoints of Cuneiform Literature' IEJ 12 (1962), pp. 13–26; Harbsmeier, 'Der Dienst der historisch-kritischen Exegeses-Predigt' EvTh 23 (1963), pp. 42–55; Kraus, 'Zur Geschichte des Überlieferungsbegriffs in der at. Wissenschaft' EvTh 16 (1956), pp. 371–87; Kuhl, 'Die Wiederaufnahme—ein literarkritisches Prinzip?' ZAW 64 (1952), pp. 1–11; Noth, *Developing Lines of Theological Thought in Germany* (Fourth Annual Bibliographical Lecture, 1963, Union Theological Seminary in Virginia), pp. 3–10, 19–21; Spadafora, *Saggi di critica ed esegesi biblica* (1962); Stoebe, 'Grenzen der Literarkritik im AT' ThZ 18 (1962), pp. 385–400; Zimmerli, 'Die historisch-kritische Bibelwissenschaft und die Verkündigungsaufgabe der Kirche' EvTh 23 (1963), pp. 17–31.

p. 2, n. 1, Bratton, 'Precursors of Biblical Criticism' JBL 50 (1931), pp. 176–85 [Origen, Ibn Ezra, Spinoza]; Jepsen, 'Ludwig Diestel als Greifswalder Theologe' *Hanna Jursch-Festschr.* (1963), pp. 1–18.

p. 2, n. 3, Hailperin, *Rashi and the Christian Scholars* (1963).

p. 2, n. 4, Brookes, 'The influence of the Franco-Spanish Commentator and Grammarian David Kimchi (1160–1235) on Biblical Study' XXV ICO Vol. I (1962), pp. 391–5.

p. 2, n. 5, Amsler, *L'AT dans l'Église* (1960); Bardtke, 'Gedanken zur Arbeit an der Geschichte der at. Wissenschaft' Estudios Eclesiásticos 34 (1960), pp. 367–79; Hornig, *Die Anfänge der historisch-kritischen Theologie: Johann Salomo Semler's Schriftverständnis und seine Stellung zu Luther* (1961).

p. 2, n. 6, Bamberger, 'The Early Editions of Spinoza's "Tractatus Theologico-Politicus"' Studies in Bibliography and Booklore 5 (1961), pp. 9–33; Rosalie L. Colie, 'Spinoza in England, 1665–1730' Proc. Am. Philos. Soc. 107 (1963), pp. 183–219; Stuermann, 'Benedict Spinoza: A Pioneer in Biblical Criticism' PAAJR 29 (1960/61), pp. 133–79; Zac, 'Les avatars de l'interprétation de l'Écriture chez Spinoza' RHPhR 42 (1962), pp. 17–37.

p. 7, n. 11, Brownlee, 'Edh-Dheeb's Story of his Scroll Discovery' RQ 3 (1961/62), pp. 483–94.

§ 2. GENERAL CONSIDERATIONS

Anonymous, *Los géneros literarios de la Sagrada Escritura* (1957); H. M. and N. K. Chadwick, *The Growth of Literature*, I (1932), II (1936), III (1940); Childs, *Memory and Tradition in Israel* (1962); Culley, 'An Approach to the Problem of Oral Tradition' VT 13 (1963), pp. 113–25; Feldman, 'Biblical Motives and Sources' JNESt 22 (1963), pp. 73–103; Galbiati, 'I generi letterari nella teoria del P. G. M. Lagrange e nell'Enciclica "Divino afflante Spiritu"' La scuola cattolica 75 (1947), pp. 177–86, 282–92; Gerhardsson, *Memory and Manuscript. Oral Tradition and Written Transmission in Rabbinic Judaism and Early Christianity* (1961); 'Mündliche und schriftliche Tradition der Prophetenbücher' ThZ 17 (1961), pp. 216–20; Vansina, *De la tradition orale. Essai de méthode historique* (Kon. Mus. voor Midden-Afrika, Tervuren, Belgie, Annalen-Reeks 36, 1961); Widengren, 'Tradition and Literature in Early Judaism and in the Early Church' Numen 10 (1963), pp. 42–83.

§ 3. SPEECHES, SERMONS, PRAYERS

Ackroyd, 'The Vitality of the Word of God in the OT. A Contribution to the Study of Transmission and Exposition of the OT Material' ASTI 1 (1962), pp. 7–23; Bickerman, 'Bénédiction et prière' RB 69 (1962), pp. 524–32; Blank, 'Some Observations concerning Biblical Prayer' HUCA 32 (1961), pp. 75–90; Cazemier, 'Das Gebet in den Pyramidentexten' JEOL 15 (1957/58), pp. 47–65; Haspecker, 'Israels Gespräch mit Gott. Bittgebete aus den erzählenden Schriften des AT' Bibel und Leben 2 (1961), pp. 81–92.

p. 14, line 7, Boling, 'And who is Š-K-M?' (Judges ix, 28)' VT 13 (1963), pp. 479–82.

p. 14, line 9 from end, Malamat, 'Kingship and Council in Israel and Sumer: A Parallel' JNESt 22 (1963), pp. 247–53.

p. 15, n. 4, Cazelles, 'Trois asiatismes possibles dans Anastasi I' GLECS 9 (1960/63), pp. 1–3; Posener, 'La mésaventure d'un Syrien et le nom égyptien de l'ours' Or 13 (1944), pp. 193–204. Cf. Kramer, *Sumerische literarische Texte aus Nippur*, Vol. I: *Mythen, Epen, Weisheitsliteratur und andere Literaturgattungen* (1961), pp. 15–18, Nos. 36–44, Pls. LXXX–C: Disputationen; Lambert, 'La littérature sumérienne à propos d'ouvrages récents' RA 55 (1961), pp. 177–96; 56 (1962), pp. 81–90, 214.

p. 16, n. 6, Emerton, 'Priests and Levites in Deuteronomy' VT 12 (1962), pp. 129–38.

p. 17, line 2 from end, Gamper, 'Die heilsgeschichtliche Bedeutung des salomonischen Tempelweihegebets' ZKTh 85 (1963), pp. 55–61.

§ 4. RECORDS

p. 18, n. 1, Alt, 'Die geschichtliche Bedeutung der neuen phönikischen Inschriften aus Kilikien' FuF 24 (1948), pp. 121–4; 'Die Götter in den phönikischen Inschriften von Karatepe' ThLZ 75 (1950), cols. 513–22; 'Die Opfer in den phönikischen Inschriften von Karatepe' ThLZ 75 (1950), cols. 571–6; Barnett, 'Karatepe, The Key to the Hittite Hieroglyphs' AnSt 3 (1953), pp. 53–95; Dahood, 'Karatepe Notes' Bibl 44 (1963), pp. 74–5; Friedrich, 'Zur Interpretation von Satz XVI der phönizischbildhethitischen Bilinguis von Karatepe' Or 31 (1962), pp. 223–4; Grégoire, 'Azitawadda-Estwed' NC 1/2 (1949/50), pp. 122–7; Lévy, 'Les inscriptions de Karatepe' NC 1/2 (1949/50), pp. 105–21; Liverani, 'Bar-Guš e Bar-Rakib' RStOr 36 (1961), pp. 185–7; Machteld J. Mellink, 'Karatepe. More Light on the Dark Ages' BiOr 7 (1950), pp. 141–50; Matthiae, *Studi sui relievi di Karatepe* (1963); O'Callaghan, 'The Phoenician Inscriptions on the King's Statue at Karatepe' CBQ 11 (1949), pp. 233–48; Pedersen, 'The Phoenician Inscription of Karatepe' AcOr[H] 21 (1953), pp. 33–56; von Soden, 'Azitawadda = Mattî von Atunna; KTK and Kasku' OLZ 56 (1961), cols. 576–9.

p. 18, n. 2, Finkelstein, 'Ammiṣaduqa's Edict and the Babylonian "Law Codes" ' JCSt 15 (1961), pp. 91–104.

§ 4a. CONTRACTS

Alberti, *Matrimonio e Divorzio nella Bibbia* (1962); Bengtson, *Die Verträge der griechisch-römischen Welt von 700 bis 338 v. Chr. Die Staatsverträge des Altertums*, ed. Bengtson, Vol. II (1962); Bikerman, 'Couper une Alliance' Archives d'Histoire du Droit Oriental 5 (1950/51), pp. 133–56; Edel, 'Zur Schwurgötterliste des Hethitervertrages' ZÄS 90 (1963), pp. 31–5; Gross, 'Der Sinai-Bund als Lebensform des auserwählten Volkes im AT' Trierer ThSt 15 (1962), pp. 1–15; Annie Jaubert, *La notion d'alliance dans le Judaïsme aux abords de l'ère chrétienne* (1963); Jepsen, 'Berith. Ein Beitrag zur Theologie der Exilszeit' *Rudolph-Festschr.* (1961), pp. 161–79; Kienast, *Die altassyrischen Texte des orientalischen Seminars der Universität Heidelberg und der Sammlung Erlenmeyer-Basel* (Ergänzungsbände zu ZA 1, 1960); Loewenstamm, 'From this time forth and evermore' Tarbiz 32 (1962/63), pp. 313–16; McCarthy, *Treaty and Covenant* (AnBibl 21, 1963); Moran, 'De Foederis Traditione' VD 40 (1962), pp. 3–17; Newman, *The People of the Covenant* (1962); Noth, *Die Ursprünge des alten Israel im Licht neuer Quellen* (AFLNW Fasc. 94, 1961); Nougayrol, 'Documents du Ḫabur' Syria 37 (1960), pp. 205–14, cf. pp. 205–9: Une nouvelle tablette du Ḫana; 'Guerre et Paix à Ugarit' Iraq 25 (1963), pp. 110–23; Smend, *Die Bundesformel* (ThSt 68, 1963); Whitley, 'Covenant and Commandment in Israel' JNESt 22 (1963), pp. 37–48.

p. 19, n. 4, Borger, 'Zu den Asarhaddon-Verträgen aus Nimrud' ZA 54 (1961), pp. 173–196; Frankena, 'Nogmaals het verdrag van Asarhaddon' Phoenix 6 (1963), pp. 19–31; Korošec, 'Quelques traités de l'époque néo-assyrienne' Romanitas, Rio de Janeiro 3 (1961), pp. 261–77; 'Staatsverträge aus neuassyrischer Zeit' [Serbian, German summary] ZZR 29 (1959), pp. 135–45, 145–7.

p. 19, n. 5, *Excavations at Nuzi VIII* (Lacheman) (1962); Elena Cassin, 'Tablettes inédites de Nuzi' RA 56 (1962), pp. 57–80; 'L'influence babylonienne à Nuzi' JESHO 5 (1962), pp. 113–38; Jankowska, 'Zur Geschichte der hurritischen Gesellschaft (Auf Grund von Rechtsurkunden aus Arrapḫa und Alalaḫ)' XXV ICO Vol. I (1962), pp. 226–32; Lacheman, 'The Word *sudutu* in the Nuzi Tablets' XXV ICO Vol. I (1962), pp. 233–8; Speiser, 'The Wife-Sister Motif in the Patriarchal Narratives' *Biblical and Other Studies* ed. Altmann (1963), pp. 15–28.

p. 19, n. 6, Lüddeckens, *Ägyptische Eheverträge* (Ägyptol. Abh. I, 1960).

p. 20, n. 7, Fensham, 'Clauses of Protection in Hittite Vassal-Treaties and the OT' VT 13 (1963), pp. 133–43; Klengel, 'Der Schiedsspruch des Muršili II. hinsichtlich Barga und seine Übereinkunft mit Duppi-Tešup von Amurru' (KBo III, 3)' Or 32 (1963), pp. 32–55; Korošec, 'Les Hittites et leurs vassaux syriens à la lumière des nouveaux textes d'Ugarit (PRU IV)' RHA 18 (1960), pp. 65–79; Otten, 'Ein althethitischer Vertrag mit Kizzuwatna' JCSt 5 (1951), pp. 129–32; 'Neue Quellen zum Ausklang des hethitschen Reiches' MDOG 94 (1963), pp. 1–23; Sugi, 'Der Vertrag des Tudḫalijaš IV. mit Ištarmuwaš von Amurru' Orient 1 (1960), pp. 1–22.

p. 20, n. 8, Brekelmans, 'Sefire I A 29–30' VT 13 (1963), pp. 225–8; Cantineau, 'Remarques sur la stèle araméenne de Sefiré-Soudjin' RA 28 (1931), pp. 167–76; Dupont-Sommer, 'Une inscription araméenne inédite de Sfiré' BMB 13 (1956), pp. 23–41, Pls. I–VI; 'Une stèle araméenne inédite de Sfiré (Syrie) du VIIIᵉ siècle avant J.-C.' CRAI (1957), pp. 245–9; 'Un traité araméen du VIIIᵉ siècle avant J.-C.' CRAI (1958), pp. 177–82; 'Trois Stèles Araméennes provenant de Sfiré: Un Traité de vassalité du VIIIᵉ siècle avant J.-C.' Ann. Arch. Syrie 10 (1960), pp. 21–54, Pls. I–X; Fensham, 'The Wild Ass in the Aramean Treaty between Bar Ga'ayah and Mati'el' JNESt 22 (1963), pp. 185 f.; Fitzmyer, 'The Aramaic Inscriptions of Sefire I and II' JAOS 81 (1961), pp. 178–222; Garbini, 'Sefire I A 28' RStOr 36 (1961), pp. 9–11; Liverani (cf. § 126 on p. 18, n. 1); Moran, 'A Note on the Treaty Terminology of the Sefîre Steles' JNESt 22 (1963), pp. 173–6; Noth, 'Der historische Hintergrund der Inschriften von *Sefîre*' ZDPV 77 (1961), pp. 118–72; Picard, 'Le rite magique des εἴδωλα de cire brûlés, attesté sur trois stèles araméennes de Sfiré vers le milieu du VIIIᵉ s. av. notre ère' Rev. Arch. (1961), pp. 85–7; Sacchi, 'Osservazioni storiche sulla prima iscrizione di Sfire' AANL Ser. VIII, Vol. XVI (1961), pp. 175–91; Segert, 'Zur Schrift und Orthographie der altaramäischen Stelen von Sfire' ArOr 32 (1964), pp. 110–28; von Soden (cf. § 126 on p. 18, n. 1); Tocci, 'Un frammento di stele aramaica da Tell Sifr' Oriens Antiquus 1 (1962), pp. 21–2; Veenhof, 'An Aramaic Curse with a Sumero-Akkadian Prototype' BiOr 20 (1963), pp. 142–4. Lit. p. 24, n. 24; § 126 on p. 24, n. 24.

p. 20, n. 9, Korošec, 'Quelques remarques juridiques sur deux traités internationaux d'Alalaḫ' *Mélanges Lévy-Bruhl* (1959), pp. 171–8; Mendelsohn, 'On Marriage in Alalakh' *Essays Baron* (1959), pp. 351–7.

p. 21, n. 11, Callaway, 'Burials in Ancient Palestine: From the Stone Age to Abraham' BA 26 (1963), pp. 74–91; McKenzie, 'Judicial Procedure at the Town Gate' VT 14 (1964), pp. 100–4.

p. 21, n. 14, Pestman, *Marriage and Matrimonial Property in Ancient Egypt* (1961).

p. 21, n. 15, van Dijk, 'Neusumerische Gerichtsurkunden in Bagdad' ZA 55 (1962), pp. 70–90, see pp. 70–7: 1. Ehescheidungsprozess; Paterson, 'Divorce and Desertion in the OT' JBL 51 (1932), pp. 161–70; Yaron, 'A Royal Divorce at Ugarit' Or 32 (1963), pp. 21–31.

§ 4b. LETTERS

Baer, 'An Eleventh Dynasty Farmer's Letter to his Family' JAOS 83 (1963), pp. 1–19; Cıvil, 'The "Message of Lu-dingir-ra to His Mother" and a Group of Akkado-Hittite

"Proverbs" ' JNESt 23 (1964), pp. 1–11; Goetze, 'Fifty Old Babylonian Letters from Harmal' Sumer 14 (1958), pp. 3–78, Pls. 1–24; Luck, 'Brief und Epistel in der Antike' Das Altertum 7 (1960), pp. 77–84.

p. 22, nn. 16–19, Klengel, 'Zum Brief eines Königs von Ḫanigalbat (IBoT I 34)' Or 32 (1963), pp. 280–91.

p. 22, n. 16, Barnett, 'Hamath and Nimrud. Shell Fragments from Hamath and the Provenance of the Nimrud Ivories' Iraq 25 (1963), pp. 81–5, Pls. XV–XVIII; Hulin, 'The Inscriptions on the Carved Throne-Base of Shalmaneser III' Iraq 25 (1963), pp. 48–69; Laessøe and Knudsen, 'An Old Babylonian Letter from a Hurrian Environment' ZA 55 (1962), pp. 131–7; Mallowan, 'Where the most splendid Assyrian Ivories ever known have been found: The King's Residence in Fort Shalmaneser, Nimrud; and a foretaste of magnificence yet to be published' ILN 234 (1959), pp. 99–100; 'The "Mona Lisa" of Nimrud' Iraq 25 (1963), pp. 1–5, Pl. I; Oates, 'The Excavations at Nimrud (Kalḫu), 1960–1961' Iraq 23–4 (1961/62); 'The First Great Assyrian Military Headquarters to be Completely Revealed: Fort Shalmaneser, Nimrud. Excavations and Discoveries—Part 1' ILN 241 (1962), pp. 834–837; 'The Most Spectacular Discovery to be Made in Fort Shalmaneser. The King's Throne Base and its Vivid Reliefs—Part 2' ILN 241 (1962), pp. 879–81; 'The Excavations at Nimrud (Kalḫu), 1962' Iraq 25 (1963), pp. 6–37, Pls. II–VIII; Reade, 'A Glazed-Brick Panel from Nimrud' Iraq 25 (1963), pp. 38–47, Pl. IX; Saggs, 'The Nimrud Letters, 1952—Part VI' Iraq 25 (1963), pp. 70–80, Pls. XI–XIV; Stearns, *Reliefs from the Palace of Ashurnasirpal II* (AfO Beih. 15, 1961); Youngblood, 'Amorite Influence in a Canaanite Amarna Letter (EA 96)' BASOR 168 (1962), pp. 24–7.

p. 22, n. 17, Finet, 'Une lettre de récriminations au vice-roi de Mari, Iasmaḫ-Addu' AIPhHOS 15 (1960), pp. 17–32; Klengel (cf. § 126 on p. 188, n. 11); Malamat, 'Mari and the Bible: Some Patterns of Tribal Organization and Institution' JAOS 82 (1962), pp. 143–50, see pp. 147–50: The Patrimony as a Tribal Institution.

p. 22, n. 19, Malamat, 'Campaigns of Amenhotep II and Thutmose IV to Canaan' Scripta Hieros. VIII (1961), pp. 218–31: Akkadian letters from Taanach and Gezer. According to PEQ 94 (1962), p. 99, cuneiform tablets from the Amarna period (presumably letters) have come to light in Shechem.

p. 22, n. 20, Esteban, 'Una fórmula de cortesía epistolar de Ugarit, repetida en una carta judeo-aramea del siglo V a. C.' Sefarad 22 (1962), pp. 101–2; Laroche, 'Lettre d'un préfet du roi hittite' RHA 18 (1961), pp. 81–8; Otten, 'Die inschriftlichen Funde' (MDOG 88, 1955: *Bericht über die Ausgrabungen in Bogazköy im Jahre 1954*), pp. 33–6; 'Hethitische Schreiber in ihren Briefen' MIOF 4 (1956), pp. 179–89; Liane Rost, 'Die außerhalb von Bogazköy gefundenen hethitischen Briefe' MIOF 4 (1956), pp. 328–50.

p. 23, line 4, Frank, 'A Note on II Kings xix, 10, 14' CBQ 25 (1963), pp. 410–14.

p. 23, line 10, Rendtorff, 'Botenformel und Botenspruch' ZAW 74 (1962), pp. 165–77.

p. 23, n. 24, Benveniste (cf. § 126 on p. 551, line 7. See below); Couroyer, 'Le Temple de Yahô et l'orientation dans les papyrus araméens d'Éléphantine' RB 68 (1961), pp. 525–40; Dupont-Sommer, ' "Bêl et Nabû, Šamaš et Nergal" sur un ostracon araméen inédit d'Éléphantine' RHR 128 (1944), pp. 28–39; 'Le syncrétisme religieux des Juifs d'Éléphantine d'après un Ostracon araméen inédit' RHR 130 (1945), pp. 17–28; 'Sabbat et Parascève à Éléphantine d'après des ostraca araméens inédits' MDSAI XV, 1 (1960), pp. 67–88; 'Un ostracon araméen inédit d'Éléphantiné (Collection Clermont-Ganneau no. 44)' *Studies Driver* (1963), pp. 53–8, 1 Pl.; Erichsen, *Eine demotische Schenkungsurkunde aus der Zeit des Darius* (AAMz 1962, No. 6, 1963); Esteban, 'Una fórmula de cortesía epistolar de Ugarit, repetida en una carta judeo-aramea del siglo V. a. C.' Sefarad 22 (1962), pp. 101–2; Hammershaimb, 'Om jødisk bosættelse uden for Palæstina i gammeltestamentlig tid' DTT 25 (1962), pp. 36–47; Hoftijzer, 'Ein Papyrus-fragment aus El-Hibeh' VT 12 (1962), pp. 341–2; Hoftijzer and Pestman, 'Hereditary Rights as laid down in the Marriage Contract Krael. 2' BiOr 19 (1962), pp. 216–19; Liverani, 'Antecedenti dell' onomastica aramaica antica' RStOr 37 (1962), pp. 65–76; Porten, 'The Structure and Orientation of the Jewish Temple at Elephantine' JAOS 81 (1961), pp. 38–42; Ricke, *Die Tempel Nektanebos' II. in Elephantine* (1960); Sauneron, *Inscriptions romaines au temple de Khnoum à Éléphantiné* (Beiträge zur ägyptischen

Bauforschung und Altertumskunde, Heft 6, 1960); Yaron, *Introduction to the Law of the Aramaic Papyri* (1961). Lit. p. 20, n. 8, § 126 on p. 20, n. 8. An Aramaic letter from the middle of the seventh century B.C. found in Assyria: Dupont-Sommer, 'L'ostracon araméen d'Assour' Syria 24 (1944/45), pp. 24–61.

p. 24, n. 26, Hartman, 'The Great Tree and Nabuchodonosor's Madness' *Gruenthaner Mem. Vol.* (1962), pp. 75–82.

§ 4c. LISTS

Edda Bresciani, 'Un papiro aramaico dell'età tolomaica' AANL XVI (1961), pp. 258–64; Labat, *Elam and Western Persia c. 1200–1000 B.C.* (CAH Rev. Ed. 23, 1964); Mazar, 'The Military Elite of King David' VT 13 (1963), pp. 310–20; Mertens, 'Völkerwanderungen im österlichen Mittelmeer am Ende des 2. Jahrtausends v. Chr.' Das Altertum 10 (1964), pp. 3–13; Schifman, 'Aus der Geschichte des phönizischen Handels mit Griechenland in der zweiten Hälfte des zweiten Jahrtausends und zu Beginn des ersten Jahrtausends v. Chr.' *TJU-MENV-Festschrift* (1963), pp. 89–94; Wainwright, 'A Teucrian at Salamis in Cyprus' JHSt 83 (1963), pp. 146–51; Wente, 'Shekelesh or Shasu?' JNESt 22 (1963), pp. 167–72.

p. 24, line 2 from end, on Albright cf. Freedman, 'Portrait of an Archaeologist' Presbyterian Life (Dec. 15, 1961), pp. 5–11. Albright, 'Toward a More Conservative View' Christianity Today 7 (1963), pp. 3–5.

p. 25, n. 29, Albright, 'The End of Calneh in Shinar' JNESt 3 (1945), pp. 254 f.: on x, 10, וְכַלְנֶה; Andrews, 'The Mycaenean Name of the land of the Achaians' RHA 13 (1955), pp. 1–19; Attema, *Arabië en de Bijbel* (Exegetica III, 4, 1961); Benoit, 'Les fouilles d'Alésia et l'expansion Hellénique en occident' CRAI (1962), pp. 159–73; Bérard, *La colonisation grecque de l'Italie méridionale et de la Sicile dans l'antiquité* (²1957); *L'expansion et la colonisation grecques jusqu'aux Guerres médiques* (1960); Borger, 'Die Aussprache des Gottesnamens Ninurta' Or 30 (1961), p. 203: on x, 8 f. Nimrod; Culican, 'Aspects of Phoenician Settlement in the West-Mediterranean' Abr-Nahrain 1 (1961), pp. 36–55; Dossin, 'Le site de Reḥôbôt-'Ir et de Resen' Muséon 47 (1934), pp. 107–21: on x, 11 f.; Elderkin, *Migration in the Mycenaean Age* (1963); Février, 'Alashia – Élise' JA 248 (1960), p. 259: on x, 4 Elis; Garbini, 'L'espansione fenicia nel Mediterraneo' Cultura e scuola 7 (1963), pp. 92–7; Gibson, 'Observations on Some Important Ethnic Terms in the Pentateuch' JNESt 20 (1961), pp. 217–38; Goetze, 'The Linguistic Continuity of Anatolia as shown by its Proper Names' JCSt 8 (1954), pp. 74–81; 'Cilicians' JCSt 16 (1962), pp. 48–58; Grohmann, *Arabien* (Handbuch d. Altertumswissenschaft Abt. III, 1963); Hauschild, 'Die indogermanischen Völker und die Sprachen Kleinasiens' FuF 37 (1963), pp. 111–13; Jehasse, 'Les fouilles d'Alésia' CRAI (1962), pp. 363–79; Junker, 'Die Zerstreuung der Völker nach der biblischen Urgeschichte' Trierer ThZ 70 (1961), pp. 182–5; Labat, *Elam c. 1600–1200 B.C.* (CAH Rev. Ed. 16, 1963); Mayani, *The Etruscans Begin to Speak* (1963); Mertens, 'Les Peuples de la Mer' Chronique d'Égypte 35 (1960), pp. 65–88; Otten, 'Neue Quellen zum Ausklang des Hethitischen Reiches' MDOG 94 (1963), pp. 1–23; Pesce, *Sardegna punica* (1961); Rathjens, 'Die alten Welthandelsstrassen und die Offenbarungsreligionen' Oriens 15 (1962), pp. 115–29; Rowe, 'A History of Ancient Cyrenaica' Suppl. aux Ann. du Serv. des Ant. de l'Égypte 12 (1948), pp. 3–50; Schachermeyr, 'Das Keftiu-Problem und die Frage des ersten Auftretens einer griechischen Herrenschicht im minoischen Kreta' Jahresbericht des Österreichischen Archäologischen Instituts in Wien, Vol. XLV (Hauptblatt 1960), pp. 44–68; Wagner, *Die Stammtafel des Menschengeschlechtes nach der babylonisch-biblischen Ur-Überlieferung dargestellt und ethnographisch gedeutet* (²1947); Wainwright, 'The Teresh, the Etruscans and Asia Minor' AnSt 9 (1959), pp. 197–213.

p. 25, n. 31, Boecker, 'Erwägungen zum Amt des Mazkir' ThZ 17 (1961), pp. 212–16.

p. 25, n. 32, Pritchard, 'Excavating a Biblical Site in Jordan: Joshua's and Solomon's Zarethan Identified' ILN 244 (1964), pp. 487–90: on I Kings iv, 12.

§ 4d. LAWS

Hentschke, *Satzung und Setzender. Ein Beitrag zur israelitischen Rechtsterminologie* (BWANT 5, F.3, 1963); Kupiczewski, 'In memoriam Jacob J. Rabinowitz' The Journal of Juristic Papyrology = Rocznik papirologii prawniczej 13 (1961), pp. 29–32; Rabinowitz, 'Neo-Babylonian Legal Documents and Jewish Law' *ib.*, pp. 131–75; Sikkema, *De Lening in het OuT* (Diss. jur. Leiden, 1957).

p. 27, n. 36, Fensham, 'The Possibility of the Presence of Casuistic Law Material at the Making of the Covenant at Sinai' PEQ 93 (1961), pp. 143–6; Kilian, 'Apodiktisches und kasuistisches Recht im Licht ägyptischer Analogien' BZ 7 (1963), pp. 185–202.

p. 27, n. 37, Nober, 'Nota ad "Codicem Ur-Nammu" ' VD 31 (1953), pp. 65–9; 32 (1954), p. 257, n. 26.

p. 27, n. 38, Borger, 'Kleinigkeiten zur Textkritik des Kodex Ḫammurapi' Or 31 (1962), pp. 364–6; Bracker, *Das Gesetz Israels verglichen mit den altorientalischen Gesetzen der Babylonier, der Hethiter und der Assyrer* (1962); Gonzalo Maeso 'La législación mosaica y el Código de Hammurabi' Cult Bíbl 20 (1963), pp. 89–108; Haase, *Die keilschriftlichen Rechtssammlungen in deutscher Übersetzung* (1963); Rivkah Harris, 'The *nadītu* Laws of the Code of Hammurapi in Praxis' Or 30 (1961), pp. 163–9; Klíma, 'Le droit élamite au IIème millénaire av. n. è. et sa position envers le droit babylonien' ArOr 31 (1963), pp. 287–309; Korošec, 'Le Code de Ḫammurabi et les droits antérieurs' RIDA 8 (1961), pp. 11–27; Leemans, *Legal and Administrative Documents of the Time of Ḫammurabi and Samsuilana* (SLB 1, 3, 1960); Szlechter, 'Le colonat partiaire à Suse et le Code de Hammurapi' RA 55 (1961), pp. 113–34; Wiseman, 'The Laws of Hammurabi again' JSSt 7 (1962), pp. 161–72; Yaron, 'Forms in the Laws of Eshnunna' RIDA 9 (1962), pp. 137–53; 'Matrimonial Mishaps at Eshnunna' JSSt 8 (1963), pp. 1–16.

p. 28, n. 40, Cavaignac, 'Notes sur deux articles du Code Hittite (§ 163, 162)' RHA 13 (1955), pp. 35–7; Friedrich, 'Zum letzten Satze der zweiten Tafel der hethitischen Gesetze' RHA 18 (1960), pp. 33–5; Güterbock, 'Further Notes on the Hittite Laws' JCSt 16 (1962), pp. 17–23; Haase, 'Zur Systematik der zweiten Tafel der hethitischen Gesetze' RIDA 7 (1960), pp. 51–4; 'Zu den hethitischen Gesetzen' ZA 54 (1961), pp. 100–4; 'Über Noxalhaftung in der hethitischen Rechtssammlung' ArOr 29 (1961), pp. 419–21; 'Regelt § 9 der hethitischen Rechtssammlung eine leichte Leibesverletzung?' BiOr 19 (1962), pp. 114–16; 'Über neue Vorschläge zur Erklärung der hethitischen Formel *parnaššeia šuuaizzi*' BiOr 19 (1962), pp. 117–22; Annelies Kammenhuber, 'Zur Textüberlieferung der II. Tafel der hethitischen Gesetze' BiOr 18 (1961), pp. 124–7; Korošec, 'Le droit hittite parmi les droits cuneiformes' XXV ICO Vol. I (1962), pp. 282–90; 'Les lois Hittites et leur évolution' RA 57 (1963), pp. 121–44; 'L'évolution du chatiment d'homicide dans le droit hittite' [Serbian, French sum.] Zbornik Pravnog Fakulteta u Zagrebu 12 (1962), pp. 241–57, 257–9; Petschow, 'Zur Noxalhaftung im hethitischen Recht' ZA 55 (1962), pp. 237–50; Riemschneider, 'Zu den Körperverletzungen im hethitischen Recht' ArOr 29 (1961), pp. 177–82; Soušek, 'Einige Bemerkungen zum hethitischen Strafrecht' Orientalia Pragensia I (1960), pp. 3–11; 'Einige Bemerkungen zur kritischen Bearbeitung der hethitischen Gesetze' OLZ 56 (1961), cols. 453–68.

p. 28, n. 41, Gevirtz, 'West-Semitic Curses and the Problem of the Origins of Hebrew Law' VT 11 (1961), pp. 137–69.

p. 28, n. 42, Klíma, 'Bibliographisches zum Keilschriftrecht V' The Journal of Juristic Papyrology = Rocznik papirologii prawniczej 13 (1961), pp. 269–90.

p. 29, n. 43, Elena Cassin, 'Nouvelles données sur les relations familiales à Nuzi' RA 57 (1963), pp. 113–19.

§ 4e. CULTIC ORDINANCES

p. 30, n. 44, Loss, 'Olocausto e sacrificio pacifico' Salesianum 24 (1962), pp. 525–33.

p. 31, line 13, Speiser, 'Unrecognized Dedication' IEJ 13 (1963), pp. 69–73: on Num. xviii.

p. 31, n. 47, Caquot, 'Un sacrifice expiatoire à Ras Shamra' RHPhR 42 (1962), pp. 201–211; Février, 'L'évolution des rites sacrificiels à Carthage' Bulletin Archéologique du comité des travaux historiques et scientifiques Années 1959–1960 (1962), pp. 22–7; Fuchs, 'Archäologische Forschungen und Funde in Sardinien' Archäologischer Anzeiger (1963), cols. 278–327, see cols. 312 f.; Pesce, *Sardegna Punica* (1961), pp. 68 ff.; Sznycer, 'Sur l'inscription néopunique "Tripolitaine 27" ' Semitica 12 (1962), pp. 45–50.

p. 31, n. 51, Milgrom, 'The Biblical Diet Laws as an Ethical System' Interpret. 17 (1963), pp. 288–301; Rodinson, 'Quelques idées sur les prohibitions alimentaires chez les Sémites' XXV ICO Vol. I (1962), pp. 362–6.

p. 31, n. 52, Ibn Ḥibbān al-Bustī, *'Al Musnad aṣ-ṣaḥīḥ 'alā t-taqāsīm wa-l-anwā'*, ed. A. M. Šākir, vol. I (1952 ff.); *Mašāhīr'ulamā' al-amṣār*, ed. Fleischhammer (1959); Kister, 'A booth like the booth of Moses . . .: a study of an early *ḥadith*' BSOASt 25 (1962), pp. 150–5; Rendtorff, *Die Gesetze in der Priesterschrift* (FRLANT N.F. 44, ²1963); Wensinck, *Handbook of Early Muhammadan Tradition* (1927 (1960)); Wensinck *et al.*, *Concordance et Indices de la Tradition Musulmane*, I–IV (1932/64).

§ 5a. POETIC NARRATIVES

Anwander, 'Prolegomena zu einer Mythosmonographie' Münchener ThZ 13 (1962), pp. 52–5; Auerbach, *Mimesis: Dargestellte Wirklichkeit in der abendländischen Literatur* (1946); E.T. *Mimesis: the representation of reality in western literature* (1953); Cox, *History and Myth. The World around us and the World within* (1961); Green, 'The Norms of Epic' Comparative Literature XIII (1961), pp. 193–207; Hartlich and Sachs, *Der Ursprung des Mythosbegriffes in der modernen Bibelwissenschaft* (1952); Knevels, 'Wesen und Sinn des Mythos. Untersuchung zur Eliminierung und Existenzialiserung des Mythos' Part I StG 15 (1962), pp. 668–86; Obenauer, *Das Märchen. Dichtung und Deutung* (1959); Perry, 'Fable' StG 12 (1959), pp. 17–37; de Vries, *Forschungsgeschichte der Mythologie* (1961).

Caspari, 'Der Stil des Eingangs der israelitischen Novelle' ZWTh 53 (1911), pp. 218–53; Eissfeldt (FRLANT 36, 1923), I, pp. 56–77 = *Kl. Schr.* I (1962), pp. 84–104; Gibson, 'Light from Mari on the Patriarchs' JSSt 7 (1962), pp. 44–62; Gordon, 'The Patriarchal Narratives' JNESt 13 (1954), pp. 56–9; 'The Mediterranean Factor in the OT' SVT IX (1963), pp. 19–31; 'Hebrew Origins in the Light of Recent Discovery' *Biblical and Other Studies* ed. Altmann (1963), pp. 3–14; 'Newest Frontier in Biblical Studies' Christianity Today 7 (1962/63), pp. 575–80; Jacob, 'Abraham et sa signification pour la foi chrétienne' RHPhR 42 (1962), pp. 148–56; Koole, 'Het litterair genre van Genesis i–iii' GThT 62 (1963), pp. 81–122; Kramer, *Sumerian Mythology* (1961 (²1962); (1961) (cf. § 126 on p. 15, n. 4), pp. 14 f., Nos. 27–35, Pls. LXIV–LXXIX; Parrot, *Abraham et son temps* (CAB 14, 1962); Renckens, *De Godsdienst van Israël* (1962), pp. 51–81: Israëls vaderen; von Rad, 'History and the Patriarchs' ET 72 (1961), pp. 213–16; Seeligmann, 'Aetiological Elements in Biblical Historiography' [Hebr., Engl. summary] Zion 26 (1961), pp. 114–69, I–II; 'Hebräische Erzählung und biblische Geschichtsschreibung' ThZ 18 (1962), pp. 305–25; Strobel, 'Wort Gottes und Mythos im Alten Testament' Catholica 17 (1963), pp. 180–96; Toombs, 'The Formation of the Myth Patterns in the OT' JBR 22 (1961), pp. 108–12; Ullendorff, 'Ugaritic Studies within their Semitic and Eastern Mediterranean Setting' BJRL 46 (1963/64), pp. 236–49; Weiss, 'Einiges über die Bauformen des Erzählens in der Bibel' VT 13 (1963), pp. 456–75; Widengren, 'Early Hebrew Myths and their Interpretation' *Myth, Ritual and Kingship* ed. Hooke (1958), pp. 149–203.

p. 35, n. 1, Banu, 'Le moment Prométhéen du poème Gilgamesh et son rôle dans l'histoire de l'athéisme oriental' Acta Ant. Ac. Sc. Hung. IX (1961), pp. 15–25; Elena Cassin, 'Note sur le "commerce de carrefour" en Mésopotamie ancienne' JESHO 4 (1961), pp. 164–167; Dhorme, 'Un nouveau fragment de l'épopée de Gilgamès' RA 55 (1961), pp. 153–4; Diakonoff, *L'épopée de Gilgamès* [Russian], (1961), on this cf. Lambert, RA 56 (1962), pp. 96 f.; van Dijk, 'I.M. 52; 615: Un songe d'Enkidu' Sumer 14 (1958), pp. 114–21; de Fraine, 'Gilgameš apud Ezechielem?' VD 26 (1948), pp. 49–52; 'De conceptu vitae aeternae in epopaea Gilgameš' VD 27 (1949), pp. 102–11; Frenkian, 'L'épopée de Gilgamesh et les poèmes homériques' Studia et Acta Orientalia Bukarest II (1959), pp. 89–105; Friedrich, 'Zur Einordnung hethitischer Gilgamesch-Fragmente' Or 30 (1961), pp. 90–1; Gurney, 'The Sultantepe Tablets VI: A Letter of Gilgamesh' AnSt 7 (1957), pp. 127–36; Heidel, 'A New Babylonian Gilgamesh Fragment' JNESt 11 (1952), pp. 140–3, Pl. XIV, cf. Gössmann, *Das Era-Epos* (1956); Kramer (cf. § 126 on p. 15, n. 4), p. 11, Nos. 12–14, Pls. XXVII–XLII: Gilgameš; Lambert, 'The Fifth Tablet of the Era Epic' Iraq 24 (1962), pp. 119–25, Pl. XXXVI; Matouš, 'Zur neueren Literatur über das Gilgames-Epos' BiOr 21 (1964), pp. 3–9; Nötscher, 'Die Gilgamesch-Dichtung' Augustinianum 1 (1961), pp. 120–3; Nougayrol, 'Nouveaux textes de Ras-Shamra' CRAI (1960), pp. 163–71, cf. 170–1: Text 22. 421 Fragment des Gilgameš-Epos; Sandars, *The Epic of Gilgamesh* (1960); Schurr, 'Das Gilgamesch-Epos' Theologie der Gegenwart 5 (1962), pp. 173–5; Shaffer, *Sumerian Sources of Tablet XII of the Epic of Gilgameš* (Diss. Dept. of Oriental Studies, University of Pennsylvania, 1962).

p. 35, n. 2, Inez Bernhardt and Kramer, 'Enki und die Weltordnung' WZ Jena 6 (1959/60), pp. 231–56, 18 Pls.; Brandon, 'The Propaganda Factor in Some Ancient Near Eastern Cosmogonies' *Essays Hooke* (1963), pp. 20–35; *Creation Legends of the Ancient Near East* (1963); Kramer, 'Sumerian Literature: A General Survey' *Essays Albright* (1961), pp. 249–266; (1961) (cf. § 126 on p. 15, n. 4), p. 9, No. 1, Pls. I–XI: Enki und die Weltordnung; 'Die Suche nach dem Paradies. Dilmun und die Indus-Zivilisation' WZ Halle 12 (1963), pp. 311–17; Landsberger and Wilson, 'The Fifth Tablet of *Enuma Eliš*' JNESt 20 (1961), pp. 154–79; Matouš, 'Zur Datierung von Enūma eliš' ArOr 29 (1961), pp. 30–4; Meier, 'Ein neues Bruchstück des babylonischen Schöpfungsmythus' AfO 20 (1963), p. 82; Speiser, 'Mesopotamian Motifs in the Early Chapters of Genesis' Expedition Vol. V, No. 1 (1962), pp. 18–19, 43; Weiser, 'Die biblische Geschichte vom Paradies und Sündenfall' Deutsche Theologie (1937), pp. 9–37 = *Glaube und Geschichte im AT* (1961), pp. 228–57; Wohlstein, 'Der Gott Anu in den Urzeitmythen' RStOr 36 (1961), pp. 159–83.

p. 36, n. 3, Classen, 'Anaximander' Hermes 90 (1962), pp. 159–72; Herrmann, 'Die Naturlehre des Schöpfungsberichtes. Erwägungen zur Vorgeschichte von Genesis i' ThLZ 86 (1961), cols. 413–24; Schwabl, 'Die griechischen Theogonien und der Orient' in *Éléments orientaux dans la religion grecque ancienne* (1960), pp. 39–56; 'Weltschöpfung' RE Suppl IX (1962), cols. 1433–1582; Young, 'The Days of Genesis ii' WThJ 25 (1963), pp. 143–72.

p. 36, n. 8, Cooke, 'The Sons of (the) God(s)' ZAW 76 (1964), pp. 22–47.

p. 37, n. 14, Herrmann, *Phèdre et ses fables* (1950); Swoboda, 'De Phaedro Aesopi Aemulatore' Eos 52 (1962), pp. 323–36.

p. 37, n. 15, Civil, 'The Home of the Fish. A New Sumerian Literary Composition' Iraq 23 (1961), pp. 154–75; Ebeling, 'Fabel' RLA III, 1 (1957), pp. 1–2; Gordon, 'Animals as represented in the Sumerian proverbs and fables, a preliminary study' *Drewnij Mir [Ancient World]. Festschr. Struwe* (1962), pp. 226–49; Nougayrol, 'Une fable hittite' RHA 18 (1961), pp. 117–19.

p. 38, n. 17, Rost, 'Die Tierkapellen von Tell Halaf' Theologia Viatorum IX (1964), pp. 175–80.

p. 38, n. 19, Montet, *Das alte Ägypten und die Bibel* (1960), pp. 20–32 *et pass.*

p. 38, n. 24, Childs, 'A Study on the Formula "Until this Day" ' JBL 82 (1963), pp. 279–292; Eissfeldt, ' "Gut Glück!" in semitischer Namengebung' JBL 82 (1963), pp. 195–200; Key, 'The Giving of Proper Names in the Old Testament' JBL 83 (1964), pp. 55–9; Lohfink, 'Genesis ii f. als "Geschichtliche Ätiologie" ' Scholastik. Vierteljahrschrift für Theologie und Philosophie 38 (1963), pp. 321–34; Moran, 'The Hebrew Language in its Northwest Semitic Background' *Essays Albright* (1961), pp. 54–72, cf. p. 62 on Naphtali.

p. 40, n. 30, de Vine, 'The Sin of Onan, Gen. xxxviii, 8–10' CBQ 4 (1942), pp. 323–40.

p. 40, n. 31, Brongers, *De Jozefgeschiedenis bij Joden, Christenen en Mohammedanen* (1962); Rowe, 'The Famous Solar-City of On' PEQ 94 (1962), pp. 133–48, Pls. XXIX–XXX.

p. 42, line 29, Ilona Oppelt, 'Das Grab des Riesen Goliath (mit einer Kartenskizze)' JbAC 3 (1960), pp. 17–23: on I Sam. xvii.

p. 42, line 10 from end, Schreiber, 'Samson uprooting a Tree' JQR 50 (1959/60), pp. 176–80; 'Further Parallels to the Figure of Samson the Tree-Uprooter' JQR 52 (1961/62), pp. 35–40.

p. 43, line 8, Lindblom, 'Theophanies in Holy Places in Hebrew Religion' HUCA 32 (1961), pp. 23–52.

p. 43, line 22, Delorme, 'À propos du songe de Jacob' *Mémorial Gelin* (1961), pp. 47–54.

p. 43, n. 37, Keller, 'Die Wallfahrt von Sichem nach Bethel' Kirchenbl. f. d. ref. Schweiz 111 (1955), pp. 163–5.

p. 44, line 4 from end, Hoenig, 'Circumcision: The Covenant of Abraham' JQR 53 (1952/53), pp. 322–34.

p. 44, n. 39, Scheiber, 'Ihr sollt kein Bein dran zerbrechen' VT 13 (1963), pp. 95–7: on Exod. xii, 46, Num. ix, 12, Jub. xlix, 13.

p. 46, line 5, Caquot, 'Aḥiyya de Silo et Jéroboam Ier' Semitica 11 (1961), pp. 17–27: on I Kings xi, 29–39, xiv, 1–18.

§ 5b. HISTORICAL NARRATIVES

Adinol, 'Storiografia biblica et storiografia classica' Riv Bibl 9 (1961), pp. 42–58; Barr, 'Revelation through History in the OT and in Modern Theology' Interpretation 17 (1963), pp. 192–205; Bernhardt, 'Elemente mythischen Stils in der at. lichen Geschichtsdarstellung' WZ Rostock 12 (1963), pp. 295–7; Curtis, 'A Suggested Interpretation of the Biblical Philosophy of History' HUCA 34 (1963), pp. 115–23; Dihle, *Studien zur griechischen Biographie* (AAG 3. F. 37, 1956); Erbse, 'Zur Geschichtsbetrachtung des Thukydides' Antike und Abendland X (1961), pp. 19–34; Feldmann, 'Biblical Motives and Sources' JNESt 34 (1963), pp. 73–103; Guthrie, *God and History in the OT* (1960); Haag, *Homer, Ugarit und das Alte Testament* (Bibl. Beiträge N.F.2, 1962); Hempel, *Geschichten und Geschichte im Alten Testament bis zur persischen Zeit* (1964); Helene Homeyer, 'Zu den Anfängen der griechischen Biographie' Philologus 106 (1962), pp. 75–85; Honecker, 'Zum Verständnis der Geschichte in Gerhard von Rads Theologie des Alten Testaments' EvTh 23 (1963), pp. 143–68; Jacoby, *Abhandlungen zur griechischen Geschichtsschreibung*, ed. by Bloch (1956); Maly, 'The Nature of Biblical History' The Bible Today 1 (1962/63), pp. 276–85; Meister, 'Motive und Formen der römischen Geschichtsschreibung' Das Altertum 10 (1964), pp. 13–26; Merkelbach (§ 126 on p. 507, n. 4); Moore, 'Die Eigenart der hebräischen Geschichtsschreibung im alttestamentlichen Zeitalter' 28. Bericht der Lehranstalt für die Wissenschaft des Judentums (1910), pp. 65–74; Mowinckel, 'Israelite Historiography' ASTI 2 (1963), pp. 4–26; Pannenberg, 'Kerygma und Geschichte' Festschr. von Rad (1961), pp. 129–40; Pannenberg, Rendtorff, Wilckens, *Offenbarung als Geschichte* (KuD, 1. Beiheft, 1961); Rendtorff, 'Geschichte und Überlieferung' Festschr. von Rad (1961), pp. 81–94; 'Geschichte und Wort im AT' EvTh 22 (1962), pp. 621–49; Ridderbos, 'Het Oude Testament en de Geschiedenis' GThT 57 (1957), pp. 112–20; 58 (1958), pp. 1–9; Schwartz, 'Über das Verhältnis der Hellenen zur Geschichte' Logos 9 (1920), pp. 171–87 = Ges. Schr. I (1938), pp. 47–66; 'Geschichtsschreibung und Geschichte bei den Hellenen' Die Antike 4 (1928), pp. 14–30 = Ges. Schr. I (1938), pp. 67–87; *Griechische Geschichtsschreiber* (1957); Seeligmann (cf. § 126 on § 5a); 'Menschliches Heldentum und göttliche Hilfe. Die doppelte Kausalität im alttestamentlichen Geschichtsdenken' ThZ 19 (1963), pp. 385–411; Soggin, 'Atliche Glaubenszeugnisse und geschichtliche Wirklichkeit' ThZ 17 (1961), pp. 385–98; Wright, 'Cult and History. A Study of a Current Problem in OT Interpretation' Interpr. 16 (1962), pp. 3–20.

p. 48, n. 47, Wilson, 'The Assembly of a Phoenician City' JNESt 4 (1945), p. 245: on Wen-Amon II, 70–1.

p. 48, n. 48, Laessøe, *The Shemsharā Tablets. A Preliminary Report* (1959); on this cf. Falkenstein, ZA 54 (1961), pp. 286–8.

p. 50, line 16, Crown, 'A Reinterpretation of Judges ix in the Light of its Humour' Abr-Nahrain 3 (1961/62), pp. 90–8.

p. 50, n. 56, Edzard, 'Neue Inschriften zur Geschichte von Ur III unter Susūen' AfO 19

(1959/60), pp. 1–32, Pls. I–IV; Goetze, 'Hittite and Anatolian Studies' *Essays Albright* (1961), pp. 316–27; Kramer (1961) (§ 126 on p. 15, n. 4), pp. 14f., Nos. 27–35, Pls. LXIV–LXXIX: Historiographische Texte; van Proosdij, 'De opbouw der geschiedschrijving van Voor-Azië' JEOL 15 (1957/58), pp. 177–83; Kraus, 'Alt-babylonische Quellensammlungen zur altmesopotamischen Geschichte' AfO 20 (1963), pp. 153–5; Lambert, 'A New Fragment of the King of Battle' AfO 20 (1963), pp. 1–82; Otten, 'Aitiologische Erzählung von der Überquerung des Taurus' ZA 55 (1962), pp. 156–8; Weidner, 'Assyrische Epen über die Kassiten-Kämpfe' AfO 20 (1963), pp. 113–16, Pl. V.

p. 51, n. 57, Borger, *Die Inschriften Asarhaddons, Königs von Assyrien* (AfO Beih. 9, 1956); Edzard, 'Eine Inschrift des Kudurmabuk von Larsa aus Nippur' AfO 20 (1963), pp. 159–61; Grayson, 'The Walters Art Gallery Sennacherib Inscription' AfO 20 (1963), pp. 83–96, Pls. I–IV; Hallo, 'The Royal Inscriptions of Ur: a Typology' HUCA 33 (1962), pp. 1–43; Hirsch, 'Die Inschriften der Könige von Agade' AfO 20 (1963), pp. 1–82; Hulin, 'Another Esarhaddon Cylinder from Nimrud' Iraq 24 (1962), pp. 116–18; Nougayrol, 'Notes Épigraphiques' Syria 39 (1962), pp. 188–92, see pp. 190–2: Fragment de stèle d'Asarhaddon (?) provenant du Ghâb.

p. 51, n. 59, Ahlström, 'Die Königsideologie in Israel. Ein Diskussionsbeitrag' ThZ 18 (1962), pp. 205–10; Amsler, *Roi et Messie. La tradition davidique dans l'Ancien Testament* (Cahiers Théologiques 49, 1963); Coppens, 'L'espérance messianique. Ses origines et son développement' RSR 37 (1963), pp. 113–49; Frankfort, *Kingship and the Gods* (4th Impr. 1962); Gross, *Weltherrschaft als religiöse Idee im Alten Testament* (BBB 6, 1953); Harrelson, 'Nonroyal Motifs in the Royal Eschatology' *Essays Muilenburg* (1962), pp. 147–65; Kline, 'Divine Kingship—and Genesis vi, 1–4' WThJ 24 (1962), pp. 187–104; Lohse, 'Der König aus Davids Geschlecht. Bemerkungen zur messianischen Erwartung der Synagoge' *Festschr. Otto Michel* (1963), pp. 337–45; Malamat, 'Kingship and Council in Israel and Sumer: A Parallel' JNESt 22 (1963), pp. 247–53; Massaux et al., *La Venue du Messie. Messianisme et Eschatologie* (1962); Michel and Betz, 'Von Gott gezeugt' BZNW 26 (1960), pp. 3–23; Morgenstern, 'The King-God among the Western Semites and the Meaning of Epiphanes' VT 10 (1960), pp. 138–97; Soggin, 'Regalità divina in Ugarit ed in Israele' Protestantesimo 17 (1962), pp. 85–9; Thornton, 'Charismatic Kingship in Israel and Judah' JThSt 14 (1963), pp. 1–11; Wallis, 'Die Anfänge des Königtums in Israel' WZ Halle 12 (1963), pp. 239–47; Whybray, 'Some Historical Limitations of Hebrew Kingship' ChQR 163 (1961/62), pp. 136–50; Zeitlin, 'The Origin of the Idea of the Messiah' *Essays Silver* (1963), pp. 447–59.

p. 52, n. 61, Allam and Morenz, 'Warum hieß Sesostris Sesostris?' FuF 36 (1962), pp. 8–9, cf. 9; Barns, *The Ashmolean Ostracon of Sinuhe* (1952); Caminos, *The Chronicle of Prince Osorkon* (An. Or. 37, 1958); on this cf. Leclant, Orientalia 30 (1961), pp. 407–15; Fecht, 'Der Moskauer "literarische Brief" als historisches Dokument' ZÄS 87 (1962), pp. 12–31; Grapow, *Der stilistische Bau der Geschichte des Sinuhe* (VIOF 10, 1952); Kees, 'Zu der Annaleninschrift des Hohenpriesters Osorkon vom 11. Jahre Takeloths II' MIOF 2 (1954), pp. 353–62; Wessetzky, 'Sinuhe's Flucht' ZÄS 90 (1963), pp. 124–7.

p. 52, n. 64, Altheim and Stiehl, 'New Fragments of Greek Philosophers' East and West, N.S. 12 (1961), pp. 3–18, cf. pp. 10–12; Grelot, 'Les proverbes araméens d'Aḥiqar' RB 68 (1961), pp. 178–94.

p. 54, n. 67, Newman, 'The Prophetic Call of Samuel' *Essays Muilenburg* (1962), pp. 86–97: on I Sam. iii, 1–iv, 1a, etc.; Richter, 'Traum und Traumdeutung im AT. Ihre Form und Verwendung' BZ 7 (1963), pp. 202–20.

§ 6. THE LOGICAL AND METRICAL STRUCTURE OF HEBREW POETRY

Alonso-Schökel, 'Quid scimus hodie de rhythmo poetico hebraico?' VD 40 (1962), pp. 109–22; *Estudios de Poetica Hebrea* (1963); Altheim and Stiehl, *Die Araber in der Alten Welt* (1964), pp. 608–22: Äthiopische Verskunst (comments on two books by Anton Schall); Blenkinsopp, 'Stylistics of Old Testament Poetry' Bibl 44 (1963), pp. 352–8: on Alonso-Schökel (1963); Boling, ' "Synonymous" Parallelism in the Psalms' JSSt 5 (1960), pp. 221–255; Fecht, 'Mitteilung über Untersuchungen zur altägyptischen Metrik' XXV ICO Vol. I

(1962), pp. 161–6; Fück, 'Bemerkungen zur altarabischen Metrik' ZDMG 111 (1962), pp. 464–9; Gevirtz, *Patterns in the Early Poetry of Israel* (Studies in Ancient Oriental Civilization 32, 1963); Melamed, 'Break-up in Biblical Poetry' Scripta Hieros. VIII (1961), pp. 115–53; Schall, *Zur äthiopischen Verskunst* (1961); Weil, *Grundri und System der altarabischen Metren* (1958).

The following comments are from Ernst Vogt (dated 24th October 1961) on § 6, and in particular with reference to the assessment there of Ley's *Grundzügen* (1875) and his *Leitfaden* (1887):

'(1) Above all, it appears to me that the real significance of Ley has not been brought out. Rather than express my own opinions, I cite those of other scholars. Briggs, *The Book of Psalms* I (1907), p. xxxix: "To Ley, more than to any other scholar, is due the credit of leading to a correct conception of the measures of Hebrew poetry." Similarly T. H. Robinson in ZAW 54 (1936), pp. 37 f., and in *Bertholet-Festschrift* (1950,) p. 450; likewise Segert in Archiv Or. (1953), p. 502.

'(2) On p. 61 Ley is described as "the originator of the theory which reckoned with an anapaestic rhythm". It is true that Ley frequently stresses that the Hebrew language possesses an ascending accentuation, but he never makes the anapaest into a metrical principle. I thought that I had read the word anapaest in Ley, but in spite of repeated searching I cannot find it, and I now believe that Ley never used it. It was Sievers who first introduced the anapaest as a metrical principle, and this in explicit contrast to Ley, and he calls Ley's "verse foot" which is the word itself as it is naturally constructed together with its accent, an "accumulation of syllables whose form and length is of no significance for the rhythm" (I, p. 85). Ley fully anticipated this charge, in *Grundzüge* (p. 22), and in *Leitfaden* (pp. 8 f.): the example of Deut. xxxii, 1, in *Grundzüge* (p. 131) may further be compared here. It appears to me that Sievers, in spite of other merits in his works, contributed nothing to metrical studies by his introduction of the anapaest. The same is further true of Mowinckel's iambics. If I read Ps. cxxxvii, 1–3, following Mowinckel's scansion, it horrifies me, for there is no poetry left in it. How differently the rhythm of the same verses grips the reader if they are read following Ley's principles and the words are given their natural structure: *'al-nahᵃrót Babél, šam-yašábnu gambakínu bᵉẓokrenu et-Siyyon*. The poet has deliberately chosen long rhythmic units and depicts the long, sad hours of the exiles. I think that we should go back much more to Ley, even though not all his pioneer work is to be accepted.

'(3) On p. 61: Ley in *Grundzüge* (1875), pp. 52 f., does describe the lines 3 + 2 as "elegiac pentameters"; but in *Leitfaden* (1887), p. 16, he avoids this expression, and presumably deliberately. He uses the more satisfactory phrase: "The Pentameter is used predominantly in the elegies"; the line is of course deliberately used also in other compositions.

'(4) Up to the present, of Hebrew statements concerning metrics we know only Ecclus. xliv, 5 (*'al ḥoq*), xlvii, 9 (*tiqqen*), and Eccles. xii, 9 f. (*'iẓẓen, tiqqen mᵉšalim* as an expression for the metrical balance of the lines; cf. Akkad. *mašâlu* 'be equal', *mišlu* 'half'; Arab., Aram., Ethiop. *mšl*. 'compare, be like'). It would now be interesting—in reference to p. 57—to compare IQH I, 28–9, where the metre is probably explicitly mentioned: *wattášem dᵉbarím 'al-qáu, umabbaʿ rûaḥ šᵉfatáyim* bᵉmiddá, *wattoṣéʿ* qauwim. . . . In view of the parallel *in mensura, qau* here appears actually to mean "line, verse".'

p. 58, n. 4, Albright, 'The Role of the Canaanites in the History of Civilisation' *Essays Albright* (1961), pp. 328–62, cf. pp. 339 f.

p. 59, n. 10, de Liagre Böhl, 'De Tocht van de Godin Isjtar naar het Dodenrijk' JEOL 15 (1957/58), pp. 154–259.

p. 64, n. 15, Enciso Viana, 'El Salmo ix–x' Est Bíbl 19 (1960), pp. 201–14.

p. 64, n. 16, Bauer, 'Ps. cxix, 105a, als Lämpcheninschrift?' ZAW 74 (1962), p. 324; Houston Smith, 'The Household Lamps of Palestine in Old Testament Times' BA 27 (1964), pp. 1–31, see p. 11: on Ps. cxix, 105; BA 27 (1964), pp. 101–24 (to be concluded).

§ 7. SAYINGS OF VARIOUS KINDS

p. 65, line 10, Lehming, 'Zur Erzählung von der Geburt der Jakobssöhne' VT 13 (1963), pp. 74–81: on Gen. xxix, 31–xxx, 24.

p. 67, line 16, Dahood, 'Two Textual Notes on Jeremia' CBQ 23 (1961), pp. 462–4: on xiii, 18, xxii, 18.

p. 67, line 4 from end, Gradwohl, 'Zum Verständnis von Ex. xvii, 15 f.' VT 12 (1962), pp. 491–4.

p. 67, n. 9, Grønbæk, 'Juda og "den Hellige Krig" ' DTT 25 (1962), pp. 82–97.

p. 68, n. 10, Seebass, 'Zu Num. x, 33 f.' VT 14 (1964), pp. 111–13.

§ 8. LEGAL SAYINGS

Boecker, *Redeformen des Rechtslebens im Alten Testament* (WMANT 14, 1963); Cazelles, 'Ex. xxxiv, 21, traite-t-il du Sabbat?' CBQ 23 (1961), pp. 223–6; Dus, 'Das zweite Gebot. Zum Sieg der heiligen Lade über das Schnitzbild in Bethel' CV 4 (1961), pp. 37–50; Ettisch, 'Die monotheistische Symbolik der Bundestafeln' VT 14 (1964), pp. 211–15; Gerstenberger, *Wessen und Herkunft des sog. apodiktischen Rechtes im AT* (Diss. theol. Bonn, 1961); Gordon, 'A Note on the Tenth Commandment' JBR 31 (1963), pp. 208–9; Guttmann, 'The "Second Commandment" and the Image in Judaism' HUCA 32 (1961) pp. 161–78; Heinemann, *Untersuchungen zum apodiktischen Recht* (Diss. theol. Hamburg, 1958); Horst, *Kahle-Festschr.* (1935), pp. 19–28 = *Gottes Recht* (1961), pp. 167–75; 'Das Eigentum nach dem AT' Kirche im Volk, Heft 2 (1949), pp. 87–102 = *Gottes Recht* (1961), pp. 203–21; 'Naturrecht und AT' EvTh 10 (1950/51), pp. 253–73 = *Gottes Recht* (1961), pp. 235–59; 'Recht und Religion im Bereich des AT' EvTh 16 (1956), pp. 49–75 = *Gottes Recht* (1961), pp. 260–91; EvTh 17 (1957), pp. 366–84 = *Gottes Recht* (1961), pp. 292–314; Jonsen, 'The Decalogue: Command and Presence' Thought 38 (1963), pp. 421–46; Kremers 'Die Stellung des Elterngebotes im Dekalog' EvTh 21 (1961), pp. 145–61; Kruyswijk, '*Geen gesneden beeld*' (Ac. Proefschr. Vrije Un. Amsterdam, 1962); Lohfink, 'Das Hauptgebot im Alten Testament' Geist und Leben 36 (1963), pp. 270–81; Neuenschwander, 'Das sechste Gebot' SThU 31 (1961), pp. 89–103; Otten, 'Die Eidesleistung des Ašḫapala' RHA 18 (1960), pp. 121–7; von Rad, *Moses* (1960); Renaud, *Je suis un Dieu jaloux. Évolution sémantique et signification théologique de qin'ah* (Lectio divina 36, 1963); Graf Reventlow, *Gebot und Predigt im Dekalog* (1962); 'Kultisches Recht im Alten Testament' ZThK 60 (1963), pp. 267–304; Rowley, 'Mose und der Monotheismus' ZAW 69 (1957), pp. 1–21 = 'Moses and Monotheism' *From Moses to Qumran* (1963), pp. 35–63; BJRL 34 (1951/52), pp. 81–118 = *Men of God* (1963), pp. 1–36; Scholder, 'Was heißt: Du sollst den Feiertag heiligen?' EvTh 21 (1961), pp. 284–9; Stamm, *Le Décalogue à la lumière des recherches contemporaines* (1959); 'Dreißig Jahre Dekalogforschung' ThR 27 (1961), pp. 189–239, 281–305; *Der Dekalog im Lichte der neueren Forschung* (²1961); Watts, 'Infinitive Absolute as Imperative and the Interpretation of Exodus xx, 8' ZAW 74 (1962), pp. 141–5; Zimmerli, *Bertholet-Festschr.* (1950), pp. 550–63 = *Ges. Aufs.* (1963), pp. 234–50.

p. 70, line 16, Krebs, 'Zur kultischen Kohabitation mit Tieren im Alten Orient' FuF 37 (1963), pp. 19–21: on Exod. xxii, 8 etc.

p. 70, n. 1, Barreca, 'Su alcune epigrafi puniche di Nora' Acc. Naz. dei Lincei, Rend. mor. (1961), pp. 298–305, Pls. I–II; Février, 'Le rite de substitution dans les textes de N'Gaous' JA 250 (1962), pp. 1–10; Reyniers, 'Notes sur le sanctuaire punique d'El Hofra' Recueil des notices et mémoires de la Société Archéologique, Historique et Géographique de Constantine Vol. LXX (1957-58-59), pp. 119–23; Schaeffer, *Ugaritica* IV (1962), pp. 77–83; de Vaux (§ 126 on p. 145, n. 1), pp. 49–81: Sacrifices humains en Israël; E.T., pp. 63–90.

p. 70, n. 3, Kosmala, 'The so-called *Ritual Decalogue*' ASTI 1 (1962), pp. 31–61: on Exod. xxxiv, 5–26*; Torralba, 'Decálogo ritual, Ex. xxxiv, 10–26' Est Bibl 20 (1961), pp. 407–21.

§ 9. CULTIC SAYINGS

van Ass, *Skuldbelydenis en genadverkondiging in die OuT* (1961); Brichto, *The Problem of 'Curse' in the Hebrew Bible* (JBL Mon. xiii, 1963); Fensham, 'Malediction and Benediction in Ancient Near Eastern Vassal Treaties and the OT' ZAW 74 (1962), pp. 1–9; Hempel, ZDMG 79 (1925), pp. 20–110 = BZAW 81 (1961), pp. 30–113; Horst, 'Segen und Segenshandlungen in der Bibel' EvTh 7 (1947/48), pp. 23 7 = *Gottes Recht* (1961), pp. 188–202;

Lambert, 'The Babylonian *tamītu* Texts' XXV ICO Vol. I (1962), pp. 205–6; Lindblom, •Lot-casting in the OT' VT 12 (1962), pp. 164–78.

p. 72, line 22, Kraft, 'A Note on the Oracle of Rebecca (Gen. xxv, 23)' JThSt 13 (1962), pp. 318–20.

p. 72, n. 1, Schenke, 'Orakelwesen im alten Ägypten' Das Altertum 9 (1963), pp. 67–77; Struwe, 'Die Frage der Existenz eines Pfeilorakels in Sumer' XXV ICO Vol. I (1962), pp. 178–86.

p. 72, n. 2, Zimmerli, *Alt-Festschr.* (1953), pp. 179–209 = *Ges. Aufs.* (1963), pp. 311–40; Buss, 'The Language of the Divine "I" ' JBR 29 (1961), pp. 102–7.

p. 73, n. 3, Dentan, 'The Literary Affinities of Exodus xxxiv, 6 f.' VT 13 (1963), pp. 34–51.

p. 74, line 15, Dahood, 'A Note on Psalm xv, 4 (xiv, 4)' CBQ 16 (1954), p. 302; Koch, 'Tempeleinlaßliturgien und Dekalog' *Festschr. von Rad* (1961), pp. 45–60: on Ps. xv, Deut. xxvi, Ps. xxiv, 3–6, etc.; Koole, 'Psalm xv—eine königliche Einzugsliturgie?' OTS 13 (1963), pp. 98–111.

p. 76, n. 6, Dekkers, 'Des ordalies en droit romain' RIDA Année 2, Tome 2 (1949), pp. 55–78; Dossin, 'Un cas d'ordalie par le dieu fleuve d'après une lettre de Mari' *Studia et Documenta ad iura Orientis Antiqui pertinentia* II (1939), pp. 112–18; 'L'ordalie à Mari' CRAI (1958), pp. 387–92; Montet, 'À propos des ordalies suméro-hittites et préhelléniques' RArch 1961, tome III (1961), pp. 1–4; Picard, 'Ordalies suméro-hittites et préhelléniques' RHA 18 (1960), pp. 129–42.

p. 76, n. 7, Bowman, 'Arameans, Aramaic and the Bible' JNESt 7 (1948), pp. 65–90; Brekelmans, 'Het "historische Credo" van Israël' Tijdschrift voor theologie 3 (1963), pp. 1–11; Dupont-Sommer, *Les Araméens* (1949); 'Sur les débuts de l'histoire araméenne' SVT I (1953), pp. 40–9; Koopmans, 'De Literatuur over het Aramees na 1940' JEOL 15 (1957/ 1958), pp. 125–32.

§ 10. PROPHETIC SAYINGS

Alonso-Schökel, 'Genera litteraria prophetica (Ad librum recentem Cl. Westermann)' VD 39 (1961), pp. 185–92; Baumgärtel, 'Die Formel *nᵉᵘ um jahwe*' ZAW 73 (1961), pp. 277–90; Fensham, 'Common Trends in Curses of the Near Eastern Treaties and Kudurru-Inscriptions Compared with Maledictions of Amos and Isaiah' ZAW 75 (1963), pp. 155–75; Gerstenberger, 'The Woe-Oracles of the Prophets' JBL 81 (1962), pp. 249–63; Gibson, 'Life and Society at Mari and in Old Israel' Transact. Glasgow Or. Soc. 18 (1959/60), pp. 15–29, cf. pp. 23–7; Harvey, 'Le "Rîb-Pattern", réquisitoire prophétique sur la rupture de l'alliance' Bibl 43 (1962), pp. 172–96; Hempel, 'Jahwegleichnisse der israelitischen Propheten' ZAW 42 (1924), pp. 74–104 = BZAW 81 (1961), pp. 1–29; 'Prophet and Poet' JThSt 40 (1939), pp. 113–32 = 'Prophet und Dichter' BZAW 81 (1961), pp. 287–307; Hertzberg, ThLZ 75 (1952), cols. 219–26 = *Beiträge* (1962), pp. 81–90; Johnson, *The Cultic Prophet in Ancient Israel* (²1962); Lindblom, 'Die Vorstellung vom Sprechen Jahwes zu den Menschen im AT' ZAW 75 (1963), pp. 263–88; Núñez, *Profetas, sacerdotes y reyes en el antiguo Israel. Problemas de adaptión del Yahvismo en Canaan* (1962); Eva Osswald, *Falsche Prophetie im AT* (SGV 237, 1962); Rendtorff, 'Erwägungen zur Frühgeschichte des Prophetentums in Israel' ZThK 59 (1962), pp. 145–67; Ridderbos (1955) = *Exegetica* II, 1; Rowley, JSSt 1 (1956), pp. 338–60 = *From Moses to Qumran* (1963), pp. 111–38; von Waldow, *Der traditionsgeschichtliche Hintergrund der prophetischen Gerichtsreden* (BZAW 85, 1963); Westermann, *Grundformen prophetischer Rede* (Beitr. EvTh 31, 1960); Würthwein, 'Kultpolemik oder Kultbescheid? Beobachtungen zu dem Thema "Prophetie und Kult" ' *Weiser-Festschr.* (1963), pp. 115–31; Zimmerli (1954) = *Ges. Aufs.* (1963), pp. 41–119; *Mél. Bibl. Robert* (1957), pp. 154–64 = *Ges. Aufs.* pp. 120–32.

§ 11. PROVERB, RIDDLE AND WISDOM SAYINGS

de Boer, 'The Counsellor' SVT III (1955), pp. 42–71; Browne, *The Wisdom of Israel. An Anthology* (³1945); Cazelles, 'Les débuts de la sagesse en Israël' SPOA (1963), pp. 27–40;

Forman, 'The Context of Biblical Wisdom' Hibbert Journal 60 (1962), pp. 125–32; Gaster, 'Samaritan Proverbs' *Studies Neuman* (1962), pp. 228–42; Gemser, 'The Spiritual Structure of Biblical Aphoristic Wisdom. A Review of Recent Standpoints and Theories' Homiletica en Biblica 21 (1962), pp. 3–10; Harrington, 'The Wisdom of Israel' Irish ThQ 30 (1963), pp. 311–25; van Imschoot, 'Sagesse et l'Esprit dans l'AT' RB 47 (1938), pp. 23–49; Montgomery, 'Wisdom as Gift. The Wisdom Concept in Relation to Biblical Messianism' Interpret. 16 (1962), pp. 43–57; Murphy, 'The Concept of Wisdom Literature' *Gruenthaner Mem. Vol.* (1962), pp. 46–54; 'Where is the Wise Man?' The Bible Today 1 (1962), pp. 30–7; Nádor, 'Über einen Aphorismentyp und seine antiken Vorläufer' Das Altertum 8 (1962), pp. 8–12; Paterson, *The Wisdom of Israel* (1960); Ziegler, *Chokma, Sophia, Sapientia* (Würzburger Universitätsreden 32, 1961); Zimmerli, 'Ort und Grenze der Weisheit im Rahmen der alttestamentlichen Theologie' SPOA (1963), pp. 121–37.

p. 83, n. 2, Schaeffer, 'Nouvelles Découvertes à Ras Shamra-Ugarit' CRAI (1962), pp. 232–6, see p. 236: Textes litteraires, "Sagesses" ou maximes, sous forme de conseils d'un père à son fils.

p. 83, n. 3, Sumero-akkadian Wisdom: Castellino, 'Nota a un proverbio accadico' RStOr 37 (1962), pp. 49 f.; *Sapienza babilonese* (1962); Couturier, 'Sagesse Babylonienne et Sagesse Israélite' Sciences Ecclésiastiques 14 (1962), pp. 293–309; Gemser, BiOr 19 (1962), pp. 151–3: on Gordon (1960); Kramer (§ 126 on p. 15, n. 4), pp. 18 f. Nos. 45–52, Pls. CI–CVIII: Sprichwörter; 'Literary Texts from Ur VI, Part II' Iraq 25 (1963), pp. 171–6: Wisdom Compositions; Lambert, 'Celibacy in the World's Oldest Proverb' BASOR 169 (1963), pp. 63 f.; Nougayrol, 'Nouveaux textes accadiens de Ras-Shamra' CRAI (1960), pp. 163–71, cf. pp. 169–80: Text 22. 439 Sayings and Counsels; 'Les Sagesses babyloniennes: Études récentes et textes inédits' SPOA (1963), pp. 41–51, see pp. 47–51: Wisdom Texts from Ugarit; Yvonne Rosengarten, 'Le nom et la fonction de "sage" dans les pratiques religieux de Sumer et d'Akkad' RHR 162 (1962), pp. 133–46.

Egyptian Widsom: Barucq, 'Une veine de spiritualité sacerdotale et sapientielle dans l'Égypte ancienne' *Mémorial Gelin* (1961), pp. 193–202; Bleeker, 'L'idée de l'ordre cosmique dans l'ancienne Égypte' RHPhR 42 (1962), pp. 193–200; Brunner, 'Eine neue Entlehnung aus der Lehre des Djedefhor' *Kees-Festschrift* (1956)=MDAI Kairo 14 (1956), pp. 17–19; 'Der "Gottesvater" als Erzieher des Kronprinzen' ZÄS 86 (1961), pp. 90–100, Pl. III; 'Ptaḥḥotep bei den koptischen Mönchen' ZÄS 86 (1961), pp. 145–7; 'Der freie Wille Gottes in der ägyptischen Weisheit' SPOA (1963), pp. 103–20; *Die Lehre des Cheti, Sohnes des Duauf* (Ägyptologische Forschungen Bd. 13, 1963); Capart, 'Une sagesse démotique d'après le livre récent d'Aksel Volten' Bull. Ac. Belg (1942), pp. 50–83; Daumas, 'La naissance de l'humanisme dans la littérature de l'Égypte ancienne' Oriens Antiquus 1 (1962), pp. 155–84; Gardiner, *Hieratic Papyri in the British Museum. Third Series. Chester Beatty Gift* (1935); Kees, 'Zu den Lebensregeln des Amonspriesters Nebneteru (Kairo Cat. 42225)' ZÄS 88 (1962), pp. 24–6; Leclant, 'Documents nouveaux et points de vue récents sur les Sagesses de l'Égypte Ancienne' SPOA (1963), pp. 5–26; Montet, 'Des fruits défendus et la confession des péchés' SPOA (1963), pp. 53–62; Morenz, Ägyptologische Beiträge zur Erforschung der Weisheitsliteratur Israels' SPOA (1963), pp. 63–71; Pirenne, 'La morale dans l'Égypte antique'. Ac. Belg. 5e Série, Tome XLVIII (1962), pp. 112–29; Posener and Sainte Fare Garnot, 'Sur une Sagesse Égyptienne de base époque (Papyrus Brooklyn nos. 47, 218, 135)' SPOA (1963), pp. 153–7; Posener, 'Sur un papyrus didactique inédit de basse époque conservé en Musée de Brooklyn' XXV ICO Vol. I (1962), pp. 116–7; Théodoridès, 'La "Satire des Métiers" et les marchands' AIPhHOS XV ([1958/59], 1960), pp. 39–69; Vergote, 'La notion de Dieu dans les livres de sagesse égyptiens' SPOA (1963), pp. 159–90; Volten, 'Der Begriff der Maat in den ägyptischen Weisheitstexten' SPOA (1963), pp. 73–101; *Studien zum Weisheitsbuch des Anii* (Danske Vid. Selskab. XXIII, 3, 1938); *Kopenhagener Texte zum demotischen Weisheitsbuch* (Analecta Aegyptiaca I, 1940); *Das demotische Weisheitsbuch. Studien und Bearbeitung* (Analecta Aegyptiaca II, 1941); 'Die moralischen Lehren des demotischen Pap. Louvre 2414' *Studi Ippolito Rosellini*, Vol. II (1955), pp. 269–80, 2 Pls.; Walcot, 'Hesiod and the Instructions of Onchsheshonqy' JNESt 21 (1962), pp. 215–19; 'Hesiod and the Didactic Literature of the

Near East' REG 75 (1962), pp. 13–36; van de Walle, 'Problèmes relatifs aux méthodes d'enseignement dans l'Égypte ancienne' SPOA (1963), pp. 191–207.

p. 84, n. 4, Altheim and Stiehl, 'New Fragments of Greek Philosophers' East and West N.S. Vol. 12 (1961), pp. 3–18, cf. pp. 10–12.

p. 85, n. 7, Porter, 'Samson's Riddle: Judges xiv, 18' JThSt 13 (1962), pp. 106–9.

p. 85, n. 8, Roth, 'The Numerical Sequence x/x + 1 in the OT' VT 12 (1962), pp. 300–11 Sauer (§ 126 on p. 475, n. 16).

p. 87, n. 12, Franz Altheim and Ruth Stiehl, 'Neue Fragmente Fenons von Kition aus dem Arabischen' FuF 36 (1962), pp. 12–14; Audet, 'La Sagesse de Ménandre l'Égyptien' RB 59 (1952), pp. 55–81; Gorler, *Menandrou gnomai* (1963); Kraemer, 'Arabische Homerverse' ZDMG 106 (1956), pp. 259–316; Riessler, *Altjüdisches Schrifttum außerhalb der Bibel* (1928), pp. 1047–57, 1328 f.; Ullmann, *Die arabische Überlieferung der sogenannten Menandersentenzen* (AKM 34, 1, 1961); Widengren, 'The Status of the Jews in the Sassanian Empire' Iranica Antiqua 1 (1961), pp. 117–62.

§ 12. SONGS OF WORK AND HARVEST, DRINKING SONGS, SONGS OF MARRIAGE AND LOVE, WATCHMAN'S SONGS

Hatto, 'Das Tagelied in der Weltliteratur' Deutsche Vierteljahrsschrift für Literaturwissenschaft und Geistesgeschichte 36 (1962), pp. 489–506.

p. 88, n. 2, Koenig, 'Sourciers, Thaumaturges et Scribes' RHR 164 (1963), pp. 17–38, 165–80.

p. 89, line 4 from end, on סְמָדַר S. of Sol. ii, 13, 15, vii, 13, cf. Yadin, *Haẓor II* (1960), pp. 73 f., Pl. XCV, 4.

p. 90, line 25. According to Ezek. iii, 17, xxxiii, 7, Ezekiel knew himself to have been appointed by Yahweh as a צֹפֶה *watchman* (A note from Ackroyd).

§ 13. MOCKING SONGS AND FUNERAL DIRGES

Kramer, *Two Elegies on a Pushkin Museum Tablet. A New Sumerian Literary Genre* (1960).

p. 95, line 28, Guillaume, 'The Meaning of כדמה in Ezek. xxvii, 32' JThSt 13 (1962), pp. 324 f. Lit. p. 96, n. 7; § 126 on p. 378, nn. 29, 30.

§ 14. ROYAL SONGS AND VICTORY SONGS

p. 99, n. 3, Kutsch, *Salbung als Rechtsakt im AT und im Alten Orient* (BZAW 87, 1963), pp. 63–5; Tournay, 'Les affinités du Ps. xlv avec le Cantique des Cantiques et leur interprétation messianique' SVT IX (1963), pp. 168–212.

p. 100, line 7 from end, On זֶה סִינַי in v. 5, cf. Moran, 'The Hebrew Language in its Northwest Semitic Background' *Essays Albright* (1961), pp. 54–72, cf. p. 61.

p. 100, n. 4, Blenkinsopp, 'Ballad Style and Psalm Style in the Song of Deborah' Bibl 42 (1961), pp. 61–71; Haupt, 'Die Schlacht von Taanach' BZAW 27 (1914), pp. 191–245; Nielsen, 'La Guerre considérée comme une religion et la Religion comme une guerre. Du chant de Débora au Rouleau de la guerre de Qoumran' StTh 15 (1961), pp. 93–112; Schreiner (§ 126 on p. 703, n. 7); Seale, 'Deborah's Ode and the Ancient Arabian Qasida' JBL 81 (1962), pp. 343–7; Speier, 'On צדקת פרזנו, Judg. v, 11' JBL 82 (1963), p. 216.

§ 15. CULTIC SONGS

Barucq, *L'expression de la Louange divine et de la Prière dans la Bible et en Égypte* (Institut français d'archéologie orientale. Bibliothèque d'étude Tome XXXIII, 1962); Dus, 'Die altisraelitische amphiktyonische Poesie' ZAW 75 (1963), pp. 45–54; Mowinckel, 'Bemerkinger til salmenen i den norske bibeloversettelse' NTT 63 (1962), pp. 129–270; Wallert, *Die Psalmen im Alten Ägypten* (Münchener Ägyptol. Studien 1, 1962); Wolff, 'Der Aufruf zur Volksklage' ZAW 76 (1964), pp. 48–56.

p. 102, n. 1, Crim, *The Royal Psalms* (1962).

p. 103, line 15, Kaiser, 'Erwägungen zu Psalm ci' ZAW 74 (1962), pp. 195–205.

p. 103, n. 4, Schilling, ' ". . . wider Gott und seinen Gesalbten". Davidssohn—Gottessohn—Heilsbringer. Auslegung von Ps. ii' Bibel und Leben 2 (1961), pp. 261–77.

p. 103, n. 5, Beek, 'De exegetische moelijkheden van Psalm cx' Vox Theol. 15 (1944), pp. 94–6; Krinetzki, 'Psalm cx (cix). Eine Untersuchung seines dichterischen Stils' ThGl 51 (1961), pp. 110–21; Linton, 'The trial of Jesus and the Interpretation of Psalm cx' NTSt 7 (1960/61), pp. 258–62; Nober, 'De torrente in via bibet' VD 26 (1948), pp. 351–3; Schedl, 'Aus dem Bache am Wege' ZAW 73 (1961), pp. 290–7; Vis, 'Is Ps. cx een Messiaanse Psalm?' Vox Theol. 15 (1944), pp. 91–3.

p. 103, n. 6, Moriarty, 'Reges Tharsis et insularum' VD 26 (1948), pp. 172–6; Pautrel, 'Le style de cour et le Psaume lxxii' *Mémorial Gelin* (1961), pp. 157–64.

p. 104, n. 8, Falkenstein, 'Sumerische religiöse Texte' ZA 49 (1950), pp. 80–150; 50 (1952), pp. 61–91; 52 (1957), pp. 58–75, 2 Pls.; 55 (1962), pp. 11–67; Kraus, 'De babylonisch-assyrische poëzie' Forum de Letteren III, No. 4 Leiden (1962), pp. 198–216; Lambert (1961) (§ 126 on p. 15, n. 4), pp. 191–6.

p. 105, n. 10, Ullendorff (§ 126 on § 5b), pp. 238–42.

p. 106, n. 11, Holzmeister, 'Tria Cantica N.T.' VD 26 (1948), pp. 356–64.

p. 106, n. 12, Flusser, 'Sanktus und Gloria' *Festschr. Michel* (1963), pp. 129–52.

p. 106, n. 14, Driver, 'The Resurrection of Marine and Terrestrial Creatures' JSSt 7 (1962), pp. 12–22; Kruse, 'Archetypus Psalmi civ' VD 29 (1951), pp. 31–43; Lanczkowski, 'Eine jüdische Ausstrahlung altägyptischer Glaubensformen. Bemerkungen zur Religion der Kaffitscho' Saeculum 12 (1961), pp. 131–9.

p. 107, n. 16, Kremer, 'Kommet, lasset uns jauchzen dem Herrn! Anregungen zur Meditation über Psalm xcv (xciv)' Bibel und Leben 3 (1962), pp. 131–7.

p. 109, n. 22, Grill, 'Der Berg Salmon Ps. lxviii, 15' ThZ 17 (1961), pp. 432–4; Guillaume, 'A Note on Psalm lxviii, 5' JThSt 13 (1962), pp. 322 f.

p. 109, n. 23, viii, xix, xxix Deissler, 'Zur Datierung und Situierung der "kosmischen" Hymnen Pss. viii, xix, xxix' *Junker-Festschr.* (1961), pp. 47–58; viii Cazelles, 'Note sur le Psaume viii' *Hommage à Mgr. Weber* (1962), pp. 79–91; Hempel, 'Mensch und König. Studie zu Psalm viii und Hiob' FuF 35 (1961), pp. 119–23; xix Eisler, 'Jahves Hochzeit mit der Sonne. Ein Neumonds- und Hüttenfestlied Davids aus dem salomonischen Buch der Lieder (Zu Psalm xix, 2–7 und I Kön. viii, 12 f. [53 LXX])' MVAG 22 (1917), pp. 21–70; Budde, 'Psalm xix, 2–7, "Jahves Hochzeit mit der Sonne?"' OLZ 22 (1919), cols. 257–66; Eisler, 'Nochmals zum neunzehnten Psalm' JSOR 11 (1927), pp. 21–46; xix Szekeres, 'Is Psalm xix een natuurpsalm?' Veritatem in caritate (1962), pp. 47–64; xxix Cazelles, 'Une relecture du psaume xxix' *Mémorial Gelin* (1961), pp. 119–28; Pax, 'Studien zur Theologie von Psalm xxix' BZ 6 (1962), pp. 93–100; Ridderbos, 'Enkele aspecten van Psalm xxix' GThT 60 (1960), pp. 64–9; Rivera, 'Anotationes al Salmo xxix' Rev Bibl 23 (1961), pp. 9–14; Werner Schmidt, *Königtum Gottes in Ugarit und Israel* (BZAW 80, 1961), pp. 46–9; xlvi Junker, 'Der Strom, dessen Arme die Stadt Gottes erfreuen (Ps. xlvi, 5)' Bibl 43 (1962), pp. 197–201; Krinetzki, 'Der anthologische Stil des xlvi. Psalms und seine Bedeutung für die Datierungsfrage' Münchener ThZ 12 (1961), pp. 52–71; ' "Jahwe ist uns Zuflucht und Wehr." Eine stilitisch-theologische Auslegung von Psalm xlvi (xlv)' Bibel und Leben 3 (1962), pp. 26–42; Kruse, 'Fluminis impetus laetificat Civitatem Dei' VD 27 (1949), pp. 23–7; Weiss, 'Wege der neuen Dichtungswissenschaft in ihrer Anwendung auf die Psalmenforschung (Methodologische Bemerkungen, dargelegt am Beispiel von Ps. xlvi)' Bibl 42 (1961), pp. 255–302; lxv Wiesmann, 'Zu Ps. lxv (lxiv), v. 10–14' BZ 23 (1935/36), pp. 242–3; lxvii Jefferson, 'The Date of Psalm lxvii' VT 12 (1962), pp. 201–5; lxxvi Montagnini, 'Illuminans tu mirabiliter a montibus aeternis' VD 40 (1962), pp. 258–63; lxxxvii Schmuttermayr, 'Um Psalm lxxxvii (lxxxvi), 5' BZ 7 (1963), pp. 104–10.

p. 110, line 18, Fichtner, 'Jes lii, 7–10, in der christlichen Verkündigung' *Rudolph-Festschr.* (1961), pp. 51–66.

p. 110, n. 24, Kapelrud, 'Nochmals *Jahwä mālāk*' VT 13 (1963), pp. 229–31; Lipiński, 'Yāhweh mâlāk' Bibl 44 (1963), pp. 405–60.

p. 110, n. 29, Eissfeldt, ZAW 46 (1928), pp. 81–105 =*Kl. Schr.* I (1962), pp. 172–93.

p. 111, n. 32, Gonzalez, 'Le Psaume lxxxii' VT 13 (1963), pp. 293–309.

p. 111, n. 33, Jefferson, 'Psalm lxxvii' VT 13 (1963), pp. 87–91.

p. 112, line 8 from end, Köbert, 'Ibn at-Taiyib's Erklärung von Psalm xliv' Bibl 43 (1962), pp. 338–48.

p. 112, n. 34, Emerton, 'Notes on Three Passages in Psalms Book III' JThSt 14 (1963), pp. 374–81, see pp. 374–7: I. Ps. lxxiv, 5; pp. 377–80: II. Ps. lxxiv, 11.

p. 112, n. 35, Glombitza, 'Betende Bewältigung der Gottesleugnung. Versuch einer existentialen Interpretation der drei Psalmen lxxix, xciv, cxxxvii' NThT 14 (1960), pp. 329–49.

p. 112, n. 36, Eissfeldt, 'Ps. lxxx und Ps. lxxxix' WdO III, 1 (1963), pp. 27–31.

p. 112, n. 37, Dequeker, 'Les *qedôšîm* du Ps. lxxxix à la lumière des croyances sémitiques' EThL 39 (1963), pp. 469–84; Eissfeldt, 'Ps. lxxx und Ps. lxxxix' WdO III, 1 (1963), pp. 27–31; Mowan, 'Quatuor Montes Sacri in Ps. lxxxix, 13?' VD 41 (1963), pp. 11–20; Nötscher, 'Zum emphatischen Lamed' VT 3 (1953), pp. 372–80, cf. p. 379: Ps. lxxxix 19 . . .: "Denn fürwahr Jahwe (ליהוה) ist unser Schild und der Heilige Israels וְלִקְדוֹשׁ unser König" ; Sarna, 'Ps. lxxxix: A Study in Inner Biblical Exegesis' *Biblical and Other Studies* ed. Altmann (1963), pp. 29–46; Ward, 'The Literary Form and Liturgical Background of Psalm lxxxix' VT 11 (1961), pp. 321–39; van der Woude, 'Zwei alte cruces im Psalter: Ps. xxxii, 6 und Ps. lxxxix, 20' OTS 13 (1963), pp. 130–6.

p. 115, n. 44, iii, vi Botterweck, 'Klage und Zuversicht der Bedrängten, Auslegung der Psalmen iii und vi' Bibel und Leben 3 (1962), pp. 184–93; v Krinetzki, 'Psalm v. Eine Untersuchung seiner dichterischen Struktur und seines theologischen Gehaltes' ThQ 142 (1962), pp. 23–46; vi Coppens, 'Les psaumes vi et xli dépendent-ils du livre de Jérémie?' HUCA 32 (1961), pp. 217–26; xvii Schedl, ' "Die Pfade des Rechtsbrechers" *'orḥôt pārîṣ* (Ps. xvii, 4)' BZ 6 (1962), pp. 100–2; xxii Frost, 'Psalm xxii: An Exposition' Canadian JTh 8 (1962), pp. 102–15; Magne, 'Le texte du Psaume xxii et sa restitution sur deux colonnes' Semitica 11 (1961), pp. 29–41; Martin-Achard, 'Remarques sur le Psaume xxii' Verbum Caro 65 (1963), pp. 78–87; Nober, 'Notae philologicae' VD 39 (1961), pp. 109–13; (a) Me-alu (pp. 109–10), (b) *Yᵉhud* (Aram.) =Jerusalem? (pp. 110–11), (c) Ps.xxii, 30 'vernae Inferorum' (?) (pp. 111–13); xxvi Snijders, 'Psaume xxvi et l'innocence' OTS 13 (1963), pp. 112–30; Vogt, 'Psalm xxvi, ein Pilgergebet' Bibl 43 (1962), pp. 328–37; xxviii Rabinowitz, 'The Alleged Orphism of 11 Q Ps. xxviii, 3–12' ZAW 76 (1964), pp. 193–200; xxxv Winton Thomas, 'Psalm xxxv, 15 f.' JThSt 12 (1961), pp. 50 f.; xlii + xliii Amstutz, 'Unser Gottesdienst' SThU 31 (1961), pp. 225–42; Bauer, 'Ad Deum qui laetificat iuventutem meam' VD 40 (1962), pp. 184–9: on Ps. xliii, 4, etc.; li Beaucamp, 'Justice divine et pardon' *Mémorial Gelin* (1961), pp. 129–44; Bonnard, 'Le vocabulaire du miserere' *Mémorial Gelin* (1961), pp. 145–56; Botterweck, 'Sei mir gnädig, Jahwe, nach deiner Güte' Bibel und Leben 2 (1961), pp. 136–42; Dalglish, *Psalm Fifty-One in the Light of Ancient Near Eastern Patternism* (1962); lxi, lxii, lxiii Asensio, 'Teologia bíblica de un triptico: Salmos lxi, lxii y lxiii' Est Bíbl 21 (1962), pp. 111–25; lxix Vogt, ' "Ihr Tisch werde zur Falle" (Ps. lxix, 23)' Bibl 43 (1962), pp. 79–82; cix Guillaume, 'A Note on Psalm cix, 10' JThSt 14 (1963), pp. 92–3; Kaddary, 'חלל ='bore', 'pierce'. Note on Ps. cix, 22' VT 13 (1963), pp. 486–9; cxxvi Cazelles, 'L'expression hébraïque *šubʰ šebʰ ut* viendrait-elle de l'accadien d'Assarhaddon?' GLECS 9 (1960/63), pp. 57–60: on Ps. cxxvi, 1, etc.; Babylonian-Assyrian Laments: Castellino, 'Urnammu, three Religious Texts' ZA 52 (1957), pp. 1–57, 2 Pls.; 53 (1959), pp. 106–32.

p. 120, line 10 from end, Pascual, 'Dos notas al Salterio' Est Ecl 34 (1960), pp. 645–55, Pl. XXIX–XXX [Hermon mons].

p. 120, n. 54, Boehmer, 'Der Reichtum von Psalm xxiii (Vulg. xxii)' BZ 23 (1935/36), pp. 166–70; Müller, 'Der gute Hirte' ZÄS 86 (1961), pp. 126–44; Winton Thomas, 'צַלְמָוֶת in the OT' JSSt 7 (1962), pp. 191–200: on xxiii, 4.

p. 120, n. 56, Asensio (§ 126 on p. 115, n. 44).

p. 123, line 7, Krinetzki, 'Ps. xxx (xxix) in stilistisch-exegetischer Betrachtung' ZKTh 83 (1961), pp. 345–60.

p. 123, line 15, van der Woude, 'Zwei alte cruces im Psalter: Ps. xxxii, 6 und lxxxix, 20' OTS 13 (1963), pp. 131–6.

p. 123, line 4 from end, Koch, 'Denn seine Güte währet ewiglich' EvTh 21 (1961), pp. 531–44.

p. 123, n. 69, Carmignac and Guilbert, *Les Textes de Qumrân* I, (1961), pp. 127–80; Maier, *Die Texte vom Toten Meer* (1960), I, pp. 71–122; II, pp. 63–110.

§ 16. WISDOM POEMS

Murphy, 'A Consideration of the Classification "Wisdom Psalms"' SVT IX (1963), pp. 153–64.

p. 124, n. 2, Houston Smith (§ 126 on p. 64, n. 16), p. 7: on Prov. xxxi, 18.

p. 124, n. 3, Keller, 'Les "Béatitudes" de l'AT' *Hommage à W. Vischer* (1960), pp. 88–100.

p. 125, n. 4, Arbez, 'A Study of Psalm i' CBQ 7 (1945), pp. 398–404.

p. 125, n. 6, van der Ploeg, 'Notes sur le Psaume xlix' OTS 13 (1963), pp. 137–72.

p. 125, n. 7, Schilling, 'Leidensfrage und Gottesgemeinschaft' Bibel und Leben 2 (1961), pp. 25–39.

p. 125, n. 8, Emerton, 'Notes on three Passages in Psalms Book III' JThSt 14 (1963), pp. 374–81, see p. 381: III. Psalm lxxviii, 41 and the Syriac Verb '*br* 'to be angry'; Liebreich, 'The Liturgical Use of Psalm lxxviii, 38' *Studies Neuman* (1962), pp. 365–74; Rothstein, 'Psalm lxxviii ein Zeuge für die jahwistische Gestalt der Exodustradition und seine Abfassungszeit' ZWTh 43 (1900), pp. 532–85; Schildenberger, 'Psalm lxxviii (lxxvii) und die Pentateuchquellen' *Junker-Festschr.* (1961), pp. 231–56.

p. 125, n. 11, Pascual (§126 on p. 120, line 10 from end).

p. 125, n. 12, Baumgärtel and Westermann, ' " Lehre uns bedenken, daß wir sterben müssen " ' MPTh 50 (1961), pp. 425–39.

p. 125, n. 13, Scriba, 'Via dolorosa. Zur theologischen Auslegung des cxxxix. Psalms' *Mitzenheim-Festschr.* (1961), pp. 50–9.

p. 126, n. 14, Braumann, 'Zum traditionsgeschichtlichen Problem der Seligpreisungen Mt. v, 3–12' NT 4 (1960), pp. 253–60.

§ 18. THE HISTORICAL BOOKS

Eissfeldt, ThBl 6 (1927), cols. 333–7 = *Kl. Schr.* I (1962), pp. 123–49; Nübel, *Davids Aufstieg in der Frühe israelitischer Geschichtsschreibung* (Diss. theol. Bonn 1959, 1959).

p. 135, n. 6, Albright, 'A Trial Excavation in the Mound of Bethel' BASOR 29 (1928), pp. 9–11; Jamme and van Beek, 'The South-Arabian Clay Stamp from Bethel Again' BASOR 163 (1961), pp. 15–18; Kelso, 'The Fourth Campaign at Bethel' BASOR 164 (1962), pp. 5–19; 'Béthel' RB 69 (1962), pp. 254 f.; Weippert, 'Archäologischer Jahresbericht' ZDPV 79 (1963), pp. 164–79, see pp. 170–1: *bētīn*.

p. 136, n. 9, Aharoni, 'The Land of Gerar' [Hebr., Engl. summary] Eretz-Israel 3 (1954), pp. 108–11, V, Pl. 5, Fig. 5: Gerar = Tell Abu Hureirah; Albright, 'Abram the Hebrew' BASOR 163 (1961), pp. 36–54, cf. p. 48: Gerar = Tell Abu Hureirah; Alt, 'Beiträge zur historischen Geographie und Topographie des Negeb' JPOS 11 (1931), pp. 204–21; 12 (1932), pp. 126–41; 15 (1935), pp. 294–324; 17 (1937), pp. 218–35; 18 (1938), pp. 149–60 = *Kl. Schr.* III (1959), pp. 382–472: Gerar = Tell eš-šerī'a.

p. 138, line 3, Gordon, 'David the Dancer' *Kaufmann Jub. Vol.* (1960), pp. 46–9: on II Sam. vi.

p. 138, line 15, Donner, 'Der "Freund des Königs"' ZAW 73 (1961), pp. 269–77: on II Sam. xv, 37, xvi, 16 f., I Chron. xxvii, 33, I Kings iv, 5.

p. 138, n. 12, O'Ceallaigh, 'And *so* David did to *all the cities* of Ammon' VT 12 (1962), pp. 179–89.

p. 138, line 22, Garbini, 'Osservazioni linguistiche a I Sam. cap. i–iii' Bi e Or 5 (1963), pp. 47–52.

p. 141, lines 10–12, Driver, 'Plurima mortis imago' *Studies and Essays Abraham A. Neuman* (1962), pp. 128–43: on II Sam. xviii, 9–14, xx, 1–13 and on וַיִּשְׁכַּב עָם אֲבוֹתָיו, etc.

p. 141, line 22, Yadin, *Haẓor* II (1960), p. 37, n. 1, on I Kings xv, 20.

§ 19. THE COLLECTIONS (CORPORA) OF LAW

Audet, 'Origines comparées de la double tradition de la loi et de la sagesse dans le Proche-Orient ancien' XXV ICO Vol. I (1962), pp. 352–7; Daube, 'Error and Accident in the Bible' RIDA 2 (1949), pp. 189–213; 'Direct and Indirect Causation in Biblical law' VT 11 (1961), pp. 246–69; Morgenstern, 'The Book of the Covenant. Part IV—The *Miṣwôt*' HUCA 33 (1962), pp. 59–105; Neufeld, '*Ius redemptionis* in Ancient Hebrew Law' RIDA 8 (1961), pp. 29–40; Neufeld, 'Inalienability of Mobile and Immobile. Pledges in the Laws of the Bible' RIDA 9 (1962), pp. 33–44; Preiser, 'Vergeltung und Sühne im altisraelitischen Strafrecht' *Festschr. Eberhard Schmidt* (1961), pp. 7–38; J. M. P. Smith, *The Origin and History of Hebrew Law* (New impression 1960); Zimmerli, ThLZ 85 (1960), cols. 481–98 = *Ges. Aufs.* (1963), pp. 249–76; *Das Gesetz und die Propheten. Zum Verständnis des Alten Testaments* (1963); Zingg, 'Das Schuld- und Vollstreckungsrecht . . . nach Moses' Judaica 16 (1960), pp. 72–90, 156–71, 207–15; 'Das Strafrecht nach den Gesetzen Moses' Judaica 17 (1961), pp. 106–19; 'Israels Privatrecht nach den Gesetzen Moses' Judaica 18 (1962), pp. 129–38.

p. 145, n. 1, Sirad, 'Sacrifices et rites sanglants dans l'Ancien Testament' Sciences ecclésiastiques 15 (1963), pp. 173–97; de Vaux, *Les Sacrifices de l'Ancien Testament* (Cahiers de RB 1, 1964), pp. 28–48: Holocaustes et sacrifices de communion; pp. 82–100: Sacrifices expiatoires; E.T. *Studies in OT Sacrifice* (1964), pp. 27–51, 91–112.

§ 20. THE PROPHETIC AND APOCALYPTIC BOOKS

Haufe, 'Entrückung und eschatologische Funktion im Spätjudentum' ZRGG 13 (1961), pp. 105–33.

p. 151, n. 1, Herrmann, 'Prophetie in Israel und Ägypten. Recht und Grenze eines Vergleichs' SVT IX (1963), pp. 47–65; Lanczkowski, *Altägyptischer Prophetismus* (Ägyptol. Abh. 4. 1960).

p. 151, n. 2, Daumas, 'Littérature prophétique et exégétique égyptienne et commentaires esséniens' *Mémorial Gelin* (1961), pp. 203–22.

p. 152, n. 4, Altheim, 'Das alte Iran' *Propyläen-Weltgeschichte* II (1962), pp. 137–235, cf. pp. 198 f.: Apokalypse; Dodds, 'New Light on the "Chaldaean Oracles"' HThR 54 (1961), pp. 263–73; Eddy, *The King is Dead. Studies in the Near Eastern Resistance to Hellenism 334–31 B.C.* (1961); Kroll, *De oraculis chaldaicis* (1961) (reprint from Breslauer Philol. Abh. VII, 1, 1894); Lewy, *Chaldaean Oracles and Theurgy; Mysticism, Magic and Platonism in the later Roman Empire* (Publications de l'Institut français d'archéologie orientale. Recherches d'archéologie, de philologie et d'histoire. Vol. 13, 1956).

§ 21. THE POETIC AND DIDACTIC BOOKS

Audet (§ 126 on § 19).

p. 152, lines 15–18, Arens, 'Hat der Psalter seinen "Sitz im Leben" in der Synagogalen Lehrordnung des Pentateuch?' OBL IV (1962), pp. 107–31.

p. 153, n. 4, Ferguson and Echols, 'Critical Bibliography of Spoken Arabic Proverb Literature' Journal of American Folklore 65 (1952), pp. 67–84; Goitein, 'The Origin and Historical Significance of the Present-day Arabic Proverb' Islamic Culture 26 (1952), pp. 169–79; Kraemer, 'Arabische Homerverse' ZDMG 106 (1956), pp. 259–316, cf. pp. 302–316; Riessler, *Altjüdisches Schrifttum ausserhalb der Bibel* (1928), pp. 1047–57, 1328 f.; Sellheim, Review in Oriens 13/14 (1960/61), pp. 469–71; 'Eine unbekannte Sprichwörtersammlung des Abū l-Hasan al Baihaqī' Der Islam 39 (1964), pp. 226–32; Ullmann, *Die arabische Überlieferung der sogenannten Menandersentenẓen* (AKM 34, 1, 1961).

§ 22. THE PENTATEUCH: NAME AND CONTENTS

(a) ATD: Noth, Exod. E.T. (1962); Lev. (1962), E.T. (1965); Biblia Comentada: Colunga, Pentateuco (1960); BOuT: de Fraine, Gen. (1963); Vink, Lev. (1962); Drubbel, Num. (1963); Camb.-B: Ryle, Gen. (1914); Driver, Exod. (1911); Chapman, Streane, Lev. (1914); Smith, Deut. (1918); CIB: Steinmann, Gen. (1963); Auzou, Exod. (1963); Steinmann, Deut. (1961); HK: Gunkel, Gen. (⁵1963); Jerusalem-B: de Vaux, Gen. (2nd rev. ed. 1962; ³1963); LBC: Fritsch, Gen. (1960); Napier, Exod. (1962); PBS: McEleney, *Introduction to the Pentateuch* (1960); Hunt, Gen. (1960); Murphy, Exod. (1960); Moriarty, Num. (1960); Glanzman, Deut. (1960); Pismo Święte Starego Testamentu: Łach, Gen. (1962); Sources Bibliques: Buis and Leclercq, *Le Deutéronome* (1963); Torch-B: Herbert, Gen. xii–l (1962).
(b) Goldman, *The Book of Human Destiny. From Slavery to Freedom* (1958): on Exod. i–xx. Emerton, 'Commentaries on Exodus' Theology 66 (1963), pp. 453–6.

p. 156, line 27, Loss, 'La partecipazione dei laici al rito dell'olocausto secondo Lv. i, 3–13' Salesianum 23 (1961), pp. 353–62.

p. 157, line 18 from end, Gispen, 'De gelofte' GThT 61 (1961), pp. 4–13, 37–45, 65–73, 93–107.

p. 157, line 6 from end, Speiser (§ 126 on p. 31, line 13): on Num. xviii, 7.

§ 23. THE PENTATEUCH AS A WHOLE, WITH PARTICULAR REFERENCE TO THE NARRATIVE

Albright, 'Jethro, Hobab and Reuel in Early Hebrew Tradition' CBQ 25 (1963), pp. 1–11; Braun, *The Work of Père Lagrange* (1963); Cazelles, 'Pentateuque' Suppl. Dict. Bible VII (1964), cols. 687–858; Mowinckel, *Tetrateuch, Pentateuch, Hexateuch* (BZAW 90, 1964); Murphy, 'Moses and the Pentateuch' CBQ 11 (1959), pp. 165–78; Naville, 'La composition et les sources de la Genèse' RHR 78 (1918), pp. 1–38; Eva Osswald, *Das Bild des Mose in der kritischen alttestamentlichen Wissenschaft seit Julius Wellhausen* (1963); Porter, *Moses and Monarchy: A Study in the Biblical Tradition of Moses* (1963); Ridderbos, 'Het boek Numeri: Ontstaan en historische betrouwbaarheid. Beschouwingen over de bronnensplitsing' GThT 61 (1961), pp. 141–50; Seebass, *Mose und Aaron, Sinai und Gottesberg* (AETh 2, 1962); Segal, 'The Composition of the Pentateuch—A Fresh Examination' Scripta Hieros. VIII (1961), pp. 68–114; de Vries, 'The Hexateuchal Criticism of Abraham Kuenen' JBL 82 (1963), pp. 31–57.

p. 159, n. 2, Bull, 'A Re-examination of the Shechem Temple' BA 23 (1960), pp. 101, 110–19; 'The Architectural Recording of the Shechem Excavation' BA 23 (1960), pp. 120–6; Campbell, 'Excavations at Shechem 1960' BA 23 (1960), pp. 102–10; Campbell and Ross, 'The Excavation of Shechem and the Biblical Tradition' BA 26 (1963), pp. 2–27; Cross, 'An Inscribed Seal from Balâṭah (Shechem)' BASOR 167 (1962), pp. 14–15; Delcor, 'Vom Sichem der hellenistischen Epoche zum Sychar des NT' ZDPV 78 (1962), pp. 34–48; Horn, 'Scarabs from Shechem' JNESt 21 (1962), pp. 1–14, Pl. I; Jonas, 'A Diadem of the Cult of Kybele from the Neapolis Region (Samaria)' PEQ 94 (1962), pp. 118–28, Pls. XXVII–XXVIII; Sellers, 'Coins of the 1960 Excavation at Shechem' BA 25 (1962), pp. 87–96; Toombs, 'Sichem' RB 70 (1963), pp. 425–33; Toombs and Wright, 'The Third Campaign at Balâṭah (Shechem)' BASOR 161 (1961), pp. 11–54; 'The Fourth Campaign at Balâṭah (Shechem)' BASOR 169 (1963), pp. 1–60; Vilar, 'El Templo de Baal Berit en Siquem' Est Bíbl 21 (1962), pp. 65–7; Wright, 'Archaeological Finds and Strata' BA 25 (1962), pp. 34–40; 'Selected Seals from the Excavations at Balâṭah (Shechem)' BASOR 167 (1962), pp. 5–13; 'From the Hebrew Patriarchs to Alexander the Great and John Hyrcanus: 1600 Years of Shechem and its Pillars of the Covenant' ILN 243 (1963), pp. 204–8; Wright and Toombs, 'Sichem' RB 69 (1962), pp. 257–70.

p. 163, line 22, Bardtke, 'Franz Delitzsch' ThLZ 88 (1963), cols. 161–70.

p. 163, n. 18, Hupfeld, 'W. M. Leberecht de Wette und Hermann Hupfeld. Ein Briefwechsel' NZSTh 5 (1963), pp. 54–96.

p. 164, n. 23, Hupfeld (§ 126 on p. 163, n. 18).

p. 164, n. 29, Caquot, 'L'alliance avec Abram (Genèse xv)' Semitica 12 (1962), pp

51–66; Cazelles, 'Connections et structure de *Gen.* xv' RB 69 (1962), pp. 321–49; Seebass, 'Gen. xv, 2b' ZAW 75 (1963), pp. 317–19; 'Zu Genesis xv' Wort und Dienst 7 (1963), pp. 132–49.

p. 165, n. 31, Perlitt, *Geschichtsphilosophie und historiographische Voraussetzungen für die Darstellung der Religion und Geschichte Israels durch Wilhelm Vatke und Julius Wellhausen* (BZAW 94, 1965); Rendtorff, 'Alttestamentliche Theologie und israelitisch-jüdische Religionsgeschichte' *Festschr. Karl Kupisch* (1963), pp. 208–22, see pp. 217–21.

p. 166, line 2 from end, Jules Halévy, *Recherches Bibliques. L'Histoire des Origines d'après la Genèse. Texte, Traduction et Commentaire.* I. (Genèse i–xxv) (Paris, 1895), dedicated 'À la mémoire d'Auguste Dillmann'; II. (Genèse xxv, 19–l, 26) (Paris, 1901). Halévy regards Genesis, to which the study is restricted, as a unified work compiled at the beginning of the reign of Solomon and making use of older materials. Cf. II, pp. I–II Preface: 'La Genèse est l'œuvre d'une seule école qui, en se servant d'anciennes chroniques ou de notes détachées de quelques cahiers anonymes, a rédigé ce recueil d'après les principes religieux qu'elle voulait populariser sous une forme historique. Et comme la rédaction d'une œuvre si considérable doit répondre à un besoin pressant et suppose en même temps une époque de paix et de prospérité nationale, on voit aussitôt qu'il faut nécessairement s'arrêter au début du règne de Salomon, qui forme l'apogée de la puissance hébraïque. C'est aussi à cette époque, marquée par la centralisation du culte monothéiste à Jérusalem, que la rédaction d'un code rituel pour le nouveau sanctuaire a été une affaire d'actualité urgente. Chez toutes les nations du monde, les codes religieux et rituels se placent à l'aube de leur développement civilisateur. Déroger à cette règle générale pour faire du document A une composition pédantesque de l'époque exilique, où la foi dans le rétablissement de la nationalité et du sanctuaire de Jérusalem s'était éteinte dans la masse populaire (Ézéchiel, xxxvii), n'est-ce pas le plus arbitraire? A cause de la haute importance de cette question, j'ai d'ailleurs cru nécessaire de lui consacrer diverses études supplémentaires, ainsi que des monographies substantielles sur la relation du code sacerdotal avec les écrits prophétiques et le Deutéronome. Enfin, le cadre de ces recherches a été élargi par des considérations sur certains documents de l'ancienne époque littéraire qui jettent une vive lumière sur l'état religieux d'alors. Ces diverses études ont paru successivement dans la *Revue Sémitique* entre 1896 et 1900; la matière s'est tellement accrue que sa réunion en un volume ne me paraît plus pouvoir être retardée' (p. II).

p. 166, n. 43, Cassuto, *A Commentary on the Book of Genesis. Part I: From Adam to Noah. Gen. i–vi,* 8, transl. by Abrahams (1961 (1962)); *The Documentary Hypothesis and the Composition of the Pentateuch,* transl. by Abrahams (1961 (1962)).

p. 169, n. 54, Bruston, 'Les cinq documents de la Loi mosaïque' ZAW 12 (1892), pp. 177–211.

p. 170, line 6 from end, Caquot, 'Remarques sur la fête de la "néoménie" dans l'ancien Israël' RHR 158 (1960/61), pp. 1–18, cf. pp. 4–9: on Ps. lxxxi; Loewenstamm, 'The Bearing of Psalm lxxxi upon the Problem of Exodus' [Hebr., Engl. summary] Eretz-Israel 5 (1958), pp. 80–2, 88*.

§ 24. THE PROBLEM OF DEUTERONOMY

Lohfink, 'Die Bundesurkunde des Königs Josias (Eine Frage an die Deuteronomiumsforschung)' Bibl 44 (1963), pp. 261–88, 461–98; Nicholson, 'The Centralisation of the Cult in Deuteronomy' VT 13 (1963), pp. 380–8; Minette de Tilesse, 'Sections "tu" et sections "vous" dans le Deutéronome' VT 12 (1962), pp. 29–87; Yeivin, 'Die Zeit des Deuteronomiums' [Hebr.] *Studies in the History of Israel and its Country* (1960), pp. 213–35.

p. 175, line 9, Verdam, ' "On ne fera point mourir les enfants pour les pères "en droit biblique' RIDA 3 (1949), pp. 393–416: on xxiv 16.

§ 25. AN ASSESSMENT OF THE DEVELOPMENT OF PENTATEUCHAL CRITICISM

p. 177, n. 1, Evans, 'Synoptic Criticism since Streeter' ET 72 (1960/61), pp. 295–9.

p. 177, n. 2, Cassuto, *The Documentary Hypothesis* (1962), pp. 9–12: Homer and

Pentateuchal criticism; Gordon, 'Newest Frontier in Biblical Studies' Christianity Today 7 (1962/63), pp. 575–80, see pp. 577 f.; Myres, *Homer and his Critics,* ed. by Dorothea Gray (1958); Schadewaldt, *Hellas und Hesperien* (1960), pp. 9–41: Homer.

p. 179, n. 3, Glueck, 'Five Years of Archaeological Exploration in the Negev' Antiquity and Survival II, 2/3 (1957), pp. 273–86, 10 Pls.; 'Archaeological Exploration of the Negev' BASOR 159 (1960), pp. 3–14; 'The Archaeological History of the Negev' HUCA 32 (1961), pp. 11–18; 'Where Political Stability . . . Exploration of the Negev—Part I' ILN 238 (1961), pp. 880–83; 'Prosperity and Recession in the Ancient Negev . . . Exploration of the Negev—Part II' ILN 238 (1961), pp. 934–7; *A Bibliography* (1962); Kapelrud 'Hvem var Abraham?' NTT 64 (1963), pp. 163–74; Speiser, 'The wife-sister motif in the patriarchal narratives' *Biblical and Other Studies* ed. Altmann (1963), pp. 15–28.

§ 26. ANALYSIS OF THE PENTATEUCHAL NARRATIVE: THE ARGUMENTS FOR ANALYSIS

p. 182, n. 2, Dothan, 'Excavations at Horvat Beter (Beersheba)' 'Atiqot I (1959), pp. 1–42, Pls. I–VII; Perrot, 'Les VIe er VIIe campagnes de fouilles a Béersheba' CRAI (1959), pp. 133–40, with a note by Dhorme (pp. 140 f.) on the Horites, Deut. ii, 12.

p. 183, n. 3, Raymond Abba, 'The Divine Name Yahweh' JBL 80 (1961), pp. 320–8; Cross, 'Yahweh and the God of the Patriarchs' HThR 55 (1962), pp. 225–59; Eissfeldt, 'Jahwe, der Gott der Väter' ThLZ 88 (1963), cols. 481–90; 'Jakobs Begegnung mit El und Moses Begegnung mit Jahwe' OLZ 58 (1963), cols. 325–31; Kosmala, 'The Name of God (YHWH and HU')' ASTI 2 (1963), pp. 103–6; Lauterbach, 'Substitutes for the Tetragrammaton' PAAJR 2 (1930/31 [1931]), pp. 39–67; MacLaurin, 'YHWH, the Origin of the Tetragrammaton' VT 12 (1962), pp. 439–63; Mowinckel, 'The Name of the God of Moses' HUCA 32 (1961), pp. 121–33; Vergote, 'Une théorie sur l'origine égyptienne du nom de Yahweh' EThL 39 (1963), pp. 447–52; Walker, 'The Riddle of the Ass's Head and the Question of a Trigram' ZAW 75 (1963), pp. 205–27.

p. 184, line 28, Beirne, 'A Note on Numbers xi, 4' Bibl 44 (1963), pp. 201–3.

p. 186, n. 9, Koenig (§ 126 on p. 88, n. 2).

p. 188, line 15, Driver, 'A Lost Colloquialism in the OT' JThSt 8 (1957), pp. 272 f: on Gen. xviii, 10, 14, I Sam, xxv, 6, II Kings iv, 16, 17; Loretz, 'K't ḥyh—"wie jetzt ums Jahr" Gen. xviii, 10' Bibl 43 (1962), pp. 75–8; Yaron, 'Ka'eth ḥayyah and koh leḥay' VT 12 (1962), pp. 500–1.

p. 188, n. 11, Albright, 'Zur Zähmung des Kamels' ZAW 62 (1950), p. 315; Forbes, *Studies in Ancient Technology* II (1955), pp. 187–208; Gordon, 'Abraham of Ur' *Studies Driver* (1963), pp. 77–84, see p. 83, n. 5; (§ 126 on p. 258, n. 7), pp. 9–10; Klengel, 'Zu einigen Problemen des altvorderasiatischen Nomadentums' ArOr 30 (1962), pp. 585–96; Kuz'mina, 'Die älteste figürliche Darstellung des Kamels aus dem Gebiet von Orenburg und das Problem der Domestikation durch die Baktrier' Sovjetskaja Archeologija (1963), pp. 38–46; Nagel, 'Frühe Tierwelt in Südwestasien' ZA 55 (1963), pp. 169–222, Pls. I–XIV: Kamel; Parrot, *Abraham et son temps* (CAB 14, 1962), p. 88; Pohl, 'Das Kamel in Mesopotamien' Or 19 (1950), pp. 251–3; 'Nochmals das Kamel in Mesopotamien' Or 21 (1925) pp. 373–4; 'Zur Zähmung des Kamels' Or 23 (1954), pp. 453 f.; Walz, 'Zum Problem der Domestikation der altweltlichen Cameliden' ZDMG 101 (1951), pp. 29–51; 'Beiträge zur ältesten Geschichte der altweltlichen Cameliden unter besonderer Berücksichtigung des Problems des Domestikationszeitpunktes' Actes IVe Congr. Anthropologique, Part III (1956) pp. 190–204; de Vaux, 'Les patriarches Hébreux et les découvertes modernes VII–VIII' RB 56 (1949), pp. 5–36, cf. pp. 7–16.

§ 27. ANALYSIS OF THE PENTATEUCHAL NARRATIVE: THE RESULTS

p. 189, line 1, MacLaurin, 'Shaddai' Abr-Nahrain 3 (1961/62, 1963), pp. 99–118; Weippert, 'Erwägungen zur Etymologie des Gottesnamens El Šaddaj' ZDMG 111 (1962), pp. 42–62: on Gen. xvii, 1.

p. 189, line 5, Redford, 'Exodus i, 11' VT 13 (1963), pp. 401–18.

p. 189, line 8, Morgenstern, *The Fire upon the Altar* (1963): on Lev. ix, 24; Gradwohl, 'Das "fremde Feuer" von Nadab und Abihu' ZAW 75 (1963), pp. 288–96: on Lev. x, 1 f., xvi, 1, Num. iii, 4, xxvi, 61; Bertman, 'Tasseled Garments in the Ancient East Mediterranean' BA 24 (1961), pp. 119–28: on Num, xv, 37–41, Deut. xxii, 12; Perath, 'De bewening van Nadab en Abihu' NedThT 16 (1961/62), pp. 47–8.

p. 189, n. 3, Dumermuth, 'Moses strahlendes Gesicht' ThZ 17 (1961), pp. 240–8.

p. 189, n. 4, Lehming, 'Versuch zu Num. xvi' ZAW 74 (1962), pp. 291–321.

p. 189, n. 5, Moran, 'Moses und der Bundesschluß am Sinai' Stimmen der Zeit 170 (1961/62), pp. 120–33.

p. 189, n. 6, Albright, 'The Home of Balaam' JAOS 35 (1915), pp. 386–90; Gross, ' "Ein Zepter wird sich erheben aus Israel" (Num. xxiv, 17). Die messianische Hoffnung im AT' Bibel und Kirche 17 (1962), pp. 34–7; Guillaume, 'A Note on Numbers xxiii, 10' VT 12 (1962), pp. 335–7; Roth, 'Star and Anchor: Coin Symbolism and the End of Days' Eretz-Israel 6 (1960), pp. 13*–15*: on Num. xxiv, 17, 24.

p. 190, n. 7, Engnell, 'Pæsaḥ-Maṣṣot and the Problem of "Patternism" ' Or Suec 1 (1952), pp. 39–50; Fohrer, *Überlieferung und Geschichte des Exodus. Eine Analyse von Exodus i-xv* (BZAW 91, 1964); Weiss, 'A Note on אֹתָם in Ex. x, 11' ZAW 76 (1964), p. 188.

p. 192, n. 14, Kosmala, 'The "Bloody Husband" ' VT 12 (1962), pp. 14–28: on Exod. iv, 24–6; Morgenstern, 'The "Bloody Husband" (?) (Exod, iv. 24–26) Once again' HUCA 34 (1963), pp. 35–70.

§ 28. THE PENTATEUCH SOURCE L

p. 194, line 2 from end, Krieger, 'Der Schrecken Isaaks' Judaica 17 (1961), pp. 193–5: on Gen. xxxi, 42, 53. Torczyner, 'Zu נַחֻשְׁתִּי Gen. xxx, 27' OLZ 20 (1917), cols. 10–12.

p. 195, n. 5, 'Recent Discoveries in the Sinai Peninsula. A Preliminary Note' Antiquity and Survival II 2/3 (1957), pp. 287–98: I. Aharoni, 'Results of the Archaeological Investigations' (pp. 287–96), II. Avi-Yonah, 'St. Catherine, Sinai and its Library' (pp. 297–8); Champdor, *Le Mont Sinai et le monastère Sainte-Cathérine* (1963); Gerster, *Sinai* (1961); Gunneweg, 'Mose in Midian' ZThK 61 (1964), pp. 1–9; König, 'La localisation du Sinaï et les traditions des scribes' RHPhR 43 (1963), pp. 2–31; 44 (1964), pp. 200–35; Seebass, *Mose und Aaron. Sinai und Gottesberg* (AETh 2, 1962).

p. 197, n. 8, de Langhe, 'Les études bibliques de Mgr. Ryckmans' EThL 39 (1963), pp. 418–31; Pirenne, 'L'œuvre d'épigraphiste de Mgr. Ryckmans' EThL 39 (1963), pp. 423–46.

p. 198, n. 9, Armerding, 'The Last Words of Jacob: Gen. xlix' BS 112 (1955), pp. 320–9; Blenkinsopp, 'The Oracle of Judah and the Messianic Entry' JBL 80 (1961), pp. 55–64; Dahood, '*mkrtyhm* in Genesis xlix, 5' CBQ 23 (1961), pp. 54–6; Good, 'The "Blessing" on Judah, Gen. xlix, 8–12' JBL 82 (1963), pp. 427–32; Smyth, 'Gen. xlix, 8–12' CBQ 7 (1945), pp. 290–305.

§ 29. THE PENTATEUCH SOURCES J AND E

Wolff, 'Heilsgeschichte—Weltgeschichte im AT' Der ev. Erzieher 14 (1962), pp. 129–36 [on J].

p. 199, n. 2, Sandmel, 'Genesis iv, 26b' HUCA 32 (1961), pp. 19–29.

p. 199, n. 4, Gordon, 'Abraham of Ur' *Studies Driver* (1963), pp. 77–84.

p. 199, n. 7, Eising, 'Die ägyptischen Plagen' *Junker-Festschr.* (1961), pp. 75–87.

p. 200, line 20, Waterhouse, 'A Land Flowing with Milk and Honey' Andrews University Seminary Studies I (1963), pp. 152–66.

p. 201, line 1, Donner, 'Zu Gen. xxviii, 22' ZAW 74 (1962), pp. 68–70.

p. 201, line 3, Morgenstern, 'The Elohist Narrative in Exodus iii, 1–15' AJSL 37 (1920/21), pp. 242–62.

p. 201, n. 14, Soggin, 'Die Geburt Benjamins, Genesis xxxv, 16–20 (21)' VT 11 (1961), pp. 432–40; Tsevat, 'Studies in the Book of Samuel II' HUCA 33 (1962), pp. 107–18.

p. 201, n. 16, Faley, *The Kingdom of Priests* (1960); Fohrer, ' "Priesterliches Königtum", Ex. xix, 6' ThZ 19 (1963), pp. 359–62; Moran, ' "A Kingdom of Priests" ' Saint Mary's Theology Studies 1 = *Memorial Gruenthaner* (1962), pp. 7–20.

p. 202, n. 17, Gradwohl, 'Die Verbrennung des Jungstiers, Ex. xxxii, 20' ThZ 19 (1963), pp. 50–3.

p. 203, lines 23–4, Napier, *Song of the Vineyard. A Theological Introduction to the OT* (1962), pp. 26 f.: 'J . . . seems to have originated in the south (*Judah*) . . ., E . . . in the north (*Ephraim*).'

p. 204, n. 19, Eissfeldt, ZAW 58 (1940/41), pp. 190–215 = *Kl. Schr.* II (1963), pp. 282–305.

§ 30. THE PENTATEUCH SOURCE P

Haran, 'Shilo and Jerusalem' [Hebr., Engl. summary] Tarbiz 31 (1961/62), pp. 317–25, V; 'Shilo and Jerusalem: The Origin of the Priestly Tradition in the Pentateuch' JBL 81 (1962), pp. 14–24; Schmidt, 'מִשְׁכָּן als Jerusalemer Kultsprache' ZAW 75 (1963), pp. 91–2; Steinmann, *Code Sacerdotale I, Genèse–Exode* (CIB, 1962); Zimmerli, ThZ 16 (1960), pp. 268–88 = *Ges. Aufs.* (1963), pp. 205–16.

p. 205, n. 6, Bönhoff, 'Die mutmaßliche Grundgestalt der priesterlichen Geschichtsquelle im Hexateuch' Die Studierstube 14 (1916), pp. 290–311.

p. 205, n. 8, Bauer, 'Sir. xv, 14 et Gen. i, 1' VD 41 (1963), pp. 243–4; Eichrodt, 'In the Beginning' *Essays Muilenburg* (1962), pp. 1–10; Humbert, 'Encore le premier mot de la Bible' ZAW 76 (1964), pp. 121–31.

p. 206, n. 12, Hertzberg, *Festschr. Rendtorff* (1958), pp. 130–6 = *Beiträge* (1962), pp. 126–33; O'Rourke, 'The Passover in the OT' The Bible Today 1 (1962/63), pp. 302–9; Segal, *The Hebrew Passover from the Earliest Times to A.D. 70* (London Oriental Series, Vol. 12, 1963), on this cf. Winton Thomas, BSOASt 26 (1963), pp. 652 f.; de Vaux (§ 126 on p. 145, n. 1), pp. 7–27: Le sacrifice pascal, E.T. pp. 1–26.

p. 206, n. 13, Cleveland, 'Cherubs and the "Tree of Life" in Ancient South Arabia' BASOR 172 (1963), pp. 55–60; Dumermuth, 'Josua in Ex. xxxiii, 7–11' ThZ 19 (1963), pp. 161–8; Haran, 'The Uses of Incense in the Ancient Israelite Ritual' VT 10 (1960), pp. 113–29; 'The Complex of Ritual Acts performed inside the Tabernacle' Scripta Hieros. VIII (1961), pp. 272–302; 'The Disappearance of the Ark' IEJ 13 (1963), pp. 46–58; de Vaux, 'Arche d'alliance et Tente de réunion' *Mémorial Gelin* (1961), pp. 55–70: on Exod. xxxiii, 7–11; 'Les chérubins et l'arche d'alliance. Les sphinx gardiens et les trônes divins dans l'ancien Orient' MUB 37 (1961/62), pp. 93–124, Pls. I–V.

§ 31. THE INTERRELATIONSHIP OF THE STRANDS L J E AND P AND THEIR COMBINING

p. 209, lines 15–16, Greenberg, 'Another Look at Rachel's Theft of the Teraphim JBL 81 (1962), pp. 239–48.

§ 32. AMPLIFICATIONS OF THE NARRATIVE STRANDS

Copisarow, 'The ancient Egyptian, Greek and Hebrew Concept of the Red Sea' VT 12 (1962), pp. 1–13; Dahood, '*nâdâ* "to hurl" in Ex. xv, 16' Bibl 43 (1962), pp. 248 f.; Lauha, 'Das Schilfmeermotiv im AT' SVT IX (1963), pp. 32–46.

Albright, 'Abram the Hebrew: A New Archaeological Interpretation' BASOR 163 (1961), pp. 36–54; Loren R. Fisher, 'Abraham and his Priest-King' JBL 81 (1962), pp. 264–70; Hamp, 'Melchisedech als Typus' *Pro Mundi Vita. Festschr. z. Eucharist. Weltkongr. 1960* (1960), pp. 7–20; Hauer, 'Who was Zadok?' JBL 82 (1963), pp. 89–94; Hertzberg, 'Die Melchisedek-Traditionen' JPOS 8 (1928), pp. 169–79 = *Beiträge* (1962), pp. 36–44; Lack, 'Les origines de 'Elyon, le Très-Haut, dans la tradition cultuelle d'Israël' CBQ 24 (1962), pp. 44–64; Lohfink, 'De Moysis epinicio (Ex. xv, 1–18)' VD 41 (1963), pp. 277–89; Milik, ' "Saint Thomas de Phordêsa" et Gen. xiv, 17' Bibl 42 (1961), pp. 78–84.

p. 211, line 17, Weiss, 'Some Problems of the Biblical "Doctrine of Retribution" '
[Hebr., Engl. summary] Tarbiz 31 (1961/62), pp. 236–63, I–II; 32 (1962–63), pp. 1–18,
I–II: on Gen. xviii, 22–3, Num. xvi, 22, II Sam. xiv, 17 etc.

p. 211, n. 1, Liverani, 'Ḫurri e Mitanni' Oriens Antiquus 1 (1962), pp. 253–7.

§ 33. THE BOOK OF THE COVENANT

L'Hour, 'L'Alliance de Sichem' RB 69 (1962), pp. 5–36, 161–84, 350–68; van Selms, 'Die
Bondsboek en de reg van Gosen' HTSt 16 (1961), pp. 329–43.

p. 213, n. 2, Hardy, *Blood Feuds and the Payment of Blood Money in the Middle East*
(1963); Heinisch, 'Das Sklavenrecht in Israel und im Alten Orient' StC 11 (1934/35), pp.
201–18, 276–90: on xxi, 2–6.

p. 214, line 8, Radin, 'The Kid and its Mother's Milk' AJSL 40 (1923/24), pp. 209–18:
on xxiii, 19.

p. 215, n. 8, Renaud, *Je suis un dieu jaloux. Évolution sémantique et signification théologique
de qinᵉʾah* (Lectio divina 36, 1963).

p. 217, n. 12, Fensham, '*D* in Exodus xxii, 12' VT 12 (1962), pp. 337–9.

p. 218, line 3, Fensham, 'Widow, Orphan and the Poor in Ancient Near Eastern Legal
and Wisdom Literature' JNESt 21 (1962), pp. 129–39: on xxii, 21–24, xxiii, 6, etc.

§ 34. DEUTERONOMY

Bächli, *Israel und die Völker. Eine Studie zum Deuteronomium* (AThANT 41, 1962); Blair,
'An Appeal to Remembrance. The Memory Motif in Deuteronomy' Interpr. 15 (1961),
pp. 41–7; Emerton, 'Priests and Levites in Deuteronomy' VT 12 (1962), pp. 129–38;
Granild, 'Jeremia und das Deuteronomium' StTh 16 (1962), pp. 153–4; Kline, *Treaty of
the Great King; The Covenant Structure of Deuteronomy* (1963); L'Hour, 'Une législation
criminelle dans le Deutéronome' Bibl 44 (1963), pp. 1–28; Lohfink, 'Die Bundesurkunde
des Königs Josias (Eine Frage an die Deuteronomiumsforschung)' Bibl 44 (1963), pp. 461–
498; Maarsingh, *Onderzoek naar de Ethiek van de Wetten in Deuteronomium* (Diss. Utrecht,
1961); Myers, 'The Requisites for Response. On the Theology of Deuteronomy' Interpr.
15 (1961), pp. 14–31; Ormann, 'Die Stilmittel im Deuteronomium' *Baeck-Festschr.* (1938),
pp. 39–53; von Rad, 'The Preaching of Deuteronomy and our Preaching' Interpr. 15
(1961), pp. 3–13; Weinfeld, 'The Origin of Humanism in Deuteronomy' JBL 80 (1961),
pp. 241–7; 'The Change in the Conception of Religion in Deuteronomy' [Hebr., Engl.
summary] Tarbiz 31 (1961/62), pp. 1–17, I–III.

p. 221, n. 5, Grelot, 'La racine *hwn* en Deut. i, 41' VT 12 (1962), pp. 198–201; Lohfink,
'Wie stellt sich das Problem Individuum—Gemeinschaft in Deut. i, 6–iii, 29?' Scholastik
35 (1960), pp. 403–7; 'Mandatum magnum in Dtn v–xi' VD 41 (1963), pp. 73–7;
Das Hauptgebot. Eine Untersuchung literarischer Einleitungsfragen zu Dtn v–xi (AnBibl 20,
1963); Moran, 'The End of the Unholy War and the Anti-Exodus' Bibl 44 (1963), pp. 333–
342; 'The Ancient Near Eastern Background of the Love of God in Deuteronomy' CBQ
25 (1963), pp. 77–87.

p. 224, n. 7, Roifer, 'The Breaking of the Heifer's Neck' [Hebr., Engl. summary]
Tarbiz 31 (1961/62), pp. 119–43, I.

p. 224, n. 8, Weidner, 'Eine Erbteilung in mittelassyrischer Zeit' AfO 20 (1963), pp.
121–4.

p. 224, n. 9, Welles et al., *The Parchments and Papyri* (*The Excavations at Dura-
Europos. Final Report* V, Part I, 1959), pp. 160–6, No. 31, Pl. XIV: Divorce (A.D. 204);
pp. 166–9, No. 32, Pls. XXVI, XXVII, 3: Divorce (A.D. 254).

p. 227, line 15, Müller (§ 126 on p. 260, line 17): on I Sam. iv, 4–8.

p. 227, n. 14, Meyer, 'Die Bedeutung von Deuteronomium xxxii, 8 f., 43 (4 Q) für die
Auslegung des Moseliedes' *Rudolph-Festschr.* (1961), pp. 197–209; Moran, 'Some Remarks
on the Song of Moses' Bibl 43 (1962), pp. 317–27; Walker, 'Concerning *hû* and '*anî hû*'
ZAW 74 (1962), pp. 205 f.: on Deut. xxxii, 39; Isa. xli, 4; xliii, 10, 13; xlvi, 4; xlviii, 12;
Winter, 'Nochmals zu Deuteronomium xxxii, 8' ZAW 75 (1963), pp. 218–23; Wright, 'The

Lawsuit of God; A Form-Critical Study of Deuteronomy xxxii' *Essays Muilenburg* (1962), pp. 26–67.

p. 228, line 4, Freedman, 'The Original Name of Jacob' IEJ 13 (1963), pp. 125–6: on xxxiii, 28.

p. 228, n. 16, Seeligmann, 'A Psalm from Pre-Regal Times' VT 14 (1964), pp. 75–92.

p. 228, n. 17, Baeck, 'סנה und סיני' MGWJ 46 (1902), pp. 299–301; 'Der im Dornbusch Wohnende' *Aus drei Jahrtausenden* (²1958), pp. 240–42: on xxxiii, 16 ; Boehmer, 'Der Gottesberg Tabor' BZ 23 (1935/36), pp. 333–41: on xxxiii, 19; Eissfeldt, 'Der Gott Tabor' ARW 31 (1934), pp. 14–41 = *Kl. Schr.* II (1963), pp. 29–54: on xxxiii, 19; Goebel, *Ethnica. Pars Prima. De Graecarum civitatum proprietatibus proverbio notatis* (Diss. phil. Breslau 1915); Moran, 'The Hebrew Language in its Northwest Semitic Background' *Essays Albright* (1961), pp. 54–72, cf. pp. 60 f.: on xxxiii, 11.

p. 230, line 4, Eissfeldt (1958) (p. 227, n. 14), pp. 43–54: on xxvii–xxxiv; Lohfink, 'Der Bundesschluß im Land Moab. Rechtsgeschichtliches zu Dt. xxviii, 69–xxxii, 47' BZ 6 (1962), pp. 32–54.

p. 230, n. 22, L'Hour (§ 126 on § 33); Lewy, 'The Puzzle of Dt. xxvii: Blessings announced, but curses noted' VT 12 (1962), pp. 207–11.

§ 35. THE HOLINESS CODE

Kilian, *Literarkritische und formgeschichtliche Untersuchung des Heiligkeitsgesetzes* (BBB 19, 1963).

p. 234, n. 4, Montefiore, 'Thou shalt love thy Neighbour as Thyself' NT 5 (1962), pp. 157–70.

§ 37. THE BOOKS OF JOSHUA, JUDGES, SAMUEL AND KINGS

Harrington, 'A Biblical View of History' Irish ThQ 28 (1962), pp. 207–22; Jenni, 'Zwei Jahrzehnte Forschung an den Büchern Josua bis Könige' ThR 27 (1961), pp. 1–32, 97–146; Soggin, 'Der judaische *'am-ha'areṣ* und das Königtum in Juda. Ein Beitrag zum Studium der deuteronomischen Geschichtsschreibung' VT 13 (1963), pp. 187–95.

p. 242, n. 2, Haag, 'Von Jahwe geführt. Auslegung von Ri i, 1–20' Bibel und Leben 4 (1963), pp. 103–15. On Petra, cf. also Hammond, 'Petra. The Excavation of the Main Theatre' The American Scholar 32 (1962/63), pp. 93–116; Diana Kirkbride, 'A short Account of the Excavations at Petra in 1953–1956' Ann. Dep. Ant. Jordan 4/5 (1960), pp. 117–22; 'Seyl Aclat, a Pre-Pottery-Neolithic Village near Petra—which fills in the Background to the Earliest Jericho and Hacilar' ILN 242 (1963), pp. 82–4; Millard, 'A Seal from Petra' PEQ 93 (1961), p. 136, Pl. XVIII B; Parr, 'Nabataean Sculpture from Khirbet Brak' Ann. Dep. Ant. Jordan 4/5 (1960), pp. 134–6; 'Le "Conway High Place" à Pétra. Une nouvelle interprétation' RB 69 (1962), pp. 64–79, Pls. I–IV; 'Petra, the Famous Desert City of the Nabataeans, Archaeologically Examined: The Discovery of the Earliest Buildings—Part I' ILN 241 (1962), pp. 746–9; 'Beautiful Nabataean Pottery and Figurines: Discoveries from the First Systematic Excavations at Petra—Part II' ILN 241 (1962), pp. 798–891; Wright, 'Structure of the Qasr Bint Far'un' PEQ 93 (1961), pp. 8–37, Pls. I–II, 1 folding plan; 'Petra—The Arched Gate, 1959–60' PEQ 93 (1961), pp. 124–35, Pls. XVII, XVIII A.

§ 38. THE BOOK OF JOSHUA

CIB: Fourmond and Steinmann (1960); PBS: de Vault (1960).

Amiran and Ben-Arieh, 'Sedentarization of Beduin in Israel' IEJ 13 (1963), pp. 161–81; Dus, 'Das Sesshaftwerden der nachmaligen Israeliten im Lande Canaan' CV 6 (1963), pp. 263–75; Hoftijzer, 'Enige opmerkingen rond het israëlitische 12-stammensysteem' NedThT 14 (1959/60), pp. 241–63; Kallai (Kleinmann), *The Allotments of the Tribes of Israel and their Boundaries* (Abstract of Thesis submitted for the Degree 'Doctor of Philosophy' to the Senate of the Hebrew University on 12th June 1963, 1963); Mazar,

'Topographical Studies VI: The Cities in the Tribal Area of Dan: Jos. xix, xxi' [Hebr., Engl. summary] BIES 24 (1959/60), pp. 8–16, III; Mendenhall, 'The Hebrew Conquest of Palestine' BA 25 (1962), pp. 66–86; Orlinsky, 'The Tribal System of Israel and Related Groups in the Period of the Judges' Oriens Antiquus 1 (1962), pp. 11–20; Smend, *Jahwekrieg und Stämmebund* (FRLANT 84, 1963); Yeivin (ed.). *Studies in the History of Israel and its Country* [Hebr.] (1960), pp. 135–77.

p. 249, line 4, Lohfink, 'Die deuteronomistische Darstellung des Übergangs der Führung Israels von Moses auf Josue' Scholastik 37 (1962), pp. 32–44: on Josh. i.

p. 249, line 18, Malamat, 'The Ban in Mari and in the Bible' [Hebr.] *Kaufmann Jub. Vol.* (1960), pp. קמט-קנח: on ch. vii; Noth, 'Lehrkursus 1954' ZDPV 71 (1955), pp. 1–59, cf. pp. 42–55: 'Die Ebene Achor': on vii, 24, 26.

p. 249, last line, North, ' 'Ap(h)eq(a) and 'Azeqa' Bibl 41 (1960), pp. 41–63: on x, 10–11; Tadmor, ' 'Azeqa in Judah in a Royal Assyrian Inscription' [Hebr., Engl. summary] BIES 24 (1959/60), pp. 22–32, III–IV: on x, 10–11.

p. 249, n. 1, Elena Cassin (§ 126 on p. 35, n. 1); Koch, 'Der Spruch "Sein Blut bleibe auf seinem Haupt" ' VT 12 (1962), pp. 396–416; Müller (§ 126 on p. 260, line 17).

p. 249, n. 3, Ruth Amiran, 'Myths of the Creation of Man and the Jericho Statues' BASOR 167 (1962), pp. 23–5; Anati, 'Prehistoric Trade and the Puzzle of Jericho' BASOR 167 (1962), pp. 25–31; Bar-Adon, 'Another Ivory Bull's Head from Palestine' BASOR 165 (1962), pp. 46 f.; Cleveland, 'An Ivory Bull's Head from Ancient Jericho' BASOR 163 (1961), pp. 30–6; 'Acknowledgement of the Bull's Head from Khirbet Kerak' BASOR 165 (1962), p. 47; Delcor, 'Le Trésor de la maison de Yahweh' VT 12 (1962), pp. 353–377: on vi, 19, etc.; Kathleen M. Kenyon, *Archaeology in the Holy Land* (1960); Vincent, 'Jéricho. Une hypothèse' MUB 37 (1961/62), pp. 81–90.

p. 249, n. 6, Grintz, ' "Ai which is beside Beth-Aven". A Re-examination of the Identity of 'Ai' Bibl 42 (1961), pp. 201–16; Roth, 'Hinterhalt und Scheinflucht' ZAW 75 (1963), pp. 296–304.

p. 249, n. 8, Campbell, 'Archaeological News and Views' RA 26 (1963), pp. 27–34, cf. pp. 27–30: Gibeon; Dajani, 'An Iron Age Tomb at al-Jib' Ann. Dep. Ant. Jordan 2 (1953), pp. 66–74; Pritchard, *The Water System of Gibeon* (Museum Monographs, 1961); *Gibeon, where the Sun stood still* (1962); 'Gabaon' RB 69 (1962), pp. 255–66, Pl. XXXIX; 'Two Thousand Years of Gibeon: Bronze Age Tombs and Iron Age Walls Revealed in Continued Excavations' ILN 241 (1962), pp. 440–3; 'Civil Defense at Gibeon' Expedition Vol. V, No. 1 (1962), pp. 10–17; 'Gabaon' RB 70 (1963), pp. 423–5, Pls. XVI, XVIIb; Weipert, 'Archäologischer Jahresbericht' ZDPV 79 (1963), pp. 173 f.: *eǧ-ǧīb*.

p. 250, n. 9, Tadmor, 'The Babylonian Liver Model from Hazor' IEJ 11 (1961), p. 85; Täubler, 'Chazor in den Briefen von Tell el-Amarna' *Baeck-Festschr.* (1938), pp. 4–30; Tocci, 'Hazor nell'età del Medio e Tardo Bronzo' RStOr 37 (1962), pp. 59–64; Tournay, 'Note sur l'inscription akkadienne de Haṣor' RB 69 (1962), p. 475; Yadin etc., *Hazor* III–IV (Plates) (1964).

p. 250, n. 10, Delekat, *Katoche, Hierodulie und Adoptionsfreilassung* (Münchener Beiträge zur Papyrusforschung und antiken Rechtsgeschichte 47, 1964); *Asylie und Schutzorakel am Zionheiligtum* (1965).

p. 251, line 21, Herrmann, 'Issakar' FuF 37 (1963), pp. 21–6: on xix, 17–23; Koch, 'Zur Lage von Şemarajim' ZDPV 78 (1962), pp. 19–29, Pl. 1A–3A: on xviii, 22; Schunck, 'Bemerkungen zur Ortsliste von Benjamin (Jos. xviii, 21–8)' ZDPV 78 (1962), pp. 143–58; Wallis, 'Thaanath-Silo' ZDPV 77 (1961), pp. 38–45, Pl. 3: on xvi, 6.

p. 251, n. 12, Fensham, 'The Treaty between Israel and the Gibeonites' BA 27 (1964), pp. 96–100; Grintz, 'The Treaty with the Gibeonites' [Hebr., Engl. summary] Zion 26 (1961), pp. 69–84, I; Klengel, 'Zur Sklaverei in Alalah' Acta Ant. Ac. Sc. Hung. 11 (1963), pp. 1–15; Levine, 'The Netinim' JBL 82 (1963), pp. 207–12; Liver, 'The Literary History of Joshua ix' JSSt 8 (1963), pp. 227–43; Mendelsohn, *Slavery in the Ancient Near East* (1949), see index under Temple Slave; Zeitlin, 'Slavery during the Second Commonwealth and the Tannaitic Period' JQR 53 (1952/53), pp. 185–218.

p. 251, n. 14, Fohrer, 'Eisenzeitliche Anlagen im Raume südlich von *nāʿūr* und die

Südwestgrenze von Ammon' ZDPV 77 (1961), pp. 56–71; Landes, 'The Material Civilisation of the Ammonites' BA 24 (1961), pp. 66–86; Lapp (§ 126 on p. 677, n. 24), p. 24: on Ramath Mizpeh, xiii, 26; Reventlow, 'Das Ende der ammonitischen Grenzbefestigungskette' ZDPV 79 (1963), pp. 127–37, Pl. 11; Schmitt, 'Zwei Untersuchungen im *wādi nāʿūr*' ZDPV 77 (1961), pp. 46–55, Pls. 4, 5 B; Schunk, 'Erwägungen zur Geschichte und Bedeutung von Mahanaim' ZDMG 113 (1963), pp. 34–40: on Mahanaim, xiii, 26.

p. 251, n. 16, Applebaum, 'Beth-Shean' IEJ 10 (1960), pp. 126 f., 263; 'Beth Shean' RB 69 (1962), pp. 408–10, Pl. XLV; 'Where Saul and Jonathan perished: Beth Shean in Israel—The Roman Theatre and a Greek Statue Discovered' ILN 242 (1963), pp. 380–3: on xvii, 11; Avi-Yonah, 'Scythopolis' IEJ 12 (1962), pp. 123–34; Heller, 'Noch zu Ophra, Ephron und Ephraim' VT 12 (1962), pp. 339–41; Lapp, 'Palestine: Known But Mostly Unknown' BA 26 (1963), pp. 121–34, see pp. 125, 130–2: on תַּעְנָךְ Josh, xvii, 11, Judg. i, 27, I Chron. vii, 29; Negev, 'Beth-Shean' IEJ 12 (1962), p. 151; Israel Exploration Society, 'The Valley of Beth-Shan' IEJ 11 (1962), pp. 198–201: on xvii, 11; *The Beth-Shean Valley* [Hebr.] (1962).

p. 252, line 22, Pritchard (Lit. § 126 on p. 25, n. 32): on iii, 16.

p. 252, n. 17, Klein (1934/35) = מחקרים ארצי ישראליים (Palästina-Studien, III, 4, 1934).

p. 252, n. 19, Gevirtz, 'Jericho and Shechem' VT 13 (1963), pp. 52–62.

p. 254, line 3, Hertzberg, 'Adonibezeq' JPOS 6 (1926), pp. 213–21 = 'Adonibesek' *Beiträge* (1962), pp. 28–35: on Judg. i, 5–7.

p. 255, line 17, Bülow and Mitchell, 'An Iron Age II Fortress on Tel Nagīla' IEJ 11 (1961), pp. 101–10, Pls. 26, 27: on Gath, xi, 22; Campbell, 'Archaeological News and Views' BA 26 (1963), pp. 27–34, see pp. 30–2; In Search of the Philistines, on xi, 22, Ashdod; Freedman, 'The Second Season at Ancient Ashdod' BA 26 (1963), pp. 134–39: on xi, 22.

p. 255, n. 24, Berg, *Die Ältesten Israels im AT* (Diss. Hamburg, 1959); Dus, 'Die "Ältesten Israels"' CV 3 (1960), pp. 232–42; Hallo, 'A Sumerian Amphictyony' JCSt 14 (1960), pp. 88–115; L'Hour, 'L'Alliance de Sichem' RB 69 (1962), pp. 5–36, 161–84, 350–68; van der Ploeg, 'Les anciens dans l'AT' *Junker-Festschr.* (1961), pp. 175–91; Schmidt, *Der Landtag von Sichem* (Diss. theol. Tübingen, 1961), cf. ThLZ 87 (1962), col. 788.

p. 256, n. 25, Cross, 'The Discovery of the Samaria Papyri' BA 26 (1963), pp. 109–21; Delcor, 'Hinweise auf das Samaritanische Schisma im AT' ZAW 74 (1962), pp. 281–91; Macdonald, *The Theology of the Samaritans* (1964); Rowley, 'The Samaritan Schism in Legend and History' *Essays Muilenburg* (1962), pp. 208–22; Wright, 'The Samaritans at Shechem' HThR 55 (1962), pp. 357–66.

§ 39. THE BOOK OF JUDGES

CIB Steinmann (1961); LBC: Rust (1961); PBS: King (1960).
Alonso-Schökel, 'Erzählkunst im Buche der Richter' Bibl 42 (1961), pp. 143–72; Beyerlin, 'Gattung und Herkunft des Rahmens im Richterbuch' *Weiser-Festschr.* (1964), pp. 1–29; Dus, 'Die "Sufeten Israels"' ArOr 31 (1963), pp. 444–69; Haag, 'Die Zeit der Richter' Bibel und Leben 4 (1963), pp. 31–8; Kaufmann, סֵפֶר שֹׁפְטִים (1962); Orlinsky (§ 126 on § 38); Richter, *Traditionsgeschichtliche Untersuchungen zum Richterbuch* (BBB 18, 1963); Robertson, BJRL 30 (1946), pp. 91–114 = *The OT Problem* (1950), pp. 159–82; Yeivin (§ 126 on § 38); van Zyl (ed.), *Book of Judges* (Papers OuTWP, 1959, 1959).

p. 258, n. 1, Alt, 'Neue Erwägungen über die Lage von Mizpa, Ataroth, Beeroth und Gibeon' ZDPV 69 (1953), pp. 1–27; Hertzberg, 'Mizpa' ZAW 47 (1929), pp. 161–96; McCown and Wampler, *Tell en-Naṣbeh*, Vol. I, II (1947); Muilenburg, 'Mizpah of Benjamin' StTh 8 (1955), pp. 25–42; Schunck, *Benjamin. Untersuchungen zur Entstehung und Geschichte eines israelitischen Stammes* (BZAW 86, 1963).

p. 258, n. 2, van Zyl, *The Moabites* (Pr.O.S. III, 1960).

p. 258, n. 3, Beyerlin, 'Geschichte und heilsgeschichtliche Traditionsbildung im AT (Richter vi–viii)' VT 13 (1963), pp. 1–25; Davies, 'Judges viii, 22–23' VT 13 (1963), pp. 151–7.

p. 258, n. 4, Fensham, 'Salt as Curse in the OT and the Ancient Near East' BA 24 (1962), pp. 48–50; Gevirtz, 'Jericho and Shechem' VT 13 (1963), pp. 52–62.

p. 258, n. 6, Eva Danelius, 'Shamgar ben 'Anath' JNESt 22 (1963), pp. 191–3; Finkelstein, ' "Mesopotamia" in Cuneiform Sources' XXV ICO Vol. I (1962), pp. 219–25; Yeivin, 'Topographic and Ethnic Notes II. E. The Five Kushite Clans in Canaan' 'Atiqot 3 (1961), pp. 176–80: cf. Judg. iii, 7–11.

p. 258, n. 7, Fensham, 'Shamgar ben 'Anath' JNESt 20 (1961), pp. 197 f.; Giveon, 'A Ramesside "Semitic" Letter' RStOr 37 (1962), pp. 167–73, see pp. 168–9; Gordon, 'Hebrew Origins in the Light of Recent Discovery' *Biblical and Other Studies* ed. Altmann (1963), pp. 3–14, see p. 13.

p. 260, line 17, Müller, 'Die kultische Darstellung der Theophanie' VT 14 (1964), pp. 183–91: on vii, 16–22.

p. 260, lines 25–30, Blenkinsopp, 'Structure and Style in Judges xiii-xvi' JBL 82 (1963), pp. 65–76.

p. 260, n. 11, C(ampbell), 'Archaeological News and Views' BA 26 (1963), pp. 27–34, see pp. 30–4: In Search of the Philistines.

p. 261, n. 13, Noth, 'The Background of Judges xvii–xviii' *Essays Muilenburg* (1962), pp. 68–85.

p. 263, n. 15, Hertzberg, ThLZ 79 (1954), cols. 285–90 = *Beiträge* (1962), pp. 118–25; Kraus, *Gottesdienst in Israel* (²1962).

p. 264, line 31, Franken, 'The Excavations at Deir 'Allā in Jordan' VT 10 (1960), pp. 386–93, Pls. 1–16; 11 (1961), pp. 361–72, Pls. 1–23; 12 (1962), pp. 378–82; 14 (1964), pp. 417–22, 10 Pls.; 'Clay tablets from Deir 'Alla, Jordan' VT 14 (1964), pp. 377–9, 1 Pl.; Yoyotte, 'Un souvenir du "Pharaon" Taousert en Jordanie' VT 12 (1962), pp. 464–9: on סֻכּוֹת Gen. xxxiii, 17; Josh. xiii, 27; Judg. viii, 5–8.

p. 264, line 33, Curtis, 'East is East . . .' JBL 90 (1961), pp. 355–63; on viii, 1–3, xi, 26, xii, 1–6.

§ 40. THE BOOKS OF SAMUEL

(a) LBC: Rust (1961); Segal [Hebr.] (1956); Torch-B: McKane (1963); ATD: Hertzberg, E.T. (1964).

(b) de Boer, 'Als David moeste vluchten voor Saul den Tyran' NedThT 17 (1963), pp. 283–297; Buccellati, 'La "carriera" di David e quella di Idrimi, re di Alalac' Bi e Or 4 (1962), pp. 95–9; Donner, 'Der "Freund des Königs" ' ZAW 73 (1961), pp. 269–77; Goslinga, 'De parallele teksten in ded boeken Samuel en Kronieken' GThT 61 (1961), pp. 108–16; Johnson, *Die hexaplarische Rezension des I. Samuelbuches der Septuaginta* (StTh 22, 1963); on this cf. Soisalon-Soininen, STKv 39 (1963), pp. 171–3; Malamat (ed.), *The Kingdoms of Israel and Judah* [Hebr., Engl. summary] (1961); Mildenberger, *Die vordeuteronomische Saul-David-überlieferung* (Diss. theol. Tübingen, 1962), cf. ThLZ 87 (1962), cols. 778 f.; Nübel, *Davids Aufstieg in der Frühe israelitischer Geschichtsschreibung* (Diss. theol. Bonn, 1959); Tsevat, 'Studies in the Book of Samuel' HUCA 32 (1961), pp. 191–216; 33 (1962), pp. 107–18; 'Studies in the Book of Samuel III. The Steadfast House: What was David promised in II Sam. vii, 11b–16?' HUCA 34 (1963), pp. 71–82; Weiser, *Samuel. Seine geschichtliche Aufgabe und religiöse Bedeutung. Traditionsgeschichtliche Untersuchungen zu 1 Samuel vii–xii* (FRLANT 81, 1962); van Zyl (ed.), *Books of Samuel* (Papers OuTWP 1960, 1961).

p. 269, n.3, Loren R. Fisher, 'The Temple Quarter' JSSt 8 (1963), pp. 34–41, see pp. 39–41: Jerusalem; Fohrer, 'Zion—Jerusalem im AT' ThWNT VII, 5/6 (1961), pp. 291–318; Kathleen M. Kenyon, 'In Search of Ancient Jerusalem: A First Account of the Beginning of Excavation Designed to Reveal the Early History of the Site—Part I' ILN 240 (1962), pp. 578–90; 'The Holy City from Today to 1800 B.C.: First Findings of Planned Series of Excavations in and around the Old City of Jerusalem—Part II' ILN 240 (1962), pp. 619–21; McKenzie, 'The City and Israelite Religion' CBQ 25 (1963), pp. 60–70; Mazar, 'David's Reign in Hebron and the Conquest of Jerusalem' *Essays Silver* (1963), pp. 235–44; Schreiner, *Sion-Jerusalem Jahwes Königssitz*, 3 Vols.: I. *Theologie der Heiligen Stadt im AT* (StANT

7, 1963); Scott, 'A Further Trace of the Sukenik-Mayer "Third Wall" ' BASOR 169 (1963), pp. 61 f.

p. 269, n. 4, Ciasca, 'Un deposito di statuette da Tell Gat' Oriens Antiquus 2 (1963), pp. 45–63; Mazar, 'The Military Élite of King David' VT 13 (1963), pp. 310–20.

p. 269, line 23, Garbini 'Osservacioni linguistiche a I Sam, cap. i-iii' Bi e Or 5 (1963), pp. 47–52; Noth, 'Samuel und Silo' VT 13 (1963), pp. 390–400.

p. 269, n. 10, Kline, WThJ 19 (1956/57), pp. 1–24 is continued on pp. 172–84; 20 (1957–58), pp. 46–70. Cf. also Borger, 'Das Problem der *'apīru* ("Ḥabiru")' ZDPV 74 (1958), pp. 121–32; Bottéro, *Le problème des Ḥabiru à la 4ᵉ rencontre assyriologique internationale* (Cahiers Société asiatique XII, 1954); Cazelles, 'Hébreu, Ubru et Hapiru' Syria 35 (1958), pp. 198–217; Gray 'The Ḥābirū-Hebrew Problem in the Light of the Source Material Available at Present' HUCA 29 (1958), pp. 135–202; Greenberg, *The Ḥab/piru* (1955); Jepsen, 'Die "Hebräer" und ihr Reich' AfO 15 (1945/51), pp. 55–68; Otten, 'Zwei althethitische Belege zu den Ḥapiru (SA.GAZ)' ZA 52 (1957), pp. 216–23; Pohl, 'Einige Gedanken zur Habiru-Frage' WZKM 54 (1957), pp. 157–60; Yeivin, 'The Origin and Disappearance of the Khab/piru' XXV ICO Vol. I (1962), pp. 439–41. Grayson, 'Kurze Wörterstudien' Bi e Or 5 (1963), pp. 86, 110: on I xiii, 1. Robertson, 'The 'urīm and tummīm; what were they' VT 14 (1964), pp. 67–74.

p. 271, n. 12, Gadd, *Ideas of Divine Rule in the Ancient Near East* (Schweich Lectures 1945, 1948), pp. 88 f.; Vieyra, 'Les noms du "mundus" en hittite et en assyrien et la pythonisse d'Endor' RHA 19 (1961), pp. 47–55.

p. 271, n. 14, Buber, 'How Saul was made King' [Hebr.] Tarbiz 22 (1950/51), pp. 1 20. 65–84; Hallevy, 'Charismatic Kingship in Israel' [Hebr., Engl. summary] Tarbiz 30 (1960/61), pp. 231–41, 314–40, V–VII; Robertson, BJRL 28 (1944), pp. 175–206 = *The OT Problem* (1950), pp. 105–36; Soggin, 'Charisma und Institution im Königtum Sauls' ZAW 75 (1963), pp. 54–65.

p. 273, line 38, Naor and Kallai, 'Fountain which is in Jezreel' [Hebr., Engl. summary] BIES 25 (1961), pp. 251–56, II: on I xxix, 1.

p. 274, n. 22, Mazar, 'The "Perfume Factory" of King Josiah; and a Canaanite "High Place" of 5000 Years ago—Recent Discoveries at Engedi, by the Dead Sea' ILN 242 (1963), pp. 546–7; Mazar, Dothan, Dunayewski, ' 'Ein Gedi. Archaeological Excavations 1961–62' [Hebr.] BIES 27 (1963), pp. 1–134, Pls. 1–37; Mazar, Dunayevsky, Trude Dothan, 'En-gedi' IEJ 12 (1962), pp. 145–6; Weippert, 'Archäologischer Jahresbericht' ZDPV 79 (1963), pp. 164–79, see p. 172: Engedi.

p. 274, n. 27, (Anonymous), 'I Sam. xiii, 1' Bi e Or 5 (1963), p. 29.

p. 275, n. 29, Gratiane Offner, 'Jeux corporels en Sumer' RA 56 (1962), pp. 31–8.

p. 275, n. 31, Biram, 'The Northern Limit of David's Kingdom' [Hebr.] *Kaufmann Jub. Vol.* (1960), pp. סה–פד; M.F. ' 'Ein-Gev' AfO 20 (1963), pp. 260 f.; Malamat, 'Aspects of Foreign Policies of David and Solomon' JNESt 22 (1963), pp. 1–17; Mazar, 'The Aramean Empire and its Relations with Israel' BA 25 (1962), pp. 98–120; 'Ein Gev' RB 69 (1962), pp. 399–401, Pl. XLIV c, d; Mazar et al., 'Ein-Gev' IEJ 11 (1961), pp. 192 f.; Tadmor, 'The Southern Border of Aram' IEJ 12 (1962), pp. 114–22.

p. 279, n. 41, Bentzen, 'The Cultic Use of the Story of the Ark' JBL 67 (1948), pp. 37–53; Delcor, 'Jahwe et Dagon ou le Jahwisme face à la religion des Philistines, d'après I Sam. v' VT 14 (1964), pp. 136–54; Dus, 'Noch zum Brauch der "Ladewanderung" ' VT 13 (1963), pp. 126–32; 'Die Erzählung über den Verlust der Lade' VT 13 (1963), pp. 333–7; 'Der Beitrag des benjaminitischen Heidentums zur Religion Israels (Zur ältesten Geschichte der heiligen Lade)' CV 4 (1963), pp. 61–80; Haran, 'The Removal of the Ark of the Covenant' [Hebr.] BIES 25 (1961), pp. 211–23; Trencsenyi-Waldapfel, 'Der Mäusegott bei Homer' Acta Univers. Carolinae. Philosophica et Historica I (1963), pp. 211–23.

p. 280, line 3, Ap-Thomas, 'Saul's "Uncle" ' VT 11 (1961), pp. 241–5: on I x, 14–16; 'Saul's Uncle (I Samuel x, 13–16)' XXV ICO Vol. I (1962), pp. 437–41.

p. 280, n. 44, Amsler, *David, Roi et Messie* (Cahiers théologiques 49, 1963); Caquot, 'La prophétie de Nathan et ses échos lyriques' SVT IX (1963), pp. 213–24; Enciso Viana, 'La vocación de Natanael y el Salmo xxiv' Est Bíbl 19 (1960), pp. 229–36; Gese, 'Der

Davidsbund und die Zionserwählung' ZThK 61 (1964), pp. 10–26; Kutsch, 'Die Dynastie von Gottes Gnaden' ZThK 58 (1961), pp. 137–53; Loretz, 'The *Perfektum Copulativum* in 2 Sm vii, 9–11' CBQ 23 (1961), pp. 294–6; Tsevat (§ 126 on § 4b).

p. 281, n. 45, Yeivin, 'The High Place at Gibeon' RHJE I (1947), pp. 143–7.

p. 281, n. 47, de Boer, 'Confirmatum est cor meum. Remarks on the Old Latin text of the Song of Hannah' OTS 13 (1963), pp. 173–95.

§ 41. THE BOOKS OF KINGS

(a) ATD; Würthwein (1963); BK; Noth (1964–); UAHC: Honor, *Kings* I (1962); Gray, *I and II Kings, A Commentary* (The Old Testament Library, 1963).

(b) Bickermann, *Chronologie* (²1963); Finegan, *Handbook of Biblical Chronology* (1963); Freedman and Campbell, 'The Chronology of Israel and the Ancient Near East' *Essays Albright* (1961), pp. 203–28; Jepsen, 'Zur Chronologie der Könige von Israel und Juda' in Jepsen and Hanhart, *Untersuchungen zur israelitisch-jüdischen Chronologie* (BZAW 88, 1963), pp. 1–48; Malamat (§ 126 on § 40); Morgenstern, 'The New Year for Kings' *Gaster Anniversary Vol.* (1936), pp. 439–59; Schedl, 'Textkritische Bemerkungen zu den Synchronismen der Könige von Israel und Juda' VT 12 (1962), pp. 88–116; Tadmor, 'The Campaigns of Sargon II of Assur: A Chronological History Study' JCSt 12 (1958), pp. 22–40, 77–100; 'The Last Three Decades of Assyria' [Russ.] XXV ICO Vol. I (1962), pp. 240 f.; Thiele, 'The Synchronisms of the Hebrew Kings—a Re-Evaluation' Andrews University Seminary Studies 1 (1963), pp. 121–8; Yeivin (§ 126 on § 38), pp. 178–302.

p. 283, n. 9, Albright, 'The Elimination of King "So" ' BASOR 171 (1963), p. 66; Goedicke, 'The End of "So, King of Egypt" ' BASOR 171 (1963), pp. 64–6.

p. 284, line 9, Feuillet, 'Les villes de Juda au temps d'Ozias' VT 11 (1961), pp. 270–91; Tadmor, 'Azriyau di Yaudi' Scripta Hieros. VIII (1961), pp. 232–71.

p. 284, n. 17, Rowley, 'Hezekiah's Reform and Rebellion' BJRL 44 (1961/62), pp. 395–431 = *Men of God* (1963), pp. 98–132.

p. 285, line 31, Cook, 'Pekah' VT 14 (1964), pp. 121–35.

p. 285, n. 19, Schedl, 'Nochmals das Jahr der Zerstörung Jerusalems 587 oder 586 vChr' ZAW 74 (1962), pp. 209–13.

p. 285, n. 21, Heathcote, *Israel to the Time of Solomon* (1960).

p. 287, line 6, Tadmor, 'Que and Muṣri' IEJ 11 (1961), pp. 143–50: on I x, 28, II vii; Israel Exploration Society, *Elath. The 18th annual convention of the Israel Exploration Society, 1962* (1963).

p. 287, line 16, Finkelstein, 'Mesopotamia' JNESt 21 (1962), pp. 73–92: on I v, 4.

p. 287, n. 28, Aharoni, 'Tamar and the Roads to Elath' IEJ 13 (1963), pp. 30–42; Evans, 'The Incidence of Labour-service in the Old Babylonian Period' JAOS 83 (1963), pp. 20–6; 'The Incidence of Labour-Service at Mari' RA 57 (1963), pp. 65–78; Gichon, 'The Defences of the Solomonic Kingdom' PEQ 95 (1963), pp. 113–26; Mendelsohn, 'On Corvée Labor in Ancient Canaan and Israel ["light shed on the use of corvée labor in ancient Canaan and Israel by the Alalakh and Ugaritic documents, as well as by the recently discovered Hebrew letter from the seventh century B.C."]' BASOR 167 (1962), pp. 31–5: on I ix, 15 etc.

p. 288, line 40, Reymond, 'Le rêve de Salomon (I Rois iii, 4–15)' *Hommage à W. Vischer* (1960), pp. 210–15.

p. 289, line 21, Mashal, 'A Casemate Wall at Ezion-Geber' [Hebr., Engl. summary] BIES 25 (1961), pp. 157–9, III: on I ix, 26.

p. 289, n. 33, Ap-Thomas, 'Excavations in Jerusalem (Jordan), 1962' ZAW 74 (1962), pp. 321 f.; Hertzberg, 'Der heilige Fels und das AT' JPOS 12 (1932), pp. 32–42 = *Beiträge* (1962), pp. 45–53; Kathleen M. Kenyon, 'Excavations in Jerusalem, 1961' PEQ 94 (1962), pp. 72–90, Pls. XVII–XXV; 'Excavations at Jerusalem, 1961' Antiquity 36 (1962), pp. 93–6; 'Excavations in Jerusalem, 1962' PEQ 95 (1963), pp. 7–21, Pls. I–X; 'Biblical Jerusalem' Expedition, Vol. I, No. 1 (1958), pp. 32–5; Kornfeld, 'Der Symbolismus der Tempelsäulen' ZAW 74 (1962), pp. 50–7; Möhlenbrink, *Der Tempel Salomos* (BWANT 59, 1932); Pritchard (§ 126 on p. 25, n. 32): on I vii, 45–6; Saller, 'Jerusalem and its Surroundings in the

Bronze Age' Studii Biblici Franciscani Liber Annuus 12 (1961/62), pp. 147–76; Scheja, 'Hagia Sophia und Templum Salomonis' Istanbuler Mitteilungen 12 (1962), pp. 44–58, Pls. 10–11; Hans Schmidt, *Der heilige Fels in Jerusalem. Eine archäologische und religionsgeschichtliche Studie* (1933); de Vaux, 'Jérusalem' RB 70 (1963), pp. 416–9, Pl. XV; Weidhaas, 'Aufgaben und erkennbarer gegenwärtiger Stand der Forschung über in Holz und Stein kombinierte Baukonstruktionen im Altertum' WZ Weimar 6 (1956/57), pp. 149–66, 235–47, 317–28; Weippert, 'Archäologischer Jahresbericht' ZDPV 79 (1963), pp. 164–79, see pp. 174–6: Jerusalem; Yeivin, 'Jachin and Boaz' [Hebr., Engl. summary] Eretz-Israel 5 (1958), pp. 97–104, 89*, Pl. ‏ב "ר-י‎).

p. 289, n. 35, van Beek, 'South Arabian History and Archaeology' *Essays Albright* (1961), pp. 229–48; Pirenne, *Le royaume Sud-Arabe de Qatabân* (1961); Ullendorff, 'The Queen of Sheba' BJRL 45 (1962/63), pp. 486–504.

p. 290, n. 36, Rothenberg, 'Cades Barné' Bible et Terre Sainte 32 (1960), pp. 4–14; 'Ancient Copper Industries in the Western Arabah' PEQ 94 (1962), pp. 5–71, Pls. I–XVI; Wright, 'More on King Solomon's Mines' BA 24 (1961), pp. 59–62.

p. 290, n. 37, Casson, *Les marins de l'antiquité. Explorateurs et combattants sur la Méditerranée d'autrefois.* Texte français de L. Galhi-Kahic (1961); Joseph, 'Ophir of the Bible: Identification' Tamil Culture. Journal of the Academy of Tamil Culture 10 (1963), pp. 48–70; Maisler, 'Two Hebrew Ostraca from Tell Qasîda' JNESt 10 (1951), pp. 265–7, Pls. XI, XII; Yeivin, 'Did the Kingdom of Israel have a Maritime Policy?' JQR 50 (1959/60), pp. 193–228.

p. 290, n. 39, van der Woude, 'I Reg xx, 34' ZAW 76 (1964), pp. 188–91.

p. 291, n. 45, (Anonymous), 'I Reg. xviii, 20' Bi e Or 5 (1963), pp. 10–13; Gevarjahu ‏סיידל ספר לחקר תולדות מלחמת הנבאים בפולחן הבעל‎ (1962), pp. 334–65; Hayman, 'A Note on I Kings xviii, 27' JNESt 10 (1951), pp. 57–8; Mowinckel, 'The verb $\hat{si}^ah$ and the nouns $\hat{si}^ah$, $\hat{si}\hat{ha}$' StTh 15 (1961), pp. 1–10; Rowley, BJRL 43 (1960/61), pp. 190–219 = *Men of God* (1963), pp. 37–65; Würthwein, 'Die Erzählung vom Gottesurteil auf dem Karmel' ZThK 59 (1962), pp. 131–44.

p. 292, n. 49, Schmidt, 'Ein "Haus Omris" bei Samaria?' ZDPV 78 (1962), pp. 30–3.

p. 294, line 28, Tom, ' "Kaalkop, ga op! Kom op!" of: "vaar op!" ' GThT 59 (1959), pp. 249–51: on II ii, 23.

p. 295, n. 54, Kuschke, 'Das $\underline{k}rijtn$ der Mesa-Stele' ZDPV 77 (1961), pp. 24–31; Reed and Winnett, 'A Fragment of an Early Moabite Inscription from Kerak' BASOR 172 (1963), pp. 1–9; Segert, 'Die Sprache der moabitischen Königsinschrift' ArOr 29 (1961), pp. 197–267; on this cf. Dupont-Sommer, CRAI (1962), pp. 50 f.

p. 296, n. 57, Tadmor, 'The Southern Border of Aram' [Hebr.] BIES 25 (1961), pp. 201–210. Lit., p. 275, n. 31; § 126 on p. 275, n. 31.

p. 296, n. 58, Adontz, *Histoire d'Arménie, les origines du Xe siècle au VIe* (1946): on II Kings xix, 37 ‏אֶרְךָ‎; Bright, 'Le problème des campagnes de Sennacherib en Palestine' *Hommage à W. Vischer* (1960), pp. 20–31; Freedman, 'The Chronology of Israel' *Essays Albright* (1961), pp. 203–14, 225–8, cf. pp. 211 f.; Ginsberg, ' "Roots below and fruit above" and related matters' *Studies Driver* (1963), pp. 72–6: on II Kings xix, 36, Isa. xiv, 29, xxxvii, 31, Ezek. xvii, 9, Hos. ix, 16, Amos ii, 9; Goossens, 'Taharqa le conquérant' Chronique d'Égypte 22 (1947), pp. 239–44; Grayson, 'The Walters Art Gallery Sennacherib Inscription' AfO 20 (1963), pp. 83–96; Leclant, 'Kashta, Pharaon, en Égypte' ZÄS 90 (1963), pp. 74–81; Mazar, 'The Aramean Empire and its Relations with Israel' BA 25 (1962), pp. 98–120; Ullendorff, 'The Knowledge of Language in the OT' BJRL 44 (1961/62), pp. 455–65, cf. pp. 456–9: on II xviii, 26; Williams, 'Preliminary Report on the Excavations at Tell Rifa'at' Iraq 23 (1961), pp. 68–87, Pls. XXXI–XLI: on Arpad, II xviii, 34; xix, 13.

p. 300, n. 67, Laessøe, 'Building Inscriptions from Fort Shalmaneser, Nimrud' Iraq 21 (1959), pp. 38–41; Rinaldi, 'Una nova iscrizioni di Salmanassar III di Assiria = Iraq 21, 38–40, pl. xii' Bi e Or 3 (1961), pp. 64–5; Wilson, 'The Kurba il Statue of Shalmaneser III' Iraq 24 (1962), pp. 90–115, Pls. XXX–XXXV.

p. 301, line 7, Kingsbury, 'A Seven Day Ritual in the Old Babylonian Cult at Larsa' HUCA 34 (1963), pp. 1–34: on II Kings viii, 65–66.

p. 301, line 12, Driver, 'Geographical Problems' Eretz-Israel 5 (1958), pp. 16*–20*, cf. pp. 18*–20*: II Kings xvii, 24, מִבָּבֶל וּמִכּוּתָה וּמֵעַוָּה וּמֵחֲמָת וּסְפַרְוָיִם.

§ 42. GENERAL CONSIDERATIONS CONCERNING THE BOOKS OF ISAIAH, JEREMIAH, EZEKIEL AND THE TWELVE MINOR PROPHETS

Bishop, *Prophets of Palestine. The Local Background to the Preparation of the Way* (1962); Blank, 'Il Profeta e Dio' Studi e materiali di Stori delle Religioni 32 (1961), pp. 1–20; Buccellati, 'Gli Israeliti di Palestina al tempo dell'esilio' Bi e Or 2 (1960), pp. 199–210; Burrows, 'Prophecy and the Prophets at Qumrân' *Essays Muilenburg* (1962), pp. 223–32; Donner, 'Die soziale Botschaft der Propheten im Lichte der Gesellschaftsordnung in Israel' Oriens Antiquus 2 (1963), pp. 229–45; *Israel unter den Völkern. Die Stellung der klassischen Propheten des 8. Jahrhunderts v. Chr. zur Aussenpolitik der Könige von Israel und Juda* (SVT XI, 1964); Fohrer, 'Remarks on Modern Interpretation of the Prophets' JBL 80 (1961), pp. 309–19; 'Zehn Jahre Literatur zur at. Prophetie (1951–1960)' ThR 28 (1962), pp. 1–75, 235–97, 301–74; Freedman, 'The Law and the Prophets' SVT IX (1963), pp. 250–65; González-Núñez, *Profetas, sacerdotes y reyes en el antiguo Israël* (1962); Heaton, *The OT Prophets* (²1961); Hempel, 'Jahwegleichnisse der israelitischen Propheten' ZAW 42 (1924), pp. 74–104 = BZAW 81 (1961), pp. 1–29; 'Prophet and Poet' JThSt 40 (1939), pp. 113–32 = 'Prophet und Dichter' BZAW 81 (1961), pp. 287–307; Hertzberg, 'Die prophetische Kritik am Kult' ThLZ 75 (1950), cols. 219–26 = *Beiträge* (1962), pp. 81–90; 'Sind die Propheten Fürbitter?' *Weiser-Festschr.* (1963), pp. 63–74; Heschel, *The Prophets* (1962); 'Prophetic Inspiration: An Analysis of Prophetic Consciousness' Judaism 11 (1962), pp. 3–13; Hylander, 'Die "Schrift"-Prophetie' *Bulmerincq-Gedenkschrift* (1938), pp. 69–81; Jacob, 'Les prophètes bibliques sont-ils des révolutionnaires ou des conservateurs?' Christianisme social (1963), pp. 287–97; Jenni, *Die alttestamentliche Prophetie* (Theologische Studien 67, 1963); Kaiser, 'Wort der Propheten und Wort Gottes. Ein hermeneutischer Versuch' *Weiser-Festschr.* (1963), pp. 75–92; Kapelrud, *Fra Israels profeter til de vise menn* (1961); Kirkpatrick, *The Doctrine of the Prophets* (³1901, 1958); Koch, 'Gibt es ein Vergeltungsdogma im AT?' ZThK 52 (1955), pp. 1–42, cf. pp. 1–16; Lindblom, *Prophecy in Ancient Israel* (1962); Lubscyk, *Der Auszug Israels aus Ägypten. Seine theologische Bedeutung in prophetischer und priesterlicher Überlieferung* (Erfurter Theol. Studien 11, 1963); Mathews, *Prophets of the King*, I, II (1960); Mayer, 'Sünde und Gericht in der Bildersprache der vorexilischen Propheten' BZ 8 (1964), pp. 22–44; Milne, 'Prophet, Priest and King and their Effect on Religion in Israel' Abr-Nahrain II (1962), pp. 55–67; Noth, ' "Geld und Geist" im Kult des alten Israel' *Freundesgabe für Ernst Hellmut Vits* (1963), pp. 185–203, see pp. 197–203; Penna, *I Profeti* ('Ut unum sint' 8, 1959); Porteous, 'The Prophets and the Problem of Continuity' *Essays Muilenburg* (1962), pp. 11–25; 'Actualization and the Prophetic Criticism of the Cult' *Weiser-Festschr.* (1963), pp. 93–105; Rendtorff, 'Tradition und Prophetie' Theologia Viatorum VIII (1962), pp. 216–26; Graf Reventlow, 'Prophetenamt und Mittleramt' ZThK 58 (1961), pp. 269–84; Robertson, 'The Rôle of the Early Hebrew Prophet' BJRL 42 (1959/60), pp. 412–31; Ross, 'The Prophet as Yahweh's Messenger' *Essays Muilenburg* (1962), pp. 98–107; Schedl, *Geschichte des AT*. Vol. IV: *Das Zeitalter der Propheten* (1962); Sjöberg, 'De förexiliska profeternas förkunnelse. Några synpunkter' SEA 14 (1949), pp. 7–42; Synave and Benoit, *Prophet and Inspiration* (1961); Tresmontant, *Sittliche Existenz bei den Propheten Israels*. Transl. by Schaad (1962); Vawter, *The Conscience of Israel; Pre-exilic Prophets and Prophecy* (1961, 1962); Vellas, Θρησκευτικαὶ προσωπικότητες τῆς ΠΔ I (²1957), II (²1963); Westermann, *Grundformen prophetischer Rede* (Beitr. EvTh 31, 1960); Whitley, *The Prophetic Achievement* (1963); Zimmerli, *Die Botschaft der Propheten heute* (Calwer Hefte 44, 1961); (§126 on § 19).

§ 43. ISAIAH I–XXXIX

ATD: Kaiser (xiii–xxxix) (1963); ClB: Steinmann, i–xxxix (1960); PBS: Huesman (1961); Sacra Bibbia: Penna (1958); Torch-B: Mauchline: i–xxxix (1962); ZBK: Fohrer, I (i–xxiii) (1961), II (xxiv–xxxix) (1962).
Eaton, 'Commentaries on Isaiah' Theology 60 (1957), pp. 451–5; Fey, *Amos und Jesaja. Abhängigkeit und Eigenständigkeit des Jesaja* (WMANT 12, 1963); Fohrer, 'The Origin, Composition and Tradition of Isaiah i–xxxix' ALUOS 3 (1961/62), pp. 3–38; Gozzo, *La dottrina teologica del libro di Isaia* (1962); Leslie, *Isaiah—chronologically arranged, translated and understood* (1963); Marshall, 'The Structure of Isaiah i–xii' Biblical Research 7 (1962), pp. 19–32; Milgrom, 'Did Isaiah Prophesy during the Reign of Uzziah?' VT 14 (1964), pp. 164–82; Rondeleux, *Isaïe et le prophétisme* (Maîtres spirituels 24, 1961); Tur-Sinai, 'A Contribution to the Understanding of Isaiah i–xii' Scripta Hieros. VIII (1961), pp. 154–88; Virgulin, *La 'Fede' nella Profezia d'Isaia* (1961); Vriezen, 'Essentials of the Theology of Isaiah' *Essays Muilenburg* (1962), pp. 128–46; *Jahwe en zijn stad* (1962); Wildberger, 'Jesajas Verständnis der Geschichte' SVT IX (1963), pp. 83–117.

p. 304, n. 5, Garofalo, *La nozione profetica del 'Resto d'Israele'* (1942).

p. 305, n. 10, Eissfeldt, PJB 27 (1931), pp. 58–66 = *Kl. Schr.* I (1962), pp. 239–46.

p. 305, n. 11, Kedar-Kopfstein, 'A Note on Isaiah xiv, 31' Textus II (1962), pp. 143–5.

p. 306, n. 15, Labushagne, 'Ugaritic *blt* and *bilti* in Is. x, 4' VT 14 (1964), pp. 97–9.

p. 307, line 39, Ackroyd, 'A Note on Isaiah ii, 1' ZAW 75 (1963), pp. 320–1.

p. 309, line 15, Winton Thomas, 'A Lost Hebrew Word in Isaiah ii, 6' JThSt 13 (1962), pp. 323 f.; 'The Text of Jesaja ii, 6, and the Word שׁפק' ZAW 75 (1963), pp. 88–90.

p. 309, n. 22, Fohrer, 'Jesaja i als Zusammenfassung der Verkündigung Jesajas' ZAW 74 (1962), pp. 251–68; Stuiber, 'Die Wachhütte im Weingarten' JbAC 2 (1959), pp. 86–9: on i, 8.

p. 309, n. 24, Schoneveld, 'Jesaia i, 18–20' VT 13 (1963), pp. 342–4.

p. 309, n. 26, Scheiber, 'Zwei Bemerkungen zu Jesaja' VT 11 (1961), pp. 455 f.: on iii, 15; xxi, 12.

p. 309, n. 27, van den Branden, 'I giaielli delle donne di Gerusalemme secondo Isaia iii, 18–21' Bi e Or 5 (1963), pp. 87–94.

p. 310, n. 30, Gnilka, *Die Verstockung Israels. Isaias vi, 9–10, in der Theologie der Synoptiker* (StANT III, 1961); Schmidt, 'Wo hat die Aussage: Jahwe "der Heilige" ihren Ursprung?' ZAW 74 (1962), pp. 62–6; Walker, 'Disagion versus Trisagion' NTSt 7 (1961), pp. 170–1.

p. 310, n. 32, Coppens, 'L'interprétation d'Is., vii, 14 à la lumière des études les plus récentes' *Junker-Festschr.* (1961), pp. 31–45; Criado, 'El valor de *laken* (Vg "propter") en Is. vii, 14. Contribución al estudio del Emmanuel' Estudios Eclesiásticos 34 (1960), pp. 741–51; Dequeker, 'Isaïe vii, 14: וקרא את שמו עמנו אל' VT 12 (1962), pp. 331–5; Prado, 'La Madre del Emanuel: Jes vii, 14' Sefarad 21 (1961), pp. 85–114; Rehm, 'Das Wort *'almāh* in Is. vii' BZ 8 (1964), pp. 89–101; Schulz, ' 'Alma' BZ 23 (1935/36), pp. 229–41, cf. pp. 239–41; Wolff, *Frieden ohne Ende. Jes. vii, 1–17 und ausgelegt ix, 1–6* (BSt 35, 1962).

p. 311, line 19, Lohfink, 'Isaias viii, 12–14' BZ 7 (1963), pp. 98–104.

p. 311, n. 36, Sæbø, 'Zur Traditionsgeschichte von Jesaja viii, 9–10' ZAW 76 (1964), pp. 132–44.

p. 313, n. 41, Wright, 'The Eighth Campaign of Sargon II of Assyria (714 B.C.)' JNESt 2 (1943), pp. 173–86; Helene von Zeissl, *Äthiopen und Assyrer in Ägypten. Beiträge zur Geschichte der ägyptischen Spätzeit* (Ägyptolog. Forschungen 14, ²1963).

p. 314, n. 42, Helene von Zeissl (§ 126 on p. 313, n. 41).

p. 314, n. 43, Dothan, 'The First Controlled Excavation of a City of the Philistines: Revealing the Past of Ancient Ashdod—Part I' ILN 243 (1963), pp. 904–6; 'The Philistines in Decline: Ashdod Babylonian, Persian, Hellenistic and Maccabaean—Part II' ILN 243 (1963), pp. 944–6; Saggs, 'Assyrian Warfare in the Sargonid Period' Iraq 25 (1963), pp. 145–58.

p. 314, n. 45, Guillaume, 'A Note on the Meaning of Isaiah xxii, 5' JThSt 14 (1963), pp. 383–5.

p. 315, n. 50, Fullerton, 'The Stone of the Foundation' AJSL 37 (1920/21), pp. 1–50: on Isa. xxviii, 16; Virgulin, 'Il significato della pietra di fondazione in Is xxviii, 16' Riv Bibl 7 (1959), pp. 208–20.

p. 317, line 29, Harel, 'Desert Landscapes in Isaiah's Prophecy' Interpr. 17 (1963), pp. 319–23.

p. 318, n. 61, Cannawurf, 'The authenticity of Micah iv, 1–4' VT 13 (1963), pp. 26–33; Junker, 'Sancta Civitas, Jerusalem Nova. Eine formkritische und überlieferungsgeschichtliche Studie zu Is ii' Trierer ThSt 15 (1962), pp. 17–33.

p. 318, n. 62, Coppens, 'Le roi idéal d'Is. ix, 5–6 et xi, 1–5 est-il une figure messianique?' *Mémorial Gelin* (1961), pp. 85–108.

p. 318, n. 63, Haspecker, 'Is ix, 1–6—ein prophetisches Weihnachtslied?' Bibel und Leben 3 (1962), pp. 249–57; Müller, 'Uns ist ein Kind geboren. Jes. ix, 1–6 in traditionsgeschichtlicher Sicht' EvTh 21 (1961), pp. 408–419; Wolff, 'Bibelarbeit über Jesaja ix, 6' *Fragen d. wiss. Erforsch. d. Hl. Schrift* (1962), pp. 24–46; § 126 on p. 310, n. 32.

p. 319, last line, Labat, 'Kaštariti, Phraorte et les débuts de l'histoire Mède' JA 249 (1961), pp. 1–12; Cavaignac, 'À propos du début de l'histoire des Mèdes (R. Labat, JA (1961), pp. 1–12)' JA 249 (1961), pp. 153–62.

p. 319, n. 65, Verhoef, 'Die Dag van die Here' Exegetica II, 3 (1956), pp. 28–49.

p. 320, n. 68, Hitzig, *Des Propheten Jonas Orakel über Moab kritisch vindicirt und durch Übersetzung nebst Anmerkungen erläutert* (1931); Rudolph, 'Jesaja xv–xvi' *Studies Driver* (1963), pp. 130–43.

p. 321, n. 71, Guillaume, 'A Note on Isaiah xix, 7' JThSt 14 (1963), pp. 382–3.

p. 322, n. 73, Galling, 'Jesaia xxi im Licht der neuen Nabonidtexte' *Weiser-Festschr.* (1963), pp. 49–62.

p. 323, n. 76, Anderson, 'Isaiah xxiv–xxvii Reconsidered' SVT IX (1963), pp. 118–26; Fohrer, 'Der Aufbau der Apokalypse des Jesajabuches (Is xxiv–xxvii)' CBQ 25 (1963), pp. 34–45; van Zyl, 'Isaiah xxiv–xxvii: Their Date of Origin' OuTWP 1962 (1963), pp. 44–57.

p. 324, n. 79, Alonso-Schökel, 'La canción de la viña, Is xxvii, 2–5' Est Bíbl 34 (1960), pp. 764–74.

p. 325, n. 81, de Liagre Böhl, 'De verwoestingen van Babylon door Darius I en Xerxes in het licht van babylonische en bijibelse bronnen' HTSt 16 (1961), pp. 261–78; 'Die babylonischen Prätendenten zur Zeit des Xerxes' BiOr 19 (1962), pp. 110–14.

§ 44. ISAIAH XL–LV

ATD: Westermann [xl–lxvi] (1966); North (1964).

Aalders, 'Jeruzalem in de OT periode tweemal verwoest?' GThT 57 (1957), pp. 98–105; Anderson, 'Exodus Typology in Second Isaiah' *Essays Muilenburg* (1962), pp. 177–95; Barsotti, 'Onias vittima e sacerdote' Humanitas X, 8 (1955), pp. 745–61; Begrich, *Studien zu Deutero-Jesaja,* ed. by Zimmerli (Theol. Bücherei 20, 1963); (1938)=BWANT 77; Buber, 'Jesus und der "Knecht" ' *Pro Regno Pro Sanctuario van der Leeuw* (1950), pp. 21–78; Coppens, 'Miscellanées Bibliques' EThL 39 (1963), pp. 87–121, cf. pp. 104–14: XXI. Le serviteur de Yahvéh et le fils d'homme daniélique sont-ils des figures messianiques?; Davidson, 'Universalism in Second Isaiah' SJTh 16 (1963), pp. 166–85; Haran, *Between RI'SHONÔT (Former Prophecies) and HADASHÔT (New Prophecies). A Literary-Historical Study in the Group of Prophecies Isaiah xl–xlviii* [Hebr.] (1963); 'The Literary Structure and Chronological Framework of the Prophecies in Is. xl–xlviii' SVT IX (1963), pp. 127–55; Hempel, ZSTh 7 (1929/30), pp. 631–60=BZAW 81 (1961), pp. 174–97; Jackson, 'The Prophetic Vision. The Nature of the Utterance in Isaiah xl–lv' Interpr. 16 (1962), pp. 65–75; Kapelrud, *Et folk på hjemferd. 'Trøsteprofeten'—den annen Jesaja—og hans budskap* (1964); Katzmann, 'Die Heilszukunft in ihrer Beziehung zur Heilsgeschichte nach Jes. xl–lv' Bibl 32 (1951), pp. 65–89, 141–72; Lassalle, 'Le grand prêtre Onias, est-il le Serviteur d'Isaïe?' Bulletin du Cercle Ernest Renan No. 73 (June 1960), pp. 1–4; Manson,

The Servant Messiah (1953, 1961); Morgenstern, 'The Suffering Servant—a New Solution' VT 11 (1961), pp. 292–320, 406–31; 'Two Additional Notes to "The Suffering Servant—a New Solution" ' VT 13 (1963), pp. 321–32; Moriarty, 'The Suffering Servant' The Way (1962), pp. 121–34; Mowinckel, *He That Cometh* (1956), pp. 187–257; Orlinsky, 'The So-called "Suffering Servant" in Isaiah lii–liii and alleged ancient Near Eastern Parallels' XXV ICO Vol. I (1962), p. 357; Reinwald, *Cyrus im 2. Teil des Buchs Isaias Kap. xl–lv* (1956); Rese, 'Überprüfung einiger Thesen von Joachim Jeremias zum Thema des Gottesknechtes im Judentum' ZThK 20 (1963), pp. 21–41; Rowley, OTS 8 (1950), pp. 100–36 = *The Servant of the Lord* (1952), pp. 59–88; Schroten, 'Het gerundium in Deutero Jesaja' NThT 17 (1962) pp. 54–8; Vogt, 'Die Ebed-Jahwe-Lieder und ihre Ergänzungen' Estudios Eclesiásticos 34 (1960), pp. 775–88; Whitley, 'Textual Notes on Deutero-Isaiah' VT 11 (1961), pp. 457–61; Zimmerli, 'Der "neue Exodus" in der Verkündigung der beiden grossen Exilspropheten' *Ges. Aufs.* (1963), pp. 192–204; 'Der Wahrheitserweis Jahwes nach der Botschaft der beiden Exilspropheten' *Weiser-Festschr.* (1963), pp. 133–51; Zimmerli and Jeremias, *The Servant of God* (Studies in Biblical Theology 20, 1957).

p. 333, n. 5, Allen, 'Isaiah liii, 11 and its Echoes' Vox Evangelica (1962), pp. 24–8; Coppens, 'Miscellanées Bibliques' EThL 39 (1963), pp. 87–121, cf. pp. 114–119: XXXII. La finale du quatrième chant du serviteur (Is. liii, 10–12); pp. 120–1: Annexe. Le texte d'Is. liii, 10–11; Hertzberg, 'Die "Abtrünnigen" und die "Vielen". Ein Beitrag zu Jesaja liii' *Rudolph-Fetsschr.* (1961), pp. 97–134; Wolff, 'Wer ist der Gottesknecht in Jes. liii?' EvTh 22 (1962), pp. 338–42.

p. 337, line 1, Johns, 'A Note on Isaiah xlv, 9' Andrews University Seminary Studies 1 (1963), pp. 62–4.

p. 337, line 2, Morgenstern, ' "The Oppressor" of Isa. li, 13—Who was He?' JBL 81 (1962), pp. 25–34.

p. 337, line 25, Klengel, 'Babylon zur Zeit der Perser, Griechen und Parther' Staatliche Museen zu Berlin. Forschungen und Berichte, Vol. 5 (1962), pp. 40–53.

p. 337, n. 14, Eissfeldt, 'The Promises of Grace to David in Isaiah lv, 1–5' *Essays Muilenburg* (1962), pp. 196–207.

p. 339, n. 19, Kuyper, 'The Meaning of חסדו Isa. xl, 6' VT 13 (1963), pp. 489–92.

p. 340, line 27, Guillaume, 'A Note on the Meaning of בין' JThSt 13 (1962), pp. 109–111: on xliv, 4, Jer. xlviii, 45, Ezek. xlvii, 18.

§ 45. ISAIAH LVI–LXVI

Zimmerli, SThU 20 (1950), pp. 110–22 = *Ges. Aufs.* (1963), pp. 217–33.

p. 343, n. 5, Rinaldi, 'Gli "scampati" di Is. lxvi, 18–22' *Mémorial Gelin* (1961), pp. 109–118.

p. 344, lines 4–5, Grelot, 'L'exégèse messianique d'Isaïe, lxiii, 1–6' RB 70 (1963), pp. 371–80; Rubinstein, 'Word-substitution in Isaiah lxiii, 5 and lix, 16' JSSt 8 (1963), pp. 52–5.

§ 46. JEREMIAH

CIB: Steinmann (1961); LBC: Kuist (1961).

Blank, *Jeremiah, Man and Prophet* (1961); Dahood, 'Two Textual Notes on Jeremiah' CBQ 23 (1961), pp. 465–74; Gerstenberger, 'Jeremiah's Complaints' JBL 82 (1963), pp. 393–408; Granild (§ 126 on § 34); Holladay, 'Jeremiah's Lawsuit with God' Interpr. 17 (1963), pp. 280–7; Klein, 'Commentary on Jeremiah' AThR 45 (1963), pp. 121–58, 284–309; Neher, *Jeremias*. German transl., Rauch (1961); Reventlow, *Liturgie und prophetisches Ich bei Jeremia* (1963); Rowley, OTS 8 (1950), pp. 100–36 = *The Servant of the Lord* (1952), pp. 59–88; 'The Early Prophecies of Jeremiah in their Setting' BJRL 45 (1962/63), pp. 198–234 = *Men of God* (1963), pp. 133–68; StOTPr (1950), pp. 157–74 = *From Moses to Qumran* (1963), pp. 187–208; Smith, 'The Decalogue in the Preaching of Jeremias' CBQ 4 (1942), pp. 197–209; Tannert, 'Zum Begriff "thora" bei Jeremia und Deuterojesaja' *Festgabe Sommerlath* (1960), pp. 25–32; Winton Thomas, 'The Age of Jeremiah in the Light of Recent Archaeological Discovery' PEQ 82 (1950), pp. 1–15.

p. 349, lines 13–15, Cross, *The Ancient Library of Qumrân* (1958), p. 139.

p. 350, line 31, Wächter, 'Überlegungen zur Umnennung von Pašḥūr in Māgôr Missābīb in Jeremia xx, 3' ZAW 74 (1962), pp. 57–62.

p. 351, line 10, Prijs, 'Jeremia xx 14 ff.: Versuch einer neuen Deutung' VT 14 (1964), pp. 104–8.

p. 351, line 26, Bach, 'Bauen und Pflanzen' *Festschr. von Rad* (1961), pp. 7–32: on i. 10.

p. 352, n. 16, Soggin, ' "La tua condotta nella valle". Nota a Geremia ii, 23a' RStOr 36 (1961), pp. 207–11.

p. 357, last line, Dahood, 'Philological Notes on Jer. xviii, 14–15' ZAW 74 (1962), pp. 207–9.

p. 357, n. 28, Holladay, 'Jeremiah's Lawsuit with God' Interpr. 17 (1963), pp. 280–7.

p. 359, line 7, Holladay, 'The so-called "deuteronomic gloss" in Jer. viii, 19b' VT 12 (1962), pp. 494–8.

p. 359, line 31, Ackroyd, 'Jeremiah x, 1–16' JThSt 14 (1963), pp. 385–90.

p. 361, n. 38, Coppens, 'La Nouvelle Alliance en Jér. xxxi, 31–34' CBQ 25 (1963), pp. 12–21; Feuillet, 'Note sur la traduction de Jér. xxxi, 3c' VT 12 (1962), pp. 122–4; Hertzberg, ThLZ 77 (1962), cols. 595–602 = *Beiträge* (1962), pp. 91–100; Martin-Achard, 'La nouvelle alliance, selon Jérémie' RThPh 12 (1962), pp. 81–92; Schoneveld, 'Jeremia xxxi 29. 30' VT 13 (1963), pp. 339–41.

p. 361, n. 30, May, 'Individual Responsibility and Retribution' HUCA 32 (1961), pp. 107–20: on xxxi, 29–30; Schedl, ' "Femina circumdabit virum" oder "via salutis"? Textkritische Untersuchungen zu Jer. xxxi, 22' ZKTh 83 (1961), pp. 431–42.

p. 362, line 2, Vincent, 'Jérusalem. Ville Sainte (Jér. xxxi, 38–40)' JJPES ([1934/35] 1934), pp. III–XVI.

p. 363, n. 44, Kuschke, 'Jeremia xlviii, 1–8. Zugleich ein Beitrag zur historischen Topographie Moabs' *Rudolph-Festschr.* (1961), pp. 181–96.

p. 364, line 8, Quinn, 'Alcaeus 48 (B 16) and the Fall of Ascalon (604 B.C.)' BASOR 164 (1962), pp. 19–20: on xlvii, 5–7.

§ 47. EZEKIEL

CIB: Steinmann et al. (1961); LBC: Howie (1962); PBS: Siegman (1961); Ironside (1959). Eichrodt, 'Der Sabbat bei Hesekiel. Ein Beitrag zur Nachgeschichte des Prophetentextes' *Junker-Festschr.* (1961), pp. 65–74; Junker, 'Ein Kernstück der Predigt Ezechiels. Studie über Ez xviii' BZ 7 (1963), pp. 173–85; Miller (§ 46); O'Doherty, 'Ezechiel Today' The Bible Today 1 (1962/63), pp. 387–91; von Rabenau, 'Das prophetische Zukunftswort im Buch Hesekiel' *Festschr. von Rad* (1961), pp. 61–80; Graf Reventlow, *Wächter über Israel. Ezechiel und seine Tradition* (BZAW 82, 1962); Rowley, BJRL 36 (1953/54), pp. 146–90 = *Men of God* (1963), pp. 169–210; Tannert (§ 46); Tournay, 'À propos des babylonismes d'Ézéchiel' RB 68 (1961), pp. 388–93; de Vries, 'Remembrance in Ezekiel' Interpr. 16 (1962), pp. 58–64; Zimmerli, ThZ 13 (1957), pp. 494–508 = *Ges. Aufs.* (1963), pp. 178–91; 'Das Gotteswort des Ezechiel' *Ges. Aufs.* (1963), pp. 133–47; cf. also § 126 on §§ 44, 47; van Zyl, ed. *Studies on the Book of Ezekiel* (Papers OuTWP 1961, 1961).

p. 367, n. 6, Kramer, 'The Death of Dumuzi (Tammuz). A newly Restored Sumerian Poem' XXV ICO Vol. I (1962), pp. 169–73.

p. 369, n. 10, Gurney, 'Tammuz Reconsidered: Some Recent Developments' JSSt 7 (1962), pp. 147–60.

p. 373, line 12, Eichrodt, 'Das prophetische Wächteramt. Zur Exegese von Hesekiel xxxiii' *Weiser-Festschr.* (1963), pp. 31–41.

p. 373, line 14, Bar Derōmā' (p. 330): on xlvii, 15.

p. 374, n. 18, Liverani (§ 126 on p. 18 n. 1), pp. 186 f.

p. 376, n. 23, Margalioth, 'The Laws of the Priests and the Sacrifices in Ezechiel' [Hebr.] Tarbiz 22 (1950/51), pp. 21–7.

p. 376, n. 24, Zimmerli, ZAW 66 (1955), pp. 1–26 = *Ges. Aufs.* (1963), pp. 148–77.

p. 378, n. 29, Ruger, *Das Tyrusorakel E₃ xxvii* (Diss. theol. Tübingen, 1961), cf. ThLZ 87 (1962), col. 284. Lit. p. 96, n. 7; § 126 on p. 95, line 28.

p. 378, n. 30, Heltzer, 'La Phénicie à la limite des VIIe–VIe siècles avant notre ère' [Russ., French summary] Instituta Narodow Asii 46 (1962), pp. 188–201; Jensen, 'Royal Purple of Tyre' JNESt 22 (1963), pp. 114–18; Millard, 'Ezekiel xxvii, 19: The Wine Trade of Damascus' JSSt 7 (1962), pp. 201–3. Lit. § 126 on p. 96, n. 7; § 126 on p. 95, line 28.

p. 378, n. 31, May, 'The King in the Garden of Eden: A Study of Ezekiel xxviii, 12–14' *Essays Muilenburg* (1962), pp. 166–76.

p. 378, n. 32, Dumermuth, 'Zu Ez. xiii, 18–21' VT 13 (1963), pp. 228 f.; Torczyner, מְצוֹדְדוֹת נְפָשׁוֹת לְפוֹרְחוֹת JJPES ([1934/35,] 1934), pp. 257–60: on xiii, 18, 20.

p. 379, line 2, Caspari, 'Die Stellung und Bedeutung von Hez. xviii innerhalb des geschichtlichen Stufenganges der biblischen Religion' *Festschr. ₃. 50 jährigen Stiftungsfest des Theol. Stud. Vereins, Erlangen* (1910), pp. 299–328; May (§ 126 on p. 361, n. 30): on xviii; Rappaport, *Fathers and Children. Collective and Individual Responsibility in Jewish Thought* (1963).

p. 379, line 3, Guthrie, 'Ezekiel xxi, 1' ZAW 74 (1962), pp. 268–81.

p. 379, line 6, Dahood, 'An Allusion to Koschar in Ezekiel xxxiii, 32' Bibl 44 (1963), pp. 531–2.

p. 379, n. 35, Eissfeldt, PJB 27 (1931), pp. 58–66 = *Kl. Schr.* I (1962), pp. 239–46; JPOS 16 (1936), pp. 286–92 = *Kl. Schr.* II (1963), pp. 101–6; Fitzmyer, 'A Note on Ez. xvi 30' CBQ 23 (1961), pp. 460–2.

p. 379, n. 38, Remboy, 'Le thème du berger dans l'œuvre d'Ézéchiel' Liber Annuus Studii Biblici Franciscani 11 (1960/61), pp. 113–44.

§ 48. THE BOOK OF THE TWELVE PROPHETS

ClB: Steinmann and Hanon, Mic, Zeph, Joel, Nah, Hab (1962); Epworth Preacher's Commentaries: Edgar, Joel, Ob, Jon, Nah.—Mal. (1962); LBC: Myers, Hos.—Jon. (1960); Gailey, Mic—Mal (1962); Pirot and Clamer: Deissler and Delcor, Hos.—Jon. (1961); Sacra Bibbia: Rinaldi, Hos, Joel, Ob, Jon. (1960); Torch-B: Eaton, Ob, Nah, Hab, Zeph. (1961); Jones, Joel, (1964); Jones, Hag. Zech. Mal. (1962).
Single Commentaries: Bič, Zech. (1962); Unger, Zech. (1963).

Frost, *Patriarchs and Prophets* (1963); Krause, *Studien ₃u Luthers Auslegung der kleinen Propheten* (BHTh 32, 1961); Morgan, *The Minor Prophets. The men and their messages* (1960); Napier, *Prophets in Perspective* (1963); Wellhausen, *Die kleinen Propheten* (⁴1963).

§ 49. HOSEA

Caquot, 'Osée et la Royauté' RHPhR 41 (1961), pp. 123–46; Eichrodt, ' "The Holy One in Your Midst." The Theology of Hosea' Interpr. 15 (1961), pp. 259–73; Francisco, 'Evil and Suffering in the Book of Hosea' Southwestern J Th 5 (1962/63), pp. 33–41; Jacob, 'L'Héritage cananéen dans le livre du prophète Osée' RHPhR 43 (1963), pp. 250–9; Rowley, BJRL 39 (1955/57), pp. 200–33 = *Men of God* (1963), pp. 66–97; Rudolph, 'Präparierte Jungfrauen?' ZAW 75 (1963), pp. 65–73: on Hos. i; Wiéner and Colson, *Un roi fit des noces à son fils* (1962); Wolff, 'Guilt and Salvation. A Study of the Prophecy of Hosea' Interpr. 15 (1961), pp. 274–85; 'Guds lidenskap i rettstriden med Israel. Om særpreget i Hoseas forkynnelse' TTKi 33 (1962), pp. 74–82.

p. 385, n. 1, Lohfink, 'Zu Text und Form von Os iv, 4–5' Bibl 42 (1961), pp. 303–32.

p. 386, line 8, Cazelles, 'The Problem of the Kings in Osee viii, 4' CBQ 11 (1949), pp. 14–25.

p. 386, line 9, Dorothea Ward Harvey, 'Rejoice not, O Israel' *Essays Muilenburg* (1962), pp. 116–27: on ix, 1.

p. 386, line 17, Lohfink, 'Hate and Love in Osee ix, 15' CBQ 25 (1963), p. 417.

p. 386, line 24, Glanzman, 'Two Notes: Amos iii, 15 and Osee xi, 8–9' CBQ 23 (1961), pp. 227–33; King, ' "When Israel was a Child . . ." ' 8 The Bible Today 1 (1962/63), pp. 286–93; Ritschl, 'God's Conversion. An Exposition of Hosea xi' Interpr. 15 (1961), pp. 286–303.

p. 386, n. 7, von Kölichen, 'Der "Lehrer der Gerechtigkeit" und Hos x, 12, in einer rabbinischen Handschrift des Mittelalters' ZAW 74 (1962), pp. 324–7; McCarthy, 'Hosea xii, 2: Covenant by Oil' VT 14 (1964), pp. 215–21.

p. 386, n. 9, Ginsberg, 'Hosea's Ephraim, More Fool than Knave. A New Interpretation of Hosea xii, 1–14' JBL 80 (1961), pp. 339–47.

p. 387, last line, Guillaume, 'A Note on Hosea ii, 23, 24 (21, 22)' JThSt 15 (1964), pp. 57–58.

p. 387, n. 11, Ackroyd, 'Hosea and Jacob' VT 13 (1963), pp. 245–59.

§ 50. JOEL

Bič, *Das Buch Joel* (1960); Kutsch, 'Heuschreckenplage und Tag Jahwes in Joel i und ii' ThZ 18 (1962), pp. 81–94; Myers, 'Some Considerations Bearing on the Date of Joel' ZAW 74 (1962), pp. 177–95; Wolff, *Die Botschaft des Buches Joel* (Theol. Existenz heute N.F. 109, 1963).

p. 392, n. 3, Roth, 'The Teacher of Righteousness and the Prophecy of Joel' VT 13 (1963), pp. 91–95.

p. 393, n. 6, Besnand, *Le mystère du Nom. Quiconque invoquera le nom du Seigneur sera sauvé. (Joel iii, 5, Mc. xvi, 16)* (Lectio divina 35, 1962).

§ 51. AMOS

Fey (§ 126 on § 43); Gese, 'Kleine Beiträge zum Verständnis des Amosbuches' VT 12 (1962), pp. 417–38; Honeycutt, *Amos and his Message* (1963); Graf Reventlow, *Das Amt des Propheten bei Amos* (FRLANT 80, 1962); Smend, 'Das Nein des Amos' EvTh 23 (1963), pp. 404–23; Terrien, 'Amos and Wisdom' *Essays Muilenburg* (1962), pp. 108–15.

p. 396, n. 3, Eissfeldt, ' "Juda" in II Könige xiv, 28 und "Judäa" in Apostelgeschichte ii, 9' WZ Halle 12 (1963), pp. 229–38; ' "Juda" und "Judäa" als Bezeichnungen nordsyrischer Bereiche' FuF 38 (1964), pp. 20–5; Gordon, *Introduction to OT times* (1953), p. 209 and *The World of the OT* (1958), p. 219; see also in JBL 70 (1951), pp. 161 f. Cf. also the note in *Introduction*, p. 214, n. 9 = *The World of the OT*, p. 224, n. 13: on Amos iii, 12: 'This confirms the statement in Kings that Jeroboam's empire included Aram.'

p. 397, n. 7, Cohen, 'Amos *was* a Navi' HUCA 32 (1962), pp. 175–8.

p. 398, n. 11, Dahood, 'To pawn one's cloak' Bibl 42 (1961), pp. 359–66: on Amos ii, 7–8; Prov. xx, 16; xxvii, 13; xxiii, 27–8.

p. 398, n. 14, Černý, *The Day of Yahwe and Relevant Problems* (1948); Verhoef, *Die Dag van die Here* (Exegetica II, 3, 1956).

p. 400, line 9, Glanzmann, 1961 (§ 126 on p. 386, line 24).

p. 400, n. 19, Moeller, 'Ambiguity at Amos iii, 12' BT 15 (1964), pp. 31–4.

§ 52. OBADIAH

Neiman, 'Sefarad: The Name of Spain' JNESt 22 (1963), pp. 128–32.
Lit., p. 242, n. 2; § 126 on p. 242, n. 2.

§ 53 JONAH

Ellul, *Le livre de Jonas* (Cahiers bibliques de "Foi et Vie", 1952); Haller, *Die Erzählung von dem Propheten Jona* (Theol. Existenz heute 65, 1958); Jacob, 'Le livre du prophète Jonas' Rencontres pédagogiques (1963), pp. 5–15; Marion Lawrence, 'Ships, Monsters and Jonah' AJA 66 (1962), pp. 289–96, Pls. 77–8; Loretz, *Gotteswort und menschliche Erfahrung. Eine Auslegung der Bücher Jona, Rut, Hoheslied, Qohelet* (1963); Schildenberger,' Der Sinn des Buches Jonas' Erbe und Auftrag 38 (1962), pp. 93–102; Schreiner, 'Eigenart, Aufbau, Inhalt und Botschaft des Buches Jonas' Bibel und Kirche 17 (1962), pp. 8–14; Steffen, *Das Mysterium von Tod und Auferstehung. Formen und Wandlungen des Jona-Motivs* (1963);

Stommel, 'Zum Problem der frühchristlichen Jonasdarstellungen (mit drei Tafelabbildungen)' JbAC 1 (1958), pp. 112–15, Pl. 8; Vaccari, 'Il genere letterario del libro di Giona in recenti pubblicazione' Divinitas 5 (1961), pp. 1–28.

p. 406, line 8, Lohfink, 'Jona ging zur Stadt hinaus (Jon iv, 5)' BZ 5 (1961), pp. 185–203.

§ 54. MICAH

Beyerlin, 'Kultische Tradition in Michas Prophetie. Ein Beitrag zum Problem Kultus und Prophet' Vox Theologica 31 (1960), pp. 2–12; Eissfeldt, 'Ein Psalm aus Nord-Israel (Micha vii, 7–20)' ZDMG 112 (1963), pp. 259–68; Hammershaimb, 'Einige Hauptgedanken in der Schrift des Propheten Micha' StTh 15 (1961), pp. 11–34; Kapelrud, 'Eschatology in the Book of Micah' VT 11 (1961), pp. 392–405.

p. 408, line 28, Gottlieb, 'Den tærskende kvie Mi iv, 11–12' DTT 26 (1963), pp. 167–171; Schwantes, 'A Note on Micah v, 1 (Hebrew iv, 14)' Andrews University Seminary Studies 1 (1963), pp. 105–7.

§ 55. NAHUM

Balabán, 'Proto-Nahum und die Geschichtsphilosophie' CV 5 (1962), pp. 234–40.

p. 414, n. 2, Morenz in a note dated 25th January 1962 comments on van Doorslaer's view: 'I have become more and more convinced that while Thebes is certainly called No Amon in Nahum, what the town name is in fact intended to represent is Egypt. This would account for the picture of the land which is to be associated with the Delta region. We may note the parallel Ḥikuptaḥ =Memphis, which later became the term for the whole land (Aegyptos).'

§ 56. HABAKKUK

Brownlee, 'The Placarded Revelation of Habakkuk' JBL 82 (1963), pp. 319–25; Strobel, *Untersuchungen zum eschatologischen Verzögerungsproblem auf Grund der spätjüdischurchristlichen Geschichte von Habakuk ii, 2 ff.* (SNT II, 1961).

p. 420, line 32, Jung, 'Hab ii, 5: κατοινωμένος oder κατοιόμενος?' Bibl 32 (1951), pp. 564–6.

p. 420, n. 4, Eaton, 'The Origin and Meaning of Habakkuk iii' ZAW 76 (1964), pp. 144–71.

§ 57. ZEPHANIAH

Williams, 'The Date of Zephaniah' JBL 82 (1963), pp. 77–88.

p. 423, line 7 from end, Winton Thomas, 'A Pun on the Name Ashdod in Zeph. ii, 4' ET 74 (1962/63), p. 63.

p. 423, n. 1, Lit., p. 319, n. 65; p. 398, n. 14; § 126 on p. 319, n. 65; p. 398, n. 14.

§ 58. HAGGAI

Galling, *Studien zur Geschichte Israels im persischen Zeitalter* (1964); Hesse, 'Haggai' *Rudolph-Festschr.* (1961), pp. 109–34.

p. 426, n. 1, Franz Altheim and Ruth Stiehl, 'Gaumāta—der Magier—die erste Bewegung mazdakitischen Charakters' *Sozialökonomische Verhältnisse im Alten Orient und im Klassischen Altertum.* Edited by Günther and Schrot (1961), pp. 1–24; Dandamaev, 'L'inscription de Behistoun et les auteurs antiques sur Bardija–Gaumata' [Russ., French summary] Instituta Narodow Asii 46 (1962), p. 252–8; Hinz, 'Zu § 14 der Behistun-Inschrift' ZDMG 113 (1963), pp. 231–5; Klíma, 'Gaumāta der Magier' ArOr 31 (1963), pp. 119–21; Nylander, 'Bemerkungen zu einem Inschriftfragment in Pasargardae' Or Suec 11 (1962), pp. 121–5: 'Cambyses, the Great King, the Son of Cyrus, the Achaemenid, who built (this building) 530–526 . . . Spring 525 . . . attack upon Egypt'.

§ 59. ZECHARIAH I–VIII

Galling, 'Serubbabel und der Wiederaufbau des Tempels in Jerusalem' *Rudolph-Festschr.* (1961), pp. 67–96; (§ 126 on § 58); Johns, 'The Military Strategy of Sabbath Attacks on the Jews' VT 13 (1963), pp. 482–6: on II Kings xxv, 8–9; Uffenheimer, *The Visions of Zechariah. From Prophecy to Apocalyptic* [Hebr., Engl. summary] (1961); on this cf. Schubert, BZ 8 (1964), pp. 131–4.

p. 430, n. 4, Randellini, 'Satana nell' Antico Testamento' Bi e Or 5 (1963), pp. 127–32.
p. 430, n. 5, Houston Smith (§ 126 on p. 64, n. 16), p. 5: on Zech. iv, 2.
p. 430, n. 9, Eissfeldt, ARW 28 (1930), pp. 1–30 = *Kl. Schr.* I (1962), pp. 206–34, cf. pp. 19 f. (222 f.).

§ 60. ZECHARIAH IX–XIV

Jones, 'A Fresh Interpretation of Zechariah ix–xi' VT 12 (1962), pp. 241–59; Lamarche, *Zacharie ix–xiv. Structure littéraire et Messianisme* (1961); Lassalle, 'Le Deutéro-Zacharie date du temps des Macchabées' Bulletin Renan 87 (1962), pp. 1–4; Otzen, *Studien über Deuterosacharja* (Acta Theologica Danica VI, 1964); Treves, 'Conjectures concerning the date and authorship of Zechariah ix–xiv' VT 13 (1963), pp. 196–207.

p. 436, line 31, Otzen would regard chs. ix–x as coming from the time of Josiah, ch. xi from the period immediately before the fall of the southern kingdom of Judah, chs. xii–xiii from the early exilic period, and ch. xiv from the late post-exilic period.
p. 436, n. 6, Grotius in fact attributed the prophecies of chs. ix–xiv to the Zechariah of the sixth century B.C., but saw them as fulfilled in Alexander the Great's attack on Syria and Palestine. Cf. also Otzen (§ 126 on § 60), p. 13, n. 9.
p. 437, n. 8, Dahood, 'Zacharia ix, 1, 'ên 'ādām' CBQ 25 (1963), pp. 123–4; Tadmor, 'Azriyau of Yaudi' Scripta Hieros. VIII (1961), pp. 232–71, cf. 266–71: 'The Word of YHWH in the Land of Hadrach'.
p. 437, n. 10, Torrey, ' "Yawan" and "Hellas" as Designations of the Seleucid Empire' JAOS 25 (1904), pp. 302–11: on ix, 3.
p. 440, n. 15, Roth, 'The Cleansing of the Temple and Zechariah xiv, 21' NT 4 (1960), pp. 174–81.

§ 61. MALACHI

Elliger, 'Maleachi und die biblische kirchliche Tradition' *Weiser-Festschr.* (1963), pp. 43–8.

p. 441, line 3 from end, Tsevat, 'Studies in the Book of Samuel' HUCA 32 (1961), pp. 191–216, cf. pp. 214–16: 'Excursus 2 Mal. ii. 3 LXX.'
p. 441, n. 2, Rehm, 'Das Opfer der Völker nach Mal i, 11' *Junker-Festschr.* (1961), pp. 193–208.

§ 62. THE ORDER OF THE 'WRITINGS'

Henshaw, *The Writings. The Third Division of the Old Testament Canon* (1963).

§ 63. THE PSALTER

ATD: Weiser (E.T.) (1962); Jerusalem-B.: Gelineau (1961); KV: Ridderbos, I (i–xli), (1962); LBC: Rhodes (1960); PBS: King, Psalms, Parts 1, 2 (1962); North, Psalms, Parts 3, 4 (1963); Epworth Preacher's Commentaries: Rodd, Pss. i–lxxii (1963); UAHC: Freehof (1962); van der Ploeg, De Psalmen (1963).
Alleman, 'Devotional Studies based on Psalms' *Biblical Studies Alleman* (1960), pp. 4–62; Anderson, 'Israel's Creed: Sung, not Signed' SJTh 16 (1963), pp. 277–85; Barth, *Einführung in die Psalmen* (BSt 32, 1961); de Boer ed., *Studies on Psalms* (OTS XIII, 1963); Brongers, 'Die Rache- und Fluchpsalmen im AT' OTS XIII (1963), pp. 21–42; Bückers, 'Zur Verwertung der Sinaitraditionen in den Psalmen' Bibl 32 (1951), pp. 401–22; Buss, 'The Psalms of Asaph and Korah' JBL 82 (1963), pp. 382–92; Clements, 'Temple and Land: A Significant Aspect of Israel's Worship' Glasgow Or. Soc. Transact. 19 (1961/62), pp. 16–28; Coppens, 'Les Saints dans le Psautier' EThL 39 (1963), pp. 485–500; Crim, *The*

Royal Psalms (1962); Dahood, 'The Divine Name 'Elî in the Psalms' ThSt [USA] 14 (1953), pp. 452–7; Henton Davies, 'The Ark in the Psalms' *Essays Hooke* (1963), pp. 51–61; Donald, 'The Semantic Field of "Folly" in Proverbs, Job, Psalms and Ecclesiastes' VT 13 (1963), pp. 285–92; Drijvers, *Über die Psalmen. Eine Einführung in Geist und Gehalt des Psalters* (1961); Enciso Viana, 'Los Salmos—prólogos' Est Ecl 34 (1960), pp. 621–31; 'Cómo se formó la primera parte del libro de los Salmos?' Bibl 44 (1963), pp. 129–48; Gelin, *La Prière des Psaumes* (1961); Gemser, 'Gesinnungsethik im Psalter' OTS 13 (1963), pp. 1–20; Gese, 'Zur Geschichte der Kultsänger im zweiten Tempel' *Festschr. Michel* (1963), pp. 222–34; Hauret, 'Un problème insoluble? La chronologie des psaumes' RSR 35 (1961), pp. 225–56; Holm-Nielsen, 'The Importance of Late Jewish Psalmody for the understanding of the OT Psalmodic Tradition' StTh 14 (1960), pp. 1–53; Hruby, 'Geschichtlicher Überblick über die Anfänge der synagogalen Liturgie und ihre Entwicklung' Judaica 18 (1962), pp. 193–214; 19 (1963). pp. 1–25; Jones, 'The Cessation of Sacrifice after the Destruction of the Temple in 586 B.C.' JThSt 14 (1963), pp. 12–31, cf. pp. 23–31; Kaminka, 'The Meaning of some Difficult Passages in the Psalter' *Gaster Anniversary Vol.* (1936), pp. 283–94; Koch (§ 126 on § 42), pp. 16–22; Kunz, 'Untersuchungen zur Textstruktur solistischer Psalmen' Kirchenmusikalisches Jahrbuch 45 (1961), pp. 1–37; 'Zur Liedgestalt der ersten fünf Psalmen' BZ 7 (1963), pp. 261–70; Lassalle, 'Onias III et les Psaumes macchabéens' Bulletin Renan 85 (1961), pp. 7–9; Luyten, 'Het zelfbeklag in de Psalmen' EThL 39 (1963), pp. 501–38; Mowinckel, *The Psalms in Israel's Worship* (1962); ThLZ 87 (1962), cols. 32–9: on Michel (1960); (OBL IV, 1962) *Le Psautier. Ses origines. Ses problèmes. Son influence. Études présentées aux XIIᵉ Journées Bibliques* (29–31 août 1960); Pax, 'Studien zum Vergeltungsproblem der Psalmen' Liber Annuus Studii Biblici Franciscani 11 (1960/61), pp. 56–112; Rimaud and Gelineau, *Le Guide du Psautier de la 'Bible de Jerusalem'* (1962); Ridderbos, 'The Psalms: style-figures and structure' OTS 13 (1963), pp. 43–76; Ringgren, *The Faith of the Psalmists* (1963); Schneider, 'Die Psalterteilung in Fünfziger- und Zehnergruppen' *Festschrift Stohr* (1960), pp. 36–47; 'Die Psalmen im Gottesdienst des Alten Bundes. Ein Diskussionsbeitrag zum gleichnamigen Buch von A. Arens' ThRev 58 (1962), cols. 225–34; Seierstad, 'Teologisk Revy: Hovedspørmål i den Kultiske tolkning av Salmene i det gamle testamente' TTKi 34 (1963), pp. 33–46; Szörényi, *Psalmen und Kult im AT (Zur Formgeschichte der Psalmen)* (1961); Thierry, 'Remarks on various passages of the Psalms' OTS 13 (1963), pp. 77–97; Winton Thomas, *The Text of the Revised Psalter* (1963); Tur-Sinai, 'On Some Obscure Passages in the Book of Psalms i–xxxv' *Essays Silver* (1963), pp. 433–46; Westermann, 'Zur Sammlung des Psalters' Theologia Viatorum VIII (1962), pp. 278–84, cf. ZDMG 111 (1962), pp. 388 f.; Wolverton, 'The Psalmist's Belief in God's Presence' Canadian JTh 9 (1963), pp. 82–94; Worden, *The Psalms are Christian Prayer* (1962).

p. 448, last line, González, 'El Salmo lxxv y el Juicio escatológico' Est Bíbl 21 (1962), pp. 5–22.

p. 448, n. 8, Schilling, ' "Vergeß ich Dich je, Jerusalem". Ergriffen und ergrimmt. Auslegung von Ps. cxxxvii (cxxxvi)' Bibel und Leben 2 (1961), pp. 157–87.

p. 450, n. 14, Abramowski, 'Zur Theologie Theodors von Mopsuestia' ZKG 72 (1961), pp. 263–93; Greer, *Theodore of Mopsuestia: Exegete and Theologian* (1961); Pirot, *L'œuvre exégétique de Théodore de Mopsueste* (1913); Sages, 'Does Seventh-Day Adventist Theology Owe a Debt to Theodore of Mopsuestia?' Andrew University Seminary Studies 1 (1963), pp. 81–90; Tying, 'Theodore of Mopsuestia as an Interpreter of the OT' JBL 50 (1931), pp. 298–303.

p. 451, n. 15, Aileen Guilding, *The Fourth Gospel and Jewish Worship* (1960), pp. 24–44; Porter, 'The Pentateuch and the Triennial Lectionary Cycle: An examination of a Recent Theory' *Essays Hooke* (1963), pp. 163–74; Thirtle, *The Titles of the Psalms* (²1905); Visser, 'De geheimenissen van de Griekse opschriften der Psalmen ontsluiert. Gregorius van Nyssa's "In inscriptiones psalmorum" ' NThT 18 (1963/64), pp. 14–29

p. 453, n. 22, Schedl, ' "Die Heiligen" und die "Herrlichen" in Psalm xvi, 1–4' ZAW 76 (1964), pp. 171–5.

p. 453, n. 23, Hickmann, *45 siècles de musique dans l'Égypte ancienne à travers la sculpture,* *la peinture, l'instrument* (1956); 'Vorderasien und Ägypten im musikalischen Austausch' ZDMG 111 (1962), pp. 23–41; *Ägypten. Musikgeschichte in Bildern*, ed. by Besseler and Schneider, II, I (1961); Husmann, *Grundlagen der antiken und orientalischen Musikkultur* (1961); Kaltenbach, *Le livre qui chante la gloire de Dieu. Études sur les psaumes* (1949); Wegener, *Griechenland* (*Musikgeschichte in Bildern* II, 4, 1964).

p. 454, n. 28, Sarna, 'The Psalm for the Sabbath Day (Ps. xcii)' JBL 81 (1962), pp. 155–168.

§ 64. JOB

CIB: Steinmann (1961); COuT: Kroeze (1961); KAT: Fohrer (1963); Commentaire de L'AT: Terrien (1963); LBC: Kelly (1962); UAHC: Freehof (1962). Bourke, *The Book of Job*, Part 2 (1963).

Anderson, 'Another Perspective on the Book of Job' Transact. Glasgow Or. Soc. 18 (1959/60), pp. 53–6; Carstensen, *Defense of Honor* (³1963); Croatto, 'El problema del dolor' Rev Bibl 24 (1962), pp. 129–35; Dahood, 'Northwest Semitic Philology and Job' *Gruenthaner Mem. Vol.* (1962), pp. 55–74; Donald (§ 126 on § 63); Fohrer, *Studien zum Buche Hiob* (1963); 'Das Hiobproblem und seine Lösung' WZ Halle 12 (1963), pp. 249–58; '4 Q Or Nab, II Q Tg Job und die Hioblegende' ZAW 75 (1963), pp. 93–97; Gemser, BiOr 19 (1962), pp. 175–7, on Tur-Sinai (1957); Goldsmith, 'The Healing Scourge' Interpr. 17 (1963), pp. 271–9; Guillaume, 'The Arabic Background of the Book of Job' *Essays Hooke* (1963), pp. 106–27; Hempel, 'Was nicht im Buche Hiob steht' *Festschr. Hirsch* (1963), pp. 134–6; ZSTh 6 (1929), pp. 621–89 = BZAW 81 (1961), pp. 114–73; Irwin, 'Job's Redeemer' JBL 81 (1962), pp. 217–29; Jaspers, 'Hiob' *Gerhard Krüger-Festschr.* (1962), pp. 86–106; Jepsen, *Das Buch Hiob und seine Deutung* (1963); Koch (§ 126 on § 42), pp. 32–37; Pope, *The Book of Job: A New Translation with Introduction and Notes* (Anchor Bible Series, 1964); Rowley, BJRL 41 (1958/59), pp. 167–207 = *From Moses to Qumran* (1963), pp. 141–83; Sarna, 'The Mythological Background of Job xviii' JBL 82 (1963), pp. 315–8; Skehan, 'Strophic Patterns in the Book of Hiob' CBQ 23 (1961), pp. 125–42; Torrance, 'Why Does God Let Man Suffer?' Interpr. 15 (1961), pp. 157–63; Vischer, 'God's Truth and Man's Lie. A Study of the Message of the Book of Job' Interpr. 15 (1961), pp. 131–46; Weiser, 'Das Problem der sittlichen Weltordnung im Buche Hiob' ThBl 2 (1923), cols. 154–64 = *Ausg. Schr.* (1961), pp. 9–19; Wood, 'The Idea of Life in the Book of Job' Transact. Glasgow Or. Soc. 18 (1959/60), pp. 29–37; Zimmerli, 'Gott—Schicksal oder Anrede'? EvTh 21 (1961), pp. 193–208.

p. 456, line 15, Kelly, 'Truth in Contradiction. A Study of Job xx and xxi' Interpr. 15 (1961), pp. 147–56; Loretz, 'Ḥbr in Jb. xvi 4' CBQ 23 (1961), pp. 293–4.

p. 457, line 21, Guillaume, 'An Archaeological and Philological Note on Job xxxii, 19' PEQ 93 (1961), pp. 147–50.

p. 457, line 31, Heras, 'The Standard of Job's Immortality' CBQ 11 (1949), pp. 263–79: on xxix, 18.

p. 457, line 32, Winton Thomas, 'Job xl. 29b : Text and Translation' VT 14 (1964), pp. 114–16.

p. 457, n. 10, Gordis, 'Elihu the Intruder. A Study of the Authenticity of Job (Chapters xxxii–xxxiii)' *Biblical and Other Studies* ed. by Altmann (1963), pp. 60–78.

p. 458, line 11, Priest, 'Where is Wisdom to be Placed?' JBR 31 (1963), pp. 276–82.

p. 458, n. 15, Fohrer, 'Gottes Antwort aus dem Sturmwind Hiob xxxviii–xli' ThZ 18 (1962), pp. 1–24; Ward, *Out of the Whirlwind* (1958).

p. 459, line 8, Klotz, 'Notes on the Unicorn' Concordia Theol. Monthly 32 (1961), pp. 286–7: on רְאֵם xxxix, 9, 10.

p. 461, n. 25, Snaith, 'The Hebrew Root G'L (I)' ALUOS 3 (1961), pp. 60–7.

p. 463, n. 30, Gordis (§ 126 on p. 457, n. 10).

p. 463, n. 31, Hulsbosch, 'Sagesse créatrice et éducatrice' Augustinianum 1 (1961), pp. 217–35, 433–51; 2 (1962), pp. 5–39; 3 (1963), pp. 5–27 = *Sagesse créatrice et éducatrice* (Bibliotheca Augustiniana N.S. Sectio Biblica I 1963).

p. 464, n. 32, Bishai, 'Notes on HSKN in Job xxii, 21' JNESt 20 (1961), pp. 258–9.

p. 469, n. 48, Williams, 'Reflections on the *Lebensmüde*' XXV ICO Vol. I (1962), pp. 80–95.

p. 469, n. 51, Gadd, 'Two Sketches from the Life at Ur' Iraq 25 (1963), pp. 177–88, cf. pp. 181–8: At the Cleaner's; Gurney, 'The Sultantepe Tablets V. The Tale of the Poor Man of Nippur' AnSt 6 (1956), pp. 145–64; 7 (1957), p. 136; Gurney and Finkelstein, *The Sultantepe Tablets* I (1957), p. 4, Pls. L–LIII, Nos. 38, 39; Lambert, *Babylonian Wisdom Literature* (1960), pp. 21–62.

§ 65. THE PROVERBS OF SOLOMON

ATD: Ringgren (1962); Herder-B: Schneider (1962); PBS: Forestell (1960); Sources Bibliques: Barucq (1963); Torch-B: Jones (1962); Tyndale OT Commentaries: Kidner (1964); UAHC: Plaut, *Book of Proverbs* (1961).

Buber, 'Das Buch der Gleichsprüche' *Die Schriftwerke verdeutscht* (1962), pp. 211–73; *Zur Verdeutschung des letzten Bandes der Schrift* (Supplement to *Die Schriftwerke verdeutscht*) (1962), pp. 10–13; Dahood, *Proverbs and Northwest Semitic Philology* (Scripta Pontificii Instituti Biblici, 113, 1963); Donald (§ 126 on § 63); Forman, 'The Context of Biblical Wisdom' Hibbert Journal 60 (1961/62), pp. 125–32; Koch (§ 126 on § 42), pp. 2–10; Montgomery, 'Wisdom as Gift. The Wisdom Concept in Relation to Biblical Messianism' Interpr. 16 (1962), pp. 43–57; Nötscher, 'Biblische und babylonische Weisheit' BZ 6 (1962), pp. 120–6; Skladny, *Die ältesten Spruchsammlungen in Israel* (1961); Whybray, *The Concept of Wisdom in Prov. i–ix* (Diss. Oxford, 1961); Zimmerli, 'Ort und Grenze der Weisheit im Rahmen der alttestamentlichen Theologie' SPOA (1963), pp. 121–37 = *Ges. Aufs.* (1963), pp. 300–15.

p. 472, line 1, Winton Thomas, 'אַל in Prov. xxxi, 4' VT 12 (1962), pp. 499–500.

p. 472, n. 3, Dahood, 'Ugaritic *drkt* and Biblical *derek*' ThSt [USA] 15 (1945), pp. 627–631: on Hos. x, 13; Jer. iii, 13; Prov. xxxi, 3; Ps. cxxxviii, 4–5.

p. 472, n. 4, Hulsbosch (§ 126 on p. 463, n. 31).

p. 472, n. 7, Irwin, 'Where Shall Wisdom be Found?' JBL 80 (1961), pp. 133–48: on viii, 22–31; Moriarty, ' "Cum eo eram cuncta componens" Prov. viii, 30' VD 27 (1949), pp. 291–3; de Savignac, 'La sagesse en Proverbes viii, 22–31' VT 12 (1962), pp. 211–15; Vischer, 'Der Hymnus der Weisheit in den Sprüchen Salomos, viii, 22–31' EvTh 22 (1962), pp. 309–26.

p. 473, n. 9, Dahood, 'To pawn one's cloak' Bibl 42 (1961), pp. 359–66: on xx, 16; xxvii, 13; xxiii, 27–8; Amos ii, 7–8; Emerton, 'A Note on Proverbs xii, 26' ZAW 76 (1964), pp. 191–3; Winton Thomas, 'A Note on דַּעַת in Proverbs xxii, 12' JThSt 14 (1963), pp. 93–4.

p. 474, n. 10, Couroyer, 'Amenemopé I, 9; III, 13: Égypte ou Israël?' RB 68 (1961), pp. 394–400; 'L'origine égyptienne de la Sagesse d'Amenemope' RB 70 (1963), pp. 208–44; Drioton, 'Une colonie israélite au Moyenne Égypte à la fin du VIIe siècle av. J.-C.' *Mémorial Gelin* (1961), pp. 181–91; 'L'apologue des deux arbres' *Drewnij Mir* [*Ancient World*]. *Festschr. Struwe* (1962), pp. 76–80: on Amenemope c. 4; Jer. xvii, 5–8; Ps. i, 1–4; Posener, 'Aménémopé 21, 13 et bt ʾt.t au sens d'oracle' ZÄS 90 (1963), pp. 98–102; van Wijngaarden, 'Amen-em-ope en de oudere Egyptische Wijsheid' MEOL 1 (1934), pp. 44–54; Williams, 'The Alleged Semitic Original of the Wisdom of Amenemope' JEA 47 (1961), pp. 100–6.

p. 475, n. 16, Sauer, *Die Sprüche Agurs. Untersuchungen zur Herkunft, Verbreitung und Bedeutung einer biblischer Stilform unter besonderer Berücksichtigung von Proverbia c. xxx* (BWANT 84, 1963).

p. 476, line 12, Lowenstamm, 'יָפַח ,יָפֵחַ ,יָפִיחַ לְשׁוֹנֵנוּ' 26 (1962), pp. 205–8: on Prov. vi, 16–19, xii, 17, xiv, 5, 25, xix, 5, 19.

§ 66. THE BOOK OF RUTH

HAT: Würthwein (²1964); LBC: Rust (1961); Kafiḥ, חמש מגילות...עם פירושים עתיקים (1963); Segert et al., Pět Svátečních Svitků: Rut (1958); Stephenson, *A Commentary on the Five Scrolls* (1963).

Loretz (§ 126 on § 53).

p. 483, n. 7, Haag, 'Die biblischen Wurzeln des Minjan' *Festschr. Otto Michel* (1963), pp. 235–42: on iv, 2.

§ 67. THE SONG OF SONGS

BK: Gerleman (1963); BOuT: van den Oudenrijn (1962); EB: Robert et Tournay avec le concours de Feuillet (1963); HAT: Würthwein (²1963); Herder-B: Schneider (1962); KAT: Rudolph (²1962).
Kafiḥ (§ 126 on § 66); Segert et al. (§ 126 on § 66): Píseň Písní (1958); Stephenson (§ 126 on § 66).
Albright, 'Archaic survivals in the text of Canticles' *Studies Driver* (1963), pp. 1–7; Barnes, *The Song of Songs* (1961); Broadribb, 'Thoughts on the Song of Solomon' Abr-Nahrain 3 [1961/62] (1963), pp. 11–36; Feuillet, 'Le Cantique des Cantiques et l'Apocalypse' RSR 49 (1961), pp. 321–53; Gerleman, 'Die Bildsprache des Hohenliedes und die altägyptische Kunst' ASTI 1 (1962), pp. 24–30; Grelot, 'Le sens du Cantique des Cantiques' RB 71 (1964), pp. 42–56; Hanfmann, 'A Syrian from Sounion' Hesperia 31 (1952), pp. 236 f., Pl. 85; Herrmann, 'Gedanken zur Geschichte des altorientalischen Beschreibungsliedes' ZAW 75 (1963), pp. 176–97; Horst, *Festschr. Littmann* (1935), pp. 43–54 = *Gottes Recht* (1961), pp. 176–87; Kaske, 'The *Canticum Canticorum* in the *Miller's Tale*' Studies in Philology 59 (1962), pp. 479–500; Kramer, 'The Biblical Song of Songs and Sumerian Love Songs' Expedition Vol. V, No. 1 (1962), pp. 25–31; Loretz (§ 126 on § 53); Mowinckel, *Salomas høysang. Gammelhebraiske kjærlighetsdikte* (1961); Segal, 'The Song of Songs' VT 12 (1962), pp. 470–90; Steinmann, *Poésie Biblique. Isaïe, Jérémie, Job, Cantique des Cantiques* (1961); Ulanov, 'The Song of Songs: The Rhetoric of Love' The Bridge. A Yearbook, Volume IV (1962), pp. 89–118; Vaccari, 'Cantici Canticorum latine a s. Hieronymo recensit emendatio' Bibl 44 (1963), pp. 74–5; Wifstrand, JThSt 12 (1961), pp. 291–8: on Langerbeck (1960); Winandy, *Le Cantique des cantiques. Poème d'amour mué en écrit de sagesse* (Bible et Vie Chrétienne, 1960).

p. 486, n. 5, Simke, 'Cant. i, 7 f. in altchristlicher Auslegung' ThZ 18 (1962), pp. 256–7.
p. 488, n. 12, Held, 'A Faithful Lover in an Old Babylonian Dialogue' (JCSt 15, pp. 1–12). Addenda et Corrigenda' JCSt 16 (1963), pp. 37–9.
p. 490, line 14, Krinetzki, 'Die Macht der Liebe. Eine ästhetisch-exegetische Untersuchung zu Hl. viii, 6–7' MThZ 13 (1962), pp. 256–79.
p. 490, line 28, Rundgren, 'אפריון "Tragsessel, Sänfte"' ZAW 74 (1962), pp. 70–2.
p. 490, n. 26, de Vaux, 'Les Fouilles de Tell el Far'ah (Jordanie), campagnes de 1959–60' CRAI (1962), pp. 288–98; 'Les Fouilles de Tell-el-Far'ah' RB 69 (1962), pp. 212–53, Pls. XVI–XXXVIII.
p. 490, n. 28, Albright (§ 126 on § 67), p. 1: 'There is not a single Greek loanword . . . *Appiryôn* is also Iranian.'

§ 68. ECCLESIASTES (KOHELETH)

Herder-B: Schneider (1962).
Ginsberg, 'Koheleth' (*A New Commentary on the Torah, the prophets, and the Holy Writings,* ed. by Mazar) [Hebr.] (1961); Kafiḥ (§ 126 on § 66); Segert et al. (§ 126 on § 66): Kóhelet (1958); Stephenson (§ 126 on § 66).
Dahood, 'Qoheleth and Northwest Semitic Philology' Bibl 43 (1962), pp. 349–65; Donald (§ 126 on § 63); Eddy (§ 126 on p. 152, n. 4), p. 381, Index; Eichhorn, *Musings of the Old Professor. The Meaning of Kohelet. A New Translation of a Commentary on the Book of Ecclesiastes* (1963); Ellermeier, 'Das Verbum חוּשׁ in Koh ii, 25. Eine exegetische, auslegungsgeschichtliche und semasiologische Untersuchung' ZAW 75 (1963), pp. 197–217; 'Die Entmachtung der Weisheit im Denken Qohelets. Zu Text und Auslegung von Qoh vi, 7–9' ZThK 60 (1963), pp. 1–20; Gese, 'Die Krisis der Weisheit bei Kohelet' SPOA (1963), pp. 139–51; Ginsberg, 'The Quintessence of Koheleth' *Biblical and Other Studies* ed. by Altmann (1963), pp. 47–59; Koch (§ 126 on § 42), pp. 32–7; Kroeber, *Qoheleth. Untersuchungen zu Entstehungsgeschichte, Form und Sinngehalt eines antiken hebräischen*

Literaturwerkes (Diss. phil. Leipzig, 1960), cf. ThLZ 87 (1962), cols. 714–16; *Der Prediger. Hebräisch und Deutsch* (Schriften und Quellen der Alten Welt 13, 1963); Laue, *Das Buch Koheleth und die Interpolationshypothese Siegfried's* (1900); on this cf. Siegfried, ZWTh 43 (1900), pp. 299 f.; Loretz (§ 126 on § 53); 'Zur Darbietungsform der "Ich-Erzählung" im Buche Qohelet' CBQ 25 (1963), pp. 46–59; Murphy 1961) (§ 67); McNeile, *Introduction to Ecclesiastes* (1904); Popma, *Heersende te Jeruzalem* (1961); Wölfel, *Luther und die Skepsis. Eine Studie zur Kohelet-Exegese Luthers* (Forsch. z. Gesch. u. Lehre d. Protestantismus X, 12, 1958).

p. 492, n. 1, Ullendorf, 'The Meaning of קהלת' VT 12 (1962), p. 215.

p. 494, n. 10, Garbini, 'Note semitiche' Annali dell Istituto Orientale di Napoli 4 (1962), pp. 85–93: on גוּמָץ x, 8.

p. 494, n. 14, Bell and Barns, 'Early Coptic Hymn Fragments' JThSt 13 (1962), pp. 99–105, cf. pp. 99–103.

p. 495, n. 19, Carrière, 'À propos d'un grand livre et d'un petit papyrus' REG 75 (1962), pp. 37–44; *Theognis, Poèmes élégiaques* (²1962); Miriam Lichtheim, 'The Song of the Harpers' JNESt 4 (1945), pp. 178–212, Pls. I–VII; Peretti, *Teognide nella tradizione gnomologica* (Univ. Pisa, Stud. class. e orient., Vol IV, 1953); Wente, 'Egyptian "Make Merry" Songs Reconsidered' JNESt 21 (1962), pp. 118–28, Pls. XVI–XIX.

§ 69. LAMENTATIONS

HAT: Plöger (²1964).
Kafih (§ 126 on § 66); Segert et al. (§ 126 on § 66): Žalozpevy (1958); Stephenson (§ 126 on § 66).
Albrektson, *Studies in the Text and Theology of the Book of Lamentations. With a Critical Edition of the Peshitta Text* (Studia Theologica Lundensia 21, 1963); Treves, 'Conjectures sur les dates et les sujets des Lamentatons' Bulletin du Cercle Ernest Renan 95 (1963), pp. 1–3; Χαστούπη, Χαρακτὴρ τῆς Ἀλεξανδρινῆς μεταφράσεως τοῦ βιβλίου ὧν θρήνων (1963).

p. 504, n. 8, Gadd, 'The second lamentation for Ur' *Studies Driver* (1963), pp. 59–71; Kramer, 'Literary Texts from Ur VI, Part II' Iraq 25 (1963), pp. 171–6, cf. pp. 171–2: Lamentations.

§ 70. ESTHER

Camb-B.: Streane (1907); KAT: Bardtke (²1963); LBC: Kelly (1962).
Kafih (§ 126 on § 66); Segert et al. (§ 126 on § 66): Éster (1958); Stephenson (§ 126 on § 66).
Cazelles, 'Note sur la composition du rouleau d'Esther' *Junker-Festschr.* (1961), pp. 17–29; Eddy (§ 126 on p. 152, n. 4), p. 381, Index; Gan, 'The Book of Esther in the Light of the Story of Joseph in Egypt' [Hebr., Engl. summary] Tarbiz 31 (1961/62), pp. 144–9, I–II; Haenchen, 'Hamans Galgen und Christi Kreuz' *Festschr. Hirsch* (1963), pp. 113–33; Rudolf Mayer, 'Iranischer Beitrag zu Problemen des Daniel- und Esther-Buches' *Junker-Festschr.* (1961), pp. 127–35; Metzger, 'The John Rylands Megillah and Some other Illustrated Megilloth of the XVth to XVIIth Centuries' BJRL 45 (1962/63), pp. 148–84, Pls. I–IV; 'A Study of Some Unknown Hand-Painted Megilloth of the Seventeenth and Eighteenth Centuries' BJRL 46 (1963/64), pp. 84–126, Pls. I–IV; Schedl, 'Das Buch Esther und das Mysterium Israel' Kairos 5 (1963), pp. 3–17; Talmon ' "Wisdom" in the Book of Esther' VT 13 (1963), pp. 419–55.

p. 507, line 11, McKane, 'A Note on Esther ix and I Samuel xv' JThSt 12 (1961), pp. 260 f.

p. 507, n. 4, Merkelbach, *Roman und Mysterium in der Antike* (1962); on this cf. Turcan, 'Le roman "initiatique": à propos d'un livre récent' RHR 163 (1963), pp. 149–99; and also Morenz, ZDMG 113 (1963), pp. 240–4.

§ 71. DANIEL

ATD: Porteous E.T. (1965); COuT: Aalders (1962); LBC: Howie (1962).
Eddy (§ 126 on p. 152, n, 4), p. 381, Index; Gruenthaner, 'The Last King of Babylon' CBQ

11 (1949), pp. 406–27; Heichelheim, *Chronological Table from 323–30 B.C.* (1962); Koch,
'Spätisraelitisches Geschichtsdenken am Beispiel des Buches Daniel' HZ 163 (1961), pp. 1–
32; Lassalle, 'Le Messianisme au temps des Macchabées' Cahiers Renan 8, 30 (1961), pp. 1–16;
Rudolf Mayer (§ 126 on § 70); Rosén, 'On the Use of the Tenses in the Aramaic of Daniel'
JSSt 6 (1961), pp. 183–203; Täubler, 'Die weltgeschichtliche Stellung des jüdischen Staates
während der hellenistischen und römischen Zeit' 30. Bericht der Lehranstalt für die Wissen-
schaft des Judentums (1912), pp. 73–92; Weidner, 'Astrologische Geographie im Alten
Orient' AfO 20 (1963), pp. 117–21, Pl. VI.

p. 513, n. 2, Dequeker, *Wereldrijk en Godsrijk in Dan ii en vii* (Diss. Leuwen, 1959).

p. 514, n. 5, de Guglielmo, 'Dan. v, 25—An Example of Double Literal Sense' CBQ 11
(1949), pp. 202–6.

p. 514, n. 10, Coppens, 'Miscellanées Bibliques' EThL 39 (1963), pp. 87–121, cf. pp. 87–94:
XXVIII. Le chapitre vii de Daniel; pp. 84–100: XXIX. Les Saints du Très-Haut sont-ils à
identifier avec les Milices célestes?; pp. 100–4: XXX. L'origine du symbole 'Fils d'homme';
§ 126 on § 44; Coppens and Dequeker, *Le Fils de l'homme et les Saints du Très-Haut en
Daniel vii dans les Apocryphes et dans le Nouveau Testament* (ALBO III, 23, ²1961); Gaster,
'The Son of Man and the Theophany in Daniel, Ch. vii: a New Interpretation' Search I
(1931), pp. 15–30; Rhodes, 'The Kingdom of Men and the Kingdom of God. A Study of
Daniel vii, 1–14' Interpr. 15 (1961), pp. 411–30.

p. 515, n. 11, Vaucher, 'Daniel viii en Occident jusqu'au Cardinal Nicolas de Cusa'
Andrews University Seminary Studies 1 (1963), pp. 139–51.

p. 517, n. 18, Eva Osswald, 'Zum Problem der vaticinia ex eventu' ZAW 75 (1963),
pp. 27–44.

p. 520, n. 28, Girbáu, 'Sóbre la fecha de la muerte de Antiocho IV Epifanes en I Mac'
Est Bíbl 21 (1962), pp. 69–74.

p. 521, line 11, Schedl, 'Mystische Arithmetik oder geschichtliche Zahlen? Daniel viii,
14, xii, 11–13' BZ 8 (1964), pp. 101–5.

p. 521, n. 32, Horn, Review of Gordon, *The world of the OT*, JBL 78 (1959), pp. 370–2,
cf. p. 371.

p. 523, n. 35, Ben-Zvi, 'Les origines de l'établissement des tribus d'Israël en Arabie'
Muséon 74 (1961), pp. 143–90; 'The Levites among the Arabian Tribes' Essays Silver
(1963), pp. 129–35; R. Meyer, *Das Gebet des Nabonid. Eine in den Qumran-Handschriften
wiederentdeckte Weisheitserzählung* (BAL 107, 3, 1962); Ryckmans, 'Zudarabische Koloni-
zatie' JEOL 15 (1957/58), pp. 239–48. Lit. p. 322, n. 74; p. 663, n. 5.

p. 525, n. 42, Weidner, 'Astrologische Geographie im Alten Orient' AfO 20 (1963),
pp. 116–21, Pl. VI.

p. 525, n. 45, Bickerman, *Institutions des Séleucides* (1938), pp. 236–57: Le cult mon-
archique; Dohrn, *Die Tyche von Antiochia* (1961); cf. on this Horn and Franke, Gnomon 35
(1963), pp. 404–10; Downey, *A History of Antioch in Syria from Seleucus to the Arab
Conquest* (1961); Hopkins, 'A Stele from Seleucia on the Tigris' MUB 37 (1960/61), pp.
235–46; Jepsen and Hanhart (§ 126 on § 41); Lifshitz, 'Sur le culte dynastique des Séleucides'
RB 70 (1963), pp. 75–81; Samuel, *Ptolemaic Chronology* (Münchener Beiträge zur Papyrus-
forschung und antiken Rechtsgeschichte 43, 1962); Schmidt, *Untersuchungen zur Geschichte
Antiochos' des Grossen und seiner Zeit* (1963); Silvestre, 'L'Ultimatum de Popillius à
Antiochus Épiphane relaté dans le "De novissimis" du ms. Bamberg can. 10' Revue Bénédic-
tine, Abbaye de Maredsou 71 (1961), pp. 399–400; Swain, 'Antiochus Epiphanes and Egypt'
Classical Philology 39 (1944), pp. 73–94; Wilcken, *Griechische Geschichte im Rahmen der
Altertumsgeschichte* (⁹1962), pp. 236–322, 351–58: XI. Alexander der Grosse, XII. Die
hellenistische Zeit; Will, 'Les premières années du règne d'Antiochos III (223–219 av.
J.-C.)' REG 75 (1962), pp. 72–129.

p. 526, n. 47, Ashby, 'The Coming of the Son of Man' ET 72 (1960/61), pp. 360–3;
Black, 'The Son of Man Problem in Recent Research and Debate' BJRL 45 (1962/63),
pp. 305–18; Borsch, 'The Son of Man' AThR 45 (1963), pp. 174–90; Hodgson, 'The
Son of Man and the Problem of Historical Knowledge' JR 41 (1961), pp. 91–108; Manson,
BJRL 32 (1949/50), pp. 171–93 =*Studies in the Epistles and Gospels* (1962), pp. 123–45;

Moe, 'Menneskesønnen og Urmennesket' TTKi 32 (1961), pp. 65–73; Scheifler, 'El hijo del hombre en Daniel' Est Ecl 34 (1960), pp. 789–804; Sjöberg, 'בן אדם und בר אנש im Hebräischen und Aramäischen' AcOr[H] 24 (1953), pp. 57–65, 91–107; Thompson, 'The Son of Man—Some further Considerations' JThSt 12 (1961), pp. 203–9.

p. 528, line 38, Rowley, 'The Meaning of Daniel for Today' Interpr. 15 (1961), pp. 387–97.

p. 529, line 17, Driver, 'Sacred Numbers and Round Figures' Essays Hooke (1963), pp. 62–90: on Dan. ix, 24–27.

§ 72. THE BOOKS OF CHRONICLES

Freedman, 'The Chronicler's Purpose' CBQ 23 (1961), pp. 436–42; North, 'Theology of the Chronicler' JBL 82 (1963), pp. 369–81; Randellini, 'Il libro delle cronache nel' Decennio 1950–1960' RivBibl 10 (1962), pp. 136–55; Stinespring, 'Eschatology in Chronicles' JBL 80 (1961), pp. 209–19; Torrey, 'The Chronicler's History of the Return under Cyrus' AJSL 37 (1920/21), pp. 81–100.

p. 531, n. 5, Del Medico, 'Zahav Parwayim. L'Or Fructifère dans la Tradition Juive' VT 13 (1962), pp. 158–86, cf. pp. 161–8: on II Chron. iii, 6 etc.; Morgenstern, The Fire upon the Altar (1963): on II Chron. vii, 1 etc.

p. 531, n. 6, Cross, The Ancient Library of Qumrân and Modern Biblical Studies (1958), p. 32; Milik, Ten Years of Discovery in the Wilderness of Judaea (1959), p. 25.

p. 532, line 14, Rinaldi, 'Quelques remarques sur la politique d'Azarias (Ozias) de Juda en Philistie (2. Chron. xxvi 6 ss)' SVT IX (1963), pp. 225–35.

p. 532, n. 7, Donner and Kutsch, 'Archäologische Bemerkungen zu Etam' ZDPV 79 (1963), pp. 113–26, Pls. 9, 10.

p. 534, n. 16, Gertner, 'Terms of Scriptural Interpretation: a Study in Hebrew Semantics' BSOASt 25 (1926), pp. 1–27: on midrāš; 'Midrashim in the New Testament' JSSt 7 (1962), pp. 267–92; Hallewy, 'Biblical Midrash and Homeric Exegesis' [Hebr., Engl. summary] Tarbiz 31 (1961/62), pp. 157–69, III–IV, 264–80, III.

p. 535, n. 18, Katzenstein, 'Some Remarks on the Lists of the Chief Priests of the Temple of Solomon' JBL 81 (1962), pp. 377–84: on I Chron. v, 34–41, Ezra vii, 1–3, etc.

p. 540, n. 25, Avi-Yonah, 'A List of Priestly Courses from Caesarea' IEJ 12 (1962), pp. 137–42.

p. 540, n. 27, Giblet, 'Eupolème et l'historiographie du Judaisme héllénistique' EThL 39 (1963), pp. 539–54; Wacholder, 'Pseudo-Eupolemos' Two Greek Fragments on the Life of Abraham' HUCA 34 (1963), pp. 83–113.

§ 73. EZRA AND NEHEMIAH

LBC: Kelly (1962); La Sacra Bibbia: Pelaia (1957).

Bickerman, From Ezra to the Last of the Maccabees: Foundations of Postbiblical Judaism (1962); Galling (§ 126 on § 58); Grosheide, De terugkeer uit de ballingschap (Exegetica II, 4, 1957); Ezra, Nehemia. Verklaard. I. Ezra (1963); Leeseberg, 'Ezra and Nehemiah: a Review of the Return and Reform' Concordia Theological Monthly 33 (1962), pp. 79–90; Mezzacasa, 'Esdras, Nehemias y el Año Sabático' Revista Biblica 23 (1961), pp. 1–8, 82–96; Morgenstern, 'The Dates of Ezra and Nehemiah' JSSt 7 (1962), pp. 1–11; von Rad, 'Die Nehemia-Denkschrift' ZAW 76 (1964), pp. 176–87.

p. 543, line 5, Goettsberger, 'Über das III. Kapitel des Ezrabuches' JSOR 10 (1926), pp. 270–80.

p. 543, n. 6, Cameron, 'The Elamite Version of the Bisitun Inscription' JCSt 14 (1960), pp. 59–68.

p. 545, n. 15, Aharoni, 'Excavations at Ramat Raḥel, 1954' IEJ 6 (1956), pp. 102–11, 137–57, Pls. 9B–14, 21–7; 'Excavations at Ramat Raḥel' BA 24 (1961), pp. 98–118; 'Ramat Raḥel' IEJ 11 (1961), pp. 193–5; Excavations at Ramat Raḥel, Seasons 1959 and 1960 (Serie Arch. 2, 1962); 'Ramat Rahel' RB 69 (1962), pp. 401–4, Pls. XLIVa; Ciasca, 'Un ipocausto a Ramat Raḥel?' RStOr 36 (1961), pp. 13–17, Pls. I–IV; 'I capitelli a voluti in Palestina' RStOr 36 (1961), pp. 189–97; Garbini, 'Sul nome antico di Ramat Raḥel' RStOr 36 (1961), pp. 199–205; Matthiae, 'L'ostrakon dipinto di Ramat Rahel' AANL XVII (1962), pp. 265–77; Monteverdi, Moscati, Ciasca, Garbini, *Il Colle di Rachele (Ramat Raḥel). Missione archaeologica nel Vicino Oriente* (1960); Moscati, 'Riflessioni su Ramat Raḥel' Ac. dei Lincei, Rend. XVI (1961), pp. 255–60.

p. 545, n. 17, Nober, 'Notae philologicae' VD 39 (1961), pp. 109–13, cf. pp. 110 f.: on Ezra v, 8 יְהוּד.

p. 546, n. 22, Campbell, 'In Search of the Philistines' BA 26 (1963), pp. 30–32: on Ashdod etc.; Dothan, 'Ashdod' IEJ 12 (1962), pp. 147 f.; (§ 126 on p. 314, n. 43); Freedman (§ 126 on p. 255, line 17); Ullendorff, 'The Knowledge of Languages in the OT' BJRL 44 (1961/62), pp. 455–65, cf. pp. 459–61.

p. 551, line 7, Benveniste, 'Eléments Perses en Araméen d'Égypte' JA 242 (1954), pp. 297–310, cf. p. 303: on Ezra v, 3, 9, אֲשַׁרְנָא. On Tattenai, cf. Ungnad, ZAW 58 (1940/41), pp. 240–3; Olmstead, JNESt 3 (1944), 4 p.6; Caquot, Syria 32 (1955), p. 267.

p. 556, n. 39, Szemerenyi, 'Sogdicismus in der Avesta' Altheim, *Aus Spätantike und Christentum* (1951), pp. 153–66, cf. p. 163: on *āsparnā*'.

THE CANON

THE HISTORY OF THE CANON

Hesse, 'Das ZT als Kanon' NZSTh 3 (1961), pp. 315–27; Lacoque, 'L'insertion du Cantique des Cantiques dans le Canon' RHPhR 42 (1962), pp. 38–44; Margolis, *The Hebrew Scriptures in the Making* (³1948); *La Formation de la Bible Hébraïque* (1953); Robinson, *Inspiration and Revelation in the OT* (1946 (1962)).

§ 75. THE FORMATION OF THE CANON

Eybers, 'Some Light on the Canon of the Qumran Sect.' OuTWP 1962 (1963), pp. 1–14; Ravenna, 'I Maccabei nella letteratura talmudica' RivBibl 10 (1962), pp. 384–91; Roberts, 'The Old Testament Canon: A Suggestion' BJRL 46 (1963/64), pp. 164–78.

p. 564, n. 8, Weil, 'L'Archétype du Massoret ha-Massoret d'Élie Lévita' RHPhR 41 (1961), pp. 147–58; *Élie Lévita, Humaniste et Masorète (1469–1549)* StPb VII (1963).

p. 567, n. 12, Shutt, *Studies in Josephus* (1961).

p. 568, n. 13, Legasse, 'Scribes et disciples de Jésus' RB 68 (1961), pp. 321–45, cf. pp. 328–33.

§ 76. APOCRYPHA AND PSEUDEPIGRAPHA:
GENERAL CONSIDERATIONS

Enslin ed., *The Apocrypha* (²1962).

Bousset, 'Die Himmelsreise der Seele' ARW 4 (1901), pp. 136–69, 229–73 (²1961); Brockington, *Ideas of Mediation between God and Man in the Apocrypha* (1962); Eddy (§ 126 on p. 152, n. 4); Glasson, *Greek Influence in Jewish Eschatology. With special Reference to the Apocalypses and Pseudepigraphs* (1961); Grelot, 'Le Messie dans les Apocryphes de l'AT', *La venue du Messie* = Recherches Bibliques VI (1962), pp. 19–52; Hadas, *Hellenistic Culture, Fusion and Diffusion* (1959); on this cf. Schneider, Gnomon 33 (1961), pp. 307–9; Kosmala, ' "At the End of the Days" ' ASTI 2 (1963), pp. 27–37; Maag, 'Eschatologie als Funktion des Geschichtserlebnisses' Saeculum 12 (1961), pp. 123–30; Maier, 'Das Gefährdungsmotiv bei der Himmelsreise in der jüdischen Apokalyptik und "Gnosis" ' Kairos (1963), pp. 18–40; Plöger, *Theokratie und Eschatologie* (WMANT 2, ²1962); Roessler, *Gesetz und Geschichte. Untersuchungen zur Theologie der jüdischen Apokalyptik und der pharisaischen Orthodoxie* (WMANT 3, ²1962); Sint, *Pseudonymität im Altertum. Ihre Formen und ihre Gründe* (1960); Tcherikover, *Jewish Apologetic Literature Reconsidered* (Eos 48, 1956, fasc. 3) = *Symbolae Raphaeli Taubenschlag dedicatae* III (1956), pp. 169–93.

§ 77. III ESDRAS (I ESDRAS)

Hammershaimb, 'Tredje Esdrasbog', *Translations of the Pseudepigraphical literature with introduction and notes* by Hammershaimb et al. (1963), pp. 341–80.

p. 575, n. 2, Lommatzsch, 'Die Stärksten Dinge' Jb. Ak. Mainz (1961), pp. 236–8.

§ 78. THE FIRST BOOK OF MACCABEES

Camb.-B: Fairweather and Black (1897); Pismo Swiete Starego Testamentu: Gryglewicz (1961). Tedesche, *The Book of Maccabees*, (1962).

Eddy (§ 126 on § 71); Hanhart, 'Zur Zeitrechnung des I und II Makkabäerbuches', Jepsen and Hanhart, *Untersuchungen zur israelitischjüdischen Chronologie* (BZAW 88, 1964), pp. 49–96; Kreissig, 'Der Makkabäeraufstand. Zur Frage seiner sozialökonomischen Zusammenhänge und Wirkungen' Studii Classici 4 (1962), pp. 143–75; Lassalle, 'L'Histoire des temps macchabéens reconstituée à l'aide de citations d'Isaïe' Cahiers Renan 10, 34 (1962), pp. 1–20; Täubler (§ 126 on § 71); Wibbing, 'Zur Topographie einzelner Schlachten des Judas Makkabäus' ZDPV 78 (1962), pp. 159–70, Pls. 14 A, B, 15 A, B; Zeitlin, *The Rise and Fall of the Judaean State* I (1962).

p. 577, n. 2, Carmignac, *Christ and the Teacher of Righteousness* (1962).

p. 578, n. 8, Ginsburg, 'Sparta and Judaea' Classical Philology 29 (1934), pp. 117–22.

§ 79. THE SECOND BOOK OF MACCABEES

Pismo Swiete Starego Testamentu: Gryglewicz (1961).

Adinolfi, 'Le apparizioni di 2 Mac. v, 2–4 e x, 29–30' RivBibl 11 (1961), pp. 167–85; Hanhart, *Zum Text des 2. und 3. Makkabäerbuches* (NAG 13, 1961, 1961); Kraeling, 'The Jewish Community at Antioch' JBL 51 (1932), pp. 130–60: on iv. 9,

p. 580, line 19, Finkelstein, 'The Family of the High Priest Menelaus' HThR 36 (1943), pp. 33–43.

§ 80. THE THIRD BOOK OF MACCABEES

Baars, 'Eine neue griechische Handschrift des 3. Makkabäerbuches' VT 13 (1963), pp. 82–7; Hanhart (§ 126 on § 79); Loewe, 'A Jewish Counterpart to the Acts of the Alexandrians' JJSt 12 (1961), pp. 105–22; Tscherikover, 'The Third Book of Maccabees as a Historical Source of Augustus' Time' Scripta Hieros. VII (1961), pp. 1–25.

§ 81. THE BOOK OF TOBIT

Scazzocchio, ' "Ecclesiastico", "Tobia", "Sapienza di Salomone" alla luce dei testi di Qumran' RStOr 37 (1962), pp. 199–209.

§ 82. THE BOOK OF JUDITH

Haag, 'Die besondere Art des Buches Judith und seine theologische Bedeutung' Trierer ThZ 71 (1962), pp. 288–301; *Studien zum Buch Judith* (1963); Skehan, 'The Hand of Judith' CBQ 25 (1963), pp. 94–110.

p. 586, n. 4, Free, 'Dothan' RB 69 (1962), pp. 266–70, Pl. XL.

p. 587, line 18, Skehan, 'Why Leave Out *Judith*?' CBQ 24 (1962), pp. 147–54.

p. 587, n. 9, Zeitlin, 'Queen Salome and King Jannaeus Alexander' JQR 51 (1960/61), pp. 1–33.

§ 83. THE PRAYER OF MANASSEH
(ORATIO MANASSIS)

p. 588, line 11, Schneider, 'Die biblischen Oden im christlichen Altertum, seit dem VI. Jahrhundert, in Jerusalem und Konstantinopel, im Mittelalter, im hexaplarischen Psalter' Bibl 30 (1949), pp. 28–65, 239–72, 433–53, 479–500; 40 (1959), pp. 199–200 [SBO I (1959), pp. 65–75].

§ 84. THE ADDITIONS TO DANIEL

Wurmbrand, 'A Falasha Variant of the Story of Susanna' Bibl 44 (1963), pp. 29–35.

§ 87. THE LETTER OF JEREMIAH (EPISTULA JEREMIAE)

p. 595, n. 3, Baillet, Milik, de Vaux, Les 'Petites Grottes' de Qumrân (1962), p. 143, No. 2, Pl. XXX: EpJer 43–4 (7 Q 2 1).

§ 88. THE WISDOM OF JESUS BEN SIRA (ECCLESIASTICUS)

Fang-Che-Yong, 'Ben Sira de novissimis hominis' VD 41 (1963), pp. 21–38; Hartmann, 'Sirach in Hebrew and in Greek' CBQ 23 (1961), pp. 443–51; Rivkin, 'Ben Sira and the Non-existence of the Synagogue: A Study in Historical Method' Essays Silver (1963), pp. 320–54; Scazzocchio (§ 126 on § 81); Snaith, 'The Importance of Ecclesiasticus (The Wisdom of Ben Sira)' ET 75 (1963/64), pp. 66–9; Vaccari, 'Ecclesiastico xxxvii, 10–11: critica ed esegesi' Est Ecl 34 (1960), pp. 505–13; Ziegler, Die Münchener griechische Sirach-Handschrift 493. Ihre textgeschichtliche Bedeutung und erstmalige Edition durch den Augsburger Humanisten David Hoeschel (1604) (SAM, 1962, 4, 1962).

p. 598, line 14, Germann, 'Jesus ben Siras Dankgebet und die Hodayot' ThZ 19 (1963), pp. 81–7.

p. 598, line 21, Bickerman, 'The Civic Prayer of Jerusalem' HThR 55 (1962), pp. 163–185, cf. pp. 180–5: (I Macc. xii, 11, II Macc. i, 6), Ecclus. l, 19—national prayer.

p. 599, n. 14, Goitein, 'What would Jewish and General History Benefit by a Systematic Publication of the Documentary Geniza Papers?' PAAJR 23 (1954), pp. 29–39; 'The Cairo Geniza as a Source for the History of Muslim Civilization' Studia Islamica 3 (1955), pp. 75–91; 'The Documents of the Cairo Geniza as a Source for Mediterranean Social History' JAOS 80 (1960), pp. 91–100; 'Geniza Papers of a Documentary Character in the Gaster Collection of the British Museum' JQR 51 (1960/61), pp. 34–46; 'Slaves and Slave-girls in the Cairo Geniza Records' Arabica 9 (1962), pp. 1–20; 'The Local Jewish Community in the Light of the Cairo Geniza Records' JJSt 12 (1961), pp. 133–58; 'The Medical Profession in the Light of the Cairo Geniza Documents' HUCA 34 (1963), pp. 176–84; Katsh, 'Hebrew and Judeo-Arabic MSS in the Collections of the USSR' XXV ICO Vol. I (1962), pp. 421–30, cf. pp. 427–30: D. The Antonin Genizah Collection in Leningrad; Marx, 'The Importance of the Geniza for Jewish History' PAAJR 16 (1946/47), pp. 183–204; Scheiber, 'Ein Brief an Schelomo nach Damietta in Sachen eines Lehrers aus der Kaufmann-Genisa' AcOr [B] 14 (1962), pp. 231–9; Šer, 'Handscriften der Kairener Geniza in Ungarn' [Hungarian] AcOr [B] 14 (1962), pp. 291–300.

p. 599, n. 17, Baillet, Milik, de Vaux, Les 'Petites Grottes' de Qumrân (1962), pp. 75–7, No. 18, Pl. XV: i, 19–20 (?) (2 Q 18 1); vi, 14–15 (?) (2 Q 18 1); vi, 20–31 (2 Q 18 2); di Lella, 'Qumrân and the Geniza Fragments of Sirach' CBQ 24 (1962), pp. 245–67; 'Authenticity of the Geniza Fragments of Sirach' Bibl 44 (1963), pp. 171–200; Shaked, A Tentative Bibliography of Geniza Documents (Études Juives 5, 1965).

§ 89. THE WISDOM OF SOLOMON (SAPIENTIA SALOMONIS)

Torch-B.: Geyer (1963).

Braun, 'Saint Jean, la Sagesse et l'histoire' Cullmann-Festschr. (1962), pp. 123–33; Delcor, 'L'immortalité de l'âme dans le Livre de la Sagesse et dans les documents de Qumrân' NRTh 77 (1955), pp. 614–30; Grelot, 'L'eschatologie de la Sagesse et les apocalypses juives' Mémorial Gelin (1961), pp. 165–80; Annie Jaubert, La notion d'alliance dans le Judaïsme aux abords de l'ère chrétienne (1963); Scazzacchio (§ 126 on § 81).

p. 600 line 6 from end, Grelot, 'Sagesse x 21 et le Targum de l'Exode' Bibl 42 (1961), pp. 49–60.

p. 600, line 5 from end, Murphy, ' "To Know Your Might is the Root of Immortality" (Wis xv, 3)' CBQ 25 (1963), pp. 88–93; Vanhoye, 'Mesure ou démesure en Sag. xii, 22?' RSR 50 (1962), pp. 530–7.

p. 601, line 9, Smith, 'De interpretatione Sap xiii, 9' VD 27 (1949), pp. 287–90.

p. 602, n. 8, Pflaum, 'Les sodales Antoniniani' CRAI (1962), pp. 118–21.

p. 602, n. 11, Skehan, 'Notes on the Latin Text of the Book of Wisdom' CBQ 4 (1942), pp. 230–43.

§ 90. THE LETTER OF ARISTEAS

Franz Altheim and Ruth Stiehl, 'New Fragments of Greek Philosophers. II. Porphyry in Arabic and Syriac Translation' East and West 13 (1962), pp. 3–15; Bikerman, 'Notes sur la chancellerie des Lagides' RIDA 9 (1962), pp. 251–67; Bonner, 'A Supplementary Note on the Opening of Melito's Homily' HThR 36 (1943), pp. 317–19; Gooding, 'Aristeas and Septuagint Origins: A Review of Recent Studies' VT 13 (1963), pp. 357–79; Hanhart, 'Fragen um die Entstehung der LXX' VT 12 (1962), pp. 139–63; Jellicoe, 'Aristeas, Philo and the Septuagint *Vorlage*' JThSt 12 (1961), pp. 261–71; Parsons, *The Alexandrian Library. Glory of the Hellenic World* (1952), pp. 83–105: 'The Founding of the Museum and the Library. Ptolemy Soter and Demetrius of Phaleron'; Pelletier, *Flavius Josèphe adaptateur de la 'Lettre d'Aristée': une réaction atticisante contre la Koiné* (Études et commentaires 45, 1962); *Lettre d'Aristée à Philocrate* (Sources Chrétiennes 89, 1962); Schaller, 'Hekataios von Abdera über die Juden' ZNW 54 (1963), pp. 15–31; Zuntz, 'On the Opening Sentence of Melito's Paschal Homily' HThR 36 (1943), pp. 299–315.

p. 605, n. 4, Sollberger, 'Graeco-Babyloniaca' Iraq 24 (1962), pp. 63–72, Pls. XXV–XXVI.

§ 91. THE BOOK OF JUBILEES

Baars and Zuurmond, 'The Project for a New Edition of the Ethiopic Book of Jubilees JSSt 9 (1964), pp. 67–74; Baumgarten, 'The Calendar of the Book of Jubilees and the Bible' [Hebr., Engl. Summary] Tarbiz 32 (1962/63), pp. 317–28, I–II; Cazelles, 'Sur les origines du calendrier des Jubilés Bibl 43 (1962), pp. 202–16; Derrett, 'A Problem in the Book of Jubilees and an Indian Doctrine' ZRGG 14 (1962) pp. 247–63; Ettisch, 'Das Buch Henoch und die vier Kardinalpunkte des Sonnenlaufes' VT 11 (1961), pp. 444 f.; van Goudoever, *Biblical Calendars* (²1961); Hilgert, 'The Jubilees Calendar and the Origin of Sunday Observance' Andrews University Seminary Studies 1 (1963), pp. 44–51; Kutsch, 'Die Solstitien im Kalender des Jubiläenbuches und in äth. Henoch lxxii' VT 12 (1962), pp. 205–7; Noack, 'The Day of Pentecost in Jubilees, Qumran and Acts' ASTI 1 (1962), pp. 73–95.

p. 608, n. 4, Baillet, Milik, de Vaux, *Les 'Petites Grottes' de Qumrân* (1962), pp. 77–9, Nos. 19, 20, Pl. XV: Jub. xxiii, 7–8 (2 Q **19** 1); xlvi, 1–3 (2 Q 20 1).

§ 92. THE MARTYRDOM AND ASCENSION OF ISAIAH
(MARTYRIUM ET ASCENSIO ISAIAE)

Flemming-Duensing, 'Die Himmelfahrt des Jesaja' in Hennecke, *Neutestamentliche Apokryphen* II (³1964), pp. 454–68 (E.T. 1965).

§ 93. THE PSALMS OF SOLOMON

Baars, 'A New Fragment of the Greek Version of the Psalms of Solomon' VT 11 (1961) pp. 441–44; Bammel, 'The Organization of Palestine by Gabinius' JJSt 12 (1961), pp. 158–162.

p. 611, n. 2, Baars, 'A Note on Ode of Solomon xi, 14' VT 12 (1962), p. 196; Bauer, 'Die Oden Salomos' in Hennecke, *Neutestamentliche Apokryphen* II (³1964), pp. 576–625 (E.T. 1965); Carmignac, 'Recherches sur la langue originelle des Odes de Salomon' RQ 4 (1963/64), pp. 429–32; Fabbri, 'El Simbolo de la Leche en las Odas de Salmon' Ciencia y Fe 17 (1961), pp. 273–87; Philonenko, 'Conjecture sur un verset de la onzième Ode de Salomon' ZNW 53 (1962), p. 264; Sanders (§ 126 on p. 683, n. 17), p. 15; Schneider (§ 126 on § 83).

p. 612, n. 3, Rizzo, *Le Fonti per la Storia della Conquista Pompeiana della Siria* (1963).
p. 613, line 9, Wolfson (p. 473, n. 9): on xvii, 43.

§ 94. THE FOURTH BOOK OF MACCABEES

Kraeling (§ 126 on § 79); Perler, 'Das vierte Makkabäerbuch, Ignatius von Antiochien und die ältesten Märtyrerberichte' Rivista di Archeologia Cristiana 25 (1949), pp. 47–72.

§ 95. THE SIBYLLINE ORACLES

Buchheim, *Die Orientpolitik des Triumvirn M. Antonius* (AAH 1960, 3, 1960); Knibbe 'Die Gesandtschaftsreise des jüngeren Scipio Africanus im Jahre 140 v. Chr., ein Höhepunkt der Weltreichspolitik Roms im 2 Jahrhundert.' Jahreshefte des Österreichischen Archäologischen Instituts in Wien, Bd. XLV, Hauptblatt (1960), pp. 36–8; Kocsis, 'Ost-West Gegensatz in den jüdischen Sibyllinen' NT 5 (1962), pp. 105–10; Kurfess, 'Christliche Sibyllinen' in Hennecke, *Neutestamentliche Apokryphen* II (³1964), pp. 498–528 (E.T. 1965); Mras, 'Eine neuentdeckte Sibyllen-Theosophie' Wiener Stud. 28 (1906), pp. 43–83; ' "Babylonische" und "erythräische" Sibylle' Wiener Stud. 29 (1907), pp. 25–49; Noack, 'Er essæerne omtalt i de sibyllinske orakler?' DTT 25 (1962), pp. 176–89.

§ 96. THE ETHIOPIC BOOK OF ENOCH

Kutsch (§ 126 on § 91); Ullendorff, 'An Aramaic "Vorlage" of the Ethiopic text of Enoch?' Atti del Convegno Internazionale di Studi Etiopici, Roma (1960), pp. 259–68.

p. 619, line 8 from end, Landau, 'A Greek Inscription from Acre' IEJ 11 (1961), pp. 118–26; Lozinski, *The Original Homeland of the Parthians* (1959); Schwartz, 'Note complémentaire (à propos d'une inscription grecque de St. Jean d'Acre)' IEJ 12 (1962), pp. 135 f.: on the Parthians.

p. 619, line 3 from end, Ettisch, 'Das Buch Henoch und die vier Kardinalpunkte des Sonnenlaufes' VT 11 (1961), pp. 444 f.: on lxxii.

p. 621, n. 12, Doeve, 'Lamech's achterdocht in 1 Q Genesis Apokryphon' NedThT 15 (1960/61), pp. 401–15.

§ 97. THE SLAVONIC BOOK OF ENOCH

Rubinstein, 'Observations on the Slavonic Book of Enoch' JJSt 13 (1962), pp. 1–21.

p. 622, line 3 from end, Böhlig, 'Religionsgeschichtliche Probleme aus einer Schrift von Nag Hamadi' WZ Halle 10 (1961), pp. 1325–7, cf. p. 1326: on xii, 1; xv, 1.

§ 98. THE ASSUMPTION OF MOSES (ASSUMPTIO MOSIS)

de Santo, 'The Assumption of Moses and the Christian Gospel' Interpr. 16 (1962), pp. 305–10.

p. 623, n. 1, Allon, 'The Attitude of the Pharisees to the Roman Government and the House of Herod' Scripta Hieros, VII (1961), pp. 53–78; Harder, 'Herodes-Burgen und Herodes-Städte im Jordangraben' ZDPV 78 (1962), pp. 49–63, Pls. 3 B–6 B; Perowne, *The Later Herods, the Political Background of the NT* (1958); Schalit, 'Die frühchristliche Überlieferung über die Herkunft der Familie des Herodes. Ein Beitrag zur Geschichte der politischen Invektive in Judäa' ASTI 1 (1962), pp. 109–60; Stern, 'A. Schalit's Herod' JJSt 11 (1960), pp. 49–58; Wacholder, *Nicolaus of Damascus* (University of California Publications in History 75, 1962); Wirgin, 'On King Herod's Messianism' IEJ 11 (1961), pp. 153–4.

p. 624, n. 3, Licht, 'Taxo, or the Apocalyptic Doctrine of Vengeance' JJSt 12 (1961), pp. 95–103.

§ 99. IV EZRA (II ESDRAS)

p. 625, n. 1, Duensing, 'Das fünfte und sechste Buch Esra' in Hennecke, *Neutestamentliche Apokryphen* II (³1964), pp. 488–98 (E.T. 1965).

§ 100. THE SYRIAC APOCALYPSE OF BARUCH

Baars, 'Neue Textzeugen der syrischen Baruchapokalypse' VT 13 (1963), pp. 476–8; Zimmermann, 'Translation and Mistranslation in the Apocalypse of Baruch' *Studies Neuman* (1962), pp. 580–7.

p. 629, n. 2, Philonenko, 'Remarques sur un hymne essénien de caractère gnostique' Semitica 11 (1961), pp. 43–54; 'Une paraphrase du cantique d'Anne' RHPhR 42 (1962), pp. 157–68.

§ 102. THE TESTAMENTS OF THE XII PATRIARCHS

Delcor, 'Un roman d'amour d'origine thérapeute: Le Livre de Joseph et Asénath' Bull. de littérature Ecclésiastique 63 (1962), pp. 3–27; Gnilka, 'II Cor vi, 14–vii, 1 im Lichte der Qumranschriften und der Zwölf-Patriarchen-Testamente' *Festschr. Joseph Schmid* (1963), pp. 86–94; de Jonge, 'Christian Influence in the Testaments of the Twelve Patriarchs' NT 4 (1960), pp. 182–235; 'Once more: Christian Influence in the Testaments of the Twelve Patriarchs' NT 5 (1962), pp. 311–9; 'Christelijke elementen in de Vitae prophetarum' NedThT 16 (1962), pp. 161–78; Uricchio, 'De Lege et Messia in ordine ad iustificationem in "Testamentis XII Patriarcharum"' VD 25 (1948), pp. 98–103, 152–62, 304–10; Widengren, 'Royal Ideology and the Testaments of the Twelve Patriarchs' *Essays Hooke* (1963), pp. 202–12.

§ 103. THE LIFE OF ADAM AND EVE
(VITA ADAE ET EVAE. APOCALYPSIS MOSIS)

Leder, 'Sundenfallerzählung und Versuchungsgeschichte: zur Interpretation von Mc i, 12f.' ZNW 54 (1963), pp. 188–216; Jeremias, 'Nachwort zum Artikel von H.-G. Leder (oben S.188 ff.)' ZNW 54 (1963), pp. 278–9.

§ 104. A SURVEY OF THE DISCOVERIES OF TEXTS MADE IN THE WILDERNESS OF JUDAEA SINCE 1947

(a) Baillet, Milik, de Vaux, *Les 'Petites Grottes' de Qumrân. Exploration de la falaise. Les grottes 2 Q, 3 Q, 5 Q, 6 Q, 7 Q, à 10 Q. Le rouleau de cuivre (Discoveries in the Judaean Desert of Jordan* III) (1962).

(b) (i) Carmignac, Cothenet and Lignée, *Les Textes de Qumran. Traduits et Annotés* II (1963); Dupont-Sommer, *The Essene Writings from Qumrân*, transl. by Vermès ([2]1962); Vermès, *The Dead Sea Scrolls in English* (1962). (ii) Brownlee, *The Meaning of the Qumrân Scrolls for the Bible* (1964); Cross, *The Ancient Library of Qumrân and Modern Biblical Studies* (rev. ed., 1962); La Sor, 'Historical Framework. The Present Status of Dead Sea Scrolls Study' Interpr. 16 (1962), pp. 259–79; van der Ploeg, 'Les Manuscrits du Désert de Juda. Publications récentes' BiOr 20 (1963), pp. 220–8.

(c) Burchard, *Bibliographie zu den Handschriften vom Toten Meer* II (BZAW 88, 1963); La Sor, 'Bibliography' RQ 4 (1962/63), pp. 139–59, 311–20; 4 (1963/64), pp. 467–80; Nober, 'Elenchus bibliographicus' Bibl 44 (1963), Nos. 851–972; 45 (1964), Nos. 448–588; Stier, IZBG 8 (1961/62), Nos. 1204–79; 9 (1962/63), Nos. 1385–1521, 2170.

p. 638, n. 1, Brownlee (§ 126 on p. 7, n. 11); 'Some New Facts concerning the Discovery of the Scrolls of 1 Q' RQ 4 (1963/64), pp. 417–20.

p. 638, n. 3, Bardtke, 'Qumran und seine Funde' ThR 29 (1963), pp. 162–92 (to be continued).

p. 639, n. 5, Aharoni, 'The Caves from Naḥal Ḥever' 'Atiqot 3 (1961), pp. 148–62, Pls. XX–XXIII; Avigad, Aharoni, Bar-Adon, Yadin et al., 'Les grottes du Désert de Juda' RB 69 (1962), pp. 381–4, Pl. XLI; 'The Expedition to the Judean Desert 1961' IEJ 12 (1962) pp. 167–262, Pls. 15–48; Aviram, Avigad, Aharoni et al., 'The Judean Desert Caves' [Hebr.] BIES 26 (1962), pp. 139–242, Pls. א-לל; Bardtke, *Die Handschriftenfunde in der Wüste Juda* (1962), pp. 27–50, 56–63, Figs. 4, 5–15; Leibel, 'On the Fragment of Psalms from Naḥal Ḥever' [Hebr., Engl. summary] BIES 25 (1961), pp. 248, II; Levin and Horovitz,

'The Textile Remains from the Caves of Naḥal Ḥever' 'Atiqot 3 (1961), pp. 163–4, Pl. XXIV; Lifshitz, 'The Greek Documents from Naḥal Ṣeelim and Naḥal Mishmar' IEJ 11 (1961), pp. 53–62, 205; 'Papyrus grecs du désert de Juda' Aegyptus 42 (1962), pp. 240–56; Nathan, 'The Skeletal Material from Naḥal Ḥever' 'Atiqot 3 (1961), pp. 165–75, Pls. XXV–XXVII; Schwartz, 'Remarques sur des fragments grecs du Désert de Juda' RB 69 (1962), pp. 61–3; Yadin, 'Psalms on Scroll Finds at Masada' The Observer, London (Nov. 24, 1963).

p. 639, n. 6, Abramsky, Bar-Kochba, Prince of Israel [Hebr.] (1961); Amoussine, 'Le contrat araméen de 134 ap. notre ère provenant des environs de la Mer Morte' [Russ.] Drewnij Mir [Ancient World]. Festschr. Struwe (1962), pp. 202–13; Bar-Adon, 'Dead Sea Finds of Bar Kochba's and Chalcolithic Times: the Extraordinary Copper Treasure from the Treasure Cave of Nahal Mishmar' ILN 239 (1961), pp. 972–4; Bardtke, Die Handschriften-funde in der Wüste Juda (1962), pp. 16–26, 81–93, 97–110, Fig. 3; Borchensius, The Son of the Star (1960); Brand, 'Some Notes on the Bar Kokhba Letters' [Hebr., Engl. summary] Tarbiz 32 (1962/63), pp. 225–31, II–III; Cross (§ 126 on § 114, 2); Kutscher, 'מחוז = Harbour in the DSS' [Hebr., Engl. summary] BIES 25 (1961), pp. 160–1, III; Elisabeth Koffmann, 'Die "Restitutionsklausel" in den aramäischen Vertragsurkunden von Murabba'at' RQ 4 (1963/ 1964), pp. 421–7; Lehmann, 'Studies in the Murabba'ât and Naḥal Ḥever Documents' RQ 4 (1962/63), pp. 53–81; Rudolf Meyer, 'Die vier Höhlen von Murabba'ât' ThLZ 88 (1963), cols. 19–28; Nötscher, 'Bar Kochba, Ben Kotsba: Der Sternsohn, der Prächtige' VT 11 (1961), pp. 449–51; Philonenko, 'Un titre messianique de Bar Kokheba' ThZ 17 (1961), pp. 34–5; Schoneveld, 'Nieuwe gegebens over de opstand van Bar Kochba' Veritatem in caritate (1961), pp. 91–7; Segert, 'Zur Orthographie und Sprache der aramäischen Texte von Wadi Murabba'ât' ArOr 31 (1963), pp. 122–37; Yadin, 'Finding Bar Kochba's Despatches' ILN 239 (1961), pp. 772–5; 'New Archives of the Revolt of Bar Kochba' ILN 239 (1961), pp. 820–2; The Finds from the Bar-Kokhba Period in the 'Cave of Letters' [Hebr.] (1963); Yaron, 'The Murabba'at Documents' JJSt 11 (1960), pp. 157–71; Zeitlin, 'The Fiction of the Bar Kokba Letters' JQR 51 (1960/61), pp. 265–74.

p. 640, n. 7, Bardtke, Die Handschriftenfunde in der Wüste Juda (1962), pp. 51–3: Die Funde in chirbet mird; Grohmann ed., Arabic Papyri from Hirbet el-Mird (1963).

p. 640, n. 8, Díez Macho, 'La lengua hablada por Jesucristo' Oriens antiquus 2 (1963), pp. 95–132; Emerton, 'Did Jesus speak Hebrew?' JThSt 12 (1961), pp. 189–202; Perrot, 'Un fragment christo-palestinien découvert à Khirbet Mird (Act., x, 28–29; 32–41)' RB 70 (1963), pp. 506–55, Pls. XVIII–XIX; Rabinowitz, ' "Be opened" = 'Εφφαθά (Mark vii, 34): Did Jesus speak Hebrew?' ZNW 53 (1962), pp. 229–38; Rosen, 'Palestinian κοινή in Rabbinic Illustration' JSSt 8 (1963), pp. 56–72; Schulz, 'Maranatha und Kyrios Jesus' ZNW 53 (1962), pp. 125–44.

p. 642, n. 12, Laperrousaz, 'Études de quelques problèmes concernant "L'archéologie de la Mer Morte". À propos d'un livre récent' Semitica 12 (1962), pp. 67–104; Poole and Read, 'The "Tannery" of 'Ain Feshkha' PEQ, 93 (1961), pp. 114–23, Pl. XVI; Williams, 'An Early Coin from Qumran' NTSt 8 (1962), pp. 334–5: A bronze coin from the period of Antiochus Epiphanes (175-145 B.C.) with the head of Antiochus on the obverse, and a female figure and ΒΑΣΙΛΕΩΣ ΑΝΤΙΟΧΟΥ on the reverse.

p. 642, n. 12, Audet, 'Qumrân et la notice de Pline sur les Esséniens' RB 68 (1961), pp. 346–87; Black, The Essene Problem (1961); Buchanan, 'The Role of Purity in the Structure of the Essene Sect' RQ 4 (1963/64), pp. 397–406; Burchard, 'Pline et les Esséniens. À propos d'un article récent' RB 69 (1962), pp. 533–69; Laperrousaz, ' "Infra hos Engadda." Notes à propos d'un article récent' RB 69 (1962), pp. 369–80; Lindeskog, 'Die Essenerfrage in Geschichte und Gegenwart' ASTI 1 (1962), pp. 96–108; Vermès 'Essenes and Thera-peutai' RQ 3 (1961/62), pp. 495–504).

p. 643, n. 14, Zeitlin, 'The Fallacy of the Antiquity of the Hebrew Scrolls once more exposed' JQR 52 (1961/62), pp. 346–66.

p. 643, n. 16, Roth, 'The Pharisees in the Jewish Revolution of 66–73' JSSt 7 (1962), pp. 63–80.

p. 643, n. 17, Brandon, 'Jesus and the Zealots' ALUOS 2 (1961), pp, 11–25; Hahn,

'Zwei dunkle Stellen in Josephus' AcOr [B] XIV (1962), pp. 131–8, cf. pp. 135–8: on *Bell. Jud.* II § 142 and CD XII 6–8; Roth, 'Melekh ha-'olam: Zealot influence in the Liturgy?' JJSt 11 (1960), pp. 173–5; Zeitlin, 'Zealots and Sicarii' JBL 81 (1962), pp. 395–8.

§ 105. THE MANUAL OF DISCIPLINE

Carmignac, Cothenet and Lignée (§ 126 on § 104), pp. 11–27, 31–42 (Carmignac).

p. 645, n. 1, Burchard (§ 104) (1957, [2]1959), pp. 3, 115, proposes the Siglum 1 Q IV for the 'Genesis Apocryphon' described in § 111, the fourth of the scrolls previously in the possession of Mar. Athanasius Samuel.

p. 648, lines 11–19, Baillet, Milik, de Vaux, *Les 'Petites Grottes' de Qumrân* (1962), pp. 180–3, Nos. 11, 13, Pls. XXXVIII, XXXIX, XL (5 Q 11 1 1; 5 Q 11 1 11; 5 Q 13 4 2–3).

§ 106. THE DASMASCUS DOCUMENT

Carmignac, Cothenet and Lignée (§ 126 on § 104), pp. 131–204 (Cothenet).

p. 650, lines 9–10, Baillet, Milik, de Vaux, *Les 'Petites Grottes' de Qumrân* (1962), pp. 128–31, No. 15, Pl. XXVI (6 Q 15 1, 6 Q 15 2, 6 Q 15 3, 6 Q 15 4); p. 181, No. 12, Pl. XXXVIII (5 Q 12 1).

p. 650, n.3, Delcor, 'Le docteur de Justice, Nouveau Moïse dans les Hymnes de Qumrân' OBL IV (1962), pp. 407–23; Roth, 'The Teacher of Righteousness and the Prophecy of Joel' VT 13 (1963), pp. 91–5.

p. 650, n. 6, Jeremias, *Der Lehrer der Gerechtigkeit* (1963).

p. 652, n. 8, Rowley, BJRL 44 (1961/62), pp. 111–56 = *From Moses to Qumran* (1963), pp. 239–79.

§ 107. THE WAR SCROLL

Nielsen (§ 126 on p. 100, n. 4).

§ 108. THE HYMN SCROLL AND SIMILAR COLLECTIONS OF SONGS AND PRAYERS

Baillet, 'Psaumes, Hymnes, cantiques et prières dans les manuscrits de Qumrân' OBL IV (1962), pp. 389–405; Delcor, *Les Hymnes de Qumrân (Hodayot). Texte Hébreu, Introduction, Commentaire* (1962); Morawe, 'Vergleich des Aufbaus der Danklieder und hymnischen Bekenntnislieder (1 Q H) von Qumran mit dem Aufbau der Psalmen im AT und in Spätjudentum' RQ 4 (1963/64), pp. 323–56; Sveinar, 'Salmer og Salmedikting i Qumran' NTT 64 (1963), pp. 99–111; Barbara Thiering, 'The Poetic Forms of the Hodayot' JSSt 8 (1963), pp. 189–209.

p. 657, n. 6, Carmignac, Cothenet and Lignée (§ 126 on § 104), pp. 311–20 (Carmignac).
p. 657, n. 10, Carmignac, Cothenet and Lignée (§ 126 on § 104), pp. 299–301 (Carmignac).

§ 109. THE HABBAKUK 'COMMENTARY' AND SIMILAR 'COMMENTARIES'

Carmignac, 'Notes sur les Pesharim' RQ 3 (1961/62), pp. 505–38; Carmignac, Cothenet and Lignée (§ 126 on § 104), pp. 93–117 (Carmignac); Dupont-Sommer, *Observations sur le Commentaire d'Habacuc découvert près de la Mer Morte* (1950); Finkel, 'The Pesher of Dreams and Scriptures' RQ 4 (1963/64), pp. 357–70.

p. 658, n. 1, van der Ploeg, *Bijbelverklaring te Qumran* (Med. Ned. Ak. N.R. 23, no. 8, 1960).

p. 659, n. 5, Carmignac, Cothenet and Lignée (§ 126 on § 104), pp. 65–76 (Carmignac).
p. 659, n. 6, Carmignac, Cothenet and Lignée (§ 126 on § 104), pp. 77–81 (Carmignac).
p. 659, n. 7, Carmignac, Cothenet and Lignée (§ 126 on § 104), pp. 82–4 (Carmignac).
p. 659, n. 8, Allegro, 'More Unpublished Pieces of a Qumran Commentary on Nahum (4 Q p Nah)' JSSt 7 (1962), pp. 304–8, Pls. I–III; Amoussine, 'Éphraïm et Manassé dans le Pêshèr de Nahum (4 Q p Nahum)' RQ 4 (1963/64), pp. 389–96; Carmignac, Cothenet

and Lignée (§ 126 on § 104), pp. 85–92 (Carmignac); Dupont-Sommer, 'Observations sur le Commentaire de Nahum découvert près de la Mer Morte' Journal des Savants (1963), pp. 201–27; Licht, 'Additional Columns to the Nahum Pesher' [Hebr.] Molad 19 (1961), pp. 454–6.

p. 660, n. 9, Carmignac, Cothenet and Lignée (§ 126 on § 104), p. 118 (Carmignac).

p. 660, n. 10, Carmignac, Cothenet and Lignée (§ 126 on § 104), pp. 119–26 (Carmignac); Stegemann, 'Der Pešer Psalm xxxvii aus Höhle 4 von Qumran' RQ 4 (1963), pp. 235–70.

p. 660, n. 11, Carmignac, Cothenet and Lignée (§ 126 on § 104), pp. 127, 128 (Carmignac).

p. 660, n. 13, Carmignac, Cothenet and Lignée (§ 126 on § 104), pp. 285–8 (Carmignac).

p. 661, n. 14, Carmignac, Cothenet and Lignée (§ 126 on § 104), pp. 279–84 (Carmignac).

p. 661, n. 15, Carmignac, Cothenet and Lignée (§ 126 on § 104), pp. 263–7 (Carmignac); Lindars, 'Second Thoughts IV. Books of Testimonies' ET 75 (1963/64), pp. 173–5; Prigent, Les Testimonia dans le christianisme primitif: l'Épître de Barnabé i–xvi et ses sources (1961).

§ 110. THE APOCALYPSES

p. 662, n. 1, Carmignac, Cothenet and Lignée (§ 126 on § 104), pp. 255–61 (Carmignac).

p. 663, n. 5, Carmignac, Cothenet and Lignée (§ 126 on § 104), pp. 289–94 (Carmignac).

§ 111. HAGGADIC NARRATIVE WORKS

On the Siglum 1 Q IV for the 'Genesis Apocryphon' cf. § 126 on p. 645, n. 1. Carmignac, Cothenet and Lignée (§ 126 on § 104), pp. 207–53 (Lignée); Rowley, 'Notes on the Aramaic of the Genesis Apocryphon' Studies Driver (1963), pp. 116–29.

p. 664, line 16, Grelot, 'Parwaïm, des Chroniques à l'Apocryphe de la Genèse' VT 11 (1961), pp. 30–8; 'Retour au Parwaïm VT 14 (1964), pp. 155–69; Del Medico, 'Zahav parwayim. L'or fructifère dans la tradition juive' VT 13 (1963), pp. 158–86; Meyer, 'URUK. KI und 'EREK. MAT (Genesis-Midrasch II, 23)' RQ 3 (1961/62), pp. 553–8.

p. 664, n. 2, Carmignac, Cothenet and Lignée (§ 126 on § 104), pp. 247–53 (Carmignac); Wacholder (§ 126 on p. 540, n. 27).

p. 666, line 19, Laperrousaz, 'Remarques sur l'origine des rouleaux de cuivre découverts dans la Grotte 3 de Qumrân' RHR 159 (1961), pp. 147–72, cf. p. 167: '...l'hypothèse la plus plausible consiste à voir dans cette liste les endroits où Bar Kokeba ... a dissimulé son trésor' ('... the most plausible hypothesis is to regard this list as containing the places where Bar Kochba ... concealed his treasures').

p. 666, n. 9, Allegro, 'The Copper Scroll from Qumrân' Transact. Glasgow Univ. Or. Soc. XVIII (1961), pp. 56–65; Rengstorf, Hirbet Qumrân and the problem of the Library of the Dead Sea Cave (1963); Rowley, 'Comparison and Contrast. Qumran and the Early Church' Interpr. 16 (1962), pp. 292–304; Review of Discoveries in the Judaean Desert of Jordan III (1963), The Heythrop Journal 4 (1963), pp. 408–11.

p. 666, n. 11, Milik, 'Le rouleau de Cuivre provenant de la grotte 3 Q (3 Q 15)' (Discoveries in the Judaean Desert of Jordan III (1962), pp. 199–302, Pls. XLIII–LXXI).

§ 112. PARENETIC AND DIDACTIC WRITINGS. JURIDICAL AND ASTROLOGICAL WORKS

p. 667, n. 1, Carmignac, Cothenet and Lignée (§ 126 on § 104), pp. 295–7 (Carmignac).

§ 114. BOOKS AND WRITING

1. Books

Bruce, The Books and the Parchments. Some Chapters on the Transmission of the Bible (³1963); Cardascia, Les Archives de Murašu (1961); Evans, 'An Old Babylonian Soldier: Notes on the Archive of Ubarrum' JCSt 14 (1960), pp. 34–42; Funke, Buchkunde (²1963); Goossens, 'Introduction à l'archivéconomie à l'Asie antérieure' RA 46 (1952), pp. 98–107; 'Classement des Archives Royales de Mari' RA 46 (1952), pp. 137–54; Gordon, 'Towards a Grammar of Minoan' Or 32 (1963), pp. 292–7; Gurney and Hulin, *The Sultantepe Tablets* II (1964); Hunger et al., *Geschichte der Textüberlieferung der antiken und mittelalterlichen Literatur*. I: *Antikes und mittelalterliches Buch- und Schriftwesen* (1961); on this cf. Zuntz, *Gnomon* 35 (1963), pp. 1–10; Kramer, 'New Literary Catalogue from Ur' RA 55 (1961), pp. 169–76; Lambert, 'Ancestors, Authors, and Canonicity' JCSt 11 (1957), pp. 1–14, 112; 'A Catalogue of Texts and Authors' JCSt 16 (1962), pp. 59–77; Landsberger 'Remarks on the Archive of the Soldier Ubarum' JCSt 9 (1955), pp. 121–31; Lange, *Das Buch im Wandel der Zeiten* (⁶1951); Sollberger, 'Thirty-two Dated Tablets from the Reign of Abīešuḫ' JCSt 5 (1951), pp. 77–97; Szlechter, 'Les tablettes juridiques datées du règne d'Abī-ešuḫ conservées au Musée d'Art et d'Histoire de Genève' JCSt 7 (1953), pp. 81–99.

p. 671, n. 1, E. J. Wein and Ruth Opificius, *7000 Jahre Byblos* (1963).

p. 672, n. 3, Dunand, 'Histoire d'une source' MUB 37 (1961), pp. 39–53, Pls. I–II, cf pp. 50–53.

2. Writing

Franz Altheim and Ruth Stiehl, 'Die zweite (aramäische) Inschrift aus Mcḫet'a' *Die aramäische Sprache unter den Achaimeniden* I (1963), pp. 243–61, 312; Altheim, *Geschichte der Hunnen* IV (1962), pp. 8–23; Albright, 'The Early Alphabetic Inscriptions from Sinai and their Decipherment' BASOR 110 (1948), pp. 6–22; Avdiev, 'L'origine de l'écriture en Ancienne Égypte' XXV ICO Vol. I (1962), pp. 117–25; van den Branden, 'L'origine des alphabets protosinaïtique, arabes préislamiques et phénicien' BiOr 19 (1962), pp. 198–206; 'Les inscriptions protosinaïtiques' Oriens Antiquus 1 (1962), pp. 197–214; Brice and Grumach, 'Studies in the Structure of Some Ancient Scripts' BJRL 45 (1962/63), pp. 15–57; British Museum, *Writing in Ancient Western Asia. Its origins and Development from Pictures to Letters* (1963); Cross, 'Epigraphic Notes on Hebrew Documents of the Eighth–Sixth Centuries B.C.: I. A New Reading of a Place Name in the Samaria Ostraca' BASOR 163 (1961), pp. 12–14; 'II. The Murabba'ât Papyrus and the Letter found near Yabneh-Yam' BASOR 165 (1962), pp. 34–46; 'III. The Inscribed Jar Handles from Gibeon' BASOR 168 (1962), pp. 18–23; 'The Discovery of the Samaria Papyri' BA 26 (1963), pp. 109–21; Diringer, *Writing* (1962); 'Some Problems of "Semitic Epigraphy"' XXV ICO Vol. I (1962), pp. 329–336; Doblhofer, *Voices in Stone: The Decipherment of Ancient Scripts and Writings* (1961); Ettisch, 'The Monumental Pictorial Script of the Hebrews' JQR 54 (1963/64), pp. 28–57; Falkenstein, 'Die babylonische Schule' Saeculum 4 (1953), pp. 125–37; Friedrich, 'Der Werdegang der Schrift' Saeculum 14 (1963), pp. 123–40; Gelb, *Old Akkadian Writings and Grammar* (²1961); *A Study of Writing* (²1963); Gordon, 'The Dreros Bilingual' JSSt 8 (1963), pp. 76–9; Hoftijzer, 'Kanttekeningen bij het onderzoek van de westsemitische epigrafie' JEOL 15 (1957/58), pp. 112–25; Jeffery, *The Local Scripts of Archaic Greece* (1961); 'Writing' in Wace and Stubbings, *A Companion to Homer* (1962), pp. 545–59; Labat, 'Le rayonnement de la langue et de l'écriture akkadiennes au deuxième millénaire avant notre ère' Syria 39 (1962), pp. 1–27; Lambert, 'Le travail des scribes aux premiers âges de l'écriture' XXV ICO Vol. I (1962), pp. 187–9; Lange, *Schriftfibel* (³1951); Martin, 'A Twelfth Century Bronze Palimpsest' RStOr 37 (1962), pp. 175–97, Pl. I; 'Revision and Reclassification of the Proto-Byblian Signs' Or 31 (1962), pp. 250–71, 339–63; Mieses, *Die Gesetze der Schriftgeschichte. Konfession und Schrift im Leben der Völker* (1919); Millard, Alphabetic Inscriptions on Ivories from Nimrud' Iraq 24 (1962), pp. 41–51, Pls. XXIII–XXIV; Jacqueline Pirenne, 'La Grèce et Saba, une nouvelle base pour la chronologie sud-arabe' MDSAI XV 1 (1960), pp. 89–196, Pls. I–IX; 'Aux origines de la graphie Syriaque' Syria 40 (1963), pp. 101–37, Pls. I–II; Reed and Winnett (§ 126 on p. 295, n. 54); Segert, DLZ 83 (1962), cols. 100–103: on Cohen (1953); Tsevat, 'A Chapter on Old West Semitic Orthography' *Bloch Memorial Vol.* (1960), pp. 82–91; Virolleaud, 'L'alphabet sénestrogyre de Ras-Shamra (Ugarit)' CRAI (1960), pp. 85–90; Weidmüller, 'Der Buchstabe M. Formenwandel und Verbreitung' Börsenblatt für den deutschen Buchhandel, Frankfurter Ausgabe No. 89 (8 Nov. 1960), pp. 3–11; 'Alpha-Aleph-Ochsenkopf?' *ib.* No. 67 (20 Aug. 1963, special issue 12 pp.); Wemyss, *The Language of the World Ancient and Modern. The Alphabets, and Other Written Characters, in Sound and Symbol* (1950).

p. 674, line 10, Yeivin, 'Das geistige Leben in Jerusalem zur Zeit des ersten Tempels' *Studies in the History of Israel and its Country* [Hebr.] (1960), pp. 302–18.

p. 674, n. 9, Segal, *'yrḥ* in the Gezer "Calendar" ' JSSt 7 (1962), pp. 212–21, Pls. I–IV; Talmon, 'The Gezer Calendar and the Seasonal Cycle of Ancient Canaan' JAOS 83 (1963), pp. 177–87.

p. 674, n. 10, On the raising of the tribute imposed by Tiglathpileser V upon Menahem (cf. II Kings xv, 19–20), from the Israelite landowners, cf. Ras Shamra tablet 19, 17 in Virolleaud, 'Les nouvelles tablettes alphabéthiques de Ras-Shamra (XIXᵉ campagne, 1955)' CRAI (1956), pp. 63–7, cf. pp. 63 f., and in Schaeffer, *Ugaritica* IV (1962), pp. 73, 75.

p. 674, n. 11, Aharoni, 'The Samaria Ostraca—an Additional Note' IEJ 12 (1962), pp. 67–69; Cross (§ 126 on § 114, 2); Kaufman, 'A Note on the Place Name *Spr* and the Letter *Samek* in the Samaria Ostraca' BASOR 172 (1963), pp. 60–1; Rainey, 'Administration in Ugarit and the Samaria Ostraca' IEJ 12 (1962), pp. 62 f.; Sznycer, 'Nouveaux Ostraca de Nisa' Semitica 12 (1962), pp. 105–26; Yadin, 'A Further Note on the Samaria Ostraca' IEJ 12 (1962), pp. 64–6.

p. 675, line 3, Naveh, 'Old Hebrew Inscriptions in a Burial Cave' IEJ 13 (1963), pp. 74–92, Pls. 9–13.

p. 675, n. 12, Dothan, 'An Inscribed Jar from Azor' 'Atiqot 3 (1961), pp. 181–4, Pls. XXVIII, 4, 5; 'Excavations at Azor, 1960' IEJ 11 (1961), pp. 171–5, Pls. 33–5, cf. pp. 174 f., Pl. 35, 6; Lapp, 'Ptolemaic Stamped Handles from Judah' BASOR 172 (1963), pp. 22–35; Yadin, 'The Fourfold Division of Judah' BASOR 163 (1961), pp. 6–12.

p. 675, n. 14, Aharoni, 'Excavations at Ramat Raḥel' BA 24 (1961), pp. 98–118, cf. pp. 104–12.

p. 675, n. 16, Avigad, 'The Jotham Seal from Elath' BASOR 163 (1961), pp. 18–22; 'A Seal of "Manasseh Son of the King" ' IEJ 13 (1963), pp. 133–6, Pl. 18 C; Cross, 'An Archaic Inscribed Seal from the Valley of Aijalon' BASOR 168 (1962), pp. 12–18; Giveon, 'Two New Hebrew Seals and their Iconographic Background' PEQ 93 (1961), pp. 38–42, Pls. III–IV; Horn, 'An Early Aramaic Seal with an Unusual Design' BASOR 167 (1962), pp. 16–18; Millard, 'A Seal from Petra' PEQ 93 (1961), p. 136, Pl. XVIII B; Moscati, 'On Ancient Hebrew Seals' JNESt 11 (1952), pp. 164–8; Scott, 'The Seal of *Šmrjw*' VT 14 (1964), pp. 108–10.

p. 675, n. 18, Aharoni and Ruth Amiran, 'Tel Arad' IEJ 12 (1962), pp. 144 f.; Brand, 'Remarks on the Hashavyahu Letter' [Hebr.] Yediot [BIES 27] (1962/63), p. 206; Cross (§ 126 on § 114, 2); Naveh, 'More Hebrew Inscriptions from Meṣad Hashavyahu' IEJ 12 (1962), pp. 27–32, Pls. 5–6; 'The Excavations at Meṣad Ḥashavyahu' IEJ 12 (1962), pp. 89–113, Pls. 9–12; 'A Hebrew Letter from the Time of Jeremiah' Archaeology 15 (1962), pp. 108–11; Yeivin, 'The Judicial Petition from Mezad Hashavyahu' BiOr 19 (1962), pp. 3–10, Pl. I. According to PEQ 94 (1962), p. 99, Hebrew letters on ostraca, including one of fifteen lines from one Yenaḥemyahu, have been found in Tell 'Arad in the eastern Negeb.

p. 676, n. 22, Kadman, *Corpus Nummorum Palaestinensium*, IV (1961); *The Coins of Akko Ptolemais* (1961); Kadman and Kindler, *Coins in Palestine throughout the ages* [Hebr.] (1963); Kanael, 'Ancient Jewish Coins and their Historical Importance' BA 26 (1963), pp. 38–62; 'Additions and Corrections to BA XXVI, 2' BA 26 (1963), p. 140; Meshorer, 'An Attic Archaic Coin from Jerusalem' 'Atiqot 3 (1961), p. 185; Reifenberg, *Ancient Jewish Coins* (³1963); Roth, 'The Historical Implications of the Jewish Coinage of the First Revolt' IEJ 12 (1962), pp. 33–46.

p. 677, n. 24, Brett, 'The Qaṣr el-'Abd: A Proposed Reconstruction' BASOR 171 (1963), pp. 39–45; Dorothy Kent Hill, 'The Animal Fountain of 'Arâq el-Emîr' BASOR 171 (1963), pp. 45–55; Lapp, 'Soundings at 'Arâq el-Émîr (Jordan)' BASOR 165 (1962), pp. 16–34; 'The Second and Third Campaigns at 'Arâq el-Émîr' BASOR 171 (1963), pp. 8–39; ''Arâq el-Émîr' RB 70 (1963), pp. 411–16, Pl. XIV; Stern, 'Notes on the Story of Joseph the Tobiad (Josephus, Antiquities XII, 154 ff.)' [Hebr., Engl. summary] Tarbiz 32, (1962/63), pp. 35–47, III; Weippert, 'Archäologischer Jahresbericht' ZDPV 79 (1963), pp. 164–79, cf. pp. 165–9: 'araḳ el-emîr.

THE MASORETIC TEXT (𝔐)

Kahle, 'Hebreo premasorético' Sefarad 21 (1961), pp. 240–50; 'Pre-Massoretic Hebrew, Textus 2 (1962), pp. 1–7; Leibel, 'A Note regarding the Development of Biblical Orthography' [Hebr., Engl. summary] Tarbiz 32 (1962/63), pp. 114–19, I–II; Robertson, 'Points of Interest in the Massoretic Text' JNESt 2 (1943), pp. 35–9; Seeligmann, 'Researches into the Criticism of the Massoretic Text of the Bible' [Hebr., Engl. summary] Tarbiz 25 (1955/56), pp. 118–39, I–II; Talmon, 'The Three Scrolls of the Law that were found in the Temple Court' Textus 2 (1962), pp. 14–27; Weil, 'Propositions pour une étude de la tradition massorétique Babylonienne' Textus 2 (1962), pp. 103–19; 'La Massorah Magna Babylonienne des Prophètes' Textus 3 (1963), pp. 163–70, 1 Pl.; 'Quatre Fragments de la Massorah Magna Babylonienne' Textus 3 (1963), pp. 74–120, Pls. I–VIII; Weingreen, 'A Rabbinic Type Gloss in the LXX Version of I Samuel i, 18' VT 14 (1964), pp. 225–8

§ 115. THE CONSONANTAL TEXT

Baillet, Milik, de Vaux, Les 'Petites Grottes' de Qumrân (Discoveries in the Judaean Desert of Jordan III) (1962), p. 303: Index des Textes Bibliques; Freedman, 'The Masoretic Text and the Qumran Scrolls: A Study in Orthography' Textus 2 (1962), pp. 87–102; Hempel, Weitere Mitteilungen über Text und Auslegung der am Nordwestende des Toten Meeres gefundenen hebräischen Handschriften (NAG 1961, No. 10, 1961) = Die Texte von Qumran in der heutigen Forschung (1962); Mansoor, 'The Massoretic Text in the Light of Qumran' SVT IX (1963), pp. 305–21; Wernberg-Møller, 'The Hodayoth and Biblical Textual Criticism' XXV ICO Vol. I (1962), pp. 386–7.

p. 680, n. 2, Stegemann and Becker, 'Zum Text von Fragment 5 aus Wadi Murabba'ât' RQ 3 (1961/62), pp. 443–8.

p. 681, n. 5, Flusser, 'The Text of Isa. xlix, 17, in the DSS' Textus 2 (1962), pp. 140–2; Talmon, 'DSIᵃ as a Witness to Ancient Exegesis of the Book of Isaiah' ASTI 1 (1962), pp. 62–72.

p. 683, n. 11, Hempel, 'Zu 4 Q Deut. xxxii, 8' ZAW 74 (1962), p. 70.

p. 683, n. 14, Brownlee, 'The Literary Significance of the Bisection of Isaiah in the Ancient Scroll of Isaiah from Qumran' XXV ICO Vol. I (1962), pp. 431–7.

p. 683, n. 15, Brownlee, 'The Scroll of Ezekiel from the eleventh Qumran Cave' RQ 4 (1962/63), pp. 11–28, Pls. I–II.

p. 683, n. 16, Weiss, 'A Comparison between the Massoretic and the Qumran Texts of Nahum iii, 1–11' RQ 4 (1963/64), pp. 433–9.

p. 683, n. 17, Brownlee, 'La form poétique du Psaume cli de la grotte 11' RQ 4 (1963/1964), pp. 371–85; Leibel, 'On the Fragment of Psalms from Naḥal Ḥever' [Hebr., Engl. summary] BIES 25 (1961), p. 248, II; Rabinowitz (§ 126 on p. 115, n. 44); Sanders, 'The Scroll of Psalms (11 Q Pss) from Cave 11: A Preliminary Report' BASOR 165 (1962), pp. 11–15; 'Ps. cli in 11 Q Pss' ZAW 75 (1963), pp. 73–86; 'Two non-canonical Psalms in 11 Q Psᵃ' ZAW 76 (1964), pp. 57–75; 'Responsum' ZAW 76 (1964), p. 200; Skehan, 'The Apocryphal Psalm cli' CBQ 25 (1963), pp. 407–9.

p. 686, line 9, Barthélemy, 'Les tiqquné sopherim et la critique textuelle de l'Ancien Testament' SVT IX (1963), pp. 285–304.

§ 116. THE POINTING OF THE TEXT

Franz Altheim and Ruth Stiehl, Ein asiatischer Staat. Feudalismus unter den Sasaniden und ihren Nachbarn (1954), pp. 175–89: 'Kodifikation'; Dietrich, Neue palästinisch punktierte Bibelfragmente veröffentlicht und auf Text und Punktation hin untersucht (Duplicated Diss., Tübingen, 1960); Massorah ... Vol. I (1964); Díez Macho, 'A new list of the so-called "Ben-Naftali" manuscripts preceded by an inquiry into the true character of these manuscripts' Studies Driver (1963), pp. 16–52; Goshen-Gottstein, 'Biblical Manuscripts in the United States' Textus 2 (1962), pp. 28–59, 1 Pl.; 'The Rise of the Tiberian Bible Text' Studies and Texts of the Philip W. Lown Institute of Advanced Judaic Studies I, ed. by Altmann (1963), pp.

79–122; Lehmann, *The Damascus Pentateuch and its Manuscript Tradition according to Ben Naphtali* (1962); Lipschuetz, 'Mishael ben Uzziel's Treatise on the Differences between Ben Asher and Ben Naphthali' [Hebr., Engl. summary] Textus 2 (1962), pp. א–נה; Millás-Vallicrosa, 'Un antiguo glossario hispano-hebraico con transcripciones pretiberiensias' Sefarad 21 (1961), pp. 219–39; Murtonen, 'Von einigen weniger bekannten hebräischen Punktationssystemen' Das Altertum 8 (1962), pp. 114–23; Rüger, 'Ein neues Fragment des Richterbuches mit babylonischer Punktation' ZAW 75 (1963), pp. 223–5; 'Zwei neue Fragmente zu Mischael Ben Uzziels כתאב אלכלף aus der Kairo-Geniza' VT 13 (1963), pp. 231–5; 'Ein neues Genesis-Fragment mit komplizierter babylonischer Punktation aus der Kairo-Geniza' VT 13 (1963), pp. 235–7; Snaith, 'The Ben Asher Text' Textus 2 (1962), pp. 8–13; Weil (§ 126 on p. 564, n. 8); 'Un fragment de *Okhlah* palestinienne' ALUOS 3 (1961/62), pp. 68–80; 'Le développement de l'œuvre massorétique' Bulletin d'Information de l'Institut de Recherche et d'Histoire des Textes No. 11 (1962), pp. 43–67; 'Propositions pour une étude de la tradition massorétique babylonienne' Textus 2 (1962), pp. 103–19; 'Quatre Fragments de la Massorah Magna Babylonienne' Textus 3 (1963), pp. 74–120, Pls. I–VIII; 'Massorah Magna Babylonienne des Prophètes' Textus 3 (1963), pp. 163–70, 1 Pl.; Yeivin, 'A Babylonian Fragment of the Bible in the Abbreviated System' Textus 2 (1962), pp. 120–39.

p. 690, n. 4, Hempel, 'Der Hebräische Text zweier Wolfenbütteler Fragmente' NGW (1962), pp. 155–71; Rudolf Meyer, 'Die Bedeutung des Kodex Reuchlinianus für die Hebräische Sprachgeschichte. Dargestellt am Dageš-Gebrauch' ZDMG 113 (1963), pp. 51–61.

p. 691, line 34, Rubinstein, 'Singularities in the Massorah of the Leningrad Codex (B 19a)' JJSt 12 (1961), pp. 123–31.

p. 692, n. 9, Weil, 'La Bible de l'Université hébraïque de Jérusalem' RHPhR 43 (1963), pp. 193–9.

p. 692, n. 10, Goshen-Gottstein, 'The Aleppo Codex and Ben Būyā'ā the Scribe' [Hebr., Engl. summary] Tarbiz 33 (1963), pp. 149–52, 2 Pls. On the Aleppo Codex cf. Barnes (§ 126 on § 67), Appendix 7: A lost page of Genesis of the Ben Asher Aleppo Codex; Yeivin, 'The Vocalization of Qere-Kethiv in A' Textus 2 (1962), pp. 146–9.

§ 117. GENERAL CONSIDERATIONS. TRANSLATIONS. THE POLYGOTS

Biblia Sacra Polyglotta. Ed. by Waltonus, 6 Vols. Reprint of the edition of 1657 (1963); Ayuso Marazuela, 'La Biblio Visigótica de San Isidoro de León' Est Bíbl 19 (1960), pp. 5–24, 167–200; 20 (1961), pp. 5–43, 243–59, 359–406; Rabin, 'The Ancient Versions and the Indefinite Subject' Textus 2 (1962), pp. 60–76.

p. 694, nn. 3–5, Wallis, Detailed discussion of the *Polyglotta Matritensia*, ThLZ 88 (1963), cols. 419–21.

§ 118. THE SAMARITAN PENTATEUCH

Baillet, 'Une feuille du Pentateuque Samaritain à l'abbaye de Beuron' RB 70 (1963), pp. 225–42, Pls. III–IV; Ben-Ḥayyim, *The Literary and Oral Tradition of Hebrew and Aramaic amongst the Samaritans* I. II (1957), III, 1 (1961) [Hebr.]; on this cf. Baillet, 'La récitation de la Loi chez les Samaritans' RB 69 (1962), pp. 570–87; Pérez Castro, 'Fragmento inédito del Séfer Abisa'' Sefarad 21 (1961), pp. 3–8; Robertson, VT 12 (1962), pp. 228–35: on Pérez Castro, *Séfer Abiša'* (1959); *Catalogue of the Samaritan Manuscripts in the John Rylands Library Manchester*. Vol. II: *The Gaster Manuscripts* (1962), pp. 1–42, Pls. 1–5; Talmon, 'Some Unrecorded Fragments of the Hebrew Pentateuch in the Samaritan Version' Textus 3 (1963), pp. 60–73.

§ 119. THE TARGUMS

Goldberg, 'Die spezifische Verwendung des Terminus Schekhinah im Targum Onkelos als Kriterium einer relativen Datierung' Judaica 19 (1963), pp. 43–61; Goshen-Gottstein,

Aramaic Bible Versions. Comparative selections and glossary (1963); Grelot, 'Les Targums du Pentateuque—Étude comparée d'après Genèse, iv, 3–16' Semitica 9 (1959), pp. 59–88; Kadari, 'Studies in the Syntax of Targum Onkelos' [Hebr., Engl. summary] Tarbiz 32 (1962/63), pp. 232–51, III–IV; Katsh, 'S. Baer's Unpublished Targum Onkelos Text' *Studies Neuman* (1962), pp. 329–42; Komlosh, 'The Aggada in the Targumim of Jacob's Blessing' [Hebr., Engl. summary] Bar-Ilan. Annual of Bar-Ilan University Studies in Judaica and Humanities 1 (1963), pp. 195–206, XLIV; Le Déaut, 'Traditions targumiques dans le Corpus Paulinien' Bibl 42 (1961), pp. 28–48; Martin, 'The Babylonian Tradition and Targum' OBL IV (1962), pp. 425–51; Rudolf Meyer, ' "Elia" und "Ahab" ' (Tg. Ps.–Jon. zu Deut. xxxiii, 11)' *Festschr. Michel* (1963), pp. 356–68; Schulz, 'Die Bedeutung der neuen Targumforschung für die synoptische Tradition' *Festschr. Michel* (1963), pp. 425–36; Stauffer, 'Der Methurgeman des Petrus' *Festschr. Joseph Schmid* (1963), pp. 283–93; Vermès, 'The Targumic Versions of Genesis iv, 3–16' ALUOS 3 (1961/62), pp. 81–114; 'Haggadah in the Onkelos Targum' JSSt 8 (1963), pp. 159–69; Vööbus, *Peschitta und Targumim des Pentateuchs. Neues Licht zur Frage der Herkunft der Peschitta aus dem altpalästinischen Targum* (1958); Wernberg-Møller, 'An Inquiry into the Validity of the Text-Critical Argument for an Early Dating of the Recently Discovered Palestinian Targum' VT 12 (1962), pp. 312–30; 'Prolegomena to a Re-Examination of the Palestinian Targum Fragments of the Book of Genesis Published by P. Kahle, and their Relationship to the Peshitta' JSSt 7. (1962), pp. 253–66.

p. 696, n. 1, van der Ploeg, *Le Targum de Job de la Grotte 11 de Qumran* (MAA N.R. 25, 9, 1962); van der Woude, 'Das Hiobtargum aus Qumrân-Höhle XI' SVT IX (1963), pp. 322–31.

p. 697, n. 3, Kadari, 'ד-clauses in Targum Onkelos' Textus 3 (1963), pp. 36–59.

p. 698, n. 8, Diaz, 'Palestinian Targum and New Testament' NT 6 (1963), pp. 75–80; Le Déaut, 'Goûter le calice de la mort' Bibl 43 (1963), pp. 82–6; Martin, 'Palaeography of Neofiti 1' Textus 3 (1963), pp. 1–35.

p. 698, n. 10, Speier, ' "Das Kosten des Todeskelches" im Targum' VT 13 (1963), pp. 344–5.

§ 120. THE PESHIṬTA AND OTHER OLD SYRIAC TRANSLATIONS

(a) The Peshiṭta Institute, *Peshiṭta . . . Specimen edition* (1964); *Vetus Testamentum Syriace et Neosyriace* (Reprint, London, 1954).

(b) *List of OT Peshiṭta Manuscripts* ed. by the Peshiṭta Institute of the University of Leiden (1961); 'Peshiṭta Institute Communications I. II. III' VT 12 (1962), pp. 127–8, 237–9, 351 f.; Albrektson (§ 126 on § 69); Baars, 'Description of three Syriac OT Manuscripts' VT 13 (1963), pp. 260–8; Dirksen, 'A sixth-century palimpsest of Judges reconstructed' (Peshiṭta Institute Communications IV) VT 13 (1963), pp. 285–92; Emerton, 'Unclean Birds and the Origin of the Peshitta' JSSt 7 (1962), pp. 204–11; Moss, *Catalogue of Syriac Printed Books and Related Literature in the British Museum* (1962); on this cf. de Boer, VT 12 (1962), pp. 504–7; Tisserant, 'Le plus ancien manuscrit biblique daté' RB 8 (1911), pp. 85–92; Vööbus, 'Completion of the Vetus Syra Project' Biblical Research, Chicago 7 (1962), pp. 48–56; (§ 126 on § 119); Wernberg-Møller, 'Some Observations on the Relationship of the Peshitta Version of the Book of Genesis to the Palestinian Targum Fragments Published by Professor Kahle, and to Targum Onkelos' StTh 15 (1961), pp. 128–80.

§ 121. THE SEPTUAGINT

(b) Hanhart (§ 126 on § 90); Kahle, 'Die von Origenes verwendeten griechischen Bibelhandschriften' StP IV (1961), pp. 107–17; Maldfeld, 'Der Beitrag ägyptischer Papyruszeugen für den frühen griechischen Bibeltext' Mitteilungen aus der Papyrussammlung der Österreichischen Nationalbibliothek, Neue Serie, V. Folge (1956), pp. 79–84; Tritton, 'Some Notes on the Septuagint' Transact. Glasgow Univ. Or. Soc. XVIII (1962), pp. 49–52;

Ziegler, 'In memoriam Dr. Peter Katz (Cambridge)' ThLZ 87 (1962), cols. 794–6; *Die Septuaginta. Erbe und Auftrag* (Würzburger Universitätsreden 33, 1962).

p. 703, n. 7, Schreiner, 'Textformen und Urtext des Deboraliedes in der Septuaginta' Bibl 42 (1961), pp. 173–200; 'Zum B-Text des griechischen Canticum Deborae' Bibl 42 (1961), pp. 333–58.

p. 704, n. 23, Ziegler, 'Die Vokabel-Varianten der *O*-Rezension im griechischen Sirach' *Studies Driver* (1963), pp. 172–90.

p. 704, n. 24, Bickermann (1956): on Gen. xxxiv, 12 and Exod. xxii, 4; 'The Septuagint as a Translation' PAAJR 28 (1959), pp. 1–39.

p. 705, line 16, Smit Sibinga, *The Old Testament Text of Justin Martyr. I. The Pentateuch* (1963).

p. 706, n. 31, Ant. Pap. II contains as No. 51 (p. 1, Pl. IV), No. 52 (pp. 1–2) and No. 53 (pp. 3–6) fragments of Ps. lxxi (lxxii), Isa. i and Jer. xxviii–xxxii, from the sixth century.

p. 710, line 13, Davison, 'The Transmission of the Text' in Wace and Stubbings, *A Companion to Homer* (1962), pp. 215–33; Erbse, 'Über Aristarchs Iliasausgaben' Hermes 87 (1959), pp. 275–303.

p. 710, n. 59, Johnson, *Die hexaplarische Rezension des 1. Samuelbuches der Septuaginta* (StTh 22, 1963).

p. 711, n. 64, de Boer, 'A Syro-Hexaplar Text of the Song of Hannah; I Samuel ii, 1–10' *Studies Driver* (1963), pp. 8–15; Johnson, *Die hexaplarische Rezension des 1. Samuelbuches der Septuaginta* (StTh 22, 1963); Rudolf Meyer, 'Bemerkungen zu den Mailänder Hexapla-fragmenta' *Festgabe Hanna Jursch* (1963), pp. 122–31; 'Aus der Sekunda des Origenes' *Hebräisches Textbuch* (1960), pp. 68–71.

p. 712, line 7, Wallace-Hadrill, *Eusebius of Caesarea* (1960), pp. 59–99.

p. 712, line 12, Jellicoe, 'The Hesychian Recension Reconsidered' JBL 82 (1963), pp. 409–18.

p. 712, n. 66, Metzger, 'Lucian and the Lucianic Recension of the Greek Bible' NTSt 8 (1962), pp. 189–203.

p. 713, n. 70, Gryglewicz, 'Le codex Alexandrinus du premier livre des Macchabées' Roczniki Teologiczno-Kanoniczne 8 (1961), pp. 23–37.

p. 713, n. 71, Junack, 'Constantin Tischendorf und die neutestamentliche Kritik' Das Altertum 2 (1956), pp. 48–56; Lauch, 'Nichts gegen Tischendorf' *Festgabe Sommerlath* (1960), pp. 15–64.

p. 713, n. 73 (second section), Böhlig, *Codex Proverbiorum* (1963); *Proverbien-Kodex. Die Sprüche Salomos* (1963); Filson, 'The Bodmer Papyri' BA 22 (1959), pp. 48–51; 'New Greek and Coptic Gospel Manuscripts' BA 24 (1961), pp. 2–18; 'More Bodmer Papyri' BA 25 (1962), pp. 50–7, cf. pp. 50–1; Kasser, *Papyrus Bodmer III. Évangile de Jean et Genèse i, 1–iv, 2 en bohaïrique* (CSCO 177/178, 1958); *Papyrus Bodmer VI. Livre des Proverbes* (CSCO 194, 1960); 'Le papyrus Bodmer III et les versions bibliques coptes' Muséon 74 (1961), pp. 423–33; *Papyrus Bodmer XVIII. Deutéronome i–x, 7 en sahidique* (1962); 'Origine de quelques variantes dans la version sahidique des Proverbes' EThR 36 (1962), pp. 359–66; *Papyrus Bodmer XXI. Jos. vi, 16–25; vii, 6–xi, 23; xxii, 1–2, 19–xxiii, 7, 15–xxiv, 23 en sahidique* (1963); Shore, *Joshua i–vi and other passages in Coptic, ed. from a fourth-century Sahidic Codex in the Chester Beatty Library, Dublin* (1963); Zandee, 'Iosephus contra Apionem. An Apocryphal Story of Joseph in Coptic' Vigiliae Christianae 15 (1961), pp. 193–213, 10 Pls.

p. 714, n. 75, Ecker, *Die arabische Job-Übersetzung des Gaon Sa'adja Ben Josef al-Fajjûmî* (Studien zum A und NT 4, 1962); Henninger, 'Arabische Bibelübersetzungen von Früh-mittelalter bis zum 19. Jahrhundert' NZMW 17 (1961), pp. 201–33; Melamed, 'The Targum Yehonathan and an Arabic Tafsīr to the Song of Deborah' [Hebr.] Eretz-Israel 3 (1954), pp. 198–206; Shunari, 'An Arabic *Tafsīr* of the Song of Deborah' Textus 2 (1962), pp. 77–86; Zucker, *Rav Saadya Gaon's Translation of the Thora* [Hebr.] (1958); on this cf. Hirschberg [Hebr., Engl. summary] Tarbiz 31 (1961/62), pp. 414–22, IV.

§ 122. THE TRANSLATIONS OF AQUILA, THEODOTION AND SYMMACHUS

Barthélemy, *Les devanciers d'Aquila* (SVT X, 1963); Reider and Turner, *An Index to Aquila* (SVT XII, 1964).

§ 123. THE OLD LATIN (VETUS LATINA)

(a) *Vetus Latina, Die Reste der altlateinischen Bibel* ... XXIV, fasc. 1, *Epist. ad Eph* (1962); *Vetus Latina*. Vol. I: Fischer, *Verzeichnis der Sigel* (²1963).
(b) Ayuso Marazuela (§ 126 on § 117); Boscherini, 'Sulla lingua delle primitive versioni latine dell' Antico Testamento' Atti e Memorie dell'Accademia Toscana di Szienze e Lettere La Colombaria, Vol. XXVI (1961/62), pp. 205–229; de Boer (§ 126 on p. 281, n. 47); Cantera, 'Origin, familias y fuentes de la Vetus Latina' Sefarad 22 (1962), pp. 296–311; La Bonnardière, *Biblia Augustiniana*. AT Vol. II (1960); Smit Sibinga (§ 126 on p. 705, line 16); Vaccari, 'Les traces de la *Vetus Latina* dans le *Speculum* de Saint Augustin' StP IV (1961), pp. 228–33.

§ 124. THE VULGATE

La Bonnardière, *Biblia Augustiniana*. OT. Livres historiques (1960); Les Douze Petits Prophètes (1964); Fang Che-Yong, 'Sir vii, 36 (Vulg. vii, 40) iuxta hebraicam veritatem' VD 40 (1962), pp. 18–26; Fischer, 'Codex Amiatinus und Cassiodor' BZ 6 (1962), pp. 56–79; Rost, 'Geschichte und Bedeutung der Vulgata' Bibel und Kirche 18 (1963), pp. 55–9; Sutcliffe, 'Notes on St. Jerome's Hebrew Text' CBQ 11 (1949), pp. 139–43; Weber, *Psalterii secundum Vulgatam Bibliorum Versionem Nova Recensio [pro manuscripto]* (Clervaux, 1961).

§ 125. THE EVALUATION OF THE MATERIAL OF TEXTUAL CRITICISM. CONJECTURAL EMENDATIONS

Dahood, 'Ugaritic Studies and the Bible' Gregorianum 43 (1962), pp. 55–79; Goshen-Gottstein, 'Theory and Practice of Textual Criticism. The Text-critical use of the Septuagint' Textus 3 (1963), pp. 130–58; Jepsen, 'Von den Aufgaben der alttestamentlichen Textkritik' SVT IX (1963), pp. 332–41; Koenig, 'L'activité herméneutique des scribes dans la transmission du texte de l'Ancien Testament II' RHR 162 (1962), pp. 1–43; 'Les methodes herméneutiques des scribes d'après la tradition du texte d'Isaïe' École Pratique des Hautes Études, IVe section, Annuaire 1962/63 (1962), pp. 245–8; Mirsky, 'Biblical Variants in Mediaeval Hebrew Poetry' Textus 3 (1963), pp. 159–62; Weingreen, 'Exposition in the Old Testament and Rabbinic Literature' *Essays Hooke* (1963), pp. 187–201; Weiss, 'On Ligatures in the Hebrew Bible (בּ‑כּ)' JBL 82 (1963), pp. 188–94; Zeitlin, 'Some Reflections on the Text of the Pentateuch' JQR 51 (1960/61), pp. 321–31.

p. 721, line 3, Weil, 'La nouvelle édition de la Massorah' (BHK IV) et l'histoire de la Massorah' SVT IX (1963), pp. 266–84.

I REFERENCE INDEX

OLD TESTAMENT

(a) *Canonical Books*

(b) *Apocrypha*

(c) *Pseudepigrapha*

(d) *Qumran Writings*

ANCIENT NEAR EASTERN AND EGYPTIAN SOURCES

846

INDEX OF AUTHORS

Ruwet, Johann, 559
Ryan, J. K., 575
Ryckmans, Gonzague, 197
Ryckmans, Jacques, 768
Rylaarsdam, J. Coert, 155, 471
Ryle, Herbert Edward, 541, 588, 741, 757
Rypins, Stanley Israel, 669
Rypka, J., 485
Ryssel, Victor, 155, 505, 541, 588, 591, 596, 627, 630
Ryzach, Alois, 615

Saarisalo, Aapeli, 697
Sabatier, Petrus, 716
Sacchi, P., 724
Sachau, Eduard, 495
Sachs, Abraham Joseph, 513, 577
Sachs, Walter, 728
Sæbø, Magne, 311, 491, 755
Sage, R. A., 763
Saggs, H. W. F., 22, 199, 331, 369, 725, 755
Sainte Fare-Garnot, Jean, 735
Šākir, Aḥmad Muḥamad, 728
Saliby, Nessib, 25
Saller, S., 752
Salmon, Petrus, 718
Salomies, Ilmari, 857
Salonen, Armas, 437
Samuel, A. E., 768
Šanda, Albert, 281
Sandars, N. K., 729
Sander-Hansen, C. E., 52
Sanders, G. B., 514
Sanders, Henry Arthur, 671, 706
Sanders, J. A., 656, 773, 781
Sandmel, Samuel, xxiv, 744
Sant, C., 158
de Santo, Charles, 774
Sarfatti, G. B., 302
Sarna, Nahum M., 455, 738, 764
Sauer, F., xxiii
Sauer, Georg, 445, 765
Sauneron, S., 53, 725
de Savignac, Jean, 103, 161, 324, 473, 765
Saydon, Pierre-Paul, 1, 39, 76, 129, 253, 331, 585, 673
Scarlett, William, 382
Scarpat, G., 718, 719
Scazzocchio, L., 771, 772
Schaad, H. P. M., 754
Schachermeyr, Fritz, 525
Schadewaldt, Wolfgang, 177, 743
Schaeder, Hans Heinrich, 31, 541, 543, 544, 549, 556, 707
Schaeffer, Claude Frederic-Armand, 48, 49, 733, 735, 780
Schäfer, Karl Th., 717
Schäfers, Joseph, 714
S(c)halit, Abraham, 525, 574, 624, 774
Schall, Anton, 731, 732
Schaller, B., 773

Scharbert, Joseph, 12, 71, 73, 331
Scharf, A. M., 452
Schärf, Rosa Riwkah, 430
Scharff, Alexander, 84
Schaumberger, Johannes B., 404, 513, 577
Schechter, Solomon, 599, 646, 649, 650
Schedl, Claus, 452, 737, 738, 752, 754, 758, 763, 767, 768
Scheiber, Alexander, 322, 688, 730, 755, 772
Scheifler, J. R., 769
Scheja, Georg, 753
Schelbert, Georg, 698
Schelhaas, J., 269, 308
Schelkle, K. H., 559
Schenke, Hans-Martin, 734
Scherer, Paul, 454
Schiefer, F. Walther, 625
Schifman, I. S., 726
Schild, E., 183
Schildenberger, Johannes B., 99, 120, 196, 268, 505, 591, 717, 720, 739, 760
Schilling, Othmar, 107, 596, 737, 739, 763
Schimmel, A., 31
Schirmann, J., 596
Schlatter, Adolf, 577, 578
Schleifer, J., 713
Schloerb, Rolland Walter, 470
Schmid, Christian Friedrich, 569
Schmid, Wilhelm, 540
Schmidt, Carl, 706
Schmidt, Eberhard, 740
Schmidt, Erich F., 543
Schmidt, Hans, 33, 69, 85, 102, 109, 113, 119, 121, 126, 173, 210, 235, 303, 311, 334, 346, 354, 365, 382, 384, 430, 432, 444, 450, 455, 460, 463, 500, 753
Schmidt, Hatto H., 768
Schmidt, Johannes, 81, 494
Schmidt, Karl Ludwig, 97
Schmidt, Martin Anton, 366, 371
Schmidt, Nathaniel, 617, 622
Schmidt, Werner, 51, 111, 737, 745, 749, 753, 755
Schmidtke, Friedrich, 25, 283
Schmitt, Ernst, 455
Schmitt, Götz, 749
Schmitz, Otto, 125, 339
Schmökel, Hartmut, 26, 69, 200, 283, 469, 484, 489
Schmuttermayr, Georg, 737
Schnabel, Paul, 523
Schnapp, Friedrich, 631, 634
Schneider, Carl, 771
Schneider, Heinrich, 85, 155, 541, 588, 592, 680, 699, 700, 717, 718, 763, 764, 765, 766, 770, 771
Schneider, Max, 763
Schoene, Alfred, 371
Schoeps, Hans-Joachim, 609, 611, 658, 715
Schofield, John Noel, 277, 360
Scholder, Klaus, 733

III INDEX OF ABBREVIATIONS

Commentaries

ATD = Das Alte Testament Deutsch, ed. (HERNTRICH and) WEISER, Göttingen.
BK = Biblischer Kommentar, Neukirchen.
BOuT = De Boeken van het Oude Testament, Roermond en Maaseik.
Camb.-B = Cambridge-Bible for Schools and Colleges, Cambridge.
Cent.-B = Century-Bible, London.
Charles = *The Apocrypha and Pseudepigrapha of the OT in English* ... edited in Conjunction with many Scholars by R. H. CHARLES (London 1913, 1963).
Clamer-B s. Pirot & Clamer.
ClB = Connaître la Bible, Bruges.
COuT = Commentar op het Oude Testament, Kampen.
CSS = Cursus Scripturae Sacrae, Paris.
EB = Études Bibliques, Paris.
Echter-B = Die Heilige Schrift in deutscher Übersetzung, Würzburg (Echter-Verlag).
EH = Exegetisches Handbuch zum AT, Münster.
EK = Einzelkommentar.
ΕΠΔ = 'Ερμηνεία Παλαιᾶς Διαθήκης, Athens.
Expositor's B = Expositor's Bible, London.
Fritzsche-Grimm = FRITZSCHE and GRIMM, *Kurzgefaßtes exegetisches Handbuch zu den Apokryphen des AT* (Leipzig 1851–1860).
Hammershaimb = HAMMERSHAIMB et al., De gammeltestamentig Pseudepigrafer i Oversættelse med Inledning (Copenhagen 1953 ff.).
Harper's B = Harpers Annotated Bible, New York.
Hartum = HARTUM, הַסְּפָרִים הַחִיצוֹנִים, (Yavne (Israel) 1958 ff.).
HAT = Handbuch zum AT, Tübingen.
Herder-B = Herders Bibelkommentar, Freiburg i. Br.
HK = Handkommentar zum AT, Göttingen.
HS = *Die Heilige Schrift des AT*, ed. FELDMANN and HERKENNE, Bonn.
HSAT = Die Heilige Schrift des AT (KAUTZSCH) (4th edn. 1922/23), ed. BERTHOLET, Tübingen.
IB = The Interpreter's Bible, New York, Nashville (Tenn.).
ICC = The International Critical Commentary, Edinburgh.
Jerusalem-B = La Sainte Bible traduite en français sous la direction de l'École Biblique de Jérusalem, Paris.
JewApocrLit = ZEITLIN et al., Jewish Apocryphal Literature (New York, 1950, ff.).
Kahana = KAHANA, הַסְּפָרִים חַחִיצוֹנִים, Tel-Aviv (²1956).
KAT = Kommentar zum AT, Leipzig, Gütersloh.
Kautzsch = *Die Apokryphen und Pseudepigraphen des AT in Verbindung mit anderen übersetzt u. herausgegeben*, KAUTZSCH (Tübingen 1900 (1921)).
KD = Biblischer Commentar über das AT, ed. KEIL and DELITZSCH, Leipzig.
KeH = Kurzgefaßtes exegetisches Handbuch zum AT, Leipzig.
KHC = Kurzer Hand-Commentar zum AT (Freiburg i. Br., Leipzig), Tübingen.
KV = Korte Verklaring der Heilige Schrift, Kampen.
LBC = Layman's Bible Commentary, London.
LD = Lectio Divina, Paris.
Montserrat-B = La Bíblia. Versió dels textos originals i comentari pels monjos de Montserrat Montserrat.
PBS = Pamphlet Bible Series, New York.
Pirot & Clamer = L. PIROT & A. CLAMER, La Sainte Bible, Paris.
Riessler = RIESSLER, *Altjüdisches Schrifttum außerhalb der Bibel, übersetzt und erläutert* (Augsberg 1928).
SAT = Die Schriften des AT (GUNKEL, GRESSMANN), Göttingen.

SB, Sa Bi	=	La Sacra Bibbia, Turin.
SBOT	=	The Sacred Books of the OT, ed. PAUL HAUPT, Leipzig, Baltimore (Md.).
Soncino-B	=	The Soncino Books of the Bible, Bournemouth.
SZ	=	Kurzgefaßter Kommentar zu den heiligen Schriften Alten und Neuen Testamentes, ed. STRACK and ZÖCKLER (Nördlingen), München.
Torch-B	=	Torch Bible Commentaries, London.
TU	=	Tekst en Uitleg, Den Haag, Groningen.
UAHC	=	Union of American Hebrew Congregations: Jewish commentary for Bible readers, New York.
WC	=	The Westminster Commentaries, London.
ZBK	=	Zürcher Bibelkommentare, Zürich, Stuttgart.
Zöckler	=	ZÖCKLER, *Die Apokryphen des AT nebst einem Anhang über die Pseudepigraphenliteratur* (in SZ, A. Altes Testament, 9. Abt.), München (1891).

*Journals and Composite Works**

A XXIV IOK	=	Akten des XXIV. Internationalen Orientalistenkongresses, München 1957, ed. H. FRANKE (Wiesbaden 1959).
AAB	=	Abhandlungen der Deutschen (Preußischen) Akademie der Wissenschaften zu Berlin, Berlin.
AAG, AGA	=	Abhandlungen der Akademie der Wissenschaften in Göttingen, Göttingen.
AAH	=	Abhandlungen der Heidelberger Akademie der Wissenschaften, Heidelberg.
AAM	=	Abhandlungen der Bayrischen Akademie der Wissenschaften, München.
AAMz	=	Abhandlungen der Akademie der Wissenschaften und der Literatur in Mainz, Wiesbaden.
AANL	=	Atti della Accademia Nazionale dei Lincei, Rome.
AASOR	=	Annual of the American Schools of Oriental Research, New Haven (Conn.).
ABR	=	Australian Biblical Review, Melbourne.
AcAn[B]	=	Acta Antiqua Academiae Scientiarum Hungaricae, Budapest.
AcOr[B]	=	Acta Orientalia Academiae Scientiarum Hungaricae, Budapest.
AcOr[(L)H]	=	Acta Orientalia, (Leiden) Havniae = Kopenhagen.
ADAI Abt. Kairo	=	Abhandlungen des Deutschen Archäologischen Instituts, Abt. Kairo, Glückstadt.
AER	=	American Ecclesiastical Review, Washington (D.C.).
AETh	=	Abhandlungen zur evangelischen Theologie, Bonn.
ÄZ, ZÄS	=	Zeitschrift für ägyptische Sprache und Altertumskunde (Leipzig), Berlin.
AFLNW	=	Veröffentlichungen der Arbeitsgemeinschaft für Forschung des Landes Nordrhein-Westfalen, Köln und Opladen.
AfK, AKG	=	Archiv für Kulturgeschichte, Köln, Graz.
AfO	=	Archiv für Orientforschung (Berlin), Graz.
AGGW	=	Abhandlungen der Gesellschaft der Wissenschaften zu Göttingen, Berlin.
AIPhHOS	=	Annuaire de l'Institut de Philologie et d'Histoire Orientales et Slaves, Brüssel.
AJA	=	American Journal of Archaeology (Norwood [Mass.], Concord [N.H.]), Baltimore (Md.).
AJSL	=	American Journal of Semitic Languages and Literatures, Chicago (Ill.).
AJTh	=	American Journal of Theology, Chicago (Ill.).
AKM, AKML	=	Abhandlungen zur Kunde des Morgenlandes (Leipzig) Wiesbaden.
ALBO	=	Analecta Lovaniensia Biblica et Orientalia, Louvain.
ALUOS	=	Annual of Leeds University Oriental Society.
AMz Jahrbuch	=	Akademie der Wissenschaften und der Literatur in Mainz, Jahrbuch, Wiesbaden.
AnBibl	=	Analecta Biblica, Rome.
ANEP	=	*The Ancient Near East in Pictures relating to the Old Testament*, ed. by J. B. PRITCHARD (Princeton (New Jersey), 1954).
ANET	=	*Ancient Near Eastern Texts relating to the Old Testament*, ed. by J. B. PRITCHARD (Princeton (New Jersey), ²1955).
AnSt	=	Anatolian Studies, London.
ANVAO	=	Avhandlinger utgitt av det Norske Videnskaps-Akademi i Oslo, Oslo.
AO	=	Der Alte Orient. Gemeinverständliche Darstellungen, Leipzig.

* For the publications of learned societies, reference is always to the monographs and reports of their philosophical/historical sections.

AOB   = *Altorientalische Bilder zum AT*, ed. GRESSMANN (Berlin und Leipzig ²1927).
AOT   = *Altorientalische Texte zum AT*, ed. GRESSMANN (Berlin und Leipzig ²1926).
ArOr   = Archiv Orientální, Prag.
Ar. Doc.   = G. R. DRIVER, *Aramaic Documents of the Fifth Century B.C.* (Oxford 1954).
ARM   = *Archives Royales de Mari. Transcriptions et Traductions*, publiées sous la direction de PARROT et DOSSIN, Paris.
Ar.Pap. (C.)   = A. COWLEY, *Aramaic Papyri of the Fifth Century B.C.* (Oxford 1923).
Ar. Pap. (K.)   = EMIL G. KRAELING, *The Brooklyn Museum Aramaic Papyri. New Documents of the Fifth Century B.C.* (New Haven (Conn.) 1953).
ARW   = Archiv für Religionswissenschaft, Leipzig, Berlin.
AST   = MARK LIDZBARSKI, *Altsemitische Texte*, I (Giessen 1907).
ASTI   = Annual of the Swedish Theological Institute in Jerusalem, Leiden.
ATA   = Alttestamentliche Abhandlungen, Münster.
AThANT   = Abhandlungen zur Theologie des Alten und Neuen Testaments, Zürich.
'Atiqot   = 'Atiqot. Journal of the Israel Department of Antiquities, Jerusalem.
AThR   = Anglican Theological Review, Evanston (Ill.).
AWAT   = Archiv für wissenschaftliche Erforschung des AT, ed. MERX, 1–2 (Halle 1869–1872).
BA   = The Biblical Archaeologist, New Haven (Conn.).
Bab. u. Ass.   = MEISSNER, *Babylonien und Assyrien* (Heidelberg), I (1920); II (1925).
Bab.-Ass. Lit.   = MEISSNER, *Die Babylonisch-Assyrische Literatur* (Wildpark-Potsdam 1928).
BAH   = Bibliothèque Archéologique et Historique, Paris.
BAL   = Berichte über die Verhandlungen der Sächsischen Akademie der Wissenschaften zu Leipzig, Berlin.
BASOR   = Bulletin of the American Schools of Oriental Research, New Haven (Conn.), Baltimore (Md.).
BBB   = Bonner Biblische Beiträge, Bonn.
BEThL   = Bibliotheca Ephemeridum Theologicarum Lovaniensium, Paris, Gembloux.
BFChrTh   = Beiträge zur Förderung christlicher Theologie, Gütersloh.
BHET   = Bulletin d'Histoire et d'Exégèse de l'Ancien Testament, Leuven-Louvain.
BHK   = Biblia Hebraica ed. KITTEL.
BHTh   = Beiträge zur Historischen Theologie, Tübingen.
Bibl   = Biblica, Rome.
Bibl Or, BiOr   = Bibliotheca Orientalis, Leiden.
Bi e Or   = Bibbia e Oriente, Milano.
BIES   = Bulletin of the Israel Exploration Society = ועתיקותיה ידיעות החברה לחקירת ארץ־ישראל, Jerusalem.
Bijdragen   = Bijdragen. Tijdschrift voor Filosofie en Theologie, Nijmegen, Brugge.
BJPES   = Bulletin of the Jewish Palestine Exploration Society =ארץ־ישראל ועתיקייתיה ידיעות החברה העברית לחקירת, Jerusalem.
BJRL   = Bulletin of the John Rylands Library, Manchester.
BMB   = Bulletin du Musée de Beyrouth, Beyrouth.
The Bridge   = The Bridge. A Yearbook of Judaeo-Christian Studies, Newark (N.Y.).
BRL   = KURT GALLING, *Biblisches Reallexikon* (Tübingen 1937).
BS   = Bibliotheca Sacra, Dallas (Texas).
BSOASt   = Bulletin of the School of Oriental and African Studies, University of London, London.
BSt   = Biblische Studien, Neukirchen.
BT   = The Bible Translator, London.
BWA(N)T   = Beiträge zur Wissenschaft vom Alten (und Neuen) Testament (Leipzig), Stuttgart.
ByZ   = Byzantinische Zeitschrift (Leipzig), München.
BZ   = Biblische Zeitschrift (new series from 1957), (Freiburg i. Br.), Paderborn.
BZAW   = Beihefte zur Zeitschrift für die Alttestamentliche Wissenschaft (Gießen), Berlin.
BZNW   = Beihefte zur Zeitschrift für die Neutestamentliche Wissenschaft (Gießen), Berlin.
CAB   = Cahiers d'Archéologie Biblique, Neuchâtel.
CahSi   = Cahiers Sioniens, Paris.
CanadianJTh   = Canadian Journal of Theology, Toronto.
CBQ   = Catholic Biblical Quarterly, Washington (D.C.).
CG   = KAHLE, *The Cairo Geniza* (Oxford ²1959).

ChQR = Church Quarterly Review, London.
CivCatt = La Civiltà Cattolica, Rome.
COOKE, NSI s. NSI.
COWLEY, Ar. Pap. s. Ar. Pap. (C).
CRAI = Comptes Rendus de l'Académie des Inscriptions et Belles-Lettres, Paris.
Crozer Q = Crozer Quarterly, Chester (Pa.).
CSCO = Corpus scriptorum christianorum orientalium, Paris.
CultBíbl = Cultura Bíblica, Segovia.
CuW = Christentum und Wissenschaft, Dresden.
CV = Communio Viatorum, Prague.
DOTT = WINTON THOMAS, Documents from Old Testament Times (London 1958).
DTT = Dansk Teologisk Tidsskrift, Kopenhagen.
ELKZ = Evangelisch-Lutherische Kirchenzeitung, Berlin.
Erbe und
  Auftrag = Erbe und Auftrag. Benedictinische Monatsschrift, Beuron.
Eripainos = Eripainos teoksesta. Talenta quinque: Commentationes in honorem Ilmari Salomies,
  teoksesta Eino Sormunen, E. G. Gulin, Rafael Gyllenberg, G. O. Rosenqvist (Helsinki
  1953).
Essays Irwin = A Stubborn Faith. Papers on OT and Related Subjects, printed to honour
  William Andrew Irwin, ed. E. C. Hobbs (1956).
Est Bíbl = Estudios Bíblicos, Madrid.
ET = The Expository Times, Edinburgh.
E.T. = English Translation.
EThL = Ephemerides Theologicae Lovanienses, Leuven-Louvain.
EThR = Études Théologiques et Religieuses, Montpellier.
EvTh = Evangelische Theologie, München.
EV(V) = English Version(s).
Exp = Expositor, London.
FRLANT = Forschungen zur Religion und Literatur des Alten und Neuen Testaments,
  = Göttingen.
FuF = Forschungen und Fortschritte, Berlin.
GGA = Göttingische Gelehrte Anzeigen, Göttingen.
GJV = EMIL SCHÜRER, Geschichte des Jüdischen Volkes im Zeitalter Jesu Christi, I–III,
  (Leipzig ⁴1901–11). E.T. of ed. 2 (1897).
GLECS = Comptes Rendus du Groupe Linguistique d'Études Chamito-Sémitiques, Paris.
GM = BENOIT, MILIK, DE VAUX, Les Grottes de Murabba'ât (Discoveries in the Judaean
  Desert, II) (Oxford 1960).
GThT = Gereformeerd Theologisch Tijdschrift (Baarn, Aalten), Kampen.
HdO = Handbuch der Orientalistik, hrsg. von BERTOLD SPULER (Leiden, Köln, 1952 ff.).
Heil. Land = Das Heilige Land, Köln.
HJ = Historisches Jahrbuch der Görres-Gesellschaft, München.
HThR = Harvard Theological Review, Cambridge (Mass.).
HTSt = Hervormde Teologiese Studies, Pretoria.
HUCA = Hebrew Union College Annual, Cincinnati (Ohio).
HZ = Historische Zeitschrift, München, Berlin.
IEJ = Israel Exploration Journal, Jerusalem.
ILN = Illustrated London News, London.
Interpr. = Interpretation, Richmond (Virginia).
Irish ThQ = Irish Theological Quarterly, Maynooth.
IZBG = Internationale Zeitschriftenschau für Bibelwissenschaft und Grenzgebiete,
  Düsseldorf.
JA = Journal Asiatique, Paris.
JAOS = Journal of the American Oriental Society (Boston [Mass.]), New Haven (Conn.).
JbAC = Jahrbuch für Antike und Christentum, Münster.
Jb.Ak.Mainz = s. AMz Jahrbuch.
Jb. Jüd.-Lit.
  Ges. = Jahrbuch der Jüdisch-Literarischen Gesellschaft, Frankfurt/Main.
JBL = Journal of Biblical Literature (New York, New Haven ([Conn.]), Philadelphia
  (Pa.).
JBR = Journal of Bible and Religion, Boston (Mass.).
JCSt = Journal of Cuneiform Studies, New Haven (Conn.).

JDTh = Jahrbücher für Deutsche Theologie, Stuttgart, Gotha.
JEA = Journal of Egyptian Archaeology, London.
JEOL = Jaarbericht van het Voorziatisch-Egyptisch Gezelschap (Genootschap) 'Ex
= Oriente Lux', Leiden.
JESHO = Journal of Economic and Social History of the Orient.
Jew Rev = The Jewish Review, London.
JJPES = Journal of the Jewish Palestine Exploration Society = ארץ-ישראל ועתיקותיה
קובץ החברה העברית לחקרית, Jerusalem.
JJSt = Journal of Jewish Studies, London.
JKlF = Jahrbuch für Kleinasiatische Forschung, Heidelberg.
JNESt = Journal of Near Eastern Studies, Chicago (Ill.).
JPOS = Journal of the Palestine Oriental Society, Jerusalem.
JpTh = Jahrbücher für protestantische Theologie, Leipzig.
JQR = Jewish Quarterly Review, Philadelphia (Pa.).
JR = Journal of Religion, Chicago (Ill.).
JRAS = Journal of the Royal Asiatic Society of Great Britain and Ireland, London.
JSOR = Journal of the Society of Oriental Research, Toronto.
JSSt = Journal of Semitic Studies, Manchester.
JThSt = Journal of Theological Studies, Oxford.
Kern- = Kernmomenten der antieke beschaving en haar moderne beleving (MEOL
momenten No. 7), Leiden 1947.
Klio = Kkio. Beiträge zur Alten Geschichte, Leipzig.
Kl. Schr. = Kleine Schriften.
KlT = Kleine Texte für theologische und philosophische Vorlesungen, begun by
LIETZMANN, ed. ALAND.
KRAELING, Ar. Pap. s. Ar. Pap. (K.).
KuD = Kerygma und Dogma, Göttingen.
LUA = Lunds Universitets Årsskrift, Lund.
MAA = Mededeelingen der Koninklijke Akademie van Wetenschappen te Amsterdam,
Amsterdam. (N.R. = Nieuwe Reeks (New Series)).
MAOG = Mitteilungen der Altorientalischen Gesellschaft, Leipzig.
MDAI Kairo = Mitteilungen des Deutschen Archäologischen Instituts, Abt. Kairo, Wiesbaden.
MDOG = Mitteilungen der Deutschen Orient-Gesellschaft, Berlin.
MDS,MDSAI = Mémoires présentés par divers savants à l'académie des inscriptions et belles-
lettres, Paris.
MEOL = Mededeelingen en Verhandelingen van het Voor-Aziatisch Egyptisch Gezel-
schap (Genootschap) 'Ex Oriente Lux', Leiden.
MGkK = Monatsschrift für Gottesdienst und kirchliche Kunst, Göttingen.
MGWJ = Monatsschrift für Geschichte und Wissenschaft des Judentums, Breslau.
MIOF = Mitteilungen des Instituts für Orientforschung, Berlin.
Misc. Bibl. = *Miscellanea Biblica edita a Pontificio Instituto Biblico ad celebrandum annum XXV
ex quo conditum est institutum* (Rom), I, II (1934).
MO = Le Monde Oriental, Uppsala.
MPTh = Monatsschrift für Pastoraltheologie, Göttingen.
MUB = Mélanges de (la Faculté Orientale de) l'Université Saint-Joseph, Beyrouth
(Libanon).
MThZ = Münchener Theologische Zeitschrift, München.
MV(Ä)G = Mitteilungen der Vorderasiatisch(-Ägyptisch)en Gesellschaft (Berlin), Leipzig.
NA(W)G,
  NG(A)W = Nachrichten (von) der Akademie der Wissenschaften in Göttingen, Göttingen.
NC = La Nouvelle Clio, Bruxelles.
NedThT = Nederlands Theologisch Tijdschrift, Wageningen.
NGG(W) = Nachrichten von der Gesellschaft der Wissenschaften zu Göttingen, Göttingen.
NKZ = Neue Kirchliche Zeitschrift, Erlangen, Leipzig.
NRTh = Nouvelle Revue Théologique, Paris.
NSI = G. A. COOKE, *A Text-Book of North-Semitic Inscriptions* (Oxford 1903).
NT = Novum Testamentum, Leiden.
NTA = Neutestamentliche Abhandlungen, Münster.
NThSt = Nieuwe Theologische Studiën, Groningen, Den Haag.
NThT = Nieuw Theologisch Tijdschrift, Haarlem.

NTS(t)	=	New Testament Studies, Cambridge.
NTT	=	Norsk Teologisk Tidsskrift, Oslo.
NZMW	=	Neue Zeitschrift für Missionswissenschaft, Beckenried (Schweiz).
NZSTh	=	Neue Zeitschrift für Systematische Theologie, Berlin.
OBL	=	Orientalia et Biblica Lovaniensia, Louvain.
OIP	=	The Oriental Institute Publications, Chicago (Ill.).
OLZ	=	Orientalistische Literaturzeitung (Leipzig), Berlin.
Op. Min.	=	Opera Minora.
Or	=	Orientalia, Rom.
OrChr	=	Oriens Christianus (Leipzig), Wiesbaden.
Orient.Neerl.	=	Orientalia Neerlandica, Leiden.
Or Suec	=	Orientalia Suecana, Uppsala.
OTMSt	=	*The Old Testament and Modern Study*, by H. H. ROWLEY (Oxford 1951).
OTS	=	Oudtestamentische Studiën, Leiden.
OuTWP	=	Die Ou Testamentiese Werkgemeenskap in Suid-Afrika, Pretoria.
P XXII CO	=	Proceedings of the Twenty Second Congress of Orientalists held in Istanbul, 1951. Vol. II: Communications, Leiden 1957.
PAAJR	=	Proceedings of the American Academy for Jewish Research, Philadelphia (Pa.).
PBA	=	Proceedings of the British Academy, London.
PEFQSt	=	Palestine Exploration Fund. Quarterly Statement, London.
PEQ	=	Palestine Exploration Quarterly, London.
PIHAN	=	Publications de l'Institut historique et archéologique Néerlandais de Stamboul, Leiden.
PJ	=	Preußische Jahrbücher, Berlin.
PJB	=	Palästinajahrbuch, Berlin.
PRE	=	*Realencyklopädie für protestantische Theologie und Kirche* (Leipzig ³1896–1913).
Pr.O.S.	=	Pretoria Oriental Series, Pretoria.
PRU	=	*Le Palais Royal d'Ugarit* (Paris).
PSBA	=	Proceedings of the Society of Biblical Archaeology, Bloomsbury (London).
PW s. RE		
QC I, II, etc.	=	BARTHÉLEMY and MILIK, *Qumran Cave, I, II,* etc. (*Discoveries in the Judaean Desert, I, II,* etc.) (Oxford 1955 ff).
Quantula-cumque	=	*Studies presented to Kirsopp Lake* (London 1937).
RA	=	Revue d'Assyriologie et d'Archéologie Orientale, Paris.
RB	=	Revue Biblique (Vol. 50–52 = Vivre et Penser 1, 1941; 2, 1942; 3, 1945), Paris.
RBiLit	=	Revista Bíblica con Sección Litúrgica, Buenos Ayres.
RCuBíbl	=	Revista de Cultura Bíblica, Rio de Janeiro.
RE	=	Paulys Realencyclopädie der classischen Altertumswissenschaft, Stuttgart. Neue Bearbeitung, beg. von Wissowa.
REG	–	Revue des Études Grecques, Paris.
REJ	=	Revue des Études Juives, Paris.
RES	=	Revue des Études Sémitiques, Paris.
RES Bab	=	Revue des Études Sémitiques et Babyloniaca, Paris.
Rev. Arch.	=	Revue Archéologique, Paris.
Rev Bénédict	=	Revue Bénédictine, Abbaye de Maredsous.
RevBíbl	=	Revista Bíblica, Villa Calzada (Argentina).
RevEcclLiège	=	Revue Ecclésiastique Liège, Liège.
Rev Ét Anc	=	Revue des Études Anciennes, Bordeaux.
RGG	=	Die Religion in Geschichte und Gegenwart, Tübingen.
RHA	=	Revue Hittite et Asianique, Paris.
RHPhR	=	Revue d'Histoire et de Philosophie Religieuses, Strasbourg, Paris.
RHR	=	Revue de l'Histoire des Religions, Paris.
Ric Rel	=	Ricerche Religiose, Rom.
RIDA	=	Revue International des Droits de l'Antiquité, Louvain.
RivBibl	=	Rivista Biblica, Rom.
RLA	=	*Reallexikon der Assyriologie*, ed. EBELING and MEISSNER (Berlin, Leipzig), I (1932); II (1938); III, 1. 2 (1957/9).
RQ	=	Revue de Qumrân, Paris.
RS(c)PhTh	=	Revue des Sciences Philosophiques et Théologiques (Le Saulchoir), Paris.
RSR	=	Recherches de Science Religieuse, Paris.

RStO(r)   = Rivista degli Studi Orientali, Rom.
RThPh   = Revue de Théologie et de Philosophie (Montauban), Lausanne.
SAB   = Sitzungsberichte der Deutschen (Preußischen) Akademie der Wissenschaften zu Berlin, Berlin.
SAH   = Sitzungsberichte der Heidelberger Akademie der Wissenschaften, Heidelberg.
SAM   = Sitzungsberichte der Bayrischen Akademie der Wissenschaften, München.
SAW   = Sitzungsberichte der Österreichischen Akademie der Wissenschaften in Wien (Leipzig), Wien.
SBO   = Studia Biblica et Orientalia, Rom I–III, 1959.
SCHÜRER, GJV s. GJV
Scripta
  Hieros.   = Scripta Hierosolymitana. Publications of the Hebrew University, Jerusalem.
SEA   = Svensk Exegetisk Årsbok, Lund.
Sefarad   = Revista de la Escuela de Estudios hebraicos del Instituto Arias Montano, Madrid.
SGV   = Sammlung gemeinverständlicher Vorträge aus dem Gebiet der Theologie und Religionsgeschichte, Tübingen.
SJTh   = Scottish Journal of Theology, Edinburgh.
SKG   = Schriften der Königsberger Gelehrten Gesellschaft, Halle/Saale.
SLB   = *Studia ad Tabulas cuneiformes collectas a F. M. Th de Liagre Böhl pertinentia* (Leiden 1960).
SNT   = Supplements to Novum Testamentum, Leiden.
SNVAO   = Skrifter utgitt av Det Norske Videnskaps-Akademi i Oslo, Oslo.
SPOA   = François Weidel et al., *Les sagesses du Proche-Orient Ancien, Colloque de Strasbourg 1962* (1963).
StANT   = Studien zum Alten und Neuen Testament, München.
Starine   = Jugoslavenska alcademija znanosti i umjetnosti Zayrebu.
StC   = Studia Catholica, Nijmegen.
StEv   = *Studia Evangelica. Papers presented to the International Congress on „The Four Gospels in 1957" held at Christ Church, Oxford 1957* = TU 73, 1959.
StG   = Studium Generale, Heidelberg.
SThU   = Schweizerische Theologische Umschau, Bern.
SThZ   = Schweizerische Theologische Zeitschrift, Zürich.
StMSR   = Studi e Materiali di Storia delle Religioni (Rom), Bologna.
StOr   = Studia Orientalia, Helsinki.
StOTPr   = *Studies in Old Testament Prophecy presented to Th. H. Robinson*, ed. by H. H. ROWLEY (Edinburgh 1950).
StP   = Studia Patristica I–VI = TU 63, 64, 78–81.
StPb   = Studia Postbiblica, Leiden.
StT   = Studi e Testi, Rom.
StTh   = Studia Theologica, cura ordinum theologorum Scandinavicorum edita, Lund, Aarhus.
StTh[Riga]   = Studia Theologica, Riga.
Stud. Anselm = Studia Anselmiana, Rom.
SupplDict
  Bible   = *Dictionnaire de la Bible*. Supplément, Paris.
SVT   = Supplements to Vetus Testamentum, Leiden.
S(v)TK(v)   = Svensk Teologisk Kvartalskrift, Lund.
SyBU   = Symbolae Biblicae Upsalienses, Uppsala.
Syria   = Syria. Revue d'Art Oriental et d'Archéologie, Paris.
ThBl   = Theologische Blätter, Leipzig.
ThD   = Theology Digest, Saint Mary's (Canada).
Theol. Ex.   = Theologische Existenz heute, München.
ThF   = Theologische Forschung. Wissenschaftliche Beiträge zur kirchlich-evangelischen Lehre, Hamburg-Volksdorf.
ThGl   = Theologie und Glaube, Paderborn.
ThLBl   = Theologisches Literaturblatt, Leipzig.
ThLZ   = Theologische Literaturzeitung, Leipzig, Berlin.
ThPQ   = Theologisch-Praktische Quartalschrift, Linz.
ThQ   = Theologische Quartalschrift, Tübingen, Stuttgart.
ThR   = Theologische Rundschau, Tübingen.
ThRv   = Theologische Revue, Münster.

ThSt	=	Theologische Studiën, Utrecht.
ThSt[B]	=	Theologische Studien, hrsg. von K. BARTH (und M. GEIGER), Zürich.
ThSt[USA]	=	Theological Studies, Woodstock (Md.).
ThStKr	=	Theologische Studien und Kritiken (Hamburg, Gotha, Leipzig), Berlin.
ThT	=	Theologisch Tijdschrift, Leiden.
ThToday	=	Theology of Today, Princeton (N.Y.).
ThWNT	=	*Theologisches Wörterbuch zum Neuen Testament*, begun by G. KITTEL, ed. G. FRIEDRICH (Stuttgart, 1932 ff.).
ThZ	=	Theologische Zeitschrift, Basel.
TriererThSt	=	Trierer Theologische Studien, Trier.
TriererThZ	=	Trierer Theologische Zeitschrift, Trier.
TSt	=	Texts and Studies, Cambridge.
TTKi	=	Tidsskrift for Teologi og Kirke, Oslo.
TU	=	Texte und Untersuchungen zur Geschichte der altchristlichen Literatur, Leipzig, Berlin.
TuA Beuron	=	Texte und Arbeiten, hrsg. durch die Erzabtei Beuron, Beuron.
Ug. Lit.	=	C. H. GORDON, *Ugaritic Literature. A Comprehensive Translation of the Poetic and Prose Texts* (Rome 1949).
Ug. Manual	=	C. H. GORDON, *Ugaritic Manual* (Rome 1955).
VAA	=	Verhandelingen der Koninklijke Akademie van Wetenschappen te Amsterdam, Amsterdam.
VD	=	Verbum Domini, Rom.
Vie Spirit.	=	La Vie Spirituelle, Paris.
VigChr	=	Vigiliae Christianae, Amsterdam.
VIOF	=	Veröffentlichungen des Instituts für Orientforschung, Berlin.
Vivre et Penser	=	Vivre et Penser 1, 2, 3(= Vol. 50–52 de la Revue Biblique), Paris 1941–45.
Vox Theol.	=	Vox Theologica, Assen, Utrecht.
VT	=	Vetus Testamentum, Leiden.
WdO	=	Die Welt des Orients. Wissenschaftliche Beiträge zur Kunde des Morgenlandes (Wuppertal, Stuttgart), Göttingen.
WMANT	=	Wissenschaftliche Monographien zum Alten und Neuen Testament, Neukirchen.
W(estminster) ThJ	=	Westminster Theological Journal, Philadelphia (Pa.).
WuD	=	Wort und Dienst. Jahrbuch der Theologischen Schule Bethel, Bielefeld.
WZ	=	Wissenschaftliche Zeitschrift.
WZKM	=	Wiener Zeitschrift für die Kunde des Morgenlandes, Wien.
ZA	=	Zeitschrift für Assyriologie (Leipzig), Berlin.
ZÄS, ÄZ	=	Zeitschrift für Ägyptische Sprache und Altertumskunde (Leipzig), Berlin.
ZAW	=	Zeitschrift für die Alttestamentliche Wissenschaft (Gießen), Berlin.
ZDMG	=	Zeitschrift der Deutschen Morgenländischen Gesellschaft (Leipzig), Wiesbaden.
ZDPV	=	Zeitschrift des Deutschen Palästina-Vereins (Leipzig, Stuttgart), Wiesbaden.
ZdZ	=	Zeichen der Zeit, Berlin.
ZevE	=	Zeitschrift für evangelische Ethik, Gütersloh.
ZKG	=	Zeitschrift für Kirchengeschichte, Stuttgart.
ZKTh	=	Zeitschrift für Katholische Theologie, Innsbruck.
ZKWL	=	Zeitschrift für Kirchliche Wissenschaft und Kirchliches Leben, Leipzig.
ZLThK	=	Zeitschrift für die gesamte Lutherische Theologie und Kirche, Leipzig.
ZMR	=	Zeitschrift für Missionskunde und Religionswissenschaft, Berlin.
ZNW	=	Zeitschrift für die Neutestamentliche Wissenschaft (Gießen), Berlin.
ZRGG	=	Zeitschrift für Religions- und Geistesgeschichte, Köln.
ZS	=	Zeitschrift für Semitistik und verwandte Gebiete, Leipzig.
ZSavRG	=	Zeitschrift der Savigny-Stiftung für Rechtsgeschichte, Weimar.
ZSTh	=	Zeitschrift für Systematische Theologie (Gütersloh), Berlin.
ZThK	=	Zeitschrift für Theologie und Kirche (Freiburg i. Br., Leipzig), Tübingen.
ZWTh	=	Zeitschrift für Wissenschaftliche Theologie, Jena, Halle, Leipzig.
ZZR	=	Zbornik znanstvenik razprav.